TEACHER'S EDITION

James West Davidson

Pedro Castillo

PRENTICE HALL

Printed in the United States of America.

ISBN 0-13-434904-0

1 2 3 4 5 6 7 8 9 10 03 02 01 00 99

Upper Saddle River, New Jersey Needham, Massachusetts

Contents

Chapter Managers

Show students how history affects

- **Student Edition**
- **Teacher's Edition**
- **Teaching Resources With Test Bank CD-ROM**

  Vocabulary Builder
  Practice Your Skills
  Critical Thinking and Writing
  Map Mystery
  Connecting History and Literature
  Biography Flashcards
  Section Quizzes
  Chapter Tests (Forms A & B)
  Test Bank CD-ROM
  Alternative Assessment Booklet
  Lesson Planner Book
  Classroom Manager Book
  Why Study History? Book
  Why Study History? Poster
  Document-Based Discovery Book
  Citizenship for Life Book
  Interdisciplinary Connections Book
  Nystrom Atlas of Our Country

- **Student Performance Pack**

  Interactive Student Tutorial CD-ROM
  Guide to the Essentials of American History
  (Available in English and Spanish)
  Guide to the Essentials Teacher's Guide
  Guided Reading Audiotapes
  Guided Reading Audiotapes (Spanish)
  Standardized Test Prep Handbook

- **The American Nation Transparencies**
- **The American Nation on Audiotapes**
- **Classroom Literature Library**
- **Listening to Literature Audiotapes**
- **Listening to Music, *The American Experience* Audio CD**
- **Interdisciplinary Explorations**
- **TCI History Alive!® Activity Pack**
- **Voices of Freedom: Sources in American History**
- **American History Customized Reader**
- **American History Historical Outline Map Book**
- **Constitution Study Guide**
- **Constitution Study Guide/Teacher's Manual**
- **Resource Pro® With Planning Express® CD-ROM**
- **American Heritage® History of the United States CD-ROM and Teacher's Guidebook (Windows/Macintosh)**
- **United States History Video Collection™**

  Videodiscs (10) with Guidebook
  Videotapes (20) with Guidebook

PROGRAM HIGHLIGHTS

- solid content
- captivating, age-appropriate narrative
- outstanding skill instruction
- innovative ways to make history meaningful
- strong focus on geography
- a special civics overview chapter
- up-to-date content

their lives today with...

THE AMERICAN NATION'S COMPLETE PACKAGE

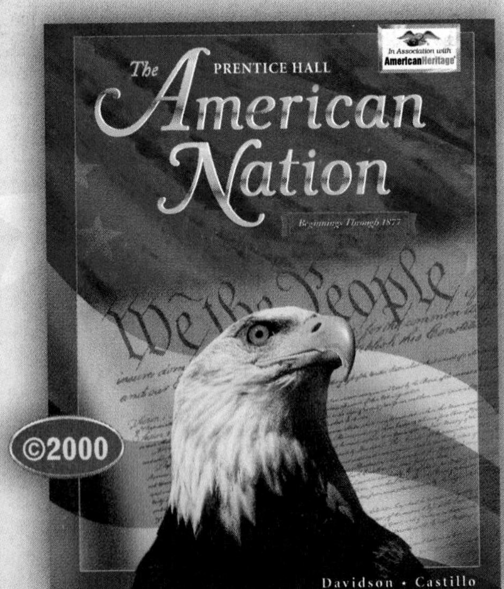

More ways than any other program to show students why history matters.

Introducing the new edition of the country's leading middle grades program.

WHY STUDY HISTORY?

This breakthrough feature connects with students again and again—whether it's showing them how Supreme Court decisions affect their lives or showing what role they will have in choosing the leaders of tomorrow. The Teacher's Edition includes WHY STUDY HISTORY?, FAST FACTS and BIBLIOGRAPHY highlights. In addition, a complete WHY STUDY HISTORY? teaching pack of hands-on resources supports each Student Edition chapter and is part of our innovative Teaching Resources package.

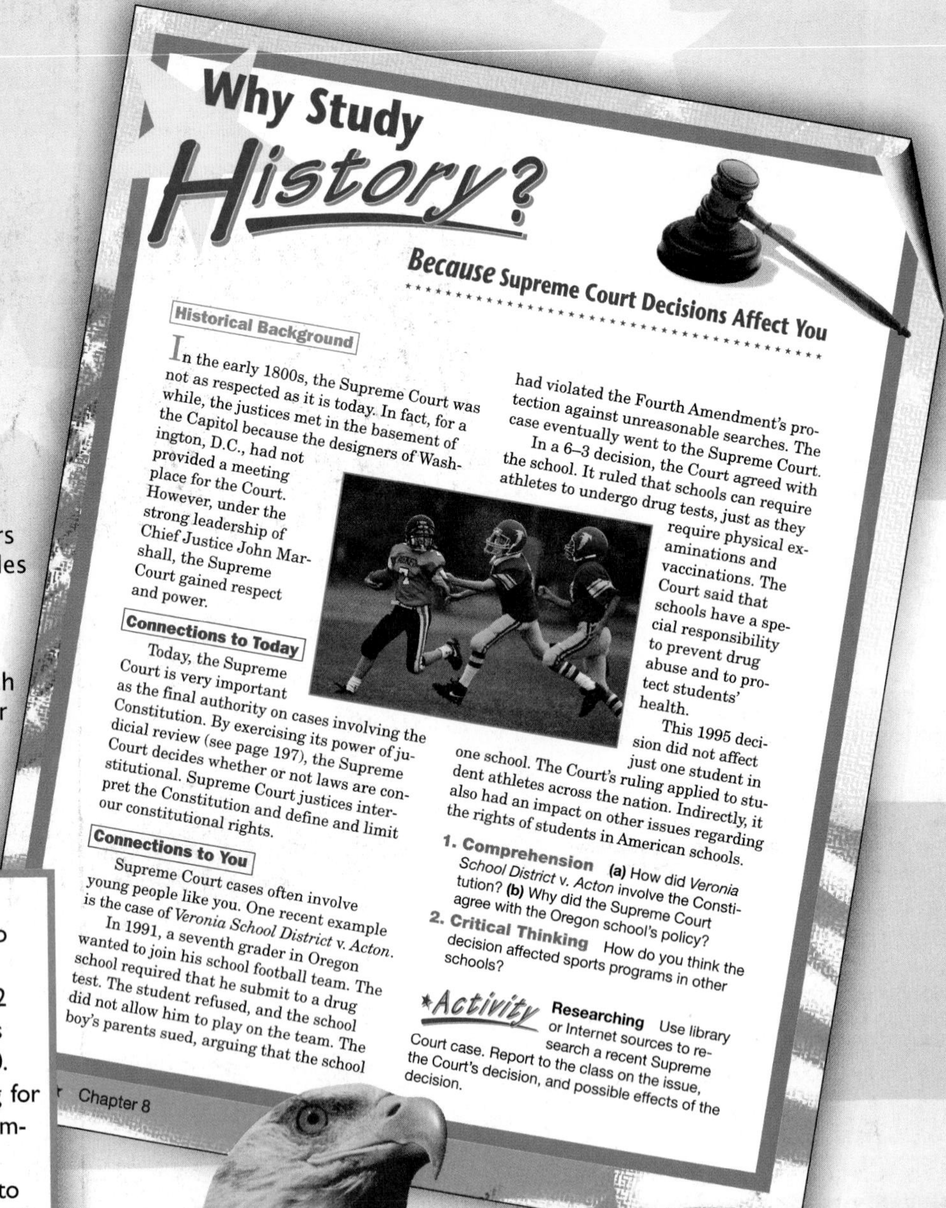

Fast Facts

★ The generation gap is nothing new to the Supreme Court. Joseph Story was appointed to the Court at the age of 32 in 1811. In 1932, Oliver Wendell Holmes retired from the Court at the age of 90.

★ Lawyers can spend months preparing for a Supreme Court case but are usually limited to 30 minutes of oral argument.

★ Of the thousands of cases appealed to the Court each year (nearly 8,000 in 1996), the Court agrees to hear only about 150.

Why Study History?

Because Supreme Court Decisions Affect You

Historical Background

In the early 1800s, the Supreme Court was not as respected as it is today. In fact, for a while, the justices met in the basement of the Capitol because the designers of Washington, D.C., had not provided a meeting place for the Court. However, under the strong leadership of Chief Justice John Marshall, the Supreme Court gained respect and power.

Connections to Today

Today, the Supreme Court is very important as the final authority on cases involving the Constitution. By exercising its power of judicial review (see page 197), the Supreme Court decides whether or not laws are constitutional. Supreme Court justices interpret the Constitution and define and limit our constitutional rights.

Connections to You

Supreme Court cases often involve young people like you. One recent example is the case of *Veronia School District v. Acton*.

In 1991, a seventh grader in Oregon wanted to join his school football team. The school required that he submit to a drug test. The student refused, and the school did not allow him to play on the team. The boy's parents sued, arguing that the school had violated the Fourth Amendment's protection against unreasonable searches. The case eventually went to the Supreme Court.

In a 6–3 decision, the Court agreed with the school. It ruled that schools can require athletes to undergo drug tests, just as they require physical examinations and vaccinations. The Court said that schools have a special responsibility to prevent drug abuse and to protect students' health.

This 1995 decision did not affect just one student in one school. The Court's ruling applied to student athletes across the nation. Indirectly, it also had an impact on other issues regarding the rights of students in American schools.

1. **Comprehension** (a) How did *Veronia School District v. Acton* involve the Constitution? (b) Why did the Supreme Court agree with the Oregon school's policy?
2. **Critical Thinking** How do you think the decision affected sports programs in other schools?

★Activity **Researching** Use library or Internet sources to research a recent Supreme Court case. Report to the class on the issue, the Court's decision, and possible effects of the decision.

Chapter 8

Since its introduction by Prentice Hall, *The American Nation* has been the standard by which all other middle grades American history programs have been judged. Over 12 million copies are being used by teachers today. This brand-new edition builds on the lively narrative and more relevant approach that continue to set it apart.

HISTORY & YOU

These activities encourage students to become active learners through assuming the roles of historical figures and completing thoughtful writing activities.

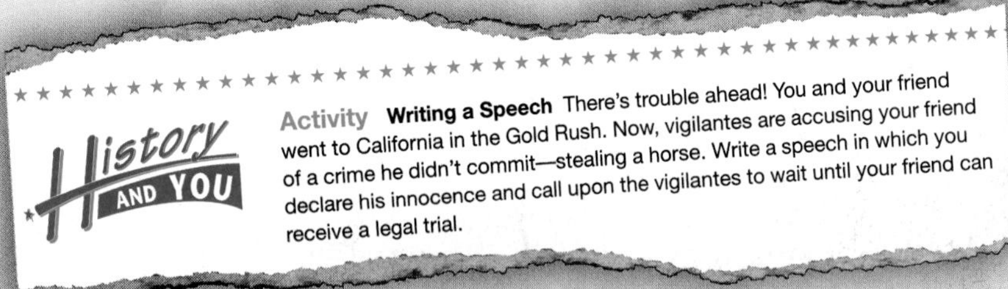

History AND YOU
Activity **Writing a Speech** There's trouble ahead! You and your friend went to California in the Gold Rush. Now, vigilantes are accusing your friend of a crime he didn't commit—stealing a horse. Write a speech in which you declare his innocence and call upon the vigilantes to wait until your friend can receive a legal trial.

LINKING PAST AND PRESENT

LINKING PAST AND PRESENT is a highly visual feature that helps students make the connection between past events and events today.

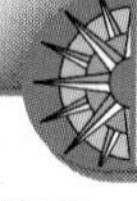

Linking Past and Present

Past

Trial by Jury

Trial by jury is part of the nation's English heritage. Yet in colonial times, British officials sometimes suspended jury trials. Therefore, many Americans wanted the new Constitution to guarantee this right. The members of a jury promise to give an impartial verdict based on evidence. ★ **Turn to the Reference Section and read the Sixth Amendment. List three rights guaranteed to Americans accused of crimes.**

ACTIVITY BANK

Interdisciplinary Activity

Exploring Science Working with a partner, give a presentation on how a geologic feature of the West influenced history. For example, you might choose the Rio Grande, the Great Salt Lake, the Rocky Mountains, the Central Valley of California, or the gold in California.

Career Skills Activity

City Planner You are a city official of San Francisco in 1849. You know that thousands of people will be moving to your city over the next few years. Write a report in which you propose a plan for growth.

Citizenship Activity

Exploring Immigration Like Californians, most Americans today are immigrants or descended from immigrants. Do you know when any of your ancestors first came to this country? If so, prepare a chart tracing your ancestors back to the first people in your family to come to the United States.

Internet Activity Use the Internet to find sites dealing with the early history of the Mormons. Take notes on what you find and use them to compose a two-paragraph report on early Mormon history.

Connections With Science

Acting as botanist for the expedition, Meriwether Lewis collected and preserved many plants. He carefully dried and pressed each specimen. Of the more than 200 specimens Lewis brought back, 39 still remain at the Academy of Natural Sciences in Philadelphia.

ACTIVITY BANK

This is a high-interest way to encourage student participation. As with all the program's activities, guided instruction helps you with assessment.

INTERDISCIPLINARY CONNECTIONS

In-text notes appear at least twice in every chapter. Team teaching strategies and an INTERDISCIPLINARY CONNECTIONS book in the Teaching Resources provide you with a wealth of resources.

Now *The American Nation* of the country's premier

The American Nation has remained the middle grades leader for a very good reason—we constantly listen to teachers and incorporate their most exciting suggestions. The latest example of this innovation is that now students and teachers alike will have the opportunity to benefit from the vast archives and scholarship of *American Heritage* magazine and classic books. This groundbreaking arrangement means that now you can experience exclusive benefits.

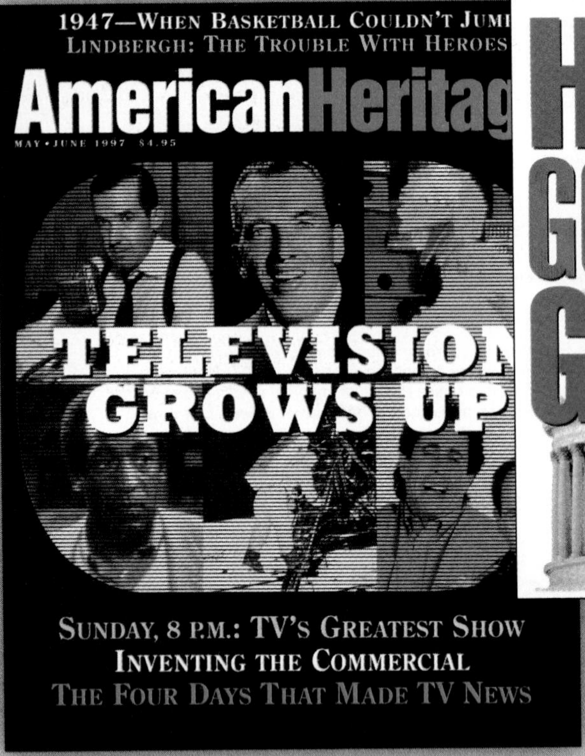

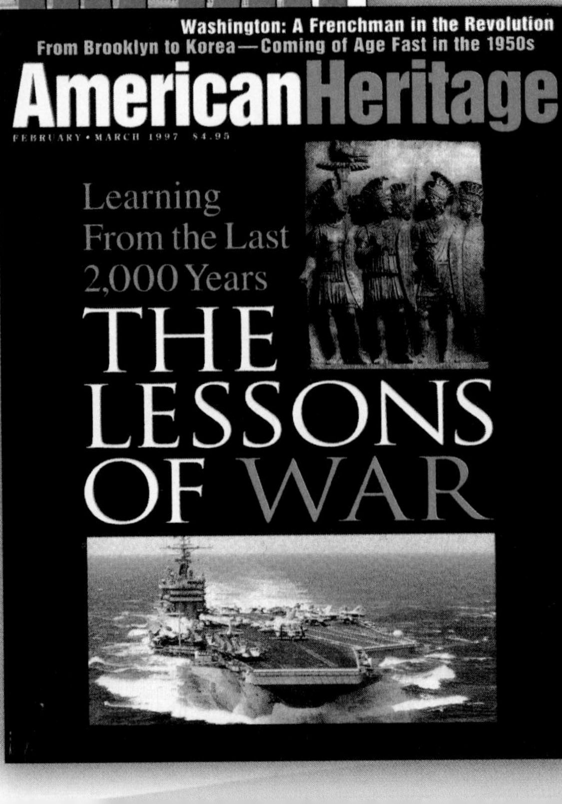

American Heritage Magazine

American Heritage magazine features compelling accounts and historical scholarship that add a whole new dimension to the way your students perceive their American history studies.

s infused with the vitality American history magazine.

AmericanHeritage
MAGAZINE

HISTORY HAPPENED HERE

The USS Constitution

The USS Constitution *became known as "Old Ironsides" because British cannonballs often bounced off her thick wooden hull. In 1905, the ship was docked in Boston and opened to the public. In 1997, the ship underwent major restoration. Today, the United States Navy invites you to come aboard and tour "Old Ironsides." In the nearby museum, you can relive history by commanding a ship, hoisting a sail, or firing a cannon.*

★ ***To learn more about this historic ship, write:*** *USS* Constitution *Museum, Charlestown Navy Yard, Charlestown, MA 02129.*

HISTORY HAPPENED HERE

These lively features are integrated throughout *The American Nation* and are based on the popular HISTORY HAPPENED HERE features in *American Heritage* magazine.

FROM THE ARCHIVES OF
AmericanHeritage®

The early government bureaucracy
In the early years, the Treasury Department was the largest of the federal departments. At the end of 1789, it had 39 employees. By 1801, 78 people worked in the Washington office and 1,615 others worked in the field, collecting taxes and import duties.

Source: Bernard A. Weisberger, "What Made the Government Grow," *American Heritage* magazine, September 1997.

POINT-OF-USE TEACHING NOTES

Point-of-use teaching notes from *American Heritage* magazines and books are woven throughout to help your class see history as they've never seen it before!

AMERICAN HERITAGE® THE HISTORY OF THE UNITED STATES CD-ROM

AMERICAN HERITAGE® HISTORY OF THE UNITED STATES CD-ROM gives you an interactive, in-depth program that features a wide array of multimedia, including nearly 30 minutes of live-action video, almost 1,000 photographs, and over two hours of audio and music.

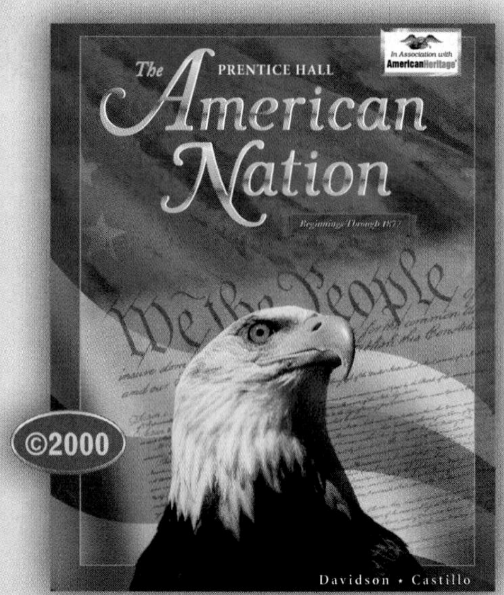

Prentice Hall's *Student* student success in three

Not offered by any other program, this specially developed *Student Performance Pack* for *The American Nation* provides the resources students need to enhance their performance in the areas of reading, test taking, and English language development.

STUDENT PERFORMANCE PACK

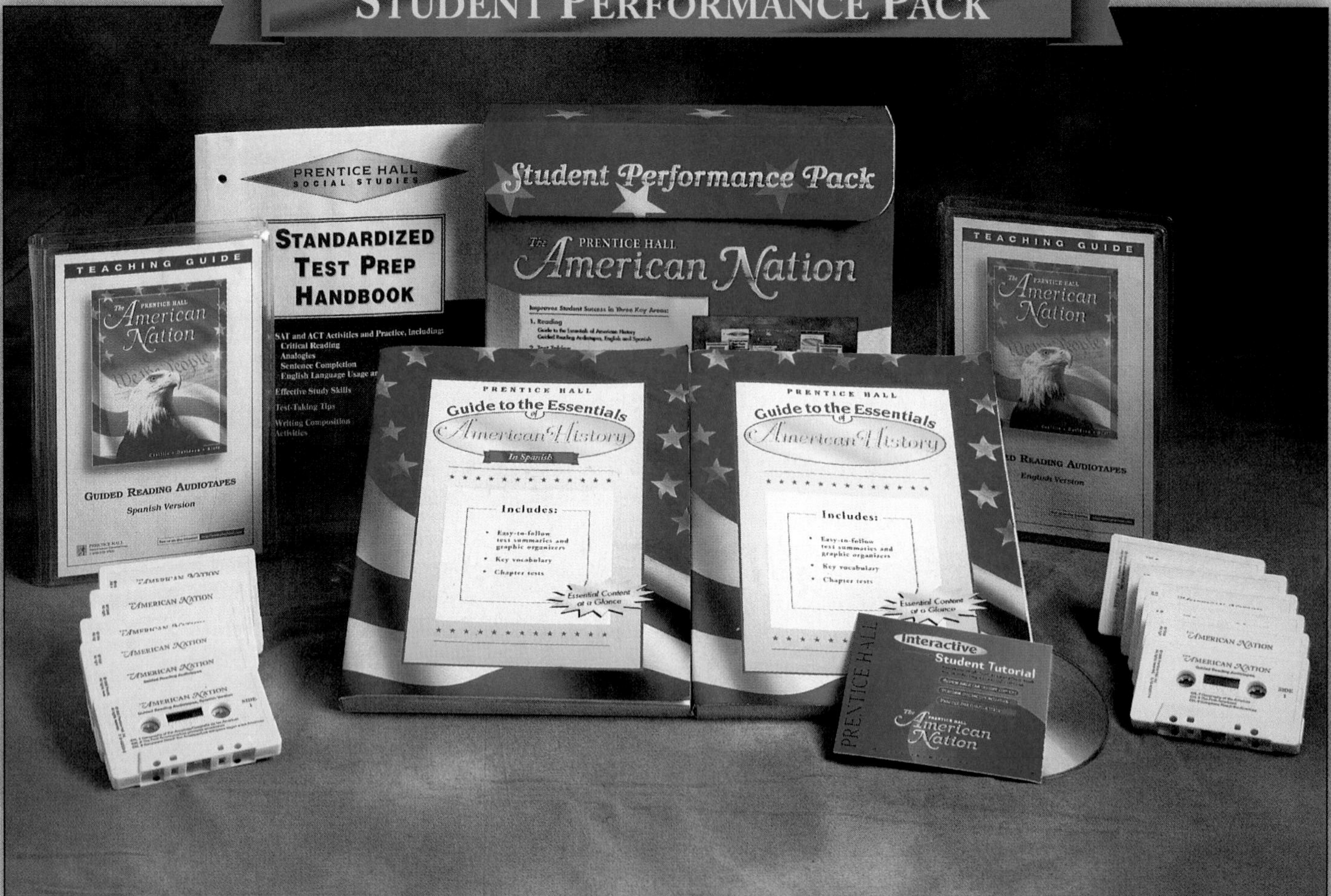

Performance Pack improves key areas.

1. READING

- GUIDE TO THE ESSENTIALS OF AMERICAN HISTORY reviews critical content for every section of the student text. Section and chapter reviews help assess student comprehension.
- GUIDED READING AUDIOTAPES, ENGLISH & SPANISH provide section-by-section summaries. The tapes can be used in conjunction with the *Guide to the Essentials of American History* book.

2. TEST TAKING

- INTERACTIVE STUDENT TUTORIAL CD-ROM allows students to actively review American history content, perform interactive activities, and take practice chapter tests.
- STANDARDIZED TEST PREP HANDBOOK helps prepare students for standardized tests and other critical assessment with study tips and practice tests.

3. ENGLISH LANGUAGE DEVELOPMENT

- GUIDE TO THE ESSENTIALS OF AMERICAN HISTORY provides a review of critical content for every section of the student book in English and Spanish. Plus, section and chapter reviews help assess student comprehension.

A program that helps your students

At Prentice Hall we know that students need to master skills that they will use not only in school but throughout their lives. In *The American Nation* we provide numerous opportunities for students to learn, practice, and apply skills.

Skills for Life

Skills for Life help your students prepare for the 21st century. Students go beyond the basic map and graph skills to develop critical thinking, information management, and communication skills.

Practice Your Skills worksheets in the Teaching Resources and Skills for Life Mini Lessons in the Teacher's Edition extend the skills taught in the student book.

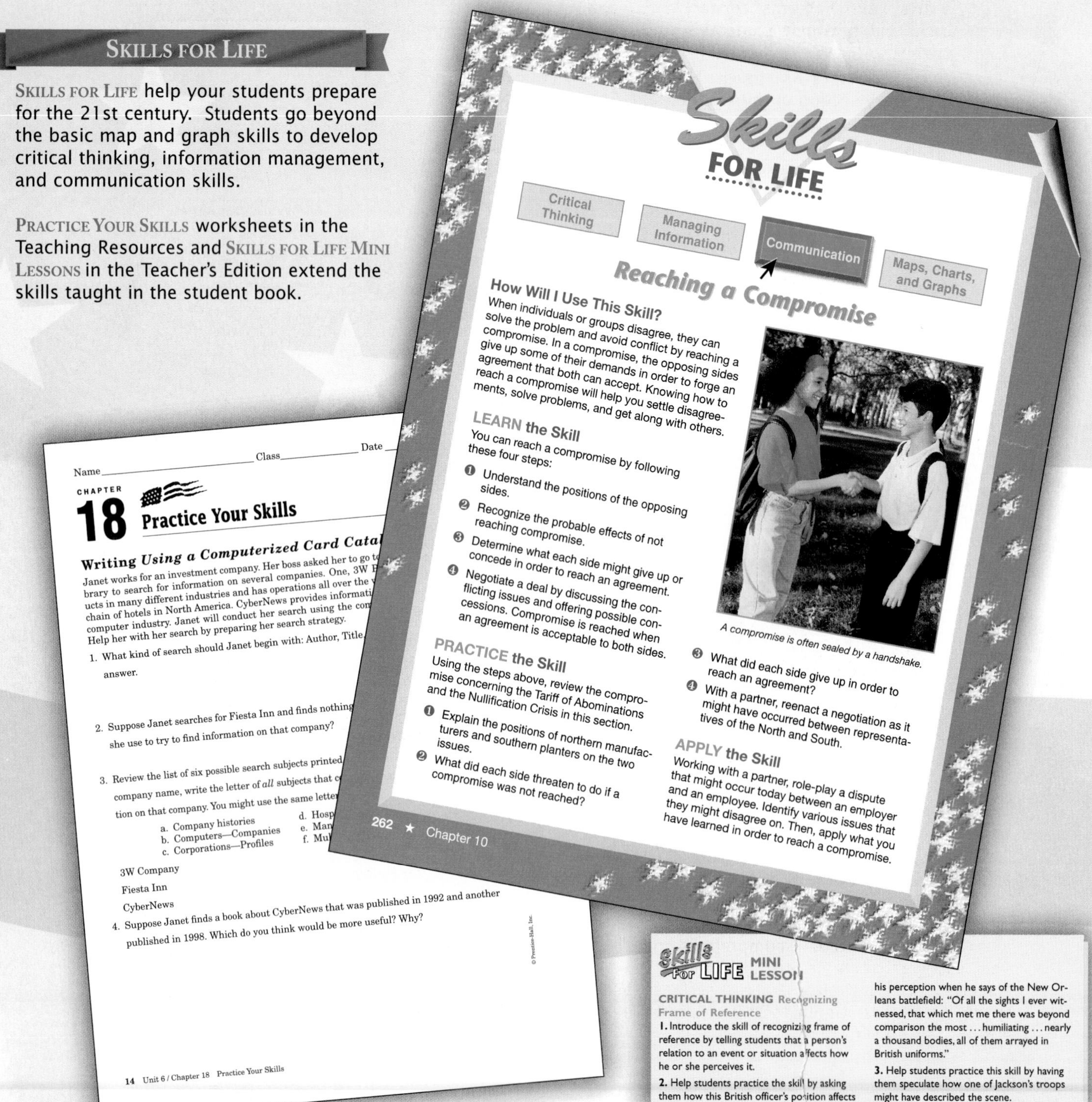

Skills FOR LIFE

Critical Thinking | Managing Information | Communication | Maps, Charts, and Graphs

Reaching a Compromise

How Will I Use This Skill?
When individuals or groups disagree, they can solve the problem and avoid conflict by reaching a compromise. In a compromise, the opposing sides give up some of their demands in order to forge an agreement that both can accept. Knowing how to reach a compromise will help you settle disagreements, solve problems, and get along with others.

LEARN the Skill
You can reach a compromise by following these four steps:

1. Understand the positions of the opposing sides.
2. Recognize the probable effects of not reaching compromise.
3. Determine what each side might give up or concede in order to reach an agreement.
4. Negotiate a deal by discussing the conflicting issues and offering possible concessions. Compromise is reached when an agreement is acceptable to both sides.

PRACTICE the Skill
Using the steps above, review the compromise concerning the Tariff of Abominations and the Nullification Crisis in this section.

1. Explain the positions of northern manufacturers and southern planters on the two issues.
2. What did each side threaten to do if a compromise was not reached?
3. What did each side give up in order to reach an agreement?
4. With a partner, reenact a negotiation as it might have occurred between representatives of the North and South.

A compromise is often sealed by a handshake.

APPLY the Skill
Working with a partner, role-play a dispute that might occur today between an employer and an employee. Identify various issues that they might disagree on. Then, apply what you have learned in order to reach a compromise.

262 ★ Chapter 10

Name________________ Class__________ Date____

CHAPTER 18 **Practice Your Skills**

Writing *Using a Computerized Card Catal*

Janet works for an investment company. Her boss asked her to go t… brary to search for information on several companies. One, 3W … ucts in many different industries and has operations all over the … chain of hotels in North America. CyberNews provides informati… computer industry. Janet will conduct her search using the co… Help her with her search by preparing her search strategy.

1. What kind of search should Janet begin with: Author, Title… answer.
2. Suppose Janet searches for Fiesta Inn and finds nothing… she use to try to find information on that company?
3. Review the list of six possible search subjects printed… company name, write the letter of *all* subjects that c… tion on that company. You might use the same lette…
   a. Company histories
   b. Computers—Companies
   c. Corporations—Profiles
   d. Hosp…
   e. Man…
   f. Mul…

   3W Company
   Fiesta Inn
   CyberNews
4. Suppose Janet finds a book about CyberNews that was published in 1992 and another published in 1998. Which do you think would be more useful? Why?

© Prentice-Hall, Inc.

14 Unit 6 / Chapter 18 Practice Your Skills

Skills for LIFE MINI LESSON

CRITICAL THINKING Recognizing Frame of Reference

1. Introduce the skill of recognizing frame of reference by telling students that a person's relation to an event or situation affects how he or she perceives it.

2. Help students practice the skill by asking them how this British officer's position affects his perception when he says of the New Orleans battlefield: "Of all the sights I ever witnessed, that which met me there was beyond comparison the most . . . humiliating . . . nearly a thousand bodies, all of them arrayed in British uniforms."

3. Help students practice this skill by having them speculate how one of Jackson's troops might have described the scene.

build lifelong skills.

Graphic Organizer Skills

Graphic organizers in every chapter summarize key information. Cause-and-effect charts, flow charts, Venn diagrams, concept maps, and other diagrams help students visualize the connections among historical events.

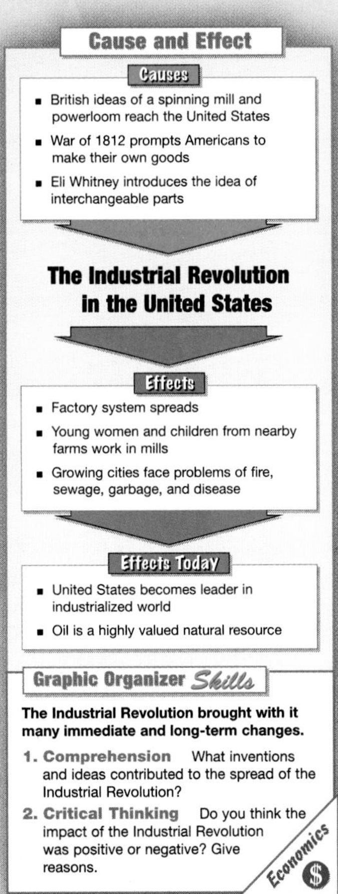

Cause and Effect
Causes
British ideas of a spinning mill and powerloom reach the United States
War of 1812 prompts Americans to make their own goods
Eli Whitney introduces the idea of interchangeable parts
The Industrial Revolution in the United States
Effects
Factory system spreads
Young women and children from nearby farms work in mills
Growing cities face problems of fire, sewage, garbage, and disease
Effects Today
United States becomes leader in industrialized world
Oil is a highly valued natural resource
Economics

Graphic Organizer Skills

The Industrial Revolution brought with it many immediate and long-term changes.

1. **Comprehension** What inventions and ideas contributed to the spread of the Industrial Revolution?
2. **Critical Thinking** Do you think the impact of the Industrial Revolution was positive or negative? Give reasons.

Map, Chart, and Graph Skills

More than 125 clear and colorful maps, graphs, charts, and graphic organizers in the student book help students learn essential content. The caption for every graphic includes questions that help students practice and apply their skills.

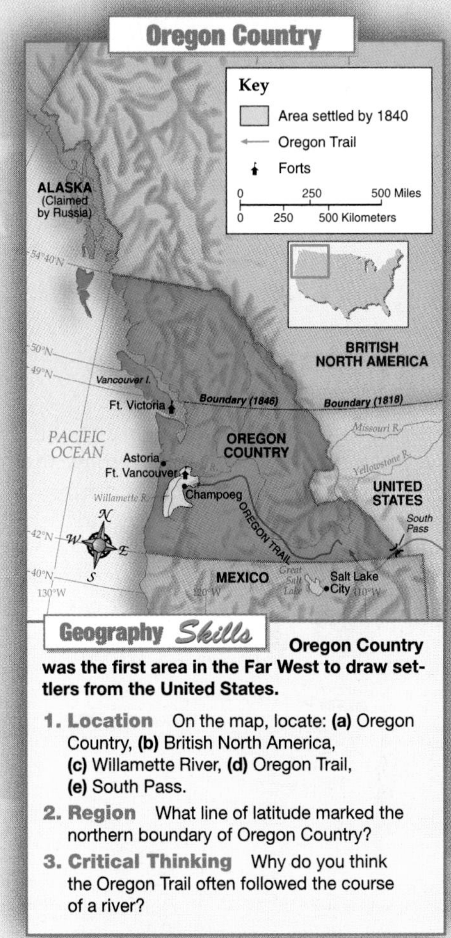

Geography Skills **Oregon Country was the first area in the Far West to draw settlers from the United States.**

1. **Location** On the map, locate: **(a)** Oregon Country, **(b)** British North America, **(c)** Willamette River, **(d)** Oregon Trail, **(e)** South Pass.
2. **Region** What line of latitude marked the northern boundary of Oregon Country?
3. **Critical Thinking** Why do you think the Oregon Trail often followed the course of a river?

Reading and Writing Skills

The Student Edition includes extensive opportunities for students to develop reading and writing skills. The Teacher's Edition provides Reading Actively and Writing Actively strategies designed by reading specialists. These strategies engage students before, during, and after reading.

Reading Actively

Before Reading Before reading the section, have students turn the main headings into main topics of an outline. Then, as they read, have them record two or three important subtopics for each main topic.

A complete array of resources to help

The American Nation provides numerous opportunities to assess your students' progress. The program includes both traditional and alternative means of assessment.

Section Assessment

Every section in the student book concludes with a comprehensive section review. In addition, the Teaching Resources provides a quiz for every section of every chapter in the student book. You can use these traditional assessment tools to gauge student comprehension and provide students with regular feedback.

Name ________________ Class ________ Date ________

CHAPTER 15 **Section 2 Quiz**

A Long, Difficult Struggle (pages 381–386)

Reviewing Key People and Places

From the box below, choose the person or place that matches the underlined phrase. Write the letter of the answer in the space provided.

a. Battle of Fredericksburg	d. Stonewall Jackson
b. Battle of Antietam	e. George McClellan
c. Battle of Shiloh	f. Ulysses S. Grant

1. The Confederate general who held his ground at the Battle of Bull Run gained a reputation for courage.
2. The commander of the Union armies in 1861 was a cautious person.
3. Neither side won a clear victory at the battle that took place in Maryland in September 1862.
4. One of the bloodiest battles of the war took place in a small village on the Tennessee River.
5. The Union general who captured Fort Henry and Fort Donelson made progress for the Union in the West.
6. In one of the Union's worst defeats, General Burnside ordered his men to charge six times.

Understanding the Main Ideas

From the box below, choose the place or term that best completes each sentence. Write the letter of the answer in the space provided.

a. Richmond	c. blockade	e. ironclad
b. Bull Run	d. defensive	f. Mississippi

1. One of the Union strategies was to ________ southern ports, cutting off the South's supply of manufactured goods from Europe.
2. The Union planned to seize control of the ________ River to keep the South from using the river to supply its troops.
3. Union generals wanted to seize ________ and capture the Confederate government there.
4. The Confederate strategy was to make the northerners tired of fighting by waging a/an ________ war.
5. Northerners were sure of a quick victory until the Battle of ________ showed that the war would be long and bloody.
6. The use of ________ ships such as the *Monitor* and the *Merrimack* changed naval warfare.

Unit 5 / Chapter 15 Section 2 Quiz 19

Chapter Assessment

The Review and Activities pages found at the end of every chapter help students review the chapter, practice geography skills, perform critical thinking and writing practice, and analyze different points of view.

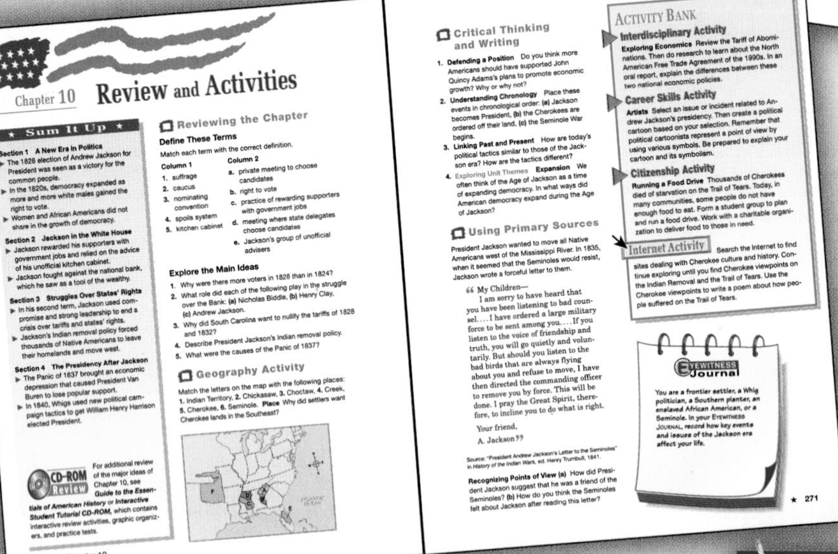

Chapter 10 **Review and Activities**

★ Sum It Up ★

Section 1 A New Era in Politics
- The 1828 election of Andrew Jackson for President was seen as a victory for the common people.
- In the 1820s, democracy expanded as more and more white males gained the right to vote.
- Women and African Americans did not share in the growth of democracy.

Section 2 Jackson in the White House
- Jackson rewarded his supporters with government jobs and relied on the advice of his unofficial kitchen cabinet.
- Jackson fought against the national bank, which he saw as a tool of the wealthy.

Section 3 Struggles Over States' Rights
- In his second term, Jackson used compromise and strong leadership to end a crisis over tariffs and states' rights.
- Jackson's Indian removal policy forced thousands of Native Americans to leave their homelands and move west.

Section 4 The Presidency After Jackson
- The Panic of 1837 brought an economic depression that caused President Van Buren to lose popular support.
- In 1840, Whigs used new political campaign tactics to get William Henry Harrison elected President.

CD-ROM Review For additional review of the major ideas of Chapter 10, see ***Guide to the Essentials of American History*** or ***Interactive Student Tutorial CD-ROM,*** which contains interactive review activities, graphic organizers, and practice tests.

Reviewing the Chapter

Define These Terms

Match each term with the correct definition.

Column 1	Column 2
1. suffrage	a. private meeting to choose candidates
2. caucus	b. right to vote
3. nominating convention	c. practice of rewarding supporters with government jobs
4. spoils system	d. meeting where state delegates choose candidates
5. kitchen cabinet	e. Jackson's group of unofficial advisers

Explore the Main Ideas

1. Why were there more voters in 1828 than in 1824?
2. What role did each of the following play in the struggle over the Bank: **(a)** Nicholas Biddle, **(b)** Henry Clay, **(c)** Andrew Jackson.
3. Why did South Carolina want to nullify the tariffs of 1828 and 1832?
4. Describe President Jackson's Indian removal policy.
5. What were the causes of the Panic of 1837?

Geography Activity

Match the letters on the map with the following places: **1.** Indian Territory, **2.** Chickasaw, **3.** Choctaw, **4.** Creek, **5.** Cherokee, **6.** Seminole. **Place** Why did settlers want Cherokee lands in the Southeast?

270 ★ Chapter 10

Critical Thinking and Writing

1. **Defending a Position** Do you think more Americans should have supported John Quincy Adams's plans to promote economic growth? Why or why not?
2. **Understanding Chronology** Place these events in chronological order: **(a)** Jackson becomes President, **(b)** the Cherokees are ordered off their land, **(c)** the Seminole War begins.
3. **Linking Past and Present** How are today's political tactics similar to those of the Jackson era? How are the tactics different?
4. Exploring Unit Themes **Expansion** We often think of the Age of Jackson as a time of expanding democracy. In what ways did American democracy expand during the Age of Jackson?

Using Primary Sources

President Jackson wanted to move all Native Americans west of the Mississippi River. In 1835, when it seemed that the Seminoles would resist, Jackson wrote a forceful letter to them.

> "My Children—
> I am sorry to have heard that you have been listening to bad counsel.... I have ordered a large military force to be sent among you.... If you listen to the voice of friendship and truth, you will go quietly and voluntarily. But should you listen to the bad birds that are always flying about you and refuse to move, I have then directed the commanding officer to remove you by force. This will be done. I pray the Great Spirit, therefore, to incline you to do what is right.
> Your friend,
> A. Jackson"

Source: "President Andrew Jackson's Letter to the Seminoles" in *History of the Indian Wars*, ed. Henry Trumbull, 1841.

Recognizing Points of View (a) How did President Jackson suggest that he was a friend of the Seminoles? **(b)** How do you think the Seminoles felt about Jackson after reading this letter?

Activity Bank

Interdisciplinary Activity

Exploring Economics Review the Tariff of Abominations. Then do research to learn about the North American Free Trade Agreement of the 1990s. In an oral report, explain the differences between these two national economic policies.

Career Skills Activity

Artists Select an issue or incident related to Andrew Jackson's presidency. Then create a political cartoon based on your selection. Remember that political cartoonists represent a point of view by using various symbols. Be prepared to explain your cartoon and its symbolism.

Citizenship Activity

Running a Food Drive Thousands of Cherokees died of starvation on the Trail of Tears. Today, in many communities, some people do not have enough food to eat. Form a student group to plan and run a food drive. Work with a charitable organization to deliver food to those in need.

Internet Activity Search the Internet to find sites dealing with Cherokee culture and history. Continue exploring until you find Cherokee viewpoints on the Indian Removal and the Trail of Tears. Use the Cherokee viewpoints to write a poem about how people suffered on the Trail of Tears.

Eyewitness Journal

You are a frontier settler, a Whig politician, a Southern planter, an enslaved African American, or a Seminole. In your Eyewitness Journal, record how key events and issues of the Jackson era affect your life.

★ 271

Interactive Student Tutorial CD-ROM

The Interactive Student Tutorial CD-ROM is a breakthrough tool for test practice. This dual-platform CD-ROM provides review of essential content in American history. Students can perform interactive exercises and practice for chapter tests.

assess student progress.

CHAPTER TESTS WITH TEST BANK CD-ROM

This book contains tests A and B with multiple-choice questions and short critical thinking and writing activities. It also includes three opportunities per chapter for students to analyze historical sources.

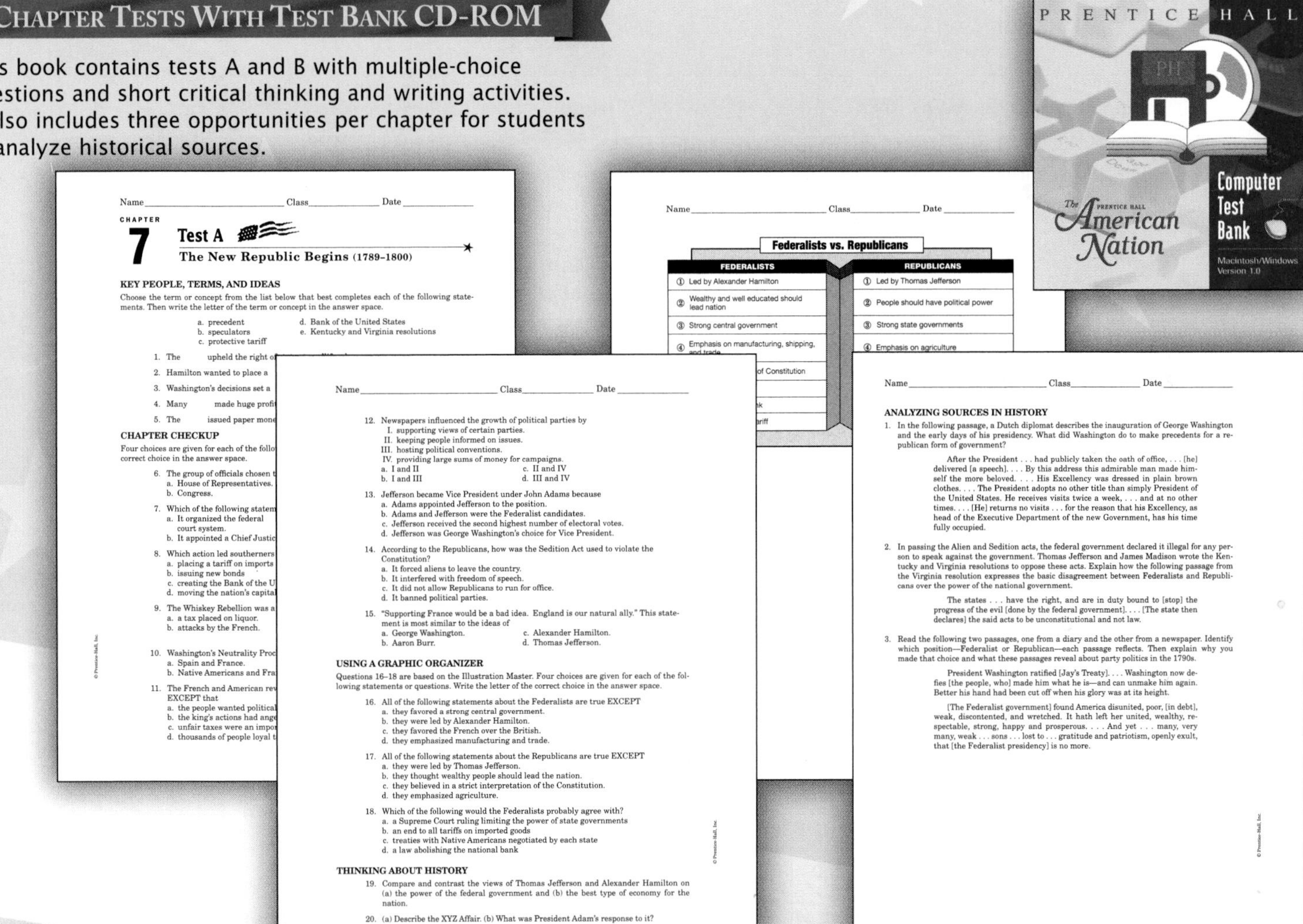

Name__________ Class__________ Date__________

CHAPTER 7 Test A

The New Republic Begins (1789–1800)

KEY PEOPLE, TERMS, AND IDEAS

Choose the term or concept from the list below that best completes each of the following statements. Then write the letter of the term or concept in the answer space.

a. precedent
b. speculators
c. protective tariff
d. Bank of the United States
e. Kentucky and Virginia resolutions

1. The ___ upheld the right o
2. Hamilton wanted to place a
3. Washington's decisions set a
4. Many ___ made huge profit
5. The ___ issued paper mone

CHAPTER CHECKUP

Four choices are given for each of the follo correct choice in the answer space.

6. The group of officials chosen t
a. House of Representatives.
b. Congress.
7. Which of the following statem
a. It organized the federal court system.
b. It appointed a Chief Justic
8. Which action led southerners
a. placing a tariff on imports
b. issuing new bonds
c. creating the Bank of the U
d. moving the nation's capita
9. The Whiskey Rebellion was a
a. a tax placed on liquor.
b. attacks by the French.
10. Washington's Neutrality Proc
a. Spain and France.
b. Native Americans and Fra
11. The French and American re EXCEPT that
a. the people wanted politica
b. the king's actions had ang
c. unfair taxes were an impo
d. thousands of people loyal t

Name__________ Class__________ Date__________

Federalists vs. Republicans

FEDERALISTS	REPUBLICANS
① Led by Alexander Hamilton	① Led by Thomas Jefferson
② Wealthy and well educated should lead nation	② People should have political power
③ Strong central government	③ Strong state governments
④ Emphasis on manufacturing, shipping, and trade	④ Emphasis on agriculture
of Constitution	

Name__________ Class__________ Date__________

12. Newspapers influenced the growth of political parties by
I. supporting views of certain parties.
II. keeping people informed on issues.
III. hosting political conventions.
IV. providing large sums of money for campaigns.
a. I and II
b. I and III
c. II and IV
d. III and IV

13. Jefferson became Vice President under John Adams because
a. Adams appointed Jefferson to the position.
b. Adams and Jefferson were the Federalist candidates.
c. Jefferson received the second highest number of electoral votes.
d. Jefferson was George Washington's choice for Vice President.

14. According to the Republicans, how was the Sedition Act used to violate the Constitution?
a. It forced aliens to leave the country.
b. It interfered with freedom of speech.
c. It did not allow Republicans to run for office.
d. It banned political parties.

15. "Supporting France would be a bad idea. England is our natural ally." This statement is most similar to the ideas of
a. George Washington.
b. Aaron Burr.
c. Alexander Hamilton.
d. Thomas Jefferson.

USING A GRAPHIC ORGANIZER

Questions 16–18 are based on the Illustration Master. Four choices are given for each of the following statements or questions. Write the letter of the correct choice in the answer space.

16. All of the following statements about the Federalists are true EXCEPT
a. they favored a strong central government.
b. they were led by Alexander Hamilton.
c. they favored the French over the British.
d. they emphasized manufacturing and trade.

17. All of the following statements about the Republicans are true EXCEPT
a. they were led by Thomas Jefferson.
b. they thought wealthy people should lead the nation.
c. they believed in a strict interpretation of the Constitution.
d. they emphasized agriculture.

18. Which of the following would the Federalists probably agree with?
a. a Supreme Court ruling limiting the power of state governments
b. an end to all tariffs on imported goods
c. treaties with Native Americans negotiated by each state
d. a law abolishing the national bank

THINKING ABOUT HISTORY

19. Compare and contrast the views of Thomas Jefferson and Alexander Hamilton on (a) the power of the federal government and (b) the best type of economy for the nation.

20. (a) Describe the XYZ Affair. (b) What was President Adam's response to it?

38 Unit 3 / Chapter 7 Test A

Name__________ Class__________ Date__________

ANALYZING SOURCES IN HISTORY

1. In the following passage, a Dutch diplomat describes the inauguration of George Washington and the early days of his presidency. What did Washington do to make precedents for a republican form of government?

> After the President . . . had publicly taken the oath of office, . . . [he] delivered [a speech]. . . . By this address this admirable man made himself the more beloved. . . . His Excellency was dressed in plain brown clothes. . . . The President adopts no other title than simply President of the United States. He receives visits twice a week, . . . and at no other times. . . . [He] returns no visits . . . for the reason that his Excellency, as head of the Executive Department of the new Government, has his time fully occupied.

2. In passing the Alien and Sedition acts, the federal government declared it illegal for any person to speak against the government. Thomas Jefferson and James Madison wrote the Kentucky and Virginia resolutions to oppose these acts. Explain how the following passage from the Virginia resolution expresses the basic disagreement between Federalists and Republicans over the power of the national government.

> The states . . . have the right, and are in duty bound to [stop] the progress of the evil [done by the federal government]. . . . [The state then declares] the said acts to be unconstitutional and not law.

3. Read the following two passages, one from a diary and the other from a newspaper. Identify which position—Federalist or Republican—each passage reflects. Then explain why you made that choice and what these passages reveal about party politics in the 1790s.

> President Washington ratified [Jay's Treaty]. . . . Washington now defies [the people, who] made him what he is—and can unmake him again. Better his hand had been cut off when his glory was at its height.

> [The Federalist government] found America disunited, poor, [in debt], weak, discontented, and wretched. It hath left her united, wealthy, respectable, strong, happy and prosperous. . . . And yet . . . many, very many, weak . . . sons . . . lost to . . . gratitude and patriotism, openly exult, that [the Federalist presidency] is no more.

42 Unit 3 / Chapter 7 Analyzing Sources in History

© Prentice-Hall, Inc.

ALTERNATIVE ASSESSMENT BOOK

There are opportunities throughout the program to use alternative means of assessment. The ALTERNATIVE ASSESSMENT book contains rubrics and evaluation guides for every type of activity-based assessment contained in the student book.

10 • Alternative Assessment

Name __________ Date __________
Class __________

Analyzing a Primary Source Rubric

	Exemplary	Adequate	Minimal	Attempted
Analysis of Document	Offers in-depth analysis and interpretation of the document; distinguishes between fact and opinion; explores reliability of author; compares and contrasts author's point of view with views of others	Offers accurate analysis of the document	Demonstrates only a minimal understanding of the document	Reiterates one or two facts from the document but does not offer any analysis or interpretation of the document
Knowledge of Historical Context	Shows evidence of thorough knowledge of period in which source was written; relates primary source to specific historical context in which it was written	Uses previous general historical knowledge to examine issues included in document	Limited use of previous historical knowledge without complete accuracy	Barely indicates any previous historical knowledge
Identification of Key Issues/Main Points	Identifies the key issues and main points included in the primary source; shows understanding of author's goal(s)	Identifies most but not all of the key issues and main points in the primary source	Describes in general terms one issue or concept included in the primary source	Deals only briefly and vaguely with the key issues and main points in the document
Resources	Uses several outside resources in addition to primary source	Uses 1–2 outside resources in addition to primary source	Relies heavily on the material/information provided	Relies exclusively on the material/information provided; no evidence of outside resources
Identification of Literary Devices	Analyzes author's use of literary devices such as repetition, irony, analogy, and sarcasm	Mentions author's use of literary devices but does not develop fully	Does not discuss author's use of literary devices	Does not discuss author's use of literary devices
Understanding of Audience	Shows strong understanding of author's audience	Shows some understanding of author's audience	Shows little understanding of author's audience	Shows no understanding of author's audience

ALTERNATIVE ASSESSMENT

Topic	See Prentice Hall Literature. Timeless Voices, Timeless Themes*
Unit 1 • Early Heritage of the Americas	
Skills for Life: Listening, page 40 (Native American folklore)	Zuni, The Girl Who Hunted Rabbits (folk tale), Unit 1 Part 1
People of the Southwest, pages 39–41 (ways of life)	Zuni retold by Richard Erdoes and Alfonso Ortiz, Coyote Steals the Sun and Moon (creation story), Unit 10 Part 1, and Mourning Dove, The Spirit Chief Names the Animal People (creation story), Unit 10 Part 1
Columbus Reaches the Americas, pages 62–64	Joaquin Miller, Columbus (Poem), Unit 2 Part 1
Governing New Spain, pages 68–70 (Spanish settlement in the Americas)	Roberto Felix Salazar, The Other Pioneers (poem), Unit 2 Part 1
Pilgrims Seek Religious Freedom, pages 88–89	William Bradford, The Pilgrim's Landing and First Winter (nonfiction), Unit 2 Part 1
Unit 2 • A Nation Is Born	
Lexington and Concord, pages 154–155 (Paul Revere)	Henry Wadsworth Longellow, Paul Revere's Ride (poem), Unit 3 Part 2
Declaration of Independence, pages 166–168	John Adams, Jefferson Is Selected to Write the Declaration of Independence (nonfiction), Unit 3 Part 2, and Thomas Jefferson, Getting Advice From Ben Franklin (nonfiction), Unit 3 Part 2
Civic Values, page 235	Edward Everett Hale, The Man Without a Country (short story), Unit 4 Part 1
Unit 3 • The Nation Takes Shape	
To the Mississippi, pages 301–302 (moving westward)	Rosemary Carr Benét, Johnny Appleseed (poem), Unit 10, and Davy Crockett, Davy Crockett's Dream (tall tale) and Tussle With a Bear (tall tale), Unit 10 Part 2
Steam Transport, pages 303–305 (steamboats)	Mark Twain, Cub Pilot on the Mississippi (nonfiction), Unit 2

* The references to Prentice Hall Literature: Timeless Voices, Timeless Themes are from the Silver edition.

Connections With Literature

Unit 4 • The Nation Expands

Topic	See Prentice Hall Literature. Timeless Voices, Timeless Themes*
The Lure of Oregon, page 346	Carl Sandburg, Paul Bunyan of the North Woods (tall tale), Unit 10 Part 2
Wagon Trains West, pages 349–350	Stephen Vincent Benét, Western Wagons (poem), Unit 2 Part 1
A Mix of Cultures in the Southwest, page 364	José Griego y Maestas and Rudolfo A. Anaya, Chicoria (Mexican American cuento), Unit 10 Part 1
Life Without Freedom, pages 390–393 (African American folk tales)	Jackie Torrence, Brer Possum's Dilemma (African American tale), Unit 10 Part 1, and Zora Neale Hurston, How the Waves Got Whitecaps (African American tale), Unit 10 Part 1
The Underground Railroad, pages 405–407 (Harriet Tubman)	Ann Petry, Harriet Tubman: Guide to Freedom (nonfiction), Unit 2 Part 1
New Opportunities, pages 410–411 (new careers for women)	Eve Merriam, Elizabeth Blackwell (poem), Unit 3 Part 2
American Storytellers, pages 412–413 (Edgar Allan Poe)	Edgar Allan Poe, The Tell-Tale Heart (short story), Unit 6 Part 1
Poetic Voices, pages 414–415 (Henry Wadsworth Longfellow)	Henry Wadsworth Longfellow, The Wreck of the Hesperus (poem), Unit 9 Part 1
Poetic Voices, pages 414–415 (Walt Whitman)	Walt Whitman, Poets to Come (poem), Unit 1 Part 2

Unit 5 • Division and Reunion

Topic	See Prentice Hall Literature. Timeless Voices, Timeless Themes*
The War in the West, page 458 (Battle of Shiloh)	Ray Bradbury, The Drummer Boy of Shiloh (short story), Unit 1
The Emancipation Proclamation, pages 459–461	Russell Freedman, Emancipation from Lincoln: A Photobiography (nonfiction), Unit 3 Part 1
The Hard Life of Soldiers, page 463	Ambrose Bierce, The Horseman in the Sky (short story), Unit 6 Part 1
Lincoln is Assassinated, pages 480–481	Walt Whitman, O Captain! My Captain! (poem), Unit 3 Part 1
Postwar Problems, pages 478–479	Arna Bontemps, Southern Mansion (poem), Unit 5 Part 2

Topic	See Prentice Hall Science Explorer
Unit 1 • Early Heritage of the Americas	
Maps and Mapmaking, pages 8–13	***Earth's Changing Surface,*** **Chapter 1.3, Mapping the Earth's Surface**
Physical Regions of North America, pages 14–17	***Environmental Science,*** **Chapter 2.4, Earth's Biomes**
Types of Landforms, page 14	***Earth's Changing Surface,*** **Chapter 1.2, Landforms and Landscapes**
Rivers and Lakes, pages 17–18	***Earth's Water,*** **Chapter 2.1, Streams and Rivers, and Chapter 2.2, Ponds and Lakes**
Weather and Climate, pages 19–21	***Weather and Climate,*** **Chapter 4.1, What Causes Climate?**
North American Climates, pages 21–23	***Weather and Climate,*** **Chapter 4.2, Climate Regions**
The First English Colonies, page 86 (tobacco)	***Human Biology and Health,*** **Chapter 5.2, Integrating Health: Smoking**
Unit 2 • A Nation Is Born	
The Spread of New Ideas, pages 121–122 (gravity)	***Motion, Forces, and Energy,*** **Chapter 2.3, Friction and Gravity**
Because National Symbols Unite Us, page 207 (eagle population)	***Environmental Science,*** **Chapter 1.3, Integrating Mathematics: Changes in Population**
The Executive Branch, pages 228–230 (National Aeronautics and Space Administration)	***Astronomy,*** **Chapter 1.3, Integrating Technology: Into Space**
The Executive Branch, pages 228–230 (Department of Transportation)	***Environmental Science,*** **Chapter 5.1, Sources of Air Pollution**
Unit 3 • The Nation Takes Shape	
Jefferson Plans An Expedition, page 272 (mapping)	***Earth's Changing Surface,*** **Chapter 1.3, Mapping the Earth's Surface**
The Lewis and Clark Expedition, pages 272–275 (wildlife)	***Animals,*** **Chapter 4.4, Kinds of Mammals**
Because Technology Continues to Change Our Lives, page 298 (computer)	***Electricity and Magnetism,*** **Chapter 4.3, Computers**
Growing Cities, page 299–300 (fire hazards)	***Chemical Interactions,*** **Chapter 1.4, Fire and Fire Safety**
Steam Transport, pages 303–305 (travel velocity)	***Motion, Forces, and Energy,*** **Chapter 1.1, Describing and Measuring Motion**

Connections With Science

Topic	See Prentice Hall Science Explorer
Unit 4 • The Nation Expands	
Early Years in California, page 356 (climate)	*Weather and Climate,* Chapter 4.2, Climate Regions
A Refuge for the Mormons, pages 365–366 (irrigation systems)	*Earth's Water,* Chapter 3.2, Balancing Water Needs
New Machines, page 374 (farming inventions)	*From Bacteria to Plants,* Chapter 5.5, Feeding the World
The Telegraph, page 375	*Electricity and Magnetism,* Chapter 4.2, Electronic Communication
Because the Fight Against Alcohol Abuse Continues, page 400	*Human Biology and Health,* Chapter 7.4, Integrating Health: The Effects of Alcohol and Other Drugs
Unit 5 • Division and Reunion	
Naval Action, pages 456–457 (ironclad ships)	*Motion, Forces, and Energy,* Chapter 2.3, Floating and Sinking
Hard Life of Soldiers, page 463 (disease)	*Human Biology and Health,* Chapter 6.1, Infectious Disease
The Southern Economy, pages 466–467 (famine)	*Human Biology and Health,* Chapter 3.1, Why You Need Food
Industry and the "New South," pages 492–493	*Inside Earth,* Chapter 4.2, Mineral Resources

Topic	See Prentice Hall Middle Grades Mathematics
Unit 1 • Early Heritage of the Americas	
Exact Location, page 4 (latitude and longitude)	**Course 3, Graphing on the Coordinate Plane, Lesson 10-7**
Maps and Mapmaking, pages 8–13	**Course 2, Exploring Maps and Scale Drawings, Lesson 6-5**
Time Zones, pages 12–13	**Course 1, Modeling Subtraction of Integers, Lesson 10-4**
Physical Regions of North America, pages 14–17	**Course 3, Units of Measurement, Lesson 6-2**
Reading a Line Graph, page 71	**Course 1, Making Bar and Line Graphs, Lesson 1-6**
Reading a Pie Graph, page 101	**Course 1, Data and Circle Graphs, Lesson 7-10**
Unit 2 • A Nation Is Born	
Organizing the Northwest Territory, pages 190–191 (townships and sections)	**Course 1, Estimating Area, Lesson 9-1**
The Three-Fifths Compromise, page 196	**Course 1, Using Fraction Models, Lesson 5-8**
The Legislative Branch, page 225	**Course 1, Patterns and Number Sense, Lesson 2-1**
Unit 3 • The Nation Takes Shape	
Battling the National Debt, pages 245–246	**Course 3, Solving Proportions, Lesson 6-3**
Hamilton's Plan, pages 246–247 (speculation)	**Course 1, Investigating Fractions, Lesson 5-9**
Building Up the Economy, pages 247–249 (bar graph)	**Course 2, Interpreting Graphs, Lesson 10-7**
Limits on Trade, page 278 (United States exports)	**Course 3, Organizing and Displaying Data, Lesson 1-1**
Growing Cities, pages 299–300 (urbanization)	**Course 1, Percents, Fractions, and Decimals, Lesson 7-7**
Protection From Foreign Competition, pages 309–310 (protective tariffs)	**Course 1, Finding the Percent of a Number, Lesson 7-9**

Topic	See Prentice Hall Middle Grades Mathematics
Unit 4 • The Nation Expands	
More Voters, page 326 (expanding suffrage)	**Course 1, Percents, Fractions, and Decimals, Lesson 7-7**
Wagon Trains West, pages 349–350 (converting miles to kilometers)	**Course 1, Metric Units of Length, Lesson 3-8**
Dividing Oregon, page 360 (latitude and longitude)	**Course 3, Graphic Points, Lesson 4-1**
The First Railroads, page 376 (determining distance)	**Course 3, Formulas, Lesson 3-4**
Cotton Gin, Cotton Boom, pages 383–384	**Course 2, Interpreting Graphs, Lesson 10-7**
Unit 5 • Division and Reunion	
The Election of 1860, page 440 (reading circle graphs)	**Course 2, Using Data to Persuade, Lesson 1-8**
Strengths and Weaknesses, pages 448–450 (reading a table)	**Course 1, Make a Table, Lesson 1-2**
Early Plan for Reconstruction, page 484 (Ten Percent Plan)	**Course 1, Percent Sense Using Models, Lesson 7-6**
Johnson Is Impeached, pages 484–485 (two-thirds majority)	**Course 2, Percents, Fractions, and Decimals, Lesson 6-7**
Election of 1876, pages 491–492 (popular and electoral votes)	**Course 2, Circle Graphs, Lesson 7-8**

Block Scheduling help throughout

The American Nation program provides help to meet your block scheduling needs. Flexibility is key to your success. The Teacher's Edition, Teaching Resources, Student Performance Pack, Resource Pro® and additional integrated technology provide the opportunity for you to expand coverage of every topic or to cover essential content in limited time.

Classroom Manager

Choose which resources you need to provide varied activities in longer instructional periods. The Classroom Manager provides a chapter-by-chapter guide to resources at your fingertips. Critical thinking and writing correlations help you meet social studies standards.

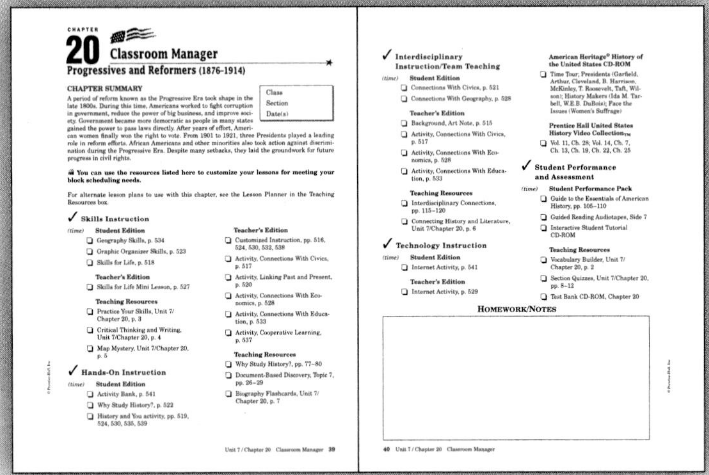

CHAPTER 20 **Classroom Manager**

Progressives and Reformers (1876–1914)

Class
Section
Date(s)

CHAPTER SUMMARY

A period of reform known as the Progressive Era took shape in the late 1800s. During this time, Americans worked to fight corruption in government, reduce the power of big business, and improve society. Government became more democratic as people in many states gained the power to pass laws directly. After years of effort, American women finally won the right to vote. From 1901 to 1921, three Presidents played a leading role in reform efforts. African Americans and other minorities also took action against discrimination during the Progressive Era. Despite many setbacks, they laid the groundwork for future progress in civil rights.

You can use the resources listed here to customize your lessons for meeting your block scheduling needs.

For alternate lesson plans to use with this chapter, see the Lesson Planner in the Teaching Resources box.

✓ **Skills Instruction**

(time) **Student Edition**
- ❑ Geography Skills, p. 534
- ❑ Graphic Organizer Skills, p. 523
- ❑ Skills for Life, p. 518

Teacher's Edition
- ❑ Skills for Life Mini Lesson, p. 527

Teaching Resources
- ❑ Practice Your Skills, Unit 7/Chapter 20, p. 3
- ❑ Critical Thinking and Writing, Unit 7/Chapter 20, p. 4
- ❑ Map Mystery, Unit 7/Chapter 20, p. 5

Teacher's Edition
- ❑ Customized Instruction, pp. 516, 524, 530, 532, 538
- ❑ Activity, Connections With Civics, p. 517
- ❑ Activity, Linking Past and Present, p. 520
- ❑ Activity, Connections With Economics, p. 528
- ❑ Activity, Connections With Education, p. 533
- ❑ Activity, Cooperative Learning, p. 537

Teaching Resources
- ❑ Why Study History?, pp. 77–80
- ❑ Document-Based Discovery, Topic 7, pp. 26–29
- ❑ Biography Flashcards, Unit 7/Chapter 20, p. 7

✓ **Hands-On Instruction**

(time) **Student Edition**
- ❑ Activity Bank, p. 541
- ❑ Why Study History?, p. 522
- ❑ History and You activity, pp. 519, 524, 530, 535, 539

Unit 7 / Chapter 20 Classroom Manager 39

✓ **Interdisciplinary Instruction/Team Teaching**

(time) **Student Edition**
- ❑ Connections With Civics, p. 521
- ❑ Connections With Geography, p. 528

Teacher's Edition
- ❑ Background, Art Note, p. 515
- ❑ Activity, Connections With Civics, p. 517
- ❑ Activity, Connections With Economics, p. 528
- ❑ Activity, Connections With Education, p. 533

Teaching Resources
- ❑ Interdisciplinary Connections, pp. 115–120
- ❑ Connecting History and Literature, Unit 7/Chapter 20, p. 6

✓ **Technology Instruction**

(time) **Student Edition**
- ❑ Internet Activity, p. 541

Teacher's Edition
- ❑ Internet Activity, p. 529

American Heritage® History of the United States CD-ROM
- ❑ Time Tour; Presidents (Garfield, Arthur, Cleveland, B. Harrison, McKinley, T. Roosevelt, Taft, Wilson); History Makers (Ida M. Tarbell, W.E.B. DuBois); Face the Issues (Women's Suffrage)

Prentice Hall United States History Video Collection™
- ❑ Vol. 11, Ch. 28; Vol. 14, Ch. 7, Ch. 13, Ch. 19, Ch. 22, Ch. 25

✓ **Student Performance and Assessment**

(time) **Student Performance Pack**
- ❑ Guide to the Essentials of American History, pp. 105–110
- ❑ Guided Reading Audiotapes, Side 7
- ❑ Interactive Student Tutorial CD-ROM

Teaching Resources
- ❑ Vocabulary Builder, Unit 7/Chapter 20, p. 2
- ❑ Section Quizzes, Unit 7/Chapter 20, pp. 8–12
- ❑ Test Bank CD-ROM, Chapter 20

Homework/Notes

40 Unit 7 / Chapter 20 Classroom Manager

Point-of-Use Block Scheduling Activities

Point-of-use activity suggestions in the Teacher's Edition meet your need to engage students' interest, using a variety of techniques.

★ Activity ★

Connections With Arts

Describing a geographic setting Discuss the importance of setting in literature. Give an example of a story with an interesting setting, such as a mountain. Ask students to write a 3-paragraph story using a particular geographic setting. Then have them rewrite the story in a new setting. Ask students to discuss how their ... and why. (average)

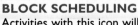

★ Customized Instruction ★

Extroverted Learners

Conducting an interview Point out to students that although the Embargo Act of 1807 was very unpopular, the Republicans won the presidential election of 1808. Have students suppose that it is several weeks before the 1808 election. Ask them to take the role of journalists interviewing the Republican candidate, James Madison. Have students work in pairs to prepare questions for Madison such as "How do you feel about the effects of the Embargo Act ... intercourse Act on Americans?" ... do you plan to stop violations ... neutrality?" Have partners take ... of interviewer and candidate in ... and-answer session. (*challengin*...

★ Activity ★

Connections With Mathematics

Counting troops In the Union Army: 10 companies = 1 regiment; 4 regiments = 1 brigade; 4 brigades = 1 division; 1–2 divisions = one army corps. On paper, a regiment had about 1,000 troops. Ask: How many soldiers were in a company? *(100)* Brigade? *(4,000)* Division? *(16,000)* Corps of 2 divisions? *(32,000)* (basic)

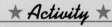

BLOCK SCHEDULING
Activities with this icon will help you meet Block Scheduling needs.

the program.

PACING GUIDE FOR AMERICAN HISTORY

You can use this pacing guide to plan your course in American History. It is based on two semesters of 44 days per semester for a total of 88 days of instruction. This guide is just a model. You may need to modify it to meet the needs of your class or your block schedule configuration.

UNIT OF STUDY	PERIODS
Focus on Geography (Prehistory–Present)	4
The First Americans (Prehistory–1600)	3
A Meeting of Different Worlds (1100–1700)	5
The 13 English Colonies (1630–1750)	6
The Road to Revolution (1745–1775)	4
The American Revolution (1775–1783)	6
Creating a Republic (1776–1791)	4
Civics Overview: The Constitution at Work (1789–Present)	6
The New Republic Begins (1789–1800)	6
The Age of Jefferson (1801–1816)	4
Industry and Growth (1790–1825)	4
Democracy in the Age of Jackson (1824–1840)	4
Westward Expansion (1820–1860)	6
The Worlds of North and South (1820–1860)	4
An Era of Reform (1820–1860)	4
A Dividing Nation (1820–1861)	5
The Civil War (1861–1865)	6
The Reconstruction Era (1864–1877)	4
Linking Past to Present (1877–Present)	3

RESOURCE PRO® CD-ROM

Plan your lessons to fit your block scheduling needs. Award-winning RESOURCE PRO® WITH PLANNING EXPRESS® CD-ROM lets you customize and create daily lesson plans at the touch of a button.

Easy-to-use integrated technology.

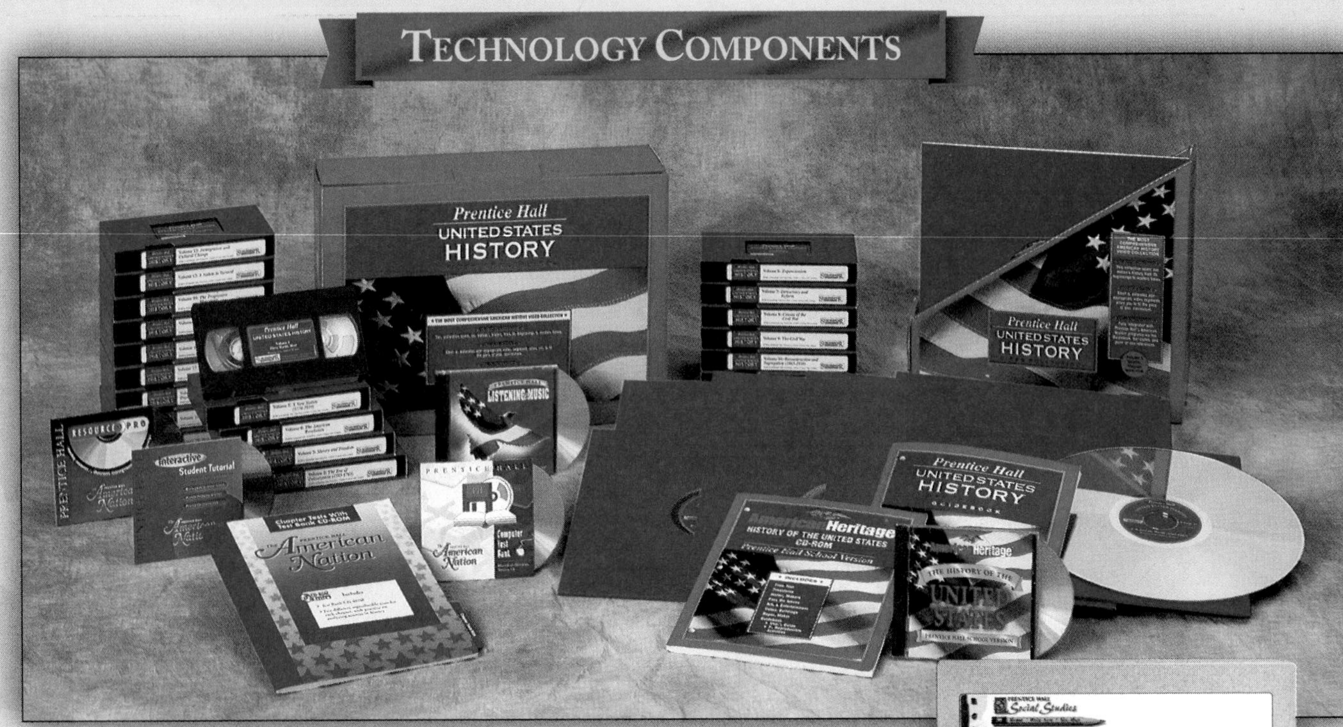

PRENTICE HALL SCHOOL WEB SITE

This comprehensive social studies INTERNET WEB SITE—at www.phschool.com—helps you stay current on key issues. It provides you with the tools to link past and present to students' lives. The site has discussion groups that let you share ideas, receive professional development, and much more.

www.phschool.com

THE AMERICAN NATION TECHNOLOGY PROGRAM

- Interactive Student Tutorial CD-ROM
- Guided Reading Audiotapes (English and Spanish)
- Book on Audiotapes
- Listening to Music CD
- Listening to Literature Audiotapes
- Resource Pro® With Planning Express® CD-ROM
- American Heritage® History of the United States CD-ROM
- Prentice Hall United States History Video Collection™

Use these bar codes to control your videodisc player when using the Prentice Hall United States History Video Collection™.

English

Spanish

Play

Pause

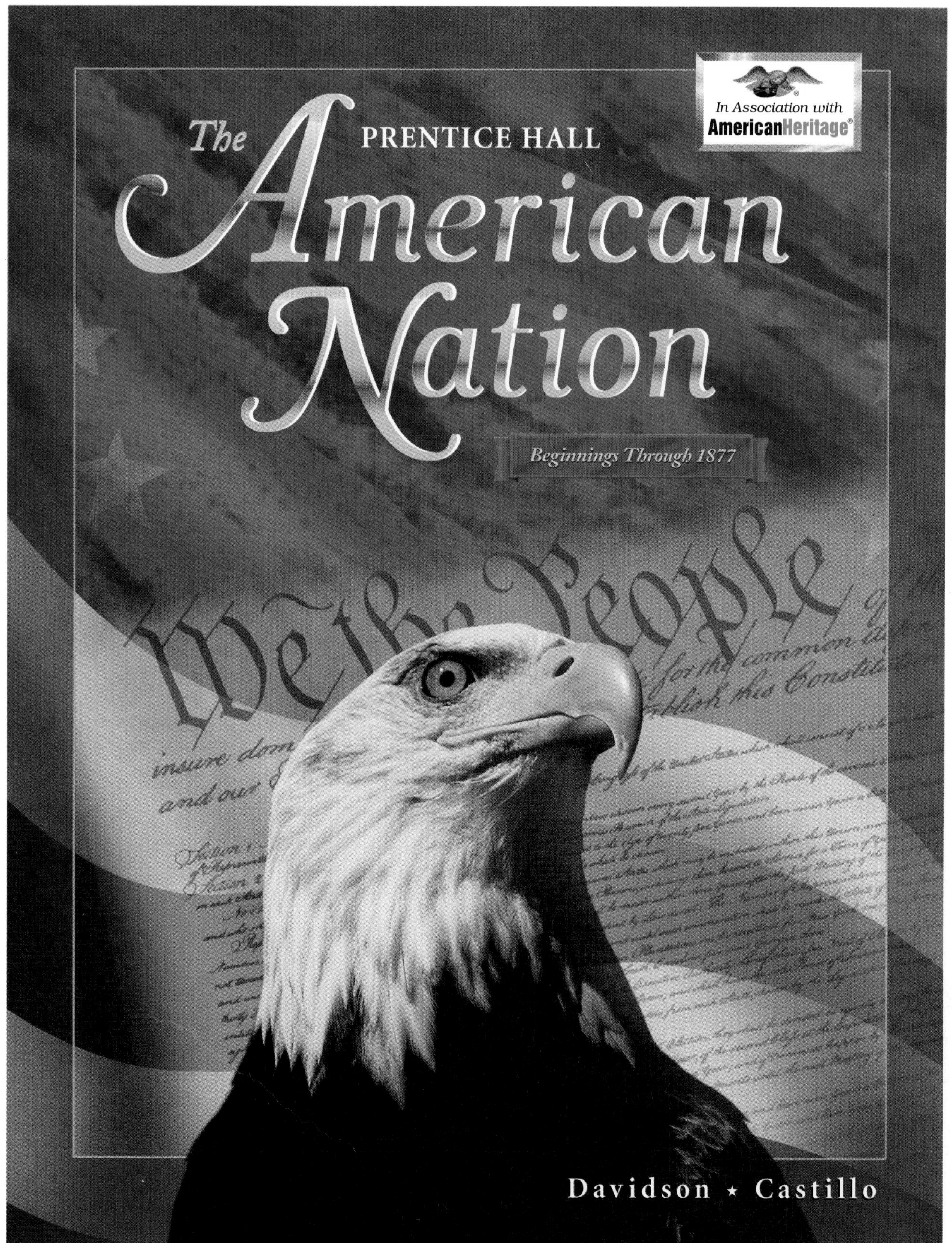

PRENTICE HALL
Upper Saddle River, New Jersey
Needham, Massachusetts

Authors

James West Davidson is coauthor of *After the Fact: The Art of Historical Detection* and *Nation of Nations: A Narrative History of the American Republic.* Dr. Davidson has taught at both the college and high school levels. He has also consulted on curriculum design for American history courses. Dr. Davidson is an avid canoeist and hiker. His published works on these subjects include *Great Heart,* the true story of a 1903 canoe trip in the Canadian wilderness.

Pedro Castillo teaches American history at the University of California, Santa Cruz, where he also co-directs the Chicano-Latino Research Center. He has earned a Rockefeller Foundation Research Fellowship and two Senior Fulbright-Hayes Lectureships in Latin America. Dr. Castillo's published works on American history and Chicano Latino history include *Mexico en Los Angeles* and *An Illustrated History of Mexican Los Angeles.*

AmericanHeritage® *American Heritage* magazine was founded in 1954, and it quickly rose to the position it occupies today: the country's preeminent magazine of history and culture. Dedicated to presenting the past in incisive, entertaining narratives underpinned by scrupulous scholarship, *American Heritage* today goes to more than 300,000 subscribers and counts the country's very best writers and historians among its contributors. Its innovative use of historical illustration and its wide variety of subject matter have gained the publication scores of honors across more than forty years, among them the National Magazine Awards.

Acknowledgments and Illustration Credits begin on page 652.

PRENTICE HALL

Printed in the United States of America.

ISBN 0-13-434902-4

1 2 3 4 5 6 7 8 9 10   02 01 00 99 98

Upper Saddle River, New Jersey   Needham, Massachusetts

Program Reviewers

Academic Consultants

David Beaulieu, Ph.D.
Director of Office of Indian Education
U.S. Department of Education
Washington, D.C.

Richard Beeman, Ph.D.
Professor of History
University of Pennsylvania
Philadelphia, Pennsylvania

William Childs, Ph.D.
Associate Professor of History
Ohio State University
Columbus, Ohio

Heidi Hayes Jacobs, Ed.D.
President, Curriculum Designs, Inc.
Rye, New York
Adjunct Professor of Curriculum and Teaching
Columbia University
New York, New York

Tetsuden Kashima, Ph.D.
Associate Professor of American Ethnic Studies
University of Washington
Seattle, Washington

Emma Lapsansky, Ph.D.
Professor of History and Curator of Special Collections
Haverford College
Haverford, Pennsylvania

Lyn Reese
Director, Women in World History Curriculum
Berkeley, California

Joel Silbey, Ph.D.
Professor of History
Cornell University
Ithaca, New York

Teacher Reviewers

Buckley Bangert
Social Studies Teacher
Ortega Middle School
Alamosa, Colorado

Clement R. Brown, III
Social Studies Teacher
Madison Junior High School
Naperville, Illinois

Lynn Castiaux
Social Studies Teacher/Mentor
Sylvan Middle School
Citrus Heights, California

Leslie Clark
Team Teacher
Lincoln Middle School
Hawthorne, New Jersey

Sandra Lee Eades, Ph.D.
Social Studies Content Leader
Ridgely Middle School
Lutherville, Maryland

Beverly Hooper
Social Studies Teacher
Dartmouth School
San Jose, California

Joseph Mancusi
Assistant Principal
Westhill School
Stamford, Connecticut

Bill McElree
Social Studies Teacher
Vista Compana Middle School
Apple Valley, California

Denis O'Rourke
Chairman, Dept. of Social Studies
Hommocks Middle School
Larchmont, New York

Sharon L. Pope
Secondary Social Studies Coordinator
Spring Branch Independent School District
Houston, Texas

Jill Schumacher
Social Studies Teacher
Brown Middle School
McAllen, Texas

Reading Specialist

Bonnie Armbruster, Ph.D.
Professor of Education
University of Illinois at Urbana–Champaign
Champaign, Illinois

Accuracy Panel

Esther Ratner
Greyherne Information Services
With Marvin Beckerman, Ph.D., University of Missouri–St. Louis

Muriel Beckerman, University of Missouri–St. Louis

Lynn D. Hoover, The Hoover Associates

Jane B. Malcolm, Professional Research Services

Bennet J. Parstek, Ed.D., St. John's University, New York

Alice Radosh, Ph.D., Academy of Educational Development

Lorraine Rosenberg, Baldwin School District, New York (Ret.)

Cathy S. Zazueta, California State University, Los Angeles

UNIT 1 Early Heritage of the Americas xvi

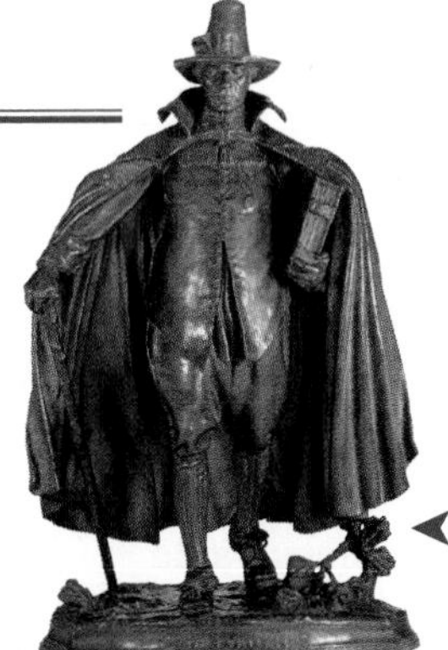

Statue of a New England Puritan

Chapter Source Readings

Anasazi pottery

UNIT 2 A Nation Is Born 128

Early American flag

Chapter Source Readings

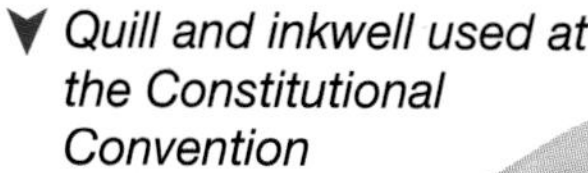

Quill and inkwell used at the Constitutional Convention

UNIT 3 The Nation Takes Shape 240

Thomas Jefferson

The Louisiana Purchase

Women factory workers

Unit 4 The Nation Expands 320

African American preacher

Chapter Source Readings

Conestoga wagon

Unit 5 Division and Reunion 420

Civil War army caps

Chapter Source Readings

Emancipation Proclamation

Reference Section

Special Features

★ *With the editors of* American Heritage *magazine as your guides, you see and read about special sites where American history happened.*

HISTORY HAPPENED HERE

▲ *The Erie Canal*

Linking ...

★ *The Linking features use engaging visuals to make historical connections.*

Linking Past and Present

Linking History and Technology

Linking United States and the World

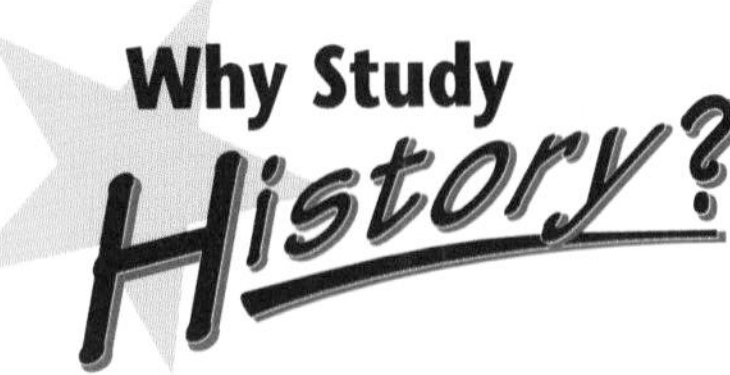

★ *These high-interest features show how history is relevant to American life today and to your life in particular.*

▲ *Because you will choose our nation's leaders*

Viewpoints: Source Readings in American History

★ *Eyewitness accounts, historical documents, and literature selections provide you with different viewpoints on American history.*

Eyewitness Accounts

Historical Documents

Literature

★ *Learn and practice valuable skills: Critical Thinking; Managing Information; Communication; and Maps, Charts, and Graphs.*

▲ *Using the Internet*

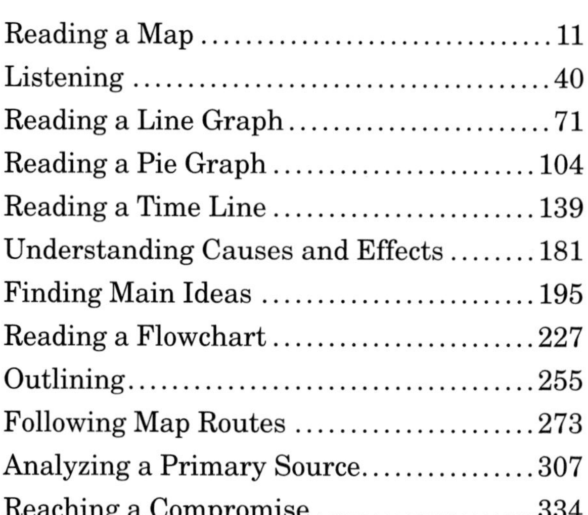

Charts, Graphs, and Time Lines

Continued

Charts, Graphs, and Time Lines (continued)

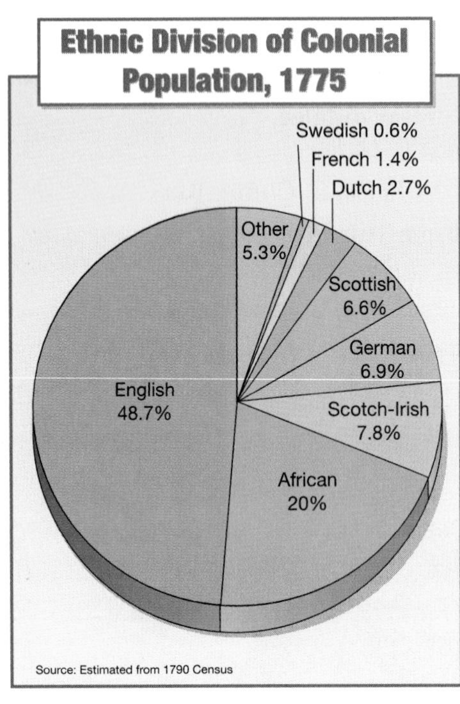

Graphic Organizers

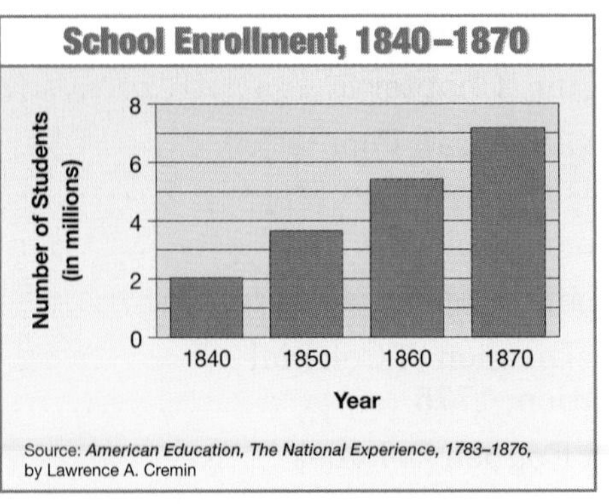

Maps and Geography Activities

Geography Activities

Geographic Atlas

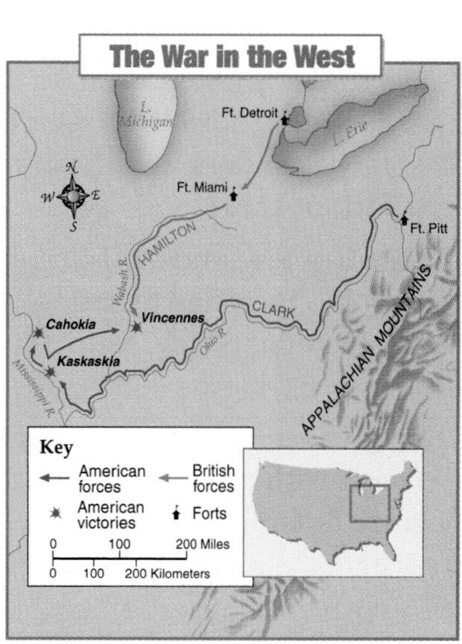

About This Book

The American Nation is organized into 9 units and 30 chapters. The Table of Contents lists units, chapters, sections, and special features.

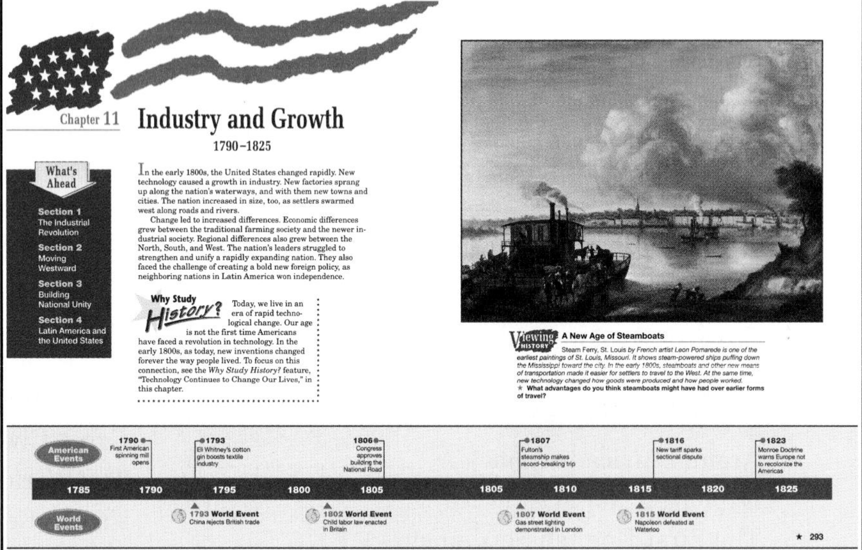

Chapter 11

Industry and Growth

1790–1825

What's Ahead

Section 1 The Industrial Revolution

Section 2 Moving Westward

Section 3 Building National Unity

Section 4 Latin America and the United States

In the early 1800s, the United States changed rapidly. New technology caused a growth in industry. New factories sprang up along the nation's waterways, and with them new towns and cities. The nation increased in size, too, as settlers swarmed west along roads and rivers.

Change led to increased differences. Economic differences grew between the traditional farming society and the newer industrial society. Regional differences also grew between the North, South, and West. The nation's leaders struggled to strengthen and unify a rapidly expanding nation. They also faced the challenge of creating a bold new foreign policy, as neighboring nations in Latin America won independence.

Why Study History? Today, we live in an era of rapid technological change. Our age is not the first time Americans have faced a revolution in technology. In the early 1800s, as today, new inventions changed forever the way people lived. To focus on this connection, see the *Why Study History?* feature, "Technology Continues to Change Our Lives," in this chapter.

Viewing History A New Age of Steamboats

Steam Ferry, St. Louis by French artist Leon Pomarede is one of the earliest paintings of St. Louis, Missouri. It shows steam-powered ships puffing down the Mississippi toward the city. In the early 1800s, steamboats and other new means of transportation made it easier for settlers to travel to the West. At the same time, new technology changed how goods were produced and how people worked.

★ **What advantages do you think steamboats might have had over earlier forms of travel?**

American Events

1790 First American spinning mill opens

1793 Eli Whitney's cotton gin boosts textile industry

1806 Congress approves building the National Road

1807 Fulton's steamship makes record-breaking trip

1816 New tariff sparks sectional dispute

1823 Monroe Doctrine warns Europe not to recolonize the Americas

1785 1790 1795 1800 1805 1805 1810 1815 1820 1825

World Events

1793 World Event China rejects British trade

1802 World Event Child labor law enacted in Britain

1807 World Event Gas street lighting demonstrated in London

1815 World Event Napoleon defeated at Waterloo

★ 293

In Each Unit

- **Unit Opener** a two-page introduction to the contents and major theme of the unit.
- **History Through Literature** a two-page excerpt from a work of American literature.

In Each Chapter

- **Chapter Opener** a two-page introduction that includes a time line and chapter summary.
- **As You Read** an introduction to each section, including questions to guide your reading and lists of vocabulary terms and people.
- **Section Reviews** questions and activities that test your understanding of each section.
- **Skills for Life** a lesson that helps you to learn, practice, and apply a useful skill.
- **Linking...** Past and Present, or United States and the World, or History and Technology is a visual feature that shows interesting connections.
- **Biographies** portraits of and information about key people in American history.
- **Interdisciplinary Connections** footnotes that give connections to Geography, Economics, Civics, Arts, or Science.
- **Maps, Graphs, and Charts** visual tools that help you understand history and practice important skills.
- **Chapter Review and Activities** two pages to help you review key terms and ideas and practice valuable skills, with these special features:
  - *Using Primary Sources,* a primary source excerpt with questions that help you recognize different points of view.
  - *Activity Bank,* includes Interdisciplinary, Career Skills, Citizenship, and Internet activities.
  - *Eyewitness Journal,* writing activity that lets you take on different historical roles.
  - *Critical Thinking and Writing,* questions and exercises that go beyond simple recall.

Special Features

- **Why Study History?** This feature demonstrates the relevance of historical ideas and events to American life today and to your life in particular.
- **AmericanHeritage® Magazine History Happened Here** The editors of *American Heritage* magazine are your guides to interesting historic sites throughout the nation.

Reference Section

- Includes an Atlas, a Gazetteer, a Glossary, the Declaration of Independence, the Constitution of the United States, documents, information about the fifty states, information about the Presidents of the United States, and an Index.

Researching on the Internet

THE INTERNET

The **Internet** includes millions of business, governmental, educational, and individual computers on the World Wide Web. Using programs called browsers, Internet users can find out what sites are available on the Web and then access those sites.

SEARCHING THE INTERNET

There are two basic ways to find information on the Internet. The first is to go directly to the Net site that contains the information you want. Each site has an address, called a **URL,** or Universal Resource Locator. (For example, http://www.phschool.com is the URL of the Prentice Hall Web site.) Of course, this method works only if you know the appropriate URL.

The second way is to use a **search engine,** such as Infoseek or Yahoo! Type the key words representing the topic you want to research. The search engine will then scan the Internet and list sites that pertain to your topic.

Whichever method you choose, you will encounter sites containing **hyperlinks.** These appear as colored or underlined text or as icons. Hyperlinks act as doorways to other documents at the same Web site or others. When you click your mouse on hyperlinked text or graphics, an entirely new document appears on your screen.

Pay careful attention to the source of the information you find. Is the source a government agency, or a university, or a private company, or an individual? Not all sources are equally accurate or reliable in what they present.

TIPS FOR SUCCESSFUL SEARCHES

Focus your search. Because the Internet contains so much, it is easy to "wander off" into other parts of the Internet and forget about the information that you are trying to locate. To avoid this problem, establish a specific research goal before you begin.

Make bookmarks for useful Web sites. A bookmark is a note to your computer to "remember" the location of a Web site. Later, you can reach any bookmarked site with a simple click of your mouse.

Use specific key words. If your key words are too general, your search might turn up thousands of Net sites. Make your key words specific. Many search engines have useful tips on searching with key words.

Seek guidance from teachers and parents. Ask a teacher, parent, or librarian for help in evaluating whether Web sites and information are reliable and appropriate to your research.

See us on the Internet

http://www.phschool.com

At Prentice Hall's Web site, you will find current event updates, social studies links, and other resources to help you learn about American history.

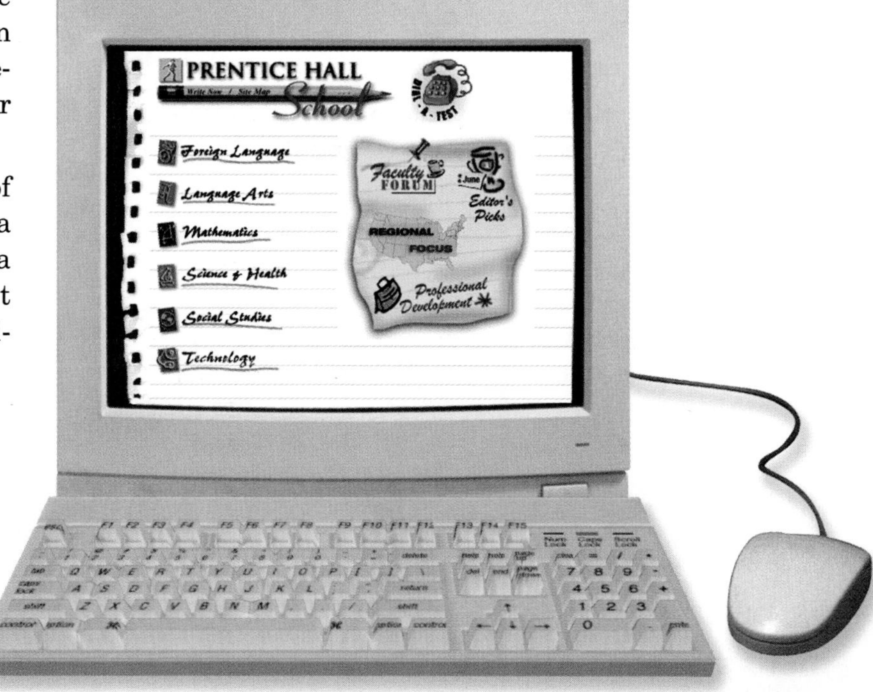

Unit 1

Early Heritage of the Americas

Thematic Overview

The United States today is a unique blend of peoples and cultures. This unit relates the early, often difficult, phases of the blending process.

Chapter 1 looks at the geography of the United States and the profound effect it has had on American history. (See pp. 2–27.) **Chapter 2** explores the cultures and civilizations of Native American groups that once thrived in the Americas. It also tells what happened when Europeans first encountered these ancient peoples. (See pp. 28–57.) **Chapter 3** examines European colonization of the Americas, its impact on Native Americans, the introduction of enslaved Africans to the Americas, and European rivalries in North America. (See pp. 58–91.) **Chapter 4** discusses the formation and development of the original 13 English colonies and shows how their governments laid the foundation for American government today. (See pp. 92–125.)

ANSWERS

Possible answers: Africans and Asians. For more information on this artist, see the Background Art Note at the bottom of this page.

RESOURCE DIRECTORY

Teaching Resources
Document-Based Discovery
• Origins, pp. 2–5

Unit 1

Early Heritage of the Americas

What's Ahead

Viewing Unit Themes **A Meeting of Different Cultures**
George Catlin, an American artist of the 1800s, painted LaSalle Claiming Louisiana for France, April 9, 1682. *As Native Americans watch, newly arrived French explorers gather around a flag and a cross. Encounters and exchanges between Europeans and Native Americans helped form the roots of American society.* ★ **In addition to Europeans and Native Americans, what other people have helped shape American society?**

★ *Background* ★
Art Note

A Meeting of Different Cultures In the 1820s, while still a young lawyer, George Catlin saw a delegation of Native Americans pass through Philadelphia on their way back from Washington. He vowed to become a historian and recorder of Native American cultures. In his wide travels and explorations of Native American life, he lived with 48 different peoples. As part of his quest to preserve their culture, he produced almost 600 paintings, including more than 500 portraits, and amassed a vast collection of cultural artifacts, like pipes, utensils, and tools.

Unit Theme Origins

Over thousands of years, Native Americans formed diverse societies throughout North America. In the 1500s and 1600s, Europeans and Africans began to arrive in the Americas. The blending and clashing of these three cultures helped shape the nature of modern American life.

Along the Atlantic coast of North America, settlers from England established 13 colonies. English political traditions would form the basis for the American government today.

How did people of the time view American origins? They can tell you in their own words.

Viewpoints on American Origins

"Roots have spread out from the Tree of the Great Peace, one to the north, one to the east, one to the south, and one to the west."

Treaty forming an alliance among Iroquois nations (1500s)

"The people are a collection of diverse nations in Europe as French, Dutch, Germans, Swedes, Danes, Finns, Scotch, Irish, and English."

William Penn, founder of Pennsylvania (1685)

"A democracy... is when... power is lodged in a council consisting of all the members and where every member has the privilege of a vote. ...Every man has the privilege freely to deliver his opinion concerning the common affairs."

John Wise, Massachusetts minister (1717)

Activity Writing to Learn The peoples who first settled in North America came from many different backgrounds. Think about your school and your community. Then, make a list of the things that can help different people to live together without conflict.

Viewpoints on American Origins

★ **The Iroquois League** strove to establish "peace, civil authority and righteousness" among the Indian tribes.

★ **William Penn,** an English Quaker, based the government of the Commonwealth of Pennsylvania on freedom of worship and the rights of English people.

★ **John Wise,** a Congregational minister born in Massachusetts, held liberal views regarding both civil and church governments.

CRITICAL THINKING Despite differences in cultures and religious beliefs, the authors of these three quotations believed in the distribution of power among—and the peaceful coexistence of—disparate groups. How might they judge the effectiveness of our government in dealing with the wide diversity of cultures present in the United States today?

Guided Instruction

Encourage students to think about the types of situations that cause conflicts. Then have them brainstorm ways to avoid these conflicts. Consider what individuals can do and what actions groups or organizations can take.

ASSESSMENT See the rubrics in the Alternative Assessment booklet in the Teaching Resources.

★ Background ★

Historians Debate

Doing justice to the past Historians once saw Columbus's voyage as the progress of civilization. In *Admiral of the Ocean Sea*, Samuel E. Morison focuses on Columbus as a daring sailor and explorer. Since the 1960s, however, historians have raised disturbing questions about the impact of the European "discovery" of the Americas on Native American societies. The quincentenary of 1492 sparked a debate about celebrating an event that led to the deaths of millions of Native Americans. Kirkpatrick Sales takes this harsh view in *The Conquest of Paradise: Christopher Columbus and the Columbian Legacy,* indicting Columbus and Europeans for their greed and cruelty. To do justice to the past, writes historian James Axtell, we must avoid replacing one myth with another and reject simplistic labels.

Technology

AmericanHeritage® History of the United States CD-ROM

Access the Time Tour "A Meeting of Different Worlds" to accompany Unit 1.

Chapter 1 Manager

SECTION OBJECTIVES	TEACHING RESOURCES	ADDITIONAL RESOURCES
1 Five Themes of Geography (pp. 4–7) **Objectives** 1. Identify the five themes of geography. 2. Describe how people and their natural environment interact. 3. List some causes and effects of the movement of people.	**Lesson Planner,** p. 1 (average) .... 60 mins. **Unit 1/Chapter 1** • Critical Thinking and Writing: Applying Information, p. 4 (basic) .... 20 mins. • Biography Flashcard: Lady Bird Johnson, p. 7 (average) .... 20 mins. • Section 1 Quiz, p. 8 (average) .... 15 mins. **Interdisciplinary Connections** • Main Idea: The American Land, pp. 2, 6 (average) .... 20 mins.	**Prentice Hall Literature Library** • Literature of the American Southwe
2 Maps and Mapmaking (pp. 8–13) **Objectives** 1. Identify the different types of maps people use. 2. Describe how latitude and longitude help us to locate places. 3. Explain why today's maps are more accurate than maps of the past.	**Lesson Planner,** p. 2 (average) .... 90 mins. **Unit 1/Chapter 1** • Practice Your Skills: Reading a Map, p. 3 (average) .... 20 mins. • Section 2 Quiz, p. 9 (average) .... 15 mins.	
3 American Lands and Climates (pp. 14–23) **Objectives** 1. Describe the eight physical regions of the United States. 2. Explain the importance of lakes and rivers to the United States. 3. Identify the major climates of North America.	**Lesson Planner,** p. 3 (average) .... 90 mins. **Unit 1/Chapter 1** • Vocabulary Builder, p. 2 (basic) .... 15 mins. • Map Mystery: Many Rivers to Cross, p. 5 (average) .... 15 mins. • Connecting History and Literature: This Land Is Your Land, p. 6 (average) .... 15 mins. • Section 3 Quiz, p. 10 (average) .... 15 mins. **Why Study History?** • We All Need Water, pp. 3–6 (average) .... 90 mins. **Interdisciplinary Connections** • Main Idea: The American Land, pp. 3–5 (average) .... 20 mins. **Chapter Tests,** pp. 1–6 (average) .... 45 mins.	**Voices of Freedom** • America the Beautiful, p. 13 (average) • A European View of North America, pp. 14–15 (average) • An Indian Prayer for the Sun, p. 16 (average) **Customized Reader** • Exploring the Coast of Florida With John Hawkins in 1565, article IB-2 (challenging) • A Walk in the Desert, article XB-7 (average) • A Fur Trader Describes Southeastern Alaska, article IVB-5 (average) **Historical Outline Map Book** • Physical Regions of the United States, p. 2 (average) • Climates of the United States, p. 3 (average) • Physical United States, p. 83 (average) • Regional maps, pp. 86–92 (average) **Interdisciplinary Explorations** • Where River Meets Sea: America's Estuaries at Risk (challenging)

Assessment Options

Teaching Resources
- Alternative Assessment booklet
- Section Quizzes, Unit 1, Chapter 1, pp. 8–10
- Chapter Tests, Chapter 1, pp. 1–6
- Test Bank CD-ROM

Student Performance Pack
- Guide to the Essentials of American History, Chapter 1 Test, p. 10
- Standardized Test Prep Handbook
- Interactive Student Tutorial CD-ROM

Interdisciplinary Connections

Teaching Resources
- Map Mystery, Unit 1, Chapter 1, p. 5
- Connecting History and Literature, Unit 1, Chapter 1, p. 6
- Interdisciplinary Connections, pp. 1–6

Interdisciplinary Explorations
- Where River Meets Sea: America's Estuaries at Risk

Voices of Freedom, pp. 13–16

Customized Reader, articles IB-2, IVB-5, XB-7

Historical Outline Map Book, pp. 2, 3, 83, 86–92

Prentice Hall Literature Library
- Literature of the American Southwest

Technology

Interactive Student Tutorial CD-ROM

Test Bank CD-ROM

Color Transparencies
- Plate Collisions, p. B-33
- The United States, p. 1-51
- Regional maps, pp. 1-57, 1-61, 1-65, 1-69, 1-73, 1-77, 1-81, 1-85

Guided Reading Audiotapes
(English/Spanish), side 1

Listening to Music CD
- Aaron Copland, from *Appalachian Spring*

Resource Pro® CD-ROM

Prentice Hall Home Page
www.phschool.com

Student Performance Pack

Guide to the Essentials of American History
- Ch. 1, pp. 7–10
(Available in English and Spanish)

Guided Reading Audiotapes (English/Spanish), side 1

Standardized Test Prep Handbook

Interactive Student Tutorial CD-ROM

BLOCK SCHEDULING
Activities with this icon will help you meet your Block Scheduling needs.

ENGLISH LANGUAGE LEARNERS
Activities with this icon are suitable for English Language Learners.

TEAM TEACHING
Activities and Background Notes with this icon present starting points for Team Teaching.

Teachers' Bibliography

From the Archives of **American Heritage®**

Don't miss the special American Heritage® teaching notes found in this chapter.

Contact Teachers' Curriculum Institute to learn more about History Alive!® resources on American geography. See History Alive!® unit: The Geography of America From Past to Present, Section 1, "Reviewing Basic Geography," and Section 2, "Learning the Physiographic Features of the United States."

Explore your library to find these issues related to Chapter 1: *Mississippi River,* March 1990; *Historic Parks,* July 1991; *The Grand Canyon,* June 1980.

Prentice Hall Web Site You can access a structured, on-line environment that allows you to preview curriculum-related resources and receive updated information on groundbreaking events from around the nation and the world. (www.phschool.com)

Chapter 1

Focus on Geography
Prehistory–Present

Introducing the Chapter

Have students preview the main ideas of this chapter by looking over the visuals. Suggest they look for ways in which mapmakers show land and water.

Using the Time Line Introduce students to the chapter time lines in their textbook with questions such as these: **(1)** What two kinds of events are shown on this time line? *(American events and world events)* **(2)** Which set of events is placed above the time line? *(American events)* Below the time line? *(world events)* **(3)** Where can you find the most recent events on the time line? *(to the far right)* **(4)** How many centuries are marked off on the time line? *(five, from 1500 to the present)* **(5)** How were the world events linked to the American events during the 1500s? *(Europeans met Native Americans as they explored the Americas.)*

Ask students to recall instances when they used the natural environment for pleasure, such as skiing, hiking, or boating. Have the class brainstorm a list of ways that land, water, and climate are valuable for both recreational and economic uses. Refer to the list during the study of American lands and climates later in the chapter.

For additional *Why Study History?* support, see p. 20.

Chapter 1

Focus on Geography
Prehistory–Present

What's Ahead

The United States of America is blessed with a beautiful, diverse, and valuable natural environment. In this chapter, you will study geography in general and the geography of our nation in particular. You will learn about the landforms, physical regions, natural resources, and climates of the United States.

Several tools will aid you in your study. Geographers have developed five themes to help you understand the relationship between geography and history. Various kinds of maps will also prove useful.

Why Study History? In the months ahead, you will see how geography has influenced the history, the government, and the economy of the United States. You will also study how people's actions affect the natural environment. You can learn about the vital importance of one natural resource and how you can help preserve it by reading this chapter's *Why Study History?* feature, "We All Need Water."

American Events

1500s Early encounters between Europeans and Native Americans

1600s Growing numbers of enslaved Africans in the Americas

Prehistory | 1500 | 1600 | 1700

World Events

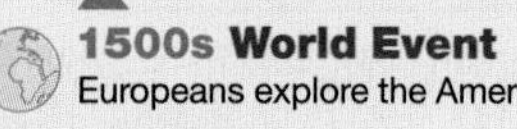

1500s World Event Europeans explore the Americas

Viewing History **The View From Space**

This picture was taken by a satellite in orbit around the Earth. You are looking directly at North America. The colors are enhanced to highlight the Earth's physical features. Green represents lowlands and orange represents highlands.

★ **What other continents are visible in this satellite photograph?**

1700	1800	1900	Present
	1800s Migration to the Pacific Coast increases	**1900s** Industrialization affects the natural environment	**Present** Efforts to protect the environment increase

1700s World Event European states struggle for control of North America 

1800s World Event Millions of immigrants move to the United States

★ Background ★
Art Note

The View From Space Satellite photography began in 1960 when the U.S. Space Agency launched its first weather satellite. Images of the atmosphere were clear enough for scientists to locate a dangerous typhoon. Early satellite photos showed only sections of the Earth surface, but by the 1970s, they could show whole Earth images like the one above. T

Documents and Literature

On pp. 524–527, you will find two readings to enrich this chapter:

1. Eyewitness Account "The Mountains of California," John Muir's description of the natural beauty of the Sierra Nevada in the 1800s. (Use with Section 3.)

2. Literature "America the Beautiful," Katharine Lee Bates's song praising the natural bounty of the land and American devotion to liberty. (Use with Section 3.)

Writing Actively 

Responding to Art Tell students that astronauts have photographed views of Earth similar to the one on this page. Some astronauts have described how beautiful Earth appeared and how the sight affected their feelings toward their home planet. After students have studied the picture, have them suppose they are astronauts in space. Tell them to write diary entries describing this view of Earth and their feelings about it at that moment.

parts of South America, Asia, Africa, and Europe

Section 1
Five Themes of Geography

LESSON PLAN

Objectives

★ Identify the five themes of geography.
★ Describe how people and their natural environment interact.
★ List some causes and effects of the movement of people.

1 Engage

Warm Up Write the words *geography* and *history* on the chalkboard. Ask: "How might the 2 terms be related?" and "Why does a study of history begin with a review of geography?"

Activating Prior Knowledge Have students list some impressive geographic features they have seen in person or in pictures. Then have them compare their choices and file their lists for future reference.

Reading Actively

Before Reading Direct students to the questions under Explore These Questions. Tell them to find answers to these questions as they read. Note that the last 2 questions relate to 2 of the 5 themes of geography.

2 Explore

Ask students to read the section. For homework, have them research the theme of place as it applies to their own community.

RESOURCE DIRECTORY

Teaching Resources
Lesson Planner, p. 1
Unit 1/Chapter 1
• Critical Thinking and Writing: Applying Information, p. 4

1 Five Themes of Geography

As You Read

Explore These Questions
- What are the five themes of geography?
- How do people and their natural environment interact?
- What are some causes and effects of the movement of people?

Define
- geography
- history
- latitude
- longitude
- irrigate

SETTING the Scene If you read almost any newspaper, you will find stories about the land around you. One story might argue that building a dam will be harmful to a river. Another might announce the discovery of oil. To understand these and other issues, we need to understand geography.

Geography and History

Geography is the study of people, their environments, and their resources. Geographers ask how the natural environment affects the way we live and how we, in turn, affect the environment. By showing how people and the land are related, geography helps to explain both the past and the present.

Geography is closely linked to history. **History** is an account of what has happened in the lives of different peoples. Both historians and geographers want to understand how the characteristics of a place affect people and events.

To help show the connection between geography and history, geographers have developed five themes. The themes are location, place, interaction between people and their environment, movement, and region.

Location

Where did this event happen? Where is this place? Both historians and geographers often ask such questions. Finding the answers involves the geographic theme of location.

Exact location

As you study American history, you will sometimes need to know the absolute, or exact, location of a place. For example, where, exactly, is Washington, D.C., the nation's capital?

To describe the exact location of Washington, D.C., geographers use a grid of numbered lines on a map or globe that measure latitude and longitude. Lines of **latitude** measure distance north and south from the Equator. Lines of **longitude** measure distance east and west from the Prime Meridian, which runs through Greenwich (GREHN ihch), England.

The exact location of Washington, D.C., is 39 degrees (°) north latitude and 77 degrees (°) west longitude. In writing, this location is often shortened to 39°N/77°W. The Gazetteer in the Reference Section of this book provides the exact location of many important places in American history.

Relative location

Sometimes it is more useful to know the relative location of a place, or its location in relation to some other place. Is Washington, D.C., on the east or west coast of the United States? Is it north or south of Richmond, Virginia? These questions involve relative location.

Knowing relative locations will help you see the relationship between places. Is a place located near a lake, river, or other source of water and transportation? Is it inland or on the coast? Answers to such ques-

★ ***Background*** ★

Our Diverse Nation

Scholarly geographer Ellen Churchill Semple (1863–1932) of Louisville, Kentucky, chose geography over the carefree life of a socialite. She studied geography in Germany under Friedrich Ratzel, who believed that human development is determined by physical environment. Returning to the United States, Semple explored and developed Ratzel's theory in the backcountry of Kentucky. Her book *Influences of Geographic Environment* helped make geography a serious field of study in the United States. T

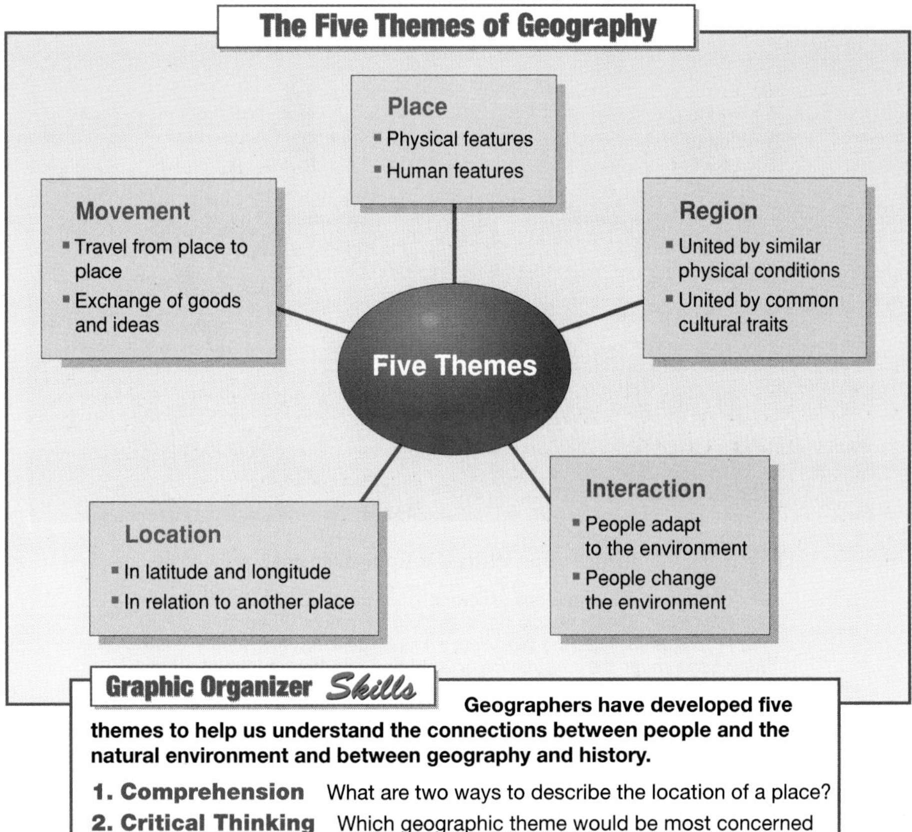

Graphic Organizer Skills **Geographers have developed five themes to help us understand the connections between people and the natural environment and between geography and history.**

1. **Comprehension** What are two ways to describe the location of a place?
2. **Critical Thinking** Which geographic theme would be most concerned with international trade?

tions help explain why cities grew where they did. Chicago, Illinois, for instance, developed at the center of water, road, and railroad transportation in the Midwest.

Place

A second geography theme is place. Geographers generally describe a place in terms of both physical and human features.

The physical features of a place include climate, soil, plant life, animal life, and bodies of water. For example, New England has a hilly terrain, a rocky coast, and many deep harbors. Because of these physical features, early Native Americans of the region turned to fishing for a living.

People help to shape the character of a place through their ideas and actions. The human features of a place include the kinds of houses people build as well as their means of transportation, ways of earning a living, languages, and religions.

Think of the human features of the American frontier. In the forests of the frontier, early settlers built log cabins. On the grassy plains, where trees were scarce, some settlers built their homes out of sod, clumps of earth, and grass.

★ Activity ★
Connections With Geography

Mapping trade routes Small groups should brainstorm a list of foreign goods that Americans buy. Ask: "Where do the goods originate?" Refer students to the Reference Section. Have them draw a global map, label the area of each product's origin, and use arrows to show the product's route to the U.S. (*basic*) T

Ask them to consider physical features, human features, or both. Students should share their findings with the class.

3 Teach

Write this passage on the chalkboard and tell students it describes an event that they will study during the year. "In the 1840s, 15,000 Mormons traveled more than 1,000 miles from Illinois to Utah. They settled in the Great Salt Lake valley. The valley was a hot, dry desert, but [they] built an irrigation system that let them grow crops in the desert. They also built Salt Lake City at 41°N/112°W. In Utah, the Mormons preserved their own religion and way of life." Have students discuss this passage in terms of the 5 themes of geography.

4 Assess

To close the lesson, have students complete the section review. Or, divide the class into 5 groups, giving each group one theme of geography. Have each group illustrate its theme with a drawing, chart, diagram, or map. Have groups present their illustrations to the class and discuss how their theme relates to people and events today or in the past.

★ ★ ★ ★ ★ ★ ★ ★ ★ ★ ★ ★ ★ ★ ★ ★ ★

Graphic Organizer Skills

ANSWERS **1.** latitude and longitude; in relation to another place **2.** movement, which includes the exchange of goods

Reading Actively

During Reading Have students list the five themes of geography and then answer the question: "How could each geographical theme relate to the study of history?"

ANSWER

Possible answer: Pollution from lakeshore cities could affect water quality and wildlife.

Writing Actively

After Reading Refer students to the list of geographic features they created as they began the chapter. Have them select one feature from the list and write a paragraph relating it to one or more of the five themes of geography.

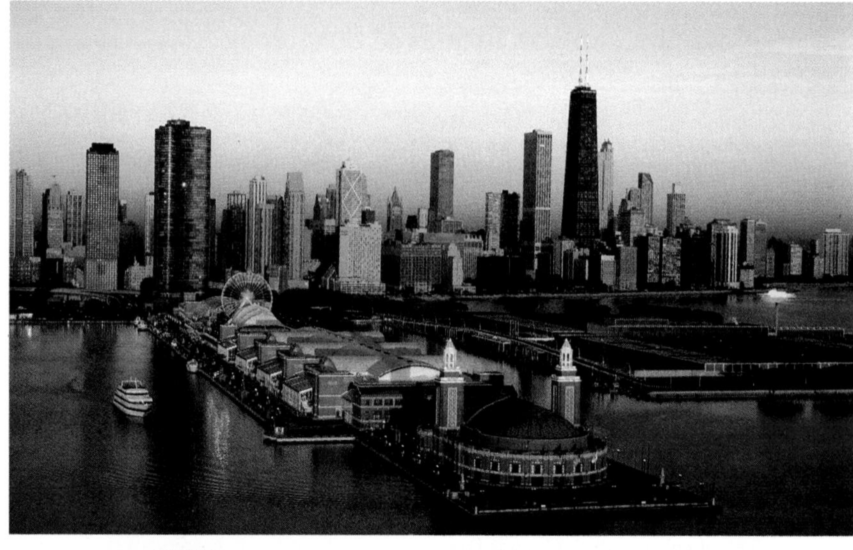

Viewing History **Interaction With the Environment**

Chicago is one of several major cities that dot the shores of Lake Michigan. Before people interacted with the natural environment, only dense forests encircled the lake. Notice how Chicago has extended into Lake Michigan through the construction of large piers. ★ **How might lakeshore cities like Chicago have a negative impact on the natural environment?**

Interaction

Interaction between people and their environment is a third theme of geography. Throughout history, people have adapted to and changed their natural environment.

For example, ancient hunters in the Americas learned to plant seeds and grow food crops. This adaptation greatly affected their lives. No longer did they have to move from place to place in search of food.

Agriculture was impossible in the arid Imperial Valley of southeastern California until irrigation canals were built in the 1900s. The canals bring water from the Colorado River. Today, the Imperial Valley is a very productive farming region.

Later, Native Americans in the Southwest found ways to **irrigate,** or bring water to, the desert. They dug ditches that channeled water from the Salt and Gila rivers. In this way, they were able to change arid, unproductive land into farmland.

In the 1860s, railroad builders in the United States changed the natural environment in order to improve transportation. They wanted to link the Atlantic and Pacific coasts. The railroad workers blasted through mountains and built bridges across rivers. When the project was completed, a railroad line stretched across the nation, linking the eastern and western parts of the United States.

Today, advanced technology allows people to alter their environment dramatically. People have invented ways to take oil from beneath the ocean floor. They have cut down forests to build communities. They have

★ Customized Instruction ★
Visual Learners

Creating a comparison chart Divide the class into pairs and have the teams select two states that interest them. Tell partners to prepare a chart comparing the physical and cultural features of the states they have chosen. Suggest they compare landforms, bodies of water, climate, cities, roads, farms, and other key features. Remind them to classify each entry on their chart as either a physical or a cultural feature. Encourage partners to include small illustrations. Refer them to such classroom resources as almanacs, atlas maps, and encyclopedias. Have students title their charts using words related to the five themes. (*average*)

RESOURCE DIRECTORY

Teaching Resources
Unit 1/Chapter 1
- Biography Flashcard: Lady Bird Johnson, p. 7
- Section 1 Quiz, p. 8

Interdisciplinary Connections
- Main Idea: The American Land pp. 2, 6

wiped out pests that destroy crops. Such changes have brought great benefits. They have also created new problems, such as air and water pollution.

Movement

A fourth geographic theme involves the movement of people, goods, and ideas. Movement occurs because people and resources are scattered unevenly around the globe. To get what they need or want, people travel from place to place. As they meet other people, they exchange ideas and technology as well as goods.

History provides many examples of the movement of people and ideas. The first people who came to the Americas were hunters following animal herds. Much later, people from all over the world moved to the United States in search of political and religious freedom. They brought with them customs and beliefs that have helped shape American life.

Today, the movement of goods links the United States with all parts of the world. For example, American producers ship goods such as grain and computers to Europe and Africa. Meanwhile, we rely on materials such as oil and tin from other parts of the world.

Region

Geographers study regions. A region is an area of the world that has similar, unifying characteristics. The characteristics of a region may be physical, such as its climate or landforms. For example, the Great Plains is considered a region because it has fairly level land, very hot summers, very cold winters, and little rainfall. The Pacific Coast region, meanwhile, is known for its rugged mountains, dense forests, and scenic ocean shore.

A region's characteristics may also be human and cultural. San Francisco's Chinatown is a region because Chinese Americans there have preserved their language and culture. In New York City, Broadway is a theater district where many plays are performed. In Chicago, the Loop is a downtown area where there are office buildings and museums.

A region can be any size. It can be as large as the United States or as small as a neighborhood. Within one city, there could be several regions. For example, there may be a parkland area known for its natural beauty. There may be a residential area where people live in homes and apartments. There also may be a business district, occupied mostly by office buildings and stores.

★ Section 1 Review ★

Recall

1. **Define** **(a)** geography, **(b)** history, **(c)** latitude, **(d)** longitude, **(e)** irrigate.

Comprehension

2. Briefly describe the five themes of geography.
3. **(a)** Describe two examples of how the natural environment can affect the way people live. **(b)** Give two examples of problems that can result when people change the natural environment.
4. How has the movement of people helped shape American life?

Critical Thinking and Writing

5. **Synthesizing Information** How does the picture of the New England coast on page 17 illustrate the theme of place?
6. **Understanding Causes and Effects** How does modern technology affect the movement of people, goods, and ideas?

Activity **Using Geographic Themes** Use the five themes of geography to describe the neighborhood, community, or state in which you live. Develop your description by writing one or two sentences for each of the five themes.

FROM THE ARCHIVES OF AmericanHeritage®

Wetland or wasteland? Even in this century, conservationists supported the draining of swamps and marshes. They considered them to be "nature's failures" and felt that the land could be better used for farms and buildings. Today, wetlands and the many wildlife habitats they house are vigorously protected by law.

Source: William B. Meyer, "When Dismal Swamps Became Priceless Wetlands," *American Heritage* magazine, May/June 1994.

★ Section 1 Review ★

ANSWERS

1. (a)–(d) p. 4, **(e)** p. 6

2. Location: either a place's exact position on Earth or its position relative to another place; Place: physical and human features; Interaction: how people have adapted to or altered their environment; Movement: why people, goods, and ideas move from place to place; Region: area that has similar, unifying characteristics.

3. Possible answers: **(a)** Coastal New England: Native Americans fished; forests: settlers built log cabins. **(b)** air/water pollution

4. Immigrants: with their customs

5. Physical features: a rocky, rugged coast, the ocean; human feature: the lighthouse

6. Possible answer: Air travel moves people and goods quickly. Telephones, faxes, and computers quickly spread news and ideas.

Activity

Guided Instruction
Give students these examples of how the 5 themes can be used: Location: 20 miles west of the state capital; Place: a dry plain; Interaction: humans clearing trees for farms; Movement: East Coast natives settling an area in the 1800s; Region: part of the corn belt

ASSESSMENT See the rubrics in the Alternative Assessment booklet in the Teaching Resources.

Section 2

Maps and Mapmaking

LESSON PLAN

Objectives

★ Identify the different types of maps people use.

★ Describe how latitude and longitude help us to locate places.

★ Explain why today's maps are more accurate than maps of the past.

1 Engage

Warm Up Ask students what kinds of maps they have seen. Have them list the different kinds and indicate the kinds of information found on each map.

Activating Prior Knowledge Divide the class into small groups. Have students select a map from the lists they created and tell other group members how using the map influenced the student's life on a specific occasion. Students may cite actual instances or create hypothetical but realistic events.

Reading Actively

Before Reading Have students skim the major headings in the section and turn each into a question, such as "What do maps and globes show?" Tell students to look for answers to these questions as they read the section.

2 Explore

Ask students to read the section. For a homework assignment, have

RESOURCE DIRECTORY

Teaching Resources
Lesson Planner, p. 2

Maps and Mapmaking

As You Read

Explore These Questions

- What different types of maps do people use?
- How do latitude and longitude help us to locate places?
- Why are today's maps more accurate than maps of the past?

Define

- globe
- cartographer
- map projection
- hemisphere
- standard tlme zone

Identify

- Equator
- Prime Meridian

SETTING the Scene In a tiny Indian fishing village in the early 1600s, a small group gathered around Samuel de Champlain. They watched closely as the French explorer pointed to the shore and then drew a sweeping line on a deerskin spread out on the ground. The line represented the coastline where they stood. Quickly, the Native American chief drew other lines on the informal map. A young man added piles of rocks to represent the village and nearby settlements.

Champlain and the Native Americans he met on Cape Ann in Massachusetts did not understand each other's languages. Yet they found a way to communicate. Together, they created a map of the local area. Champlain later used the map to aid him in exploring the Massachusetts coast. People today use maps, too, to help them locate places, judge distances, and follow routes.

Maps and Globes

To locate places, geographers use maps and globes. A map is a drawing of the Earth's surface. A **globe** is a sphere with a map of the Earth printed on it. Because a globe is the same shape as the Earth, it shows sizes and shapes accurately.

Geographers often use flat maps rather than globes.

A globe is a map of the world.

Unlike a globe, a flat map of the world allows you to see all of the Earth's surface at one time. It is easier to handle and can show more detail. Still, a flat map has the disadvantage that it distorts, or misrepresents, some parts of the Earth.

Map Projections

Mapmakers, or **cartographers**, have developed dozens of different map projections. **Map projections** are ways of drawing the Earth on a flat surface.

Each map projection has benefits and disadvantages. Some projections show the sizes of landmasses correctly but distort their shapes. Others give continents their true shapes but distort their sizes. Still other projections distort direction or distances.

Mercator projection

In 1569, Gerardus Mercator developed the Mercator projection, the best map of its day. For hundreds of years, sailors depended on the Mercator map. Mercator himself boasted of his map:

> "If you wish to sail from one port to another, here is a chart, and a straight line on it, and if you follow this line carefully you will certainly arrive at your destination."

★ *Background* ★

Turning Points

Mercator makes sea travel safer Thanks to Gerardus Mercator, ocean seafarers could accurately chart long voyages for the first time. Mercator thought of the Earth as shaped like an orange. The lines of longitude were like vertical cuts made in the rind. If the orange were peeled and the segments of the rind were lined up side by side, the sphere could be flattened out. Because the tops and bottoms of the segments did not touch, Mercator widened each section of his flattened globe at the top and bottom so that it formed a rectangle. By doing so, Mercator sacrificed accuracy at the areas around the poles, which accounts for the enlargement of landmasses at the top and bottom of the Mercator projection. T

A Mercator map shows the true shapes of landmasses, but it distorts size, especially for places that are far from the Equator. On a Mercator map, for example, Greenland appears as big as all of South America, even though South America is more than eight times larger!

Robinson projection

Today, many geographers use the Robinson projection. It shows the correct sizes and shapes of landmasses for most parts of the world. The Robinson projection also gives a fairly accurate view of the relationship between landmasses and water.

Kinds of Maps

Maps are part of our daily lives. You have probably read road or bus maps. On television, you have seen weather maps and maps of places in the news.

As you study history, you will use various maps. Examine the Geographic Atlas in the Reference Section of this book. There, you will find maps showing national and state boundaries as well as the physical features and natural resources of the United States.

Each kind of map serves a specific purpose. A political map shows boundaries that people have set up to divide the world into countries and states. A physical map shows natural features, such as mountains and rivers. A population map lets you see how many people live in a particular area. An economic map shows how people of a certain region make a living. A natural resource map helps you see links between the resources of an area and the way people use the land.

Still other kinds of maps include election maps, product maps, and battle maps. These maps also help you to see the connections between geography and history.

Map Projections

Robinson Projection

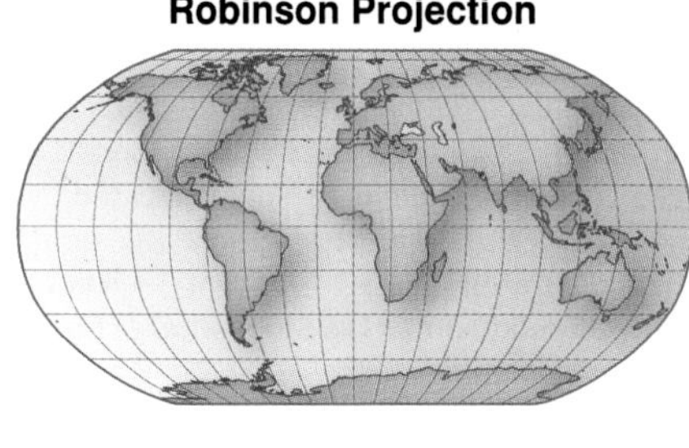

Mercator Projection

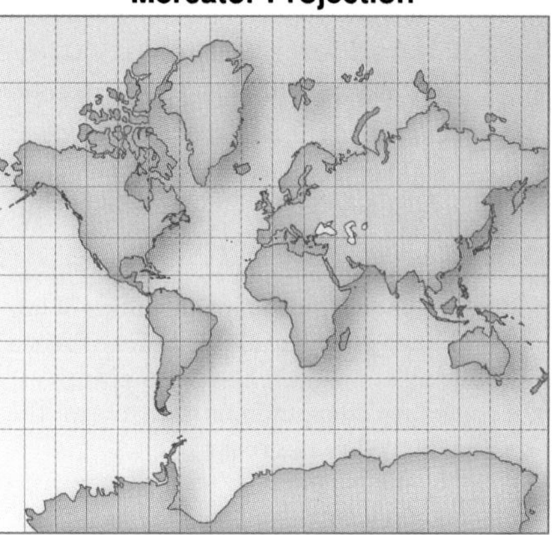

Geography Skills **Map projections make it possible for mapmakers to show a round world on a flat map.**

1. **Location** Use the map on page 10 to locate: **(a)** North America, **(b)** Africa, **(c)** Asia.
2. **Place** How does North America appear differently on the two projections?
3. **Critical Thinking** On the Mercator map, which areas are most distorted?

them use atlases, almanacs, or other sources to find a map of world time zones. Tell students to locate a city that would have daylight while their community is in darkness. Ask students to share findings with the class.

3 Teach

Have students look closely at the three modern maps in the section. Review what kind of map each one is, what kind of information each map shows, and how much detail it includes. Use the Skills for Life lesson in this section to review the different parts of a map: title, key, and symbols. Then have students find three different kinds of maps in later chapters and repeat the process with them.

4 Assess

To close the lesson, have students complete the section review. As an alternative, direct students to the Geographic Atlas in the Reference Section at the end of the book. Have them write two sentences for each map, telling what information the map gives about their local area.

★ ★ ★ ★ ★ ★ ★ ★ ★ ★ ★ ★ ★ ★ ★ ★ ★ ★

Geography Skills

ANSWERS **1.** Review locations with students. **2.** Possible answer: The Robinson projection gives a more accurate picture of the size of North America than the Mercator projection. **3.** areas farthest from the Equator

FROM THE ARCHIVES OF **AmericanHeritage**®

Technology changes landscape Thomas Jefferson predicted it would take a thousand years for American settlements to reach the Pacific Ocean. He could not have foreseen the technological revolution that would speed the pace of frontier settlement and permanently alter the American landscape.

Source: John Steel Gordon, "The American Environment," *American Heritage* magazine, October 1993.

Reading Actively

During Reading After students read the section on Kinds of Maps on the preceding page, have them list six different kinds of maps. Then ask them to write a sentence that answers the question: "How does a natural resource map differ from a physical map?"

Geography Skills

ANSWERS **1.** Review locations with students. **2.** Moscow **3.** North America, Europe, continental Asia

The World

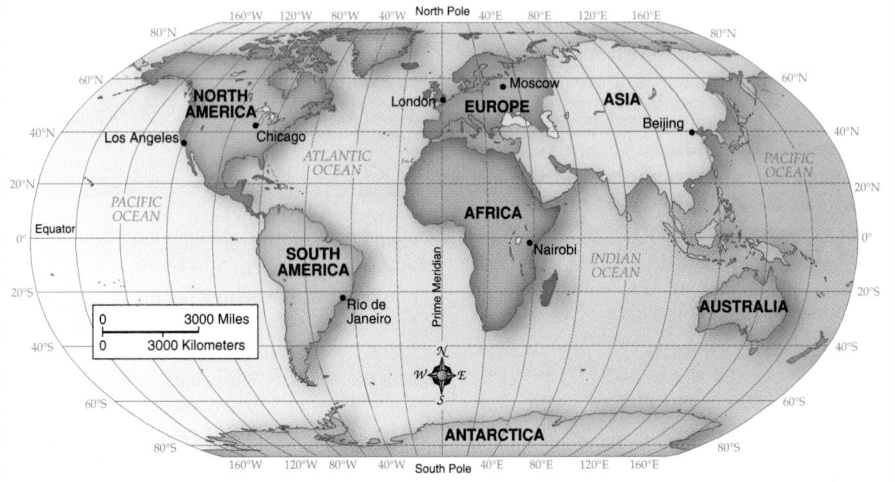

Geography Skills **By using lines of latitude and lines of longitude, one can locate any specific place in the world.**

1. **Location** On the map, locate: **(a)** Atlantic Ocean, **(b)** Pacific Ocean, **(c)** Europe, **(d)** North America, **(e)** Africa.
2. **Location** Which city is located at about 55°N/35°E?
3. **Critical Thinking** Which continents lie entirely in the Northern Hemisphere?

Latitude and Longitude

Most maps and globes include lines of latitude and lines of longitude. The lines form a grid, making it possible to locate places exactly. Each latitude and longitude line on the grid is measured in degrees (°).

Latitude

Look at the map of the world, above. Notice that lines of latitude run east and west. As you have read, lines of latitude measure distances north and south from the Equator.

The **Equator** is an imaginary line that lies at 0° latitude. It divides the Earth into two halves, called **hemispheres.**

The Northern Hemisphere lies north of the Equator. In the Northern Hemisphere, lines of latitude are numbered from 1°N to 90°N, where the North Pole is located.

The Southern Hemisphere lies south of the Equator. There, lines of latitude are numbered from 1°S to 90°S, where the South Pole is located.

Longitude

Lines of longitude on a map or globe run north and south between the two poles. They measure distances east and west from the **Prime Meridian,** which lies at 0° longitude and runs through the Royal Observatory in Greenwich, England. Unlike lines of latitude, lines of longitude are not parallel to each other. They converge at the North Pole and South Pole. The distance between longitude lines is greatest at the Equator. The distance

★ Customized Instruction ★
English Language Learners

Mapping native regions To help make maps more relevant and understandable to English language learners, have students use classroom or library resources to copy a physical map of their native region. Tell them to show as many physical features as possible—rivers, lakes, mountains, plains. Students should also include relative references, such as the Equator, North or South poles, latitude, and longitude.

As the text introduces geographic terms, ask students to associate each term with its equivalent in their primary language, and help them to write a brief definition in English. *(average)* ELL T

Resource Directory

Teaching Resources
Unit 1/Chapter 1
- Practice Your Skills: Reading a Map, p. 3

Skills FOR LIFE

Critical Thinking | Managing Information | Communication | **Maps, Charts, and Graphs**

Reading a Map

How Will I Use This Skill?

Maps are not used just to study history and geography. They can also help you plan a trip, understand current events, or find out about the weather. Knowing how to read a map can keep you from getting lost, or help you find your way again.

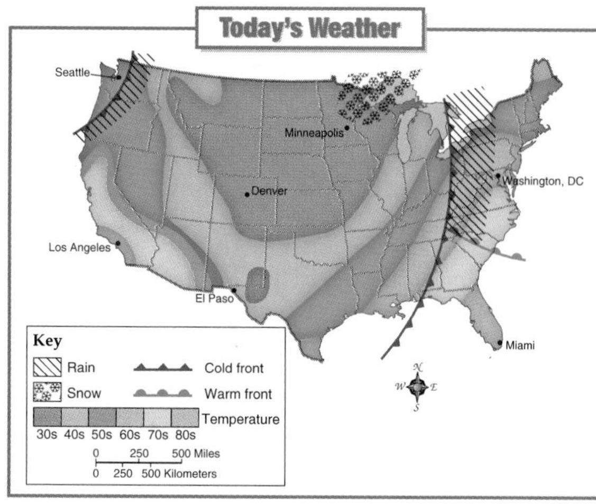

LEARN the Skill

You can read a map by following these three steps:

1. Identify the topic of the map. The **title** will tell you the subject of the map. The **key** explains the meanings of the map's symbols and colors.
2. Look at a map's **scale** to determine distances between places. The scale shows you how many inches on the map equal how many actual miles or kilometers.
3. Study the **directional arrow** to identify north, south, east, and west on a map.

PRACTICE the Skill

Use the steps above and the map on this page to answer the following questions.

1. (a) What is the title of the map? (b) How is a cold front shown on the map? (c) According to the color key, what is today's temperature in Los Angeles? In Denver?
2. (a) On the scale, how many miles are represented by 3/4 of an inch? (b) What is the approximate distance from Washington, DC, to Miami in miles? In kilometers?
3. (a) What is the northernmost city shown on the map? (b) What direction would you travel from El Paso to reach a place where it is snowing?

APPLY the Skill

With a group of classmates, create a map of your classroom. Include a title, plus a key that explains what symbols represent doors, windows, desks, and other features. Use a compass or the sun to determine north, south, east, and west. Use a tape measure to measure the room and create a scale.

Skills FOR LIFE

PRACTICE the Skill

ANSWERS

1. **(a)** Today's Weather **(b)** blue triangles **(c)** Los Angeles, 80s; Denver, 30s
2. **(a)** about 500 miles **(b)** about 1,000 miles; about 1,600 kilometers
3. **(a)** Seattle **(b)** northeast

APPLY the Skill

Guided Instruction

If possible, show students floor plan maps or other indoor map models. Have students first make rough maps before drawing their final maps on graph paper. You may want to pair students with spatial relation skills with those who have difficulty in this area.

ASSESSMENT See the rubrics in the Alternative Assessment booklet in the Teaching Resources.

★ Activity ★
Connections With Mathematics

Comparing distances To show how maps can distort distances, bring a globe to class. Have students use string to measure the distance between the North Pole and Miami and between Moscow and New York. Then have them calculate and compare the same distances using an atlas map. (*basic*) ELL T

★ Activity ★
Connections With Geography

Applying map skills Refer students to the Reference Section. Ask: "What is the exact location of a large American city in the Gazetteer?" and "Using the U.S. map in the Geographic Atlas, what is that city's location relative to two other American cities? To your own community?" (*average*) T

Viewing History ANSWER

Possible answer: Geographers have more accurate data about the size and shape of continents; mapmakers have developed new projections to show rounded areas on flat surfaces.

Writing Actively

After Reading After students have read the section, have them write three or four main ideas for the section. Then direct them to Section 2 under Sum It Up at the end of the chapter. Have students compare their statements with those at the end of the chapter.

Early Map of the Americas

This 1595 map distorts the true shapes of North America and South America. Gerardus Mercator, the map's creator, refers to the Americas as New India. Maps of the 1500s may not have been totally accurate, but they were very artistic. ★ **Why are today's maps much more accurate than those of several centuries ago?**

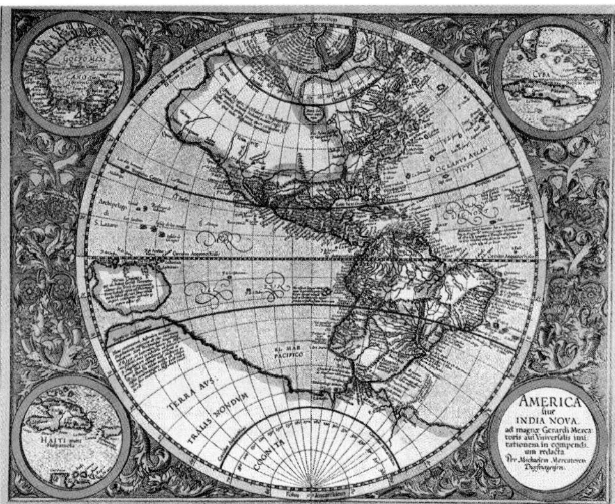

between the lines decreases as they approach and finally meet at the poles.

Lines of longitude are numbered from 1° to 179° east or west longitude. The line of longitude at 180° lies on the opposite side of the world from the Prime Meridian.

The circle formed by the Prime Meridian and 180° divides the Earth into the Eastern and Western hemispheres. The Eastern Hemisphere includes most of Europe, Africa, and Asia. The Western Hemisphere includes North America and South America.

Locating places

To locate places, you must combine latitude and longitude. Look at the map on page 10. Chicago is located north of the Equator at about 42°N latitude. It lies west of the Prime Meridian at about 88°W longitude. Its location is 42°N/88°W. Use the United States map in the Reference Section to find the exact location of your state capital.

Time Zones

Lines of longitude are also used to help us know what time it is around the world. When it is 11 A.M. in Miami, Florida, it is 8 A.M. in Portland, Oregon. In Lagos, Nigeria, it is 5 P.M.

Why does time differ from place to place? The answer is that the Earth rotates on its axis. As the Earth moves, the sun appears to rise in some places and to set in others. Throughout the world, people determine time by this rising and setting of the sun.

To make it easier to tell time around the world, a system of **standard time zones** was set up in 1884. Under this system, the world was divided into 24 times zones. Standard time is measured from the Prime Meridian, which runs through Greenwich, England.

When it is noon in Greenwich, it is before noon (A.M.) in places west of Greenwich. It is after noon (P.M.) in places east of Greenwich.

$ Connections With Economics

In the United States, the Daylight Saving Time system provides people with more usable hours of daylight. From April to October, clocks are set ahead one hour. The total amount of daylight remains the same, but more daylight hours are available for outdoor activities in the late afternoon and evening.

★ Background ★

Did You Know?

Map facts Interest in maps is ancient:

- Ptolemy (A.D. 90–168) established the practice of orienting maps with north at the top and east on the right.
- Maps showing Earth as a sphere date as far back as the second century A.D.
- *Latitude* comes from the Latin word for *wide,* thus latitude refers to the Earth's "width" on maps. T

★ Activity ★

Cooperative Learning

Evaluating map projections Divide the class into small groups. Tell students that they are cartographers who have been asked to create a map of the world. Have each group list what it would need to make an accurate map. Have students examine the two map projections in the section and decide which type to use, listing reasons for and against each. (*average*) T

RESOURCE DIRECTORY

Teaching Resources
Unit I/Chapter I
- Section 2 Quiz, p. 9

12 ★ Chapter 1

If you travel east from Greenwich across Europe, Africa, or Asia, you add one hour as you move through each time zone.

Making Accurate Maps

The oldest surviving map in the world today was created by an ancient cartographer on a clay tablet sometime around 2300 B.C. Ever since, geographers have worked to make maps more accurate.

Early mapmaking

Early cartographers relied on information from sailors and travelers as well as legends to create their maps. As a result, their maps included many errors. Five hundred years ago, European mapmakers did not even know that North America and South America existed!

Since the 1500s, mapmaking has improved greatly. Daring sailors gained information about uncharted lands. Explorers studied ocean currents and wind patterns around the world. Scientists learned more about the Earth itself.

Using satellites

Today, mapmakers depend on computers and satellites. By taking photographs from space, satellites provide information that no one on the ground can furnish. As a result, maps are more accurate than ever before.

Launched in 1972, Landsat 1 was the first satellite specially designed to study the Earth's surface from space. The unmanned spacecraft took pictures from about 570 miles (900 km) above the Earth. Each photo showed a land area that an airplane would need 1,000 pictures to depict. Within two years, Landsat photographed more than 80 percent of the Earth's surface.

Images from Landsat 1 and later satellites provided extraordinary help to mapmakers. They revealed uncharted islands. They enabled scientists to see entire mountain ranges and drainage basins at a single glance. They allowed surveys of remote areas, such as the polar regions and oceans. Based on these images, cartographers corrected old maps and mapped some places for the first time.

Today, geographers rely on satellites for more and more information about the Earth. Geographers can use satellite information to chart changes in population density and economic activity. They can also learn more about weather patterns, vegetation, pollution, and mineral resources.

★ Section 2 Review ★

Recall

1. **Locate** (a) North America, (b) South America, (c) Asia, (d) Arctic Ocean.
2. **Identify** (a) Equator, (b) Prime Meridian.
3. **Define** (a) globe, (b) cartographer, (c) map projection, (d) hemisphere, (e) standard time zone.

Comprehension

4. Why does a globe show the Earth more accurately than a flat map?
5. How can we use latitude and longitude to find the exact location of a place?
6. How have satellites made maps more accurate than ever before?

Critical Thinking and Writing

7. **Applying Information** Describe some of the special features of a road map.
8. **Understanding Causes and Effects** Before the 1500s, why were European maps of the world very inaccurate?

Activity **Making a Weather Map** You are the meteorologist for a local television news program. Make a map of your region, showing your forecast for tomorrow's weather conditions. You may wish to use the map on page 11 as a model.

★ Section 2 Review ★

ANSWERS

1. See map, p. 10
2. (a)–(b) p. 10
3. (a)–(c) p. 8, (d) p. 10, (e) p. 12
4. A globe is the same shape as Earth so can represent it accurately.
5. Latitude: position relative to the Equator; Longitude: position relative to the Prime Meridian; both used to locate points on Earth
6. They show geographic features difficult to see from the ground.
7. Possible answers: Location and names of highways and interstates; distances between towns or cities noted; color coding of roads
8. European scientists and cartographers knew little about many parts of the Earth and had to rely on travelers' stories or legends.

Activity

Guided Instruction

Suggest that students begin with an outline of their own and a few neighboring states. Have them refer to newspaper or TV weather forecasts for their area for the next day. Tell students to show air masses or fronts and to use patterns to show rain, snow, wind, or other weather conditions. They can use color for temperature ranges. Remind them to provide a key with their map.

ASSESSMENT See the rubrics in the Alternative Assessment booklet in the Teaching Resources.

★ Background ★ Linking Past and Present

Earth and beyond Early satellites photographed Earth, but today's satellites are also photographing the surfaces of other planets, especially Mars and Mercury. Mars, with its ancient volcanoes, craters, and sand dunes, resembles the landscape of Mexico and California. Mountains have been mapped on Mercury. T

★ Background ★ Recent Scholarship

Map biases Many believe that maps are a very reliable source of information. Mark Monmonier's *How to Lie With Maps* suggests otherwise. Monmonier says maps reflect a cartographer's unconscious biases. Mapmakers may conceal or misrepresent information. Monmonier's book also explores how maps are created today. T

Section 3
American Lands and Climates

LESSON PLAN

Objectives

★ Describe the eight physical regions of the United States.
★ Explain the importance of lakes and rivers to the United States.
★ Identify the major climates of North America.

1 Engage

Warm Up Have students list and define in their own words any terms they have heard on local TV or radio weather reports.

Activating Prior Knowledge Have students use the climate map in this section to describe the climate in your area. Ask them to identify the kinds of severe weather that their community sometimes experiences. During the discussion, ask these questions: "What weather emergencies have you experienced? What warnings, if any, did you have? How long did the emergency last?"

Reading Actively

Before Reading Review the first and last questions under Explore These Questions. Have students list the eight physical regions and seven major climates as they read the section.

Resource Directory

Teaching Resources
Lesson Planner, p. 3
Unit 1/Chapter 1
- Connecting History and Literature: This Land is Your Land, p. 6

Interdisciplinary Connections
- Main Idea: The American Land, p. 5

Transparencies
Interdisciplinary Connections
- Plate Collisions, p. B-33

3 American Lands and Climates

As You Read

Explore These Questions
- What are the eight physical regions of the United States?
- How are rivers and lakes important to the United States?
- What are the major climates of North America?

Define
- isthmus
- mountain
- elevation
- hill
- plain
- plateau
- tributary
- weather
- climate
- precipitation
- altitude
- El Niño

Setting the Scene North America is the world's third largest continent. As the World map in the Reference Section shows, the Atlantic Ocean washes the eastern shore of North America. The Pacific Ocean laps at its western shore. To the north lies the icy Arctic Ocean. To the south, an **isthmus** (IHS muhs), or narrow strip of land, links North America to South America.

North America has many different features. For example, one of the world's highest mountains, Mount McKinley, is in Alaska. Yet one of the lowest points on the Earth is in Death Valley, California. You will find many examples of contrast as you read more about the American land.

Types of Landforms

North America has many landforms, or natural features. There are high mountains, rolling hills, and long rivers. There are grassy plains, dense forests, and barren deserts. Within these different landscapes are four basic landforms: mountains, hills, plains, and plateaus (pla TOHZ).

Mountains are high, steep, rugged land. They rise to an **elevation,** or height, of at least 1,000 feet (300 m) above the surrounding land. Few people live on steep mountainsides. Yet people often settle in valleys between mountains.

Hills are areas of raised land that are lower and more rounded than mountains. Farming is often possible on hilly land. Therefore, more people live in hilly areas than on mountains.

Plains are broad areas of fairly level land. Few plains are totally flat. Most are gently rolling. Plains do not usually rise much above sea level. People often settle on plains because it is easy to build farms, roads, and cities on the level land.

Plateaus are plains that range from a few hundred to many thousand feet above sea level. With enough rain, plateaus can be good for farming. Mountains surround some plateaus. Such plateaus are often very dry because the mountains cut off rainfall.

Mountains, hills, plains, and plateaus are only a few of the special words that geographers use. For definitions of other geographic terms, you may refer to the Dictionary of Geographic Terms on pages 24–25.

Physical Regions of North America

The landforms of North America form seven major physical regions. The United States also includes an eighth region, the Hawaiian Islands in the Pacific Ocean. (See the map on page 19.)

The seven physical regions of North America offer great

The red fox is native to North America.

MINI LESSON

MAPS, CHARTS, AND GRAPHS

Interpreting a Physical Map

1. Introduce the skill by explaining that physical, or topographical, maps depict natural features and provide extensive detail on elevations for an area.

2. Help students practice the skill by examining the Physical Features map of the United States in the Geographic Atlas in the Reference Section. Ask them to use the color key showing elevations as they read the map.

3. Help students apply the skill by asking these questions: At what elevation are most of the Rocky Mountains? *(7,000–10,000 feet)* Which plains region has elevations ranging from 0 to 3,000 feet? *(Interior Plains)* Which physical regions are closest to sea level? *(Coastal Plains)* (*basic*) T contrasts. In some regions, the land is fertile. There, farmers plant crops and reap rich harvests. Other regions have natural resources such as coal and oil.

Pacific Coast

The westernmost region of North America is the Pacific Coast. It includes high mountain ranges that stretch from Alaska to Mexico. In the United States, some of these western ranges hug the Pacific Ocean. The Cascades and Sierra Nevada* stand a bit farther inland. Some important cities of the Pacific Coast are Seattle, Portland, San Francisco, and Los Angeles.

An important feature of the Pacific Coast region is the San Andreas Fault. This is a 600-mile (970 km) fracture in the Earth's crust. It runs through California from northwest to southeast. Movement of the Earth's crust along this fault causes earthquakes.

In 1906, a powerful earthquake shook the city of San Francisco. The tremors and fires that followed destroyed thousands of buildings and killed some 700 people. In 1994, another strong earthquake caused significant damage and loss of life in Los Angeles.

Intermountain region

East of the coast ranges is the Intermountain region. It is a very rugged region of mountain peaks, high plateaus, deep canyons, and deserts. The Grand Canyon, which is more than 1 mile (1.6 km) deep, and the Great Salt Lake are natural features of this region. Salt Lake City and Phoenix are among the few major cities of the Intermountain region.

*Sierra (see EHR uh) is the Spanish word for mountain range. Nevada is Spanish for snowy. Spanish explorers were the first to see these snow-covered mountains.

Viewing HISTORY **Mount Rainier**

The beauty of the Cascade Mountains can be seen at Mount Rainier National Park in the state of Washington. In spring, colorful wildflowers and evergreen trees contrast sharply with Mount Rainier's snowcap. ★ **In what physical region are the Cascades located?**

★ Activity ★

Connections With Science and Technology

Researching Earth's history Have students prepare an illustrated report on the shaping of Earth's crust. They should include theories about supercontinents and continental drift. The maps and diagrams could show plate tectonics, fault lines, or how some landmasses fit together like pieces of a puzzle. (*challenging*) T

2 Explore

Ask students to read the section. For a homework assignment, have them find and bring in recent weather maps from news sources. Have students compare the weather maps to the climates of the United States map in this section. Ask: "How do the two types of maps differ? When might you use a climate map? A weather map? What features of your climate region do the weather maps support?"

3 Teach

Divide the class into eight groups and assign each group one of the physical regions of the United States. Have each group prepare and present a brief oral report describing the physical characteristics of their region. As part of each report, tell students to identify one state in their physical region and describe its relative location and climate.

4 Assess

To close the lesson, have students complete the section review. As an alternative, have students write brief essays in which they **(a)** describe the course of a major American river from its source to its mouth; **(b)** list some of its tributaries; and **(c)** name the physical regions and climates through which it flows.

★ ★ ★ ★ ★ ★ ★ ★ ★ ★ ★ ★ ★ ★ ★ ★ ★

ANSWER

The Cascades are located in the Pacific Coast region.

 ANSWER

It is flat and covered with grass, which is good for grazing.

Rocky Mountains

The Rocky Mountains stretch from Alaska through Canada into the United States. They include the Bitterroot Range in Idaho and Montana, the Big Horn Mountains in Wyoming, and the Sangre de Cristo Mountains in Colorado and New Mexico. In Mexico, the Rocky Mountains become the Sierra Madre (MAH dray), or mother range.

The Rockies include some of the highest peaks in North America. Many peaks are more than 14,000 feet (4,200 m) high. Throughout history, people have described the mountains' rugged beauty and grandeur.

The Rockies, however, were a serious barrier to settlement of the United States. When settlers moved west in the 1800s, crossing the Rockies posed great hardships. Some people decided to stay and live in the Rockies. Today, Denver is a major city in the region.

Interior Plains

Between the Rockies in the West and the Appalachian Mountains in the East is a large lowland area called the Interior Plains. The dry western part of the Interior Plains is called the Great Plains. The eastern part is called the Central Plains.

According to scientists, a great inland sea once covered the Interior Plains. Today, some parts are rich in coal and petroleum.* Other parts offer fertile soil for farming and grassland for raising cattle. Chicago and Dallas are major cities on the Interior Plains.

Appalachian Mountains

The Appalachian Mountains run along the eastern part of North America. They stretch from Canada in the North to Georgia and Mississippi in the South. The Appalachians have different names in different places. For example, the Green Mountains, Alleghenies, and Great Smokies are all part of the Appalachian Mountains.

The Appalachians are lower and less rugged than the Rockies. The highest Appalachian peak is Mt. Mitchell in North Carolina, which is 6,684 feet (2,037 m) high. Still, early European settlers had a hard time crossing these heavily forested mountains.

Canadian Shield

The Canadian Shield is a lowland area that lies mostly in eastern Canada. The

*The Natural Resources map in the Reference Section shows where natural resources are located.

Viewing History: Interior Plains

Plains cover much of the central United States. They stretch from the Mississippi River to the Rocky Mountains and from Texas (shown at right) to Montana. The region is ideal for raising cattle. ★ **Why is this region ideal for raising cattle?**

▼ *Texas longhorn*

★ *Background* ★

Did You Know?

Badlands and bones In South Dakota, which is part of the Interior Plains, lies the Badlands—a barren area with little drinkable water and steep, craggy walls of soft stone eroded into odd shapes. The area has yielded many fossils, or remains, of ancient mammals, including giant piglike creatures and three-toed horses that walked the Earth 33 million years ago. T

★ *Activity* ★

Community Involvement

Working for clean water Divide the class into small groups and have each group research pollution or other problems affecting a major river system or lake in the United States. Tell them to find out what steps have been taken to solve the problems, then brainstorm additional solutions. Have each group present its findings and recommendations to the class. (*average*) T

RESOURCE DIRECTORY

Teaching Resources
Unit 1/Chapter 1
- Map Mystery: Many Rivers to Cross, p. 5

Interdisciplinary Connections
- Main Idea: The American Land, pp. 3–4

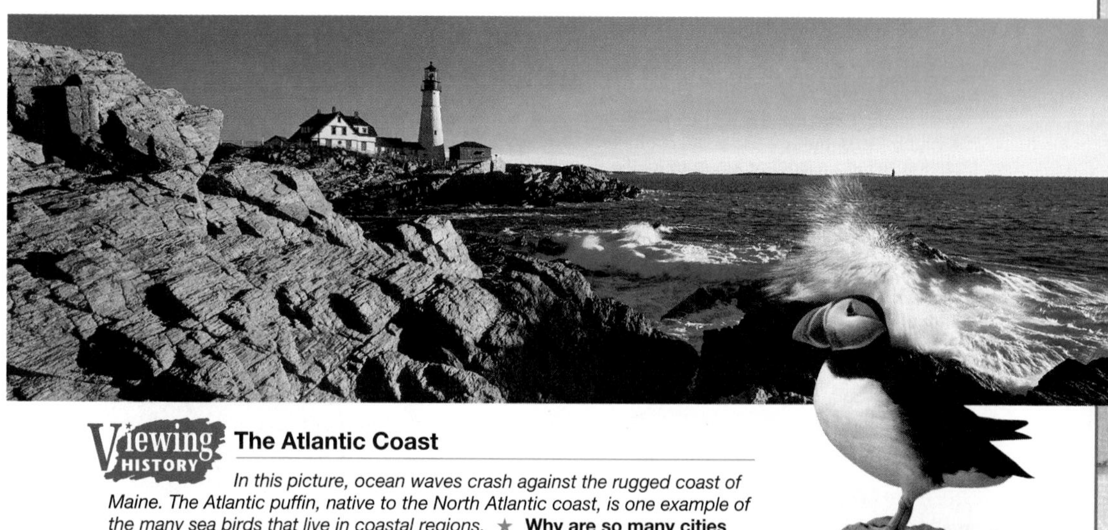

Viewing HISTORY **The Atlantic Coast**

In this picture, ocean waves crash against the rugged coast of Maine. The Atlantic puffin, native to the North Atlantic coast, is one example of the many sea birds that live in coastal regions. ★ **Why are so many cities built near an ocean?**

Atlantic puffin ➤

southern part extends into the United States. The region was once an area of high mountains. The mountains were worn away to low hills and plains. The Canadian Shield lacks topsoil for farming, but it is rich in minerals.

Coastal Plains

The region called the Coastal Plains is a fairly flat, lowland area that includes the Atlantic Plain and the Gulf Plain. The Atlantic Plain lies between the Atlantic Ocean and the foothills of the Appalachians. The Atlantic Plain is narrow in the North, where Boston and New York City are located. It broadens in the South to include all of Florida.

Another part of the Coastal Plains is the Gulf Plain, which lies along the Gulf of Mexico. The Gulf Plain has large deposits of petroleum. New Orleans and Houston are major cities of the Gulf Plain.

Hawaiian Islands

The Hawaiian Islands lie far out in the Pacific, about 2,400 miles (3,860 km) west of California. There are eight large islands and many small islands.

The islands are the visible tops of volcanoes that erupted through the floor of the Pacific Ocean. Some volcanoes are still active. Mauna Loa, on the island of Hawaii, is an active volcano that rises 13,680 feet (4,170 m) above sea level.

Rivers and Lakes

Great river systems crisscross North America. They collect runoff water from rains and melting snows and carry it into the oceans.

The mighty Mississippi

The Mississippi and Missouri rivers make up the longest and most important river system in the United States. This river system carries water through the Interior Plains into the Gulf of Mexico.

Many **tributaries,** or streams and smaller rivers, flow into the Mississippi-Missouri river system. Among these tributaries are the Ohio, Tennessee, Arkansas, and Platte rivers. These and other rivers provide water for the rich farmlands of the Interior Plains.

The Mississippi River also serves as a means of transportation. Today, barges carry freight up and down the river. As in the past, people travel by boat on the river.

Viewing HISTORY ANSWER

They are conveniently located for shipping goods overseas; they were the places newcomers reached when they first arrived in this country.

Reading Actively

During Reading Have students find the statement on this page that "The Mississippi and Missouri rivers make up the longest and most important river system in the United States." Ask students to look for evidence to support this statement as they read the section.

★ *Customized Instruction* ★

Kinesthetic Learners

Making topographical maps To help students appreciate the variety of landforms in North America, have them construct their own three-dimensional topographical maps. Divide the class into small groups. Give each group a copy of a relief map of North America. Have them glue the maps to firm cardboard and use clay to build and shape the various landforms. Each group member should be responsible for creating one landform for the model. When the clay has dried, students can paint their landscapes, using four or more colors to indicate the different landforms. Each map should include a color key. Display the maps in the classroom. (*average*)

Technology

Listening to Music CD
- Aaron Copland, from *Appalachian Spring*

Biography
ANSWER

As a landscape photographer, Adams probably wanted to see the natural environment preserved and protected.

Biography Ansel Adams

Ansel Adams (1902–1984) is well known for his sharply focused black-and-white photographs of American landscapes. In 1946, the native Californian founded the California School of Fine Arts in San Francisco. From 1936 to 1973, he served as director of the Sierra Club, a group devoted to conservation of the natural environment. ★ **Why do you think Adams was so interested in conservation of the environment?**

◀ *Ansel Adams took this photo of the Grand Canyon.*

The mighty Mississippi has inspired many admiring descriptions. Among them is this one from the 1937 film *The River:*

> “The Mississippi River runs to the Gulf.
> Carrying every drop of water, that flows down two thirds of the continent,
> Carrying every brook and rill, rivulet and creek,
> Carrying all the rivers that run down two thirds of the continent.
> The Mississippi runs to the Gulf of Mexico.”

The Colorado River

The Colorado River is another important river. It begins in the Rocky Mountains and flows through Colorado, Utah, Arizona, and Nevada. It forms the border between California and Arizona as it flows toward the Gulf of California. Smaller rivers feed into the Colorado. These include the Green River and the San Juan River.

The Colorado River created the Grand Canyon in Arizona. For millions of years, the river rushed over layers of rock, carving a deeper and deeper channel. Today, the Grand Canyon is one mile (1.6 km) deep and 18 miles (29 km) wide in some places.

There are several dams along the course of the Colorado River. These dams hold back the flow of the river. They help provide water and electricity to the people of the Southwest.

International borders

The Rio Grande and the St. Lawrence River serve as political boundaries. The Rio Grande is part of the border between the United States and Mexico. The St. Lawrence is part of the border with Canada.

Five large lakes, called the Great Lakes, also form part of the border between the United States and Canada. The Great Lakes are Superior, Michigan, Huron, Erie, and Ontario. Today, canals connect the Great Lakes, forming a major inland waterway that is important for commerce.

★ *Background* ★

Recent Scholarship

Boring into global warming mysteries
Climate records reveal that average temperatures on Earth have risen about 0.5°C during this century. The records extend back only about 100 years, however. Scientists need figures for a much longer period of time if they are to judge whether global warming stems from the Earth's natural warming-and-cooling cycles or from industrial pollution.

In their March 14, 1997, *Science* report "Borehole Temperatures and a Baseline for 20th-Century Global Warming Estimates," Robert N. Harris and David S. Chapman show that boring holes into the ground provides good data about climate in earlier times. Tests in Utah suggest that global warming began during the late 1800s and did not occur naturally. T

Resource Directory

Transparencies
Geography and History
- The United States, p. 1-51
- Regional maps, pp. 1-57, 1-61, 1-65, 1-69, 1-73, 1-77, 1-81, 1-85

Weather and Climate

North America has a variety of weather patterns and climates. **Weather** is the condition of the Earth's atmosphere at any given time and place. It may be hot or cold, rainy or dry, or something in between.

Climate is the average weather of a place over a period of 20 to 30 years. Two main aspects of climate are temperature and **precipitation** (pree sihp uh TAY shuhn), or water that falls in the form of rain, sleet, hail, or snow.

Several factors affect climate. One factor is distance from the Equator. Lands near the Equator usually are hot and wet all year. Lands near the North and South poles are cold all year. **Altitude,** or height above sea

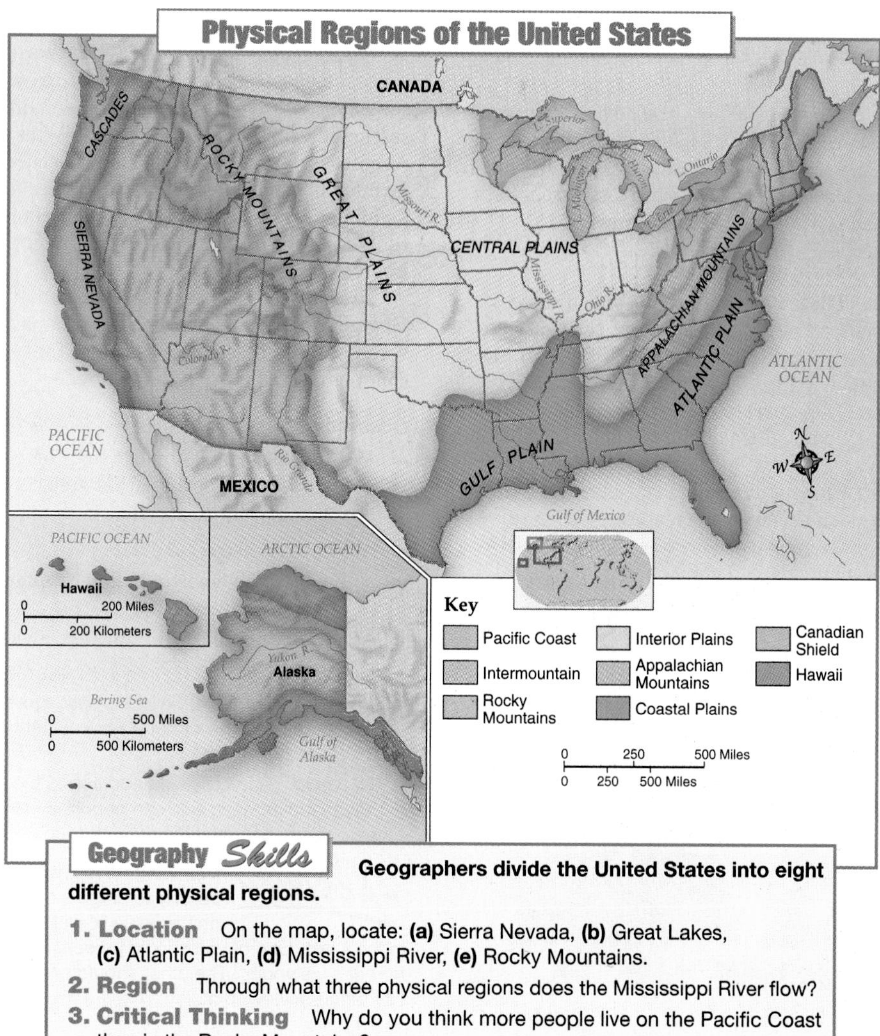

Geography *Skills* **Geographers divide the United States into eight different physical regions.**

1. **Location** On the map, locate: **(a)** Sierra Nevada, **(b)** Great Lakes, **(c)** Atlantic Plain, **(d)** Mississippi River, **(e)** Rocky Mountains.
2. **Region** Through what three physical regions does the Mississippi River flow?
3. **Critical Thinking** Why do you think more people live on the Pacific Coast than in the Rocky Mountains?

Geography *Skills*

ANSWERS **1.** Review locations with students. **2.** Canadian Shield, Central Plains, Gulf Plain **3.** The high elevations of the Rocky Mountains make the region a more difficult place to live than the Pacific Coast.

★ *Background* ★

Did You Know?

Utah's saltwater lake Utah's Great Salt Lake is actually an inland sea. However, it is saltier than any ocean because, as its waters evaporate, they leave behind salts that are trapped in the lake and do not run off into streams and rivers. The rate of evaporation varies so the lake shrinks and expands; but, on average, it is about 75 miles (120k) long and 30 miles (48k) wide. T

Why Study History?

ANSWERS

1. The growing population has made the demand for water much greater than it was when the agreements were made. **2.** Possible answers: collect rainwater to water plants, take showers instead of baths

★Activity

Guided Instruction
Have students who take the role of the city official research how farmers use water and how much water they use. For instance, they could find out how farmers irrigate their fields, how much water for agriculture goes to waste, what percentage of the water in the West is used by farmers and by cities. Students taking the role of farmers should investigate water usage and waste in cities. Both sides should consider the effects of recycling and pollution. Give students a specific amount of time in which to present their arguments.

ASSESSMENT See the rubrics in the Alternative Assessment booklet in the Teaching Resources.

RESOURCE DIRECTORY

Teaching Resources
Why Study History?
• We All Need Water, pp. 3–6

Why Study History?

Because We All Need Water

Historical Background

In the past century, the demand for water has risen greatly. More and more water is diverted from rivers to serve people's needs. As a result, some major rivers throughout the world have begun to run dry.

Connections to Today

The Colorado River is one of those rivers. (See page 18.) Today, the Colorado rarely empties into the Pacific Ocean. Instead, it gradually shrinks until its last traces evaporate in the desert heat of Mexico.

Today, the demand for Colorado River water is greater than the supply. In 1922, an agreement divided the river's water among seven western states. Other agreements guaranteed water rights to Native Americans and Mexico. Now, more than 20 million people rely on the Colorado River.

In California, this poster urges young people to conserve water.

Colorado River water disputes are often settled in court. Large cities such as Los Angeles and San Diego frequently accuse farmers of wasting water through old-fashioned irrigation methods. The farmers reply that cities are overbuilding and drawing too much water.

According to California Congressman George Miller, "The heart of the West is water. . . . It will be the most important commodity in dictating the future."

Connections to You

We all need water. You can help save water by taking these and other steps.

- Take short showers.
- Fix leaky faucets.
- Do only full loads in the dishwasher and clothes washer.
- Wash automobiles and water lawns infrequently.

1. **Comprehension** Why do past agreements on sharing Colorado River water not meet today's needs?
2. **Critical Thinking** In addition to the ideas above, what else can people do to help conserve water?

Debating Work with a partner to stage a debate on the issue of water rights in the West. One of you should present a farmer's viewpoint. The other should present a city official's viewpoint.

Fast Facts

★ Each year up to 18,000 people thrill to "running the rapids" of the Colorado River through the Grand Canyon.
★ To clear the Colorado River of silt and rebuild its banks' ecological systems, the government deliberately flooded it in 1995 by releasing water from Glen Canyon Dam.
★ To prevent water wars, the Texas government owns Colorado River waters within its borders. It apportions water rights to farmers and other users.

Bibliography

To read more about this topic:

1. *John Wesley Powell,* Roger A. Bruns (Enslow Publishers, 1997). Powell's exploration of the Colorado River and conservation efforts.
2. *Drought,* Edward F. Dolan (Franklin Watts, 1990). An account of water shortages and human efforts to combat them.
3. Internet. Colorado River water use at crwua.mwd.dst.ca.us/tcr/crwua_tcr.htm.

Linking United States and the World

The Philippines

United States

Weather Connections

Conditions around the world can affect your weather. Mount Pinatubo (above, left), a volcano in the Philippines, erupted in 1991. Gases and dust blocked some of the sun's rays and lowered temperatures in much of the world. In North America, though, the eruption led to a milder than average winter. ★ **What is the average winter like in the area where you live?**

level, also affects climate. In general, highlands are cooler than lowlands. Other factors that influence climate include ocean currents, wind currents, and mountains.

In the Pacific Ocean, wind and ocean currents interact to create the cyclical phenomenon called the **El Niño** (ehl NEEN yoh) Southern Oscillation. The temperature of Pacific Ocean water plays a major role in the phenomenon. During an El Niño period, the surface water of the eastern Pacific Ocean warms. During a La Niña (lah NEEN yah) period, ocean surface temperatures cool.

The Southern Oscillation affects weather patterns in nearly three quarters of the world. In the United States, for example, the warm ocean water of an El Niño helps to cause frequent and powerful storms in California and the Southwest. In Northeastern states, meanwhile, El Niño usually contributes to milder than normal winters.

North American Climates

The United States has 10 major climates. Look at the map on page 22 to see the locations of these climates.

Marine

The strip of land from southern Alaska to northern California is sometimes called the Pacific Northwest. This region has a mild, moist marine climate, with warm summers and cool winters. Moist winds from the Pacific Ocean bring mild temperatures and moisture that condenses and falls as rain or snow. The Pacific Northwest has many forests. This makes it the center of the lumber industry.

Mediterranean

Much of California has a Mediterranean climate. Winters are mild and wet. Summers are hot and dry. Farmers and fruit growers

Internet Activity

Tracing El Niño Have students visit the Midwestern Climate Center at www.mcc.sws.uiuc.edu/elnino.html and answer these questions: Who named El Niño? How does El Niño affect Midwestern winters? How often did El Niño occur between 1951 and 1991? Given the changing nature of the Internet, you may wish to preview this site before directing students to it. (*average*) T

Linking United States and the World

ANSWER Review with students average winter temperatures and precipitation in your area.

Writing Actively

After Reading After students have read the section, have them create three appropriate bumper stickers to sell to tourists who visit a particular physical region, climate region, and river (or lake) in the United States.

Geography Skills

ANSWERS **1.** Review locations with students. **2.** Washington, Oregon, California, Arizona, Colorado, Utah, Alaska **3. (a)** southern parts of California, as well as parts of Nevada, Utah, Arizona, New Mexico, Colorado and southwestern Texas **(b)** All these areas have desert climates in which water is scarce.

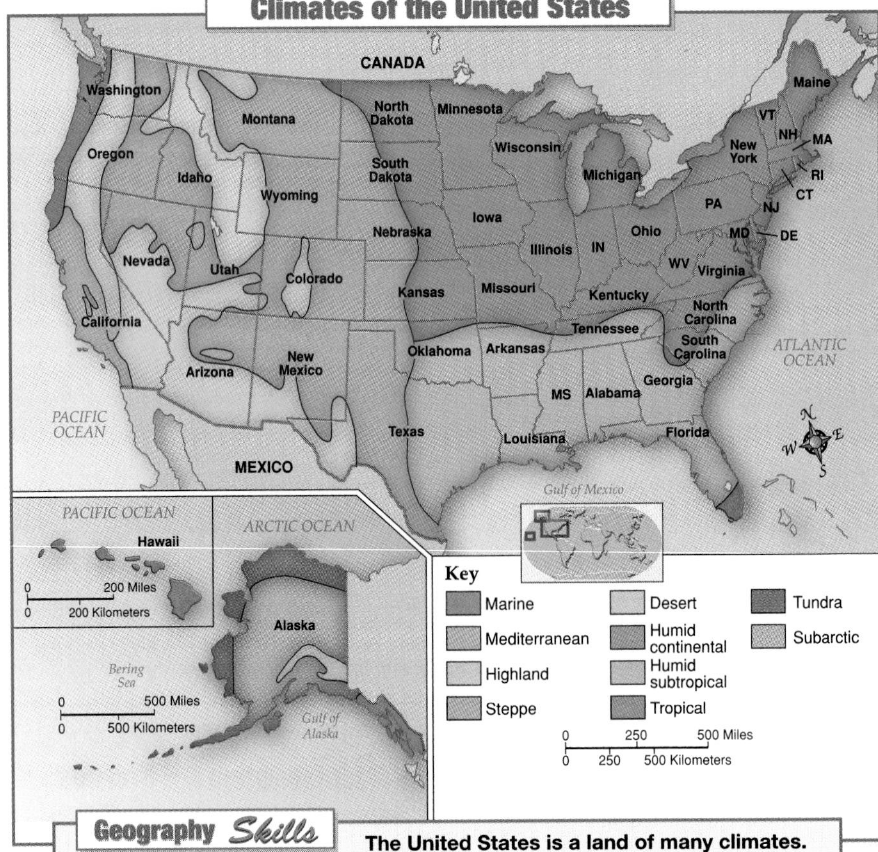

Geography Skills **The United States is a land of many climates.**

1. **Location** On the map, locate: **(a)** New York, **(b)** Ohio, **(c)** Arizona.
2. **Place** What states have three or more different climates?
3. **Critical Thinking** **(a)** Identify a state or part of a state where water is probably scarce. **(b)** Why is water in such short supply there?

must often irrigate the land. Because of the climate, this region produces crops that cannot be grown anywhere else in the country. For example, it produces almost all the nation's almonds, walnuts, olives, apricots, dates, and figs.

Highland

In the Cascades, Sierra Nevada, and Rocky Mountains, a highland climate brings cooler temperatures. Conditions in a highland climate vary according to altitude. For example, Mount Rainier in the state of Washington, at over 14,000 feet (4,200 m) above sea level, is snow-capped all year. During the spring and summer, runoff from melting snows provides water to the major rivers of the West. Many people vacation in the mountains so they can participate in winter sports. In summer, vacationers come to the mountains to escape the heat and enjoy the cool highland temperatures.

★ Background ★
Did You Know?

Weather wisdom Before the National Weather Service was established in the late 1800s, almanacs and diaries kept by sailors and farmers were the best sources for weather and climate information. Farmers' knowledge was especially useful because they had observed nature—often with a respectable level of accuracy—over a long period of time. Their crops and livelihood depended on the weather. A great deal of weather "knowledge" from the past, however, is folklore. Many Native Americans, for example, believed that rainbows were bridges to the spirit world. On a similar subject, English settlers claimed that "It's bad luck to point at a rainbow." T

Resource Directory

Teaching Resources
Unit 1/Chapter 1
- Vocabulary Builder, p. 2
- Section 3 Quiz, p. 10

Chapter Tests, pp. 1–6

Desert and steppe

Much of the southwestern United States has a desert climate, with hot days and cold nights. This dry region stretches as far east as the Rockies. In the deserts of Nevada, Arizona, and southeastern California, there is almost no rainfall. In many areas, people irrigate the land so that they can grow crops.

East of the Rockies are the Great Plains. They have a steppe climate with limited rainfall. Summers are hot and winters are cold. Huge herds of buffaloes once grazed on the short grasses of the Great Plains. In the 1800s, settlers brought cattle to graze on the plains.

Humid continental

The Central Plains and the northeastern United States have a humid continental climate. This climate, with mild summers and cold winters, has more precipitation than the steppe. Tall prairie grasses once covered the Central Plains. Today, American farmers raise much of the world's food in this region.

At one time, the humid continental climate supported forests that covered much of the northeastern United States. Early European settlers cleared forests to build settlements and to grow crops. However, many forests remain, and the lumber industry thrives in some areas.

Tropical and humid subtropical

Southern Florida and Hawaii, located near the Equator, have tropical climates. The hot, humid conditions make these regions good for growing such crops as pineapples and citrus fruits. The warm tropical temperatures are also ideal for the tourism industry.

The southeastern United States has a humid subtropical climate. Warm temperatures and regular rainfall make this region ideal for growing crops such as cotton, soybeans, and peanuts.

Tundra and subarctic

Northern and western coastal regions of Alaska have a tundra climate. It is cold all year round. The rest of Alaska and northern Canada have a subarctic climate with long, cold winters and short summers. Farming is limited to a small fertile valley in southern Alaska. Almost one third of Alaska is covered by forest. Therefore, logging and the production of paper pulp are important industries.

★ Section 3 Review ★

Recall

1. **Locate** **(a)** North America, **(b)** Pacific Coast, **(c)** Intermountain region, **(d)** Rocky Mountains, **(e)** Interior Plains, **(f)** Appalachian Mountains, **(g)** Mississippi River, **(h)** Great Lakes.
2. **Define** **(a)** isthmus, **(b)** mountain, **(c)** elevation, **(d)** hill, **(e)** plain, **(f)** plateau, **(g)** tributary, **(h)** weather, **(i)** climate, **(j)** precipitation, **(k)** altitude, **(l)** El Niño.

Comprehension

3. Name the eight physical regions of the United States and describe one feature of each region.
4. How do rivers and lakes benefit the economy of the United States?
5. Describe the climate of the region where you live.

Critical Thinking and Writing

6. **Drawing Conclusions** Do you think more people live in the Appalachian Mountains or in the Rocky Mountains? Why?
7. **Making Decisions** If you could live anywhere in the United States, which physical region and climate would you choose? Explain.

Activity **Making a Chart** You are the graphic designer for a popular vacation and travel magazine. Create a chart that lists and describes the 10 major climates of the United States.

★ Activity ★
Connections With Geography

Diagramming orographic precipitation
Have students use library sources to research orographic (mountain-induced) precipitation and the rain shadow effect. Have them diagram or illustrate the process and share the results in class. Discuss how the process affects two climates in the Northwest. (*average*) T

★ Section 3 Review ★

ANSWERS

1. See map, p. 19, and Geographic Atlas in the Reference Section.

2. (a)–(f) p. 14, **(g)** p. 17, **(h)–(k)** p. 19, **(l)** p. 21

3. Possible answers: Pacific Coast and Rocky Mountains—high mountain ranges; Intermountain—high mountain peaks; Interior Plains—lowland area; Appalachian Mountains—lower, less rugged than the Rockies; Canadian Shield—lowlands, rich in minerals; Coastal Plains—lowland area; Hawaiian Islands—tops of underwater volcanoes

4. by providing water for people and serving as shipping routes

5. Students should describe average temperatures and precipitation.

6. Possible answer: More people live in the Appalachians because they are lower and less rugged.

7. Answers should be based on the descriptions in the section.

Guided Instruction
Charts should describe the temperature and precipitation for each climate. Encourage students to use colors or pictures for the different climates. If possible, have students enhance computer skills by creating their charts using a pagemaking or word processing program.

ASSESSMENT See the rubrics in the Alternative Assessment booklet in the Teaching Resources.

CD-ROM
Test Bank CD-ROM, Ch. 1
Interactive Student Tutorial

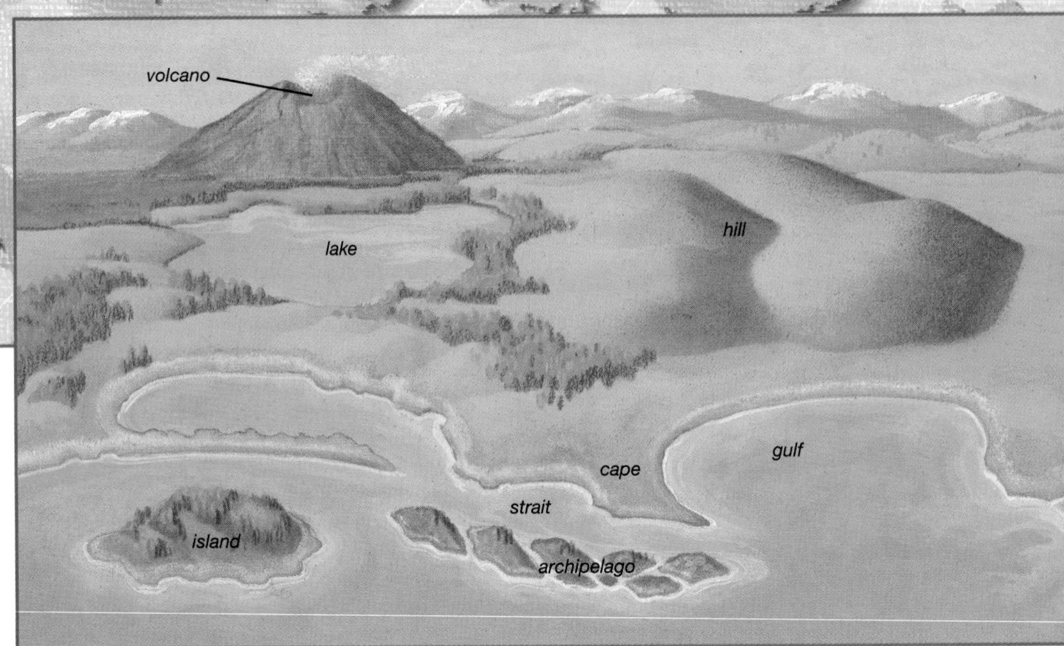

Dictionary of Geographic Terms

The list below includes important geographic terms and their definitions. Sometimes, the definition of a term includes an example in parentheses. An asterisk (*) indicates that the term is illustrated above.

altitude height above sea level.

***archipelago** chain of islands. (Hawaiian Islands)

basin low-lying land area that is surrounded by land of higher elevation; land area that is drained by a river system. (Great Basin)

***bay** part of a body of water that is partly enclosed by land. (San Francisco Bay)

canal waterway made by people that is used to drain or irrigate land or to connect two bodies of water. (Erie Canal)

***canyon** deep, narrow valley with high, steep sides. (Grand Canyon)

***cape** narrow point of land that extends into a body of water. (Cape Cod)

climate pattern of weather in a particular place over a period of 20 to 30 years.

***coast** land that borders the sea. (Pacific Coast)

coastal plain lowland area lying along the ocean. (Gulf Plain)

continent any of seven large landmasses on the Earth's surface. (Africa, Antarctica, Asia, Australia, Europe, North America, South America)

continental divide mountain ridge that separates river systems flowing toward opposite sides of a continent.

***delta** land area formed by soil that is deposited at the mouth of a river. (Mississippi Delta)

desert area that has little or no moisture or vegetation. (Painted Desert)

directional arrow arrow on a map that always points north.

downstream in the direction of a river's flow; toward a river's mouth.

elevation the height above sea level.

fall line place where rivers drop from a plateau or foothills to a coastal plain, usually marked by many waterfalls.

foothills low hills at the base of a mountain range.

***gulf** arm of an ocean or sea that is partly enclosed by land, usually larger than a bay. (Gulf of Mexico)

hemisphere half of the Earth. (Western Hemisphere)

***hill** area of raised land that is lower and more rounded than a mountain. (San Juan Hill)

***island** land area that is surrounded by water. (Puerto Rico)

★ Activity ★
Our Diverse Nation

Translating terms Have students review the Dictionary of Geographic Terms. Then ask English language learners to give equivalents in their language for some terms. Students may note similarities and differences. For example, the English word *canyon* comes from the Spanish word *cañón,* but the English word *sea* is unrelated to the Spanish *mar.* (*basic*) ELL

★ Activity ★
Connections With Arts

Describing a geographic setting Discuss the importance of setting in literature. Give an example of a story with an interesting setting, such as a mountain. Ask students to write a 3-paragraph story using a particular geographic setting. Then have them rewrite the story in a new setting. Ask students to discuss how their stories changed and why. (*average*) T

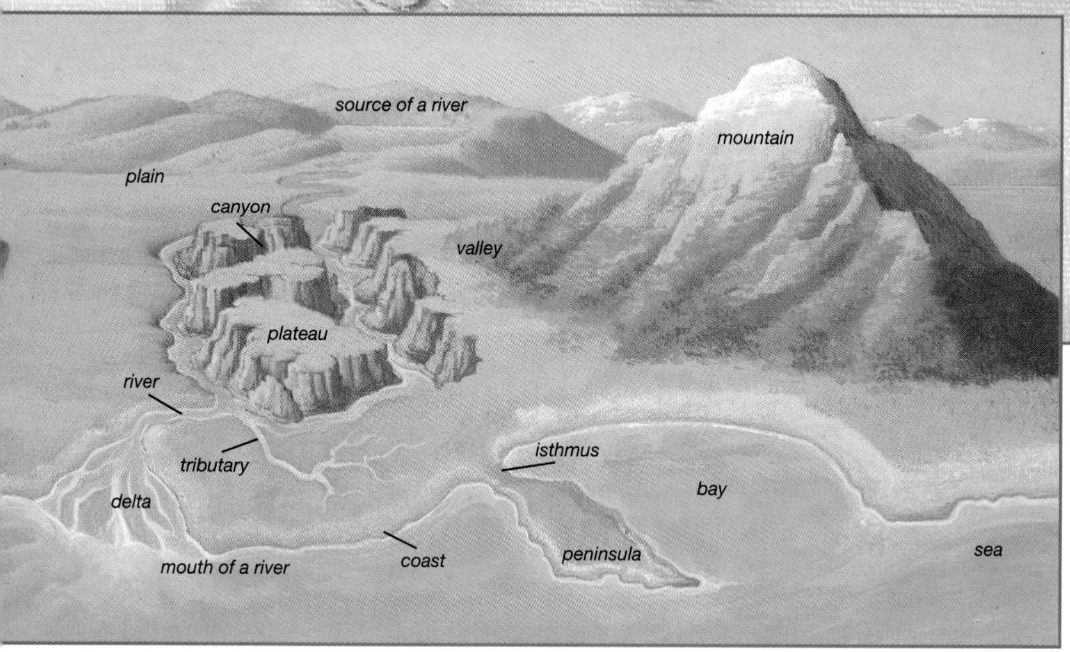

***isthmus** narrow strip of land joining two large land areas or joining a peninsula to a mainland. (Isthmus of Panama)

***lake** body of water surrounded entirely by land. (Lake Superior)

latitude the distance in degrees north and south from the Equator.

longitude the distance in degrees east or west from the Prime Meridian.

marsh lowland with moist soils and tall grasses.

***mountain** high, steep, rugged land that rises sharply above the surrounding land. (Mount McKinley)

mountain range chain of connected mountains. (Allegheny Mountains)

***mouth of a river** place where a river or stream empties into a large body of water.

ocean any of the four largest bodies of salt water on the Earth's surface. (Arctic, Atlantic, Indian, and Pacific Oceans)

***peninsula** piece of land that is surrounded by water on three sides. (Delmarva Peninsula)

piedmont rolling land along the base of a mountain range.

***plain** broad area of fairly level land that is generally close to sea level.

***plateau** large area of high, flat, or gently rolling land.

prairie large area of natural grassland with few or no trees or hills.

***river** large stream of water that empties into an ocean or lake or another river. (Pecos River)

***sea** large body of salt water that is smaller than an ocean. (Caribbean Sea)

sea level average level of the ocean's surface from which the height of land or depth of the ocean is measured.

***source of a river** place where a river begins.

steppe flat, treeless land with limited moisture.

***strait** narrow channel that connects two larger bodies of water. (Straits of Florida)

***tributary** stream or small river that flows into a larger stream or river.

upstream in the direction that is against a river's flow; toward a river's source.

***valley** land that lies between hills or mountains. (Shenandoah Valley)

***volcano** cone-shaped mountain formed by an outpouring of lava—hot, liquid rock—from a crack in the Earth's surface. (Mount St. Helens or Mauna Loa)

weather condition of the air at any given time and place.

★ *Activity* ★

Cooperative Learning

Charting examples of natural features Divide the class into small groups. Ask a student in each group to be the recorder. Have recorders turn a sheet of paper sideways and write the following terms along the top: *bay, canal, desert, island, mountain.* Have the students in each group take turns naming specific bays, canals, deserts, and so on in the United States. Tell students that they may use the maps in their textbooks, if necessary. Recorders should write each example under the appropriate heading. After a suitable length of time, have each team share its chart with the class. Encourage students to discuss what they know about each place named in their charts. (basic)

Chapter 1

Review and Activities

Reviewing the Chapter

Define These Terms

1. d **2.** c **3.** a **4.** b **5.** e

Explore the Main Ideas

1. Geographers describe place in terms of physical and human features.

2. Possible answers: People interact with their environment by growing crops, irrigating deserts, building roads, cutting down forests.

3. Flat maps cannot accurately show all parts of the Earth, which is spherical.

4. Pacific Coast—tall mountain ranges; Intermountain, east of the Pacific coast—high plateaus, deserts, canyons; Rocky Mountains, north-south range in the western U.S.—high peaks that impeded movement westward; Interior Plains, between the Rockies and the Appalachians—large lowland area; Appalachian Mountains, eastern U.S.—lower and less rugged than the Rockies; Canadian Shield, mostly in eastern Canada—lowland area rich in minerals; Coastal Plains, eastern and southern coasts—lowland area; Hawaiian Islands, in the South Pacific—tops of underwater volcanoes that rise above sea level.

5. Many tributaries flow into the Mississippi River system; it is an important source of water and a major transportation route.

6. Marine, from southern Alaska to northern California—mild, warm, and wet; Mediterranean, much of California—wet, mild winters and hot, dry summers; highland, mountains—colder; desert and steppe, southwestern U.S.—dry, hot; humid continental, Central Plains, northeast U.S.—mild summers, cold winters, more rain; tropical and humid subtropical, southern Florida, Hawaii—hot, humid; tundra and subarctic, Alaska—cold winters, short summers.

Chapter 1 Review and Activities

★ Sum It Up ★

Section 1 Five Themes of Geography

- Geography is the study of people, their environments, and their resources.
- The five themes of geography help show the connection between geography and history.
- The five themes of geography are location, place, interaction, movement, and region.

Section 2 Maps and Mapmaking

- Each type of map projection has advantages and disadvantages.
- Latitude and longitude lines on maps enable us to locate places exactly.
- The use of computers and satellites has made modern mapmaking more accurate than the mapmaking of centuries ago.

Section 3 American Lands and Climates

- Mountains, plains, and many other types of landforms can be found in North America.
- There are eight major physical regions in the United States.
- Rivers and lakes provide many benefits to the people of the United States.
- A variety of factors interact to produce weather and climate conditions.
- The United States has 10 major climates.
- The climate of a region helps to determine some of the economic activities that take place in the region.

For additional review of the major ideas of Chapter 1, see ***Guide to the Essentials of American History*** or ***Interactive Student Tutorial CD-ROM,*** which contains interactive review activities, graphic organizers, and practice tests.

Reviewing the Chapter

Define These Terms

Match each term with the correct definition.

Column 1	Column 2
1. history	**a.** lines measuring distance east and west from the Prime Meridian
2. latitude	**b.** a mapmaker
3. longitude	**c.** lines measuring distance north and south from the Equator
4. cartographer	**d.** an account of what has happened in people's lives
5. precipitation	**e.** water that falls as rain, sleet, or snow

Explore the Main Ideas

1. How do geographers generally describe place?
2. How do people interact with their environment?
3. Why do all flat maps distort the shapes of continents and oceans?
4. Locate and describe three physical regions of the United States.
5. Why is the Mississippi River such an important waterway?
6. Locate and describe three climates found in the United States.

Geography Activity

Match the letters on the map with the following places: **1.** North America, **2.** South America, **3.** Atlantic Ocean, **4.** Pacific Ocean, **5.** Isthmus of Panama, **6.** Great Lakes.
Location What ocean lies to the east of North America?

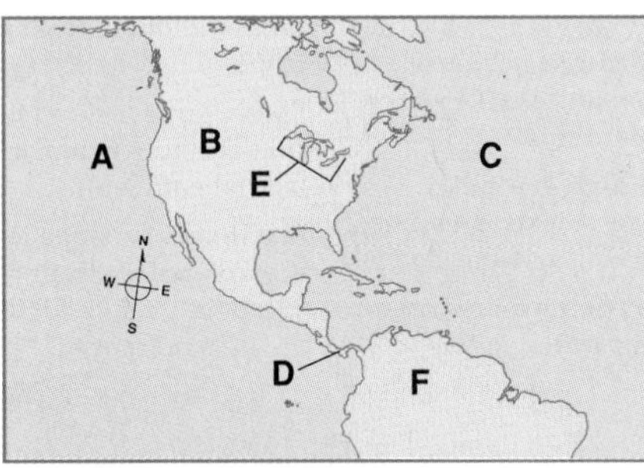

Geography Activity

1. B **2.** F **3.** C **4.** A **5.** D **6.** E

Location Atlantic Ocean

Critical Thinking and Writing

1. (a) Student answers should use geographic and climate terms from the text. **(b)** Possible answers: irrigated for farmland; built roads

2. The later map is more reliable because of increased geographic knowledge and advances in mapping methods.

3. (a) Pacific Coast **(b)** mild and moist marine climate

4. Possible answer: Climate can affect farming methods, how and when construction is done, materials used in construction, demands for fuel, water, and other resources.

Using Primary Sources

(a) Hastings expected people to clear forests, introduce herds of cattle, and plant crops in the "wild" lands of the West. **(b)** He was excited about the changes, which he saw as "improvements."

Critical Thinking and Writing

1. **Applying Information** Using the themes of geography, **(a)** describe the special geographic characteristics of the place where you live, **(b)** describe an example of how people in your community have adapted to or changed the natural environment.
2. **Evaluating Information** Which is more reliable: a map of North America from the 1500s or a map of North America from the 1900s? Explain the reasons for your choice.
3. **Synthesizing Information** Look at the picture of Mount Rainier that appears in Section 3 of this chapter. **(a)** Describe the physical region in which Mount Rainier is located. **(b)** Describe the climate of that region.
4. **Exploring Unit Themes** **Origins** How can the climate of a region affect people's economic activities in that region?

Using Primary Sources

In 1845, Lansford W. Hastings wrote a guide for people traveling to the West. In it he made the following predictions:

> "The time is not distant, when those wild forests, trackless plains, untrodden valleys . . . will present one grand scene of continuous improvements . . . when those vast forests shall have disappeared before the hardy pioneer; those extensive plains shall abound with innumerable herds of domestic animals; those fertile valleys shall groan under the weight of their abundant products."

Source: *The Emigrants' Guide to Oregon and California*, Lansford W. Hastings, 1845.

Recognizing Points of View **(a)** What changes did Hastings expect from human interaction with the environment? **(b)** How did he feel about the predicted changes?

Activity Bank

Interdisciplinary Activity

Exploring the Arts Do research to find a song or poem about an American river. Read or sing the composition to the class. Then lead a group discussion on what the song or poem says about the river.

Career Skills Activity

Cartographers On a large sheet of paper, create a map of the United States. On the map, draw and label the 50 states. Then label the major physical regions and landforms of the United States.

Citizenship Activity

Using a Political Map Find a map that shows the Congressional districts in your state. Identify the district in which you live. Through research, find out the name of your district's representative in Congress. If an issue or question concerns you, you can write about it to your Congressperson and ask for a response.

Internet Activity

Use the Internet to find the official site of NASA (National Aeronautics and Space Administration). There you will find images of the Earth taken by satellites orbiting the Earth. Select a picture that interests you and, if possible, print it out. In a written report, describe what the picture shows and explain why the picture might be useful to a cartographer.

EYEWITNESS Journal
You are traveling across the United States from somewhere on the Atlantic Coast to somewhere on the Pacific Coast. List all the states that you are traveling through. Also, list and describe all the physical regions that you are crossing.

Activity Bank

ASSESSMENT To assess the activities on this page, see the rubrics in the Alternative Assessment booklet in the Teaching Resources. You might want to share the rubrics with your students before they begin work.

Interdisciplinary Activity

1. Suggest students start their research by picking a river and then consulting songbooks in a library to find a song about it. Students might brainstorm a list of famous rivers and river songs they already know (e.g., "Old Man River").
2. Tell students to research their river, checking an encyclopedia or other source to try to find out how the song relates to some aspect of the river.
3. Students could perform the songs at an "American River Songfest."

Career Skills Activity

1. Suggest that students use the maps in the Reference Section of the textbook to do the activity.
2. Tell students that state borders need not be exact, but maps should reflect the approximate shapes and relative sizes of states.
3. Have students select several clear and accurate maps for classroom display.

Citizenship Activity

1. Districts are supposed to be drawn up to provide equal representation based on population within a state. Have students compare Congressional districts to population maps of their state.
2. If possible, have a state official visit the class and explain how Congressional districts in your state were determined.
3. To extend the activity, have students draw district maps of their own that ensure equal representation.

Eyewitness Journal

1. Refer students to their answers to question 4 under Explore the Main Ideas, which include descriptions of the physical regions of the U.S.
2. Encourage students to describe an actual cross-country trip they may have made.
3. Have students use encyclopedias to research and list exciting geographic features they might see in each state.

Internet Activity

1. Have students go to www.phschool.com, which contains updated information on a variety of topics.
2. One site you may find useful for this activity is Earth from Space at earth.jsc.nasa.gov.
3. Given the changing nature of the Internet, you may wish to preview this site before directing students to it.

Chapter 2 Manager

SECTION OBJECTIVES	TEACHING RESOURCES	ADDITIONAL RESOURCE
1 Early People and Cultures (pp. 30–35) **Objectives** 1. Explain where the first people to reach America came from. 2. Explain how archaeologists learn about the past. 3. Describe how early peoples adapted to the desert Southwest.	**Lesson Planner,** p. 4 (average) .... 60 mins. **Unit 1/Chapter 2** • Map Mystery: Who Were the Cliff Dwellers? p. 14 (basic) .... 15 mins. • Section 1 Quiz, p. 17 (average) .... 15 mins.	**Historical Outline Map Book** • Hunters Reach America, p. 1
2 People of North America (pp. 36–45) **Objectives** 1. Explain why many different cultures developed in North America. 2. Describe the different ways of life Native Americans developed. 3. Explain the role religion played in the lives of Native Americans.	**Lesson Planner,** p. 5 (average) .... 45 mins. **Unit 1/Chapter 2** • Practice Your Skills: Listening, p. 12 (average) .... 30 mins. • Critical Thinking and Writing: Comparing Information on a Chart, p. 13 (basic) .... 20 mins. • Connecting History and Literature: The Girl Who Hunted Rabbits, p. 15 (average) .... 20 mins. • Biography Flashcard: Dekanawida, p. 16 (average) .... 20 mins. • Section 2 Quiz, p. 18 (average) .... 15 mins. **Interdisciplinary Connections** • Main Idea: Native American Life, pp. 7–12 (average) .... 20 mins.	**Voices of Freedom** • An Arapaho Legend, pp. 16–17 (average) • Keeping a Heritage Alive, pp. 18–19 (average) • Founding of the League of the Iroquois, pp. 19–20 (average) **Historical Outline Map Book** • Native American Cultures, p. 4 **Customized Reader** • The Legend of Devil's Tower, article IA-5 (average) • The Good Twin and the Evil Twin, article IA-6 (average) • When Grizzlies Walked Upright, article IA-7 (average) **Prentice Hall Literature Libra** • Literature of the Southwest
3 Great Civilizations in the Americas (pp. 46–51) **Objectives** 1. Identify where the Mayan, Aztec, and Incan civilizations flourished. 2. Describe the main achievements of these civilizations. 3. Explain how religion and learning were linked in Aztec society.	**Lesson Planner,** p. 6 (average) .... 45 mins. **Unit 1/Chapter 2** • Section 3 Quiz, p. 19 (average) .... 15 mins.	**Voices of Freedom** • Farming Methods of the Incas, p. 21 (average) **Historical Outline Map Book** • Great Empires of the Americas, p. 5
4 After 1492 (pp. 52–55) **Objectives** 1. Explain how the 1492 encounter with Europeans affected Native Americans. 2. Describe the Columbian Exchange. 3. Identify elements of Native American culture that Europeans adopted.	**Lesson Planner,** p. 7 (average) .... 90 mins. **Unit 1/Chapter 2** • Vocabulary Builder, p. 11 (basic) .... 15 mins. • Section 4 Quiz, p. 20 (average) .... 15 mins. **Why Study History?** • Sports Are Important in Our Culture, pp. 7–10 (average) .... 90 mins. **Chapter Tests,** pp. 7–12 (average) .... 45 mins.	**Voices of Freedom** • Columbus Lands in America, pp. 24–26 (challenging) **Customized Reader** • Viking Saga of the Discovery of Vinland, article IB-6

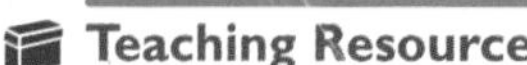

Assessment Options

Teaching Resources
- Alternative Assessment booklet
- Section Quizzes, Unit 1, Chapter 2, pp. 17–20
- Chapter Tests, Chapter 2, pp. 7–12
- Test Bank CD-ROM

Student Performance Pack
- Guide to the Essentials of American History, Chapter 2 Test, p. 15
- Standardized Test Prep Handbook
- Interactive Student Tutorial CD-ROM

Interdisciplinary Connections

Teaching Resources
- Map Mystery, Unit 1, Chapter 2, p. 14
- Connecting History and Literature, Unit 1, Chapter 2, p. 15
- Interdisciplinary Connections, pp. 7–12

Voices of Freedom, pp. 16–21, 24–26

Customized Reader, articles IA-5, IA-6, IA-7, IB-6

Prentice Hall Literature Library
- Literature of the Southwest

Technology

AmericanHeritage® History of the United States CD-ROM
- Time Tour: The First Americans in a Meeting of Different Worlds
- Arts and Entertainment: Books
- Virtual Buildings: Iroquois Longhouse

Interactive Student Tutorial CD-ROM

Test Bank CD-ROM

Color Transparencies
- Celestial Germinators, p. D-25
- Native American Handcrafts, p. D-27
- The Americas and the World, 1300–1600, p. E-13
- Native American Dwellings, p. H-23

Guided Reading Audiotapes (English/Spanish), side 1

Listening to Literature Audiocassettes: The American Experience, Navajo Night Chant, side 1; From the Houses of Magic, side 1; Spring Song, side 1; Song Concerning a Dream of the Thunderbirds, side 1; From the Walam Olum, side 1

Resource Pro® CD-ROM

Prentice Hall United States History Video Collection™ (Spanish track available on disk version.) Vol. 1, Ch. 7

Prentice Hall Home Page
www.phschool.com

Student Performance Pack

Guide to the Essentials of American History
- Ch. 2, pp. 11–15
  (Available in English and Spanish)

Guided Reading Audiotapes (English/Spanish), side 1

Standardized Test Prep Handbook

Interactive Student Tutorial CD-ROM

BLOCK SCHEDULING
Activities with this icon will help you meet your Block Scheduling needs.

ENGLISH LANGUAGE LEARNERS
Activities with this icon are suitable for English Language Learners.

TEAM TEACHING
Activities and Background Notes with this icon present starting points for Team Teaching.

Teachers' Bibliography

From the Archives of AmericanHeritage®

Don't miss the special American Heritage® teaching notes found in this chapter.

Contact Teachers' Curriculum Institute to learn more about History Alive!® resources on Native Americans. See History Alive!® unit: Geography of America From Past to Present, Section 3, "Adapting to the Environment: Native Americans."

Explore your library to find these issues related to Chapter 2: *Diné: The People of the Navajo Nation,* July 1987; *Pueblo Indians,* November 1984; *Cherokee Indians,* February 1984.

Prentice Hall Web Site You can access a structured, on-line environment that allows you to preview curriculum-related resources and receive updated information on groundbreaking events from around the nation and the world. (www.phschool.com)

Chapter 2

The First Americans
Prehistory–1600

Introducing the Chapter

Have students preview the main ideas of this chapter by looking over the visuals. Suggest they look for examples of cultural differences among the first Americans.

Using the Time Line To provide students with practice using the time line, ask questions such as these: **(1)** When did Mayan cities flourish in Mexico and Central America? *(A.D. 300–900)* **(2)** In the 1300s, what West African kingdom reached its height? *(Mali)* **(3)** Whose was the largest empire in the Americas at the time of Columbus? *(Incas)* **(4)** When was the Iroquois League formed? *(1570s)*

Ask students to name as many sports and games as they can that are important to Americans today. Have students speculate about where and why these sports developed—for example, target shooting and archery sharpened hunting skills.

For additional *Why Study History?* support, see p. 54

Chapter 2

The First Americans

Prehistory–1600

What's Ahead

Thousands of years ago, hunters from Asia followed herds of wild animals to the Americas. As they gradually spread through North and South America, they developed a variety of cultures. The economic activities, religious beliefs, and societies of these first Americans reflected the environments in which they lived, from the icy north to the dry desert of the Southwest. Farther south, in Mexico and Central and South America, several great civilizations arose.

The world of these first Americans changed dramatically after Europeans reached American shores. At the same time, aspects of Native American culture spread to other parts of the globe.

Why Study History? European settlers adapted many Native American customs. These included sports, such as lacrosse. Today, as in the past, sports play a role in society that goes far beyond just having fun. To focus on this connection, see this chapter's *Why Study History?* feature, "Sports Are Important in Our Culture."

American Events

300–900 Mayan cities flourish in Mexico and Central America

1100–1200 Anasazis build cliff dwellings in Southwest

Prehistory | 1000 | 1200

World Events

30,000–15,000 Years Ago World Event Hunters from Asia cross land bridge to the Americas

1013 World Event Danish Vikings conquer England

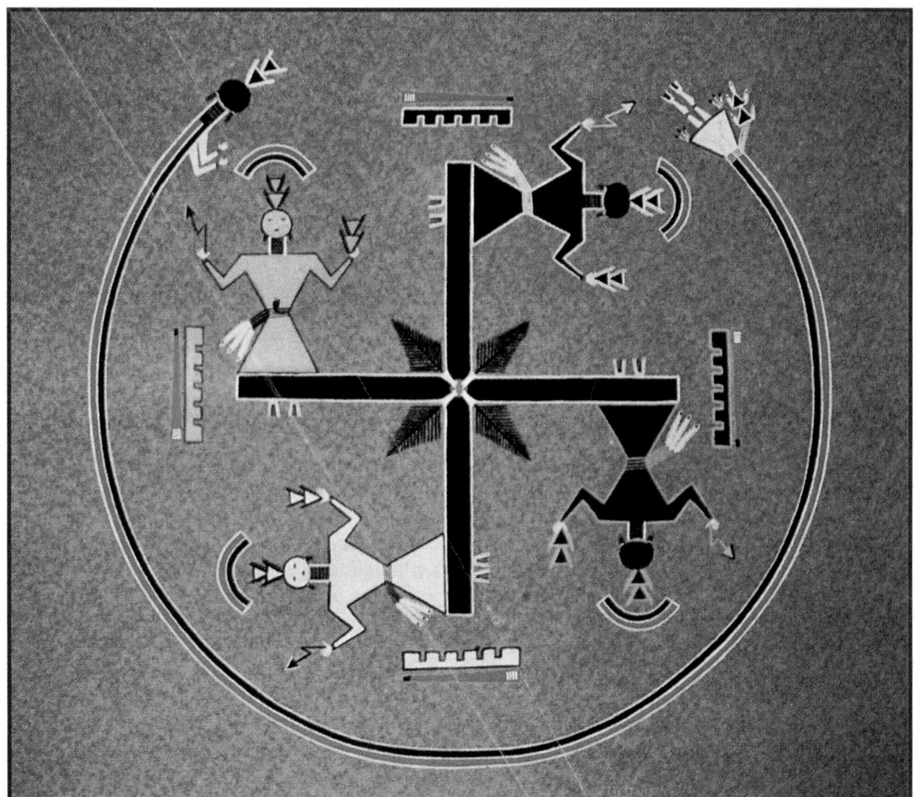

Viewing HISTORY **Native American Art**

The Navajos used sand paintings in healing and religious ceremonies. This painting shows a whirlwind, or tornado, as people on spinning logs. Navajo culture arose in the American Southwest. Dozens of other Native American cultures emerged in the varied environments of North and South America. ★ **How does this painting reflect the desert environment of the Navajos?**

1400s Aztecs build powerful empire in Mexico

Early 1500s Incas control the largest empire in the Americas

1570s Peoples of the Eastern Woodlands form the Iroquois League to promote peace

1200 — 1400 — 1600

1300s World Event West African kingdom of Mali reaches its height

1492 World Event Columbus reaches the Americas

★ Background ★
Art Note

Native American Art To the Navajos, the universe is a balance of good and evil spiritual elements. Should the equilibrium be disturbed, even accidentally, disasters occur. Religious rituals known as chants are used to restore universal harmony. When a chanter, or singer, creates a sand painting during such a ritual, the sacred images are erased as soon as the ceremony concludes. T

Documents and Literature

On pp. 527–530, you will find two readings to enrich this chapter:

1. Literature "The Spider Woman," Navajo folk tale, relates how Navajo women learned to weave. (Use with Section 2.)

2. Eyewitness Account "A Description of Montezuma," excerpt from the memoirs of Spanish soldier Bernal Díaz, relating his observations of Montezuma during an early visit. (Use with Section 3.)

Writing Actively 

Responding to Art Ask students to examine the sand painting on this page. Read the caption aloud and discuss the caption's meaning. Then have students write a poem about tornadoes that uses the same images as the painting.

Viewing HISTORY ANSWER

Students should recognize that the Navajos used sand, which was plentiful in the desert, and they illustrated a natural phenomenon of their region—a tornado.

Technology

Videodiscs/Videotapes
Show the *Prentice Hall United States History Video Collection*™ segments for this chapter. The videodisc version has a Spanish track. Press audio until you get the left channel for English or the right channel for Spanish, or use the bar codes in the Guidebook.

AmericanHeritage® History of the United States CD-ROM
- Time Tour: The First Americans in a Meeting of Different Worlds (*average*)

Section 1
Early People and Cultures

LESSON PLAN

Objectives

★ Explain where the first Americans came from.

★ Explain how archaeologists learn about the past.

★ Describe how early peoples adapted to the desert Southwest.

1 Engage

Warm Up Write the word *culture* on the chalkboard. Ask students to list words or phrases that they associate with modern American culture. On the chalkboard, record student responses.

Activating Prior Knowledge In small groups, have students identify elements from other cultures they know of or have studied. Have groups categorize the aspects of American or other cultures to discover common elements, such as food, clothing, shelter, religion, customs, and government, and create a list of those elements.

Reading Actively

Before Reading Have students examine the headings, visuals, and captions in the section. Have them list three groups they will study in this section.

RESOURCE DIRECTORY

Teaching Resources
Lesson Planner, p. 4

Transparencies
Time Lines
- The Americas and the World, 1300–1600, p. E-13

Early People and Cultures

As You Read

Explore These Questions
- Where did the first Americans come from?
- How do archaeologists learn about the past?
- How did early people adapt to the desert Southwest?

Define
- glacier
- artifact
- archaeology
- culture
- adobe
- pueblo
- drought

Identify
- Native American
- Mound Builder
- Hohokam
- Anasazi

SETTING the Scene Crouched low, the small band of hunters crept slowly forward. Ahead, a herd of bison grazed at the edge of a swamp. At a signal, the hunters leaped up, shouting loudly. The startled herd stampeded into the swamp. As the bison struggled in the deep mud, the hunters hurled their spears.

Scenes much like this one took place on the Great Plains more than 10,000 years ago. Tracking herds of bison or woolly mammoths, skillful hunters were among the first people to settle the Americas. Over many thousands of years, their descendants spread out across two continents. In the process, they developed many different ways of life.

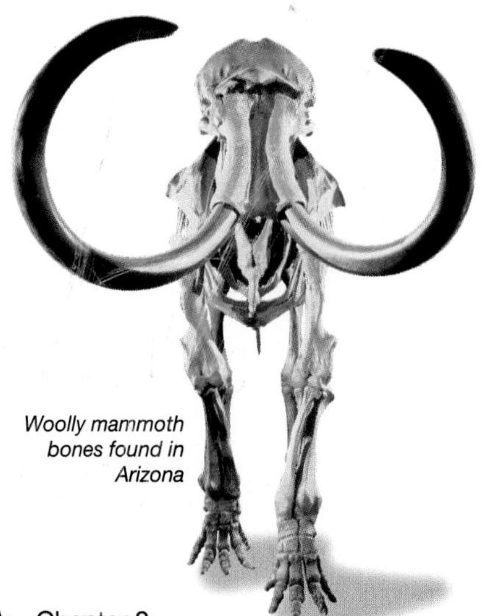

Woolly mammoth bones found in Arizona

The First Americans Migrate From Asia

Like other early people, the first Americans left no written records to tell us where they came from or when they arrived. However, scientists have found evidence to suggest that the first people reached the Americas sometime during the last ice age.

The last ice age

According to geologists, the Earth has gone through four ice ages. The last one took place between 100,000 and 10,000 years ago.

During the last ice age, thick sheets of ice, called **glaciers,** spread out from the arctic regions. Almost one third of the Earth was buried under these sheets of ice. In North America, glaciers stretched across Canada and reached as far south as Kentucky.

As they moved, glaciers changed the lands they covered. They pushed soil, rocks, and huge boulders across the land. They created islands such as Long Island, New York, as well as Nantucket and Martha's Vineyard off the coast of Massachusetts. Water from melting glaciers drained into channels, creating rivers such as the Missouri.

Crossing the land bridge

Because glaciers locked up water from the oceans, sea levels fell. As a result, land that had been under water was uncovered. In the far north, a land bridge joined Siberia in northeastern Asia to Alaska in North

★ ***Customized Instruction*** ★

English Language Learners

Making a picture dictionary Visual images of unfamiliar words may help ELL students grasp difficult concepts. Have ELL students start a picture dictionary of words associated with Native American customs, artifacts, and buildings. Students can use descriptions and context clues from the text, as well as from other reference books on Native Americans. By illustrating these words, students will gain a better understanding of their meaning and can create a reference product that could be part of the class library. Have students begin with words such as *mound, adobe,* and *pueblo* in this section and then add terms such as *igloo, kayak, potlatch, hogan, tepee, travois, long house,* and *chinampas* as they read the rest of the chapter. *(average)* ELL T

America. Today, this land bridge is under the Bering Strait.

Scientists think that the first Americans were probably hunters. Traveling in small bands, they followed herds of woolly mammoth, bison, and other game across the land bridge. Some groups may have wandered along the southern coast of the land bridge, catching fish and sea mammals.

Experts date the arrival of these first Americans anywhere from 30,000 to 15,000 years ago. Once they reached the Americas, the continuing search for better hunting grounds led the newcomers across the land. Over thousands of years, they spread out through North America, Central America, and South America.

Adapting to new conditions

About 12,000 years ago, the ice age ended. Temperatures rose around the globe. Glaciers melted, and the ocean once more covered the land bridge. At about the same time, the woolly mammoths and mastodons died out.

The people of the Americas adapted to the new conditions. They hunted smaller animals, gathered wild berries and grains, and caught fish.

Then, about 5,000 years ago, some people learned to grow crops such as corn, beans, and squash. Farming changed those people's lives. People who farmed no longer had to move constantly in search of food. Instead, they built the first permanent villages in the Americas. As farming methods improved, villagers produced more food. In turn, the increased food supply allowed populations to grow.

Studying the First Americans

Today, experts in many fields are working to develop a clearer picture of the first Americans. Some are studying the remains of ancient people of northeast Asia. They hope to learn how these Asian people might be related to the first Americans.

Other experts are analyzing the languages of Native American groups today. **Native Americans** are the descendants of the

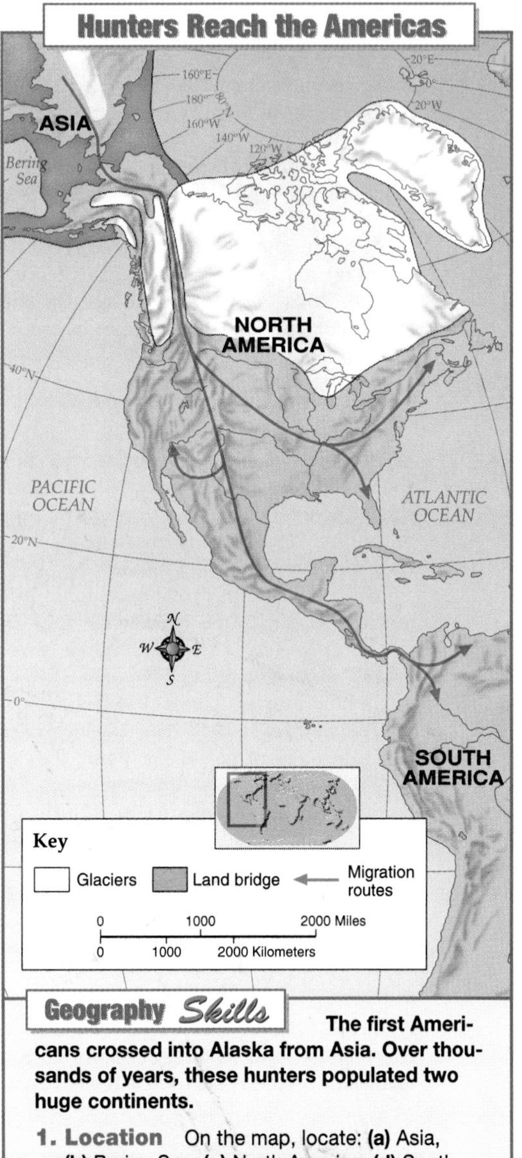

Geography Skills **The first Americans crossed into Alaska from Asia. Over thousands of years, these hunters populated two huge continents.**

1. **Location** On the map, locate: **(a)** Asia, **(b)** Bering Sea, **(c)** North America, **(d)** South America.
2. **Movement** In which direction did early hunters travel from Asia to reach North America?
3. **Critical Thinking** Why do you think many of the first Americans continued to travel southward after crossing the land bridge?

2 Explore

Ask students to read the section. For a homework assignment, have them research and report on one group, such as the Mound Builders, Hohokams, or Anasazis.

3 Teach

Review with students the cultural categories they previously identified. Add any of the following that they have not identified: food, clothing, shelter, government, customs and behavior, ideas, religion and beliefs, and education/skills. Have students use these categories to make a chart for each culture studied in this section.

4 Assess

To close the lesson, have students complete the section review. Or have them write essays about the distinct features of each culture. Encourage them to illustrate major points.

★ ★ ★ ★ ★ ★ ★ ★ ★ ★ ★ ★ ★ ★ ★ ★ ★ ★

Geography Skills

ANSWERS

1. Review locations with students. **2.** southeast **3.** Possibly they followed animal herds. Also, the region near the land bridge was very cold and difficult to live in.

★ Background ★ Historiography

Prehistorical mystery tour In *The Great Journey: The Peopling of Ancient America,* Brian M. Fagan explores various theories about the first migrations to the Americas. Fagan's great advantage as "tour guide" is a broad knowledge of disciplines, ranging from botany, genetics, and meteorology, to geology and oceanography.

Videodiscs/Videotapes
Prentice Hall United States History Video Collection™, Vol. 1, Ch. 7, "The First Americans," 5 mins (average) ELL

first people to reach the Americas thousands of years ago. Through the study of Native American languages, scholars are trying to trace how these people spread out across the Americas.

Still other scholars are examining stone tools, weapons, baskets, and carvings found across the Americas. Objects such as these made by humans are called **artifacts** (AHRT uh faktz). Artifacts are the building blocks of **archaeology** (ahr kee AHL uh jee), the study of evidence left by early people in order to find out about their way of life.

Artifacts provide valuable clues

By studying artifacts, archaeologists can learn much about the people who made them. A finely carved arrowhead suggests that a people knew how to make weapons and hunt. Woven plant fibers suggest that they were skilled basket makers.

Each object can provide valuable information. At the same time, each new find raises questions such as, "When was it made?" and "Who made it?"

In laboratories, experts use technology to analyze new finds. By testing the level of carbon in a piece of pottery or bone, they can date it to within a few hundred years. They might study kernels of ancient corn through a microscope to find out about the climate in which it grew. They might compare clay pots from different areas to find out about the people who made them.

Forming theories about ancient cultures

From artifacts and other evidence, archaeologists form theories about the cultures of ancient people. A **culture** is the entire way of life that a people has developed. It includes their homes, clothing, economy, arts, and government. It also includes the customs, ideas, beliefs, and skills that they pass on from generation to generation.

Often, very little evidence survives about an ancient people. Sometimes, archaeologists find evidence in unexpected places, through sheer luck. A flood might wash away a river bank and uncover ancient bones. A bulldozer clearing land might dig up a buried campsite. Each new find or new method of studying ancient artifacts helps to fill in the story of early Americans.

In their search for evidence about the past, archaeologists often dig up ancient sites. In recent years, however, they have grown more aware of the need to respect Native American landmarks and traditions. Government officials, too, have become more respectful of Native American concerns. Some laws have been passed to protect Native American burial grounds.

Connections With Geography

In the southwestern United States, geography has helped archaeologists study early cultures. The dry climate has preserved baskets, bags, sandals, nets, and other items dating back approximately 2,000 years. In a damper climate, many of these items might have rotted away.

The Mound Builders

Among the artifacts that archaeologists have found in North America are thousands of earthen mounds. The mounds are scattered across a region stretching from the Appalachian Mountains to the Mississippi Valley and from Wisconsin to Florida. Scholars call the people who built these earthworks **Mound Builders.** The Mound Builders lived at various times from about 3,000 years ago until the 1700s. The two main groups were the Hopewells and the Mississippians.

Purpose of the mounds

The mounds served different purposes. The first mounds were burial grounds, probably for important leaders. Inside the mounds, archaeologists have found carved pipes, stone sculptures, and copper weapons, tools, and ornaments. They have also found shells from the Gulf of Mexico and turquoise from the Southwest. This evidence shows that the Mound Builders traded with people from other parts of North America.

Some mounds were used for religious ceremonies. They are shaped like pyramids

MINI LESSON

COMMUNICATION Writing an Essay

1. To introduce the skill of writing an essay, tell students that an essay has a title that suggests its topic, a thesis statement that presents the main point, body paragraphs that support the main point, and a conclusion that summarizes the topic.

2. To help students practice the skill, guide them through these steps: **(a)** Pick a topic, decide on the main point, write a thesis statement, support the main point with examples and facts, organize the support logically, write a summary, pick a title. **(b)** Draft the essay. **(c)** Revise, polish, and proofread.

3. Have students apply the skill by using the steps to write an essay about the first Americans or the Mound Builders.

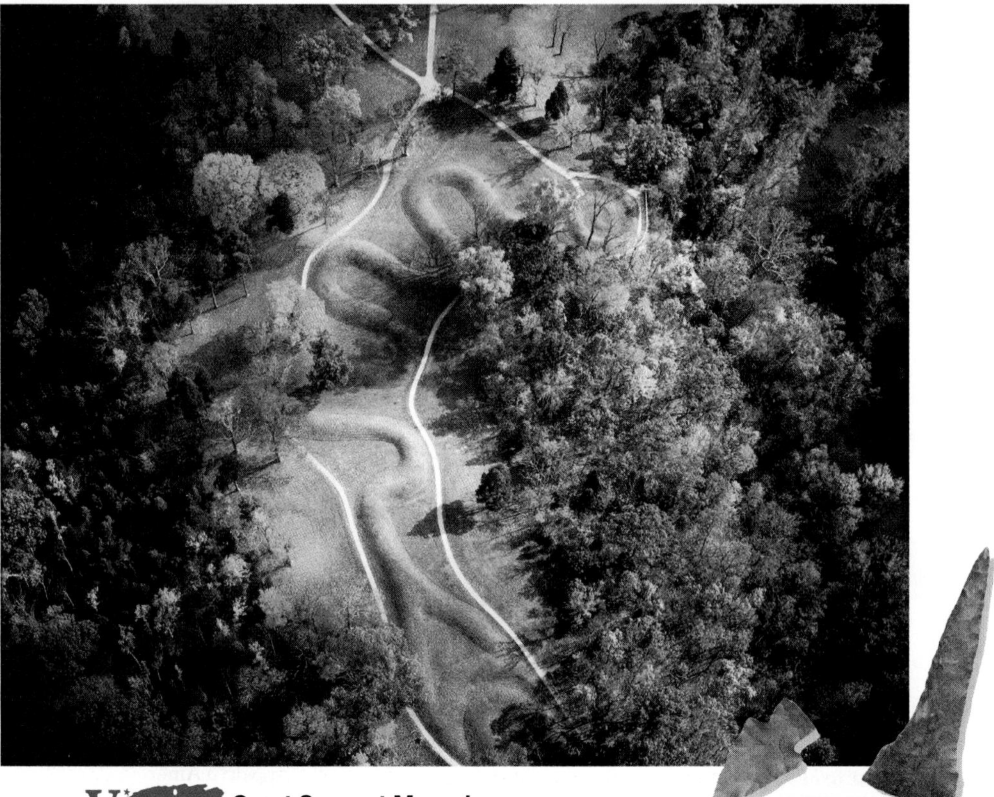

Viewing HISTORY Great Serpent Mound

The ancient Americans known as the Mound Builders left behind thousands of mounds. One of the largest is the Great Serpent Mound, shown here. It twists across the Ohio landscape for more than 1,200 feet (365 m). ★ **Why do you think present-day archaeologists are eager to examine early burial mounds?**

▲ *Flints found at Great Serpent Mound*

with flat tops. On the flat surfaces, the people built temples and homes for the ruling class.

More than 2,000 years ago, Hopewell builders created the twisting Great Serpent Mound in present-day Ohio. From above, it looks like a snake with a coiled tail. The meaning of this and other animal-shaped mounds remains a mystery.

Monk's Mound

Some time between 700 and 1500, the Mississippians built a large city at Cahokia (kah HOH kee ah), in present-day Illinois. As many as 30,000 people may have lived there at one time. Over the years, the Cahokians moved tons of soil, basketload by basketload, to build Monk's Mound. This vast platform mound covers 16 acres—equal to 14½ football fields! Hundreds of other smaller mounds stand nearby.

The Mississippians built a wooden fence around Cahokia. Beyond this fence, they placed circles of evenly spaced posts. Some archaeologists think the posts served as a kind of calendar. From the top of Monk's Mound, rulers could see the shadows cast by the posts. Shorter shadows announced the

Viewing HISTORY ANSWER

Possible answer: The artifacts found in the mounds can provide important clues about the way of life of early Americans.

FROM THE ARCHIVES OF AmericanHeritage®

Mounds of mystery The great mounds have long intrigued Americans. In the 1700s and 1800s, people speculated that the mounds had been built by ancients from such widely diverse areas as Wales, Greece, or Peru—or even by the lost tribes of Israel. Thomas Jefferson and later explorer John Wesley Powell each proposed that the mounds were built by Native Americans.

Source: Michael S. Durham, "Mound Country," *American Heritage* magazine, April 1995.

★ *Background* ★

Recent Scholarship

Fighting science In his book *Red Earth, White Lies: Native Americans and the Myth of Scientific Fact* (Scribner, 1997), Vine DeLoria criticizes the scientific approach to evaluating ancient peoples and their origins. DeLoria believes that the study of oral traditions and religious beliefs of Native Americans is a more reliable indicator of their cultural prehistory.

AmericanHeritage
MAGAZINE

Mesa Verde National Park
To learn more about this site on the Internet, go to www.mesaverde.org.

Reading Actively 

During Reading Ask students to prepare a graphic organizer comparing and contrasting the Mound Builders and the Anasazis.

Writing Actively 

After Reading Have students use the following topic sentence to begin a paragraph linking the environment and the first Americans: "The environment affected the first Americans in many ways." Have students complete the paragraph with at least three sentences that support the topic sentence.

AmericanHeritage
MAGAZINE

HISTORY HAPPENED HERE

Mesa Verde National Park

The cliff dwellings at Mesa Verde were abandoned more than 700 years ago. Yet these spectacular buildings still stand. They remind us of the skill of Native Americans who carved entire villages out of the canyons and cliffs of southwest Colorado. Cliff Palace (left) is the largest complex at Mesa Verde. It contains more than 200 rooms, with sections up to four stories tall. The park also has a museum where you can see many Anasazi artifacts.

★ ***To learn more about this historic site, write:*** *Superintendent, Mesa Verde National Park, Colorado 81330.*

Clay cup from Mesa Verde

coming of spring. Longer ones showed that autumn was near. To farming people like the Mississippians, knowing when to plant and when to harvest crops was important.

Early Cultures of the Southwest

Through careful study, archaeologists have also learned much about the early people of the American Southwest. This desert region may seem like a poor place to farm. Annual rainfall is only 5 to 10 inches (13 to 25 cm). In the daytime, temperatures can soar above 100° Fahrenheit (38°C). Cactus and sagebrush cover the desert floor.

Still, at least 3,000 years ago, people in the Southwest learned to grow crops such as corn. In time, several major farming societies, including the Hohokams (hoh HOH kahmz) and Anasazis (ah nuh SAH zeez), made their homes there.

The **Hohokams** lived in present-day southern Arizona. About 2,000 years ago, they developed ways to turn the dry desert into fertile farmland. They dug a vast system of irrigation ditches to bring water to dry land. The irrigation ditches channeled water from the Salt and Gila rivers into fields that then produced corn, squash, and beans.

In the late 1800s, archaeologists began to study thousands of abandoned stone buildings that dotted the Southwest. Most were built between 750 and 1300.

Who built these structures? Archaeologists asked the Navajos, the Native Americans who live in the region today. The Navajos replied that the mounds were built by the Anasazis. In the Navajo language, Anasazi means "ancient one."

Anasazi pueblos

As the Hohokams did, the **Anasazis** farmed the desert by using irrigation. The Anasazis built large, multistoried houses.

★ *Background* ★

Linking Past and Present

Ancient ancestors Archaeologists and historians believe that the modern Pima and Papago peoples are descendants of the Hohokams. Both peoples lived on the same land that the Hohokams had called home; both peoples also were farmers. Elements of their language and ceremonies suggest an ancient link with the Aztecs as well.

★ *Background* ★

Did You Know?

Architectural excellence The ruins of cliff dwellings at the Chaco Culture National Park in northwestern New Mexico are a testimony to the great building skills of the Anasazis. The park covers 53 square miles. The older buildings seem to have a unique local style, while some of the more recent structures show Mexican influences.

RESOURCE DIRECTORY

Teaching Resources
Unit 1/Chapter 2
- Map Mystery: Who Were the Cliff Dwellers? p. 14
- Section 1 Quiz, p. 17

Walls were made of stone and sun-dried bricks, called **adobe.** When the Spanish explored the Southwest in the early 1500s, they called these houses **pueblos** (PWEHB lohz), or villages. Similar in some ways to modern apartment buildings, pueblos could shelter hundreds of families.

Anasazi pottery

At Pueblo Bonito, in New Mexico's Chaco Canyon, a giant house was once home to 1,000 people. Its 800 rooms are tiny, but the Anasazis spent much of their time in sunny, outdoor courtyards. The house has no stairways or hallways. To reach rooms on the upper floors, people climbed steep ladders.

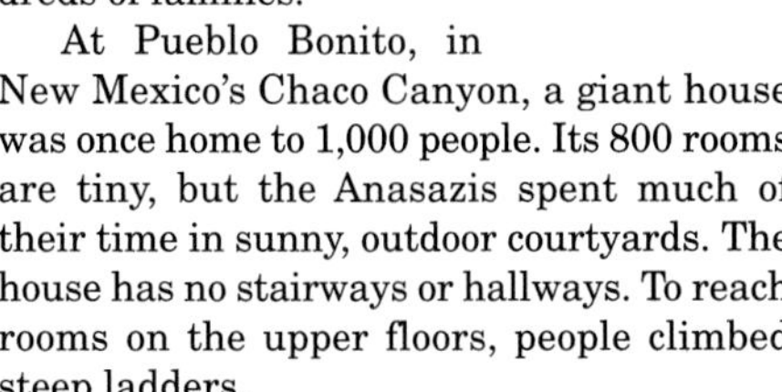

Cliff dwellings

Sometime between 1,000 and 800 years ago, some Anasazis sought protection from warlike neighbors. To make their villages harder to attack, they built adobe houses along the cliffs that dotted the region. Toeholds cut into the rock let the Anasazis climb up and down the cliff walls. On top of the cliffs, they planted corn and other crops.

A network of roads connected Anasazi villages. Along these roads, traders carried cotton, sandals made from yucca leaves, and blankets woven from turkey feathers. Some Anasazi traders headed into present-day Mexico to trade with people there.

In the late 1200s, the Anasazis abandoned most of their villages. Archaeologists think that a **drought,** or long dry spell, hit the region. One legend speaks of such a disaster:

> "Snow ceased in the north and the west; rain ceased in the south and the east; the mists of the mountains above were drunk up; the waters of the valleys below were dried up.... Our ancients who dwelt in the cliffs fled ... when the rain stopped long, long ago."

Later, some of the Anasazis may have gone back to their homes. Most, however, became part of other cultures. Today, descendants of these early people preserve traditions of the ancient Anasazi culture.

★ Section 1 Review ★

Recall

1. **Identify** **(a)** Native American, **(b)** Mound Builder, **(c)** Hohokam, **(d)** Anasazi.
2. **Define** **(a)** glacier, **(b)** artifact, **(c)** archaeology, **(d)** culture, **(e)** adobe, **(f)** pueblo, **(g)** drought.

Comprehension

3. How did ancient people first arrive in the Americas?
4. Describe three kinds of evidence that archaeologists study.
5. **(a)** How did the Hohokams farm the desert? **(b)** Why did the Anasazis abandon their villages?

Critical Thinking and Writing

6. **Applying Information** Review the subsection The First Americans Migrate From Asia on page 30. How does the information in this subsection support the idea that geography affects history?
7. **Recognizing Points of View** Why have archaeologists and Native Americans sometimes clashed over the digging up of burial grounds?

Activity **Writing a Survival Plan** Unplug that computer! Circumstances have forced you to live for a year in the desert Southwest. Write a plan explaining how you might adapt to your environment, as early Native Americans did. Consider all your options!

★ Section 1 Review ★

ANSWERS

1. (a) p. 31, **(b)** p. 32, **(c)–(d)** p. 34

2. (a) p. 30, **(b)–(d)** p. 32, **(e)–(g)** p. 35

3. They crossed a land bridge that joined Asia and North America.

4. Possible answers: tools, weapons, baskets, carvings, bones, food, pottery

5. (a) by digging irrigation ditches to bring water from the Salt and Gila rivers to their fields **(b)** probably because of a drought

6. The land bridge formed during the last ice age let people from Asia migrate overland into North America.

7. Possible answer: They contain artifacts that archaeologists can study to learn about the Mound Builders. But to Native Americans, the burial grounds are sacred and should not be disturbed.

Activity

Guided Instruction

Have students begin by listing basic needs *(food, shelter, clothing)*. Then have them brainstorm for natural items that could supply these needs. *(Food: plants such as wild berries and nuts; shelter: a cave; clothing: animal skins)*

ASSESSMENT See the rubrics in the Alternative Assessment booklet in the Teaching Resources.

★ Activity ★

Connections With Science and Technology

Planning a museum exhibit While Thomas Jefferson is best known as an American political leader, scientists consider him the founder of American archaeology. Have small groups of students research Jefferson's archaeological work and plan a museum exhibit about his contributions to American archaeology. Display possibilities include murals, glass cases with artifacts, illustrated time lines, touch talks, and maps. Display descriptions should identify the work presented and its significance to the field. Each group should include a detailed diagram or layout for its exhibit. *(challenging)* ELL T

Section 2 People of North America

LESSON PLAN

Objectives

★ Explain why many different cultures developed in North America.

★ Describe the different ways of life Native Americans developed.

★ Explain the role religion played in the lives of Native Americans.

1 Engage

Warm Up On the chalkboard, write *desert, forest, arctic ice,* and *grassy plains.* Have students discuss what challenges they might face if they lived in any of those environments.

Activating Prior Knowledge Have small groups choose one culture area from the map on p. 39. Using what they learned in Chapter 1, have them list aspects of daily life that people in their area would have had to adapt to their environment, such as housing needs based on climate.

Reading Actively

Before Reading Ask students to turn the section heading into a question. As they read, have them jot down notes to answer the question.

RESOURCE DIRECTORY

Teaching Resources
Lesson Planner, p. 5
Interdisciplinary Connections
• Main Idea: Native American Life, pp. 7–12

People of North America

As You Read

Explore These Questions
- Why did many different cultures develop in North America?
- What ways of life did Native Americans develop?
- What role did religion play in the lives of Native Americans?

Define
- culture area
- tribe
- igloo
- kayak
- potlatch
- kiva
- hogan
- travois
- tepee
- long house
- clan
- sachem

Identify
- Inuit
- Pueblo
- kachina
- Apache
- Navajo
- Natchez
- Iroquois
- League of the Iroquois

SETTING the Scene When Italian explorer Christopher Columbus reached the Americas in 1492, he thought he had reached the East Indies, a group of islands off the coast of Asia. He called the people he met "los Indios," or "the Indians." Soon, all Europeans were calling the people of the Americas Indians. By the time they realized Columbus's error, they were used to the term.

The name Indian is misleading for another, more important, reason. Native Americans do not belong to a single group. In Columbus's time, as now, Native Americans included many different people with many distinct cultures. In North America alone, Native Americans spoke hundreds of languages. Their cultures also varied greatly, from simple to highly complex.

Culture Areas and Tribes

The map on page 39 shows the 10 major culture areas of North America, north of Mexico. A **culture area** is a region in which people share a similar way of life.

Within each culture area, there were many different tribes. A **tribe** is a group of villages or settlements that shares common customs, language, and rituals. Members of a tribe saw themselves as a distinct people who shared the same origin. Throughout history, tribal organizations have played an important role in Indian life.

The tribe felt a strong bond with the land, plants, and animals in the region where they lived. As they hunted animals or raised crops or gathered wild plants, members of the tribe tried to keep a balance with the forces of the natural world. Their religious ceremonies and daily customs were designed to help them maintain that balance.

People of the Far North

Two culture areas, the Arctic and Subarctic, stretched across the far northern part of North America. In both regions, people adapted to harsh climates. In the Arctic, winter temperatures drop to –30° Fahrenheit (–34° C). Snow stays on the ground much of the year.

Arctic

Frozen seas and icy, treeless plains made up the world of the **Inuits,** the people of the Arctic.* The Inuits used all the limited re-

*Inuit, meaning "humans," was the Arctic people's name for themselves. Neighboring people, the Crees, called the Inuits "Eskimos," or "Eaters of Raw Meat."

★ *Customized Instruction* ★

Kinesthetic Learners

Portraying ancient peoples Divide the class into groups, and assign each group one of the Native American peoples discussed in the section. Tell each group to keep its identity secret. Each group should then create a pantomime or dialogue to illustrate an activity of their people, as described in the text. For example, the Inuit group could mime hunting whales or building an igloo. Have other groups identify the people portrayed. Conclude with a discussion of how the activities show the interaction of people with their environment. (*basic*) ELL T sources of their environment in order to survive. In summer, they collected driftwood from the ocean shores to make tools and shelters. In winter, they built **igloos,** or houses of snow and ice. Lamps filled with seal oil kept the igloos warm even in the most bitter cold. Inuit women made warm clothing out of furs and waterproof boots out of sealskins.

Because food was scarce, the Inuits could not live in the same place all year round. In winter, large bands set up camp at a favorite spot near the sea. There on the thick sea ice, they hunted for seals. In spring, they paddled **kayaks** (KI aks), or small skin boats, to spear seals, whales, or walruses. When the summer came, they moved inland in smaller bands to hunt caribou or to fish in inland rivers and lakes.

Inuit religious beliefs reflected their close ties to the natural world. Inuits believed that each animal had a spirit. Before the hunt, they offered gifts to the animal they hoped to catch. After a successful hunt, they sang songs of praise and thanks to the animals.

Subarctic

Like their Arctic neighbors, the people of the Subarctic faced a severe environment. They, too, moved from place to place, hunting moose and caribou or fishing in rivers and

Viewing History **In the Frozen Arctic**

In the Arctic region, Inuit hunters moved across an icy landscape in search of food. Inuit carvings reflect the importance of the seals, walruses, and polar bears they depended on for survival. ★ **How did Inuits find shelter during the Arctic winter?**

Inuit carving of a walrus

2 Explore

Ask students to read the section. For a homework assignment, have them research and report on a specific people discussed in the section.

3 Teach

Ask students to take the role of someone traveling across North America in 1491. Have students create a journal record of the Native American groups that the person might meet. Encourage students to write in the first person.

4 Assess

To close the lesson, have students complete the section review. As an alternative, have students play a "Jeopardy"-style game. Choose several students to give information relating to various Native American groups. Call on volunteers to create appropriate questions. Award points for good "answers" and accurate "questions."

★ ★ ★ ★ ★ ★ ★ ★ ★ ★ ★ ★ ★ ★ ★ ★ ★ ★

Viewing History ANSWER

They built igloos out of ice.

★ *Background* ★

Did You Know?

Inuit information

- The Inuit called their southern neighbors *itqilit,* meaning lousy, or full of lice.
- Coastal Inuit were primarily whale, walrus, and seal hunters; interior Inuit were primarily caribou hunters.
- Shamans, some of whom were women, performed magic, secured revenge, and cured illness.

oceans. They fashioned caribou and rabbit skins into robes and leggings. When Europeans arrived, many Subarctic peoples supplied furs to traders.

People of the Northwest Coast

The people of the Northwest Coast enjoyed a favorable climate and abundant food supplies. They gathered rich harvests of fish from the sea. Sea creatures provided more than just food. In some areas, people caught shellfish, called dentalia, to use as money. The longer the string of dentalia shells, the greater was the value.

In autumn, the rivers were full of salmon. To show their gratitude, the people returned salmon skeletons to the water. They believed that the Salmon Beings would grow new bodies and continue to provide food. The fishers of one Northwest Coast group, the Kwakiutls (kwah kee OOT 'lz), chanted this prayer of thanks when they caught their first fish of the year:

> "We have come to meet alive,
> Swimmer,
> do not feel wrong about what I have
> done to you,
> friend Swimmer,
> for that is the reason why you came,
> that I may spear you,
> that I may eat you,
> Supernatural One, you, Long-Life-
> Giver, you Swimmer.
> Now protect us, me and my wife."

The Northwest Coast people also benefited from nearby forests. They cut down tall cedar trees and floated the timber by water to their villages. There, they split the tree trunks into planks for houses and canoes. From the soft inner bark, they made rope, baskets, and clothes. The forests also were home to deer, moose, and bears that the people hunted for meat and hides.

With plenty of food, the people of the Pacific Northwest could stay in one place. They built permanent villages and prospered from trade with nearby groups.

Within a village, families gained status according to how much they owned. Families sometimes competed for rank. To improve their standing, they held a **potlatch,** or ceremonial dinner, to show off their wealth. The family invited many guests and gave everyone presents. The more the family gave away, the more respect it earned. At one potlatch, which took years for the family to prepare, gifts included 8 canoes, 54 elk skins, 2,000 silver bracelets, 7,000 brass bracelets, and 33,000 blankets!

Other People of the West

Climates and resources varied in other parts of the West. As people adapted to these environments, they developed very different cultures.

Great Basin

The Great Basin lies in the dry Intermountain region of the United States. With little water, few plants or animals survived. As a result, Great Basin people like the Utes (yootz) and Shoshones (shoh SHOH neez) had to spend most of their time looking for food. They hunted rabbits or dug for roots in the desert soil.

Because the land offered so little, only a few related families traveled together in search of food. They had few possessions beyond digging sticks, baskets, and other tools or weapons needed for hunting. When they camped, they built temporary shelters out of willow poles and reeds.

Plateau

The people of the Plateau lived between two mountain ranges: the Rocky Mountains to the east and the Cascades to the west. Their main source of food was fish from rivers, like the Columbia and Fraser, or from smaller streams. They also hunted and gathered roots, nuts, and berries. In winter, they lived in earth houses that were partly underground. In summer, they set up lodges, temporary shelters made by placing rush mats over cottonwood frames.

Some groups traded with the Northwest Coast people and were influenced by their way of life. Others, like the Nez Percés (NEHZ PER sihz), adopted customs from the peoples of the Great Plains.

RESOURCE DIRECTORY

Teaching Resources
Unit 1/Chapter 2
- Connecting History and Literature: The Girl Who Hunted Rabbits, p. 15

Transparencies
Fine Art
- Native American Handcrafts, p. D-27

★ *Background* ★

Recent Scholarship

Ending a myth In *Daughters of the Earth* (Collier Macmillan, 1996), Carolyn Niethammer disputes the image of Native American women as oppressed and submissive. Niethammer studied legends, ceremonies, and songs, as well as the writings of early anthropologists, and she interviewed Native American women of today. She followed the women from various Native American peoples from childbirth to death, portraying them as strong, proud individuals—guardians of the home, rulers, warriors, and people of stature within their cultures.

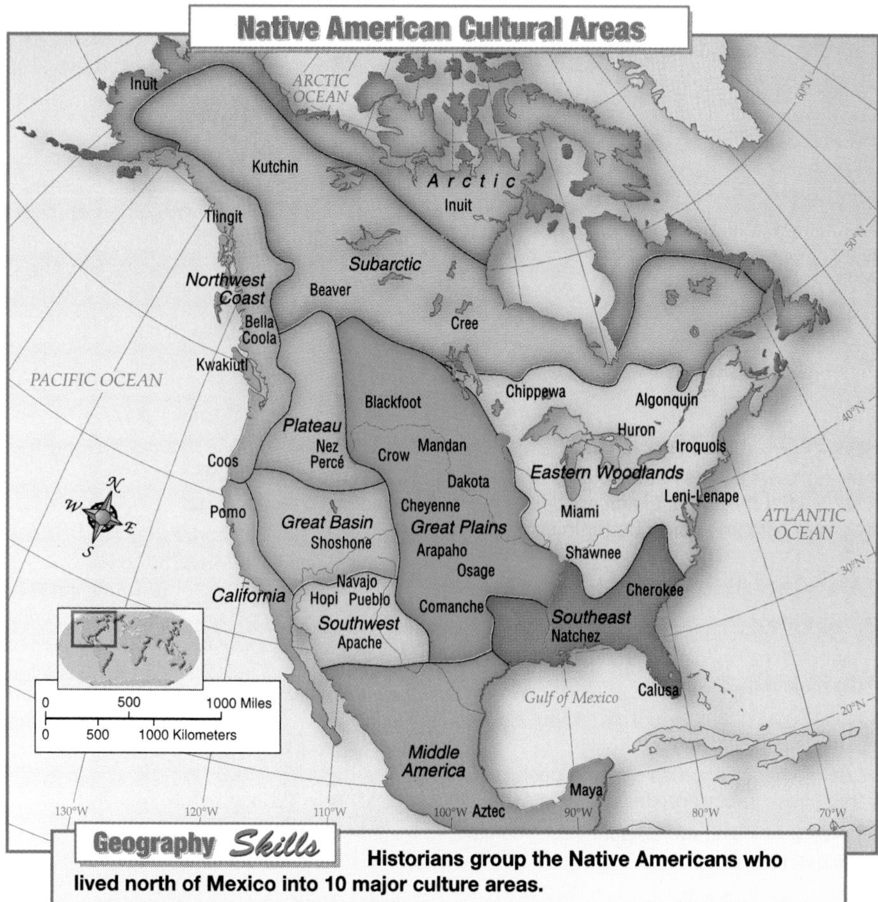

Geography Skills **Historians group the Native Americans who lived north of Mexico into 10 major culture areas.**

1. **Location** On the map, locate the areas inhabited by the following groups: **(a)** Iroquois, **(b)** Inuit, **(c)** Pomo, **(d)** Hopi, **(e)** Shoshone.
2. **Place** Name two groups that lived in the coldest regions of North America.
3. **Critical Thinking** In which culture areas could Native Americans probably depend on the sea for food? Explain.

California

Differences in climate and resources helped create diverse cultures in California. Coastal people fished in the ocean and rivers. In the northern valleys, people hunted deer, rabbits, and elk or collected berries and nuts. In the southeast desert, small bands lived much like the people of the Great Basin.

For many Californians, like the Pomos, acorns were the basic food. Women harvested the nuts in autumn and later pounded them into flour. Both women and men among the Pomos were skilled at weaving baskets, which they decorated with fine designs.

People of the Southwest

The **Pueblos,** the Spanish name for people of the Southwest, were descended from the Anasazis. They included such groups as the Hopis, Acomas, Zuñis, and Lagunas. By

★ *Activity* ★

Connections With Geography

Giving an oral presentation Divide the class into small groups and assign each a Native American people. Have groups research the types of clothing their people wore and the materials and methods they used to make them. Have the groups also research what effects the environment had on these types of clothing. Ask each group to prepare an oral presentation that describes the link between the environment and the clothing (including seasonal or other variations) used by their people. Groups should prepare illustrations or models for each type of clothing to accompany their presentations and help explain how the clothes were designed and made. (challenging) ELL T

Geography *Skills*

ANSWERS **1.** Review locations with students. **2.** Inuit, Kutchin **3.** any culture area bounded by the sea, especially the Eastern Woodlands, Southeast, Northwest Coast, and California

Skills FOR LIFE

PRACTICE the Skill
ANSWERS

1. why the rabbit has long ears

2. Possible answer: You hear the story from the point of view of the rabbit, the eagle, and a neutral speaker.

3. Answers will vary depending on how the student partner who is reading the story acts out the tale.

4. They summarize the main point set out in the first sentence of the story and add to it.

APPLY the Skill
Guided Instruction

Remind students to listen closely to the description their partners give and try to introduce them as accurately as possible. Suggest that students first practice their introductions on their own or with another student who is not their partner.

ASSESSMENT See the rubrics in the Alternative Assessment booklet in the Teaching Resources.

Critical Thinking | Managing Information | **Communication** | Maps, Charts, and Graphs

Listening

How Will I Use This Skill?
Listening is not as easy as it sounds. Statistics show that most people miss much of what they hear. Listening clearly will help you follow directions, get along with people, and do better in school and on the job.

LEARN the Skill
Use these steps to practice listening skills:

1. Listen to the opening words to determine the main topic.
2. Notice how changes in the speaker's voice emphasize certain ideas.
3. Look for facial expressions and gestures that stress important ideas.
4. Listen for closing remarks that summarize the main point.

PRACTICE the Skill
Native American groups passed along tales like the one at right. Work with a partner. One partner reads the tale aloud, while the other listens and answers the following questions.

1. What is the main topic of the story?
2. What changes in voice helped you understand the story?
3. Did the speaker use any gestures?
4. How do the closing words summarize the story?

APPLY the Skill
Select a partner. Give each other brief descriptions of yourselves. Then, introduce your partner to the class. See how accurate you are.

"Listen, and learn why the rabbit has long ears. When the world was new, the rabbit had short ears. Back then, many, many moons ago, the rabbit and the eagle argued a lot. One day, in anger, the eagle grabbed the rabbit and flew it to her nest high in the trees. She gave the rabbit to her baby eagles as a toy.

The baby eagles enjoyed chasing and tugging at the rabbit. One time, the rabbit got hurt. In a fit of rage, he killed all the baby eagles. The rabbit became frightened. He knew the mother eagle would look for him. He tried to disguise himself by taking feathers from the tiny eagles and stuffing them in his ears, stretching them very long. He then ran away and tried to hide himself in a hole of a fallen birch tree.

When the eagle saw what happened, she searched for the rabbit for revenge. She saw the ears showing out of the tree and was ready to attack when she remembered an old tradition of covering the dead with birch bark. She thought the rabbit was dead, and so she flew away.

Later, the eagle realized her mistake. To this day, the eagle still hunts the rabbit. Now you know why the rabbit has long ears and hides from the eagle."

★ Activity ★
Our Diverse Nation

Analyzing myths Invite students to research and read some folk tales or myths of a Native American group. You may wish to provide materials for classroom use. Myths offer many possibilities, as do stories that feature Coyote or Raven, both tricksters. Have each student share a tale or myth with classmates and explain what he or she thinks it shows about the culture or environment of a particular group. For example, does the story value honesty or cleverness? What elements of nature are mentioned? What religious beliefs does the story suggest? Ask students to compare and contrast these stories. (*average*) T

RESOURCE DIRECTORY

Teaching Resources
Unit 1/Chapter 2
- Practice Your Skills: Listening, p. 12

Transparencies
Fine Art
- Celestial Germinators, p. D-25

Viewing History **Kachina Dolls**

To the Hopis of the Southwest, kachina dolls represented the spirits of the natural world. To create figures like these required great skill and care. For example, the kachina on the left is made of wood, cotton, fur, horsehair, feathers, shell, horn, and stone. ★ **Why do you think Hopi craftworkers took such care to create kachina dolls?**

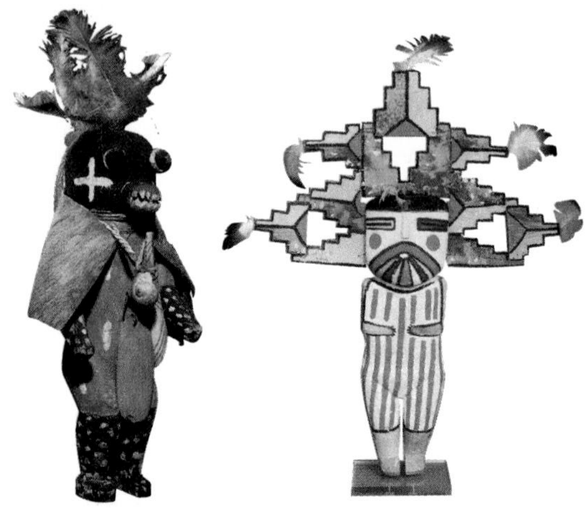

1500, only the Hopis still farmed on clifftops as the Anasazis had done. Other groups lived in villages along the Rio Grande and its tributaries.

Pueblo way of life

Like their ancestors, the Pueblos built adobe houses and grew corn, beans, and squash. Their religious beliefs reflected the importance of farming. Most Pueblo villages had a **kiva,** or underground chamber, where men held religious ceremonies. Through prayers and other rituals, they tried to please the spirits of nature, such as wind, rain, and thunder.

At planting or harvest time, the Hopis and Zuñis held ceremonies to ensure rainfall and good crops. In the villages, cries rang out: "The kachinas are coming!" **Kachinas,** or masked dancers, represented the spirits. If the dance was pleasing to the spirits, they would return as rain to water the next season's crops.

The Pueblos traced their family lines through their mothers. This custom gave women special importance. When a man married, he went to live with his wife's family. Also, Pueblo wives owned most of the family property.

Navajos and Apaches

About 1500, two new groups reached the Southwest: the **Apaches** and the **Navajos.** Both groups lived as hunters, but they often raided Pueblo fields for food.

In time, the Navajos accepted many Pueblo ways. They began to farm and to build **hogans,** or houses made of mud plaster over a framework of wooden poles. The Apaches, however, continued to follow herds of buffalo and the other game they hunted. They traded dried buffalo meat and animal skins to the Pueblos in exchange for corn and woven cloth.

VI People of the Great Plains

Centuries ago, vast grasslands extended across the Great Plains from the Rocky Mountains to the Mississippi River. Because there were few trees, Plains people built their homes of sod, chunks of thickly matted grass.

Farming and hunting

Some Plains people farmed along river banks. In spring, women broke up the soft ground using hoes made from animal bones. They then planted corn, beans, squash, and sunflowers.

Large herds of animals grazed on the Plains, including buffalo, antelope, elk, deer, and bighorn sheep. Plains people hunted the animals on foot. In winter, men hunted near the village. In summer, however, they often traveled for miles in search of buffalo and other animals. They carried their belongings with them on a **travois** (truh VOY), or sled, pulled by dogs.

Each village had a ruling council that included the best hunters. The chief was respected by other council members because he spoke well and judged wisely.

Viewing History ANSWER

Possible answer: The kachinas represented the spirits who controlled the lives of the Hopis. Craftworkers wanted to please these spirits to ensure rainfall and good crops.

FROM THE ARCHIVES OF AmericanHeritage®

Almost a forgotten people The pueblo-building Mimbres vanished around A.D. 1150, but evidence of their advanced building and farming techniques and their extensive trading has been left behind on their painted bowls. Elegant designs and strong images of people, animals, plants, and mythical creatures line the inner surfaces of these bowls.

Source: Rebecca Carrier, "A Mimbres Painted Bowl," *American Heritage* magazine, July–August 1995.

Technology

Listening to Literature Audiocassettes
The American Experience
- Navajo Night Chant, side 1
- From the Houses of Magic, side 1

Reading Actively

During Reading Have students note the following statement on this page: "During the 1700s, the way of life of the Plains people changed." Ask students to find evidence to support this statement as they read the section.

Viewing History ANSWER

They used buffalo hides to make tepees.

RESOURCE DIRECTORY

Transparencies

Exploring Technology

- Native American Dwellings, p. H-23

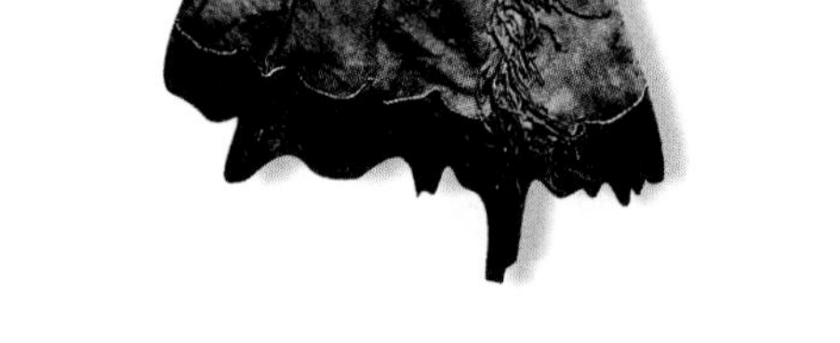

Viewing History — Clothing From the Great Plains

On the Great Plains, Comanche hunters followed herds of deer and antelope. They ate the deer meat and used the hides to make clothing, like this woman's buckskin dress. ★ **In what other ways did Plains people make use of the animals they hunted?**

A new way of life

During the 1700s, the way of life of the Plains people changed. They began to catch and tame wild horses that appeared on the Plains. These horses descended from animals brought to the Southwest by Spanish settlers some 200 years earlier. Until then, there had been no horses in North America. A Blackfoot tale describes their reaction to seeing horses for the first time:

> "After a time, a woman said, 'Let's put a travois on one of them just like we do on our small dogs.' They made a larger travois and attached it to one of the gentler horses. It didn't kick or jump. They led the horse around with the travois attached. Finally, a woman mounted the horse and rode it."

Soon, Plains people became skillful riders. Because they could travel farther and faster than before, they raised fewer crops. They hunted more, moving often to follow huge herds of buffalo that roamed the plains. They also began to live in **tepees,** cone-shaped tents made of buffalo hides that could be carried easily on a travois.

People of the Southeast

The Southeast was home to more Native Americans than any other region. A warm climate, fertile soil, and plentiful rain helped Southeast people produce good crops.

Most people lived in villages and farmed nearby land. They built their homes from saplings, or young trees. They split the trees into strips and wove them to make a frame for walls. Then, they plastered the walls with a mixture of clay and dry grass.

Farming and religion

Men and women had clearly defined roles in the community. Men cleared the land and hunted deer and other animals. Women planted, weeded, and harvested the crops. Among rows of corn, they planted beans that climbed up the cornstalks. They also grew squash, pumpkins, and sunflowers.

Most religious ceremonies were linked to farming. The most important, the Green Corn Ceremony, took place in midsummer, when the corn ripened. It marked the end of the year. Celebrations lasted several days. The highlight, on the last day, was the lighting of the sacred fire followed by a dance around its flames. With this event, the new year began.

Natchez society

One Southeast group, the **Natchez** (NACH ihz), hunted, fished, and farmed along the fertile coast of the Gulf of Mexico. They divided the year into 13 months. Each month

Connections With Civics

While warrior chiefs led most Plains Indian societies, the Cheyennes had a complex civil, or nonmilitary, government. The ruling council included representatives from the 10 main Cheyenne bands. Any warrior chief sent to the council had to resign his military power.

★ *Background* ★

Our Diverse Nation

The value of horses The first documentation of Native Americans on horseback comes from northern Mexico in the late 1500s. It is likely that the use of horses spread across the Plains as the result of trading among various groups.

Horses quickly became a valued commodity. Some Native American groups began to use horses as a measure of wealth—the more horses, the greater the prosperity. Some groups even used horses to measure time: Before the coming of the horse, the people lived in the "dog days"—the time when dogs were used to haul gear from one campsite to another.

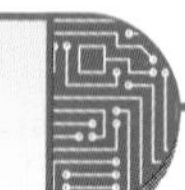

Linking History and Technology

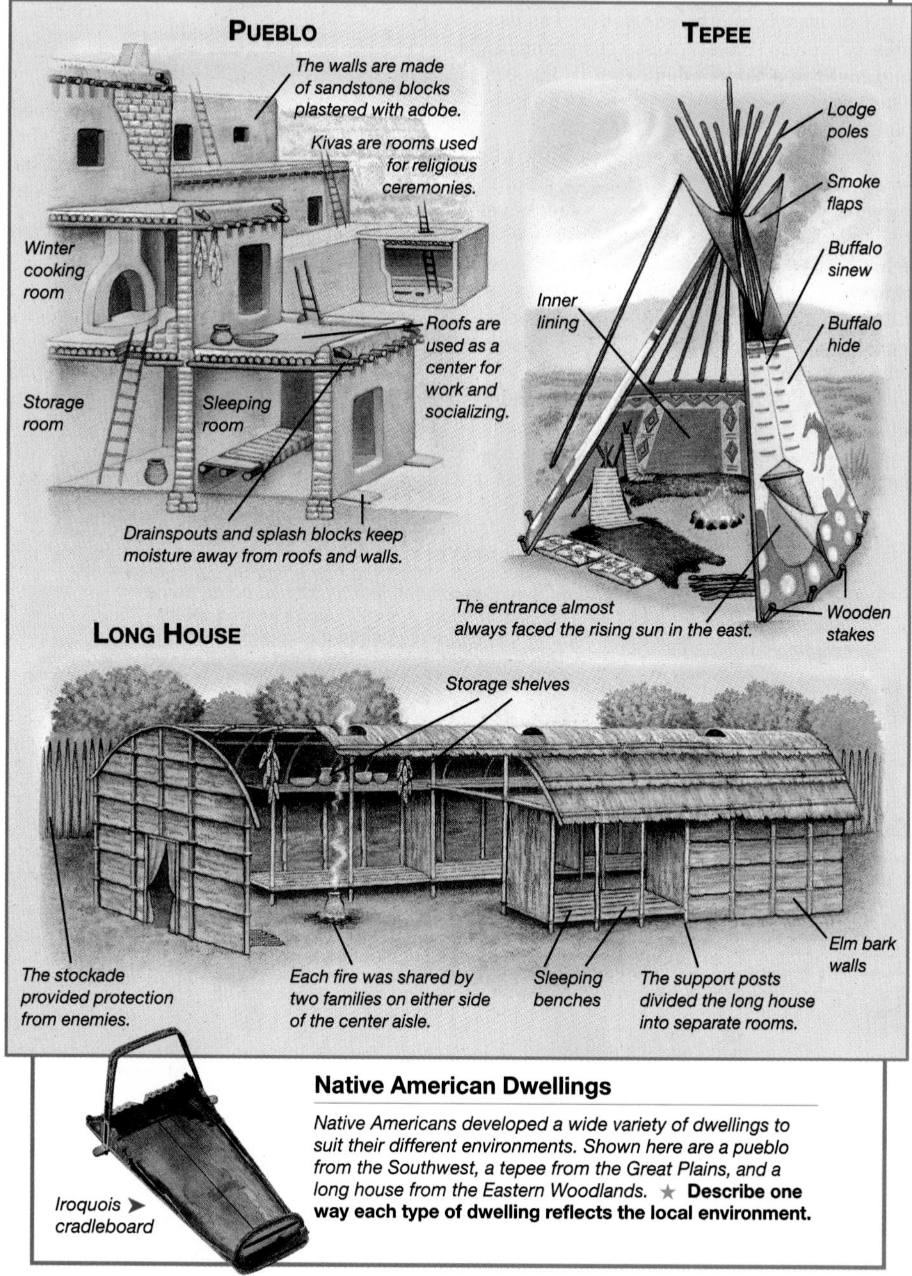

Pueblo
The walls are made of sandstone blocks plastered with adobe.
Kivas are rooms used for religious ceremonies.
Winter cooking room
Roofs are used as a center for work and socializing.
Storage room
Sleeping room
Drainspouts and splash blocks keep moisture away from roofs and walls.
Tepee
Lodge poles
Smoke flaps
Buffalo sinew
Buffalo hide
Inner lining
The entrance almost always faced the rising sun in the east.
Wooden stakes
Long House
Storage shelves
Elm bark walls
The stockade provided protection from enemies.
Each fire was shared by two families on either side of the center aisle.
Sleeping benches
The support posts divided the long house into separate rooms.
Iroquois ➤ cradleboard

Native American Dwellings

Native Americans developed a wide variety of dwellings to suit their different environments. Shown here are a pueblo from the Southwest, a tepee from the Great Plains, and a long house from the Eastern Woodlands. ★ **Describe one way each type of dwelling reflects the local environment.**

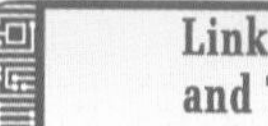

Linking History and Technology

ANSWER The pueblo was built of sandstone and adobe, or mud brick, materials found in the desert. The tepee, used by the Plains people who hunted buffalo, was made from buffalo hide and sinew. The long house was made from the abundant trees of the Eastern Woodlands.

★ *Background* ★

Did You Know?

Just not townsfolk Although the Navajos, or Diné as they call themselves, were influenced by Pueblo ways, they never built villages. They would sometimes gather their hogans into small family groups of mothers and married daughters—this was as close as they came to village living. More often, Navajo hogans and their summer dwellings of brush were widely scattered.

Technology

AmericanHeritage® History of the United States CD-ROM
- Virtual Buildings: Iroquois Longhouse (*average*)
- Arts and Entertainment: Books (*average*)

Listening to Literature Audiocassettes
The American Experience
- Spring Song, side 1
- Song Concerning a Dream of the Thunderbirds, side 1

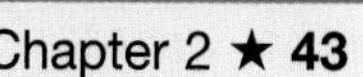

Writing Actively

After Reading Ask students to write two or three main ideas summarizing Section 2. Ask volunteers to read their summaries aloud. Then have students read the Section 2 Sum It Up at the end of the chapter.

ANSWER

Eastern Woodlands

was named after a food or animal that the Natchez harvested or hunted. Months included Strawberry, Little Corn, Mulberry, Deer, Turkey, and Bear.

Natchez religious beliefs centered on worship of the sun. Priests kept a fire going day and night in a temple dedicated to the sun. The Natchez believed that fire came from the sun.

The Natchez ruler, the Great Sun, was worshipped as a god. He lived atop a giant pyramid mound. The Great Sun's feet never touched the ground. He either was carried in a litter or walked on mats. Below the Great Sun were other members of his family, called Little Suns. Next came Nobles, then Honored People, and finally Stinkards, or commoners, who were the majority of the people.

Marriage laws ensured that membership in each class kept changing. By law, noble men and women had to marry Stinkards. Even the Great Sun chose a Stinkard as a wife. In this way, no one family could hold the position of Great Sun forever. In time, even descendants of a Great Sun became Stinkards.

People of the Eastern Woodlands

Many groups lived in the Eastern Woodlands. In the forests and open lands, they hunted deer, moose, and other game. They also planted crops of corn, pumpkins, and squash.

The Iroquois: a complex society

The most powerful people of this region were the **Iroquois** (IHR uh kwoi). They lived in present-day New York State.

The Iroquois called themselves House Builders. They built **long houses** out of wood poles sided with bark. A typical long house was about 150 feet (46 m) long and 20 feet (7 m) wide. A hallway, with small rooms

Viewing History **Iroquois Women at Work**

In several Native American cultures, including the Iroquois, women were responsible for growing and gathering food. Here, Iroquois women collect sap to make maple sugar. ★ **In what culture region did the Iroquois live?**

★ Background ★
Religion and Ethics

More Sun Each daybreak, the Natchez Great Sun went to the Temple to greet "the rising of his elder brother" (the sun). Little Suns held important positions in the Great Sun's village, or were chiefs of villages owing allegiance to the Great Sun. The Great Sun was considered to be so important that, at his death, his wife and servants were executed to escort him into the afterlife. T

★ Background ★
Did You Know?

The False Face Society Among the Iroquois, the False Face Society played an important role in fighting illness.

- The society took its name from the masks members wore in the ceremonies.
- Members had the power to cure all sorts of ailments.
- Anyone cured by the False Face Society became a member.

RESOURCE DIRECTORY

Teaching Resources
Unit 1/Chapter 2
- Critical Thinking and Writing: Comparing Information on a Chart, p. 13
- Biography Flashcard: Dekanawida, p. 16
- Section 2 Quiz, p. 18

on either side, ran the length of the long house. Each room was home to one family. Families living across from each other shared a fireplace in the hallway.

Women had a special place in Iroquois society. They owned all household property and were in charge of planting and harvesting. Like a Pueblo man, an Iroquois man moved in with his wife's family when he married. Iroquois women also shared in political power because they chose clan leaders. A **clan** was a group of two or more related families. If a clan leader did not do his job well, the women could remove him from his position.

League of the Iroquois

The Iroquois included five nations: the Mohawk, Seneca, Onondaga (ahn uhn DAW guh), Oneida (oh NI duh), and Cayuga (kay YOO guh). Each nation had its own ruling council.

Constant warfare disrupted the Iroquois nations. Around 1570, the nations formed an alliance to end the fighting. According to legend, a religious leader named Dekanawida (deh kan ah WEE dah) inspired Hiawatha, a Mohawk, to organize the alliance. It became known as the **League of the Iroquois.** According to Iroquois tradition, the founders of the League of the Iroquois made this promise:

> "We bind ourselves together by taking hold of each other's hands.... Our strength shall be in union, our way the way of reason, righteousness, and peace.... Be of strong mind, O chiefs. Carry no anger and hold no grudges."

Later, a sixth nation, the Tuscarora (tuhs kuh ROR uh), joined the League.

A council of 50 **sachems,** or specially chosen tribal leaders, met once a year to make decisions for the League. Again, Iroquois women chose the sachems. At meetings, the council discussed problems and voted on ways to solve them. Each nation had one vote. The council could take action only if all of the nations agreed. The League helped end warfare among the Iroquois nations, and gave them a united defense against their enemies.

★ Section 2 Review ★

Recall

1. **Identify** **(a)** Inuit, **(b)** Pueblo, **(c)** kachina, **(d)** Apache, **(e)** Navajo, **(f)** Natchez, **(g)** Iroquois, **(h)** League of the Iroquois.
2. **Define** **(a)** culture area, **(b)** tribe, **(c)** igloo, **(d)** kayak, **(e)** potlatch, **(f)** kiva, **(g)** hogan, **(h)** travois, **(i)** tepee, **(j)** long house, **(k)** clan, **(l)** sachem.

Comprehension

3. **(a)** Name two Native American cultures that developed in North America. **(b)** Explain how each adapted to its environment.
4. How did cultures that relied on farming for food differ from those that were mainly hunters?
5. How did religion play a major role in the everyday life of most Native American cultures?

Critical Thinking and Writing

6. **Synthesizing Information** Review the feature Linking History and Technology on page 43. **(a)** Which of the three kinds of home shown here would you expect to find in a culture that relied on hunting for its way of life? Explain. **(b)** Which would be most suited to a settled farming community? Explain.
7. **Linking Past and Present** The Iroquois League helped settle disputes and keep the peace. What institutions perform this role in American society today?

Activity **Writing a Chant** Write a chant celebrating your links with the natural world. For example, you could express gratitude for the foods you eat, or for the type of weather you most enjoy. For one example of a chant, see the Kwakiutl chant on page 38.

★ Section 2 Review ★

ANSWERS

1. (a) p. 36, **(b)** p. 39, **(c)–(e)** p. 41, **(f)** p. 42, **(g)** p. 44, **(h)** p. 45

2. (a)–(b) p. 36, **(c)–(d)** p. 37, **(e)** p. 38, **(f)–(h)** p. 41, **(i)** p. 42, **(j)** p. 44, **(k)–(l)** p. 45

3. (a) Possible answers: Inuits, Arctic; Natchez, Southeast **(b)** The Inuits used driftwood to make tools and shelters in summer; built houses of snow and ice in winter. The Natchez farmed in the Southeast's warm, wet climate and fertile soil; they used trees, clay, and grass to build homes.

4. Hunters moved in search of food; farmers lived in settled villages.

5. Most tried to live in harmony with nature and used religious ceremonies to please the spirits.

6. (a) tepees, because they were portable **(b)** long houses or pueblos, because they were more permanent dwellings

7. Possible answers: the courts, the FBI, police departments

Guided Instruction
Have students reread the chant in this section. Point out that the chant gives thanks, personifies the salmon, and apologizes for its death. Suggest students use similar themes in their chants.

ASSESSMENT See the rubrics in the Alternative Assessment booklet in the Teaching Resources.

★ *Background* ★
Turning Points

Welcome back In 1712, Europeans drove the Tuscarora, an Iroquoian people, out of North Carolina. When the Tuscarora came north looking for a new home, the Five Nations welcomed them, saying, "[T]hey were of us and went from us long ago, and now are returned." The Great League gave them land and a council seat. Thus, the League of Five Nations became Six Nations.

Listening to Literature Audiocassettes
The American Experience
• From the Walam Olum, side 1

Section 3

Great Civilizations in the Americas

LESSON PLAN

Objectives

★ Identify where the Mayan, Aztec, and Incan civilizations flourished.

★ Describe the main achievements of these civilizations.

★ Explain how religion and learning were linked in Aztec society.

1 Engage

Warm Up Have students discuss a variety of responses to complete this statement: When I call a place *civilized,* I mean that _____.

Activating Prior Knowledge Have students create a dictionary entry for *civilization.* Have them include the syllabic division, pronunciation, and part of speech, as well as the definition. Ask a volunteer to verify the class definition in a dictionary.

Reading Actively

Before Reading Have students read the questions under Explore These Questions. Tell students that as they read, they should jot down notes that help answer each question.

RESOURCE DIRECTORY

Teaching Resources
Lesson Planner, p. 6

3 Great Civilizations in the Americas

As You Read

Explore These Questions

- Where did the Mayan, Aztec, and Incan civilizations flourish?
- What were the main achievements of these civilizations?
- How were religion and learning linked in Aztec society?

Define

- civilization
- hieroglyphics
- causeway
- chinampas
- absolute power
- terrace
- aqueduct
- surplus

Identify

- Maya
- Olmec
- Aztec
- Tenochtitlán
- Inca
- Cuzco

SETTING the Scene Some 1,500 years ago, large oceangoing canoes sped along the Caribbean coast of Mexico. Cutting swiftly through the blue waters of the Caribbean Sea, the canoes made an impressive sight. Even more impressive were the riches inside the canoes. Traders carried jade statues, turquoise jewelry, parrot feathers, cocoa beans, and other valuable goods across a wide area.

The canoes belonged to the **Mayas,** a people who flourished in Mexico and Central America. The Mayas were one of several Native American people who built great, complex societies in the ancient Americas.

The Earliest American Civilizations

A civilization is an advanced culture. Historians identify several basic features of early civilizations. Perhaps the most important is the building of cities. Other features include a well-organized government, a system of social classes, specialized jobs, a complex religion, and some method of keeping records.

The earliest known American civilization was that of the **Olmecs.** The Olmecs emerged in the forests along the Gulf of Mexico, around 3,500 years ago. Archaeologists know very little about the Olmecs. However, rich tombs and temples suggest a powerful class of priests and nobles stood at the top of Olmec society.

The most dramatic Olmec artifacts are the giant carved stone heads found near a religious center. Without the use of pack animals or wheeled vehicles, the Olmecs moved these colossal 40-ton stones from distant quarries. Olmec temples were decorated with designs of grinning snakes and dragons. Similar designs in later buildings suggest that the Olmec civilization influenced the later, more advanced Mayan civilization.

Vase showing a Mayan king

Mayan Civilization

Mayan civilization emerged about 3,000 years ago. It grew up in the rain forests of present-day Mexico and Guatemala. The rain forests were difficult and dangerous places to live. Poisonous snakes hung from trees. Jaguars and other wild animals prowled the forest floor. Disease-carrying insects infested the swamps.

From earlier people, the Mayas learned to grow corn and to build stone structures. With much work, they cleared the jungle and drained the swamps.

★ *Background* ★

Religion and Ethics

Powerful influence The Olmecs of Mexico's Gulf Coast jungles produced the first major civilization of the New World. Their sculptures are both impressive and instructive. At least 10 gods are represented in various forms of Olmec art, ranging from small figurines to monumental statues and reliefs. Jaguar-like features or masklike expressions typify the rigid stone images. These sculptures and the ruins of Olmec religious buildings suggest a powerful religion in which priestly rulers dominated the people through rituals intended to control weather and jungle spirits. The Olmecs' religious culture strongly influenced later Middle American civilizations. T

On the cleared land, they grew corn to feed a growing population. They lived in simple homes with mud walls and thatched roofs.

Great cities

In time, the Mayas built great cities in many parts of Mexico and Central America. Two of these cities were Tikal and Copán. Each city had its own ruler. Although rival cities sometimes fought, they also enjoyed times of peaceful trade. Roads that cut through the jungle linked inland cities to the coast.

Towering above the cities were huge stone pyramids. Atop each pyramid stood a temple. There, priests performed ceremonies to please the Mayan gods.

Social classes

Priests were at the top of Mayan society. Only priests had the knowledge to perform the ceremonies that the Mayas believed were necessary to guarantee good harvests and victory in battle.

Nobles, government officials, and warriors also enjoyed high rank. A visitor to a Mayan city could easily spot priests and nobles. They wore gold jewelry, fine headdresses, and colorful cotton garments. While most rulers were men, Mayan records and carvings indicate that sometimes women governed on their own or in the name of young sons.

Near the bottom of Mayan society was a large class of peasant farmers. Lowest of all were slaves. Slaves were generally prisoners of war.

Advances in learning

Mayan priests paid careful attention to the passage of time and to the pattern of daily events. By studying the sun and the stars, they tried to predict the future. In that way, they could honor the gods who controlled events, including harvests, trade, and hunts.

Concern with time and the seasons led the Mayas to explore astronomy and mathematics. With the knowledge they gained, they created an accurate 365-day calendar. They also developed an advanced number system that included the concept of zero.

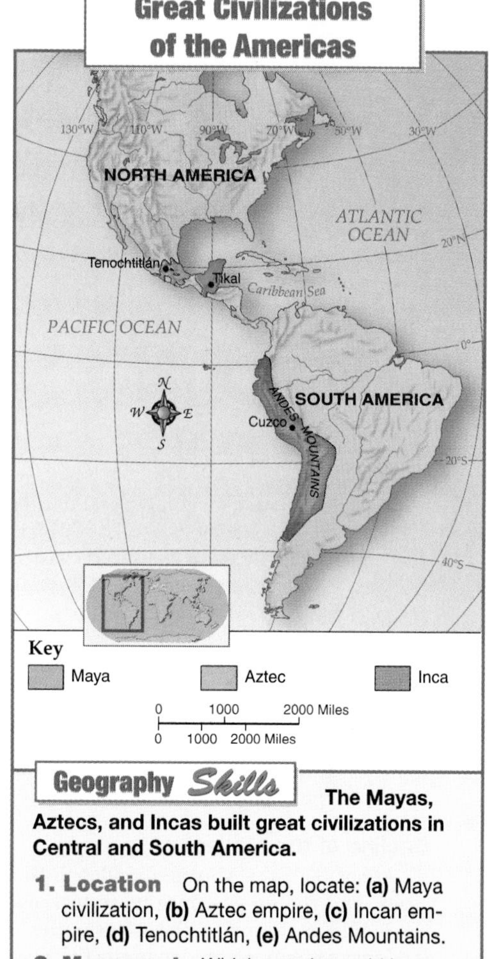

Geography *Skills* **The Mayas, Aztecs, and Incas built great civilizations in Central and South America.**

1. **Location** On the map, locate: **(a)** Maya civilization, **(b)** Aztec empire, **(c)** Incan empire, **(d)** Tenochtitlán, **(e)** Andes Mountains.
2. **Movement** Which people would have been able to travel by way of the Caribbean Sea?
3. **Critical Thinking** Why might the Incas have had trouble keeping their empire united?

To record their findings, Mayan priests invented a system of **hieroglyphics,** or writing that uses pictures to represent words and ideas. Not until recent years have scholars deciphered Mayan hieroglyphics. The Mayas carved records on stone columns or painted them on paper made from bark.

2 Explore

Ask students to read the section. For a homework assignment, have them research and report on two or three facts about the Olmecs, Mayas, Aztecs, or Incas not in the text.

3 Teach

Provide students with these statements: **(a)** The Mayas settled in swampland that bred mosquitoes and disease. **(b)** The Aztec capital was often in danger of attack. **(c)** The Incas needed to communicate with all parts of their empire. **(d)** Earthquakes posed a threat to Incan temples. **(e)** Incan farmers lived on steep slopes where rain could wash away soil and crops. For each statement, have students explain how the problem was solved and then discuss what these solutions say about each civilization.

4 Assess

To close the lesson, have students complete the section review. Or have students create graphic organizers to compare the **(a)** cities, **(b)** class systems, and **(c)** religions of the three great empires of Central and South America.

★ ★ ★ ★ ★ ★ ★ ★ ★ ★ ★ ★ ★ ★ ★ ★ ★ ★ ★

Geography *Skills*

ANSWERS **1.** Review locations with students. **2.** Mayas, Aztecs **3.** The empire covered a huge and mostly mountainous area.

★ *Background* ★

Did You Know?

Mayan mathematics The Mayas were sophisticated mathematicians and astronomers. Their system of arithmetic had a base of 20 rather than a base of 10. Mayan astronomers used observations of the moon, sun, and Venus to create a calendar. Their calendar was divided into 19 months—18 months of 20 days each and 1 month of 5 days. T

ANSWER

Parents teach many skills to their children. In addition, children learn skills at school and by reading books, watching television, using computers, and observing other people.

Viewing History **Aztec Education**

Pictures in an Aztec book show how Aztec parents taught their children needed skills. At left, a father teaches his son how to gather firewood, paddle a canoe, and fish. The mother, at right, instructs her daughter in grinding grain and weaving cloth. ★ **How do we pass on important skills to young people today?**

Decline of the Mayas

About 850, the Mayas abandoned their cities, and the forests once more took over the land. For centuries, these "lost cities" of the Mayas remained hidden in the thick rain forests of Central America.

We are unsure why the cities were left to decay. Perhaps peasants rebelled against heavy taxes imposed by their rulers. Maybe farming wore out the soil. Even though their cities declined, the Mayan people survived. Today, more than 2 million people in southern Mexico and Guatemala speak Mayan languages.

Aztec Civilization

To the north of the Mayan cities, the **Aztecs** built a powerful empire. Until the 1300s, the Aztecs were wanderers, moving from place to place in search of food. Then, according to legend, a god told the Aztecs to look for a sign. They were to search for an eagle perched on a cactus with a snake in its beak.* On that spot, the god instructed, the Aztecs should build their capital. After more wandering, the Aztecs found the eagle in swampy Lake Texcoco (tay SKOH koh), in central Mexico.

Tenochtitlán

The Aztecs built their capital, **Tenochtitlán** (tay noch tee TLAHN), on an island in the middle of Lake Texcoco. Aztec engineers built **causeways,** or raised roads, out of packed earth. Aztec causeways connected the island to the mainland.

Farmers learned to grow crops on the swampland. They dug canals and filled in

*Today, the eagle, snake, and cactus remain symbols of Mexico and appear on the Mexican flag.

★ *Activity* ★

Cooperative Learning

Creating a barter system Discuss with the class how a barter economy works. Divide students into small groups. Tell students in each group to assume that they are economists who have been hired to convert the U.S. monetary economy into a barter system. Ask each group to list items frequently purchased, classifying them as *Needs* or *Wants*. Next, they should assign relative values to each item, setting rates of exchange among the various goods. Have each group post its list; then allow groups to barter with one another. Remind students to consider the importance of needs and wants. Afterward, discuss with students the advantages and disadvantages of a barter system and what they learned about the relative values of items. (*challenging*) T parts of the lake. With long stakes, they attached reed mats to the swampy lake bottom. Then, they piled mud onto the mats and planted their crops. Aztec farmers harvested as many as seven crops a year on these **chinampas,** or floating gardens.

In the 1400s, the Aztecs expanded their power by conquering neighboring people. They adopted many beliefs and ideas from these defeated people.

Riches from trade and conquest turned Tenochtitlán into a large, bustling city. City marketplaces offered an abundance of goods. "There are daily more than 60,000 people bartering and selling," wrote a Spanish visitor in the 1500s.

Canoes darted up the canals that crisscrossed the city. Soldiers and merchants traveled the causeways between Tenochtitlán and the mainland. Drawbridges on the roads could be raised in case of attack.

Religion

Religion was central to Aztec life. Young men and women attended special schools where they trained to become priests and priestesses. Like the Mayas, Aztec priests studied the heavens and developed advanced calendars. They used these calendars to determine when to plant or harvest and to predict future events. The priests divided the year into 18 months. Each month was governed by its own god. Aztec books contained knowledge about the gods as well as special prayers and hymns.

The sun god was especially important. Each day, the Aztecs believed, the sun battled its way across the heavens. They compared the sun's battles to their own, calling themselves "warriors of the sun." To ensure a successful journey across the sky, the sun required human sacrifices. The Aztecs sacrificed tens of thousands of prisoners of war each year to please their gods.

A powerful empire

By 1500, the Aztecs ruled millions of people from the Gulf of Mexico to the Pacific Ocean. The emperor had **absolute power,** that is, he had total authority over the people he ruled. The Aztec emperor was treated

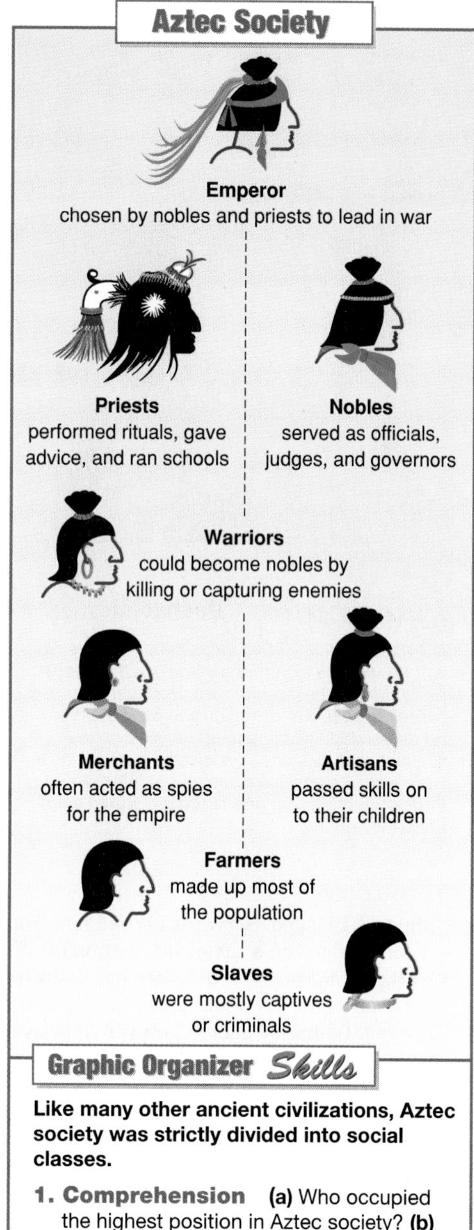
Aztec Society
Emperor
chosen by nobles and priests to lead in war
Priests
performed rituals, gave advice, and ran schools
Nobles
served as officials, judges, and governors
Warriors
could become nobles by killing or capturing enemies
Merchants
often acted as spies for the empire
Artisans
passed skills on to their children
Farmers
made up most of the population
Slaves
were mostly captives or criminals

Graphic Organizer Skills

Like many other ancient civilizations, Aztec society was strictly divided into social classes.

1. **Comprehension** **(a)** Who occupied the highest position in Aztec society? **(b)** Which classes of people were equal to one another?
2. **Critical Thinking** How does this graphic organizer suggest the importance of warfare in Aztec society? Give two examples.

Reading Actively 

During Reading Refer students to the graphic organizer on this page. As they read, have them look for additional information about the classes in Aztec society. Have students use that information to write a paragraph summarizing the roles of as many classes as possible.

Graphic Organizer Skills

ANSWERS **1. (a)** the emperor **(b)** Nobles and priests were equal to one another, as were merchants and artisans. **2.** The emperor was chosen to lead in war. Successful warriors could rise to the class of nobles.

Internet Activity

Exploring Aztec religion Have students learn more about Aztec religion at the Aztec Student Teacher Resource Center at http://members.aol.com/spdtom/index.html. Have students report three new pieces of information they learned and download graphs for visual presentations. Given the changing nature of the Internet, you may wish to preview this site. (*average*)

★ Background ★
Religion and Ethics

Paying homage to the gods Human sacrifice was not the only way in which the Aztecs honored their gods. Throughout the year, ceremonies with dances, songs, processions, offerings, and dramas were held. In addition, Aztec priests managed the temple lands and educated children. To the Aztecs, these tasks all expressed respect for their gods.

Writing Actively

After Reading Have students compare the Aztecs and Incas by completing the following structured paragraph: Aztecs and Incas are similar in several ways. Both made technical advances in _______ and _______. Both had strong _______ beliefs. Finally, in both Aztec and Incan religions, the _______ god was especially important.

Biography

ANSWER

Possible answer: Having a single language would make it easier for people in all parts of the Incan empire to communicate with one another, and it would make administration of the vast empire easier.

RESOURCE DIRECTORY

Teaching Resources
Unit 1/Chapter 2
• Section 3 Quiz, p. 19

Biography **Pachacuti**

In 1438, Pachacuti rallied Incan forces to drive off an invasion. The Incas soon made him their leader. As founder of the Incan empire, Pachacuti devoted himself to uniting all the lands and people of Peru. He demanded that conquered people all speak one language, Quechua. He also turned the city of Cuzco into a magnificent capital. ★ **Why would Pachacuti think that one language would help unite his empire?**

almost like a god. Servants carried him from place to place on a litter. If the emperor did walk, nobles scattered flower petals in his path so that his feet never touched the ground. Ordinary people lowered their eyes when he passed.

Heavy taxes and the demand for human sacrifices fueled revolts among the neighboring people conquered by the Aztecs. Powerful Aztec armies, however, put down any uprising, taking even more prisoners to be sacrificed to the gods. One Aztec poet boasted:

> “Who could conquer Tenochtitlán? Who could shake the foundation of heaven?”

In fact, the "foundation of heaven" was not as strong as the poet thought. As you will read in Chapter 3, in the 1520s, enemies of the Aztecs would help to destroy Tenochtitlán and end the Aztec empire.

Incan Civilization

Far to the south of the Aztec empire, the **Incas** united the largest empire in the Americas. By 1492, the Incan empire stretched for almost 3,000 miles (4,800 km) along the western coast of South America. (See the map on page 47.)

The Incan capital at **Cuzco** (KOOS koh) was high in the Andes Mountains. From there, the Incas ruled more than 10 million people living in coastal deserts, lowland jungles, and high mountains.

Farming

Like the Mayas and Aztecs, the Incas adapted customs and ideas from earlier cultures. Among them were the Moche, who lived along the Pacific coast of South America between about 250 and 700, and the Chimu people, who came after them.

Expanding on farming methods of these earlier Andean peoples, the Incas carved **terraces,** land shaped like wide steps, into the steep mountainsides. Sturdy stone walls kept the rains from washing the soil off the terraces. Stone **aqueducts,** or raised channels, carried water to the terraces from distant rivers. Most gardens produced two crops a year, including more than 100 varieties of potatoes.

The emperor, known as the Sapa Inca, controlled all the land and riches of the empire. Officials kept records of what each family in the empire produced. The government stored their **surplus,** or extra, crops in warehouses owned by the emperor. Incan officials used much of the food in these warehouses to feed the sick or victims of famine.

Engineering and medicine

The Incas perfected highly advanced building techniques. Their huge stone temples and forts showed their expert engineering skills. With only human labor, ropes, and wooden rollers, the Incas moved into place massive stones that weighed as much as 200 tons.

50 ★ Chapter 2

★ Customized Instruction ★

Visual Learners

Creating study aids Have students work in small groups to create flashcards to use as section study aids. Use construction paper or large index cards. On one side, flashcards should show large pictures or single-word clues that suggest each empire discussed in the section and on the other the correct identification. Viewers should be able to identify the civilization from the picture. For example, a 365-day calendar should elicit the response "Maya." Have groups exchange flashcards and use them to review the section. (basic) ELL

Stonemasons chiseled each block so that it fit tightly to the next without any kind of cement. Even a knife blade could not fit between blocks. Incan buildings survived hundreds of earthquakes. Some remain standing today.

To unite and control their sprawling empire, the Incas built a complex network of roads. More than 19,000 miles (30,000 km) of roads linked all parts of the empire. Incan engineers carved roads through rock mountains and stretched rope bridges across deep gorges.

Teams of runners carried royal commands and news quickly across the empire. A runner from Cuzco, for example, would carry a message to a nearby village. From there, another runner would race to the next relay station. This system helped the emperor to control his people. If a runner brought news of a revolt, Incan armies could move swiftly along the network of roads to crush it.

Besides their success as farmers and engineers, the Incas made several important advances in medicine. They used quinine to treat malaria, performed successful brain surgery, and also discovered medicines to lessen pain.

Incan gold earrings

Religious beliefs

Like the Aztecs, the Incas worshipped the sun. The emperor, they believed, was descended from the sun god. A specially trained class of "chosen women of the sun" attended the emperor and performed religious rituals. To honor the sun, the Incas lined the walls of palaces and temples with sheets of gold. They called gold "the sweat of the gods." Nobles and priests adorned themselves with golden ornaments.

Very little Incan gold has survived. In the 1530s, as you will read, the Spanish rode up Incan highways to the golden city of Cuzco. The Incas, weakened by civil war and disease, were unable to fight off the invaders. The newcomers melted down the golden treasures of the Incan empire and sent them to Europe.

★ Section 3 Review ★

Recall

1. **Locate** **(a)** Mexico, **(b)** Guatemala, **(c)** Tikal, **(d)** Aztec empire, **(e)** Andes Mountains, **(f)** Incan empire.
2. **Identify** **(a)** Maya, **(b)** Olmec, **(c)** Aztec, **(d)** Tenochtitlán, **(e)** Inca, **(f)** Cuzco.
3. **Define** **(a)** civilization, **(b)** hieroglyphics, **(c)** causeway, **(d)** chinampas, **(e)** absolute power, **(f)** terrace, **(g)** aqueduct, **(h)** surplus.

Comprehension

4. **(a)** What civilizations emerged in present-day Mexico? **(b)** Where did the Incas build their civilization?
5. Describe one achievement of each of the following: **(a)** Mayas, **(b)** Aztecs, **(c)** Incas.
6. How was religion central to Aztec life?

Critical Thinking and Writing

7. **Synthesizing Information** Review the definition of a civilization on page 46. Then, choose one of the groups discussed in this section and explain why it should be considered a civilization.
8. **Comparing** Compare the major features of two of the civilizations discussed in the section. How are they similar? How are they different?

★ ★

Activity **Writing a Travel Plan** Next stop—Tenochtitlán! You are planning a trip through time to the Aztec capital. Write a list of the sights you want to see and the things you most want to do.

★ Section 3 Review ★

ANSWERS

1. See map, p. 47, and the Geographic Atlas map in the Reference Section.

2. (a)–(b) p. 46, **(c)–(d)** p. 48, **(e)–(f)** p. 50

3. (a) p. 46, **(b)** p. 47, **(c)** p. 48, **(d)–(e)** p. 49, **(f)–(h)** p. 50

4. (a) Olmec, Maya, Aztec **(b)** the Andes Mountains, along the western coast of South America

5. Possible answers: **(a)** Mayas: hieroglyphics **(b)** Aztecs: an advanced calendar **(c)** Incas: sophisticated building methods

6. Possible answers: Its priests determined when to plant or harvest crops; humans were sacrificed to please the sun god.

7. Possible answer: The Mayas built cities; had a complex government, social system, and religion; and recorded their accomplishments in writing.

8. Possible answer: Both the Mayas and the Aztecs cleared the jungle and built great cities, and their priests were powerful. But the Aztecs were more warlike.

Activity

Guided Instruction
Have students reread the text description of the city and then try to visualize what it was like.

ASSESSMENT See the rubrics in the Alternative Assessment booklet in the Teaching Resources.

★ *Background* ★

Linking Past and Present

Present-day Incas? The Incas drew conquered people into their empire. Settlers from older parts of the empire were moved into the conquered areas, carrying the official language, Quechua, to the new people. Twenty-eight languages of the Quechua family are still spoken by the Native Americans in the Andean highlands.

Section 4

After 1492

★ ★ ★ ★ ★ ★ ★ ★ ★ ★ ★ ★ ★ ★ ★ ★ ★

LESSON PLAN

Objectives

★ Explain how the 1492 encounter with Europeans affected Native Americans.

★ Describe the Columbian Exchange.

★ Identify elements of Native American culture that Europeans adopted.

1 Engage

Warm Up Tell students that you have a puzzle for them. Ask: "What do these everyday foods have in common: corn, potatoes, squash, and peanuts?" If students cannot guess, tell them that all these foods originated in the Americas.

Activating Prior Knowledge Write the name *Christopher Columbus* on the chalkboard. Have the class create a word web with everything they know about Columbus.

Reading Actively

Before Reading Ask students to skim the section, looking at the illustrations and headings. Ask them to write two or three sentences predicting what the section will be about. Have them verify or correct their predictions as they read.

RESOURCE DIRECTORY

Teaching Resources
Lesson Planner, p. 7

4 After 1492

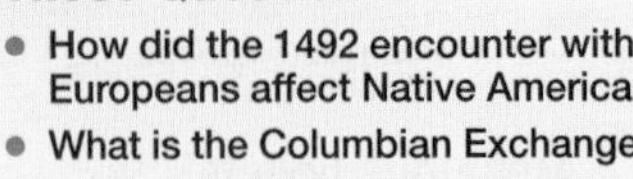

As You Read

Explore These Questions

- How did the 1492 encounter with Europeans affect Native Americans?
- What is the Columbian Exchange?
- What elements of Native American culture did Europeans adopt?

Identify

- Viking
- Leif Erickson
- Vinland
- Christopher Columbus
- Taíno
- Columbian Exchange

SETTING the Scene Approximately 1,000 years ago, a group of seafaring men and women sailed across the Atlantic Ocean to settle on an island they called Vinland. There, they met local traders, who carried packs made of fur and skins. A witness wrote:

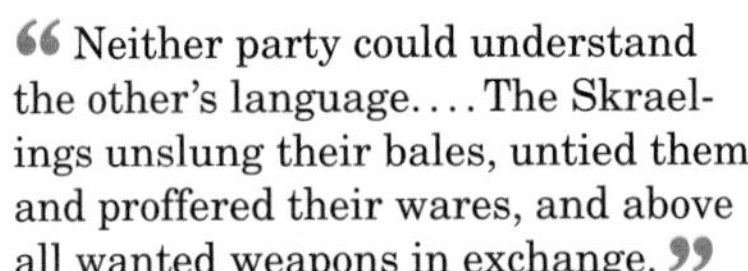

> "Neither party could understand the other's language.... The Skraelings unslung their bales, untied them, and proffered their wares, and above all wanted weapons in exchange."

This meeting was one of the earliest encounters between Native Americans and Europeans. The "Skraelings" were Inuits. The settlers were **Vikings,** seafaring people from Scandinavia in Northern Europe.

The Viking settlement was brief and had no long-term effect on Native Americans. Then, in 1492, an expedition from Spain sailed into the Caribbean Sea. This time, the arrival of Europeans would have a dramatic impact on people throughout the Americas.

Early Contacts

For thousands of years, Native Americans had little knowledge of the world beyond their shores. Early contacts with outsiders were limited.

In 1001, Viking sailors led by **Leif Erickson** reached the northern tip of North America. They settled for a brief time in a flat, wooded territory they called **Vinland.** Today, many archaeologists believe that the Viking settlement was located in present-day Newfoundland, in Canada. The Vikings did not stay in Vinland long. No one is sure why they left. Viking stories, however, describe fierce battles with the Inuits.

Figurehead of a Viking ship

There are also many stories about seafaring people from Asia reaching the Americas. Most experts agree that such voyages were very rare, if they occurred at all. Still, some believe that even after the last ice age ended, people continued to cross the Bering Sea from Asia into North America. Others claim that fishing boats from China and Japan blew off course and landed on the western coast of South America.

Encounter in 1492

If these early contacts did in fact take place, they had little impact either on Native Americans or the rest of the world. The encounter in 1492, however, changed history. Italian-born sailor **Christopher Columbus** led a Spanish fleet into the Caribbean. The voyage set off a chain of events whose effects are still felt throughout the world today. (You will read more about Christopher Columbus and other Europeans in Chapter 3.)

Columbus first landed in the Americas on a small Caribbean island. Friendly relations with the **Taínos** (TI nohz), the Native Ameri-

★ ***Customized Instruction*** ★

Introverted Learners

Locating Native American influences Discuss with the class the many states and cities that have Native American names. Assign pairs of students a region of the United States, and provide a map of the area assigned. Have partners locate three states, towns, or rivers (or other place names) that they think might be of Native American origin. Have them use the library or the Internet to find the meanings of the names chosen and to identify the Native American group that named each one. On a large outline map of the United States, ask students to write their place names, name origins, and English translations. (*challenging*) ELL T cans he met there, did not last. Columbus and the Europeans who followed him were convinced that their culture was superior to that of the Indians. They claimed Taíno lands for themselves. They forced Taínos to work in gold mines, on ranches, or in Spanish households. Many Taínos died from harsh conditions. Others died from European diseases. Within 100 years of Columbus's arrival, the entire Taíno population had been destroyed.

The Taínos' experience with Europeans set a tragic pattern for Native Americans. That pattern was repeated again and again throughout the Americas.

Cultural Exchange

The 1492 encounter between Native Americans and Europeans had other effects. It started a worldwide exchange of goods and ideas that transformed people's lives around the globe. Because it began with Columbus, this transfer is known as the **Columbian Exchange.** It covered a wide range of areas, including food, medicine, government, technology, the arts, and language.

The exchange went in both directions. Europeans learned much from Native Americans. At the same time, Europeans contributed in many ways to the culture of the Americas. They introduced domestic animals such as chickens and horses. They also taught Native Americans how to use metals to make copper pots and iron knives.

Tragically, Europeans also brought new diseases to the Americas. Millions of Native Americans died of smallpox and other diseases to which they had no resistance.

Native American Influences

For their part, Native Americans introduced Europeans to new customs and ideas. Beginning with the encounter in 1492, elements of Native American culture gradually spread around the world.

Food and farming

Over thousands of years, Native Americans had learned to grow a variety of crops. After 1492, they introduced Europeans to valuable food crops such as corn, potatoes, beans, tomatoes, manioc (a root vegetable), squash, peanuts, pineapples, and blueberries. Today, almost half the world's food crops come from plants that were first grown in the Americas.

Europeans carried the new foods with them as they sailed around the world. Everywhere, people's diets changed and populations increased. In South Asia, people used American hot peppers and chilies to spice their curries, or stews. Millions of Chinese peasants began growing sweet potatoes. Italians made sauces from tomatoes. People in West Africa grew manioc and maize.

Viewing History **Potato Farming in South America**

Farmers in the Andes first raised potatoes about 2,000 years ago. As a result of the Columbian Exchange, the potato has become an important part of people's diets around the world. ★ **Identify two other food crops that were first grown in the Americas.**

2 Explore

Ask students to read the section. For a homework assignment, have them research the Columbian Exchange. Ask them to summarize how Europeans and Native Americans affected each other.

3 Teach

Have students, as a class, choose the most important idea in each subsection. Write their consensus ideas on the chalkboard, and have students copy them onto a piece of paper, adding a few phrases of explanation to each.

4 Assess

To close the lesson, have students complete the section review. As an alternative, have them assume the role of Native Americans or Europeans. Ask them to write letters to a newspaper that argue the positive or negative results of the Columbian Exchange.

Viewing History ANSWER

Possible answers: squash, beans, corn, manioc, tomatoes, peanuts, pineapples, blueberries

★ *Background* ★

Did You Know?

Sour grapes? The Vikings reported that they had discovered "wine berries" in Vinland—presumably, grapes. It seems, however, that the Vikings used this term for all berries. Because some historians doubt that grapes could have grown that far north, they think the fruit actually may have been the cranberries or gooseberries that grow in northeastern North America.

Why Study *History?*

ANSWERS

1. (a) It taught young men the skills needed to be successful in their society—hunting and fighting. **(b)** Boys became part of a team at birth; ceremonies ensured that the game would be a part of their culture. **2.** Accept all reasonable answers. For example, basketball teaches teamwork, aim, cooperation, coordination.

★Activity

Guided Instruction
Direct students to library resources on sports and their rules, or have them research such games on the Internet. Ask them to be specific about the rules of the game. They might also find magazine articles about their sport that suggest why it is popular.

ASSESSMENT See the rubrics in the Alternative Assessment booklet in the Teaching Resources.

Writing Actively

After Reading Have students use the Identify terms from the beginning of the section to write a paragraph summarizing the importance of the events that began in 1492.

RESOURCE DIRECTORY

Teaching Resources
Unit 1/Chapter 2
- Vocabulary Builder, p. 11
- Section 4 Quiz, p. 20
- Chapter Tests, pp. 7–12

Why Study History?
- Sports Are Important in Our Culture, pp. 7–10

Why Study *History?*

Because Sports Are Important in Our Culture

Historical Background

The athletes lined the playing field—nearly 1,000 young men in all. Each held a long pole topped with a web of leather netting. As the game began, they rushed up and down the mile-long field, trying to pass a ball over the other team's goal. Play was fast, dangerous, and exhausting. It might last well into the next day!

The players were Iroquois. They called the game baggataway. You know it by its French name: lacrosse.

The game was more than fun. The game taught young men agility, quick thinking, and teamwork—skills they would need as hunters or warriors. In fact, some called the game "the little brother of war." Each boy was assigned to a team at birth. The night before a match, villages held ceremonies with music, dancing, and speeches to cheer their team to victory.

Connections to Today

Today, lacrosse is popular in many American schools. Other sports we enjoy today were played by Native Americans. Field hockey and ice hockey developed partly from a sport known as the shinny game. Like Native Americans, we also compete in kayaking, canoeing, archery, swimming, wrestling, and foot races.

Connections to You

For us, as for Native Americans, sports are more than just fun. Athletics can improve your health and physical fitness.

Modern lacrosse player

School pep rallies, like the pregame ceremonies of the Iroquois, encourage a sense of pride and community. Sports can also teach skills that you will use later in life. Today's sports emphasize teamwork, responsibility, and fair play.

1. **Comprehension** **(a)** Why did the Iroquois consider baggataway important? **(b)** How did they make sure each new generation learned the game?
2. **Critical Thinking** Choose a sport that is popular at your school. What kind of skills can that sport teach?

Reporting on Sports Research the modern rules of lacrosse or one of the other sports mentioned above. Report on how that sport is played and why you think it has remained so popular today.

Fast Facts

Ball games are nothing new in the Americas.
★ The Mayas engaged in complex ceremonial games performed on large, elaborate stone courts.
★ Aztec games involved getting a rubber ball through a vertical stone hoop.
★ The Inuits played an unstructured form of kickball.
★ The Algonquins are generally credited with inventing lacrosse. The ball was made of tightly packed deerskin.

Bibliography

To read more about this topic:

1. *American Sports: From the Age of Folk Games to the Age of Televised Sports,* Benjamin G. Rader (Prentice Hall, 1996). Covers colonial times to the present.
2. *Chronicle of the Olympics, 1896–2000* (D K Publishing Inc., 1998). Provides all medal winners plus games information through those scheduled at Sydney in 2000.
3. Internet. All-Web guide to sports sites around the world at www.sport-hq.com.

Language

Native American influences also show up in language. Europeans adopted words for clothing (poncho, moccasin, parka), trees (pecan, hickory), and inventions (toboggan, hammock). In an essay titled "The Indian All Around Us," historian Bernard DeVoto noted:

> "Depending on what part of the country you are in, you may see a chipmunk, muskrat, woodchuck, or coyote. The names of all these animals are Indian words. . . . Twenty-six of our states have Indian names."

Massachusetts, Alabama, Texas, Michigan, and Missouri are all Native American words. Many rivers bear Native American names, including the Mississippi, the Potomac, and the Monongahela.

Technology and medicine

Native Americans helped European settlers survive in North America. Besides showing the newcomers how to grow foods such as corn, Indians taught them hunting skills suitable to the American land. They led explorers on foot along Indian trails and paddled them up rivers in Indian canoes.

In the North, Indians showed Europeans how to use snowshoes and trap fur-bearing animals. Europeans also learned to respect Native American medical knowledge. Indians often treated the newcomers with medicines unknown to Europeans.

Other influences

As time went on, Native American cultures influenced the arts, sports, and even government. Today, Indian designs in pottery and leather work are highly prized. Americans play versions of such Indian games as lacrosse.

Some early leaders of the United States studied Native American political structures. Benjamin Franklin saw the League of the Iroquois as a model and urged Americans to unite in a similar way.

In time, all Native Americans felt the effects of European conquest. Still, despite attacks on their culture, Native Americans survived throughout the two continents. They preserved many traditions, including a respect for nature. Native Americans sought to live in harmony with the natural world. If that harmony was disrupted, they believed, misfortune would result. Today, many people have come to admire and share this concern for nature.

★ Section 4 Review ★

Recall

1. **Identify** **(a)** Viking, **(b)** Leif Erickson, **(c)** Vinland, **(d)** Christopher Columbus, **(e)** Taíno, **(f)** Columbian Exchange.

Comprehension

2. How did the arrival of Columbus affect the Taínos?
3. Describe two effects of the Columbian Exchange on Native Americans.
4. Name three ways that Native Americans influenced our culture today.

Critical Thinking and Writing

5. **Analyzing Information** Some historians think that Asians explored the Americas years before Columbus arrived. What kinds of evidence might prove that these historians are correct?
6. **Defending a Position** Do you think that the world was harmed or enriched by the Columbian Exchange? Defend your position.

Activity **Examining Exchange** List three items or activities in your life that were part of the Columbian Exchange. Write one or two sentences explaining how your life would be different without each item or activity.

★ Activity ★

Turning Points

Creating a bulletin board display Have students work in small groups to create a bulletin board display of the Columbian Exchange. One group might prepare an outline map of Europe and the Americas, showing the path of exchanges. Some groups can research and illustrate specific exchanges of plants, animals, medicines, clothing, language, or technology. Other groups can prepare a balance sheet evaluating which groups benefited most from exchanges in particular areas or overall. The Columbian Exchange extended from Europe to Africa to the Americas to Asia. Have students include African and Asian impacts as well. (*average*) ELL

★ Section 4 Review ★

ANSWERS

1. (a)–(e) p. 52, **(f)** p. 53

2. Europeans took over Taíno lands and enslaved the people. Within 100 years, European diseases had wiped out the Taínos.

3. Possible answers: Native Americans began using European domestic animals, tools, and weapons; many died from European diseases.

4. Possible answers: Native American words and place names; games such as lacrosse; and the influence of Native American political structures on some early colonial leaders who shaped our system of government

5. Possible answers: Asian artifacts in Native American cultures of the same period; written records describing contact

6. Possible answers: Enriched: spread new foods and ideas around the world; Harmed: Native American cultures, because many were completely destroyed

Activity

Guided Instruction
Give students the examples of food such as potatoes (used in French fries), tomatoes (used in pizza), and peanuts (used in peanut butter and in candy). Have students also consider items brought to the Americas by Europeans.

ASSESSMENT See the rubrics in the Alternative Assessment booklet in the Teaching Resources.

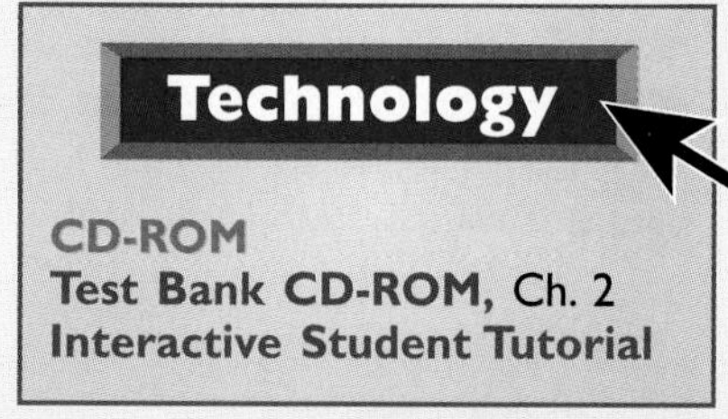

CD-ROM
Test Bank CD-ROM, Ch. 2
Interactive Student Tutorial

Chapter 2

Review and Activities

Reviewing the Chapter

Define These Terms

1. d **2.** a **3.** b **4.** e **5.** c

Explore the Main Ideas

1. Possible answer: shells from the Gulf of Mexico and turquoise from the Southwest in sites of the Mound Builders

2. Ceremonies were intended to honor the forces of nature.

3. Women owned all household property, were in charge of planting and harvesting, and elected the sachems.

4. The Aztecs sacrificed prisoners of war to the sun god.

5. Possible answers: **(a)** Native Americans learned to use metals to make copper pots and iron knives. **(b)** tomatoes, corn

Geography Activity

1. D **2.** B **3.** F **4.** A **5.** C **6.** E

Interaction They dug canals and created chinampas, or floating gardens, with mats staked to the lake bottom and filled with mud for growing crops.

Critical Thinking and Writing

1. (a) the crossing of the land bridge; the height of the Mayan culture; the arrival of Columbus; the founding of the League of Iroquois **(b)** Tomatoes were not brought to Europe until after Columbus reached the Americas.

2. Possible answer: Both have the same goal—rapid communication. But the Incas relied on human muscle and energy; today we rely on electronic technology.

3. Possible answers: **(a)** Class boundaries were not permanently defined. **(b)** People could move up in society through marriage, but not through merit. By its very nature, a class system is unequal.

4. Possible answer: Yes, because even America's early history can help us understand the United States today and give us guidance for the future. For instance, understanding the Iroquois political system may enhance insight into our own, since some colonial leaders were influenced by it. Understanding how Native Americans lived in harmony with the environment may help us do the same.

Using Primary Sources

(a) The Yguazes chased a deer until it tired and they could catch it. **(b)** The Yguazes were tireless and remained in good spirits even in times of extreme hunger.

Chapter 2 Review and Activities

★ Sum It Up ★

Section 1 Early People and Cultures

- The first Americans crossed a land bridge from Asia between 30,000 and 15,000 years ago.
- The first Americans adapted to the desert Southwest by learning to grow crops under dry conditions and building adobe houses.

Section 2 People of North America

- Native American cultures varied widely depending on geography.
- The religious beliefs of Native Americans reflected their close ties with the natural world.
- In the Eastern Woodlands, the five Iroquois nations formed a league to end warfare.

Section 3 Great Civilizations in the Americas

- The Mayan civilization boasted skill in astronomy, mathematics, and writing.
- The Aztecs of Mexico ruled a huge empire with millions of people.
- In South America, the Incas perfected advanced building techniques and built roads and bridges to unite their empire.

Section 4 After 1492

- Contact with Europeans had tragic consequences for Native Americans, as millions died of European diseases.
- The Columbian Exchange brought new products, technology, and ideas both to the Americas and to the rest of the world.

For additional review of the major ideas of Chapter 2, see ***Guide to the Essentials of American History*** or ***Interactive Student Tutorial CD-ROM,*** which contains interactive review activities, graphic organizers, and practice tests.

Reviewing the Chapter

Define These Terms

Match each term with the correct definition.

Column 1	Column 2
1. culture	**a.** group of villages or settlements that share common customs
2. tribe	**b.** advanced culture
3. civilization	**c.** object made by humans
4. hieroglyphics	**d.** complete way of life
5. artifact	**e.** writing that uses pictures

Explore the Main Ideas

1. What evidence suggests that early Native Americans traded with one another?
2. What was one important purpose of the religious ceremonies of Native Americans?
3. What role did women play in Iroquois society?
4. How did the Aztecs treat people captured in warfare?
5. **(a)** Describe one skill Native Americans learned from Europeans. **(b)** Identify two American products that Europeans adopted.

Geography Activity

Match the letters on the map with the following places: **1.** Mayan civilization, **2.** Aztec empire, **3.** Incan empire, **4.** Tenochtitlán, **5.** Tikal, **6.** Cuzco. **Interaction** How were the Aztecs able to grow crops on swampland?

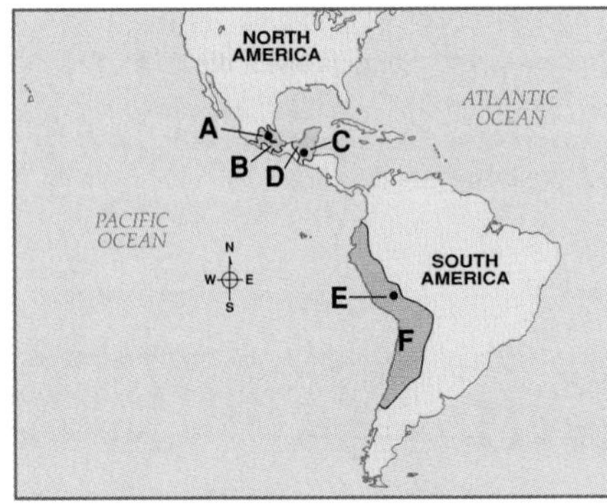

Critical Thinking and Writing

1. **Understanding Chronology** **(a)** Place the following in correct chronological order: the height of the Mayan culture; the arrival of Columbus; the crossing of the land bridge; the founding of the League of the Iroquois. **(b)** How do you know that Columbus never ate tomato sauce when he was a boy?
2. **Linking Past and Present** Compare the communication technology of the Incas with our communication technology today.
3. **Analyzing Ideas** Review what you have read about Natchez society. **(a)** What was one advantage of the Natchez rule regarding marriage? **(b)** What was one disadvantage?
4. Exploring Unit Themes **Origins** Is it valuable for Americans to study early American cultures? Support your answer by citing examples from this chapter.

Using Primary Sources

Alvar Nuñez Cabeza de Vaca was an early Spanish explorer. He described the Yguazes people of the Gulf Coast region in this way:

> "These Indians are so accustomed to running that without rest or fatigue they follow a deer from morning to night. In this way they kill many. They pursue them until [the deer are] tired down, and sometimes overtake them in the race. Their houses are of matting, placed upon four hoops. They carry them on the back, and [move] every two or three days in search of food. . . . They are a merry people, considering the hunger they suffer; for they never cease, notwithstanding, to observe their festivities."

Source: *Original Narratives of Early American History: Spanish Explorers in the Southern United States*, 1959.

Recognizing Points of View **(a)** How did the Yguazes catch deer? **(b)** What does the writer think is interesting or surprising about the Yguazes?

Activity Bank

Interdisciplinary Activity

Exploring the Arts Do research on traditional Native American designs from your region of the country. Then, use one of these designs in your own work of art.

Career Skills Activity

Engineers Do research on Incan engineering. Make a model or draw a diagram of an Incan bridge. Prepare a report in which you compare the bridge with a modern bridge.

Citizenship Activity

Forming a League Forming the League of the Iroquois required cooperation, organization, and commitment. Sketch out a plan for a league that would meet a need in your school. Suggest what kind of body would make decisions and what groups would need to be represented.

Internet Activity

Use the Internet to find sites dealing with Native Americans in your state. Save the information you have found as a text file. Work with other members of your class to print out and bind the text files in an attractive format.

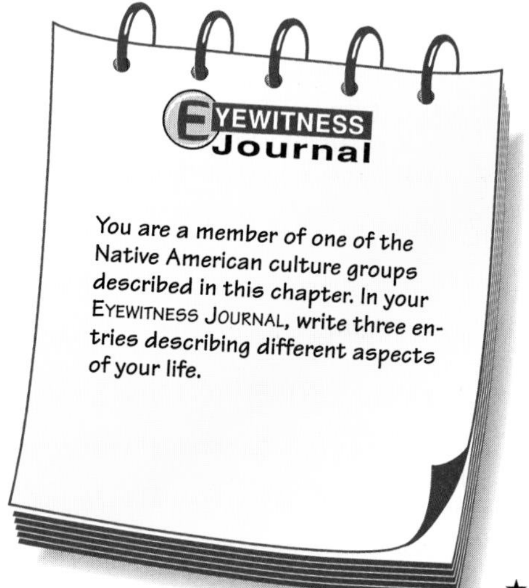

EYEWITNESS Journal
You are a member of one of the Native American culture groups described in this chapter. In your EYEWITNESS JOURNAL, write three entries describing different aspects of your life.

Activity Bank

ASSESSMENT To assess the activities on this page, see the rubrics in the Alternative Assessment booklet in the Teaching Resources. You might want to share the rubrics with your students before they begin work.

Interdisciplinary Activity

1. Have students visit local libraries for books on Native American art and museums to see actual examples.
2. Point out that Native American art may feature common design elements such as geometric patterns or animal figures.
3. Display student artwork in the classroom. Award prizes for the most inventive piece and the most genuine copy of Native American art.

Career Skills Activity

1. Tell students that the Incas made both stone bridges and suspension bridges. Either could be contrasted with modern bridges.
2. You may wish to have students work in teams to do research on and model the bridges and to prepare their reports.
3. Arrange for students to present their reports to the class.

Citizenship Activity

1. Before students begin, have them brainstorm for school needs and possible projects.
2. Encourage students to find ways to link the school and the community—for example, by working with a variety of community groups.
3. Point out that the league would be most effective if it relied on some kind of elections.

Eyewitness Journal

1. Help students focus with this list of events they could include: hunt, religious ritual, battle, meals, encounter with Europeans, courting of a prospective mate.
2. Encourage students to turn a description of an event into a poem.
3. Ask for volunteers to share their entries with the class.

Internet Activity

1. Have students look at www.phschool.com, which contains updated information on a variety of topics.
2. The answer service and metasearch engine Ask Jeeves, at www.aj.com, will return hits from many other search engines. Have students try combinations of their inquiry.
3. Given the changing nature of the Internet, you may wish to preview these sites.

Chapter 3 Manager

SECTION OBJECTIVES	TEACHING RESOURCES	ADDITIONAL RESOURCE
1 Europeans Reach the Americas (pp. 60–64) **Objectives** 1. Explain how the Crusades and the Renaissance changed Europe. 2. Explain why Europeans looked for new sea routes to Asia. 3. Describe the effects of Columbus's voyages.	**Lesson Planner,** p. 8 (average) . . . . .90 mins. **Unit 1/Chapter 3** • Section 1 Quiz, p. 27 (average) . . . . .15 mins. **Why Study History?** • You Live in a Shrinking World, pp. 11–14 (average) . . . . .90 mins. **Interdisciplinary Connections** • Main Idea: Columbian Exchange, pp. 14, 16–18 (average) . . . . .20 mins.	**Voices of Freedom** • Marco Polo on the Wealth of Asia, pp. 23–24 (challenging) **Historical Outline Map Book** • Voyages of Discovery, p. 8 (average) **Customized Reader** • Columbus Lands in the Americas, article IB-3 (challenging)
2 Spain Builds an Empire (pp. 65–72) **Objectives** 1. Describe how Spain interacted with Native American empires. 2. Explain how Spain governed its lands in the Americas. 3. Explain why life was difficult for the Native Americans who lived under Spanish rule.	**Lesson Planner,** p. 9 (average) . . . . .45 mins. **Unit 1/Chapter 3** • Practice Your Skills: Reading a Line Graph, p. 22 (average) . . . . .30 mins. • Critical Thinking and Writing: Analyzing Information, p. 23 (basic) . . . . . .20 mins. • Biography Flashcard: Doña Marina, p. 26 (average) . . . . .20 mins. • Section 2 Quiz, p. 28 (average) . . . . .15 mins.	**Voices of Freedom** • Rescued by Indians, pp. 26–27 (average) **Historical Outline Map Book** • Spanish Explorers in North America, p. 9 (average) **Customized Reader** • Montezuma, article IA-1 (challenging) • A Spanish Colony in Florida, article IB-7 (average)
3 Africans Come to the Americas (pp. 73–77) **Objectives** 1. Explain why African states were prosperous. 2. Describe how the African slave trade changed in the 1500s. 3. Identify the Middle Passage.	**Lesson Planner,** p. 10 (average) . . . . .90 mins. **Unit 1/Chapter 3** • Section 3 Quiz, p. 29 (average) . . . . .15 mins. **Interdisciplinary Connections** • Main Idea: Columbian Exchange, p. 15 (average) . . . . .20 mins. **Document-Based Discovery** • Origins, pp. 2–5 (average) . . . . .90 mins.	**Voices of Freedom** • Hardships of the Atlantic Crossing, pp. 30–31 (average)
4 Colonizing North America (pp. 78–83) **Objectives** 1. Explain how competition grew among European nations. 2. Describe how trappers and missionaries helped New France to grow. 3. Explain how the arrival of Europeans affected Native Americans in North America.	**Lesson Planner,** p. 11 (average) . . . . .90 mins. **Unit 1/Chapter 3** • Section 4 Quiz, p. 30 (average) . . . . .15 mins.	**Voices of Freedom** • Marquette and Joliet, pp. 32–33 (challenging) **Historical Outline Map Book** • Search for a Northwest Passage, p. 10 (average) **Customized Reader** • A Voyage Down the Mississippi, article IIA-8 (challenging) • Dutch Customs in Old New York, article IIA-15 (average)
5 The First English Colonies (pp. 84–89) **Objectives** 1. Describe how representative government took root in Virginia. 2. Explain why the Piligrims started a colony in North America. 3. Describe how Native Americans helped the Plymouth Colony to survive.	**Lesson Planner,** p. 12 (average) . . . . .45 mins. **Unit 1/Chapter 3** • Vocabulary Builder, p. 21 (basic) . . . . .15 mins. • Map Mystery: What Happened to John Smith?, p. 24 (basic) . . . . .15 mins. • Connecting History and Literature: Of Plymouth Plantation, p. 25 (average) . . .20 mins. • Section 5 Quiz, p. 31 (average) . . . . .15 mins. **Chapter Tests,** Unit 1, Chapter 3, pp. 13–18 (average) . . . . .45 mins.	**Voices of Freedom** • Skills Needed in the New World, pp. 28–29 (average) • A Virginia Colonist's Despair, p. 34 (average) • Pilgrims and Indians Make Peace, pp. 35–36 (challenging) **Customized Reader** • Returning to Roanoke Colony, article IB-4 (challenging)

Assessment Options

Teaching Resources
- Alternative Assessment booklet
- Section Quizzes, Unit 1, Chapter 3, pp. 27–31
- Chapter Tests, Chapter 3, pp. 13–18
- Test Bank CD-ROM

Student Performance Pack
- Guide to the Essentials of American History, Chapter 3 Test, p. 21
- Standardized Test Prep Handbook
- Interactive Student Tutorial CD-ROM

Interdisciplinary Connections

Teaching Resources
- Map Mystery, Unit 1, Chapter 3, p. 24
- Connecting History and Literature, Unit 1, Chapter 3, p. 25
- Interdisciplinary Connections, pp. 13–18

Voices of Freedom, pp. 23–24, 26–36

Customized Reader, articles IA-1, IB-3, IB-4, IB-7, IIA-8, IIA-15, IIA-17

Technology

AmericanHeritage® History of the United States CD-ROM
- Time Tour: Europeans Reach the Americas in A Meeting of Different Worlds
- History Makers: Christopher Columbus, John Smith, Pocahontas

Interactive Student Tutorial CD-ROM

Test Bank CD-ROM

Color Transparencies
- Columbian Exchange, p. B-37
- The Americas and the World, 1300–1600, p. E-13
- The Americas and the World, 1600–1800, p. E-15
- Exploration of the Americas, p. F-13
- When Worlds Collide, p. G-13

Guided Reading Audiotapes (English/Spanish), side 1

Resource Pro® CD-ROM

Prentice Hall United States History Video Collection™ (Spanish track available on disc version.) Vol. 1, Chs. 10, 13, 16, 19, 22, 25; Vol. 2, Chs. 7, 10, 13

Prentice Hall Home Page
www.phschool.com

Student Performance Pack

Guide to the Essentials of American History
- Ch. 3, pp. 16–21
  (Available in English and Spanish)

Guided Reading Audiotapes (English/Spanish), side 1

Standardized Test Prep Handbook

Interactive Student Tutorial CD-ROM

BLOCK SCHEDULING
Activities with this icon will help you meet your Block Scheduling needs.

ENGLISH LANGUAGE LEARNERS
Activities with this icon are suitable for English Language Learners.

TEAM TEACHING
Activities and Background Notes with this icon present starting points for Team Teaching.

Teachers' Bibliography

From the Archives of AmericanHeritage®

Don't miss the special American Heritage® teaching notes found in this chapter.

Contact Teachers' Curriculum Institute to learn more about History Alive!® resources on the meeting of different cultures in North America. See History Alive!® unit: Geography of America From Past to Present, Section 4, "Adapting to the Environment: Colonial Settlers," and Colonial Life and the American Revolution, Section 2, "Slavery in the Colonies."

Explore your library to find these issues related to Chapter 3: *St Augustine: America's Oldest City,* November 1995; *Jamestown,* April 1994; *Pilgrims to a New World,* November 1989.

Prentice Hall Web Site You can access a structured, on-line environment that allows you to preview curriculum-related resources and receive updated information on groundbreaking events from around the nation and the world. (www.phschool.com)

Chapter 3

A Meeting of Different Worlds 1100–1700

Introducing the Chapter

Have students preview the main ideas of this chapter by looking over the visuals. Suggest they look for examples of cultural differences.

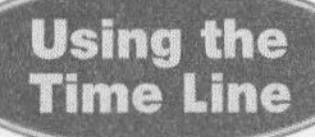

To reinforce student understanding of the sequence of events in this chapter, ask them to look at the time line on these pages. Ask questions such as these: **(1)** What European nation was the first to found a colony in the Americas? *(Spain)* **(2)** When did the Pilgrims reach Plymouth? *(1620)* **(3)** What event occurred in Europe during the same century that saw the fall of the Aztec and Incan empires to Spain? *(Protestant Reformation)* **(4)** Did the French explore the Mississippi River before or after the founding of Jamestown? *(after)*

Ask students to think about recent purchases they and other members of their families have made of food, clothing, electronics, and other goods. Students should list any that were imported and then share their lists with the class.

For additional *Why Study History?* support, see p. 63.

Chapter 3

A Meeting of Different Worlds 1100–1700

What's Ahead

In the late 1400s, Europeans in search of trade sailed across the Atlantic and made contact with Native Americans. Soon, Spain and other nations established settlements in the Americas. The Europeans also began to bring enslaved Africans there. Gradually, Native American, European, and African peoples and cultures interacted to form a new way of life.

By the early 1600s, the nations of Europe were competing eagerly for wealth in the Americas. The Spanish built a large empire that spread over both North and South America. The French, Dutch, and English sought territory in North America. The English who settled at Jamestown and Plymouth brought with them traditions of political rights and freedoms.

Why Study History? Today, we take contact among different parts of the world for granted. You can look at African art in European museums, or eat tacos in Japan. In the modern world, the pace of global exchange is much faster than it was 500 years ago. To focus on this connection, see this chapter's *Why Study History?* feature, "You Live in a Shrinking World."

American Events

1493 Columbus founds Spanish colony on Hispaniola

1521 Aztec empire falls to the Spanish

1100 | 1400 | 1500

World Events

1100–1300s World Event Christians go on Crusades to Holy Land

1400s World Event Prince Henry encourages exploration by sea

Viewing HISTORY **Crossing the Atlantic**

This illustration by Johann Theodor de Bry shows Portuguese ships in an ocean filled with flying fish and sea monsters. Beginning in the late 1400s, European explorers and conquerors set sail across the Atlantic Ocean. Their voyages had a lasting impact, not only on Europe and the Americas, but on West Africa as well.

★ **How do you think illustrations like this affected European sailors as they sailed out into the Atlantic Ocean?**

1535 Incan empire is controlled by the Spanish

1607 Jamestown is founded by British colonists

1620 Pilgrims arrive at Plymouth

1673 French explore the Mississippi River

1500 **1600** **1700**

1500s World Event Protestant Reformation causes religious conflicts

1600s World Event British East India Company trades in India

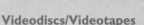

Writing Actively

Responding to Art Ask students to assume the role of a passenger or crew member aboard this Portuguese ship voyaging across the Atlantic Ocean. Have students describe the hopes and fears of the voyager and the real and imagined hazards he or she faced.

Viewing HISTORY ANSWER

Possible answer: Such illustrations may have frightened inexperienced sailors and made them reluctant to venture far into the Atlantic.

★ Background ★

Art Note

Crossing the Atlantic This picture is by engraver, printmaker, and publisher Johann de Bry, who was born in Liege in what is today Belgium. De Bry, who lived from 1561 to 1623, assisted his father, Theodor de Bry, in publishing an illustrated series on European travels and voyages of discovery called *Collectiones peregrinationum*. T

Documents and Literature

On pp. 531–533, you will find two readings to enrich this chapter:

1. Eyewitness Account "Two Descriptions of the Middle Passage," excerpts give two views on slave ship conditions. (Use with Section 3.)

2. Document "The Mayflower Compact," text of the agreement the English colonists drew up to govern themselves by rule of law. (Use with Section 5.)

Technology

Videodiscs/Videotapes

Show the *Prentice Hall United States History Video Collection*™ segments for this chapter. The videodisc has a Spanish track. Press audio until you get the left channel for English or the right channel for Spanish, or use the bar codes in the Guidebook.

American Heritage® History of the United States CD-ROM

- Time Tour: Europeans Reach the Americas in A Meeting of Different Worlds (*average*)

Section 1

Europeans Reach the Americas

LESSON PLAN

Objectives

★ Explain how the Crusades and the Renaissance changed Europe.
★ Explain why Europeans looked for new sea routes to Asia.
★ Describe the effects of Columbus's voyages.

1 Engage

Warm Up Tell students to suppose that they will be the first ones to travel beyond the solar system. Ask: "What are your thoughts and feelings? What might you encounter on the voyage?"

Activating Prior Knowledge Have students list reasons for U.S. space exploration in the twentieth century. List the reasons on the chalkboard. Later, compare them with the reasons for European exploration in the 1400s and 1500s.

Reading Actively

Before Reading Ask: "Why did Europeans begin their voyages of exploration?" Ask students to jot down at least three reasons as they read, to share their reasons with the class, and to rank them in order of importance.

1 Europeans Reach the Americas

As You Read

Explore These Questions
- How did the Crusades and the Renaissance change Europe?
- Why did Europeans look for new sea routes to Asia?
- What were the effects of Columbus's voyages?

Define
- monarch
- feudalism
- manor
- serf
- magnetic compass
- astrolabe
- caravel
- colony

Identify
- Middle Ages
- Crusades
- Renaissance
- Johannes Gutenberg
- Prince Henry
- Bartholomeu Dias
- Vasco da Gama
- Christopher Columbus

SETTING the Scene During the **Middle Ages,** the period in European history from about 500 to 1350, many Europeans thought of the world as a disk floating on a great ocean. The disk was made up of only three continents: Europe, Africa, and Asia.

Most Europeans knew little about the lands beyond their small villages. Even mapmakers called the waters bordering Europe the Sea of Darkness. Sailors who strayed into these waters often returned with tales of fearsome creatures: "One of these sea monsters," swore one sailor, "has horns, flames, and huge eyes 16 or 20 feet across."

Were such tales true? The few who wondered had no way of finding out. Most Europeans were not interested in the outside world because daily life was hard and their main concern was survival.

The Middle Ages

During the Middle Ages, weak European **monarchs,** or kings and queens, divided their lands among nobles. These nobles, or lords, had their own armies and courts but owed loyalty to a monarch. This system of rule by lords who owe loyalty to a monarch is called **feudalism** (FYOOD 'l ihz uhm).

Feudal life revolved around the manors of these powerful lords. The **manor** included the lord's castle, peasants' huts, and surrounding villages or fields. Most people on the manor were **serfs,** or peasants who worked for the lord and could not leave the manor without the lord's permission.

On the manor, people had to produce for themselves nearly everything they needed. There were few merchants and traders. Few roads or towns existed.

During the Middle Ages, all Christians in Western Europe belonged to the Roman Catholic Church. As a result, the Church had great influence.

A Changing Europe

Toward the end of the Middle Ages, conditions began to change. Religious wars led to increased trade with people in Asia and Africa. There was also a revival of learning in Europe.

The Crusades

To Christians, the city of Jerusalem in the Middle East was sacred because Jesus had lived and taught there. They referred to the city and other places in Palestine as the Holy Land. Jerusalem was also a holy place to Jews and Muslims.

From about 1100 to 1300, Christians and Muslims fought a series of religious wars for control of the Holy Land. Thousands of Christians from all over Europe joined in these wars, known as the **Crusades.** In the end, however, the Europeans failed to win control of the Holy Land.

RESOURCE DIRECTORY

Teaching Resources
Lesson Planner, p. 8

Transparencies
Time Lines
- The Americas and the World, 1300–1600, p. E-13
- The Americas and the World, 1600–1800, p. E-15

★ *Background* ★

Did You Know?

Greedy for glory Although some nobles joined the Crusades out of genuine religious conviction, others were motivated by desire for financial gain, hoping to improve their fortunes through war. The Crusades attracted younger sons of feudal lords who would not inherit land from their fathers.

★ *Activity* ★

Connections With Geography

Reading a map Have students use the World Map in the Reference Section to see how Europeans might have reached the Middle East and Asia overland before 1500. After they read about Vasco da Gama, ask: "Compare his route to India with those Europeans use today." (*basic*) ELL T

Still, the Crusades had lasting effects for the Europeans. For the first time, large numbers of Europeans had traveled beyond the small towns of their birth. In the Middle East, they ate exotic foods, such as rice, oranges, and dates. They tasted ginger, pepper, and other spices that both improved the taste of food and helped preserve it. They bought shimmering silks and colorful rugs from Arab traders.

Italian merchants quickly realized that Europeans would pay handsome prices for these foreign goods. They therefore began a lively trade with Arab merchants in the Middle East.

The increase in trade led to an increase in knowledge. From the Arabs, Italian merchants learned about new instruments that made it easier to sail across large bodies of water. The **magnetic compass,** with a needle that always pointed north, helped ship captains sail a straight course. Another useful instrument was the **astrolabe** (AS troh layb). This tool made it possible for sailors to determine the positions of stars and figure out latitude at sea. Both the magnetic compass and the astrolabe helped make sailing less frightening.

A revival of learning

Increased trade and travel made Europeans curious about the wider world. Scholars translated ancient Greek, Roman, and Arab works. They then made discoveries of their own in fields such as art, medicine, astronomy, and chemistry. This burst of learning was called the **Renaissance** (REHN uh sahns), a French word meaning rebirth. It lasted from the late 1300s to about 1600.

The invention of the printing press helped to spread the Renaissance spirit. It was invented during the mid-1400s by German printer **Johannes Gutenberg** (GOOT uhn berg). Before Gutenberg's invention, there were few books because people had to copy them by hand. With the printing press, however, large numbers of books could be printed at low cost. As books became more available, more people learned to read. As reading increased, people learned more about the world around them.

Search for New Trade Routes

As trade brought new prosperity to Europe, kings and queens fought to increase their power. In England and France, rulers established greater authority over feudal lords. In Portugal and Spain, Christian monarchs drove out Arab Muslims who had conquered much of the area.

The rulers of England, France, Portugal, and Spain also looked for ways to increase their wealth. Huge profits could be made by trading with China and other Asian lands. However, Arab and Italian merchants controlled the trade routes across the Mediterranean Sea. Western European rulers would have to find another route to Asia.

Portugal led the way. In the early 1400s, **Prince Henry,** known as the Navigator, encouraged sea captains to sail south along the coast of West Africa. He founded an informal school to help sailors in their explorations.

Viewing History **Wealth and Knowledge**

In his painting The Moneylender and His Wife, *Renaissance painter Quentin Metsys captured the spirit that was changing Europe in the 1400s and 1500s. Europeans wanted new wealth and knowledge. This spirit encouraged overseas trade and voyages of exploration.*
★ **How did Metsys communicate the ideas of wealth and knowledge in this painting?**

2 Explore

Ask students to read the section. For homework, have them research and write a short biographical sketch of one explorer discussed in this section.

3 Teach

Ask students to describe how each of these developments affected European exploration: **(a)** the Crusades; **(b)** invention of the printing press; **(c)** European monarchs try to increase their power and wealth; **(d)** Portuguese open up sea routes to the spice trade in Asia.

4 Assess

To close the lesson, have students complete the section review. Or have each student list the section's main ideas and write a brief summary of the section. Have students exchange summaries and check to see that all main ideas have been discussed.

ANSWER

The coins represent wealth and the book, knowledge. The moneylender and his wife are richly dressed and possess many things.

★ *Background* ★

Did You Know?

Thanks for the memories From the fall of Rome until the Renaissance, much of the learning of ancient Greece and Rome was preserved by Arab scholars or by Christian and Jewish scholars working in Arab lands. Arab scholars also made important advances in the fields of astronomy, mathematics, medicine, science, and philosophy.

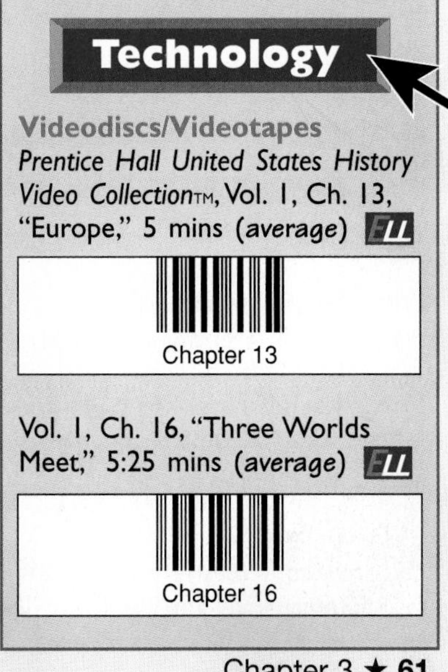

Technology

Videodiscs/Videotapes

Prentice Hall United States History Video Collection™, Vol. 1, Ch. 13, "Europe," 5 mins *(average)* ELL

Chapter 13

Vol. 1, Ch. 16, "Three Worlds Meet," 5:25 mins *(average)* ELL

Chapter 16

Biography

ANSWER

Columbus was correct. However, he did not know that the continents of North and South America lay between Europe and Asia. Also, he miscalculated the distance to Asia.

Reading Actively

During Reading Have students read to find out what developments made Portugal and Spain leaders in European exploration and how each benefited from its explorations.

Writing Actively

After Reading Have students write two or three sentences describing the events and circumstances that led up to King Ferdinand and Queen Isabella's decision to finance Christopher Columbus's voyage across the Atlantic.

▲ *Astrolabe*

Biography Christopher Columbus

Christopher Columbus grew up in Genoa, one of the busiest seaports in Italy. As a young sailor, he heard how Portuguese sea captains were trying to reach the Indies and other parts of Asia by sailing around Africa. After studying Portuguese charts, Columbus formed his own idea. He would reach the Indies not by sailing south and east, but by sailing west. ★ **Was Columbus correct in thinking that he could reach Asia by sailing west? Explain.**

Under Henry's guidance, the Portuguese designed a new type of ship, the **caravel** (KAR uh vehl). With triangular sails and a steering rudder, the caravel enabled captains to sail against the wind.

Portuguese sailors gradually established a new route from Western Europe to Asia. In 1488, **Bartholomeu Dias** reached the southern tip of Africa. Then, in 1498, **Vasco da Gama** sailed around southern Africa and continued to India. (See the map on page 75.) Gradually, Portuguese ships pressed on to the East Indies, an island chain off the southeastern coast of Asia. This was the source of the trade in spices.

Columbus Reaches the Americas

The Spanish watched the Portuguese with envy because they, too, wanted a share of the rich Asian spice trade. In 1492, King Ferdinand and Queen Isabella agreed to finance a voyage of exploration by an Italian sea captain named **Christopher Columbus.** Columbus planned to reach the East Indies by sailing west across the Atlantic.

Across the Atlantic

In August 1492, Columbus set sail with three ships and a crew of about 90 sailors. As captain, he commanded the largest vessel, the *Santa María.* The other ships were the *Niña* and the *Pinta.*

After stopping briefly at the Canary Islands, the little fleet continued west into unknown territory. Fair winds sped them along, but a month passed without the sight of land. Some sailors began to grumble. They had never been beyond the sight of land for so long. Still, Columbus sailed on.

On October 7, sailors saw flocks of birds flying southwest. Columbus changed course to follow the birds. A few days later, crew members spotted tree branches and flowers floating in the water. At 2 A.M. on October 12, the lookout on the *Pinta* spotted white cliffs shining in the moonlight. *"Tierra! Tierra!"* he shouted. "Land! Land!"

At dawn, Columbus rowed ashore and planted the banner of Spain. Columbus called the local people Indians because he was convinced that he had reached the East Indies, in Asia. In fact, as you read in Chapter 2, he had reached the island home of the Taínos, in what are now called the West Indies. The West Indies lie off the coasts of North and South America. At the time, these continents were unknown to Europeans.

Riches for Spain

For three months, Columbus explored the West Indies. To his delight, he found signs of gold on the islands. Eager to report his success, he returned home to Spain.

Columbus gave King Ferdinand and Queen Isabella gifts of pink pearls and brilliantly colored parrots. The two Spanish

Resource Directory

Teaching Resources
Why Study History?
- You Live in a Shrinking World, pp. 11–14

Interdisciplinary Connections
- Main Idea: Columbian Exchange, pp. 14, 16–18

Transparencies
Interdisciplinary Connections
- Columbian Exchange, p. B-37

★ Customized Instruction ★

Auditory Learners

Making an audiotape Christopher Columbus's account of his first voyage to the Americas was preserved by Bartolomé de Las Casas, who copied the *Santa Maria*'s log. Ask a small group of auditory learners to skim this log of the 1492 voyage and select passages that give insight into life on board ship. Once students have chosen favorite passages, they can create a radio play or sound collage of the voyage by mixing readings from the log with music, sea sounds, and other special effects. *The Diario of Christopher Columbus' First Voyage to America* by Oliver Dunn, James Kelley, and Bartolomé de Las Casas (University of Oklahoma Press, 1991) is a useful resource. (*average*) T

Why Study *History?*

Because You Live in a Shrinking World

Historical Background

Among the Aztecs in Mexico 600 years ago, a typical meal included corn porridge, beans, tortillas, and tomato or pepper sauce. In Europe, meanwhile, most people ate dark bread, cheese, and cabbage or turnip soup.

Then in the 1500s, contacts grew between the Americas and the rest of the world. Europeans got their first taste of potatoes, corn, and cocoa from the Americas. Native Americans began eating wheat bread, bananas, and citrus fruit from Europe, Africa, and Asia.

Connections to Today

Our world continues to get smaller. Today, people around the world watch American movies and television shows. They wear American styles of clothing and listen to American forms of music. At the same time, new ideas and goods travel from other lands to become part of American culture. New dance styles have come from Latin America, new clothing fashions from France, and new advances in communication from Japan. Due to modern communication and transportation, exchanges take place more quickly than ever before.

Connections to You

You can see—and taste—examples of cultural exchange in the international foods aisle of your local supermarket. The chart above lists some foods from other lands that have become popular in the United States.

Food	Description	Place of Origin
borscht	Cold beet soup	Russia, Ukraine
chutney	Sauce or relish made of fruits, herbs, and spices	India
couscous	Tiny grains of wheat cooked until fluffy	North Africa
feta cheese	White, crumbly cheese	Greece
gazpacho	Chilled tomato soup	Spain
hummus	Spread made from chickpeas	Middle East
salsa	Hot sauce made from tomatoes, chilies, peppers, herbs, and spices	Mexico
egg rolls	Shredded vegetables in fried dough wrapper	China
sushi	Raw fish and rice, often wrapped in seaweed	Japan

Plate of tacos ➤

1. **Comprehension**
   (a) Name two foods that Native Americans introduced to Europeans.
   (b) Name two Mexican foods that are popular in the United States today.
2. **Critical Thinking** How do you think communication via the Internet affects cultural exchange today?

★Activity **Planning a Food Festival** Working with other students, plan a festival of popular international foods. For ideas on what foods to include, visit your local supermarket or consult an international cookbook.

ANSWERS

1. Possible answers: **(a)** potatoes, corn **(b)** tacos, salsa **2.** Possible answer: Ideas and information can be exchanged faster and easier than ever before; people can publish on the World Wide Web and promote ideas to the entire world.

★Activity

Guided Instruction

Have students assemble a variety of foods—fruits, meats, vegetables, spices. Students should compare dishes to see similarities, even among foods from different cultures or regions. They could also research the agricultural resources of a country or region to see how such resources influence its foods.

ASSESSMENT See the rubrics in the Alternative Assessment booklet in the Teaching Resources.

Fast Facts

★ The Internet, which is helping to shrink our world through communication and information exchange, can be accessed in more than 100 countries.

★ Beets, broccoli, carrots, eggplant, lettuce, okra, onions, peas, and radishes were brought to the Americas from Europe, Africa, and Asia.

★ Salsa, a Latin American musical style, is a popular import to the U.S. that originated in Cuba and Puerto Rico.

Bibliography

To read more about this topic:

1. *Chilies to Chocolate,* Janet Alice Long (University of Arizona Press, 1992). Foods that Native Americans gave the world.
2. *Consuming Culture: Why You Eat What You Eat,* Jeremy MacClancy (Henry Holt, 1993). How culture and cultural exchange shape what humans eat.
3. Internet. Cultural food exchange, science, recipes, and gardening tips. (www.horizon.nmsu.edu/garden)

Technology

AmericanHeritage® History of the United States CD-ROM
• History Makers: Christopher Columbus (*average*)

Videodiscs/Videotapes
Prentice Hall United States History Video Collection™, Vol. 1, Ch. 19, "The Columbian Exchange," 3 mins (*average*) ELL

Chapter 19

★ Section 1 Review ★

ANSWERS

1. See the World Map in the Reference Section and the map, p. 68.

2. (a)–(b) p. 60, **(c)–(e)** p. 61, **(f)–(h)** p. 62

3. (a)–(d) p. 60, **(e)–(f)** p. 61, **(g)** p. 62, **(h)** p. 64

4. (a) The Crusades introduced Europeans to Asian goods and technology. **(b)** The Renaissance led to discoveries in fields such as medicine, astronomy, and chemistry.

5. They wanted to grow rich by bypassing the Arabs and Italians who controlled the trade routes.

6. (a) grew rich, seized colonies, found new foods **(b)** lost their lands, had to work for Europeans, died from overwork and European diseases

7. They failed to conquer the Middle East but did spark new trade.

8. Possible answer: Columbus did "discover" the Americas *for Europeans,* but Native Americans knew these lands existed, even if Europeans did not.

Activity

Guided Instruction
Have students structure their contracts as numbered lists that explain each point. Remind them that Columbus originally wanted to find a shorter route to Asia.

ASSESSMENT See the rubrics in the Alternative Assessment booklet in the Teaching Resources.

RESOURCE DIRECTORY

Teaching Resources
Lesson Planner, p. 9
Unit 1/Chapter 3
• Section 1 Quiz, p. 27

monarchs listened intently to his descriptions of tobacco, pineapples, and hammocks used for sleeping. Columbus also described the natives of the islands he had visited:

> "[They were] of a very acute intelligence . . . [but had] no iron or steel weapons. . . . Should your majesties command it, all the inhabitants could be made slaves."

The Spanish monarchs were impressed. They gave Columbus the title of Admiral of the Ocean Sea. They also agreed to finance his future voyages.

Columbus made three more voyages to the West Indies. In 1493, on an island he called Hispaniola (present-day Haiti and the Dominican Republic), he founded the first Spanish colony in the Americas. A **colony** is a group of people who settle in a distant land and are ruled by the government of their native land. Columbus also explored Cuba and Jamaica and sailed along the coasts of Central America and northern South America. Wherever he went, he claimed the lands for Spain.

Columbus's lasting impact

For years, Columbus has been remembered as the bold sea captain who "discovered America." In at least one sense, he deserves that honor. Europeans knew nothing of the Americas before Columbus brought them news about this "new world." Today, however, we also recognize that other people "discovered" America long before Columbus. Still, his daring voyages initiated lasting contact among the peoples of Europe, Africa, and the Americas.

For Native Americans, though, the contact begun by Columbus resulted in tragedy. Columbus and other Europeans who came after him seized Indian lands. They forced native people to work in mines or on farms. Over the next 50 years, hundreds of thousands of Caribbean Indians died from harsh working conditions and European diseases.

For better or for worse, the voyages of Columbus signaled a new era for the Americas. Curious Europeans wanted to explore the lands across the Atlantic. They saw the Americas as a place where they could settle, trade, and grow rich.

★ Section 1 Review ★

Recall

1. **Locate** **(a)** Europe, **(b)** Middle East, **(c)** Asia, **(d)** Mediterranean Sea, **(e)** East Indies, **(f)** West Indies.
2. **Identify** **(a)** Middle Ages, **(b)** Crusades, **(c)** Renaissance, **(d)** Johannes Gutenberg, **(e)** Prince Henry, **(f)** Bartholomeu Dias, **(g)** Vasco da Gama, **(h)** Christopher Columbus.
3. **Define** **(a)** monarch, **(b)** feudalism, **(c)** manor, **(d)** serf, **(e)** magnetic compass, **(f)** astrolabe, **(g)** caravel, **(h)** colony.

Comprehension

4. Describe how each of the following changed life in Europe: **(a)** the Crusades, **(b)** the Renaissance.
5. Why did Western European rulers want to find new routes to Asia?
6. How did Columbus's voyages affect **(a)** Europeans, **(b)** Native Americans?

Critical Thinking and Writing

7. **Drawing Conclusions** In what way were the Crusades both a success and a failure?
8. **Recognizing Points of View** For many years, American schoolchildren were taught that Columbus "discovered America." In what way is this an accurate statement? In what way is the statement inaccurate?

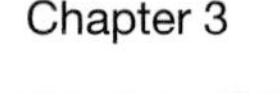

Activity **Writing a Contract** You are a legal expert in service to King Ferdinand and Queen Isabella. Draw up a contract explaining what your monarchs will provide to Christopher Columbus and what they expect from him in return.

★ Background ★
Recent Scholarship

Illuminating Columbus Some scholars today praise Columbus as a superb mariner and visionary. Others see him as an agent for the genocide of Native Americans. In *Columbus Then and Now: A Life Reexamined,* Miles Davidson analyzes sources from the 1400s and 1500s and finds "shared misconceptions and errors" that shape current views of Columbus.

★ Activity ★
Our Diverse Nation

Holding a debate In the U.S., the second Monday in October is a legal holiday—Columbus Day. Some Native American groups protest celebrating this day because of its tragic consequences for Native American cultures. Others disagree. Have students research and develop a class debate on this issue: "Columbus Day should be observed." (*average*)

Spain Builds an Empire

As You Read

Explore These Questions

- How did Spain interact with Native American empires?
- How did Spain govern its lands in the Americas?
- Why was life difficult for the Native Americans who lived under Spanish rule?

Define

- conquistador
- pueblo
- presidio
- mission
- peninsulare
- creole
- mestizo
- encomienda
- plantation

Identify

- Vasco Núñez de Balboa
- Ferdinand Magellan
- Montezuma
- Hernando Cortés
- Francisco Pizarro
- Spanish borderlands
- Laws of the Indies
- Juan de Oñate
- Eusebio Francisco Kino
- Bartolomé de Las Casas

SETTING the Scene "What a troublesome thing it is to discover new lands. The risks we took, it is hardly possible to exaggerate." Thus said Bernal Díaz del Castillo, one of the many Spanish **conquistadors** (kahn KEES tuh dorz), or conquerors, who marched into the Americas in the 1500s. When asked why they traveled to the Americas, Díaz responded, "We came here to serve God and the king and also to get rich."

In their search for glory and gold, the conquistadors made Spain one of the richest nations in Europe. Soon, Spanish colonists followed the conquistadors and created a vast new empire in the Americas. However, the building of Spain's empire meant suffering and even death for Aztecs, Incas, and other Native Americans.

Spanish sailing ship of the 1400s

Early Explorations

After Columbus reached the West Indies, the Spanish explored and settled other islands in the Caribbean Sea. By 1511, they had conquered Puerto Rico, Jamaica, and Cuba. They also explored the eastern coasts of North America and South America. Like Columbus, these explorers were searching for a western route to Asia.

Then, in 1513, an adventurer named **Vasco Núñez de Balboa** (bal BOH uh) plunged into the jungles of the Isthmus of Panama. Native Americans had told him that a large body of water lay to the west. With a party of Spanish and Indians, Balboa reached the Pacific Ocean after about 25 days. He stood in the crashing surf and claimed the ocean for Spain.

The Spanish had no idea how wide the Pacific was until a sea captain named **Ferdinand Magellan** (muh JEHL uhn) sailed across it. The expedition left Spain in 1519. After much hardship, it rounded the very stormy southern tip of South America and entered the Pacific Ocean. Crossing the Pacific, the sailors were forced to eat rats and sawdust when they ran out of food. Magellan himself was killed in a battle with the local people of the Philippine Islands off the coast of Asia.

Of five ships and about 250 crew members, only one ship and 18 sailors returned to Spain in 1522, three years after they set out.

★ Background ★

Did You Know?

Sailing for Spain When Magellan left Spain in 1519, he was seeking a sea route to the Spice Islands by sailing westward. Although he was Portuguese, he sought Spanish support for this voyage. Portugal would not outfit ships to seek a western route to Asia that went around or through South America because Spain would dominate such a route.

Section 2 Spain Builds an Empire

LESSON PLAN

Objectives

★ Describe how Spain interacted with Native American empires.

★ Explain how Spain governed its lands in the Americas.

★ Explain why life was difficult for the Native Americans who lived under Spanish rule.

1 Engage

Warm Up Write the words *explorer* and *conqueror* on the chalkboard. Ask students what the differences are in the meanings of these two words. Have students name some historical figures who have been both.

Activating Prior Knowledge Have students discuss what they know about life in the Aztec and Incan empires before the coming of the Spanish. Record answers on the chalkboard.

Reading Actively

Before Reading Before reading the section, have students turn the main headings into the main topics of an outline. Then, as they read, have them record two or three important subtopics for each main topic.

2 Explore

Ask students to read the section. For homework, have them pick one explorer from the section, research his route, and explain how his explorations increased European knowledge of the Americas.

3 Teach

Conduct a classroom trial focusing on this question: "Were the conquistadors—Cortés and Pizarro—justified in their treatment of the Aztecs and Incas?" Assign students to serve as judge, lawyers for each side, witnesses, and jury. After the evidence has been presented, have the jury deliberate and reach a verdict.

4 Assess

To close the lesson, have students complete the section review. As an alternative, ask them to list the benefits and costs of the conquest for Native Americans and for the Spanish. Ask: "For which group was exploration of the Americas a 'win-win' situation?"

★ ★ ★ ★ ★ ★ ★ ★ ★ ★ ★ ★ ★ ★ ★ ★ ★ ★

ANSWER

The Spanish had gunpowder and metal armor, while the Aztecs used spears and small shields.

Viewing History: Conquering the Aztecs

This illustration depicts one episode in the Spanish conquest of the Aztecs. In 1520, a unit of Spanish soldiers attacked a group of Aztecs as they were participating in a religious celebration. Unprepared for battle, the Aztecs suffered heavy losses. ★ **How did the military equipment of the Spaniards differ from the equipment used by the Aztecs?**

◀ *Steel breast plate of a conquistador*

These survivors were the first men to circumnavigate, or sail around, the world. In doing so, they had found an all-water western route to Asia. Their voyage made Europeans aware of the true size of the Earth.

Spanish Conquistadors

Meanwhile, Spanish colonists in the Caribbean heard rumors of gold and other riches in nearby Mexico. Spanish conquistadors began to dream of new conquests. The rulers of Spain gave conquistadors permission to establish settlements in the Americas. In return, conquistadors agreed to give Spain one fifth of any gold or treasure they captured.

Cortés conquers the Aztecs

In 1519, messengers brought disturbing news to **Montezuma** (mahn tuh ZYOO muh), the Aztec emperor who ruled over much of Mexico. They said that they had seen a large house floating on the sea. It was filled with white men with long, thick beards.

Montezuma thought that these strangers might be messengers of gods. Aztec sacred writings predicted that a powerful white-skinned god would come from the east to rule the Aztecs. The white strangers did come from the east, and they were certainly powerful. They wore metal armor and had weapons that spit fire. As the strangers neared Tenochtitlán (tay nawch tee TLAHN), the capital of the Aztec empire, Montezuma decided to welcome them as his guests.

The Spanish leader, **Hernando Cortés** (kor TEHZ), took advantage of Montezuma's invitation. Like other conquistadors, Cortés wanted power and riches. An Indian woman the Spanish called Doña Marina had told him about Aztec gold. With only about 600 soldiers and 16 horses, Cortés set out to seize the Aztecs' gold. On November 8, 1519, Cortés marched into Tenochtitlán. For the next six months, he held Montezuma prisoner.

Finally, the Aztecs attacked and drove out the Spanish, but the victory was brief. Aided by people whom the Aztecs had conquered, Cortés recaptured Tenochtitlán. In the end, the Spanish killed Montezuma and destroyed Tenochtitlán. The mighty Aztec empire had fallen.

Pizarro conquers the Incas

Another bold conquistador, **Francisco Pizarro** (pee ZAR oh), heard about the fabulous Incan empire while marching with Balboa across Panama. Pizarro decided to sail down the Pacific coast of South America with fewer than 200 Spanish soldiers. In 1532, he captured the Incan emperor Atahualpa (at ah WAHL pa) and much of his army. An Incan historian described the surprise attack:

> "The Spaniards killed them all—with horses, with swords, with guns.... From more than 10,000 men, there did not escape 200."

Later, the Spanish executed Atahualpa. The following year, Pizarro's army attacked

★ *Background* ★

Viewpoints

Astounding cities Bernal Díaz, a soldier in Cortés's army, was much impressed by his first view of Tenochtitlán. He wrote, "When we saw all those cities and villages built in the water and other great towns on dry land, and that straight and level causeway leading to Mexico, we were astounded.... Indeed, some of our soldiers asked whether it was not all a dream."

★ *Background* ★

Did You Know?

Montezuma's treasure The story persists that more than $10 million in gold and jewels belonging to Montezuma is hidden somewhere in Mexico or in the southwestern United States. Supposedly, in 1520, Montezuma had the treasure buried at a site just north of Tenochtitlán. All attempts to find it have failed.

RESOURCE DIRECTORY

Teaching Resources
Unit 1/Chapter 3
- Critical Thinking and Writing: Analyzing Visual Information, p. 23
- Biography Flashcard: Doña Marina, p. 26

Cuzco, the Incan capital in present-day Peru. Without the leadership of Atahualpa, Incan resistance collapsed. By 1535, Pizarro controlled much of the Incan empire.

Reasons for Spanish victories

With only a handful of soldiers, the Spanish had conquered two great empires. There were several major reasons for the remarkable success that the Spanish enjoyed.

First, the Spanish had superior military equipment. They were protected by steel armor and had guns. Meanwhile, the Aztecs and Incas relied on clubs, bows and arrows, and spears. Also, the Native Americans had never seen horses. As a result, they were frightened by mounted Spanish soldiers.

Another factor was that the Native Americans offered weak resistance. The Aztecs were slow to fight because they thought the Spanish might be gods. The Incas were weak from fighting among themselves over control of their government.

Finally, the Indians fell victim to European diseases. Large numbers of Indians died from chicken pox, measles, and influenza. Some historians believe that disease alone would have ensured Spanish victory over the Indians.

Seeking Riches in the North

The Spanish search for treasure extended beyond the lands of the Aztecs and Incas. Moving north, conquistadors explored the area known as the **Spanish borderlands.** The borderlands spanned the present-day United States from Florida to California.

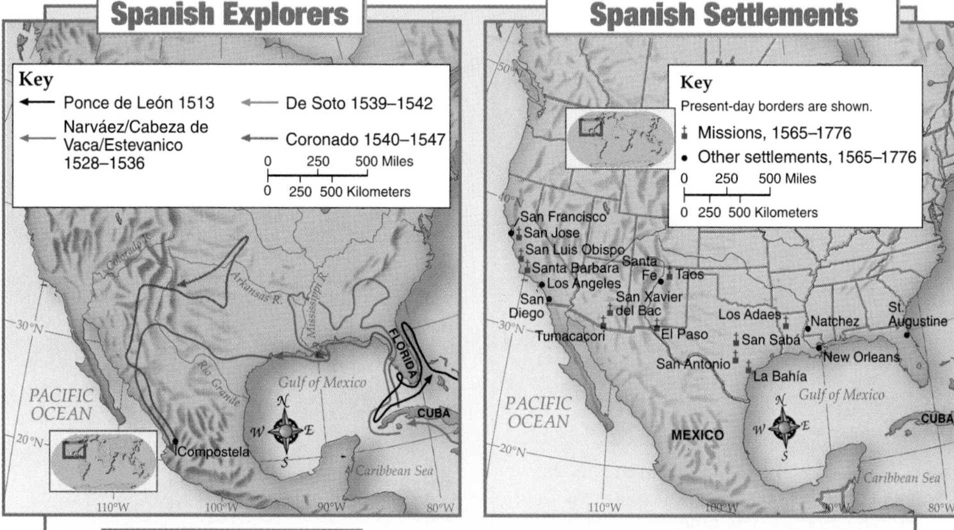

Geography Skills **Spanish conquistadors explored and conquered parts of North America in the 1500s. They mapped the routes that Spanish settlers later followed.**

1. **Location** On the maps, locate: **(a)** Coronado's route, **(b)** De Soto's route, **(c)** St. Augustine, **(d)** San Antonio, **(e)** Santa Fe, **(f)** Los Angeles, **(g)** San Francisco.
2. **Region** What is the easternmost Spanish settlement shown on the maps?
3. **Critical Thinking** In what states of the present-day United States would you expect Spanish influence to be strong?

Geography Skills

ANSWERS **1.** Review locations with students. **2.** St. Augustine **3.** Florida, Texas, California, and the states in the American Southwest

★ *Background* ★

Turning Points

Deadly greed unrecognized The Incan ruler Atahualpa badly misjudged the Spaniards. He believed they wanted only gold, failing to perceive their lust for power and empire. As a hostage, he offered a huge ransom in gold in exchange for his release. Pizarro agreed. Once they got their gold, however, the Spanish killed Atahualpa.

★ *Activity* ★

Our Diverse Nation

Writing journal entries Ask students to research Native American inhabitants of some part of the Spanish borderlands and the impact of Spanish rule on them. Ask students to take the viewpoint of a Native American in that region and write journal entries describing changes brought by the Spanish and their feelings about those changes. (*average*)

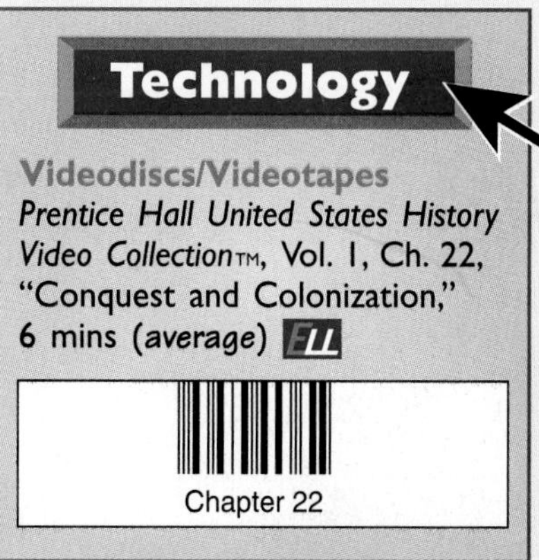

Reading Actively

During Reading Have students read to find out how the Spanish used the Laws of the Indies to govern their new empire.

Geography Skills

ANSWERS **1.** Review locations with students. **2.** Viceroyalty of New Spain **3.** Spain held colonies there, and it needed to control the Caribbean Sea route between Spain and the Americas.

Juan Ponce de León (PAWN suh day lay AWN) traveled through parts of Florida in 1513, looking for a legendary fountain of youth. Indians claimed that anyone who bathed in its magical water would remain young forever. Ponce de León found no such fountain.

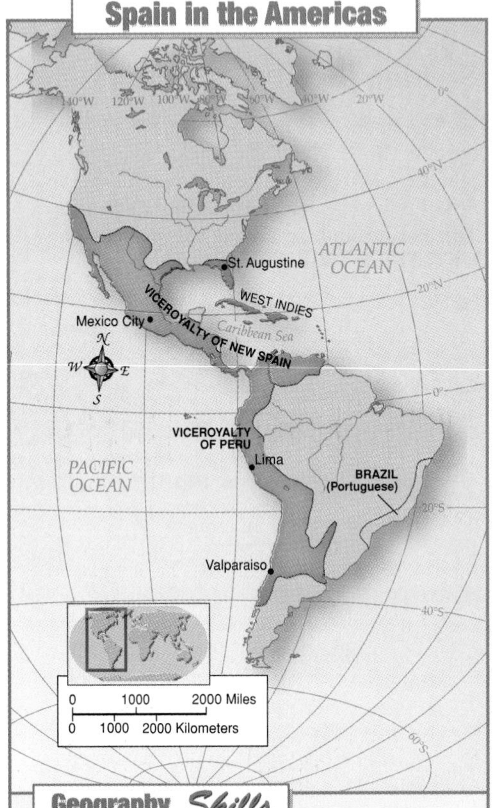

Geography Skills **In the 1500s, Spain established a system for ruling its American colonies. The colonies were divided into the Viceroyalty of New Spain and the Viceroyalty of Peru.**

1. **Location** On the map, locate: **(a)** Brazil, **(b)** West Indies, **(c)** Mexico City, **(d)** Lima.
2. **Region** Which viceroyalty included Mexico and Florida?
3. **Critical Thinking** Why was control of the Caribbean Sea important to Spain?

In 1528, Panfilo Narváez (nar VAH ehs) led an expedition that ended in disaster. A storm struck his fleet in the Gulf of Mexico. Narváez and many others were lost at sea. The rest landed on an island near present-day Texas. Native Americans captured the few survivors and held them prisoner. Álvar Núñez Cabeza de Vaca assumed leadership of the group, which included an enslaved African named Estevanico.

In 1533, Cabeza de Vaca, Estevanico, and two others finally escaped their captors. The four went searching for a Spanish settlement. Their astonishing journey did not end until 1536, when they reached a town in Mexico. They had traveled by foot more than 1,000 miles through the Southwest. (See the map on page 67.) They learned much about Native American ways. They also heard amazing tales about seven cities whose streets were paved with gold.

From 1539 to 1542, Hernando De Soto explored Florida and other parts of the Southeast. He was looking for the cities of gold and other treasures. In 1541, he reached the Mississippi River. De Soto died along the riverbank, without finding the riches he sought.

The conquistador Francisco Coronado (koh roh NAH doh) also heard about the seven cities of gold. In 1540, he led an expedition into the southwestern borderlands. He traveled through Mexico to present-day Arizona and New Mexico. Some of his party went as far as the Grand Canyon. Still, the Zuñi villages he visited had no golden streets.

Governing New Spain

The Spanish king decided to set up a strong system of government to rule his growing empire in the Americas. In 1535, the king divided his lands into New Spain and Peru. The borderlands were part of New Spain. He put a viceroy in charge of each region to rule in his name.

The viceroys enforced the **Laws of the Indies,** a code of laws that stated how the colonies should be organized and ruled. The Laws of the Indies provided for three kinds of settlements in New Spain: pueblos, presidios (prih SIHD ee ohz), and missions. Sometimes,

★ Activity ★
Linking Past to Present

Finding evidence Have students use the maps in this section to identify present-day states where Spanish influence is likely to be strongest. (*FL, AZ, NM, CA, TX*) Have them find data on Spanish language use, place names, popularity of Spanish cuisine, music, and architectural styles in those states today and then present a report to the class. (challenging) ELL T

★ Background ★
Did You Know?

Golden dreams Spanish explorers were tantalized by tales of the Seven Golden Cities of Cibola in North America. Cabeza de Vaca heard that city buildings were studded with gold and turquoise. His stories paralleled South American tales of Eldorado ("The Gilded One"), a kingdom so rich in gold that the king, covered in gold dust, would bathe in a sacred lake.

HISTORY HAPPENED HERE

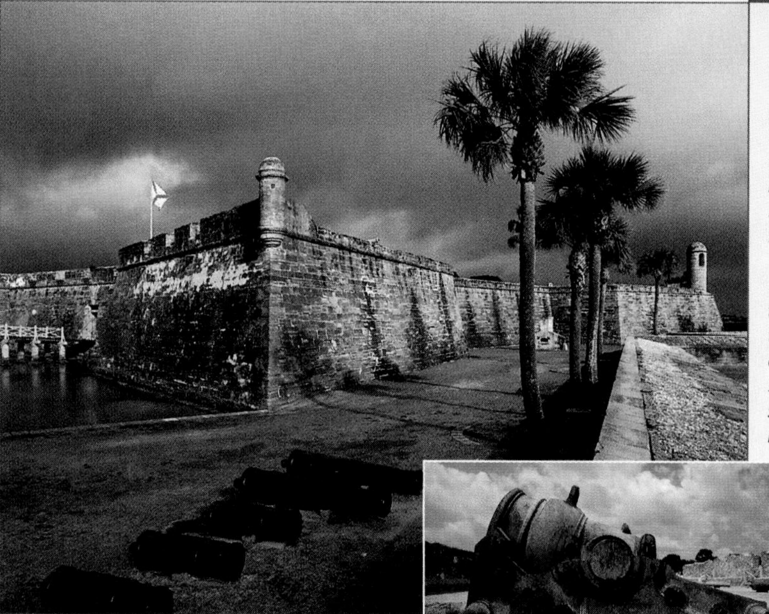

Cannon at Castillo de San Marcos ➤

Castillo de San Marcos

Castillo de San Marcos was the tenth fort built to protect the town of St. Augustine. The first nine were built of wood. The Spanish decided to build a stone fortress after a pirate attack in 1668. The fort was completed in 1695 and survived its first major test in 1702 when it was attacked by the British. Today, you can cross a moat to Castillo de San Marcos and stand atop the stone walls that defended Spanish settlers some 300 years ago.

★ ***To learn more about this historic site, write:*** *Castillo de San Marcos National Monument, 1 South Castillo Drive, St. Augustine, FL 32084.*

a large community included all three types of settlements.

Pueblos, or towns, were centers of farming and trade. In the middle of the town was a plaza, or public square. Here, townspeople and farmers gathered on important occasions. They also came to worship at the church. Shops and homes lined the four sides of the plaza.

Spanish rulers took control of Indian pueblos and built new towns as well. In 1598, **Juan de Oñate** (oh NYAH tay) founded the colony of New Mexico among the adobe villages of the Pueblo Indians. He used brutal force to conquer the Native Americans of the region. In 1609, Don Pedro de Paralta founded Santa Fé as the Spanish capital of New Mexico.

Presidios were forts where soldiers lived. Inside the high, thick walls of a presidio were shops, stables for horses, and storehouses for food. Most soldiers lived in large barracks. Soldiers protected the farmers who settled around the presidios. The first presidio in the borderlands was built in 1565 at St. Augustine, Florida. (See History Happened Here above.)

Missions were religious settlements run by Catholic priests and friars. Like other Europeans in the Americas, the Spanish believed they had a duty to convert Indians to Christianity. They often forced Indians to live and work on the missions.

Missionaries gradually moved into various parts of the Spanish borderlands. The first mission in Texas was founded at El Paso in 1659. In 1691, Father **Eusebio Francisco Kino** (KEE noh) crossed into present-day Arizona. He eventually set up 24 missions in the area. Missionaries also moved into California. By the late 1700s, a string of missions dotted the California coast from San Diego to San Francisco. (See the map on page 67.)

AmericanHeritage
MAGAZINE

Castillo de San Marcos To learn more about the Castillo de San Marcos on the Internet, go to the National Park Service's Web site at www.nps.gov/casa/index.htm.

Internet Activity

Visit an Arizona mission In "Images of the Southwest" at dizzy.library.arizona.edu/images/swf/mission.shtml, the University of Arizona Library has information on Father Kino and his Arizona missions. Have students choose a mission and write a paragraph describing it. Given the changing nature of the Internet, you may wish to preview this site. (*average*)

Biography

ANSWER

Creoles, mestizos, and Indians had fewer rights and privileges than Spanish-born peninsulares.

RESOURCE DIRECTORY

Teaching Resources
Unit 1/Chapter 3
- Practice Your Skills: Reading a Line Graph, p. 22

Biography **Sor Juana**

Juana Inés de la Cruz was one of the most talented poets of New Spain. Because she was a girl, she was refused admission to the university in Mexico City. She entered a convent at age 16 and devoted herself to studying and writing poetry. She also wrote a spirited defense of women's right to an education. ★ **Besides women, what other people in New Spain were denied equal rights?**

Society in New Spain

The Laws of the Indies divided the people in Spanish colonies into four social classes: peninsulares (puh nihn suh LAH rayz), creoles (KREE ohlz), mestizos (mehs TEE zohz), and Indians.

Four social classes

At the top of the social scale were the **peninsulares.** Born in Spain, the peninsulares held the highest jobs in the colonial government and the Catholic Church. They also owned large tracts of land as well as rich gold and silver mines.

Below the peninsulares were the **creoles.** Creoles were people born in the Americas to Spanish parents. Many creoles were wealthy and well educated. They owned farms and ranches, taught at universities, and practiced law. However, they could not hold the jobs that were reserved for peninsulares.

Below the creoles were the **mestizos,** people of mixed Spanish and Indian background. Mestizos worked on farms and ranches owned by peninsulares and creoles. In the cities, they worked as carpenters, shoemakers, tailors, and bakers.

The lowest class in the colonies was the Indians. The Spanish treated them as a conquered people. Under New Spain's strict social system, Indians were kept in poverty for hundreds of years.

A blending of cultures

By the mid-1500s, a new way of life had begun to take shape in New Spain. It blended Spanish and Indian ways.

Spanish settlers brought their own culture to the colonies. They introduced their language, laws, religion, and learning. In 1539, a printer in Mexico City produced the first European book in the Americas. In 1551, the Spanish founded the University of Mexico.

Native Americans also influenced the culture of New Spain. As you have read in Chapter 2, colonists adopted items of Indian clothing, such as the poncho and moccasins. Indians also introduced Spanish colonists to new foods, including potatoes, corn, tomatoes, and chocolate.

With the help of Indian workers, Spanish settlers built many fine libraries, theaters, and churches. The Indians used materials they knew well, such as adobe bricks. Sometimes, Spanish priests allowed Indian artists to decorate the church walls with paintings of harvests and local traditions.

Harsh Life for Indians

The colonists who came to the Americas needed workers for their ranches, farms, and mines. To help them, the Spanish government gave settlers **encomiendas** (ehn koh mee EHN dahz), or the right to demand labor or taxes from Native Americans living on the land.

Working in mines and plantations

During the 1500s, mines in Mexico, Peru, and other areas of the Americas made Spain

★ Customized Instruction ★
English Language Learners

Building vocabulary Point out that many Define terms in this section are words of Spanish origin: *conquistador, pueblo, presidio, peninsulare, creole, mestizo.* If the first language of any of your ELL students is Spanish, have volunteers pronounce these words for the class as they are spoken in Spanish. If students are familiar with the meanings of these words or have visited pueblos or presidios settled in colonial times, have them share this knowledge as well. Encourage your Spanish-speaking students to pronounce and explain to the class other Spanish words that have entered the English language such as *plaza, fiesta, rodeo,* and *tornado.* You might also ask Spanish speakers to work with other ELL students to help them understand these terms. (*average*) ELL

FOR LIFE

Critical Thinking | Managing Information | Communication | **Maps, Charts, and Graphs**

Reading a Line Graph

How Will I Use This Skill?

Graphs present statistics, or number facts, in a visual way. A line graph can show you at a glance how statistics change over time—from the population of the world to your batting average.

LEARN the Skill

You can read a line graph by following these four steps:

1. Use the title to identify the subject of the graph. The source line will tell you where the information was found.
2. Study the labels on the graph. The horizontal (or side-to-side) axis usually tells you the time period covered by the graph. The vertical (or up-and-down) axis tells you what is being measured.
3. Practice reading the information on the graph. Line up the points on the graph with the horizontal and vertical axes to determine how much or how many of something there was at a given time.
4. Draw conclusions about the information presented on the graph.

PRACTICE the Skill

Use the line graph on this page to answer the following questions.

1. (a) What is the subject of the line graph? (b) What is the source of the information?
2. (a) What time period is covered by the graph? (b) What is being measured?
3. About how many Native Americans lived in central Mexico before 1520? In 1580?
4. Using the information on the graph, make a generalization about the Indian population of central Mexico.

Native American Population of Central Mexico

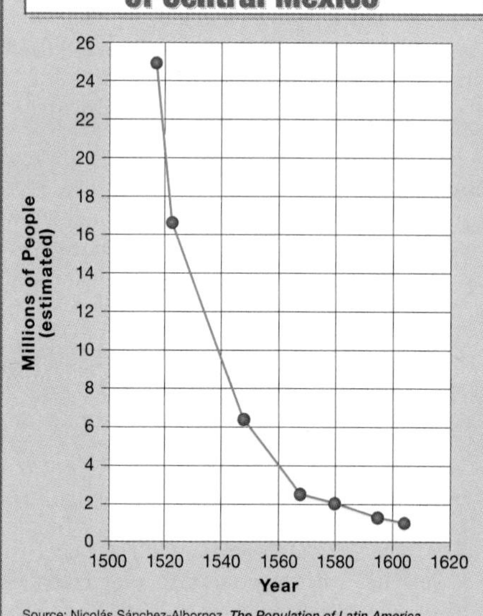

Source: Nicolás Sánchez-Albornoz, *The Population of Latin America*

APPLY the Skill

For the next week, keep track of the number of hours you spend each day performing a certain activity. Use your statistics to make a line graph.

Skills FOR LIFE

PRACTICE the Skill ANSWERS

1. (a) Native American population of Central Mexico **(b)** Nicolás Sánchez-Albornoz, *The Population of Latin America*

2. (a) 1500–1620 **(b)** millions of people

3. about 25 million; about 2 million

4. Possible answer: Between 1500 and 1600, Central America's Native American population fell dramatically.

APPLY the Skill

Guided Instruction

Students should pick a daily activity such as doing homework or watching television. In a notebook, students should write the days of the week. As they perform the activity, they should write the time spent on it next to the day. Provide graph paper for students to use in preparing their graphs.

ASSESSMENT See the rubrics in the Alternative Assessment booklet in the Teaching Resources.

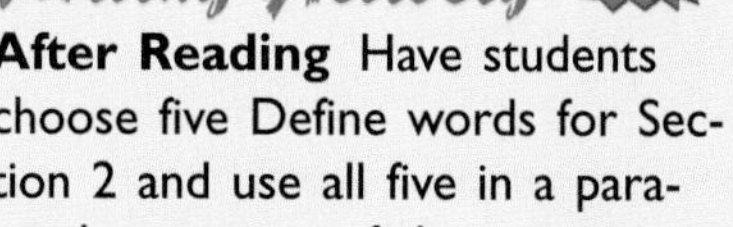

After Reading Have students choose five Define words for Section 2 and use all five in a paragraph summary of the section.

★ *Background* ★

Did You Know?

The tenth muse Sor Juana Inés de la Cruz was a creole. A highly respected poet, she was called the Tenth Muse. She saw some of her poems set to music by the chapel masters of the Mexico City Cathedral. At the convent, Sor Juana often welcomed the viceroy and other officials who sought her company and learned conversation.

★ Section 2 Review ★

ANSWERS

1. See maps, pp. 67, 68.

2. (a)–(b) p. 65, **(c)–(e)** p. 66, **(f)** p. 67, **(g)** p. 68, **(h)–(i)** p. 69, **(j)** p. 72

3. (a) p. 65, **(b)–(d)** p. 69, **(e)–(h)** p. 70, **(i)** p. 72

4. superior weapons such as steel armor and guns; horses that frightened Native Americans; sometimes weak resistance; European diseases that devastated their populations

5. organized colonies into three types of settlements; regulated the social system; was a law code

6. (a) Native Americans were forced to work in mines and on plantations; millions died from overwork and diseases. **(b)** asked the Spanish king to protect the Indians; suggested that Africans replace the Indians as laborers

7. Possible answer: It ruled its American empire for its own profit.

8. Possible answer: They needed workers and felt entitled to make conquered Indians work for them.

Activity

Guided Instruction
Have students reread the relevant material of the text before beginning. Suggest students use a diagram or graphic organizer to display the information.

ASSESSMENT See the rubrics in the Alternative Assessment booklet in the Teaching Resources.

RESOURCE DIRECTORY

Teaching Resources
Lesson Planner, p. 10
Unit 1/Chapter 3
• Section 2 Quiz, p. 28

rich. Spanish treasure ships laden with thousands of tons of gold and silver sailed regularly across the Atlantic.

The Spanish forced Native Americans to work in the gold and silver mines. In flickering darkness, Indians labored in narrow tunnels where they hacked out rich ores. Many died when tunnels caved in.

Meanwhile, on the islands of the West Indies, large numbers of Indians worked on **plantations,** or large estates farmed by many workers. They grew sugar cane and tobacco, which plantation owners sold in Spain at a huge profit.

Thousands of Native Americans died from overwork in mines and on plantations. As you have read, European diseases killed millions more. (See the graph on page 71.)

Las Casas seeks reform

These harsh conditions led one priest, **Bartolomé de Las Casas** (day lahs KAH sahs), to seek reform. Traveling through New Spain, Las Casas witnessed firsthand the deaths of Indians due to hunger, disease, and mistreatment. He was horrified by the terrible conditions that he saw:

> “The Indians were totally deprived of their freedom. . . . Even beasts enjoy more freedom when they are allowed to graze in the field.”

Las Casas journeyed to Spain and asked the king to protect the Indians. In the 1540s, the royal government did pass laws prohibiting the enslavement of Native Americans. The laws also allowed Indians to own cattle and grow crops. However, few officials in New Spain enforced the new laws.

As the death toll among Native Americans rose, the Spanish looked for a new source of labor. Las Casas, still seeking to help the Indians, suggested that Africans be brought as slaves to replace Indian laborers. Unlike Indians, Africans did not catch European diseases, he said. Besides, they were used to doing hard farm work in their homelands. In the years ahead, Las Casas would regret the results of his suggestion.

★ Section 2 Review ★

Recall

1. **Locate** **(a)** Pacific Ocean, **(b)** Gulf of Mexico, **(c)** Florida, **(d)** New Spain.
2. **Identify** **(a)** Vasco Núñez de Balboa, **(b)** Ferdinand Magellan, **(c)** Montezuma, **(d)** Hernando Cortés, **(e)** Francisco Pizarro, **(f)** Spanish borderlands, **(g)** Laws of the Indies, **(h)** Juan de Oñate, **(i)** Eusebio Francisco Kino, **(j)** Bartolomé de Las Casas.
3. **Define** **(a)** conquistador, **(b)** pueblo, **(c)** presidio, **(d)** mission, **(e)** peninsulare, **(f)** creole, **(g)** mestizo, **(h)** encomienda, **(i)** plantation.

Comprehension

4. Why were a handful of Spanish soldiers able to conquer the empires of the Aztecs and Incas?
5. How did the Laws of the Indies regulate life in New Spain?
6. **(a)** In what ways was life harsh for Native Americans under Spanish rule? **(b)** How did Bartolomé de Las Casas try to help Indians?

Critical Thinking and Writing

7. **Making Generalizations** Based on what you have read in this section, make a generalization about the way Spain governed its colonies in the Americas.
8. **Recognizing Points of View** Why do you think the Spanish felt they had the right to force the Indians to work for them?

Activity **Creating a Chart** One of your friends has asked you for help understanding the social classes of Spain's American colonies. Help your friend by creating a chart that accurately illustrates the social structure that existed in New Spain.

★ Background ★
Turning Points

Without resistance The first epidemic of Old World diseases in the Americas began in late 1518 or early 1519 in Santo Domingo. The disease, apparently smallpox, was accompanied by other diseases such as measles and respiratory illnesses. The epidemic became pandemic, spreading rapidly through the Greater Antilles, Mexico, Central America, and possibly Peru.

Africans Come to the Americas

Explore These Questions
- Why were African states prosperous?
- How did the African slave trade change in the 1500s?
- What was the Middle Passage?

Define
- city-state
- kinship network
- Middle Passage

Identify
- Swahili
- Mansa Musa
- Affonso

Setting the Scene In the late afternoon, the distant sound of a horn, blown repeatedly, interrupted the peace of a small West African village. Children ran toward the sound. *"Batafo! Batafo!"* they cried. "Traders!"

Soon the caravan arrived. The long line of porters and camels carried precious goods. Some brought sacks of salt or fish. Others had gold, fine fabrics, or jewelry. Some pushed slaves toward the village.

Trade had long played a vital role in African life. Complex trade routes across the Sahara, a vast desert, linked African villages and kingdoms. At first, Europeans played little or no role in this trade. After the 1400s, however, new trading patterns developed. They drew Africa into closer contact with both Europe and the Americas.

West African ivory carving, showing Portuguese traders

African States

Africa is a vast continent, the second largest on Earth. Across the continent, a wide variety of societies and cultures developed. By the 1400s, there were prosperous trading states in both East Africa and West Africa.

East Africa

On the coast of East Africa, where there were natural harbors, small villages grew into busy trading centers. Gold from Zimbabwe, a powerful inland state, made its way to coastal cities such as Mogadishu, Kilwa, and Sofala. From the coastal cities, ships carried the gold and other valuable products up the African coast as well as to India. (See the map on p. 75.)

The profits from trade helped local rulers build strong city-states in East Africa. A **city-state** is a large town that has its own independent government.

As East Africans mingled with merchants from other lands, a rich variety of cultures developed. From Arab traders, many East Africans adopted the religion of Islam. The blend of cultures also gave rise to **Swahili,** a new language that used both Arab and African words.

West Africa

Several major trading states also emerged south of the Sahara in West Africa. Of these, two of the most important were Mali and Songhai.

Between 1200 and 1400, the kingdom of Mali reached its height. Its most famous ruler was the emperor **Mansa Musa.** In 1324, Mansa Musa journeyed from Mali across North Africa to Egypt and the Middle East. His wealth dazzled the Egyptians, who spread tales of his splendor as far as Europe. A Spanish map of the period shows a powerful Mansa Musa on his throne. The

★ *Background* ★

Did You Know?

Golden giveaway Mali ruler Mansa Musa was a devout Muslim who made a pilgrimage to Mecca in 1324. His journey attracted much attention. On the way, Mansa Musa stopped in Cairo with his train of a hundred camels loaded with gold. He spent gold so lavishly that it was reported the value of gold in Cairo dropped for more than a decade.

Section 3 Africans Come to the Americas

LESSON PLAN

Objectives

★ Explain why African states were prosperous.
★ Describe how the African slave trade changed in the 1500s.
★ Identify the Middle Passage.

1 Engage

Warm Up Ask students how they think the immigrant experience for people forced to move to a country against their will would differ from that of those who move voluntarily.

Activating Prior Knowledge Have students recall what they learned about the death rate among Native Americans after Europeans arrived. Have them speculate on how European colonists might have responded to the loss of cheap local labor.

Reading Actively

Before Reading Have students note the statement on this page that "trade had long played a vital role in African life." Have them find evidence to support this statement as they read the section.

2 Explore

Ask students to read the section. For a homework assignment, have them research and bring to class additional information on Mansa Musa, Mali, or Songhai.

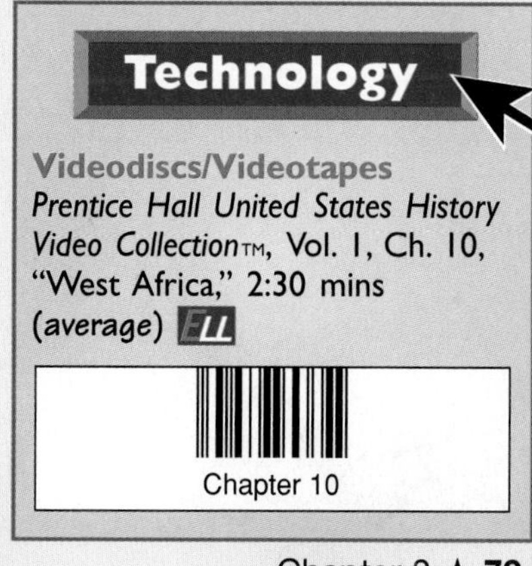

Technology

Videodiscs/Videotapes
Prentice Hall United States History Video Collection™, Vol. 1, Ch. 10, "West Africa," 2:30 mins (average) ELL

Chapter 10

3 Teach

Have students identify the causes of each of the following developments. Then have them pick one development and create a graphic organizer showing its causes and effects: **(a)** Affonso protests the slave trade. **(b)** Las Casas suggests that Africans be brought to New Spain as slaves. **(c)** Spanish colonists begin importing Africans as slaves. **(d)** Some Africans on the West African coast participate in the slave trade.

4 Assess

To close the lesson, have students complete the section review. As an alternative, ask them to write three or four questions about the section. Have students trade questions and answer each other's questions.

★ ★ ★ ★ ★ ★ ★ ★ ★ ★ ★ ★ ★ ★ ★ ★ ★

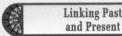

Linking Past and Present

ANSWER

They are wearing clothing of traditional African design.

Linking Past and Present

Past

Present

African Art

In many African societies, elaborate masks were used in political, religious, and social ceremonies. At left is a mask of a West African king, carved by African artists several hundred years ago. At right, a similar mask is present during an American family's celebration of Kwanzaa. ★ **How else does this American family show pride in its African roots?**

mapmaker praised Mansa Musa's great wealth by writing these words on the map:

> "So abundant is the gold in his country that he is the richest and most noble king in all the land."

Later, in the 1400s, Songhai (SAWNG hi) became the most powerful kingdom in West Africa. Timbuktu, located on the Niger River, was one of Songhai's thriving cities. Timbuktu boasted over 100 schools, including a university.

Connections With Economics

Captain Theodore Canot, a European slave trader, witnessed the busy economy of the West African town of Timbo: "They weave cotton, work in leather, fabricate iron, . . . engage diligently in agriculture, and, whenever not laboriously employed, devote themselves to reading and writing."

Village and Family Life

Throughout Africa, most people lived in small villages and made a living by herding or farming. Many farmers worked the same land as their parents and grandparents before them. In rain forests close to the coast, farmers grew yams and other crops. In the grasslands, they raised millet, rice, and other grains. During the 1500s, Africans also began to grow corn, which had been introduced from the Americas.

Family relations played an important part in African life. Children had duties not only to their parents but also to aunts, uncles, and cousins. Grandparents received special respect. These kinds of close family ties are called a **kinship network.** Kinship ties encouraged a strong sense of community and cooperation.

African religions helped to stress the importance of kinship. Religious ceremonies honored ancestors and the spirits of the Earth. Farmers believed that by farming the

Skills For LIFE MINI LESSON

MAPS, CHARTS, AND GRAPHS

Drawing Conclusions From a Map

1. Introduce the skill of drawing conclusions from a map by noting that one can use map information to make reasoned judgments. Have students describe the types of information the map on p. 75 provides.

2. Help students practice the skill by using the map and their earlier reading in the chapter to draw conclusions about how Da Gama's route to Asia might have led to increased European contact with Africa.

3. Have students apply the skill by using the map and their reading of the section to determine what the ancient kingdoms of Mali and Songhai, which were powerful in sequence, had in common *(much the same area)*, and suggest why Europeans knew little or nothing about them *(located inland from coast)*.

land properly, they brought honor to their families.

The African Slave Trade

In Africa, as elsewhere around the world, slavery had been part of the social and economic system since ancient times. Most slaves in Africa were people who had been captured in war. African traders often transported and sold slaves as laborers. Muslim merchants also carried African slaves into Europe and the Middle East.

In many African societies, slaves were part of the community. They were treated as servants rather than property. According to a saying of the Ashanti people, "A slave who knows how to serve inherits his master's property." In time, slaves or their children might become full members of the society.

Around Africa to Asia

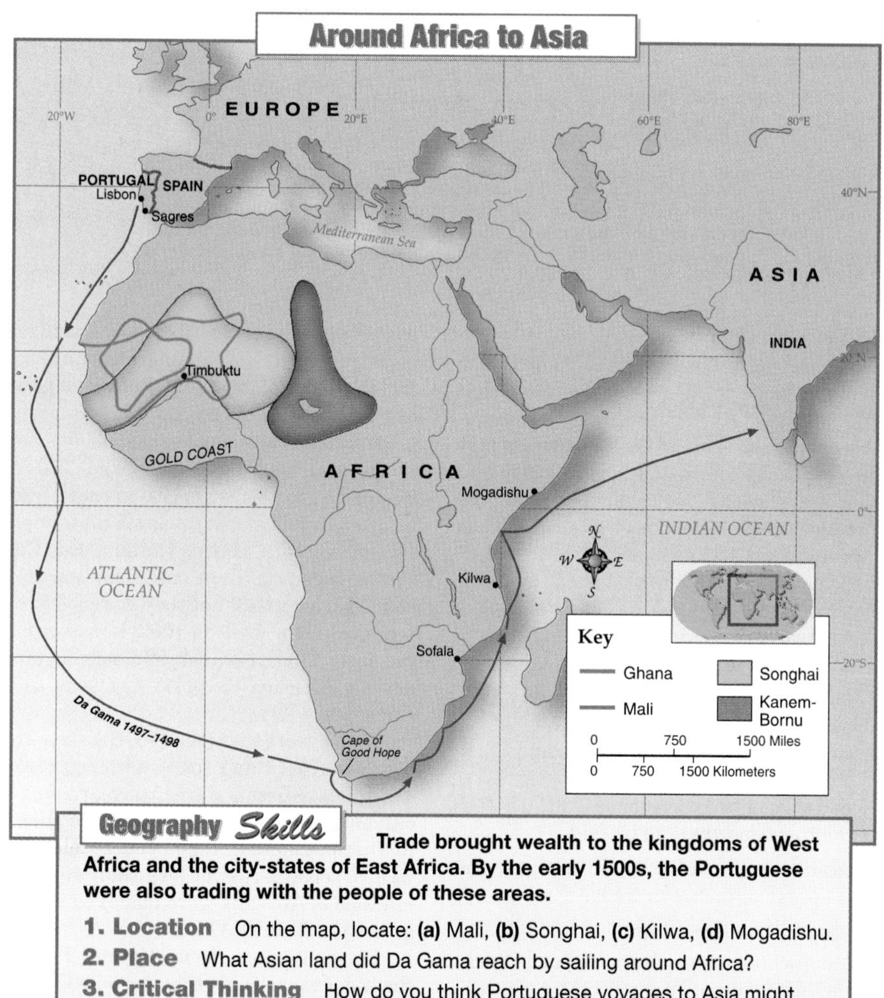

Geography *Skills* **Trade brought wealth to the kingdoms of West Africa and the city-states of East Africa. By the early 1500s, the Portuguese were also trading with the people of these areas.**

1. **Location** On the map, locate: **(a)** Mali, **(b)** Songhai, **(c)** Kilwa, **(d)** Mogadishu.
2. **Place** What Asian land did Da Gama reach by sailing around Africa?
3. **Critical Thinking** How do you think Portuguese voyages to Asia might have benefited the coastal city-states of East Africa?

Reading Actively

During Reading Have students read to find out how slavery changed in Africa as Europeans built overseas empires. Have them write several sentences describing the changes.

Geography *Skills*

ANSWERS **1.** Review locations with students. **2.** India **3.** Portuguese ships stopped at the coastal city-states to trade and buy supplies.

★ *Background* ★

Recent Scholarship

Atlantic slave trade Hugh Thomas's *The Slave Trade: The Story of the Atlantic Slave Trade, 1440–1870* exhaustively documents the 430-year history of the forced migration of Africans to the Americas. Thomas sheds new light on the economic role of slavery in all countries and regions involved in the Atlantic slave trade.

Viewing HISTORY ANSWER

The owners of plantations needed workers. As the Native American population declined, planters imported increasing numbers of enslaved Africans. As the plantation system spread, it increased demand for workers and made the slave trade very profitable.

Writing Actively

After Reading Have students write a paragraph explaining how the colonization of the Americas by Spain, Portugal, and other European countries fueled the growth of the African slave trade.

RESOURCE DIRECTORY

Teaching Resources
Unit 1/Chapter 3
- Section 3 Quiz, p. 29

Document-Based Discovery
- Origins, pp. 2–5

Interdisciplinary Connections
- Main Idea: Columbian Exchange, p. 15

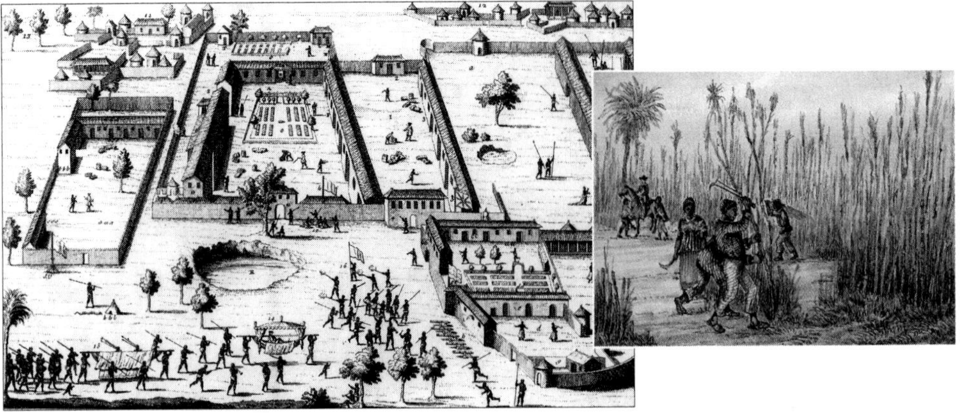

Viewing HISTORY The African Slave Trade

Along the coast of West Africa, the Portuguese, French, Dutch, and English built forts from which they could participate in the profitable slave trade. African traders became wealthy by selling captives to the Europeans. The inset picture shows enslaved Africans in the West Indies, doing the backbreaking work of harvesting sugar cane. ★ **How did the plantation system in the Americas affect the African slave trade?**

Europeans participate

During the 1400s, the slave trade took a dramatic new turn. It was at this time that the Portuguese started trading with communities along the African coast. At first, they were primarily interested in gold, ivory and other trade goods. However, by 1500, the Portuguese were also buying as many as 2,500 enslaved Africans each year.

Some African leaders protested the growing slave trade. **Affonso,** a Christian king of the Central African kingdom of Kongo, wrote to the king of Portugal:

> ❝ Merchants are taking every day our natives, sons of the land and sons of our nobles and vassals and our relatives, because the thieves and men of bad conscience... grab them and get them to be sold. ❞

Such protests, however, could not stop the rapid spread of the slave trade.

Slavery in the Americas

Meanwhile, as you have learned, Spain was building a great empire in the Americas. Portugal too had established a colony—in the present-day country of Brazil in South America. For a while, Spanish and Portuguese colonists forced Native Americans to work in mines and on plantations. Before long, however, thousands of Indians were dying from mistreatment and disease.

As you have read (see page 72), Bartolomé de Las Casas suggested that Africans be brought to New Spain as slaves to replace Indian laborers. Unlike Indians, Las Casas said, Africans did not catch European diseases. He also said that they were used to doing hard farm work in their homelands. In the early 1500s, Spanish colonists began importing Africans to work as slaves in the Americas.

In the years that followed, the slave trade between Africa and the Americas grew. By the 1600s, African slaves were arriving not only in Spanish and Portuguese colonies but in Dutch, English, and French colonies as well. Over a period of less than 400 years, millions of Africans were enslaved and sent across the Atlantic Ocean.

Slave traders from Spain, Portugal, Britain, France, and other western European nations set up posts along the West African coast. They offered guns and other goods in

★ Customized Instruction ★

Extroverted Learners

Presenting a play Olaudah Equiano wrote a gripping narrative about being kidnapped and sent across the Atlantic on a slave ship. It appears in many anthologies and can be found in *Crossing the Danger Water,* edited by Deirdre Mullane. Have extroverted learners select portions of this narrative to perform as a play or pantomime. One student can serve as narrator to read aloud portions of Equiano's story to the class, while other students pantomime the events described. Students should look up unfamiliar words in a dictionary, and they may need to paraphrase parts of the narrative in order to move the action along. (*average*) exchange for slaves. As the demand for slaves increased, Africans who lived along the coast made raids into the interior, seeking captives to sell to the Europeans. They marched their captives to the coast. There, the slaves were loaded aboard European ships headed for the Americas.

Some scholars today estimate that more than 10 million enslaved Africans were transported to the Americas between the 1500s and 1800s. The vast majority came from West Africa and most were sent to Brazil or the Caribbean. However, a total of more than 500,000 enslaved Africans would eventually arrive in the British colonies of North America. (You will read about the English colonies in Chapter 4.)

The Middle Passage

In the 1700s, English sailors began referring to the passage of slave ships west across the Atlantic Ocean as the **Middle Passage.** Below the decks of the slave ships, slaves were crammed tightly together on shelves. One observer noted that they were "rammed like [fish] in a barrel." They were "chained to each other hand and foot, and stowed so close, that they were not allowed above a foot and a half for each in breadth." The captives were allowed above deck to eat and exercise in the fresh air only once or twice a day.

Many enslaved Africans resisted, but only a few escaped. Some fought for their freedom during the trip. Others refused to eat or even jumped overboard to avoid a life of slavery. Olaudah Equiano (oh LAW dah ehk wee AH noh), an enslaved African, recalled an incident from his Middle Passage:

> "One day... two of my wearied countrymen who were chained together... jumped into the sea; immediately another... followed their example.... Two of the wretches were drowned, but [the ship's crew] got the other, and afterwards flogged him unmercifully for thus attempting to prefer death to slavery."

Records of slave ships show that about 10 percent of Africans loaded aboard ship for passage to the Americas died during the voyage. Many died of illnesses that spread rapidly in the filthy, crowded conditions inside a ship's hold. Others died of mistreatment. The Atlantic slave trade would last about 400 years. During that time, it may have caused the deaths of as many as 2 or 3 million Africans.

★ Section 3 Review ★

Recall

1. **Locate** (a) Mogadishu, (b) Kilwa, (c) Mali, (d) Songhai, (e) Timbuktu.
2. **Identify** (a) Swahili, (b) Mansa Musa, (c) Affonso.
3. **Define** (a) city-state, (b) kinship network, (c) Middle Passage.

Comprehension

4. (a) How did trade affect the culture of East Africa? (b) What were some of the achievements of Songhai?
5. How did the slave trade change after Europeans arrived in Africa?
6. Describe conditions on the Middle Passage.

Critical Thinking and Writing

7. **Comparing** How do traditional African kinship networks compare to American family ties today?
8. **Drawing Conclusions** Why do you think the antislavery protests of King Affonso and others were ignored by both Africans and Europeans?

Activity **Writing a Short Story** Write a short story about a young African who is captured by slavers and transported across the Atlantic to the Americas. In your story, also describe the life that the African was forced to leave behind.

★ Section 3 Review ★

ANSWERS

1. See map, p. 75.
2. **(a)–(b)** p. 73, **(c)** p. 76
3. **(a)** p. 73, **(b)** p. 74, **(c)** p. 77
4. **(a)** It linked diverse cultures, carried Islam to East Africa, and financed the rise of strong city-states. **(b)** It was a wealthy, powerful kingdom; the city Timbuktu had 100 schools and its own university.
5. Europeans wanted slaves; African slave traders raided the interior to meet this demand; enslaved Africans were sent across the Atlantic.
6. Africans were crammed into small, filthy spaces below deck; disease spread rapidly, causing many deaths. Some jumped overboard.
7. African: stronger ties that extend across generations and families; American: more individualistic and less family-centered
8. Possible answer: Profits outweighed moral arguments. African slave traders wanted guns and other European goods. Many Europeans at the time saw Africans as inferior.

Activity

Guided Instruction
Remind students of the elements of fiction: character, plot, and setting. Have them create a believable plot about one historically likely incident (e.g., an escape attempt).

ASSESSMENT See the rubrics in the Alternative Assessment booklet in the Teaching Resources.

★ Background ★
Turning Points

Slavery and sugar The European sweet tooth played a part in establishing slavery in the Americas. Producing sugar, which became a highly profitable crop, required huge numbers of workers. As more sugar plantations were set up in Brazil and the Caribbean, the demand for slaves soared. To Europeans, the Caribbean islands became known as the Sugar Islands.

★ Activity ★
Connections With the Arts

Giving a book report Invite interested students to read a novel about the slave trade called *Middle Passage* by Charles Johnson, a National Book Award winner in 1990. The story takes place mostly on a slave ship, the *Republic*. Review the book first, and then have students report on it to the class. (challenging)

Section 4
Colonizing North America

LESSON PLAN

Objectives

★ Explain how competition grew among European nations.

★ Describe how trappers and missionaries helped New France to grow.

★ Explain how the arrival of Europeans affected Native Americans in North America.

1 Engage

Warm Up Ask students why they think many American places, including cities and states, are named *New*. Then, make a list on the chalkboard of place names that begin with *New* and speculate on the origin of these names.

Activating Prior Knowledge Have students describe what Spain gained from its explorations in the Americas. Ask: "How did Spain's successes affect other European powers' view of the Americas?"

Reading Actively

Before Reading Have students examine the map and the subheads in the section and identify the European countries that became rivals in North America during this period. As students read, have them note the reasons for these rivalries.

RESOURCE DIRECTORY

Teaching Resources
Lesson Planner, p. 11

Transparencies
Cause and Effect
• Exploration of the Americas, p. F-13

Colonizing North America

As You Read

Explore These Questions
- How did competition grow among European nations?
- How did trappers and missionaries help New France grow?
- How did the arrival of Europeans affect Native Americans in North America?

Define
- northwest passage
- Protestant Reformation
- missionary

Identify
- Jacques Cartier
- Henry Hudson
- Samuel de Champlain
- coureur de bois
- Jacques Marquette
- Robert de La Salle
- Peter Minuit
- New Netherland
- Algonquin

Setting the Scene In August 1497, the court of King Henry VII of England buzzed with excitement. Italian sea captain Giovanni Caboto and a crew of sailors from England had just returned from a 79-day Atlantic voyage. Caboto, called John Cabot by the English, reported that he had reached a "new-found island" in Asia where fish were plentiful.

Cabot was one of many Europeans who explored North America in the late 1400s and early 1500s. England, France, and the Netherlands all envied Spain's new empire. They wanted American colonies of their own.

Search for a Northwest Passage

Throughout the 1500s, European nations continued looking for new ways to reach the riches of Asia. They felt that Magellan's route around South America was too long. They wanted to discover a shorter **northwest passage,** or waterway through or around North America. (See the map on page 79.)

As you read above, John Cabot was confident he had found such a passage in 1497. He was mistaken. His "new-found island" off the Asian coast in fact lay off the shore of North America. Today, it is called Newfoundland and is the easternmost province of Canada.

In 1524, the French sent Giovanni da Verrazano (vehr rah TSAH noh), another Italian captain, in search of a northwest passage. Verrazano journeyed along the North American coast from the Carolinas to Canada. During the 1530s, **Jacques Cartier** (KAR tee YAY), also sailing for the French, sailed a good distance up the river that is now known as the St. Lawrence.

In 1609, the English sailor **Henry Hudson** sailed for the Dutch. His ship, the *Half Moon,* entered what is today New York harbor. Hudson continued some 150 miles (240 km) up the river that now bears his name.

The following year, Hudson made a voyage into the far north—this time for the English. After spending a harsh winter in what is now called Hudson Bay, Hudson's crew rebelled. They put Hudson, his son, and seven loyal sailors into a small boat and set it adrift. The boat and its crew were never seen again.

All these explorers failed to find a northwest passage to Asia. However, they succeeded in mapping and exploring many parts of North America. The rulers of western Europe began thinking about how to profit from the region's rich resources.

European Rivalries

As European nations began to compete for riches around the world, religious differences also heightened their rivalry. Until the 1500s, the Roman Catholic Church was the

★ Customized Instruction ★
Introverted Learners

Making an historical marker Besides the people discussed in this section, many other explorers searched for a northwest passage, including James Cook, John Davis, Martin Frobisher, William Baffin, and Roald Amundsen. In 1905, Amundsen became the first to complete a northwest passage through Arctic waters to the Pacific Ocean. Ask introverted learners to choose one of these explorers and research his goals, routes, and successes or failures. Then have them design an historical marker to commemorate the explorer's efforts. The marker should indicate a date, place, and event related to the explorer. Students should include a map showing where their marker should be placed. (*average*) T only church in western Europe. After that, however, a major religious reform movement split the Catholic Church and sharply divided Christians.

Catholics and Protestants

In 1517, a German monk named Martin Luther challenged many practices of the Catholic Church. Luther believed that the Church had become too worldly and greedy. He opposed the power of popes. He also objected to the Catholic teaching that believers needed to perform good works to gain eternal life. Luther argued that people could be saved only by their faith in God.

Luther's supporters became known as Protestants because of their protests against the Church. The **Protestant Reformation,** as the new movement was known, divided Europe. Soon, the Protestants themselves split, forming many different Protestant churches.

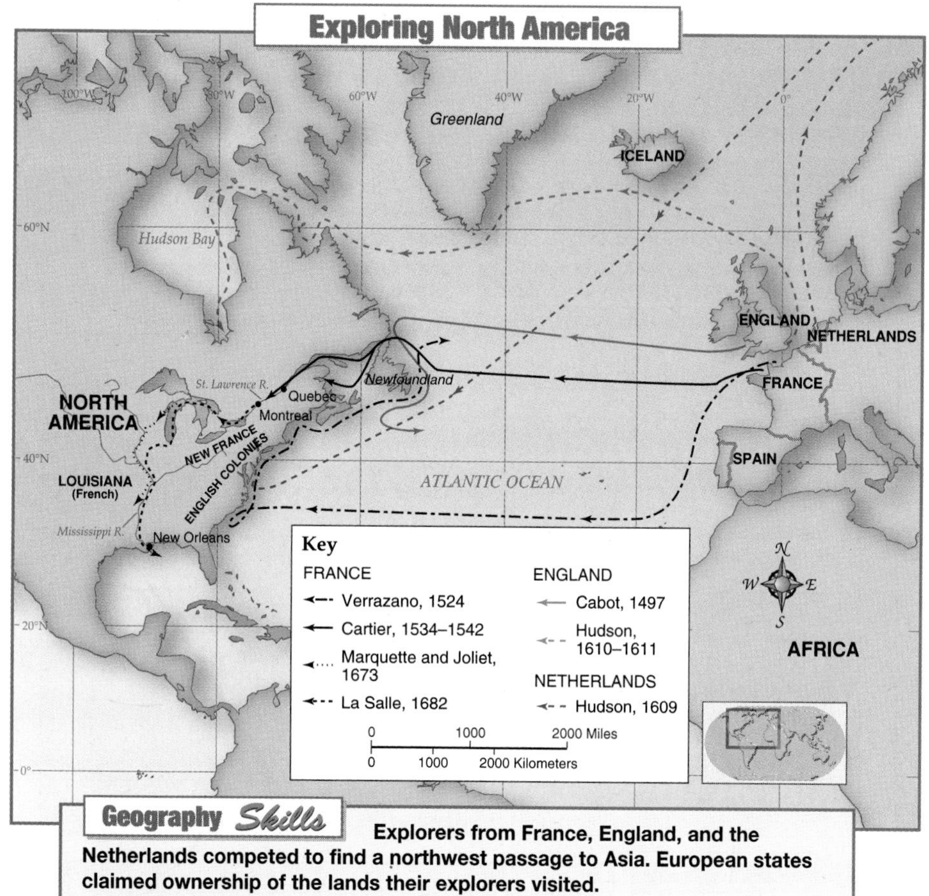

Geography *Skills* **Explorers from France, England, and the Netherlands competed to find a northwest passage to Asia. European states claimed ownership of the lands their explorers visited.**

1. **Location** On the map, locate: **(a)** English Colonies, **(b)** New France.
2. **Region** What waterway was most important for travel through Louisiana?
3. **Critical Thinking** Why might you expect conflict between the French and English in North America?

From the Archives of AmericanHeritage®

Cabot vanishes In 1497, John Cabot became the first European since Viking days to set foot in North America. Cabot made a second voyage west in 1498, but no one knows what happened to him. One source claims that his ship sank; others have him exploring Greenland or reaching Cape Cod.

Source: Frederic D. Schwarz, "The Time Machine," *American Heritage* magazine, May/June 1997.

2 Explore

Ask students to read the section. For homework, have them research and write a short biography of one explorer in this section. Have the class list traits they associate with an explorer. *(risk-taker, curiosity, courage, determination)*

3 Teach

Have students make a six-column chart with these headings: Nationality, Sponsor (Country), Area Explored, Dates, Goal, and Results. In the first column, have them list the explorers discussed in this section. Students can also determine if any of these explorers visited their area or state.

4 Assess

To close the lesson, have students complete the section review. Or have them write a brief essay comparing the efforts of France and the Netherlands to build colonies in North America.

★ ★ ★ ★ ★ ★ ★ ★ ★ ★ ★ ★ ★ ★ ★ ★ ★ ★ ★ ★

Geography *Skills*

ANSWERS **1.** Review locations on map with students. **2.** Mississippi River **3.** Possible answer: Because there were no strict boundaries separating their North American territories, border disputes might result.

Technology

Videodiscs/Videotapes

Prentice Hall United States History Video Collection™, Vol. 1, Ch. 25, "Europe and North America," 2:15 mins *(average)* ELL

Chapter 25

Vol. 2, Ch. 7, "Europe's North American Colonies," 2:15 mins *(average)* ELL

Chapter 7

Chart *Skills*

ANSWERS **1. (a)** John Cabot, Henry Hudson **(b)** Robert de La Salle **2.** Possible answers: One country might have offered Hudson better terms or might have been willing to outfit more ships. Hudson might have had a dispute with one of the countries.

As a result, religion divided the states of western Europe. In the late 1500s, Roman Catholic monarchs ruled Spain and France. Elizabeth I, a Protestant queen, ruled England. In the Netherlands, the Dutch people were mostly Protestant.

Rivalries in the Americas

As Europeans spread to the Americas, they brought their religious conflicts with them. Queen Elizabeth encouraged English adventurers to raid Spanish colonies and capture the treasure fleets of Catholic Spain.

European Explorers

Explorer	Achievements
For Portugal	
Bartolomeu Dias 1487–1488	Sailed around the southern tip of Africa
Vasco da Gama 1497–1498	Sailed around Africa to India
Pedro Álvares Cabral 1500	Reached Brazil
For Spain	
Christopher Columbus 1492–1504	Explored the West Indies and the Caribbean
Vasco Núñez de Balboa 1513	Sighted the Pacific Ocean
Juan Ponce de León 1508–1509, 1513	Explored Puerto Rico Explored Florida
Ferdinand Magellan 1519–1522	Led first expedition to sail around the world
Pánfilo de Narváez/Cabeza de Vaca/ Estevanico 1528–1536	Traveled in the Spanish borderlands
Francisco Coronado 1540–1542	Explored southwestern North America
Hernando De Soto 1516–1520, 1539–1542	Explored Central America Led expedition to the Mississippi River
Juan Cabrillo 1542–1543	Explored west coast of North America
For England	
John Cabot 1497–1501(?)	Explored east coast of North America
Henry Hudson 1610–1611	Explored Hudson Bay
For the Netherlands	
Henry Hudson 1609	Explored east coast of North America and the Hudson River
For France	
Giovanni da Verrazano 1524	Explored east coast of North America, including present-day New York harbor
Jacques Cartier 1534–1542	Explored St. Lawrence River
Samuel de Champlain 1603–1615	Explored St. Lawrence River valley Founded Quebec
Jacques Marquette/Louis Joliet 1673	Explored along the Mississippi River
Robert de La Salle 1679–1682	Explored Great Lakes Reached the mouth of the Mississippi River

Chart *Skills* **Starting in the late 1400s, western European nations sent explorers to find new trades and to establish new colonies.**

1. **Comprehension** **(a)** Name two explorers who worked for England. **(b)** What Frenchman explored the Great Lakes?
2. **Critical Thinking** What theory can you offer to explain why Henry Hudson sailed for two different countries?

★ *Background* ★
Did You Know?

Patriotic piracy The rivalry between England and Spain led Queen Elizabeth to support Francis Drake and other "sea dogs" who attacked Spanish shipping. The queen gave them ships and a share in the loot they seized. In 1581, when King Philip II of Spain demanded that Drake be punished for piracy, Elizabeth responded by knighting Drake.

★ *Activity* ★
Viewpoints

Writing a report The Spanish initially viewed the Native Americans they met as prospective laborers; they tried to enslave them and convert them to Christianity. The French saw Indians as prospective trading partners. Have students write a report that compares Spain and France in their treatment of Native Americans in the Americas. (*challenging*)

Protestant England also competed with Catholic France for lands in North America.

Not all rivalries were religious, however. The Netherlands and England struggled against each other even though both were Protestant. They competed for control of land in North America and for economic markets all over the world.

New France

The first permanent French settlements, in what became known as New France, were founded by **Samuel de Champlain** (sham PLAYN). The first colony took root at Port Royal, Nova Scotia, in 1605. Three years later, Champlain led another group of settlers along the route Cartier had pioneered. On a rocky cliff high above the St. Lawrence River, Champlain built a trading post known as Quebec (kwi BEHK).

Economy of New France

Unlike Spain's empire in the Americas, the French empire had little gold or silver. Instead, the French profited from fishing, trapping, and trading.

Most French colonists were traders and trappers. Those who lived and worked in the woods became known as **coureurs de bois** (koo RYOOR duh BWAH), or runners of the woods. The French brought knives, kettles, cloth, and other items for trade with Native Americans. In return, the Native Americans gave them beaver skins and other furs that sold for high prices in Europe.

Coureurs de bois established friendly relations with the Native Americans. Many married Indian women. They learned trapping and survival skills from Native Americans. For example, Indians taught them how to make valuable tools such as snowshoes and canoes.

Missionary work

Catholic missionaries often came from Europe and traveled with the fur traders. The missionaries were determined to convert Native Americans to Christianity. They set up missions, drew maps, and wrote about the lands they explored. Life was difficult, especially in winter. One priest recalled traveling through deep snow using Indian snowshoes:

> "If a thaw came, dear Lord, what pain!... I was marching on an icy path that broke with every step I took; as the snow softened...we often sunk in it up to our...waist."

Viewing History **"Runner of the Woods"**

To be a successful hunter and trapper in New France, a coureur de bois, or "runner of the woods," often relied on Native American skills and technology. For example, the snowshoes that Indians invented made it easier to travel through deep snow. ★ **What other skills did coureurs de bois learn from Indians?**

Expansion to the Mississippi

French trappers followed the St. Lawrence deep into the heart of North America. Led by Indian guides, they reached the Great Lakes. Here, Indians spoke of a mighty river, which they called Mississippi, or "Father of the Waters."

In 1673, a French missionary, Father **Jacques Marquette** (mar KEHT), and a fur trader, Louis Joliet (JOH lee eht), set out with

Reading Actively

During Reading As students read, ask them to take notes on how the French tried to make their North American empire profitable even though it lacked the gold that produced such wealth for the Spanish.

Viewing History ANSWER

They learned how to trap, how to build and use canoes, and how to survive in the wilderness.

★ *Background* ★

Did You Know?

False hopes Marquette and Joliet set out on March 17, 1673, and were thrilled to reach the Mississippi River, believing they had found a passage to Asia. But by July 17, they had followed the Mississippi to the Arkansas River, and Marquette concluded that the Mississippi flowed into the Gulf of Mexico, not the Pacific Ocean. At this point, the men turned back.

ANSWER

Today, Manhattan Island, part of New York City, has skyscrapers, roads, and sidewalks, plus almost 2 million residents.

Writing Actively

After Reading Have students write two paragraphs. One should describe the reasons for rivalries among European nations in Europe; the other should describe the causes of their rivalries in North America.

RESOURCE DIRECTORY

Teaching Resources
Unit 1/Chapter 3
- Section 4 Quiz, p. 30

Viewing History **A View of Manhattan**

The Dutch built New Amsterdam on the southern tip of Manhattan Island. From a small town of fewer than 30 houses, the settlement grew into a busy port visited by ships from around the world. This painting shows New Amsterdam as it appeared in the 1600s. ★ **What does Manhattan Island look like today?**

Indian guides to reach the Mississippi. They followed the river for more than 700 miles (1,100 km) before turning back. In 1682, another explorer, **Robert de La Salle,** completed the journey to the Gulf of Mexico. La Salle named the region Louisiana in honor of the French king, Louis XIV.

To keep Spain and England out of Louisiana, the French built forts along the Mississippi. One fort, at the mouth of the river, was named New Orleans. New Orleans soon grew into a busy trading center. The French also built forts in the north along the Great Lakes. Among them was Fort Detroit, built by Antoine Cadillac near Lake Erie.

Government of New France

New France was governed much like New Spain. The French king controlled the government directly, and people had little freedom. A council appointed by the king made all decisions.

King Louis XIV was concerned that too few French were moving to the territories of New France. In the 1660s, therefore, he sent about a thousand farmers to the colony. The newcomers included many young women.

Despite Louis's efforts to increase the population of New France, the colony grew slowly. By 1680, only about 10,000 settlers lived in the colony. Of those, one third lived on farms along the St. Lawrence. Many more chose the life of the coureurs de bois, who lived largely free of government control.

New Netherland

Like the French, the Dutch hoped to profit from their discoveries in the Americas. In 1626, **Peter Minuit** (MIHN yoo wiht) led a group of Dutch settlers to the mouth of the Hudson River. There, he bought Manhattan Island from local Indians. Minuit called his settlement New Amsterdam. Other Dutch colonists settled farther up the Hudson River. The entire colony was known as **New Netherland.**

By the mid-1600s, New Amsterdam grew into a busy port. The Dutch welcomed people of many nations and religions to their colony. One Dutch governor boasted that more than 15 languages could be heard in the streets of New Amsterdam.

In 1655, the Dutch enlarged New Netherland by taking over the colony of New Sweden. The Swedes had established New Sweden along the Delaware River some 15 years earlier.

★ *Background* ★

Our Diverse World

Cajun country In the 1700s, many French settlers in Acadia, known today as Nova Scotia, were forced out by the British, who had gained control of the area. Acadians moved to Louisiana, then still under French rule. There, they kept their French language and customs; later they became known as *Cajuns*, a local form of the word *Acadian*.

★ *Activity* ★

Connections With Geography

Analyzing a map On a modern U.S. map, ask students to locate areas claimed by France in the 1600s and to list French place names in these areas. The French built forts and settlements along the Mississippi and St. Lawrence rivers, and the Great Lakes. Have students suggest reasons for this pattern. (*average*) ELL T

Rivalry over furs

Dutch traders sent furs to the Netherlands. The packing list for the first shipment included "the skins of 7,246 beaver, 853 otter, 81 mink, 36 cat lynx, and 34 small rats."

The Dutch and French became rivals in the fur trade. In this rivalry, the French were helped by the **Algonquin** (al GAHN kwihn) Indians. The Dutch made friends with the Iroquois. For many years, fighting raged among the Europeans and their Indian allies.

Dutch ways in North America

The Dutch brought many of their customs to New Netherland. They liked to ice-skate, and in winter the frozen rivers and ponds filled with skaters. Every year on Saint Nicholas's birthday, children put out their shoes to be filled with all sorts of presents. Later, "Saint Nick" came to be called Santa Claus.

Some Dutch words entered the English language. A Dutch master was a "boss." The people of New Amsterdam sailed in "yachts." Dutch children munched on "cookies" and went for rides through the snow on "sleighs."

Impact on Native Americans

The coming of Europeans to North America brought major changes for Native Americans. Once again, as in New Spain, European diseases killed millions of Indians. Rivalry over the fur trade increased Indian warfare because European settlers encouraged their Indian allies to attack one another. The scramble for furs also led to overtrapping. By 1640, trappers had almost wiped out the beavers on Iroquois lands in upstate New York.

The arrival of European settlers affected Native Americans in other ways. Missionaries tried to convert Indians to Christianity. Indians eagerly adopted European trade goods, such as copper kettles and knives, as well as muskets and gunpowder for hunting. Alcohol sold by European traders had a harsh effect on Native American life.

The French, Dutch, and English all waged warfare to seize Indian lands. As Indians were forced off their lands, they moved westward onto lands of other Indians. The conflict between Native Americans and Europeans would continue for many years.

★ Section 4 Review ★

Recall

1. **Locate** (a) Newfoundland, (b) St. Lawrence River, (c) Hudson Bay, (d) Quebec, (e) Mississippi River, (f) Louisiana.
2. **Identify** (a) Jacques Cartier, (b) Henry Hudson, (c) Samuel de Champlain, (d) coureur de bois, (e) Jacques Marquette, (f) Robert de La Salle, (g) Peter Minuit, (h) New Netherland, (i) Algonquin.
3. **Define** (a) northwest passage, (b) Protestant Reformation, (c) missionary.

Comprehension

4. Why did European nations compete for control of lands in North America?
5. (a) How did French trappers get along with Native Americans? (b) Why did missionaries often travel with the coureurs de bois?
6. How did competition between the French and Dutch affect the Algonquins and Iroquois?

Critical Thinking and Writing

7. **Comparing** (a) Describe one way in which New France was similar to New Spain. (b) Describe one way in which they were different.
8. **Inferring** How did missionaries help New France expand?

Activity **Making a Map** Suppose you can send a map back through time to French explorers of the 1600s. On your map, show how they can travel by land and water from Newfoundland through New France to the mouth of the Mississippi.

★ Section 4 Review ★

ANSWERS

1. See map, p. 79.
2. **(a)–(b)** p. 78, **(c)–(e)** p. 81, **(f)–(h)** p. 82, **(i)** p. 83
3. **(a)** p. 78, **(b)** p. 79, **(c)** p. 81
4. The nations all wanted a share of North America's wealth.
5. **(a)** They got along well by trading with Native Americans and by learning their way of life. **(b)** to convert Native Americans to Christianity
6. They were drawn into the French-Dutch rivalry, and Indian warfare increased.
7. Possible answers: **(a)** The monarchs directly controlled the colonists; Christian missionaries tried to convert Native Americans. **(b)** The French focused on trade, not plantations; Spain's settlements were larger than France's.
8. They set up missions, drew maps, and wrote about the lands they explored, opening lands for future settlement.

Activity

Guided Instruction

Refer students to the map on p. 79 to locate Newfoundland and the mouth of the Mississippi. Encourage students to include written directions for the route.

ASSESSMENT See the rubrics in the Alternative Assessment booklet in the Teaching Resources.

★ Background ★
Did You Know?

New York! New York! The Dutch West India Company wanted a settlement at the mouth of the Hudson River to protect its fur trade. When Minuit bought Manhattan Island for this purpose, he paid the Indians $24 worth of beads, ribbons, and other trade goods. The Dutch settlement, New Amsterdam, was later renamed New York by the English.

★ Activity ★
Linking Past and Present

Mapping history New Amsterdam's main street—the "broad way"—would become Manhattan's most famous: Broadway. Have students research the origins of at least two street names in their own area. Have the class create a map of their area, with legends explaining the historical significance of each named street. *(average)* T

Section 5
The First English Colonies

LESSON PLAN

Objectives

★ Describe how representative government took root in Virginia.
★ Explain why the Pilgrims started a colony in North America.
★ Describe how Native Americans helped the Plymouth Colony to survive.

1 Engage

Warm Up Have the class brainstorm and list rules they would enact if they were establishing a colony.

Activating Prior Knowledge Have students describe the challenges Spain faced in establishing and governing its colonies and then speculate whether or not the English would face similar problems in North America.

Reading Actively

Before Reading Have students read Explore These Questions. As they read, have them jot down notes to answer each question.

2 Explore

Ask students to read the section. For a homework assignment, have them research what can be seen on a visit to the site of the Jamestown colony today.

RESOURCE DIRECTORY

Teaching Resources
Lesson Planner, p. 12
Unit 1/Chapter 3
• Map Mystery: What Happened to John Smith?, p. 24

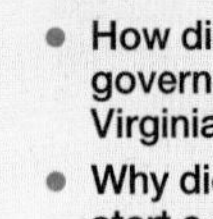

The First English Colonies

As You Read

Explore These Questions
- How did representative government take root in Virginia?
- Why did the Pilgrims start a colony in North America?
- How did Native Americans help the Plymouth Colony to survive?

Define
- charter
- representative government
- Magna Carta
- Parliament
- Mayflower Compact

Identify
- Sir Walter Raleigh
- John Smith
- Powhatan
- Pocahontas
- House of Burgesses
- Pilgrims
- Squanto

SETTING the Scene "If England possesses these places in America, Her Majesty will have good harbors, plenty of excellent trees for masts, good timber to build ships . . . all things needed for a royal navy, and all for no price."

Richard Hakluyt wrote these words to persuade Queen Elizabeth I of England to set up colonies in North America. Hakluyt explained a total of more than 30 arguments in favor of settlement. "We shall," Hakluyt concluded, "[stop] the Spanish king from flowing over all the face . . . of America."

Hakluyt's pamphlet, written in 1584, appealed to English pride. England's rival, Spain, had built a great empire in the Americas. England was determined to win a place there, too.

Settlement at Roanoke

The man who encouraged Hakluyt to write his pamphlet was **Sir Walter Raleigh,** a favorite of Queen Elizabeth. With the queen's permission, Raleigh raised money to outfit a colony in North America. In 1585, seven ships and about 100 men set sail across the Atlantic.

The colonists landed on Roanoke (ROH uh nohk), an island off the coast of present-day North Carolina. Within a year, the colonists ran short of food and quarreled with neighboring Native Americans. When an English ship stopped in the harbor, the weary settlers climbed aboard and sailed home.

In 1587, Raleigh asked John White, one of the original colonists, to return to Roanoke with a new group of settlers. This time, women and children went along, too. In Roanoke, one of the women gave birth to a baby girl named Virginia Dare. She was the first English child born in North America.

When supplies ran low, White returned to England, leaving behind 117 colonists. White planned to return in a few months. In England, however, he found the whole nation preparing for war with Spain. It was three years before he returned to Roanoke.

When White did reach Roanoke, he found the settlement strangely quiet. Houses stood empty. Vines twined through the windows and pumpkins sprouted from the earthen floors. White found the word CROATOAN, the name of a nearby island, carved on a tree.

Connections With Science

In 1998, researchers from the University of Arkansas and the College of William and Mary theorized that the Roanoke settlers were victims of the region's worst drought in eight centuries. Their theory was based on the study of moisture-sensitive tree rings from 800-year-old cypress trees.

★ *Customized Instruction* ★

Kinesthetic Learners

Performing a play The disappearance of the Roanoke colonists has long been a subject of debate. Some scholars argue that the settlers were murdered by hostile Native Americans, killed by the Spanish, or intermarried with the Croatoans, with their descendants living in North Carolina today. Have kinesthetic learners research various theories about the "lost colonists," including the theory discussed in the Connections With Science note on this page. Then have them write and present a short play about the fate of the colonists. The play should include explanations for clues found in the deserted colony, such as the word CROATOAN carved on a tree. (*average*) T

White was eager to investigate, but a storm was blowing up and his crew refused to make the trip. The next day, White stood sadly on board as the captain set sail for England. To this day, the fate of Roanoke's settlers remains a mystery.

Jamestown Colony

Nearly 20 years passed before England tried again to plant a colony. Then, in 1606, the Virginia Company of London received a charter from King James I. A **charter** is a legal document giving certain rights to a person or company. The charter gave the Virginia Company the right to settle lands to the north of Roanoke, between North Carolina and the Potomac River. The land was called Virginia. The charter guaranteed colonists of Virginia the same rights as English citizens.

A difficult start

In the spring of 1607, 105 colonists arrived in Virginia. They sailed into Chesapeake Bay and began building homes along the James River. They named their tiny outpost Jamestown, after their king, James I.

The colonists soon discovered that Jamestown was located in a swampy area. The water was unhealthy, and mosquitoes spread malaria. Many settlers suffered or died from disease.

Governing the colony also proved difficult. The Virginia Company had chosen a council of 13 men to rule the settlement. Members of the council quarreled with one another and did little to plan for the colony's future. By the summer of 1608, the Jamestown colony was near failure.

Starvation and recovery

Another major problem was starvation. Captain **John Smith,** a 27-year-old soldier and explorer, observed that the colonists were not planting enough crops. He complained that people wanted only to "dig gold, wash gold, refine gold, load gold." As they searched in vain for gold, the colony ran out of food.

Smith helped to save the colony. He set up stern rules that forced colonists to work if they wished to eat. He also visited nearby Indian villages to trade for food. **Powhatan** (pow uh TAN), the most powerful chief in the area, agreed to sell corn to the English.

Peaceful relations between the English and Native Americans of the region were short-lived, however. Whenever the Indians did not agree to supply food voluntarily, the colonists used force to seize what they needed. On one occasion John Smith aimed a gun at Powhatan's brother until the Indians provided corn to buy his freedom. Incidents such as these led to frequent and bloody warfare. Peace was restored, for a brief time only, when the colonist John Rolfe married **Pocahontas,** daughter of Powhatan.

While the English were enjoying the peace, their economic difficulties resumed.

Biography **Pocahontas**

Pocahontas, daughter of Powhatan, brought food to starving colonists at Jamestown. According to John Smith, she also saved him from an execution that her father had ordered. Later, Pocahontas converted to Christianity, married colonist John Rolfe, and moved to England. There, an artist painted this portrait of her in English dress.

★ **Why do you think the story of Pocahontas remains so popular today?**

From the Archives of American Heritage®

Admission price In 1624, Captain John Smith detailed a list of items required of settlers in Virginia, plus fees they had to pay for passage and shipping. Exactly 365 years later, a history professor from Kansas priced modern equivalents of all items and services. His total cost: $6,449.00.

Source: James B.M. Schick, "John Smith's Bill: Then and Now." *American Heritage* magazine, November 1989.

3 Teach

Draw a two-column chart on the chalkboard. Label the columns "Problems" and "Solutions." Have students suggest problems the Jamestown colony faced in its early years and describe how colonists tried to solve each problem. Have students repeat this process for the Plymouth colony. Then have students compare these early English settlements.

4 Assess

To close the lesson, have students complete the section review. Or have students work in pairs to write four questions about the section. Have pairs exchange and answer each other's questions.

Biography ANSWER

Possible answer: Her life seems like a romantic adventure story.

Technology

AmericanHeritage® History of the United States CD-ROM

- History Makers: John Smith, Pocahontas (*average*)

 ANSWER

men without property, women, and nonwhites

Viewing History: Representative Government

Virginia's House of Burgesses, shown at left, first met in 1619. It consisted of 22 representatives elected by "freemen" of the colony. In their first session, the burgesses passed laws against drunkenness and gambling and required colonists to attend church each Sunday. ★ **What people in Virginia could not elect burgesses?**

Problems arose soon after John Smith returned to England in 1609. For the next few years, the colony suffered terribly. Desperate settlers cooked "dogs, cats, snakes, [and] toadstools" to survive. To keep warm, they broke up houses to burn as firewood.

Tobacco and economic success

The Jamestown economy finally got on a firm footing after 1612, when colonists began growing tobacco. Europeans had learned about tobacco and pipe smoking from Native Americans. Although King James I considered smoking "a vile custom," the new fad caught on quickly. By 1620, England was importing more than 30,000 pounds (13,500 kg) of tobacco a year. At last, Virginians had found a way to make their colony succeed.

Representative Government

With Jamestown's economy improving, the Virginia Company took steps to establish a stable government in Virginia. In 1619, it sent a governor with orders to consult settlers on all important matters. Male settlers were allowed to elect burgesses, or representatives. The burgesses met in an assembly called the **House of Burgesses.** Together with the governor, they made laws for the colony.

The House of Burgesses marked the beginning of **representative government** in the English colonies. A representative government is one in which voters elect representatives to make laws for them.

The idea that people had political rights was deeply rooted in English history. In 1215, English nobles had forced King John to sign the **Magna Carta,** or Great Charter. This document said that the king could not raise taxes without first consulting the Great Council of nobles and church leaders. The Magna Carta established the principle, or basic idea, that English monarchs had to obey the laws of the land.

Over time, the rights won by nobles were extended to other English people. The Great Council grew into a representative assembly, called **Parliament.** By the 1600s, Parliament was divided into the House of Lords, made up of nobles, and an elected House of Commons. Only a few rich men had the right to vote. Still, the English had established that their king or queen must consult Parliament on money matters and must respect the law.

At first, free Virginians had even greater rights than citizens in England. They did not have to own property in order to vote. In 1670, however, the colony restricted the vote to free, male property owners.

Despite these limits, representative government remained important in Virginia. The idea took root that settlers should have a say in the affairs of the colony.

★ *Background* ★

Turning Points

A model for government The Magna Carta established the principle that the monarch must obey the law. Much later it helped lay the groundwork for Britain's slowly evolving system of representative government. As such, this famous document is often seen as a milestone in the evolution of our own democratic traditions.

★ *Activity* ★

Connection With Civics

Writing a report Ask students to compare and contrast the governments of Jamestown and New Spain. Students might consider differences in English and Spanish political traditions and how these differences influenced government in the American colonies of each nation. Have students present their findings in a report. (*challenging*)

New Arrivals in Virginia

Virginia needed more people in order for the colony to grow and thrive. During the early years of the Jamestown Colony, only a few women chose to make the journey from England. There was also a need for more workers to help raise tobacco and other crops.

Women in Virginia

In 1619, the Virginia Company sent about 100 women to Virginia to help "make the men more settled." This first shipload of women quickly found husbands in Jamestown. The Virginia Company profited from the marriages because it charged each man who found a wife 150 pounds (68 kg) of tobacco.

Women did make the colony more settled. Still, life in Virginia remained a daily struggle. Women in Virginia were not allowed the right to vote throughout the colonial period. Women had to make everything from scratch—food, clothing, even medicines. Hard work and childbirth killed many at a young age.

The first Africans arrive

In 1619, a Dutch ship arrived at Jamestown with about 20 Africans. The Dutch sold the Africans to Virginians who needed laborers for growing tobacco. The colonists valued the agricultural skills that the Africans brought with them.

Two of the Africans, Antoney and Isabella, married after they arrived in Virginia. In 1624, they had a son, William. He was the first child of African descent to be born in the English colonies.

By 1644, about 300 Africans lived in Virginia. Some of them were slaves for life. Others worked as servants and expected one day to own their own farms. Some Africans did become free planters. For a time, free Africans in Virginia could own property, testify in court, and vote in elections. In 1651, Anthony Johnson owned 250 acres of land and employed five servants to help him work it.

Later in the 1600s, Virginia set up a system of laws allowing white colonists to enslave Africans. As slavery expanded, free Africans also lost rights. By the early 1700s, free African property owners could not vote.

Cause and Effect

Causes

- Europeans want more goods from Asia
- Muslims gain control of trade between Europe and Asia
- Rulers of European nations seek ways to increase their wealth
- European nations look for a sea route to Asia
- Columbus reaches the Americas

Exploration of the Americas

Effects

- Spain builds an empire in the Americas
- English, French, and Dutch set up colonies in North America
- Millions of Native Americans die from "European" diseases
- Slave traders bring enslaved Africans to the Americas
- Foods from the Americas are introduced into Europe

Effects Today

- The United States is a multicultural society today
- American foods, such as corn and potatoes, are important to people's diets around the world

Graphic Organizer *Skills*

Several hundred years ago, European exploration of the Americas affected Native Americans, Africans, and Europeans. The impact of this period is still felt today.

1. **Comprehension** How did economic factors lead to European exploration?
2. **Critical Thinking** Name some of the languages that are spoken by the people of North America and South America today.

Graphic Organizer *Skills*

ANSWERS **1.** Desire for Asian goods and wealth led Europeans to seek a sea route to Asia.
2. Possible answers: English, Spanish, French, Portuguese, Native American languages

Reading Actively

During Reading Have students read to see which different groups of people were settling the first English colonies.

★ ***Background*** ★

Did You Know?

Wives wanted The shortage of women colonists remained a serious impediment to the growth and stability in the southern colonies, especially the newer ones, for many years. As a result, recruiters in Europe often used rosy advertisements to appeal directly to women. One newspaper ad for the Carolinas boldly declared: "If any maid or single woman have a desire to go over, they will think themselves in the Golden Age; when men paid a dowry for their wives; for if they be but civil, and under 50 years of age, some honest man or other, will purchase them for their wives."

Technology

Videodiscs/Videotapes
Prentice Hall United States History Video Collection™, Vol. 2, Ch. 10, "The English in the New World," 4 mins (*average*) ELL

Geography Skills

ANSWERS **1.** Review locations on map with students. **2.** Wampanoags, Narragansetts **3.** Cape Cod forms a protected bay in which ships can seek safety from ocean storms.

Writing Actively

After Reading Ask students to review the graphic organizer in this section and write a short essay on the causes and effects of European exploration of the Americas.

Pilgrims Seek Religious Freedom

In 1620, another band of English settlers, the **Pilgrims,** sailed for the Americas. Unlike the Virginians or the Spanish, these colonists sought neither gold nor silver. All they wanted was to practice their religion freely.

In England, the Pilgrims belonged to a religious group known as Separatists. They were called that because they wanted to separate from the official church, the Church of England. The English government bitterly opposed this and took action against the Separatists. Separatists were fined, jailed, and sometimes even executed.

The First English Settlements

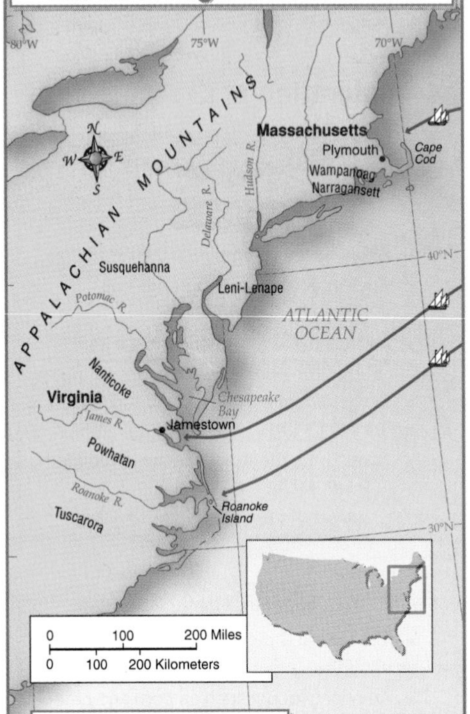

Geography Skills In the late 1500s and early 1600s, English settlers established colonies in Roanoke, Jamestown, and Plymouth.

1. **Location** On the map, locate: **(a)** Roanoke Island, **(b)** Jamestown, **(c)** Plymouth, **(d)** Virginia, **(e)** Massachusetts.
2. **Region** What Native American peoples lived in the area around Plymouth?
3. **Critical Thinking** How did the shape of the land around Plymouth provide a natural harbor for ships?

The Pilgrims' journey

In the early 1600s, a group of Separatists left England for Leyden, a city in the Netherlands. The Dutch allowed the newcomers to worship freely. Still, the Pilgrims missed their English way of life. They also worried that their children were growing up more Dutch than English.

A group of Pilgrims returned to England. Along with some other English people, they won a charter to set up a colony in Virginia. In September 1620, more than 100 men, women, and children set sail aboard a small ship called the *Mayflower.*

After a stormy two-month voyage, the Pilgrims landed on the cold, bleak shore of Cape Cod, in present-day Massachusetts. It was November 1620. Exhausted by the difficult sea voyage, the Pilgrims decided to travel no farther.

The Mayflower Compact

Before going ashore, the Pilgrims decided to establish rules for their new settlement. They gathered together and drew up the **Mayflower Compact.** The 41 men who signed it agreed to consult one another about laws for the colony and promised to work together to make the colony succeed:

> "We, whose names are underwritten... Having undertaken for the Glory of God, and Advancement of the Christian Faith... a voyage to plant the first colony in the northern parts of Virginia... do enact, constitute, and frame, such just and equal Laws... as shall be thought most [fitting] and convenient for the general Good of the Colony."

Resource Directory

Teaching Resources
Unit 1/Chapter 3
- Vocabulary Builder, p. 21
- Connecting History and Literature: Of Plymouth Plantation, p. 25
- Section 5 Quiz, p. 31
- Chapter Tests, pp. 13–18

Transparencies
Political Cartoons
- When Worlds Collide, p. G-13

★ Activity ★ Cooperative Learning

Designing an historic site Tell students that Plimoth Plantation, which re-creates the first Massachusetts colony, is a popular tourist attraction today. Have them research its features and layout (www.plimoth.org). Working in groups, have students design a similar attraction for another colonial settlement, with appropriate buildings and events. (*average*) ELL

★ Activity ★ Community Involvement

Helping those in need Americans have always helped one another. In 1621, the Pilgrims received help from Native Americans. This tradition of mutual support continues today. Have students conduct a food drive to support a local outreach program or participate as a class in the work of a local soup kitchen, community garden, or hot meal program. (*basic*) ELL T

Early hardships

The Pilgrims named the colony Plymouth. They built their settlement on the site of a Native American village that had been abandoned because of disease. The colonists even found baskets filled with corn that they were able to eat.

However, the corn was not enough to get the Pilgrims through their first winter. The harshly cold season was also difficult to survive because the Pilgrims had not had enough time to build proper shelters. Nearly half the settlers perished of disease or starvation. The Pilgrims' religious faith was strong, however. They believed that it was God's will for them to remain in Plymouth.

▲ *The Pilgrims wore beaver hats such as this.*

Help from Native Americans

In the spring, the Pilgrims received help from neighboring Indians. A Pemaquid Indian, Samoset, had learned English from earlier explorers sailing along the coast. He introduced the Pilgrims to Massasoit (MAS uh soit), chief of the local Wampanoag (wahm puh NOH ahg) Indians.

The Wampanoag who helped the Pilgrims most was named **Squanto.** Squanto brought the Pilgrims seeds of native plants—corn, beans, and pumpkins—and showed them how to plant them. He also taught the settlers to stir up eels from river bottoms and then snatch them with their hands. The grateful Pilgrims called Squanto "a special instrument sent of God."

In the fall, the Pilgrims had a very good harvest. Because they believed that God had given them this harvest, they set aside a day for giving thanks. In later years, the Pilgrims celebrated after each harvest season with a day of thanksgiving. Americans today celebrate **Thanksgiving** as a national holiday.

★ Section 5 Review ★

Recall

1. **Locate** (a) Roanoke Island, (b) Jamestown, (c) Cape Cod, (d) Plymouth.
2. **Identify** (a) Sir Walter Raleigh, (b) John Smith, (c) Powhatan, (d) Pocahontas, (e) House of Burgesses, (f) Pilgrims, (g) Squanto.
3. **Define** (a) charter, (b) representative government, (c) Magna Carta, (d) Parliament, (e) Mayflower Compact.

Comprehension

4. (a) What were the origins of representative government in the English colonies? (b) Which Virginia colonists were denied equal rights?
5. Why did the Pilgrims come to the Americas?
6. Describe two ways in which Squanto helped the Plymouth colonists.

Critical Thinking and Writing

7. **Linking Past and Present** In the 1600s, there was representative government in Jamestown. How do we have representative government in the United States today?
8. **Comparing** How were the reasons for founding Jamestown different from the reasons for founding Plymouth?

★ ★

Activity **Creating an Advertisement** You are an investor in the Virginia Company, and you want to encourage people to move to Virginia. Create an advertisement describing and illustrating the advantages of life in Virginia.

★ Section 5 Review ★

ANSWERS

1. See map, p. 88.
2. (a) p. 84, (b)–(d) p. 85, (e) p. 86, (f) p. 88, (g) p. 89
3. (a) p. 85, (b)–(d) p. 86, (e) p. 88
4. (a) the Magna Carta and Parliament (b) men without property, women, nonwhites
5. to practice their religion freely
6. He showed the Pilgrims how to grow corn, beans, and pumpkins and how to catch eels for food.
7. We elect representatives to local, state, and national legislatures.
8. Jamestown was founded to create wealth for the Virginia Company, whereas Pilgrims went to Plymouth for religious reasons.

History and You Activity

Guided Instruction

Advertisements often mix rational arguments with messages and images designed to produce a positive emotional reaction. Have students brainstorm for both logical reasons to come to Virginia and images or "soundbites" that appeal to the emotions.

ASSESSMENT See the rubrics in the Alternative Assessment booklet in the Teaching Resources.

★ *Background* ★

Linking Past and Present

The Wampanoag The Wampanoags, whose name has been translated as "People of the Dawn" or "People of the First Light," still live in southeastern Massachusetts and on the island of Martha's Vineyard. They own 3,400 acres of land on the island, and their autonomous reservation is home to approximately 40 percent of the 800-person Wampanoag Tribe. The Wampanoags recently revived a yearly celebration of Moshup, their creator. Through narration, music, and acting, they tell the story of Moshup's life and his creation of Martha's Vineyard and the surrounding area.

Technology

Videodiscs/Videotapes

Prentice Hall United States History Video Collection™, Vol. 2, Ch. 13, "Pilgrims and Puritans," 5 mins (average) ELL

Chapter 13

CD-ROM

Test Bank CD-ROM, Ch. 3

Interactive Student Tutorial

Chapter 3

Review and Activities

Reviewing the Chapter

Define These Terms

1. d **2.** e **3.** a **4.** c **5.** b

Explore the Main Ideas

1. Crusades: It sparked desire for goods from Asia and the Middle East; increased trade and travel. Renaissance: It made Europeans eager to learn more about the wider world.

2. for gold, for Spain, and to spread Christianity

3. As Native Americans died from disease and mistreatment, the Spanish brought enslaved Africans to work their plantations.

4. (a) taught the French how to trap fur-bearing animals and how to survive in the wilderness; traded with and guided French explorers **(b)** showed the Pilgrims how to grow local crops and find other food

5. (a) Virginia's House of Burgesses reflected the English tradition of representative government. **(b)** The Mayflower Compact established the rule of one law for all, as had the Magna Carta.

Geography Activity

1. D **2.** F **3.** E **4.** G **5.** B **6.** A **7.** C **Region** to trade for spices

Critical Thinking and Writing

1. Possible answers: Native American influences: attitudes toward the environment, foods, traditions, arts, language; African influences: arts, foods, traditions, music, language; European influences: religion, government, language

2. b, a, d, c

3. (a) approved, because Las Casas tried to help Native Americans **(b)** critical, because Las Casas attacked the planters' treatment of Native Americans **(c)** approved, because Las Casas's suggestion to replace Native Americans with Africans would increase a slave trader's wealth **(d)** angry, because Las Casas wanted to end Native American suffering by having his people suffer instead

4. Answers will vary but should be supported by information from the chapter.

Using Primary Sources

(a) The French planned to surround the Iroquois; wreck their fields; burn their villages; capture their women, children, and old men; and drive their warriors into the woods, where other Native Americans would kill them. **(b)** The French respected the Iroquois's fighting skills, as shown by the use of such words as "brave, active, more skilled in the use of the gun than our Europeans" to describe them.

Chapter 3

Review and Activities

★ Sum It Up ★

Section 1 Europeans Reach the Americas

- During the Renaissance, Europeans grew interested in the world beyond Europe.
- European voyages to the Americas started a global exchange of products and ideas.

Section 2 Spain Builds an Empire

- Spanish conquistadors conquered the Aztecs and Incas and built a Spanish empire in the Americas.
- In time, the Spanish and Native American cultures began to blend together.

Section 3 Africans Come to the Americas

- By the 1400s, there were thriving trading communities in both East and West Africa.
- African and European traders worked together to supply millions of enslaved Africans for labor in the Americas.

Section 4 Colonizing North America

- European states, such as France and the Netherlands, were rivals for wealth and power in the Americas.
- Native Americans traded with Europeans, but also suffered from warfare and loss of lands.

Section 5 The First English Colonies

- The first English colonies in North America were at Jamestown and Plymouth.
- People in English colonies enjoyed English traditions of rights and freedoms.
- Native Americans helped the settlers of the Plymouth Colony survive their first difficult years in North America.

For additional review of the major ideas of Chapter 3, see ***Guide to the Essentials of American History*** or ***Interactive Student Tutorial CD-ROM,*** which contains interactive review activities, graphic organizers, and practice tests.

Reviewing the Chapter

Define These Terms

Match each term with the correct definition.

Column 1	Column 2
1. Parliament	**a.** town that has its own independent government
2. presidio	**b.** legal document giving rights to a person or company
3. city-state	**c.** waterway through or around North America to Asia
4. northwest passage	**d.** English law-making body
5. charter	**e.** fort where Spanish soldiers lived

Explore the Main Ideas

1. How did the Renaissance and Crusades cause Europeans to look beyond Europe?
2. Why did Spanish conquistadors go to the Americas?
3. How did the transatlantic African slave trade begin?
4. What role did Native Americans play in the building of **(a)** New France, **(b)** Plymouth Colony?
5. How did English political traditions affect government in **(a)** Virginia, **(b)** Plymouth?

Geography Activity

Match the letters on the map with the following places: **1.** Africa, **2.** Asia, **3.** Europe, **4.** North America, **5.** East Indies, **6.** West Indies, **7.** South America. **Region** Why did Europeans want to reach Asia?

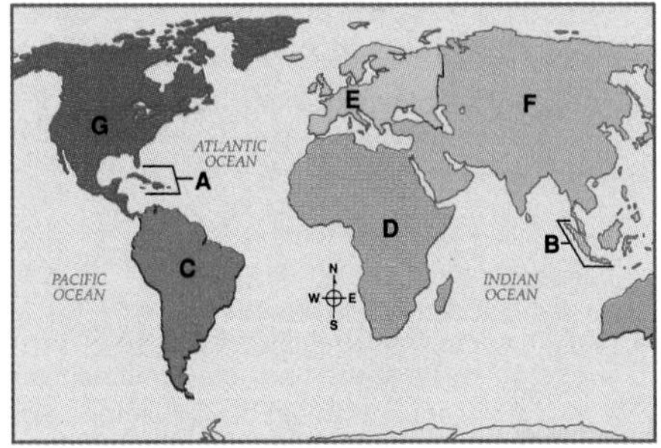

Critical Thinking and Writing

1. **Linking Past and Present** How are Native American, African, and European influences evident today in the society and culture of the United States?
2. **Understanding Chronology** Place the following events in chronological order: **(a)** Columbus crosses the Atlantic, **(b)** the Renaissance begins, **(c)** Spain builds missions in borderlands, **(d)** Cortés conquers Aztecs.
3. **Recognizing Points of View** Describe how you think each of the following people might have felt about Bartolomé de Las Casas: **(a)** an enslaved Native American in New Spain, **(b)** a Spanish plantation owner, **(c)** a Portuguese slave trader, **(d)** King Affonso of Kongo.
4. **Exploring Unit Themes Origins** Choose one event or development discussed in this chapter. Explain why you think that event or development had an impact on the present-day United States.

Using Primary Sources

In their rivalry for power in North America, Europeans enlisted the aid of Native American warriors. In 1687, the French planned an attack on the Iroquois, who were allies of the English.

> "The Iroquois force consists of two thousand picked warriors—brave, active, more skillful in the use of the gun than our Europeans and all well armed. . . . If they be [surrounded] on both sides, all their plantations of Indian corn will be destroyed, their villages burnt, their women, children, and old men captured, and their warriors driven into the woods, where they will be pursued and [destroyed] by the other Indians."

Source: *Memoir for the Marquis de Seignelay*, 1687, Department of Alfa-Information, University of Groningen, 1996.

Recognizing Points of View (a) How did the French plan to destroy the Iroquois? **(b)** Did the French respect the Iroquois? Explain.

Activity Bank

Interdisciplinary Activity

Exploring the Arts Do research on Native American, European, or African art of the 1600s. In a presentation, display one or more copies of sample artwork. Explain how the art was created and discuss the meaning or symbolism of the art.

Career Skills Activity

Biologists Prepare a fact sheet on an animal species that was hunted in the North American fur trade. Include information such as the animal's diet, habitat, and whether it is endangered today. Create drawings to illustrate your fact sheet.

Citizenship Activity

Exploring Local Government In New Spain, the Spanish king appointed viceroys to make laws. In Virginia, the House of Burgesses made laws. Do research to learn how local laws are made in your community today. Present your findings in a chart.

Internet Activity

Review the maps on page 67. Some Spanish missions, pueblos, and presidios still stand today and are open to explore. Find Internet home pages dealing with those sites today. List the Internet addresses of the most interesting and informative sites. Share your list so others can visit, too.

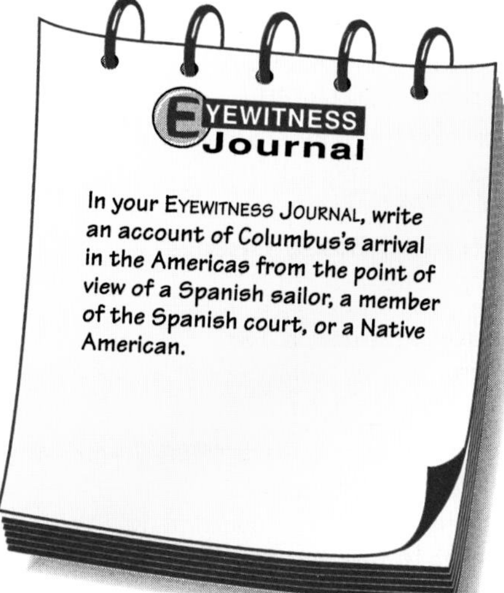

Eyewitness Journal
In your Eyewitness Journal, write an account of Columbus's arrival in the Americas from the point of view of a Spanish sailor, a member of the Spanish court, or a Native American.

Activity Bank

ASSESSMENT To assess the activities on this page, see the rubrics in the Alternative Assessment booklet in the Teaching Resources. You might want to share the rubrics with your students before they begin work.

Interdisciplinary Activity

1. If possible, invite an art teacher to class to suggest some research ideas and art history resources.
2. If applicable, have students focus on how their artwork reflects the encounters taking place at this time among Africans, Native Americans, and Europeans.
3. Allow students to work in teams if they wish.

Career Skills Activity

1. Remind students that fact sheets should be well organized and provide an overview of each animal's habitat and survival techniques. Any technical terms should be defined.
2. Students might consult encyclopedias and books on North American wildlife.
3. Extend the activity by asking interested students to build dioramas showing the habitat of a selected animal.

Citizenship Activity

1. Suggest that students call their local or city offices for information or research the topic in the town library.
2. Students might find a local city or town manager who is willing to speak about how local laws are made.
3. Extend the activity by having students create a diagram or graphic organizer of how local or state laws are made.

Eyewitness Journal

1. Have students begin by reviewing the relevant passages of their textbooks.
2. Suggest students do more research before they write.
3. Ask students to read their accounts aloud if time permits.

Internet Activity

1. Have students look at www.phschool.com, which contains updated information on a variety of topics.
2. One site you may find useful for this activity is Mission San Juan Capistrano at sanjuancapistrano.com/MissionSJC/.
3. Given the changing nature of the Internet, you may wish to preview this site.

Chapter 4 Manager

SECTION OBJECTIVES	TEACHING RESOURCES	ADDITIONAL RESOURCE
1 The New England Colonies (pp. 94–99) **Objectives** 1. Explain why the Puritans set up the Massachusetts Bay Colony. 2. Identify the founders of Connecticut and Rhode Island. 3. Describe what life was like in the New England colonies.	**Lesson Planner,** p. 13 (average) . . . . **90 mins.** **Unit 1/Chapter 4** • Map Mystery: Where to Plant Colonies, p. 35 (average) . . . . **20 mins.** • Connecting History and Literature: Upon the Burning of Our House, p. 36 (challenging) . . . . **20 mins.** • Section 1 Quiz, p. 38 (average) . . . . **15 mins.** **Interdisciplinary Connections** • Main Idea: American Ingenuity, p. 20 (average) . . . . **20 mins.**	**Voices of Freedom** • Slave's Ballad on an Indian Attack, pp. 37–38 (average) **Historical Outline Map Book** • The New England Colonies, p. 16 (average) **Customized Reader** • A Letter From a Massachusetts Settler, article IIB-11 (average) • The Examination and Trial of an Accused Witch, article IIB-9 (challenging)
2 The Middle Colonies (pp. 100–105) **Objectives** 1. Explain why William Penn started a colony in North America. 2. Explain why the Middle Colonies were known as the Breadbasket Colonies. 3. Describe backcountry life.	**Lesson Planner,** p. 14 (average) . . . . **45 mins.** **Unit 1/Chapter 4** • Practice Your Skills: Reading a Pie Graph, p. 33 (average) . . . . **20 mins.** • Section 2 Quiz, p. 39 (average) . . . . **15 mins.** **Document-Based Discovery** • Origins, pp. 2–5	**Historical Outline Map Book** • The Middle Colonies, p. 17 (average) **Customized Reader** • William Penn's Regulations for Settlers in Pennsylvania, article IIB-14 (challenging)
3 The Southern Colonies (pp. 106–111) **Objectives** 1. Explain why the Southern Colonies were founded. 2. Describe the two ways of life that developed in the Southern Colonies. 3. Explain why slavery became important in the South.	**Lesson Planner,** p. 15 (average) . . . . **90 mins.** **Unit 1/Chapter 4** • Biography Flashcard: Olaudah Equiano, p. 37 (average) . . . . **20 mins.** • Section 3 Quiz, p. 40 (average) . . . . **15 mins.** **Interdisciplinary Connections** • Main Idea: American Ingenuity, pp. 21, 24 (average) . . . . **20 mins.** **Document-Based Discovery** • Origins, pp. 2–5	**Voices of Freedom** • Bacon Rebels, pp. 41–42 (average **Historical Outline Map Book** • The Southern Colonies, p. 18 (average) **Customized Reader** • Petition From North Carolina "Regulators," article IIB-8 (averag **Interdisciplinary Explorations** • The Wreck of the Henrietta Mari (average)
4 Governing the Colonies (pp. 112–116) **Objectives** 1. Explain why England passed the Navigation Acts. 2. Describe what colonial governments were like. 3. Summarize the rights English colonists enjoyed.	**Lesson Planner,** p. 16 (average) . . . . **45 mins.** **Unit 1/Chapter 4** • Section 4 Quiz, p. 41 (average) . . . . **15 mins.** **Why Study History?** • You Have a Say in Government, pp. 15–18 (average) . . . . **90 mins.**	**Historical Outline Map Book** • The Thirteen Colonies, p. 15 (average)
5 A Changing Colonial Culture (pp. 117–123) **Objectives** 1. Describe features of the Great Awakening. 2. Explain how colonists educated their children. 3. Describe how new ideas spread through the colonies.	**Lesson Planner,** p. 17 (average) . . . . **75 mins.** **Unit 1/Chapter 4** • Vocabulary Builder, p. 32 (basic) . . . . **15 mins.** • Critical Thinking and Writing: Analyzing Visual Evidence, p. 34 (challenging) . . . . . . **20 mins.** • Section 5 Quiz, p. 42 (average) . . . . **15 mins.** **Chapter Tests,** pp. 19–24 (average) . . . . . **45 mins.** **Interdisciplinary Connections** • Main Idea: American Ingenuity, pp. 22–23 (average) . . . . **20 mins.**	**Voices of Freedom** • A Critical View of Philadelphia, pp. 46–47 (average) • The Wisdom of Benjamin Franklin, pp. 50–51 (average) **Customized Reader** • Letter From an Indentured Servant to Her Father, article IIA-10 (challenging)

Assessment Options

Teaching Resources
- Alternative Assessment booklet
- Section Quizzes, Unit 1, Chapter 4, pp. 38–42
- Chapter Tests, Chapter 4, pp. 19–24
- Test Bank CD-ROM

Student Performance Pack
- Guide to the Essentials of American History, Chapter 4 Test, p. 27
- Standardized Test Prep Handbook
- Interactive Student Tutorial CD-ROM

Interdisciplinary Connections

Teaching Resources
- Map Mystery, Unit 1, Chapter 4, p. 35
- Connecting History and Literature, Unit 1, Chapter 4, p. 36
- Interdisciplinary Connections, pp. 19–24

Interdisciplinary Explorations,
- The Wreck of the Henrietta Marie

Voices of Freedom, pp. 37–38, 41–42, 46–47, 50–51

Customized Reader, articles IIA-10, IIB-8, IIB-9, IIB-11, IIB-14

Historical Outline Map Book, pp. 15–18

BLOCK SCHEDULING
Activities with this icon will help you meet your Block Scheduling needs.

ENGLISH LANGUAGE LEARNERS
Activities with this icon are suitable for English Language Learners.

TEAM TEACHING
Activities and Background Notes with this icon present starting points for Team Teaching.

Technology

AmericanHeritage® History of the United States CD-ROM
- Time Tour: The Thirteen English Colonies in a Meeting of Different Worlds
- History Makers: Anne Hutchinson, William Penn, Benjamin Franklin
- Arts and Entertainment: Books

Interactive Student Tutorial CD-ROM

Test Bank CD-ROM

Color Transparencies
- How Lightning Works, p. B-39
- Ethnic Division of the Colonial Population, 1775, p. C-11
- The Sargent Family, p. D-29
- The Americas and the World, 1600–1800, p. E-15
- 13 Colonies, p. I-17
- New England States, p. I-57
- Middle Atlantic States, p. I-61
- Southeastern States, p. I-65

Guided Reading Audiotapes (English/Spanish), side 2

Resource Pro® CD-ROM

Prentice Hall United States History Video Collection™ (Spanish track available on disc version.) Vol. 2, Chs. 13, 16, 19, 25; Vol. 3, Chs. 7, 10, 13, 16, 19, 28

Prentice Hall Home Page www.phschool.com

Student Performance Pack

Guide to the Essentials of American History
- Ch. 4, pp. 22–27
  (Available in English and Spanish)

Guided Reading Audiotapes (English/Spanish), side 2

Standardized Test Prep Handbook

Interactive Student Tutorial CD-ROM

Teachers' Bibliography

Don't miss the special American Heritage® teaching notes found in this chapter.

Contact Teachers' Curriculum Institute to learn more about History Alive!® resources on colonial life. See History Alive!® units: Geography of America from Past to Present, Section 4, "Adapting to the Environment: Colonial Settlers," and Colonial Life and the American Revolution, Section 1, "Examining Colonial Society," and Section 2, "Slavery in the Colonies."

Explore your library to find these issues related to Chapter 4: *Deerfield, A Colonial Perspective,* September 1995; *The Antislavery Movement,* February 1993; *Folk Art,* August 1991; *Colonial Crafts,* June 1990; *The People of Williamsburg,* February 1990; *Daniel Boone,* June 1988; *Witchcraft,* October 1986; *Chesapeake Bay,* September 1986.

PRENTICE HALL School

Prentice Hall Web Site You can access a structured, on-line environment that allows you to preview curriculum-related resources and receive updated information on groundbreaking events from around the nation and the world. (www.phschool.com)

Chapter 4

The 13 English Colonies 1630–1750

Introducing the Chapter

Have students preview the main ideas of this chapter by looking over the visuals. Suggest they look for examples of the new ways of life that developed in the English colonies in North America.

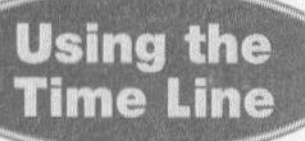

To provide students with practice in understanding chronology, ask questions such as these: **(1)** In what year did William Penn found the colony of Pennsylvania? *(1682)* **(2)** What happened in England seven years later? *(William and Mary signed the English Bill of Rights.)* **(3)** Was the colony of Georgia founded before, during, or after the Great Awakening? *(during)* **(4)** During the period shown on this time line, which colony was the first to be founded? *(Massachusetts.)*

Ask students to name as many voting opportunities that Americans have as they can think of. Elicit from them that they themselves vote for student body officers and club officials. Discuss with students the advantages of electing representatives rather than having officers appointed by rulers, monarchs, or other leaders.

For additional *Why Study History?* support, see p. 115.

Chapter 4

The 13 English Colonies

1630–1750

In the 1600s and 1700s, English settlers founded 13 colonies on the eastern coast of what is now the United States. Many colonists came in search of new homes or a chance to earn a living. Others sought religious freedom. Over time, the various colonies developed different economies and ways of life.

Despite their differences, English settlers in all of the colonies came to develop an independent spirit and a tradition of self-government. This independence was strengthened by a religious movement called the Great Awakening and by new social and political ideas from Europe.

The United States grew from the 13 English colonies. As a result, many of our traditions have English roots. One of the most important is representative government—the right to elect the people who govern us. To focus on this connection, see the *Why Study History?* feature, "You Have a Say in Government," in this chapter.

American Events

1630 Puritans from England set up colony in Massachusetts

1675 Metacom leads Native Americans against settlers in New England

1682 William Penn founds colony of Pennsylvania

1630 — 1650 — 1670 — 1690

World Events

1660 World Event Britain passes Second Navigation Act

1689 World Event William and Mary sign English Bill of Rights

Viewing HISTORY **Colonial Life in Needlework**

In England's North American colonies, women skilled at needlework recorded details of their daily life. This sampler shows wealthy Bostonians in the mid-1700s. By this time, different ways of life had developed across the 13 English colonies. ★ **Do you think this sampler gives an accurate picture of colonial life? Why or why not?**

1700s Plantations in the Southern Colonies rely on slave labor

1730s Religious movement, known as the Great Awakening, sweeps through the colonies

1732 Georgia is founded as refuge for people jailed for debt

1690 **1710** **1730** **1750**

1700s World Event Age of Enlightenment begins

1725 World Event British Quakers speak out against slavery

Writing Actively

Responding to Art Have students examine the sampler on this page. Then have students write short paragraphs explaining what they can learn about colonial life from this piece of needlework.

Viewing HISTORY ANSWER

Students should recognize that the picture probably depicts certain details accurately, such as style of dress. However, it does not accurately portray all of colonial life because it shows only wealthy Bostonians.

★ *Background* ★

Art Note

Colonial Life in Needlework Colonial women and girls often worked on samplers during the evening when the family gathered to read from the Bible or from respected writers of the time. Their samplers sometimes included excerpts from these texts, which were then framed with decorative borders. **T**

Documents and Literature

On pp. 533–537, you will find two readings to enrich this chapter:

1. Historical Document "Attracting Settlers to the Carolinas," excerpts from a pamphlet circulated by the Carolina Lord Proprietors. (Use with Section 3.)

2. Eyewitness Account "How I Became a Printer," excerpt from Ben Franklin's *Autobiography* describing his apprenticeship. (Use with Section 5.)

Technology

Videodiscs/Videotapes

Show the *Prentice Hall United States History Video Collection*™ segments for this chapter. The videodisc version has a Spanish track. Press audio until you get the left channel for English or the right channel for Spanish, or use the bar codes in the Guidebook.

AmericanHeritage® History of the United States CD-ROM

- Time Tour: The 13 English Colonies in A Meeting of Different Worlds (*average*)

☆ Section 1
The New England Colonies

LESSON PLAN

Objectives

★ Explain why the Puritans set up the Massachusetts Bay Colony.

★ Identify the founders of Connecticut and Rhode Island.

★ Describe what life was like in the New England colonies.

1 Engage

Warm Up Ask: "What might make you and your whole family move to another country?" Have students brainstorm answers. Ask: "Which reasons might have applied to people living in the 1600s and 1700s?"

Activating Prior Knowledge Help students locate New England on a U. S. map. Then ask: "Why do you think this region was named *New England?*"

Reading Actively

Before Reading Have volunteers read Explore These Questions and take notes to answer each question.

2 Explore

Have students read the section. For homework, have them do research on conflicts between

RESOURCE DIRECTORY

Teaching Resources
Lesson Planner, p.13
Unit 1/Chapter 4
- Map Mystery: Where to Plant Colonies, p. 35
- Connecting History and Literature: Upon the Burning of Our House, p. 36

Transparencies
Time Lines
- The Americas and the World, 1600–1800, p. E-15

The New England Colonies

As You Read

Explore These Questions
- Why did the Puritans set up the Massachusetts Bay Colony?
- Who founded the colonies of Connecticut and Rhode Island?
- What was life like in the New England colonies?

Define
- toleration
- common
- Sabbath
- town meeting

Identify
- John Winthrop
- Puritans
- General Court
- Great Migration
- Thomas Hooker
- Fundamental Orders of Connecticut
- Roger Williams
- Anne Hutchinson
- Metacom

April and May 1630 were cold, stormy months in the North Atlantic. Huddled below deck, colonists aboard the ship *Arbella* wondered if they had been foolish to sail to a new land. Their leader, however, had no doubts. **John Winthrop,** a lawyer and a devout Christian, assured them that their new colony would set an example to the world:

> "The Lord will make our name a praise and glory, so that men shall say of succeeding [colonies]: 'The Lord make it like that of New England.' For we must consider that we shall be like a City upon a Hill. The eyes of all people are on us."

The passengers on the *Arbella* were among more than 1,000 people who left England in 1630 to settle in North America. They set up their colony on Massachusetts Bay, north of Plymouth. Over the next 100 years, English settlers would build towns and farms throughout New England.

Puritans in Massachusetts

John Winthrop and his followers were part of a religious group known as **Puritans.** Unlike the Pilgrims, the Puritans did not want to separate entirely from the Church of England. Instead, they hoped to reform the church by introducing simpler forms of worship. They wanted to do away with many practices inherited from the Roman Catholic church, such as organ music, finely decorated houses of worship, and special clothing for priests.

Leaving England

The Puritans were a powerful group in England. Many were well-educated and successful merchants or landowners. Some sat in the House of Commons.

Charles I, who became king in 1625, disapproved of the Puritans and their ideas. He canceled Puritan business charters and had Puritans expelled from universities. He even had a few Puritans jailed.

By 1629, some Puritan leaders were convinced that England had fallen on "evil and declining times." They persuaded royal officials to grant them a charter to form the Massachusetts Bay Company. The company's bold plan was to build a new society in New England. They vowed to base their new society on biblical laws and teachings. Far from the watchful eye of the king, Puritans would run their colony as they pleased.

Some settlers joined the Massachusetts colonists for economic rather than religious reasons. In wealthy English families, the oldest son usually inherited his father's estate. With little hope of owning land, younger sons

94 ★ Chapter 4

★ Background ★

Did You Know?

John Winthrop An attorney and government official in England, John Winthrop lost his position to anti-Puritan policies. When the Puritans resolved to create a new society in the Americas, he embraced the cause and exhorted his fellow Puritans to make their colony a model for others. Winthrop was so well respected that he was elected governor of the colony 12 times.

★ Background ★

Turning Points

Victims of enclosure From the 1500s through the 1800s, many English farmers were victims of the enclosure movement, in which wealthy landowners fenced off or enclosed what previously had been common land. The enclosure movement forced many small farmers and farm workers off the land. Some looked to North America, which seemed to have limitless, cheap land.

sought opportunity elsewhere. They were attracted to Massachusetts Bay because it offered cheap land or a chance to start a business.

Governing the colony

In 1629, the Puritans sent a small advance party to North America. John Winthrop and his larger party arrived the following year. Winthrop was chosen first governor of the Massachusetts Bay Colony, as the Puritan settlement was called.

Once ashore, Winthrop set an example for others. Although he was governor, he worked hard to build a home, clear land, and plant crops. One colonist wrote, "He so encouraged us that there was not an idle person to be found in the whole colony."

Under the charter, only stockholders who had invested money in the Massachusetts Bay Company had the right to vote. Most settlers, however, were not stockholders. They resented taxes and laws passed by a government in which they had no say.

Winthrop and other stockholders quickly realized that the colony would run more smoothly if a greater number of settlers could take part. At the same time, Puritan leaders sought to keep non-Puritans out of government. As a result, they granted the right to vote for governor to all men who were church members. Later, male church members also elected representatives to an assembly called the **General Court.**

Under the firm leadership of Winthrop and other Puritans, the Massachusetts Bay Colony grew and prospered. Between 1629 and 1640, some 15,000 men, women, and children made the journey from England to Massachusetts. This movement of people is known as the **Great Migration.** Many of the newcomers settled in Boston, which grew into the colony's largest town.

Settling Connecticut

In May 1636, a Puritan minister named **Thomas Hooker** led about 100 settlers out

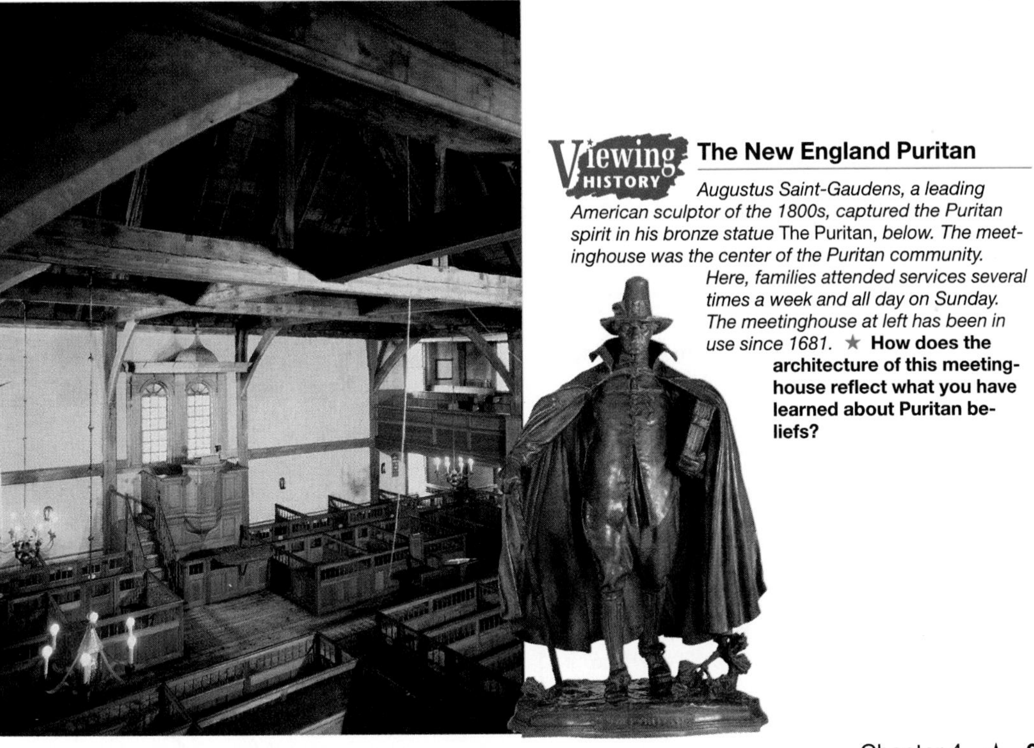

Viewing HISTORY **The New England Puritan**

Augustus Saint-Gaudens, a leading American sculptor of the 1800s, captured the Puritan spirit in his bronze statue The Puritan, *below. The meetinghouse was the center of the Puritan community. Here, families attended services several times a week and all day on Sunday. The meetinghouse at left has been in use since 1681.* ★ **How does the architecture of this meetinghouse reflect what you have learned about Puritan beliefs?**

Native Americans and the English in the 1600s. Have students present their findings to the class.

3 Teach

Have the class run a panel discussion about the settling of New England. Assign one student to be moderator and others to be John Winthrop, Thomas Hooker, Roger Williams, Anne Hutchinson, and Metacom. Remaining students can prepare questions for the panelists, focusing on the roles of government and religion in colonial life and on the conflict between settlers and Native Americans.

4 Assess

To close the lesson, have students complete the section review. Or have students write an essay suggesting how each New England colony contributed to the ideals behind our government today.

★ ★ ★ ★ ★ ★ ★ ★ ★ ★ ★ ★ ★ ★ ★ ★ ★ ★

Viewing HISTORY ANSWER

The Puritans wanted to reform the Church of England by simplifying its worship service. The wood-frame architecture reflects this simplicity; the building lacks ornaments and stained glass windows.

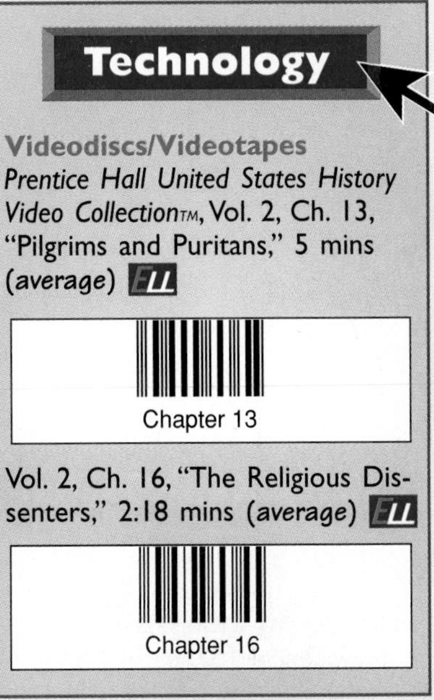

Technology

Videodiscs/Videotapes

Prentice Hall United States History Video Collection™, Vol. 2, Ch. 13, "Pilgrims and Puritans," 5 mins (*average*) ELL

Chapter 13

Vol. 2, Ch. 16, "The Religious Dissenters," 2:18 mins (*average*) ELL

Chapter 16

Geography *Skills*

ANSWERS **1.** Review locations with students. **2.** Massachusetts, Rhode Island, Connecticut **3.** It had many harbors, forests to supply wood, and fish and whales offshore.

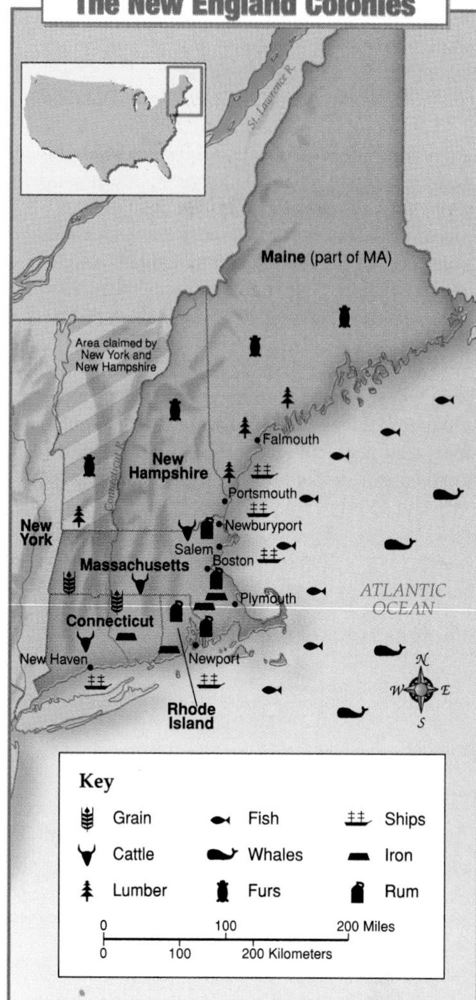

Geography *Skills* **The New England colonies were among the first English settlements in North America. Major economic activities in the region included shipbuilding, fishing, and fur trapping.**

1. **Location** On the map, locate: **(a)** Massachusetts, **(b)** Connecticut, **(c)** Rhode Island, **(d)** New Hampshire, **(e)** Boston, **(f)** Plymouth.
2. **Interaction** In which colonies did settlers mine iron ore?
3. **Critical Thinking** How did New England's geography encourage the growth of shipbuilding?

of Massachusetts Bay. Pushing west, they drove their cattle, goats, and pigs along Indian trails that cut through the forests. When they reached the Connecticut River, they built a town, which they called Hartford.

Hooker left Massachusetts Bay because he believed that the governor and other officials had too much power. He wanted to set up a colony in Connecticut with strict limits on government.

In 1639, the settlers wrote a plan of government called the **Fundamental Orders of Connecticut.** It created a government much like that of Massachusetts. There were, however, two important differences. First, the Fundamental Orders gave the vote to all men who were property owners, including those who were not church members. Second, the Fundamental Orders limited the governor's power. In this way, the Fundamental Orders expanded the idea of representative government in the English colonies.

In 1662, Connecticut became a separate colony, with a new charter granted by the king of England. By then, 15 towns were thriving along the Connecticut River.

Settling Rhode Island

Another Puritan who challenged the leaders of Massachusetts Bay was **Roger Williams.** A young minister in the village of Salem, Williams was gentle and good-natured. Most people, including Governor Winthrop, liked him. Williams's ideas, however, alarmed Puritan leaders.

Williams believed that the Puritan church had too much power in Massachusetts. In Williams's view, the business of church and state should be completely separate. The role of the state, said Williams, was to maintain order and peace. It should not support a particular church.

Williams also believed in religious toleration. **Toleration** means a willingness to let others practice their own beliefs. In Puritan Massachusetts, non-Puritans were not permitted to worship freely.

Puritan leaders viewed Williams as a dangerous troublemaker. In 1635, the Gen-

★ *Background* ★
Viewpoints

Religious toleration Rhode Island founder Roger Williams once wrote, "The government extends no further than over the bodies and goods of their subjects, not over their souls, and [so] they may not undertake to give laws unto the souls and consciences of men." Such religious toleration made Rhode Island a haven for people of many religious backgrounds.

★ *Background* ★
Our Diverse Nation

First synagogue In Newport, Rhode Island, Jewish immigrants from Spain and Portugal began meeting in 1658. For a century, they worshipped in private homes. In 1759, however, the Jewish citizens of Newport decided to build a house of worship. Touro Synagogue was the result. It was named after Isaac Touro, the congregation's respected rabbi.

Resource Directory

Transparencies
Geography and History
- New England States, p. I-57

96 ★ Chapter 4

eral Court ordered him to leave Massachusetts. Fearing that the court would send him back to England, Williams fled to Narragansett Bay, where he spent the winter with Indians. In the spring, the Indians sold him land for a settlement. After a few years, it became the English colony of Rhode Island.

In Rhode Island, Williams put into practice his ideas about toleration. He allowed complete freedom of religion for all Protestants, Jews, and Catholics. He did not set up a state church or require settlers to attend church services. He also gave all white men the right to vote. Before long, settlers who disliked the strict Puritan rule of Massachusetts flocked to Providence and other towns in Rhode Island.*

Anne Hutchinson

Among those who fled to Rhode Island was **Anne Hutchinson.** A devout Puritan, Hutchinson regularly attended church services. After church, she and her friends gathered at her home to discuss the minister's sermon. At first, Hutchinson merely related what the minister had said. Later, she began to express her own views. Often, she seemed to criticize the minister's teachings.

Puritan leaders grew angry. They believed that Hutchinson's opinions were full of religious errors. Even worse, they said, a woman did not have the right to explain God's law. In November 1637, Hutchinson was ordered to appear before the General Court.

At her trial, Hutchinson answered all the questions put to her by General Winthrop and other members of the court. Time after time, she revealed weaknesses in their arguments. They could not prove that she had broken any Puritan laws or disobeyed any religious teachings.

Then, after two days of questioning, Hutchinson made a serious mistake. She told the court that God spoke directly to her, "By the voice of His own spirit to my soul." Members of the court were shocked. Puritans believed that God spoke only through the Bible, not directly to individuals. The court declared that Hutchinson was "deluded by the Devil" and ordered her out of the colony.

In 1638, Hutchinson, along with her family and some friends, went to Rhode Island. The Puritan leaders had won their case. For later Americans, however, Hutchinson became an important symbol of the struggle for religious freedom.

*In 1763, Jewish settlers in Rhode Island built Touro Synagogue, the first Jewish house of worship in North America. It still stands today.

Biography **Anne Hutchinson**

Anne Hutchinson was the respectable wife of a wealthy Boston merchant. She worked as a midwife, helping to deliver babies, and had 14 children of her own. When she questioned the authority of Puritan ministers, though, she was banished from the colony. Although Puritan leaders denounced her "bold spirit," today she is admired for her brave stand. ★ **How did Anne Hutchinson anger Puritan officials?**

Conflict With Native Americans

From Massachusetts Bay, settlers fanned out across New England. Some built trading and fishing villages along the coast north of

Reading Actively

During Reading Have students note the statement on the facing page that Roger Williams "believed in religious toleration." Ask students to find evidence to support this statement as they read the section.

Biography

ANSWER

She discussed and even criticized the minister's sermons; she questioned the teachings of the male religious leaders.

★ Activity ★

Linking Past and Present

Locating colonial landmarks Indians later killed Anne Hutchinson and her family near present-day Pelham Bay Park in the Bronx, New York. The Hutchinson River Parkway is named after her. Have students use maps of states in the Northeast to list the places and geographic features that may date back to colonial times, then research to confirm. (*average*) ELL

Technology

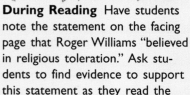

AmericanHeritage® History of the United States CD-ROM

• History Makers: Anne Hutchinson (*average*)

Viewing History ANSWER

It helped New England become a center of shipbuilding. The many fish and whales in New England's coastal waters also led to the growth of the whaling industry.

Writing Actively

After Reading Ask students to write two or three main ideas for this section before having them read Sum It Up at the end of the chapter. Then have them compare their main ideas with those in Sum It Up for Section 1.

Viewing History Colonial Boston

This engraving shows a street near Boston harbor in the 1660s. By this time, fishing was already a vital part of the New England economy. The cod was so important that it even appeared in home decoration. ★ **Identify two other ways the sea played an important role in the economy of New England.**

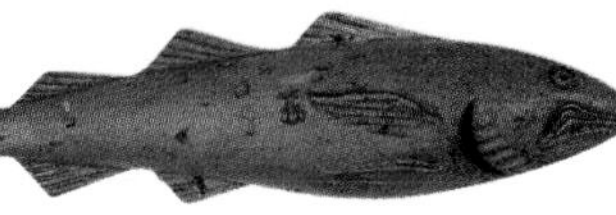

Wooden cod from a Massachusetts home

Boston. In 1680, the king made these coastal settlements into a separate colony called New Hampshire.

As more colonists settled in New England, they took over Native American lands. As a result, fighting broke out between white settlers and Indian nations of the region.

The largest conflict came in 1675. Wampanoag Indians, led by their chief, **Metacom,** attacked villages throughout New England. Other Indian groups soon allied themselves with the Wampanoags. Fighting lasted 14 months. Metacom and his allies destroyed 12 towns and killed more than 600 European settlers.

In the end, however, Metacom was captured and killed. The English sold his family and about 1,000 other Indians into slavery in the West Indies. Other Indians were forced from their homelands. Many of them died of starvation.

The pattern of English expansion followed by war between colonists and Indians was repeated throughout the colonies. It would continue for many years to come.

Life in New England

Puritans believed that people should worship and tend to local matters as a community. As a result, New England became a land of tightly knit towns and villages.

At the center of each village was the **common,** an open field where cattle grazed. Nearby stood the meetinghouse, where Puritans worshipped and held town meetings. Wooden houses with steep roofs lined the town's narrow streets.

Religion and family

The Puritans took their **Sabbath,** or holy day of rest, very seriously. On Sundays, no one was allowed to play games or visit taverns to joke, talk, and drink. The law required all citizens to attend church services, which on Sunday lasted all day.

During the 1600s, women sat on one side of the church and men cn the other. Blacks and Indians stood in a balcony at the back. Children had separate pews, where an adult watched over them. If they "sported and played," they were punished.

The Puritans taught that children were a blessing of God. The average family had seven or eight children. The healthy climate allowed New Englanders to live long lives. Many reached the age of 70. As a result, children often grew up knowing both their parents and their grandparents.

Government

At **town meetings,** settlers discussed and voted on many issues. What roads should be built? How much should the

RESOURCE DIRECTORY

Teaching Resources
Unit 1/Chapter 4
- Section 1 Quiz, p. 38

Interdisciplinary Connections
- Main Idea: American Ingenuity, p. 20

Transparencies
Fine Art
- The Sargent Family, p. D-29

★ Customized Instruction ★

Kinesthetic Learners

Building a model Have students choose one aspect of New England life described in this section and then depict it in a three-dimensional model. Students may use papier-mâché, found objects, cloth, or clay to create their scenes from colonial life. Possibilities include a Puritan village; a church service; a town meeting; and economic activities, such as maple syrup production or fishing. Encourage students to research their topic and remind them to make their work accurate. Have students write a brief explanation of their model on an index card to be placed near their work. Display finished models around the classroom. (*average*) ELL schoolmaster be paid? Town meetings gave New Englanders a chance to speak their minds. This early experience encouraged the growth of democratic ideas in New England.

Puritan laws were strict. About 15 crimes carried the death penalty. One crime punishable by death was witchcraft. In 1692, Puritans in Salem Village executed 20 men and women as witches.

Economy

New England was a difficult land for colonists. The Puritans, though, believed that daily labor honored God as much as prayer. With hard work, they built a thriving way of life.

New England's rocky soil was poor for farming. After a time, however, settlers learned to grow many Native American crops, such as Indian corn, pumpkins, squash, and beans.

Although the soil was poor, the forests were full of riches. Settlers hunted wild turkey and deer, as well as hogs that they let roam free in the woods. In the spring, colonists collected sweet sap from sugar maple trees. Settlers also cut down trees and floated them to sawmills near ports such as Boston, Massachusetts, or Portsmouth, New Hampshire. These cities grew into major shipbuilding centers.

Other New Englanders fished the coastal waters for cod and halibut. When the fish were running, fishers worked tirelessly, seldom taking time to eat or sleep. Shellfish in New England were especially large. Oysters sometimes grew to be a foot long. Lobsters stretched up to 6 feet!

In the 1600s, New Englanders also began to hunt whales. Whales supplied oil for lamps, as well as ivory and other products. In the 1700s and 1800s, whaling grew into a big business.

Decline of the Puritans

During the 1700s, the Puritan tradition declined. Fewer families left England for religious reasons. Ministers had less influence on the way colonies were governed. Even so, the Puritans stamped New England with their distinctive customs and their dream of a religious society.

★ Section 1 Review ★

Recall

1. **Locate** (a) Massachusetts, (b) Connecticut, (c) Rhode Island, (d) New Hampshire.
2. **Identify** (a) John Winthrop, (b) Puritans, (c) General Court, (d) Great Migration, (e) Thomas Hooker, (f) Fundamental Orders of Connecticut, (g) Roger Williams, (h) Anne Hutchinson, (i) Metacom.
3. **Define** (a) toleration, (b) common, (c) Sabbath, (d) town meeting.

Comprehension

4. How did the Puritans govern the Massachusetts Bay Colony?
5. Explain why each of the following left the Massachusetts Bay Colony: (a) Thomas Hooker, (b) Roger Williams, (c) Anne Hutchinson.
6. How did the New England colonists make a living?

Critical Thinking and Writing

7. **Making Generalizations** Make a generalization about the role of religion in the Massachusetts Bay Colony. Give two examples to support your generalization.
8. **Making Inferences** Why do you think the Puritan leaders felt threatened by settlers who voiced opposing views?

Activity **Writing a Letter** Go back in time! You are a young person living in Puritan New England about 1650. Write a letter to a friend in England, explaining what you like and what you do not like about life in New England.

★ Section 1 Review ★

ANSWERS

1. See map, p. 96.
2. **(a)–(b)** p. 94, **(c)–(e)** p. 95, **(f)–(g)** p. 96, **(h)** p. 97, **(i)** p. 98
3. **(a)** p. 96, **(b)–(d)** p. 98
4. Male Puritan church members elected the governor and representatives to the General Court.
5. **(a)** to set up a colony that limited the government's power; **(b)** to escape being expelled for his religious/political views; **(c)** expelled for her religious views
6. farmed, hunted, fished, and set up businesses such as shipbuilding
7. Possible answer: Religion controlled government. Examples: Only male church members could vote; opposing Puritan ways could lead to expulsion from the colony.
8. Possible answer: The colony was built on religious doctrines, so they felt that to question their authority threatened their world.

Activity

Guided Instruction
Have students review the text before writing and then make two lists about New England life: the advantages and the disadvantages.

ASSESSMENT See the rubrics in the Alternative Assessment booklet in the Teaching Resources.

Internet Activity

Salem witch trials Encourage students to research and report on the Salem witch trials. One site they might consult is www.nationalgeographic.com/feature/97/salem, which offers an interactive feature on the Salem witch hysteria. Given the changing nature of the Internet, you may wish to preview this site before sending students to it. *(average)*

Technology

Videodiscs/Videotapes
Prentice Hall United States History Video Collection™, Vol. 2, Ch. 19, "The Indian Wars," 1:45 min *(average)* ELL

Chapter 19

AmericanHeritage® History of the United States CD-ROM
- Arts and Entertainment: Books *(average)*

Section 2 The Middle Colonies

LESSON PLAN

Objectives

★ Explain why William Penn started a colony in North America.

★ Explain why the Middle Colonies were known as the Breadbasket Colonies.

★ Describe backcountry life.

1 Engage

Warm Up Have students look at a physical map of the Middle Colonies and New England. Ask: "What geographic features could make living in the Middle Colonies easier than living in New England?"

Activating Prior Knowledge Have students brainstorm to list items or ideas that they associate with New York, New Jersey, Pennsylvania, and Delaware. Record their ideas on the chalkboard.

Reading Actively

Before Reading Have students read the section headings and look at the visuals. Ask them to write a few sentences predicting what the section will be about. Then have them correct their predictions.

2 Explore

Ask students to read the section. For homework, have them do research on one of these topics: Peter Stuyvesant, patroons, Quakers, William Penn, manufacturing in

RESOURCE DIRECTORY

Teaching Resources
Lesson Planner, p. 14

Transparencies
Our Multicultural Heritage
• Ethnic Division of the Colonial Population, 1775, p. C-11

2 The Middle Colonies

As You Read

Explore These Questions
- Why did William Penn start a colony in North America?
- Why were the Middle Colonies known as the Breadbasket Colonies?
- What was life like in the backcountry?

Define
- patroon
- proprietary colony
- proprietor
- royal colony
- cash crop
- backcountry

Identify
- Peter Stuyvesant
- William Penn
- Quakers
- Pennsylvania Dutch
- Breadbasket Colonies
- Great Wagon Road

SETTING the Scene In the summer of 1744, a doctor from the colony of Maryland traveled north to Philadelphia. Doctor Hamilton was amazed at the wide variety of people he met during his stay in that city. He wrote:

> "I dined at a tavern with a very mixed company of different nations and religions. There were Scots, English, Dutch, Germans, and Irish. There were Roman Catholics, Church [of England] men, Presbyterians, Quakers, . . . Moravians, . . . and one Jew."

By 1700, England had four colonies in the region directly south of New England. These colonies became known as the Middle Colonies because they were located between New England and the Southern Colonies. As Doctor Hamilton observed, the Middle Colonies had a much greater mix of people than either New England or the Southern Colonies.

New Netherland Becomes New York

As you read, the Dutch set up the colony of New Netherland along the Hudson River. In the colony's early years, settlers traded with Indians for furs and built the settlement of New Amsterdam into a thriving port.

To encourage farming in New Netherland, Dutch officials granted large parcels of land to a few rich families. A single land grant could stretch for miles. Indeed, one grant was as big as Rhode Island! Owners of these huge estates were called **patroons.** In return for the grant, each patroon promised to settle at least 50 European farm families on the land. Few farmers wanted to work for the patroons, however. Patroons had great power and could charge whatever rents they pleased.

Most settlers lived in the trading center of New Amsterdam. They came from all over Europe. Many were attracted by the chance to practice their religion freely.

Dutch colonists were mainly Protestants who belonged to the Dutch Reformed Church. Still, they permitted members of other religions—including Roman Catholics, French Protestants, and Jews—to buy land. "People do not seem concerned what religion their neighbor is," wrote a shocked visitor from Virginia. "Indeed, they do not seem to care if he has any religion at all."

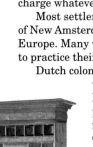

Dutch-style writing desk from colonial New York

By 1664, the rivalry between England and the Netherlands for trade and colonies was at its height. In August of that year, English

★ Background ★
Linking Past and Present

Colonial gold mine The Episcopal Parish of Trinity Church, at the western end of Wall Street in New York City, is among the wealthiest parishes in the world. Established in 1697 by royal charter, Trinity was given an income, ownership of any whales that washed up in New York Province, and—in 1705—a nearby area known as Queen Anne's farm. When New York began to boom in the mid-1800s, the increase in property values allowed Trinity to prosper through rents. Today the land is worth billions. The church has used its wealth to endow over 1,600 institutions and gives to hundreds of worthy causes. Trinity, although legally exempt, voluntarily pays real estate taxes on its income-producing properties as a contribution to the city.

warships entered New Amsterdam's harbor. **Peter Stuyvesant** (STI vuh sehnt), the governor of New Netherland, swore to defend the city. However, he had few weapons and little gunpowder. Also, Stuyvesant had made himself so unpopular with his harsh rule and heavy taxes that the colonists refused to help him. In the end, he surrendered without firing a shot.

King Charles II of England then gave New Netherland to his brother, the Duke of York. He renamed the colony New York in the duke's honor.

New Jersey

At the time of the English takeover, New York stretched as far south as the Delaware River. The Duke of York realized that it was too big to govern easily. He gave some of the land to friends, Lord Berkeley and Sir George Carteret. They set up a proprietary (proh PRI uh tuhr ee) colony, which they called New Jersey.

In setting up a **proprietary colony,** the king gave land to one or more people. These **proprietors** were free to divide the land and rent it to others. They made laws for the colony but had to respect the rights of colonists under English law.

Like New York, New Jersey attracted people from many lands. English Puritans mingled with French Protestants, Scots, Irish, Swedes, and Finns.

In 1702, New Jersey became a **royal colony,** that is, a colony under control of the English crown. The colony's charter protected religious freedom and the rights of an assembly that voted on local matters.

Pennsylvania

South of New Jersey, **William Penn** founded the colony of Pennsylvania in 1682. Penn came from a wealthy English family. King Charles II was a personal friend. At age 22, however, Penn shocked family and friends by joining the **Quakers,** one of the most despised religious groups in England.

The Quakers

Like Pilgrims and Puritans, Quakers were Protestant reformers. Their reforms went further than those of other groups, however. Quakers believed that all people—men and women, nobles and commoners—were equal in God's sight. They allowed women to preach in public and refused to bow or remove their hats in the presence of the nobility. Quakers spoke out against war and refused to serve in the army.

To most English people, Quaker beliefs seemed wicked. In both England and New England, Quakers were arrested, fined, or even hanged for their ideas. Penn became convinced that the Quakers must leave England. He turned to the king for help.

Charles II made Penn proprietor of a large tract of land in North America. The king named the new colony Pennsylvania, or Penn's woodlands.

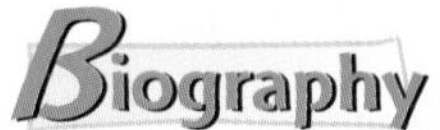

Peter Stuyvesant

Peter Stuyvesant lost a leg fighting in the Caribbean. He fought just as hard when he became governor of New Netherland. Given almost total power, he imposed heavy taxes and punished lawbreakers with public whippings. When colonists demanded a voice in government, he replied that his authority came "from God." Still, Stuyvesant was powerless to stop England from taking over the colony. ★ **What are some advantages and disadvantages of having a strong ruler like Stuyvesant?**

the Middle Colonies, or relations with Indians in the Middle Colonies.

3 Teach

Ask students to create flags, coins, or seals for one Middle Colony. Suggest they use important events, products, or typical livelihoods as design symbols. Display student work and give students time to explain the symbols they used.

4 Assess

To close the lesson, have students complete the section review. Or have them write one effect for each cause: **(a)** England and the Netherlands compete for power. *(war between them in Europe; England seizes New Netherland)* **(b)** The Duke of York thinks that New York is too big to govern easily. *(He gives some land to friends, who set up the colony of New Jersey.)* **(c)** Penn sends pamphlets about his colony to Europe. *(Settlers arrive from England, Scotland, Wales, the Netherlands, France, and Germany.)* **(d)** Farms and homes spread far apart in the Middle Colonies. *(Counties, not villages, become centers of local government.)*

★ ★ ★ ★ ★ ★ ★ ★ ★ ★ ★ ★ ★ ★ ★ ★ ★

Biography ANSWER

Possible answers: Advantages: Such rulers can inspire others and act quickly when needed. Disadvantages: Such rulers can refuse to compromise or can ignore people's rights.

★ *Background* ★ Religion and Ethics

Defenseless The Quaker commitment to nonviolence eventually became a problem for Pennsylvania. Because they controlled the government, Quakers refused to raise an army—even for defense. After Indian attacks on western Pennsylvania's colonists in 1755 flooded eastern Pennsylvania towns with refugees, non-Quakers forced the Quakers to relinquish government control.

Technology

AmericanHeritage® History of the United States CD-ROM
- History Makers: William Penn (*average*)

Reading Actively

During Reading Have students refer to the items they had associated with the Middle Colonies when activating prior knowledge at the beginning of the section. As they read, students should look for evidence of these items.

Geography Skills

ANSWERS

1. Review locations with students. **2.** by river; by land along the Great Wagon Road **3.** It had access to the ocean and was a starting point for the Great Wagon Road to the backcountry.

RESOURCE DIRECTORY

Teaching Resources
Document-Based Discovery
• Origins, pp. 2–5

Transparencies
Geography and History
• Middle Atlantic States, p. I-61

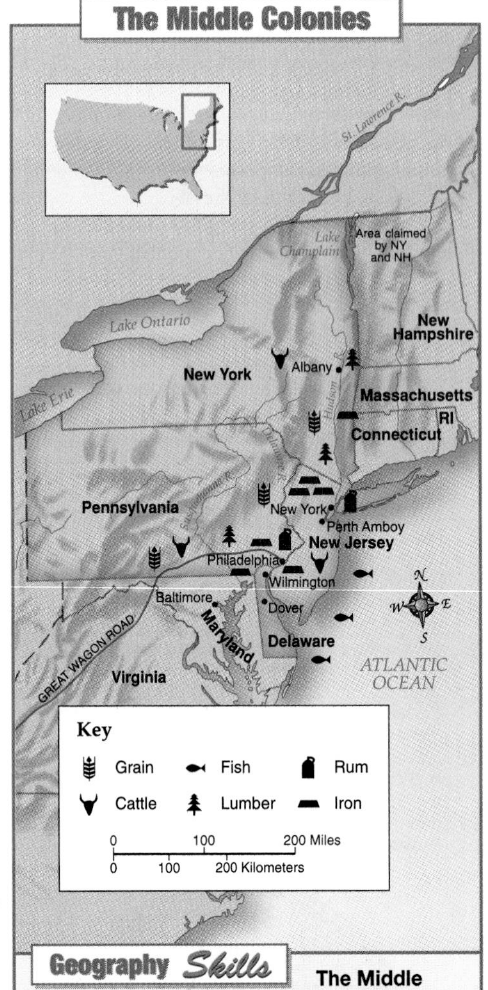

Geography Skills The Middle Colonies were located to the south and west of New England and north of the Southern Colonies.

1. **Location** On the map, locate: **(a)** New York, **(b)** New Jersey, **(c)** Pennsylvania, **(d)** Delaware, **(e)** Hudson River, **(f)** Philadelphia, **(g)** Great Wagon Road.
2. **Movement** Identify two ways settlers could have traveled inland from the Atlantic Coast.
3. **Critical Thinking** Based on the map, why do you think Philadelphia would become a major trading center?

A policy of fairness

Penn thought of his colony as a "holy experiment." He wanted it to be a model of religious freedom, peace, and Christian living. Protestants, Catholics, and Jews went to Pennsylvania to escape persecution. Later, English officials forced Penn to turn away Catholic and Jewish settlers.

Penn's Quaker beliefs led him to speak out for fair treatment of Native Americans. Penn believed that the land belonged to the Indians. He said that settlers should pay for the land. Native Americans respected Penn for this policy. As a result, colonists in Pennsylvania enjoyed many years of peace with their Indian neighbors. One settler later remarked:

> "And as [Penn] treated the Indians with extraordinary humanity, they became very civil and loving to us. . . . As in other countries, the Indians were [angered] by hard treatment, which hath been the [cause] of much bloodshed, so the [opposite] treatment here hath produced love and affection."

The colony grows

Penn sent pamphlets describing his colony all over Europe. Soon, settlers from England, Scotland, Wales, the Netherlands, France, and Germany began to cross the Atlantic Ocean to Pennsylvania.

Among the new arrivals were large numbers of German-speaking Protestants. They became known as **Pennsylvania Dutch** because people could not pronounce the word Deutsch (DOICH), which means German.

Penn carefully planned a capital city along the Delaware River. He named it Philadelphia, a Greek word meaning "brotherly love." Philadelphia grew quickly. By 1710, a visitor wrote that it was "the most noble, large, and well-built city I have seen."

Delaware

For a time, Pennsylvania included some lands along the lower Delaware River. The region was known as Pennsylvania's Lower Counties.

★ Customized Instruction ★

English Language Learners

Creating an illustrated dictionary Visual images may help English language learners grasp difficult or unfamiliar words and concepts. Have ELL students create an illustrated dictionary of social studies terms that they can add to throughout the year. Have them write the words listed in the Define columns plus these additional terms: *Quaker, pamphlet, grain, iron ore.* Students can use descriptions and context clues in the text as well as reference books to prepare illustrated definitions. Encourage students to write the definition in their native language as well as in English. (*average*) ELL T

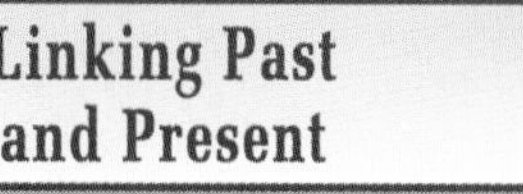

Linking Past and Present

Past

Present

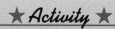

A Simple Country Life

Today, in certain parts of Pennsylvania, horses and buggies are still a common sight, as they were in colonial days. The Amish, a Christian sect, came to Pennsylvania in the 1700s. Today, Amish families farm the land, use horses, and dress as plainly as their ancestors did.
★ **Why do you think the Amish chose Pennsylvania as their home?**

Settlers in the Lower Counties did not want to send delegates to a faraway assembly in Philadelphia. In 1701, Penn allowed them to elect their own assembly. Later, the Lower Counties broke away to form the colony of Delaware.

Life in the Middle Colonies

Farmers found more favorable conditions in the Middle Colonies than in New England. The broad Hudson and Delaware river valleys were rich and fertile. Winters were milder than in New England, and the growing season lasted longer.

A thriving economy

On such promising land, farmers in the Middle Colonies produced surpluses of wheat, barley, and rye. These were **cash crops,** or crops that are sold for money at market. In fact, the Middle Colonies exported so much grain that they became known as the **Breadbasket Colonies.**

Farmers of the Middle Colonies also raised herds of cattle and pigs. Every year, they sent tons of beef, pork, and butter to the ports of New York and Philadelphia. From there, the goods went by ship to New England and the South or to the West Indies, England, and other parts of Europe.

Encouraged by William Penn, skilled German craftsworkers set up shop in Pennsylvania. In time, the colony became a center of manufacturing and crafts. One visitor reported that workshops turned out "hardware, clocks, watches, locks, guns, flints, glass, stoneware, nails, [and] paper."

Settlers in the Delaware River valley profited from the region's rich deposits of iron ore. Heating the ore in furnaces, they purified it and then hammered it into nails, tools, and parts for guns.

Middle Colony homes

Farms in the Middle Colonies were generally larger than those in New England.

Linking Past and Present

ANSWER Pennsylvania was tolerant of religious differences.

★ Activity ★

Connections With Mathematics

Calculating distance Have students calculate distances between places in the Middle Colonies—for example, between the Delaware border and Philadelphia or between two cities. Ask: "How long do you think it would take to travel each distance by the various means available to people in the 1700s?" (*average*) T

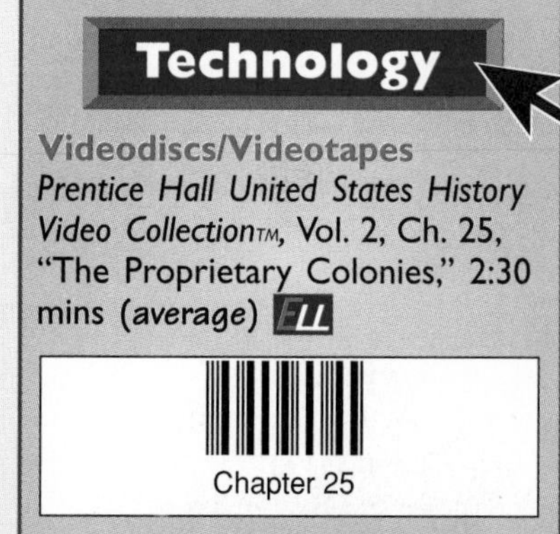

PRACTICE the Skill

ANSWERS

1. (a) Ethnic Division of Colonial Population, 1775 **(b)** the colonial population in 1775

2. (a) English, Swedish, French, Dutch, Scottish, German, Scotch-Irish, and African **(b)** No, there is a group labeled "Other."

3. (a) English **(b)** 0.6% **(c)** African

APPLY the Skill

Write the months of the year and the total number of students in the class on the chalkboard. Call out the name of each month and have students raise their hands if they were born in that month. Beside each month, tally the numbers and then have student volunteers compute each month's percentage of the whole. Have other volunteers work together to create a pie chart of the data.

ASSESSMENT See the rubrics in the Alternative Assessment booklet in the Teaching Resources.

Writing Actively

After Reading Ask students to use the information in the map in this section as the basis for a short essay on economic activities in the Middle Colonies.

RESOURCE DIRECTORY

Teaching Resources
Unit 1/Chapter 4
- Practice Your Skills: Reading a Pie Graph, p. 33
- Section 2 Quiz, p. 39

Skills FOR LIFE

Critical Thinking | Managing Information | Communication | Maps, Charts, and Graphs

Reading a Pie Graph

How Will I Use This Skill?

When you read textbooks, newspapers, or magazines, you will often find important statistics presented as part of a pie graph. A pie graph is in the shape of a circle that represents 100% of the group you are examining. Pie graphs present statistics in wedges, like pieces of a pie. The wedges represent percentages of the whole, helping you better compare the groups.

LEARN the Skill

You can learn to understand pie graphs by using the steps below.

1. Identify the topic of the pie graph. Remember that the circle represents 100% of the group you are examining.
2. Identify which groups are represented by the various wedges of the pie. Some groups which are few in number or not easily identified may be shown as "others."
3. Compare the sizes of the various groups. The largest wedge will correspond to the largest group.

PRACTICE the Skill

Use the steps below to read the pie graph. The graph does not include Indians.

1. (a) What is the topic of this graph? (b) What entire group does the circle as a whole represent?
2. (a) List the population groups represented by the wedges. (b) Are all groups identified individually on the graph?

Ethnic Division of Colonial Population, 1775

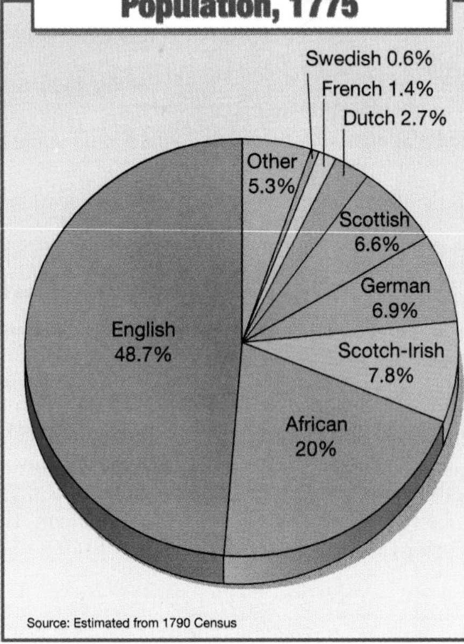

Source: Estimated from 1790 Census

3. (a) Which group made up the largest percentage of the colonial population? (b) What percentage of the population had Swedish roots? (c) What was the largest non-European group shown here?

APPLY the Skill

Take a poll to determine in which month each member of your class was born. Turn the numbers into percentages and show the information on a pie graph. To figure out percentages, divide the number in each group by the total number of the class.

★ Activity ★

Linking Past and Present

Comparing Have students compare the challenges faced by immigrants to the United States today and by those who came to the English colonies in the 1600s and early 1700s. Consider such questions as: "What resources did immigrants have to help them get started?" "What opportunities existed for economic improvement?" "How were they received by native-born Americans?" *(average)* ELL

Because houses tended to be far apart in the Middle Colonies, towns were less important. Counties, rather than villages, became centers of local government.

The different groups who settled the Middle Colonies had their own favorite ways of building. Swedish settlers introduced log cabins to the Americas. The Dutch used red bricks to build narrow, high-walled houses. German settlers developed a wood-burning stove that heated a home better than a fireplace, which let blasts of cold air leak down the chimney.

The Backcountry

In the 1700s, thousands of German and Scotch-Irish settlers arrived in Philadelphia. From there, they traveled west into the **backcountry,** the area of land along the eastern slopes of the Appalachian Mountains. Settlers followed an old Iroquois trail that became known as the **Great Wagon Road.**

To farm the backcountry, settlers had to clear thick forests. From Indians, settlers learned how to use knots from pine trees as candles to light their homes. They made wooden dishes from logs, gathered honey from hollows in trees, and hunted wild animals for food. German gunsmiths developed a lightweight rifle for use in forests. Sharpshooters boasted that the "Pennsylvania rifle" could hit a rattlesnake between the eyes at 100 yards.

Many of the settlers who arrived in the backcountry moved onto Indian lands. "The Indians . . . are alarmed at the swarm of strangers," one Pennsylvania official reported. "We are afraid of a [fight] between them for the [colonists] are very rough to them." On more than one occasion, disputes between settlers and Indians resulted in violence.

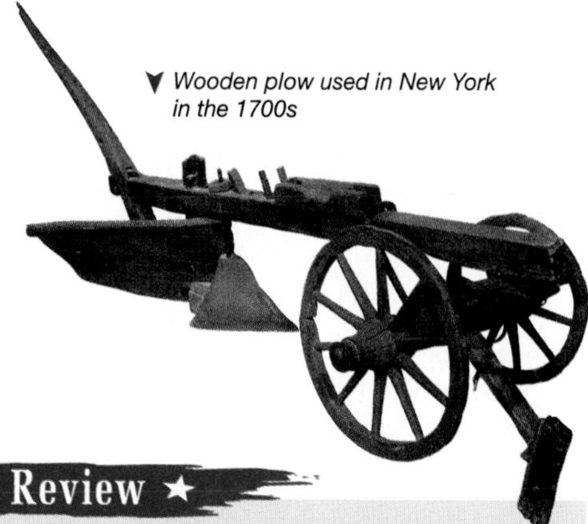

Wooden plow used in New York in the 1700s

★ Section 2 Review ★

Recall

1. **Locate** **(a)** New York, **(b)** New Jersey, **(c)** Pennsylvania, **(d)** Philadelphia, **(e)** Delaware.
2. **Identify** **(a)** Peter Stuyvesant, **(b)** William Penn, **(c)** Quakers, **(d)** Pennsylvania Dutch, **(e)** Breadbasket Colonies, **(f)** Great Wagon Road.
3. **Define** **(a)** patroon, **(b)** proprietary colony, **(c)** proprietor, **(d)** royal colony, **(e)** cash crop, **(f)** backcountry.

Comprehension

4. What policies did William Penn follow in the Pennsylvania colony?
5. How did the land and climate help Middle Colonies farmers to prosper?
6. What did settlers have to do in order to farm the backcountry?

Critical Thinking and Writing

7. **Comparing** **(a)** How was Penn's "holy experiment" like the Puritan idea of a "city upon a hill"? **(b)** How was it different?
8. **Understanding Causes and Effects** Why do you think many settlers moved westward into the backcountry?

★ ★

Activity **Creating a Pamphlet** Did you ever think about a career in advertising? Make up a pamphlet advertising the settlement of Pennsylvania like the ones that Penn sent to countries all over Europe. Encourage people to move to Pennsylvania by describing its economy and society.

★ Background ★

Recent Scholarship

Who, why, where, when, what? In his book *Immigration,* L. Edward Purcell explores trends in American immigration from the 1600s to the present. He delves into who came and why, where and when they settled, what they brought, and what they found. Purcell examines both the legal and social aspects of immigration and how immigrants have shaped this nation.

★ Section 2 Review ★

ANSWERS

1. See map, p. 102.
2. **(a)–(c)** p. 101, **(d)** p. 102, **(e)** p. 103, **(f)** p. 105
3. **(a)** p. 100, **(b)–(d)** p. 101, **(e)** p. 103, **(f)** p. 105
4. tolerated religious diversity, said colonists should pay the Indians for land
5. Fertile land in the Hudson and Delaware river valleys and a relatively mild climate helped farmers produce cash crops.
6. clear thick forests
7. **(a)** Possible answer: Each was meant to be a model. **(b)** Penn supported tolerance and religious freedom, whereas the Puritans wanted a refuge for themselves, not tolerance for others.
8. Possible answers: cheap land; independence

Activity

Guided Instruction
Remind students that the pamphlet should be based on facts from the text, but encourage them to make the description positive and convincing.

ASSESSMENT See the rubrics in the Alternative Assessment booklet in the Teaching Resources.

The Southern Colonies

Explore These Questions
- Why were the Southern Colonies founded?
- What two ways of life developed in the Southern Colonies?
- Why did slavery become important in the South?

Define
- indigo
- debtor
- buffer
- plantation
- slave code
- racism

Identify
- Mason-Dixon Line
- Lord Baltimore
- Act of Toleration
- Bacon's Rebellion
- James Oglethorpe
- Mary Musgrove
- Tidewater

SETTING the Scene In 1763, two English mathematicians, Charles Mason and Jeremiah Dixon, began to survey the 244-mile boundary between Pennsylvania and Maryland. The boundary had been in dispute since 1681.

For four years, Mason and Dixon carefully laid stone markers on the border between the two colonies. The sides of the markers facing Pennsylvania were inscribed with the letter *P*. The sides facing Maryland were inscribed with the letter *M*. In 1767, the two men completed the **Mason-Dixon Line.**

The Mason-Dixon Line was more than just the boundary between Pennsylvania and Maryland. It also divided the Middle Colonies from the Southern Colonies. Below the Mason-Dixon Line, the Southern Colonies developed a way of life different in many ways from that of the other English colonies.

Maryland

In 1632, Sir George Calvert persuaded King Charles I to grant him land for a colony in the Americas. Calvert had ruined his career in Protestant England by becoming a Roman Catholic. Now, he planned to build a colony where Catholics could practice their religion freely. He named the colony Maryland in honor of Queen Henrietta Maria, the king's wife.

Calvert died before his colony could get underway. His son Cecil, **Lord Baltimore,** pushed on with the project.

Settling the colony

In the spring of 1634, 200 colonists landed along the upper Chesapeake Bay, across from England's first southern colony, Virginia. The land was rich and beautiful. In the words of one settler:

> "The soil is dark and soft, a foot in thickness, and rests upon a rich and red clay. Every where there are very high trees.... An abundance of springs afford water.... There is an [endless] number of birds.... There is [nothing] wanting to the region."

Maryland was truly a land of plenty. Chesapeake Bay was full of fish, oysters, and crabs. Across the bay, Virginians were already growing tobacco for profit. Maryland's new settlers hoped to do the same.

Remembering the early problems at Jamestown, the newcomers avoided the swampy lowlands. They built their first town, St. Mary's, in a healthful location.

As proprietor of the colony, Lord Baltimore appointed a governor and a council of advisers. He gave colonists a role in government by creating an elected assembly. Eager to attract settlers to Maryland, Lord Baltimore made generous land grants to anyone who brought over servants, women, and children.

A few women took advantage of Lord Baltimore's offer of land. Two sisters, Margaret and Mary Brent, arrived in Maryland in

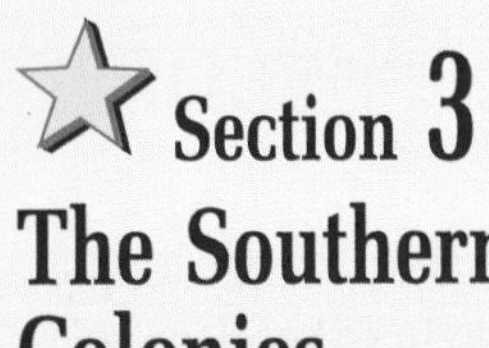

Section 3 The Southern Colonies

LESSON PLAN

Objectives

★ Explain why the Southern Colonies were founded.

★ Describe the two ways of life that developed in the Southern Colonies.

★ Explain why slavery became important in the South.

1 Engage

Warm Up Write the word *tobacco* on the chalkboard. Tell students that while many people today consider tobacco undesirable, settlers in the Southern Colonies, unaware of its health risks, considered it a highly desirable, profitable crop.

Activating Prior Knowledge Have students who have visited the South (or another U.S. region if your school is in the South) share their opinions about how the South differs from the other regions of the United States.

Reading Actively

Before Reading Have students use the main headings as the topics of an outline. As they read, have them record 2–3 important subtopics for each main topic.

2 Explore

Have students read the section. Point out that Bacon's Rebellion encouraged planters to rely more

RESOURCE DIRECTORY

Teaching Resources
Lesson Planner, p. 15
Interdisciplinary Connections
• Main Idea: American Ingenuity, p. 21

Transparencies
Geography and History
• Southeastern States, p. I-65

Skills For LIFE MINI LESSON

MAPS, CHARTS, AND GRAPHS
Using Thematic Maps

1. Introduce the skill by explaining that thematic maps have a special purpose, indicated by the map's title. Explain that colors and symbols are very important on this type of map.
2. Help students practice the skill by studying the map on the facing page, paying close attention to all the information in the key.
3. Help students apply the skill by asking: "What is the purpose of this map?" *(to show economic activities in the Southern Colonies)* "How do you know?" *(map title and key)* "What symbol represents lumber-producing areas?" *(a tree)* "In which colonies was indigo grown?" *(Georgia, the Carolinas)* "Which two colonies had the most varied economies?" *(North Carolina, South Carolina)* ELL T

1638 with nine male servants. In time, they set up two plantations of 1,000 acres each. Later, Margaret Brent helped prevent a rebellion among the governor's soldiers. The Maryland assembly praised her efforts, saying that "the colony's safety at any time [was better] in her hands than in any man's."

Religious toleration

To ensure Maryland's continued growth, Lord Baltimore welcomed Protestants as well as Catholics to the colony.

Later, Lord Baltimore came to fear that Protestants might try to deprive Catholics of their right to worship freely. In 1649, he asked the assembly to pass an **Act of Toleration.** The act provided religious freedom for all Christians. As in many colonies, this freedom did not extend to Jews.

Bacon's Rebellion

Meanwhile, settlers continued to arrive in Virginia, lured by the promise of profits from tobacco. Wealthy planters, however, controlled the best lands near the coast. Newcomers had to push farther inland, onto Indian lands.

As in New England, conflict over land led to fighting between settlers and Indians. After several bloody clashes, settlers called on the governor to take action against Native Americans. The governor refused. He was unwilling to act, in part because he profited from his own fur trade with Indians. Frontier settlers were furious.

Finally, in 1676, Nathaniel Bacon, an ambitious young planter, organized angry men and women on the frontier. He raided Native American villages. Then, he led his followers to Jamestown and burned the capital.

The uprising, known as **Bacon's Rebellion,** lasted only a short time. When Bacon died suddenly, the revolt fell apart. The governor hanged 23 of Bacon's followers. Still, he could not stop English settlers from moving onto Indian lands along the frontier.

The Carolinas

South of Virginia and Maryland, English colonists settled in a region which they called

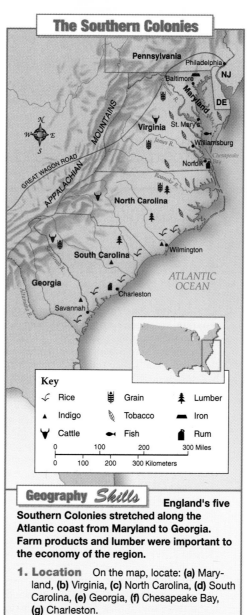

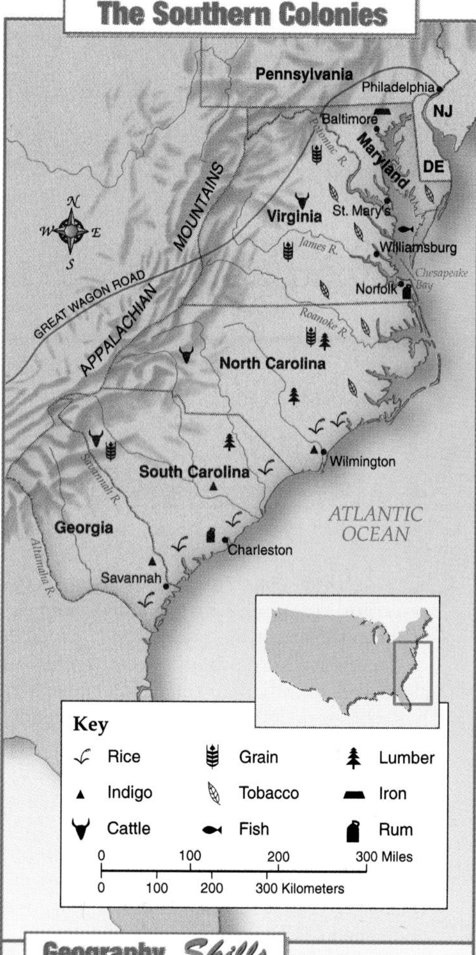

Geography Skills England's five Southern Colonies stretched along the Atlantic coast from Maryland to Georgia. Farm products and lumber were important to the economy of the region.

1. **Location** On the map, locate: **(a)** Maryland, **(b)** Virginia, **(c)** North Carolina, **(d)** South Carolina, **(e)** Georgia, **(f)** Chesapeake Bay, **(g)** Charleston.
2. **Place** Describe the area where cattle herding took place.
3. **Critical Thinking** Compare this map to the maps on pages 96 and 102. **(a)** What crops were grown only in the Southern Colonies? **(b)** Why do you think such products were not grown farther north?

on slave labor than on white European servants. The rebellion showed that former servants who moved to the backcountry could become a dangerous force. Suggest that students explore other reasons for slavery's important role in the southern economy.

3 Teach

Tell students that a fictional New England newspaper has published an article entitled "Why the Southern Colonies Will Not Survive." Have them write letters to the editor that agree or disagree with this viewpoint and that justify their opinion. Have volunteers read their letters aloud in class.

4 Assess

To close the lesson, have students complete the section review. Or have them create a "Race to Colonize" board game. The game pieces can be thick cardboard cut into the shape of each Southern Colony. A path can lead from start to finish, with directions along the way such as "Jamestown is burned by rebellious settlers—Lose one turn." Encourage students to use information from the section.

★ ★ ★ ★ ★ ★ ★ ★ ★ ★ ★ ★ ★ ★ ★ ★ ★

Geography Skills

ANSWERS

1. Review locations with students.
2. inland, along the eastern edges of the Appalachian Mountains
3. (a) rice, indigo, tobacco **(b)** They probably required a warmer climate or a longer growing season.

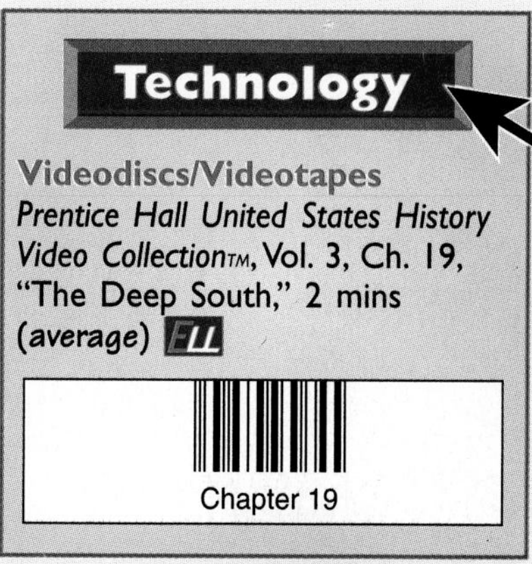

Technology
Videodiscs/Videotapes
Prentice Hall United States History Video Collection™, Vol. 3, Ch. 19, "The Deep South," 2 mins (average) ELL
Chapter 19

ANSWER

The picture shows that many trees had to be cleared before Savannah could be built.

Reading Actively

During Reading Ask students to read to find out why the Southern Colonies were settled. Then have them write a paragraph summarizing the reasons.

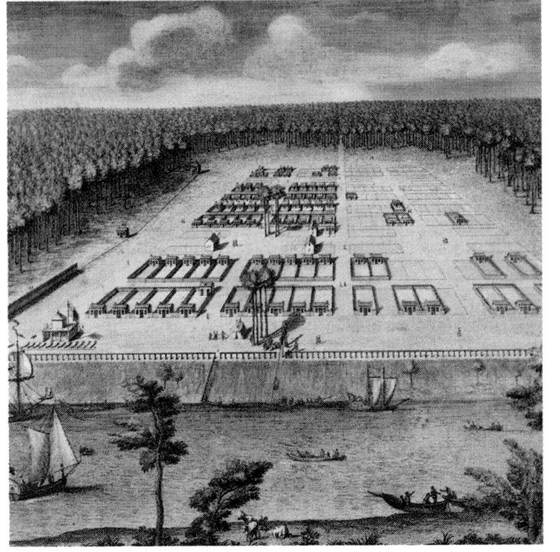

Viewing History **Settling Georgia**

This engraving from 1734 is the earliest known picture of Savannah, Georgia. English colonists carved the settlement out of a forest on the banks of the Savannah River. ★ **Based on this picture, how can you tell that building Savannah was hard work?**

the Carolinas. Settlement took place in two separate areas, one in the north and the other in the south.

In the northern part of the Carolinas, settlers were mostly poor tobacco farmers who had drifted south from Virginia. They tended to have small farms.

Farther south, a group of eight English nobles set up a larger colony. As proprietors, they received a grant of land from King Charles II in 1663. The largest settlement, Charles Town, grew up where the Ashley and Cooper rivers met. Later, Charles Town was shortened to Charleston.

Most early settlers in Charleston were English people who had been living in Barbados, a British colony in the Caribbean. Later, other immigrants arrived, including Germans, Swiss, French Protestants, and Spanish Jews.

Around 1685, a few planters discovered that rice grew well in the swampy lowlands along the coast. Before long, Carolina rice was a valuable crop traded around the world. Settlers in southern Carolina later learned to raise **indigo,** a plant used to make a valuable blue dye.

Carolina planters needed large numbers of workers to grow rice. At first, they tried to enslave local Indians. Many Indians died of disease or mistreatment, however. Others escaped into the forests. Planters then turned to slaves from Africa. By 1700, the majority of people coming to Charleston were African men and women brought there against their will.

The northern area of Carolina had fewer slaves. Differences between the two areas led to division of the colony into North Carolina and South Carolina in 1712.

Georgia

The last of England's 13 colonies was carved out of the southern part of South Carolina. **James Oglethorpe,** a respected English soldier and energetic reformer, founded Georgia in 1732. He wanted the new colony to be a place where **debtors,** or people who owed money they could not pay back, could make a new start.

A haven for debtors

Under English law, the government could imprison debtors until they paid what they owed. If they ever got out of jail, debtors often had no money and no place to live. Oglethorpe offered to pay for debtors and other poor people to travel to Georgia. "In America," he said, "there are enough fertile lands to feed all the poor of England."

In 1733, Oglethorpe and 120 colonists built the colony's first settlement at Savan-

Connections With Geography

Indigo was first grown in South Carolina by 17-year-old Eliza Lucas. She ran the family plantation while her father, an army colonel, served overseas. While away, Colonel Lucas sent his daughter seeds from all over the world. Eliza Lucas found that the West Indian indigo plant grew well in land that was bad for planting rice.

★ Background ★

Did You Know?

Influences of geography The south Atlantic coast was a perfect haven for pirates. Shifting sandbars and shallow sounds provided effective hiding places for pirate ships.

The most famous pirate of the early 1700s was Edward Teach, more popularly known as Blackbeard. Blackbeard captured many trading ships in the waters off South Carolina, but when he ventured up the coast of Virginia, he ran into trouble. In November 1718, Virginians set off in two armed ships to find Blackbeard and get rid of him once and for all. Lieutenant Robert Maynard's ship finally trapped the pirate, killing him and many of his crew. Maynard and his men tied Blackbeard's head to the bow of their ship and sailed home in triumph. T

RESOURCE DIRECTORY

Teaching Resources

Interdisciplinary Connections

- Main Idea: American Ingenuity, p. 24

nah, above the Savannah River. Oglethorpe set strict rules for the colony. Farms could be no bigger than 500 acres, and slavery was forbidden.

At first, Georgia grew slowly. Later, however, Oglethorpe changed the rules to allow large plantations and slave labor. After that, the colony grew more quickly.

Rivalry with Spain

England hoped that Georgia would act as a buffer between the Carolinas and Spanish Florida. A **buffer** is a land located between two larger lands that reduces the possibility of conflict between them. Spain and England both claimed the land between South Carolina and Florida. Spain, aided by Creek allies, tried to force the English out. Oglethorpe and the Georgians held their ground.

A woman known as **Mary Musgrove** greatly helped Oglethorpe during this time. The daughter of a Creek mother and an English father, Musgrove spoke both Creek and English. She helped to keep peace between the Creeks and the settlers in Georgia. Musgrove's efforts did much to allow the colony of Georgia to develop in peace.

Two Ways of Life

Today, we often think of the colonial South as a land where wealthy planters lived in elegant homes, with large numbers of enslaved African Americans toiling in the fields. In fact, this picture is only partly true. As the Southern colonies grew, two distinct and different ways of life emerged—one along the Atlantic coast and another in the backcountry.

Tidewater plantations

The Southern Colonies enjoyed warmer weather and a longer growing season than the colonies to the north. Virginia, Maryland, and parts of North Carolina all became major tobacco-growing areas. Settlers in South Carolina and Georgia raised rice and indigo.

Colonists soon found that it was most profitable to raise tobacco and rice on large plantations. As you recall, a **plantation** is a large estate farmed by many workers. On these southern plantations, anywhere from 20 to 100 slaves did most of the work. Most slaves worked in the fields. Some were skilled workers, such as carpenters, barrel

Viewing History **Two Ways of Life**

These pictures from the 1700s show two vastly different ways of life in the Southern Colonies. At left, wealthy planters enjoy a life of elegant leisure. At right, a woman in the backcountry fetches water for her daily chores. ★ **Who do you think fetched the water for the wealthy planters shown here?**

ANSWER

enslaved African Americans

★ *Background* ★

Our Diverse Nation

Sorrowful journey The voyage of ships bringing enslaved Africans to the Americas became known as the Middle Passage. The trip was so named because it fell between the First Passage, which was the captives' journey from the interior of Africa to the coast, and the Third Passage, which was the heartbreaking sale of enslaved Africans to owners in the Americas.

ANSWER

Sierra-Leon; as slaves, possibly in or around Charlestown

Writing Actively

After Reading Ask students to write two or three main ideas for this section before having them read Sum It Up at the end of the chapter. Then have them compare their main ideas with those for Section 3 in Sum It Up.

Viewing History: Slavery in the South

As the poster shows, colonial law permitted Africans to be bought and sold as property. The growth of slavery allowed southern colonists to work large plantations. The painting at right shows rows of slave cabins on a plantation in the Southern Colonies. ★ **Where did the slaves advertised on the poster come from? Where would they end up?**

makers, or blacksmiths. Still other slaves worked in the main house as cooks, servants, or housekeepers.

The earliest plantations were located along rivers and creeks of the coastal plain. Because the land was washed by ocean tides, the region was known as the **Tidewater.** The Tidewater's gentle slopes and rivers offered rich farmland for plantations.

Farther inland, planters settled along rivers. Rivers provided an easy way to move goods to market. Planters loaded crops onto ships bound for the West Indies and Europe. On the return trip, the ships carried English manufactured goods and other luxuries for planters and their families.

Most Tidewater plantations had their own docks, and merchant ships picked up crops and delivered goods directly to them. For this reason, few large seaport cities developed in the Southern Colonies.

Only a small percentage of white southerners owned large plantations. Yet, planters set the style of life in the South. Life centered around the Great House, where the planter's family lived. The grandest homes had elegant quarters for the family, a parlor for visitors, a dining room, and guest bedrooms.

In the growing season, planters decided which fields to plant, what crops to grow, and when to harvest the crops and take them to market. Planters' wives kept the household running smoothly. They directed house slaves and made sure daily tasks were done, such as milking cows.

The backcountry South

West of the Tidewater, life was very different. Here, at the base of the Appalachians, rolling hills and thick forests covered the land. As in the Middle Colonies, this inland area was called the backcountry. Attracted by rich soil, settlers followed the Great Wagon Road into the backcountry of Maryland, Virginia, and the Carolinas.

The backcountry was more democratic than the Tidewater. Settlers there were more likely to treat one another as equals. Men

RESOURCE DIRECTORY

Teaching Resources
Unit 1/Chapter 4
- Biography Flashcard: Olaudah Equiano, p. 37
- Section 3 Quiz, p. 40

Document Based Discovery
- Origins, pp. 2–5

★ Customized Instruction ★
Extroverted Learners

Counseling immigrants Have students assume the role of counselors helping people to decide whether or not to immigrate to America and in which colony to settle. Students can work in small groups, with partners, or individually to develop a list of questions to ask potential immigrants before they leave Europe. The questions should be designed to provide information that the counselors can use to help guide the potential immigrants. Have students create skits with dialogue between the counselor and potential immigrant, asking and answering the questions. Using the potential immigrant's answers, the counselor can decide whether or not the person should go to America and, if so, to which colony. (*average*) ELL

110 ★ Chapter 4

tended smaller fields of tobacco or corn or hunted game. Women cooked meals and fashioned simple, rugged clothing out of wool or deerskins.

The hardships of backcountry life brought settlers closer together. Families gathered to husk corn or help one another build barns. Spread out along the edge of the Appalachians, these hardy settlers felled trees, grew crops, and changed the face of the land.

Growth of Slavery

In the early years, Africans in the English colonies included free people and servants as well as slaves. Indeed, during the 1600s, even those Africans who were enslaved enjoyed some freedom. In South Carolina, for example, some enslaved Africans worked without supervision as cowboys, herding cattle to market.

Planters rely on slavery

On plantations throughout the Southern Colonies, enslaved Africans used farming skills they had brought from West Africa. They showed English settlers how to grow rice. They also knew how to use wild plants unfamiliar to the English. They made water buckets out of gourds, and they used palmetto leaves to make fans, brooms, and baskets.

By 1700, plantations in the Southern Colonies had come to rely on slave labor. Slaves cleared the land, worked the crops, and tended the livestock.

Limiting rights

As the importance of slavery increased, greater limits were placed on the rights of slaves. Colonists passed laws that set out rules for slaves' behavior and denied slaves their basic rights. These **slave codes** treated enslaved Africans not as human beings but as property.

Most English colonists did not question the justice of owning slaves. They believed that black Africans were inferior to white Europeans. The belief that one race is superior to another is called **racism.** Some colonists claimed that they were helping slaves by introducing them to Christianity.

A handful of colonists saw the evils of slavery. In 1688, Quakers in Germantown, Pennsylvania, became the first group of colonists to call for an end to slavery.

★ Section 3 Review ★

Recall

1. **Locate** **(a)** Maryland, **(b)** Virginia, **(c)** North Carolina, **(d)** South Carolina, **(e)** Georgia.
2. **Identify** **(a)** Mason-Dixon Line, **(b)** Lord Baltimore, **(c)** Act of Toleration, **(d)** Bacon's Rebellion, **(e)** James Oglethorpe, **(f)** Mary Musgrove, **(g)** Tidewater.
3. **Define** **(a)** indigo, **(b)** debtor, **(c)** buffer, **(d)** plantation, **(e)** slave code, **(f)** racism.

Comprehension

4. Why did their founders set up the colonies of **(a)** Maryland, and **(b)** Georgia?
5. How was life in the Tidewater different from life in the backcountry South?
6. What role did slaves play in the economy of the Southern Colonies by 1700?

Critical Thinking and Writing

7. **Applying Information** Review the definition of religious toleration. Did Maryland's Act of Toleration provide true religious toleration? Explain.
8. **Analyzing Ideas** How did the passage of slave codes in the colonies reflect racism?

Activity **Creating Flashcards** Do you get confused about the 13 English colonies? Use the text, including the maps and charts, to create 13 flashcards. On one side, write the name of a colony. On the other, write three facts about that colony. You may later use these cards for review.

★ Section 3 Review ★

ANSWERS

1. See map, p. 107.

2. **(a)–(b)** p. 106, **(c)–(d)** p. 107, **(e)** p. 108, **(f)** p. 109, **(g)** p. 110

3. **(a)–(b)** p. 108, **(c)–(d)** p. 109, **(e)–(f)** p. 111

4. **(a)** to provide Catholics with a safe place to practice their religion **(b)** to provide a haven for people jailed for debt in England to make a fresh start

5. Tidewater: rich land for wealthy planters' plantations; lived in comfort with slaves to work their fields; backcountry: smaller farms; life was harder and rougher but more democratic

6. Slaves cleared land, planted and harvested crops, tended livestock.

7. No, because it limited religious freedom to Christians.

8. Possible answer: Because Europeans regarded blacks as inferior, they treated enslaved Africans as property without human rights.

Guided Instruction
Encourage students to use symbols or visual images as well as written information on their flashcards. Have students exchange cards and compare their facts.

ASSESSMENT See the rubrics in the Alternative Assessment booklet in the Teaching Resources.

★ *Activity* ★
Cooperative Learning

Planning an advertising campaign Tell students to suppose they work for the governor of a southern colony who is eager to attract more settlers. Have them work in groups to design an advertising campaign to attract settlers to the colony. Students might wish to include slogans, jingles, handbills, posters, employment opportunity ads, real estate ads, and feature stories for newspapers or magazines that present the colony in a positive light. Groups should assign specific writing, editing, and illustration tasks to individual members. (*average*)

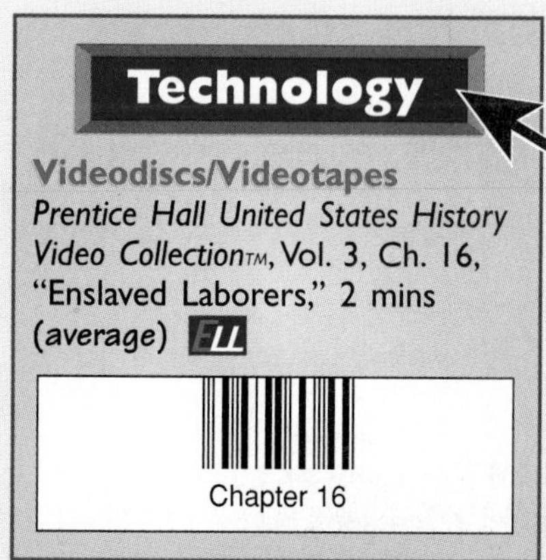

Technology
Videodiscs/Videotapes
Prentice Hall United States History Video Collection™, Vol. 3, Ch. 16, "Enslaved Laborers," 2 mins (*average*)
Chapter 16

Section 4
Governing the Colonies

LESSON PLAN

Objectives

★ Explain why England passed the Navigation Acts.
★ Describe what colonial governments were like.
★ Summarize the rights English colonists enjoyed.

1 Engage

Warm Up Ask: "Why do we have the secret ballot in the United States?" and "What problems might arise if people had to vote in public?" Point out to students that in colonial America, voters announced their selections aloud.

Activating Prior Knowledge Have students discuss whether English leaders in the early 1700s would have seen their American colonies as successes or failures.

Reading Actively

Before Reading Ask students to turn the section heading into a question. As they read, have them jot down notes to help them answer the question.

2 Explore

Ask students to read the section. For homework, have them do research to find out how Rhode Island and Connecticut were able to elect their own governors.

RESOURCE DIRECTORY

Teaching Resources
Lesson Planner, p. 16

Transparencies
Geography and History
• 13 Colonies, p. I-17

Governing the Colonies

As You Read

Explore These Questions
- Why did England pass the Navigation Acts?
- What were colonial governments like?
- What rights did English colonists enjoy?

Define
- mercantilism
- import
- export
- triangular trade
- legislature
- bill of rights

Identify
- Navigation Acts
- Yankee
- Glorious Revolution
- English Bill of Rights

SETTING the Scene Philadelphia bustled with activity in 1750. Young farmers drove cattle, pigs, and sheep to market along narrow cobblestone streets. On the docks, sailors unloaded barrels of molasses from the West Indies, wines from Spain and Portugal, Dutch and English cloth, as well as spices, leather goods, tea, and coffee.

Philadelphia was the largest and busiest seaport in the colonies. Yet, by the 1700s, trade flourished all along the Atlantic coast. As trade increased, England began to take a new interest in its colonies.

England Regulates Trade

Like other European nations at the time, England believed that colonies existed for the benefit of the home country. This belief was part of an economic theory known as **mercantilism** (MER kuhn tihl ihz uhm). According to this theory, a nation became strong by building up its gold supply and expanding trade.

Because exports help a country earn money, mercantilists thought that a country should export more than it imports. **Imports** are goods brought into a country. **Exports** are goods sent to markets outside a country.

Beginning in the 1650s, the English Parliament passed a series of **Navigation Acts** that regulated trade between England and its colonies. The purpose of these laws was to ensure that only England benefited from colonial trade.

Under the new laws, only colonial or English ships could carry goods to and from the colonies. The Navigation Acts also listed certain products, such as tobacco and cotton, that colonial merchants could ship only to England. In this way, Parliament created jobs for English workers who cut and rolled tobacco or spun cotton into cloth.

The Navigation Acts helped the colonies as well as England. For example, the law encouraged colonists to build their own ships. As a result, New England became a prosperous shipbuilding center. Also, because of the acts, colonial merchants did not have to compete with foreign merchants because they were sure of having a market for their goods in England.

Still, many colonists resented the Navigation Acts. In their view, the laws favored English merchants. Colonial merchants often ignored the Navigation Acts or found ways to get around them.

Trading in Rum and Slaves

The colonies produced a wide variety of goods, and ships moved up and down the Atlantic coast in an active trade. Merchants from New England dominated colonial trade. They were known as **Yankees,** a nickname that implied they were clever and hardworking. Yankee traders earned a reputation for profiting from any deal.

Colonial merchants developed many trade routes. One route was known as the **triangular trade** because the three legs of

★ ***Customized Instruction*** ★

Visual Learners

Mapping the colonies Students who learn visually might enjoy making a map of the 13 English colonies. Distribute an outline map or ask students to trace the eastern United States. Refer students to the maps in this chapter and to the atlas maps in the Reference Section of their books. Have them: **(a)** locate and label the 13 colonies; **(b)** locate Concord, Boston, Providence, Hartford, New York, Trenton, Philadelphia, Baltimore, Dover, Norfolk, Raleigh, Charleston, Savannah; **(c)** label the Atlantic Ocean, Chesapeake Bay, Appalachian Mountains; **(d)** color New England one shade, the Middle Colonies another, and the Southern Colonies a third; **(e)** create a title and a legend for their maps. *(average)* ELL T the route formed a triangle. On the first leg, ships from New England carried fish, lumber, and other goods to the West Indies. There, Yankee traders bought sugar and molasses, a dark-brown syrup made from sugar cane. The ships then sailed back to New England, where colonists used the molasses and sugar to make rum.

On the second leg of the journey, ships carried rum, guns, gunpowder, cloth, and tools from New England to West Africa. In Africa, merchants traded these goods for slaves. On the final leg, ships carried enslaved Africans to the West Indies. With the profits from selling the enslaved Africans, traders bought more molasses.

Many New England merchants grew wealthy from the triangular trade. In doing so, they often disobeyed the Navigation Acts. Traders were supposed to buy sugar and molasses only from English colonies in the West Indies. However, the demand for molasses

The 13 English Colonies

Colony / Date Founded	Leader	Reasons Founded
New England Colonies		
▪ Massachusetts Plymouth / 1620 Massachusetts Bay / 1630	William Bradford John Winthrop	Religious freedom Religious freedom
▪ New Hampshire / 1622	Ferdinando Gorges John Mason	Profit from trade and fishing
▪ Connecticut / 1636	Thomas Hooker	Expand trade; religious and political freedom
▪ Rhode Island / 1636	Roger Williams	Religious freedom
Middle Colonies		
▪ New York / 1624	Peter Minuit	Expand trade
▪ Delaware / 1638	Swedish settlers	Expand trade
▪ New Jersey / 1664	John Berkeley George Carteret	Expand trade; religious and political freedom
▪ Pennsylvania / 1682	William Penn	Profit from land sales; religious and political freedom
Southern Colonies		
▪ Virginia / 1607	John Smith	Trade and farming
▪ Maryland / 1632	Lord Baltimore	Profit from land sales; religious and political freedom
▪ The Carolinas / 1663 North Carolina / 1712 South Carolina / 1712	Group of eight proprietors	Trade and farming; religious freedom
▪ Georgia / 1732	James Oglethorpe	Profit; home for debtors; buffer against Spanish Florida

Chart *Skills* **English settlers founded 13 separate colonies along the Atlantic coast of North America.**

1. **Comprehension** **(a)** Identify two colonies founded by people seeking religious freedom. **(b)** Identify two colonies founded to expand trade.
2. **Critical Thinking** How long did it take for England to establish its American colonies?

3 Teach

Have students use index cards to create a flashcard for each colony that includes information from the table on this page and information about the government of each colony. Students can then use the flashcards to test one another on the material in the section.

4 Assess

To close the lesson, have students complete the section review. Or have them suppose they were elected to the lower house of a colonial legislature. Ask them to write a journal entry about why they ran for office, how they were elected, and what responsibilities they have.

★ ★ ★ ★ ★ ★ ★ ★ ★ ★ ★ ★ ★ ★ ★ ★ ★ ★

Chart *Skills*

ANSWERS **1. (a)** Possible answers: Massachusetts, Rhode Island, Connecticut, New Jersey, Pennsylvania, Maryland, the Carolinas **(b)** Possible answers: New Hampshire, Connecticut, New York, New Jersey, Delaware, Virginia, the Carolinas **2.** about 125 years

FROM THE ARCHIVES OF AmericanHeritage®

Source of discontent British customs officials trying to enforce the Navigation Acts in the 1770s provoked Rhode Islanders. When the British schooner H.M.S. *Gaspee,* known for confiscating the goods of even small merchants' vessels, ran aground in 1772, Providence merchants boarded it, captured the crew, and burned the ship.

Source: Robert G. Athearn, *American Heritage Illustrated History of the United States* Vol. 2, 1989.

Technology

Videodiscs/Videotapes

Prentice Hall United States History Video Collection™, Vol. 3, Ch. 7, "The Atlantic World," 1:45 min (average) ELL

Chapter 7

Prentice Hall United States History Video Collection™, Vol. 3, Ch. 10, "The Sugar Islands," 4 mins (average) ELL

Chapter 10

Reading Actively

During Reading Have students note the statement on p. 112 that the "Navigation Acts helped the colonies as well as England." Ask students to find evidence to support this statement.

Graphic Organizer Skills

ANSWERS **1. (a)** rum, guns, gunpowder, cloth, tools **(b)** West Indies **2.** New England merchants gained sugar and molasses, while the South profited from the labor of enslaved Africans.

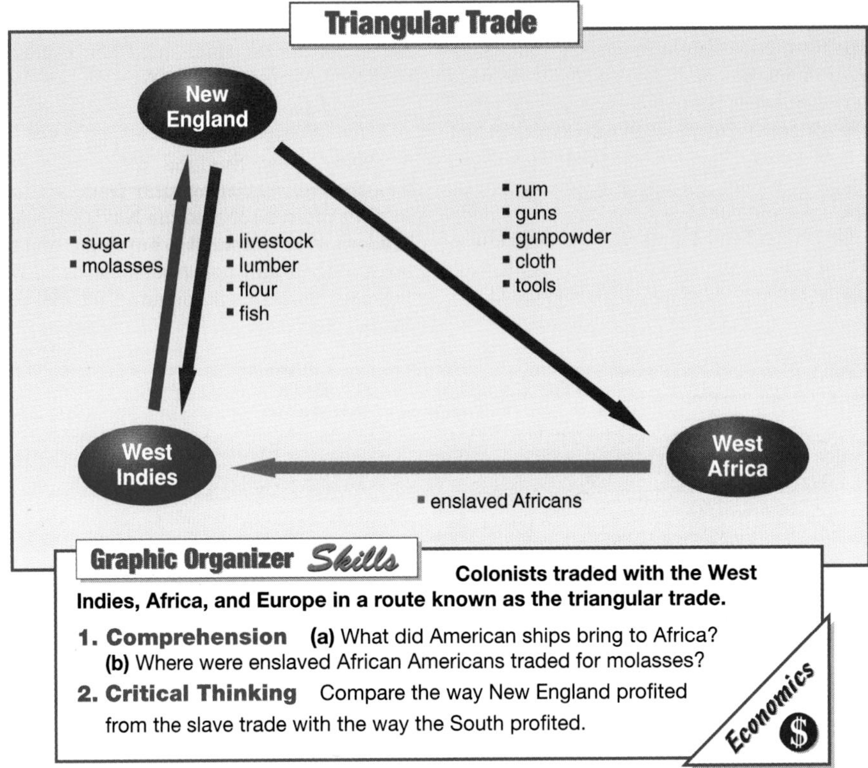

Graphic Organizer Skills **Colonists traded with the West Indies, Africa, and Europe in a route known as the triangular trade.**

1. **Comprehension** **(a)** What did American ships bring to Africa? **(b)** Where were enslaved African Americans traded for molasses?
2. **Critical Thinking** Compare the way New England profited from the slave trade with the way the South profited.

Economics $

was so high that New Englanders smuggled in cargoes from the Dutch, French, and Spanish West Indies, too. Bribes made customs officials look the other way.

Political Life

Although each colony developed its own government, the governments had much in common. A governor directed the colony's affairs and enforced the laws. Most governors were appointed, either by the king or by the colony's proprietor. In Rhode Island and Connecticut, however, colonists elected their own governors.

Elected assemblies

Each colony also had a legislature. A **legislature** is a group of people who have the power to make laws. In most colonies, the legislature had an upper house and a lower house. The upper house was made up of advisers appointed by the governor.

The lower house was an elected assembly. It approved laws and protected the rights of citizens. Just as important, it had the right to approve any taxes the governor asked for. This "power of the purse," or right to raise or spend money, was an important check on the governor's power. Any governor who ignored the assembly risked losing his salary.

The right to vote

Each colony had its own rules about who could vote. By the 1720s, however, all the colonies had laws that restricted the right to vote to white Christian men over the age of 21. In some colonies, only Protestants or members of a particular church could vote. All voters had to own property. Colonial leaders believed that only property owners knew what was best for a colony.

★ Background ★ Turning Points

Connecticut leads the way In 1639, Puritan settlers drew up the first colonial constitution—the Fundamental Orders of Connecticut. It included:

- a representative assembly
- popular election of lawmakers from each town to serve in the assembly
- popular election of a governor and judges

Other colonies later wrote constitutions.

Resource Directory

Teaching Resources
Why Study History?
- You Have a Say in Government, pp. 15–18

Why Study History?

Because You Have a Say in Government

Historical Background

In 1295, King Edward I of England needed money for a war with France. To get the funds, he summoned Parliament, including representatives of the "common people," lords, and clergy. "What touches all should be approved by all," the king said. Over the years, the power of Parliament grew.

The idea of representative government passed on to England's American colonies. In 1619, King James I gave the Virginia colonists the right to form the House of Burgesses. Other colonies developed their own legislatures. Finally, the colonies became the United States of America. The English tradition of electing officials to make laws became the basis of American democracy.

Connections to Today

Today, Americans participate in government at many levels. On the national level, citizens elect representatives to Congress. Each state has its own legislature. In counties, cities, and towns, residents elect councils and boards to pass laws and make regulations. In some small towns, especially in New England, citizens still come together at town meetings to make their own laws.

Connections to You

Representative government affects you in a direct way. Do you attend a public school? If so, an elected school board probably governs your school district. School boards make decisions that affect everything from the books you use to your school's dress code and code of conduct.

You may also participate in representative government right now, by electing or serving on the student council. A student council may seem a long way from the English Parliament. Yet they are part of the same proud tradition.

1. Comprehension **(a)** How did the English tradition of representative government come to the colonies? **(b)** List two types of representative government in the United States today.

2. Critical Thinking "What touches all should be approved by all," said King Edward I. How do the king's words reflect one basic idea behind representative government?

★**Activity** **Writing a Speech** You have decided to run for a seat on your school's student council. Write a campaign speech. Describe what policies you would support. Explain why other students should elect you to be their representative.

Student Council Election

VOTE TODAY!

Representative government begins early.

Fast Facts

★ Greece spawned democracy—the term combines the Greek words *demos* ("people") and *kratia* ("rule")—about 500 B.C.

★ A Carolina colonist observed in 1706: "For this last election, Jews, Strangers, Sailors, Servants, Negroes & almost every French Man in Craven & Berkly county came down to elect, & their votes were taken."

★ In 1665, almost half the members of Virginia's House of Burgesses were former indentured servants.

Bibliography

To read more about this topic:

1. *Politics and Government (Legacies),* Richard Wood (Thomson Learning, 1995). Illustrated history of political societies.

2. *We Hold These Truths: From Magna Carta to the Bill of Rights,* James Avers (Viking Press, 1977). How American rights evolved.

3. Internet. See the Magna Carta manuscript in Britain at www.bl.uk; click on "Digital Library."

ANSWERS

1. (a) King James I gave the Virginia colonists the right to form a legislature, and other colonies followed suit. **(b)** Possible answers: On the national level, citizens elect representatives to Congress. On the local level, citizens elect school boards. **2.** Since everyone should have a say in legislation, representative governments allow citizens to elect legislators to represent them in the process of law making.

★**Activity**

Guided Instruction

Before students begin to write a speech, have them survey students to find out about important school issues. Have them use the results to determine what issues need to be addressed. Students could listen to recorded campaign speeches for style and format. Remind students to practice their speeches before presenting them.

ASSESSMENT See the rubrics in the Alternative Assessment booklet in the Teaching Resources.

Writing Actively 

After Reading Ask students to use the graphic organizer on the facing page and their reading to write a short essay on who benefited from the triangular trade.

★ Section 4 Review ★

ANSWERS

1. (a)–(b) p. 112, **(c)–(d)** p. 116

2. (a)–(d) p. 112 **(e)** p. 114, **(f)** p. 116

3. England: ensured its control over colonial shipping; certain products could be shipped only to England, creating jobs for workers; colonies: led colonists to build ships; protected colonial merchants from foreign competition

4. A governor, appointed by the monarch or colony's proprietor, directed the colony and enforced the laws. Most colonial legislatures had a governor-appointed upper house and an elected lower house.

5. After the 1720s, white male Christian property owners over 21 could vote. In some colonies, only Protestants or members of a particular church could vote.

6. Possible answer: The colonists might have resented restrictions on their rights despite the benefits that resulted from these Acts.

7. They reflected England's Parliament and let colonists elect representatives to handle local affairs.

Activity

Guided Instruction
Have students review the material on the colonial economies and governments. Suggest they write about a particular region.

ASSESSMENT See the rubrics in the Alternative Assessment booklet in the Teaching Resources.

RESOURCE DIRECTORY

Teaching Resources
Lesson Planner, p. 17
Unit 1/Chapter 4
• Section 4 Quiz, p. 41

On election day, voters and their families gathered in towns and villages. Smiling candidates shook hands with voters and slapped them heartily on the back. In some areas, they offered to buy them drinks. When things quieted down, the sheriff called the voters together. One by one, he read out their names. Each man announced his vote aloud:

> “*Sheriff:* Mr. Blair, whom do you vote for?
> *Mr. Blair:* John Marshall.
> *Mr. Marshall:* Your vote is appreciated, Mr. Blair.”

A bill of rights

Colonists took great pride in their elected assemblies. They also valued the rights the Magna Carta gave them as English subjects. (See page 86.)

Colonists won still more rights as a result of the **Glorious Revolution** of 1688. Parliament removed King James II from the throne and asked William and Mary of the Netherlands to rule. In return for Parliament's support, William and Mary signed the **English Bill of Rights** in 1689. A **bill of rights** is a written list of freedoms the government promises to protect.

The English Bill of Rights protected the rights of individuals and gave anyone accused of a crime the right to a trial by jury. Just as important, the English Bill of Rights said that a ruler could not raise taxes or an army without the approval of Parliament.

Limits on liberties

In many ways, English colonists in the Americas enjoyed more freedoms than the English themselves. More ordinary men could vote. Over time, colonial legislatures increased their power.

Still, the rights of English citizens did not extend to everyone in the colonies. Women had more rights in the colonies than in Europe, but far fewer rights than did free white males. A woman's father or husband was supposed to protect her. A married woman could not start her own business or sign a contract unless her husband approved it.

In most colonies, unmarried women and widows had more rights than married women. They could make contracts and sue in court. In Maryland and the Carolinas, women settlers who headed families could buy land on the same terms as men.

Africans and Native Americans in the colonies had almost no rights. Sadly, slavery existed side by side with the English liberties so many colonists held dear. The conflict between liberty and slavery would not be resolved until the 1860s.

★ Section 4 Review ★

Recall

1. **Identify** (a) Navigation Acts, (b) Yankee, (c) Glorious Revolution, (d) English Bill of Rights.
2. **Define** (a) mercantilism, (b) import, (c) export, (d) triangular trade, (e) legislature, (f) bill of rights.

Comprehension

3. List two ways that the Navigation Acts benefited (a) England, and (b) the colonies.
4. How were colonial governments organized?
5. Which colonists had the right to vote?

Critical Thinking and Writing

6. **Predicting Consequences** How do you think the Navigation Acts might affect future relations between England and the colonies? Explain.
7. **Analyzing Ideas** How did colonial legislatures reflect the tradition of self-rule?

Activity **Making a Decision** The time is 1750. You are a young person in Britain looking for success and freedom, so you plan to move to the American colonies. Write a letter to your parents explaining the reasons for your decision.

★ Activity ★

Connections With Civics

Charting governments Have students create a chart to compare colonial governments with their own state government today. Columns should be headed: Colonial Government and State Government. Rows should be labeled: Chief Executive, Executive Functions, Lawmaking Bodies, Functions of Lawmakers, Voting Rights, Other Rights, and Limits on Liberties. Have students use their textbooks and library resources to complete their charts. Ask students to use their charts to write several paragraphs discussing similarities and differences between colonial and modern state governments. (*average*) T

A Changing Colonial Culture

As You Read

Explore These Questions
- What was the Great Awakening?
- How did colonists educate their children?
- How did new ideas spread through the colonies?

Define
- gentry
- middle class
- indentured servant
- public school
- tutor
- apprentice
- dame school
- libel

Identify
- Gullah
- Great Awakening
- Jonathan Edwards
- George Whitefield
- Enlightenment
- Benjamin Franklin
- John Peter Zenger

SETTING the Scene Benjamin Franklin of Philadelphia was a writer, scientist, businessman, and community leader. In 1743, he called on his fellow colonists to expand their cultural horizons:

> "The first drudgery of settling new colonies . . . is now pretty well over, and there are many in every province . . . [who have time] to cultivate the finer arts, and improve the common stock of knowledge."

Franklin invited colonists to join a society to promote "USEFUL KNOWLEDGE." Thus, the American Philosophical Society was born.

Franklin's new society was only one sign that the colonies were coming of age. By the mid-1700s, they had developed a culture that was truly new and American.

Social Classes

For the most part, colonists enjoyed more social equality than people in England did. Still, class differences existed. Like Europeans, colonial Americans thought it was only natural that some people ranked more highly than others.

Powdered wigs like this were the fashion for men of the gentry.

The gentry and the middle class

At the top of society stood the **gentry.** The gentry included wealthy planters, merchants, ministers, successful lawyers, and royal officials. They could afford to dress elegantly in the latest fashions from London.

Below the gentry were the **middle class.** The middle class included farmers who worked their own land, skilled craftsworkers, and some tradespeople. Nearly three quarters of all white colonists belonged to the middle class. They prospered because land in the colonies was plentiful and easy to buy. Also, laborers were in demand, and skilled workers received good wages.

Indentured servants

The lowest social class included hired farmhands, indentured servants, and slaves. **Indentured servants** signed contracts to work without wages for four to seven years for anyone who would pay their ocean passage to the Americas. When their term of service was completed, indentured servants received "freedom dues": a set of clothes, tools, and 50 acres of land. Because there were so few European women in the colonies, female indentured servants often shortened their terms of service by marrying.

★ *Background* ★

Did You Know?

Wig fashions A well-dressed colonial man usually sported a fashionable wig. Barbers were kept busy dressing these hairpieces. A gentleman had many wig styles to choose from—including the "pigeon's wing," "comet," "cauliflower," "rose," and "snail back." After choosing a wig, a gentleman could then instruct his barber to sprinkle it with gray or blue perfumed powder.

Section 5
A Changing Colonial Culture

LESSON PLAN

Objectives

★ Describe features of the Great Awakening.
★ Explain how colonists educated their children.
★ Describe how new ideas spread through the colonies.

1 Engage

Warm Up Ask students to think about what their lives might have been like if they had lived in colonial times. Have students as a class write a day's schedule for a colonial boy and girl of their own ages.

Activating Prior Knowledge Ask: "What was colonial life like?" and "What are the possible sources of your images of colonial life?" Do students think their images are accurate? Why or why not?

Reading Actively

Before Reading Have students read Explore These Questions. As they read, have them jot down notes to help them answer each question. Later, they can use these notes to answer the Comprehension questions in the section review.

2 Explore

Have students read the section. For homework, have them find out more about one of these topics:

Technology

Videodiscs/Videotapes
Prentice Hall United States History Video Collection™, Vol. 3, Ch. 13, "Indentured Servants," 4:35 mins (average) ELL

Chapter 13

indentured servants, African influences on colonial society, the Great Awakening, or travel during colonial times.

3 Teach

Write the following statements on the chalkboard: **(a)** Puritans wanted their children to read the Bible. **(b)** Formal education was considered less important for girls than for boys. **(c)** During the Great Awakening, preachers encouraged people to examine their own lives. Have students explain how each of these views shaped colonial life.

4 Assess

To close the lesson, have students complete the section review. As an alternative, have them write an essay explaining how each visual in this section illustrates some aspect of colonial culture.

★ ★ ★ ★ ★ ★ ★ ★ ★ ★ ★ ★ ★ ★ ★ ★ ★

ANSWER

Possible answers: milking cows, feeding farm animals, helping in the fields

RESOURCE DIRECTORY

Teaching Resources
Unit 1/Chapter 4
- Critical Thinking and Writing: Analyzing Visual Evidence, p. 34

Interdisciplinary Connections
- Main Idea: American Ingenuity, pp. 22–23

Viewing HISTORY New England Mother and Child

Throughout the colonies, women had major household responsibilities such as spinning, preparing meals, and raising children. This 1674 painting shows a mother and daughter in Boston. Generally, the clothing worn by colonial children was just a miniature version of what their parents wore. ★ **What additional duties might a farm woman have?**

◄ *Colonial spinning wheel*

Thousands of men, women, and children came to North America as indentured servants. After completing their terms, some became successful and rose into the middle class.

Women's Work in the Colonies

From New Hampshire to Georgia, colonial women did many of the same tasks. A wife took care of her household, husband, and family. By the kitchen fire, she baked the family's meals. She milked cows, watched the children, and made clothing.

In the backcountry, wives and husbands often worked side by side in the fields at harvest time. With so much to be done, no one worried whether harvesting was proper "woman's work." A visitor described a backcountry woman's activities:

> ❝ She will carry a gunn in the woods and kill deer, turkeys &c., shoot down wild cattle, catch and tye hoggs, knock down [cattle] with an ax, and perform the most manfull Exercises as well as most men. ❞

In cities, women sometimes worked outside the home. A young single woman from a poorer family might work as a maid, a cook, or a nurse for one of the gentry. Other women were midwives, delivering babies. Still others sewed fine hats or dresses to be sold to women who could afford them. Learning such skills required many years of training.

Some women learned trades from their fathers, brothers, or husbands. They worked as butchers, shoemakers, or silversmiths. Quite a few women became printers. A woman might take over her husband's business when he died.

African Cultural Influences

By the mid-1700s, the culture of Africans in the colonies varied greatly. On rice plantations in South Carolina, slaves saw few white colonists. As a result, African customs

Connections With Economics

In 1733, some women in New York cited their economic achievements in a newspaper notice: "We are house keepers, pay our taxes, carry on trade and most of us are she merchants, and as we . . . contribute to the support of the government, we ought to be entitled to some of the sweets of it."

★ *Background* ★

Historiography

Costume change The painting above shows Elizabeth Freake and her daughter Mary. In 1981, surface radiography of the painting revealed that this portrait was actually painted on top of an older one. In the original portrait, Elizabeth's dress was black and of a different style. The baby Mary did not appear at all in the original version. Instead, Elizabeth's hands rested in her lap. Experts suggest that the rising social status of the Freakes, who may have heard about updated clothing styles in England, prompted the changes. **T**

remained strong. For example, parents often chose African names for their children, such as Quosh or Juba or Cuff. In some coastal areas, African Americans spoke a distinctive combination of English and West African languages, known as **Gullah.**

In Charleston and other South Carolina port towns, more than half the population had African roots. Many of them worked along the docks, making rope or barrels or helping to build ships. Skilled craftsworkers made fine wooden cabinets or silver plates and utensils. Many of their designs reflected African artistic styles. Although most Africans in these towns were enslaved, many opened their own shops or stalls in the market. Some used their earnings to buy their own and their family's freedom.

In Virginia and Maryland, African traditions were weaker. Africans in the Chesapeake region were less isolated from white farmers and planters. Also, by the 1750s, the number of new slaves arriving in the region each year had begun to decline. Even so, many old customs survived. One traveler observed an African-style funeral. Mourners took part in a ceremony to speed a dead man's spirit to his home, which they believed was in Africa.

Fewer Africans lived in the Middle Colonies and New England. Most lived in such cities as Philadelphia, New York, and Newport. Often, the men outnumbered the women. As a result, the number of African families remained small.

Viewing History **Preserving African Culture**

In the colonies, African craftsworkers created much fine wooden furniture. Many of their works, such as this detail from a fireplace, were inspired by traditional African designs.
★ **In what colonies did African influences remain strongest?**

The Great Awakening

In the 1730s and 1740s, a religious movement known as the **Great Awakening** swept through the colonies. Its drama and emotion touched women and men of all backgrounds and classes.

Powerful preachers

A New England preacher, **Jonathan Edwards,** set off the Great Awakening. In powerful sermons, Edwards called on colonists, especially young people, to examine their lives. He preached of the sweetness and beauty of God. At the same time, he warned listeners to heed the Bible's teachings. Otherwise, they would be "sinners in the hands of an angry God," headed for the fiery torments of hell. Edwards thundered:

> "O sinner! Consider the fearful danger you are in: it is a great furnace of wrath [anger], a wide and bottomless pit. . . . You hang by a slender thread, with the flames of divine wrath flashing about it, and ready every moment to singe it, and burn it asunder."

In 1739, when an English minister named **George Whitefield** arrived in the colonies, the movement spread like wildfire. Whitefield drew huge crowds to outdoor meetings from Massachusetts to Georgia. His voice rang with feeling as he called on sinners to repent. After hearing Whitefield speak, Jonathan Edwards's wife reported, "I have seen upwards of a thousand people hang on his words with breathless silence, broken only by an occasional half-suppressed sob."

Viewing History **ANSWER**

the Carolinas

★ *Background* ★

Recent Scholarship

Rave reviews George Whitefield was a wildly popular speaker. In *'Pedlar in Divinity': George Whitefield and the Transatlantic Revivals, 1737–1770,* historian Frank Lambert argues that Whitefield's real importance lay not in his preaching but in his marketing methods. Lambert sees Whitefield's use of print media and advance publicity teams as inaugural events in the commercialization of religion.

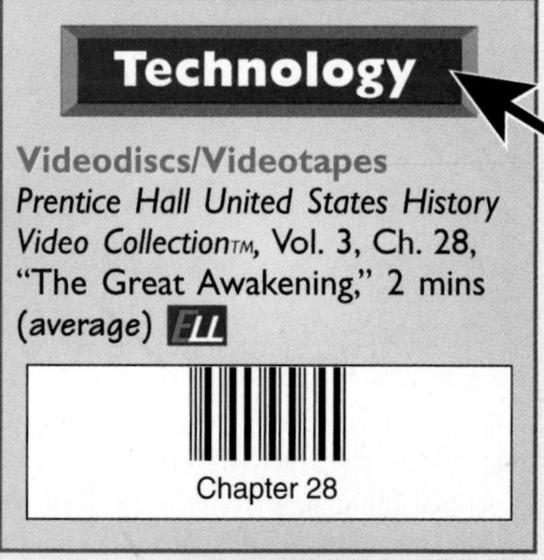

Technology

Videodiscs/Videotapes
Prentice Hall United States History Video Collection™, Vol. 3, Ch. 28, "The Great Awakening," 2 mins (average) ELL

Chapter 28

Reading Actively

During Reading As students read, ask them to see how education differed in New England, the Middle Colonies, and the Southern Colonies. Then have them write two or three sentences describing the differences.

ANSWER

Possible answer: They may have felt that preachers like Whitefield appealed primarily to listeners' emotions, not their reason.

RESOURCE DIRECTORY

Transparencies

Interdisciplinary Connections

- How Lightning Works, p. B-39

Biography George Whitefield

George Whitefield's preaching drew huge crowds throughout the colonies. One witness reported, "He looked as if he was clothed with authority from the great God, and my hearing him preach gave me a heart wound." Whitefield also encouraged the building of American colleges such as Princeton.

★ **Why did some Americans oppose preachers like Whitefield?**

Impact of the Awakening

The Great Awakening aroused bitter debate. People who supported the movement often split away from their old churches to form new ones. Opponents warned that the movement was too emotional. Still, the growth of so many new churches forced colonists to become more tolerant of people with different beliefs.

The Great Awakening contributed in another way to the spread of democratic feelings in the colonies. Many of the new preachers were not as well educated as most ministers. They argued that book learning was less important than a heart filled with the holy spirit. Such teachings encouraged a spirit of independence. Many believers felt more free to challenge authority when their liberties were at stake. In years to come, many of the same colonists were willing to challenge the authority of British officials.

A Tradition of Education

Among the colonists, New Englanders were the most concerned about education. Puritans taught that all people had a duty to study the Bible. If colonists did not learn to read, how would they fulfill this duty?

New England

In 1647, the Massachusetts assembly passed a law ordering all parents to teach their children "to read and understand the principles of religion." They also required all towns with 50 or more families to hire a schoolteacher. Towns with 100 families or more also had to set up a grammar school to prepare boys for college.

In this way, Massachusetts set up the first **public schools,** or schools supported by taxes. Public schools allowed both rich and poor children to receive an education.

The first New England schools had only one room for students of all ages. Parents paid the schoolteacher with corn, peas, or other foods. Each child was expected to bring a share of wood to burn in the stove. Students who forgot would find themselves seated in the coldest corner of the room!

Middle and Southern Colonies

In the Middle Colonies, churches and individual families set up private schools. Because pupils paid to attend, only wealthy families could afford to educate their children.

In the Southern Colonies, people lived too far from one another to bring children together in one school building. Some planters engaged **tutors,** or private teachers. The wealthiest planters sent their sons to school in England. As a rule, slaves were denied education of any kind.

Apprentices and dame schools

Boys whose parents wished them to learn a trade or craft served as apprentices (uh PREHN tihs ehz). An **apprentice** worked for a master to learn a trade or a craft. For

★ *Activity* ★

Connections With Education

Making a time line Remind students that religion was part of all teaching in the first public schools. Ask them to consult books on government and the Constitution to find out how the idea of separation of church and state came to be applied to public schools. Have them summarize their findings in a time line that extends from the 1600s, when the first public schools were established, to today. Time lines should include important Supreme Court decisions, such as *Engel v. Vitale,* which outlawed prayer in public schools in 1962, declaring the practice unconstitutional. (*challenging*) T example, when a boy reached age 12 or 13, his parents might apprentice him to a master glassmaker. The young apprentice lived in the glassmaker's home for six or seven years. The glassmaker gave him food and clothing. He was also supposed to teach the boy how to read and write and provide him with religious training.

In return, the apprentice worked without pay in the glassmaker's shop and learned the skills he needed to set up his own shop. Boys were apprenticed in many trades, including papermaking, printing, and tanning.

In New England, some girls attended **dame schools,** or private schools run by women in their own homes. Most schools in the colonies accepted only boys, however. Girls learned skills from their mothers, who taught them to spin wool, weave, and embroider. A few learned to read and write.

An Age of Reason

During the 1600s, European scientists tried to use reason and logic to understand the world. They developed theories and then performed experiments to test them. In doing so, they discovered many laws of nature. The English scientist Isaac Newton, for example, explained the law of gravity.

The Enlightenment spreads

European thinkers of the late 1600s and 1700s believed that reason and scientific methods could be applied to the study of society. They tried to discover the natural laws that governed human behavior. Because these thinkers believed in the light of human reason, the movement that they started is known as the **Enlightenment.**

In the 13 colonies, the Enlightenment spread among better educated colonists. They included wealthy merchants, lawyers, ministers, and others who had the leisure to read the latest books from Europe.

Benjamin Franklin

The best example of the Enlightenment spirit in the 13 colonies was **Benjamin Franklin.** Franklin was born in 1706, the son of a poor Boston soap and candle maker. Although he had only two years of formal schooling, he used his spare time to study literature, mathematics, and foreign languages.

At age 17, Franklin made his way to Philadelphia. There, he built up a successful printing business. His most popular publication was *Poor Richard's Almanac.* Published yearly, it contained useful information and clever quotes, such as "Early to bed, early to rise, makes a man healthy, wealthy, and wise."

T Young *Timothy* Learnt Sin to fly.
U *Vaſhti* for Pride, Was ſet aſide.
W *Whales* in the Sea, GOD's Voice obey.
X *Xerxes* did die, And ſo muſt I.
Y While Youth do cheer Death may be near.
Z *Zaccheus* he Did climb the Tree, Our Lord to ſee.

WHO was the firſt Man? *Adam.*
Who was the firſt Woman? *Eve.*
Who was the firſt Murderer? *Cain.*
Who was the firſt Martyr? *Abel.*
Who was the firſt tranſlated? *Enoch.*
Who was the oldeſt Man? *Methuſelah.*
Who built the Ark? *Noah.*
Who was the patienteſt Man? *Job.*
Who was the meekeſt Man? *Moſes.*
Who led *Iſrael* into *Canaan*? *Joſhua.*
Who was the ſtrongeſt Man? *Samſon.*
Who kill'd *Goliah*? *David.*
Who was the wiſeſt Man? *Solomon.*
Who was in the Whale's Belly? *Jonah.*
Who ſaves loſt Men? *Jeſus Chriſt.*
Who is *Jeſus Chriſt*? *The Son of God.*
Who was the Mother of Chriſt? *Mary.*
Who betray'd his Maſter? *Judas.*
Who deny'd his Maſter? *Peter.*
Who was the firſt Chriſtian Martyr? *Stephen.*
Who was chief Apoſtle of the Gentiles? *Paul.*

Viewing History — Education in the Colonies

Education and values were closely linked in the colonies. The picture at left shows apprentices learning beekeeping and carpentry. The writing around the picture praises the value of work. The New England primer, above, taught Bible tales and moral lessons along with the alphabet.

★ **Examine the page from the primer. What moral lesson is taught with the letter *Y*? What does this suggest about the Puritan attitude toward childhood?**

Viewing History ANSWER

It teaches that death is not that far away from birth and that there is no time for play. Puritans felt that children should realize the seriousness of life—and death.

★ Customized Instruction ★

Kinesthetic Learners

A colonial drama Divide the class into three groups to represent New England, the Middle Colonies, and the Southern Colonies. Have each group do research on the rights granted to and withheld from citizens, the role of religion, and attitudes toward education in their region. Have students use their research to create skits showing how these ideas shaped everyday life in their region and suggesting how these ideas would change in the future. Encourage students to use quotations from primary sources as well as costumes and props appropriate to the period. After each performance, allow time for students to discuss the skits. (*challenging*) T

Technology

American Heritage® History of the United States CD-ROM

- History Makers: Benjamin Franklin (*average*)
- Arts and Entertainment: Books (*average*)

AmericanHeritage
MAGAZINE

Colonial Williamsburg To learn more about Colonial Williamsburg on the Internet, go to www.history.org/welcome.html.

Writing Actively

After Reading Have students complete the following paragraph: New __________ spread quickly through the colonies, beginning first in the thriving ________ and then spreading to the countryside. __________ soon appeared, and by the 1750s, most colonies had at least one weekly. As the demand for news grew, a concern arose over freedom of the _________. The trial of _________ laid the foundation for this basic American right.

Resource Directory

Teaching Resources
Unit 1/Chapter 4
- Vocabulary Builder, p. 32
- Section 5 Quiz, p. 42
- Chapter Tests, pp. 19–24

AmericanHeritage
MAGAZINE

HISTORY HAPPENED HERE

Colonial Williamsburg

In the 1700s, Williamsburg was one of the most important cities in Virginia. Today, it is one of the state's most popular attractions. As you walk down the restored streets, you can watch people bake bread, print newspapers, or make shoes as they did in colonial times.

★ ***To learn more about this historic site, write:*** *Colonial Williamsburg Foundation, P.O. Box 627, Williamsburg, VA 23187.*

◄ A wigmaker in Colonial Williamsburg demonstrates her trade.

Like other Enlightenment thinkers, Franklin wanted to use reason to improve the world around him. He invented practical devices such as a lightning rod, a smokeless fireplace, and bifocal glasses. As a community leader, Franklin persuaded Philadelphia officials to pave streets, organize a fire company, and set up the first lending library in the Americas. Franklin's inventions and his public service earned him worldwide fame.

Colonial Cities and the Spread of Ideas

While most colonists lived on farms, towns and cities strongly influenced colonial life. Through the great ports of Philadelphia, New York, Boston, and Charleston, merchants shipped products overseas. Towns and cities also served as the center of a busy trade between the coast and the growing backcountry.

Culture flourished in the cities. By the mid-1700s, all major colonial cities had their own theaters. City dwellers found entertainment at singing societies, traveling circuses, carnivals, and horse races.

Communication and the growth of newspapers

The growth of colonial cities helped new ideas to spread. The newest ideas from Europe appeared first in city drawing rooms and taverns. In 1704, John Campbell founded the *Boston News-Letter,* the first regular weekly newspaper in the English colonies. Within 50 years, each of the colonies except New Jersey and Delaware had at least one weekly paper.

The growth of colonial newspapers led to a dispute over freedom of the press. **John Peter Zenger** published the *Weekly Journal*

FROM THE ARCHIVES OF AmericanHeritage®

The history of Williamsburg The economy of 18th-century Williamsburg relied on colonial government and the Virginians who came to the city for the meetings of the General Court. After the Virginia government moved to Richmond in 1780, the town declined. Starting in 1926, John D. Rockefeller, Jr., helped to restore it.

Source: Walter Karp, "'My Gawd, They've Sold the Town,'" *American Heritage* magazine, August/September 1981.

in New York City. In 1734, he was arrested for publishing stories that criticized the governor. Zenger was put on trial for **libel**, the act of publishing a statement that may unjustly damage a person's reputation. Zenger's lawyer argued that, since the stories were true, his client had not committed libel. He told the jury:

> "By your verdict, you will have laid a noble foundation for securing to ourselves, our descendants, and our neighbors, the liberty both of exposing and opposing tyrannical power by speaking and writing truth."

▲ *Connecticut tavern sign*

The jury agreed and freed Zenger. Freedom of the press would later become recognized as a basic American right.

Improved travel

Newspapers often took several months to travel from one colony to another. Travel was often slow and difficult. Roads were rough and muddy, and there were few bridges over streams and rivers. Worst of all, there were no road signs. Most colonists stayed close to home.

Colonists set up a postal system, but it was slow. In 1717, it took one month for a letter to travel from Boston to Williamsburg, Virginia. In the winter, delivery could take twice as long.

As the colonies grew, roads and mail service improved. Families built taverns along main roads and in towns and cities. Travelers stopped to rest and to exchange news and gossip with local people.

Along with the growth of cities, improved travel and communication created an active colonial culture. In cities, large numbers of people exchanged news and ideas that eventually spread throughout the colonies. In the years ahead, these ideas would help shape a revolution.

★ Section 5 Review ★

Recall

1. **Identify** **(a)** Gullah, **(b)** Great Awakening, **(c)** Jonathan Edwards, **(d)** George Whitefield, **(e)** Enlightenment, **(f)** Benjamin Franklin, **(g)** John Peter Zenger.
2. **Define** **(a)** gentry, **(b)** middle class, **(c)** indentured servant, **(d)** public school, **(e)** tutor, **(f)** apprentice, **(g)** dame school, **(h)** libel.

Comprehension

3. How did the Great Awakening contribute to the spread of democratic feelings in the colonies?
4. Why did the Puritans support public education?
5. In what ways was Benjamin Franklin an example of the Enlightenment spirit?

Critical Thinking and Writing

6. **Making Inferences** Why do you think there was greater social equality in the colonies than in England?
7. **Linking Past and Present** How did New England public schools compare with public schools today?

Activity **Delivering an Editorial** You are a television reporter with a time machine. You have gone back to 1734 to report on the trial of John Peter Zenger. Write and deliver a one-minute editorial explaining why you think he should or should not be found guilty.

★ Section 5 Review ★

ANSWERS

1. (a)–(d) p. 119, **(e)–(f)** p. 121, **(g)** p. 122

2. (a)–(c) p. 117, **(d)–(f)** p. 120, **(g)** p. 121, **(h)** p. 123

3. The rise of new churches led to more religious tolerance. Preachers argued that the holy spirit was a more reliable guide to living than books, thus encouraging people to challenge authority.

4. so children could read the Bible

5. He used reason/logic to understand and improve his world.

6. Possible answer: In Massachusetts, the schools educated rich and poor, lowering class barriers. Settlers often faced the same problems, so they learned to work together.

7. Possible answer: New England: emphasis on reading/Christian doctrine; one teacher, paid with goods rather than cash, taught children of all ages in one room. Today: no religious teaching in public schools; each student age group has its own teachers, who receive regular salaries.

Guided Instruction

Have students watch the local news for examples of TV editorials and then work together in pairs.

ASSESSMENT See the rubrics in the Alternative Assessment booklet in the Teaching Resources.

★ Activity ★
Linking Past and Present

Writing an essay Ask students to write an essay comparing mail delivery in colonial times and today. Students should discuss delivery times and methods, especially the wide range of modern services. They should conclude by hypothesizing about how changes in mail service have affected our society and government. (*average*) T

CD-ROM
Test Bank CD-ROM, Ch. 4
Interactive Student Tutorial

Chapter 4

Review and Activities

Reviewing the Chapter

Define These Terms

1. c **2.** a **3.** e **4.** b **5.** d

Explore the Main Ideas

1. Connecticut gave the vote to all men who were property owners and limited the governor's power.

2. Proprietary colony: was owned by one or more people; was not under direct control of the crown; royal colony: was under direct control of the crown

3. Catholics: to practice their religion freely; debtors: to escape imprisonment and make a new start

4. the rights guaranteed by the English Bill of Rights, such as the right to trial by jury; the right to approve local taxes through elected colonial legislatures

5. upper class, or gentry, of planters, merchants, ministers, lawyers, and royal officials; middle class of farmers, skilled craftworkers, and some tradespeople; lowest class of hired farmhands, indentured servants, and slaves

Geography Activity

1. A **2.** B **3.** C **4.** F **5.** E **6.** D

Region Maryland, Virginia, North Carolina, South Carolina, Georgia

Critical Thinking

1. (a) The Puritans wanted religious freedom, but only for themselves. **(b)** They were not tolerant of other faiths or of the questioning of their own.

2. (a) Jamestown is founded; colonists begin to plant tobacco; Virginia settlers move inland, Georgia is founded. **(b)** Virginia settlers moving inland caused Bacon's Rebellion.

3. Americans today use the secret ballot and do not have to say how they voted; candidates do not necessarily know who voted for them.

4. Possible answers: representative government because it was the foundation of our political system; right to a trial by jury because it protects individuals from arbitrary government actions

Using Primary Sources

(a) to persuade someone to capture and return Winifred Thomas to her master **(b)** indentured servant and convict possibly sentenced to indentured servitude for her crime **(c)** Pierce considered Thomas his property; the gunpowder mark may be his "brand."

Chapter 4 Review and Activities

★ Sum It Up ★

Section 1 The New England Colonies

- The Puritans went to New England to form a society where they could practice their religious beliefs.
- Life in New England was based on farming, hunting, and fishing.

Section 2 The Middle Colonies

- The Middle Colonies had a diverse mix of people, in part because they offered settlers religious freedom.
- The economy of the Middle Colonies was based on farming, but grew to include manufacturing as well.

Section 3 The Southern Colonies

- Two distinct ways of life emerged on Tidewater plantations and backcountry farms.
- As a plantation economy grew, slavery became firmly established in the Southern Colonies.

Section 4 Governing the Colonies

- The British passed laws to control colonial trade.
- Democratic traditions grew in the colonies, including representative government and protection of individual rights.

Section 5 A Changing Colonial Culture

- The Great Awakening inspired religious feeling and beliefs about equality.
- New England offered public education, while schools in the Middle and Southern colonies were usually private.

For additional review of the major ideas of Chapter 4, see ***Guide to the Essentials of American History*** or ***Interactive Student Tutorial CD-ROM,*** which contains interactive review activities, graphic organizers, and practice tests.

Reviewing the Chapter

Define These Terms

Match each term with the correct definition.

Column 1	**Column 2**
1. toleration	**a.** owner of a huge estate in New Netherland
2. patroon	**b.** theory that a nation becomes strong by building its gold supply and expanding trade
3. debtor	**c.** willingness to let others practice their own beliefs
4. mercantilism	**d.** someone who promises to work for four to seven years in exchange for passage
5. indentured servant	**e.** someone who owes money

Explore the Main Ideas

1. How did the Fundamental Orders of Connecticut differ from the plan of government in Massachusetts?
2. How did a proprietary colony differ from a royal colony?
3. Why did Catholics and debtors want to move to North America?
4. What rights did English colonists have?
5. Describe the main social classes in the colonies.

Geography Activity

Match the letters on the map with the following places: **1.** New England Colonies, **2.** Middle Colonies, **3.** Southern Colonies, **4.** Massachusetts, **5.** Pennsylvania, **6.** Virginia. **Region** Name the five Southern Colonies.

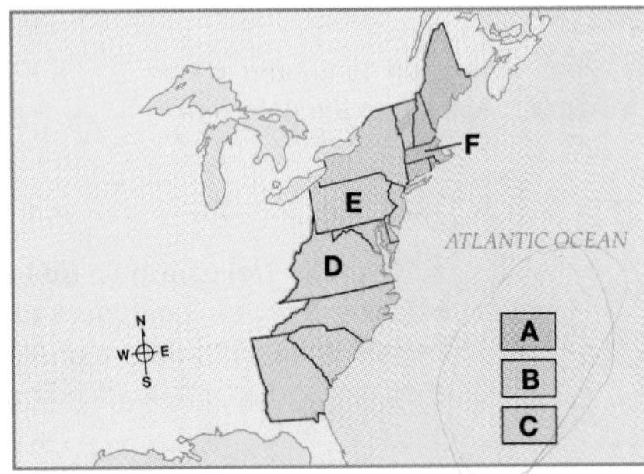

Critical Thinking and Writing

1. **Analyzing Ideas** "The Puritans came to America in search of religious freedom." **(a)** In what sense is this statement accurate? **(b)** In what sense is this statement inaccurate?
2. **Understanding Chronology** **(a)** Place the following events in the correct chronological order: Georgia is founded; colonists begin to plant tobacco; Jamestown is founded; Virginia settlers move inland. **(b)** Which of these events was the direct cause of Bacon's Rebellion?
3. **Linking Past and Present** **(a)** Reread the description of voting in the colonies on page 116. How does it differ from the way Americans vote today?
4. **Exploring Unit Themes** **Origins** What do you think are the two most important traditions the United States got from England? Explain your reasoning.

Using Primary Sources

The following notice appeared in Southern newspapers sometime in the 1730s:

> "Ran away some time in June last, from William Pierce of Nansemond County, . . . a convict servant woman named Winifred Thomas. She is a Welsh woman, short, black-haired and young; marked on the inside of her right arm with gunpowder, W.T., and the date of the year underneath. She knits and spins, and is supposed to be gone into North Carolina by the way of Cureatuck and Roanoke Inlet. Whoever brings her to her master shall be paid a [gold coin] besides what the law allows."

Source: *A Documentary History of American Industrial Society,* 1910.

Recognizing Points of View **(a)** What is the purpose of this advertisement? **(b)** Based on your reading, was Winifred Thomas a slave or an indentured servant? **(c)** What was Pierce's attitude toward Thomas?

ACTIVITY BANK

Interdisciplinary Activity

Exploring Sciences Do research on the inventions of Benjamin Franklin. Create a display that explains how one of his inventions worked.

Career Skills Activity

Playwrights Read more about the life of women in the British colonies. Write a short play in which a city woman, a backcountry woman, and the mistress of a plantation meet and compare their lives.

Citizenship Activity

Learning About Education In this chapter you read about the beginnings of public education. One of the responsibilities of citizens is being informed about education in the community. Arrange to visit a meeting of a local school board or parent-teacher association. Write a report on your visit.

Internet Activity

Use the Internet to find sites dealing with William Penn. After you have done research to find out more about him, write a letter from Penn to the President of the United States today, advising the President on how to handle some of the challenges facing our nation. Use information from your research in your letter.

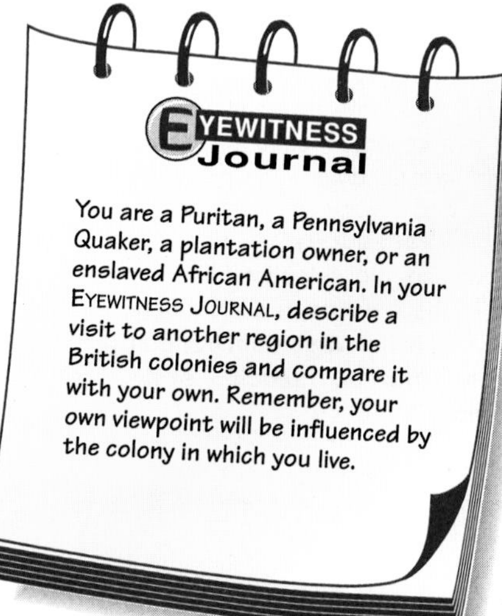

EYEWITNESS Journal
You are a Puritan, a Pennsylvania Quaker, a plantation owner, or an enslaved African American. In your EYEWITNESS JOURNAL, describe a visit to another region in the British colonies and compare it with your own. Remember, your own viewpoint will be influenced by the colony in which you live.

ACTIVITY BANK

ASSESSMENT To assess the activities on this page, see the rubrics in the Alternative Assessment booklet in the Teaching Resources. You might want to share the rubrics with your students before they begin work.

Interdisciplinary Activity

1. Suggest that students consult biographies of Franklin or histories of science and invention in the United States.

2. Explain to students that the model need not be a *working* model, but they should show and explain how the invention worked through diagrams or labels.

3. Encourage students to extend the activity by researching later scientific developments or inventions based on Franklin's work.

Career Skills Activity

1. Have students look for primary sources about colonial women on the Internet or in local libraries. Emphasize that good writers study original sources to give their writing authenticity.

2. Encourage students to include detail about colonial life in their dialogue without making it sound unnatural.

3. Ask students to read or act out their work for the class.

Citizenship Activity

1. Help students arrange to visit a school board or parent–teacher meeting in small groups or as a class. Have a volunteer call to request permission to attend such meetings.

2. Afterward, select several students to share their reports with the class.

3. Have students extend the activity by forming a student committee to offer recommendations to the school board or parent-teacher group.

EYEWITNESS Journal

1. Encourage students to review and make notes on their person's home region before looking at the region he/she will visit.
2. Remind students to review the differences between various colonial regions to choose a region their character will visit.
3. Have pairs of students whose characters are visiting each other's regions compare notes.

Internet Activity

1. Have students look at www.phschool.com, which contains updated information on a variety of topics.
2. One site you may find useful for this activity is the American Studies Department of the University of Virginia's Penn site at xroads/virginia.edu/~cap/penn/pnhome.html.
3. Given the changing nature of the Internet, you may wish to preview this site.

Hiawatha the Unifier

Iroquois Folk Tale

Author Note

The Iroquois people The Iroquois called themselves Ongwanonsionni, or "We of the Extended Lodge." This name reflects the Iroquois's reliance on both the extended family and the idea of the common good. The Iroquois held property in common, even food. This prompted one French Jesuit priest to write, "Their kindness, humanity and courtesy not only makes them liberal with what they have, but causes them to possess hardly anything except in common."

Build Vocabulary

Have students look up and discuss *untutored, eternal, devastation, tranquil, counselors, orators, recoil, strife,* and *innumerable* before they read. Ask: "Why might the word *untutored* be a good way to describe an enemy?" and "Which words might be applied to a war or a time of trouble?"

Prereading Focus

You might have students reread Section 2 in Chapter 2 to review the discussion about the peoples of the Eastern Woodlands.

Connect Your Experience

Have students recall a time when they felt threatened or uncomfortable. Ask: "What caused your discomfort?" and "How did you handle the situation?"

Purpose-Setting Question

Ask: "Have you ever heard the saying 'There's safety in numbers'? What do you think this saying means?"

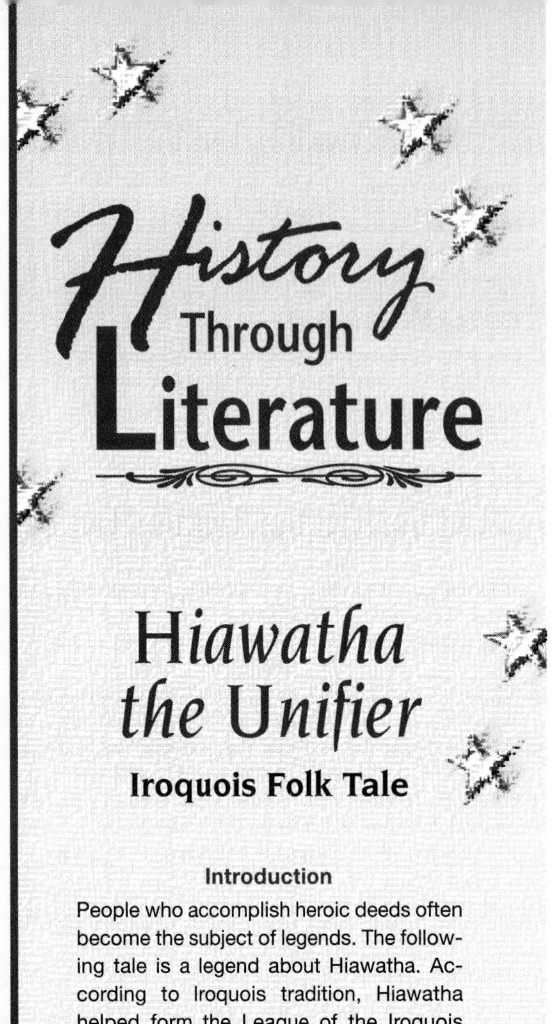

Hiawatha the Unifier

Iroquois Folk Tale

Introduction

People who accomplish heroic deeds often become the subject of legends. The following tale is a legend about Hiawatha. According to Iroquois tradition, Hiawatha helped form the League of the Iroquois around 1570. The following traditional tale appeared in a collection called *American Indian Myths and Legends.*

Vocabulary

Before you read the selection, find the meanings of these words in a dictionary: **untutored, eternal, devastation, tranquil, counselors, orators, recoil, strife, innumerable.**

From out of the north beyond the Great Lakes came wild tribes, fierce, untutored nations who knew nothing of the eternal law;* peoples who did not plant or weave baskets or fire clay into cooking vessels. All they knew was how to prey on those who planted and reaped the fruits of their labors. Fierce and pitiless, these strangers ate their meat raw, tearing it apart with their teeth. Warfare and killing were their occupation. They burst upon Hiawatha's people like a flood, spreading devastation wherever they went. Again the people turned to Hiawatha for help. He advised all the nations to assemble and wait his coming.

And so the five tribes came together at the place of the great council fire, by the shores of a large and tranquil lake where the wild men from the north had not yet penetrated. The people waited for Hiawatha one day, two days, three days. On the fourth day his gleaming white magic canoe appeared, floating, gliding above the mist....

When the sachems, elders, and wise men had seated themselves in a circle around the sacred fire, Hiawatha came before them and said:

"My children, war, fear, and disunity have brought you from your villages to this sacred council fire. Facing a common danger, and fearing for the lives of your families, you have yet drifted apart, each tribe thinking and acting only for itself. Remember how I took you from one small band and nursed you up into many nations. You must reunite now and act as one. No tribe alone can withstand our savage enemies, who care nothing about the eternal law, who sweep upon us like the storms of winter, spreading death and destruction everywhere.

"My children, listen well. Remember that you are brothers, that the downfall of one means the downfall of all. You must have one fire, one pipe, one war club....

"Onondagas, you are a tribe of mighty warriors. Your strength is like that of a giant pine tree whose roots spread far and deep so that it can withstand any storm. Be you the protectors. You shall be the first nation.

*The eternal law refers to the need to keep a balance between people and nature.

126 ★ Unit 1

Critical Reading

1. What was the result of the meeting of the five tribes? *(The League of the Five Nations was formed.)*

2. How does Hiawatha convince the tribes to unite? *(He tells them that no tribe alone can win against the enemy, but that if they join together, they can prevail.)*

3. What do you think is meant by the "great sea of the east" referred to in the passage? *(probably the Atlantic Ocean)*

Background for Understanding

When the League of the Iroquois was formed, tribes agreed not to declare war unless all members approved. During the American Revolution, however, the league released tribes from that promise and let each decide independently; most sided with the British. The Iroquois continued to think of themselves as an independent nation even after the United States was established.

"Oneida, your men are famous for their wisdom. Be you the counselors of the tribes. You shall be the second nation.

"Seneca, you are swift of foot and persuasive in speech. Your men are the greatest orators among the tribes. Be you the spokesmen. You shall be the third people.

"Cayuga, you are the most cunning. You are the most skilled in the building and managing of canoes. Be you the guardians of our rivers. You shall be the fourth nation.

"Mohawk, you are foremost in planting corn and beans and in building longhouses. Be you the nourishers.

"Your tribes must be like the five fingers of a warrior's hand joined in gripping the war club. Unite as one, and then your enemies will recoil before you back into the northern wastes from whence they came. Let my words sink deep into your hearts and minds. Retire now to take counsel among yourselves, and come to me tomorrow to tell me whether you will follow my advice."

On the next morning the sachems and wise men came to Hiawatha with the promise that they would from that day on be as one nation. Hiawatha rejoiced. He gathered up the dazzling white feathers which the great mystery bird of the sky had dropped and gave the plumes to the leaders of the assembled tribes. "By these feathers," he said, "you shall be known as the Ako-no-shu-ne: the Iroquois." Thus with the help of Hiawatha, the Great Unifier, the mighty League of the Five Nations was born and its tribes held sway undisturbed over all the land between the great river of the west and the great sea of the east.

The elders begged Hiawatha to become the chief sachem of the united tribes, but he told them: "This can never be, because I must leave you. Friends and brothers, choose the wisest women in your tribes to be the future clan mothers and peacemakers. Let them turn any strife rising among you into friendship. Let your sachems be wise enough to go to such women for advice when there are disputes. Now I have finished speaking. Farewell."

At that moment there came to those assembled the sweet sound like the rush of rustling leaves and the song of innumerable birds. Hiawatha stepped into his white mystery canoe, and instead of gliding away on the waters of the lake, it rose slowly into the sky and disappeared into the clouds. Hiawatha was gone, but his teachings survive in the hearts of the people.

Viewing History **Cap of an Iroquois Leader**

Wooden caps like this one were traditionally worn by important members of the Iroquois League. The six-sided design on the band may symbolize the six nations that belonged to the League after the Tuscarora joined. ★ **What was the chief purpose of the Iroquois League?**

Analyzing Literature

1. Why did the Five Nations seek Hiawatha's help?
2. According to Hiawatha, why was each of the Five Nations important to the League as a whole?
3. **Synthesizing Information** **(a)** What final advice did Hiawatha give the sachems? **(b)** Based on your reading, did they follow this advice?

Viewing History ANSWER

The chief purpose of the Iroquois League was to bring peace to the warring Iroquois tribes so they could better defend against their common enemies.

Analyzing Literature

ANSWERS

1. The Five Nations sought Hiawatha's help because they were under attack by fierce tribes from the north.
2. The Onondaga were important because they were strong warriors, the Oneida because they were wise, the Seneca because they were fast runners and persuasive speakers, the Cayuga because they were skilled in building and managing canoes, the Mohawk because they were excellent farmers and builders of long houses.
3. (a) Hiawatha advised the sachems to appoint women to act as clan mothers and peacemakers for the League of the Five Nations. **(b)** Yes, Iroquois women owned all household property, managed the farming, and chose the sachems.

Teaching Alternatives

Team Teaching: Language Arts

Work with a language arts teacher to help students understand the term *oratory*. Ask students to review Hiawatha's speech in the excerpt. Then discuss other types of oratory, such as the speeches given by attorneys during trials and by members of Congress during debates. Point out that the chief goal of most oratory is to persuade to a certain point of view, and discuss how that goal is usually achieved.

Connections With Arts

Iroquois artwork, such as this striking cap, used various designs rich in symbolism. The hexagon represented the council fire; scroll designs, like the scalloped edge of the metal encircling the cap, suggested good luck. Traditional Iroquois caps, or *gustowehs*, like this one marked an individual as an important member of the tribe.

Unit 2

A Nation Is Born

Thematic Overview

Dissatisfaction with British rule led American colonists to declare independence from Great Britain and to fight a long, hard, but ultimately successful, battle for freedom. Americans soon realized that their young nation needed a more secure foundation than that which their first constitution, the Articles of Confederation, provided.

Chapter 5 examines the issues and events that led American colonists to the point of rebelling against Britain. (See pp. 130–157.) **Chapter 6** describes the American Revolution from its early battles to the Declaration of Independence and the final defeat of the British. (See pp. 158–185.) **Chapter 7** considers the problems of the young republic and the work of American leaders to craft an enduring framework for government, the Constitution of the United States. (See pp. 186–211.) **Chapter 8** explores the Constitution in detail and explains how it structures our government and protects the rights of Americans today. (See pp. 212–237.)

ANSWERS

Possible answers: freedom of speech, freedom of the press, freedom of petition, and freedom of assembly. The Background Art Note on this page gives information on quilting.

RESOURCE DIRECTORY

Teaching Resources
Document-Based Discovery
- Rights and Liberties, pp. 6–9

Unit 2 A Nation Is Born

What's Ahead

Viewing Unit Themes — Freedom of Religion: A Basic American Right

Since colonial days, American women have used the craft of quilt-making to express their values and depict their daily life. This detail from a New England quilt from the late 1700s portrays a church as the center of the community. Americans of the time expected their new government to safeguard freedom of religion. ★ **List two other freedoms that Americans enjoy.**

★ Background ★ Art Note

Freedom of Religion: A Basic American Right It is not surprising that a church would get "top billing" in the quilt design above. Quilts in the late 1700s were rarely made for strictly practical purposes. Rather, quilt making gave busy colonial women both a creative outlet and an opportunity to socialize. Gradually, quilting bees became forums in which women exchanged their views on such subjects as politics and religion. Quilt designs from the period often reflect the views and principles of the quilters. By the mid-1800s, women were raising funds for political causes by raffling their quilts.

Unit Theme Rights and Liberties

In 1776, the 13 colonies declared their independence from Britain. One major reason was colonists' belief that Britain had violated their basic rights.

Later, American leaders worked to create a government. Many people in the United States demanded that the new government protect basic liberties, such as freedom of religion, freedom of the press, and the right to trial by jury.

How did Americans of the time feel about basic rights and liberties? They can tell you in their own words.

Viewpoints on Rights and Liberties

"If we separate from Britain, what code of laws will be established? How shall we be governed so as to retain our liberties?"

Abigail Adams, wife of John Adams (1775)

"By reason of long bondage and hard slavery, we have been deprived of the profits of our labor or the advantage of inheriting estates from our parents as our neighbors the white people do."

Paul Cuffe, African American ship owner (1783)

"Were it left to me to decide whether we should have a government without newspapers, or newspapers without a government, I should not hesitate a moment to prefer the latter."

Thomas Jefferson, Virginia political leader (1787)

History AND YOU **Activity** **Writing to Learn** Turn to the First Amendment in the Reference Section and read the Constitution. List the freedoms guaranteed by the First Amendment. Then, choose one of those freedoms. Write a skit showing what life might be like if that freedom were not protected.

★ *Background* ★

Historians Debate

Examining the founders Washington, Adams, Jefferson, Madison, and other founders of the republic often appear larger than life. How were their ideas about rights and liberties formed and engraved into the Constitution? Charles Beard's *Economic Interpretation of the Constitution of the United States* (1913) spurred a generation of historians to study the financial accounts of delegates to the Constitutional Convention. In *We The People*, Forrest McDonald shows how Beard's book may be flawed. Historian Garry Wills in *Explaining America: The Federalist* has examined the intellectual background of the founders, while Richard B. Morris focused more on their creative statesmanship.

Viewpoints on Rights and Liberties

★ **Abigail Adams,** a prolific letter writer and avid historian, supported women's rights and opposed slavery.

★ **Paul Cuffe,** a successful shipowner and son of a slave, worked for the rights of free African Americans.

★ **Thomas Jefferson,** third President of the United States, believed in religious freedom and campaigned for free public education.

CRITICAL THINKING These three historical figures, who achieved prosperity and success themselves, believed strongly in helping others succeed. Why do you think that protecting the rights of the individual was so important to all three speakers?

Guided Instruction
Suggest that students read the margin notes beside the First Amendment in the Reference Section to ensure comprehension. You might have pairs or small groups work together on the skits and present them to the class.

ASSESSMENT See the rubrics in the Alternative Assessment booklet in the Teaching Resources.

Technology

AmericanHeritage® History of the United States CD-ROM
Access the Time Tour "From Revolution to Republic" to accompany Unit 2.

Chapter 5 Manager

SECTION OBJECTIVES	TEACHING RESOURCES	ADDITIONAL RESOURCES
1 Rivalry in North America (pp. 132–134) **Objectives** 1. Name the European nations that competed for land in North America. 2. Explain why the French built a system of forts. 3. Explain why Indian nations became involved in the struggle between France and England.	**Lesson Planner,** p. 18 (challenging) .... 45 mins. **Unit 2/Chapter 5** • Biography Flashcard: Jean Baptiste Pointe du Sable, p. 7 (average) .... 20 mins. • Section 1 Quiz, p. 8 (average) .... 15 mins.	**Customized Reader** • A Prophetic Warning About the United States, article IIIA-1 (average)
2 The French and Indian War (pp. 135–141) **Objectives** 1. Explain why the British and French went to war in North America. 2. Describe the advantages each side had in the war. 3. Describe how the Treaty of Paris affected North America.	**Lesson Planner,** p. 19 (challenging) .... 45 mins. **Unit 2/Chapter 5** • Practice Your Skills: Reading a Time Line, p. 3 (average) .... 20 mins. • Map Mystery: Why Fort Niagara? p. 5 (average) .... 20 mins. • Section 2 Quiz, p. 9 (average) .... 15 mins.	**Voices of Freedom** • Washington Meets With the French, p. 54 (average) • Wolfe and Montcalm: The Last Battle, pp. 55–56 (average) **Historical Outline Map Book** • The French and Indian War, p. 21 (average) • North America in 1763, p. 22 (average)
3 A Crisis Over Taxes (pp. 142–149) **Objectives** 1. Explain the goal of the Proclamation of 1763. 2. Describe how colonists protested British taxes. 3. Explain what the Boston Massacre was.	**Lesson Planner,** p. 20 (average) .... 90 mins. **Unit 2/Chapter 5** • Connecting History and Literature: Speech Against Writs of Assistance, p. 6 (challenging) .... 20 mins. • Section 3 Quiz, p. 10 (average) .... 15 mins. **Why Study History?** • You Pay Taxes, pp. 19–22 (average) .... 90 mins. **Interdisciplinary Connections** • Main Idea: Growing Tensions With Britain, pp. 28–29 (average) .... 20 mins. **Document-Based Discovery** • Origins, pp. 2–5 (average) .... 90 mins.	**Voices of Freedom** • Paul Revere on the Boston Massacre, pp. 57–58 (average) **Customized Reader** • "I Heard the Word 'Fire'": The Boston Massacre, article IIB-4 (average)
4 The Fighting Begins (pp. 150–155) **Objectives** 1. Explain why Americans protested the Tea Act. 2. Describe how Britain responded to the Boston Tea Party. 3. Explain why fighting broke out at Lexington and Concord.	**Lesson Planner,** p. 21 (average) .... 45 mins. **Unit 2/Chapter 5** • Vocabulary Builder, p. 2 (basic) .... 10 mins. • Critical Thinking and Writing: Making Decisions, p. 4 (average) .... 20 mins. • Section 4 Quiz, p. 11 (average) .... 15 mins. **Chapter Tests** pp. 25–30 (average) .... 45 mins. **Interdisciplinary Connections** • Main Idea: Growing Tensions With Britain, pp. 26–27, 30 (average) .... 20 mins.	**Historical Outline Map Book** • Lexington and Concord, p. 23 (average)

Assessment Options

Teaching Resources
- Alternative Assessment booklet
- Section Quizzes, Unit 2, Chapter 5, pp. 8–11
- Chapter Tests, Chapter 5, pp. 25–30
- Test Bank CD-ROM

Student Performance Pack
- Guide to the Essentials of American History, Chapter 5 Test, p. 32
- Standardized Test Prep Handbook
- Interactive Student Tutorial CD-ROM

Interdisciplinary Connections

Teaching Resources
- Map Mystery, Unit 2, Chapter 5, p. 5
- Connecting History and Literature, Unit 2, Chapter 5, p. 6
- Interdisciplinary Connections, pp. 25–30

Voices of Freedom, pp. 54–58

Customized Reader, article IIB-4, IIIA-1

Historical Outline Map Book, pp. 21–23

Listening to Music CD
- Chester, side 2

Technology

AmericanHeritage® History of the United States CD-ROM
- Time Tour: The Road to Revolution in From Revolution to Republic
- History Makers: Abigail Adams, Patrick Henry

Interactive Student Tutorial CD-ROM

Test Bank CD-ROM

Color Transparencies
- The Boston Massacre, p. B-41
- The American Revolution, p. F-15
- Colonial Printing Press, p. H-29
- North Central States, p. I-73

Guided Reading Audiotapes (English/Spanish), side 2

Listening to Literature Audiocassettes: The American Experience
- Speech in the Virginia Convention, Patrick Henry, side 2

Listening to Music CD
- Chester, side 2

Resource Pro® CD-ROM

Prentice Hall United States History Video Collection™ (Spanish track available on disk version.) Vol. 2, Chs. 28, 31, 34; Vol. 4, Chs. 7, 13, 16

Prentice Hall Home Page www.phschool.com

Student Performance Pack

Guide to the Essentials of American History
- Ch. 5, pp. 28–32 (Available in English and Spanish)

Guided Reading Audiotapes (English/Spanish), side 2

Standardized Test Prep Handbook

Interactive Student Tutorial CD-ROM

BLOCK SCHEDULING
Activities with this icon will help you meet your Block Scheduling needs.

ENGLISH LANGUAGE LEARNERS
Activities with this icon are suitable for English Language Learners.

TEAM TEACHING
Activities and Background Notes with this icon present starting points for Team Teaching.

Teachers' Bibliography

From the Archives of AmericanHeritage®

Don't miss the special American Heritage® teaching notes found in this chapter.

HISTORY ALIVE!®

Contact Teachers' Curriculum Institute to learn more about History Alive!® resources on the events leading up to the American Revolution. See History Alive!® unit: Colonial Life and the American Revolution, Section 3, "Growing Conflict With England."

Explore your library to find these issues related to Chapter 5: *The Boston Massacre,* March 1980; *Daniel Boone,* June 1988; *The French and Indian War,* April 1991.

Prentice Hall Web Site You can access a structured, on-line environment that allows you to preview curriculum-related resources and receive updated information on groundbreaking events from around the nation and the world. (www.phschool.com)

Chapter 5

The Road to Revolution 1745–1775

Introducing the Chapter

Have students preview the main ideas of this chapter by looking over the visuals. Suggest they look for examples of potential or actual conflicts in British North America in the mid-1700s.

Using the Time Line To provide students with practice in reading a time line, play a game of "before" and "after" by asking students to complete sentences such as these: **(1)** Settlers started moving across the Appalachian Mountains __________ the French and Indian war. *(before)* **(2)** Parliament passed the Tea Act __________ the Proclamation of 1763. *(after)* **(3)** Fighting at Lexington and Concord occurred __________ the British captured Quebec. *(after)*

Have students list some additional services that they would like their school to provide. Examples might be busing for fans to after-school games, individual tutors, or exercise machines. Then ask students to consider ways to pay for these services, concluding that money would have to be raised. Have them decide if they want the services enough to contribute their own money to obtain them.

For additional *Why Study History?* support, see p. 146.

Chapter 5

The Road to Revolution

1745–1775

What's Ahead

Between 1754 and 1760, competition for land led to a conflict between England and France that is now known as the French and Indian War. The British, with the help of American colonists and Indian allies, put an end to French power in North America.

After the war, Britain angered colonists by taxing them without giving them representation in Parliament. Over the next years, colonial protests grew stronger. Finally, in April 1775, British troops and colonial farmers clashed at the villages of Lexington and Concord in Massachusetts. The battles marked the start of the American Revolution.

"Taxation without representation is tyranny!" This protest sparked a revolution in the 13 colonies. Today, American citizens have representation. Still, attempts to raise taxes always stir heated debate. To focus on this connection, look at the *Why Study History?* feature, "You Pay Taxes," in this chapter.

American Events

1740s Settlers cross Appalachian Mountains

1754 French and Indian War begins

1759 British capture of French Quebec is turning point of war

1745 | 1750 | 1755 | 1760

World Events

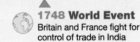

1748 World Event Britain and France fight for control of trade in India

1756 World Event Seven Years' War begins in Europe

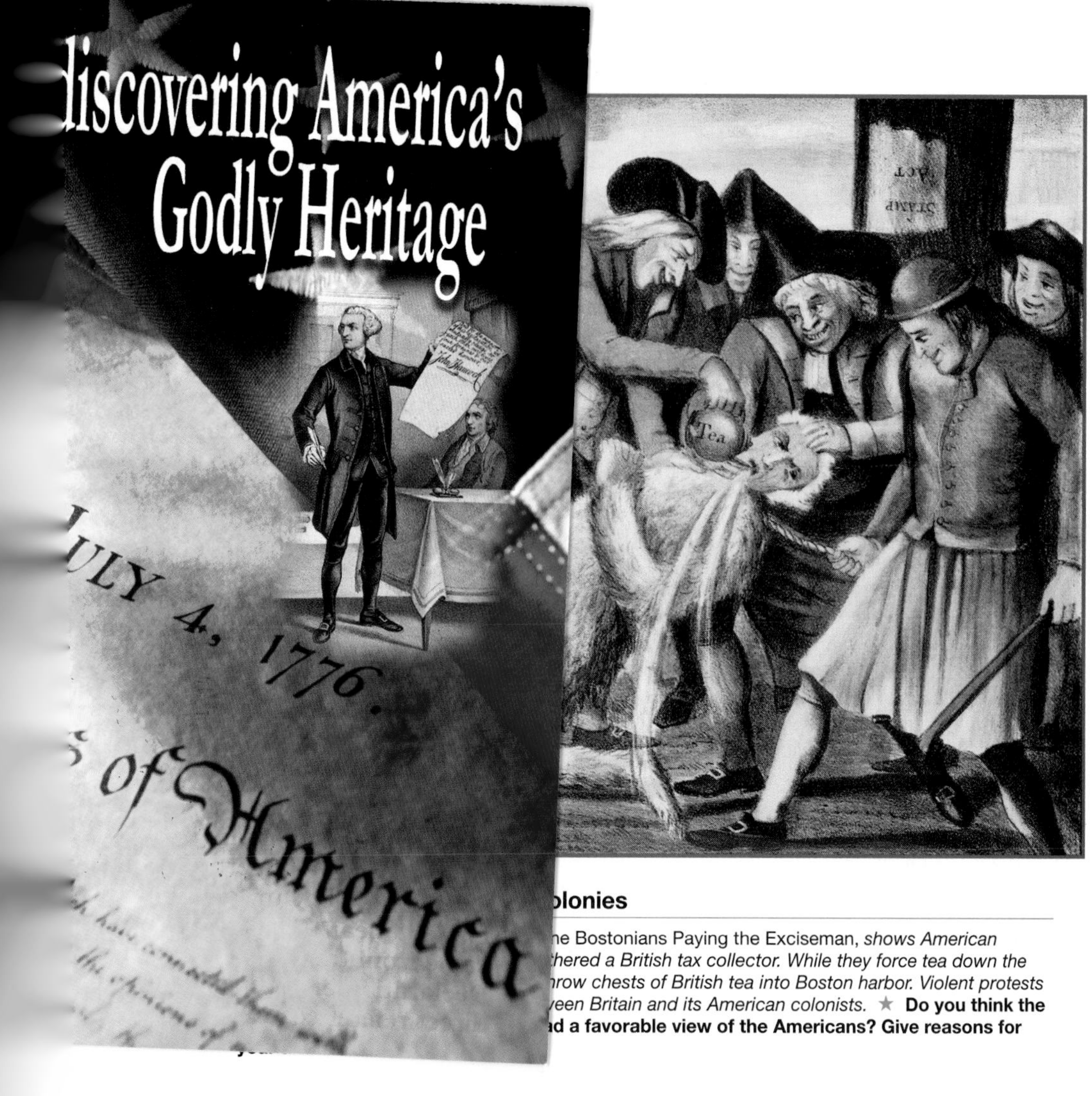

olonies

he Bostonians Paying the Exciseman, shows American
thered a British tax collector. While they force tea down the
hrow chests of British tea into Boston harbor. Violent protests
veen Britain and its American colonists. ★ **Do you think the**
d a favorable view of the Americans? Give reasons for

	1763 Proclamation of 1763 closes western lands to further settlement	**1773** Boston Tea Party is punished by the Intolerable Acts	**1775** Fighting breaks out at Concord and Lexington
1760	**1765**	**1770**	**1775**

1763 World Event Treaty of Paris ends French power in North America

1773 World Event British Parliament passes Tea Act

Writing Actively 

Responding to Art After students have studied the engraving and its caption, have them write a report that the British tax collector might have sent to the governor of Massachusetts. Students may assign a date for the incident and name the colonists involved. Have students try to describe what happened from the tax collector's point of view.

Viewing HISTORY ANSWER

Possible answer: No, the expressions on their faces make them look brutal, and they are shown committing violent acts.

★ *Background* ★ Art Note

Protests in the Colonies Cartoons and other depictions of events of the 1770s appeared in both colonial and British publications. Benjamin Franklin published one of the first colonial cartoons in 1754 (shown in Section 2), but he gave up his printing career in 1758 to take a diplomatic post in London. Paul Revere began publishing revolutionary cartoons in 1774. T

Documents and Literature

On pp. 538–541, you will find two readings to enrich this chapter:

1. Eyewitness Account "Exploring the Ohio Valley," excerpts from diplomat/soldier George Croghan's descriptive journal as he explored the territory won from France. (Use with Section 2.)

2. Literature "Revolutionary Tea," song about how colonists viewed Britain and the Tea Act of 1773. (Use with Section 4.)

Technology

Videodiscs/Videotapes
Show the *Prentice Hall United States History Video Collection*™ segments for this chapter. The videodisc version has a Spanish track. Press audio until you get the left channel for English or the right channel for Spanish, or use the bar codes in the Guidebook.

AmericanHeritage® History of the United States CD-ROM
- Time Tour: The Road to Revolution in From Revolution to Republic (*average*)

Section 1 Rivalry in North America

LESSON PLAN

Objectives

★ Name the European nations that competed for land in North America.

★ Explain why the French built a system of forts.

★ Explain why Indian nations became involved in the struggle between France and England.

1 Engage

Warm Up Write the term *territory* on the chalkboard. Ask students what a nation today must do to prove its control of a certain territory.

Activating Prior Knowledge Ask students what groups of people lived in North America in the 1750s. *(French, Spanish, Native Americans, Africans, English)* Have students work in small groups to list unique features of the English colonies.

Reading Actively

Before Reading Have students read the headings in the section and turn each heading into a question. Tell them to look for answers as they read.

2 Explore

Ask students to read the section. For homework, have them do research and a report on the conflict between the Iroquois nations

RESOURCE DIRECTORY

Teaching Resources
Lesson Planner, p. 18
Unit 2/Chapter 5
- Biography Flashcard: Jean Baptiste Pointe du Sable, p. 7

Transparencies
Geography and History
- North Central States, p. I-73

1 Rivalry in North America

As You Read

Explore These Questions
- What European nations competed for land in North America?
- Why did the French build a system of forts?
- Why did Indian nations become involved in the struggle between France and England?

Identify
- Hurons
- Joseph Brant

SETTING the Scene In June 1749, the governor of New France sent a group of men down the Ohio River. The men stopped from time to time to nail an engraved lead plate to a tree or to set one in the ground. These plates proclaimed that the fertile land of the Ohio Valley belonged to France.

About the same time, Christopher Gist, a Virginia fur trader, was also roaming the Ohio Valley. Gist worked for the Ohio Company, a group of English investors. King George II had given the company a huge tract of land in the valley. They sent Gist to find a good spot for settlement.

Gist chose a site where the Ohio and Allegheny rivers meet. On a rock beside the water, he carved these words:

> The Ohio Company
> FEBy 1751
> By Christopher Gist

Clearly, with two great powers claiming the same land, the stage was set for conflict. At stake was more than control of the Ohio River valley. France and England each hoped to drive the other nation out of North America altogether.

Competing Claims

By the mid-1700s, the major powers of Europe were locked in a worldwide struggle for empire. England, France, Spain, and the Netherlands competed for trade and colonies in far-flung corners of the globe. The English colonies in North America soon became caught up in the contest.

By the late 1600s, England had already taken over New York from the Dutch. Its two remaining rivals in North America were Spain and France. The major threat from Spain was in the West Indies and along the border between Georgia and Spanish Florida. England and Spain clashed often in these areas.

Spain also had settlements in present-day New Mexico, Texas, and Arizona. However, these settlements were located far away from England's colonies on the Atlantic coast. As a result, the English paid little attention to them.

The threat from France was much more serious to the English colonies. France claimed a vast area that stretched from the St. Lawrence River westward to the Great Lakes and southward to the Gulf of Mexico. To protect their land claims, the French built an extensive system of forts. (See the map on page 133.)

Connections With Geography

As the French explored and settled North American lands, they gave French names to forts, towns, and natural features. Familiar examples of these French names include *Detroit* (narrow water passage), *Des Moines* (belonging to the monks), *Baton Rouge* (red stick), and *Vermont* (green mountain).

★ Customized Instruction ★

English Language Learners

Reinforcing information English language learners may need help to understand the important content in this section. Pair English language learners with English-proficient volunteers. Have ELL students read the text aloud, one segment at a time. At the end of each segment, have them orally summarize the content, with feedback from their partners. Use these questions as summary guides: **(1)** How did both the French and English establish claims in the Ohio valley? **(2)** Why was France a greater threat to the English than Spain? **(3)** Why did the English-French rivalry heat up after 1740? **(4)** How did the Indians respond to the French-English rivalry in Ohio? *(average)* ELL

Conflict in the Ohio Valley

At first, most English settlers were content to remain along the Atlantic coast. By the 1740s, however, traders from New York and Pennsylvania were crossing the Appalachian Mountains in search of furs. Pushing into the Ohio Valley, they tried to take over the profitable French trade with the Indians.

France was determined to stop the English from intruding on their territory. The Ohio River was especially important to the French because it provided a vital link between their lands in Canada and the Mississippi River. In 1751, the French government sent the following orders to its officials in New France:

> "Drive from the Ohio River any European foreigners, and do it in a way that will make them lose all taste for trying to return."

Native Americans Choose Sides

Native Americans had hunted animals and grown crops in the Ohio Valley for centuries. They did not want to give up the land to European settlers, French or English. One Native American protested to an English trader:

> "You and the French are like the two edges of a pair of shears. And we are the cloth which is to be cut to pieces between them."

Still, the growing conflict between England and France was too dangerous to ignore. Some Native Americans decided that the only way to protect their way of life was to take sides in the struggle.

Allies for the French

At the same time, both France and England tried to make Indian allies. The French expected the Indians to side with them. Most French in North America were trappers and traders, not farmers like the English. The French generally did not destroy Indian hunting grounds by clearing forests for farms. Also, many French trappers married Native American women and adopted their ways.

France built strong alliances with several Native American groups. As you read, the French gained the support of the Algonquins. (See page 83.) They also built friendly relations with the **Hurons.** The Hurons often served as negotiators between French traders and other Indian nations.

North America in 1753

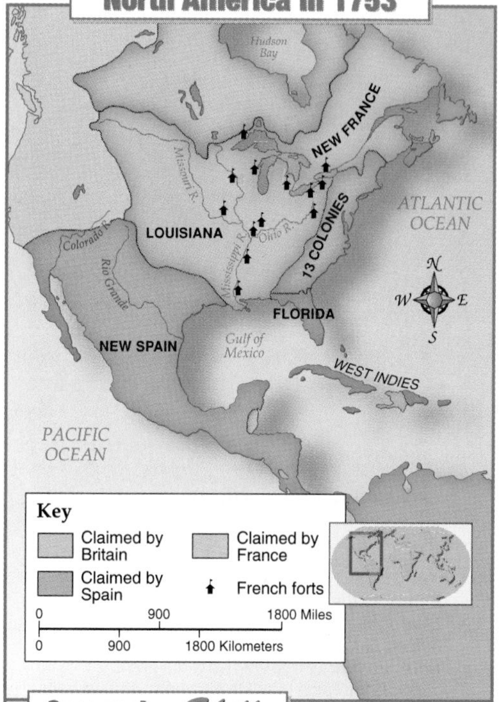

Geography *Skills* **In 1753, France and Spain claimed land to the north, south, and west of the 13 English colonies.**

1. **Location** On the map, locate: **(a)** New France, **(b)** Louisiana, **(c)** Florida, **(d)** Mississippi River, **(e)** Ohio River.
2. **Region** Which nation controlled Florida in 1753?
3. **Critical Thinking** Note the location of the French forts in 1753. Why do you think France built forts at these locations?

and the Algonquins and Hurons, and how that conflict was related to Europeans.

3 Teach

Write this statement on the chalkboard: "By the late 1740s, both the French and the British knew that a struggle for control of North America was inevitable—it had to happen." Have students decide as a class if they agree or disagree with the statement, using evidence from the section.

4 Assess

To close the lesson, have students complete the section review. Or have them work in small groups to prepare "map talks," using the map on this page to explain how the stage for conflict in North America was set by 1753.

★ ★ ★ ★ ★ ★ ★ ★ ★ ★ ★ ★ ★ ★ ★ ★ ★ ★

Geography *Skills*

ANSWERS **1.** Review locations with students. **2.** Spain **3.** Students should note that forts were located along rivers and on the Great Lakes to protect New France from English settlers who might travel west by water.

Writing Actively

After Reading Ask students to write a short essay on the causes and effects of rivalry in North America in the mid-1700s.

★ *Activity* ★

Connections With Geography

Mapping the Ohio-Mississippi River route On U.S. outline maps, have students draw and label the: **(1)** 2 rivers that form the Ohio R., **(2)** Ohio R., **(3)** Mississippi R., **(4)** Great Lakes, **(5)** Missouri R. Have them label New Orleans and Pittsburgh and then trace in red the Canadian–New Orleans water route. *(average)* ELL T

★ Section 1 Review ★

ANSWERS

1. (a) p. 133, **(b)** p. 134

2. Spain, France

3. forts and alliances with Indians

4. (a) French trappers/traders did not clear forests for farms or destroy hunting grounds; some married Indian women and adopted their ways. **(b)** to get help against their Algonquin enemies; because English trade goods were cheaper than French goods

5. They were competing globally for trade and colonies.

6. Possible answers: **(a)** French-English rivalry would hurt Indians. **(b)** No, Europeans ("shears") would destroy Indians ("cloth").

Activity

Guided Instruction
Tell students they may have to explain away the problems that Britain caused Indians. Have them review the section before drafting the speech.

ASSESSMENT See the rubrics in the Alternative Assessment booklet in the Teaching Resources.

ANSWER
Possible answer: His blanket and hair reflect Native American styles, but he wears a European-style shirt and carries a gun.

RESOURCE DIRECTORY

Teaching Resources
Lesson Planner, p. 19
Unit 2/Chapter 5
• Section 1 Quiz, p. 8

Biography **Joseph Brant**

Known to the British as Joseph Brant, the Mohawk chief Thayendanegea was a valuable ally. He helped persuade the Iroquois nations to side with Britain in their struggle against the French. In later years, Brant became a Christian and helped translate the Bible into the Mohawk language. ★ **How does this painting show that Brant combined Native American and English cultures?**

Allies for the English

In contrast to the French, English settlers were mostly farm families. They ignored Indian rights when they cleared land for crops. Nor did they respect Indian ways. As the English moved onto their lands, the Indians fought back.

Still, in the end, England also found allies among Native Americans. The English won over the powerful Iroquois nations, who were old enemies of the Algonquins and the Hurons.

An English trader and official, William Johnson, helped gain Iroquois support for England. The Iroquois respected Johnson, and they listened carefully when he urged them to side with the English. Johnson was one of the few English settlers who had an Indian wife, Molly Brant. She was the sister of the Mohawk chief Thayendanegea, known to the English as **Joseph Brant.** Brant became a valuable ally for the English.

Some Indians supported the English because they charged lower prices for trade goods than the French did. Many Indians began to buy goods from English rather than French traders. The loss of Indian trade angered the French, who were determined to defend their claims in the Ohio Valley.

★ Section 1 Review ★

Recall

1. **Identify** **(a)** Hurons, **(b)** Joseph Brant.

Comprehension

2. Who were England's two main rivals in North America?
3. What steps did France take to protect its lands in North America?
4. **(a)** Why did the French expect Native Americans to side with them? **(b)** Why did some Indians side with the English?

Critical Thinking and Writing

5. **Applying Information** How did the rivalry among England, France, and Spain in North America reflect their worldwide struggle for power?
6. **Recognizing Points of View** Reread the statement by the Native American to the English trader on page 133. **(a)** What did the speaker mean by these words? **(b)** Do you think he felt that Native Americans could hold out against the British and French? Explain.

Activity **Writing a Speech** You are William Johnson. Write a speech in which you explain to the Iroquois why they should help the English instead of the French.

★ Background ★

Viewpoints

Enough is enough! The dim view many Native Americans took of the English grew out of their own history as well as unfair treatment at the hands of the English. In the late 1600s, for example, the Iroquois established sovereignty over the Leni-Lenape in Pennsylvania and began selling Leni-Lenape lands to English colonists. Dispossessed, many Leni-Lenape moved from Pennsylvania to Ohio, much of which was unclaimed by any Native American group at that time. When the Iroquois granted Ohio land to the English, many Native Americans remembered the past and welcomed French resistance to the English presence there.

The French and Indian War

As You Read

Explore These Questions

- Why did the British and French go to war in North America?
- What advantages did each side have in the war?
- How did the Treaty of Paris affect North America?

Identify

- George Washington
- French and Indian War
- Albany Plan of Union
- Edward Braddock
- William Pitt
- James Wolfe
- Marquis de Montcalm
- Plains of Abraham
- Treaty of Paris

SETTING the Scene Captain Joncaire had just sat down to dinner on December 4, 1753, when a tall young man strode into the room. He introduced himself as Major **George Washington.** He said he had a letter from the English lieutenant governor of Virginia, Robert Dinwiddie, to the commander of the French forces in the Ohio Valley.

Joncaire told his visitor where the commander could be found. The captain then politely invited Washington to dine. As they ate, Joncaire boasted that France was determined to take full possession of the Ohio River valley. The remark made Washington pause. He knew that in the letter he was carrying, Dinwiddie warned the French to get out of the Ohio Valley!

For years, tensions had been building between the French and the English. By the 1750s, armed conflict seemed certain. The war that followed would forever change the balance of power in North America.

Fighting Begins

Three times between 1689 and 1748, France and Great Britain* had fought for power in Europe and North America. Each war ended with an uneasy peace.

In 1754, fighting broke out for a fourth time. The struggle that followed lasted until 1760. English settlers called the conflict the **French and Indian War** because it pitted them against France and its Native American allies.

Scuffles between France and Britain in the Ohio River valley triggered the opening shots of the French and Indian War. Young George Washington played a major role in this early phase of the conflict.

George Washington

At the time, George Washington was only 22 years old, but he was an able and brave soldier. Washington had grown up on a plantation in Virginia, the son of wealthy parents. Gifted at mathematics, he began working as a land surveyor at the age of 15. His job took him to frontier lands in western Virginia. In 1753, when Lieutenant Governor Dinwiddie wanted to warn the French out of Ohio, Washington offered to deliver the message. On this dangerous mission, the young officer narrowly escaped death.

After Washington returned, Dinwiddie promoted him to colonel. He also sent the young man west again. At the time, some wealthy Virginians claimed land in the upper Ohio Valley. To protect their claims, they urged the governor of Virginia to build a fort where the Monongahela and Allegheny rivers meet. (See the map on page 138.) Dinwiddie ordered Washington to take a party of 150 men and build the fort.

* In 1707, England and Scotland were officially joined into the United Kingdom of Great Britain. After that date, the terms *Great Britain* and *British* were used to describe the country and its people. However, the terms *England* and *English* were still used throughout much of the 1700s.

★ Background ★

Did You Know?

Follow the horn! Soldiers in the 1750s carried gunpowder in hollowed-out cow or ox horns. Many British soldiers, however, carried powder horns on which artisans engraved maps of war zones. The horns were popular souvenirs of the soldiers' tour of duty in North America, but they may also have been their best guides through the wilderness.

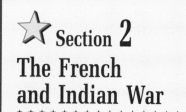

Section 2
The French and Indian War

LESSON PLAN

Objectives

★ Explain why the British and French went to war in North America.

★ Describe the advantages of each side in the war.

★ Describe how the Treaty of Paris affected North America.

1 Engage

Warm Up Write this headline on the chalkboard: "ENGLAND AND FRANCE AT WAR: Both Claim Native American Lands." Have students write responses.

Activating Prior Knowledge Remind students that the French-Indian link resulted from the fur trade and that the British had ties to the Iroquois. Ask: "If you wanted to be on the winning side, which side would you join? Why? What might happen if your ally lost?"

Reading Actively

Before Reading Have students read the section to answer the questions in Explore These Questions.

Technology

Videodiscs/Videotapes
Prentice Hall United States History Video Collection™, Vol. 2, Ch. 28, "The Colonial Wars," 4 mins (*average*) ELL

Chapter 28

Vol. 2, Ch. 31, "The French and Indian War," 1:26 min (*average*) ELL

Chapter 31

2 Explore

Have students read the section. For homework, ask them to find out about the Acadians and how the French and Indian War affected them. Some students may enjoy reading Henry Wadsworth Longfellow's poem about the Acadians, "Evangeline."

3 Teach

Tell students to assume the role of war correspondents for a newspaper in a neutral country. As you progress through the section, have them compose a headline and two sentences summarizing the significance of each major event.

4 Assess

To close the lesson, have students complete the section review. Or have students work in small groups and divide up these roles: George Washington, Captain Joncaire, Governor Dinwiddie, Benjamin Franklin, Edward Braddock, William Pitt, James Wolfe, Marquis de Montcalm. Other group members are reporters who interview the person before and/or after major events described in the section.

★ ★ ★ ★ ★ ★ ★ ★ ★ ★ ★ ★ ★ ★ ★ ★ ★

Biography

ANSWER

Possible answer: Students may already know that Washington commanded the army in the American Revolution and that he was the first President of the United States.

Conflict at Fort Necessity

In April 1754, Washington and his party headed for Ohio country. Along the way, they heard that the French had just completed Fort Duquesne (doo KAYN) at the fork of the Monongahela and Allegheny rivers. This was the very spot where Dinwiddie had ordered Washington to build a fort.

Determined to carry out his orders, Washington journeyed on. Indian allies revealed that a French scouting party was camped in the woods ahead. Marching quietly through the night, Washington surprised and scattered the French.

Washington's success was short-lived, however. Hearing that the French were planning to counterattack, he and his men quickly built a makeshift stockade. They named it Fort Necessity. A huge force of French and Indians surrounded the fort. Trapped and heavily outnumbered, the Virginians were forced to surrender. Soon after, the French released Washington, and he returned home to Virginia.

Despite Washington's defeat, the British quickly saw the importance of the skirmish. "The volley fired by this young Virginian in the forests of America," a British writer noted, "has set the world in flames."

Biography George Washington

Like many wealthy young Virginians, George Washington enjoyed dancing and horseback riding. At the same time, he worked hard managing the family plantation and later as a surveyor. After his defeats in the French and Indian War, Washington wrote, "I have been on the losing [side] ever since I entered the service." Little did he know that he would one day lead his country to independence.

★ **List two facts you know about Washington.**

The Albany Congress

While Washington was defending Fort Necessity, delegates from seven colonies gathered in Albany, New York. The delegates to the Albany Congress met for two reasons. They wanted to persuade the Iroquois to help them against the French. They also wanted to plan a united colonial defense.

The Iroquois refuse

Iroquois leaders listened patiently to the delegates, but they were wary of the request for help. The British and French "are quarreling about lands which belong to us," pointed out Hendrik, a Mohawk chief. "And such a quarrel as this may end in our destruction." In addition, the Iroquois believed that the French were stronger and had more forts than the British.

In the end, the Iroquois left without agreeing to help the British. At the same time, they did not join the French either.

Franklin's plan of union

The delegates in Albany knew that the colonists had to work together to defeat the French. Benjamin Franklin, the delegate from Pennsylvania, proposed the **Albany Plan of Union.** The plan was an attempt to create "one general government" for the 13 colonies. It called for a Grand Council made up of representatives from each colony. The council would make laws, raise taxes, and set up the defense of the colonies.

The delegates voted to accept the Plan of Union. When the plan was submitted to the colonial assemblies, however, not one ap-

★ *Background* ★

Did You Know?

Washington, the homebody Three years before the French and Indian War began, young George Washington took his first and last trip outside the area that would later become the United States. In 1751, he accompanied his older half brother, Lawrence, on a voyage to the Caribbean island of Barbados. They hoped the tropical climate would cure Lawrence's tuberculosis.

★ *Background* ★

Did You Know?

Necessary but not sufficient When the French attacked General Braddock, George Washington moved quickly to protect his forces by building a makeshift stockade called Fort Necessity. The fort was far from ideal because it was built in a soggy creek bottom. Even worse, it was surrounded on three sides by thickly wooded hills, making it easy for the French and Indians to attack.

proved it. None of the colonies wanted to give up any of its powers to a central council. The largest colony, Virginia, had not even sent a delegation to the Albany Congress! A disappointed Benjamin Franklin expressed his frustration at the failure of his plan:

> “Everyone cries a union is necessary. But when they come to the manner and form of the union, their weak noodles are perfectly distracted.”

The Two Sides

At the start of the French and Indian War, the French had several advantages over the British. Because the English colonies could not agree on a united defense, 13 separate colonial assemblies had to approve all decisions. New France, on the other hand, had a single government that could act quickly when necessary. Also, the French had the support of many more Indian allies than the British did.

Britain, however, also had strengths. At the time, the population of the English colonies was about 15 times greater than that of New France. The English colonies were clustered along the coast, so they were easier to defend than the widely scattered French settlements. In addition, while most Indians sided with the French, the British did have some Indian allies. Finally, the British navy ruled the seas.

Early English Defeats

In 1755, General **Edward Braddock** led British and colonial troops in an attack against Fort Duquesne. Braddock was a stubborn man, called “Bulldog” behind his back. He knew how to fight a war in the open fields of Europe. However, he knew little about how to fight in the wilderness of North America. Still, the general boasted that he would sweep the French from the Ohio Valley.

Disaster for “Bulldog” Braddock

Braddock’s men moved slowly because they had to clear a road through thick forests for their cannons and other heavy gear. George Washington, who went with Braddock, was upset by the slow pace. Indian scouts warned Braddock that he was headed for trouble. He ignored them.

As the British neared Fort Duquesne, the French and their Indian allies launched a surprise attack. Sharpshooters hid in the forest and picked off British soldiers, whose bright-red uniforms made them easy targets. Washington later wrote to his mother:

> “Our [forces] consisted of about 1,300 well-armed troops, chiefly of the English soldiers, who were struck with such a panic that they behaved with more cowardice than it is possible to conceive. The officers behaved gallantly in order to encourage their

Viewing History **A Call for Union**

In 1754, Benjamin Franklin printed this famous cartoon in the Pennsylvania Gazette. *That year, Franklin drew up the Albany Plan of Union. However, his hopes for political unity among the 13 colonies did not succeed.*

★ **Summarize the main point of Franklin’s cartoon in your own words.**

◄ *Model of Ben Franklin*

Reading Actively

During Reading Have students create a “Winner-Loser” graphic organizer for battles of the French and Indian War from Fort Duquesne to Quebec. Their organizers should list battles in chronological order, include British and/or French commanders, and note any special outcomes besides who won and lost.

ANSWER

Possible answer: Unless the colonies unite, they would not be able to defeat the French or organize a united defense.

★ Activity ★

Connections With Mathematics

Estimating population About 100,000 people lived in New France in 1754, but there were 15 times as many English colonists at the time. Ask: “How many English colonists were there?” *(1,500,000)* Have students compare population densities using the areas of New France and the colonies. *(average)* ELL T

★ Background ★

Turning Points

Defeat and revelation In *Braddock at the Monongahela*, Paul E. Kopperman contends that General Braddock’s defeat had far-reaching impact by helping raise public opinion of George Washington to nearly divine status, and by convincing colonists that Britain could not protect them. It thus planted early seeds of discontent that would lead to revolt and independence.

Geography *Skills*

ANSWERS **1.** Review locations with students. **2.** about 800 miles **3.** Yes, most British advances were by water. The taking of Quebec was accomplished by river.

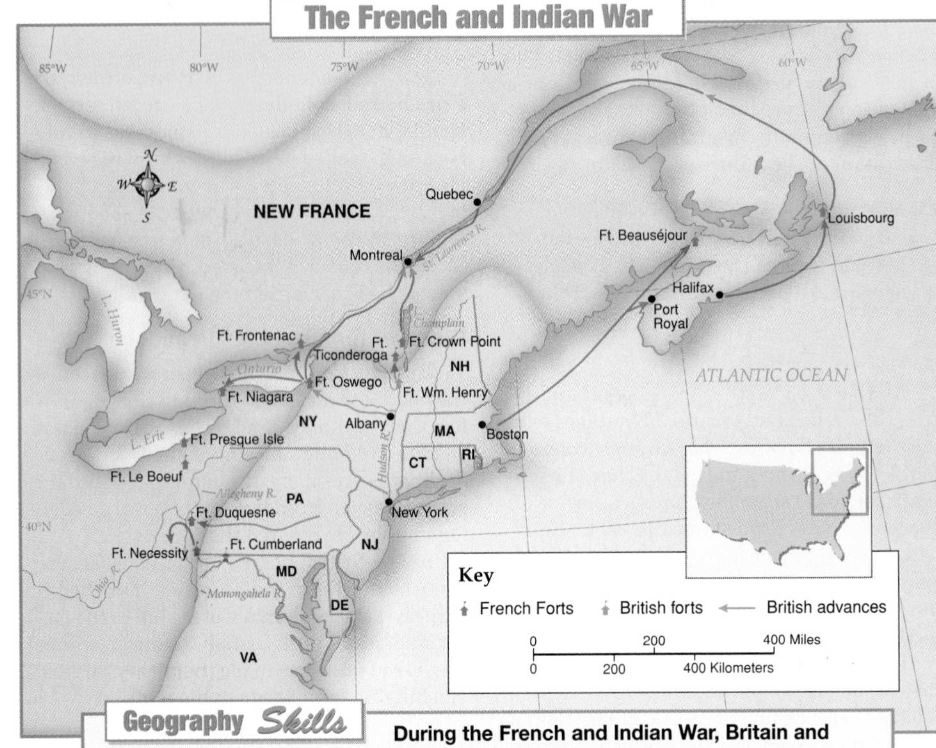

Geography *Skills* **During the French and Indian War, Britain and France battled for control of North America. The conflict began in the Ohio River valley.**

1. **Location** On the map, locate: **(a)** Fort Necessity, **(b)** Fort Duquesne, **(c)** Louisbourg, **(d)** Quebec, **(e)** Albany.
2. **Movement** About how many miles did advancing British forces travel from Louisbourg to Quebec?
3. **Critical Thinking** Based on the map, do you think naval power was important in fighting the French and Indian War? Explain.

men, for which they suffered greatly, there being nearly 60 killed or wounded—a large proportion out of the number we had! ❞

Braddock himself had five horses shot out from under him before he fell, fatally injured. Washington was luckier. He later reported that he "escaped without a wound, although I had four bullets through my coat."

Almost half the British were killed or wounded. Washington and other survivors returned to Virginia with news of Braddock's defeat. Washington was now put in command of a small force of men. For the rest of the war, he had the almost impossible task of guarding the long Virginia frontier against Indian attack.

Further British setbacks

During the next two years, the war continued to go badly for the British. British attacks against several French forts ended in failure. Meanwhile, the French won important victories, capturing Fort Oswego on Lake Ontario and Fort William Henry on

★ *Customized Instruction* ★

Visual Learners

Creating three-dimensional battle maps
Divide students into small groups and have each one select a battle covered in this section. Have them research the geographic features of the site of their battle. Then have them construct a three-dimensional terrain map of the battle site. They may use clay, salt dough, miniatures, food coloring, color markers, or other materials to create their maps. When the maps are completed, have groups demonstrate how geographic features affected the battle. Remind them to consider the impact of location such as the accessibility of Fort Louisbourg to the British navy. (*average*) ELL T

RESOURCE DIRECTORY

Teaching Resources
Unit 2/Chapter 5
- Practice Your Skills: Reading a Time Line, p. 3

Critical Thinking | Managing Information | Communication | **Maps, Charts, and Graphs**

Reading a Time Line

How Will I Use This Skill?

A time line is a graphic organizer that lists events in chronological, or time, order. Using a time line can help you understand sequences and see relationships between events. You might find time lines, not only in history books, but also in magazine and newspaper articles about current events.

LEARN the Skill

At the start of each chapter in this book, you will find a two-page horizontal time line. It is organized from left to right, with the earliest date on the left. Some events may take place over several years. This will be indicated on the time line.

Time lines are divided into equal time periods. The total period of time from beginning to end is called the time span. Use the following steps to read a time line:

1. Look at the first and last dates on the time line to determine the complete time span.
2. Notice the intervals, or divisions, on the time line.
3. Look at the specific events and dates listed.
4. Determine if there is any relationship between events.

PRACTICE the Skill

Use the time line below to answer the following questions.

1. (a) What is the earliest event shown? (b) What is the latest event? (c) What is the time span of the time line?
2. How many years are there between dates on the time line?
3. (a) What took place in 1755? (b) When did the fighting in North America end?
4. (a) How would you describe the success of the British in the early years of the war? (b) What relation did the events of 1758 have to the events of 1760?

APPLY the Skill

Make a time line of important events in your life. Use your life up to this point as the time span. Include at least six events that you feel made a major difference in your life.

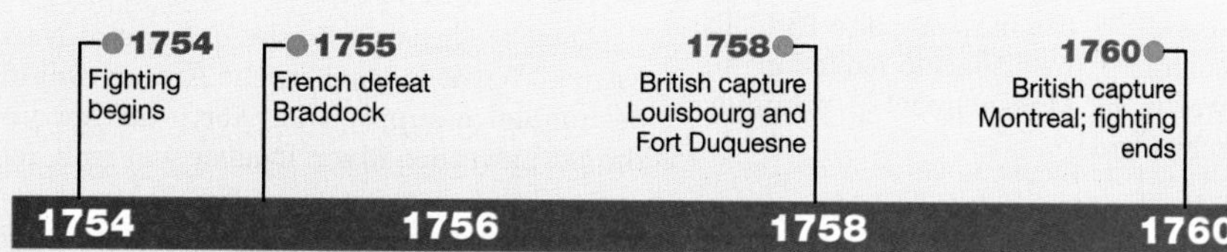

1754 Fighting begins
1755 French defeat Braddock
1758 British capture Louisbourg and Fort Duquesne
1760 British capture Montreal; fighting ends
1754
1756
1758
1760

Skills FOR LIFE

PRACTICE the Skill ANSWERS

1. (a) 1754—Fighting begins **(b)** 1760—British capture Montreal; fighting ends **(c)** about 6 years

2. 2 years

3. (a) French defeat Braddock **(b)** 1760

4. (a) Britain had little success in the early years of the war. **(b)** The British victories in 1758 turned the tide of the war, leading to the final French defeat.

APPLY the Skill

Guided Instruction

Remind students to choose even intervals, possibly one- or two-year divisions. Suggest they might extend their time line beyond their current age and include some future goals and dates. Encourage students to write a summary of what their time line might reveal to others who read it.

ASSESSMENT See the rubrics in the Alternative Assessment booklet in the Teaching Resources.

★ Background ★ Viewpoints

No respect In the French and Indian War, British troops did most of the fighting and left all of the support tasks to the colonial militias. The British were condescending and arrogant toward the Americans. One British colonel described them as "sufficient to work our boats, drive our Waggons, and…do the Work that in inhabited Countrys are performed by Peasants." Colonials were subjected to ridicule. In 1755, an English army surgeon supposedly penned new words to an old tune. They mocked a colonial named "Yankee Doodle" who rode to town on a pony, stuck a feather in his hat, and "call[ed] it macaroni." *Macaroni* was a scornful term used for dandies, who slavishly followed the latest fashions in French clothing.

Technology

Videodiscs/Videotapes

Prentice Hall United States History Video Collection™, Vol. 2, Ch. 34, "America in 1763," 2:20 mins (*average*) ELL

Chapter 34

Writing Actively

After Reading Have students state one important fact from each of the six subsections in this section.

Geography Skills

ANSWERS **1.** Review locations with students. **2.** Britain and Spain; Russia had some land claims in the Northwest. **3.** The treaty vastly reduced French power in North America.

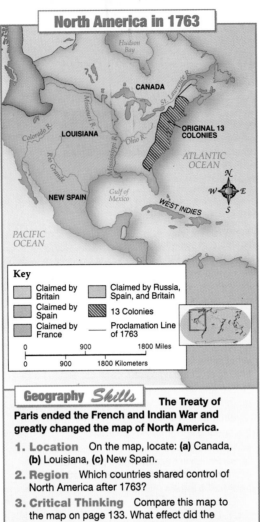

RESOURCE DIRECTORY

Teaching Resources
Unit 2/Chapter 5
- Map Mystery: Why Fort Niagara? p. 5
- Section 2 Quiz, p. 9

North America in 1763

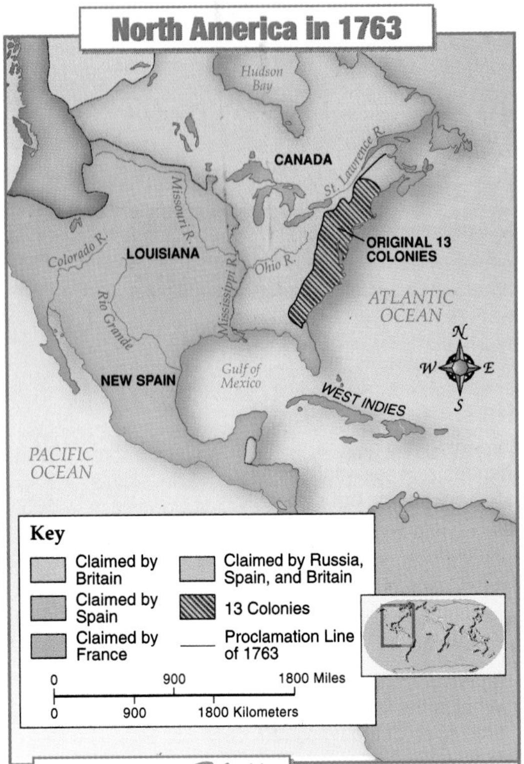

Geography Skills **The Treaty of Paris ended the French and Indian War and greatly changed the map of North America.**

1. **Location** On the map, locate: **(a)** Canada, **(b)** Louisiana, **(c)** New Spain.
2. **Region** Which countries shared control of North America after 1763?
3. **Critical Thinking** Compare this map to the map on page 133. What effect did the Treaty of Paris have on French power in North America?

Lake George. (See the map on page 138.) To English colonists, the situation looked grim. In the words of Massachusetts minister Jonathan Edwards:

> “God indeed is remarkably frowning upon us every where; our enemies get up above us very high, and we are brought down very low: They are the Head, and we are the Tail. . . . What will become of us God only knows.”

The Tide of Battle Turns

In 1757, **William Pitt** became the new head of the British government. Pitt was a bold leader. “I believe that I can save this nation and that no one else can,” he declared with great confidence.

Pitt set out to win the war in North America. Once that goal was achieved, he argued, the British would be free to focus on victory in other parts of the world.* Pitt sent Britain's best generals to North America. To encourage colonists to support the war, he promised large payments for military services and supplies.

Under Pitt's leadership, the tide of battle turned. In 1758, Major General Jeffrey Amherst captured Louisbourg, the most important fort in French Canada. That year, the British also won more Iroquois support.

The Iroquois persuaded the Delawares at Fort Duquesne to abandon the French. Without the Delawares, the French could no longer hold the fort. Acting quickly, the British seized Fort Duquesne, which they renamed Fort Pitt after the British leader. The city of Pittsburgh later grew up on the site of Fort Pitt.

The Fall of New France

The British enjoyed even greater success in 1759. By summer, they had pushed the French from Fort Niagara, Crown Point, and Fort Ticonderoga (ti kahn duh ROH guh). Now, Pitt sent General **James Wolfe** to take Quebec, capital of New France.

Battle for Quebec

Quebec was vital to the defense of New France. Without Quebec, the French would be unable to supply their forts farther up the St. Lawrence River. Quebec was well de-

* By 1756, fighting between the French and British had broken out in Europe. There, it became known as the Seven Years' War. The British and the French also fought in India. In the early years of the war, the British suffered setbacks on every front.

★ **Activity** ★

Cooperative Learning

Creating diary entries Divide students into three groups. Tell the members of one group to suppose they are French soldiers during the French and Indian War. The second group will represent British soldiers; the third group, American colonists fighting alongside the British. Have students in each group collaborate to write diary entries showing their group's point of view about these events: **(a)** General Braddock's attack on Fort Duquesne, **(b)** the battle for Quebec, and **(c)** the British capture of Montreal. Remind students to include facts about each event as well as thoughts and feelings of participants. Invite each group to share its diary with the class and compare the different points of view. (*average*) fended, though. The city sat atop a steep cliff high above the St. Lawrence. An able French general, the **Marquis de Montcalm,** was prepared to fight off any British attack.

General Wolfe devised a bold plan to capture Quebec. He knew that Montcalm had only a few soldiers guarding the cliff because the French thought that it was too steep to climb. Late one night, Wolfe ordered British troops to move quietly in small boats to the foot of the cliff. Under cover of darkness, the soldiers swarmed ashore and scrambled to the top.

The next morning, Montcalm awakened to some shocking news. A force of 4,000 British troops were drawn up on the **Plains of Abraham,** a grassy field just outside the city.

Montcalm quickly marched out his own troops to meet the enemy. A fierce battle followed. When it was over, both Montcalm and Wolfe were dead. Moments before Wolfe died, a soldier gave him the news that the British had won. Wolfe reportedly whispered, "Now, God be praised, I will die in peace." On September 17, 1759, Quebec surrendered to the British.

Treaty of Paris

The fall of Quebec sealed the fate of New France. In 1760, the British took Montreal, and the war in North America ended. Fighting dragged on in Europe for several more years. Finally, in 1763, Britain and France signed the **Treaty of Paris,** officially bringing the long conflict to an end.

The Treaty of Paris marked the end of French power in North America. Under the treaty, Britain gained Canada and all French lands east of the Mississippi River. France was allowed to keep two islands in the Gulf of St. Lawrence, as well as its rich sugar-growing islands in the West Indies. Spain, which had entered the war on the French side in 1762, gave up Florida to Britain. In return, Spain received all French land west of the Mississippi. In addition, Spain gained the vital port city of New Orleans. Spain retained control of its vast empire in Central and South America.

After years of fighting, peace returned to North America. Yet, in a few short years, a new conflict would break out. This time, the struggle would pit Britain against its own 13 colonies.

★ Section 2 Review ★

Recall

1. **Locate** **(a)** Fort Necessity, **(b)** Fort Duquesne, **(c)** Louisbourg, **(d)** Quebec.
2. **Identify** **(a)** George Washington, **(b)** French and Indian War, **(c)** Albany Plan of Union, **(d)** Edward Braddock, **(e)** William Pitt, **(f)** James Wolfe, **(g)** Marquis de Montcalm, **(h)** Plains of Abraham, **(i)** Treaty of Paris.

Comprehension

3. What were the causes of the French and Indian War?
4. **(a)** List two strengths of the French in the French and Indian War. **(b)** List two strengths of the British.
5. **(a)** What lands did Britain gain under the Treaty of Paris? **(b)** How did the treaty affect French power in North America?

Critical Thinking and Writing

6. **Analyzing Ideas** **(a)** How would the Albany Plan of Union have helped the colonies fight the French? **(b)** Why do you think colonists rejected the Plan of Union?
7. **Linking Past and Present** How might your life be different if France, not England, had won the French and Indian War?

Activity **Creating a Battle Plan** You are a British commander at the start of the French and Indian War. You know all of your strengths and weaknesses and those of your enemy. Examine the map on page 138. Then, write up a brief statement explaining why you think you should attack the French fort at Louisbourg.

★ Section 2 Review ★

ANSWERS

1. See map, p. 138.

2. **(a)–(b)** p. 135, **(c)** p. 136, **(d)** p. 137, **(e)–(f)** p. 140, **(g)–(i)** p. 141

3. Long-term cause: the French-English struggle over North America; immediate cause: control of the Ohio Valley

4. **(a)** New France had a unified government that could act quickly; the French had more Indian allies than the British. **(b)** The coastal English colonies were easier to defend and had a much larger population than New France.

5. **(a)** Canada; all lands east of the Mississippi River **(b)** ended French power in North America

6. **(a)** created a united defense **(b)** Individual colonies refused to give up power to a central council.

7. Possible answers: With France controlling North America, French would be the chief language of North America and French law and models of government might have shaped the United States.

Guided Instruction
Have students begin by reviewing the map. Remind them to consider the importance Louisbourg might have had for the French.

ASSESSMENT See the rubrics in the Alternative Assessment booklet in the Teaching Resources.

Section 3

A Crisis Over Taxes

★ ★ ★ ★ ★ ★ ★ ★ ★ ★ ★ ★ ★ ★ ★ ★ ★

LESSON PLAN

Objectives

★ Explain the goal of the Proclamation of 1763.

★ Describe how colonists protested British taxes.

★ Identify the Boston Massacre.

1 Engage

Warm Up Ask students to complete this sentence in appropriate ways: A citizen is someone who __________. Discuss the various rights, privileges, and responsibilities suggested by student responses.

Activating Prior Knowledge Remind students that after 1763, the Atlantic coast and Ohio Valley were inhabited only by British colonists and Native Americans. Have students predict how attitudes and expectations of the colonists, Indians, and British government might change as a result.

Reading Actively

Before Reading Read aloud this sentence, which appears at the end of Setting the Scene on this page: "Despite their differences, colonists began to move toward unity." Have students find evidence to support this statement as they read the section.

RESOURCE DIRECTORY

Teaching Resources
Lesson Planner, p. 20

Transparencies
Cause and Effect
• The American Revolution, p. F-15

3 A Crisis Over Taxes

As You Read

Explore These Questions
- What was the goal of the Proclamation of 1763?
- How did colonists protest British taxes?
- What was the Boston Massacre?

Define
- petition
- boycott
- repeal
- writ of assistance
- nonimportation agreement
- committee of correspondence

Identify
- Pontiac's War
- Proclamation of 1763
- Stamp Act
- Townshend Acts
- Sons of Liberty
- Daughters of Liberty
- Samuel Adams
- John Adams
- Mercy Otis Warren
- Patrick Henry
- Boston Massacre

As Britain celebrated the victory over France, a few officials expressed concern. Now that the French were no longer a threat, would the 13 colonies become too independent? Might they even unite one day against Britain? Benjamin Franklin scoffed at such an idea. He recalled the failure of the colonies to agree to his Albany Plan of Union:

> ❝ If [the colonies] could not agree to unite for their defense against the French and Indians, . . . can it reasonably be supposed there is any danger of their uniting against their own nation? . . . I will venture to say, a union amongst them for such a purpose is not merely improbable, it is impossible. ❞

Franklin was wrong. After the French and Indian War, new British policies toward the colonies aroused angry cries from Massachusetts to Georgia. Despite their differences, colonists began to move toward unity.

New Troubles on the Frontier

By 1760, the British had driven France from the Ohio Valley. Their troubles in the region were not over, however. For many years, fur traders had sent back glowing reports of the land beyond the Appalachian Mountains. With the French gone, English colonists eagerly headed west to claim the lands for themselves.

Clashes with Native Americans

Many Native American nations lived in the Ohio Valley. They included the Senecas, Delawares, Shawnees, Ottawas, Miamis, and Hurons. As British settlers moved into the valley, they often clashed with these Native Americans.

In 1762, the British sent Lord Jeffrey Amherst to the frontier to keep order. French traders had always treated Native Americans as friends, holding feasts for them and giving them presents. Amherst refused to do this. Instead, he raised the price of goods traded to Indians. Also, unlike the French, Amherst allowed English settlers to build farms and forts on Indian lands.

Discontented Native Americans found a leader in Pontiac, an Ottawa chief who had fought on the side of the French. An English trader remarked that Pontiac "commands more respect amongst these nations than any Indian I ever saw." In April 1763, Pontiac spoke out against the British, calling them "dogs dressed in red, who have come to rob [us] of [our] hunting grounds and drive away the game."

★ *Customized Instruction* ★

Kinesthetic Learners

Role-playing viewpoints on the Proclamation of 1763 Divide the class into discussion groups of four members each. Have members assume the roles of a fur trapper, colonial farmer, British official, and an Ottawa Indian. Tell students to discuss the different points of view, for and against the Proclamation, that the four characters might take. Instruct each group to create a map showing the frontier area and the proclamation line, the Great Lakes, Detroit, and other British forts. Have students use the map to highlight relevant discussion points. Then have them script an appropriate dialogue for the four characters and perform it for the class. (*average*)

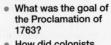

Pontiac's War

Soon after, Pontiac led an attack on British troops at Fort Detroit. He then called on other Indians to join the fight. A number of other nations responded. In a few months, they captured most British forts on the frontier. British and colonial troops struck back and regained much of what they had lost.

Pontiac's War, as it came to be called, did not last long. In October 1763, the French informed Pontiac that they had signed the Treaty of Paris. Because the treaty marked the end of French power in North America, the Indians could no longer hope for French aid against the British.

One by one, the Indian nations stopped fighting and returned home. "All my young men have buried their hatchets," Pontiac reportedly observed. By December, the British controlled the frontier.

Proclamation of 1763

Pontiac's War convinced British officials that they should stop British subjects from settling on the western frontier. To do this, the government issued the **Proclamation of 1763.** The proclamation drew an imaginary line along the crest of the Appalachian Mountains. Colonists were forbidden to settle west of the line. All settlers already west of the line were "to remove themselves" at once.

To enforce the law, Britain sent 10,000 troops to the colonies. Few troops went to the frontier, however. Most stayed in cities along the Atlantic coast.

The proclamation angered colonists. Some colonies, including New York, Pennsylvania, and Virginia, claimed lands in the West. Also, colonists had to pay for the additional British troops that had been sent to enforce the law. In the end, many settlers simply ignored the proclamation and moved west anyway.

One colonist who defied the Proclamation of 1763 was Daniel Boone. In 1767, Boone explored Kentucky, west of the Appalachians. Later, he led settlers through the Cumberland Gap along an old Indian path, renamed the Wilderness Road. Boone fought a number of battles against the Indians.

Britain Imposes New Taxes

The French and Indian War had plunged Britain deeply into debt. As a result, the tax bill for citizens in Britain rose sharply. The British prime minister, George Grenville, decided that colonists in North America should help share the burden. After all, he reasoned, it was the colonists who had gained most from the war.

Sugar Act

In 1764, Grenville asked Parliament to approve the Sugar Act, which put a new tax on molasses. Molasses, you will recall, was a valuable item in the triangular trade. (See page 114.)

Pontiac's War

Despite a hard-fought struggle, Indian forces under Pontiac were unable to drive English settlers out of the Ohio Valley. More than 100 years later, Frederic Remington imagined this scene of Pontiac's warriors attacking Fort Detroit. Remington was a painter and sculptor who specialized in scenes of the American West. ★ **Why did Pontiac want to drive out the British?**

2 Explore

Ask students to read the section. For homework, have them research the settlement of Kentucky to learn where Boonesborough was located, which Indians lived in Kentucky, and why the settlers fought so hard to protect Boonesborough.

3 Teach

On the chalkboard or bulletin board, draw a chart with three columns entitled: Act, Purpose, Effect. Under Act, list Proclamation of 1763, Sugar Act of 1764, Stamp Act of 1765, and Townshend Acts. Call on volunteers to complete the chart.

4 Assess

To close the lesson, have students complete the section review. Or have groups of students write answers to identify key people, places, and events from the section on 3x5 cards. Have groups exchange answers and write an appropriate question on the reverse side of each card.

★ ★ ★ ★ ★ ★ ★ ★ ★ ★ ★ ★ ★ ★ ★ ★ ★

ANSWER

The British were building forts on Indian lands and driving away the game.

Videodiscs/Videotapes

Prentice Hall United States History Video Collection™, Vol. 4, Ch. 7, "The People Get Political," 3 mins (*average*)

Chapter 7

The Sugar Act replaced an earlier tax, which had been so high that any merchant who paid it would have been driven out of business. As a result, most colonial merchants simply avoided the tax by smuggling molasses into the colonies. Often, they bribed tax collectors to look the other way. The Sugar Act of 1764 lowered the tax. At the same time, the law made it easier for British officials to bring colonial smugglers to trial. Grenville made it clear that he expected the new tax to be paid.

Stamp Act

Grenville also persuaded Parliament to pass the **Stamp Act** of 1765. The act placed new duties on legal documents such as wills, diplomas, and marriage papers. It also taxed newspapers, almanacs, playing cards, and even dice.

All items named in the law had to carry a stamp showing that the tax had been paid. Stamp taxes were used in Britain and other countries to raise money. However, Britain had never required American colonists to pay such a tax.

"No Taxation Without Representation!"

When British officials tried to enforce the Stamp Act, they met with stormy protests. Riots broke out in Boston, New York City, Newport, and Charleston. Angry colonists threw rocks at agents trying to collect the unpopular tax. Some tarred and feathered the agents. In Boston, a mob burned an effigy, or likeness, of the English tax collector and then destroyed his home. John Adams, a Massachusetts lawyer, wrote:

> "Our presses have groaned, our pulpits have thundered, our legislatures have resolved, our towns have voted, the crown officers everywhere trembled."

The fury of the colonists shocked the British. After all, Britain had spent a great deal of money to protect the colonies against the French. Besides, people living in Britain were paying much higher taxes than the colonists were. Why, the British asked, were colonists so angry about the Stamp Act?

Colonists replied that the taxes imposed by the Stamp Act were unjust. The taxes, they claimed, went against the principle that there should be no taxation without representation. That principle was rooted in English traditions dating back to the Magna Carta. (See page 86.)

Colonists insisted that only they or their elected representatives had the right to pass taxes. Since the colonists did not elect representatives to Parliament, Parliament had no right to tax them. The colonists were willing to pay taxes—but only if the taxes were passed by their own colonial legislatures.

Moving toward unity

The Stamp Act crisis brought a sense of unity to the colonies. Critics of the law called for delegates from every colony to meet in New York City. There, the delegates would consider actions against the hated Stamp Act.

In October 1765, nine colonies sent delegates to what became known as the Stamp Act Congress. The delegates drew up petitions to King George III and to Parliament. A **petition** is a formal written request to someone in authority, signed by a group of people. In these petitions, the delegates rejected the Stamp Act and asserted that Parliament had no right to tax the colonies. Parliament paid little attention.

The colonists took other steps to change the law. They joined together to boycott British goods. To **boycott** means to refuse to buy certain goods and services. The boycott of British goods took its toll. Trade fell off by 14 percent. British merchants suffered. So, too, did British workers who made goods for the colonies.

Finally, in 1766, Parliament **repealed,** or canceled, the Stamp Act. At the same time, though, it passed a law asserting that Parliament had the right to raise taxes in "all cases whatsoever."

The Townshend Acts

In May 1767, Parliament reopened the debate over taxing the colonies. In a fierce exchange, George Grenville, now a member

RESOURCE DIRECTORY

Teaching Resources
Unit 2/Chapter 5
- Connecting History and Literature: Speech Against Writs of Assistance, p. 6

Internet Activity

Visiting the Stamp Act Congress Send students to the Northwestern University site douglass.speech.nwu.edu/stam_a53.htm. Have them read the Stamp Act Congress's Declarations and write an essay on how they show that colonists were loyal to Britain in 1765. Given the changing nature of the Internet, you may wish to preview this site. (*challenging*)

★ *Background* ★

Did You Know?

Captain Boycott While colonists did boycott British goods, they must have used a different word to describe it. The word *boycott*, meaning a refusal to buy goods, entered the English language only in the 1800s after Irish farmers ended all dealings with Captain Charles C. Boycott, an English rent collector who refused to lower rents after severe crop failures. T

British tax stamp

Teapot protesting the Stamp Act

Viewing History **Protesting the Stamp Act**

Tax collectors hoped to make a good living distributing stamps. Instead, they found themselves targets of violence. Here, protesters tie a tax collector to a pole and drive him through the streets on a cart. ★ **Why do you think many Americans were dismayed by the tactics used by tax protesters?**

of Parliament, clashed with Charles Townshend, the official in charge of the British treasury. "You are cowards, you are afraid of the Americans, you dare not tax America!" Grenville shouted.

"Fear? Cowards?" Townshend snapped back. "I dare tax America!"

The next month, Parliament passed the **Townshend Acts,** which taxed goods such as glass, paper, paint, lead, and tea. The taxes were low, but colonists still objected. The principle, they felt, was the same: Parliament did not have the right to tax them without their consent.

The Townshend Acts also set up new ways to collect taxes. Customs officials were sent to American ports with orders to stop smuggling. Using legal documents known as **writs of assistance,** the officers would be allowed to inspect a ship's cargo without giving a reason.

Colonists protested that the writs of assistance violated their rights as British citizens. Under British law, an official could not search a person's property without a good reason for suspecting the owner of a crime. Arguing against the writs, Massachusetts lawyer James Otis commented:

> "Now, one of the most essential branches of English liberty is the freedom of one's house. A man's house is his castle; and while he is quiet, he is as well guarded as a prince in his castle. This writ, if it should be declared legal, would totally [destroy] this privilege. Customhouse officers may enter our houses when they please."

Colonial protests widen

Colonists responded swiftly and strongly to the Townshend Acts. From north to south, colonial merchants and planters signed **nonimportation agreements.** In these agreements, they promised to stop importing goods taxed by the Townshend Acts. The colonists hoped that the new boycott would win repeal of the Townshend Acts.

To protest British policies, some angry colonists formed the **Sons of Liberty.** From Boston to Charleston, Sons of Liberty staged

Viewing History ANSWER

Students should recognize that many people would have considered acts such as the destruction of property and attacks on officials to be unjustified and illegal acts of violence.

Reading Actively

During Reading Have students create a graphic organizer comparing and contrasting colonial objections to the Stamp Act and the writs of assistance provision of the Townshend Acts.

MINI LESSON

CRITICAL THINKING Learning from Art

1. Introduce the skill of learning from art by explaining that art fulfills many purposes. Cartoons entertain and make a point. Pictures may illustrate, inform, shock, or just be enjoyed for their beauty.

2. Help students practice the skill by studying the picture on this page and identifying instances of anger in the scene. Ask: "How does the scene reveal anger?" *(raised arms, tied up tax collector being paraded around)* "What are the women at the far right doing?" *(observing)*

3. Have students apply the skill by deciding what the artist's purpose was. *(probably to illustrate and inform others about colonial protests; perhaps to show that the colonists have the upper hand)* T

ANSWERS

1. Possible answers: The government wastes tax money; taxes are too high; the poor pay too much, the rich too little; the tax system is too complicated. **2.** Possible answers: Benefits: Taxes pay for defense, health care for the poor and elderly, transportation, education, and other government services. Disadvantages: Many taxpayers do not use these programs; taxes always seem to go up, not down; tax money is sometimes misspent.

Guided Instruction
Have students begin by researching how tax money is raised and spent in their community. Find out what is taxed (income, property, goods) and at what rates. Encourage students to contact local officials to learn about the town budget. Students should consider which programs paid by town taxes they would be willing to give up to reduce taxes.

ASSESSMENT See the rubrics in the Alternative Assessment booklet in the Teaching Resources.

Why Study History?

Because You Pay Taxes

Government by the People: NO NEW TAXES

Many Americans protest that their taxes are too high.

Historical Background

In the 1760s and 1770s, colonists charged that taxes levied on them by the British government were unfair because Americans did not elect representatives to Parliament. "No taxation without representation!" American patriots cried. In protest, they boycotted British goods and attacked tax collectors. They even tarred and feathered a few agents. The furor over taxes helped cause the American Revolution.

Connections to Today

Fortunately, we no longer tar and feather tax collectors, but many people do still object to taxes. The most frequent complaint is that taxes are too high. In the mid-1990s, the average American worked from January to May just to pay taxes!

The size of the tax bill is not the only complaint. Some people charge that the tax system is unfair. They say that the poor pay too much while the rich pay too little. Others say that the tax system is too complicated and that the rules are hard to understand. Recently, one sentence in a tax instruction was 436 words long—longer than the entire Gettysburg Address. As a result, nearly half of all Americans pay someone else to prepare their taxes.

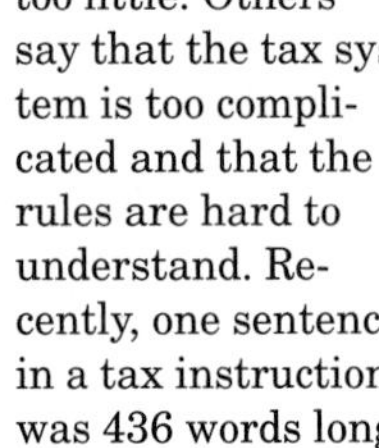

Taxes pay for essential services, such as fire protection.

Connections to You

If your state has a sales tax, you already pay taxes whenever you buy a taxable item. When you get a job, you will pay income taxes. Some day, you may pay property taxes on a home. As a voter, you will help to choose the legislators who decide our nation's tax laws.

Do you think taxes should be drastically reduced? Before you decide, remember that taxes pay for important services. Tax cuts could mean less money for national defense, health care, education, and transportation. There would also be less money for fire and police protection, recreation facilities, and the environment. So when you consider taxes, consider carefully.

1. **Comprehension** Describe three reasons some Americans complain about taxes today.
2. **Critical Thinking** Taxes spread the cost of services across the entire population. What are the benefits of this system? What are the disadvantages?

★Activity **Debating** Organize a classroom debate on taxes. One side should argue in favor of lower tax rates and the benefits to be gained from them. The other side should oppose tax cuts because of the possible negative effects on the community.

Fast Facts

★ The Internal Revenue Service (IRS) collects and processes federal income taxes. This federal agency employs 102,000 people and has a budget of $7.8 billion.
★ In fiscal year 1996, the IRS processed 205 million tax returns, assisting 99 million taxpayers by telephone and 6.3 million at walk-in offices nationwide.
★ When the U.S. enacted an income tax in 1862, the maximum rate was 5 percent; in 1997, the top rate was 39.6 percent.

Bibliography

To read more about this topic:

1. *Taxes and Government Spending (Economics for Today),* Andrea Lubov (Lerner, 1990). Illustrated explanation of how all levels of government collect and spend money.
2. *Taxation: Paying for Good Government,* Charles Hirsch (Raintree/Steck Vaughn, 1992). How and why taxation works.
3. Internet. See the IRS's amusing and helpful tax magazine at www.irs.gov.

RESOURCE DIRECTORY

Teaching Resources
Why Study History?
• You Pay Taxes, pp. 19–22
Document-Based Discovery
• Origins, pp. 2–5

mock hangings of cloth or straw effigies dressed like British officials. The hangings were meant to show tax collectors what might happen to them if they tried to collect the unpopular taxes.

Some women joined the **Daughters of Liberty.** They paraded, signed petitions, and organized a boycott of fine British cloth. They urged colonial women to raise more sheep, prepare more wool, and spin and weave their own cloth. A slogan of the Daughters of Liberty declared, "It is better to wear a Homespun coat than to lose our Liberty."

Some Sons and Daughters of Liberty also used other methods to support their cause. They visited merchants and urged them to sign the nonimportation agreements. A few even threatened people who continued to buy British goods.

New Leaders Emerge

As the struggle over taxes continued, new leaders emerged in all the colonies. Men and women in New England and Virginia were especially active in the colonial cause.

In Massachusetts

Samuel Adams of Boston stood firmly against Britain. Sam Adams seemed an unlikely leader. He was a failure in business and a poor public speaker. Still, he loved politics. He was always present at Boston town meetings and Sons of Liberty rallies. Adams's greatest talent was organizing people. He knew how to work behind the scenes, arranging protests and stirring public support.

Sam's cousin John was another important Massachusetts leader. **John Adams** was a skilled lawyer. More cautious than Sam, he weighed evidence carefully before acting. His knowledge of British law earned him much respect.

Mercy Otis Warren also aided the colonial cause. Warren published plays that made fun of British officials. She formed a close friendship with Abigail Adams, the wife of John Adams. The two women used their pens to spur the colonists to action. They also called for greater rights for women in the colonies.

In Virginia

Virginia contributed many leaders to the struggle against taxes. In the House of Burgesses, George Washington joined other Virginians to protest the Townshend Acts.

A young lawyer, **Patrick Henry,** became well known as a violent critic of British policies. His speeches in the House of Burgesses moved listeners to both tears and anger. Once, Henry attacked Britain with such fury that some listeners cried out, "Treason!" Henry boldly replied, "If this be treason, make the most of it!"

Britain Takes Action

Port cities such as Boston and New York were centers of protest. In New York, a dispute arose over the Quartering Act. Under

Biography **Mercy Otis Warren**

Mercy Otis Warren's anger was inflamed when her brother, James Otis, was struck on the head by an English officer and suffered permanent brain damage. Warren used her pen and sharp wit to stir feelings against the British. In plays like The Blockheads, *she ridiculed British officials. Warren's home in Massachusetts became a meeting place for colonists who opposed British policies.* ★ **How do writers influence public opinion today?**

Biography
ANSWER

Possible answers: through newspaper and magazine columns and editorials; books; plays; movie and television scripts

★ *Background* ★
Our Diverse Nation

A dramatic approach to public opinion Mercy Otis Warren wrote her first play dealing with American-British relations in 1772. In four later plays, she used humor to make the British look ridiculous. She also wrote a serious history of the struggle for independence, a three-volume work published in 1805.

Technology

AmericanHeritage® History of the United States CD-ROM
- History Makers: Abigail Adams, Patrick Henry (*average*)

Listening to Literature Audiocassettes
The American Experience
- Speech in the Virginia Convention, Patrick Henry, side 2

Listening to Music CD
- Chester, side 2

Writing Actively

After Reading Have students write a letter that Sam Adams might have sent to a friend about why boycotts were more effective than petitions.

ANSWER

Paul Revere wanted to stir up anti-British feeling.

Viewing History **The Boston Massacre**

Paul Revere's engraving of the Boston Massacre helped whip up colonial fury against the British. In fact, the picture is very inaccurate. No British officer ever gave an order to fire, as shown here. The redcoats, faced with an unruly mob, fired on their own. Revere also shows seven American dead, when there were actually five. ★ **Why do you think Revere distorted the event in his engraving?**

that law, colonists had to provide housing, candles, bedding, and beverages to soldiers stationed in the colonies. When the New York assembly refused to obey the law, Britain dismissed the assembly in 1767.

Britain also sent two regiments to Boston to protect customs officers from local citizens. To many Bostonians, the soldiers were a daily reminder that Britain was trying to bully them into paying unjust taxes. When British soldiers walked along the streets of Boston, they risked insults or even beatings. The time was ripe for disaster.

The Boston Massacre

On the night of March 5, 1770, a crowd gathered outside the Boston customs house. Colonists shouted insults at the "lobsterbacks," as they called the redcoated British who guarded the building. Then the Boston crowd began to throw snowballs, oyster shells, and chunks of ice at the soldiers.

The crowd grew larger and rowdier. Suddenly, the soldiers panicked. They fired into the crowd. When the smoke from the musket volley cleared, five people lay dead or dying. Among the first to die was Crispus Attucks, a black sailor who was active in the Sons of Liberty.

Colonists were quick to protest the incident, which they called the **Boston Massacre**. Boston silversmith Paul Revere stirred up anti-British feeling with an engraving that showed British soldiers firing on unarmed colonists. Sam Adams wrote letters to other colonists to build outrage about the shooting.

RESOURCE DIRECTORY

Teaching Resources
Unit 2/Chapter 5
- Section 3 Quiz, p. 10

Interdisciplinary Connections
- Main Idea: Growing Tensions With Britain, pp. 28–29

Transparencies
Interdisciplinary Connections
- The Boston Massacre, p. B-41

★ Background ★
Recent Scholarship

Bad management, bad product In *For Good and Evil: The Impact of Taxes on the Course of Civilization,* Charles Adams sees the Revolution as a product of Britain's bad government and its failure to protect colonists' rights. Worse still, many British officials were corrupt. Canada, which happened to have an upright colonial governor, stayed out of the conflict.

FROM THE ARCHIVES OF AmericanHeritage®

A desirable tax? The Boston committee of correspondence in 1772 actually campaigned to pay a tax. Britain planned to discontinue having colonists pay colonial judges. Instead, it would pay the judges from the royal treasury to make up for depreciated colonial currency. Patriots wanted to pay the salaries from local taxes to avoid British control of judges.

Source: Frederic D. Schwarz, "The Time Machine," *American Heritage* magazine, November 1997.

The soldiers were arrested and tried in court. John Adams agreed to defend them, saying that they deserved a fair trial. He wanted to show the world that the colonists believed in justice, even if the British government did not. At the trial, Adams argued that the crowd had provoked the soldiers. His arguments convinced the jury. In the end, the heaviest punishment any soldier received was a branding on the hand.

Samuel Adams later expanded on the idea of a letter-writing campaign like the one he had used to arouse colonists after the Boston Massacre. Adams formed a **committee of correspondence.** Members of the committee regularly wrote letters and pamphlets reporting on events in Massachusetts. Before long, committees of correspondence became a major tool of protest in every colony.

Samuel Adams

A Temporary Calm

By chance, on the very day of the Boston Massacre, Parliament voted to repeal most of the Townshend Acts. English merchants, harmed by the nonimportation agreements, had pressured Parliament to end the taxes. Still, King George III asked Parliament to retain the tax on tea. "There must always be one tax to keep up the right [to tax]," he argued. Parliament agreed.

News of the repeal delighted the colonists. Most people dismissed the remaining tax on tea as not important and ended their boycott of British goods. For a few years, calm returned. Yet the underlying issue—Britain's power to tax the colonies—remained unsettled. For the first time, the colonists were thinking more clearly about their political rights.

★ Section 3 Review ★

Recall

1. **Identify** **(a)** Pontiac's War, **(b)** Proclamation of 1763, **(c)** Stamp Act, **(d)** Townshend Acts, **(e)** Sons of Liberty, **(f)** Daughters of Liberty, **(g)** Samuel Adams, **(h)** John Adams, **(i)** Mercy Otis Warren, **(j)** Patrick Henry, **(k)** Boston Massacre.
2. **Define** **(a)** petition, **(b)** boycott, **(c)** repeal, **(d)** writ of assistance, **(e)** nonimportation agreement, **(f)** committee of correspondence.

Comprehension

3. **(a)** Why did Britain issue the Proclamation of 1763? **(b)** How did colonists respond to the Proclamation?
4. **(a)** What argument did the colonists use against British taxes? **(b)** How did colonists protest the taxes?
5. Describe the key events leading up to the Boston Massacre.

Critical Thinking and Writing

6. **Understanding Causes and Effects** Why did the French defeat in North America doom Pontiac's efforts to drive English settlers out of the Ohio Valley?
7. **Defending a Position** Do you think Britain had the right to tax the colonies? Defend your position.

Activity **Writing a Letter** Spread the word! You are a member of Sam Adams's committee of correspondence. Write a letter to other colonists in which you remind them of the injustice of British taxes and the actions of British officials and troops, and call for further protests.

★ *Activity* ★

Connections With Arts

Writing headlines Divide students into groups of three. Tell some groups they represent Patriots, others pro-British colonists, and others neutral observers. Have each group write headlines describing the Boston Massacre from its assigned perspective. Groups should research additional information on the Boston Massacre and prepare several headlines before selecting one to write on the chalkboard. When each group has contributed a headline, have the class decide which headline best represents the perspective of each category—Patriots, pro-British colonists, and neutral observers. (*average*) T

★ Section 3 Review ★

ANSWERS

1. (a)–(b) p. 143, **(c)** p. 144, **(d)–(e)** p. 145, **(f)–(j)** p. 147, **(k)** p. 148

2. (a)–(c) p. 144, **(d)–(e)** p. 145, **(f)** p. 149

3. (a) to stop further frontier settlement and avoid conflict with the Indians **(b)** They were angry; many simply ignored it and moved west anyway.

4. (a) Since they did not elect representatives to Parliament, they could not be taxed "without representation." **(b)** attacked tax collectors; boycotted British goods

5. A crowd shouted insults and threw things at soldiers guarding the customs house. When the crowd grew larger and rowdier, panicked soldiers fired, leaving five people dead or dying.

6. Without French aid, the Indians could not hold back the settlers.

7. Possible answers: Yes, Britain defended the colonies and they should help pay for it. No, they had no representation in Parliament so were being unjustly taxed.

Activity

Guided Instruction
Suggest that students first outline the major events of the section. Have them think of creative actions the colonists could take.

ASSESSMENT See the rubrics in the Alternative Assessment booklet in the Teaching Resources.

Section 4 The Fighting Begins

LESSON PLAN

Objectives

★ Explain why Americans protested the Tea Act.

★ Describe how Britain responded to the Boston Tea Party.

★ Explain why fighting broke out at Lexington and Concord.

1 Engage

Warm Up Work with students to formulate a definition of *intolerable*. Ask them to name actions they would find intolerable.

Activating Prior Knowledge Write "1770" on the chalkboard. Have students recall two key events of 1770 *(Boston Massacre, repeal of the Townshend Acts except for tea tax)*. Have students speculate on the chances for peace between the colonists and Britain.

Reading Actively

Before Reading Ask students to turn the section title into a question. Have them jot down answers as they read.

2 Explore

Have students read the section. For homework, have students find out who Lord Frederick North was and what attitude he held toward the American colonists.

RESOURCE DIRECTORY

Teaching Resources

Lesson Planner, p. 21

Interdisciplinary Connections

• Main Idea: Growing Tensions With Britain, pp. 26–27, 30

4 The Fighting Begins

As You Read

Explore These Questions

- Why did Americans protest the Tea Act?
- How did Britain respond to the Boston Tea Party?
- Why did fighting break out at Lexington and Concord?

Define

- militia
- minuteman

Identify

- British East India Company
- Tea Act
- Boston Tea Party
- Intolerable Acts
- First Continental Congress

One night in July 1774, John Adams stopped at a tavern in eastern Massachusetts. After riding for more than 30 miles, he was hot and dusty, and his body ached with fatigue.

Adams asked the innkeeper for a cup of tea. The innkeeper, however, refused his request. She did not serve tea, she informed him. He would have to drink coffee instead.

Adams later praised the innkeeper's conduct. In a letter to his wife, Abigail, he wrote that tea must be given up by all colonists. He promised to break himself of the habit as soon as possible.

Why did colonists like John Adams give up tea? The answer was taxes. When Parliament decided to enforce a tea tax in 1773, a new crisis exploded. This time, colonists began to think the unthinkable. Perhaps the time had come to reject British rule and declare independence.

Uproar Over Tea

Tea was tremendously popular in the colonies. By 1770, at least one million Americans brewed tea twice a day. People "would rather go without their dinners than without a dish of tea," a visitor to the colonies noted.

Parliament passes the Tea Act

Most tea was brought to the colonies by the **British East India Company.** The company bought tea in southern Asia and sold it to colonial tea merchants. The merchants then sold the tea to the colonists. To make a profit, the merchants sold the tea at a higher price than they had paid for it.

In the 1770s, however, the British East India Company found itself in deep financial trouble. More than 15 million pounds of its tea sat unsold in British warehouses. Britain had kept a tax on tea as a symbol of its right to tax the colonies. The tax was a small one, but colonists resented it. They refused to buy English tea.

Parliament tried to help the East India Company by passing the **Tea Act** of 1773. The act let the company bypass the tea merchants and sell directly to colonists. Although colonists would still have to pay the tea tax, they would not have to pay the higher price charged by tea merchants. As a result, the tea itself would cost less than ever before.

To the surprise of Parliament, colonists protested the Tea Act. Tea merchants were angry because they had been cut out of the

American physicians joined the protest against tea. They spread stories warning about tea's adverse effects on health. One doctor claimed that drinking tea would make one an invalid for life. Another said that tea weakened "the tone of the stomach, and therefore of the whole system, inducing tremors and spasmodic affections."

★ Background ★

Recent Scholarship

Taxes or sovereignty? Alan Brinkley's *Unfinished Nation* suggests that different opinions about sovereignty were more at issue than taxes. Colonial arguments that England could legislate for its empire but not for its colonies split sovereignty between the colonies and Britain. To the British, any system must have only one, ultimate authority.

★ Background ★

Did You Know?

Harbors or teapots? The Boston Tea Party inspired other harbor "parties." In Annapolis, Maryland, Patriots burned a British vessel before its full cargo of tea could be unloaded. New York Patriots, like those in Boston, wore Indian dress as they dumped a cargo of tea into the East River. Virginians staged a similar party.

Viewing History: Boston Tea Party

Disguised as Indians, some 50 or 60 Bostonians attacked British tea ships. A crowd watched silently as the colonists dumped tea into Boston harbor. British officials called the Boston Tea Party "the most wanton and unprovoked insult offered to the civil power that is recorded in history."

★ **Why did colonists attack the tea ships?**

◄ *Colonial tea caddy*

tea trade. If Parliament ruined tea merchants today, they warned, what would prevent it from turning on other businesses tomorrow?

Even tea drinkers, who would have benefited from the law, scorned the Tea Act. They believed that it was a British trick to make them accept Parliament's right to tax the colonies.

A new boycott

Once again, colonists responded to the new tax with a boycott. One colonial newspaper warned:

> "Do not suffer yourself to sip the accursed, dutied STUFF. For if you do, the devil will immediately enter into you, and you will instantly become a traitor to your country."

Daughters of Liberty and other women led the boycott. They served coffee or made "liberty tea" from raspberry leaves. At some ports, Sons of Liberty enforced the boycott by keeping the British East India Company from unloading cargoes of tea.

Boston Tea Party

Three ships loaded with tea reached Boston harbor in late November 1773. The colonial governor of Massachusetts, Thomas Hutchinson, insisted that they unload their cargo as usual.

Sam Adams and the Sons of Liberty had other plans. On the night of December 16, they met in Old South Church. They sent a message to the governor, demanding that the ships leave the harbor. When the governor rejected the demand, Adams stood up and declared, "This meeting can do nothing further to save the country."

Adams's words seemed to be a signal. As if on cue, a group of men burst into the meetinghouse. Dressed like Mohawk Indians, they waved hatchets in the air. From the gallery above, voices cried, "Boston harbor a teapot tonight! The Mohawks are come!"

The disguised colonists left the meetinghouse and headed for the harbor. Others joined them on the way. In the cold, crisp night, under a nearly full moon, the men boarded the ships, split open the tea chests, and dumped the tea into the harbor. By 10 P.M., the **Boston Tea Party,** as it was later called, was over. Its effects would be felt for a long time to come.

Britain Strikes Back

Colonists had mixed reactions to the Boston Tea Party. Some cheered the action. Others worried that it would encourage lawlessness in the colonies. Even those who condemned the Boston Tea Party, though, were shocked at Britain's response.

Punishing Massachusetts

The British were outraged by what they saw as Boston's lawless behavior. In 1774, Parliament, encouraged by King George III,

3 Teach

Divide the class into four groups to represent committees of correspondence from Boston, Philadelphia, Virginia, and South Carolina. Have each group write to the other committees, describing and reacting to specific events in the section. A messenger can deliver the letters, to which recipients should respond.

4 Assess

To close the lesson, have students complete the section review. Or work with students to create a classroom time line for this section.

Viewing History ANSWER

They wanted to protest the tax on tea and Parliament's right to tax them at all.

FROM THE ARCHIVES OF AmericanHeritage®

Britain's "helpful" blunder To Britain, bypassing colonial merchants while retaining the tea tax seemed ideal. It would help the East India Company, give colonial consumers cheap tea, and maintain British sovereignty. The Tea Act, however, angered wealthy American merchants, prompting their alliance, which became a decisive and powerful force for revolution.

Source: Frederic D. Schwarz, "The Time Machine," *American Heritage* magazine, October 1997.

Technology

Videodiscs/Videotapes

Prentice Hall United States History Video Collection™, Vol. 4, Ch. 13, "The Boston Tea Party," 1:30 min (*average*) ELL

Chapter 13

Linking History and Technology

ANSWER

Each letter had to be put in place; the forms were inked by hand; one page was printed at a time and hung up to dry.

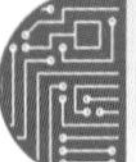

Linking History and Technology

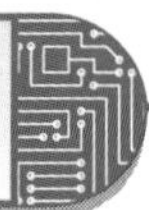

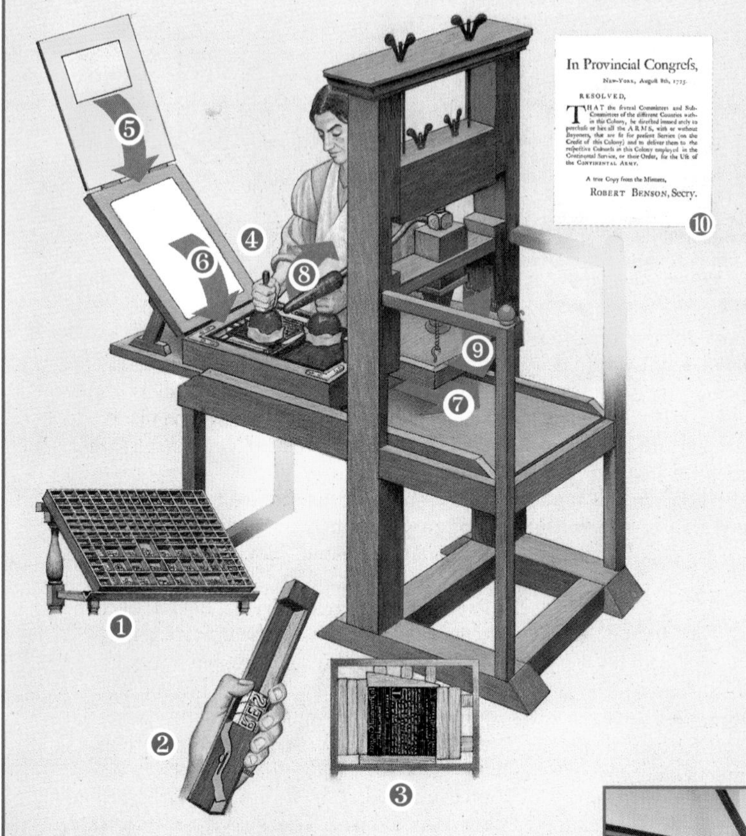

❶ *The type case held metal letters.*

❷ *Letters were placed in a composing stick to create lines of type.*

❸ *Lines of type were locked in a form to create a sheet of text.*

❹ *The form was inked with ink balls.*

❺ *The frisket kept the margins of the paper clean. It folded onto the tympan.*

❻ *The tympan held the paper. It folded onto the form.*

❼ *The form was slid under the platen.*

❽ *The press bar was pulled to lower the platen.*

❾ *The platen pressed the inked form against the paper.*

❿ *The printed page was removed and hung on a drying rack.*

Colonial Printing Press

Colonial printers played a vital role in uniting colonists against the British. Besides publishing newspapers and magazines, they also printed letters and pamphlets that kept colonists informed of such developments as the Intolerable Acts. The drawing shows how a printing press of the time worked. ★ **Why would printing a document with this press be very time-consuming?**

Printing press owned by Benjamin Franklin ➤

★ Customized Instruction ★

Extroverted Learners

Dramatizing a colonial printer's dilemma Have students suppose they own a printing shop in the 1770s. Discuss the issues they might face. Would they be approached by British officials to print new laws for the colonies? Would they create pamphlets for the Sons and Daughters of Liberty? Would they print pamphlets for the local committee of correspondence? How would they justify involvement in the Patriot cause? Appoint several students to record their classmates' responses. Then have students work in small groups to create a short play about the colonial printer's dilemma. Each group should write one scene. Have students perform their play for other classes. (*average*)

RESOURCE DIRECTORY

Teaching Resources
Unit 2/Chapter 5
- Critical Thinking and Writing: Making Decisions, p. 4

Transparencies
Exploring Technology
- Colonial Printing Press, p. H-29

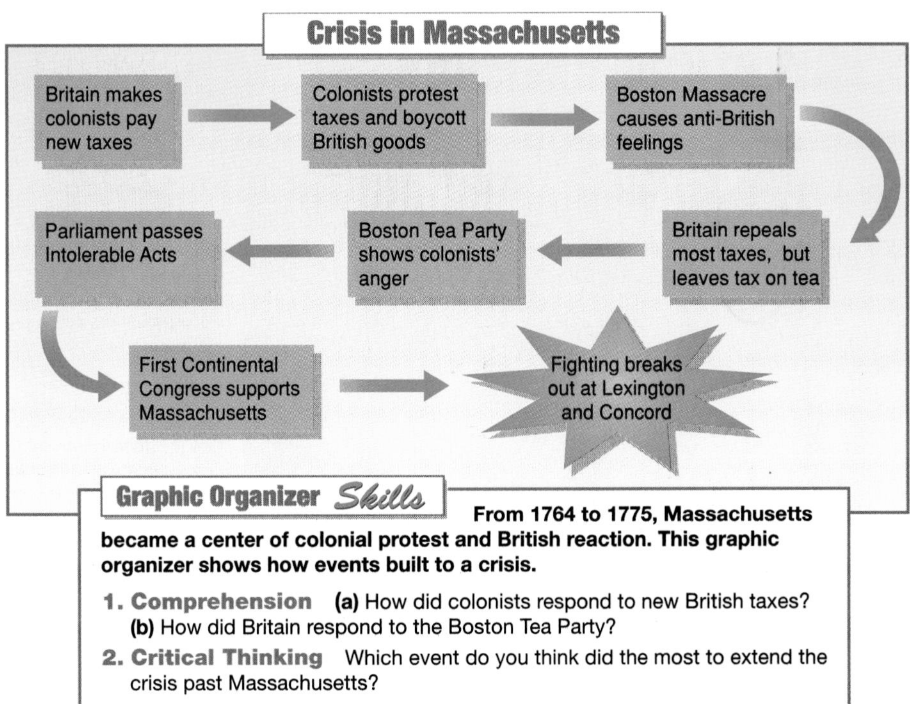
Crisis in Massachusetts
Britain makes colonists pay new taxes
Colonists protest taxes and boycott British goods
Boston Massacre causes anti-British feelings
Britain repeals most taxes, but leaves tax on tea
Boston Tea Party shows colonists' anger
Parliament passes Intolerable Acts
First Continental Congress supports Massachusetts
Fighting breaks out at Lexington and Concord

Graphic Organizer *Skills* **From 1764 to 1775, Massachusetts became a center of colonial protest and British reaction. This graphic organizer shows how events built to a crisis.**

1. **Comprehension** **(a)** How did colonists respond to new British taxes? **(b)** How did Britain respond to the Boston Tea Party?
2. **Critical Thinking** Which event do you think did the most to extend the crisis past Massachusetts?

acted to punish Massachusetts. Colonists called the four laws they passed the **Intolerable Acts** because they were so harsh.

First, Parliament shut down the port of Boston. No ship could enter or leave the harbor—not even a small boat. The harbor would remain closed until the colonists paid for the tea.

Second, Parliament forbade Massachusetts colonists to hold town meetings more than once a year without the governor's permission. In the past, colonists had called town meetings whenever they wished.

Third, Parliament provided for customs officers and other officials charged with major crimes to be tried in Britain instead of in Massachusetts. Colonists protested that a dishonest official could break the law in the colonies and avoid punishment "by being tried, where no evidence can pursue him."

Fourth, Parliament passed a new Quartering Act. No longer would redcoats camp in tents on Boston Common. Instead, British commanders could force citizens to house troops in their homes.

Other colonies support Boston

The committees of correspondence spread news of the Intolerable Acts. They warned that the people of Boston faced hunger while their port was closed. People from other colonies responded quickly. Carts rolled into the city with rice from South Carolina, corn from Virginia, and flour from Pennsylvania.

In the Virginia assembly, a young lawyer named Thomas Jefferson suggested that a day be set aside to mark the shame of the Intolerable Acts. The royal governor of Virginia rejected the idea and dismissed the assembly. The colonists went ahead anyway. On June 1, 1774, church bells tolled slowly. Merchants closed their shops. Many colonists prayed and fasted all day.

In September 1774, colonial leaders called a meeting in Philadelphia. Delegates from 12 colonies gathered in what became

Graphic Organizer *Skills*

ANSWERS **1. (a)** with protests and boycotts **(b)** by passing the Intolerable Acts **2.** Possible answer: the Intolerable Acts, because they caused the colonies to rally around Boston and begin working together against the British

Reading Actively

During Reading After students read the subsection entitled Punishing Massachusetts, have them summarize the purpose and the provisions of the Intolerable Acts.

★ *Activity* ★

Connections With the World

Negotiating Divide students into three groups: Patriots, British, and Neutrals. Put Patriots and British in separate parts of the room. Tell students that the Intolerable Acts have just been passed. Have each group discuss this question: "Can war be avoided?" Have British and Patriot groups make two lists: **(1)** benefits of preserving peace; **(2)** reasons for going to war. Have Neutrals list reasons why both sides should seek peace. Then have the British and Patriot groups write proposals for settling the conflict. Neutrals can carry proposals and responses or information on the progress of negotiations between groups. Set a time limit for negotiations and see if groups can avoid armed conflict. (*average*)

AmericanHeritage
MAGAZINE

Concord To learn more about Concord, go to the Minute Man National Historic Site on the Internet, through the National Park Service's Web site at www.nps.gov/mima/.

Writing Actively

After Reading Have students complete a paragraph with specific examples to support this topic sentence: "A buildup of arms and troops preceded the first shots in the American Revolution."

RESOURCE DIRECTORY

Teaching Resources
Unit 2/Chapter 5
- Vocabulary Builder, p. 2
- Section 4 Quiz, p. 11

Chapter Tests, pp. 25–30

AmericanHeritage
MAGAZINE

HISTORY HAPPENED HERE

Concord

The old North Bridge in Concord looks peaceful now. On April 19, 1775, though, this quiet spot was a scene of turmoil and bloodshed. It was here that colonial minutemen met and drove back three companies of redcoats. Today, you can walk across the restored bridge and view the stone monument shown here. Nearby, an 1873 statue by sculptor Daniel Chester French honors the heroic minutemen who fired "the shot heard round the world."

★ ***To learn more about this historic site, write:*** *Minute Man National Historical Park, P.O. Box 160, 174 Liberty Street, Concord, MA 01742.*

◄ The Minute Man, *by Daniel Chester French*

known as the **First Continental Congress.** Only Georgia did not send delegates.

After much debate, the delegates passed a resolution backing Massachusetts in its struggle. They agreed to boycott all British goods and to stop exporting goods to Britain until the Intolerable Acts were repealed. The delegates also urged each colony to set up and train its own militia (muh LIHSH uh). A **militia** is an army of citizens who serve as soldiers during an emergency.

Before leaving Philadelphia, the delegates agreed to meet again in May 1775. Little did they know that before then an incident in Massachusetts would change the fate of the colonies forever.

Lexington and Concord

In Massachusetts, newspapers called on citizens to prevent what they called "the Massacre of American Liberty." Volunteers known as **minutemen** trained regularly. Minutemen got their name because they kept their muskets at hand, prepared to fight at a minute's notice. Meanwhile, Britain built up its forces. More troops arrived in Boston, bringing the total number in that city to 4,000.

Early in 1775, General Thomas Gage, the British commander, heard a rumor that minutemen had a large store of arms in Concord, a village about 18 miles (29 km) from Boston. Gage planned a surprise march to Concord to seize the arms. (See the map on page 162.)

Sounding the alarm

On April 18, about 700 British troops quietly left Boston under cover of darkness. The Sons of Liberty were watching. As soon as the British set out, the Americans hung two lamps from the Old North Church in Boston. This signal meant that the redcoats were on the move.

★ Background ★ Did You Know?

Visiting heroes Delegates traveling to the First Continental Congress in Philadelphia had a chance to see the other colonies and meet fellow Patriots. It took John Adams and the other Massachusetts delegates 20 days to reach their destination. En route, the group was met in New Haven, Connecticut, with the ringing of church bells.

★ Background ★ Linking Past and Present

Remembering the Revolution The battle sites at Lexington and Concord, located about 10 miles apart, are now national historical parks visited by many tourists. To this day, Massachusetts celebrates Patriot's Day on the third Monday in April to commemorate these battles. The Boston Marathon also commemorates the battles.

Colonists who were waiting across the Charles River saw the signal. Messengers mounted their horses and galloped through the night toward Concord. One midnight rider was Paul Revere. "The British are coming! The British are coming!" shouted Revere as he passed through each sleepy village along the way.

"The shot heard round the world"

At daybreak on April 19, the redcoats reached Lexington, a town near Concord. On the village green, some 70 minutemen were waiting, commanded by Captain John Parker. The British ordered the minutemen to go home.

Outnumbered, the colonists began to leave. Suddenly, a shot rang out through the chill morning air. No one knows who fired it. In the brief struggle that followed, eight colonists were killed and one British soldier was wounded.

The British pushed on to Concord. Finding no arms in the village, they turned back to Boston. On a bridge outside Concord, they met 300 minutemen. Again, fighting broke out. This time, the British were forced to retreat. As they withdrew, colonial sharpshooters took deadly aim at them from the woods and fields. Local women also fired at the British from their windows. By the time they reached Boston, the redcoats had lost 73 men. Another 200 British soldiers were wounded or missing.

News of the battles at Lexington and Concord spread swiftly. To many colonists, the fighting ended all hope of reaching an agreement with Britain. Only war would decide the future of the 13 colonies.

More than 60 years after the battles of Lexington and Concord, a well-known New England poet, Ralph Waldo Emerson, wrote a poem honoring the minutemen. Emerson's "Concord Hymn" begins:

> "By the rude bridge that arched
> the flood,
> Their flag to April's breeze unfurled,
> Here once the embattled farmers
> stood,
> And fired the shot heard round the
> world."

The "embattled farmers" faced long years of war. At the war's end, though, the 13 colonies would stand strong and free as a new, independent nation.

★ Section 4 Review ★

Recall

1. **Locate** (a) Boston, (b) Concord, (c) Lexington.
2. **Identify** (a) British East India Company, (b) Tea Act, (c) Boston Tea Party, (d) Intolerable Acts, (e) First Continental Congress.
3. **Define** (a) militia, (b) minuteman.

Comprehension

4. (a) Why did Britain pass the Tea Act? (b) Why did the act anger colonists?
5. How did the Intolerable Acts help to unite the colonies?
6. Describe the events that led to the fighting at Lexington.

Critical Thinking and Writing

7. **Making Inferences** Do you think the organizers of the Boston Tea Party would have ended their protests against Britain if Parliament had repealed the tax on tea? Explain.
8. **Identifying Alternatives** (a) Do you think Parliament should have passed the Intolerable Acts in response to the Boston Tea Party? (b) What other actions might Parliament have taken in this situation?

Activity **Writing a Poem** Today, as in the past, writers like Mercy Otis Warren often use their skills to comment on current events. You are a poet living in colonial Boston. Write a poem in which you tell about the Boston Tea Party, the Intolerable Acts, or the events of April 19, 1775.

★ Background ★
Our Diverse Nation

Paul who? Paul Revere is one of the most famous Sons of Liberty, but few people know that his father fled from France to the colonies to escape religious persecution. Once here, he changed his name from Rivoire to one that caused English-speakers less trouble: Revere. If he had not, we might speak instead of "the midnight ride of Apollos Rivoire."

★ Section 4 Review ★

ANSWERS

1. See map, p. 162.

2. (a)–(b) p. 150, **(c)** p. 151, **(d)** p. 153, **(e)** p. 154

3. (a)–(b) p. 154

4. (a) so the East India Company could sell directly to colonists **(b)** because it tried to make them accept Britain's right to tax them

5. The other colonies decided to help Boston; the First Continental Congress resulted.

6. British troops went to Concord to seize weapons and met some minutemen, who began to leave. Someone fired. Fighting began.

7. Possible answer: No, these radical colonists may already have wanted to end British rule.

8. Possible answers: **(a)** No: they were too harsh and punished a city for the crime of a few. Yes: they showed who was boss. **(b)** repealed the Tea Act or started negotiations

Activity

Guided Instruction

A full version of "Concord Hymn" is in *The Concord Hymn and Other Poems* (Dover, 1996). Suggest students use free or rhymed verse. Let volunteers share their poems.

ASSESSMENT See the rubrics in the Alternative Assessment booklet in the Teaching Resources.

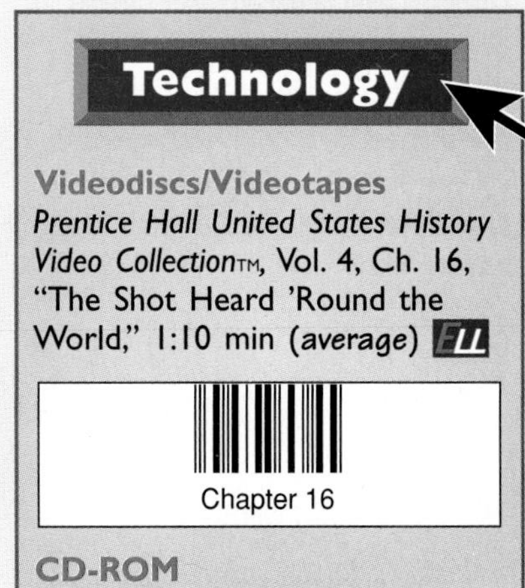

Technology
Videodiscs/Videotapes
Prentice Hall United States History Video Collection™, Vol. 4, Ch. 16, "The Shot Heard 'Round the World," 1:10 min (average) ELL
Chapter 16
CD-ROM
Test Bank CD-ROM, Ch. 5
Interactive Student Tutorial

Chapter 5

Review and Activities

Reviewing the Chapter

Define These Terms

1. b **2.** a **3.** d **4.** e **5.** c

Explore the Main Ideas

1. It provided a vital link between Canada and the Mississippi River.

2. Britain's Lord Amherst raised the price of goods traded to Native Americans and let colonists settle on their lands.

3. They paraded, signed petitions, and boycotted British goods.

4. The port of Boston was closed, creating hardships and food shortages.

5. The British were forced to retreat; it ended many colonists' desire to reach agreement.

Geography Activity

1. A **2.** D **3.** E **4.** B **5.** C

Location the Mississippi River

Critical Thinking and Writing

1. Possible answer: It would have made colonists reluctant to fight.

2. English, not French, was the chief language after France lost its empire in North America. Also, because Native Americans were killed or later pushed onto reservations, their languages declined.

3. Americans consent to taxation through elected representatives at all levels of government.

4. Possible answer: the ban on town meetings held without the governor's permission, because it limited the colonists' right to self-government

Chapter 5 Review and Activities

★ Sum It Up ★

Section 1 Rivalry in North America

- By the mid-1700s, England, France, Spain, and the Netherlands were competing for land and trade in North America.
- Native Americans were drawn into the struggle between the French and British in the Ohio Valley.

Section 2 The French and Indian War

- In 1754, the French and Indian War pitted the British against the French and their Indian allies.
- As a result of the French and Indian War, Britain won control of French land claims in North America.

Section 3 A Crisis Over Taxes

- Colonists objected to the Proclamation of 1763 because it forbade them to settle in lands west of the Appalachian Mountains.
- American colonists objected to Parliament's attempts to tax them without their consent.
- Colonists were outraged when British soldiers shot and killed Americans in the Boston Massacre.

Section 4 The Fighting Begins

- Conflict over taxes gradually increased until colonists staged the Boston Tea Party and Britain passed the Intolerable Acts.
- In April 1775, fighting between British troops and colonial minutemen marked the start of the American Revolution.

For additional review of the major ideas of Chapter 5, see ***Guide to the Essentials of American History*** or ***Interactive Student Tutorial CD-ROM,*** which contains interactive review activities, graphic organizers, and practice tests.

Reviewing the Chapter

Define These Terms

Match each term with the correct definition.

Column 1	Column 2
1. petition	**a.** refusal to buy certain goods and services
2. boycott	**b.** formal written request
3. repeal	**c.** army of citizens who serve as soldiers during an emergency
4. committee of correspondence	**d.** cancel
5. militia	**e.** group that wrote letters and pamphlets reporting events in the colonies

Explore the Main Ideas

1. Why was the Ohio River especially important to the French before 1754?
2. Why did Pontiac call for war against British settlers?
3. How did the Daughters of Liberty protest the Tea Act?
4. How did the Intolerable Acts affect the port of Boston?
5. Describe the outcome of the battles of Lexington and Concord.

Geography Activity

Match the letters on the map with the following locations: **1.** Spanish lands in 1763, **2.** British lands in 1763, **3.** Original 13 English colonies, **4.** Mississippi River, **5.** Ohio River.

Location What body of water formed the western boundary of British lands in North America in 1763?

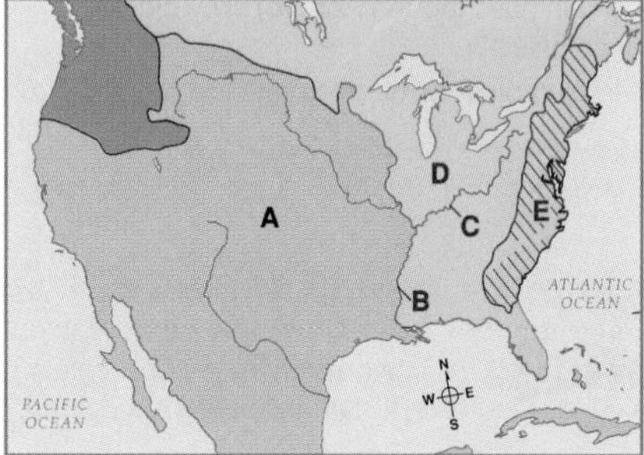

Using Primary Sources

(a) boys, mob **(b)** He thinks that crying "liberty" is merely an excuse to plunder and destroy property. **(c)** Possible answer: Adams would have argued that the people were protesting against unjust rule and that the papers burned were tax records.

Critical Thinking and Writing

1. **Understanding Chronology** In 1763, Britain banned settlement west of the Appalachian Mountains. Why do you think it did not issue such a proclamation before the French and Indian War?
2. **Linking Past and Present** Why is English the most widely spoken language in the United States and Canada today?
3. Exploring Unit Themes **Origins** The principle that people must give their consent before they pay taxes goes back to ancient British law. How is it reflected in our government today?
4. **Ranking** Which of the Intolerable Acts do you think would have been most alarming to the Americans throughout the colonies? Explain your reasoning.

Using Primary Sources

In August 1765, Francis Bernard, the governor of Massachusetts, reported to England on a Stamp Act riot in Boston:

> “Toward evening some boys began to light a bonfire before the Town House, which is a usual signal for a mob. Before it was quite dark a great company of people gather together crying liberty and property, which is the usual notice of their intention to plunder and pull down a house. . . . They went to the house of Mr. Story, . . . broke into it and tore it all to pieces; and took out all the books and papers, among which were all the records of the Court of the Admiralty, and carried them to the bonfire and burned them.”

Source: *The Annals of America,* Volume 2, 1976.

Recognizing Points of View (a) In the first sentence, what words does Bernard use to describe the protesters? **(b)** How does he view the protesters' use of the word *liberty*? **(c)** How do you think Samuel Adams would have responded to the governor's report?

Activity Bank

Interdisciplinary Activity

Exploring the Arts List five reasons for the colonists' anger with Britain. Based on your list, write a song of protest against British treatment. You can make up your own melody or write new words to an existing tune. Sing or play your song for the class.

Career Skills Activity

Scriptwriters Write a script dramatizing one of the events you have read about in this chapter. With a small group of students, perform your skit for the class.

Citizenship Activity

Testing Alternative Courses of Action Review the events of the Boston Tea Party. List reasons for citizens of the colonies to support the actions of the protesters. Then, list reasons for citizens to condemn the protesters' actions.

Internet Activity

Use the Internet to find sites dealing with one of the people you have read about in this chapter. Write a mini-biography of the person you have chosen. If possible, illustrate your biography with a picture downloaded from the Web site.

Eyewitness Journal
You are one of the following: a Native American in the Ohio Valley in 1750; Major George Washington in the 1750s; a Son or Daughter of Liberty in 1770; a minuteman on April 19, 1775. In your Eyewitness Journal, describe the events of the time that have had the greatest effect on you.

★ 157

Activity Bank

ASSESSMENT To assess the activities on this page, see the rubrics in the Alternative Assessment booklet in the Teaching Resources. You might want to share the rubrics with your students before they begin work.

Interdisciplinary Activity

1. Allow students to use an existing melody if they wish, but have them write new lyrics.

2. Remind students that their songs should mention reasons for the colonists' feelings and convey their angry mood.

3. If possible, schedule performance time outside of regular class hours. Invite students who play musical instruments to accompany themselves.

Career Skills Activity

1. Have students outline the sequence of events or actions in their scene.

2. Remind students that their dialogue should be original. Have them conduct more research on the event to make their scripts more realistic.

3. If possible, videotape performances so students can watch them later.

Citizenship Activity

1. You may wish to conduct this activity with the class as a whole.

2. Have students list reasons on the chalkboard for and against the protesters. If students have trouble opposing the protesters, have them think of reasons in these categories: ethical, practical, and political.

3. If you wish, have students brainstorm for reasons in small groups first.

Eyewitness Journal

1. Have students begin by listing the main events mentioned in the chapter that would have affected their characters.
2. Have students use these lists to make a chronological narrative.
3. Remind students to explain how the event affected their characters, rather than simply describe the event.

Internet Activity

1. Have students go to www.phschool.com, which contains updated information on a variety of topics.
2. One useful site is Yahoo's Web site on Revolutionary figures at www.yahoo.com/Arts/Humanities/History/U_S_History/18th_Century/Revolutionary_War/People/.
3. Given the changing nature of the Internet, you may wish to preview this site.

Chapter 6 Manager

SECTION OBJECTIVES	TEACHING RESOURCES	ADDITIONAL RESOURCE
1 Early Battles (pp. 160–164) **Objectives** 1. Explain how Americans pursued both war and peace in 1775. 2. Describe the advantages of each side as they entered the war. 3. Explain how the Continental Army gained control of Boston.	**Lesson Planner,** p. 22 (average) . . . . .90 mins. **Unit 2/Chapter 6** • Map Mystery: Refugees of the Revolution, p. 15 (average) . . . . .20 mins. • Connecting History and Literature: To His Excellency, General Washington, p. 16 (challenging) . . . . .20 mins. • Section 1 Quiz, p. 18 (average) . . . . .15 mins.	**Historical Outline Map Book** • The Revolutionary War: An Overview, p. 24 (average) • The Revolutionary War in the Northeast, p. 25 (average) **Customized Reader** • A Frontier Scout in Vermont During the Revolution, article IIIB-9 (average)
2 Declaring Independence (pp. 165–168) **Objectives** 1. Explain how *Common Sense* influenced the colonists. 2. Describe how American Patriots responded to the Declaration of Independence. 3. Summarize the main ideas of the Declaration of Independence.	**Lesson Planner,** p. 23 (challenging) . . . . .90 mins. **Unit 2/Chapter 6** • Practice Your Skills: Understanding Causes and Effects, p. 13 (average) . . . . . .20 mins. • Critical Thinking and Writing: Distinguishing Fact From Opinion, p. 14 (average) . . . . .20 mins. • Section 2 Quiz, p. 19 (average) . . . . .15 mins. **Why Study History?** • We Celebrate Our Independence, pp. 23–26 (average) . . . . .90 mins.	**Voices of Freedom** • How the Declaration Was Written, pp. 60–62 (average) **Customized Reader** • Diary of a Quaker and a Tory, article IIIA-6 (average)
3 Fighting in the Middle States (pp. 169–173) **Objectives** 1. Describe defeats and hardships the Americans suffered in the Middle States. 2. Explain why the Battle of Saratoga was a turning point in the war. 3. Describe the help the United States received from other nations.	**Lesson Planner,** p. 24 (challenging) . . . . .90 mins. **Unit 2/Chapter 6** • Section 3 Quiz, p. 20 (average) . . . . .15 mins. **Interdisciplinary Connections** • Main Idea: The American Revolution, pp. 31–36 (average) . . . . .20 mins.	**Voices of Freedom** • Lafayette's Impressions of America, p. 63 (average)
4 Other Battlefronts (pp. 174–177) **Objectives** 1. Describe the major action in the West. 2. Explain how the South became the major battlefield of the war. 3. Explain how women and African Americans took part in the war.	**Lesson Planner,** p. 25 (average) . . . . .45 mins. **Unit 2/Chapter 6** • Biography Flashcard: Juan de Miralles, p. 17 (average) .20 mins. • Section 4 Quiz, p. 21 (average) . . . . .15 mins.	**Historical Outline Map Book** • The Revolutionary War in the West, p. 26 (average) **Customized Reader** • Nancy Ward, Beloved Woman of t Cherokees, article IIIA-11 (averag • A Black Man's Request for His Revolutionary Pension, article IIIA- (average) • A Woman's Experience in the American Revolution, article IIIA-2 (average)
5 Winning the War (pp. 178–183) **Objectives** 1. Explain how the Americans began to win battles in the South. 2. Explain how the Americans and French defeated the British at Yorktown. 3. Describe the terms of the Treaty of Paris.	**Lesson Planner,** p. 26 (average) . . . . .45–90 mins. **Unit 2/Chapter 6** • Vocabulary Builder, p. 12 (basic) . . . . .10 mins. • Section 5 Quiz, p. 22 (average) . . . . .15 mins. **Chapter Tests,** pp. 31–36 (average) . . . . .45 mins.	**Historical Outline Map Book** • The Revolutionary War in the Sout p. 27 (average) • North America in 1783, p. 28 (average) **Voices of Freedom** • An Eyewitness at Yorktown, pp. 65–67 (average)

Assessment Options

Teaching Resources
- Alternative Assessment booklet
- Section Quizzes, Unit 2, Chapter 6, pp. 18–22
- Chapter Tests, Chapter 6, pp. 31–36
- Test Bank CD-ROM

Student Performance Pack
- Guide to the Essentials of American History, Chapter 6 Test, p. 38
- Standardized Test Prep Handbook
- Interactive Student Tutorial CD-ROM

Interdisciplinary Connections

Teaching Resources
- Map Mystery, Unit 2, Chapter 6, p. 15
- Connecting History and Literature, Unit 2, Chapter 6, p. 16
- Interdisciplinary Connections, pp. 31–36

Voices of Freedom, pp. 60–63, 65–67

Customized Reader, articles IIIA-1, IIIA-2, IIIA-6, IIIA-11, IIIB-9

Historical Outline Map Book, pp. 24–28

BLOCK SCHEDULING
Activities with this icon will help you meet your Block Scheduling needs.

ENGLISH LANGUAGE LEARNERS
Activities with this icon are suitable for English Language Learners.

TEAM TEACHING
Activities and Background Notes with this icon present starting points for Team Teaching.

Technology

AmericanHeritage® History of the United States CD-ROM
- Time Tour: The American Revolution in From Revolution to Republic
- Arts and Entertainment: Patriotic Songs

Interactive Student Tutorial CD-ROM

Test Bank CD-ROM

Color Transparencies
- The Battle of Yorktown, p. B-43
- Battle of Bunker Hill, p. D-31
- The American Revolution, p. F-15
- Middle Atlantic States, p. I-61
- South Central States, p. I-69
- North Central States, p. I-73

Guided Reading Audiotapes (English/Spanish), side 2

Listening to Literature Audiocassettes: The American Experience:
- To His Excellency, General Washington, side 2

Resource Pro® CD-ROM

Prentice Hall United States History Video Collection™ (Spanish track available on disc version.) Vol. 4, Chs. 19, 25, 28, 31

Prentice Hall Home Page
www.phschool.com

Student Performance Pack

Guide to the Essentials of American History
- Ch. 6, pp. 33–38
  (Available in English and Spanish)

Guided Reading Audiotapes (English/Spanish), side 2

Standardized Test Prep Handbook

Interactive Student Tutorial CD-ROM

Teachers' Bibliography

From the Archives of AmericanHeritage® Don't miss the special American Heritage® teaching notes found in this chapter.

Contact Teachers' Curriculum Institute to learn more about History Alive!® resources on the American Revolution. See History Alive!® unit: Colonial Life and the American Revolution, Section 4, "Toward Independence."

Explore your library to find these issues related to Chapter 6: *Patriotic Tales of the Revolution,* September 1983; *Loyalists of the Revolution,* August 1987; *Thomas Jefferson,* September 1989; *George Washington,* April 1992; *Benjamin Franklin,* September 1992; *The Adams Family,* November 1993.

Prentice Hall Web Site You can access a structured, on-line environment that allows you to preview curriculum-related resources and receive updated information on groundbreaking events from around the nation and the world. (www.phschool.com)

Chapter 6

The American Revolution
1775–1783

Introducing the Chapter

Have students preview the main ideas of this chapter by looking over chapter visuals. Suggest they look for examples of major events of the American Revolution.

Using the Time Line To reinforce student understanding of the sequence of events in this chapter, ask them to look at the time line on these pages. Ask questions such as these: **(1)** What years does the time line cover? *(1775–1783)* **(2)** In what year did France recognize American independence? *(1778)* **(3)** What was the chronological order of these battles—King's Mountain, Saratoga, Bunker Hill, Yorktown? *(Bunker Hill, Saratoga, King's Mountain, Yorktown)* **(4)** What treaty agreement ended the war? *(Treaty of Paris, 1783)*

Ask students to describe the reasons Americans celebrate the Fourth of July as a national holiday as well as the various ways their families and communities celebrate this holiday.

For additional *Why Study History?* support, see p. 167.

Chapter 6

The American Revolution
1775–1783

After Lexington and Concord, representatives of the colonies tried, without success, to find a peaceful solution to the conflict with Britain. In 1776, as the fighting spread, they called for separation from Britain. With the bold words of the Declaration of Independence, the United States became a nation.

The Americans now fought a life-and-death struggle for liberty. From New England, the major operations of the war gradually spread to the Middle States and the South. With help from France and other nations, the Americans defeated the British and won their war for independence.

Why Study History? On July 4, 1776, Americans declared their independence from British rule. Today, on every Fourth of July, we celebrate the Declaration of Independence and the ideals it proclaims. To learn more about how and why we celebrate, see this chapter's *Why Study History?* feature, "We Celebrate Our Independence."

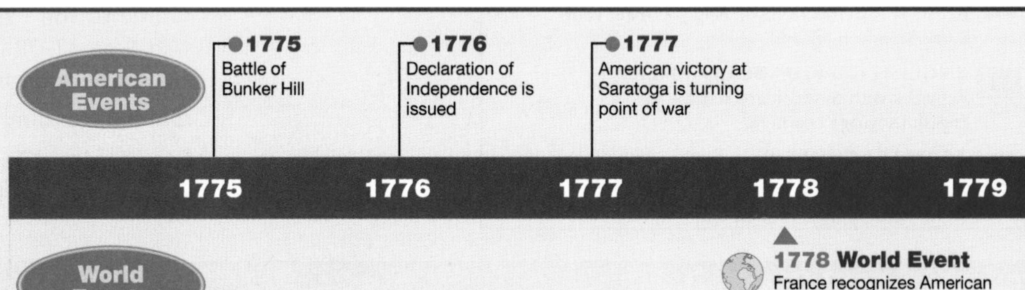

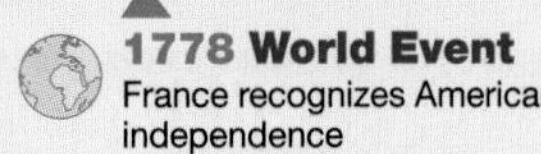

Writing Actively

Responding to Art Ask students to take on the role of a British soldier in the painting on this page. Students should assume that they have fought the colonists for several years before this event. Have students write a letter home to family in England, describing their thoughts and feelings at this moment of surrender.

Viewing History ANSWER

Possible answer: The colonies provided Great Britain with wealth, territory, and power.

Viewing History: A Nation Wins Its Independence

This painting, Surrender of Lord Cornwallis, *is by John Trumbull, one of the greatest early American artists. It shows British troops surrendering to an American army at Yorktown, Virginia, in 1781. The Battle of Yorktown marked the end of the American Revolution. The six-year struggle freed the 13 colonies from British rule.*

★ **Why do you think Britain was unwilling to give up its colonies?**

1780 Patriots' victory at King's Mountain boosts morale

1781 British surrender at Yorktown

1783 Britain recognizes American independence in the Treaty of Paris

1779 | 1780 | 1781 | 1782 | 1783

1779 World Event Spain enters the war against Britain

1782 World Event War between British and Marāthā people of India ends

★ Background ★
Art Note

A Nation Wins Its Independence Early in the war, artist John Trumbull served as an aide to General Washington. He resigned his position in 1777 to paint full-time. Encouraged by Thomas Jefferson, in 1784, he began a series of paintings on the nation's history. His paintings record such events as the Battle of Bunker Hill and Burgoyne's surrender at Saratoga. T

Documents and Literature

On pp. 541–544, you will find two readings to enrich this chapter:

1. Historical Document "Common Sense," excerpts from Thomas Paine's pamphlet supporting independence. (Use with Section 2.)

2. Eyewitness Account "Letters on Independence," excerpts from letters between Abigail and John Adams about women's rights. (Use with Section 2.)

Technology

Videodiscs/Videotapes
Show the *Prentice Hall United States History Video Collection*™ segments for this chapter. The videodisc version has a Spanish track. Press audio until you get the left channel for English or the right channel for Spanish, or use the bar codes in the Guidebook.

AmericanHeritage® History of the United States CD-ROM
- Time Tour: The American Revolution in From Revolution to Republic (*average*)

Section 1
Early Battles

LESSON PLAN

Objectives

★ Explain how Americans pursued both war and peace in 1775.
★ Describe the advantages of each side as they entered the war.
★ Explain how the Continental Army gained control of Boston.

1 Engage

Warm Up Write this John Adams statement on the chalkboard: "The Revolution was in the minds of the people, and this was effected from 1760 to 1775... before a drop of blood was drawn at Lexington." Ask students: "What did Adams mean?"

Activating Prior Knowledge Have students discuss why colonists were willing to fight Britain by 1775.

Reading Actively

Before Reading Have students turn the main headings into main topics of an outline. Then, as they read, have them record two or three important subtopics for each main topic.

2 Explore

Ask students to read the section. For homework, have them do research and a report on Benedict Arnold's early military career.

RESOURCE DIRECTORY

Teaching Resources
Lesson Planner, p. 22
Unit 2/Chapter 6
- Map Mystery: Refugees of the Revolution, p. 15
- Connecting History and Literature: To His Excellency, General Washington, p. 16

Early Battles

As You Read

Explore These Questions
- How did Americans pursue both war and peace in 1775?
- What were the advantages of each side as they entered the war?
- How did the Continental Army gain control of Boston?

Define
- refugee
- blockade
- mercenary

Identify
- Ethan Allen
- Green Mountain Boys
- Continental Army
- Olive Branch Petition
- Patriots
- Loyalists
- Battle of Bunker Hill
- Benedict Arnold

Setting the Scene The events of April 19, 1775, left the British stunned. How had a handful of rebels forced 700 redcoats to retreat? That night, British soldiers grew even more uneasy as they watched rebels set up campfires all around Boston.

In the months ahead, the campfires remained. They were a clear sign that the quarrel between Britain and its colonies had blazed into war. Many colonists clung to hopes for a peaceful solution. Others were ready and eager to fight.

War or Peace?

On May 10, 1775, just a few weeks after the battles at Lexington and Concord, delegates from the colonies met at the Second Continental Congress in Philadelphia. Most who attended still hoped to avoid a final break with Britain. However, while they were meeting, the fighting spread.

Rebels take Ticonderoga

Ethan Allen, a blacksmith known for his fierce temper, followed a course of action rather than talk. Allen decided to lead a band of Vermonters, known as the **Green Mountain Boys,** in a surprise attack on Fort Ticonderoga, located at the southern tip of Lake Champlain. (See the map on page 162.) Allen knew that inside the fort were many cannons which the colonies badly needed.

In early May, the Green Mountain Boys crept quietly through the morning mists to Fort Ticonderoga. They quickly overpowered the guard on duty and entered the fort. Allen rushed to the room where the British commander slept. "Come out, you old rat!" he shouted. The commander demanded to know by whose authority Allen acted. "In the name of the Great Jehovah and the Continental Congress!" Allen replied.

The British commander surrendered Ticonderoga. With the fort, the Green Mountain Boys won a valuable supply of cannons and gunpowder. Allen's success also gave the Americans control of a key route into Canada.

Setting up an army

Then, in June, the Second Continental Congress took the bold step of setting up the **Continental Army.** John Adams proposed that George Washington of Virginia be appointed commander:

> "I [have] in mind for that important command... a gentleman whose skill and experience as an officer, whose independent fortune, great talents, and excellent universal character would command the [approval] of all America."

Tall and dignified, George Washington commanded the respect of all the delegates. They promptly voted to approve him as commander. Without wasting any time, the new

★ Background ★

Did You Know?

Traitor? In 1775, when Ethan Allen tried to take Quebec, Canada, he was captured by the British and held until 1778. Back in Vermont, he tried to get the Continental Congress to grant Vermont statehood. When Congress refused, he talked to the British about making Vermont a British province. Although accused of treason, his guilt was never proven.

★ Activity ★

Cooperative Learning

Making and analyzing a map Have students work in groups to research the importance of geography at Fort Ticonderoga, the Battle of Bunker Hill, or the attack on Quebec. Some students can make physical maps of the battle sites, while others write captions about how geographic features affected the outcome of events. (*average*) ELL T general left Philadelphia to take charge of the forces around Boston.

A peace petition

Even though the delegates had created an army, they were not eager for war. After much debate, Congress decided to try to patch up the quarrel with Britain by sending the **Olive Branch Petition,** written by John Dickinson of Pennsylvania. In it, they declared their loyalty to King George and asked him to repeal the Intolerable Acts.

George III was furious when he heard about the petition. The colonists, he raged, were trying to begin a war "for the purpose of establishing an independent empire!" He blamed "wicked and desperate persons" in the colonies for the growing conflict. Rejecting the Olive Branch Petition, the king vowed to bring the rebels to justice.

The Opposing Sides

The rebels that King George III spoke of called themselves **Patriots.** They opposed aspects of British rule that they considered harsh and unjust. Most of the American colonists were Patriots.

In their war with Britain, the Patriots faced a powerful foe. They also had to struggle against a large number of colonists who chose to remain loyal British subjects.

American Patriots

It would take a great effort for the Patriots to overcome their disadvantages. Colonial forces were poorly organized and untrained. They had few cannons, little gunpowder, and no navy.

Yet the Patriots had some important advantages. Many Patriots owned rifles and were good shots. Also, they had a brilliant commander in George Washington. Another strength was that they would fight hard to defend their homes and property. Reuben Stebbins of Massachusetts was typical of many patriotic farmers. When the British approached, he rode off to battle. "We'll see who's goin' t' own this farm!" he cried.

The British

The British were a powerful foe. They had highly trained, experienced troops. Their navy was the best in the world. British ships could move soldiers quickly up and down the Atlantic coast. In addition, many colonists still supported the British.

Still, Britain was not without problems. Britain's armies were 3,000 miles (4,800 km) from home. News and supplies took months to travel from Britain to North America. Also, British soldiers risked attacks by colonists once they marched out of the cities into the countryside.

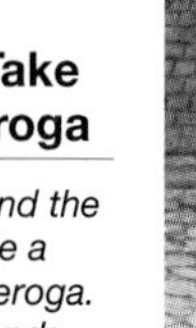

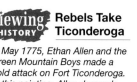

Rebels Take Ticonderoga

In May 1775, Ethan Allen and the Green Mountain Boys made a bold attack on Fort Ticonderoga. In this painting, Allen demands that the British commander surrender. ★ **Why was Fort Ticonderoga an important prize?**

3 Teach

Have students create a chart on the chalkboard of American and British strengths and weaknesses. Have them evaluate the performance of each side at Ticonderoga, Bunker Hill, and in Canada as well as each side's leadership, morale, and degree of popular support for the war. Have students use the completed chart to decide on the greatest strengths and weaknesses of each side.

4 Assess

To close the lesson, have students complete the section review. As an alternative, have students work in pairs to select the most important main ideas from each subsection. For each main idea, have students write two supporting statements.

ANSWER

It provided the Americans with cannons and gunpowder, and it gave them control of a route into Canada.

★ *Background* ★

Did You Know?

Loyal subjects About 500,000 colonists were Loyalists. In no colony did Loyalists outnumber Patriots, but in the Middle Colonies of New York and New Jersey, many tenant farmers and Dutch settlers supported George III. In Pennsylvania, many Germans and Quakers wanted no part of the Revolution. When forced to choose sides, they generally supported the British.

Reading Actively

During Reading Have students read to learn the outcome of the Battle of Bunker Hill and what it indicated about the American and British forces.

Geography Skills

ANSWERS

1. Review locations with students. **2. (a)** Arnold sailed north to Maine, then marched northward overland to Quebec. **(b)** Montgomery left Fort Ticonderoga, traveling north by water across Lake Champlain, then marched northward overland to Montreal, then northeast to Quebec paralleling the St. Lawrence River. **3.** Possible answer: Arnold had a longer route and also had to march through wintry, mountainous Maine woods, whereas Montgomery traveled by boat through the mountains and then followed what was probably a well-traveled land route between Montreal and Quebec.

The War for Independence Begins

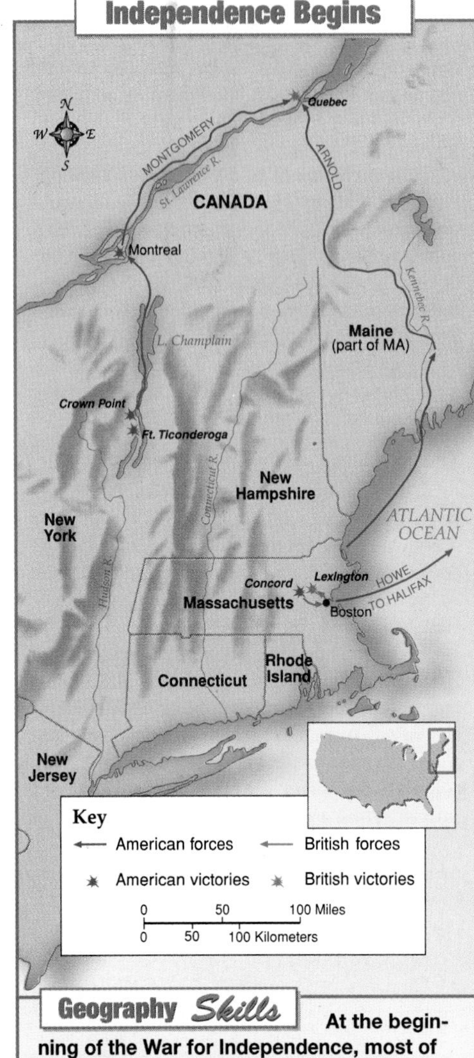

Geography Skills **At the beginning of the War for Independence, most of the fighting took place in the northern colonies and in Canada.**

1. **Location** On the map, locate: **(a)** Lexington, **(b)** Concord, **(c)** Boston, **(d)** Fort Ticonderoga, **(e)** Quebec.
2. **Movement** **(a)** Describe Arnold's route to Canada. **(b)** Describe Montgomery's route from Crown Point to Quebec.
3. **Critical Thinking** Based on the map, which American commander would have a harder time reaching Quebec? Explain.

American Loyalists

American colonists who remained loyal to Britain were known as **Loyalists** or Tories. It is estimated that they made up about 20 percent of the colonists. They included wealthy merchants and former officials of the royal government. However, some farmers and craftsworkers were also Loyalists. There were more Loyalists in the Middle States and the South than in New England.

Loyalists faced tough times during the American Revolution. Patriots tarred and feathered people known to favor the British. Many Loyalists fled to England or Canada. Others found shelter in cities controlled by the British. Those who fled lost their homes, stores, and farms.

The Fight for Boston

During the first year of conflict, much of the fighting was centered around Boston. About 6,000 British troops were stationed there. Colonial militia surrounded the city and prevented the British from marching out.

Battle of Bunker Hill

Even before Washington reached Boston, the Patriots took action. On June 16, 1775, Colonel William Prescott led 1,200 minutemen up Bunker Hill, across the river from Boston. From there, they could fire on British ships in Boston harbor. Prescott, however, noticed that nearby Breed's Hill was an even better position. He ordered his men to move there and dig defensive trenches.

At sunrise, the British general, William Howe, spotted the Americans. He ferried about 2,400 redcoats across the harbor to attack the rebels' position. Slowly, the British began to climb Breed's Hill. Each soldier carried a heavy pack that weighed about 125 pounds. Many of the British troops were exhausted even before the fighting began.

The Americans waited patiently as the British approached. The Patriots held their fire because they had very little gunpowder. Their commanders warned, "Don't shoot until you see the whites of their eyes!"

When the Americans finally fired, the British were forced to retreat. A second British attack was also turned back. On the

★ Customized Instruction ★

Visual Learners

Creating a cartoon While the Battle of Bunker Hill was a British victory, it was a promising beginning for the inexperienced American soldiers. Have visual learners create political cartoons about this event. Ask some students to draw cartoons for a British newspaper or magazine. The others can take the perspective of the Patriot cause. Before students begin their work, display examples of political cartoons on current issues and point out techniques cartoonists use to express their points of view. Have students create titles for their cartoons. Post their finished products on the bulletin board and have students take turns deciding which perspective each cartoon reflects. (*average*)

RESOURCE DIRECTORY

Transparencies
Fine Art
• Battle of Bunker Hill, p. D-31

Viewing History **The Fight for Boston**

In this painting of the Battle of Bunker Hill, British ships bombard the village of Charlestown, across the river from Boston. Meanwhile, British troops make the long march up Breed's Hill to attack the waiting Americans. ★ **Why was the Battle of Bunker Hill important to Americans?**

Drum carried at Bunker Hill

third try, the British succeeded in pushing over the top. They took both Bunker Hill and Breed's Hill, but paid a high price for their victory. More than 1,000 redcoats lay dead or wounded. American losses numbered only about 400.

The **Battle of Bunker Hill** was the first major battle of the Revolution. It proved that the Americans could fight bravely. However, it also showed that the British would not be easy to defeat.

The British leave Boston

Washington finally reached Boston a few weeks after the Battle of Bunker Hill. There, he found about 16,000 troops camped in huts and tents at the edge of the city. Their weapons ranged from rifles to swords made by local blacksmiths.

General Washington quickly began to turn raw recruits into a trained army. His job was especially difficult because soldiers from different colonies mistrusted one another. "Connecticut wants no Massachusetts men in her corps," he wrote. And "Massachusetts thinks there is no necessity for a Rhode Islander to be introduced into her [ranks]." Slowly, Washington won the loyalty of his troops. They, in turn, learned to take orders and work together.

In January 1776, Washington had a stroke of good fortune. Soldiers arrived outside Boston with cannons they had dragged across the mountains from Fort Ticonderoga.

Writing Actively 

After Reading Have students write a short essay describing the early battles of the war and what impact an American victory or defeat seemed to have on the Patriot cause.

Viewing History ANSWER

It was the first major battle of the Revolution. While it showed that the Americans could fight bravely, it also showed that the British would not be easy to defeat.

★ Background ★

Our Diverse Nation

Not like us Continental soldiers from different colonies did not want to serve in the same regiments at first. New Englanders mistrusted Virginians, whom they called "buckskins" for the fringed hunting shirts they wore. Pennsylvanians were suspicious of "Yankees," or New England residents. General Washington tried hard to create a sense of unity among his fighting forces.

Technology

Listening to Literature Audiocassettes
The American Experience
- To His Excellency, General Washington, side 2 (*average*)

★ Section 1 Review ★

ANSWERS

1. See map, p. 162.

2. (a)–(c) p. 160, **(d)–(e)** p. 161, **(f)** p. 162, **(g)** p. 163, **(h)** p. 164

3. (a)–(c) p. 164

4. (a) sent Olive Branch Petition to George III **(b)** set up Continental Army, made Washington its commander

5. (a) a highly trained, experienced army; a powerful navy **(b)** fighting to defend their homes; many owned rifles and were good shots; they had a brilliant leader in George Washington.

6. put cannons on Dorchester Heights, overlooking Boston Harbor; made General Howe realize he could not hold Boston

7. They were weakened by bad weather and cold; they lacked French support in Quebec.

8. Possible answer: feared persecution or death if they stayed

Activity

Guided Instruction
Help students understand what a difficult choice colonists had. Remind them that success was far from certain, and that rebellion was a radical step. Have them consider why disloyalty to King George might have been a moral, as well as political, issue.

ASSESSMENT See the rubrics in the Alternative Assessment booklet in the Teaching Resources.

RESOURCE DIRECTORY

Teaching Resources
Lesson Planner, p. 23
Unit 2/Chapter 6
- Section 1 Quiz, p. 18
- Critical Thinking and Writing: Distinguishing Fact From Opinion, p. 14

Washington had the cannons placed on Dorchester Heights, overlooking the harbor.

Once General Howe saw the American cannons in place, he knew that he could not hold Boston. In March 1776, he and his troops sailed from Boston to Halifax, Canada. About 1,000 American Loyalists went with the British. The Loyalists of Boston became **refugees,** people who flee their homes to seek refuge from war, persecution, or other hardships.

Although the British left New England, they had not given up. King George III ordered a **blockade** of all colonial ports. A blockade is the shutting off of a port to keep people or supplies from moving in or out. The king also used Hessian **mercenaries,** or troops for hire, from Germany to help fight the colonists.

March on Canada

While Washington's army was winning control of Boston, other Americans were launching an attack on Canada. The Americans hoped to get help from French Canadians, who were unhappy under British rule.

In the fall of 1775, two American armies moved north into Canada. (See the map on page 162.) Richard Montgomery led one army from Fort Ticonderoga to Montreal. He seized that city in November 1775. He then moved toward Quebec. **Benedict Arnold** led the second army north through Maine. He was supposed to join forces with Montgomery in Quebec.

Arnold and his troops had a terrible journey through the Maine woods in winter. Rainstorms followed by freezing nights coated their clothes with ice. Supplies ran so low that soldiers survived only by eating boiled bark and shoe leather. Finally, Arnold reached Quebec. However, he was disappointed to learn that most French Canadians did not support the Americans.

In a blinding snowstorm on December 31, 1775, the Americans attacked Quebec. Montgomery was killed, and Arnold was wounded. The Americans failed in their attempt to take the city. They stayed outside Quebec until May 1776, when the British landed new forces in Canada. At last, weakened by disease and hunger, the Americans withdrew, leaving Canada to the British.

★ Section 1 Review ★

Recall

1. **Locate** **(a)** Fort Ticonderoga, **(b)** Boston, **(c)** Montreal, **(d)** Quebec.
2. **Identify** **(a)** Ethan Allen, **(b)** Green Mountain Boys, **(c)** Continental Army, **(d)** Olive Branch Petition, **(e)** Patriots, **(f)** Loyalists, **(g)** Battle of Bunker Hill, **(h)** Benedict Arnold.
3. **Define** **(a)** refugee, **(b)** blockade, **(c)** mercenary.

Comprehension

4. **(a)** How did the Second Continental Congress pursue a peaceful settlement with Britain? **(b)** What steps did the Congress take to prepare for war with Britain?
5. **(a)** What advantages did the British have over the Patriots? **(b)** What advantages did the Patriots have?
6. How did Washington force the British to leave Boston?

Critical Thinking and Writing

7. **Understanding Causes and Effects** Explain two reasons for the American failure to capture Quebec.
8. **Making Inferences** Why did the Boston Loyalists feel that they had to go with the British to Canada?

Activity **Making a Decision** You are an American in 1775. War between the rebels and the British seems certain! Decide whether you will become a Loyalist or a Patriot. Explain the facts and ideas that led to your decision.

★ Activity ★
Connections With Technology

Writing a report Weapons of war in the 1770s were very different from those of today. Officers relayed 22 separate commands to soldiers as they loaded, then fired, their muskets. Have students research and report on how warfare evolved with inventions such as the Colt revolver, Gatling gun, armored tank, and radar. (*average*)

★ Background ★
Turning Points

Already satisfied Because French Canadians were satisfied with the Quebec Act, they did not openly support the Americans during the Revolution. The Quebec Act, passed in 1774, was seen by American colonists as one of the Intolerable Acts. The Quebec Act protected the rights, religion, and language of the French in Quebec.

Declaring Independence

As You Read

Explore These Questions
- How did *Common Sense* influence the colonists?
- How did American Patriots respond to the Declaration of Independence?
- What are the main ideas of the Declaration of Independence?

Define
- traitor
- preamble
- natural rights

Identify
- *Common Sense*
- Thomas Paine
- Richard Henry Lee
- Thomas Jefferson
- Declaration of Independence

Many Americans had come to believe that Parliament did not have the right to make laws for the 13 colonies. After all, they argued, the colonists had their own elected legislatures. At the same time, however, most Americans still felt strong bonds of loyalty to Britain. Especially, they felt they owed allegiance to the king.

Then, in January 1776, a pamphlet titled ***Common Sense*** appeared on the streets of Philadelphia. "I offer nothing more than simple facts, plain arguments, and common sense," wrote its author, **Thomas Paine.** Though Paine had only recently arrived from England, he strongly supported the colonists in their quarrel with the king. In blunt words, he boldly urged the colonies to declare their independence.

Common Sense

In *Common Sense,* Thomas Paine tried to convince the colonists that they did not owe loyalty to George III or any other monarch. The very idea of setting up kings and queens was wrong, he said.

> "In England a King hath little more to do than to make war and give away [jobs]; which in plain terms, is to impoverish the nation.... Of more worth is one honest man to society and in the sight of God, than all the crowned ruffians that ever lived."

Americans did not owe anything to England, either, Paine went on. If the English had helped the colonists, they had done so for their own profit. It could only hurt the Americans to remain under British rule:

> "Everything that is right or reasonable pleads for separation.... 'Tis time to part."

Common Sense won many colonists to the idea of independence. In six months, more than 500,000 copies of the pamphlet were printed and sold. "*Common Sense* is working a powerful change in the minds of men," George Washington observed.

Moving Toward Independence

Paine's *Common Sense* affected many members of the Continental Congress. In June 1776, **Richard Henry Lee** of Virginia offered a resolution stating that "these United Colonies are, and of right ought to be, free and independent States."

Delegates faced a difficult decision. There could be no turning back once

COMMON SENSE;

ADDRESSED TO THE

INHABITANTS

OF

AMERICA,

On the following interesting

SUBJECTS.

PHILADELPHIA;

Printed, and Sold, by R. BELL, in Third-Street.

MDCCLXXVI.

Common Sense by Thomas Paine

Section 2
Declaring Independence

LESSON PLAN

Objectives

★ Explain how *Common Sense* influenced the colonists.

★ Describe how American Patriots responded to the Declaration of Independence.

★ Summarize the main ideas of the Declaration of Independence.

1 Engage

Warm Up Ask students what kinds of information they would put in a document that declares a colony's independence from the country that rules it.

Activating Prior Knowledge Have students give reasons why the colonists might favor or oppose separation from Britain.

Reading Actively

Before Reading Have students read to find out what was "revolutionary" about the Declaration of Independence.

2 Explore

Ask students to read the section. For homework, have some students do research on the early life and career of Thomas Jefferson up to 1776, while others do research on Thomas Paine's early life and career. The class can compare these two revolutionary Thomases.

★ *Background* ★
Recent Scholarship

American made In *American Scripture: Making the Declaration of Independence,* historian Pauline Maier breaks controversial new ground by putting the Declaration of Independence squarely within the tradition of colonial discontent. Maier sees the Declaration as a natural extension of prior colonial protests rather than a document whose ideas came mainly from Europe.

3 Teach

Divide the class into three groups. Ask each group to prepare a dialogue between a delegate to the Continental Congress and a newspaper reporter on one of these topics: **(a)** how and why the Declaration of Independence was written; **(b)** the origin and meaning of natural rights, and how this concept is reflected in the Declaration; **(c)** the contents of the Declaration. After each dialogue, have the speakers answer additional questions on their topics from the class.

4 Assess

To close the lesson, have students complete the section review. Or ask each student to write a brief essay describing the ideas that helped shape the Declaration of Independence.

★ ★ ★ ★ ★ ★ ★ ★ ★ ★ ★ ★ ★ ★ ★ ★ ★

ANSWER

to explain why the colonies were separating from Britain and declaring independence

Reading Actively

During Reading Have students note the statement under Moving Toward Independence that "[d]elegates faced a difficult decision." Ask them to look for evidence to support this statement as they read.

RESOURCE DIRECTORY

Teaching Resources
Unit 2/Chapter 6
- Practice Your Skills: Understanding Causes and Effects, p. 13

Why Study History?
- We Celebrate Our Independence, pp. 23–26

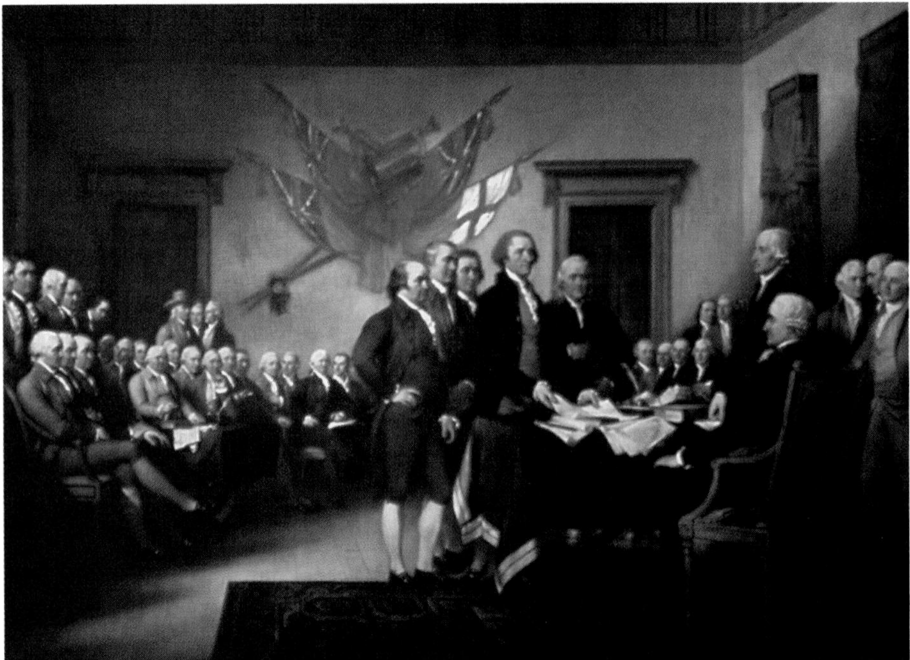

Viewing History **Signing the Declaration**

Thomas Jefferson labored many hours perfecting the Declaration of Independence. Here, Jefferson and other committee members present the Declaration to the Continental Congress. This painting, like the one on page 159, is by John Trumbull. ★ **What was the purpose of the Declaration of Independence?**

they declared independence. If they fell into British hands, they would be hanged as traitors. A **traitor** is a person who betrays his or her country.

The Congress took a fateful step. They chose a committee to draw up a declaration of independence. The committee included John Adams, Benjamin Franklin, Thomas Jefferson, Robert Livingston, and Roger Sherman. Their job was to tell the world why the colonies were breaking away from Britain.

The committee asked Jefferson to write the document. **Thomas Jefferson** was one of the youngest delegates. A quiet man, he spoke little at formal meetings. Among friends, however, he liked to sprawl in a chair with his long legs stretched out and talk for hours. His ability to write clearly and gracefully had earned him great respect.

The Declaration of Independence

In late June, Jefferson completed the declaration, and it was read to the Congress. On July 2, the Continental Congress voted that the 13 colonies were "free and independent States." Two days later, on July 4, 1776, the delegates accepted Jefferson's **Declaration of Independence,** making only a few minor changes.

John Hancock, president of the Continental Congress, signed the Declaration first. He penned his signature boldly, in large, clear letters. "There," he said, "I guess King George will be able to read that."

Copies of the Declaration were distributed throughout the colonies. Across the colonies, those who were Patriots greeted the

★ Customized Instruction ★

English Language Learners

Paraphrasing Pair English language learners with students more proficient in English to examine the concept of natural rights in the Declaration of Independence. Pairs can begin by copying the first part of the Declaration on a sheet of paper and circling such unfamiliar words and phrases as *self-evident, endowed, unalienable,* and *pursuit of happiness.* ELL students can use a dictionary to find definitions appropriate to the context and then write a similar concept in their native language. Have pairs take turns putting each phrase in the first part of the Declaration into their own words. As one person paraphrases the document, the other can record it. Have groups read their versions aloud to the class. (*average*) ELL

Why Study History?

Because We Celebrate Our Independence

Independence Day fireworks over Washington, D.C.

Historical Background

John Adams reacted proudly to the signing of the Declaration of Independence. He declared that the event "ought to be solemnized with pomp and parade, with shows, games, sports, guns, bells, bonfires, and illuminations, from one end of this continent to the other, from this time forward, forevermore."

In 1777, on the first anniversary of the Declaration of Independence, Philadelphia overflowed with excitement. A navy ship on the Delaware River sounded a 13-gun salute. Bells rang all day, bonfires burned in the streets, and fireworks lit up the evening sky. Following a dinner attended by members of Congress, American soldiers paraded through the city's streets.

Connections to Today

Throughout the nation, we celebrate Independence Day in much the same way that people did in 1777. John Adams would feel right at home with our parties, picnics, athletic games, patriotic speeches, and American flags. Today's televised concerts, parades of large, decorated floats, and massive displays of community-sponsored fireworks would have been beyond his imagination, but certainly in keeping with his spirit.

Connections to You

How do you commemorate the Fourth of July? You may celebrate the day at the beach, at the park, or in your own backyard. Yet, no matter how you spend the Fourth of July, the reason for celebration remains the same—to honor the foresight and courage of our founders.

The Declaration of Independence that they issued spoke of equality. It also discussed the rights and freedoms that all people have and the responsibility of government to protect those rights and freedoms. During the Revolutionary War, Americans fought and died for those ideas. Today, you enjoy a democratic way of life based on those ideas.

1. **Comprehension** Describe three things that Philadelphians did in 1777 to commemorate Independence Day.
2. **Critical Thinking** How do the ideas in the Declaration of Independence still live on today?

★ ***Activity*** It is 1776 and you are a member of the Continental Congress. Review the ideas contained in the Declaration of Independence. Write a short speech explaining to the Congress (your classmates) why they should sign it.

Why Study History?

ANSWERS

1. rang bells, set bonfires, lit fireworks; members of Congress dined out; soldiers paraded in the streets **2.** Possible answers: They live on in our government and our attitudes about democracy and freedom worldwide.

★ Activity

Guided Instruction
Encourage students to review their texts and list ideas in the Declaration to use in their speeches. Suggest that they practice their speeches on their own or with a friend before giving them in class. Point out that they might want to save their best reason for last (or else use it first), but they should be sure to use it effectively.

ASSESSMENT See the rubrics in the Alternative Assessment booklet in the Teaching Resources.

Writing Actively

After Reading Ask students to write a newspaper editorial explaining to colonists in 1776 why the Declaration of Independence was written and why protecting natural rights was important.

Fast Facts

★ Nations that celebrate a July Independence Day include France (July 14, Bastille Day) and Canada (July 1, Canada Day), as well as Venezuela, Argentina, Belgium, and Peru.
★ Congress declared July 4 a national legal holiday in 1941.
★ The first public reading of the Declaration took place on July 8th in Philadelphia's Independence Square as church bells pealed and crowds cheered.

Bibliography

To read more about this topic:
1. *Celebrate America,* Jess Brallier and Sally Chabert (Berkley, 1995). Holiday traditions, famous fourths, songs.
2. *Celebrating the Fourth,* Len Travers (Univ. of Massachusetts Press, 1997). How the Fourth shaped our national identity.
3. Internet. For patriotic music, fireworks, and more, consult www.holidays.net/independence/index.

Technology

Videodiscs/Videotapes
Prentice Hall United States History Video Collection™, Vol. 4, Ch. 19, "The Declaration of Independence," 4:20 mins (*average*)
ELL

Chapter 19

★ Section 2 Review ★

ANSWERS

1. (a)–(c) p. 165, **(d)–(e)** p. 166

2. (a) p. 166, **(b)–(c)** p. 168

3. Possible answers: Americans did not owe loyalty to Britain; monarchs are useless; Britain was motivated only by desire for profit; it hurt Americans to remain under British rule; it was time to separate.

4. They celebrated; New York Patriots tore down a statue of George III.

5. Preamble: introduction; part 2: outlines the rights of people; part 3: lists wrongs committed by Britain; part 4: announces independence.

6. Possible answers: A king is useless, if not harmful; separation is reasonable and necessary.

7. Possible answer: Cite the statement that "all men are created equal" and endowed with "certain unalienable rights," including liberty.

Activity

Guided Instruction

Have students use a dictionary and the glossary in the margin of the Declaration of Independence in the Reference Section to help them paraphrase the document. Have them read their versions to their friends.

ASSESSMENT See the rubrics in the Alternative Assessment booklet in the Teaching Resources.

RESOURCE DIRECTORY

Teaching Resources
Lesson Planner, p. 24
Unit 2/Chapter 6
• Section 2 Quiz, p. 19

Transparencies
Geography and History
• Middle Atlantic States, p. I-61

news of independence with joyous celebrations. In New York, Patriots tore down a statue of King George III. In Boston, the sound of cannons could be heard for hours.

The Declaration of Independence consists of a **preamble,** or introduction, followed by three main parts. (The complete Declaration of Independence is printed in the Reference Section.)

Natural rights

The first part of the Declaration stresses the idea of **natural rights,** or rights that belong to all people from birth. In bold, ringing words, Jefferson wrote:

> "We hold these truths to be self-evident, that all men are created equal, that they are endowed by their Creator with certain unalienable rights, that among these are life, liberty, and the pursuit of happiness."

According to the Declaration of Independence, people form governments in order to protect their natural rights and liberties. Governments can exist only if they have the "consent of the governed." If a government fails to protect the rights of its citizens, then it is the people's "right [and] duty, to throw off such government, and provide new guards for their future security."

British wrongs

The second part of the Declaration lists the wrongs committed by Britain. Jefferson condemned King George III for disbanding colonial legislatures and for sending troops to the colonies in times of peace. He complained about limits on trade and about taxes that had been imposed without the consent of the people. Jefferson listed many other wrongs to show why the colonists had the right to rebel. He also pointed out that the colonies had petitioned the King to correct these injustices. Yet they remained.

Independence

The last part of the Declaration announces that the colonies had become the United States of America. All political ties with Britain were cut. As a free and independent nation, the United States had the power to make alliances and trade with other countries.

★ Section 2 Review ★

Recall

1. **Identify** **(a)** *Common Sense,* **(b)** Thomas Paine, **(c)** Richard Henry Lee, **(d)** Thomas Jefferson, **(e)** Declaration of Independence.
2. **Define** **(a)** traitor, **(b)** preamble, **(c)** natural rights.

Comprehension

3. What arguments did Thomas Paine offer in favor of independence?
4. How did American Patriots react to the Declaration of Independence?
5. Describe the four parts of the Declaration of Independence.

Critical Thinking and Writing

6. **Analyzing Primary Sources** Review the excerpts from Thomas Paine's *Common Sense* that appear on page 165. Explain the meaning of those excerpts in your own words.
7. **Synthesizing Information** After the Declaration of Independence was issued, enslaved Africans sent petitions to state legislatures asking for freedom. How might they have used the Declaration of Independence to support their demands?

Activity **Writing a Document** You are Thomas Jefferson. Reports are coming in that many people cannot understand the Declaration of Independence because the language is too complex. Try to help them by rewriting the preamble, or first paragraph, in simpler language.

★ *Activity* ★

Connections With Civics

Analyzing a primary source John Locke, an English philosopher of the late 1600s, wrote that people had natural rights and oppressed people had the right to revolt against an unjust government. Have students find one or more passages in the Declaration of Independence that suggest Locke's influence on Jefferson's thinking. Remind them to review all parts of the Declaration and analyze direct statements as well as the way an argument is made. Have students explain their choices. (*challenging*)

Fighting in the Middle States

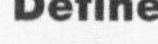

As You Read

Explore These Questions
- What defeats and hardships did the Americans suffer in the Middle States?
- Why was the Battle of Saratoga a turning point in the war?
- What help did the United States receive from other nations?

Define
- ally
- cavalry

Identify
- Battle of Long Island
- Nathan Hale
- Battle of Trenton
- John Burgoyne
- Battle of Saratoga
- Marquis de Lafayette
- Friedrich von Steuben
- Thaddeus Kosciusko

Setting the Scene It was early one morning in late June of 1776. Daniel McCurtin glanced out his window at New York harbor. He was amazed to see "something resembling a wood of pine trees trimmed." He watched the forest move across the water. Then, he understood. The trees were the masts of ships!

Continental Army medicine chest

> "I could not believe my eyes... the whole bay was full of shipping as ever it could be. I declare that I thought all London was afloat."

Daniel McCurtin had witnessed the arrival of a large British fleet in New York. Aboard the ships were General Howe and his redcoats. Thus began a new stage in the war. Previously, most of the fighting of the American Revolution took place in New England. In mid-1776, the heavy fighting shifted to the Middle States. There, the Continental Army suffered through the worst days of the war.

The British Take New York

Washington, expecting Howe's attack, had led his forces south from Boston to New York City. His army, however, was no match for the British. Howe had about 34,000 troops and 10,000 sailors. He also had ships to ferry them ashore. Washington had fewer than 20,000 poorly trained troops. Worse, he had no navy.

In August, Howe's army landed on Long Island. In the **Battle of Long Island,** more than 1,400 Americans were killed, wounded, or captured. The rest retreated to Manhattan. The British followed. To avoid capture, Washington hurried north.

Throughout the autumn, Washington fought a series of battles with Howe's army. In November, he crossed the Hudson River into New Jersey. Pursued by the British, the Americans retreated across the Delaware River into Pennsylvania.

During the campaign for New York, Washington needed information about Howe's forces. **Nathan Hale,** a young Connecticut officer, slipped behind British lines and returned with the details. Soon after, the British captured Hale. They tried him and condemned him to death. As Hale walked to the gallows, he is said to have declared: "I only regret that I have but one life to lose for my country."

Despair and New Hope

Months of campaigning took a toll on the Continental Army. In December 1776, Washington described his troops as sick, dirty, and "so thinly clad as to be unfit for service." Every day, soldiers deserted. Washington

★ *Background* ★

Did You Know?

Dying for his country Nathan Hale was 21 years old when he was hanged by the British as an American spy. Born in 1755, he graduated from Yale in 1773 and taught school until joining the Connecticut militia and then the Continental Army. He was disguised as a Dutch school teacher when captured. Some believe that Hale's cousin, a fervent Loyalist, betrayed him.

Section 3
Fighting in the Middle States

LESSON PLAN

Objectives

★ Describe defeats and hardships the Americans suffered in the Middle States.

★ Explain why the Battle of Saratoga was a turning point in the war.

★ Describe the help the United States received from other nations.

1 Engage

Warm Up Write these Thomas Paine words on the chalkboard: "These are the times that try men's souls." Ask: "What events might make Americans wonder if declaring independence was the right decision?"

Activating Prior Knowledge Have students describe the strengths and weaknesses of each side at this point in the war.

Reading Actively

Before Reading Have students read to find out why the period covered early in this section has been described as a bleak time for the Patriots. Ask them to note why Americans felt desperate at this time.

2 Explore

Ask students to read the section. For homework, have them pick one of the Europeans who fought alongside the Patriots such as the

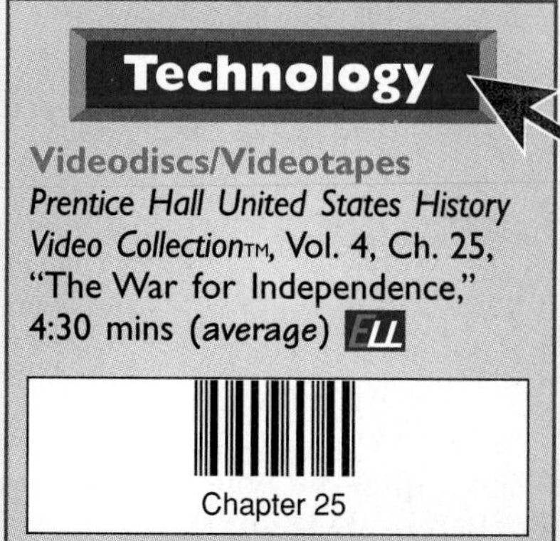

Technology

Videodiscs/Videotapes
Prentice Hall United States History Video Collection™, Vol. 4, Ch. 25, "The War for Independence," 4:30 mins (*average*) ELL

Chapter 25

Marquis de Lafayette, Friedrich von Steuben, or Thaddeus Kosciusko. Have them research and report on why that person joined the Patriots and how he contributed to the war effort.

3 Teach

Have students make a chart in their notebooks with five columns and five rows. Have them label columns: Battle, Date, Where Fought, Result, Significance. Have them label rows: Long Island, Trenton, Princeton, Brandywine/Germantown, Saratoga. After students complete their charts, let them compare answers.

4 Assess

To close the lesson, have students complete the section review. Or have them write an essay explaining why the outlook for the Patriots improved in the spring of 1778.

★ ★ ★ ★ ★ ★ ★ ★ ★ ★ ★ ★ ★ ★ ★ ★ ★

Geography *Skills*

ANSWERS

1. Review locations with students. **2.** Howe sailed south from New York, then north into Chesapeake Bay, then landed his troops so they could march overland toward Philadelphia. **3.** While Burgoyne moved south along the shore of Lake Champlain, St. Leger sailed down the St. Lawrence River and into Lake Ontario before moving onto land. In both cases, the British used the easiest land or sea route available.

RESOURCE DIRECTORY

Teaching Resources
Interdisciplinary Connections
- Main Idea: The American Revolution, pp. 31–36

The Revolutionary War, 1776–1777

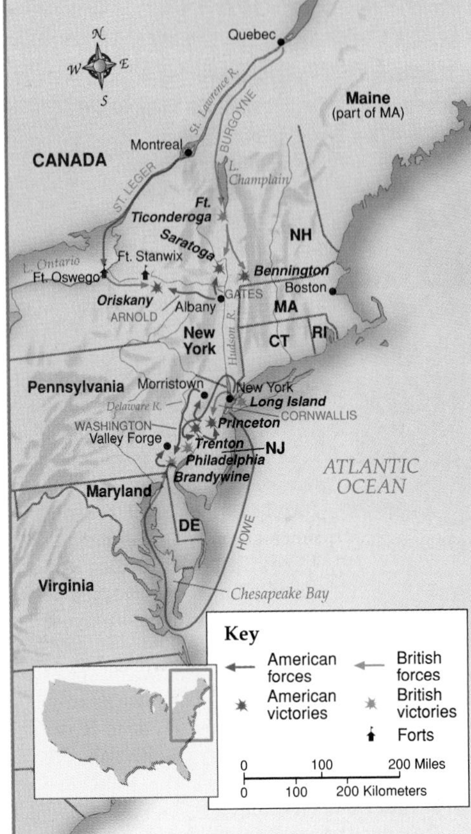

Geography *Skills* **In 1776 and 1777, the Americans and British battled over a large area. The American victory at Saratoga marked a major turning point of the war.**

1. **Location** On the map, locate: **(a)** Long Island, **(b)** New York City, **(c)** Trenton, **(d)** Hudson River, **(e)** Saratoga, **(f)** Valley Forge.
2. **Movement** How did the British use sea power to help them capture Philadelphia?
3. **Critical Thinking** How did Burgoyne and St. Leger use geography to help move their armies quickly toward Albany?

wrote to his brother: "I am wearied to death. I think the game is pretty near up."

The Crisis

Thomas Paine had retreated with the army through New Jersey. Once again, he took up his pen. This time, he wrote *The Crisis,* urging Americans to support the army.

> "These are the times that try men's souls. The summer soldier and the sunshine patriot will, in this crisis, shrink from the service of his country; but he that stands it *now* deserves the love and thanks of man and woman."

Grateful for Paine's inspiring words, Washington had *The Crisis* read aloud to his troops.

American victories in New Jersey

The Americans needed more than words to help their cause, however. General Washington decided on a bold move—a surprise attack on Trenton.

On Christmas night, Washington secretly led his troops across the icy Delaware River. Soldiers shivered as spray from the river froze on their faces. Once ashore, they marched through swirling snow. "Soldiers, keep by your officers," Washington urged.

Early on December 26, the Americans surprised the Hessian troops guarding Trenton and took most of them prisoner. An American summed up the **Battle of Trenton:** "Hessian population of Trenton at 8 A.M.—1,408 men and 39 officers; Hessian population at 9 A.M.—0."

British General Charles Cornwallis set out at once to retake Trenton and capture Washington. Late on January 2, 1777, he saw the lights of Washington's campfires. "At last we have run down the old fox," he said, "and we will bag him in the morning."

Washington fooled Cornwallis. He left the fires burning and slipped behind British lines to attack Princeton. There, the Continental Army won another victory. From Princeton, Washington moved to Morristown, where the army spent the winter. The victories at Trenton and Princeton gave the Americans new hope.

FROM THE ARCHIVES OF AmericanHeritage®

The Conway Cabal Was there a plot in 1777 to remove George Washington as Commander-in-Chief? Washington thought so. Rumors flew and harsh words were penned. Verbal sniping by fellow generals Horatio Gates, Thomas Conway, and others threatened Washington's authority; they later became known as the Conway Cabal.
Source: Preston Russell, "The Conway Cabal," *American Heritage* magazine, February/March 1995.

★ *Activity* ★
Connections With Arts

Analyzing a song Ask students: "What makes this verse from the ballad *The Battle of Trenton* patriotic?"

Our object was the Hessian band,
That dared invade fair freedom's land,
And quarter in that place.
Great Washington he led us on,
Whose streaming flag in storm or sun
Had never known disgrace. (*basic*)

Viewing History **Victory at Princeton**

This painting depicts the battle at Princeton, New Jersey, in January 1777. Victories at Trenton and Princeton boosted American morale. Still, difficult times lay ahead for Washington's troops. ★ **How was Washington able to surprise the British at Princeton?**

Turning Point of the War

In London, British officials were dismayed by the army's failure to crush the rebels. Early in 1777, General **John Burgoyne** (buhr GOIN) presented George III with a new plan for victory. If British troops cut off New England from the other colonies, he argued, the war would soon be over.

Burgoyne wanted three British armies to march on Albany, New York, from different directions. They would crush American forces there. Once they controlled the Hudson River, the British could stop the flow of soldiers and supplies from New England to Washington's army.

Britain's plan fails

Burgoyne's plan called for General Howe to march on Albany from New York City. George III, however, wanted Howe to capture Philadelphia first.

In July 1777, Howe sailed from New York to the Chesapeake Bay. (See the map on page 170.) Despite Washington's efforts to stop him, Howe captured Philadelphia. He then went on to defeat the Americans at the battles of Brandywine and Germantown. Howe then retired to comfortable quarters in Philadelphia for the winter. Washington retreated to Valley Forge, where he set up a makeshift camp.

Meanwhile, two other British armies under Burgoyne and Barry St. Leger (lay ZHAIR) marched from Canada toward Albany. St. Leger tried to take Fort Stanwix. However, Benedict Arnold drove him back with a strong American army.

Victory at Saratoga

Only Burgoyne was left to march on Albany. His army moved slowly because it had many heavy baggage carts to drag through the woods. To slow Burgoyne further, Patriots cut down trees to block the route and dammed up streams to create swampy bogs.

Despite these obstacles, Burgoyne retook Fort Ticonderoga. He then sent troops into Vermont to find food and horses. There, Patriots attacked the redcoats. At the Battle of

Reading Actively

During Reading Have students read to find out why Saratoga was a turning point in the war.

Viewing History ANSWER

Washington left campfires burning to trick the British into thinking American troops were still in camp. He then slipped behind British lines to attack Princeton.

★ *Background* ★

Recent Scholarship

Saratoga Richard Ketchum's *Saratoga: Turning Point of America's Revolutionary War* adds greatly to an understanding of why the British lost this critical battle. Ketchum focuses on how Britain's Colonial Secretary insisted that he direct military operations from London and how he failed to order General Howe to join Burgoyne at Albany.

Technology

AmericanHeritage® History of the United States CD-ROM

- Arts and Entertainment: Patriotic Songs (*average*)

Writing Actively

After Reading Ask students to use the information in the graphic organizer on this page to write a short essay on why Saratoga was a turning point in the war.

Graphic Organizer Skills

ANSWERS **1. (a)** It gave Americans money and supplies but stayed neutral. **(b)** It became an ally of the United States, provided military and naval support, and declared war on Britain. **2.** Possible answers: revenge on Britain for losses in the French and Indian War; possibly to gain some territory

Bennington, they wounded or captured nearly 1,000 British.

Burgoyne's troubles grew. The Green Mountain Boys hurried into New York to help other American forces there. At the village of Saratoga, the Americans surrounded the British. When Burgoyne tried to break free, the Americans beat him back. Realizing he was trapped, Burgoyne surrendered his entire army to the Americans on October 17, 1777.

The American victory at the **Battle of Saratoga** was a major turning point in the war. It ended the British threat to New England. It boosted American spirits at a time when Washington's army was suffering defeats. Most important, it convinced France to become an ally of the United States. Nations that are allies work together to achieve some common goal.

Help from Europe

The Continental Congress had long hoped for French aid. In 1776, the Congress had sent Benjamin Franklin to Paris. His job was to persuade Louis XVI, the French king, to help the Americans with weapons and other badly needed supplies. The Congress also wanted France to declare war on Britain. France had a strong navy that could stand up to the British.

The French were eager to hurt Britain, but they were also cautious. France and Britain were rivals for power and France was still angry about their defeat by the British in the French and Indian War. However, Louis XVI did not want to help the Americans openly until he was sure they could win.

The American victory at Saratoga convinced France and other nations that the United States could stand up to Britain. In February 1778, France became the first nation to sign a treaty with the United States. In it, Louis XVI recognized the new nation and agreed to provide military aid. Later, the Netherlands and Spain also joined in the war against Britain. France, the Netherlands, and Spain all provided loans to the Americans.

Even before European nations provided aid to the United States, individual volunteers had been coming from Europe to join the American cause. Some became leading officers in the American army.

The **Marquis de Lafayette** (lah fee YEHT), a young French noble, brought trained

Saratoga: A Turning Point

Before		After
▪ France gives American rebels money and supplies but stays neutral. ▪ French king does not want to make commitment unless he is sure Americans will win.	American Victory at Saratoga →	▪ Victory proves that Americans can win. ▪ France becomes official ally of the United States. ▪ France gives military and naval support. ▪ France declares war on Britain.

Graphic Organizer Skills **The American victory at the Battle of Saratoga was a major turning point in the War for Independence.**

1. **Comprehension** **(a)** How did France help the Americans before Saratoga? **(b)** How did France help them after Saratoga?
2. **Critical Thinking** What do you think France hoped to gain by helping the Americans win independence?

★ Customized Instruction ★

Extroverted Learners

Presenting a skit Extroverted learners can assume the roles of television war correspondents broadcasting from the Continental Army headquarters at Valley Forge. Many anthologies of primary sources, including *Voices of 1776* by Richard Wheeler, provide vivid details about the harsh conditions in the camp during the winter of 1777–1778. Have students prepare skits that feature live interviews with George Washington, ordinary soldiers, soldiers' mothers and wives back home, and "experts" on the military outlook from Valley Forge. Students can present their skits as segments in a nightly television newscast with an anchorperson introducing each segment. (*average*)

Resource Directory

Teaching Resources
Unit 2/Chapter 6
• Section 3 Quiz, p. 20

soldiers to help the Patriot cause. Lafayette, who fought at Brandywine, became one of Washington's most trusted friends.

From the German state of Prussia came **Friedrich von Steuben** (STOO buhn). He helped train Washington's Continental troops to march and drill. Von Steuben had served in the Prussian army, considered the best in Europe.

Two Polish officers also joined the Americans. **Thaddeus Kosciusko** (kahs ee UHS koh), an engineer, helped build forts and other defenses. Casimir Pulaski trained **cavalry,** or troops on horseback.

Harsh Winter at Valley Forge

The victory at Saratoga and the promise of help from Europe did much to boost American morale. Nevertheless, Washington's ragged army still faced hard times. During the long, cold winter of 1777–1778, the Continental Army suffered severe hardships at Valley Forge in Pennsylvania.

The conditions at Valley Forge were terrible. American soldiers shivered in damp, drafty huts. Many slept on the frozen ground. They had little or no warm clothing. Some soldiers stood on guard wrapped only in blankets. Many had no shoes, so they wrapped bits of cloth around their feet. As the bitter winter wore on, soldiers suffered from frostbite and disease. An army surgeon from Connecticut wrote about the suffering:

> ❝There comes a Soldier, his bare feet are seen thro his worn-out stockings, his Breeches not sufficient to cover his nakedness... his whole appearance pictures a person forsaken & discouraged.❞

As news of the suffering at Valley Forge spread, Patriots from around the nation sent help. Women collected food, medicine, warm clothes, and ammunition for the army. Some women, like Martha Washington, wife of the commander, went to Valley Forge to help the sick and wounded.

The arrival of desperately needed supplies was soon followed by warmer weather. By the spring of 1778, the army at Valley Forge was more hopeful. Washington could not know it at the time, but the Patriots' bleakest hour had passed.

★ Section 3 Review ★

Recall

1. **Locate** **(a)** New York City, **(b)** Trenton, **(c)** Princeton, **(d)** Hudson River, **(e)** Albany, **(f)** Saratoga, **(g)** Valley Forge.
2. **Identify** **(a)** Battle of Long Island, **(b)** Nathan Hale, **(c)** Battle of Trenton, **(d)** John Burgoyne, **(e)** Battle of Saratoga, **(f)** Marquis de Lafayette, **(g)** Friedrich von Steuben, **(h)** Thaddeus Kosciusko.
3. **Define** **(a)** ally, **(b)** cavalry.

Comprehension

4. What problems did the Americans face during the campaign in the Middle States?
5. Describe three results of the Battle of Saratoga.
6. Why was help from France and other nations important to the Americans?

Critical Thinking and Writing

7. **Synthesizing Information** Reread the excerpt from *The Crisis* on page 170. **(a)** What did Paine mean by the words, "These are the times that try men's souls"? **(b)** What are "sunshine patriots"? **(c)** Why do you think Washington wanted Paine's words read to the troops?
8. **Drawing Conclusions** Why do you think Burgoyne's plan to cut the colonies in two by seizing Albany ended in failure?

Activity **Reporting the News** You are a newspaper reporter during the American Revolution. Write a report on a major event or battle that took place in the Middle States. You may need to do some additional research to write an interesting and informative article.

★ Section 3 Review ★

ANSWERS

1. See map, p. 170.
2. **(a)–(b)** p. 169, **(c)** p. 170, **(d)** p. 171, **(e)–(f)** p. 172, **(g)–(h)** p. 173
3. **(a)** p. 172, **(b)** p. 173
4. many defeats; no navy; lack of food, clothing, medicine
5. ended the British threat to New England; boosted American spirits; brought French aid
6. Possible answers: They needed the French navy, weapons, supplies, and European military skills.
7. Possible answers: **(a)** Hardships test people's resolve to fight for their beliefs. **(b)** people who are Patriots only when times are good **(c)** to inspire his troops
8. Possible answers: He lacked crucial help from Howe and St. Leger; Patriots successfully harassed his march; Americans fought well.

Activity

Guided Instruction
Remind students that a newspaper article should answer these questions: *Who? What? Where? When? Why? How?* Encourage them to enliven their articles with anecdotes or quotations.

ASSESSMENT See the rubrics in the Alternative Assessment booklet in the Teaching Resources.

Internet Activity

Visiting Valley Forge Have students consult the Valley Forge Web site at www.libertynet.org/ha/valleyforge/ for weather reports from 1775 to 1782, Washington's letters, and a museum tour. Have students share two pieces of information they learned from the site. Given the changing nature of the Internet, you may wish to preview this site. (*average*)

★ Background ★
Our Diverse Nation

Prussian patriot Friedrich von Steuben was a seasoned military leader before he crossed the Atlantic. In Europe he fought in the Seven Years' War and served as an aide to Frederick the Great. He met Ben Franklin in Paris and Franklin gave him a letter of introduction to George Washington. After the war Congress awarded him a pension and several states gave him land.

Section 4
Other Battlefronts

LESSON PLAN

Objectives

★ Describe the major action in the West.
★ Explain how the South became the major battlefield of the war.
★ Explain how women and African Americans took part in the war.

1 Engage

Warm Up Ask: "How do you think fighting at sea differs from fighting on land?"

Activating Prior Knowledge Using a wall map of the U.S., show students where battles in the West and South were fought. Ask students to draw on their geographic knowledge to speculate on what challenges each side faced in fighting in these areas.

Reading Actively

Before Reading Have students examine the map and subheads in this section and identify the three battle fronts they will read about. As students read, have them note the outcome of the clashes in each area.

2 Explore

Ask students to read the section. For homework, assign each student one person from the Identify list. Have them research and report on that person's contribution to the war effort.

RESOURCE DIRECTORY

Teaching Resources
Lesson Planner, p. 25
Unit 2/Chapter 6
• Biography Flashcard: Juan de Miralles, p. 17

Transparencies
Geography and History
• South Central States, p. I-69
• North Central States, p. I-73

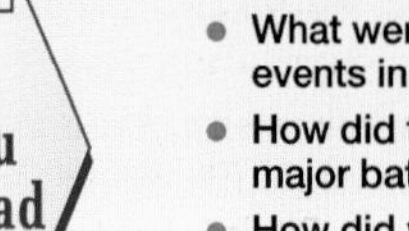

4 Other Battlefronts

As You Read

Explore These Questions
- What were the major military events in the West?
- How did the South become the major battlefield of the war?
- How did women and African Americans take part in the war?

Define
- neutral

Identify
- George Rogers Clark
- Bernardo de Gálvez
- John Paul Jones
- Betsy Ross
- Molly Pitcher
- Peter Salem

Setting the Scene Flying Crow, a Seneca chief, looked sternly at the British officers who were seated before him. "If you are so strong, Brother, and they but a weak boy, why ask our assistance?"

Like many Native American leaders, Flying Crow did not want to become involved in a war between the "weak boy"—the United States—and Britain. Yet, Native Americans could not avoid the struggle.

Americans of various backgrounds played significant roles in the Revolution. Also, the American Revolution took place on many fronts. Fighting occurred not only in the North but also in the West and South. The war was also fought at sea.

The War in the West

When the Revolution began, most Indians tried to stay **neutral,** or uninvolved in the war. The British and Patriots, however, both sought Native American aid. In the end, the British were more persuasive. They convinced many Native Americans that a Patriot victory would mean more white settlers crossing the Appalachians and taking Indian lands.

Connections With Civics

Unlike most other Iroquois, the Oneida Indians allied themselves with the Americans. The Congress thanked them in these words: "You stood forth in the cause of your friends and ventured your lives in our battles. While the sun and moon continue to give light to the world, we shall love and respect you."

Native Americans help the British

In the South, the British gained the support of the Cherokees, Creeks, Choctaws, and Chickasaws. In the summer of 1776, a Cherokee force attacked dozens of settlements on the frontier. Only after hard fighting were Patriot militia able to drive the Native Americans into the mountains. Sporadic fighting continued throughout the war.

Fighting was equally fierce on the northern frontier. In 1778, Iroquois forces led by the Mohawk leader Joseph Brant joined with Loyalists in raiding frontier settlements in Pennsylvania and New York. The next year, Patriots retaliated by invading Iroquois lands. They destroyed dozens of Iroquois villages. They also ruined thousands of acres of crops.

Victory at Vincennes

Further west, in 1778, **George Rogers Clark** led Virginia frontier fighters against the British in the Ohio Valley. With help from Miami Indians, Clark captured the British forts at Kaskaskia and Cahokia.

Clark then plotted a surprise winter attack on the British fort at Vincennes. He led a small band 150 miles (240 km) through heavy rains, swamps, and icy rivers.

★ *Customized Instruction* ★

Auditory and Visual Learners

Holding a military briefing Divide students into three groups. Assign one group the war in the West, a second group the war in the South, and a third group the role of members of the press. Tell the first two groups to assume the roles of American officers giving a military briefing. They should begin by researching one battle in their region and making a map of the battle site. Give each presenter a colored marker or pointer to use to show strategy and troop movements. Presenters can describe the military strategy of both sides, their strengths and weaknesses in the battle, the outcome, and its consequences. The press corps can then ask questions and write reports based on the briefing. (*average*)

When Clark's force reached the fort, they spread out through the woods to make their numbers appear greater than they really were. The British commander thought it was useless to fight so many Americans. He surrendered Vincennes in February 1779.

Spanish aid

On the southwestern frontier, Americans received help from New Spain. In the early years of the war, Spain was neutral. However, **Bernardo de Gálvez,** governor of Spanish Louisiana, favored the Patriots. He secretly supplied medicine, cloth, muskets, and gunpowder to the Americans. He also sent cattle from Texas to feed the Continental Army.

When Spain entered the war against Britain in 1779, Gálvez took a more active role. He seized British forts along the Mississippi River and the Gulf of Mexico. He also drove the British out of West Florida.

The War in the South

Scattered fighting had taken place in the South throughout the Revolution. In February 1776, North Carolina Patriots defeated a Loyalist army at the Battle of Moore's Creek Bridge. This battle is sometimes called the Lexington and Concord of the South.

After the British plan to conquer New York and New England failed, the South became the main battleground of the war. Sir Henry Clinton, the new British commander-in-chief, knew that many Loyalists lived in the southern backcountry. He hoped that if British troops marched through the South, Loyalists would join them.

At first, Clinton's plan seemed to work. In December 1778, the British seized Savannah, Georgia. A year and a half later, they took Charleston, South Carolina. Next, they crushed a Continental force at Camden, South Carolina. (See the map on page 179.) "I have almost ceased to hope," wrote Washington when he learned of the losses.

Fighting at Sea

At sea, the Americans could do little against the powerful British navy. British ships blockaded American ports. From time to time, however, a bold American captain captured a British ship.

The most daring American captain was **John Paul Jones.** In his most famous battle, in September 1779, Jones commanded the *Bonhomme Richard.* He was sailing in the North Sea near Britain when he spotted a large fleet of enemy merchant ships. They were guarded by a single warship, the *Serapis.* Jones attacked the *Serapis,* even though it was larger than the *Bonhomme Richard.*

In a furious battle, cannonballs ripped through the *Bonhomme Richard,* setting it on fire. The British commander called on

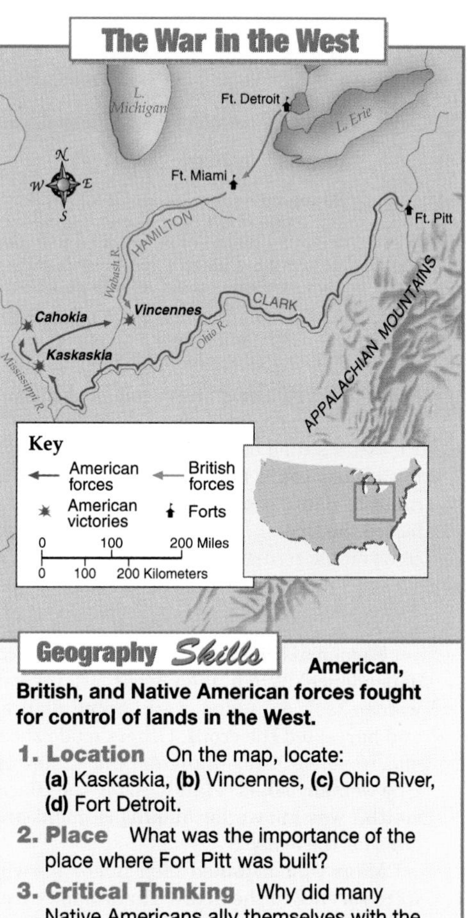

Geography *Skills* **American, British, and Native American forces fought for control of lands in the West.**

1. **Location** On the map, locate: **(a)** Kaskaskia, **(b)** Vincennes, **(c)** Ohio River, **(d)** Fort Detroit.
2. **Place** What was the importance of the place where Fort Pitt was built?
3. **Critical Thinking** Why did many Native Americans ally themselves with the British?

3 Teach

Write these statements on the chalkboard and have students identify each as true or false: **(a)** Many Native American groups sided with the Patriots. **(b)** In the West, American forces were aided by the Spanish. **(c)** Loyalists helped the British to win some early victories in the South. **(d)** Neither the British nor the Patriots won the support of African Americans. **(e)** Women made important contributions to the Patriot cause. Have students revise any false statements to make them true. Have them write two supporting statements for each true statement.

4 Assess

To close the lesson, have students complete the section review. Or ask them to write a brief report on the outcome of the fighting discussed in this section.

★ ★ ★ ★ ★ ★ ★ ★ ★ ★ ★ ★ ★ ★ ★ ★ ★ ★

Geography *Skills*

ANSWERS

1. Review locations with students. **2.** It stood at the gateway to the West, on the Ohio River. **3.** Possible answer: They felt that the British would protect them from Americans encroaching on their lands.

★ *Background* ★
Did You Know?

Fighting spirit Although Washington was discouraged by defeats in the South, many Patriots were not. The fall of Charleston spurred some to work harder. One Maryland Patriot declared, "The Fate of America is not to be decided by the Loss of a Town or Two." Patriot women in four states formed a women's group to collect money to buy shirts for needy soldiers.

Linking Past and Present

ANSWER

Possible answers: They feel a strong sense of patriotism; they like the benefits offered; they like the military discipline.

Reading Actively

During Reading Have students read to find out how women and African Americans contributed to the Patriot cause.

Writing Actively

After Reading Have students write an essay comparing and contrasting the responses of Native Americans, African Americans, and women to the struggle for independence.

Linking Past and Present
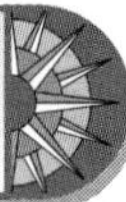

Past

Present

Women in Arms

During the American Revolution, few women took part in battle. Those who did became legendary. At left, Mary Ludwig Hays—known as "Molly Pitcher"—loads and fires a cannon. Today, thousands of American women serve on active duty in the United States military. Shown above are two female pilots aboard the aircraft carrier Eisenhower. ★ **Why do you think so many young women have volunteered to serve in the military?**

Jones to surrender. "I have not yet begun to fight!" Jones replied.

Jones sailed close to the *Serapis* so that his sailors could board the enemy ship. In hand-to-hand combat, the Americans defeated the British. Jones earned a hero's welcome on his return home.

Women in the War

Women also helped in the struggle for independence. When men went off to war, women took on added work. Some planted and harvested the crops. Others made shoes and wove cloth for blankets and uniforms. One woman, called "Handy Betsy the Blacksmith," was known for making cannons and guns for the army.

Many women joined their husbands who were serving in the army. The women cared for the wounded, washed clothes, and cooked. Martha Washington joined her husband whenever she could.

Some women achieved lasting fame for their activities in the war. **Betsy Ross** of Philadelphia sewed flags for Washington's army. Legend claims that she made the first American flag of stars and stripes.

A few women even took part in battle. During the Battle of Monmouth in 1778, Mary Ludwig Hays carried water to her husband and other soldiers. The soldiers called her Moll of the Pitcher or **Molly Pitcher.** When her husband was wounded, she took his place, loading and firing a cannon.

African Americans in the War

By 1776, more than a half million African Americans lived in the colonies. At first, the Continental Congress refused to let African Americans, whether free or enslaved, join the army. The British, however, offered freedom to any male slave who served the king. In response, Washington changed his policy and allowed free African Americans to enlist.

★ Activity ★

Our Diverse Nation

Designing a plaque Many women contributed to the war effort. Have students do research on Deborah Sampson, Phoebe Fraunces, Hardy Jane Thomas, Lydia Barrington Darragh, and Laura Wolcott. Have each student select one such revolutionary heroine and design a plaque to commemorate her contribution. Students should include a short description of the woman's accomplishments and a possible location for display of the plaque. A useful reference for this activity is *Founding Mothers* by Linda DePauw. (*average*) T

RESOURCE DIRECTORY

Teaching Resources
Unit 2/Chapter 6
- Section 4 Quiz, p. 21

Joining the fight

It is estimated that about 5,000 African Americans fought against the British. At least nine black minutemen saw action at Lexington and Concord. One of them, Prince Estabrook, was wounded. Two others, **Peter Salem** and Salem Poor, went on to fight bravely at Bunker Hill.

Some African Americans formed special regiments. Others served in white regiments as drummers, fifers, spies, and guides. Thousands of black sailors also served on American ships. Whites recognized the courage of their African American comrades, as this eyewitness account shows:

> "Three times in succession, [African American soldiers] were attacked... by well-disciplined and veteran [British] troops, and three times did they successfully repel the assault, and thus preserve our army from capture."

Enslaved African Americans faced difficult choices. If they tried to flee to the British army to gain freedom, they risked being hanged by angry Patriots. If they joined the American army or continued to work on Patriot plantations, the British might capture and sell them.

Hoping for freedom

Black Patriots hoped that the Revolution would bring an end to slavery. After all, the Declaration of Independence proclaimed that "all men are created equal." In Massachusetts and elsewhere, enslaved African Americans sent petitions to lawmakers asking for freedom.

Some white leaders also hoped the war would end slavery. James Otis wrote that "the colonists are by the law of nature free born, as indeed all men are, white or black." Quakers in particular spoke out strongly against slavery.

By the 1770s, slavery was declining in the North, where a number of free African Americans lived. During the American Revolution, several states moved to make slavery illegal, including Massachusetts, New Hampshire, and Pennsylvania. Other states also began to debate the slavery issue.

★ Section 4 Review ★

Recall

1. **Locate** (a) Kaskaskia, (b) Cahokia, (c) Vincennes.
2. **Identify** (a) George Rogers Clark, (b) Bernardo de Gálvez, (c) John Paul Jones, (d) Betsy Ross, (e) Molly Pitcher, (f) Peter Salem.
3. **Define** neutral.

Comprehension

4. Describe the role that each of the following played in the war in the West: (a) Native Americans, (b) the Spanish.
5. How did the South replace the North as the major battlefield of the Revolution?
6. (a) How did women participate in the war effort? (b) Why did some African Americans join the British army?

Critical Thinking and Writing

7. **Understanding Causes and Effects** Read the following two statements. Then decide which is the cause and which is the effect. Explain your answer. (a) Many Native Americans sided with the British. (b) During the Revolution, settlers continued to push west of the Appalachians.
8. **Drawing Conclusions** How do you think the story of John Paul Jones's victory over the *Serapis* affected the attitudes of American Patriots?

Activity **Writing a Tribute** During the American Revolution, you are a member of a special awards committee in the Congress. Choose a person or group mentioned in this section who helped the American cause. Write a tribute praising the individual's or group's accomplishments.

★ Section 4 Review ★

ANSWERS

1. See map, p. 175.

2. **(a)** p. 174, **(b)–(c)** p. 175, **(d)–(e)** p. 176, **(f)** p. 177

3. p. 174

4. **(a)** mostly fought for the British **(b)** At first, Spain was neutral, but Governor Bernardo de Gálvez of Louisiana aided the Americans. After Spain entered the war, Gálvez seized British forts and drove them out of West Florida.

5. When the British failed to take control of New York and New England, the South became the main battleground.

6. **(a)** planted and harvested crops; made weapons and supplies; some joined their husbands at the front **(b)** to gain freedom as promised by George III

7. cause: (b); effect: (a); It was because of the continued expansion of American settlers that Native Americans looked to the British for protection.

8. encouraged them; made them more determined

Activity

Guided Instruction

Remind students that their tribute should include a description of the activity that made the chosen person so worthy of praise.

ASSESSMENT See the rubrics in the Alternative Assessment booklet in the Teaching Resources.

★ Background ★ Did You Know?

Midnight rider Sybil Ludington was the 16-year-old daughter of a Patriot leader in Fredricksburg, NY. Late on April 26, 1777, a messenger came to warn her father that British troops were raiding nearby Danbury, CT, a Patriot supply center guarded by fewer than 200 Continental troops. Sybil rode 40 miles through the night to alert the militia about the attack.

★ Background ★ Our Diverse Nation

The two Salems During the Battle of Bunker Hill, black and white Patriots fought the British. Peter Salem, an African American who had fought at Concord, shot British Major Pitcairn when the latter unwisely stood to announce, "The day is ours." Later, another African American survivor of Bunker Hill, Salem Poor, was commended as "a brave and gallant soldier."

Section 5 Winning the War

LESSON PLAN

Objectives

★ Explain how the Americans began to win battles in the South.
★ Explain how the Americans and French defeated the British at Yorktown.
★ Describe the terms of the Treaty of Paris.

1 Engage

Warm Up Tell students to suppose that they command an army. Ask: "Under what circumstances might you decide to surrender rather than continue fighting?"

Activating Prior Knowledge Have students describe the war in the South in mid-1780. Ask: "Why were the British optimistic?" "Why were the Americans pessimistic?" and "Why did Washington say, 'I have almost ceased to hope'?"

Reading Actively

Before Reading Ask students to read Explore These Questions. As they read the section, have them jot down notes to answer each question.

2 Explore

Ask students to read the section. For homework, have them pick an American or British leader mentioned in this section and do research and then report on how his personal and military abilities made him an effective leader.

RESOURCE DIRECTORY

Teaching Resources
Lesson Planner, p. 26

Transparencies
Interdisciplinary Connections
• The Battle of Yorktown, p. B-43

5 Winning the War

As You Read

Explore These Questions

- How did the Americans begin to win battles in the South?
- How did the Americans and French defeat the British at Yorktown?
- What were the terms of the Treaty of Paris?

Define

- guerrilla
- siege
- ratify

Identify

- Battle of King's Mountain
- Nathanael Greene
- Daniel Morgan
- Francis Marion
- Benedict Arnold
- Comte de Rochambeau
- Admiral de Grasse
- Battle of Yorktown
- Treaty of Paris

When he was only 16 years of age, Thomas Young set out with about 900 other Patriots to capture King's Mountain in South Carolina. Although most of the Patriots were barefoot, they moved quickly up the wooded hillside, shouldering their old muskets. They were determined to take the mountain from the Loyalists dug in at the top.

Whooping and shouting, Young and his comrades dashed from tree to tree, dodging bullets as they fired their own weapons. They climbed higher and higher toward the enemy lines. Suddenly, Thomas heard the frantic cry, "Colonel Williams is shot!"

> ❝I ran to his assistance for I loved him as a father.... He revived, and his first words were, 'For God's sake boys, don't give up the hill!'... [I] returned to the field to avenge his fate.❞

Powder horn

The American Patriots in the South certainly needed the good news. General Clinton's redcoats had captured both Savannah and Charleston, forcing the American armies into retreat. Throughout the southern countryside, attacks by British troops and Loyalist militia had become especially destructive and brutal. One Loyalist officer boasted how the army was "destroying furniture, breaking windows, taking... cattle, horses, mules."

The Patriot victory at King's Mountain was only the first in a string of American victories in the South. In the months ahead, two able American generals helped to turn the tide against Cornwallis and his British army. The American generals were **Nathanael Greene** of Rhode Island and **Daniel Morgan** of Virginia.

Patriots Rally in the South

The Patriots succeeded in capturing King's Mountain on October 7, 1780. The victory boosted morale and breathed new life into the Patriot cause in the South. Jefferson called the **Battle of King's Mountain** "the turn of the tide."

Connections With Geography

Geography helped the Patriots win at King's Mountain. To reach the Loyalists atop the ridge, the Patriots climbed through a forest that protected them from enemy fire. The Loyalists had a difficult downhill line of fire. One Patriot recalled how the Loyalists "overshot us altogether, scarce touching a man except those on horseback."

Skills For LIFE MINI LESSON

MAP, GRAPH, AND CHART SKILLS
Making a Graphic Display

1. Introduce this skill by noting that graphic displays can take many forms, including flow charts, diagrams, maps, and charts. A battle map is a graphic display of military history that shows how a battle was fought.

2. Help students practice reading and creating a battle map by examining such maps in an atlas of American wars. Note how arrows and colors are used to show troop movements and positions.

3. Help students apply this skill by creating a detailed battle map for the Battle of King's Mountain in South Carolina, using information in this section plus outside research to show troop movements under American and British commanders. *(average)* T

General Greene's ability as a military leader was perhaps second only to Washington's. In 1780, Greene took command of the Continental Army in the South. Making good use of his soldiers' knowledge of the local geography, Greene chose to fight only on ground that put the British at a disadvantage. When he retreated, he followed the easiest routes. He often arranged for boats to be waiting at river crossings. General Cornwallis wore out his soldiers trying to catch Greene's army.

In January 1781, General Morgan won an important battle at Cowpens, South Carolina. Morgan used a clever tactic to defeat the British. Morgan divided his soldiers into a front line and a rear line. He ordered the front line to retreat after firing just two volleys. The British, thinking the Americans were retreating, charged forward—straight into the devastating fire of Morgan's second rank. In this way, the Americans won the Battle of Cowpens.

Greene and Morgan had combined their armies when they fought Cornwallis at Guilford Court House, near present-day Greensboro, North Carolina. The battle was one of the bloodiest of the war. Though the Americans retreated, the British sustained great losses. One Englishman observed that "another such victory would destroy the British army." Cornwallis withdrew to the coastal town of Wilmington to rest and regroup his army.

Francis Marion of South Carolina added to British frustrations. He led a small band of militia, who often slept by day and traveled by night. Marion was known as the Swamp Fox. His soldiers used **guerrilla,** or hit-and-run, tactics to harass the British. They would appear suddenly out of the swamps, quickly attack, and then retreat back into the swamps.

Victory at Yorktown

Finally, Cornwallis gave up on his plan to take the Carolinas. In the spring of 1781, he moved his troops north into Virginia. He planned to conquer Virginia and cut off the Americans' supply routes to the South.

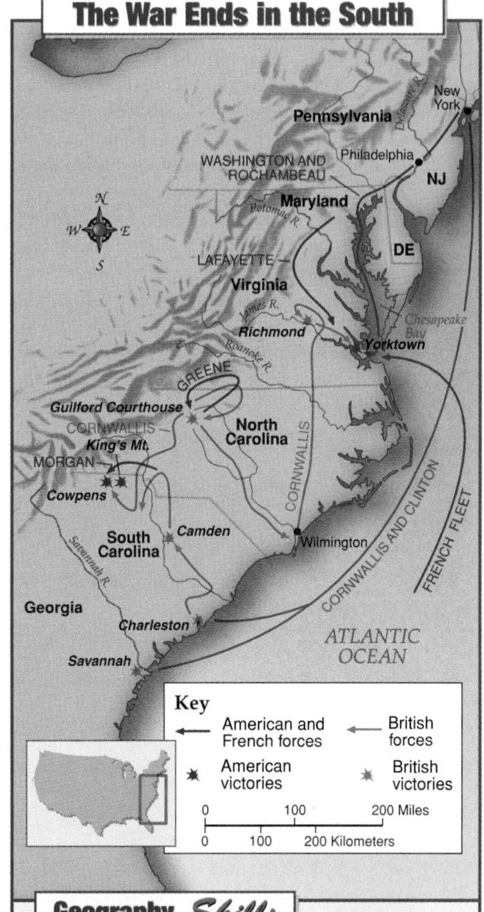

Geography *Skills* **The War for Independence came to a close in the South. After a string of defeats, the Americans gradually gained the upper hand. The last major battle was the American victory at Yorktown.**

1. **Location** On the map, locate: **(a)** Savannah, **(b)** King's Mountain, **(c)** Guilford Courthouse, **(d)** Chesapeake Bay, **(e)** Yorktown.
2. **Region** Did the British have greater control over coastal or inland regions of the South?
3. **Critical Thinking** Why was it a mistake for Cornwallis to retreat to the Yorktown peninsula?

3 Teach

Divide students into groups. Ask each group to write a news bulletin for one of these events: **(a)** Battle of King's Mountain; **(b)** siege of Yorktown; **(c)** British surrender at Yorktown; **(d)** terms of the Treaty of Paris; **(e)** Washington's farewell to his officers. Bulletins should include information about who, what, where, when, why, and the significance of the event. Have groups exchange bulletins and write a response to the event from either a Patriot or Loyalist perspective.

4 Assess

To close the lesson, have students complete the section review. Or, ask them to write an essay identifying at least three American strengths or British weaknesses that helped the Americans win the war.

★ ★ ★ ★ ★ ★ ★ ★ ★ ★ ★ ★ ★ ★ ★ ★ ★ ★

Geography *Skills*

ANSWERS

1. Review locations with students. **2.** coastal **3.** He was trapped there when the French navy blockaded the peninsula by sea while American and French troops attacked by land.

★ *Background* ★

Did You Know?

Foxy fighter Francis Marion's militia attacked British communications lines and supply depots and rescued captured Patriots. Marion's nickname, the Swamp Fox, was given to him by Banastre Tarleton, a frustrated British officer who spent much time chasing Marion.

Biography
ANSWER

Possible answers: Armistead may have appreciated Lafayette's trust in him to work for the Patriots; he may have admired Lafayette as a person and as someone who helped Americans.

An American traitor

The British had achieved some success in Virginia, even before the arrival of Cornwallis. **Benedict Arnold,** formerly one of the Americans' best generals, was now leading British troops. Arnold captured and burned the capital city of Richmond. His forces raided and burned other towns as well.

Arnold had turned traitor to the American cause in September 1780, while commanding West Point, a key fort in New York. Arnold was resentful because he felt he had not received enough credit for his victories. He also needed money. He secretly agreed to turn over West Point to the British. The plot was uncovered by a Patriot patrol, but Arnold escaped to join the British.

Biography **James Armistead**

Though enslaved, James Armistead faithfully served the Patriot cause as a spy. Under the direction of Lafayette, Armistead worked as a volunteer in the camps of Benedict Arnold and Lord Cornwallis. The information he gained contributed to the American victory at Yorktown. Later, after winning his freedom, Armistead changed his name to Lafayette. ★ **Why do you think Armistead decided to change his name to Lafayette?**

Arnold's act of treachery and his raids on towns in Connecticut and Virginia enraged the Patriots. Thomas Jefferson, governor of Virginia, offered a sizable reward in gold for his capture. Washington wrote orders that Arnold was to be hanged. Despite these efforts, Arnold was never captured.

Cornwallis trapped

Cornwallis hoped to meet with the same kind of success in Virginia that Arnold had. At first, things did go well. Cornwallis sent Loyalist troops to attack Charlottesville, where the Virginia legislature was meeting. Governor Thomas Jefferson and other officials had to flee.

American troops under Lafayette fought back by making raids against the British. Lafayette did not have enough troops to fight a major battle. Still, his strategy kept Cornwallis at bay.

Then, Cornwallis made a mistake. He refused an order from Sir Henry Clinton to send part of his army to New York. Instead, he retreated to Yorktown peninsula, a strip of land jutting into Chesapeake Bay. He felt confident that British ships could supply his army from the sea.

Washington saw an opportunity to trap Cornwallis on the Yorktown peninsula. He marched his Continental troops south from New York. With the Americans were French soldiers under the **Comte de Rochambeau** (roh shahm BOH). The combined army rushed to join Lafayette in Virginia.

Meanwhile, a French fleet under **Admiral de Grasse** was also heading towards Virginia. Once in Chesapeake Bay, De Grasse's fleet closed the trap. Cornwallis was cut off. He could not get supplies. He could not escape by land or by sea.

The British surrender

By the end of September, more than 16,000 American and French troops lay **siege** to Cornwallis's army of fewer than 8,000. A siege is the act of surrounding an enemy position in an attempt to capture it. Day after day, American and French artillery pounded the British.

For several weeks, Cornwallis held out. Finally, with casualties mounting and his

FROM THE ARCHIVES OF AmericanHeritage®

Honoring a Traitor? In the 1800s, citizens of Schuylerville, NY (formerly Saratoga), wanted to mark the great battle fought there. But they did not want to honor Benedict Arnold, one of its heroes. Near the spot where Arnold was injured is a carved stone with a booted left leg and the epaulets (shoulder symbols) of a major general—Arnold's rank—but no name.

Source: Robert Ketchum, "The Turning Point," *American Heritage* magazine, October 1997.

★ Activity ★

Cooperative Learning

Making a book Have students compile a *Who's Who in the American Revolution*. First have them list people—European, American, African American, Native American, men and women—to include. Ask each group to prepare biographical entries for several names. Develop a standard format for entries. Have students put edited entries into a single classroom reference book. (*average*) T

RESOURCE DIRECTORY

Teaching Resources
Unit 2/Chapter 6
- Vocabulary Builder, p. 12
- Section 5 Quiz, p. 22

Chapter Tests, pp. 31–36

FOR LIFE

Critical Thinking | Managing Information | Communication | Maps, Charts, and Graphs

Understanding Causes and Effects

How Will I Use This Skill?

Some causes and effects are easy to see. A frost in Florida causes the price of orange juice to rise. An accident at a busy intersection leads the town to put up a new stop sign. Recognizing the relationship between causes and effects can help you understand what has happened and predict future events.

LEARN the Skill

1. Identify the primary event or condition that you will examine.
2. Determine which events had a role in causing the primary event.
3. Determine which events occurred as a result of the primary event.
4. Explain the relationship between causes and effects.

PRACTICE the Skill

At right are a list of events and a partially filled-in cause-and-effect chart. After reading this section, answer the following questions:

1. What primary event is the focus of the chart?
2. Which events on the list would you include in the chart as causes? Why?
3. Which events on the list would you include in the chart as effects? Why?
4. (a) Why was taxation one cause of the American Revolution? (b) Do you think the United States of America could have been formed without the American Revolution?

Cause and Effect

Causes

- Parliament taxes the colonies
- ______
- ______

The American Revolution

Effects

- United States of America is formed
- ______
- ______

George Washington emerges as national leader

Proclamation of 1763 stops colonists from moving west

Intolerable Acts set up harsh rule in Massachusetts

United States borders extend to Florida and Mississippi River

APPLY the Skill

Select an event that affected you. Create a chart that identifies at least two causes and two effects of that event.

Skills FOR LIFE

PRACTICE the Skill ANSWERS

1. the American Revolution
2. Proclamation of 1763 stops colonists from moving west; Intolerable Acts punish Massachusetts harshly. These acts violated the freedom and liberties of the colonists and motivated them to rebel.
3. George Washington emerges as national leader; U.S. borders extend to Florida and Mississippi River. These events were results of the Revolution.
4. **(a)** As English citizens, colonists felt they had a right to approve taxes affecting them, but they had no direct representation in Parliament, which insisted it had the right to tax them. **(b)** Possible answer: Yes, at some point Britain might have found the colonies too difficult and expensive to rule.

APPLY the Skill

Guided Instruction

Have students present their information in a graphic organizer such as the one on this page. Encourage some students to pick the same type of event and compare causes and effects on their charts.

ASSESSMENT See the rubrics in the Alternative Assessment booklet in the Teaching Resources.

★ *Activity* ★

Connections With Geography

Analyzing a decision Have students research Cornwallis's decision to retreat to Yorktown and how this decision led to his defeat. Ask: "Could Cornwallis have avoided defeat?" Have students assume the role of a Cornwallis aide who writes him a memo proposing alternatives to his plan to go to Yorktown. (*challenging*) T

Reading Actively

During Reading Have students note the statement in the subsection entitled The Peace Treaty that "the Americans got most of what they wanted" from the Treaty of Paris. Ask them to look for evidence to support this statement as they read.

Writing Actively

After Reading Have students assume they are American soldiers who have just heard Washington bid farewell to his officers. Ask them to write a diary entry describing their thoughts on the war's end, American independence, or hopes for the future.

Geography Skills

ANSWERS

1. Review locations with students. **2.** part of what is today Minnesota; the Pacific Northwest; parts of what are today Louisiana, Mississippi, and Alabama; a small piece of what is today Quebec Province in Canada **3.** Possible answer: A new nation—the United States—exists, extending from the Atlantic to the Mississippi River.

North America in 1783

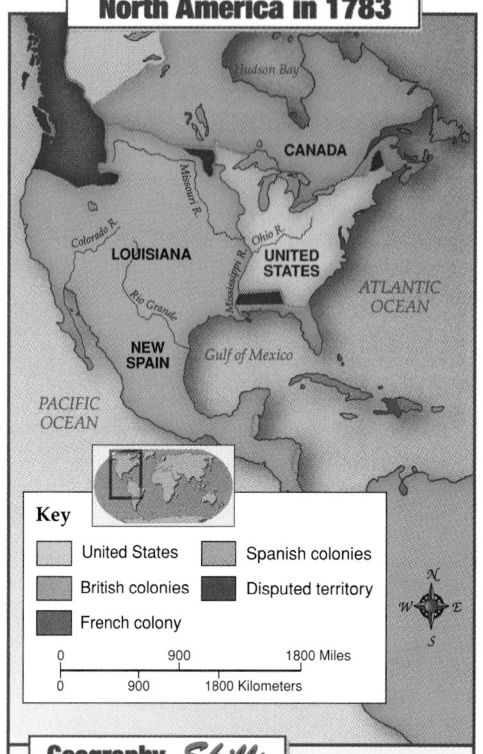

Geography Skills By the Treaty of Paris of 1783, Britain recognized the United States as an independent nation.

1. **Location** On the map, locate: **(a)** United States, **(b)** Canada, **(c)** New Spain.
2. **Interaction** What territory was claimed by both the United States and British Canada?
3. **Critical Thinking** Compare this map with the map on page 140. According to the maps, what was the major difference between North America in 1763 and North America in 1783?

supplies running low, Cornwallis decided the situation was hopeless. The British had lost the **Battle of Yorktown.**

On October 19, 1781, the British surrendered their weapons to the Americans. The French and the Americans lined up in two facing columns. As the defeated redcoats marched between the victorious troops, a British army band played the tune "The World Turned Upside Down."

The Peace Treaty

The British thought that they could settle their disputes with the American colonies through a show of massive military strength. They were mistaken. In fact, British efforts to impose their will by force served only to alienate the colonists even more. Americans who suffered at the hands of British troops usually became strong supporters of the Patriots' fight for independence. In London, however, the defeat shocked the British. "It is all over," cried the British prime minister, Lord North. Left with no other choice, he agreed to peace talks.

The talks began in Paris in 1782. Congress sent Benjamin Franklin and John Adams, along with John Jay of New York and Henry Laurens of South Carolina, to work out a treaty. Because Britain was eager to end the war, the Americans got most of what they wanted.

Under the **Treaty of Paris,** the British recognized the United States as an independent nation. The borders of the new nation extended from the Atlantic Ocean to the Mississippi River. The southern border stopped at Florida, which was returned to Spain.

On their part, the Americans agreed to ask state legislatures to pay Loyalists for property they lost in the war. In the end, however, most states ignored Loyalist claims.

On April 15, 1783, Congress **ratified,** or approved, the Treaty of Paris. It was almost eight years to the day since the battles of Lexington and Concord.

Washington's Farewell

In December 1783, General Washington bid farewell to his officers at Fraunces Tavern in New York City. Colonel Benjamin Tallmadge recalled the event:

> "Such a scene of sorrow and weeping I had never before witnessed ....[W]e were then about to part from the man who had conducted us

★ Customized Instruction ★

Auditory Learners

Presenting a radio play Have auditory learners write and tape a play depicting 1781 events leading up to and including Cornwallis's surrender at Yorktown. The play could include these characters: Lafayette, Admiral de Grasse, Comte de Rochambeau, Washington, Cornwallis, and British or American soldiers. Have scriptwriters consider these questions: What might British troops have said to each other as they retreated towards Yorktown? How might the French and Americans have acted when they first met? How might the British have behaved when they realized they must surrender? How might the Americans and their allies have reacted when they realized they had won? Actors should rehearse before taping. (*average*) T through a long and bloody war, and under whose conduct the glory and independence of our country had been achieved. ❞

All along Washington's route home to Virginia, crowds cheered the hero of American independence. The new nation faced difficult days ahead. Americans would call on Washington to lead them once again.

Reasons for the American Victory

Geography had much to do with the American victory in the Revolutionary War. It was difficult for the British to send soldiers and supplies to a war several thousand miles from home. The Patriots they sought to conquer were spread over a very wide area. When the British captured coastal cities, American forces moved inland. The Americans knew the local geography. They knew the best routes and the best places to fight.

Flag of a new nation

Assistance from other nations also contributed to the American victory. Spanish forces attacked the British along the Gulf of Mexico and in the Mississippi Valley. French money helped pay for supplies. Most important was French military aid. Without French soldiers and warships, the Americans might not have won the Battle of Yorktown.

Victory over the British was also due to the patriotic spirit, determination, and fighting skill of the Patriots. Despite many setbacks in the early years of the war, the Americans battled on. As time passed, their devotion to liberty and their fighting ability both grew. Critically important, too, was the leadership of General Washington. By war's end, Washington's ability as a general was respected by Americans and British alike.

★ Section 5 Review ★

Recall

1. **Locate** (a) King's Mountain, (b) Savannah, (c) Charleston, (d) Cowpens, (e) Guilford Courthouse, (f) Yorktown.
2. **Identify** (a) Battle of King's Mountain, (b) Nathanael Greene, (c) Daniel Morgan, (d) Francis Marion, (e) Benedict Arnold, (f) Comte de Rochambeau, (g) Admiral de Grasse, (h) Battle of Yorktown, (i) Treaty of Paris.
3. **Define** (a) guerrilla, (b) siege, (c) ratify.

Comprehension

4. For each of the American military leaders that follow, describe a tactic that the leader used to defeat the British: (a) Greene, (b) Morgan, (c) Marion.
5. How did the Americans and French achieve victory over the British at Yorktown?
6. Describe the major points of the Treaty of Paris of 1783.

Critical Thinking and Writing

7. **Analyzing Ideas** Why do you think the British played "The World Turned Upside Down" when they surrendered at Yorktown?
8. **Understanding Causes and Effects** Describe three reasons why the Americans were able to defeat the British and win the American Revolution.

Activity **Writing a Song** You are a member of a fife and drum band in the Continental Army. General Washington has asked you to write the words for a lively tune that the soldiers can march to. The General wants the song to praise the daring exploits of American soldiers in the South.

★ Background ★

Viewpoints

Focus and leadership Historian Robert Middlekauff suggests some interesting reasons for the American victory. The British lacked gifted military leaders, he argues. He considers Cornwallis the best, but he faults William Howe and Henry Clinton for lack of "strategic vision and daring." Furthermore, Middlekauff claims that the British government was not clear about its objectives in the war, and it therefore gave its military leaders neither firm direction nor stimulation. By contrast, he says, the Americans were clear from the beginning that independence was their goal. General Washington combined his talent for command with patience, prudence, and the "imagination [and] judgment [to] see that daring might sometimes be necessary."

★ Section 5 Review ★

ANSWERS

1. See map, p. 179.
2. (a)–(c) p. 178, (d) p. 179, (e)–(g) p. 180, (h)–(i) p. 182
3. (a) p. 179, (b) p. 180, (c) p. 182
4. (a) chose battle sites that put British at a disadvantage (b) made British think he was retreating at Cowpens (c) used guerrilla tactics against British
5. French fleet cut off British by sea; French and Americans blocked their escape by land.
6. Britain: recognize U.S. independence; accept its western border at the Mississippi; return FL to Spain. U.S.: ask states to pay Loyalists for property lost in the war
7. because a weak group of colonies had defeated Britain
8. familiarity with the land; French aid; determination; good leaders

Activity

Guided Instruction
Student songs could focus on one or on several figures.

ASSESSMENT See the rubrics in the Alternative Assessment booklet in the Teaching Resources.

Technology

Videodiscs/Videotapes
Prentice Hall United States History Video Collection™, Vol. 4, Ch. 28, "The World Turned Upside Down," 4 mins (*average*) ELL

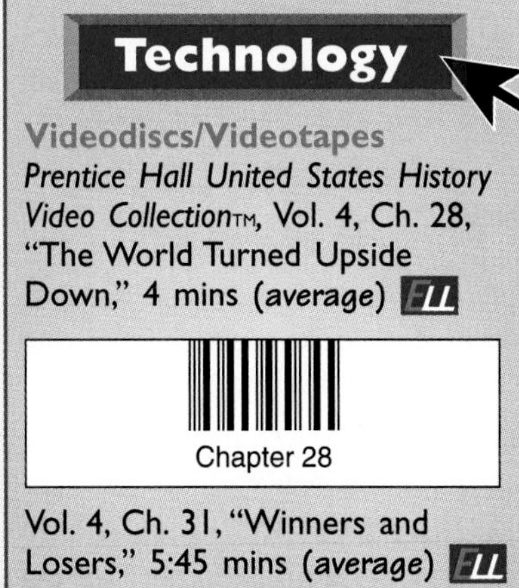
Chapter 28

Vol. 4, Ch. 31, "Winners and Losers," 5:45 mins (*average*) ELL

Chapter 31

CD-ROM
Test Bank CD-ROM, Ch. 6
Interactive Student Tutorial

Chapter 6

Review and Activities

Reviewing the Chapter

Define These Terms

1. e **2.** d **3.** b **4.** c **5.** a

Explore the Main Ideas

1. sent the Olive Branch Petition to King George but set up the Continental Army and made Washington its commander

2. (a) won many to the idea of independence **(b)** Possible answers: all men are created equal; people have certain inalienable rights; when those rights are violated, people have the right to revolt against oppression

3. to urge Americans to support the Continental Army

4. ended the British threat to New England; boosted American spirits; brought French alliance

5. Some joined the Patriots; others helped the British; they served as drummers, fifers, spies, guides, fighters, and sailors.

6. (a) a highly trained, experienced army; powerful navy **(b)** They fought on land they knew, were determined to win, had good leaders, and got aid from France.

Geography Activity

1. A **2.** C **3.** B **4.** E **5.** F **6.** D

Movement Without it, he could be—and was—trapped without supplies or an escape route.

Critical Thinking

1. Answers will vary but students should support their choices with information from the chapter.

2. when a government fails to protect the rights of citizens

3. (a) 2,3,1,4 **(b)** The American victory at Saratoga persuaded the French to enter the war. With French assistance the Americans were able to win at Yorktown. After Yorktown, the British decided to negotiate the Treaty of Paris.

Chapter 6

Review and Activities

★ Sum It Up ★

Section 1 Early Battles

- ▶ King George III rejected the Second Continental Congress's attempt to solve their conflict peacefully.
- ▶ The Americans captured Ticonderoga and Boston from the British, but lost a major battle in Canada.

Section 2 Declaring Independence

- ▶ In his pamphlet *Common Sense,* Thomas Paine argued that colonists did not owe loyalty to the king.
- ▶ The Continental Congress declared in 1776 that the American colonies had become the independent United States of America.

Section 3 Fighting in the Middle States

- ▶ The British gained contol of New York City and forced Washington's army into retreat.
- ▶ The American victory at Saratoga was the major turning point of the war.

Section 4 Other Battlefronts

- ▶ Fighting took place on many battlefronts, including the West and the high seas.
- ▶ Women aided the war effort by making needed goods, by caring for the wounded, and, in some cases, by fighting.

Section 5 Winning the War

- ▶ With help from the French, the Americans defeated the British army at Yorktown.
- ▶ By the Treaty of Paris, Britain recognized the United States as an independent nation.

For additional review of the major ideas of Chapter 6, see ***Guide to the Essentials of American History*** or ***Interactive Student Tutorial CD-ROM,*** which contains interactive review activities, graphic organizers, and practice tests.

Reviewing the Chapter

Define These Terms

Match each term with the correct definition.

Column 1	Column 2
1. traitor	**a.** to approve
2. mercenary	**b.** a friend or supporter
3. ally	**c.** not taking sides in a war
4. neutral	**d.** hired soldier who fights for a foreign country
5. ratify	**e.** person who betrays his or her country

Explore the Main Ideas

1. In 1775, how did American Patriots offer peace, but prepare for war?
2. **(a)** How did *Common Sense* affect American colonists? **(b)** Describe three ideas contained in the Declaration of Independence.
3. Why did Thomas Paine write *The Crisis*?
4. In what ways was the Battle of Saratoga a major turning point of the war?
5. What role did African Americans play during the war?
6. **(a)** What advantages did the British have in the War for Independence? **(b)** Why were Americans able to win the war?

Geography Activity

Match the letters on the map with the following places: **1.** Boston, **2.** Trenton, **3.** Saratoga, **4.** Cowpens, **5.** Savannah, **6.** Yorktown. **Movement** Why was control of the Chesapeake Bay important to Cornwallis at Yorktown?

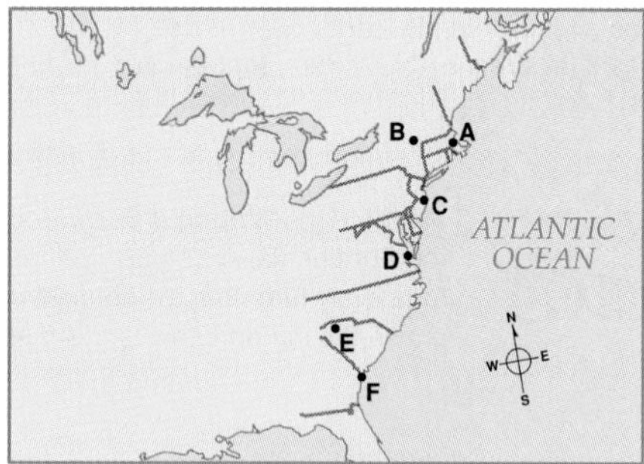

4. Possible answers: The two countries are close culturally and politically and share many common interests. Since the early 1800s, they have cooperated on many issues. Many Americans trace their ancestry to Britain.

Using Primary Sources

(a) They were well-trained, disciplined, and better armed. **(b)** They were unused to war, lacked confidence, and could be easily cowed by British troops. **(c)** Possible answers: funds and officers to train his troops; better weapons

Critical Thinking and Writing

1. **Ranking** In your opinion, what were the three biggest mistakes that British political and military leaders made between 1775 and 1783? Explain the reasons for your choices.
2. Exploring Unit Themes **Rights and Liberties** According to the Declaration of Independence, when do people have a right and duty to rebel against their government?
3. **Understanding Chronology** **(a)** Arrange the following four events in chronological order: (1) British defeat at Yorktown, (2) American victory at Saratoga, (3) French entry into the war against Britain, (4) the signing of the Treaty of Paris. **(b)** Explain how each event helped to cause the next event.
4. **Linking Past and Present** Today, the United States and Britain are close allies. Why do you think the two nations have such close ties?

Using Primary Sources

In 1776, General George Washington wrote to John Hancock, president of the Continental Congress, about the condition of the army:

> “To place any dependance upon Militia, is, assuredly, resting upon a broken staff. Men just dragged from the tender Scenes of domestick life; unaccustomed to the din of Arms; totally unacquainted with every kind of Military skill, which being followed by a want of confidence in themselves, when opposed to Troops regulary train'd, disciplined, and appointed, superior in knowledge, and superior in Arms, makes them timid, and ready to fly from their own shadows.”

Source: *The Writings of George Washington from the Original Manuscript Sources: 1745–1799.*

Recognizing Points of View **(a)** What was Washington's view of British soldiers? **(b)** What was his opinion of American militia? **(c)** What do you think Washington wanted from Congress?

Activity Bank

Interdisciplinary Activity

Exploring Sciences Do research to learn about medical treatments provided to sick and wounded soldiers of the American Revolution. Summarize your findings in a report and create illustrations of the medical instruments used at the time.

Career Skills Activity

Graphic Artist In a graphic organizer, show the role that each of the following played in the American Revolution: **(a)** Native Americans, **(b)** French, **(c)** women, **(d)** African Americans, **(e)** Spanish.

Citizenship Activity

Honoring Good Citizenship Create a "Nathan Hale Award" for a citizen of your community who has proudly made a sacrifice for the good of the United States. Working with classmates, hold a ceremony in which you explain why you are giving the award to the citizen you have chosen.

Internet Activity

Use the Internet to learn more about the activities of Nathan Hale, James Armistead Lafayette, or another spy of the Revolution. Based on what you learn, write a short fictional story about espionage in the American Revolution.

It is 1776 and you have just heard about the Declaration of Independence. Choose one of the following roles: Loyalist; Patriot; African American; Native American; British soldier; French government official; a woman whose husband, father, or son is a soldier in the war. In your EYEWITNESS JOURNAL, explain what the Declaration means for you and your future.

Activity Bank

ASSESSMENT To assess the activities on this page, see the rubrics in the Alternative Assessment booklet in the Teaching Resources. You might want to share the rubrics with your students before they begin work.

Interdisciplinary Activity

1. Reports should include explanations of symptoms and treatment for diseases such as dysentery or typhoid and descriptions of medical care given to wounded soldiers.
2. Have students give their reports as a presentation. For example, one student could take on the role of an army doctor and another a patient. They could enact a scene showing an 18th century audience of medical students how to treat a war wound.
3. Extend the activity by having students compare colonial medical knowledge to medical knowledge today.

Career Skills Activity

1. Encourage students familiar with computer pagemaking programs to use electronic composition in their projects.
2. Have students create symbols or use illustrations to represent the groups in their organizers.
3. Display completed graphic organizers for class study.

Citizenship Activity

1. Each student can choose a different citizen to honor with the award.
2. Suggest that students check with veterans groups and historical societies, or read wartime editions of local newspapers to find appropriate recipients for the award.
3. Suggest that students feature Nathan Hale's famous quote in the design of their award.

Eyewitness Journal

1. Have students write down their initial ideas, then reread their texts for relevant information.
2. Students writing in the same character may benefit from meeting in small groups to exchange ideas.
3. Encourage students to do a rewrite of their journal entries if time allows.

Internet Activity

1. Have students look at www.phschool.com, which contains updated information on a variety of topics.
2. One site you may find useful for this activity is "American Revolution: On-Line" at users.southeast.net/%7Edixe/index.htm.
3. Given the changing nature of the Internet, you may wish to preview this site.

Chapter 7 Manager

SECTION OBJECTIVES	TEACHING RESOURCES	ADDITIONAL RESOURCE
1 A Confederation of States (pp. 188–192) **Objectives** 1. Outline the ideas that guided the new state governments. 2. Describe the problems the nation faced under the Articles of Confederation. 3. Explain how the Northwest Ordinance benefited the nation.	**Lesson Planner,** p. 27 (average) . . . . .90 mins. **Unit 2/Chapter 7** • Map Mystery: Laying Out a City, p. 26 (average) . . . . .20 mins. • Connecting History and Literature: Paul Bunyan of the North Woods, p. 27 (challenging) . . . . .20 mins. • Section 1 Quiz, p. 29 (average) . . . . .15 mins. **Interdisciplinary Connections** • Main Idea: Western Lands, pp. 38–42 (average) . . . . .20 mins.	**Voices of Freedom** • Articles of Confederation, pp. 67–68 (challenging) **Historical Outline Map Book** • Western Land Claims, p. 29 (average) **Constitution Study Guide** • The Need for a New Plan of Government, pp. 17–20
2 The Constitutional Convention (pp. 193–197) **Objectives** 1. Describe how the Virginia Plan and the New Jersey Plan differed. 2. Explain how the Great Compromise satisfied both large and small states. 3. Summarize the compromises made on the issue of slavery.	**Lesson Planner,** p. 28 (average) . . . . .90 mins. **Unit 2/Chapter 7** • Practice Your Skills: Identifying Main Ideas, p. 24 (average) . . . . .30 mins. • Section 2 Quiz, p. 30 (average) . . . . .15 mins.	**Voices of Freedom** • Franklin Asks Support for the Constitution, p. 69 (average) **Constitution Study Guide** • The Constitutional Conventions, pp. 24–38
3 A More Perfect Union (pp. 198–203) **Objectives** 1. Describe the ideas that helped shape the Constitution. 2. Explain how the framers of the Constitution divided power between the national government and the states. 3. Describe how the framers limited the power of government.	**Lesson Planner,** p. 29 (average) . . . . .45 mins. **Unit 2/Chapter 7** • Section 3 Quiz, p. 31 (average) . . . . .15 mins. **Citizenship for Life** • Constitution Worksheets 3–5, pp. 11–16 (average) . . . . .20 mins.	**Constitution Study Guide** • European Influences, pp. 11–15 • The Constitution—A Living Document, pp. 46–51
4 Ratifying the Constitution (pp. 204–209) **Objectives** 1. Describe the arguments Americans raised for and against the Constitution. 2. Explain how the Constitution can be amended. 3. List the rights protected by the Bill of Rights.	**Lesson Planner,** p. 30 (average) . . . . .90 mins. **Unit 2/Chapter 7** • Vocabulary Builder, p. 23 (basic) . . . . .15 mins. • Critical Thinking and Writing: Solving Problems, p. 25 (challenging) . . . . .30 mins. • Biography Flashcard: Ann Lee, p. 28 (average) . . . . .35 mins. • Section 4 Quiz, p. 32 (average) . . . . .15 mins. **Why Study History?** • National Symbols Unite Us, pp. 27–30 (average) . . . . .90 mins. **Citizenship for Life** • Civics Worksheet 1, p. 3 (average) . . . . . .20 mins. **Chapter Tests,** pp. 37–42 (average) . . . . .45 mins.	**History Alive!® Activity Pack** • Activity 2: Constitutional Card Sort **Voices of Freedom** • A Farmer Speaks Out for the Constitution, pp. 70–71 (average) • An Antifederalist Argues His Case, p. 71 (average) **Prentice Hall Literature Library** • Southern Writers **Constitution Study Guide** • Ratification, pp. 40–42

Assessment Options

Teaching Resources
- Alternative Assessment booklet
- Section Quizzes, Unit 2, Chapter 7, pp. 29–32
- Chapter Tests, Chapter 7, pp. 37–42
- Test Bank CD-ROM

Student Performance Pack
- Guide to the Essentials of American History, Chapter 7 Test, p. 43
- Standardized Test Prep Handbook
- Interactive Student Tutorial CD-ROM

Interdisciplinary Connections

Teaching Resources
- Map Mystery, Unit 2, Chapter 7, p. 26
- Connecting History and Literature, Unit 2, Chapter 7, p. 27
- Interdisciplinary Connections, pp. 38–42

Voices of Freedom, pp. 67–71

Historical Outline Map Book, p. 29

Prentice Hall Literature Library
- Southern Writers

Technology

AmericanHeritage® History of the United States CD-ROM
- Time Tour: Creating a Republic in From Revolution to Republic
- Face the Issues: The Great Compromise of the Constitutional Convention

Interactive Student Tutorial CD-ROM

Test Bank CD-ROM

Color Transparencies
- Barter on the Western Frontier, p. B-45
- The United States and the World, 1775–1825, p. E-17
- The Need for Order, p. G-15
- Expansion of the United States, p. I-25

Guided Reading Audiotapes
(English/Spanish), side 3

Resource Pro® CD-ROM

Prentice Hall United States History Video Collection™
(Spanish track available on disc version.) Vol. 5, Chs. 7, 13, 16, 19, 25, 31

Prentice Hall Home Page
www.phschool.com

Student Performance Pack

Guide to the Essentials of American History
- Ch. 7, pp. 39–43
(Available in English and Spanish)

Guided Reading Audiotapes (English/Spanish), side 3

Standardized Test Prep Handbook

Interactive Student Tutorial CD-ROM

BLOCK SCHEDULING
Activities with this icon will help you meet your Block Scheduling needs.

ENGLISH LANGUAGE LEARNERS
Activities with this icon are suitable for English Language Learners.

TEAM TEACHING
Activities and Background Notes with this icon present starting points for Team Teaching.

Teachers' Bibliography

From the Archives of AmericanHeritage®

Don't miss the special American Heritage® teaching notes found in this chapter.

Contact Teachers' Curriculum Institute to learn more about History Alive!® resources on the early republic. See History Alive!® unit: The Constitution in a New Nation, Section 1, "The Roots of Government," Section 2, "The Creation of the Constitution," and Section 3, "The Creation of the Bill of Rights."

Explore your library to find these issues related to Chapter 7: *The Bill of Rights,* September 1991; *The Constitutional Convention,* September 1987; *The United States Senate,* November 1984; *Starting a Nation: 1780–1790,* September 1984; *The Meaning of the Constitution,* September 1982.

Prentice Hall Web Site You can access a structured, on-line environment that allows you to preview curriculum-related resources and receive updated information on groundbreaking events from around the nation and the world. (www.phschool.com)

Chapter 7

Creating a Republic
1776–1791

Introducing the Chapter

Have students preview the main ideas of this chapter by looking over the visuals. Suggest they look for key figures in the creation of the American republic.

Using the Time Line Help students see the link between the United States and the world as they read the time line. Ask questions such as these: **(1)** Why might Americans have paid little attention to news that Captain Cook had reached Hawaii? *(The American Revolution was in progress.)* **(2)** Which American and world events suggest that expansion of the United States and other nations occurred in the 1780s? *(Russians settle in Aleutian Islands off coast of Alaska; Northwest Ordinance sets up method to admit new states to the U.S.)* **(3)** Which world event took place shortly after the Constitution was ratified? *(French Revolution)*

Have students suggest images that symbolize the United States—for example, the colors red, white, and blue; the Capitol dome; and the Statue of Liberty. Then, as a class, have students think of images to serve as fitting symbols for their town.

For additional *Why Study History?* support, see p. 207.

Chapter 7

Creating a Republic

1776–1791

What's Ahead

After the American Revolution ended, the new nation struggled to create a workable government. At first, the states were knit together only by a loose set of laws. When this central government proved too weak, representatives of 12 states gathered in 1787. They created a new framework for government: the Constitution of the United States.

During nearly four exhausting months of debate, the representatives hammered out a set of laws that would make the nation strong, yet protect the rights of the people. After fiery arguments in each state, the Constitution was finally approved. It lives on as the framework of our government today.

Why Study History? While the new nation was taking shape, American leaders were also creating many symbols and traditions. Today, as in the past, emblems such as the flag and the eagle bind the American people together. To focus on this connection, see the *Why Study History* feature, "National Symbols Unite Us," in this chapter.

American Events

1777 Continental Congress completes the Articles of Confederation

1783 Treaty of Paris formally ends the American Revolution

1776 — 1780 — 1784

World Events

1778 World Event British Captain Cook becomes first European to reach Hawaii

1784 World Event Emperor Joseph II forces Cz to use German language

Viewing HISTORY **Signing the Constitution**

In 1787, representatives from 12 states gathered in Philadelphia to create a new national government. The result of their work was the Constitution, which still governs the nation today. This painting by Howard Chandler Christy shows delegates to the Constitutional Convention, including George Washington (standing right) and Benjamin Franklin (seated center). Washington served as the president of the Convention. ★ **Why do you think the representatives chose Washington as their president?**

1787 Northwest Ordinance sets up method to admit new states to the United States

1788 The Constitution is ratified

1791 Bill of Rights guarantees individual rights and freedoms

1784 | 1788 | 1792

1785 World Event Russians settle in Aleutian Islands off coast of Alaska

1789 World Event French Revolution begins

Writing Actively 

Responding to Art Have students examine the painting on this page. Then ask them to put themselves in the painting as a representative of one of the 12 states that sent representatives to Philadelphia. (Rhode Island sent none.) Then have them write a paragraph describing the event that is taking place.

Viewing HISTORY ANSWER

Washington commanded the respect and admiration of every delegate.

★ *Background* ★

Art Note

Signing the Constitution Howard Christy (1873–1952) was trained primarily as a portrait painter. That training may justify his claim of great accuracy in creating these likenesses of the men who signed the Constitution. Christy described this work as a "historical painting" rather than as a mural. The 20-by-30-foot oil painting hangs in the U.S. Capitol. T

Documents and Literature

On pp. 545–548, you will find two readings to enrich this chapter:

1. Eyewitness Account "Delegates to the Constitutional Convention," excerpts from William Pierce's character sketches of other delegates. (Use with Section 2.)

2. Historical Document "The Federalist Papers," selections by Alexander Hamilton and James Madison promoting ratification of the Constitution. (Use with Section 4.)

Technology

Videodiscs/Videotapes

Show the *Prentice Hall United States History Video Collection*™ segments for this chapter. The videodisc version has a Spanish track. Press audio until you get the left channel for English or the right channel for Spanish, or use the bar codes in the Guidebook.

AmericanHeritage® History of the United States CD-ROM

- Time Tour: Creating a Republic in From Revolution to Republic (*average*)

Section 1

A Confederation of States

LESSON PLAN

Objectives

★ Outline the ideas that guided the new state governments.

★ Describe the problems the nation faced under the Articles of Confederation.

★ Explain how the Northwest Ordinance benefited the nation.

1 Engage

Warm Up Write this question on the chalkboard: "Which do you think is more important, state or national government?" Have students write a brief response.

Activating Prior Knowledge Ask students: "How does your class make decisions?" "Does your school have a student council or other governing body?" and "How would decisions be made without that governing body?" Help students see that operating the school would be difficult if every homeroom made its own decisions. Then explain that this was part of the problem faced by the new nation.

Reading Actively

Before Reading Before they read the section, have students turn the main headings into the main topics of an outline. Then, as they read, have them record two or three important subtopics for each main topic.

RESOURCE DIRECTORY

Teaching Resources
Lesson Planner, p. 27

Transparencies
Time Lines
• The United States and the World, 1775–1825, p. E-17
Political Cartoons
• The Need for Order, p. G-15

1 A Confederation of States

As You Read

Explore These Questions
- What ideas guided the new state governments?
- What problems did the nation face under the Articles of Confederation?
- How did the Northwest Ordinance benefit the nation?

Define
- constitution
- execute
- confederation
- ordinance
- economic depression

Identify
- Articles of Confederation
- Land Ordinance of 1785
- Northwest Ordinance
- Shays' Rebellion

In 1776, the Declaration of Independence created a new nation made up of 13 independent states. The former colonies, though, had little experience working together. In the past, Britain had made the major decisions. Now, the Americans set about the business of establishing 13 state governments. Furthermore, they hoped to create a central government that all the states would follow.

State Governments

In forming a government, most states wrote a constitution. A **constitution** is a document that sets out the laws and principles of a government. States created written constitutions for two reasons. First, a written constitution would spell out the rights of all citizens. Second, it would set limits on the power of government.

The new state governments were similar to the colonial governments. The states divided political power between an executive and a legislature. The legislature was elected by the voters to pass the laws. Most legislatures had an upper house, called a senate, and a lower house. All states except Pennsylvania had a governor who **executed,** or carried out, the laws.

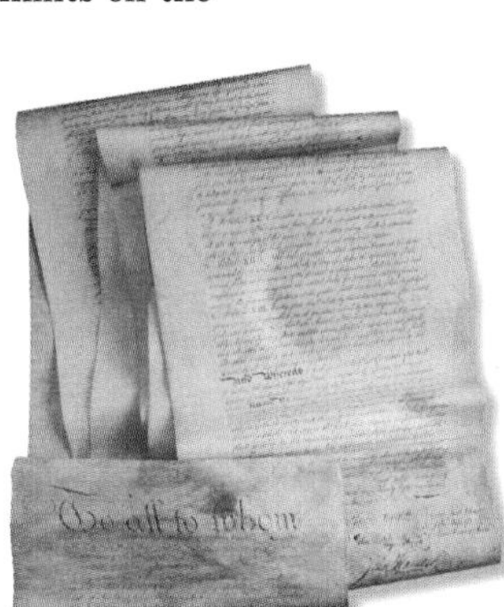
Articles of Confederation

Virginia limited government power by including a bill of rights in its constitution. A bill of rights lists freedoms that the government promises to protect. Virginia's bill of rights protected freedom of religion and freedom of the press. It also guaranteed citizens the right to a trial by jury. Other states followed Virginia's example and included bills of rights in their constitutions.

Under the state constitutions, more people had the right to vote than in colonial times. To vote, a citizen had to be white, male, and over age 21. He had to own a certain amount of property or pay a certain amount of taxes.

For a time, some women in New Jersey could vote. In a few states, free black men could vote. In no state did enslaved African Americans have the right to vote.

A Weak Confederation

In 1776, as citizens were forming state governments, the Continental Congress was drafting a plan for the nation as a whole. Delegates believed that the colonies needed to be united by a central government in order to win independence.

It was difficult to write a constitution that all of the states would approve. They

★ *Background* ★

Did You Know?

A sailing ship versus a raft According to legend, Fisher Ames, a member of Congress from Massachusetts, provided a popular description of the new democracy after the Revolution. Monarchy, he said, was like "a full-rigged ship, trim and beautiful, with all hands at their stations and the captain at the helm. It executes its maneuvers sharply and operates with the greatest efficiency, but if it hits a rock, the frail hull is crushed and the vessel sinks. Democracy is like a raft—hard to navigate, impossible to keep on course, and distressingly slow. If it runs onto a rock, it simply careens off and takes a new course."

were reluctant to give up power to a national government. In 1776, few Americans saw themselves as citizens of one nation. Instead, they felt loyal to their own states. Also, people were fearful of replacing the "tyranny" of British rule with another strong government. Still, in 1777, after much debate, the Continental Congress completed the **Articles of Confederation**—the first American constitution. It created a **confederation**, or alliance of independent states.

Government under the Articles

Under the Articles of Confederation, the states sent delegates to a Confederation Congress. Each state had one vote in Congress. Congress could declare war, appoint military officers, and coin money. It was also responsible for foreign affairs. However, these powers were few compared with those of the states.

The Articles limited the powers of Congress and preserved the powers of the states. Congress could pass laws, but at least 9 of the 13 states had to approve a law before it could go into effect.

Congress had little economic power. It could not regulate trade between states nor could it regulate trade between states and foreign countries. It could not pass tax laws. To raise money, Congress had to ask the states for it. No state could be forced to contribute funds.

The new confederation government was weak. There was no president to carry out laws. It was up to the states to enforce the laws passed by Congress. There was no system of courts to settle disputes between states. The Articles created a very loose alliance of 13 states.

Dispute over western lands

A dispute arose even before the Articles of Confederation went into effect. Maryland refused to ratify the Articles unless Virginia and other states gave up their claims to lands west of the Appalachian Mountains. Maryland wanted these western lands turned over to Congress. In this way, the "landed" states would not become too powerful.

One by one, the states gave up their western claims. Only Virginia held out. However,

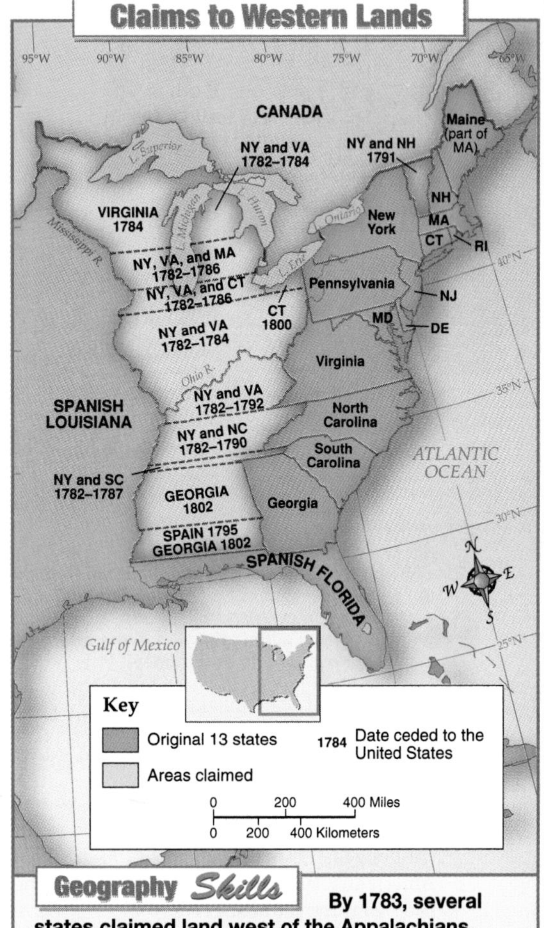

Geography Skills **By 1783, several states claimed land west of the Appalachians.**

1. **Location** On the map, locate lands claimed by both New York and Virginia.
2. **Region** Which states had no claim to western lands?
3. **Critical Thinking** Why did Thomas Jefferson, a Virginian, persuade Virginia to give up its claims to western lands?

Thomas Jefferson and other leading Virginians saw a great need for a central government. They persuaded state lawmakers to give up Virginia's claims in the West. At last, in 1781, Maryland ratified the Articles of Confederation, and the first American government went into effect.

2 Explore

Ask students to read the section. For homework, have them identify the early difficulties in the democratic process that the U.S. faced. Ask: "How could a monarchy avoid these problems?" and "Why did Americans generally reject a monarchy?" Students should share their conclusions.

3 Teach

Have students write a cause and effect for each statement: **(a)** Each state wrote its own constitution. **(b)** The Articles created a weak central government. **(c)** Virginia gave up its western lands. **(d)** The U.S. owed millions to individuals and foreign nations. **(e)** The Northwest Ordinance set up a plan for adding states to the Union.

4 Assess

To close the lesson, have students complete the section review. Or, have them write and give a speech that a member of Congress might have given on one of the following topics: ratification of the Articles of Confederation, British refusal to withdraw its troops from the Ohio Valley, settlement of western lands.

★ ★ ★ ★ ★ ★ ★ ★ ★ ★ ★ ★ ★ ★ ★ ★ ★ ★

Geography Skills

ANSWERS **1.** Review locations with students. **2.** Rhode Island, Pennsylvania, New Jersey, Delaware, Maryland **3.** The Articles would not have been ratified if Virginia held onto its lands; Jefferson wanted a national government.

★ Activity ★

Linking Past and Present

Discussing government Have students speculate about how the U.S. government today might be different if the Articles still existed. Ask: What problems might the government face? How could it solve them? Does a modern nation really *need* a chief executive? Why or why not? Could it do without a strong legislature? Why or why not? (*challenging*)

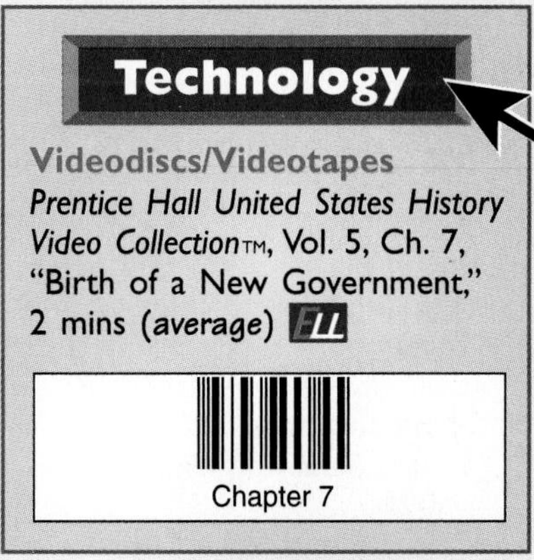

Videodiscs/Videotapes
Prentice Hall United States History Video Collection™, Vol. 5, Ch. 7, "Birth of a New Government," 2 mins (*average*)

Viewing HISTORY ANSWER

Possible answer: Trade between states would be more difficult if each state had its own system of money.

Reading Actively 

During Reading Have students note the words of Noah Webster quoted on this page. Ask them to restate his idea in their own words.

RESOURCE DIRECTORY

Teaching Resources
Unit 2/Chapter 7
- Map Mystery: Laying Out a City, p. 26
- Connecting History and Literature: Paul Bunyan of the North Woods, p. 27

Interdisciplinary Connections
- Main Idea: Western Lands, pp. 38–42

Transparencies
Interdisciplinary Connections
- Barter on the Western Frontier, p. B-45

Geography and History
- Expansion of the United States, p. I-25

Viewing HISTORY **State Banknotes**

During and after the American Revolution, each state issued its own money. The bills here came from Rhode Island and South Carolina.

★ **What problems might arise due to the fact that each state issued its own money?**

Troubles for the New Nation

By 1783, the United States had won independence. The new nation faced many challenges, however. From 1783 to 1787, Americans had reason to doubt whether their country could survive.

Conflicts between states

Despite its weaknesses, the Articles might have succeeded if the states could have put aside their differences and worked together. Many conflicts arose, however. New Hampshire and New York both claimed Vermont. Most states refused to accept the money of other states.

The Articles did not provide a way for states to settle such disputes. Noah Webster, a teacher from New England, warned:

> ❝ So long as any individual state has power to defeat the measures of the other twelve, our pretended union is but a name, and our confederation, a cobweb.❞

Money problems

As a result of borrowing during the Revolution, the United States owed millions of dollars to individuals and foreign nations. Since Congress did not have the power to tax, it had no way to repay these debts. Congress asked the states for money, but the states had the right to refuse. Often, they did.

During the Revolution, the Continental Congress solved the problem of raising funds by printing paper money. However, the money had little value because it was not backed by gold or silver. Before long, Americans began to describe any useless thing as "not worth a Continental."

As Continental dollars became worthless, states printed their own paper money. This caused confusion. How much was a North Carolina dollar worth? Was a Virginia dollar as valuable as a Maryland dollar? As a result, trade became difficult.

Other nations take advantage

Foreign countries took advantage of the confederation's weakness. Britain, for example, refused to withdraw its troops from the Ohio Valley, as it had agreed to do in the Treaty of Paris. Spain closed its port in New Orleans to American farmers. This was a serious blow to western farmers, who depended on the port to ship their products to the East.

Organizing the Northwest Territory

Despite its troubles, Congress did pass important **ordinances,** or laws, concerning the Northwest Territory, the name for lands lying north of the Ohio River and east of the Mississippi. The principles established in these laws were later applied to other areas of settlement.

Townships and sections

The **Land Ordinance of 1785** set up a system for surveying and settling the Northwest Territory. The law called for the territory to be surveyed and then divided into townships.

Each township would have 36 sections. A section was 1 square mile and contained 640

★ Customized Instruction ★

Visual Learners

Drawing political cartoons Have students work in small groups to create political cartoons for a newspaper editorial page about one of these issues: **(a)** weaknesses of the Articles of Confederation, **(b)** issue of who owns Vermont, **(c)** money problems of the U.S. government, **(d)** plan to admit new states on an equal footing with the original 13 states.

After they have finished their cartoons, have groups exchange their work. After discussing the cartoon of another group, have each group choose a spokesperson to tell the class what it thinks this cartoon says about the chosen issue. Later, post all the cartoons on a bulletin board. (*average*)

acres. (See the diagram below.) Congress planned to sell sections to settlers for $640 each. One section in every township was set aside to support public schools.

A plan for new states

Another law, passed in 1787, was the **Northwest Ordinance.** It set up a government for the Northwest Territory, guaranteed basic rights to settlers, and outlawed slavery there. It also provided for the vast region to be divided into separate territories in the future.

Once a territory had a population of 60,000 free settlers, it could ask Congress to be admitted as a new state. The newly admitted state would be "on an equal footing with the original states in all respects whatsoever."

The Northwest Ordinance was the finest achievement of the national government under the Articles. It provided a way to admit new states to the nation. It guaranteed that new states would be treated the same as the original 13 states. In time, the states of Ohio, Indiana, Illinois, Michigan, and Wisconsin were created from the Northwest Territory.

The Northwest Territory

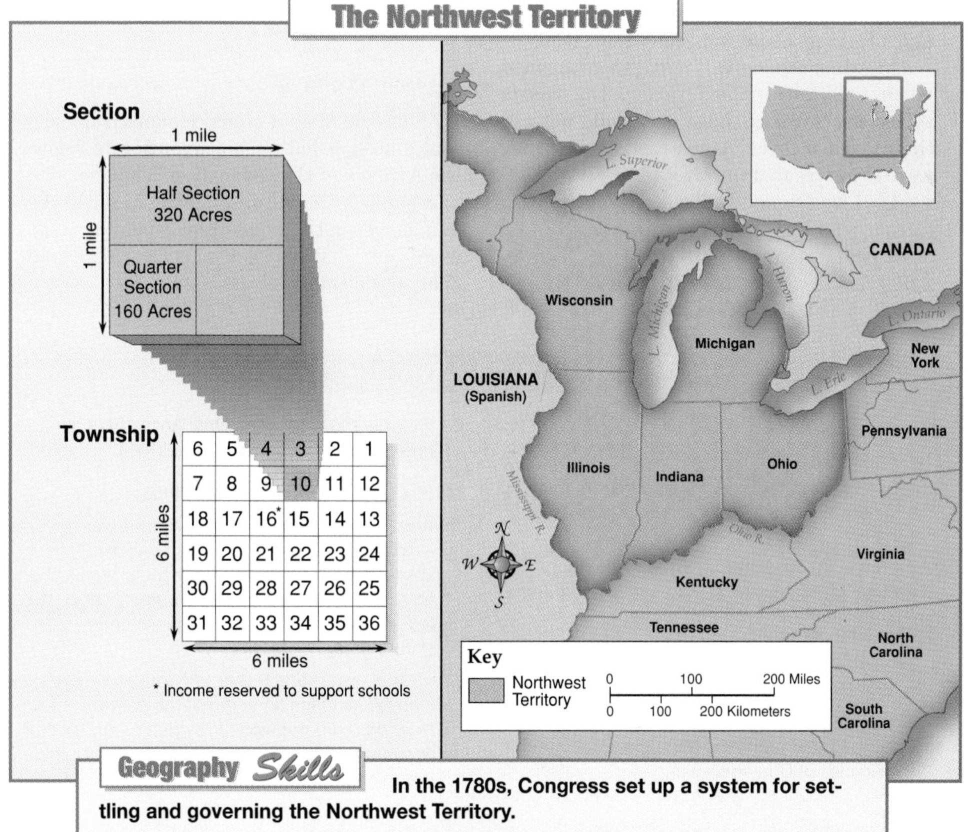

Geography *Skills* **In the 1780s, Congress set up a system for settling and governing the Northwest Territory.**

1. **Location** On the map, locate: **(a)** Ohio River, **(b)** Mississippi River, **(c)** Michigan, **(d)** Indiana, **(e)** Illinois, **(f)** Wisconsin, **(g)** Ohio.
2. **Place** What was the size of **(a)** a township, **(b)** a section?
3. **Critical Thinking** Did the state of Wisconsin have public education when it joined the Union? Explain.

Writing Actively

After Reading Ask students to use the information from the subsection Organizing the Northwest Territory and the illustration on this page as the basis for a short essay on settling and governing the Northwest Territory.

Geography *Skills*

ANSWERS **1.** Review locations with students. **2. (a)** 36 square miles **(b)** 1 square mile **3.** Yes. Wisconsin was carved out of the Northwest Territory, and every township in that territory was required to set aside funds for public schools.

★ *Background* ★
Turning Points

The grid The system established by Congress for surveying western lands dramatically affected the landscape. When crossing from Pennsylvania to Ohio—one boundary of the Northwest Territory—an airplane traveler at once notices the shift to square or rectangular plots of land. Because north–south and east–west property lines made no accommodation for topography, the system sometimes promoted soil erosion and made roads run along unnecessarily hilly routes. Despite these problems, the 1785 boundaries remain today and will no doubt last for centuries to come. T

★ Section 1 Review ★

1. See map, p. 191.

2. (a) p. 189, **(b)** p. 190, **(c)** p. 191, **(d)** p. 192

3. (a) p. 188, **(b)** p. 188, **(c)** p. 189, **(d)** p. 190, **(e)** p. 192

4. (a) Each had an executive; most had a two-house legislature. **(b)** New states were self-governing, had constitutions/bills of rights, and allowed more people to vote.

5. Possible answers: a weak national government; no executive to carry out laws; a Congress with little power

6. It provided for new states to be admitted on an equal footing with the 13 original states.

7. Possible answers: Yes; it focused attention on the problems of the Articles and forced leaders to resolve them. No; it destabilized the young nation and could have broken it apart.

8. The government's weakness hindered trade, thus handicapping the U.S., and made resolving interstate disputes difficult.

Activity

Guided Instruction
Before students start working, discuss why farmers rebelled. Have them list the reasons, then tell them to illustrate one or more reasons in the cartoon.

ASSESSMENT See the rubrics in the Alternative Assessment booklet in the Teaching Resources.

RESOURCE DIRECTORY

Teaching Resources
Lesson Planner, p. 28
Unit 2/Chapter 7
• Section 1 Quiz, p. 29

A Farmers' Revolt

While Congress dealt successfully with the Northwest Territory, it failed to solve its economic problems. After the Revolution, the nation suffered an economic depression. An **economic depression** is a period when business activity slows, prices and wages fall, and unemployment rises.

The depression hit farmers hard. During the Revolution, there had been high demand for farm products. To increase production, farmers had borrowed money for land, seed, animals, and tools. However, when the war ended and soldiers returned home, demand for farm goods weakened. Prices fell, and many farmers could not repay their loans.

In Massachusetts, matters worsened when the state raised taxes. The courts seized the farms of those who could not pay their taxes or loans. Angry farmers felt they were being treated unfairly.

In 1786, Daniel Shays, a Massachusetts farmer who had fought at Bunker Hill and Saratoga, organized an uprising. Nearly 2,000 farmers took part in **Shays' Rebellion.** They attacked courthouses and prevented the state from seizing farms. They even tried to capture an arsenal filled with guns. Finally, the Massachusetts legislature sent the militia to drive them off.

A Change Is Needed

Many Americans saw Shays' Rebellion as a sign that the Articles of Confederation did not work. George Washington warned that a terrible crisis was at hand:

> "No day was ever more clouded than the present.... I predict the worst consequences from a half-starved, limping government, always moving upon crutches and tottering at every step."

To avoid such a crisis, leaders from several states called for a convention to revise the Articles of Confederation. They decided to meet in Philadelphia in May 1787. In the end, however, this convention would do much more than just revise the Articles. It would change the course of the nation.

★ Section 1 Review ★

Recall

1. **Locate** Northwest Territory.
2. **Identify** **(a)** Articles of Confederation, **(b)** Land Ordinance of 1785, **(c)** Northwest Ordinance, **(d)** Shays' Rebellion.
3. **Define** **(a)** constitution, **(b)** execute, **(c)** confederation, **(d)** ordinance, **(e)** economic depression.

Comprehension

4. **(a)** How were the new state governments similar to the old colonial governments? **(b)** How were they different?
5. Describe three problems the nation faced under the Articles of Confederation.
6. How did the Northwest Ordinance affect the future growth of the United States?

Critical Thinking and Writing

7. **Analyzing Ideas** When Thomas Jefferson heard about Shays' Rebellion, he wrote: "The spirit of resistance to government is so valuable on occasion that I wish it to be always kept alive." Do you think Shays' Rebellion was good for the United States? Explain.
8. **Identifying Main Ideas** After only 10 years, many Americans agreed that the Articles of Confederation did not work. Why did the Articles fail to serve as a lasting constitution for the United States?

Activity **Drawing a Political Cartoon** You have been asked to create a political cartoon about Shays' Rebellion. The purpose is to help explain to younger students the reasons why farmers like Daniel Shays were angry and what happened as a result of their rebellion.

FROM THE ARCHIVES OF AmericanHeritage®

Debtors' prison The economy was so depressed in 1780s Massachusetts that valuable lands brought in only a fraction of their worth when sold. As a result, even the disposal of property could not always repay a farmer's debts. Creditors could, by law, keep debtors imprisoned indefinitely. By the end of 1786, reforms were instituted, and most debtors were released from prison.

Source: Karolyn Ide, "The Time Machine," *American Heritage* magazine, August/September 1986.

★ Activity ★

Connections With Civics

Conducting an opinion poll Have groups prepare "People on the Street" interviews about the new nation's problems. Students should write questions for passers-by (e.g., "Do you think the national government is too weak? Why or why not?") and then discuss answers. Have groups use the questions to interview one another during class. (*average*) ELL T

The Constitutional Convention

As You Read

Explore These Questions
- How did the Virginia Plan and the New Jersey Plan differ?
- How did the Great Compromise satisfy both large and small states?
- What compromises were made on the issue of slavery?

Define
- legislative branch
- executive branch
- judicial branch
- compromise

Identify
- Constitutional Convention
- James Madison
- Virginia Plan
- New Jersey Plan
- Roger Sherman
- Great Compromise
- Three-Fifths Compromise

The Liberty Bell, a symbol of freedom, originally hung in the Pennsylvania State House.

SETTING the Scene An air of mystery hung over the Pennsylvania State House in Philadelphia during the summer of 1787. Philadelphians watched as the nation's greatest leaders passed in and out of the building. Eleven years earlier, some of the same men had signed the Declaration of Independence there. What was going on now? Susannah Dillwyn wrote to her father about the excitement:

> "There is now sitting in this city a grand convention, who are to form some new system of government or mend the old one. I suppose it is a body of great consequence, as they say it depends entirely upon their pleasure whether we shall in the future have a congress."

What would this "grand convention" decide? No one knew. For almost four months, Americans waited for an answer.

The Convention Opens

On May 25, 1787, the **Constitutional Convention** opened in Philadelphia. Every state except Rhode Island sent representatives. Their mission was to revise the Articles of Confederation.

The 55 delegates gathered for the convention were a remarkable group. At age 81, Benjamin Franklin was the oldest delegate. He was wise in the ways of government and human nature. George Washington was a representative from Virginia. Washington was so well respected that the delegates at once elected him president of the Convention.

Perhaps the best-prepared delegate to the Constitutional Convention was young **James Madison** of Virginia. For months, Madison had secluded himself on his father's plantation. There, he read many books on history, politics, and commerce. He arrived in Philadelphia with a case bulging with volumes of research.

Many delegates were young men in their twenties and thirties. Among them was Alexander Hamilton of New York. During the Revolution, Hamilton served for a time as Washington's private secretary. Hamilton despised the Articles of Confederation. "The nation," he wrote, "is sick and wants powerful remedies." The powerful remedy he prescribed was a strong national government.

When the Convention began, the delegates decided to keep their talks secret. They wanted to be able to speak their minds freely. They wished to explore issues and solutions without pressures from outside.

Section 2 The Constitutional Convention

LESSON PLAN

Objectives

★ Describe how the Virginia Plan and the New Jersey Plan differed.
★ Explain how the Great Compromise satisfied both large and small states.
★ Summarize the compromises made on the issue of slavery.

1 Engage

Warm Up Have students suppose the school will hold a trivia contest pitting class against class. The number of participants will be based on class size: 1 participant for every 10 students. Ask: "Is this fair? Why or why not?"

Activating Prior Knowledge Ask: "How did most Americans feel about the central government's power after the Revolution? After Shays' Rebellion?"

Reading Actively

Before Reading Have students skim the section, check the headings and illustrations, and write 2–3 sentences predicting the section's topics. As they read, they can check their predictions.

Technology

Videodiscs/Videotapes
Prentice Hall United States History Video Collection™, Vol. 5, Ch. 16, "The Constitutional Convention," 3:50 mins (*average*) ELL

Chapter 16

Vol. 5, Ch. 13, "Shays' Rebellion" 2 mins (*average*) ELL

Chapter 13

★ Background ★

Did You Know?

Hiding out By the time the Constitutional Convention was held, the public had become extremely disgruntled with the ineffective Congress. Some members attended so rarely that obtaining a quorum was a major challenge. In 1783, Congress moved from Philadelphia to Princeton to avoid angry veterans demanding back pay. Later, it shifted to Annapolis and finally New York.

2 Explore

Ask students to read the section. Then explain that the organizers of the Constitutional Convention feared that few states would send delegates. They decided that one way to ensure participation was to seek Washington's support. At first, Washington declined, but after Shays' Rebellion, he changed his mind. Have students research Washington's view of the Articles of Confederation, Shays' Rebellion, and the Constitutional Convention.

3 Teach

Divide the class into two groups to recreate the debate over representation at the Constitutional Convention. One group should support the Virginia Plan; the other, the New Jersey Plan. Individual students should research and represent the views of particular delegates to the convention.

4 Assess

To close the lesson, have students complete the section review. Or, have them write at least two supporting facts for each of these statements: **(a)** Delegates argued over the structure of the legislature. **(b)** Northern and southern states disagreed about slavery.

★ ★ ★ ★ ★ ★ ★ ★ ★ ★ ★ ★ ★ ★ ★ ★ ★ ★

Biography ANSWER

He broke the deadlock between large and small states by working out the Great Compromise.

RESOURCE DIRECTORY

Teaching Resources
Unit 2/Chapter 7
- Practice Your Skills: Identifying Main Ideas, p. 24

Biography Roger Sherman

Roger Sherman was a shoemaker, shopkeeper, surveyor, lawyer—and one of the most respected early leaders of the United States. Thomas Jefferson once said that Sherman "never said a foolish thing in his life." Sherman was one of only four people to sign both the Declaration of Independence and the Constitution. ★ **What major contribution did Roger Sherman make to the Constitutional Convention?**

To ensure secrecy, guards stood at the door. The windows were left closed to keep passersby from overhearing the debates. The closed windows made the room very hot, however. New Englanders in their woolen suits suffered terribly in the summer heat. Southerners, with clothing more suited to warm temperatures, were less bothered.

Hopelessly Divided

Soon after the meeting began, the delegates decided to do more than revise the Articles of Confederation. They chose instead to write an entirely new constitution for the nation. They disagreed, however, about what form the national government should take.

The Virginia Plan

Edmund Randolph and James Madison, both from Virginia, proposed a plan for the new government. This **Virginia Plan** called for a strong national government with three branches. The **legislative branch** would pass the laws. The **executive branch** would carry out the laws. The **judicial branch,** or system of courts, would decide if laws were carried out fairly.

According to the Virginia Plan, the legislative branch would consist of two houses. Seats in both houses would be awarded on the basis of population. Thus, in both houses, larger states would have more representatives than smaller ones. This differed from the Articles of Confederation, which gave every state, regardless of population, one vote in Congress.

The New Jersey Plan

Small states objected strongly to the Virginia Plan. They feared that the large states could easily outvote them in Congress. In response, supporters of the Virginia Plan said that it was only fair for a state with more people to have more representatives.

After two weeks of debate, William Paterson of New Jersey presented a plan that had the support of the small states. Like the Virginia Plan, the **New Jersey Plan** called for three branches of government. However, it provided for a legislature that had only one house. Each state, regardless of its population, would have one vote in the legislature.

The Great Compromise

For a while, no agreement could be reached. With tempers flaring, it seemed that the Convention would fall apart without adopting any plan. Finally, **Roger Sherman** of Connecticut worked out a compromise that he hoped would satisfy both large and small states. A **compromise** is a settlement in which each side gives up some of its demands in order to reach an agreement.

Sherman's compromise called for a two-house legislature. Members of the lower house, known as the House of Representatives, would be elected by popular vote. As

★ Customized Instruction ★
Introverted Learners

Creating a classroom reference Ask introverted learners to research the life of Roger Sherman and his role in the new nation's history. Have students write a report about his early life, education, work experiences, how he came to sign both the Declaration of Independence and the Constitution, and any details about the Great Compromise not included in the text. Students may wish to illustrate their reports with their own artwork. They should submit reports in lightweight binders or cover them with a sturdy material so they can be used as a classroom reference. (*average*)

Skills FOR LIFE

Critical Thinking | Managing Information | Communication | Maps, Charts, and Graphs

Identifying Main Ideas

How Will I Use This Skill?

Every day you get huge quantities of information—from print materials, radio, television, the Internet, and other sources. Sometimes, excessive details make it easy to miss the main point. Learning to identify main ideas saves you time and makes it easier to understand the information you receive.

LEARN the Skill

When dealing with written information, such as in this textbook, use the structure that is provided. Take note of topic headings. In each paragraph, look for the main idea, usually found in a topic sentence at the beginning or end of the paragraph. Details and examples support the topic sentence. To identify main ideas, follow these steps.

1. Identify main topic headings and subtopic headings.
2. Identify the topic sentence found in each paragraph.
3. Identify the supporting details in each paragraph. Determine how each relates to the topic sentence.
4. Review the topic headings and main ideas of each paragraph to determine the main idea of the entire section or chapter.

PRACTICE the Skill

Review the subsection Hopelessly Divided on page 194.

1. Identify the two subtopic headings under Hopelessly Divided.
2. Identify the topic sentence of each of the five paragraphs in this subsection.
3. Identify two supporting details from the first paragraph. How does each support the main idea?
4. Review the main ideas of each paragraph. In your own words, restate the main idea of the entire subsection.

APPLY the Skill

Our mailboxes are often stuffed with business letters. Choose a letter from today's mail. Using the skills that you have learned, determine the main idea.

Quill and inkwell used at the Constitutional Convention

Skills FOR LIFE

PRACTICE the Skill ANSWERS

1. the Virginia Plan, the New Jersey Plan
2. Review the main ideas of each paragraph with students.
3. They chose instead to write an entirely new constitution for the nation—which shows that they decided to do more than revise the Articles. They disagreed, however, about what form the national government should take—which shows the problems the delegates would have.
4. Possible answer: Delegates decided to write a new constitution but disagreed about issues such as representation in the legislature.

APPLY the Skill

Guided Instruction

Suggest that students look at several letters before choosing one. Have them read and underline the topic sentence of each paragraph in the letter before determining the main idea of the letter.

ASSESSMENT See the rubrics in the Alternative Assessment booklet in the Teaching Resources.

★ Background ★ Turning Points

Scofflaw delegates? The Constitutional Convention was illegal according to the Articles of Confederation, which stated that the consent of Congress and every state's legislature was needed before that document could be altered. The Convention organizers' decision to ignore these requirements had a profound impact on the nation's subsequent history. T

★ Background ★ Recent Scholarship

Original intent In his book *Original Meanings: Politics and Ideas in the Making of the Constitution,* Jack Rakove suggests that the original intent of the Constitution can best be discovered in the delegates' notes and journals because the Convention met in secret; no agenda was set before the event; and the delegates arrived essentially uninstructed by their constituents at home.

Technology

AmericanHeritage® History of the United States CD-ROM

- Face the Issues: The Great Compromise of the Constitutional Convention (challenging)

AmericanHeritage MAGAZINE

Independence Hall To learn more about this historic site on the Internet, go to www.libertynet.org/iha/tour/_indhall.html.

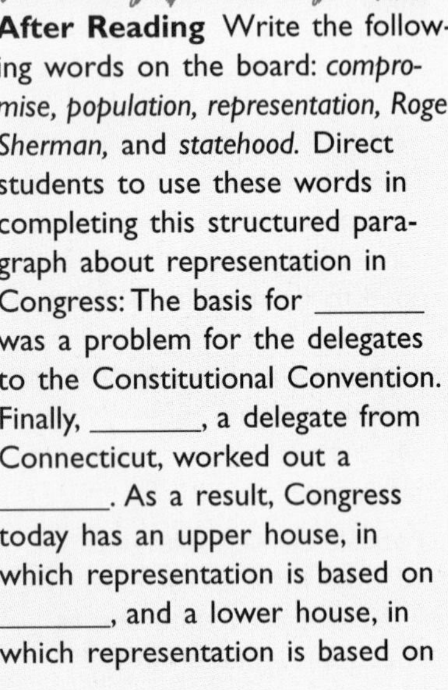

Writing Actively

After Reading Write the following words on the board: *compromise, population, representation, Roger Sherman,* and *statehood.* Direct students to use these words in completing this structured paragraph about representation in Congress: The basis for _______ was a problem for the delegates to the Constitutional Convention. Finally, _______, a delegate from Connecticut, worked out a _______. As a result, Congress today has an upper house, in which representation is based on _______, and a lower house, in which representation is based on _______.

AmericanHeritage MAGAZINE

HISTORY HAPPENED HERE

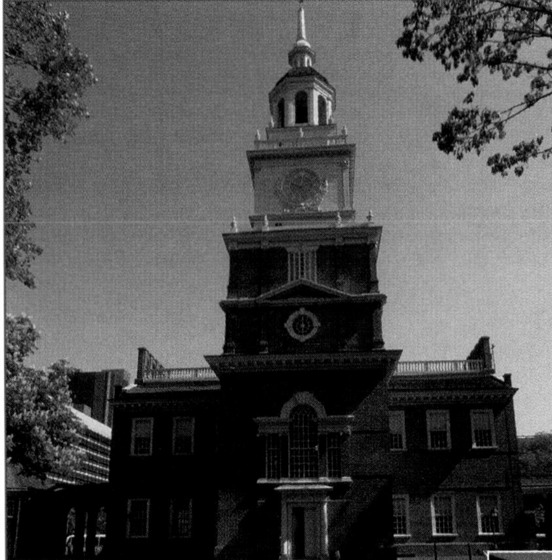

Independence Hall

For many, the birthplace of the United States is the old Pennsylvania State House, known today as Independence Hall. Here, the Declaration of Independence was signed, the Articles of Confederation were approved, and the Constitution was adopted. The site is now part of a national park. Visitors to the park can tour the building, learn about the Constitution, and see the Liberty Bell.

★ ***To learn more about this historic site, write:*** *Independence National Historical Park, 313 Walnut Street, Philadelphia, PA 19106.*

▲ Chamber where the Constitution was debated

the larger states wished, seats in the lower house would be awarded to each state according to its population.

Members of the upper house, called the Senate, would be chosen by state legislatures. Each state, no matter what its size, would have two senators. This part of Sherman's compromise appealed to the smaller states.

On July 16, the delegates narrowly approved Sherman's plan. It became known as the **Great Compromise.** Each side gave up some demands to preserve the nation.

Northern and Southern States Compromise

Just as there were disagreements between large and small states, there were also disagreements between northern and southern states. These disagreements concerned the issue of slavery. Would slaves be counted as part of a state's population? Would the slave trade continue to bring enslaved African Americans into the United States?

The Three-Fifths Compromise

Southerners wanted to include slaves in the population count even though they would not let slaves vote. If slaves were counted, southern states would have more representatives in the House of Representatives. Northerners argued that since slaves could not vote, they should not be counted.

Once again, the delegates compromised. They agreed that three fifths of the slaves in any state would be counted. In other words, if a state had 5,000 slaves, 3,000 of them would be included in the state's population count. This agreement became known as the **Three-Fifths Compromise.**

★ *Background* ★

Did You Know?

Who said anything about slavery? The words *slavery* and *slave* do not appear in the text of the Constitution. Yet counting enslaved African Americans for representation purposes was a major issue. Delegates used such phrases as "no person held in service" and "all other persons" in the Constitution, when referring to people held in slavery.

Internet Activity

The Constitution Direct students to www.nara.gov/education/teaching/constitution/home.html for more information on the Constitution. Ask students to review and rate the site on a scale from 1 to 4 and write an explanation for their rating. Given the changing nature of the Internet, you may wish to preview this site before sending students to it. (*basic*) T

RESOURCE DIRECTORY

Teaching Resources
Unit 2/Chapter 7
- Section 2 Quiz, p. 30

The slave trade

There was another disagreement over slavery. By 1787, some northern states had banned the slave trade within their borders. They urged that the slave trade be banned in the entire nation. Southerners warned that such a ban would ruin their economy.

In the end, the two sides compromised once more. Northerners agreed that Congress could not outlaw the slave trade for at least 20 years. After that, Congress could regulate the slave trade if it wished. Northerners also agreed that no state could stop a fugitive slave from being returned to an owner who claimed that slave.

Signing the Constitution

As summer drew to a close, the weary delegates struggled with other difficult questions. How many years should the President, head of the executive branch, serve? How should the courts be organized? Would members of Congress be paid?

Finally, on September 17, 1787, the Constitution was ready. Gathering for the last time, delegates listened quietly as Benjamin Franklin rose to plead that the document be accepted:

> "I doubt... whether any other Convention... may be able to make a better Constitution.... I cannot help expressing a wish, that every member of the Convention, who may still have objections to it, would with me, on this occasion, doubt a little of his own infallibility, and... put his name to this instrument."

One by one, delegates came forward to sign the document. Of the 42 delegates remaining in Philadelphia, 39 signed the document. Edmund Randolph and George Mason of Virginia, along with Elbridge Gerry of Massachusetts, refused to sign. They felt that the new Constitution gave too much power to the national government.

The Constitution required each state to hold a state convention to decide if the plan for the new government should be accepted. Once 9 of the 13 states endorsed it, the Constitution would go into effect. Before that occurred, the new Constitution was discussed and debated in all the states.

★ Section 2 Review ★

Recall

1. **Identify** (a) Constitutional Convention, (b) James Madison, (c) Virginia Plan, (d) New Jersey Plan, (e) Roger Sherman, (f) Great Compromise, (g) Three-Fifths Compromise.
2. **Define** (a) legislative branch, (b) executive branch, (c) judicial branch, (d) compromise.

Comprehension

3. Why did New Jersey and other small states oppose the Virginia Plan?
4. (a) How did the Great Compromise satisfy large states? (b) How did it satisfy small states?
5. What compromise did the North and South reach on the slave trade?

Critical Thinking and Writing

6. **Defending a Position** James Madison said that "no Constitution would ever have been adopted by the Convention if the debates had been made public." Do you agree or disagree? Defend your position.
7. **Predicting Consequences** Some historians refer to the issue of slavery as the Constitutional Convention's "unfinished business." How do you think the issue of slavery would continue to divide North and South in the years after the Convention?

Activity **Writing a Letter** You are the editor of a Philadelphia newspaper in 1787. Decide whether you agree or disagree with the Convention's decision to keep its talks secret. Explain your viewpoint in a letter to the delegates of the Constitutional Convention.

pg 193

★ Section 2 Review ★

ANSWERS

1. (a)–(b) p. 193, **(c)–(e)** p. 194, **(f)–(g)** p. 196

2. (a)–(d) p. 194

3. because under the plan, large states could easily outvote them

4. (a) by basing representation in the lower house on population **(b)** because under the plan, each state—large or small—would have two representatives in the upper house

5. that Congress could not outlaw the slave trade for at least 20 years but could regulate it after that, and that states could not stop owners from reclaiming fugitive slaves

6. Possible answer: Agree: Secrecy let delegates take uncomfortable stands in public debate; it let them compromise without losing face. Disagree: Secrecy meant the public could not contribute to or learn about the debates.

7. Possible answer: The compromise settled the issue only temporarily, but over time the issue would rise again.

Guided Instruction
Have students brainstorm occasions when secrecy is useful and when it is not. Tell them to apply those ideas in their letters.

ASSESSMENT See the rubrics in the Alternative Assessment booklet in the Teaching Resources.

★ Activity ★
Connections With Economics

Investigating coins Tell students that one of the first tasks of the new Congress was to create a currency. The first approved coin was based on a Ben Franklin design. Have students research and report on the history of U.S. coins, beginning with the first one and tracing the changes in U.S. coins to the present. *(average)* ELL T

Technology

Videodiscs/Videotapes
Prentice Hall United States History Video Collection™, Vol. 5, Ch. 19, "Am I Not a Man and Brother," 1:45 min *(average)* ELL

Chapter 19

Section 3

A More Perfect Union

LESSON PLAN

Objectives

★ Describe ideas that helped shape the Constitution.
★ Explain how the framers of the Constitution divided power between the national government and the states.
★ Describe how the framers limited the power of government.

1 Engage

Warm Up When you walk into class, tell students that the President of the United States has proclaimed a monarchy and has dismissed Congress and the Supreme Court. After students discuss the event, ask: "Could this happen in the United States? Why or why not?"

Activating Prior Knowledge Have students brainstorm a list of laws that they or their parents must obey. Write them on the board. Then ask: "Are these federal, state, or local laws?"

Reading Actively

Before Reading Have students read the questions under Explore These Questions. As they read, have them jot down notes to help them answer each question. At the end of the section, students may use these notes to answer questions in the section review.

RESOURCE DIRECTORY

Teaching Resources
Lesson Planner, p. 29

A More Perfect Union

As You Read

Explore These Questions
- What ideas helped shape the Constitution?
- How did the framers of the Constitution divide power between the national government and the states?
- How did they limit the power of government?

Define
- republic
- separation of powers
- federalism
- electoral college
- checks and balances
- bill
- veto
- override
- impeach

Identify
- Magna Carta
- English Bill of Rights
- House of Burgesses
- Mayflower Compact
- Enlightenment
- John Locke
- Montesquieu

SETTING the Scene Jonathan Smith, a Massachusetts farmer, wanted to learn the results of the Constitutional Convention. During Shays' Rebellion, he had seen how weak government could lead to violence and tyranny. Smith noted:

> "When I saw this Constitution, I found that it was a cure for these disorders. It was just such a thing as we wanted. I got a copy of it and read it over and over. I had been a member of the convention to form our state constitution, and had learnt something of the checks and balances of power; and I found them all here. I formed my own opinion, and I was pleased with this Constitution."

The framers of the Constitution had designed a **republic,** a government in which citizens rule themselves through elected representatives. The Constitution outlined a new government that would be strong. At the same time, it protected the people from excessive power in government. As Smith hoped, it also prevented any one branch of government from becoming too powerful.

Origins of the Constitution

The framers of the Constitution were well-educated men. They were familiar with the traditions of British and American government. Many of them had read the latest works of Europe's leading political philosophers. In creating the Constitution, the framers made good use of their rich knowledge and experience.

British government

As you learned in Chapter 3, the **Magna Carta** limited the power of English rulers. The Magna Carta contained two basic ideas that helped to shape both British and American government. First, it stated that English nobles had certain rights—rights that were later extended to other classes of people as well. Second, the Magna Carta made clear that English monarchs themselves had to obey the law.

When King John signed the Magna Carta, he agreed not to raise taxes without first consulting the Great Council of nobles and church officials. Eventually, the Great Council grew into the representative body known as Parliament. Parliament consisted

Connections With Civics

Benjamin Franklin admired the government formed by Indian nations in the Iroquois League. The nations in the League governed their own affairs, but joined together for mutual defense.

FROM THE ARCHIVES OF American Heritage®

Thanks to England Historical events in England and the 13 colonies made those who wrote the Constitution eager to protect citizens against government tyranny by: prohibiting religious qualifications for public office; giving the legislature checks on the powers of the executive; affirming the right of habeas corpus; narrowly defining treason.
Source: Hiller B. Zobel, "How History Made the Constitution," *American Heritage* magazine, March 1988.

of two bodies—the House of Lords and the House of Commons.

In the Magna Carta, King John was also forced to recognize that citizens had legal rights. One of the most important of these was the right to a trial by jury:

> “No freeman shall be arrested or imprisoned or dispossessed or... in any way harmed... except by the lawful judgment of his peers or by the law of the land.”

In 1689, the **English Bill of Rights** went further in limiting the monarchy and protecting the rights of citizens. The document said that parliamentary elections should be held regularly. It reaffirmed the right to a trial by jury, while protecting people from excessive fines and cruel or unjust punishment. It allowed citizens to bear arms. It also affirmed the right of habeas corpus, the idea that no person could be held in prison without first being charged with a specific crime.

The American experience

Americans enjoyed a long tradition of elected representative government. In 1619, the Virginia colonists set up the **House of Burgesses.** Eventually, each of Britain's thirteen American colonies had its own representative legislature.

Another American tradition was having written documents that clearly identified the powers and limits of government. In 1620, the Pilgrim leaders at Plymouth drew up and signed the **Mayflower Compact,** the first document of self-government in North America. They agreed to "combine ourselves together in a civil body politic" in order to establish "just and equal laws." Each of the 13 colonies had a written charter granted by the monarch or Parliament.

The framers of the Constitution also drew on their own experiences. They were very familiar with the workings of the Second Continental Congress, the Articles of Confederation, and their own state governments. Much that went into the Constitution came from either the Articles or from one of the state constitutions.

The Enlightenment

The Constitution was also based on the ideas of the European **Enlightenment.** Enlightenment thinkers believed that people could improve society through the use of reason. Many of the Constitution's framers had read the works of Enlightenment thinkers, such as John Locke and the Baron de Montesquieu (MOHN tehs kyoo).

In 1690, **John Locke** published *Two Treatises on Government.* In it, he stated two important ideas.

First, Locke declared that all people had natural rights to life, liberty, and property. Second, he suggested that government is an agreement between the ruler and the ruled. The ruler must enforce the laws and protect the people. If a ruler violates the people's natural rights, the people have a right to rebel.

Biography **Baron de Montesquieu**

Montesquieu studied European, Chinese, and Native American governments. His ideas influenced the framers of the Constitution to divide government power among three separate branches. He said that "government should be set up so that one man need not be afraid of another." ★ **Why do you think the framers of the Constitution did not want to place all power into a single branch of government?**

2 Explore

Ask students to read the section. For homework, have them research and report on one of these topics: the English Bill of Rights' protection against cruel/unjust punishment, the debates over how the President would be elected, or judicial checks on the President.

3 Teach

Tell students to suppose they are a delegate to the Constitutional Convention or a reporter. Then hold a press conference, in which delegates brief the press on the new Constitution: **(a)** delegates describe the Constitution and its origins; **(b)** delegates answer reporters' questions.

4 Assess

To close the lesson, have students complete the section review. Or, have them write short essays that support or refute these assertions: **(a)** The national government became weaker under the Constitution than under the Articles. **(b)** Each branch of the federal government has some power over the other branches. **(c)** The Constitution's framers wanted voters to elect the President directly.

★ ★ ★ ★ ★ ★ ★ ★ ★ ★ ★ ★ ★ ★ ★ ★ ★ ★ ★ ★

ANSWER

They believed a single branch could grow too strong.

★ Background ★ Viewpoints

Locke's views In *A People's History of the United States,* author Howard Zinn takes the position that Locke's "enlightened" ideas would not have seemed so bright to African Americans and the poor. Zinn writes that Locke's wealth came, in part, from the slave trade and that he firmly supported child labor. Locke felt that poor children should learn to work from the age of three.

Graphic Organizer *Skills*

ANSWERS **1.** Possible answers: **(a)** power to raise taxes; power to administer criminal justice **(b)** power to establish schools; power to make laws about marriage and divorce **2.** Possible answer: The nation needed a unified defense in times of war.

The Federal System

Powers Delegated to the National Government	Shared Powers	Powers Reserved to the States
▪ Regulate interstate and foreign trade ▪ Set standard weights and measures ▪ Create and maintain armed forces ▪ Make copyright and patent laws ▪ Establish postal offices ▪ Establish foreign policy ▪ Create federal courts ▪ Coin money ▪ Declare war ▪ Admit new states	▪ Provide for public welfare ▪ Administer criminal justice ▪ Charter banks ▪ Raise taxes ▪ Borrow money	▪ Create corporation laws ▪ Regulate trade within state ▪ Establish and maintain schools ▪ Establish local governments ▪ Make laws about marriage and divorce ▪ Conduct elections ▪ Provide for public safety

Graphic Organizer *Skills* **The system of federalism divides power between the national government and state governments.**

1. **Comprehension** **(a)** List two powers shared by national and state governments. **(b)** List two powers reserved to the states.
2. **Critical Thinking** Why do you think the power to create and maintain armed forces was delegated to the federal government?

Locke's ideas were popular among Americans. The framers of the Constitution wanted to protect people's natural rights and limit the power of government. They saw the Constitution as a contract between the people and their government.

In 1748, the French thinker Baron de **Montesquieu** published *The Spirit of the Laws.* He urged that the power of government be divided among three separate branches: the legislative, executive, and judicial. This idea, known as the **separation of powers,** was designed to keep any person or group from gaining too much power.

Montesquieu stressed the importance of the rule of law. The powers of government, he said, should be clearly defined. This would prevent individuals or groups from using government power for their own purposes. In the Constitution, the framers set out the basic laws of the nation, defining and limiting the powers of the government.

A Federal System

The framers had to decide how to divide power between the national government and the states. Under the Articles of Confederation, states had more power than Congress. Under the Constitution, states delegated, or gave up, some of their powers to the national government. At the same time, the states reserved, or kept, other powers. This division

Skills for LIFE MINI LESSON

MANAGING INFORMATION Using Note Cards

1. Introduce the skill by explaining to students that note cards can help them organize information for a research paper. Prepare a sample note card, noting title, author, publisher, copyright date, and page numbers. On the reverse side, list pertinent facts from the book. Point out that students can shuffle note cards to try out different organizations for a paper.

2. Help students practice the skill by having them prepare a model card for future use. They should follow your sample style.

3. Have students apply the skill by picking a topic related to the Constitution and locating several relevant books in the library. Students should then prepare note cards as if they were planning to write a research paper.

Resource Directory

Teaching Resources
Citizenship for Life,
- Constitution Worksheets 3–5, pp. 11–16

of power between the states and the national government is called **federalism.**

Federal powers

The Constitution spells out the powers of the federal government. For example, only the federal government can coin money or declare war. The federal government can also regulate trade between the states and with other countries.

State powers

Under the Constitution, states have the power to regulate trade within their borders. They decide who can vote in state elections. They also have power to establish schools and local governments.

In addition, the Constitution says that those powers not clearly given to the federal government belong to the states or the people. This point pleased people who were afraid that the federal government might become too powerful.

Shared powers

The Constitution lists some powers that are to be shared by federal and state governments. Both governments, for example, can build roads and raise taxes.

The framers of the Constitution had to decide how the state governments and the federal government would settle disagreements. They did so by making the Constitution "the supreme law of the land." This means that the Constitution is the final authority in any dispute between the states and the federal government.

Separation of Powers

The framers of the Constitution set up a strong federal government. However, they also took steps to prevent any one branch from becoming too powerful. James Madison said that this was necessary in order to prevent tyranny:

> "The accumulation of all powers, legislative, executive, and judiciary, in the same hands, whether one, a few, or many... may justly be pronounced the very definition of tyranny."

To prevent such a tyranny, the framers relied on Montesquieu's idea of separation of powers. In the Constitution, they created three branches of government and then defined the powers of each.

The legislative branch

The legislative branch of government is Congress. Its main function is to make laws. Congress consists of the House of Representatives and the Senate. Members of the House are elected for two-year terms. Senators are elected for six-year terms.

Under the Constitution, voters in each state elect members of the House of Representatives. Delegates to the Constitutional Convention wanted the House to represent the interests of ordinary people.

At first, the Constitution provided for senators to be chosen by state legislatures. In 1913, this was changed. Today, senators are elected in the same way as House members.

Article 1 of the Constitution sets out the powers of Congress. These include the power to collect taxes and to regulate foreign and interstate trade. In foreign affairs, Congress has the power to declare war and to "raise and support armies."

The executive branch

Article 2 of the Constitution sets up the executive branch of government. It is headed by the President. The executive branch also includes the Vice President and any advisers appointed by the President. The President and Vice President serve four-year terms.

The President is responsible for carrying out all laws passed by Congress. The President is also commander in chief of the armed forces and is responsible for directing foreign relations. Over the years, the power of the presidency has greatly increased.

The judicial branch

Article 3 of the Constitution calls for a Supreme Court. The article also allows Congress to set up other federal courts. The Supreme Court and other federal courts hear cases that involve the Constitution or any laws passed by Congress. They also hear cases arising from disputes between two or more states.

Reading Actively

During Reading Have students look at the graphic organizer on p. 200. As they read, have them look for evidence to support two of the bulleted points under each heading. For each, ask students to write a sentence in their own words further explaining the point.

★ Background ★

Recent Scholarship

Elbow room According to retired Chief Justice Warren Burger, "[T]he Constitution, remarkable as it is, fails to sharply define and limit separation of powers. . . . It did, however, create a structure that can adapt to the stresses of crises, not always efficiently and smoothly but in a way that leaves 'elbow room' to those who must act in times of crisis."

Chart *Skills*

ANSWERS **1. (a)** President **(b)** to pass laws **2.** The executive branch appoints federal judges while the judicial branch has the power to declare executive actions unconstitutional.

Writing Actively

After Reading Ask students to write two or three main ideas for this section before having them read Sum It Up at the end of the chapter. Then have them compare their main ideas with the main ideas in Section 3 of Sum It Up.

Separation of Powers

Legislative Branch (Congress)	Executive Branch (President)	Judicial Branch (Supreme Court and Other Federal Courts)
Passes laws	**Carries out laws**	**Interprets laws**
Can override President's veto	Proposes laws	Can declare laws unconstitutional
Approves treaties and presidential appointments	Can veto laws	Can declare executive actions unconstitutional
Can impeach and remove President and other high officials	Negotiates foreign treaties	
Creates lower federal courts	Serves as commander in chief of the armed forces	
Appropriates money	Appoints federal judges, ambassadors, and other high officials	
Prints and coins money	Can grant pardons to federal offenders	
Raises and supports the armed forces		
Can declare war		
Regulates foreign and interstate trade		

Chart *Skills* **The Constitution set up three branches of government. Each of the branches has its own powers.**

1. **Comprehension** **(a)** Who heads the executive branch? **(b)** What is the role of the legislative branch?
2. **Critical Thinking** Based on this chart, describe the relationship between the judicial branch and the executive branch.

Civics

Electing the President

The framers of the Constitution wanted to ensure that the President would not become too strong. Some feared that a President elected directly by the people might become too independent of Congress and the states.

Others opposed direct election because they worried that voters would not know a candidate from outside their area. In the late 1700s, news traveled slowly. New Englanders would probably know little about a candidate from the South. A candidate from Pennsylvania might be unknown to voters in Vermont or Georgia.

As a result of these concerns, the Constitution calls for an **electoral college.** It is made up of electors from every state. Every four years, the electors vote for the President and Vice President of the United States.

The framers of the Constitution expected that the electors would be well informed and familiar with the national government. They believed that such people would choose a President and Vice President wisely.

Checks and Balances

The Constitution set up a system of **checks and balances.** Under this system, each branch of the federal government has some way to check, or control, the other two branches. The system of checks and balances is another way in which the Constitution limits the power of government. (See the chart on page 220.)

★ *Customized Instruction* ★

Auditory Learners

Explaining the Constitution Tell students that understanding how the federal government works is an important step for immigrants who want to become U.S. citizens. Have students work with partners. One student can pretend that he or she has just moved to the United States from another country. The partner explains to the "new immigrant" the different powers of the three branches of government and the system of checks and balances. The "new immigrant" can ask questions to clear up any confusing details. Class members who have come from other countries may offer to explain how the American system of checks and balances resembles or differs from government practices in their countries of origin. (*average*) ELL T

Resource Directory

Teaching Resources
Unit 2/Chapter 7
• Section 3 Quiz, p. 31

Checks on Congress

To do its work, Congress passes **bills,** or proposed laws. A bill then goes to the President to be signed into law. The President can check the power of Congress by **vetoing,** or rejecting, a bill.

The Supreme Court checks the power of Congress by reviewing laws. If a law violates the Constitution, the Court can declare the law unconstitutional.

Checks on the President

After the President vetoes a bill, Congress can **override,** or overrule the veto. To override a veto, two thirds of both houses of Congress must vote for the bill again. In this way, a bill can become law without the President's signature.

Congress has other checks on the President. The President appoints officials such as ambassadors to foreign countries and federal judges. The Senate must approve these appointments. The President can negotiate treaties with other nations; however, a treaty becomes law only if two thirds of the Senate approve it.

Congress also has the power to remove a President from office if it finds the President guilty of a crime or serious misbehavior. First of all, the House of Representatives must **impeach,** or bring charges against, the President. A trial is then held in the Senate. If two thirds of the senators vote for conviction, the President must leave office.

Checks on the courts

Congress and the President have checks on the courts. The President appoints judges, who must be approved by the Senate. If judges misbehave, Congress may remove them from office. Congress establishes the number of justices in the Supreme Court. Congress can also propose changes to the Constitution to overturn Court decisions.

A Living Document

The Constitution carefully balances power among the three branches of the federal government. It also divides power between the federal government and the states. This balance has helped keep it alive for more than 200 years, longer than any other written constitution in the world. The Constitution has lasted because it is a living document. As you will read, it can be changed to meet new conditions.

★ Section 3 Review ★

Recall

1. **Identify** **(a)** Magna Carta, **(b)** English Bill of Rights, **(c)** House of Burgesses, **(d)** Mayflower Compact, **(e)** Enlightenment, **(f)** John Locke, **(g)** Montesquieu.
2. **Define** **(a)** republic, **(b)** separation of powers, **(c)** federalism, **(d)** electoral college, **(e)** checks and balances, **(f)** bill, **(g)** veto, **(h)** override, **(i)** impeach.

Comprehension

3. Describe three traditions or ideas that helped to shape the Constitution.
4. Why did the framers of the Constitution set up a system of federalism?
5. Describe one check on each of the following: **(a)** Congress, **(b)** the President, **(c)** the courts.

Critical Thinking and Writing

6. **Analyzing Ideas** On page 200, you read that the framers "...saw the Constitution as a contract between the people and their government." What do you think is meant by this statement?
7. **Comparing** Was the national government stronger under the Articles of Confederation or the Constitution? Explain.

Activity **Summarizing** You have been shipwrecked on a far-off island! The islanders want to set up a government like that of the United States. Write a summary for them in which you explain the basic ideas behind the Constitution.

★ Section 3 Review ★

ANSWERS

1. (a) p. 198, **(b)–(f)** p. 199, **(g)** p. 200

2. (a) p. 198, **(b)** p. 200, **(c)** p. 201, **(d)–(e)** p. 202, **(f)–(i)** p. 203

3. Possible answers: Locke: natural rights and the contractual theory of government; Montesquieu: separation of powers between three branches of government; England: traditions of trial by jury and representation in Parliament

4. in order to divide power between the federal and state governments in a more effective way than the Articles

5. Possible answers: **(a)** Presidents can veto bills. **(b)** Congress can impeach Presidents. **(c)** Congress can remove judges.

6. Possible answer: that people gave power to the government in return for protection and service

7. Constitution, because it gave the national government the power to tax, regulate trade, and coin money along with other powers not granted by the Articles

Activity

Guided Instruction

Have students review the section headings in order to organize their summaries and then use them as first-level headings in an outline that they then can expand on.

ASSESSMENT See the rubrics in the Alternative Assessment booklet in the Teaching Resources.

★ *Activity* ★

Linking Past and Present

Researching the Constitution today Have students clip newspaper and magazine articles that illustrate aspects of federalism, separation of powers, and/or checks and balances. For example, the President vetoes a bill or a state changes the public school curriculum. Students should be prepared to explain how their articles show the Constitution at work. Students could present their articles and explanations orally. Or you could have the class prepare a bulletin board display with the news articles and students' written explanations. (*challenging*) T

Section 4

Ratifying the Constitution

LESSON PLAN

Objectives

★ Describe the arguments Americans raised for and against the Constitution.

★ Explain how the Constitution can be amended.

★ List the rights protected by the Bill of Rights.

1 Engage

Warm Up Write on the chalkboard: "What concerns about the Constitution might citizens have had in 1787 and 1788?" Have student volunteers make suggestions.

Activating Prior Knowledge Noting what students know about the Articles of Confederation and the proposed Constitution, have them write a paragraph that explains which system they think offered the new nation the better chance to succeed and why.

Reading Actively

Before Reading Before reading the section, ask students to turn the section heading into a question. As they read, have them jot down notes to help them answer the question.

2 Explore

Ask students to read the section. For a homework assignment, have students research and report on

RESOURCE DIRECTORY

Teaching Resources
Lesson Planner, p. 30
Unit 2/Chapter 7
• Critical Thinking and Writing: Solving Problems, p. 25
Citizenship for Life
• Civics Worksheet 1, p. 3

Ratifying the Constitution

As You Read

Explore These Questions
- What arguments did Americans raise for and against the Constitution?
- How can the Constitution be amended?
- What rights does the Bill of Rights protect?

Define
- ratify
- amend
- due process

Identify
- Federalist
- Antifederalist
- *The Federalist Papers*
- Bill of Rights

SETTING the Scene In homes and in town squares across the nation, Americans discussed the new Constitution. Many supported it. Many others did not. Its critics especially worried that the Constitution had no bill of rights. In Virginia, Patrick Henry sounded the alarm:

> ❝ Show me an age and country where the rights and liberties of the people were placed on the sole chance of their rulers being good men, without a consequent loss of liberty! ❞

Was a bill of rights needed? Did the Constitution give too much power to the federal government? In the fall of 1787, citizens began to debate the document sentence by sentence. The Convention had done its work. Now the states had to decide whether or not to ratify the new frame of government.

The Constitution Goes to the Nation

The framers of the Constitution sent the document to Congress. With it, they sent a letter from George Washington, as president of the Constitutional Convention. In the letter, Washington described how the framers had struggled to make the Constitution meet the varied needs of the different states. He wrote:

> ❝ In our deliberations, we kept steadily in view... the greatest interests of every true American. That [the Constitution] will meet the full and entire [approval] of every state is not perhaps to be expected; but each will doubtless consider that had her interest been alone consulted, the consequences might have been... disagreeable or [harmful] to others. ❞

Washington warmly endorsed the document and called on Congress to support it. It was his belief, he said, that the Constitution would "promote the lasting welfare of that country so dear to us all, and secure her freedom and happiness."

The framers of the Constitution had set up a process for the states to decide on the new government. At least 9 of the 13 states had to **ratify,** or approve, the Constitution before it could go into effect. In 1787 and 1788, voters in each state elected delegates to special state conventions. These delegates then met to decide whether or not to ratify the Constitution.

Connections With Science

Today, the Constitution is publicly displayed. For protection against damage due to light, insects, and impurities in the air, each page is in a glass case filled with helium. Levels of light and humidity are carefully controlled.

★ *Background* ★

Recent Scholarship

Fish and the Bill of Rights In a 1792 letter to state governors announcing the ratification of the Bill of Rights, Thomas Jefferson first addressed the regulation of fisheries and the establishment of a post office. According to scholar Lucas A. Powe, this ordering of topics was "consistent with the view that the Bill of Rights originated in a desire to kill the Constitution." Powe believes Antifederalists like Jefferson used the original omission of a Bill of Rights strictly to drum up opposition to the Constitution. Once the Constitution was ratified, they seemed to lose interest. Says Powe, "Thus Jefferson got it right: fish were more important, and the Bill of Rights ran a poor third."

Heated Debate

In every state, heated debates took place. Supporters of the Constitution called themselves **Federalists.** They called people who opposed the Constitution **Antifederalists.**

The Federalist position

The Federalists argued that the Articles of Confederation had produced an excessively weak central government. It had placed the nation in grave danger because it left too much power with the individual states. Disputes among the states, Federalists said, had made it too difficult for the Confederation government to function.

According to the Federalists, the Constitution gave the national government the authority to function effectively. At the same time, it still protected the rights of the individual states.

Among the best-known Federalists were James Madison, Alexander Hamilton, and John Jay. They wrote a series of essays, called ***The Federalist Papers,*** defending the Constitution. They used pen names, but most people knew who they were. Today, *The Federalist Papers* remains one of the best discussions of the political theory behind the American system of government.

Biography James Madison

Historians call James Madison the "Father of the Constitution" because much of the document was based on his ideas. When the Constitution was being debated, Madison was only in his 30s. He went on to serve the nation as a member of Congress, as Secretary of State, and as the fourth President of the United States. ★ **Was Madison a Federalist or an Antifederalist?**

The Antifederalist position

Antifederalists opposed the Constitution for many reasons. They felt that it made the national government too strong and left the states too weak. They thought that the Constitution gave the President too much power. Patrick Henry was among those who voiced such concerns:

> “This Constitution is said to have beautiful features, but . . . they appear to me horribly frightful. . . . Your President may become king . . . If your American chief be a man of ambition and abilities, how easy is it for him to render himself absolute!”

Most people expected George Washington to be elected President. Antifederalists admired Washington, but they warned that future Presidents might lack Washington's honor and skill. For this reason, they said, the office should not be too powerful.

Need for a bill of rights

The chief argument used by Antifederalists against the Constitution was that it had no bill of rights. Americans had just fought a revolution to protect their freedoms. They wanted a bill of rights in the Constitution that spelled out basic freedoms such as freedom of speech and freedom of religion.

Federalists replied that the Constitution protected citizens very well without a bill of rights. Anyway, they argued, it was impossible to list all the natural rights of people. Antifederalists responded that if rights were not written into the Constitution, it would be easy to ignore them. Several state conventions refused to ratify the Constitution unless they received a firm promise that a bill of rights would be added.

why the delegates to the Constitutional Convention did not send the Constitution to state legislatures for approval. *(They feared that the legislatures would not be impartial since the states stood to lose powers under the new government. Instead, the framers sent the document straight to the people in the form of specially elected state conventions.)*

3 Teach

Have students suppose that they are delegates to a state convention, discussing whether or not to ratify the Constitution. Have one group represent Federalists; another, Antifederalists; and a third, undecided delegates. The first two groups should prepare arguments to persuade the third, while the undecided delegates should prepare questions to ask each side. Conclude the discussion by taking a vote on ratification.

4 Assess

To close the lesson, have students complete the section review. As an alternative, have students create graphic organizers that summarize the positions for or against ratification.

★ ★ ★ ★ ★ ★ ★ ★ ★ ★ ★ ★ ★ ★ ★ ★ ★

ANSWER

Madison was a Federalist and a major contributor to *The Federalist Papers.*

★ *Background* ★

Religion and Ethics

Early freedoms Freedom of religion was not guaranteed until the Bill of Rights was ratified in 1791. After George Washington became President in 1789, Quakers, Jews, Catholics, and others wrote asking him to safeguard their religious freedom. Washington responded, "Every man . . . ought to be protected in worshipping the Deity according to the dictates of his own conscience."

![Viewing History] ANSWER

Alexander Hamilton, a Federalist, had defended the Constitution and helped get it ratified.

Reading Actively

During Reading Ask students to read to find out how the Constitution was ratified. Then have them write two or three sentences summarizing the ratification struggle.

Viewing History — The Nation Celebrates

When the Constitution was ratified, celebrations were held across the nation. Shown here is a celebration parade in New York City. The three-masted ship on the float represented the "ship of state." ★ **Why do you think Alexander Hamilton's name is displayed so visibly?**

The States Vote to Ratify

One by one, states voted to ratify the Constitution. Delaware was the first, in December 1787. In June 1788, New Hampshire became the ninth state to ratify. The new government could now go into effect.

Still, the future of the United States remained in doubt. It was important that all the states support the Constitution. However, New York and Virginia, two of the largest states, had not yet ratified the plan. In both states, Federalists and Antifederalists were closely matched.

In Virginia, Patrick Henry strongly opposed the Constitution. Henry charged that the document gave the government too much power. "There will be no checks, no real balances in this government," he cried. In the end, however, Washington, Madison, and other Virginia Federalists prevailed. In late June, Virginia approved the Constitution.

In New York, the struggle went on for another month. At last, in July 1788, the state convention voted to ratify. North Carolina ratified in November 1789. Rhode Island was the last state to approve the Constitution, finally doing so in May 1790.

The Nation Celebrates

Throughout the land, Americans celebrated the news that the Constitution was ratified. The city of Philadelphia set its festival for July 4, 1788. At sunrise, church bells rang. In the harbor, the ship *Rising Sun* boomed a salute from its cannons. Horses wore bright ribbons, and bands played popular tunes.

A festive parade filed along Market Street, led by soldiers who had fought in the Revolution. Thousands cheered as six colorfully outfitted horses pulled a blue carriage shaped like an eagle. Thirteen stars and stripes were painted on the front, and the Constitution was raised proudly above it.

That night, even the skies seemed to celebrate. The northern lights, vivid bands of color, lit up the sky above the city. Benjamin Rush, a Philadelphia doctor and strong supporter of the Constitution, wrote to a friend: "'Tis done. We have become a nation."

Adding a Bill of Rights

Americans voted in the first election under the Constitution in January 1789. As

★ Activity ★

Cooperative Learning

Preparing a radio call-in Divide the class into groups. Have each group prepare a segment of a radio call-in hour on this topic: "Should the Constitution Be Ratified?" Callers should express the views of Federalists, Antifederalists, and undecideds, giving reasons for their views. If possible, provide groups with a tape recorder to record the work. (*average*)

★ Activity ★

Linking Past and Present

Researching constitutional change Have students research any currently proposed amendments to the Constitution—or the most recent amendment to the Constitution—and report their findings to the class. Possible sources of information include the *Congressional Quarterly, Congressional Record,* and Congress's Web site at www.thomas.loc.gov. (*average*)

Resource Directory

Teaching Resources
Unit 2/Chapter 7
- Biography Flashcard: Ann Lee, p. 28

Why Study History?
- National Symbols Unite Us, pp. 27–30

Why Study History?

Because National Symbols Unite Us

Historical Background

The presidential seal

The Constitution changed a loose alliance of states into a more unified nation. It takes more than a document, however, to create a nation. Shared ideals and symbols also help to bring people together. In 1782, the bald eagle was declared a symbol of the United States by Congress.

Today, the eagle and other symbols appear on the Great Seal of the United States and on the Seal of the President of the United States. On both seals, the American eagle holds an olive branch representing peace and a bundle of arrows representing military readiness. In its beak, it holds a scroll with the Latin phrase *"E pluribus Unum."* These words, which mean "Out of many, one," are our nation's motto. They refer to the union of states and to the union of the diverse American people.

Connections to Today

Almost 200 years after Congress declared it an American symbol, the American bald eagle was in serious trouble. Only about 400 breeding pairs of eagles remained in the lower 48 states. Hunting, loss of habitat, and pollution were some causes of the decline. In the 1960s, President John F. Kennedy made an urgent appeal. "The fierce beauty and proud independence of this great bird aptly symbolize the strength and freedom of America," he said, "and we shall have failed a trust if we allow the eagle to disappear."

The nation took action. Congress banned the use of DDT, an insecticide that damaged the birds' eggs. Also, it declared the eagle an endangered species. This step prohibited the hunting of eagles and protected their habitat. By the mid-1990s, the eagle population had recovered.

Connections to You

The bald eagle is only one of the emblems that represent you and all citizens of the United States. The foremost symbol of the nation is the American flag. Others include the Liberty Bell, the Statue of Liberty, and Uncle Sam. Such images have a long and interesting history as symbols of our nation.

1. **Comprehension** **(a)** Why was the bald eagle endangered in the 1960s? **(b)** How did government help the eagle to recover?
2. **Critical Thinking** Why do you think Congress chose the eagle as a symbol of the United States?

Researching and Writing Conduct research to learn about the origins and meaning of the American flag, the Liberty Bell, or other symbols of the United States. Write an essay summarizing your findings.

ANSWERS

1. (a) hunting, loss of habitat, and pollution **(b)** It banned the use of DDT, prohibited the hunting of the eagle, and protected its habitat. **2.** Possible answer: It soars free above the earth; it is proud, independent, and strong.

Guided Instruction
Encourage students to find books about American symbols. Ask them to include the history of the symbol, telling how and why it became important, what it symbolizes, and how it helps unite the nation.

ASSESSMENT See the rubrics in the Alternative Assessment booklet in the Teaching Resources.

Fast Facts

★ In 1917, photographer Arthur Mole posed 10,000 sailors to create a "living photograph" of the American flag.
★ Besides a wealth of national symbols on U.S. currency, the latest $100 bill contains microprint, watermarks, security threads, and shifting green/black ink—all to deter counterfeiters.
★ The first flag to represent the united 13 colonies was a British naval flag modified to show 13 red and white stripes.

Bibliography

To read more about this topic:

1. *Money, Money, Money: The Meaning of the Art and Symbols on United States Paper Currency,* Nancy Winslow Parker (HarperCollins, 1995). History, anecdotes.
2. *State Names, Seals, Flags and Symbols.* Benjamin and Barbara Shearer (Greenwood Press, 1994). Origins of symbols and names.
3. Internet. The Betsy Ross Home Page at www.ushistory.org/betsy/ has extensive background on the U.S. flag.

Technology

Videodiscs/Videotapes
Prentice Hall United States History Video Collection™, Vol. 5, Ch. 25, "The Promise of Freedom," 2 mins (*average*) ELL

Chapter 25

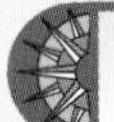
Linking Past and Present

ANSWER
right to a speedy and public trial, right to confront witnesses against the accused, right to be represented by a lawyer

Writing Actively

After Reading Ask students to review the Define terms for this section. Have them write a paragraph summary of the ratification of the Constitution using all the Define terms.

RESOURCE DIRECTORY

Teaching Resources
Unit 2/Chapter 7
• Vocabulary Builder, p. 23
• Section 4 Quiz, p. 32
Chapter Tests, pp. 37–42

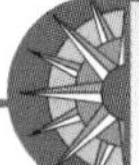
Linking Past and Present
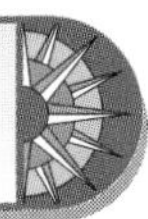

Past

Present

Trial by Jury

Trial by jury is part of the nation's English heritage. Yet in colonial times, British officials sometimes suspended jury trials. Therefore, many Americans wanted the new Constitution to guarantee this right. The members of a jury promise to give an impartial verdict based on evidence. ★ **Turn to the Reference Section and read the Sixth Amendment. List three rights guaranteed to Americans accused of crimes.**

expected, George Washington was elected President, while John Adams was chosen Vice President.

The first Congress was made up of 59 representatives and 22 senators. It met in New York City, which was chosen as the nation's first capital. The first Congress quickly turned its attention to adding a bill of rights to the Constitution.

The amendment process

The framers had set up a way to **amend,** or change, the Constitution. They did not want people to make changes lightly, however. Thus, they made the process of amending the Constitution fairly difficult.

To start the amendment process, an amendment must be proposed. This can be done in two ways. Two thirds of both houses of Congress can vote to propose an amendment, or two thirds of the states can request special conventions to propose amendments.

Next, the amendment must be ratified. Three fourths of the states must approve the amendment before it becomes part of the Constitution.

In the more than 200 years since the Constitution was adopted, only 27 amendments have been approved. Ten of those amendments were added in the first years after the Constitution was ratified.

The first 10 amendments

The first Congress proposed a series of amendments to the Constitution of the United States in 1789. By December 1791, three fourths of the states had ratified 10 amendments. Those 10 amendments became known as the **Bill of Rights.**

James Madison, who wrote the amendments, insisted that the Bill of Rights does not give Americans any rights. People already have the rights listed in the amendments. They are natural rights, said Madi-

★ *Customized Instruction* ★

English Language Learners

Creating study aids To provide listening and speaking practice, encourage English language learners to read parts of the section aloud. Once they feel comfortable, they can tape-record their reading. Then have pairs of students work together to question each other about the controversies surrounding ratification of the Constitution. Students should switch roles frequently so that each partner has a chance to ask and answer a number of questions. This questioning session can be taped too. Finally, encourage students to outline the section in writing and then to read this outline onto the tape. The finished tape can be used as a study aid for the entire class. (*average*) ELL son, that belong to all human beings. The Bill of Rights simply prevents the government from taking these rights away.

Protecting individual rights

The 10 amendments that make up the Bill of Rights ensure the basic freedoms of American citizens. The First Amendment guarantees individual liberties, including freedom of religion, freedom of speech, and freedom of the press. It also guarantees the right to assemble peacefully and the right to petition the government.

The next three amendments came out of the colonists' struggle with Britain. The Second Amendment guarantees the right of citizens to keep and bear arms. The Third Amendment was included because the framers remembered Parliament's efforts to make colonists house and feed British soldiers. The amendment prevents Congress from forcing citizens to quarter, or house, troops in their homes. The Fourth Amendment protects citizens from unreasonable searches and seizures. Before the Revolution, you will remember, British customs officials had often searched and seized the property of colonists without their permission.

The Fifth Amendment guarantees due process of law. **Due process** means that the government must follow the same fair rules in all cases brought to trial. Under the Fifth Amendment, the accused must be notified of the charges brought against him or her. The accused must also be given the chance to present a defense in court. Also, the government cannot require self-incriminating testimony nor may it try a defendant twice for the same crime if the defendant has already been acquitted.

Amendments 6 through 8 provide other protections for citizens accused of crimes. The Sixth Amendment guarantees a jury trial in criminal cases and the right to be defended by a lawyer. The Seventh Amendment requires jury trials in civil cases. The Eighth Amendment prevents judges from ordering "excessive bail" or imposing "cruel and unusual punishment" on a convicted criminal.

The Ninth Amendment assures that the rights listed in the Constitution are not the only ones that exist. The Tenth Amendment states that all powers not given to the national government and not denied to the states are reserved for the states or for the people. This assured that the power of the national government would be limited.

With the Bill of Rights in place, the new framework of government was complete. Over time, the Constitution became a living document that grew and changed along with the nation.

★ Section 4 Review ★

Recall

1. **Identify** **(a)** Federalist, **(b)** Antifederalist, **(c)** *The Federalist Papers,* **(d)** Bill of Rights.
2. **Define** **(a)** ratify, **(b)** amend, **(c)** due process.

Comprehension

3. **(a)** Why did Federalists favor ratification of the Constitution? **(b)** Why did Antifederalists oppose it?
4. Describe the process for adding amendments to the Constitution.
5. Describe three specific rights protected by the first 10 amendments to the Constitution.

Critical Thinking and Writing

6. **Defending a Position** Imagine that you are a citizen of the United States in 1789. Would you argue for or against the Constitution? How would you defend your position?
7. **Analyzing Ideas** **(a)** List five rights protected by the Bill of Rights. **(b)** Which do you think is most important? Explain.

Activity **Making Illustrations** You are the illustrator for a handbook on the rights of American citizens. Draw a series of sketches to illustrate the rights that are guaranteed by the First Amendment.

★ Section 4 Review ★

ANSWERS

1. **(a)–(c)** p. 205, **(d)** p. 208
2. **(a)** p. 204, **(b)** p. 208, **(c)** p. 209
3. **(a)** They thought the Constitution would create an effective national government and protect states' rights. **(b)** They thought it made the national government too strong, the states too weak; gave the President too much power; and needed a Bill of Rights.
4. Two thirds of either Congress or the states can propose an amendment, which three fourths of the states must ratify.
5. Possible answers: freedom of religion, speech, press, assembly
6. Possible answers: For: We need a stronger national government, the separation of powers, and a system of checks/balances. Against: the national government: too powerful; the states: too weak; no Bill of Rights protection
7. Possible answers: **(a)** freedom of religion, speech, press, assembly, and petition **(b)** Democracy will end without the freedom to speak out.

Guided Instruction
Have students reread the Bill of Rights section and then brainstorm ideas in groups. A group's best artist can create the sketch.

ASSESSMENT See the rubrics in the Alternative Assessment booklet in the Teaching Resources.

Technology

CD-ROM
Test Bank CD-ROM, Ch. 7
Interactive Student Tutorial

Chapter 7 Review and Activities

★ **Sum It Up** ★

Section 1 A Confederation of States

- During the American Revolution, most states wrote constitutions providing for a governor and legislature.
- The Articles of Confederation created a weak alliance of states.
- Under the Articles of Confederation, the government set up a system for forming and governing new territories.

Section 2 The Constitutional Convention

- The Constitutional Convention met in Philadelphia in 1787 to revise the nation's government.
- The delegates created the Constitution by making important compromises on several divisive issues.

Section 3 A More Perfect Union

- The framers of the Constitution drew ideas from British government, colonial and state governments, and the Enlightenment.
- A federal system divides power between the national and state governments.
- The separation of powers prevents any branch of government from becoming too strong.

Section 4 Ratifying the Constitution

- After many debates, the separate states approved the Constitution.
- The first 10 amendments form a Bill of Rights designed to protect the rights of individuals.

For additional review of the major ideas of Chapter 7, see ***Guide to the Essentials of American History*** or ***Interactive Student Tutorial CD-ROM,*** which contains interactive review activities, graphic organizers, and practice tests.

Reviewing the Chapter

Define These Terms

Match each term with the correct definition.

Column 1	Column 2
1. constitution	a. system of courts
2. judicial branch	b. to bring charges against
3. republic	c. nation in which voters elect representatives to govern them
4. legislative branch	d. branch that passes laws
5. impeach	e. document that sets out the laws and principles of a government

Explore the Main Ideas

1. Describe three reasons for the failure of the Articles of Confederation.
2. **(a)** Why was the Great Compromise necessary? **(b)** Why was the Three-Fifths Compromise necessary?
3. Describe three ideas that shaped the Constitution.
4. What is one benefit of a federal system of government?
5. **(a)** Describe one reason why Federalists favored the Constitution. **(b)** Describe one reason why Antifederalists opposed it.

Chart Activity

Use the chart below to answer the following questions:
1. Which state was the first to ratify the Constitution?
2. Which state was the last? **Critical Thinking** In which three states was support for the Constitution strongest?

Ratification of the Constitution

State	Date	Vote
Delaware	Dec. 7, 1787	30–0
Pennsylvania	Dec. 12, 1787	46–23
New Jersey	Dec. 19, 1787	38–0
Georgia	Jan. 2, 1788	26–0
Connecticut	Jan. 9, 1788	128–40
Massachusetts	Feb. 6, 1788	187–168
Maryland	Apr. 28, 1788	63–11
South Carolina	May 23, 1788	149–73
New Hampshire	June 21, 1788	57–46
Virginia	June 25, 1788	89–79
New York	July 26, 1788	30–27
North Carolina	Nov. 21, 1789	184–77
Rhode Island	May 29, 1790	34–32

Chapter 7 Review and Activities

Reviewing the Chapter

Define These Terms

1. e **2.** a **3.** c **4.** d **5.** b

Explore the Main Ideas

1. They did not give Congress enough power, could not solve disputes among states, and could not prevent other countries from taking advantage of the U.S.

2. (a) to settle disagreements between large and small states over representation in Congress **(b)** to settle differences between the North and South over whether or not slaves should be counted as part of a state's population

3. Possible answer: Locke's ideas of natural rights and the contractual theory of government; Montesquieu's idea of separating the powers of government among three branches; tradition of representative democracy from England

4. gives the federal government enough power to govern effectively, while protecting states' rights

5. (a) Federalists said the Constitution would let the central government function effectively. **(b)** Antifederalists said it lacked a Bill of Rights to protect individual rights.

Chart Activity

1. Delaware **2.** Rhode Island
Critical Thinking Delaware, New Jersey, Georgia

Critical Thinking and Writing

1. d, e, b, a, c

2. Possible answer: Franklin may have been unsure about whether Americans would be able to make the compromises necessary to preserve the republic.

3. Possible answer: It could violate individual rights to liberty and property.

4. Possible answer: Yes, Americans demand their rights and ask the Supreme Court to rule on issues related to the Bill of Rights.

Using Primary Sources

(a) weak **(b)** Americans intentionally made their government weak and were determined to limit its power and keep it from violating their liberties. **(c)** Because he had worked for the British, he might have been prejudiced against the Americans.

Critical Thinking and Writing

1. **Understanding Chronology** Arrange the following documents in chronological order: **(a)** the Constitution, **(b)** Articles of Confederation, **(c)** the First Amendment, **(d)** Magna Carta, **(e)** Mayflower Compact.
2. **Making Inferences** Benjamin Franklin said that Americans had a republic, if they could keep it. Why do you think Franklin was unsure whether the government would last?
3. **Predicting Consequences** What do you think might happen if the government was not required to follow due process?
4. **Exploring Unit Themes** **Rights and Liberties** The nation has changed a great deal since 1787. Does the Bill of Rights still protect individual rights in the United States today? Explain.

Using Primary Sources

During the American Revolution, Johann David Schoepf was a physician for Britain's Hessian troops. After the war, he traveled about the United States, recording his observations. Here, he comments on the government created by the Articles of Confederation:

> "The Congress has neither the necessary weight nor the necessary solidity. . . . It was to be expected of a people so enthusiastic for liberty that they should grant their Congress only a shadow of dignity, and watch its proceedings with a jealous eye."

Source: *Travels in the Confederation,* Johann David Schoepf, 1911.

Recognizing Points of View **(a)** Did Schoepf consider the new American Congress to be strong or weak? **(b)** Schoepf wrote that Americans watched Congress "with a jealous eye." What do you think he meant by this? **(c)** How do you think Schoepf's background affected his point of view?

Activity Bank

Interdisciplinary Activity

Exploring Geography Find out more about the early settlement of one of the five states carved out of the Northwest Territory. Report on how people traveled there, what obstacles they faced, and how they lived. Include a map showing geographic features of the area.

Career Skills Activity

Teachers Every immigrant who wants to become an American citizen has to learn about the Constitution. Suppose you were teaching a citizenship class. With a partner, prepare a presentation on one part the Constitution. Use visual aids such as diagrams and pictures in your presentation.

Citizenship Activity

Identifying Community Issues The process of amending the Constitution often starts with a petition—a statement signed by many members of a community and presented to lawmakers to show public support for a change. Working with others in your class, choose a problem in your community. Prepare a petition that suggests a solution.

Internet Activity

On the Internet, find information on one of the leading figures at the Constitutional Convention. Write a brief biography of the person, noting especially his role in producing the Constitution.

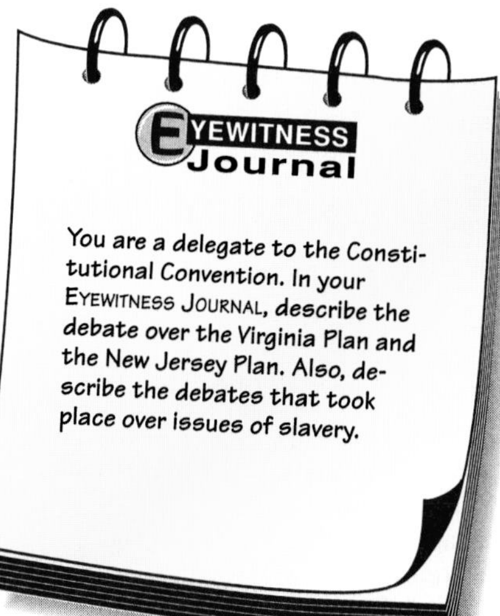

Eyewitness Journal
You are a delegate to the Constitutional Convention. In your Eyewitness Journal, describe the debate over the Virginia Plan and the New Jersey Plan. Also, describe the debates that took place over issues of slavery.

★ 211

Activity Bank

ASSESSMENT To assess the activities on this page, see the rubrics in the Alternative Assessment booklet in the Teaching Resources. You might want to share the rubrics with your students before they begin work.

Interdisciplinary Activity

1. If possible, have students use real accounts of people living then.
2. Students who reside in one of the 5 states created from the Northwest Territory may wish to visit local historical societies or libraries to find out about early settlements.
3. Extend the activity by having students compare life in the Northwest Territory to life in the early English colonies.

Career Skills Activity

1. Have students begin by choosing a part of the Constitution to teach about.
2. Students should define key government-related words in their presentations, since immigrants might be unfamiliar with this specialized vocabulary.
3. Suggest that students look through the chapter and the rest of their textbook for different kinds of visual aids.

Citizenship Activity

1. Begin by holding a discussion about local issues that students may wish to see resolved. If the class is divided, have it form groups to work on separate issues.
2. Make clear to students that no one can be forced to sign a petition and that they should accept some people's refusal to sign.
3. After you and/or school authorities have approved their petitions, have students canvass for signatures. Have them get written permission before using business locations outside stores or theaters.

Eyewitness Journal

1. Have students review the two issues. Be sure they understand the differences between the two state plans.
2. Encourage students to make their reports of the debate as lively as possible.
3. Extend the activity by asking interested students to read Madison's account of the debates and report to the class on what actually occurred.

Internet Activity

1. Have students go to www.phschool.com, which contains updated information on a variety of topics.
2. Another site you may find useful for this activity is the James Madison Museum in Orange, Virginia, at www.gemlink.com/~jmmuseum/menu.htm.
3. Given the changing nature of the Internet, you may wish to preview this site.

Chapter 8 Manager

SECTION OBJECTIVES	TEACHING RESOURCES	ADDITIONAL RESOURC
1 Goals of the Constitution (pp. 214–217) **Objectives** 1. Explain how the national government helps to unify the nation. 2. Describe the benefits of a national system of courts. 3. Explain how the Constitution protects the basic rights of the people.	**Lesson Planner,** p. 31 (average) . . . .**45 mins.** **Unit 2/Chapter 8** • Section 1 Quiz, p. 39 (average) . . . .**15 mins.** **Interdisciplinary Connections** • Main Idea: The Living Constitution, p. 46 (average) . . . .**20 mins.** **Citizenship for Life** • Civics Worksheet 1, p. 1 (average) . . . . . .**20 mins.** • Constitution Worksheet 7, p. 7 (average) . . . .**20 mins.**	
2 Five Principles of the Constitution (pp. 218–221) **Objectives** 1. Name the five basic principles of the Constitution. 2. Explain why people adopt a system of representative government. 3. Describe how the framers tried to strike a balance between too much and too little government.	**Lesson Planner,** p. 32 (average) . . . .**45 mins.** **Unit 2/Chapter 8** • Map Mystery: Shifting Power in the House, p. 36 (average) . . . .**20 mins.** • Section 2 Quiz, p. 40 (average) . . . .**15 mins.** **Interdisciplinary Connections** • Main Idea: The Living Constitution, pp. 44–45, 47–48 (average) . . . .**20 mins.** **Citizenship for Life** • Civics Worksheet 2, p. 2 (average) . . . . . .**20 mins.** • Constitution Worksheets 1–5, pp. 7–16 (average) . . . .**20 mins.**	**Constitution Study Guide** • Constitutional Principles, pp. 47–51
3 A Living Document (pp. 222–224) **Objectives** 1. Describe the formal process for changing the Constitution. 2. Explain the purpose of the Bill of Rights. 3. Identify informal changes that have been made to the Constitution.	**Lesson Planner,** p. 33 (average) . . . .**60 mins.** **Unit 2/Chapter 8** • Section 3 Quiz, p. 41 (average) . . . .**15 mins.** **Citizenship for Life** • Civics Worksheets 3–4, pp. 3–6 (average) . . . .**20 mins.** • Constitution Worksheet 6, p. 17 (average) . . . .**20 mins.**	**Constitution Study Guide** • The Amendment Process and Bill of Rights, pp. 53–56
4 The National Government at Work (pp. 225–231) **Objectives** 1. Define the roles of Congress. 2. Describe the jobs the President does. 3. Explain how the federal court system is organized.	**Lesson Planner,** p. 34 (average) . . . .**60 mins.** **Unit 2/Chapter 8** • Practice Your Skills: Reading a Flow Chart, p. 34 (average) . . . .**30 mins.** • Biography Flashcard: Sandra Day O'Connor, p. 38 (average) . . . .**35 mins.** • Section 4 Quiz, p. 42 (average) . . . .**15 mins.** **Citizenship for Life** • Constitution Worksheets 8–16, pp. 23–38 (average) . . . .**20 mins.**	**History Alive® Activity Pack** • Activity 2: Constitution Card Sort
5 Good Citizenship (pp. 232–235) **Objectives** 1. Describe how the Bill of Rights was limited. 2. Explain how the Supreme Court has used the Fourteenth Amendment to expand citizens' rights. 3. List citizens' rights and responsibilities.	**Lesson Planner,** p. 35 (average) . . . .**90 mins.** **Unit 2/Chapter 8** • Vocabulary Builder, p. 33 (basic) . . . .**15 mins.** • Section 5 Quiz, p. 43 (average) . . . .**15 mins.** **Why Study History?** • Citizens Have Responsibilities, pp. 31–34 (average) . . . .**90 mins.** **Citizenship for Life** • You Can Make a Difference Worksheets 1–11, pp. 39–60 (average) . . . .**20 mins.** **Chapter Tests,** pp. 43–48 (average) . . . . . .**45 mins.**	

Assessment Options

 **Teaching Resources**
- Alternative Assessment booklet
- Section Quizzes, Unit 2, Chapter 8, pp. 39–43
- Chapter Tests, Chapter 8, pp. 43–48
- Test Bank CD-ROM

 **Student Performance Pack**
- Guide to the Essentials of American History, Chapter 8 Test, p. 49
- Standardized Test Prep Handbook
- Interactive Student Tutorial CD-ROM

Interdisciplinary Connections

 **Teaching Resources**
- Map Mystery, Unit 2, Chapter 8, p. 36
- Interdisciplinary Connections, pp. 43–48

Technology

Interactive Student Tutorial CD-ROM

Test Bank CD-ROM

Color Transparencies
- The United States and the World, 1775–1825, p. E–17

Guided Reading Audiotapes
(English/Spanish), side 3

Resource Pro® CD-ROM

Prentice Hall United States History Video Collection™
(Spanish track available on disc version.) Vol. 5, Chs. 22, 25

Prentice Hall Home Page
www.phschool.com

Student Performance Pack

Guide to the Essentials of American History
- Ch. 8, pp. 44–49
  (Available in English and Spanish)

Guided Reading Audiotapes (English/Spanish), side 3

Standardized Test Prep Handbook

Interactive Student Tutorial CD-ROM

 **BLOCK SCHEDULING**
Activities with this icon will help you meet your Block Scheduling needs.

 **ENGLISH LANGUAGE LEARNERS**
Activities with this icon are suitable for English Language Learners.

 **TEAM TEACHING**
Activities and Background Notes with this icon present starting points for Team Teaching.

Teachers' Bibliography

Don't miss the special American Heritage® teaching notes found in this chapter.

Contact Teachers' Curriculum Institute to learn more about History Alive!® resources on the Constitution. See History Alive!® units: The Constitution in a New Nation, Section 3, "The Creation of the Bill of Rights," and Section 5, "The Constitution in Action Today."

Explore your library to find these issues related to Chapter 8: *The Bill of Rights,* September 1991; *Important Supreme Court Cases,* March 1989; *The United States Senate,* April 1984; *The Meaning of the Constitution,* September 1982.

Prentice Hall Web Site You can access a structured, on-line environment that allows you to preview curriculum-related resources and receive updated information on groundbreaking events from around the nation and the world. (www.phschool.com)

Chapter 8

The Constitution at Work
1789–Present

Introducing the Chapter
Have students preview the main ideas of this chapter by looking over the visuals. Suggest they look for ways in which the Constitution affects government at various levels and citizens in general.

Using the Time Line To provide students with practice in using the time line, ask these compare-and-contrast questions: How are the events of 1893 and 1920 similar? *(Both concern women's right to vote.)* How are the events of 1870 and 1920 alike? *(Both deal with voting rights.)* How do the events of 1870 and 1920 differ? *(Only black men, not women, won the right to vote in 1870.)* What connection can you see between the events of 1791 and 1971? *(Both involve amendments to the Constitution.)*

Have students think about personal rights and freedoms they exercise daily. Responses may include such points as freedom of speech and the right to public education. Conclude by having students choose one right they especially value and complete this sentence: Because I have the right to __________, I have the citizen's responsibility to __________.

For additional *Why Study History?* support, see p. 234.

★ CIVICS OVERVIEW ★

Chapter 8

The Constitution at Work 1789–Present

What's Ahead

The goal of the Constitution is to create a single, united nation with a fair government and system of laws. It ensures peace within the nation, provides for the defense of the country, and guarantees people's rights and liberties. The principles behind the Constitution include the people's right to rule themselves and the careful division of power among three separate branches of the government.

Changing the Constitution is not easy. For this reason, the basic framework of government has grown slowly. One key change over the centuries has been to extend the rights of citizenship to more and more Americans.

Why Study History? As you study American history, you will see how different people won greater rights. Such rights carry with them responsibilities. Americans meet their responsibilities as citizens in many ways, such as voting or serving in the military. There are also individuals who see a problem in their community and work to solve it. To meet one such person, see this chapter's *Why Study History?* feature, "Citizens Have Responsibilities."

American Events

1788 Constitution of the United States is ratified

1791 Bill of Rights is approved

1700 | 1750 | 1800 | 1850

World Events

1700s World Event Age of Enlightenment begins

1789 World Event French Revolution begins

Voting: A Right and a Responsibility

Voting is one of the most important duties of an American citizen. Two hundred years ago, only white male property owners over the age of 21 could vote in most states. Today, as this painting shows, every citizen over the age of 18 has the right to vote. ★ **List three other rights that American citizens enjoy.**

1870 Fifteenth Amendment gives African American men the right to vote

1920 Nineteenth Amendment gives women the right to vote

1971 Twenty-sixth Amendment extends voting rights to Americans 18 to 21 years old

1850 | 1900 | 1950 | 2000

1893 World Event New Zealand is first nation to give vote to women

1948 World Event United Nations approves Universal Declaration of Human Rights

Writing Actively

Responding to Art After students have studied the painting and read the caption on this page, have them write a paragraph answering this question: "Who is the American voter?" Encourage students to consider age, ethnicity, gender, individual interests, and walks of life.

ANSWER

Possible answers: rights to life, liberty, the pursuit of happiness, property; freedom of speech, religion, the press

★ Background ★
Art Note

Voting: A Right and a Responsibility Contemporary artist Mark Hess titled this realistic painting *Power to Vote.* His work celebrates the broadening of the Constitution to include all citizens, men and women, over the age of 18 as voters. The thoughtful look on each voter's face suggests the responsibilities associated with the right to vote. T

Documents and Literature

On pp. 548–551, you will find two readings to enrich this chapter:

1. Eyewitness Account "The Magna Carta," excerpts dealing with citizens' rights under the rule of law. (Use with Section 2.)

2. Eyewitness Account "The Volunteer Spirit: Three Views," passages describing the motives of Peace Corps volunteers and the feelings of someone whom the Peace Corps helped. (Use with Section 5.)

Technology

Videodiscs/Videotapes

Show the *Prentice Hall United States History Video Collection*™ segments for this chapter. The videodisc version has a Spanish track. Press audio until you get the left channel for English or the right channel for Spanish, or use the bar codes in the Guidebook.

Section 1
Goals of the Constitution

LESSON PLAN

Objectives

★ Explain how the national government helps to unify the nation.
★ Describe the benefits of a national system of courts.
★ Explain how the Constitution protects the basic rights of the people.

1 Engage

Warm Up Have students define *unconstitutional,* and name examples of possible unconstitutional actions.

Activating Prior Knowledge Remind students that by 1786, many Americans wanted fundamental changes in the national government. Have students create 3 titles for pamphlets of the 1780s that support change. Titles should suggest the reason for the change.

Reading Actively

Before Reading Have students read the headings in the section. Then have them read the questions under Explore These Questions and note which heading or headings are most likely to answer each question.

2 Explore

Ask students to read the section. For homework, tell them to find news articles that show the Con-

RESOURCE DIRECTORY

Teaching Resources
Lesson Planner, p. 31
Unit 2/Chapter 8
Interdisciplinary Connections
- Main Idea: The Living Constitution, p. 46

Transparencies
Geography and History
- The United States and the World, 1775–1825, p. E-17

Goals of the Constitution

As You Read

Explore These Questions
- How does the national government help to unify the nation?
- What are the benefits of a national system of courts?
- How does the Constitution protect the basic rights of the people?

Define
- federal
- justice
- domestic tranquillity
- general welfare
- liberty

Identify
- Preamble
- Bill of Rights

Setting the Scene In 1787, Benjamin Franklin was 81 years old. As long ago as the French and Indian War, he had urged the 13 colonies to unite for their mutual interest. Now, he was serving as the oldest delegate to the Constitutional Convention.

At the end of the convention, Franklin commented on the new Constitution. The document, he admitted, was not perfect:

> "When you assemble a number of men, to have the advantage of their joint wisdom, you inevitably assemble with those men all their prejudices, their passions, their errors of opinion, their local interests, and their selfish views. . . . It therefore astonishes me, Sir, to find this system approaching so near to perfection as it does."

Constitution of the United States

He expressed his hope that the Constitution would unite the nation and be "a blessing to the people." The Constitution has lived up to Franklin's hopes. It has remained the framework of our government for more than 200 years. It endures in part because it guarantees people their rights and liberties. Ensuring liberty is just one of the main goals of the Constitution.

Preamble to the Constitution

The opening statement, of the Constitution is called the **Preamble.** In it the American people proudly announce that they have established the Constitution to achieve certain goals:

> "We the people of the United States, in order to form a more perfect Union, establish justice, ensure domestic tranquillity, provide for the common defense, promote the general welfare, and secure the blessings of liberty to ourselves and our posterity, do ordain and establish this Constitution for the United States of America."

As you read about these six goals, think about their importance to you.

"Form a More Perfect Union"

Under the Articles of Confederation, the United States was a loose alliance of independent, quarreling states. Many states acted like separate nations. One of the main goals of the framers of the Constitution was to get the states to work together as part of a single, united nation.*

* *E pluribus unum,* the official motto of the United States, also expresses this principle of unity. The Latin phrase means, "Out of many, one."

Skills for LIFE MINI LESSON

MAPS, CHARTS, AND GRAPHS
Reading an Organization Chart

1. Introduce the skill by writing the term *Organization Chart* on the chalkboard. Explain that such graphics summarize and organize information in a way that shows relationships among data. Point out that the Contents of the Constitution chart is one such chart.

2. Help students practice the skill by asking them to name the three parts into which the chart on p. 215 divides the Constitution.

3. Have students apply the skill by answering these questions about the chart: How is the placement of the Preamble related to the Articles? *(precedes them)* How is the Bill of Rights related to the other amendments? *(It is the first 10 amendments to the Constitution.)*

To achieve this goal of unity, the Constitution gives a broad range of powers to the national government. For example, only Congress—the national legislature—has the power to tax all the people. The President—the national executive—is responsible for carrying out all the laws of the nation. And **federal,** or national, courts enforce one system of law for the entire nation.

"Establish Justice"

A second goal of the Constitution is to establish **justice,** or fairness. Justice requires that the law be applied fairly to every American, regardless of that person's race, religion, gender, country of origin, political beliefs, or financial situation. The Constitution gives this task to a federal system of courts.

Federal courts deal with a broad range of issues. They hear cases involving the Constitution, national laws, treaties, foreign ambassadors, and ships at sea. They also decide disputes between individuals, between individuals and the national government, and between the states.

When federal courts decide cases, they must often interpret, or explain, the law. The Supreme Court, the highest court in the land, can rule that a law passed by Congress or a state legislature is not permitted by the Constitution.

Why is a national system of courts necessary? Without it, state or local courts would interpret national laws. Judges in some states might refuse to enforce national laws they did not like. Disputes about the meaning of certain laws would remain unsettled. Confusion, and even injustice, might result.

"Ensure Domestic Tranquillity"

In 1786, Daniel Shays marched on a Massachusetts courthouse with hundreds of protesters. Upon hearing about Shays' Rebellion, George Washington warned, "We are fast verging to [absence of government] and confusion!" The uprising made it clear that the national government must have the power to ensure **domestic tranquillity,** or peace at home.

Contents of the Constitution

Chart *Skills* **The Constitution of the United States includes a preamble, 7 articles, and 27 amendments.**

1. **Comprehension** **(a)** What is the subject of Article 4? **(b)** On what pages would you find the Bill of Rights?
2. **Critical Thinking** **(a)** Identify as many amendments as you can that deal with voting or elections. **(b)** Why do you think so many amendments are concerned with this issue?

Civics

stitution at work today (e.g., new laws, Supreme Court decisions, or free speech issues). Have them explain how each article shows the Constitution at work.

3 Teach

Write and circle "U.S. Constitution" on the chalkboard. Then draw leader lines to 6 smaller circles below. Have students list the Constitution's goals in the smaller circles. Extend the web with another set of leaders and circles. Ask: "How does the Constitution provide for meeting its goals?" and "How might you add to or redefine the unconstitutional actions you listed earlier?"

4 Assess

To close the lesson, have students complete the section review. Or, have them give an example showing how the Constitution meets each of its 6 goals and then record each example on a separate 3x5 card. Have students swap cards with a partner, who writes the goal being met on the reverse of each card. Ask partners to swap cards again and clarify discrepancies in goal identification.

★ ★ ★ ★ ★ ★ ★ ★ ★ ★ ★ ★ ★ ★ ★ ★ ★ ★

Chart *Skills*

ANSWERS **1. (a)** Relations Among the States **(b)** pp. 606–607 **2. (a)** 12, 15, 17, 19, 20, 22–24, 26 **(b)** Possible answer: Voting is essential to a democracy. Since 1789, voting rights have gradually been extended.

★ *Activity* ★

Connections With Civics

Understanding a national motto

Explain the meaning of the motto *e pluribus unum* (Latin for "out of many, one"), found on the one-dollar bill and American coins. Have students create cartoons or drawings from earlier times or today to illustrate the motto. Have them inscribe their mottoes somewhere in their illustrations. (average) ELL T

Technology

Videodiscs/Videotapes

Prentice Hall United States History Video Collection™, Vol. 5, Ch. 22, "We the People," 2:30 mins (average) ELL

Chapter 22

Reading Actively

During Reading After students read the section entitled "Provide for the Common Defense," ask students why they think the framers of the Constitution placed the military under civilian control.

Biography

ANSWER

Kelsey's work helped "promote the general welfare" by protecting the people from a dangerous drug.

Writing Actively 

After Reading Have students rewrite the Preamble to the Constitution in their own words. Tell them to avoid using the section's Define terms. If they do use any Define term, they should include a definition of it.

Biography **Frances Kelsey**

In the early 1960s, a prescription drug named thalidomide caused birth defects in hundreds of children in Europe and Canada. Thanks to Frances Kelsey (left), the drug was never sold in the United States. As an official at the Food and Drug Administration (FDA), Kelsey refused to approve thalidomide without more tests. For her work, Kelsey received a medal from President John Kennedy (right). ★ **How did Kelsey's work fulfill one of the goals of the Constitution?**

Logo of the FDA

The Constitution gives the national government certain powers that allow it to keep the peace. State and local governments can use their own police to enforce national laws within their borders. When crime crosses state borders, however, national police agencies, such as the Federal Bureau of Investigation (FBI), can step in to help protect life and property.

Have you ever seen a news report about a civil emergency, such as a riot or a flood? If so, you probably saw the National Guard keeping the peace. The President can summon such aid if a state or community cannot or will not respond to the emergency.

"Provide for the Common Defense"

After the American Revolution, the United States had no armed forces to defend itself. Without an army, it could not force British troops to leave the western frontier. Without a navy, it could not prevent Spain from closing part of the Mississippi River to American trade.

The framers of the Constitution realized that armed forces are vital to a nation's survival. Military power helps not only to prevent attack by other nations, but also to protect economic and political interests.

The Constitution gives Congress the power to "raise and support Armies" and to "provide and maintain a Navy." Today, the armed forces include the army, navy, air force, marine corps, and coast guard.

At the same time, the Constitution establishes the principle that the military is under civilian, or nonmilitary, control. Article 2 of the Constitution states that the President is Commander in Chief of the armed forces. Thus, even the highest-ranking military officer must answer to an elected official.

"Promote the General Welfare"

The Constitution gives the national government the means to promote the **general welfare,** or well-being of all the people. The national government has the power to collect taxes. It also has the power to set aside money for programs that will benefit the people.

$ Connections With Economics

Government spending for defense and the general welfare has grown dramatically. In 1795, government outlays totaled $7.5 million for a population of 4.6 million people—an average of $1.63 per person. In 1995, the government's outlays totaled $1.5 billion for a population of 263 million people—an average of $5.70 per person.

★ Customized Instruction ★
Extroverted Learners

Producing a pageant Divide the class into six groups. Assign each group one of the six goals of the Constitution. Have students draw on what they learned in this section and their own experiences to produce a pageant illustrating each goal and its application in American life. Suggest that one student in each group act as narrator while other members present information and ideas with posters, tapes, songs, poems, costumes, artifacts, dramatizations, or other devices. Ask a volunteer to prepare and give an introduction before the six groups present their segments. (*average*) ELL

RESOURCE DIRECTORY

Teaching Resources
Unit 2/Chapter 8
- Section Quiz 1, p. 39

Citizenship for Life
- Civics Worksheet 1, p. 1
- Constitution Worksheet 7, p. 7

The workplace provides many examples of how the national government—often in cooperation with state governments—has acted to promote the general welfare. Factory owners are required to meet safety standards for work areas. Workers who are disabled or unemployed receive financial support. Thanks to the Social Security system, all workers are entitled to income upon retirement.

Another way in which the national government helps to promote the general welfare is by supporting education. Education helps to prepare people to become responsible citizens. It also provides tools and training for employment.

Support for education takes many forms. The national government pays for school nutrition programs in local school districts. Many students receive money to help pay the costs of a college education.

The national government also supports scientific research and development to improve the quality of life. For example, researchers at the National Institutes of Health lead the fight against many diseases. Scientists at the Department of Agriculture help farmers to improve their crops and develop better livestock.

"Secure the Blessings of Liberty"

Protection of liberty was a major reason that colonists fought the American Revolution. It is no wonder, then, that the framers made securing liberty a major goal of the Constitution. **Liberty** is the freedom to live as you please, as long as you obey the laws and respect the rights of others.

One way that the Constitution ensures liberty is by limiting the powers of government. For example, the **Bill of Rights,** the first 10 amendments to the Constitution, lists basic rights and freedoms that the government may not take away.

The Constitution provides yet another safeguard of liberty—the right to vote. The people select the leaders who make the laws. At the same time, they can remove from office those leaders who abuse their power.

The "blessings of liberty" have been extended to more Americans since the Constitution was written. Changes in the Constitution have been made to ensure that all Americans—no matter what their sex, religion, or race—have the same rights regarding voting, education, housing, employment, and other opportunities in life.

★ Section 1 Review ★

Recall

1. **Identify** (a) Preamble, (b) Bill of Rights.
2. **Define** (a) federal, (b) justice, (c) domestic tranquillity, (d) general welfare, (e) liberty.

Comprehension

3. (a) List two goals of the Constitution. (b) Describe one way that the national government helps to achieve each of these goals.
4. How does the national system of courts help to ensure justice for all Americans?
5. List two ways the Constitution safeguards the people's liberty.

Critical Thinking and Writing

6. **Evaluating Information** Which goal of the Constitution do you think is most important? Explain.
7. **Linking Past and Present** Are the goals of the nation today the same as those set out in the Preamble to the Constitution?

★ ★

Activity **Teaching Through Pictures** A fifth-grader in your school has to recite the Preamble to the Constitution in a speaking contest. When you hear him practice, you realize he doesn't understand what it means. Draw six pictures with captions that will explain the goals of the Constitution for him.

★ Section 1 Review ★

ANSWERS

1. (a) p. 214, (b) p. 217
2. (a)–(c) p. 215, (d) p. 216, (e) p. 217
3. Possible answers: (a) form a more perfect union, establish justice (b) To promote unity, the President carries out all the laws of the nation; the government maintains a national court system to ensure justice.
4. It ensures a uniform system of law for the entire nation.
5. Possible answers: limits the powers of government; gives citizens the right to vote
6. Accept all well-reasoned answers. Example: "Securing the blessings of liberty," because it affects all citizens everyday
7. Possible answer: Although life has changed greatly since 1787, the nation's goals set out in the Preamble to the Constitution remain largely the same.

Activity

Guided Instruction
Remind students that the headings in this section correspond to the six goals of the Preamble. Suggest that students draw one picture for each goal. If possible, have students get feedback by showing their pictures to younger students or siblings.

ASSESSMENT See the rubrics in the Alternative Assessment booklet in the Teaching Resources.

★ *Background* ★

Linking Past and Present

And proudly they still serve! Born during the Revolution, the United States Army and Navy are the oldest branches of the armed services. The Marine Corps was established as a separate service in 1798. Marines operate on land, but their actions are linked to naval operations. They also guard U.S. naval stations and embassies in other countries. The United States Coast Guard was set up in 1790 to prevent smuggling and piracy. In 1915, it was combined with the Lifesaving Service and given its present name. During war, the Coast Guard is directed by the Secretary of the Navy; in peacetime, by the Secretary of Transportation. The army directed air operations until 1947, when the United States Air Force became a separate branch of the military.

Section 2
Five Principles of the Constitution

LESSON PLAN

Objectives

★ Name the five basic principles of the Constitution.

★ Explain why people adopt a system of representative government.

★ Describe how the framers tried to strike a balance between too much and too little government.

1 Engage

Warm Up Ask students to identify by name as many elected officials as they can. Then ask: "Who is their boss?" Point out that all elected officials are accountable to the people who elected them.

Activating Prior Knowledge Tell students that many organizations post a mission statement listing their purposes and principles. Have students write a mission statement for delegates to the Constitutional Convention by completing this sentence: Our mission is to create a government that will __________, ________ and __________.

Reading Actively

Before Reading Ask students to write the five main headings of this section as the main topics for an outline. Have them leave space under each heading to add information as they read.

RESOURCE DIRECTORY

Teaching Resources
Lesson Planner, p. 32
Interdisciplinary Connections
- Main Idea: The Living Constitution, pp. 44–45, 47–48

2 Five Principles of the Constitution

Explore These Questions
- What are the five basic principles of the Constitution?
- Why do people adopt a system of representative government?
- How did the framers of the Constitution try to strike a balance between too much and too little government?

Define
- popular sovereignty
- representative government
- bill
- veto
- unconstitutional
- override

In 1787, when American leaders were struggling to create the new Constitution, every government in Europe was a monarchy. In most cases, a king or queen made, enforced, and interpreted the laws. Many European rulers would have agreed with Louis XIV, an earlier king of France. *"L'état, c'est moi,"* declared Louis. "I am the state."

Poster urging Americans to vote

The framers of the Constitution knew they had to set up a strong government. At the same time, they sought to keep power from falling into the hands of a privileged few. To achieve this delicate balance, they rested the Constitution on five basic principles: popular sovereignty, limited government, federalism, separation of powers, and checks and balances.

The People Rule

The first three words of the Constitution, "We the people," express the principle of **popular sovereignty.** According to this principle, the people hold the final authority in government.

The Constitution is a contract between the American people and their government. In it, the people grant the government the powers it needs to achieve its goals. At the same time, they limit the power of government by spelling out what the government may not do.

In a large society, not all citizens can take part directly in government. Instead, they exercise their ruling power indirectly by electing public officials to make laws and other decisions for them. This system is called **representative government.**

The people elect public officials by voting in free and frequent elections. Americans today have the constitutional right to vote for members of the House of Representatives (Article 1, Section 2) and for members of the Senate (Amendment 17). The people also elect the members of the electoral college, who, in turn, choose the President (Article 2, Section 1).

The right to vote has been gradually expanded over time. When the Constitution was ratified, only white men over age 21 who owned property could vote. Over the years, other Americans have won the right to vote. Today, all citizens are eligible to vote at the age of 18.

Limited Government

The framers of the Constitution had lived under the harsh rule of the British king. They feared tyranny, or cruel and unjust government. However, the failures of the Articles of Confederation made it clear that the national government had to be strong. How could the framers strike a balance between too much government and too little?

★ Background ★
Recent Scholarship

More than just a government? In *One United People: The Federalist Papers and the National Idea,* Edward Millican argues that proponents for ratification of the Constitution in 1787 were also setting forth the principles of the modern nation—people of shared culture living in their own state. Millican suggests that these American leaders helped to define the nation-state in an age when people were expected to be loyal to monarchs rather than to nations.

The answer was limited government. According to this principle, the government has only the powers that the people grant it. The Constitution clearly states the powers of the national government. It also states what powers the government does not have.

Guarantees of liberty

The most important limits on government are set out in the Bill of Rights. It guarantees that the government may not take away the individual freedoms of the people. These liberties include freedom of speech, freedom of the press, and freedom of religion.

The Ninth Amendment goes beyond these specific guarantees. It states that the people have rights that are not listed in the Constitution. The Tenth Amendment gives the states or the people any powers not formally granted by the Constitution to the national government.

Federalism

The framers of the Constitution created a strong central government. Yet they also wanted the states to retain much of their power. Like most Americans, they believed that state governments would best understand the special needs and concerns of their citizens. As one defender of the Constitution stated in 1788:

> “The two governments act in different manners, and for different purposes—the general government in great national concerns, in which we are interested in common with other members of the Union; the state legislature in our mere local concerns.”

The principle of federalism divides power between the federal government and state governments. The federal government has the power to deal with national issues. The states have the power to meet local needs.

The Constitution delegates, or assigns, certain powers to the national government. Other powers are reserved, or left, to the states. Still other powers, sometimes called concurrent powers, are shared by the federal and state governments. The chart on page 202 shows how government powers are divided under federalism.

Powers of the states

The Constitution does not list the powers of the states. Instead, it says that all powers not specifically granted to the federal government are reserved to the states (Tenth Amendment). At the same time, it makes clear exactly what powers the states do not have (Article 1, Section 10).

In addition to the reserved powers, the Constitution makes several guarantees to the states. All states must be treated equally in matters of trade (Article 1, Section 9). Each state must respect the laws of other states (Article 4, Section 1). Perhaps most important, all states have representation in the national government.

State License Plates

Under federalism, each state makes its own traffic laws and issues its own drivers' licenses and car registrations. At the same time, a driver's license issued by one state is valid in every other state. ★ **Name two other powers reserved to the states.**

2 Explore

Ask students to read the section. For homework, have them research and report on the number of their state's electoral votes and how that number is determined.

3 Teach

Draw a chalkboard chart with 3 columns: Principle, Definition, Examples. Have students complete the chart for the Constitution's 5 principles. In class discussion based on the text information, make sure they consider what each principle means and how it operates.

4 Assess

To close the lesson, have students complete the section review. Or, have them work in small groups to write 10 key section facts on 10 slips of paper. When all groups are done, pair groups to play a "Jeopardy"-like game. Members will draw facts from the opposing group and create relevant questions.

Reading Actively

During Reading Have students find this statement on this page: "The principle of federalism divides power between the federal ... and state governments." Ask students to find supporting evidence for this statement while reading.

ANSWER

Possible answer: meet local needs, oversee education

FROM THE ARCHIVES OF AmericanHeritage®

How big an "evil"? To the patriot Tom Paine, even the best government was a "necessary evil." What would he think of today's large government, which was born of a revolution inspired by the cry for less government and more representation, but now needs more than 3 million civilians to function?

Source: Bernard A. Weisberger, "What Made the Government Grow," *American Heritage* magazine, September 1997.

Writing Actively

After Reading Have students play the part of a delegate to the Constitutional Convention. The delegate writes a letter to his family at home, in which he explains how the Convention has created a new plan of government that safeguards the nation from tyranny.

Chart Skills

ANSWERS **1. (a)** can veto laws **(b)** can declare acts of Congress unconstitutional **2.** Possible answer: As a body of elected representatives, Congress was seen to express the will of the people.

System of Checks and Balances

Executive Branch (President carries out laws)	**Checks on the Legislative Branch** Can propose laws; Can veto laws; Can call special sessions of Congress; Makes appointments; Negotiates foreign treaties	**Checks on the Judicial Branch** Appoints federal judges; Can grant pardons to federal offenders
Legislative Branch (Congress makes laws)	**Checks on the Executive Branch** Can override President's veto; Confirms executive appointments; Ratifies treaties; Can declare war; Appropriates money; Can impeach and remove President	**Checks on the Judicial Branch** Creates lower federal courts; Can impeach and remove judges; Can propose amendments to overrule judicial decisions; Approves appointments of federal judges
Judicial Branch (Supreme Court interprets laws)	**Check on the Executive Branch** Can declare executive actions unconstitutional	**Check on the Legislative Branch** Can declare acts of Congress unconstitutional

Chart Skills **Through the system of checks and balances, each branch of government controls the powers of the other two.**

1. **Comprehension** **(a)** Name one check the President has on Congress. **(b)** How can the Supreme Court check Congress?
2. **Critical Thinking** Why do you think the framers of the Constitution gave Congress so many checks on the power of the President?

The "law of the land"

Federalism creates a working partnership between the national government and the state governments. However, when a dispute arises between them, there is no doubt where the final authority lies. The Constitution is the "supreme law of the land" (Article 6, Section 2). Only federal courts can settle the dispute.

Separation of Powers

The framers wanted to prevent the abuse of power by one person or group. To do so, the Constitution divides the national government into three branches: the legislative, the executive, and the judicial. Each branch has its own powers and responsibilities. This division of the national government is known as separation of powers.

Article 1 of the Constitution sets up the legislative branch. This branch, called Congress, makes the laws. Congress has two houses: the House of Representatives and the Senate. Its many powers include the power to tax, to coin money, and to declare war.

Article 2 describes the executive branch, which carries out the laws. The President heads the executive branch and appoints officials to help carry out the duties of the office.

★ Customized Instruction ★
Auditory Learners

Taping and interpreting the Constitution Divide the class into eight groups and assign each group one of these constitutional provisions: Article 1, Section 2; Article 1, Section 9; Article 1, Section 10; Article 2, Section 1; Article 4, Section 1; Article 6, Section 2; Amendment 1; Amendments 9 and 10. Ask each group to choose one member to read and tape-record its passage exactly as written. Other group members will then discuss and record in informal language what the provision means. Refer students to the annotated Constitution in the Reference Section. Have them use information in the section or library resources as they make their interpretations. (*average*) LL T

Resource Directory

Teaching Resources
Unit 2/Chapter 8
- Map Mystery: Shifting Power in the House, p. 36
- Section 2 Quiz, p. 40

Citizenship for Life
- Civics Worksheet 2, p. 2
- Constitution Worksheets 1–5, pp. 7–16

Article 3 creates the Supreme Court to head the judicial branch. The Supreme Court interprets and explains laws. Congress may set up lower courts as needed.

Checks and Balances

To prevent one branch of government from gaining too much power, the Constitution sets up a system of checks and balances. Each branch can check, or control, the power of the other two branches. (See the chart on page 220.)

Checks on Congress

Congress has the power to pass **bills,** or proposed laws. However, the President can influence the lawmaking process by proposing new bills or by pushing members of Congress to vote for or against a bill. The President can also check Congress by **vetoing,** or rejecting, a bill. The vetoed bill then goes back to Congress.

The Supreme Court has the power to rule whether a law is **unconstitutional,** or not permitted by the Constitution. The power to declare laws unconstitutional is one check the Supreme Court has on Congress. Any law declared unconstitutional by the Court cannot take effect.

Checks on the President

Congress has several checks on the powers of the President. For example, the President is commander in chief of the armed forces, but only Congress has the power to declare war. In addition, the President has the power to make treaties with foreign nations. However, the Senate must ratify all treaties.

Congress may also check the President by **overriding,** or setting aside, a presidential veto. In this way, a bill can become a law without the President's signature. Two thirds of each house must vote to override a veto. The Supreme Court can also check the President by declaring that an act of the President is unconstitutional.

Checks on the courts

Both the President and Congress have several checks on the power of the judicial branch. The President appoints all federal judges, while the Senate must approve the President's court appointments. In addition, Congress has the power to remove federal judges from office if they are found guilty of wrongdoing. Congress may also propose a constitutional amendment to overrule a judicial decision.

★ Section 2 Review ★

Recall

1. **Define** (a) popular sovereignty, (b) representative government, (c) bill, (d) veto, (e) unconstitutional, (f) override.

Comprehension

2. (a) Identify the five basic principles of the Constitution. (b) Describe two of them.
3. (a) Explain how representative government works. (b) Why do people in a democracy adopt this system?
4. (a) Why did the framers of the Constitution set up three branches of government? (b) How does the Constitution prevent any branch from becoming too powerful?

Critical Thinking and Writing

5. **Synthesizing Information** How are the principles of popular sovereignty and limited government related?
6. **Analyzing Ideas** Explain the following statement: The Constitution sets up a government of laws, not of people.

Activity **Making a Chart** Working with a partner or your class, create a chart that gives examples of ways in which the five basic principles of the Constitution protect you and your community.

★ Activity ★ Cooperative Learning

Debating democratic systems Like the U.S., Canada is a democracy—but with differences. Have small groups research Canada's confederation and parliamentary government. Tell half the groups to find advantages of the Canadian over the U.S. system, the rest disadvantages. In a series of exchanges, each group can debate an opposing group. *(challenging)*

★ Section 2 Review ★

ANSWERS

1. (a)–(b) p. 218, **(c)–(f)** p. 221

2. (a) popular sovereignty, limited government, federalism, separation of powers, checks and balances **(b)** Possible answers: Popular sovereignty: the people hold the final authority in government. Federalism divides power between the state and federal governments.

3. (a) People elect representatives to make laws for them. **(b)** The population is too large for everyone to take part directly in government.

4. (a) to prevent one branch's abuse of power **(b)** by setting up a system of checks and balances

5. Possible answers: The people are the source of power behind government; limited government ensures that government never robs the people of that power.

6. Possible answers: Government must operate within the Constitution and the law, and its officials and all people must obey the law.

Activity

Guided Instruction
Have students begin by thinking about what might happen if these principles did not underlie American government. Ask: "What might happen if the executive and judicial branches were combined?"

ASSESSMENT See the rubrics in the Alternative Assessment booklet in the Teaching Resources.

Section 3
A Living Document

LESSON PLAN

Objectives

★ Describe the formal process for changing the Constitution.
★ Explain the purpose of the Bill of Rights.
★ Identify informal changes that have been made to the Constitution.

1 Engage

Warm Up Write on the chalkboard: "Reasonable people can disagree." Discuss with students how this concept can apply to constitutional law and sometimes lead to battles over the interpretation of the Constitution.

Activating Prior Knowledge Ask students to create a graphic organizer around the concept "Equality in the United States." Have them enter as many examples as they can, including both negative and positive ones.

Reading Actively

Before Reading Have students draw a vertical line on a sheet of paper to divide it into 2 columns. Have them identify the 2 types of constitutional changes: Formal Changes to the Constitution and Informal Changes. Have them label each column on their papers with one type of change and jot down notes in the appropriate column as they read.

RESOURCE DIRECTORY

Teaching Resources
Lesson Planner, p. 33
Citizenship for Life
• Civics Worksheets 3–4, pp. 3–6
• Constitution Worksheet 6, p. 17

3 A Living Document

As You Read

Explore These Questions
- What is the formal process for changing the Constitution?
- What is the purpose of the Bill of Rights?
- What informal changes have been made to the Constitution?

Define
- amendment
- precedent
- Cabinet
- judicial review

Identify
- First Amendment
- Fourth Amendment
- Sixth Amendment
- Elastic Clause
- Commerce Clause

SETTING the Scene The framers of the Constitution realized that the nation would grow and change. With this in mind, they created a living Constitution—one that could be altered and improved to meet new conditions and challenges as they arose. As George Washington commented:

> "I do not think we are more inspired, have more wisdom, or possess more virtue than those who will come after us."

Formal Changes to the Constitution

The framers spelled out a process for making **amendments,** or formal written changes, to the Constitution. Amending the Constitution is not easy, however. It requires two difficult steps: proposal and ratification. (See the chart on page 223.)

Proposing an amendment

Article 5 describes two methods for proposing amendments. Two thirds of each house of Congress can vote to propose an amendment. Or two thirds of the state legislatures can demand that Congress summon a national "convention for proposing amendments."

So far, only the first method—a vote by Congress—has been used. As experts have pointed out, the Constitution does not give guidelines for a national convention. Who should set the agenda? How should delegates be selected? Such questions probably would cause much delay and confusion.

Ratifying an amendment

Article 5 also outlines two methods of ratifying a proposed amendment. Either three fourths of the state legislatures or three fourths of the states meeting in special conventions must approve the amendment. Congress decides which method of ratification to use.

So far, only the Twenty-first Amendment was ratified by state conventions. All other amendments were ratified by state legislatures. In recent years, Congress has set a time limit for ratification. The limit today is seven years, but it may be extended.

The 27 Amendments

As you can see, the amendment process is a difficult one. Since 1789, more than 9,000 amendments have been introduced in Congress. Yet, only 27 amendments have been ratified!

The Bill of Rights

The original Constitution did not list basic freedoms of the people. In fact, several states refused to ratify the Constitution until they were promised that a bill of rights would be added. Those states wanted to ensure that the national government would not be able to take away people's basic freedoms.

The Bill of Rights, the first 10 amendments to the Constitution, was ratified in 1791. (See the chart on page 215.)

★ *Customized Instruction* ★

Visual Learners

Charting the amendment process Have students collaborate in researching and illustrating the history of any amendment ratified after the Bill of Rights. Some students may be interested in researching the ERA, or Equal Rights Amendment, which was not ratified. Divide the class into groups and assign each group a different amendment. Explain that each group should determine when and how its amendment was introduced, why it was proposed, how long it took to win ratification, and how ratification—or failure to be ratified—affected the nation. Groups should present their findings as an illustrated graphic organizer. You may wish to display students' work around the classroom. (*challenging*) T

You will recognize many of the freedoms in the Bill of Rights. The **First Amendment** protects your right to worship and speak freely and to hold peaceful meetings. The **Fourth Amendment** protects you from "unreasonable" search and seizure of your home and property. The **Sixth Amendment** guarantees you the right to a trial by jury.

The protections of the Bill of Rights extend into many areas of your life. Suppose that you sent a letter to a newspaper criticizing the governor. Without the First Amendment protection of free speech, the governor might order your arrest. Without the Sixth Amendment, you might even be imprisoned for years without a trial.

Amendments 11 through 27

Only 17 amendments have been ratified since 1791. Several of these amendments reflect changing ideas about equality.

Amendments 13 through 15—the so-called Civil War amendments—were passed to protect the rights of former slaves. The Thirteenth Amendment ended slavery. The Fourteenth Amendment guaranteed citizenship and constitutional rights to African Americans. The Fifteenth Amendment guaranteed African Americans the right to vote.

Equality was also the goal of two later amendments. The Nineteenth Amendment gave women the right to vote. The Twenty-sixth Amendment set age 18 as the minimum voting age. The chart on page 215 lists Amendments 11 through 27. For more information about the amendments, refer to the page numbers shown on the chart.

Informal Changes

The language of the Constitution provides a general outline rather than specific details about the national government. Over time, this flexible language has allowed the government to adapt to the changing needs of the nation.

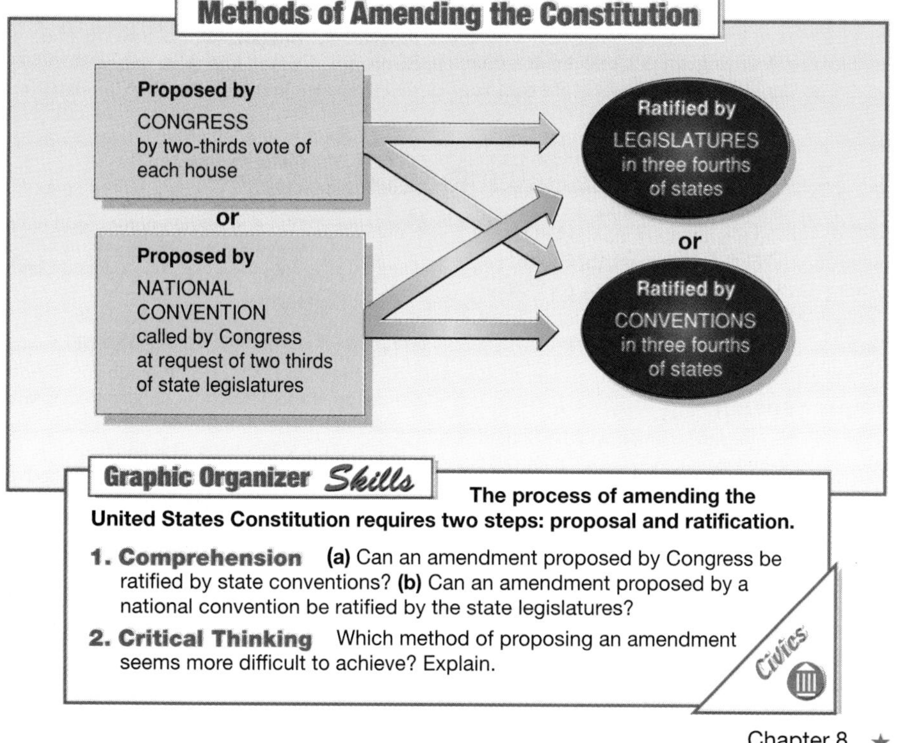

Graphic Organizer *Skills* The process of amending the United States Constitution requires two steps: proposal and ratification.

1. **Comprehension** **(a)** Can an amendment proposed by Congress be ratified by state conventions? **(b)** Can an amendment proposed by a national convention be ratified by the state legislatures?
2. **Critical Thinking** Which method of proposing an amendment seems more difficult to achieve? Explain.

Civics

2 Explore

Ask students to read the section. For homework, have them research the life and work of Justice Oliver Wendell Holmes. Tell them to look for famous quotations by or about Holmes to share with the class.

3 Teach

Review the 27 amendments in the chart on p. 215 and in the annotated Constitution in the Reference Section. Then ask students to list ways in which American life today might differ if the Constitution couldn't be amended. Ask: "Why were the framers wise to include an amendment process? Do you think the Constitution is keeping up with the times? Why or why not?"

4 Assess

To close the lesson, have students complete the section review. As an alternative, have them write an essay on how formal and informal changes are made to the Constitution.

★ ★ ★ ★ ★ ★ ★ ★ ★ ★ ★ ★ ★ ★ ★ ★ ★ ★

Writing Actively

After Reading Say: "Suppose an amendment to remove the Elastic and Commerce clauses has been proposed." Tell students to design and write a campaign advertisement in defense of each clause.

Graphic Organizer *Skills*

ANSWERS **1. (a)–(b)** yes
2. Possible answer: National Convention: It requires an extra step.

★ *Activity* ★

Connections With Civics

Creating a rights bulletin board Have students work in groups to find the Bill of Rights operating in their community today. Have them create their own illustrations, take photographs, and write their own descriptions to produce a bulletin board display entitled "The Bill of Rights Lives in Our Hometown." (*average*) T

Technology

★ Section 3 Review ★

ANSWERS

1. (a)–(c) p. 223, **(d)–(e)** p. 224

2. (a) p. 222, **(b)–(d)** p. 224

3. Proposal by two thirds of Congress or by a national convention called by Congress at the request of two thirds of state legislatures; ratified by three fourths of state legislatures or state conventions.

4. Possible answers: freedom of speech, religion, assembly; right to trial by jury

5. (a) appointed a Cabinet **(b)** expanded size and power of the executive branch to carry out economic programs

6. Possible answer: The formal process is long and difficult. Informal changes are easier to make or undo.

7. Possible answer: Yes, because the difficult amendment process can be a problem when rapid change is needed. No, because the current system ensures that amendments are carefully considered before they are enacted.

Activity

Guided Instruction
Have students review the description of these amendments in this section and in the annotated Constitution in the Reference Section. Ask for volunteers to share their essays with the class.

ASSESSMENT See the rubrics in the Alternative Assessment booklet in the Teaching Resources.

RESOURCE DIRECTORY

Teaching Resources
Lesson Planner, p. 34
Unit 2/Chapter 8
• Section 3 Quiz, p. 41

New powers for Congress

The framers knew that they could not foresee the future. To deal with this problem, Article 1, Section 8, Clause 18, gives Congress the power to make all laws that shall be "necessary and proper" to carry out the powers of the national government. This so-called **Elastic Clause** has allowed Congress to stretch its power to pass laws.

Still another clause of the Constitution has allowed Congress to extend its powers. Article 1, Section 8, Clause 3, gives Congress the power to "regulate" trade with other nations and between the states.

Armed with the **Commerce Clause** and the Elastic Clause, Congress has been able to keep pace with change. For example, it has passed laws that regulate the airline industry, television, nuclear energy, and genetic engineering.

A more powerful executive

The Constitution does not describe in detail the powers of the President. Some Presidents, however, have taken actions or made decisions that set a **precedent,** or example, for later Presidents.

George Washington set one such precedent. The Constitution does not state that the President may appoint a **Cabinet,** or group of close advisers. President Washington assumed the power to do so on his own. Every President since then has followed his lead.

In national emergencies, Presidents have expanded their constitutional role. During the Great Depression, President Franklin Roosevelt expanded the size and power of the executive branch to propose and carry out programs that would restore the national economy.

A broader role for the judiciary

The Supreme Court can decide whether acts of a President or laws passed by Congress are unconstitutional. This power is known as **judicial review.**

The Constitution does not list judicial review as a power of the judicial branch. Like the unstated powers of the President, judicial review is implied in the words and structure of the Constitution. Article 3, Section 2, states that the Supreme Court has the right to hear "all cases . . . arising under this Constitution." In the case of *Marbury* v. *Madison,* an early Supreme Court decision interpreted Article 3, Section 2, to mean that the Supreme Court has the right to decide whether any law violates the Constitution.

★ Section 3 Review ★

Recall

1. **Identify** **(a)** First Amendment, **(b)** Fourth Amendment, **(c)** Sixth Amendment, **(d)** Elastic Clause, **(e)** Commerce Clause.
2. **Define** **(a)** amendment, **(b)** precedent, **(c)** Cabinet, **(d)** judicial review.

Comprehension

3. Describe the process for amending the United States Constitution.
4. List four rights protected by the Bill of Rights.
5. **(a)** How did George Washington expand the powers of the President? **(b)** How did Franklin Roosevelt expand the President's powers during the Great Depression?

Critical Thinking and Writing

6. **Drawing Conclusions** Why do you think there have been more informal changes than formal changes to the Constitution?
7. **Defending a Position** Do you think the process of amending the Constitution should be made simpler? Defend your position.

Activity **Writing an Essay** Choose one of the amendments described in this section. In a brief essay, describe your thoughts and feelings about that amendment and what it means to you.

★ *Background* ★

Our Diverse Nation

Framers search past and present while planning for future The framers of the Constitution drew on other cultures and historical experiences as they created the new government for the United States. They looked to the ancient Roman Republic as a model for representative government. (James Madison had studied the political system of ancient Rome.) The League of the Iroquois, some historians believe, may have been one model for the Constitution's federal system. (Benjamin Franklin had studied Native American cultures closely.)

The National Government at Work

As You Read

Explore These Questions
- What are the roles of Congress?
- What jobs does the President do?
- How is the federal court system organized?

Define
- appropriate
- standing committee
- joint committee
- impeach
- constituent
- executive agreement
- appeal
- opinion
- dissenting opinion

Identify
- House of Representatives
- Senate
- Supreme Court

The Congressional Record *reports events in Congress.* ➤

SETTING the Scene On October 10, 1788, the last Congress under the Articles of Confederation transacted its final business. By September of the following year, the Presidential electors had chosen George Washington as the first President of the United States, the first Congress under the Constitution had met in New York City, and the Federal Judiciary Act had provided for the organization of the United States Supreme Court. The government of the United States, as set up by the Constitution, was in place.

More than 200 years later, Americans still live under this three-branched government set up by the Constitution. Each branch has its own clearly defined powers. Together, they provide us with a government of laws.

The Legislative Branch

Congress, the legislative branch of government, is made up of two houses: the House of Representatives and the Senate. Together, the two houses have the power to make the laws that govern all 50 states. At the same time, the states have a say in making those laws.

Two houses of Congress

The larger house, the **House of Representatives,** currently seats 435 members. The number of representatives for each state is determined according to that state's population. The more people who live in a state, the greater its number of representatives. Each state, however, is guaranteed at least one representative.*

Representatives serve for two-year terms. As a result, the entire House is up for election every even-numbered year. Congressional terms are numbered consecutively. The Congress that served from 1789 to 1791 is known as the First Congress. The Congress serving from 1999 to 2001 is the One Hundred Sixth Congress.

The **Senate,** the smaller house, has 100 members. Each state, no matter how large or small its population, has two senators. Senators serve for six-year terms. The terms are staggered, however. As a result, one third of the Senate are up for election every two years.

Powers of Congress

The chief job of Congress is to make the nation's laws. A new law first appears as a

*Guam, the Virgin Islands, American Samoa, and Washington, D.C., each elect a delegate to the House, while Puerto Rico elects a resident commissioner. However, these delegates are not voting members of the House.

★ Background ★

Did You Know?

An international beacon? Since the late 1700s, the Constitution has served as a model for other nations. Guided by U.S. occupation forces in 1947, Japan adopted a constitution with some features similar to ours. Brazil and other Latin American countries studied the U.S. Constitution when writing their own constitutions after winning independence in the 1800s.

Section 4 The National Government at Work

LESSON PLAN

Objectives

★ Define the roles of Congress.

★ Describe the jobs the President does.

★ Explain how the federal court system is organized.

1 Engage

Warm Up Write these words on the chalkboard and have students complete the sentence: "If I were President, I would . . ." Discuss student responses by asking: "Would the Constitution permit your actions?" and "Would other government branches cooperate?"

Activating Prior Knowledge Write on the chalkboard in random order the names of the current President, Vice President, senators and representatives from your state, and the Chief Justice of the Supreme Court. Have students identify each person and classify him or her as a member of the legislative, executive, or judicial branch.

Reading Actively

Before Reading Have students examine each graphic in this section. Ask them to identify the branch of government associated with each photo and each part of the graphic organizers.

2 Explore

Ask students to read the section. For a homework assignment, have them find out who is the current Speaker of the House, Senate majority leader, and Senate President *pro tem* and report on the duties of each office.

3 Teach

Have students brainstorm and then select one issue related to school life that they think should be addressed. Ask them to suppose the school is a separate nation with a government like that of the U.S. in structure and powers. Divide the class into three groups and assign each group the role of one branch of government. Have each group prepare and present a report explaining its powers and how it would work with the other branches to address the issue before the school.

4 Assess

To close the lesson, have students complete the section review. As an alternative, have students write a journal entry describing a day in the official life of each of the following: President of the U.S., a U.S. Senator, a Supreme Court Justice.

★ ★

Chart Skills

ANSWERS **1. (a)** 30, 25 **(b)** for life **2.** The Vice President takes over if anything happens to the President and so must meet the same requirements.

Resource Directory

Teaching Resources
Unit 2/Chapter 8
- Practice Your Skills: Reading a Flow Chart, p. 34

Citizenship for Life
- Constitution Worksheets 8–16, pp. 23–28

Federal Officeholders

Office	Number	Term	Selection	Requirements
Representative	At least 1 per state; based on population	2 years	Elected by voters of congressional district	Age 25 or over Citizen for 7 years Resident of state in which elected
Senator	2 per state	6 years	Original Constitution—elected by state legislature Amendment 17—elected by voters	Age 30 or over Citizen for 9 years Resident of state in which elected
President and Vice President	1	4 years	Elected by electoral college	Age 35 or over Natural-born citizen Resident of U.S. for 14 years
Supreme Court Justice	9	Life	Appointed by President	No requirements in Constitution

Chart Skills **The Constitution details the number, length of term, method of selection, and requirements for officeholders in the three branches of government.**

1. Comprehension **(a)** At what age can you be elected to the Senate? The House of Representatives? **(b)** How long may a Supreme Court Justice remain in office?

2. Critical Thinking Why do you think the requirements for President and Vice President are the same?

Civics

proposal called a bill. The bill must be passed by both houses of Congress and signed by the President to become law. The chart on page 227 shows the steps a bill must pass through before becoming a law.

Congress has another equally important power. It decides what laws or programs will receive funds. The federal government cannot spend money on any program unless Congress **appropriates** it, or sets it aside for a special purpose. In this way, Congress controls how much money the government spends, whether for military aircraft, national highways, or school lunches.

Congressional committees

During the first session of Congress, 31 bills were proposed by both houses. Today, thousands of bills are introduced every year in Congress. Clearly, it would be impossible for each member of Congress to study and make recommendations about every bill. This job is reserved for committees.

The House of Representatives and the Senate each have **standing committees.** These are permanent committees assigned to study specific issues such as agriculture, labor, and energy. They are often broken up into subcommittees that examine certain problems in depth.

Congress may sometimes create a **joint committee,** or committees that include both House and Senate members. One of the most important kinds of joint committee is the conference committee. Its task is to settle differences between the House and the Senate versions of the same bill. Members of a conference committee try to find a middle ground and to agree on the language of the bill. Compromise is often difficult.

★ Customized Instruction ★

English Language Learners

Reinforcing civics vocabulary and concepts Many civics-related terms and concepts may be especially difficult for English language learners to incorporate into their vocabulary. To build understanding of these words, you might arrange small-group sessions in which students define each term in their own words and create sentences using each in an everyday context. Have students begin this process with the Define terms for this section. As they read the section, ask ELL students to list any additional terms that cause confusion and bring their lists to follow-up small-group sessions. (*basic*) ELL

Skills
FOR LIFE

Critical Thinking | Managing Information | Communication | Maps, Charts, and Graphs

Reading a Flowchart

How Will I Use This Skill ?

A flowchart is a type of graphic organizer. It uses boxes and arrows to guide you step by step through a development or process. Learning to read a flowchart can help you understand even the most complicated processes—from programming a VCR to running for public office.

LEARN the Skill

1. Identify the process described by the flowchart.
2. Locate the starting point of the process. (This is the box with no arrow leading toward it.) Some flowcharts may have more than one starting point, since more than one part of a process is being tracked to the end point.
3. Follow the steps of the process by following the arrows to the end point.

PRACTICE the Skill

1. What process does the flowchart below describe?
2. (a) Where can a bill be introduced? (b) Why are there two starting points on this flowchart?
3. (a) What happens to a bill after it is introduced? (b) At what point in the process do the work of the Senate and the House come together? (c) What happens next?

APPLY the Skill

Create a flowchart to describe the steps of a process you know well. You might show how to play a game, how to repair something, or how to prepare a meal. Show your flowchart to some friends. See if they can understand the process by looking at your chart.

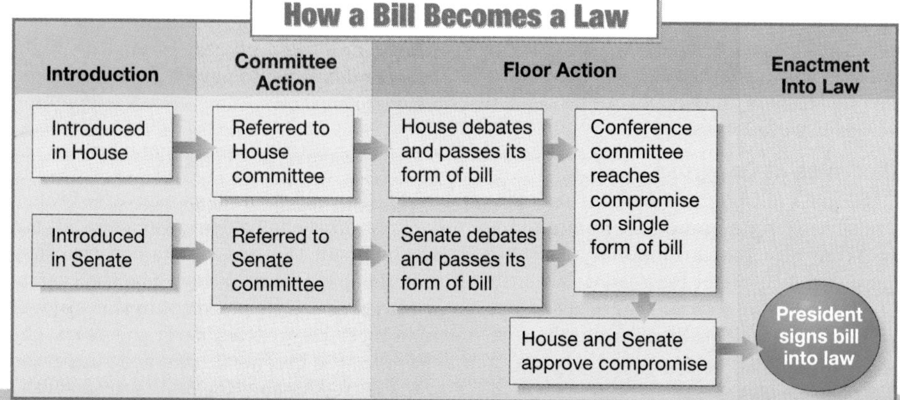
How a Bill Becomes a Law
Introduction
Committee Action
Floor Action
Enactment Into Law
Introduced in House
Referred to House committee
House debates and passes its form of bill
Introduced in Senate
Referred to Senate committee
Senate debates and passes its form of bill
Conference committee reaches compromise on single form of bill
House and Senate approve compromise
President signs bill into law

Skills
FOR LIFE

PRACTICE the Skill ANSWERS

1. how a bill gets made into a law
2. **(a)** in the House or Senate **(b)** because a bill can start in either the House or Senate
3. **(a)** It is referred to a committee. **(b)** after a bill has been passed in both the House and Senate **(c)** If necessary, a conference committee compromises on a single form of the bill and both houses approve it.

APPLY the Skill

Guided Instruction

Encourage students to include all steps in the process. Have them suppose that the people reading their final flowchart have never seen or heard of the process they are describing.

ASSESSMENT See the rubrics in the Alternative Assessment booklet in the Teaching Resources.

FROM THE ARCHIVES OF AmericanHeritage®

History in action To gain a behind-the-scenes understanding of government, people can visit Congress while it is in session in Washington, D.C. Visitors must first get a pass from their congressional representatives. Once they are admitted to the visitors' gallery, they can observe lawmakers debating contemporary issues.

Source: American Heritage editors, "History Happened Here: The Big Game," *American Heritage* magazine, November 1992.

American Heritage
M A G A Z I N E

The United States Capitol Building To learn more about the U.S. Capitol building on the Internet, go to www.aoc.gov/homepage.htm.

American Heritage
M A G A Z I N E

HISTORY HAPPENED HERE

◄ The Capitol Building in Washington, D.C.

The United States Capitol Building

History is still happening at the Capitol Building. Since November 1800, the Capitol has been the meeting place of the United States Congress. Each year, millions of people visit the parts of the Capitol open to the public. If you have a pass from your representative or senator, you can even visit the House or Senate chambers and watch lawmakers in action. Funeral ceremonies for Presidents and other outstanding Americans are held in the Great Rotunda under the famous Capitol dome.

★ ***To learn more about this historic site, write:*** *The Capitol, Washington, DC 19106.*

Passing a bill requires the cooperation of many individuals. For example, a recent trade bill was 1,000 pages long. It required the efforts of 200 members of Congress, working in 17 subcommittees, to get it passed. Most bills introduced in Congress do not meet with such success. In fact, more than 90 percent of all the bills introduced are defeated in committees.

Other roles of Congress

Members of Congress have duties other than serving on committees and making laws. They also guard the public trust. For example, the House of Representatives can **impeach,** or bring a formal charge of wrongdoing against, the President or another federal official. The Senate acts as a court to try the accused. Congress also acts as a "watchdog" by supervising the way the executive branch carries out the laws.

Members of Congress must also respond to the special needs of their states. Responsible representatives and senators must remember their **constituents,** or the people who elected them. They do this by supporting bills that have a direct impact on the people "back home." Such bills might include promoting new post offices, improving highways, and helping to pay for local education programs.

The Executive Branch

The framers created an executive branch to carry out the laws. However, they left out details about the President's powers. They thought that Congress would be the central branch of government except in times of war and other emergencies. Over the years, the powers of the President have been increased or decreased, depending on the needs of the time. Still, Americans expect the President to fill certain roles.

★ *Background* ★

Recent Scholarship

Is it time to trash the Constitution? In his book *The Frozen Republic: How the Constitution Is Paralyzing Democracy,* author Daniel Lazare claims that the Constitution is outdated. He cites the slow-moving committee system in Congress among other obstacles to democratic government. Further, Lazare blames overlapping responsibilities between federal and local law enforcement agencies for slow progress in fighting crime. An opponent of Lazare's view notes that the Constitution makes no mention of congressional committees or local law enforcement agencies and that, therefore, it is the will of the people, not the Constitution, that allows these practices. T

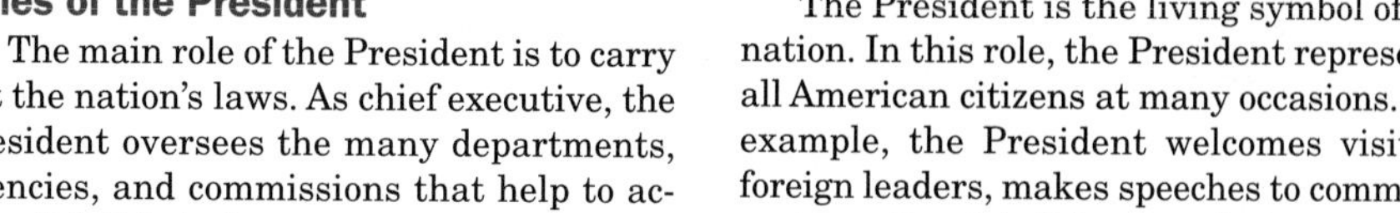

Roles of the President

The main role of the President is to carry out the nation's laws. As chief executive, the President oversees the many departments, agencies, and commissions that help to accomplish this task.

The President directs the nation's foreign policy. Three important powers allow the President to influence relations with other countries. They are the powers to appoint ambassadors, make treaties, and enter into **executive agreements.** Executive agreements are informal agreements with other heads of state, usually dealing with trade. Unlike treaties, they do not require Senate approval.

The President is the highest-ranking officer in the armed forces. As commander in chief, the President can appoint and remove top military commanders. The President may also use the armed forces to deal with crises both at home and abroad. (However, only Congress has the power to declare war on another country.)

As the nation's chief legislator, the President suggests new laws and works for their passage. In this role, the President often meets with members of Congress to win their support. Sometimes, the President campaigns for public support through television or radio speeches and press conferences. The President also can use persuasion to oppose a bill. In this case, however, the President's most powerful weapon is the power to veto a bill.

The President is the living symbol of the nation. In this role, the President represents all American citizens at many occasions. For example, the President welcomes visiting foreign leaders, makes speeches to commemorate national holidays, and gives medals to national heroes. (See the photograph on page 216.)

The American people also see the President as the chief symbol of the condition of the nation, even though this responsibility is shared with Congress and the judiciary. In describing this situation, former President Jimmy Carter declared that "When things go bad you get entirely too much blame," and "when things go good, you get entirely too much credit."

Executive agencies and departments

The nation's laws cover a broad range of concerns—defense, housing, crime, and pollution, to name a few. To carry out these laws and to perform other duties, the President needs the help of millions of government workers and assistants.

Presidents at Work

Under the Constitution, the President commands the armed forces and directs foreign policy. At left, President Bill Clinton meets with Tony Blair, prime minister of Great Britain. Above, President George Bush visits American troops in Saudi Arabia. ★ **Describe two other roles of the President.**

Reading Actively

During Reading After students read the subsection on the Roles of the President, have them create a graphic organizer illustrating the different actions Presidents can take on legislation they favor or oppose.

ANSWER

Possible answers: carries out the nation's laws, appoints ambassadors, negotiates treaties, suggests new laws

Chapter 8 ★ 229

ANSWER
Possible answers: cases regarding personal rights or interpretations of the law; disputes between states

Writing Actively

After Reading Tell students that thousands of books have been written about how the American government operates. Have students create five book titles, each title suggesting an aspect of the federal government they would like to study further. Remind them to include each of the three branches at least once in their list of titles.

The Supreme Court

Here, the 1998 Justices of the Supreme Court pose for an annual photograph. Standing, left to right, are Ruth Bader Ginsburg, David Souter, Clarence Thomas, and Stephen Breyer. Sitting, left to right, are Antonin Scalia, John Paul Stevens, Chief Justice William Rehnquist, Sandra Day O'Connor, and Anthony Kennedy.
★ **What kinds of cases does the Supreme Court hear?**

One group of assistants, the Executive Office, includes many agencies and individuals. They range from the Vice President to the Office of Management and Budget, which prepares the total budget of the United States.

The President's Cabinet, called secretaries, are the heads of executive departments. Today, the President relies on 14 executive departments—among them, the Departments of Defense, Commerce, Justice, Labor, and Energy. Each department has many concerns. For example, the Department of Agriculture deals with food quality, crop improvement, and nutrition. The Department of Transportation establishes rules for speed limits, automobile exhaust systems, and highway and vehicle safety.

More than 30 independent executive agencies also help the President carry out duties. For example, the Central Intelligence Agency (CIA) provides the President with secret information about the world's trouble spots. The National Aeronautics and Space Administration (NASA) is in charge of the nation's space program.

Eleven independent regulatory commissions enforce national laws. They establish rules, rates, and standards for trade, business, science, and transportation. For example, the Federal Trade Commission (FTC) enforced the federal law banning "false or misleading advertising" by ruling that cigarettes may not be advertised as "kind" to your throat.

Finally, there are government corporations. There are at least 60 government corporations today. They include the United States Postal Service, the Tennessee Valley Authority, and Amtrak.

The Judicial Branch

Article 3 of the Constitution gives the judicial power of the United States to the Supreme Court and to lower courts that Congress may set up. Under the Judiciary Act of 1789, Congress created the system of federal courts that still operates today.

Lower courts

Most federal cases are first heard in the district courts. These courts are located in more than 90 districts around the country. Cases brought to these courts may involve matters of criminal law, such as kidnapping and murder, or matters of civil law, such as bankruptcy and divorce. In district courts, decisions are made by either a judge or a jury, which is a panel of citizens.

Every citizen has the right to **appeal** a decision, or ask that it be reviewed by a higher court. These higher courts of appeal are called circuit, or appellate, courts. The United States has 13 circuit courts of appeal.

Circuit courts operate differently from district courts. A panel of three judges re-

★ Activity ★
Connections With Civics

Interpreting the Constitution Direct students to the presidential oath of office found in Article 2, Section 1, Clause 8 of the Constitution. Have them write an interpretation of the oath, as a Supreme Court Justice might do. Encourage them to state the duties and powers the oath does (or does not) grant the President. *(average)*

RESOURCE DIRECTORY

Teaching Resources
Unit 2/Chapter 8
- Biography Flashcard: Sandra Day O'Connor, p. 38
- Section 4 Quiz, p. 42

views each case. The judges decide if rules of trial procedure were followed in the original trial. If errors did occur, the circuit court may reverse, or overturn, the original decision. Or it may send back the case to the district court for a new trial.

Supreme Court

The **Supreme Court** is the highest court in the United States. Americans depend upon the Supreme Court to settle disputes, interpret the law, and protect their guaranteed rights. The Court is made up of a Chief Justice and eight Associate Justices. The President appoints the Supreme Court Justices, but Congress must approve the appointments. In about one out of five cases, Congress rejects the President's appointment and a new nomination must be made. Appointments to the Supreme Court are for life.

Only two kinds of cases can begin in the Supreme Court. One kind involves disputes between states. The other involves foreign ambassadors. In other cases, the Supreme Court serves as a final court of appeals. It hears cases that have been tried and appealed as far as law permits in lower courts.

The Supreme Court hears only issues about the Constitution, federal law, or treaties. It selects only about 120 cases from the 4,000 or more requests it receives each year. Most of the cases involve laws written in unclear language. The Court must decide what each law means, whom it affects, and whether it is constitutional.

A Supreme Court decision rests on a simple majority vote of at least five Justices. A member of the majority writes an **opinion**, or official statement of the legal reasons for the Court's decision. Sometimes, a member of the minority strongly disagrees with the majority ruling. That Justice may write a **dissenting opinion**, explaining the reasons for the disagreement. Justice Oliver Wendell Holmes, Jr., wrote so many dissenting opinions that he became known as the "Great Dissenter."

Supreme Court decisions are final. There are no other courts of appeal. If Congress strongly disagrees with a Supreme Court decision, however, it can take other action. It can pass a modified version of the law that will meet the Court's objections. Congress can also propose an amendment to the Constitution.

★ Section 4 Review ★

Recall

1. **Identify** (a) House of Representatives, (b) Senate, (c) Supreme Court.
2. **Define** (a) appropriate, (b) standing committee, (c) joint committee, (d) impeach, (e) constituent, (f) executive agreement, (g) appeal, (h) opinion, (i) dissenting opinion.

Comprehension

3. What are the two most important powers of Congress?
4. (a) How does the President influence legislation? (b) What three powers enable the President to direct foreign policy?
5. (a) What is the role of circuit courts? (b) What is the role of the Supreme Court?

Critical Thinking and Writing

6. **Ranking** Review the subsection "Roles of the President." List the President's roles. Then rank the roles in order of importance. Be prepared to support your ranking.
7. **Analyzing Ideas** Why is it important for Congress to approve the President's choices for Supreme Court Justices?

Activity **Making a Diagram** Make a graphic organizer with three branches. Fill in the chart to show the roles of each branch of government and the smaller parts that make them up.

Internet Activity

The Supreme Court Direct students to a Web site Oyez, Oyez, Oyez, which contains a wide range of information about the Supreme Court (http://oyez.nwu.edu/). Have them browse the site, listing the areas they find or have them create a map of the site. Ask them to name a research topic they might be able to research by using this site. (*average*)

★ Section 4 Review ★

ANSWERS

1. **(a)** p. 225, **(b)** p. 225, **(c)** p. 231
2. **(a)–(c)** p. 226, **(d)–(e)** p. 228, **(f)** p. 229, **(g)** p. 230, **(h)–(i)** p. 231
3. make laws/appropriate money
4. **(a)** suggests laws and works for their passage; uses influence to stop a bill or vetoes it **(b)** appoints ambassadors; makes treaties; enters into executive agreements with other heads of state
5. **(a)** They review lower court decisions to ensure that the rules of trial procedure were followed. **(b)** It is the final court of appeals in cases involving the Constitution, federal law, or treaties.
6. Accept rankings that show thought and are well-supported.
7. Possible answer: Its approval, part of the system of checks and balances, is important because Justices are appointed for life.

Activity

Guided Instruction

Have students review the section, taking notes on the information needed. You may wish to have groups consult with one another to make sure their charts are complete. If possible, make a master chart on the chalkboard based on work of the entire class.

ASSESSMENT See the rubrics in the Alternative Assessment booklet in the Teaching Resources.

★ Section 5
Good Citizenship

LESSON PLAN

Objectives

★ Describe how the Bill of Rights was limited.

★ Explain how the Supreme Court used the Fourteenth Amendment to expand citizens' rights.

★ List citizens' rights and responsibilities.

1 Engage

Warm Up Write this sentence on the chalkboard: "Every right carries with it a responsibility." Ask students what the statement means and how it applies to specific rights.

Activating Prior Knowledge Ask students to recall a current or past issue debated in their community. Ask them how individuals or groups responded to resolve the issue. Discuss ways in which people were exercising rights and fulfilling responsibilities in this process.

Reading Actively

Before Reading Have students read the three main headings and turn each into a question. Tell them to look for the answers as they read the section.

2 Explore

Ask students to read the section. For a homework assignment, have them research and report on local elections in your community: how

RESOURCE DIRECTORY

Teaching Resources
Lesson Planner, p. 35
Citizenship for Life
• You Can Make a Difference Worksheets 1–11, pp. 39–60

5 Good Citizenship

As You Read

Explore These Questions
- How was the Bill of Rights limited?
- How did the Supreme Court use the Fourteenth Amendment to expand citizens' rights?
- What are the rights and responsibilities of citizens?

Define
- due process

Identify
- *Gideon* v. *Wainwright*

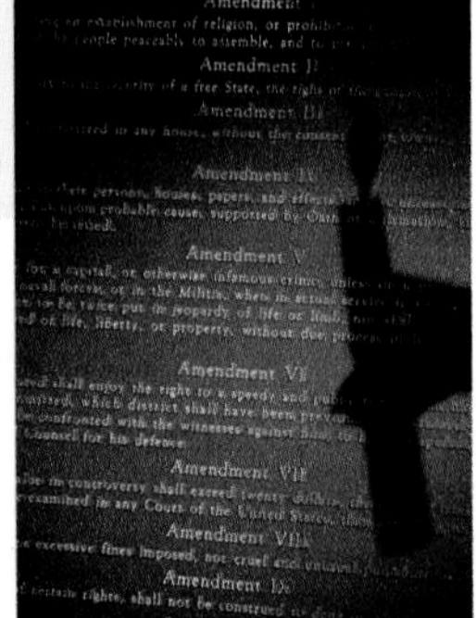

Plaque listing the Bill of Rights ➤

SETTING the Scene Americans first proclaimed their rights in the Declaration of Independence. In it, they declared boldly:

> ❝ All men are created equal; . . . they are endowed by their Creator with certain unalienable rights, that among these are life, liberty, and the pursuit of happiness. ❞

Since the birth of the nation, Americans have struggled to reach this ideal of basic rights for all. They have learned, however, that along with the rights of citizenship come responsibilities.

Citizens' Rights

The Constitution originally protected some individual rights by limiting government actions. For example, Article 6, Section 3, prevents the government from making religion a requirement for public service. Article 1, Section 9, prohibits Congress from passing a law punishing an act that was not illegal at the time it was committed.

Bill of Rights

Many Americans, however, demanded a more specific list of rights. In response, the first Congress drew up and the states ratified the Bill of Rights.

Still, the Bill of Rights applied only to the federal government. States were free to restrict or deny basic rights of many people, including women, African Americans, and Asian Americans. At times, the federal government also restricted rights through laws and court decisions.

Fourteenth Amendment

An amendment passed in 1868 paved the way for a major expansion of rights. The Fourteenth Amendment states that persons born or naturalized in the United States are citizens of both the nation and their state. No state may limit the rights of citizens or deny citizens **due process,** or a fair hearing or trial. States are also forbidden to deny citizens "equal protection of the laws."

Over the years, the Supreme Court has decided that the Fourteenth Amendment's guarantee of due process and equal protection includes rights listed in the Bill of Rights. States cannot deny citizens the protections of the Bill of Rights.

For example, in the 1960s, the Supreme Court ruled that due process includes the Sixth Amendment right to representation by a lawyer. The case of ***Gideon* v. *Wainwright*** involved a poor Florida man who had been convicted of breaking and entering. The judge hearing the case had refused the defendant's request for a lawyer. The Supreme Court ruled that a state court must appoint a lawyer for any defendant who cannot afford to hire one.

★ Customized Instruction ★
Introverted Learners

Creating a citizen's glossary Have students create an illustrated glossary of civics vocabulary, legal terms and decisions, and constitutional concepts. They may select their glossary entries from what they have read in this section, heard during class discussions, or found in outside sources. Have students collect and collate their glossaries to make pamphlets with appropriate titles and covers. Place the glossaries in the classroom resource center. Ask students to advertise the pamphlets with a poster board montage of newspaper and magazine clippings or photographs illustrating civic activities, especially local ones. (*average*) ELL T

What are basic rights?

As the Ninth Amendment states, the people have rights beyond those listed in the Constitution. Americans still strive to define these rights. Some people believe that a citizen's basic rights include the opportunity to get a good education and to find a job. Others argue that these rights are not guaranteed by the Constitution.

Citizens' Responsibilities

Like every citizen, you must do your part to safeguard your rights. At the same time, you must accept the civic responsibilities that are a part of living in a free and democratic society.

Know your rights

You cannot protect your rights unless you know what they are. Books, government pamphlets, and groups such as the League of Women Voters, the National Association for the Advancement of Colored People (NAACP), and the Legal Aid Society can give you information about your rights and the law.

You must also know the limits of your rights. A popular saying states, "Your right to swing your fist ends where my nose begins." As part of your civic responsibilities, you must respect the rights of others. After all, your rights are only as safe as your neighbor's. If you abuse or allow abuse of another citizen's rights, your own rights may be at risk someday.

Become involved

Good government depends on good leaders. Therefore, citizens have the responsibility to exercise their right to vote. A good citizen studies the candidates and the issues in order to make responsible choices.

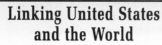

Linking United States and the World

United States

South Africa

Getting Out the Vote

Voting is both a right and a responsibility. Yet, many take this right for granted. In 1996, only 48.8 percent of Americans who were eligible to vote actually voted. In 1994, when South Africa's black majority won the right to vote for the first time (right), 86.9 percent of eligible voters cast their ballots. ★ **Why do you think South Africans were so eager to vote? What point is the cartoon on the left making?**

voters can register to vote, where the polling places are, what kinds of ballots are used, who serves as election judges, and what the judges' duties are.

3 Teach

Remind students that some Americans consider citizenship responsibilities a nuisance (for example, voting, staying informed, or serving on a jury). Divide the class into small groups. Have each group write and present a skit about a conflict between citizens who fulfill their responsibilities and those who do not. Conclude with a discussion on the meaning of citizenship.

4 Assess

To close the lesson, have students complete the section review. As an alternative, have them write newspaper editorials on voting rights and responsibilities. Tell students to use the illustrations on this page as a starting point for their editorials.

★ ★ ★ ★ ★ ★ ★ ★ ★ ★ ★ ★ ★ ★ ★ ★ ★

Linking United States and the World

ANSWER

South Africans were eager to exercise a right that had once been denied to them. The cartoon suggests that people criticize and complain about government but seldom use their civil powers, such as the vote, to bring about change.

★ *Background* ★

Did You Know?

Should patriotic Americans sing a new tune? Americans express their pride as citizens when they sing "The Star Spangled Banner" at various public gatherings. However, tone-deaf Francis Scott Key, who wrote the words in the 1800s, was no songwriter. Instead, Americans sang his lyrics to a popular British tune of the day, the tune we still use today.

Why Study *History?*

ANSWERS

1. (a) as service to one's community to help make it a better place **(b)** He had leftover food from the school cafeteria delivered to shelters and food banks. **2.** It could reduce costs because citizens would be taking on jobs without pay.

★*Activity*

Guided Instruction
Have students brainstorm a list of possible volunteer programs, including those already in operation. Encourage students to match a program to their community's needs. Their proposals should include a statement of goals, costs, and materials needed as well as setup procedures. Have the class consider the various proposals and possibly undertake one of them.

ASSESSMENT See the rubrics in the Alternative Assessment booklet in the Teaching Resources.

Writing Actively

After Reading Have students create a chart describing the provisions of the Fourteenth Amendment and its effects over time.

Why Study *History?*

Because Citizens Have Responsibilities

Historical Background

For many Americans, providing unpaid community service is an important civic responsibility. In the 1770s, cities like Boston and Philadelphia had volunteer fire departments. During the Revolution, thousands of Americans volunteered to serve in state militias. By the mid-1800s, women took a leading role in charitable organizations that cared for the sick and needy.

In April 1997, the Presidents' Summit for America's Future encouraged a national spirit of volunteerism. At the meeting, President Bill Clinton said good citizenship meant that you "serve in your community to help make it a better place."

Connections to Today

Adults are not the only volunteers. Young people can also find ways to serve their community. Consider, for example, the story of David Levitt.

David Levitt was a sixth grader in Florida when he read about Kentucky Harvest. This organization collected leftover food from restaurants and distributed it to people in need. David had an idea. He had seen how much unused food was thrown out in his school cafeteria. Why not start a similar program himself?

David presented his plan to the local school board and got permission to start a food distribution program. His first delivery was cartons of milk and bags of salad. Over the next few years, David sent more than 250,000 pounds of cafeteria leftovers to

David Levitt collects food for the needy.

shelters and food banks all over Florida. While still in middle school, he was invited to the White House and awarded a medal for his volunteer work.

Connections to You

There are many ways for you to volunteer in your community. You can participate in a food or clothing drive. You can help clean up a neighborhood park. Perhaps you would like to tutor a younger child or help at a local hospital or senior citizen center. To learn more about these and other opportunities, look up community organizations in your local telephone directory.

1. **Comprehension** **(a)** How did President Clinton define good citizenship? **(b)** How did David Levitt help his local community?
2. **Critical Thinking** How might volunteering affect the cost of government?

Writing a Proposal Decide on a volunteer program that might be helpful in your community. Describe the benefits of the program and how it could be set up. Write your plan as a formal written proposal.

Fast Facts

★ Teenagers can participate in politics through groups such as TARS, a Republican organization for teens headquartered in Manassas, Virginia.
★ Under the Helping Hands program, young people and their families can provide foster homes for baby monkeys slated for training as companions to the disabled.
★ Thirteen-year-olds help younger children with their reading under Virginia's Reading Partners program.

Bibliography

To read more about this topic:
1. *160 Ways to Help the World,* Linda Leeb Duper (Facts on File, 1996). How to find and implement service projects.
2. *Local Heroes,* Bill Berkowitz (Lexington Books, 1987). Case studies of groups and individuals who have made a difference through volunteerism.
3. Internet. Volunteers of America News at www.voa.org. Web site of a major national service organization.

RESOURCE DIRECTORY

Teaching Resources
Unit 2/Chapter 8
- Vocabulary Builder, p. 33
- Section 5 Quiz, p. 43

Why Study History?
- Citizens Have Responsibilities, pp. 31–34

Chapter Tests, pp. 43–48

The First Amendment guarantees you the freedom to speak, write, sign petitions, and meet with others freely. You can use those freedoms not only to defend your rights but also to take a stand on political and community issues. It is important to remember that such expressions should be truthful and peaceful. Supreme Court Justice Oliver Wendell Holmes, Jr., once warned:

> "The most [strict] protection of free speech would not protect a man in falsely shouting fire in a theater and causing a panic."

Responsible citizens keep informed about national and community issues. In addition to reading newspapers, you can attend local meetings. At a town council meeting, for example, you might learn about proposed solutions to local health issues or pollution problems. Groups such as the League of Women Voters may sponsor debates by candidates for political office.

The Bill of Rights guarantees citizens the right to a trial by jury. Every citizen, in turn, has the responsibility to serve on juries when called. Serving on a jury is a serious duty. Jurors must take time out from their work and personal lives. Deciding the guilt or innocence of the accused can be difficult.

Civic Values

Citizens enter into a contract with the government. They give the government the power to make certain laws. In return, they expect government to protect the well-being of society. As part of this contract, the government has the power to set penalties if laws are broken.

Like other citizens, you have a responsibility to obey the laws and respect the rights of others. For example, you should not steal, damage property, or harm someone.

Volunteer

Responsible citizens offer their time and talents to help others and to improve the community. For example, you can join or start a group to clean up parks or to serve food to senior citizens. You can also take part in a walk-a-thon or bike-a-thon to raise money for a worthy cause. Many volunteer fire departments have junior divisions.

Defend the nation

At age 18, all men must report their name, age, and address to the government. In time of war, the government may call them to serve in the armed forces. Many young citizens feel the duty to enlist in the military on their own.

★ Section 5 Review ★

Recall

1. **Identify** *Gideon* v. *Wainwright.*
2. **Define** due process.

Comprehension

3. Why were some states able to ignore the guarantees of the Bill of Rights?
4. **(a)** What does the Fourteenth Amendment guarantee? **(b)** How did the Supreme Court expand the guarantees of this amendment?
5. List three responsibilities of citizenship.

Critical Thinking and Writing

6. **Analyzing Ideas** Reread the words of Justice Holmes, above. How does this statement relate to the need to balance the rights of the individual and civic responsibility?
7. **Solving Problems** Why must a citizen of a democracy learn how to compromise?

Activity **Making a Poster** Help people in your school and community become better citizens. Create a poster that encourages people to do one of the following: know their rights, vote, become involved in government, volunteer in the community, or join the armed services.

★ Activity ★

Community Involvement

Creating a community service directory Have students research volunteer opportunities in the community by contacting local civic groups, the mayor, churches, and other groups that use volunteers. Have students create a volunteer directory. Students with computer skills can create a home page directory of volunteer programs. (*average*) T

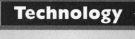

★ Section 5 Review ★

ANSWERS

1. p. 232
2. p. 232
3. It applied only to the federal government, not to states.
4. **(a)** that no state may limit the rights of citizens or deny them due process of law or equal protection of the laws **(b)** It ruled that Fourteenth Amendment protections apply to all rights in the Bill of Rights.
5. Possible answers: learn about one's rights and responsibilities, express one's views, vote, obey laws
6. Possible answer: An individual's rights extend only to the point where they might affect the rights of others. Shouting "fire" without justification in a crowded theater endangers other people.
7. Possible answer: Compromise is necessary when groups with differing views share power. Unless each compromises, or gives up some of what it wants, democracy would grind to a halt.

Activity

Guided Instruction

Have students choose the topic that most interests them. Arrange for them to display their posters in school or another public place such as the local library.

ASSESSMENT See the rubrics in the Alternative Assessment booklet in the Teaching Resources.

Technology

CD-ROM
Test Bank CD-ROM, Ch. 8
Interactive Student Tutorial

Chapter 8

Review and Activities

Reviewing the Chapter

Define These Terms

1. d **2.** a **3.** e **4.** b **5.** c

Explore the Main Ideas

1. Possible answers: collects taxes to fund social programs; creates safety standards for workers; supports disabled or unemployed workers; provides benefits for retired workers; pays for school nutrition programs; supports scientific research

2. The people grant the government certain powers in exchange for protection of their natural rights and the well-being of society.

3. It grants the right to make all laws "necessary and proper" for the government to execute its powers.

4. Possible answers: Congress approves executive judicial appointments; President can veto bills; judicial branch can declare acts of Congress unconstitutional.

5. Possible answers: the right to a trial by jury when accused of a crime; the responsibility to serve on a jury when called upon

Chart Activity

1. 50 percent, 10–30 percent

2. representative

Critical Thinking Possible answers: They don't feel they can change the way government operates. They may find themselves living under leaders they oppose with no way to change them until the next election.

Critical Thinking and Writing

1. States might not have the power to make and enforce local laws, such as regulating drivers' licenses or establishing local school systems.

2. (a) African American men; women; people 18 to 21 **(b)** people in some states who could not pay a poll tax

3. The Commerce Clause allows Congress to regulate trade between the states. Since television stations broadcast across state lines, Congress can regulate them.

4. Since citizens are expected to make decisions about how government will function, they should know about current problems and issues.

Using Primary Sources

(a) Changes in the Constitution would be necessary because societies change over time. **(b)** He approved amending the Constitution when needed.

Chapter 8 **Review and Activities**

★ Sum It Up ★

Section 1 Goals of the Constitution

- The goals of the Constitution include establishing justice, keeping peace at home, and defending the nation.
- The Constitution helps guarantee the rights and liberties of American citizens.

Section 2 Five Principles of the Constitution

- The five basic principles of the Constitution are popular sovereignty, limited government, federalism, separation of powers, and checks and balances.

Section 3 A Living Document

- The process for amending the Constitution was made difficult on purpose.
- Flexible language has allowed informal changes to the Constitution.

Section 4 The National Government at Work

- Congress, made up of the Senate and House of Representatives, makes the nation's laws.
- The duties of the President include carrying out the nation's laws, directing foreign policy, and commanding the armed forces.
- The judicial branch, headed by the Supreme Court, interprets the laws.

Section 5 Good Citizenship

- Over time, the protections of the Bill of Rights were extended to all Americans.
- Citizens have responsibilities, including obeying the law and voting.

For additional review of the major ideas of Chapter 8, see ***Guide to the Essentials of American History*** or ***Interactive Student Tutorial CD-ROM,*** which contains interactive review activities, graphic organizers, and practice tests.

Reviewing the Chapter

Define These Terms

Match each term with the correct definition.

Column 1	Column 2
1. federal	**a.** proposed law
2. bill	**b.** put money aside
3. general welfare	**c.** set aside a veto
4. appropriate	**d.** national
5. override	**e.** well-being of all the people

Explore the Main Ideas

1. How may the government promote the general welfare?
2. Describe how the Constitution is a contract.
3. How does the Elastic Clause allow for informal changes in the Constitution?
4. Give three examples of checks and balances.
5. What rights and responsibilities do citizens have in the justice system?

Chart Activity

Look at the chart and answer the following questions: **1.** What percentage of Americans vote in presidential elections? In local elections? **2.** Are people more likely to know the names of their representatives or their senators? **Critical Thinking** Why do you think so few Americans attend public meetings? What can happen if citizens do not participate in government?

Political Participation and Awareness

Percentage of Americans who...	
Vote in presidential elections	50%
Vote in congressional elections	35–40
Know name of congressional representative	36
Know names of both U.S. senators	29
Occasionally contact local officials	28
Vote in local elections	10–30
Occasionally attend public meetings	19
Give money to candidate or party	13

Source: Selected polls, including Gallup, *Denver Post* Poll, University of Michigan, and *The New York Times, 1989.*

Critical Thinking and Writing

1. Exploring Unit Themes **Rights and Liberties** How might our government be different today if there were no Tenth Amendment?
2. **Understanding Chronology** **(a)** In what order did the following groups win the right to vote: women; people 18 to 21 years old; African American men? **(b)** Who could vote for President in 1964 who could not do so in 1960?
3. **Linking Past and Present** The federal government recently adopted rules about a new type of nationwide television broadcasting that will provide sharper, clearer pictures. Explain how the government gets its power to make such rules.
4. **Defending a Position** Why is keeping informed an important responsibility of citizenship? Give reasons and examples.

Using Primary Sources

Long after the Constitution was ratified, Thomas Jefferson commented:

> "As the [human mind] becomes more developed, . . . as new discoveries are made, . . . and manners and opinions changed with the change of circumstances, [constitutions] must advance also, and keep pace with the times. We might as well require a man to wear still the coat which fitted him when a boy, as civilized society to remain ever under the [government] of their . . . ancestors."

Source: *Patterns in American History,* ed. Alexander De Conde et al., 1965.

Recognizing Points of View **(a)** What did Jefferson think happens as time goes on? **(b)** How do you think he felt about the process of amending the Constitution? Explain.

Activity Bank

Interdisciplinary Activity

Exploring the Arts Find out more about the procedure of a courtroom. If possible, visit a courthouse or watch a trial on television. Then, with several classmates, write a script and conduct a mock trial.

Career Skills Activity

Fiction Writer Write a short story about what might happen if people had no political rights. Set the story in the United States or in another country.

Citizenship Activity

Holding a Panel Discussion Organize a panel discussion to consider a proposal for a new constitutional amendment. You might examine the idea of limiting the President to a single six-year term, changing the voting age, or another issue.

Internet Activity

Use the Internet to find sites dealing with the agencies of the United States government. Choose one agency and prepare a report on its activities. Questions you should answer are: When was the agency founded? What does it do? What branch does it serve? How many employees does it have? How much money does it spend every year?

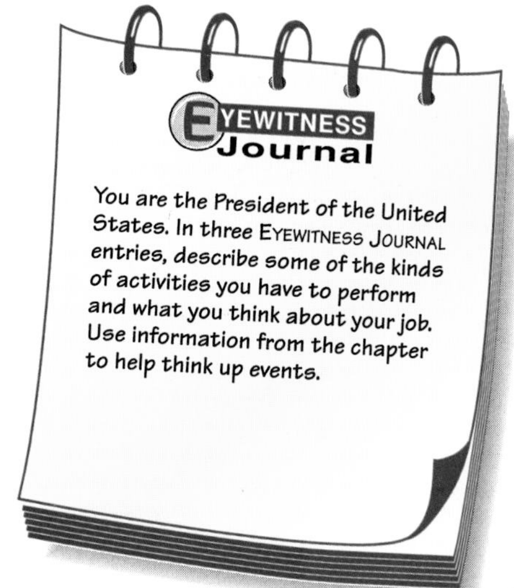

Eyewitness Journal
You are the President of the United States. In three Eyewitness Journal entries, describe some of the kinds of activities you have to perform and what you think about your job. Use information from the chapter to help think up events.

★ 237

Eyewitness Journal

1. Suggest that students structure their journal chronologically by describing a day or week in the life of a President.
2. Remind students to include as many aspects of the President's duties as they can, such as foreign policy duties, domestic duties, and commander-in-chief duties.

Internet Activity

1. Have students go to www.phschool.com, which contains updated information on a variety of topics.
2. Another site you may find useful for this activity is the WWW Virtual Library's list of links to federal agencies at www.lib.lsu.edu/gov/fedgov.html.
3. Given the changing nature of the Internet, you may wish to preview this site.

Activity Bank

ASSESSMENT To assess the activities on this page, see the rubrics in the Alternative Assessment booklet in the Teaching Resources. You might want to share the rubrics with your students before they begin work.

Interdisciplinary Activity

1. Have students call a courthouse and ask the court clerk for information about visiting a courtroom.

2. Have students research to find out about normal courtroom procedure so they can write accurate scripts.

Career Skills Activity

1. Remind students that their stories should have a conflict, a climax, and a resolution. Lack of political rights, not a peripheral issue, should be the focus of the plot.

2. Students may wish to create a literary magazine with their stories by binding them together into a magazine format.

Citizenship Activity

1. Make sure students understand what a panel discussion is—a discussion among a limited number of experts moderated by a neutral party in front of an audience that may or may not be able to participate.

2. Students may find outside political groups that might be willing to discuss an issue in a school setting. Make sure students get approval from school authorities to invite an outside group and arrange to present both sides of the issue.

Valley Forge

by Maxwell Anderson

Author Note

Maxwell Anderson Maxwell Anderson's career included five years of teaching and several years as a journalist. His first literary endeavor—*What Price Glory?*—was a play intended to portray the realities of war. Anderson's prolific work—32 plays during his career—included other tragedies, but he also produced works of comedy. The comedy *Both Your Houses,* which satirized congressional corruption, won the Pulitzer Prize in 1933. Anderson died of a stroke in 1959.

Build Vocabulary

Have students look up and discuss the words *lenient, commissary, savvy*, and *munitions* before they read the passage. Ask: "Do you think the word *lenient* often applies to the military? Are the words *commissary* and *munitions* used today?"

Prereading Focus

You might have students reread Section 3 in Chapter 6 to review what they have learned about the conditions at Valley Forge.

Connect Your Experience

Have students think about a time when they were hungry. Ask: "How long did you have to wait for food?" Help students realize how hungry soldiers at Valley Forge must have been.

Purpose-Setting Question

Ask: "Suppose you are a soldier and food is scarce. Would you risk the penalty for desertion to hunt for food or would you remain with the other troops? Why?"

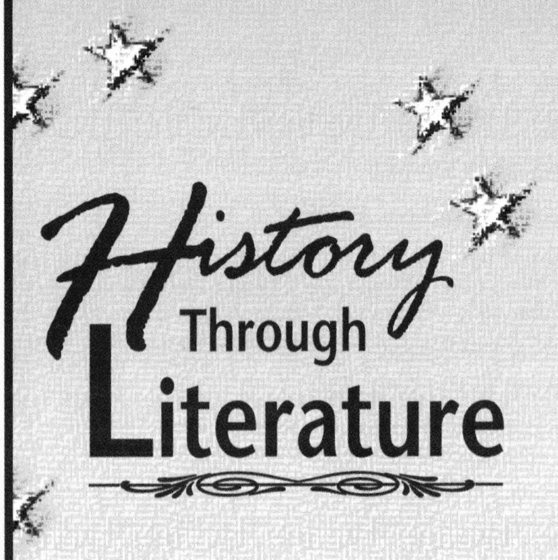

Valley Forge

by Maxwell Anderson

Introduction

For 30 years, Maxwell Anderson was one of the most respected American playwrights. Many of his dramas were based on history. His 1934 play *Valley Forge* describes the hardships the Continental Army faced during the winter of 1777–1778. In this scene, George Washington hears some of the complaints of his troops.

Vocabulary

Before you read the selection, find the meanings of these words in a dictionary: **lenient, commissary, savvy, munitions.**

TEAGUE: General Washington!

WASHINGTON: What is it?

TEAGUE: These here new regulations about men going home. Going home without leave. They say it's seventy-five lashes if they catch you now. Why is that?

WASHINGTON: The traditional penalty for desertion is shooting at sunrise. We've been more lenient here.

TEAGUE: But look, General Washington, it don't make sense. It don't stand to reason—

NICK: Do you want to talk your neck into a rope?

WASHINGTON: Let him say what's on his mind.

TEAGUE: Well, here it is: I'm going hungry here and my woman's going hungry at home. You let me go home for the winter, and you won't have to feed me, and that relieves the commissary. I rustle some wild meat for the younguns and the old woman, and they don't starve and I don't starve. More'n that, everybody knows there's two or three thousand men gone home already for that same reason, and if they was here now they'd be chewing the bark off the second-growth birch like so many cottontails. I don't hold it against you and I don't hold it against anybody because I don't know who in thunder to hold it against, but there's nothing to eat here.

ALCOCK: Stow it, will you? The dog ate the stuff, and he isn't dead yet.

TEAGUE: It ain't that I'm afraid of a good fight. A good fight's ham and eggs to me. Me and my boy here, we make for home every winter when the grub gets scarce, and we come back every spring when the fighting starts. We're coming back next spring, and every spring, till we chase the... redcoats clear out of Chesapeake Bay, and across the Atlantic Ocean and right up a lamppost in London town! Fightin's fine, but sitting here and starving down to a hide and buttons—I don't savvy it.

WASHINGTON: What is your name, sir?

TEAGUE: Teague, sir. Teague's my name.

WASHINGTON: Well, Master Teague, if they catch you they'll give you seventy-five

Critical Reading

1. Why does Washington believe he has been lenient with his troops? *(because the traditional punishment for desertion is shooting and he has changed that punishment to 75 lashes)*

2. Why did Washington set the new regulation about desertion? *(He was afraid that too many men would go home for the winter and the British would win the war.)*

3. Why has Teague joined the revolutionary cause? *(because he doesn't want to pay taxes to the king of England)*

Background for Understanding

Food at Valley Forge consisted mainly of a biscuit, called fire cake, and water. The cake, which consisted of little more than flour, was so named because it was baked on rocks in fires rather than in ovens.

While soldiers starved, nearby farmers got rich by selling their meat and grain to the British in Philadelphia. Whenever possible, Washington intercepted these shipments, seized the goods, and had the farmer imprisoned.

Viewing History: Hard Winter at Valley Forge

The March to Valley Forge by William B. Trego shows General George Washington on horseback, reviewing his troops. At Valley Forge, Washington had to plead with local merchants and farmers for food supplies. ★ **Why does Trego show one of the soldiers taking off his hat to Washington?**

lashes, and that's a good deal to take and live. On the other hand you're quite right from your own angle, and if I were you I'd feel as you do.—But this you should know, sir: if you go home, and we all go home this winter, you won't need to bother about coming back in the spring. There'll be no fighting to come back to.—General Howe will march out of Philadelphia and take over these states of ours. If he knew now how many have deserted, how many are sick, how many unfit for duty on account of the lack of food and clothes and munitions, he'd come back in force and wring our necks one by one, and the neck of our sickly little revolution along with us. . . . What are we in this war for? Do we want to quit?

THE MEN: No, sir. No.

WASHINGTON: I can't blame you if you sound a bit half-hearted about it.

TEAGUE: I'm not half-hearted about it! Not me! I'm fighting to keep King George out of my backyard! I moved west three times to get away from his . . . tax-collectors, and every time they caught up to me! I'm sick of tax-collectors, that's why I'm in it!

WASHINGTON: Then it may be you're here in error, and the sooner you discover it the better. You'll get death and taxes under one government as well as another. But I'll tell you why I'm here, and why I've hoped you were here, and why it's seemed to me worthwhile to stick with it while our guns rust out for lack of powder, and men die around me for lack of food and medicine, and women and children sicken at home for lack of clothing and the little they need to eat. . . . [W]hat I fight for is your right to do what you please with your government and with yourselves without benefit of kings.—It's for you to decide, Master Teague—you, and your son, and the rest of you. . . . But if we lose you—if you've lost interest in this cause of ours—we've lost our war, lost it completely, and the men we've left lying on our battlefields died for nothing whatever—for a dream that came too early—and may never come true. . . .

TEAGUE: I guess the old woman'll get along. She's brought in her own bear meat before.

NICK: Well, it's all right with me.

Analyzing Literature

1. What were some of the hardships that Washington's troops faced?
2. Summarize one argument Teague gives in favor of going home.
3. **Critical Thinking Comparing** How do Washington's reasons for fighting differ from Teague's?

Viewing History ANSWER

Washington was revered as the leader of the American troops. The soldier is removing his hat as a sign of respect.

Analyzing Literature

ANSWERS

1. The troops faced hunger, illness, and lack of clothes, medicine, and munitions.
2. If he goes home, he can help to feed his wife and children and won't be taking food from the other men in camp.
3. Teague's reasons are concrete and personal—he is fighting in hopes of getting relief from the heavy taxes of the British. Washington's reasons are more idealistic—he fights to win government by the people.

Teaching Alternatives

Team Teaching: Language Arts

Work with a language arts teacher to discuss with students drama as a literary genre. Ask students how setting—including props and backgrounds—contributes to the play's effect. Ask students what kind of props and backgrounds they would use to convey the situation of the soldiers at Valley Forge. Then ask if they could achieve the same effects without props.

Connections With Arts

Before he was 2 years old, William B. Trego was given calomel by a doctor to help alleviate teething pain. The medication left him paralyzed. He later recovered somewhat, but his right hand remained unusable and only the thumb and forefinger of his left hand could move. Nevertheless, he learned to paint with the brush in his right hand, guided by his left. Although he won fame for his realistic battle scenes, he remained poor. Alone and ill at the age of 51, Trego took his own life.

Unit 3

The Nation Takes Shape

Thematic Overview

The United States developed and prospered in its first 35 years. During this period, nationalism grew as Americans built a lasting government and laid the foundations for future growth.

Chapter 7 examines the problems and issues faced by the new nation as Americans launched their new government. (See pp. 170–191.) **Chapter 8** discusses Jefferson's impact as a farseeing national leader and the causes and effects of the War of 1812. (See pp. 192–219.) **Chapter 9** explores the impact of the Industrial Revolution and the determination of Americans to develop and unify their nation. (See pp. 220–245.)

Viewing UNIT THEMES ANSWER

Students might suggest that Americans were proud of having a democratic government under the Constitution. For more information about this artist, see the Background Art Note at the bottom of this page.

RESOURCE DIRECTORY

Teaching Resources
Document-Based Discovery
• Nationalism, pp. 10–13

Unit 3 The Nation Takes Shape

What's Ahead

Viewing UNIT THEMES Celebrating the Nation

American artist John Lewis Krimmel painted this election celebration in 1815. This detail shows people of all ages enjoying parades and public debate in the streets of Philadelphia. By this time, Americans had developed strong feelings of pride in their young nation. ★ **Why do you think Americans at this time felt that an election was cause for celebration?**

★ *Background* ★

Art Note

Celebrating the Nation Americans did not recognize John Lewis Krimmel's (1789–1821) talent until late in his life, but he had always found his artistic inspiration in the people and scenes of the United States. An immigrant from Germany, Krimmel left his brother's countinghouse in Philadelphia to paint for a living. Krimmel found a mirror for his own desire for creative freedom in the national desire for independence and political freedom. His work is evocative of the strong feelings many Americans had for their nation in its early years.

Unit Theme Nationalism

In the years after winning independence and adopting a new Constitution, the United States grew and prospered. As the nation took shape, so did American nationalism. Nationalism is a feeling of loyalty and devotion to one's country. Proud Americans sought to identify qualities that set the United States apart from older nations.

How did Americans of the time describe their feelings about their country? They can tell you in their own words.

Viewpoints on American Nationalism

"Britain, whose children we are, and whose language we speak, should no longer be *our* standard.... Customs, habits, and language, as well as government, should be national. America should have her *own* distinct from all the world."

Noah Webster, scholar and dictionary writer (1789)

"We have learned to love our country...because the sweat of our fathers' brows has subdued its soil;... because it embraces our fathers and mothers."

John Thornton Kirkland, Boston minister (1798)

"Our country! In her [dealings] with foreign nations, may she always be in the right; but our country, right or wrong."

Stephen Decatur, naval hero (1816)

History AND YOU

Activity **Writing to Learn** Another word for nationalism is patriotism. Many things might stir patriotic feelings, including holidays like the Fourth of July, symbols like the flag, or songs like "The Star-Spangled Banner." List 5 or 6 other things that may stir patriotic feelings. Then, choose one of the items from your list. Write a paragraph describing what you think it represents.

Viewpoints on American Nationalism

★ Noah Webster helped the United States define itself—literally—by writing the first American dictionary.

★ John Thornton Kirkland was a famous President of Harvard College.

★ Stephen Decatur led Americans to victory in many naval battles and became a military hero.

CRITICAL THINKING All three men had strong feelings for the country that had allowed them so much opportunity. However, some groups of Americans did not share in these opportunities. Would a Native American or an enslaved African American have felt such nationalistic fervor? Why or why not?

Guided Instruction
You might have the class brainstorm the list, which might include things like Thanksgiving, Olympic victories, views of American landscapes, and the Statue of Liberty. Before they begin writing, remind students to write their paragraphs using correct spelling, grammar, and punctuation.

ASSESSMENT See the rubrics in the Alternative Assessment booklet in the Teaching Resources.

★ Background ★
Historians Debate

What is an American? Since 1783, people have tried to define what makes Americans unique. Thomas Jefferson described an American as an independent idealist. Alexis de Tocqueville saw Americans in the 1830s as conformist, religious, liberty-loving, and materialistic. Some historians argue that defining an American is useless in part because it involves unworkable labels or even stereotyping. What is meant by American—the individual or a national character?

Today, some Americans define themselves in terms of ethnic or racial identity. Arthur Schlesinger, Jr., regrets this tendency in *The Disuniting of America: Reflections on a Multicultural Society* and urges a return to the "melting pot" ideal expressed in the national motto, *E Pluribus Unum*.

Technology

AmericanHeritage® History of the United States CD-ROM
Access the Time Tour "The Nation Takes Shape" to accompany Unit 3.

Chapter 9 Manager

SECTION OBJECTIVES	TEACHING RESOURCES	ADDITIONAL RESOURC
1 Launching the New Government (pp. 244–249) **Objectives** 1. Explain how Washington's actions set an example for future Presidents. 2. Describe how Hamilton planned to strengthen the nation's economy. 3. Explain why some people opposed Hamilton's economic plan.	**Lesson Planner,** p. 36 (average) . . . . .45 mins. **Unit 3/Chapter 9** • Map Mystery: Population Hot Spots in 1790–1800, p. 5 (challenging) . . . . .20 mins. • Section 1 Quiz, p. 8 (average) . . . . .15 mins. **Why Study History?** • The Debate Over Tariffs Continues, pp. 35–38 (challenging) . . . . .30 mins. **Interdisciplinary Connections** • Main Idea: Inventing a Nation, p. 51 (average) . . . . .20 mins.	
2 A Policy of Neutrality (pp. 250–252) **Objectives** 1. Describe how Americans reacted to the French Revolution. 2. Identify the policy the United States adopted when war broke out in Europe. 3. Describe how Washington's Farewell Address influenced American foreign policy.	**Lesson Planner,** p. 37 (challenging) . . . . .45 mins. **Unit 3/Chapter 9** • Biography Flashcard: Eleuthère Irénée du Pont, p. 7 (average) . . . . .20 mins. • Section 2 Quiz, p. 9 (average) . . . . .15 mins.	**Voices of Freedom** • Washington Advises Neutrality, pp. 73–74 (average) **Customized Reader** • Fur Trade With the Ojibway, article IIIA-10 (challenging)
3 The Rise of Political Parties (pp. 253–257) **Objectives** 1. Explain how political differences led to the rise of two political parties. 2. Describe the role newspapers played in politics in the late 1700s. 3. Explain how the election of 1796 increased political tensions.	**Lesson Planner,** p. 38 (average) . . . . .30 mins. **Unit 3/Chapter 9** • Practice Your Skills: Managing Information—Outlining, p. 2 (average) . . . .20 mins. • Section 3 Quiz, p. 10 (average) . . . . .15 mins. **Interdisciplinary Connections** • Main Idea: Inventing a Nation, p. 54 (average) . . . . .20 mins.	**Voices of Freedom** • Jefferson Opposes the National Bank, pp. 74–75 (challenging) • Hamilton Supports the Bank, pp. 76–77 (challenging)
4 The Second President (pp. 258–261) **Objectives** 1. Explain why many Americans favored war with France. 2. Explain why the Federalist party split in two. 3. Explain why the Alien and Sedition acts outraged many Americans.	**Lesson Planner,** p. 39 (challenging) . . . . .45 mins. **Unit 3/Chapter 9** • Vocabulary Builder, p. 2 • Critical Thinking and Writing: Understanding Causes and Effects, p. 4 (average) . . . . .15 mins. • Connecting History and Literature: Letter to Her Daughter From the New White House, p. 6 (challenging) . . . . .20 mins. • Section 4 Quiz, p. 11 (average) . . . . .15 mins. **Chapter Tests,** pp. 49–54 (average) . . . . .45 mins.	**Voices of Freedom** • A Song to Unite Americans, p. 77 (basic)

Assessment Options

Teaching Resources
- Alternative Assessment booklet
- Section Quizzes, Unit 3, Chapter 9, pp. 8–11
- Chapter Tests, Chapter 9, pp. 49–54
- Test Bank CD-ROM

Student Performance Pack
- Guide to the Essentials of American History, Chapter 9 Test, p. 54
- Standardized Test Prep Handbook
- Interactive Student Tutorial CD-ROM

Interdisciplinary Connections

Teaching Resources
- Map Mystery, Unit 3, Chapter 9, p. 5
- Connecting History and Literature, Unit 3, Chapter 9, p. 6
- Interdisciplinary Connections, pp. 49–54

Voices of Freedom, pp. 73–77

Customized Reader, article IIIA-10

Technology

AmericanHeritage® History of the United States CD-ROM
- Time Tour: The New Government Begins in The New Republic
- Presidents: George Washington, John Adams
- History Makers: Alexander Hamilton, Benjamin Banneker

Interactive Student Tutorial CD-ROM

Test Bank CD-ROM

Color Transparencies
- Martha Washington, First Lady, p. B-47

Guided Reading Audiotapes (English/Spanish), side 3

Resource Pro® CD-ROM

Prentice Hall United States History Video Collection™ (Spanish track available on disc version.) Vol. 5, Chs. 28, 34, 37

Prentice Hall Home Page
www.phschool.com

Student Performance Pack

Guide to the Essentials of American History
- Ch. 9, pp. 50–54 (Available in English and Spanish)

Guided Reading Audiotapes (English/Spanish), side 3

Standardized Test Prep Handbook

Interactive Student Tutorial CD-ROM

BLOCK SCHEDULING
Activities with this icon will help you meet your Block Scheduling needs.

ENGLISH LANGUAGE LEARNERS
Activities with this icon are suitable for English Language Learners.

TEAM TEACHING
Activities and Background Notes with this icon present starting points for Team Teaching.

Teachers' Bibliography

FROM THE ARCHIVES OF AmericanHeritage®	Don't miss the special American Heritage® teaching notes found in this chapter.
 HISTORY ALIVE!®	Contact Teachers' Curriculum Institute to learn more about History Alive!® resources on the nation's early years. See History Alive!® unit: The Constitution in a New Nation, Section 4, "The Constitution in Action, 1789–1820."
	Explore your library to find these issues related to Chapter 9: *George Washington,* April 1992; *The Two-Party System,* November 1988.
	**Prentice Hall Web Site** You can access a structured, on-line environment that allows you to preview curriculum-related resources and receive updated information on groundbreaking events from around the nation and the world. (www.phschool.com)

Chapter 9

The New Republic Begins
1789–1800

Introducing the Chapter

Have students preview the main ideas of this chapter by looking over the visuals. Suggest they look for examples of artists' use of body language to convey the expression of pride, resolution, and confidence among the people living during this period.

Using the Time Line To provide students with practice in using the time line to link the United States and the world, ask questions such as these: **(1)** How many years did George Washington serve as president? *(8 years)* **(2)** Name two American events during Washington's presidency that indicate the government's desire to avoid war. *(issuing the Neutrality Proclamation and Jay's Treaty)* **(3)** Name two world events that occurred during this same period. *(Denmark abolishes slave trade; Polish uprising)*

Ask students to recall making a purchase in which they were able to select from among domestic and foreign-made goods. Ask whether they noticed a difference in price between the foreign-made and domestic items. Tell them that the price of many foreign-made goods includes its tariff, which is a tax placed on goods imported from other countries. Explain that one purpose of tariffs is to protect domestic industries by keeping the price of imported goods equal to or greater than the price of similar domestic goods.

For additional *Why Study History?* support, see p. 248.

Chapter 9

The New Republic Begins
1789–1800

What's Ahead

In this chapter, you will learn about the early years of the United States. The new nation faced many decisions about how it would govern itself. Everything was a fresh issue, from what the President should be called to how the nation should pay its bills. The young republic also had to meet violent challenges inside its borders and on the high seas.

In these confusing times, leaders clashed over what policies to follow. Some wanted a stronger national government. Others felt the states should have more power. Before long, two political parties formed. Despite powerful feelings on both sides, the nation successfully elected its second President and moved into the 1800s.

Why Study History? Again and again, as you study American history, you will find people arguing about something called "the tariff." Tariffs may not seem very exciting. However, they can directly affect how much we pay for the things we buy. To focus on a recent issue involving tariffs, see the *Why Study History?* feature, "The Debate Over Tariffs Continues," in this chapter.

American Events

1789 George Washington becomes first President of the United States

1791 Congress creates the Bank of the United States

1793 Washington issues Neutrality Proclamation to keep the United States out of war

1788 — 1790 — 1792 — 1794

World Events

1789 World Event French Revolution begins

1792 World Event French assembly votes to end monarchy

Viewing HISTORY **Symbols of a Proud New Nation**

In the late 1700s, paper cutouts like this one were a popular form of artwork. This design shows an eagle holding a flag under the word LIBERTY—symbols of the new nation's patriotism. As President George Washington took office in 1789, Americans looked to the future with pride and hope. ★ **If you were an American in 1789, what hopes and worries might you have about the new government?**

1795 Jay's Treaty keeps peace between the United States and Britain

1797 John Adams becomes second President of the United States

1798 Sedition Act makes it a crime to criticize the government

1794 | **1796** | **1798** | **1800**

1794 World Event Thaddeus Kosciusko leads Polish uprising

1797 World Event British sailors mutiny to demand better conditions

★ Background ★

Art Note

Symbols of a Proud New Nation In the late 1700s, arts and crafts often had a patriotic theme. A popular symbol was the American bald eagle, which was declared the official emblem of the United States in 1782. This paper cutout design from the period exemplifies this use of patriotic symbols. The artist would cut such a design from a single piece of paper. T

Documents and Literature

On pp. 552–554, you will find two readings to enrich this chapter:

1. Eyewitness Account "A Description of George Washington," excerpt from a letter by Thomas Jefferson in which he describes George Washington's character. (Use with Section 1.)

2. Historical Document "Farewell Address," excerpt from Washington's Farewell Address. (Use with Section 2.)

Writing Actively

Responding to Art Tell students that the objective of the paper cutout "Liberty" was to convey and perhaps to inspire feelings of American pride and patriotism. Suggest that students look at the cover of their textbooks. Have them write a paragraph describing how the cover images represent American patriotism.

Viewing HISTORY ANSWER

Americans might hope that, under Washington, the new government would protect liberty and lead to prosperity. At the same time, they might worry that the new government would not be able to solve the problems that arose under the Articles of Confederation.

Technology

Videodiscs/Videotapes
Show the *Prentice Hall United States History Video Collection*™ segments for this chapter. The videodisc version has a Spanish track. Press audio until you get the left channel for English or the right channel for Spanish, or use the bar codes in the Guidebook.

AmericanHeritage® History of the United States CD-ROM
- Time Tour: The New Government Begins in The New Republic (*average*) ELL

Section 1
Launching the New Government

LESSON PLAN

Objectives

★ Explain how Washington's actions set an example for future Presidents.

★ Describe how Hamilton planned to strengthen the nation's economy.

★ Explain why some people opposed Hamilton's economic plan.

1 Engage

Warm Up Have students name as many of the thirteen positions in the present President's Cabinet as they can.

Activating Prior Knowledge List the Cabinet positions in a column on the chalkboard. List, in random order, the names of the people who currently fill those positions. Ask students to match the names with the positions.

Reading Actively

Before Reading Ask students to skim the section looking at the visuals and reading the headings. Then have them write two or three sentences predicting what the section will be about. As they read, have students verify or correct their predictions.

RESOURCE DIRECTORY

Teaching Resources
Lesson Planner, p. 36

Transparencies
Interdisciplinary Connections
• Martha Washington, First Lady, p. B-47

Launching the New Government

As You Read

Explore These Questions

- How did George Washington's actions set an example for future Presidents?
- How did Alexander Hamilton plan to strengthen the nation's economy?
- Why did some people oppose Hamilton's economic plan?

Define

- inauguration
- precedent
- Cabinet
- national debt
- bond
- speculator
- tariff
- protective tariff

Identify

- Judiciary Act
- District of Columbia
- Bank of the United States
- Whiskey Rebellion

SETTING the Scene The new Congress met for the first time in the spring of 1789. Vice President John Adams brought up a curious question. How should people address the President?

For three weeks, members of Congress debated the issue. Some favored the simple title "President Washington." Others felt that it lacked dignity. Instead, they suggested titles such as "His Elective Highness" or "His Highness the President of the United States and Protector of the Rights of the Same."

Finally, Washington let Congress know he was content with "President of the United States." By choosing a simple title, Washington showed he was not interested in the kind of power that European monarchs had. In this decision, like many others, Washington set an example for later Presidents.

The New Government

George Washington was inaugurated in New York City on April 30, 1789. A President's **inauguration** is the ceremony at which the President officially takes the oath of office. A witness reported that the new President looked "grave, almost to sadness." Washington no doubt was feeling the awesome responsibility of his office. He knew that Americans were looking to him to make their new government work.

As the first President, Washington had no one to imitate. While the Constitution provided a framework for the new government, it did not explain how the President should govern from day to day. Washington knew he was setting an example for future generations. "There is scarcely any part of my conduct," he said, "which may not hereafter be drawn into precedent." A **precedent** (PREHS uh dehnt) is an act or decision that sets an example for others to follow.

Washington set one important precedent at the end of his second term. In 1796, he decided not to run for a third term. Not until 1940 did any President seek a third term.

The first Cabinet

The Constitution said little about how the executive branch should be organized. It was clear, however, that the President needed talented people to help him carry out his duties.

Connections With Civics

The President who finally broke Washington's two-term precedent was Franklin D. Roosevelt. In 1940, he ran for and won a third term. Four years later, Roosevelt was elected yet again. Today, the Twenty-Second Amendment to the Constitution prohibits any President from being elected more than twice.

★ Background ★

Did You Know?

Washington sets the fashion For his inauguration, Washington wore a dark brown broadcloth suit that put American-made products in the fashion spotlight. The silver buttons on the jacket boasted the now-classic American eagle design. The coat is preserved at the Chicago Historical Society in Chicago, Illinois.

★ Background ★

Linking Past and Present

No job description Martha Washington helped create the job of First Lady. She became the President's official hostess, formally entertaining foreign and domestic leaders. As a public service, she took up the cause of needy veterans of the Revolution. Working for a public cause and serving as hostess remain part of the job today.

Viewing HISTORY **The First President**

George Washington traveled on horseback to his inauguration in New York City. Along the way, crowds gathered to cheer their new President. Here, women and children scatter flower petals in Washington's path. ★ **How can you tell this painter greatly admired Washington?**

Mug honoring President Washington's inauguration ➤

In 1789, the first Congress created five executive departments. They were the departments of State, Treasury, and War and the offices of Attorney General and Postmaster General. The heads of these departments made up the President's **Cabinet.** Members of the Cabinet gave Washington advice and directed their departments.

Washington set a precedent by carefully choosing well-known leaders to serve in his Cabinet. The two most influential were the Secretary of State, Thomas Jefferson, and the Secretary of the Treasury, Alexander Hamilton.

The federal court system

The Constitution called for a Supreme Court. Congress, however, had to organize the federal court system. In 1789, Congress passed the **Judiciary Act.** It called for the Supreme Court to have one Chief Justice and five Associate Justices.* Washington named John Jay to serve as the first Chief Justice of the United States.

The Judiciary Act also set up a system of district courts and circuit courts across the nation. Decisions made in these lower courts could be appealed to the Supreme Court, the highest court in the land.

Battling the National Debt

As Secretary of the Treasury, Alexander Hamilton wanted to build a strong economy. He faced many major problems, however. Among the most pressing was the large national debt. The **national debt** is the total sum of money a government owes to others.

* Today, the Supreme Court has eight Associate Justices.

2 Explore

Ask students to read the section. For a homework assignment, ask students to check newspapers and magazines or Internet sources for information on the current Secretary of the Treasury and on the biggest current concerns about federal finances. Have them summarize the information they find.

3 Teach

Have students work in small groups to prepare the following: **(a)** a dialogue between Hamilton and Madison on paying national and state debts; **(b)** a dialogue between Hamilton and a southern member of Congress on passing a tariff; **(c)** a dialogue between Hamilton and Washington on dealing with the leaders of the Whiskey Rebellion.

4 Assess

To close the lesson, have students complete the section review. As an alternative, ask students to write an essay that summarizes the section and mentions the issues involving money that caused problems for the new federal government. Have students describe those problems.

★ ★ ★ ★ ★ ★ ★ ★ ★ ★ ★ ★ ★ ★ ★ ★ ★ ★ ★ ★

Viewing HISTORY ANSWER

Possible answer: The painting presents Washington as a noble figure surrounded by cheering crowds. The figure of Washington is larger than anyone else in the painting.

Technology

AmericanHeritage® History of the United States CD-ROM

- Presidents: George Washington (*average*)
- History Makers: Alexander Hamilton (*average*)

Biography

ANSWER

He worked to erase the national debt, build a national bank, and have the federal government take over all state debts.

RESOURCE DIRECTORY

Teaching Resources
Unit 3/Chapter 9
- Map Mystery: Population Hot Spots in 1790–1800, p. 5

Interdisciplinary Connections
- Main Idea: Inventing a Nation, p. 51

Biography **Alexander Hamilton**

Alexander Hamilton was born on the Caribbean island of Nevis in 1755. As a boy, he faced poverty, but he worked his way up in a local trading company. He later came to New York, served as an officer in the American Revolution, and became the first Secretary of the Treasury. This portrait was painted by John Trumbull, one of the most famous early American artists.

★ **How did Alexander Hamilton help strengthen the new nation?**

During the Revolution, both the national government and the individual states needed money to pay soldiers and buy supplies. They borrowed money from foreign countries and ordinary citizens.

Then, as now, governments borrowed money by issuing bonds. A **bond** is a certificate which promises to repay the money loaned plus interest on a certain date. For example, if a person pays $100 for a bond, the government agrees to pay back $100 plus interest in five or ten years.

By 1789, most southern states had paid off their debts from the Revolution. Other states and the federal government had not. Hamilton insisted that all these debts be repaid. After all, he asked, who would lend money to the United States in the future if the country did not pay its old debts?

Hamilton's Plan

Hamilton developed a two-part plan to repay both the national and state debts. First, he wanted to buy up all the bonds issued by the national and state governments before 1789. He planned to sell new bonds to pay off those old debts. When the economy improved, the government would be able to pay off the new bonds. Second, he wanted the national government to pay off debts owed by the states.

Many people, including bankers and investors, welcomed Hamilton's plan. Others attacked it.

Madison leads the opposition

James Madison led the opposition to Hamilton's plan. Madison argued that the plan was unfair because it would reward speculators. A **speculator** is someone willing to invest in a risky venture in the hope of making a large profit.

During the Revolution, the government had paid soldiers and citizens who supplied goods with bonds. Many of these bondholders needed cash to survive. They sold their bonds to speculators. Speculators paid only 10 or 15 cents for bonds that had an original, or face, value of one dollar.

If the government repaid the bonds at face value, speculators stood to make great fortunes. Madison thought that speculators did not deserve to make such profits.

Hamilton disagreed. The United States had to repay its bonds in full, he said, in order to gain the trust and help of investors. The support of investors, he argued, was crucial for building the new nation's economy. After much debate, Hamilton convinced Congress to accept his plan of repaying the national debt.

As a southerner, James Madison also led the fight against the other part of Hamilton's plan. It called for the federal government to pay state debts. Many southern states had already paid their own debts in full. They

Skills For LIFE MINI LESSON

CRITICAL THINKING Analyzing an Argument

1. Introduce the skill of analyzing an argument by writing these steps on the chalkboard: Identify key ideas of the argument, decide if supporting statements are accurate, identify any weaknesses.

2. Help students practice the skill by having them identify Madison's first reason for rejecting Hamilton's plan (*unfair because it rewards speculators*). Ask them if supporting statements are accurate (*speculators would profit*) and whether they see any weaknesses (*fairness is open to interpretation*).

3. Help students apply this skill by identifying and analyzing Madison's second reason for rejecting Hamilton's plan.

thought other states should do the same. As a result, southerners bitterly opposed Hamilton's proposal.

Hamilton's compromise

To win support for his plan, Hamilton suggested a compromise. He knew that many southerners wanted to move the nation's capital to the South. He offered to persuade his northern friends to vote for a capital in the South if southerners supported the repayment of state debts.

Madison and other southerners accepted this compromise. In July 1790, Congress passed bills taking over state debts and providing for a new capital city.

The capital would not be part of any state. Instead, it would be built on land along the Potomac River between Virginia and Maryland. Congress called this area the **District of Columbia.** It is known today as Washington, D.C. Congress hoped that the new capital would be ready by 1800. Meanwhile, the nation's capital was moved from New York to Philadelphia.

Building Up the Economy

Hamilton's compromise with the South had resolved the problem of the national debt. Now he took steps to build up the new nation's economy.

A national bank

Hamilton called on Congress to set up a national bank. In 1791, Congress passed a bill creating the first **Bank of the United States.** The national government deposited the money it collected in taxes in the Bank. The Bank, in turn, issued paper money. The government used the paper money to make loans to farmers and businesses. By making loans to citizens, the Bank encouraged the growth of the economy.

The Bank also used the paper money to pay government bills. The new government had many expenses. It had to pay its employees, build the new capital, and keep up the army and navy.

Protecting American industry

Another part of Hamilton's economic program was designed to give American manufacturing a boost. He proposed that Congress pass a **tariff,** or tax, on all foreign goods brought into the country. Hamilton called for a very high tariff. He wanted to make imported goods more expensive to buy than goods made in the United States. Because such a tariff was meant to protect American industry from foreign competition, it was called a **protective tariff.**

In the North, where factories were growing, many people supported Hamilton's plan. Southern farmers, however, bought more imported goods than northerners did. They did not want a protective tariff that would make these goods more expensive.

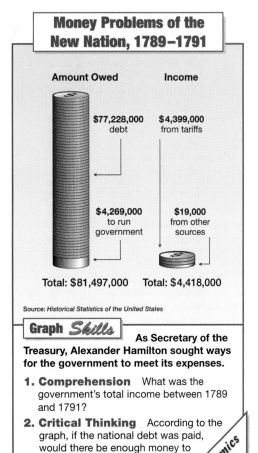

Money Problems of the New Nation, 1789–1791

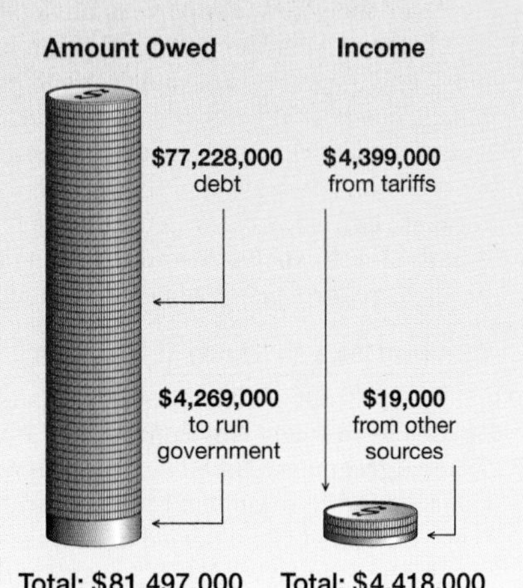

Source: *Historical Statistics of the United States*

Graph Skills **As Secretary of the Treasury, Alexander Hamilton sought ways for the government to meet its expenses.**

1. **Comprehension** What was the government's total income between 1789 and 1791?
2. **Critical Thinking** According to the graph, if the national debt was paid, would there be enough money to run the government? Explain.

Economics

Reading Actively

During Reading Have students read the subsection, A National Bank. Suggest they make a diagram or graphic organizer showing how the Bank of the United States would help build up the national economy.

Graph Skills

ANSWERS **1.** $4,418,000 **2.** Yes, without the national debt, the government's running expenses would be only $4,269,000. The government's income would cover this amount.

★ *Activity* ★

Cooperative Learning

Investigating U.S. savings bonds Have small groups research these questions about current government savings bonds and then report on their findings: What is the minimum amount a person can invest? How long does it take for a bond to mature? What is the current interest rate? For investors, what are the benefits and drawbacks? (*challenging*)

From the Archives of American Heritage®

The early government bureaucracy

In the early years, the Treasury Department was the largest of the federal departments. At the end of 1789, it had 39 employees. By 1801, 78 people worked in the Washington office and 1,615 others worked in the field, collecting taxes and import duties.

Source: Bernard A. Weisberger, "What Made the Government Grow," *American Heritage* magazine, September 1997.

Technology

Videodiscs/Videotapes

Prentice Hall United States History Video Collection™, Vol. 5, Ch. 28, "Divisions Within the Government," 4 mins (*average*) ELL

Chapter 28

American Heritage® History of the United States CD-ROM

- History Makers: Benjamin Banneker (*average*)

Why Study History?

ANSWERS

1. (a) Tariffs raise the price of overseas goods, thus making U.S. products the better buy. **(b)** Tariffs increase the cost of inexpensive goods, making them unaffordable.
2. Possible answer: Because Mexicans are paid less than Americans, it costs less to produce the item.

★Activity

Guided Instruction
Suggest that students begin by brainstorming ideas about how the tariff would affect them personally. Remind them to consider the tariff from the points of view of both the consumer and the manufacturer. Set ground rules about how long individuals can speak, in what order they can speak, whether they are allowed any response time, and so on. Make sure the "moderator" knows that a moderator's job is to remain impartial while keeping the discussion focused.

ASSESSMENT See the rubrics in the Alternative Assessment booklet in the Teaching Resources.

Writing Actively

After Reading After students finish reading the section, have them list three main ideas for this section. Then ask them to compare their list to the Sum It Up list for Section 1 in the chapter review.

RESOURCE DIRECTORY

Teaching Resources
Unit 3/Chapter 9
- Section 1 Quiz, p. 8

Why Study History?
- The Debate Over Tariffs Continues, pp. 35–38

Why Study History?

Because the Debate Over Tariffs Continues

Historical Background

In the 1790s, Alexander Hamilton wanted protective tariffs placed on imports. Other American leaders disagreed. The national debate over tariffs had begun.

Over the years, supporters have praised tariffs for raising the price of foreign imports and encouraging Americans to buy domestic goods. They say that American businesses and workers prosper as a result. Opponents, however, feel that tariffs limit competition. They want people to be free to buy the least expensive and best-made product, regardless of where it is produced.

Connections to Today

By 1993, the United States, Canada, and Mexico formed the North American Free Trade Agreement (NAFTA). The three nations agreed to remove all tariffs and other trade barriers over a period of 15 years.

Public opinion on NAFTA was divided. Supporters cheered when exports to Canada and Mexico increased. Opponents complained that American workers were losing jobs as companies moved to Mexico where labor costs were lower. Opponents also charged that Mexico did not enforce laws banning child labor, ensuring safety in the workplace, and protecting the environment.

The opponents of NAFTA and similar agreements urged consumers to boycott, or not buy, goods made in countries with unfair or unsafe labor practices. In particular, they urged consumers to boycott foreign goods made by young children.

Tariffs can increase the cost of the goods you buy.

Connections to You

In one case, students in American schools made an impact. Manufacturers in Pakistan were using children to stitch soccer balls. In protest, American and European students threatened a boycott of soccer balls made in Pakistan. As a result, the manufacturers agreed to stop using child labor.

1. **Comprehension** **(a)** Explain one argument in favor of tariffs. **(b)** Explain one argument against tariffs.
2. **Critical Thinking** It can cost less to make some products in Mexico than in the United States. Why do you think this is so?

Debating Work with other students to stage a debate on NAFTA. One group will support the treaty. Another group will oppose it. Do additional research to find information supporting your position.

Fast Facts

★ Nearly one fifth of all bicycles sold in the U.S. today are imports, subject to a tariff.
★ Tariffs are almost "as old as dirt." In the 13th century, most towns in Europe charged tariffs on goods, such as cloth, soap, flour, fruits, oil, and even jars.
★ The United States has a trade watchdog, the International Trade Commission. This independent agency keeps a watchful eye on how imports are affecting American industries.

Bibliography

To read more about this topic:

1. "Has Clinton Lost His Way?" Christopher Ogden, *Time* (June 19, 1997). President Clinton's fight for free trade agreements.
2. "Take That! And That!" Richard Lacayo, *Time* (February 28, 1994). Japanese trade barriers invite retaliatory U.S. tariffs.
3. Internet. United States International Trade Commission at www.usitc.gov, which includes numerous links related to international trade.

In the end, Congress did pass a tariff bill. However, its purpose was to raise money for operating the government, rather than protect American industries. For this reason, it was much lower than the protective tariff called for by Hamilton.

The Whiskey Rebellion

Congress also passed a bill that taxed all liquor made and sold in the United States. Hamilton wanted this tax to raise money for the Treasury. Instead, the whiskey tax led to a rebellion that tested the strength of the new government.

A hated tax

Like many other Americans, farmers in the backcountry grew corn. However, corn was bulky to haul over rough backcountry roads. Instead, farmers converted their corn into whiskey, which they could easily ship in barrels to markets in the East.

Backcountry farmers protested the whiskey tax. They compared it to the hated taxes Britain had forced on the colonies in the 1760s. Many farmers refused to pay the tax. A backcountry poet wrote:

> "Some chaps whom freedom's spirit warms
> Are threatening hard to take up arms. . . .
> Their liberty they will maintain,
> They fought for't, and they'll fight again."

In 1794, officials in western Pennsylvania tried to collect the tax. Farmers rebelled. Soon, thousands were marching through Pittsburgh. They sang Revolutionary songs and tarred and feathered tax officials.

A show of strength

Washington responded quickly to this challenge to authority. He called up the militia and sent them to Pennsylvania. When the rebels heard that 15,000 troops were marching against them, they scattered. Washington later pardoned the leaders of the rebellion.

The **Whiskey Rebellion** was a critical test of the strength of the new government. Washington had shown those who disagreed with the government that violence would not be tolerated. The President's quick response proved to Americans that their new government would act firmly in times of crisis.

★ Section 1 Review ★

Recall

1. **Identify** (a) Judiciary Act, (b) District of Columbia, (c) Bank of the United States, (d) Whiskey Rebellion.
2. **Define** (a) inauguration, (b) precedent, (c) Cabinet, (d) national debt, (e) bond, (f) speculator, (g) tariff, (h) protective tariff.

Comprehension

3. Describe one precedent that George Washington set for future governments of the United States.
4. (a) Why did Alexander Hamilton think it was important to pay off government bonds? (b) Why did James Madison oppose Hamilton's repayment plan?
5. Describe two proposals Hamilton made to raise money for the new government.

Critical Thinking and Writing

6. **Linking Past and Present** By the late 1990s, the Cabinet included the heads of 13 separate departments. Why do you think the Cabinet has grown so much since Washington's time?
7. **Forecasting** What do you think might have happened if Washington had not taken strong action to put down the Whiskey Rebellion?

Activity **Acting a Scene** The year is 1789. Your family owns government bonds, but you are not sure whether the bonds will be repaid at full value. With a partner, act out a scene between two members of the family. Discuss whether you should hold onto the bonds or sell them to a speculator.

★ Section 1 Review ★

ANSWERS

1. (a) p. 245, (b) p. 247, (c) p. 247, (d) p. 249
2. (a) p. 244, (b) p. 244, (c) p. 245, (d) p. 245, (e) p. 246, (f) p. 246, (g) p. 247, (h) p. 247
3. Possible answer: He chose well-qualified leaders for his Cabinet.
4. (a) because otherwise no one would lend the U.S. money again (b) because it rewarded speculators and penalized southern states that had already paid their debts
5. a protective tariff, a liquor tax
6. Possible answer: With growth, the nation has become more complicated and difficult to govern.
7. Possible answer: Other Americans would defy the government.

Guided Instruction
Have students reread the relevant information in the book and identify points for and against selling the bonds. Students should then develop supporting ideas for and against each position. Encourage students to conduct the discussion as a family talk, not as a debate between opponents. Pairs should act out the scene. Remember that teams presenting later in the process will have the benefit of having heard previous presentations.

ASSESSMENT See the rubrics in the Alternative Assessment booklet in the Teaching Resources.

★ Customized Instruction ★

English Language Learners

Using context clues Students who are English language learners need to make extensive use of context clues to understand unfamiliar vocabulary. To help these students focus on this strategy, write the following on the chalkboard and draw students' attention to the term *backcountry*. "Like many other Americans, farmers in the backcountry grew corn. However, corn was bulky to haul over rough backcountry roads." Explain that the use of the term *rough* to further describe *roads* provides a good clue to the meaning of "backcountry." Have students find their own examples of context clues that suggest the meanings of unfamiliar words. (basic) ELL

Section 2

A Policy of Neutrality

LESSON PLAN

Objectives

★ Describe how Americans reacted to the French Revolution.

★ Identify the policy the United States adopted when war broke out in Europe.

★ Describe how Washington's Farewell Address influenced American foreign policy.

1 Engage

Warm Up Have students define the word *neutrality* and then describe conflicts in which somebody might take a neutral position.

Activating Prior Knowledge To help students appreciate a position of neutrality, ask them to recall a time when two arguing friends both insisted that the student take a stand against the other friend.

Reading Actively

Before Reading Have students read to find cause-and-effect relationships among events and jot down their ideas as they read.

2 Explore

Ask students to read the section, summarize the main points, and consider how the storming of the Bastille appealed to many Americans, who had so recently won their own independence. Describe the factors that contributed to U.S. neutrality in the European

RESOURCE DIRECTORY

Teaching Resources
Lesson Planner, p. 37
Unit 3/Chapter 9
• Biography Flashcard: Eleuthère Irénée du Pont, p. 7

A Policy of Neutrality

As You Read

Explore These Questions
- How did Americans react to the French Revolution?
- What policy did the United States adopt when war broke out in Europe?
- How did Washington's Farewell Address influence American foreign policy?

Define
- foreign policy

Identify
- French Revolution
- Neutrality Proclamation
- Jay's Treaty
- Farewell Address

SETTING the Scene Late in 1789, French ships arriving at American seaports brought startling news. On July 14, an angry mob in Paris, France, had destroyed the Bastille (bahs TEEL), a huge fort that was being used as a prison. The attack on the Bastille was one of several events that launched the **French Revolution**.

The French Revolution broke out a few years after Americans won independence. Like the Americans, the French fought for liberty and equality. As the French Revolution grew more violent, however, it ignited political quarrels that had been smoldering in the United States.

Revolution in France

The French had many reasons to rebel against their king, Louis XVI. Peasants and the middle class paid heavy taxes, while nobles paid none. Reformers called for a constitution to limit the power of the king. They also wanted a guarantee of rights like that in the American Constitution.

Americans support the revolution

At first, most Americans supported the French Revolution. Americans knew what it meant to struggle for liberty. Then, too, France had been the first ally of the United States in the war against Great Britain. Many Americans wanted to rally behind the Marquis de Lafayette, a leading French reformer. They remembered that Lafayette had fought side by side with them in the American Revolution.

In the 1790s, however, the French Revolution entered a very violent stage. A radical group gained power. In 1793, they beheaded Louis XVI and his wife, Queen Marie Antoinette. During a "reign of terror," tens of thousands of French citizens were executed.

Violence divides American opinion

The violence in France divided Americans. Some, like Thomas Jefferson, continued to support the French. He condemned the killings of the king and queen. Still, he felt that the French had the right to use violence to win freedom.

Alexander Hamilton, John Adams, and others disagreed with Jefferson's view. They thought that the French Revolution was doomed to fail. One could no more create democracy through violence, claimed Adams, "than a snowball can exist in the streets of Philadelphia under a burning sun."

Remaining Neutral

The French Revolution shocked rulers and nobles across Europe. They feared the spread of revolutionary ideas to their own

★ *Background* ★

Viewpoints

French Revolution—valiant or despicable? Jefferson: "The liberty of the whole earth was depending on the issue of the contest, and was ever such a prize won with so little innocent blood?" (1793) Hamilton: "None can deny that the cause of France has been stained by excesses and extravagances . . . from which reason and humanity recoil." (1794)

★ *Background* ★

Did You Know?

American-inspired reformations After lending his aid to the American Revolution, Lafayette returned to France and worked to:
• Free slaves and abolish the slave trade
• Promote religious tolerance
• Give France a charter of liberties, drafting the Declaration of the Rights of Man and of the Citizen

The French Revolution

At the start of the French Revolution, famine gripped Paris. Thousands of angry women (above) marched on the palace of the king shouting, "Bread! Bread!" The statue at right honored the army of ragged peasants that rose up against long years of injustice. ★ **Why would the French expect Americans to support their revolution?**

lands. Britain, Spain, Prussia, Austria, and the Netherlands sent armies to overpower the revolutionaries in France. Europe was soon plunged into a war that continued on and off for more than 20 years.

A difficult decision

Faced with the war in Europe, Washington had to form a foreign policy for the nation. **Foreign policy** refers to the actions and stands that a nation takes in relation to other nations. An old treaty, signed during the American Revolution, allowed French ships to use American ports. As the war in Europe continued, the French wanted to use American ports to supply their ships and launch attacks on British ships.

"It is the sincere wish of United America," said the President, "to have nothing to do with . . . the squabbles of European nations." How could the United States honor its treaty with France and still remain neutral?

Divisions in the Cabinet

The issue of the treaty deepened divisions within Washington's Cabinet. Hamilton pointed out that the United States had signed the treaty with Louis XVI. Since the king was dead, he argued, the treaty was no longer valid. Jefferson, however, supported the French cause. He was suspicious of Hamilton, who wanted friendlier relations with Britain, the nation's old enemy.

After much debate, Washington issued the **Neutrality Proclamation** in April 1793. In it, he stated that the United States would not support either side in the war. It also forbade Americans to aid either Britain or France in any way.

Many viewed the Neutrality Proclamation as a defeat for Jefferson. Eventually, this and other conflicts with Hamilton caused Jefferson to leave the Cabinet.

An Unpopular Treaty

Declaring neutrality was easier than enforcing it. American merchants wanted to trade with both Britain and France. However, those warring nations ignored the rights of neutral ships. They seized American cargoes headed for each other's ports.

In 1793, the British captured more than 250 American ships trading in the French

war that began with the French Revolution.

3 Teach

Have students work in small groups. Assign one of these positions to each group: **(a)** Americans who support the French revolution; **(b)** French citizens who believe that the French should be able to use U.S. ports to attack the British; **(c)** advisers to Washington supporting U.S. neutrality. Groups will prepare a list of reasons for their positions; then a representative from each group will read its list. Compile a master list on the chalkboard.

4 Assess

To close the lesson, have students complete the section review; or ask them to create a two-column cause-and-effect chart. The first column should summarize the major events discussed in the section; the second should list the result, or effect, of each event. Events may appear in both columns.

ANSWER

Possible answers: because France had backed Americans during the Revolution; because French rebels wanted the same democratic rights that Americans favored

Writing Actively

After Reading After students read the section, have them list two U.S. policies designed to keep the U.S. out of European wars.

★ *Background* ★

Our Diverse Nation

An American reformer Treated unfairly as a Jew in France, Benjamin Nones came to the United States in 1777. This American:

- Fought in the American Revolution
- Freed his own slave in 1793
- Embraced Democratic Republican ideals
- Dedicated himself to the antislavery movement until his death in 1826

★ Section 2 Review ★

ANSWERS

1. (a) p. 250, **(b)** p. 251, **(c)** p. 252, **(d)** p. 252

2. p. 251

3. Some Americans turned against it after it turned violent. Others felt the French had the right to use violence to gain freedom.

4. He issued the Neutrality Proclamation and sent John Jay to work out a treaty.

5. He advised Americans to avoid getting involved in foreign affairs.

6. Possible answers: **(a)** People have the right to use violence to win liberty. **(b)** He valued freedom more than peace and order.

7. Students should recognize that the U.S. was partly isolated from Europe by the Atlantic Ocean.

Activity

Guided Instruction
Direct students to the index of their text to find information about Washington's career. Have them take notes as they review his role in American history. Have students develop their notes into written speeches or use them to speak extemporaneously. Collect the written speeches. Set a time limit, say 2 minutes each, for students who choose to give their speeches orally.

ASSESSMENT See the rubrics in the Alternative Assessment booklet in the Teaching Resources.

West Indies. Americans clamored for war. Washington, however, knew that the United States was too weak to fight. He sent Chief Justice John Jay to Britain for talks.

Jay worked out a treaty. It called for Britain to pay damages for American ships seized in 1793. At the same time, Americans had to pay debts to British merchants, owed from before the Revolution. Britain agreed to give up forts it still held in the Ohio Valley. However, the treaty did nothing to protect the rights of neutral American ships.

George Washington retired to Mount Vernon, his Virginia home, where he died in 1799.

Jay's Treaty sparked a storm of protest. Many Americans felt they were giving up more than Britain was. After a furious debate, the Senate finally approved the treaty in 1795. Washington accepted the treaty because he wanted to avoid war.

Washington Retires

In 1796, George Washington published his **Farewell Address**. In it, he announced he would retire. He urged the United States to remain neutral in its relations with other countries:

> "Observe good faith and justice toward all nations.... Nothing is more essential than that permanent, [habitual hatred] against particular nations and passionate attachments for others should be excluded."

Washington warned Americans to avoid becoming involved in European affairs. "'Tis our true policy to steer clear of permanent alliances with any portion of the foreign world," said the retiring President. Such alliances, he felt, would pull the United States into war. That advice guided American foreign policy for many years.

★ Section 2 Review ★

Recall

1. **Identify** **(a)** French Revolution, **(b)** Neutrality Proclamation, **(c)** Jay's Treaty, **(d)** Farewell Address.
2. **Define** foreign policy.

Comprehension

3. How did the revolution in France divide Americans?
4. Describe two actions Washington took to avoid war.
5. What advice did Washington give in his Farewell Address?

Critical Thinking and Writing

6. **Recognizing Points of View** Writing about the French Revolution, Thomas Jefferson said he was willing to see "half the earth devastated" in order to win the "liberty of the whole." **(a)** Restate Jefferson's main idea in your own words. **(b)** What does this statement tell you about Jefferson's values?
7. **Analyzing Information** How did geographic location help the United States to "steer clear of permanent alliances" with European nations for many years?

Activity **Giving an Introduction** President Washington has chosen to deliver his Farewell Address in your school auditorium. You have been asked to introduce him. Prepare a two-minute introduction naming what you consider to be Washington's greatest achievements.

★ Background ★

Linking Past and Present

Marketing celebrities Merchandisers today make profits by using the names of athletes and other celebrities on a wide variety of goods. This promotional technique is not new. George Washington was hugely popular, and his name and image were stamped on handkerchiefs, ribbons, buttons, and other items to improve sales.

★ Activity ★

Connections With the World

Identifying influences from France
Have students work in small groups to list items and events that are part of life and culture in the United States today and that reflect the influence that France and the French people have had on the United States. (*average*)

RESOURCE DIRECTORY

Teaching Resources
Lesson Planner, p. 38
Unit 3/Chapter 9
• Section 2 Quiz, p. 9

The Rise of Political Parties

As You Read

Explore These Questions
- How did political differences lead to the rise of two political parties?
- What role did newspapers play in politics?
- How did the election of 1796 increase political tensions?

Define
- faction
- unconstitutional

Identify
- Democratic Republicans
- Federalists

SETTING the Scene When President Washington took office in 1789, the United States had no political parties. In fact, most American leaders opposed the very idea of forming parties. "If I could not go to heaven but with a party," said Thomas Jefferson, "I would not go at all."

Still, deep divisions began to form in the Cabinet and Congress. Jefferson described the unpleasant mood:

> ❝ Men who have been [friends] all their lives cross streets to avoid meeting, and turn their heads another way, lest they should be obliged to touch their hats. ❞

By the time Washington left office in 1789, there were two parties competing for power.

A Distrust of Political Parties

Americans had reason to distrust political parties. They had seen how **factions,** or opposing groups within parties, worked in Britain. British factions were made up of a few people who schemed to win favors from the government. Most were more interested in personal gain than in the public good.

Americans also saw political parties as a threat to national unity. They agreed with George Washington, who warned Americans that parties would lead to "jealousies and false alarms."

Despite the President's warning, parties grew up around two members of his Cabinet, Alexander Hamilton and Thomas Jefferson. The two men differed in background, looks, and personality as well as in politics. Born in the West Indies, Hamilton had worked his way up from poverty. He dressed in fine clothes and spoke forcefully. Energetic, brilliant, and restless, Hamilton enjoyed political debate.

Jefferson was tall and lanky. Although he was a wealthy Virginia planter, he dressed and spoke informally. One senator recalled:

> ❝ His clothes seem too small for him. He sits in a lounging manner, on one hip commonly, and with one of his shoulders elevated much above the other. His face has a sunny aspect. His whole figure has a loose, shackling air.... He spoke almost without ceasing. [His conversation] was loose and rambling; and yet he scattered information wherever he went. ❞

Differing Views

Alexander Hamilton did not agree with Thomas Jefferson on many issues. At the root of their quarrels were different views about what was best for the young United States.

Manufacturing or farming

First, Hamilton and Jefferson disagreed about economic policy. Hamilton thought the United States should model itself on Britain. He felt the government should encourage

Section 3
The Rise of Political Parties

LESSON PLAN

Objectives

★ Explain how political differences led to the rise of two political parties.

★ Describe the role newspapers played in politics in the late 1700s.

★ Explain how the election of 1796 increased political tensions.

1 Engage

Warm Up Have students free-write for 3 minutes each about the images that *Democrat* and *Republican* (referring to today's political parties) bring to mind.

Activating Prior Knowledge Have students recall a recent student government election. Ask students how the different campaigns affected their own relationships with other students.

Reading Actively

Before Reading Have students turn the section title into a question (e.g., "Why did political parties arise?"). Ask them to jot down notes that answer the question.

2 Explore

Ask students to read the section, then chart how Jefferson and Hamilton differed in background, personality, and political views. Have students tell whom they would have supported for office and why.

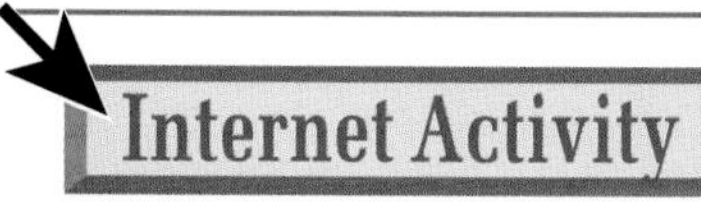

Political parties Democrats, Republicans, and Libertarians all have World Wide Web home pages (www.democrats.org/, www.rnc.org/, and www.lp.org/, respectively). Have students compare these pages and then write about the similarities and differences among the parties' messages. Because of the changing nature of the Internet, you might want to preview the sites. (*challenging*)

3 Teach

Have students draft editorials that might have appeared in 1796 in the *Gazette of the United States* and in the *National Gazette*. Use the editorials as a springboard for a discussion about the differences between the Federalists and the Democratic Republicans. Students may want to save their notes for the History and You Activity in the section review.

4 Assess

To close the lesson, have students complete the section review. As an alternative, have students choose either Hamilton or Jefferson and give a speech rallying support for that person's views on the proper powers of the federal government.

★ ★ ★ ★ ★ ★ ★ ★ ★ ★ ★ ★ ★ ★ ★ ★ ★

ANSWER

The farming scene represents Jefferson's view. The ironworker represents Hamilton's view.

Reading Actively

During Reading Before students read the subsection Strict or Loose Interpretation of the Constitution, tell them that the subsection reveals two issues upon which Hamilton and Jefferson disagreed—one specific and immediate, the other broad and far-reaching. After students have read the subsection, ask them to identify the two issues.

RESOURCE DIRECTORY

Teaching Resources
Unit 3/Chapter 9
- Practice Your Skills: Managing Information—Outlining, p. 2

Interdisciplinary Connections
- Main Idea: Inventing a Nation, p. 54

Two Views of the Nation

Federalists and Republicans disagreed. Should the new nation build its future mainly on agriculture or on manufacturing? The farmer, above, and the ironworker, right, represent these two viewpoints.
★ **Which of these pictures represents Hamilton's view? Which picture represents Jefferson's view?**

manufacturing and trade. He also favored the growth of cities and the merchant class who helped make cities prosperous.

Jefferson believed that farmers, rather than merchants, were the backbone of the new nation. "Cultivators of the earth," he wrote, "are the most valuable citizens." He feared that a manufacturing economy would corrupt the United States by concentrating power in the hands of a small group of wealthy Americans.

Federal or state governments

Hamilton and Jefferson disagreed about the power of the federal government. Hamilton wanted the federal government to have greater power than state governments. A strong federal government, he argued, could encourage the growth of commerce. It would also have the power needed to restrain unruly mobs, such as the protesters who led the Whiskey Rebellion.

In contrast, Jefferson hoped to make the government as small as possible. Then, citizens would have the freedom to act as they pleased. Jefferson feared that a strong federal government might take over powers that the Constitution gave to the states.

Strict or loose interpretation of the Constitution

These disagreements led the two leaders to clash over the Bank of the United States. Jefferson worried that a national bank would give too much power to the federal government and the wealthy investors who helped run it.

To oppose Hamilton's proposal, Jefferson argued that the law creating the bank was **unconstitutional,** that is, not permitted by the Constitution. Nowhere did the Constitution give Congress the power to create a Bank, he argued. Jefferson thought that any power not specifically given to the federal government belonged to the states.

Hamilton did not agree with Jefferson's strict interpretation of the Constitution. He preferred a looser interpretation. The Constitution gave Congress the power to make all laws "necessary and proper" to carry out

★ Background ★

Viewpoints

Controversy and the media game In the summer of 1792, the conflict between Jefferson and Hamilton started heating up. Hamilton began to write anonymous columns in newspapers friendly to his cause, in which he attacked Jefferson's character and principles. In one article, he insulted Jefferson, calling him an "intriguing incendiary." Thus began a tradition of vicious personal attacks on opponents that survives to this day in American politics.

Critical Thinking | Managing Information | Communication | Maps, Charts, and Graphs

Outlining

How Will I Use This Skill?

In school and, later, at work, you may be asked to write a report or give a presentation. You will find the job easier if you prepare an outline. An outline helps you arrange information in logical order. In addition, when you speak in public, an outline can keep you from fumbling for words!

LEARN the Skill

Make an outline by following these four steps.

1. Use the theme or topic as the title of your outline.
2. Identify and list the main ideas in order. Label them with Roman numerals.
3. Identify subtopics for each main idea. Label these with capital letters and list them under the main ideas.
4. Identify details that support each subtopic. Label and list these with Arabic numerals as shown.

PRACTICE the Skill

The sample at right is a partial outline of the subsection Differing Views. Study the sample. Then, using the steps above, make an outline of the subsection Party Rivalry.

1. Take notes as you read the subsection.
2. Using your notes and the headings in the text, write down the main ideas.
3. Using the topic sentences of the paragraphs in the text, identify the subtopics for your outline.
4. Find and list supporting details from the text.

The Clash of Jefferson and Hamilton

I. Jefferson's Views
  A. Preferred farm economy
  B. Favored strict interpretation of Constitution
    1. Against Bank of United States
      a. Too much power to federal government
      b. Unconstitutional
    2. Favored state power
  C. Favored France in foreign policy
II. Hamilton's Views
  A. Supported manufacturing economy
  B. Favored loose interpretation of Constitution
    1. Planned Bank of United States
      a. Way to collect taxes
      b. Way to pay government bills
    2. Favored federal power
  C. Supported Britain in foreign policy

APPLY the Skill

Choose a topic that interests you. Make an outline for a short talk on this subject.

Skills FOR LIFE

PRACTICE the Skill ANSWER

Possible answer:

Party Rivalry

I. Jefferson's Democratic Republicans
  A. Known as "Republicans"
  B. Supported by farmers, craftsworkers, and some planters
II. Hamilton's Federalists
  A. Wanted strong federal government
  B. Supported by merchants and manufacturers
III. Newspapers
  A. Number of papers doubled
  B. Papers supported parties
  C. Influence on public opinion
    1. Contributed to party rivalry
    2. Kept people informed

APPLY the Skill

Guided Instruction

Remind students to choose a topic that is not too broad. Encourage them to separate main ideas from supporting ideas.

ASSESSMENT

See rubrics in the Alternative Assessment booklet in the Teaching Resources.

★ *Activity* ★

Cooperative Learning

Investigating water use Have half the class list ways 18th-century farmers might use rivers and streams and the ways farming might affect the clean water supply. Tell the remaining students to make similar lists for 18th-century manufacturers. Have students discuss what each group's view of proper water-use regulation might be. (average)

Technology

Videodiscs/Videotapes

Prentice Hall United States History Video Collection™, Vol. 5, Ch. 34, "The Many or the Few?" 3:30 mins (average) ELL

Graphic Organizer *Skills*

ANSWERS **1.** Republicans opposed a national bank and a protective tariff, while Federalists favored them. **2.** The statement is closer to Federalist views. Federalists believed that the wealthy and well-educated were best qualified to lead the nation, while Republicans wanted more power in the hands of the people.

Writing Actively

After Reading Ask students to use the information in the graphic organizer as the basis for a short essay comparing and contrasting the views of Jefferson and Hamilton.

Federalists vs. Republicans

FEDERALISTS	REPUBLICANS
① Led by Alexander Hamilton	① Led by Thomas Jefferson
② Wealthy and well educated should lead nation	② People should have political power
③ Strong central government	③ Strong state governments
④ Emphasis on manufacturing, shipping, and trade	④ Emphasis on agriculture
⑤ Loose interpretation of Constitution	⑤ Strict interpretation of the Constitution
⑥ Pro-British	⑥ Pro-French
⑦ Favored national bank	⑦ Opposed national bank
⑧ Favored protective tariff	⑧ Opposed protective tariff

Graphic Organizer *Skills* **By the 1790s, there were two political parties in the United States—the Federalist party and the Republican party.**

1. **Comprehension** Describe two ways the Republicans and Federalists differed on economic issues.
2. **Critical Thinking** "The average person is far too ignorant to make wise political decisions." Do you think a Republican or a Federalist would be more likely to agree with this statement? Explain.

Civics

its duties. Hamilton argued that the Bank was necessary for the government to collect taxes and pay its bills.

Britain or France

Finally, the two leaders clashed over foreign policy. Hamilton wanted to form close ties with Britain, an important trading partner. Jefferson favored France, the first ally of the United States and a nation struggling for its own liberty.

Party Rivalry

At first, Hamilton and Jefferson clashed in private. However, when Congress began to pass many of Hamilton's programs, Jefferson and James Madison decided to organize public support for their views.

Madison and Jefferson moved cautiously at first. In 1791, they went to New York, telling people that they were going to study its wildlife. In fact, Jefferson was interested in nature and did travel far into upstate New York. Their main purpose, though, was to meet with important New York politicians like Governor George Clinton and Aaron Burr, a strong critic of Hamilton. Jefferson asked Clinton and Burr to help defeat Hamilton's program by getting New Yorkers to vote for Jefferson supporters.

Republicans and Federalists

Soon, leaders in other states began organizing to support either Hamilton or Jefferson. Jefferson's supporters called themselves **Democratic Republicans,** often shortened to Republicans.* Republicans included small farmers, craftworkers, and some wealthy planters.

*Jefferson's Republican party was not the same as today's Republican party. In fact, his party later grew into the Democratic party.

★ *Customized Instruction* ★

Extroverted Learners

Putting on a skit After students have read and discussed Section 3, have them form small groups and put on skits to demonstrate the role of newspaper publishers and reporters in the late 1700s. You may wish to suggest the following roles for students to portray: newspaper publishers, reporters, Thomas Jefferson, Alexander Hamilton, members of the Federalist party, members of the Democratic Republican party, and various members of society. After each skit, have the audience comment on the information presented and the feelings expressed during the skit. *(average)*

RESOURCE DIRECTORY

Teaching Resources
Unit 3/Chapter 9
• Section 3 Quiz, p. 10

Hamilton and his supporters were called **Federalists** because they wanted a strong federal government. Federalists drew most of their support from merchants and manufacturers in cities such as Boston and New York. They also gained the backing of some southern planters.

Newspapers take sides

In the late 1700s, the number of American newspapers more than doubled. This growth met a demand for information. A visitor from Europe noted with surprise that so many Americans could read:

> "The common people [in the United States] are on a footing, in point of literature with the middle ranks of Europe. They all read and write, and understand arithmetic; almost every little town now furnishes a circulating library."

As party rivalry grew, newspapers took sides. In the *Gazette of the United States*, publisher John Fenno printed articles in favor of Alexander Hamilton and the Federalists. Philip Freneau (frih NOH), a friend of Thomas Jefferson, started a rival paper, the *National Gazette*. Freneau vigorously supported Republicans.

Newspapers had great influence on public opinion. In stinging language, they raged against opponents. Often, articles mixed rumor and opinion with facts. Emotional attacks and counterattacks fanned the flames of party rivalry. Still, newspapers performed a needed service. They kept people informed and helped shape public opinion.

Election of 1796

Political parties played a major role in the election of George Washington's successor. In 1796, Republicans backed Thomas Jefferson for President and Aaron Burr for Vice President. Federalists supported John Adams for President and Thomas Pinckney for Vice President.

The election had an unexpected outcome, which created new tensions. Under the Constitution, the person with the most electoral votes became President. The person with the next highest total was made Vice President. John Adams, a Federalist, won office as President. The leader of the Republicans, Thomas Jefferson, came in second and became Vice President.

With the President and the Vice President from different parties, political tensions remained high. Future events would further increase the distrust between the two men. Meanwhile, John Adams took office in March 1797 as the second President of the United States.

★ Section 3 Review ★

Recall

1. **Identify** (a) Democratic Republicans, (b) Federalists.
2. **Define** (a) faction, (b) unconstitutional.

Comprehension

3. Describe two issues on which Thomas Jefferson and Alexander Hamilton disagreed.
4. How did newspapers contribute to the rivalry between political parties?
5. What role did parties play in the 1796 election?

Critical Thinking and Writing

6. **Drawing Conclusions** Why do you think political parties emerged even though most Americans opposed them?
7. **Ranking** Which of the disagreements between Jefferson and Hamilton do you think was the most serious? Explain.

Activity **Writing a Newspaper Headline** You are the publisher of either the *Gazette of the United States* or the *National Gazette*. Write three headlines about the election of 1796. Be sure your headlines express the point of view of your own newspaper.

★ Section 3 Review ★

ANSWERS

1. (a) p. 256, **(b)** p. 257

2. (a) p. 253, **(b)** p. 254

3. Possible answers: Hamilton: favored Britain and a strong federal government; Jefferson: favored France and strong states

4. Rival newspapers supported Federalists or Republicans. By mixing rumors and feelings with facts, they influenced public opinion.

5. They supported rival candidates. The Federalist Adams won the election and the Republican Jefferson became Vice President.

6. The issues that divided the supporters of Hamilton and Jefferson led to the creation of parties.

7. Possible answer: power of the federal government, because it reflects national versus local interests

Activity

Guided Instruction

Students can clarify the political positions of the *Gazette of the United States* (Federalist) and the *National Gazette* (Republican) by describing each paper's stand on: **(a)** a national bank; **(b)** strict or loose interpretation of the Constitution; **(c)** the war between Britain and France. Remind students that their headlines should reflect the political position of their paper.

ASSESSMENT See the rubrics in the Alternative Assessment booklet in the Teaching Resources.

★ Background ★ Turning Points

Extra! Extra! Read all about it! Daily newspapers produced a relative avalanche of up-to-date news on political and economic events—news that was suddenly available to the ordinary citizen. The first "daily" was the *Pennsylvania Packet and Daily Advertiser,* which started publication on September 21, 1784, in Philadelphia.

★ Background ★ Recent Scholarship

New perspective on Madison James Madison has long been thought a strict advocate of states' rights and republicanism. Lance Banning's book *The Sacred Fire of Liberty: James Madison and the Founding of the Federal Republic* argues well that Madison advocated a new federalism, which was embodied in his contributions to the Constitution.

Section 4
The Second President

LESSON PLAN

Objectives

★ Explain why many Americans favored war with France.
★ Explain why the Federalist Party split in two.
★ Explain why the Alien and Sedition acts outraged many Americans.

1 Engage

Warm Up Have students brainstorm to create a list of characteristics that they think a person would need to be a great President.

Activating Prior Knowledge Ask students to use the list from the warm up activity to judge George Washington's presidency. Remind students that John Adams was Washington's Vice President and had his own political record and reputation before he was elected President. Ask students to identify any characteristics of greatness Adams brought to his presidency.

Reading Actively

Before Reading Ask students to note the three vocabulary words: *immigrant, sedition, nullify*. Have them jot down ideas about the meaning of each word. As they come to each word in the reading, have them refine their definitions.

RESOURCE DIRECTORY

Teaching Resources
Lesson Planner, p. 39
Unit 3/Chapter 9
• Critical Thinking and Writing: Understanding Causes and Effects, p. 4

The Second President

As You Read

Explore These Questions
- Why did many Americans favor war with France?
- Why did the Federalist party split in two?
- Why did the Alien and Sedition acts outrage many Americans?

Define
- immigrant
- sedition
- nullify

Identify
- XYZ Affair
- High Federalists
- Napoleon Bonaparte
- Alien and Sedition acts
- Kentucky and Virginia resolutions

SETTING the Scene Late in his life, John Adams looked back on his career with mixed feelings. He knew that leaders such as Washington and Jefferson were more widely admired than he was. Still, Adams wrote proudly of his life's work:

> "I have done more labor, run through more and greater dangers, and made greater sacrifices than any man . . . living or dead, in the service of my country."

At the same time, Adams found it hard to boast of his achievements. In the end, he concluded: "I am not, never was, and never shall be a great man."

Although he was not a popular hero, like Washington, Adams was an honest and able leader. As President, he tried to act in the best interests of the nation, even when his actions hurt him politically.

Conflict With France

No sooner did Adams take office than he faced a crisis with France. The French objected to Jay's Treaty because they felt that it favored Britain. In 1797, French ships began to seize American ships in the West Indies, as the British had done.

Once again, Americans called for war, this time against France. Adams tried to avoid war by sending diplomats to Paris to discuss the rights of neutral nations.

The XYZ Affair

France's foreign minister, Charles Maurice de Talleyrand, did not deal directly with the Americans. Instead, he sent three secret agents to offer the Americans a deal. Before Talleyrand would begin talks, the agents said, he wanted $250,000 for himself, as well as a loan to France of $10 million. "Not a sixpence!" replied one of the American diplomats angrily.

The diplomats informed Adams about the offer. Adams, in turn, told Congress. He did not reveal the names of the French agents, referring to them only as X, Y, and Z.

Many Americans were outraged when they heard about the **XYZ Affair** in 1798. They took up the slogan, "Millions for defense, but not one cent for tribute!" They were willing to spend money to defend their country, but they refused to pay a bribe to another nation.

Adams avoids war

Despite growing pressure, Adams refused to ask Congress to declare war on France. Still, he could not ignore French attacks on American ships. He moved to strengthen the navy. Shipyards built frigates—fast-sailing ships with many guns.

This show of strength helped convince Talleyrand to stop attacking American ships. He also promised Adams that if American ambassadors came to France, they would be treated with respect.

★ *Customized Instruction* ★

Kinesthetic Learners

Creating a media campaign Form small groups to work together to create a media campaign to persuade people to support or oppose President Adams's handling of the XYZ Affair. Assign a position for each group or allow groups to choose either to support or oppose Adams. Have each group create a button, print advertisement, and a one-minute announcement to communicate its viewpoint. In planning their campaigns, students should consider the fears and concerns that arose as people learned the details of the affair. Campaigns should also take into account that although Adams was a Federalist, all Federalists did not support his decisions. (challenging)

On the Brink of War

After the XYZ Affair, many Americans called for war with France. War fever led the nation to build up its navy. At left, a cartoon shows France as a five-headed monster asking for "Money, Money, Money." At right, Americans construct a new warship. ★ **Why did the XYZ affair outrage Americans?**

The Federalist Party Splits

Many Federalists, led by Hamilton, criticized Adams's actions. They hoped a war would weaken the Republicans, supporters of France. War would also force the United States to build up its military. A stronger army and navy would increase federal power, a major Federalist goal.

Although John Adams was a Federalist, he would not give in to Hamilton. Their disagreement created a split in the Federalist party. Hamilton and his supporters were called **High Federalists**.

Over Hamilton's opposition, Adams again sent diplomats to France. When they arrived, they found an ambitious young army officer, **Napoleon Bonaparte**, in charge. Napoleon did not have time for a war with the United States. He signed an agreement to stop seizing American ships.

Like Washington, Adams kept the nation out of war. His success, however, cost him the support of many Federalists.

Alien and Sedition Acts

During the crisis with France, Federalists pushed several laws through Congress. Passed in 1798, the laws were known as the **Alien and Sedition acts**.

The Alien Act allowed the President to expel any alien, or foreigner, thought to be dangerous to the country. Another law made it harder for immigrants to become citizens. An **immigrant** is a person who enters another country in order to settle there. Before, white immigrants could become citizens after living in the United States for 5 years. Under the new law, immigrants had to wait 14 years. This law was meant to keep new settlers, who often supported the Republicans, from voting.

Republican anger grew when Congress passed the Sedition Act. **Sedition** means stirring up rebellion against a government. Under this law, citizens could be fined or jailed if they criticized the government or its officials.

2 Explore

Ask students to read the section. For a homework assignment, have them list ways that Vice President Jefferson supported or opposed President Adams. Remind students that the 1796 election was the one time in American history when the person who became Vice President had been the President's opponent during the campaign.

3 Teach

Ask students to supply factual statements in support of each generalization: **(a)** John Adams was able to resist pressure from his party to go to war with France. **(b)** The Federalists tried to limit Republican criticism of their policies. **(c)** The Republicans believed that the Alien and Sedition acts were an abuse of government power. Ask students to agree on a generalization about Adams's success as President.

4 Assess

To close the lesson, have students complete the section review. As an alternative, have them create a graphic organizer summarizing the main points presented in Section 4.

★ ★ ★ ★ ★ ★ ★ ★ ★ ★ ★ ★ ★ ★ ★ ★ ★ ★

Linking United States and the World

ANSWER

Americans were outraged that French officials would dare to demand a bribe before they would stop seizing American ships.

★ *Activity* ★
Linking Past and Present

Finding evidence Remind students that under the Sedition Act, citizens could be fined or jailed for criticizing the government or its officials. Have them find and note statements in the media that are evidence that the Sedition Act is no longer part of United States law. (*average*)

Technology

AmericanHeritage® History of the United States CD-ROM
- Presidents: John Adams (*average*)

Reading Actively

During Reading Have students read Jefferson's quotation about the Alien and Sedition acts. Ask what is meant by "If this goes down. . . ." Ask if Jefferson's predictions were based on fact or opinion. Have students consider what might have motivated Jefferson to make such a strong statement.

Biography

ANSWER

Students should recognize that women did not have the right to vote or have other political rights during Abigail Adams's time.

Writing Actively

After Reading Have students review the meanings of *immigrant, sedition,* and *nullify*. Then ask them to write three sentences, one using each word, that states a main idea in the section.

Locket given by John to Abigail Adams

Biography John and Abigail Adams

Throughout 54 years of marriage, John Adams valued the advice and support of his wife, Abigail. A brilliant woman and fine writer, Abigail Adams supported greater rights for women. They were the first President and First Lady to live in the White House. Their son, John Quincy Adams, also became President. ★ **Why would it have been hard for Abigail Adams to pursue her own political career?**

Republicans protested that the Sedition Act violated the Constitution. After all, they argued, the First Amendment protected freedom of speech and freedom of the press. Jefferson warned that the new laws threatened American liberties:

> " If this goes down, we shall immediately see attempted another act of Congress, declaring that the President shall continue in office during life, and after that other laws giving both the President and the Congress life terms in office. "

Under the Sedition Act, several Republican newspaper editors, and even members of Congress, were fined and jailed for expressing their opinions.

The Rights of States

Outraged, Jefferson urged the states to take strong action against the Alien and Sedition acts. He argued that the states had the right to **nullify,** or cancel, a law passed by the federal government. In this way, states could resist the power of the federal government.

With the help of Jefferson and Madison, Kentucky and Virginia passed resolutions in 1798 and 1799. The **Kentucky and Virginia resolutions** claimed that each state "has an equal right to judge for itself" whether a law is constitutional. If a state decides a law is unconstitutional, said the resolutions, it has the power to nullify that law within its borders.

Connections With Arts

The picture of Abigail Adams, above, is by Gilbert Stuart, one of the greatest American portrait painters. In fact, you may have a Gilbert Stuart painting in your pocket right now. His portrait of George Washington appears on the one dollar bill.

RESOURCE DIRECTORY

Teaching Resources
Unit 3/Chapter 9
- Vocabulary Builder, p. 2
- Connecting History and Literature: Letter to Her Daughter From the New White House, p. 6
- Section 4 Quiz, p. 11

Chapter Tests, pp. 49–54

★ Background ★
Turning Points

Election of 1800 The personal attacks and negative campaigning that are part of presidential elections today became commonplace in the election of 1800. Yet, in spite of strong feelings, power changed hands. Years later, Jefferson called the election "as real a revolution in the principles of our government as that of 1776 was in its form."

The Kentucky and Virginia resolutions raised a difficult question. Did a state have the right to decide on its own that a law was unconstitutional?

The question remained unanswered in Jefferson's lifetime. Before long, the Alien and Sedition acts were changed or dropped. Still, the issue of a state's right to nullify federal laws would come up again.

Election of 1800

By 1800, the cry for war against France was fading. As the election approached, the Republicans hoped to sweep the Federalists from office. Republicans focused on two issues. First, they attacked the Federalists for raising taxes to prepare for war. Second, they opposed the unpopular Alien and Sedition acts.

Republicans supported Thomas Jefferson for President and Aaron Burr for Vice President. Despite the bitter split in the Federalist party, John Adams was again named the Federalist candidate.

A deadlock

In the race for President, the Republicans won the popular vote. However, when the electoral college voted, Jefferson and Burr each received 73 votes. At the time, the electoral college did not vote separately for President and Vice President. Each Republican elector cast one vote for Jefferson and one vote for Burr.

Under the Constitution, if no candidate wins the electoral vote, the House of Representatives decides the election. The House vote, however, was also evenly split between Jefferson and Burr. After four days, and 36 votes, the tie was finally broken. The House chose Jefferson as President. Burr became Vice President.

Congress afterward passed the Twelfth Amendment. It required electors to vote separately for President and Vice President. The states ratified the amendment in 1804.

End of the Federalist era

The Republican victory set an important precedent for the nation. To this day, power continues to pass peacefully from one party to another.

After 1800, the Federalist party began to decline. Federalists won fewer seats in Congress. In 1804, the Federalist party was further weakened when their leader, Alexander Hamilton, was killed in a duel with Aaron Burr. Despite their decline, the Federalist party had helped shape the new nation. Republican Presidents eventually kept most of Hamilton's economic programs.

★ Section 4 Review ★

Recall

1. **Identify** **(a)** XYZ Affair, **(b)** High Federalists, **(c)** Napoleon Bonaparte, **(d)** Alien and Sedition acts, **(e)** Kentucky and Virginia resolutions.
2. **Define** **(a)** immigrant, **(b)** sedition, **(c)** nullify.

Comprehension

3. Why did many Americans want to declare war on France?
4. Why did John Adams lose the support of many Federalists?
5. **(a)** Why did Federalists favor the Alien and Sedition acts? **(b)** Why did Republicans oppose these laws?

Critical Thinking and Writing

6. **Applying Information** How did the Kentucky and Virginia resolutions reflect Jefferson's view of government?
7. **Analyzing Information** How did the Twelfth Amendment help prevent deadlocks like the one that took place in the election of 1800?

Activity **Drawing a Political Cartoon** Suppose that the Sedition Act of 1798 were passed by Congress today. Draw a political cartoon expressing your opinion of the law.

★ Section 4 Review ★

ANSWERS

1. (a) p. 258, **(b)–(d)** p. 259, **(e)** p. 260

2. (a) p. 259, **(b)** p. 259, **(c)** p. 260

3. It had seized U.S. ships; its officials had asked for bribes.

4. They opposed his efforts to avoid war with France.

5. (a) Alien: It delayed granting citizenship to immigrants, who tended to vote Republican. Sedition: It silenced Republicans who criticized the government. **(b)** Alien: It denied the vote to some supporters. Sedition: It violated freedom of speech and the press.

6. The resolutions said states would nullify federal law; he believed in strong state, not federal, government.

7. It prevented ties by requiring 2 ballots: for President and Vice President.

Activity

Guided Instruction
Suggest that students write a one-sentence opinion of the act to clarify their views. Ask them to pick a situation or symbol that represents their views. Tell them that what counts is their idea, not the quality of the art itself.

ASSESSMENT See the rubrics in the Alternative Assessment booklet in the Teaching Resources.

Technology

Videodiscs/Videotapes
Prentice Hall United States History Video Collection™, Vol. 5, Ch. 37, "The Revolution of 1800," 1:40 min *(average)* ELL

Chapter 37

CD-ROM
Test Bank CD-ROM, Ch. 9
Interactive Student Tutorial

FROM THE ARCHIVES OF AmericanHeritage®

Campaign ad Early political campaigns felt free to attack their opponents. A Republican campaign ad in 1800 shouted, "REPUBLICANS Turn out, . . . and save your Country from ruin! . . . DOWN WITH THE TORIES . . . Before they have it in their power to . . . reduce your families to distress by heavy taxation. . . ."

Source: Bernard A. Weisberger, "The Lives of the Parties," *American Heritage* magazine, September 1992.

★ *Background* ★

Did You Know?

Vice President indicted Aaron Burr was indicted for killing Hamilton in 1804 and was not elected Vice President for Jefferson's second term. In 1807, Burr was hunted down and tried for treason when he formed a conspiracy of rebels seeking to create a separate nation on the frontier. Aaron Burr is buried in Princeton, New Jersey.

Chapter 9

Review and Activities

Reviewing the Chapter

Define These Terms

1. e **2.** b **3.** d **4.** a **5.** c

Explore the Main Ideas

1. Many southern states had already paid their debts and thought other states should do the same.

2. Britain and France both seized cargoes belonging to merchants of the United States.

3. (a) The Federalist supporters were generally merchants and manufacturers in cities such as Boston and New York. **(b)** Republicans were small farmers and craftsworkers.

4. Adams refused to ask Congress to declare war, and he strengthened the American navy.

5. Several Republican newspaper editors, and even members of Congress, were fined and jailed for expressing their opinions.

Graph Activity

1. about 1,800 people **2.** It more than doubled. **3.** It grew because President Adams wanted to convince France to stop attacking American ships by strengthening the U.S. Navy.

Critical Thinking and Writing

1. Possible answers: **(a)** Because Washington had been the military leader of the Revolution, people in every part of the country were united in their admiration for him. **(b)** By having the federal government pay off state debts, Hamilton put more power in the hands of the national government. **(c)** Washington showed that the federal government would take strong action to enforce its policies in the states.

2. Possible answers: Yes, because the United States should not interfere in the affairs of other nations. No, because the United States is more powerful today and has economic ties all over the world.

3. Make sure students give reasons to support their opinions.

4. (a) French Revolution begins; Neutrality Proclamation; Washington's Farewell Address; XYZ Affair; Adams builds up American navy **(b)** Possible answer: The XYZ Affair led Americans to call for war against France. As a result, Adams built up the American navy.

Using Primary Sources

(a) She was unable to get firewood because there were so few people in the area that no one could be found to cut wood and bring it to her. **(b)** She was surprised because the area around the capital was covered with trees. **(c)** No, she found it lonely and lacking in comforts.

Chapter 9 Review and Activities

★ Sum It Up ★

Section 1 Launching the New Government

- George Washington set many precedents that determined how future Presidents would govern the nation.
- Alexander Hamilton formed a plan to improve the nation's finances.
- A rebellion against the national government quickly melted away when President Washington responded forcefully.

Section 2 A Policy of Neutrality

- Americans were sharply divided in their reaction to the French Revolution.
- Washington responded to war between Britain and France by declaring that the United States would remain neutral.

Section 3 The Rise of Political Parties

- Because of widely differing views on national issues, two major political parties soon formed in the new republic.
- Federalists supported a strong federal government, while Republicans opposed policies that made the national government too strong.

Section 4 The Second President

- Despite pressure, President John Adams avoided war with France.
- The unpopular Alien and Sedition acts led the states to consider ways to take power back from the federal government.
- In the election of 1800, power passed from the Federalists to the Republicans.

For additional review of the major ideas of Chapter 9, see ***Guide to the Essentials of American History*** or ***Interactive Student Tutorial CD-ROM,*** which contains interactive review activities, graphic organizers, and practice tests.

Reviewing the Chapter

Define These Terms

Match each term with the correct definition.

Column 1	Column 2
1. national debt	**a.** stirring up rebellion
2. tariff	**b.** type of tax
3. speculator	**c.** person who enters a country in order to settle there
4. sedition	**d.** someone who invests in a risky venture to make a profit
5. immigrant	**e.** total a government owes

Explore the Main Ideas

1. Why did many southerners oppose Hamilton's plan to settle state debts?
2. How did Britain and France make Washington's neutrality policy difficult to enforce?
3. Describe the people who supported: **(a)** the Federalist party; **(b)** the Republican party.
4. How did President Adams avoid war?
5. How was the Sedition Act used to silence Republicans?

Graph Activity

Look at the graph below and answer the following questions: **1.** How many people served in the navy in 1798? **2.** What had happened to the navy by 1800? **Critical Thinking** Why did the size of the navy change?

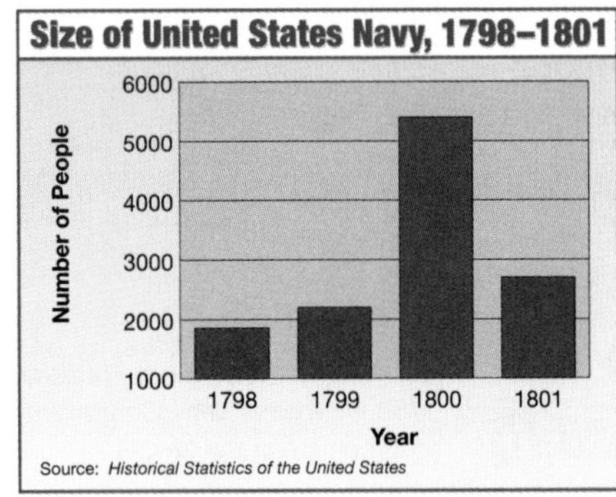

Critical Thinking and Writing

1. Exploring Unit Themes **Nationalism** How did each of the following strengthen the nation: **(a)** the presidency of Washington; **(b)** Hamilton's plan to pay off state debts; **(c)** Washington's response to the Whiskey Rebellion?
2. **Linking Past and Present** Washington urged the United States never to take sides in the world's wars. Do you think this policy would make sense in today's world? Explain.
3. **Defending a Position** Do you think the Constitution should be interpreted strictly or loosely? Give reasons for your position.
4. **Understanding Chronology** **(a)** Place the following events in chronological order: XYZ Affair; Neutrality Proclamation; French Revolution begins; Adams builds up American navy; Washington's Farewell Address. **(b)** Describe the relationship between two of these events.

Using Primary Sources

In its early years, Washington, D.C., was little more than a clearing in the wilderness. First Lady Abigail Adams described its location in a letter to a friend in 1800:

> "Woods are all you see, from Baltimore until you reach the city. . . . Here and there is a small [hut], without a glass window, [all alone] amongst the forests, through which you travel miles without seeing any human being. . . . But, surrounded with forests, can you believe that [fire]wood is not to be had, because people cannot be found to cut and cart it!"

Source: *Letters of Mrs. Adams,* edited by Charles Francis Adams, 1840.

Recognizing Points of View **(a)** Why was Abigail Adams unable to get firewood? **(b)** Why did she consider this surprising? **(c)** Do you think Abigail Adams approved of the new city? Explain.

Activity Bank

Interdisciplinary Activity

Exploring Economics Use library resources to locate information on our current national debt in newspapers or magazines. Prepare a three-minute presentation in which you explain what economic problems may arise because of the national debt.

Career Skills Activity

Reporters Early newspapers often mixed rumor and opinion with facts. Today, reporters have to keep facts and opinions apart. Practice this skill by writing a brief account of the election of 1796 as it might have appeared in a paper of the time. Then, write another account based only on facts.

Citizenship Activity

Researching Political Parties Learn about the political organizations in your area. Most groups will be glad to tell you about the rights and responsibilities of membership. Prepare a one-page data sheet covering at least two political parties. Describe their views and some of their recent or planned activities.

Internet Activity

Today, as in the 1790s, the United States has a special government bank. Use the Internet to find information about the Federal Reserve Bank. Then, write a reaction to the Federal Reserve Bank from the point of view of a Federalist or of a Democratic Republican.

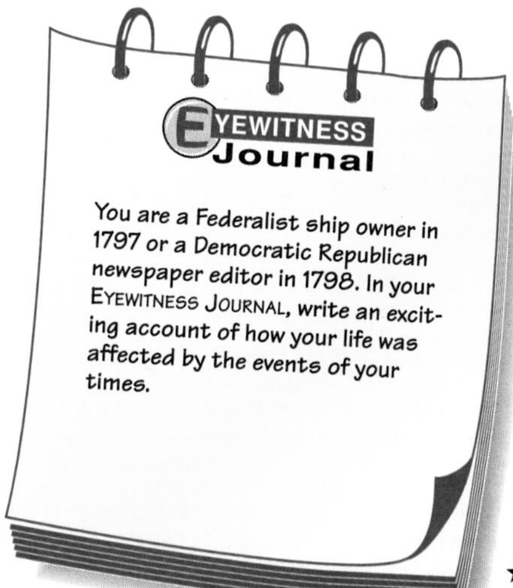

EYEWITNESS Journal
You are a Federalist ship owner in 1797 or a Democratic Republican newspaper editor in 1798. In your EYEWITNESS JOURNAL, write an exciting account of how your life was affected by the events of your times.

Activity Bank

ASSESSMENT To assess the activities on this page, see the rubrics in the Alternative Assessment booklet in the Teaching Resources. You might want to share the rubrics with your students before they begin work.

Interdisciplinary Activity

1. Direct students to guides to periodical literature such as newspaper indexes. "Balancing the budget" is another topic they could research.
2. You may ask some students to create a chart showing the variation in the national debt over time.
3. Ask students to give their reports by turns at the end of class over 3 or 4 days, or randomly choose students to give their presentation. Have the remaining students submit their reports in writing.

Career Skills Activity

1. If necessary, explain the difference between fact and opinion.
2. Suggest that students research the election to make their articles more informative. Almanacs or encyclopedias would be a good source of information.
3. Some students may wish to typeset their articles in newspaper format using a word processor. Different formats can be used for each of the articles.

Citizenship Activity

1. Suggest that students begin by consulting a telephone book to find the names of specific political parties. Such organizations as the League of Women Voters can also provide information. Encourage students to investigate parties other than the two majority parties.
2. Have students take notes of their talks with party members.
3. Direct students to use their notes as the basis of their data sheets.

Eyewitness Journal

1. Tell students a ship owner might have had cargoes seized by the French; a newspaper editor might have been jailed for sedition.
2. Have students use information on the political situation as a backdrop.
3. Encourage students to make their accounts colorful and dramatic.

Internet Activity

1. Have students go to www.phschool.com, which contains updated information on a variety of topics.
2. Another site you may find useful for this activity is the Web site of the Federal Reserve Board at www.bog.frb.fed.us/.
3. Given the changing nature of the Internet, you may wish to preview this site before directing students to it.

Chapter 10 Manager

SECTION OBJECTIVES	TEACHING RESOURCES	ADDITIONAL RESOURC
1 Republicans in Power (pp. 266–269) **Objectives** 1. Describe Jefferson's ideas about government. 2. List the ways Jefferson reduced the power of government. 3. Explain the importance of *Marbury* v. *Madison.*	**Lesson Planner,** p. 40 (average) . . . . .45 mins. **Unit 3/Chapter 10** • Critical Thinking and Writing: Comparing Information on a Chart, p. 14 (average) .30 mins. • Section 1 Quiz, p. 18 (average) . . . . .15 mins. **Why Study History?** • Supreme Court Decisions Affect You, pp. 39–42 (average) . . . . .90 mins.	**Voices of Freedom** • The First Republican President, pp. 78–79 (challenging)
2 The Louisiana Purchase (pp. 270–275) **Objectives** 1. Explain why control of the Mississippi River was important to western farmers. 2. Describe how the United States gained Louisiana. 3. Identify achievements of the Lewis and Clark expedition.	**Lesson Planner,** p. 41 (average) . . . . .90 mins. **Unit 3/Chapter 10** • Practice Your Skills: Reading Map Routes, p. 13 (average) . . . . .30 mins. • Section 2 Quiz, p. 19 (average) . . . . .15 mins. **Interdisciplinary Connections** • Main Idea: The Louisiana Purchase, pp. 57, 58, 60 (average) . . . . .20 mins.	**History Alive!® Activity Pack** • Journal Writing: Heading West With Lewis and Clark **Voices of Freedom** • The Shoshones Meet Lewis and Clark, pp. 79–80 (average) **Historical Outline Map Book** • Exploring the Louisiana Purchase p. 30 (average) **Customized Reader** • The Lewis and Clark Expedition Meet With a Sioux Tribe, article IIIB-4 (challenging)
3 New Threats From Overseas (pp. 276–278) **Objectives** 1. Describe how overseas trade grew in the late 1700s. 2. Explain how war in Europe hurt American trade. 3. Explain why the Embargo Act failed.	**Lesson Planner,** p. 42 (average) . . . . .45 mins. **Unit 3/Chapter 10** • Section 3 Quiz, p. 20 (average) . . . . .15 mins.	**Voices of Freedom** • Sympathy for Oppressed Americans, pp. 80–81 (average)
4 The Road to War (pp. 279–283) **Objectives** 1. Explain why the Prophet and Tecumseh united Native Americans. 2. Describe how fighting on the frontier led to war with Britain. 3. Explain why the War Hawks wanted war with Britain.	**Lesson Planner,** p. 43 (average) . . . . .45–90 mins. **Unit 3/Chapter 10** • Connecting History and Literature: Tecumseh Speaks Out, p. 16 (average) . . . . .30 mins. • Section 4 Quiz, p. 21 (average) . . . . .15 mins.	**Voices of Freedom** • Henry Clay Defends War With Britain, pp. 82–83 (challenging) • Tecumseh Protests Land Sale, pp. 81–82 (average) **Historical Outline Map Book** • Land Acquired From Native Americans to 1810, p. 31 (average)
5 The War of 1812 (pp. 284–289) **Objectives** 1. Explain why the United States was not ready for war with Britain. 2. List the major turning points of the war in the West. 3. Describe the results of the war.	**Lesson Planner,** p. 44 (average) . . . . .90 mins. **Unit 3/Chapter 10** • Vocabulary Builder, p. 12 (basic) . . . . .15 mins. • Map Mystery: Jackson's Trap at New Orleans, p. 15 (average) . . . . .45 mins. • Biography Flashcard: Dolley Madison, p. 17 (average) .30 mins. • Section 5 Quiz, p. 22 (average) . . . . .15 mins. **Chapter Tests,** pp. 55–60 (average) . . . . .45 mins.	**Historical Outline Map Book** • The War of 1812, p. 32 (average) **Customized Reader** • The Inspiration for "The Star-Spangled Banner," article IIIB-7 (average)

Assessment Options

Teaching Resources
- Alternative Assessment booklet
- Section Quizzes, Unit 3, Chapter 10, pp. 18–22
- Chapter Tests, Chapter 10, pp. 55–60
- Test Bank CD-ROM

Student Performance Pack
- Guide to the Essentials of American History, Chapter 10 Test, p. 60
- Standardized Test Prep Handbook
- Interactive Student Tutorial CD-ROM

Interdisciplinary Connections

Teaching Resources
- Map Mystery, Unit 3, Chapter 10, p. 15
- Connecting History and Literature, Unit 3, Chapter 10, p. 16
- Interdisciplinary Connections, pp. 55–60

Voices of Freedom, pp. 78–83

Customized Reader, articles IIIB-4, IIIB-7

Historical Outline Map Book, pp. 30–32

BLOCK SCHEDULING
Activities with this icon will help you meet your Block Scheduling needs.

ENGLISH LANGUAGE LEARNERS
Activities with this icon are suitable for English Language Learners.

TEAM TEACHING
Activities and Background Notes with this icon present starting points for Team Teaching.

Technology

AmericanHeritage® History of the United States CD-ROM
- Time Tour: The Jefferson Era (1801–1816) in The New Republic
- History Makers: John Marshall, Meriwether Lewis, William Clark, Tecumseh
- Presidents: Thomas Jefferson
- Arts and Entertainment: Music

Interactive Student Tutorial CD-ROM

Test Bank CD-ROM

Color Transparencies
- Expansion of the United States, p. I-25
- The Indian Council, p. D-37
- Lewis and Clark With Sacajawea, p. B-49
- Lands Lost by Indians, p. I-39

Guided Reading Audiotapes (English/Spanish), side 4

Resource Pro® CD-ROM

Prentice Hall United States History Video Collection™ (Spanish track available on disc version.) Vol. 5, Ch. 40; Vol. 6, Chs. 7, 10, 13

Prentice Hall Home Page
www.phschool.com

Student Performance Pack

Guide to the Essentials of American History
- Ch. 10, pp. 55–60
(Available in English and Spanish)

Guided Reading Audiotapes (English/Spanish), side 4

Standardized Test Prep Handbook

Interactive Student Tutorial CD-ROM

Teachers' Bibliography

FROM THE ARCHIVES OF AmericanHeritage®	Don't miss the special American Heritage® teaching notes found in this chapter.
 HISTORY ALIVE!®	Contact Teachers' Curriculum Institute to learn more about History Alive!® resources on the early years of the United States government. See History Alive!® unit: Manifest Destiny in a Growing Nation, Section 1, "Exploring Manifest Destiny."
	Explore your library to find these issues related to Chapter 10: *Thomas Jefferson,* September 1984; *James and Dolley Madison,* March 1996.
	**Prentice Hall Web Site** You can access a structured, on-line environment that allows you to preview curriculum-related resources and receive updated information on groundbreaking events from around the nation and the world. (www.phschool.com)

Chapter 10

The Age of Jefferson 1801–1816

Introducing the Chapter

Have students preview the main ideas of this chapter by looking over the visuals. Suggest they look for examples of how the nation changed during the age of Jefferson.

Using the Time Line To provide students with practice in using the time line to understand chronology, ask questions such as these: **(1)** Which event happened first—the Embargo Act or war between France and Britain? *(war between France and Britain)* **(2)** About how long had Thomas Jefferson been President when Lewis and Clark began to explore Louisiana? *(about 3 years)* **(3)** What world event occurred during the same decade as the war between the United States and Britain? *(Simón Bolívar led a revolt against Spanish rule in South America.)*

Have students consider what an American with a legal problem might mean by "I'll take this all the way to the Supreme Court if I have to!" Ask students to share their ideas about the Supreme Court and the kinds of cases it hears. Tell students that the role of the Supreme Court was not clearly defined in the early years of the new nation. The Court's role became clearer during Jefferson's presidency.

For additional *Why Study History?* support, see p. 268.

Chapter 10

The Age of Jefferson

1801–1816

What's Ahead

Republican Presidents in the early 1800s tried to serve the needs of ordinary Americans while limiting the role of government. During this time, events that affected France and Britain reached beyond their borders. As a result, the United States had the opportunity to double its size by purchasing the Louisiana territory from France. The young nation also faced war with Britain again. Although there was no clear winner in the war, many Americans became more proud of their growing nation.

Why Study History? During the early 1800s, each branch of the new government was learning its responsibilities and limits. It was at this time that the power and importance of the Supreme Court began to emerge. To learn more about the powerful influence of the "highest court in the land," see this chapter's *Why Study History?* feature, "Supreme Court Decisions Affect You."

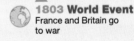

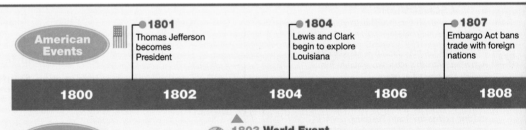

American Events

- **1801** Thomas Jefferson becomes President
- **1804** Lewis and Clark begin to explore Louisiana
- **1807** Embargo Act bans trade with foreign nations

1800 | 1802 | 1804 | 1806 | 1808

World Events

- **1803 World Event** France and Britain go to war

★ *Background* ★

Recent Scholarship

An American's American In his Jefferson studies, Joseph J. Ellis concentrates on the aspects that have made Jefferson part and parcel of the American ideal. *American Sphinx: The Character of Thomas Jefferson* reveals Jefferson as a complex man whose victories, follies, vision, and failures mirror those of the nation.

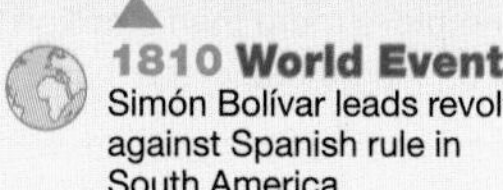

Lewis and Clark on the Lower Columbia

In 1803, President Thomas Jefferson doubled the size of the United States by purchasing the Louisiana territory. He sent Meriwether Lewis and William Clark to explore the land and establish friendship with Native Americans. In this painting by Charles M. Russell, Lewis (right) stands by the Native American Sacajawea as she addresses Chinook Indians. ★ **Do you think Native Americans welcomed Lewis and Clark? Explain.**

1811 Harrison fights Native Americans at Tippecanoe

1812 War begins between United States and Britain

1815 Jackson defeats British at New Orleans

1808	1810	1812	1814	1816

1810 World Event Simón Bolívar leads revolt against Spanish rule in South America

Writing Actively 

Direct students to the caption for the painting. Tell them that Sacajawea was traveling with Lewis and Clark to act as an interpreter. Ask them to think about what Sacajawea might be saying to the Chinook Indians. Then ask students to work with a partner to write a dialogue that might have occurred. Call on partners to present their dialogue.

Viewing History ANSWER

Possible answer: Some welcomed Lewis and Clark because of the gifts the two explorers offered. Others might have viewed them as potential rivals.

★ Background ★

Art Note

Lewis and Clark on the Lower Columbia Charles Marion Russell (1864–1926) created this painting a century after Lewis and Clark reached the Columbia River in 1805. Russell was an American painter and sculptor famous for his scenes of the West, particularly scenes of cowboy life. Russell's work is noted for its detail and authentic settings.

Documents and Literature

On pp. 555–558, you will find two readings to enrich this chapter:

1. Eyewitness Account "Traveling with Lewis and Clark," an excerpt from Sacajawea's autobiography. (Use with Section 2.)

2. Literature "The Pioneers," a selection from James Fenimore Cooper's novel of whites and Native Americans on the frontier. (Use with Section 4.)

Technology

Videodiscs/Videotapes
Show the *Prentice Hall United States History Video Collection*™ segments for this chapter. The videodisc version has a Spanish track. Press audio until you get the left channel for English or the right channel for Spanish, or use the bar codes in the Guidebook.

American Heritage® History of the United States CD-ROM
- Time Tour: The Jefferson Era (1801–1816) in The New Republic (*average*)

Section 1
Republicans in Power

LESSON PLAN

Objectives

★ Describe Jefferson's ideas about government.
★ List the ways Jefferson reduced the power of government.
★ Explain the importance of *Marbury* v. *Madison*.

1 Engage

Warm Up Have students free-write for 2 or 3 minutes the thoughts and images that they associate with the word *democratic*.

Activating Prior Knowledge Call on volunteers to share their ideas. Then organize students into small groups and ask them to describe a situation in a school setting in which democracy is practiced.

Reading Actively

Before Reading Ask students to skim the section, looking at the illustrations and reading the headings. Ask them to write two or three sentences predicting what the section will be about. As they read, have students verify or correct their predictions.

2 Explore

Ask students to read the section. For a homework assignment, ask students to search current newspapers and magazines for examples of situations involving conflict over

RESOURCE DIRECTORY

Teaching Resources
Lesson Planner, p. 40
Unit 3/Chapter 10
• Critical Thinking and Writing: Comparing Information on a Chart, p. 14

1 Republicans in Power

As You Read

Explore These Questions
- What were Jefferson's ideas about government?
- How did he reduce the power of government?
- Why was *Marbury* v. *Madison* important?

Define
- democratic
- laissez faire
- judicial review

Identify
- John Marshall
- *Marbury* v. *Madison*

SETTING the Scene When Thomas Jefferson became President of the United States in 1801, nearly nine out of ten Americans were farmers. This fact gave Jefferson confidence in the nation's future. Even though Jefferson came from a wealthy family, he believed in the importance of ordinary people, especially farmers. In a letter to James Madison, he expressed his faith in the American people:

> "Educate and inform the whole mass of the people. Enable them to see that it is their interest to preserve peace and order, and they will preserve them. . . . They are the only [ones to rely on] for the preservation of our liberty."

A More Democratic Style

As President, Jefferson tried to protect and expand the rights of ordinary citizens. He felt that the Federalists promoted the interests of the wealthy few, but neglected the needs of others. Jefferson was determined to make the government more democratic. **Democratic** means ensuring that all people have the same rights.

Jefferson's personal style matched his democratic beliefs. The new President preferred quiet dinners to the formal parties that Washington and Adams had given. He wore casual clothes and greeted people by shaking hands instead of bowing. With his informal manner, Jefferson showed that the President was an ordinary citizen.

Some Federalists worried about Jefferson's democratic beliefs. They knew that he supported the French Revolution and they feared that he might bring revolutionary change to the United States. They were also afraid that he might punish Federalists who had used the Alien and Sedition acts to jail Republicans.

In his inaugural address, Jefferson tried to quiet Federalists' fears. Though a minority, Federalists "possess their equal rights, which equal laws must protect," he told the nation. He called for an end to the political disputes of past years. "We are all Republicans, we are all Federalists," the President said. Jefferson was determined to unite the country, not divide it further.

Reduced Role of Government

Jefferson had no plan to punish Federalists. He did, however, want to change their policies. In his view, the Federalists had made the national government too large and too powerful. Jefferson wanted to reduce government power by cutting the federal budget and by reducing the federal debt.

When Jefferson became President in 1801, there were fewer than 1,000 federal employees. Today, the United States government employs more than 2 million people—not counting those in the military.

★ Customized Instruction ★
Introverted Learners

Preparing a biographical report Ask introverted learners to research the life of Thomas Jefferson and write a report for use as a class reference. Students should focus on Jefferson the man, including his early life and his accomplishments outside the political arena. Jefferson's private life and his talents as architect, scholar, scientist, and inventor are all appropriate subject matter. Encourage students to illustrate their reports with copies of architectural renderings and drawings of Jefferson's inventions. Each report should have a sturdy cover and should include the student's name and the date. Add the reports to the class reference materials. (*challenging*)

Jefferson believed in an idea known as **laissez faire** (lehs ay FAYR), from the French term for "let alone." According to laissez faire, government should play as small a role as possible in economic affairs. Laissez faire was very different from the Federalist idea of government. Alexander Hamilton, you recall, wanted government to promote trade and manufacturing.

President Jefferson tried to reduce the role of government in people's lives. He decreased the size of government departments and cut the federal budget. With the approval of Congress, he reduced the size of the army and navy. He also asked Congress to repeal the unpopular whiskey tax.

The Sedition Act expired the day before Jefferson took office. Jefferson hated the law, and he pardoned those who were in jail because of it. He also asked Congress to restore the law allowing foreign-born people to become citizens after only a five-year waiting period. Jefferson acted to change other Federalist policies as well.

Jefferson did not discard all Federalist programs, however. He kept the Bank of the United States, which he had once opposed. The federal government also continued to pay off state debts that it had taken over when Washington was President. In addition, Jefferson let many Federalists keep their government jobs.

A Stronger Supreme Court

The election of 1800 gave Republicans control of Congress. Federalists, however, remained powerful in the courts.

Several months passed between Jefferson's election and his inauguration on March 4, 1801. During that time, Federalists in the old Congress passed a law increasing the number of federal judges. President Adams then appointed Federalists to fill these new judicial positions.

One of the judges that Adams appointed was **John Marshall,** the Chief Justice of the Supreme Court. Like Jefferson, Marshall

Biography Thomas Jefferson

Jefferson, author of the Declaration of Independence and third President of the United States, was a man of many talents. A skilled architect, he designed his own home, Monticello, in the classical style of ancient Greece and Rome. Jefferson felt that it was important for citizens in a democracy to be well educated. ★ **Why do you think Jefferson placed so much value on education?**

◀ *Monticello, home of Thomas Jefferson*

the power of the federal government or over a Supreme Court ruling. Have students summarize the information; then ask them to share it with the class.

3 Teach

Have students work in small groups to prepare political cartoons that illustrate the following: **(a)** ways in which Jefferson's ideas of government differed from those of the Federalists; **(b)** ways in which President Jefferson reduced the power of the federal government.

4 Assess

To close the lesson, have students complete the section review. As an alternative, ask students to write an editorial about the Federalists which addresses questions such as "How did Jefferson attempt to end political disputes?" and "Do you think he was successful?"

Writing Actively

After Reading Have students notice the heading Reduced Role of Government. Ask them to find evidence to support the idea that Jefferson tried to reduce the role of government.

Biography

ANSWER

Possible answer: He believed that in a democracy, citizens needed education to participate in government and fulfill the responsibilities of citizenship.

★ Background ★

Did You Know?

We the People "Democratic" could hardly be used to describe the United States in the early 1800s. Voting rights, for example, were limited. In order to vote, people had to meet certain requirements:

- Maryland—own 50 acres of land
- South Carolina—believe in God
- Massachusetts—own property

Technology

AmericanHeritage® History of the United States CD-ROM

- Presidents: Thomas Jefferson (*average*)

ANSWERS

1. (a) The issue involved the Fourth Amendment's protection against unreasonable searches. **(b)** The Court said the school has a special responsibility to deter student drug abuse and to protect students' health. **2.** Possible answer: It gave all schools the right to require drug testing.

★Activity

Guided Instruction

Direct students to use guides to periodical literature such as magazines and newspaper indexes, as well as the Internet, to find Supreme Court cases. You may wish to provide a chart that students can use to fill in the details of the case. Some students may wish to present their findings in the form of a television news report.

Why Study History?

Because Supreme Court Decisions Affect You

Historical Background

In the early 1800s, the Supreme Court was not as respected as it is today. In fact, for a while, the justices met in the basement of the Capitol because the designers of Washington, D.C., had not provided a meeting place for the Court. However, under the strong leadership of Chief Justice John Marshall, the Supreme Court gained respect and power.

Connections to Today

Today, the Supreme Court is very important as the final authority on cases involving the Constitution. By exercising its power of judicial review (see page 269), the Supreme Court decides whether or not laws are constitutional. Supreme Court justices interpret the Constitution and define and limit our constitutional rights.

Connections to You

Supreme Court cases often involve young people like you. One recent example is the case of *Veronia School District* v. *Acton*.

In 1991, a seventh grader in Oregon wanted to join his school football team. The school required that he submit to a drug test. The student refused, and the school did not allow him to play on the team. The boy's parents sued, arguing that the school had violated the Fourth Amendment's protection against unreasonable searches. The case eventually went to the Supreme Court.

In a 6–3 decision, the Court agreed with the school. It ruled that schools can require athletes to undergo drug tests, just as they require physical examinations and vaccinations. The Court said that schools have a special responsibility to prevent drug abuse and to protect students' health.

This 1995 decision did not affect just one student in one school. The Court's ruling applied to student athletes across the nation. Indirectly, it also had an impact on other issues regarding the rights of students in American schools.

1. **Comprehension** **(a)** How did *Veronia School District* v. *Acton* involve the Constitution? **(b)** Why did the Supreme Court agree with the Oregon school's policy?
2. **Critical Thinking** How do you think the decision affected sports programs in other schools?

Researching Use library or Internet sources to research a recent Supreme Court case. Report to the class on the issue, the Court's decision, and possible effects of the decision.

Fast Facts

★ The generation gap is nothing new to the Supreme Court. Joseph Story was appointed to the Court at the age of 32 in 1811. In 1932, Oliver Wendell Holmes retired from the Court at the age of 90.

★ Lawyers can spend months preparing for a Supreme Court case but are usually limited to 30 minutes of oral argument.

★ Of the thousands of cases appealed to the Court each year (nearly 8,000 in 1996), the Court agrees to hear only about 150.

Bibliography

To read more about this topic:

1. "The Geography of Justice," Edward Lazarus, *US News & World Report* (July 7, 1997). Regional differences as a factor in Supreme Court decisions.

2. *The Supreme Court of the United States*, Michael Kronenwetter (Enslow Publishers, 1996). Historic Supreme Court cases.

3. Internet. Browse Teen Court TV (www.courttv.com/teens/law/). How court decisions have affected young people.

RESOURCE DIRECTORY

Teaching Resources
Unit 3/Chapter 10
• Section 1 Quiz, p. 18
Why Study History?
• Supreme Court Decisions Affect You, pp. 39–42

was a rich Virginia planter with a brilliant mind. Unlike Jefferson, however, Marshall was a Federalist. He wanted to make the federal government stronger.

The framers of the Constitution expected the courts to balance the powers of the President and Congress. However, John Marshall found the courts to be very weak. In his view, it was not clear what powers the federal courts had.

Marbury v. *Madison*

In 1803, Marshall decided a case that increased the power of the Supreme Court. The case involved William Marbury, another one of the judges appointed by Adams. Adams made the appointment on his last night as President.

The Republicans refused to accept this "midnight judge." They accused Federalists of using unfair tactics to keep control of the courts. Jefferson ordered Secretary of State James Madison not to deliver the official papers confirming Marbury's appointment.

Marbury sued Madison. According to the Judiciary Act of 1789, only the Supreme Court could decide a case that was brought against a federal official. Therefore, the case of ***Marbury* v. *Madison*** was tried before the Supreme Court.

An important precedent

In its decision, the Supreme Court ruled against Marbury. Chief Justice Marshall wrote the decision, stating that the Judiciary Act was unconstitutional. The Constitution, Marshall argued, did not give the Supreme Court the right to decide cases brought against federal officials. Therefore, Congress could not give the Court that power.

The Supreme Court's decision in *Marbury* v. *Madison* set an important precedent. It gave the Supreme Court the power to decide whether laws passed by Congress were constitutional and to reject laws that it considered to be unconstitutional. This power of the Court is called **judicial review**.

Jefferson was displeased that the decision gave more power to the Supreme Court. He felt that the decision upset the balance of power that existed among the three branches of government. Even so, the President and Congress accepted the right of the Court to overturn laws. Today, judicial review remains one of the most important powers of the Supreme Court.

★ Section 1 Review ★

Recall

1. **Identify** (a) John Marshall, (b) *Marbury* v. *Madison*.
2. **Define** (a) democratic, (b) laissez faire, (c) judicial review.

Comprehension

3. Explain how Jefferson's ideas on government differed from Federalist ideas.
4. Describe three steps Jefferson took to reduce the power of government.
5. (a) What precedent did *Marbury* v. *Madison* set? (b) How did the precedent affect the balance of power in American government?

Critical Thinking and Writing

6. **Analyzing a Primary Source** "We are all Republicans, we are all Federalists." (a) What did Jefferson mean by these words? (b) Why did he need to make such a statement?
7. **Drawing Conclusions** Today, the federal government protects consumers by regulating the quality of certain goods. Would a laissez-faire economist agree with this policy? Why or why not?

Activity **Writing a Letter** Welcome to the United States! You are a newly arrived immigrant from Europe. Write a letter to your friends in Europe describing your feelings about President Jefferson and the Republican government.

★ Section 1 Review ★

ANSWERS

1. (a) p. 267, **(b)** p. 269

2. (a) p. 266, **(b)** p. 267, **(c)** p. 269

3. Unlike the Federalists, he wanted to limit the government's power and to make government more democratic; he favored laissez-faire policies.

4. Possible answer: He reduced the size of government departments and the military, and he helped repeal the whiskey tax.

5. (a) It said the Supreme Court could rule on the constitutionality of laws passed by Congress. **(b)** It increased the Court's power.

6. (a) Both Republicans and Federalists were Americans. **(b)** to end political disputes and to ease Federalist fears of Republicans in power

7. No, because the government is interfering in the economy.

Activity

Guided Instruction

Students might consider Jefferson's desire to reduce the government's power, comparing this to the power of Europe's monarchs. They might also consider his views on education and his faith in the common people. Social status may affect the immigrant's opinion.

ASSESSMENT See the rubrics in the Alternative Assessment booklet in the Teaching Resources.

★ Background ★

Did You Know?

For whom the bell tolled During his more than 30 years as Chief Justice, John Marshall took part in about 1,000 Court decisions and personally wrote 519 of them. He died on July 6, 1835, when he was almost 80 years old. Tradition has it that the Liberty Bell cracked as it tolled for his funeral.

★ Activity ★

Cooperative Learning

Researching the Marshall Court Have small groups research the cases decided during the time that John Marshall presided over the Court. Each group should choose and research one case and prepare an oral report that summarizes arguments for both sides of the case. Each group should identify the effects of the case on Americans today. (challenging)

Technology

Videodiscs/Videotapes

Prentice Hall United States History Video Collection™, Vol. 5, Ch. 40, "The Marshall Court," 1:45 min (average) ELL

Chapter 40

AmericanHeritage® History of the United States CD-ROM

- History Makers: John Marshall (average)

Section 2

The Louisiana Purchase

LESSON PLAN

Objectives

★ Explain why control of the Mississippi River was important to western farmers.

★ Describe how the United States gained Louisiana.

★ Identify achievements of the Lewis and Clark expedition.

1 Engage

Warm Up Write "New Orleans" on the chalkboard. Ask students to describe what they think of when they hear that term.

Activating Prior Knowledge Write students' responses on the chalkboard. Next ask students why the United States in the early 1800s would be interested in the city. Then refer students to a physical map of the United States. Ask them to explain why the Mississippi River was the best route for sending goods to the East Coast. Ask students to list present-day states that might rely on the Mississippi River for the movement of goods.

Reading Actively

Before Reading As they read the section, have students list reasons why the United States purchased Louisiana. They will use the list to construct a cause-and-effect chart.

RESOURCE DIRECTORY

Teaching Resources
Lesson Planner, p. 41
Interdisciplinary Connections
- Main Idea: The Louisiana Purchase, pp. 57, 58, 60

Transparencies
Geography and History
- Expansion of the United States, p. I-25 (*average*)

The Louisana Purchase

As You Read

Explore These Questions
- Why was control of the Mississippi River important to western farmers?
- How did the United States gain Louisiana?
- What did the Lewis and Clark expedition achieve?

Define
- expedition
- Continental Divide

Identify
- Pinckney Treaty
- Toussaint L'Ouverture
- Louisiana Purchase
- Lewis and Clark
- Sacajawea
- Zebulon Pike

William Clark's journal

SETTING the Scene One day, President Jefferson received several packages. Inside, he found hides and skeletons of animals, horns of a mountain ram, and a tin box full of insects. There were also cages of live birds and squirrels, as well as gifts from the Mandan and Sioux Indians.

All of these packages were from Meriwether Lewis and William Clark. Jefferson had sent the two to explore the land west of the Mississippi River. Almost two years before, President Jefferson had purchased the territory for the United States. The packages confirmed his belief that the new lands were a valuable addition to the nation.

Control of the Mississippi

By 1800, almost one million Americans lived between the Appalachian Mountains and the Mississippi. Most were farmers.

With few roads west of the Appalachians, western farmers relied on the Mississippi to ship their wheat and corn. First, they sent their produce down the river to New Orleans. From there, oceangoing ships carried the produce to ports along the Atlantic coast.

Threats from Spain and France

Spain sometimes threatened to close the port of New Orleans to Americans. In 1795, President Washington sent Thomas Pinckney to find a way to keep the vital port open. In the **Pinckney Treaty**, Spain agreed to let Americans ship their goods down the Mississippi and store them in New Orleans. The treaty also settled a dispute over the northern border of Spanish Florida.

For a time, Americans sent their goods to New Orleans without a problem. Then, however, Spain signed a treaty with Napoleon Bonaparte, the ruler of France. The treaty gave Louisiana back to France. President Jefferson was alarmed. Napoleon had already set out to conquer Europe. Jefferson feared that Napoleon might now try to build an empire in North America.

Revolt in Haiti

President Jefferson had good reason to worry. Napoleon wanted to grow food in Louisiana and ship it to French islands in the West Indies. However, events in Haiti soon ruined Napoleon's plan.

Haiti was the richest French colony in the Caribbean. There, enslaved Africans worked sugar plantations that made French planters wealthy. Inspired by the French Revolution, the African slaves in Haiti decided to fight for their liberty. **Toussaint L'Ouverture** (too SAN loo vehr TYOOR) led the revolt. By 1801, Toussaint and his followers had nearly forced the French out of Haiti.

Napoleon sent troops to retake Haiti. Although the French captured Toussaint, they

Internet Activity

Mississippi River Have students visit www.oldmanriver.com, the river's Web site. It contains fun facts, historical information (including a time line), photos, and articles on current issues. Ask students to compare today's issues with those of Jefferson's time. Given the changing nature of the Internet, you may want to preview the site before directing students to it. (*average*) ELL

★ ***Background*** ★

Linking Past and Present

All that jazz A bustling port city even today, New Orleans also has other claims to fame. Among these claims, it is hailed as the birthplace of jazz. This original American music combines many influences, including African American music, African rhythms, and European harmonies and forms. New Orleans remains famous for its jazz clubs. T did not regain control of the island. In 1804, Haitians declared their independence. Napoleon's dream of an empire in the Americas ended with the loss of Haiti.

Buying Louisiana

Meanwhile, President Jefferson decided to try to buy the city of New Orleans from Napoleon. Jefferson wanted to be sure that American farmers would always be able to ship their goods through the port. The President sent Robert Livingston and James Monroe to buy New Orleans and West Florida from the French. Jefferson said they could offer as much as $10 million.

A surprising deal

Livingston and Monroe negotiated with Talleyrand, the French foreign minister. At first, Talleyrand showed little interest in their offer. However, changing conditions in Haiti and in Europe were causing Napoleon to alter his plans for the future.

After losing Haiti, Napoleon had abandoned his plan for an empire in the Americas. He also needed money to pay for his very costly wars in Europe. Suddenly Talleyrand asked Livingston if the United States wanted to buy all of Louisiana, not just New Orleans.

Livingston and Monroe carefully debated the matter. They had no authority to buy all of Louisiana. However, they knew that Jefferson wanted control of the Mississippi. They agreed to pay the French $15 million for Louisiana. When he signed the treaty with France, Livingston proudly declared,

> "We have lived long, but this is the noblest work of our whole lives. . . . From this day the United States take their place among the powers of the first rank."

Viewing History — A View of New Orleans

New Orleans, shown here in an 1803 painting by John L. Boqueta de Woiseri, grew prosperous by controlling trade on the Mississippi River. The city's strategic location near the Gulf of Mexico was one reason for the Louisiana Purchase.

★ **How does this 1803 painting show the prosperity of New Orleans?**

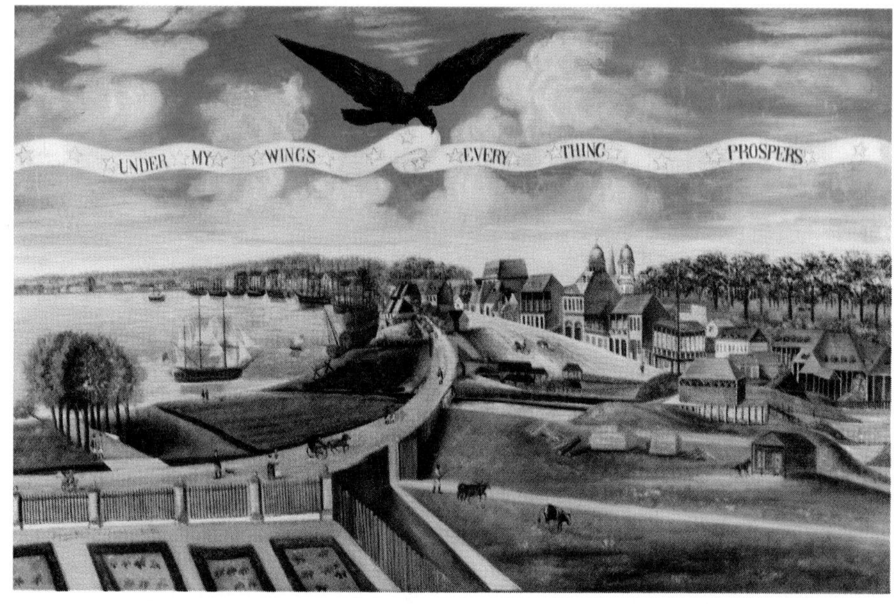
UNDER MY WINGS EVERY THING PROSPERS

2 Explore

Ask students to read the section. For a homework assignment, have them compare a recent exploration into uncharted territory (such as an unexplored deep-sea location or another planet) with the Lewis and Clark expedition. Students should indicate both similarities and differences.

3 Teach

Have students create a cause-and-effect diagram in their notebooks. At the center of the diagram, students should write the title "Louisiana Purchase." Arrows pointing toward the title should list the causes for the purchase. Arrows pointing away from the title should list the effects of the purchase. Call on students to share their diagrams.

4 Assess

To close the lesson, have students complete the section review. As an alternative, ask students to work in groups of three to prepare a talk show in which they interview Lewis and Clark. The talk show might include anecdotes about the journey as well as a description of goals the journey achieved.

Viewing History ANSWER

The many buildings and the ships in the harbor suggest that New Orleans was a thriving center of business and trade.

★ *Activity* ★

Connections With the World

Exploring Haiti Independence did not provide Haiti with a stable government. Ask students to research the history of Haiti's government from the time of its declaration of independence until the present. Students might report their findings in an illustrated time line or in an illustrated written report. (*average*)

Technology

Videodiscs/Videotapes

Prentice Hall United States History Video Collection™, Vol. 6, Ch. 7, "The Louisiana Purchase," 5 mins (*average*) ELL

Chapter 7

Reading Actively

During Reading Have students read the quotation from Thomas Jefferson on this page. Ask them to paraphrase the request as an American president would state it today.

Was the purchase constitutional?

Jefferson was pleased by the news from France, but he was not sure that he in fact had the constitutional power to purchase Louisiana. He had always insisted that the federal government had only those powers spelled out in the Constitution. The document said nothing about a President's power to buy land.

After giving it much thought, Jefferson decided that he did have the authority to buy Louisiana. The Constitution, he reasoned, allowed the President to make treaties. At his request, the Senate quickly approved a treaty making the **Louisiana Purchase.** In 1803, the United States took control of the vast lands west of the Mississippi.

Jefferson Plans an Expedition

The United States owned Louisiana now, but few Americans knew anything about the territory. In 1803, Congress provided money for a team of explorers to study the new lands. Jefferson chose Meriwether Lewis, his private secretary, to head the expedition. An **expedition** is a long journey or voyage of exploration. Lewis asked William Clark, another Virginian, to go with him. About 50 men made up the original band.

Jefferson gave Lewis and Clark careful instructions. He asked them to map a route to the Pacific Ocean. He also told them to study the climate, wildlife, and mineral resources of the new lands. The President requested a detailed report on the following:

> "Climate as characterized by the thermometer, by the proportion of rainy, cloudy, and clear days, by lightning, hail, snow, ice... by the winds prevailing at different seasons, the dates at which particular plants put forth or lose their flower, or leaf, times of appearance of particular birds, reptiles or insects."

Jefferson also instructed Lewis and Clark to learn about the Indian nations who lived in the Louisiana Purchase. For decades, these Native Americans had carried on a very busy trade with English, French, and Spanish merchants. Jefferson hoped that the Indians might trade with American merchants instead. Therefore, he urged Lewis and Clark to tell the Indians of "our wish to be neighborly, friendly, and useful to them."

The Lewis and Clark Expedition

In May 1804, **Lewis and Clark** started up the Missouri River from St. Louis. In time, their trip would take them to the Pacific Ocean. (Follow their route on the map on page 273.)

Across the plains

At first, the expedition's boats made slow progress against the Missouri's swift current. One night, the current tore away the riverbank where they were camping. The party had to scramble into the boats to avoid being swept downstream.

Lewis and Clark kept journals on their travels. They marveled at the broad, grassy plains that stretched "as far as the eye can reach." Everywhere, they saw "immense herds of buffalo, deer, elk, and antelopes."

As they traveled across the plains, the expedition met people of various Indian nations. Lewis and Clark had brought many gifts for Native Americans. They carried medals stamped with the United States seal. They also brought mirrors, beads, knives, blankets, and thousands of sewing needles and fishhooks.

During the first winter, Lewis and Clark stayed with the Mandans in present-day North Dakota. The explorers planned to continue up the Missouri in the spring. However, they worried about how they would cross the steep Rocky Mountains.

Connections With Science

Acting as botanist for the expedition, Meriwether Lewis collected and preserved many plants. He carefully dried and pressed each specimen. Of the more than 200 specimens Lewis brought back, 39 still remain at the Academy of Natural Sciences in Philadelphia.

RESOURCE DIRECTORY

Teaching Resources
Unit 3/Chapter 10
- Practice Your Skills: Reading Map Routes, p. 13

Interdisciplinary Connections
- Main Idea: The Louisiana Purchase, p. 60

Transparencies
Fine Art
- The Indian Council, p. D-37, 20 mins (*easy*)

★ *Background* ★

Turning Points

The first American outfitter? Lewis spent months selecting and inventing items for a remarkable field kit that included the following: quadrant, compass, hydrometers; rifles of his own design, muskets, cannons; blankets, hooded coats, waterproof clothing; sewing and woodworking tools; state-of-the-art medicines, medical instruments, and supplies.

From the Archives of American Heritage®

Jefferson's journals In 1791, Jefferson and his friend James Madison explored Vermont by boat and wagon. During the month-long trip, Jefferson kept journals of his observations, as he later asked Lewis and Clark to do. Years later, his granddaughter used his notes to plan a honeymoon trip to New England.

Source: Willard Sterne Randall, "Thomas Jefferson Takes a Vacation," *American Heritage* magazine, July/August 1996.

FOR LIFE

Critical Thinking | Managing Information | Communication | **Maps, Charts, and Graphs**

Following Map Routes

How Will I Use This Skill?

You can use map routes to find your way through a school or office building. With a road map, you can chart a route from home to other places. You can also give directions to others.

LEARN the Skill

You can follow a map route by using the steps below.

1. Identify the map's subject and symbols that indicate routes.
2. Use the directional arrow that identifies N, S, E, and W to determine in what direction a route goes. Recognize other directions, such as northeast (NE), the direction between N and E. Other directions are southeast (SE), southwest (SW), and northwest (NW).
3. Use the scale of miles to determine the distance of a route.
4. Choose the map route you will follow and describe it in terms of direction and distance.

The Louisiana Purchase

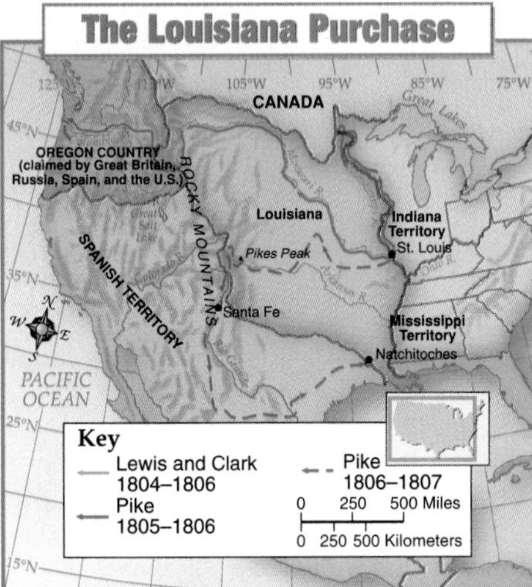

PRACTICE the Skill

Using the steps and the map above, answer the following questions.

1. What does the map show? What symbols represent routes?
2. In what general direction did Lewis and Clark travel from St. Louis?
3. About how many miles did Lewis and Clark travel in order to reach the Pacific Ocean?
4. Describe Pike's route from St. Louis to Natchitoches.

APPLY the Skill

Using a map of your community, describe the route that you follow to travel from home to school or to any other destination, such as a library or a park.

Skills FOR LIFE

PRACTICE the Skill

ANSWERS

1. Indiana Territory, Mississippi Territory, Louisiana, Spanish Territory, and Oregon Country. Routes are represented by solid red and blue lines or dotted blue lines with arrowheads.

2. northwest

3. 2,500 miles

4. west from St. Louis for approximately 750 miles; south for approximately 1,000 miles; east again for 250 miles; northeast for 500 miles

APPLY the Skill

Guided Instruction

Have students find the key, compass, and scale on a map of their own community. They should describe the route in terms of directions and distances. Students may want to use landmarks for directions.

ASSESSMENT See the rubrics in the Alternative Assessment booklet in the Teaching Resources.

★ Customized Instruction ★

English Language Learners

Giving directions You might provide English language learners with opportunities to ask for and give directions. Pair English language learners with students who are proficient in English. Suggest that ELL students work with their partners and ask for and give oral directions to local public places. As they become adept at giving directions, have the ELL students widen their focus to places of interest beyond their own local areas. Encourage partners to help each other to clarify and/or correct the directions, as needed. Finally, ask ELL students to work with their partners and give directions for places shown on the *Skills for Life* map. (*average*) ELL

Technology

Videodiscs/Videotapes

Prentice Hall United States History Video Collection™, Vol. 6, Ch. 10, "The Western Nations," 2:15 mins (*average*) ELL

Chapter 10

American Heritage® History of the United States CD-ROM

- History Makers: Meriwether Lewis, William Clark (*average*)

 **ANSWER**

Sacajawea could help Lewis and Clark communicate with various Native American groups. She knew the land and could help them find food and herbs for medicine.

Writing Actively

After Reading Refer students to the subsections Over the Rockies and To the Pacific. Discuss with students why they think Sacajawea and her husband were willing to assist Lewis and Clark in the expedition. Ask students to list character qualities they think the two must have possessed to provide the services described.

Antelope

Viewing History **The Way West**

In this painting, Lewis, Clark, and Sacajawea stand at the Great Falls of the Missouri River in 1804. Accompanying them is York, an enslaved African American in the service of Clark. After serving as a valuable member of the Lewis and Clark expedition, York was freed. He returned to the West to live with the Native Americans.

★ **Why did Lewis and Clark include Sacajawea in the expedition?**

Over the Rockies

A Shoshone woman, **Sacajawea** (sahk uh juh WEE uh), was also staying with the Mandans that winter. The Shoshones (shoh SHOH neez) lived in the Rockies. Sacajawea and her French Canadian husband agreed to accompany Lewis and Clark and serve as translators.

In early spring, the party set out. In the foothills of the Rockies, the landscape and wildlife changed. Bighorn sheep ran along the high hills. The thorns of prickly pear cactus jabbed the explorers' moccasins. One day, a grizzly bear chased Lewis while he was exploring alone.

Sacajawea contributed greatly to the success of the expedition. She gathered wild vegetables and advised the men where to fish and hunt. She knew about the healing qualities of plants and herbs, so the expedition relied on her for medical help.

In the mountains, Sacajawea recognized the lands of her people. One day, Lewis met some Shoshone leaders and invited them back to camp. Sacajawea began to "dance and show every mark of the most extravagant joy." One of the men, she explained, was her brother. The Shoshone people supplied the expedition with food and horses. The Shoshones also advised Lewis and Clark about the best route to take over the Rockies.

In the Rocky Mountains, Lewis and Clark crossed the **Continental Divide.** A continental divide is a mountain ridge that separates river systems flowing toward opposite sides of a continent. In North America,

RESOURCE DIRECTORY

Teaching Resources
Unit 3/Chapter 10
- Section 2 Quiz, p. 19

Transparencies
Interdisciplinary Connections
- Lewis and Clark With Sacajawea, p. B-49 (*average*)

★ *Background* ★

Did You Know?

Honoring Sacajawea There are many memorials in the United States dedicated to Sacajawea. Among them are Sacajawea State Park and Lake Sacajawea in Washington, and Sacajawea Monument on the Continental Divide in Idaho.

★ *Background* ★

Historiography

Very old bear tracks The work of people in other fields can illuminate or enrich our understanding of history. Naturalist Daniel Botkin studied the journals of Lewis and Clark and revisited the areas they traversed. Their detailed descriptions of the terrain let him make an educated guess about the density of the grizzly bear population in the early 1800s.

some rivers flow east from the Rockies into the Mississippi, which drains into the Gulf of Mexico. Other rivers flow west from the Rockies and empty into the Pacific Ocean.

To the Pacific

After building canoes, Lewis and Clark's party floated down the Columbia River. It carried them into the Pacific Northwest.

On November 7, 1805, Lewis and Clark finally reached their goal. Lewis wrote in his journal: "Great joy in camp. We are in view of the ocean, this great Pacific Ocean which we have been so long anxious to see." On a nearby tree, Clark carved, "By Land from the U. States in 1804 & 5."

The return trip to St. Louis took another year. In 1806, Americans celebrated the return of Lewis and Clark. The explorers brought back much useful information about the Louisiana Purchase.

Pike Explores the West

Before Lewis and Clark returned, another explorer set out from St. Louis. From 1805 to 1807, **Zebulon Pike** explored the upper Mississippi River, the Arkansas River, and parts of present-day Colorado and New Mexico. In November 1806, Pike viewed a mountain peak rising above the Colorado plains. Today, this mountain is known as Pikes Peak.

Continuing further westward into the Rocky Mountains, Pike came upon a small river. It was the Rio Grande. Pike had entered into Spanish territory. Spanish troops soon arrested Pike and his men and took them into Mexico.

After being questioned and detained for a while, the Americans were escorted through Texas back into the United States. Pike's maps and journals had been confiscated by the Spanish. Still, Pike was able to remember enough to write a report. The report greatly expanded Americans' knowledge about the Southwest.

The journeys of Zebulon Pike and Lewis and Clark excited Americans. It was a number of years, however, before settlers moved into the rugged western lands. As you will read, they first settled the region closest to the Mississippi River. Soon, the territory around New Orleans had a large enough white population for the settlers to apply for statehood. In 1812, this territory entered the Union as the state of Louisiana.

★ Section 2 Review ★

Recall

1. **Locate** **(a)** Mississippi River, **(b)** St. Louis, **(c)** Missouri River, **(d)** Rocky Mountains, **(e)** Columbia River, **(f)** Pikes Peak.
2. **Identify** **(a)** Pinckney Treaty, **(b)** Toussaint L'Ouverture, **(c)** Louisiana Purchase, **(d)** Lewis and Clark, **(e)** Sacajawea, **(f)** Zebulon Pike.
3. **Define** **(a)** expedition, **(b)** Continental Divide.

Comprehension

4. Why did western farmers oppose Spanish and French control of New Orleans?
5. Why was the United States able to buy Louisiana at a very low price?
6. Did Lewis and Clark accomplish what President Jefferson had asked them to do? Explain.

Critical Thinking and Writing

7. **Drawing Conclusions** Was Jefferson's purchase of Louisiana based on a strict or loose interpretation of the Constitution? Explain.
8. **Making Decisions** If you had been a Native American leader of the time, would you have welcomed Lewis and Clark in friendship? Explain the reasons for your decision.

Activity **Writing a Diary** Westward Ho! You are with Lewis and Clark as they travel to the Pacific. Write several diary entries describing what you see and feel as you explore Louisiana and meet the Native Americans who live there.

★ Section 2 Review ★

ANSWERS

1. See map, p. 273.
2. **(a)** p. 270, **(b)** p. 270, **(c)** p. 272, **(d)** p. 272, **(e)** p. 274, **(f)** p. 275
3. **(a)** p. 272, **(b)** p. 274
4. Farmers shipped their goods through New Orleans. They feared that either France or Spain might close the port to American shipping.
5. Napoleon had abandoned his plans for an empire in the Americas. He also needed quick money to pay for his wars in Europe.
6. Yes. They reached the Pacific Ocean, studied the Louisiana Territory and its resources, and established friendly relations with some Native American groups.
7. It was based on a loose interpretation. The Constitution does not specifically say that the president can buy land.
8. Answers will vary.

Guided Instruction
Encourage students to create a few fictional situations based on the Lewis and Clark expedition. In their diary entries, students can explain what happened and their feelings about the events. Ask for volunteers to dramatize some of the entries.

ASSESSMENT See the rubrics in the Alternative Assessment booklet in the Teaching Resources.

★ Background ★

Linking Past and Present

Reaching the peak Zebulon Pike lacked the warm clothing he needed to finish climbing the snowy Pikes Peak in November 1806, but the summit can be reached today by:

- trail
- cog railway
- automobile toll road

The Pikes Peak race—the best-known automobile hill climb in the United States—has been held there every summer since 1916.

Section 3
New Threats From Overseas

LESSON PLAN

Objectives

★ Describe how overseas trade grew in the late 1700s.
★ Explain how war in Europe hurt American trade.
★ Explain why the Embargo Act was a failure.

1 Engage

Warm Up Have students look at a map of the world to locate Tunisia, Libya, Algeria, and Morocco. Explain that they will be reading about the Barbary States, which occupied the same general area in north Africa.

Activating Prior Knowledge Ask students to review what they have learned about the American navy and American shipping during the presidencies of Washington and Adams. Volunteers can list facts from the text on these topics.

Reading Actively

Before Reading Have students preview the vocabulary words for the section. As they read, have them note the definitions of each word.

2 Explore

Ask students to read the section. As a homework assignment, have them go to the library to find articles relating to modern embargoes, such as the UN embargoes against South Africa and Iraq. Ask

RESOURCE DIRECTORY

Teaching Resources
Lesson Planner, p. 42

3 New Threats From Overseas

As You Read

Explore These Questions
- How did overseas trade grow in the late 1700s?
- How did war in Europe hurt American trade?
- Why was the Embargo Act a failure?

Define
- impressment
- embargo
- smuggler

Identify
- Barbary States
- Stephen Decatur
- Embargo Act
- Nonintercourse Act

SETTING the Scene James Brown, a young American sailor, wrote a letter. It was smuggled from a British ship and carried to the United States. The message described a desperate situation:

> "Being on shore one day in Lisbon, Portugal, I was [seized] by a gang and brought on board the [British ship] *Conqueror,* where I am still confined. Never have I been allowed to put my foot on shore since I was brought on board, which is now three years."

Brown's situation was not unusual. In the early 1800s, the British navy forced thousands of American sailors to serve on their ships. This was only one of many dangers that Americans faced as their sea trade began to thrive.

The British navy seized American sailors.

Trading Around the World

After the Revolution, American overseas trade grew rapidly. Ships sailed from New England ports on voyages that sometimes lasted three years. Everywhere they went, Yankee captains kept a sharp lookout for new goods to trade and new markets in which to sell. One clever trader sawed up the winter ice from New England ponds, packed it deep in sawdust for insulation, and carried it to India. There, he traded the ice for silk and spices.

In 1784, the *Empress of China* became the first American ship to trade with China. Before long, New England merchants built up a profitable trade with China. Yankee traders took ginseng, a plant that grew wild in New England, and exchanged it for Chinese silks and tea. The Chinese used the roots of the ginseng plant for medicines.

Yankee merchants sailed up the Pacific coast of North America in the 1790s. In fact, Yankee traders visited the Columbia River more than 10 years before Lewis and Clark. So many traders from Boston visited the Pacific Northwest that Native Americans called every white man "Boston." Traders bought furs from Native Americans. Then they sold the furs for large profits in China.

War With Tripoli

American traders ran great risks, especially in the Mediterranean Sea. For many years, pirates from nations along the coast of

★ *Background* ★

Did You Know?

Daring to the end After his exploit in Tripoli harbor, Stephen Decatur:
- Captured the British vessel HMS *Macedonia*
- Tried to run the British blockade of New York harbor in his flagship *President*
- Successfully opposed the pirates of the Barbary States in the Mediterranean area
- Died in a duel in November 1815

★ *Background* ★

Did You Know?

The pirate states Morocco, Algiers, Tunis, and Tripoli were semi-independent provinces of the Ottoman Empire. Westerners thought of them as pirate states, because they licensed sea raiders to attack and seize the ships of other nations. Americans called them the Barbary States, from the Greek word *barbaros,* meaning "foreign."

North Africa attacked vessels from Europe and the United States. The North African nations were called the **Barbary States.** To protect American ships, the United States paid a yearly tribute, or bribe, to the rulers of the Barbary States.

In the early 1800s, Tripoli, one of the Barbary States, demanded a larger bribe than usual. When President Jefferson refused to pay, Tripoli declared war on the United States. In response, Jefferson ordered the navy to blockade the port of Tripoli.

During the blockade, the American ship *Philadelphia* ran aground near Tripoli. Pirates boarded the ship and hauled the crew to prison. The pirates planned to use the *Philadelphia* to attack other ships.

Then, **Stephen Decatur,** a United States Navy officer, took action. Very late one night, Decatur and his crew quietly sailed a ship into Tripoli harbor. When they reached the captured American ship, they set it on fire so that the pirates could not use it.

In the meantime, American marines landed on the coast of North Africa. They then marched 500 miles (805 km) to launch a surprise attack on Tripoli. The war with Tripoli lasted until 1805. In the end, the ruler of Tripoli signed a treaty promising not to interfere with American ships.

American Neutrality Is Violated

During the early 1800s, American ships faced another problem. In 1803, Britain and France went to war again. At first, Americans profited from the war. British and French ships were too busy fighting to engage in trade. American merchants took advantage of the war to trade with both sides. As trade increased, American shipbuilders hurried to build new ships.

Of course, neither Britain nor France wanted the United States to sell supplies to its enemy. As in the 1790s, they ignored American claims of neutrality. Each nation tried to stop American trade with the other. Napoleon seized American ships bound for England, and the British stopped Yankee traders on their way to France. Between 1805 and 1807, hundreds of American ships were captured.

The British navy also seized American sailors and forced them to serve on British ships. This practice of forcing people into service, called **impressment,** was common in Britain. For centuries, impressment gangs had raided villages and forced young men to serve in the navy.

Because the British navy needed more men to fight France, British ships stopped and searched American vessels. British officers seized all British sailors serving on American ships. They also impressed thousands of American sailors.

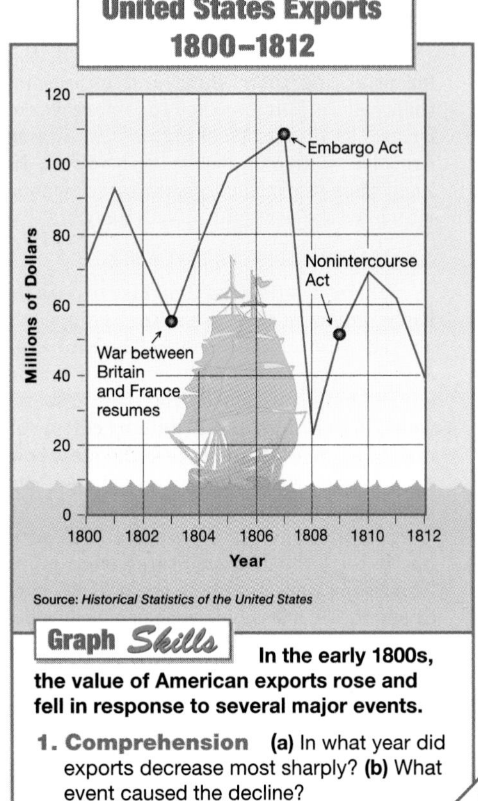

Graph Skills **In the early 1800s, the value of American exports rose and fell in response to several major events.**

1. **Comprehension** **(a)** In what year did exports decrease most sharply? **(b)** What event caused the decline?
2. **Critical Thinking** Why did United States exports increase dramatically between 1803 and 1807?

Economics

them to make notes that they can use when completing the Internet Activity in the chapter review.

3 Teach

Ask students to take on the role of a reporter who is writing an article for a foreign newspaper. They will be interviewing President Jefferson to find out what events led him to persuade Congress to pass the Embargo Act; the interview might also focus on the law's effects on U.S. citizens.

4 Assess

To close, have students complete the section review. As an alternative, have them ask and answer *who, what, where, when, why,* and *how* questions about the war with Tripoli, the violations of American neutrality during the war between Britain and France, and the Embargo and Nonintercourse acts.

Writing Actively

After Reading After they finish reading the section, students should write a paragraph summary, using all the new vocabulary words.

Graph Skills

ANSWERS **1. (a)** 1807 **(b)** Embargo Act **2.** When Britain and France went to war, they needed their merchant ships for battles, not commerce. As a result, American merchants were able to take advantage of the situation by trading with the two warring sides.

★ Activity ★
Cooperative Learning

Writing about a pirate's life Tell students that many romanticized stories and films have been created about pirates. Organize students into small groups. Ask each group to write a skit or short story that illustrates the real life of a pirate. Group members should assign researching, writing, and illustrating tasks among themselves. (*average*)

★ Section 3 Review ★

ANSWERS

1. **(a)** p. 277, **(b)** p. 277, **(c)** p. 278, **(d)** p. 278

2. **(a)** p. 277, **(b)** p. 278, **(c)** p. 278

3. looked for new markets for their goods; sent ships to distant ports in China and North Africa

4. Commerce profited until Britain and France began to seize American ships, and Britain impressed American sailors.

5. **(a)** to cut off supplies to both Britain and France **(b)** because Americans suffered more than the British and French

6. Possible answer: Benefit: A country can sell to the warring nations. Hurt: The warring nations can seize neutral ships.

7. Possible answer: It could sell exclusively to one of the warring countries if that country stopped interfering with U.S. shipping.

Activity

Guided Instruction

Have students brainstorm two lists ("No Imports" and "No Exports") and note the effects of both during an embargo. Ask: "What would not be for sale during an import embargo?" "What jobs would be affected by an export embargo?" Students can use the lists to develop ideas for their cartoons.

ASSESSMENT See the rubrics in the Alternative Assessment booklet in the Teaching Resources.

RESOURCE DIRECTORY

Teaching Resources
Lesson Planner, p. 43
Unit 3/Chapter 10
• Section 3 Quiz, p. 20

Limits on Trade

Americans were furious with the British for attacking their ships and impressing their sailors. Many wanted to declare war on Britain. Still, like Washington and Adams, President Jefferson hoped to avoid war. He knew that the small American fleet was no match for the powerful British navy.

A total ban

Jefferson persuaded Congress to pass the Embargo Act in 1807. An **embargo** is a ban on trade with another country. The **Embargo Act** forbade Americans to export or import goods. Jefferson hoped that the embargo would hurt France and Britain by cutting off needed supplies. "Our trade is the most powerful weapon we can use in our defense," one Republican newspaper wrote.

The embargo hurt Britain and France, but it hurt the United States even more. Americans were unable to get imports such as sugar, tea, and molasses. Exports dropped from $108 million in 1807 to $22 million in 1808. American sailors had no work. Farmers could not ship wheat overseas. Docks in the South were piled high with cotton and tobacco. The Embargo Act hurt New England merchants most of all.

Merchants from New England and other parts of the country protested loudly against the embargo. Some went a step further and became smugglers. A **smuggler** is a person who violates trade laws by illegally sneaking goods into or out of a country.

To stop defiance of the law, President Jefferson began using the navy and federal troops to enforce the embargo. On the border between New York and Canada, smugglers fought back. Some engaged in skirmishes with federal troops. Others, disguised as Indians, fired on federal ships.

A limited ban

After more than a year, Jefferson admitted that the Embargo Act had failed. In 1809, Congress replaced it with the less severe **Nonintercourse Act**. It allowed Americans to carry on trade with all nations except Britain and France.

The embargo was the most unpopular measure of Jefferson's years in office. Still, the Republicans remained strong. In 1808, Jefferson followed the precedent set by Washington and refused to run for a third term. James Madison, his fellow Republican, easily won the presidential election. Madison hoped that Britain and France would soon agree to stop violating American neutrality.

★ Section 3 Review ★

Recall

1. **Identify** **(a)** Barbary States, **(b)** Stephen Decatur, **(c)** Embargo Act, **(d)** Nonintercourse Act.
2. **Define** **(a)** impressment, **(b)** embargo, **(c)** smuggler.

Comprehension

3. How did American merchants expand their trading operations in the 1780s and 1790s?
4. How did war in Europe affect American overseas trade?
5. **(a)** What was the purpose of the Embargo Act? **(b)** Why did it fail?

Critical Thinking and Writing

6. **Making Generalizations** How can war both benefit and hurt the economy of a neutral nation? Explain.
7. **Predicting Consequences** What do you think the United States will do if Britain and France continue to violate American neutrality after 1809?

Activity **Drawing a Cartoon** Suppose the United States were under a limited or total embargo today. Draw a cartoon showing how such an embargo might affect you.

★ *Customized Instruction* ★

Extroverted Learners

Conducting an interview Point out to students that although the Embargo Act of 1807 was very unpopular, the Republicans won the presidential election of 1808. Have students suppose that it is several weeks before the 1808 election. Ask them to take the role of journalists interviewing the Republican candidate, James Madison. Have students work in pairs to prepare questions for Madison such as "How do you feel about the effects of the Embargo Act and the Nonintercourse Act on Americans?" and "How do you plan to stop violations of American neutrality?" Have partners take on the roles of interviewer and candidate in a question-and-answer session. (*challenging*)

The Road to War

As You Read

Explore These Questions
- Why did the Prophet and Tecumseh unite Native Americans?
- How did fighting on the frontier lead to war with Britain?
- Why did War Hawks want war with Britain?

Define
- neutral
- nationalism

Identify
- Treaty of Greenville
- Tecumseh
- the Prophet
- William Henry Harrison
- Battle of Tippecanoe
- War Hawks
- Henry Clay

In the 1790s, U.S. infantry soldiers wore coats such as the one shown here.

SETTING the Scene James Madison was a quiet, scholarly man. He had helped to write the Constitution and to pass the Bill of Rights. As President, he hoped to keep the United States out of war.

Many Americans, however, felt that Madison's approach was too timid. They argued that the United States must stand up to Native Americans and foreign countries. How could the nation grow if Native Americans stood in the way? How could the nation win respect if it allowed the British and French navies to seize American ships? The cost of war might be great, said one member of Congress. Yet, he continued, who would count in money "the slavery of our impressed seamen"?

This kind of talk aroused the nation. In the early 1800s, the United States went to war with several Native American nations. By 1812, many Americans were also calling for war with Britain.

Conflict With Native Americans

Thousands of white settlers had moved into the Northwest Territory in the 1790s. The large number of newcomers caused problems for Native Americans. The settlers ignored treaties the United States had signed with Indian nations of the region. They built farms on Indian lands. They hunted the animals that Indians depended on for food.

Fighting often broke out between the Native Americans and settlers. Isolated acts of violence led to larger acts of revenge. As a result, both sides killed innocent people who had not taken part in acts of violence. In this way, warfare spread and minor conflicts grew into larger ones.

In 1791, the Miamis of Ohio joined with other Indian nations. Little Turtle, a skilled fighter, led the Miami nation. Armed with muskets and gunpowder supplied by the British, the Miamis drove white settlers from the area.

In 1794, President Washington sent General Anthony Wayne with a well-trained army into Miami territory. The Native American forces gathered at a place called Fallen Timbers. They thought that Wayne would have trouble fighting there because fallen trees covered the land. However, Wayne's army pushed through the tangle of logs and defeated the Indians.

In 1795, leaders of the Miamis and a number of other Indian nations signed the **Treaty of Greenville.** They gave up land that would later become part of Ohio. In return, they received $20,000 and the promise of more money if they kept the peace.

Section 4 The Road to War

LESSON PLAN

Objectives

★ Explain why the Prophet and Tecumseh united Native Americans.
★ Describe how fighting on the frontier led to war with Britain.
★ Explain why the War Hawks wanted war with Britain.

1 Engage

Warm Up Write the words "hawk" and "dove" on the chalkboard. Ask students to find the terms in a dictionary and to explain how they could be used to describe a politician.

Activating Prior Knowledge Call on volunteers to share their responses. Then ask students which type of politician would favor going to war to solve a conflict. *(hawk)*

Reading Actively

Before Reading Have students read the questions under Explore These Questions. As they read, they should jot notes to help answer each question.

2 Explore

Ask students to read the section. For a homework assignment, have them use the information in the section to determine the factors that led Madison into conflicts he had hoped to avoid. Have students list these factors in the form of newspaper-article headlines.

Technology

AmericanHeritage® History of the United States CD-ROM
- Presidents: James Madison *(average)*

3 Teach

Have students work in small groups to prepare a propaganda leaflet taking the side of the War Hawks. The leaflet can include political cartoons as well as informational and persuasive articles.

4 Assess

To close the lesson, have students complete the section review. As an alternative, ask students to review the section and list the four most important facts presented. Have students share and discuss their facts as a class until they reach consensus on which four facts are most important.

★ ★ ★ ★ ★ ★ ★ ★ ★ ★ ★ ★ ★ ★ ★ ★ ★

Geography Skills

ANSWERS **1.** Review locations with students. **2.** 1784 **3.** They moved west. At the time, few American settlers were interested in the Great Plains and the lands beyond.

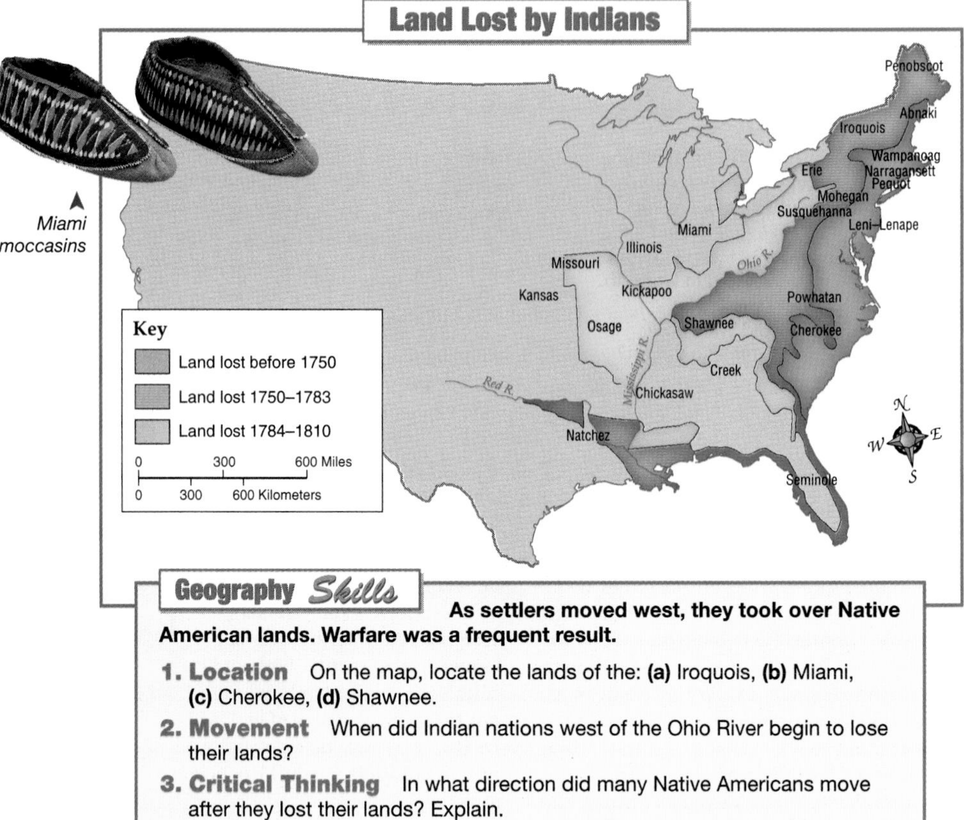

Geography Skills

As settlers moved west, they took over Native American lands. Warfare was a frequent result.

1. **Location** On the map, locate the lands of the: **(a)** Iroquois, **(b)** Miami, **(c)** Cherokee, **(d)** Shawnee.
2. **Movement** When did Indian nations west of the Ohio River begin to lose their lands?
3. **Critical Thinking** In what direction did many Native Americans move after they lost their lands? Explain.

Tecumseh's Confederation

Ohio joined the Union in 1803. By then, white settlers were pushing beyond Ohio into Indiana Territory. Many Native Americans grew angry. They wanted to keep settlers from taking more Indian land. Among those who felt this way were two Shawnee leaders: **Tecumseh** (tih KUHM suh) and his brother, called **the Prophet**.

Unity and the Old Ways

The Prophet said that he had journeyed to the spirit world. There, he learned the path that Indians must take if they were to live happily. Both the Prophet and Tecumseh said that white customs corrupted the Native American way of life. They said that many Indians depended on white trade goods, such as muskets, cloth, cooking pots, and whiskey. They believed that by returning to the old ways, Indians could gain the power to resist white invaders.

In 1808, the Prophet built a village for his followers along Tippecanoe Creek in Indiana Territory. Indians traveled from lands as far away as Missouri, Iowa, and Minnesota to hear his message. His teachings brought hope to many.

In the early 1800s, Tecumseh and the Prophet organized many Native American nations into a confederation, or league. The Prophet was the spiritual leader of the confederation and Tecumseh was its spokesperson. Tecumseh and the Prophet

Resource Directory

Teaching Resources

Unit 3/Chapter 10

- Connecting History and Literature: Tecumseh Speaks Out, p. 16

Transparencies

Geography and History

- Lands Lost by Indians, p. I-39 (*average*)

★ Activity ★

Connections With Geography

Locating Indian territories Ask students to trace the U.S. map on p. 273 and then to add labels for the locations of these Indian groups from the map on p. 280: Osage, Seminole, Cherokee, Natchez, Kickapoo, and Miami. Have students research and mark the territories for as many groups as possible. (*average*) ELL

★ Background ★

Our Diverse Nation

Culture on canvas Painter George Catlin portrayed many details of Native American life and culture in his work. Catlin was a lawyer until 1823, when he became fascinated by Native Americans and began to paint them. During nearly five decades, he created more than 500 portraits of Native Americans, including the Prophet. T persuaded Native Americans to unite against white settlers:

> “The whites have driven us from the great salt water, forced us over the mountains. . . . The way. . . to check and stop this evil is for all red men to unite in claiming a common equal right in the land.”

Tecumseh also impressed white leaders. **William Henry Harrison,** governor of Indiana Territory, grudgingly admitted, “He is one of those uncommon geniuses which spring up occasionally to produce revolutions and overturn the established order of things.”

Showdown at Tippecanoe

Rivalries among Native American nations kept Tecumseh from uniting all Indians east of the Mississippi River. Still, white settlers were alarmed at his success.

In 1811, Governor Harrison marched 1,000 soldiers against Tecumseh's town on the Tippecanoe Creek. The Prophet was in charge because Tecumseh was away organizing Indians in the South. The Prophet led a surprise night attack on Harrison's troops. Neither side won a clear victory in the battle that followed. Still, whites celebrated the **Battle of Tippecanoe** as a major victory.

Growing Conflict With Britain

The fighting with Native Americans caused relations between the United States and Britain to worsen. The British were supplying guns and ammunition to the Native Americans on the frontier. They were also encouraging Indians to attack United States' settlements.

Meanwhile, the United States and Britain also continued to disagree over trade. When the embargo against Britain and France was set to expire in 1810, the United States made a very daring offer. If either the British or French would stop seizing

Biography **Tecumseh and the Prophet**

Tecumseh (left) and the Prophet (right) felt that no Indian nation could sell land unless all other Indian nations agreed. Tecumseh said, “Sell a country! Why not sell the air, the great sea, as well as the earth?” ★ **Why did Tecumseh and the Prophet dislike the Treaty of Greenville?**

Reading Actively

During Reading Refer students to the text quote from Tecumseh. Ask volunteers to paraphrase Tecumseh's words.

Biography

ANSWER

They disliked the Treaty of Greenville because it gave a great deal of land to the white settlers.

★ *Customized Instruction* ★

Visual Learners

Writing a children's book Ask visual learners to create a picture book for young readers that illustrates the ways of life of Native Americans in the old Indiana Territory. Students should focus on how Native American groups in the area were organized and on how they chose their leaders; on how they met their needs for food, clothing, and shelter; and on their views about the land and spiritual matters. Have students use library references for their information. After they complete the research, students should write copy and create illustrations for their picture books. Give students the chance to present their work to a group of young students. (*challenging*)

Chapter 10 ★ 281

Writing Actively

After Reading Have students review the graphic organizer to write a rallying song or cheer for the War Hawks. The song or cheer should reflect the War Hawks' views about why the United States should go to war against Britain.

Graphic Organizer Skills

ANSWERS **1.** Canada and Florida **2.** Possible answer: Britain could have stopped seizing American ships and stopped giving aid to Native Americans.

Resource Directory

Teaching Resources
Unit 3/Chapter 10
• Section 4 Quiz, p. 21

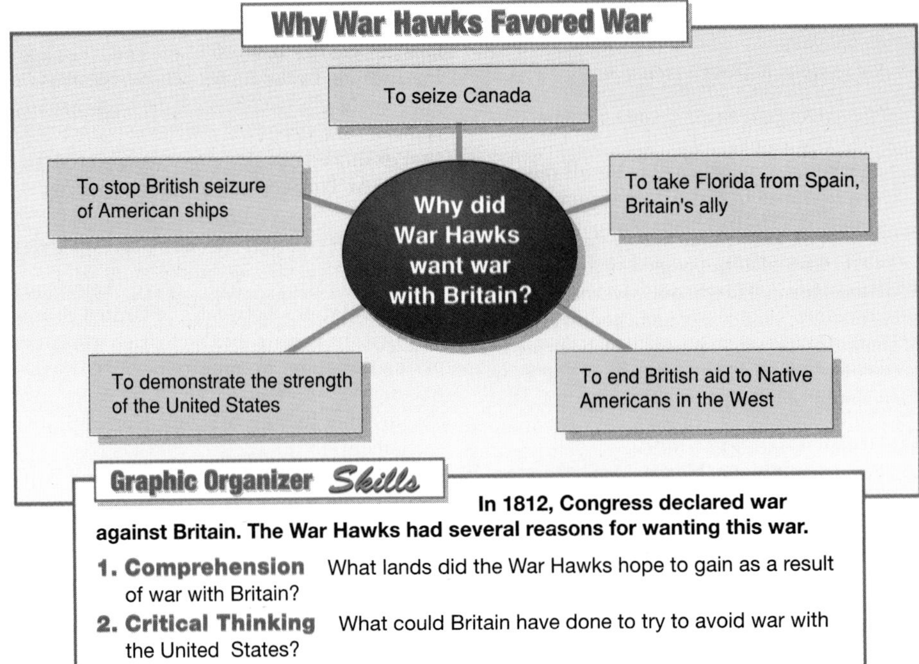

Why War Hawks Favored War
Why did War Hawks want war with Britain?
To seize Canada
To stop British seizure of American ships
To take Florida from Spain, Britain's ally
To demonstrate the strength of the United States
To end British aid to Native Americans in the West

Graphic Organizer Skills **In 1812, Congress declared war against Britain. The War Hawks had several reasons for wanting this war.**

1. **Comprehension** What lands did the War Hawks hope to gain as a result of war with Britain?
2. **Critical Thinking** What could Britain have done to try to avoid war with the United States?

American ships, the United States would halt trade with the other nation.

Seizing the chance, Napoleon quickly announced that France would respect the United States' policy of staying **neutral,** or uninvolved in the war between Britain and France. As promised, the United States continued trade with France, but stopped all shipments to Britain.

The War Hawks

While President Madison did not want war, other Americans were not as cautious. Except in New England, where many merchants wanted to restore trade with Britain, anti-British feeling ran strong. Members of Congress from the South and the West called for war with Britain. They were known as **War Hawks**.

War Hawks had a strong sense of nationalism. **Nationalism** is pride in or devotion to one's country. War Hawks felt that Britain was treating the United States as if it were still a British colony. They were willing to fight a war to defend American rights.

Arguments for war

Henry Clay of Kentucky was the most outspoken War Hawk. Clay wanted war for two reasons. He wanted revenge on Britain for seizing American ships. He also wanted to conquer Canada. "The militia of Kentucky are alone [able] to place Montreal and Upper Canada at your feet," Clay boasted to Congress. Canadians, Clay believed, would be happy to leave the British empire and join the United States.

War Hawks saw other advantages of war with Britain. South of the United States, Florida belonged to Spain, Britain's ally. If Americans went to war with Britain, War Hawks said, the United States could seize Florida from Spain.

War Hawks had yet another reason to fight Britain. They pointed out that Britain was arming Native Americans on the frontier and encouraging them to attack settlers. The War Hawks felt that winning a war against Britain would bring lasting peace and safety to American settlers on the frontier.

★ Background ★
Did You Know?

Too little, too late Napoleon didn't hesitate to strike a bargain for renewed American trade. His respect for American neutrality might not have been sincere, but it earned the prize. Britain lingered over its decision to respect the rights of the United States until 1812; it came too late to prevent war.

Congress Declares War

In 1811, the United States and Britain drifted closer to war. To prevent Americans from trading with France, British warships blockaded some American ports. The British continued to board American ships and impress American seamen. In May 1811, near New York Harbor, a brief battle broke out between an American frigate and a British warship. The Americans crippled the British ship and left 32 British dead or wounded.

The War Hawks urged that Congress prepare for a war against Britain. One of the most radical and outspoken of the War Hawks was Felix Grundy, a Congressman from Tennessee. In December 1811, he gave a very emotional speech describing what he saw as the benefits of war:

> “This war . . . will have its advantages. We shall drive the British from our continent—they will no longer have an opportunity of intriguing with our Indian neighbors.”

Grundy hoped that a war with Britain would achieve other more ambitious goals. Like most War Hawks, he dreamed of winning additional land for the United States. He closed his speech with these words: “I therefore feel anxious not only to add the Floridas to the South, but the Canadas to the North of this empire.”

Others in Congress opposed the strong views of the War Hawks. John Randolph of Virginia warned that the people of the United States would “not submit to be taxed for this war of conquest and dominion.” Representatives of New England were especially concerned. They feared that the British navy would attack New England seaports.

President Madison at last gave in to war fever. In June 1812, he asked Congress to declare war on Britain. The House voted 79 to 49 in favor of war. The Senate vote was 19 to 13. Americans soon discovered, however, that winning the war would not be as easy as declaring it.

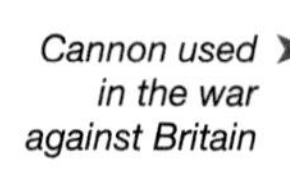

Cannon used in the war against Britain

★ Section 4 Review ★

Recall

1. **Locate** Native American lands lost **(a)** from 1750 to 1783, **(b)** from 1784 to 1810.
2. **Identify** **(a)** Treaty of Greenville, **(b)** Tecumseh, **(c)** the Prophet, **(d)** William Henry Harrison, **(e)** Battle of Tippecanoe, **(f)** War Hawks, **(g)** Henry Clay.
3. **Define** **(a)** neutral, **(b)** nationalism.

Comprehension

4. Why was there conflict between Native Americans and white settlers?
5. How did the Battle of Tippecanoe help lead to war between Britain and the United States?
6. What did the War Hawks hope to gain from a war with Britain?

Critical Thinking and Writing

7. **Identifying Main Ideas** What ideas did the Prophet and Tecumseh use to unite many Native Americans?
8. **Defending a Position** In 1812, would you have favored or opposed war with Britain? Explain the reasons for your position.

Activity **Writing a Speech** You are a Native American leader of the early 1800s. Write a speech explaining why you are against white settlement and what you think Native Americans can do to stop it. Deliver your speech to the class.

★ Section 4 Review ★

ANSWERS

1. See map, p. 280.
2. **(a)** p. 279, **(b)** p. 280, **(c)** p. 280, **(d)** p. 281, **(e)** p. 281, **(f)** p. 282, **(g)** p. 282
3. **(a)** p. 282, **(b)** p. 282
4. Whites settled on Indian lands, broke treaties, and hunted animals on which Indians depended.
5. It started a war between white settlers and Indians. War Hawks called for war, claiming the British were arming the Indians.
6. an end to both the British seizure of U.S. ships and British aid to Indians in the West; the seizure of Canada from Britain and Florida from Spain, Britain's ally
7. that uniting would allow them to protect their land from white settlers and return to traditional ways
8. Answers will vary.

Activity

Guided Instruction
Review with students the reasons for the Indians' opposition *(e.g., they lost their land and animal resources).* Students should consider violent and peaceful ends to the conflict. Speeches should have two parts: “Why I oppose white settlement” and “How we can stop it.” Students who favor violence can debate those who oppose it.

ASSESSMENT See the rubrics in the Alternative Assessment booklet in the Teaching Resources.

★ *Background* ★
Turning Points

Communication gap There might not have been a War of 1812 if telegraphs or telephones had existed at the time. Had the United States learned on June 16 that Britain had agreed to stop interfering with American shipping, it might not have declared war on June 18.

Technology

AmericanHeritage® History of the United States CD-ROM
- History Makers: Tecumseh *(average)*

Chapter 10 ★ 283

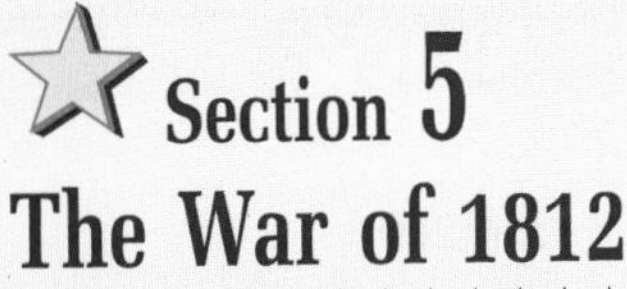

Section 5 The War of 1812

LESSON PLAN

Objectives

★ Explain why the United States was not ready for war with Britain.
★ List the major turning points of the war in the West.
★ Describe the results of the war.

1 Engage

Warm Up Write the following questions on the chalkboard for students to answer: "What might the U.S. gain from a war with Britain in 1812? What might it lose?"

Activating Prior Knowledge Encourage students to review the information in Section 3 before answering the questions. Have volunteers record their answers on the chalkboard in two lists.

Reading Actively

Before Reading Before they read the section, have students turn the main headings into main topics of an outline. Then, as they read, have them record two to three important subtopics for each main topic.

2 Explore

Ask students to read the section. For a homework assignment, have students write an essay in which they describe one thing the United States could have done to avoid

RESOURCE DIRECTORY

Teaching Resources
Lesson Planner, p. 44

The War of 1812

As You Read

Explore These Questions

- How was the United States unready for war with Britain?
- What were the major turning points of the war in the West?
- What were the results of the war?

Identify

- Oliver Hazard Perry
- Battle of Lake Erie
- Andrew Jackson
- Battle of Horseshoe Bend
- Dolley Madison
- Battle of New Orleans
- Richard Allen
- Hartford Convention
- Treaty of Ghent

SETTING the Scene Many Americans welcomed the news of war with Britain. In some cities, they fired cannons and guns and danced in the streets. One New Jersey man wrote a song calling for a swift attack on Canada:

> ❝ On to Quebec's embattled halls!
> Who will pause, when glory calls?
> Charge, soldiers, charge, its lofty walls. And storm its strong artillery. ❞

Other Americans were less enthusiastic. New Englanders, especially, talked scornfully of "Mr. Madison's war." In fact, before the war ended, some New Englanders would threaten to leave the Union and make a separate peace with Britain.

Unready for War

The American declaration of war took the British by surprise. They were locked in a bitter struggle with Napoleon, and could not spare troops to fight the United States. As the war began, however, the United States faced difficulties of its own.

Because Jefferson believed in a small federal government and had reduced spending on defense, the United States was not ready for war. The navy had only 16 ships to fight against the huge British fleet. The army was small and ill equipped. Moreover, many of the officers knew little about the military. "The state of the Army," commented a member of Congress, "is enough to make any man who has the smallest love of country wish to get rid of it."

Since there were few regular troops, the government relied on volunteers to fight the war. Congress voted to give them $124 and 360 acres of land for their service. The money was high pay at the time—equal to a year's salary for most workers.

Attracted by money and the chance to own their own farm, young men eagerly enlisted. They were poorly trained, however, and did not know how to be good soldiers. Many deserted after a few months.

Fighting at Sea

The British navy blockaded American ports to stop Americans from trading with other countries. The small American navy was unable to break the blockade. Still, several sea captains won stunning victories.

One famous battle took place early in the war, in August 1812. As he was sailing near Newfoundland, Isaac Hull, captain of the *Constitution*, spotted the British ship *Guerrière* (gai ree AIR). For nearly an hour, the two ships jockeyed for position.

At last, the guns of the *Constitution* roared into action. They tore holes in the sides of the *Guerrière* and shot off both masts. When the smoke cleared, Hull asked the British captain if he had "struck" his flag—that is, lowered his flag in surrender. "Well, I don't know," replied the stunned British captain. "Our mizzenmast is gone, our mainmast

★ *Customized Instruction* ★

Kinesthetic Learners

Researching battles Ask students to research one of the naval battles of the War of 1812 or the kinds of ships used in the war. Those interested in naval battles might research:

- Battle of Lake Erie
- Battle of the Thames
- Battle of Lake Champlain

Those interested in ships might research:

- frigates
- sloops
- corvettes

Have students draw a detailed picture of the battle or create a model of the ship they research. Display students' work. (challenging)

American Heritage MAGAZINE

HISTORY HAPPENED HERE

The USS Constitution

The USS Constitution *became known as "Old Ironsides" because British cannonballs often bounced off her thick wooden hull. In 1905, the ship was docked in Boston and opened to the public. In 1997, the ship underwent major restoration. Today, the United States Navy invites you to come aboard and tour "Old Ironsides." In the nearby museum, you can relive history by commanding a ship, hoisting a sail, or firing a cannon.*

★ ***To learn more about this historic ship, write:*** *USS* Constitution *Museum, Charlestown Navy Yard, Charlestown, MA 02129.*

is gone. And, upon the whole, you may say we *have* struck our flag."

American sea captains won other victories at sea. These victories cheered Americans, but did little to win the war.

War in the West

One goal of the War Hawks was to conquer Canada. They were convinced that Canadians would welcome the chance to throw off British rule and join the United States. The United States planned to invade Canada at three different points: Detroit, the Niagara River, and Montreal.

Invasion of Canada

General William Hull moved American troops into Canada from Detroit. The Canadians had only a few untrained troops to ward off the invasion. However, they were led by a clever and skillful British leader, General Isaac Brock.

Brock paraded his soldiers in red coats to make it appear that experienced British troops were helping the Canadians. He also let a message with false information fall into American hands. It exaggerated the number of Indians who were fighting with the Canadians. Brock's scare tactics worked. Hull retreated from Canada.

Other attempts to invade Canada also failed. Americans were wrong in thinking that the Canadians would welcome them as liberators from British rule. Instead, the Canadians fought fiercely and forced the Americans into retreat.

Battle of Lake Erie

In 1813, the Americans set out to win control of Lake Erie. Captain **Oliver Hazard Perry** had no fleet, so he designed and built his own ships. In September 1813, he sailed his tiny fleet against the British.

During the **Battle of Lake Erie**, the British battered Perry's own ship and left it

war with Britain. Call on volunteers to read their essays and discuss the viability of each suggestion.

3 Teach

Help students create a chart of major battles of the War of 1812. Draw a blank chart on the chalkboard with columns labeled "Battle," "Date," "Place," "Winner," and "Importance." Have students fill in the chart with information from the text. Ask them to determine which battle they think was the greatest triumph for the United States and which battle was the greatest defeat.

4 Assess

To close the lesson, have students complete the section review. As an alternative, play a "Jeopardy"-like game with students. Provide information from Section 5 as the answers and have students create appropriate questions.

★ ★ ★ ★ ★ ★ ★ ★ ★ ★ ★ ★ ★ ★ ★ ★ ★

American Heritage MAGAZINE

The USS *Constitution* To learn more about the USS *Constitution* Museum on the Internet, go to www.ussconstitutionmuseum.org.

★ *Background* ★

Did You Know?

Old Ironsides A nickname for the USS *Constitution* is "Old Ironsides," earned during the ship's battle with the *Guerrière*. A sailor is said to have seen shots from the British warship bounce off the sides of the *Constitution*. Amazed, the sailor exclaimed that the American ship had sides of iron.

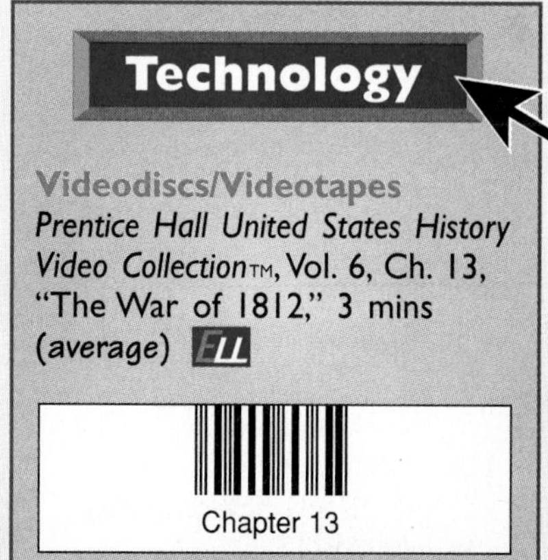

Technology

Videodiscs/Videotapes
Prentice Hall United States History Video Collection™, Vol. 6, Ch. 13, "The War of 1812," 3 mins (average) ELL

Chapter 13

Reading Actively

During Reading Have students read the subsection Native American Losses to see why the Battle of the Thames was so significant to the Native Americans.

Geography *Skills*

ANSWERS **1.** Review locations with students. **2.** south to Horseshoe Bend, southwest to Pensacola, west to New Orleans **3.** The blockade limited American trade with other nations. As a result, American merchants lost profits. Also, Americans had limited access to the foreign goods that they wanted.

The War of 1812

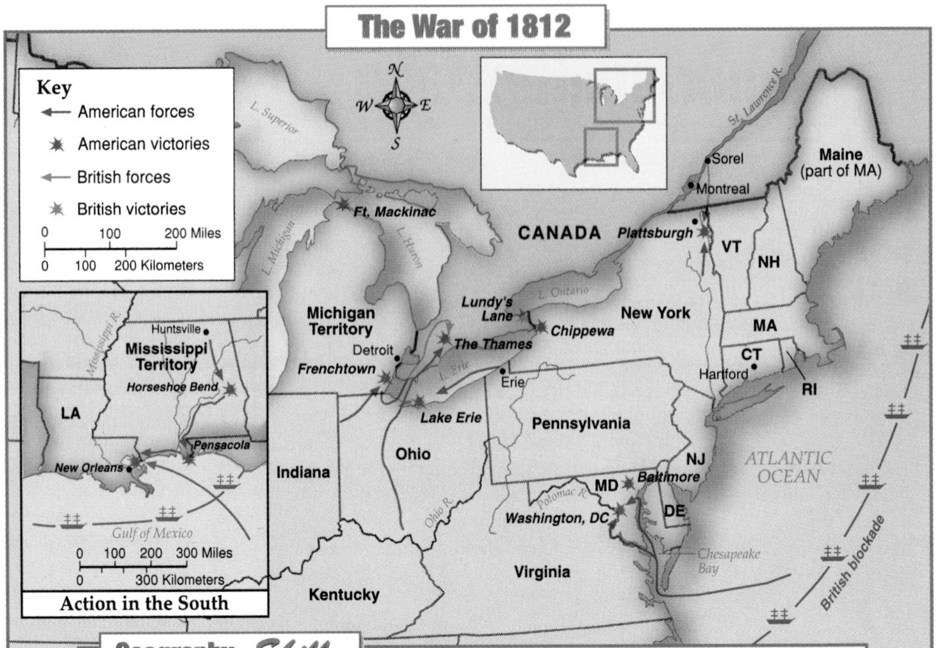

Geography *Skills*

The War of 1812 was fought on several fronts.

1. **Location** On the map, locate the following battle sites: **(a)** Plattsburgh, **(b)** Lake Erie, **(c)** The Thames, **(d)** Horseshoe Bend, **(e)** Washington, D.C., **(f)** Baltimore, **(g)** New Orleans.
2. **Movement** Using the inset map, describe the route that American forces followed from Huntsville to New Orleans
3. **Critical Thinking** How did the British blockade hurt the economy of the United States?

helpless. Perry took his flag down and rowed over to another American ship. There, he raised the colors again and continued to fight. Finally, the Americans won the battle. Captain Perry wrote his message of victory on the back of an envelope: "We have met the enemy and they are ours."

Native American losses

After losing control of Lake Erie, the British and their ally Tecumseh retreated from Detroit into Canada. General William Henry Harrison, veteran of Tippecanoe, pursued them. The Americans won a decisive victory at the Battle of the Thames. Tecumseh died in the fighting. Without Tecumseh's leadership, the Indian confederation soon fell apart.

Still, the Creeks, Tecumseh's allies in the South, continued their fight against the settlers. **Andrew Jackson,** a Tennessee officer, took command of American troops in the Creek War. In 1814, with the help of the Cherokees, Jackson won a crushing victory at the **Battle of Horseshoe Bend.** The leader of the Creeks walked alone into Jackson's camp to surrender:

> "I am in your power. Do unto me as you please. . . . If I had an army I would yet fight, and contend to the last. . . . But your people have destroyed my nation."

★ Background ★
Our Diverse Nation

Creek misfortunes Jackson allowed the Creek women and children to cross the Tallapoosa River at Horseshoe Bend to safety. Then his troops massacred 800 Creek men. His peace terms with the Native Americans forced them to give up 23 million acres of land in what is today Georgia and Alabama.

★ Background ★
Linking Past and Present

Uncle Sam During the War of 1812, Samuel "Uncle Sam" Wilson of Troy, New York, supplied meat to the American army. The barrels containing meat were marked *U.S.,* for *United States,* but many assumed that the initials stood for *Uncle Sam.* Soon, "Uncle Sam" became the nickname for the government of the United States.

Resource Directory

Teaching Resources
Unit 3/Chapter 10
- Biography Flashcard: Dolley Madison, p. 17

For the time being, the fighting ended. Once again, Native Americans had to give up land to whites.

Final Battles

In 1814, Britain and its allies defeated France. With the war in Europe over, Britain could send more troops and ships against the United States.

The British burn Washington

In the summer of 1814, British ships sailed into Chesapeake Bay and landed an invasion force about 30 miles (48 km) from Washington, D.C. American troops met the British at Bladensburg, Maryland. President Madison himself watched the battle. To his dismay, the battle-hardened British quickly scattered the untrained Americans. The British met little further resistance as they continued their march to the capital.

In the White House, **Dolley Madison** waited for her husband to return. Hastily, she scrawled a note to her sister:

> "Will you believe it, my sister? We have had a battle or skirmish near Bladensburg and here I am still within sound of the cannon! Mr. Madison comes not. May God protect us. Two messengers covered with dust come bid me fly. But here I mean to wait for him."

Soon after, British troops marched into the capital. Dolley Madison gathered up important papers of the President and a portrait of George Washington. Then, she fled south. She was not there to see the British burn the White House and other buildings.

From Washington, the British marched north toward the city of Baltimore. The key to Baltimore's defense was Fort McHenry.

Linking Past and Present

Past

Present

The White House

After capturing Washington in August 1814, the British burned the White House. Margaret Smith, a resident of the city, recalled the sad scene: "Who would have thought that this mass so solid, so magnificent, so grand... [should] be thus irreparably destroyed." In fact, the White House was not destroyed. A torrential thunderstorm put out the flames and saved the structure. Today, the White House continues to serve as the official residence of Presidents of the United States. ★ **How do you think the burning of the White House affected American morale?**

Linking Past and Present

ANSWER

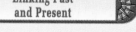

Possible answer: Angered by the British attempt to burn the White House, Americans may have been more determined than ever to fight on until the enemy had been defeated.

★ *Activity* ★

Connections With Civics

Class discussion Dolley Madison saved some important papers and a painting of George Washington as she fled the White House. Ask students to discuss whether or not they think the government would continue to exist even if the original, handwritten Constitution were destroyed. Why or why not? (*challenging*)

FROM THE ARCHIVES OF AmericanHeritage®

Rich man helps out The United States could have lost the war, were it not for the help of businessman Stephen Girard. In early 1813, the war was going badly and the Treasury was nearly empty. Girard helped the government raise over $8 million, a huge amount for that time. Girard lent more than $2 million of his own money.

Source: John Steele Gordon, "Driving a Soft Bargain," *American Heritage* magazine, September 1996.

Technology

AmericanHeritage® History of the United States CD-ROM

- Arts and Entertainment: Music (*average*)

![Viewing History] ANSWER

Word of a treaty signed in England had to come by sea. There were no quick means of communication in 1815.

Writing Actively

After Reading After students finish reading the section, have them review the goals of the War Hawks. Then ask students to make a graphic organizer showing the extent to which the goals were achieved.

Viewing History: Battle of New Orleans

In this engraving, Andrew Jackson stands atop the American defense works as he spurs his troops to victory. The Battle of New Orleans was the bloodiest engagement of the War of 1812. Neither side knew that the war had ended two weeks earlier. ★ **Why did it take so long for the news of war's end to reach New Orleans?**

From evening on September 13 until dawn on September 14, British rockets bombarded the harbor.

When the early morning fog lifted, the "broad stripes and bright stars" of the American flag still waved over Fort McHenry. The British withdrew. Francis Scott Key, who witnessed the battle, wrote a poem about the bombardment. Later, "The Star-Spangled Banner" was set to music and adopted as the national anthem of the United States.

Battle of New Orleans

In late 1814, the British prepared to attack New Orleans. From there, they hoped to sail up the Mississippi. However, Andrew Jackson was waiting for the British. Jackson had turned his frontier fighters into a strong army. He took Pensacola in Spanish Florida to keep the British from using it as a base. He then marched through Mobile and set up camp in New Orleans.

Jackson's force included thousands of frontiersmen. Many of them were expert riflemen. In addition, citizens of New Orleans joined the army to defend their city from the approaching British. Among the volunteers were hundreds of African Americans.

The American soldiers dug trenches to defend themselves. On January 8, 1815, the British attacked. Again and again, British soldiers marched toward the American trenches. More than 2,000 British fell under the deadly fire of American sharpshooters and cannons. Only seven Americans died.

All over the United States, Americans cheered the victory at the **Battle of New Orleans**. Andrew Jackson became a national hero. His fame did not dim even when Americans later learned that the battle could have been avoided. It took place two weeks after the United States and Britain had signed a treaty in Europe ending the war.

African Americans in the War

African Americans served alongside other Americans in the fight against the British. African American soldiers helped win the Battle of New Orleans. Following the British attacks on Washington and Baltimore, African American volunteers helped defend Philadelphia against a possible attack. Bishop **Richard Allen** and the Reverend Absalom Jones recruited more than 2,000 men to help build Philadelphia's fortifications. The state of New York, meanwhile, organized two regiments of black volunteers to serve in the army.

African Americans also served with distinction in the United States Navy. They helped win the Battle of Lake Erie as well as other naval battles. Commander Nathaniel Shaler praised one particular black sailor

Skills For LIFE MINI LESSON

CRITICAL THINKING Recognizing Frame of Reference

1. Introduce the skill of recognizing frame of reference by telling students that a person's relation to an event or situation affects how he or she perceives it.

2. Help students practice the skill by asking them how this British officer's position affects his perception when he says of the New Orleans battlefield: "Of all the sights I ever witnessed, that which met me there was beyond comparison the most . . . humiliating . . . nearly a thousand bodies, all of them arrayed in British uniforms."

3. Help students practice this skill by having them speculate how one of Jackson's troops might have described the scene.

RESOURCE DIRECTORY

Teaching Resources
Unit 3/Chapter 10
- Vocabulary Builder, p. 12
- Map Mystery: Jackson's Trap at New Orleans, p. 15
- Section 5 Quiz, p. 22

Chapter Tests, pp. 55–60

who was killed in battle: "When America has such [sailors], she has little to fear from the tyrants of the ocean."

Peace at Last

In the early 1800s, news took weeks to cross the Atlantic Ocean. By late 1814, Americans knew that peace talks had begun, but they did not know how they were progressing or how long they would last. As Jackson was preparing to fight the British at New Orleans, New Englanders were meeting to protest "Mr. Madison's war."

New Englanders protest

The British blockade had hurt New England's sea trade. Also, many New Englanders feared that the United States might win land in Florida and Canada. If new states were carved out of these lands, the South and the West would become more influential than New England.

Delegates from around New England met in Hartford, Connecticut, in December 1814. Most were Federalists. They disliked the Republican President and the war. The delegates to the **Hartford Convention** threatened to leave the Union if the war continued.

Then, while the delegates debated what to do, news of the peace treaty arrived. The Hartford Convention ended quickly. With the war over, the protest was meaningless.

"Nothing was settled"

The **Treaty of Ghent** was signed in the city of Ghent, Belgium, on December 24, 1814. John Quincy Adams, one of the Americans at Ghent, summed up the treaty in one sentence: "Nothing was adjusted, nothing was settled."

Britain and the United States agreed to restore prewar conditions. The treaty said nothing about impressment or neutrality. These issues had faded due to the end of the Napoleonic Wars in Europe. Other issues were settled later. In 1818, for example, the two nations settled a dispute over the border between Canada and the United States.

Looking back, some Americans felt that the War of 1812 had been a mistake. Others argued that Europe would now treat the young republic with more respect. The victories of heroes like Oliver Hazard Perry and Andrew Jackson gave Americans new pride in their country. As one Republican leader remarked, "The people are now more American. They feel and act more as a nation."

★ Section 5 Review ★

Recall

1. **Locate** (a) Lake Erie, (b) Detroit, (c) Chesapeake Bay, (d) Washington, D.C., (e) Baltimore, (f) New Orleans.
2. **Identify** (a) Oliver Hazard Perry, (b) Battle of Lake Erie, (c) Andrew Jackson, (d) Battle of Horseshoe Bend, (e) Dolley Madison, (f) Battle of New Orleans, (g) Richard Allen, (h) Hartford Convention, (i) Treaty of Ghent.

Comprehension

3. What military problems did the United States face as the War of 1812 began?
4. How did the death of Tecumseh affect the war in the West?
5. What were the results of the War of 1812?

Critical Thinking and Writing

6. **Understanding Causes and Effects** How do you think the War of 1812 helped Andrew Jackson to later become the President of the United States?
7. **Applying Information** Why did the results of the War of 1812 please some Americans, but disappoint others?

Activity **Writing a Song** Keep your head down! You are in the trenches at the Battle of New Orleans. Write a song describing what you see, hear, and feel as you help Andrew Jackson defeat the British and save New Orleans.

★ Section 5 Review ★

ANSWERS

1. See map, p. 286.
2. (a) p. 285, (b) p. 285, (c) p. 286, (d) p. 286, (e) p. 287, (f) p. 288, (g) p. 288, (h) p. 289, (i) p. 289
3. The navy had few ships; the army was small and both poorly equipped and trained. The British were blockading American ports.
4. The Indian confederation fell apart.
5. Little changed. Both sides returned to the pre-war conditions, but many Americans had more pride in their country.
6. Possible answer: His victories over the Creeks and British made him a national hero; many Americans wanted a hero as President.
7. Pleased: Some argued that the U.S. now had the respect of Europe and that Americans had a new pride in their country. Disappointed: Some felt the problems that had caused the war remained.

Guided Instruction
Ask students to take notes as they brainstorm for sensory impressions (what would they see, hear, and feel?). Suggest they write their songs to familiar tunes. Volunteers can share their songs with the class.

ASSESSMENT See the rubrics in the Alternative Assessment booklet in the Teaching Resources.

★ Activity ★

Linking Past and Present

Comparing controversial wars The War of 1812 is not the only controversial war fought by the United States. The more recent Vietnam War produced tremendous controversy. Have students research the Vietnam War and compare the location, causes, and results of that war with the War of 1812. Students might create a chart of their findings. (*challenging*)

CD-ROM
Test Bank CD-ROM, Ch. 10
Interactive Student Tutorial

Chapter 10

Review and Activities

Reviewing the Chapter

Define These Terms

1. c **2.** e **3.** a **4.** b **5.** d

Explore the Main Ideas

1. Possible answer: He felt that government should have less power over people's lives and play a very limited role in the economy.

2. The United States needed safe access to the Mississippi so American farmers could ship their produce through New Orleans.

3. They were to map a route to the Pacific, study the natural resources of Louisiana, and establish friendly relations with Native Americans.

4. At first, American merchants profited from the war. However, when France and Britain began interfering with American shipping, the American economy was hurt. The United States tried to punish the two warring nations with a trade embargo, which hurt Americans even more.

5. Native Americans united to resist the invasion of white settlers and to return to a traditional way of life.

6. (a) Possible answer: the American victory in the Battle of Lake Erie **(b)** It broke the strength of the British and their Indian allies in the North.

Geography Skills

1. E **2.** B **3.** C **4.** D **5.** A **6.** F

Chapter 10 Review and Activities

★ Sum It Up ★

Section 1 Republicans in Power

- President Jefferson tried to help ordinary citizens and limit government power.
- The Supreme Court established its power to decide if laws are constitutional.

Section 2 The Louisiana Purchase

- In 1803, the United States bought the vast western territory of Louisiana from France.
- Lewis and Clark explored Louisiana and tried to establish friendly relations with Native Americans.

Section 3 New Threats From Overseas

- American trade increased but was threatened by France and Britain.
- The Embargo Act hurt the United States more than Britain and France.

Section 4 The Road to War

- Native Americans fought to preserve their lands and culture.
- War Hawks wanted war with Britain to protect American trade and to gain new lands.

Section 5 The War of 1812

- Though poorly prepared, American forces defeated the British in key battles.
- Not all Americans supported the war. For many, however, the war brought a new sense of national pride.

For additional review of the major ideas of Chapter 10, see ***Guide to the Essentials of American History*** or ***Interactive Student Tutorial CD-ROM,*** which contains interactive review activities, graphic organizers, and practice tests.

Reviewing the Chapter

Define These Terms

Match each term with the correct definition.

Column 1	Column 2
1. laissez faire	**a.** forcing people into naval service
2. judicial review	**b.** ban on trade with another country
3. impressment	**c.** government should play a very limited role in economic affairs
4. embargo	**d.** pride in one's country
5. nationalism	**e.** Supreme Court's power to decide if laws are constitutional

Explore the Main Ideas

1. Describe two of President Jefferson's ideas about the proper role of government.
2. Why did the United States buy Louisiana from France?
3. What were the goals of the Lewis and Clark expedition?
4. How did war between Britain and France affect the United States?
5. Why did many Native Americans unite under Tecumseh and the Prophet?
6. **(a)** Describe one major turning point in the War of 1812. **(b)** Explain one result of the war.

Geography Skills

Match the letters on the map with the following places: **1.** Canada, **2.** Battle of the Thames, **3.** Battle of Horseshoe Bend, **4.** Battle of New Orleans, **5.** Baltimore, **6.** British blockade.

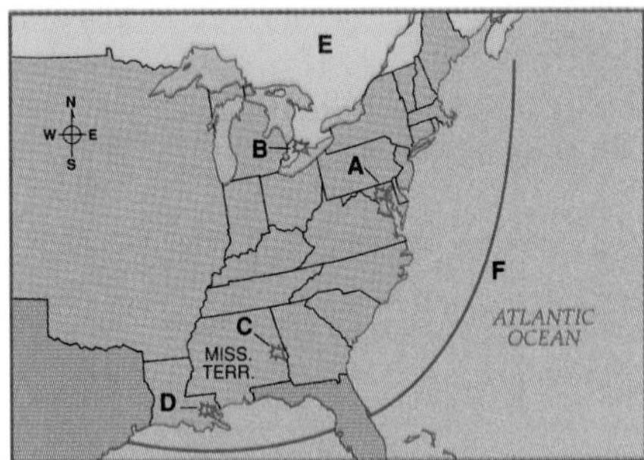

Critical Thinking and Writing

1. Answers will vary.

2. To support its war effort, Britain seized American ships and impressed American sailors, angering the United States.

3. Possible answer: Native Americans and white settlers might have agreed to share the land and coexist peacefully.

4. Possible answer: The Louisiana Purchase increased national pride by greatly enlarging the size of the United States. Andrew Jackson's victory at the Battle of New Orleans proved that the United States could defend itself against other European nations.

Using Primary Sources

(a) Hall disapproved of the embargo.
(b) Because of the embargo, Hall couldn't help his parents, who were unable to pay for their home. **(c)** Possible answer: Hall's parents might have been merchants or farmers who exported their goods to Europe. With a reduced income, they were not able to pay their rent or mortgage.

Critical Thinking and Writing

1. **Defending a Position** Do you agree or disagree with Jefferson's idea that federal power should be limited? Explain the reasons for your position.
2. **Understanding Chronology** How did a British-French war help lead to a British-American war?
3. **Solving Problems** Describe a treaty that might have satisfied both Native Americans and white settlers in the early 1800s.
4. Exploring Unit Themes **Nationalism** Describe two events or developments that caused many Americans to become more nationalistic during the Age of Jefferson.

Using Primary Sources

Soon after passage of the Embargo Act, President Jefferson received this letter from Jonathan Hall, a resident of New Hampshire:

> "Sir: I have respected your laws and your government for the United States of America and I wish to have you continue your laws and government and keep the embargo on till you see fit to take it off, though it is very trying to the people in this country about their debts. . . . I have a father and a mother and they can't take care of themselves and as times are I can't pay for their place so . . . I hope that . . . your [honor] will do a little for me, Jonathan Hall."

Source: *Jefferson Papers*. "Capt. Jonathan Hall to Jefferson." August 12, 1808.

Recognizing Points of View **(a)** Did Hall approve of the Embargo Act? **(b)** How did the embargo affect Hall? **(c)** Explain how the embargo might have caused this effect.

Activity Bank

Interdisciplinary Activity

Exploring Civics Create a chart comparing the different ideas of the Federalists and Republicans during the Age of Jefferson. Include categories such as ideas about democracy, economic policy, military policy, and foreign policy.

Career Skills Activity

Political Leaders Write a persuasive speech supporting or opposing war with Britain in 1812. The purpose of the speech is to persuade listeners to agree with your point of view. Deliver your speech to the class. Then, invite students to express their own views. If there is disagreement, you might wish to debate the issue.

Citizenship Activity

Creating a Poster "We are all Republicans, we are all Federalists," said President Jefferson. Create a poster describing and illustrating four goals you think all Americans should agree on, regardless of their political party.

Internet Activity

Use the Internet to find information about current or recent embargoes. In a written report, describe two of these modern embargoes and the reason for each. Explain whether or not each has been successful.

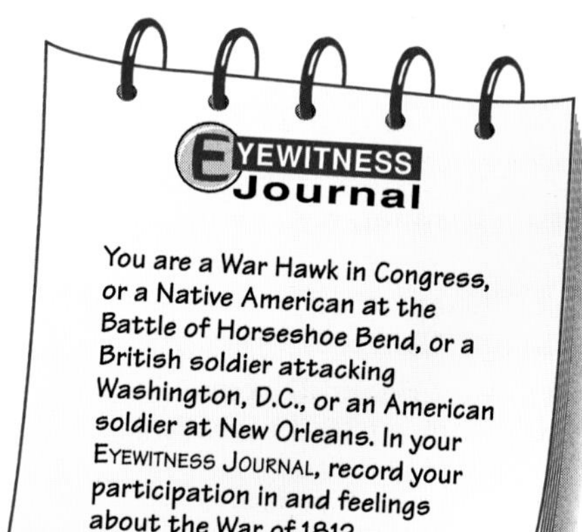

EYEWITNESS Journal
You are a War Hawk in Congress, or a Native American at the Battle of Horseshoe Bend, or a British soldier attacking Washington, D.C., or an American soldier at New Orleans. In your EYEWITNESS JOURNAL, record your participation in and feelings about the War of 1812.

★ 291

Activity Bank

ASSESSMENT To assess the activities on this page, see the rubrics in the Alternative Assessment booklet in the Teaching Resources. You might want to share the rubrics with your students before they begin work.

Interdisciplinary Activity

1. On the chalkboard, draw a sample chart with three columns and four rows. Label the columns "Ideas," "Federalists," and "Republicans." Under "Ideas," write categories such as "Democracy" and "Economic Policy."
2. Have a group of students work on one chart. Each person can gather information for a different box of the chart—for example, "Republican Economic Policy."
3. Have groups compare charts and add any new ideas that they learn from one another.

Career Skills Activity

1. Encourage each student to start with a topic sentence that expresses his or her point of view.
2. Explain that persuasive speeches often appeal to the audience's personal safety or livelihood. Students might want to include a sentence such as "What will happen to you if . . . ?"
3. Remind students that a slow, forceful delivery will add to the persuasiveness of their speeches.

Citizenship Activity

1. Suggest that students look through newspapers to get ideas for current issues, such as education, jobs, and medical care.
2. Display posters in the classroom and hallways.
3. Some students may want to plan additional ways to promote their ideas, such as newspaper editorials and letters to government representatives.

Eyewitness Journal

1. Have students select the situation with which they can identify most closely.
2. Ask students to consider how their futures will be affected by the events they are experiencing.
3. Encourage students to use information about this event to evoke ideas for the journal entry.

Internet Activity

1. Have students go to www.phschool.com, which contains updated information on a variety of topics.
2. Another useful site is the Catalog of New US Unilateral Economic Sanctions at www.usaengage.org/studies/nam2.html.
3. Given the changing nature of the Internet, you may wish to preview this site before directing students to it.

Chapter 11 Manager

SECTION OBJECTIVES	TEACHING RESOURCES	ADDITIONAL RESOURCES
1 The Industrial Revolution (pp. 294–300) **Objectives** 1. List the major effects of the Industrial Revolution. 2. Explain how the Industrial Revolution began in the United States. 3. Describe life in the early factories of the United States.	**Lesson Planner,** p. 45 (average) .... 45 mins. **Unit 3/Chapter 11** • Biography Flashcard: P.T. Barnum, p. 28 (average) .... 20 mins. • Section 1 Quiz, p. 29 (average) .... 15 mins. **Why Study History?** • Technology Continues to Change Our Lives, pp. 43–46 (average) .... 30 mins.	**Voices of Freedom** • Pros and Cons of Factory Life, pp. 83–84 (average) **Interdisciplinary Explorations** • Mill Life in the 1840s: Roots of American Industry (challenging)
2 Moving Westward (pp. 301–307) **Objectives** 1. Describe how settlers traveled westward in the early 1800s. 2. List the steps taken by Americans to improve roads. 3. Explain how steamboats and canals affected transportation.	**Lesson Planner,** p. 46 (average) .... 90 mins. **Unit 3/Chapter 11** • Practice Your Skills: Analyzing a Primary Source, p. 24 (average) .... 20 mins. • Critical Thinking and Writing: Analyzing Visual Information, p. 25 (challenging) .... 20 mins. • Map Mystery: The National Road, p. 26 (challenging) .... 20 mins. • Section 2 Quiz, p. 30 (average) .... 15 mins. **Interdisciplinary Connections** • Main Idea: The Erie Canal, pp. 61–66 (average) .... 20 mins.	**Voices of Freedom** • Mark Twain on the Lure of Steamb p. 85 (average) **Historical Outline Map Book** • The United States in 1824, p. 34 (average) • Transportation to the West, p. 33 (average) **Customized Reader** • Frontier Doctors, article IIIB-5 (challenging) • A Frontier Conversion, article IIIE (challenging)
3 Building National Unity (pp. 308–311) **Objectives** 1. Explain how Congress tried to strengthen the national economy. 2. Describe the goals of Henry Clay's American System. 3. Explain how the Supreme Court strengthened national unity.	**Lesson Planner,** p. 47 (average) .... 45 mins. **Unit 3/Chapter 11** • Section 3 Quiz, p. 31 (average) .... 15 mins. **Document-Based Discovery** • Nationalism, pp. 10–13 (challenging) .... 90 mins.	**Voices of Freedom** • A Southerner Objects to the Tari pp. 86–87 (challenging) • Americans Sing Praises of Home, p. 88 (average)
4 Latin America and the United States (pp. 312–315) **Objectives** 1. Describe how Latin American nations won independence. 2. Explain how the United States gained Florida. 3. State the purpose of the Monroe Doctrine.	**Lesson Planner,** p. 48 (average) .... 90 mins. **Unit 3/Chapter 11** • Vocabulary Builder, p. 23 (basic) .... 10 mins. • Connecting History and Literature: Letter From an American Farmer, p. 27 (average) .... 20 mins. • Section 4 Quiz, p. 32 (average) .... 15 mins. **Chapter Tests,** pp. 61–66 (average) .... 45 mins.	**Voices of Freedom** • Monroe Doctrine Declared, pp. 8 (average) **Historical Outline Map Book** • New Nations in Latin America, p. (average)

Assessment Options

Teaching Resources
- Alternative Assessment booklet
- Section Quizzes, Unit 3, Chapter 11, pp. 29–32
- Chapter Tests, Chapter 11, pp. 61–66
- Test Bank CD-ROM

Student Performance Pack
- Guide to the Essentials of American History, Chapter 11 Test, p. 65
- Standardized Test Prep Handbook
- Interactive Student Tutorial CD-ROM

Interdisciplinary Connections

Teaching Resources
- Map Mystery, Unit 3, Chapter 11, p. 26
- Connecting History and Literature, Unit 3, Chapter 11, p. 27
- Interdisciplinary Connections, pp. 61–66

Interdisciplinary Explorations
- Mill Life in the 1840s: Roots of American Industry

Voices of Freedom, pp. 83–88

Customized Reader, articles IIIB-5, IIIB-8

Historical Outline Map Book, pp. 33–35

Technology

AmericanHeritage® History of the United States CD-ROM
- Time Tour: Years of Growth and Expansion in the New Republic
- Presidents: James Monroe
- History Makers: Daniel Boone, Henry Clay

Interactive Student Tutorial CD-ROM

Test Bank CD-ROM

Color Transparencies
- Spinning Mill, p. H-31
- The Industrial Revolution in the United States, p. F-17
- Fur Traders Descending the Missouri, p. D-35
- Erie Canal, p. B-51

Guided Reading Audiotapes (English/Spanish), side 3

Resource Pro® CD-ROM

Prentice Hall United States History Video Collection™ (Spanish track available on disc version.) Vol. 6, Chs. 16, 22

Prentice Hall Home Page www.phschool.com

Student Performance Pack

Guide to the Essentials of American History
- Ch. 11, pp. 61–65 (Available in English and Spanish)

Guided Reading Audiotapes (English/Spanish), side 3

Standardized Test Prep Handbook

Interactive Student Tutorial CD-ROM

BLOCK SCHEDULING
Activities with this icon will help you meet your Block Scheduling needs.

ENGLISH LANGUAGE LEARNERS
Activities with this icon are suitable for English Language Learners.

TEAM TEACHING
Activities and Background Notes with this icon present starting points for Team Teaching.

Teachers' Bibliography

Don't miss the special American Heritage® teaching notes found in this chapter.

Contact Teachers' Curriculum Institute to learn more about History Alive!® resources on the nation's early years. See History Alive!® unit: The Constitution in a New Nation, Section 4, "The Constitution in Action, 1789–1820."

American history for kids
COBBLESTONE®

Explore your library to find these issues related to Chapter 11: *The National Road*, June 1991; *The Monroe Presidency*, September 1996.

Prentice Hall Web Site You can access a structured, on-line environment that allows you to preview curriculum-related resources and receive updated information on groundbreaking events from around the nation and the world. (www.phschool.com)

Chapter 11

Industry and Growth 1790–1825

Introducing the Chapter

Have students preview the main ideas of this chapter by looking over the visuals. Suggest they look for examples of new forms of technology, new industries, and new modes of transportation.

To reinforce student understanding of the sequence of events in this chapter, ask students to look at the time line on these pages. Ask questions such as these: **(1)** Approximately how many years does the time line cover? *(1785–1825; about 40 years)* **(2)** What world event took place the same year as Fulton's record-breaking steamboat trip? *(Gas street lighting was demonstrated in London.)* **(3)** In what year was the Monroe Doctrine issued? *(1823)*

Ask students to look around their classroom and list some of the ways in which computers affect how they spend their class time. Discuss how the widespread use of computers has changed the way people play and the way they work. Tell students that, similarly, in the early 1800s, new inventions changed American life in many ways.

For additional *Why Study History?* support, see p. 298.

Chapter 11

Industry and Growth

1790–1825

What's Ahead

In the early 1800s, the United States changed rapidly. New technology caused a growth in industry. New factories sprang up along the nation's waterways, and with them new towns and cities. The nation increased in size, too, as settlers swarmed west along roads and rivers.

Change led to increased differences. Economic differences grew between the traditional farming society and the newer industrial society. Regional differences also grew between the North, South, and West. The nation's leaders struggled to strengthen and unify a rapidly expanding nation. They also faced the challenge of creating a bold new foreign policy, as neighboring nations in Latin America won independence.

Why Study *History?* Today, we live in an era of rapid technological change. Our age is not the first time Americans have faced a revolution in technology. In the early 1800s, as today, new inventions changed forever the way people lived. To focus on this connection, see the *Why Study History?* feature, "Technology Continues to Change Our Lives," in this chapter.

American Events

1790 First American spinning mill opens

1793 Eli Whitney's cotton gin boosts textile industry

1806 Congress approves building the National Road

1785 | 1790 | 1795 | 1800 | 1805

World Events

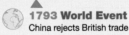

1793 World Event China rejects British trade

1802 World Event Child labor law enacted in Britain

Viewing HISTORY **A New Age of Steamboats**

Steam Ferry, St. Louis by French artist Leon Pomarede is one of the earliest paintings of St. Louis, Missouri. It shows steam-powered ships puffing down the Mississippi toward the city. In the early 1800s, steamboats and other new means of transportation made it easier for settlers to travel to the West. At the same time, new technology changed how goods were produced and how people worked.
★ **What advantages do you think steamboats might have had over earlier forms of travel?**

1807 Fulton's steamship makes record-breaking trip

1816 New tariff sparks sectional dispute

1823 Monroe Doctrine warns Europe not to recolonize the Americas

1805 | 1810 | 1815 | 1820 | 1825

1807 World Event Gas street lighting demonstrated in London

1815 World Event Napoleon defeated at Waterloo

★ Background ★
Art Note

A New Age of Steamboats French artist Leon Pomarede painted this view of St. Louis in 1832. The painting shows a steam ferry heading toward the city from the opposite bank, in Illinois. City views such as this one celebrated the growth of lively cities and the development of new American industries. T

Documents and Literature

On pp. 559–562, you will find two readings to enrich this chapter:

1. Eyewitness Account "Working in the Lowell Mills," excerpt from a book by a former Lowell girl. (Use with Section 1.)

2. Historical Document "The Monroe Doctrine," excerpt from President Monroe's State of the Union message, in which he outlined the policy later known as the Monroe Doctrine. (Use with Section 4.)

Writing Actively 

Responding to Art Ask students to think of a person who might have been traveling on the steamboat in this picture. Ask them to write a short description of that person and an explanation for his or her trip to St. Louis. Tell students to be as specific as possible.

Viewing HISTORY ANSWER

Students might predict that steamboats would be faster and could carry more goods than earlier forms of transportation. They might know that steam made it possible for boats to travel upstream, against the current.

Technology

Videodiscs/Videotapes
Show the *Prentice Hall United States History Video Collection*™ segments for this chapter. The videodisc version has a Spanish track. Press audio until you get the left channel for English or the right channel for Spanish, or use the bar codes in the Guidebook.

AmericanHeritage® History of the United States CD-ROM
- Time Tour: Years of Growth and Expansion in the New Republic (*average*)

Section 1

The Industrial Revolution

★ ★ ★ ★ ★ ★ ★ ★ ★ ★ ★ ★ ★ ★ ★ ★ ★

LESSON PLAN

Objectives

★ List the major effects of the Industrial Revolution.

★ Explain how the Industrial Revolution began in the United States.

★ Describe life in the early factories of the United States.

1 Engage

Warm Up Ask students to find an object in the classroom made entirely by hand or describe an object in their homes that is entirely handmade. Ask: What is our attitude toward handmade goods today? *(old-fashioned, unique, high quality)*

Activating Prior Knowledge Write the word *technology* on the chalkboard and ask students to discuss how new technology might have affected the lives of early Americans.

Reading Actively

Before Reading As students read the section, direct them to be alert for a cause-and-effect flow in events beginning when Samuel Slater came to the United States and ending with the growth of U.S. cities. Students should note the building of factories, the recruitment of workers for factories, and the growth of cities around mills.

RESOURCE DIRECTORY

Teaching Resources
Lesson Planner, p. 45

Transparencies
Exploring Technology
• Spinning Mill, p. H-31

The Industrial Revolution

As You Read

Explore These Questions

- What were the effects of the Industrial Revolution?
- How did the Industrial Revolution come to the United States?
- What was life like in early factories?

Define

- spinning jenny
- capitalist
- factory system
- interchangeable parts
- urbanization

Identify

- Industrial Revolution
- Samuel Slater
- Moses Brown
- Francis Cabot Lowell
- Boston Associates
- "Lowell girls"
- Eli Whitney

SETTING the Scene At dawn, the factory bell woke 11-year-old Lucy Larcom. Rising quickly, she ate her breakfast, and hurried to her job at a spinning mill in Lowell, Massachusetts. Years later, Larcom described her workplace:

> "I never cared much for machinery. The buzzing and hissing and whizzing of pulleys and rollers and spindles and flyers around me often grew tiresome.... I could look across the room and see girls moving backward and forward among the spinning frames, sometimes stooping, sometimes reaching up their arms, as their work required."

Factories and machinery were part of a revolution that reached the United States in the early 1800s. Unlike the American Revolution, this one had no battles or fixed dates. The new **Industrial Revolution** was a long, slow process which completely changed the way goods were produced.

The Industrial Revolution Begins

Before the 1800s, most people were farmers and most goods were produced by hand. As a result of the Industrial Revolution, this situation gradually began to change. Machines replaced hand tools. New sources of power, such as steam, replaced human and animal power. While most Americans continued to farm for a living, the economy began a gradual shift toward manufacturing.

New technology

The Industrial Revolution started in Britain in the mid-1700s. British inventors developed new technologies that transformed the textile industry.

Since early times, workers used spinning wheels to make thread. A spinning wheel, however, could spin only one thread at a time. In 1764, James Hargreaves developed the **spinning jenny,** a machine that could spin several threads at once. Later, Richard Arkwright invented a machine that could hold 100 spindles of thread. It was called the water frame because it required water power to turn its wheels.

Other inventions speeded up the process of weaving thread into cloth. In the 1780s, Edmund Cartwright built a loom powered by water. It allowed a worker to produce 200 times more cloth in a day than was possible before.

The factory system

New inventions led to a new method of production. Before the Industrial Revolution, most spinning and weaving took place in the home. Machines like the water frame, however, had to be housed in large mills near rivers. Water flowing downstream or over a waterfall turned a wheel that produced the power to run the machines.

To set up and operate a spinning mill required large amounts of capital, or money.

★ *Background* ★

Did You Know?

Lucy Larcom goes west Lucy Larcom, the famous mill girl, left the machinery far behind. In 1846, she moved from Lowell to Illinois, where she taught school and then attended college. She joined the faculty of Wheaton College in Norton, Massachusetts, in 1854, teaching English literature and rhetoric.

★ *Background* ★

Turning Points

Jenny does work of eight Inventor James Hargreaves could not read or write, but his invention of the spinning jenny made it possible for one worker to spin eight reels of thread at one time. Inventor Samuel Crompton used aspects of both Hargreave's spinning jenny and Arkwright's water frame to develop the spinning mule in 1779.

Linking History and Technology

❶ Wagons bring raw cotton to the mill to be spun into thread.

❷ Fast-moving water causes the water wheel to turn.

❸ The turning water wheel powers the mill's main shaft.

❹ The main shaft drives pulleys, which turn belts that drive the mill machinery.

❺ Carding machines comb the raw cotton fiber.

❻ Drawing machines pull the combed cotton fibers into ropelike strands.

❼ Spinning frames twist combed and drawn cotton strands into thread and wind them onto a bobbin.

❽ Wagons carry spun thread to weavers who use it to make cloth.

Spinning Mill

New technology in the textile industry sparked the Industrial Revolution. As shown here, rapidly moving water turned a water wheel, like the one above. The wheel produced the power to run the machines. ★ **Would your town or community have been a suitable place for a spinning mill like this one? Why or why not?**

Main shaft of a spinning mill

★ Activity ★

Cooperative Learning

Explaining the spinning mill Have students work in small groups to create a presentation that explains to a group of fifth graders how the spinning mill works. Students may use actions, gestures, jingles, or props to illustrate each of the steps in spinning thread. (*average*)

2 Explore

Ask students to read the section. For a homework assignment, ask students to check newspapers and magazines or Internet sources for descriptions of factory work today.

3 Teach

Ask students to suppose that they live in a rural area in 1820. A factory for spinning thread and weaving cloth has just been built in a nearby town. Divide the class into six groups: sheep raisers, spinners of thread, people without jobs, landowners, merchants, and town officials. Have each group discuss how the factory will change its members' lives. Have a volunteer from each group present the group's view to the class.

4 Assess

To close the lesson, have students complete the section review. As an alternative, ask students to write three questions about the material covered in the section and then exchange questions with another student. Tell students to answer their partners' questions, then to work together to review the answers.

★ ★ ★ ★ ★ ★ ★ ★ ★ ★ ★ ★ ★ ★ ★ ★ ★

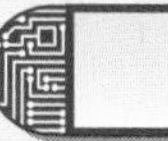

Linking History and Technology

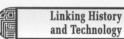

ANSWER

Answers should reflect students' knowledge of whether there are running streams or rivers near their community.

Reading Actively

During Reading Direct students' attention to the exchange of letters between Samuel Slater and Moses Brown. Ask students what they think Slater will write in his reply to Brown's invitation to come to Rhode Island.

RESOURCE DIRECTORY

Transparencies
Cause and Effect
- The Industrial Revolution in the United States, p. F-17

Capitalists supplied this money. A **capitalist** is a person who invests in a business in order to make a profit. Capitalists built factories and hired workers to run the machines.

The new **factory system** brought workers and machinery together in one place to produce goods. Factory workers earned daily or weekly wages. They had to work a set number of hours each day.

A Revolution Crosses the Atlantic

Britain wanted to keep its new technology secret. It did not want rival nations to copy the new machines. The British Parliament passed a law forbidding anyone to take plans of Arkright's water frame out of the country. It also tried to prevent factory workers from leaving Britain.

Slater breaks the law

Samuel Slater soon showed that the law could not be enforced. Slater was a skilled mechanic in one of Arkwright's mills. When he heard that Americans were offering large rewards for plans of British factories, he decided to leave England.

In 1789, Slater boarded a ship bound for New York City. He knew that British officials searched the baggage of passengers sailing to the United States. To avoid getting caught, he memorized the design of the machines in Arkright's mill. He even used a false name when he traveled.

In New York, Slater learned that **Moses Brown**, a Quaker merchant, wanted to build a spinning mill in Rhode Island. Slater wrote confidently to Brown:

> "If I do not make as good yarn as they do in England, I will have nothing for my services, but will throw the whole of what I have attempted over the bridge."

Brown replied at once: "If thou canst do what thou sayest, I invite thee to come to Rhode Island."

The first American mill

In 1790, Slater and Brown opened their first mill in Pawtucket, Rhode Island. In the following years, Slater continued to work on improvements. His wife, Hannah Slater, also contributed to the success of the mill. She discovered how to make thread stronger so that it would not snap on the spindles.

The first American factory was a huge success. Before long, other American manufacturers began to build mills using Slater's ideas.

Lowell, Massachusetts: A Model Factory Town

The War of 1812 provided a boost to American industries. The British blockade cut Americans off from their supply of foreign goods. As a result, they had to produce more goods themselves.

Francis Cabot Lowell

During the war, **Francis Cabot Lowell,** a Boston merchant, found a way to improve on British textile mills. In Britain, one factory spun thread while a second factory wove it into cloth. Why not, Lowell wondered, combine spinning and weaving under one roof?

To finance his project, Lowell joined with several partners in 1813 to form the **Boston Associates.** They built a textile factory in Waltham, Massachusetts. The new mill had all the machines needed to turn raw cotton into finished cloth.

After Lowell's death, the Boston Associates took on a more ambitious project. They built an entire factory town and named it after him. In 1821, Lowell, Massachusetts, was a village of five farm families. By 1836, it boasted more than 10,000 people. Visitors to Lowell described it as a model community made up of "small wooden houses, painted white, with green blinds, very neat, very snug, very nicely carpeted."

"Lowell girls"

To work in their new mills, the Boston Associates hired young women from nearby farms. The **"Lowell girls,"** as they came to be called, usually worked for a few years in the mills before returning home to marry. Most sent their wages home to their families. Some saved part of their wages to help set up their own homes.

★ Background ★ Turning Points

Colleges offer applied sciences With the boom in new technologies, Americans became interested in studying applied sciences like engineering. Mechanics institutes sprang up in many cities. Even colleges, such as Harvard and Yale, added applied sciences to their course offerings.

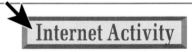

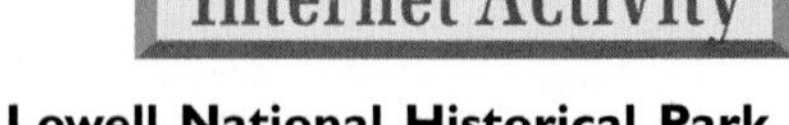

Lowell National Historical Park
Direct students to the Web site of the Lowell National Historical Park at www.nps.gov./lowe/. Ask students to browse through the site and list three exhibits or events they would like to visit, stating what they might learn from each. Given the changing nature of the Internet, you may wish to preview this site.

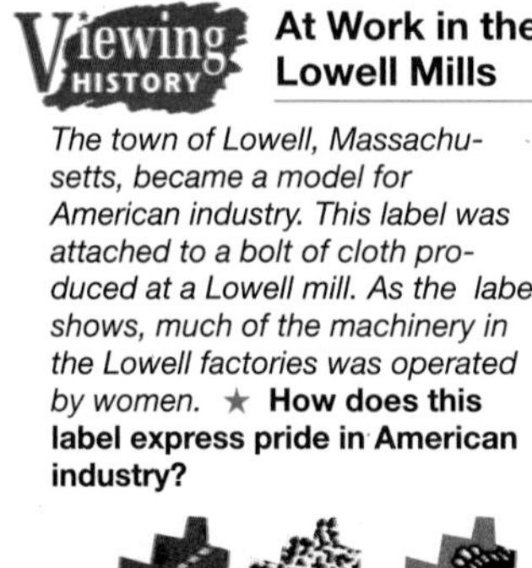

Viewing History: At Work in the Lowell Mills

The town of Lowell, Massachusetts, became a model for American industry. This label was attached to a bolt of cloth produced at a Lowell mill. As the label shows, much of the machinery in the Lowell factories was operated by women. ★ **How does this label express pride in American industry?**

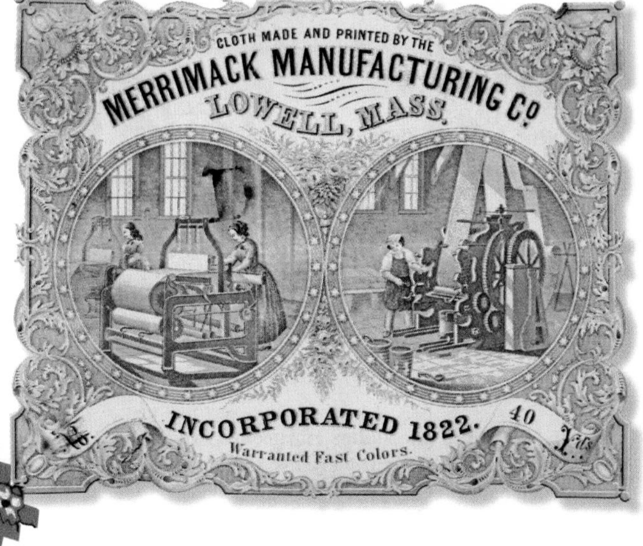

Cloth from a Lowell factory

At first, parents hesitated to let their daughters work in the mills. To reassure parents, the Boston Associates built boarding houses for their workers. The company also built a church and made rules to protect the young women.

Factory work was often tedious and hard. However, many women valued the economic freedom they got from working in the mills. The *Lowell Offering*, a magazine by and for workers in the Lowell mills, printed a song that began:

> "Despite of toil we all agree
> Out of the mills, or in,
> Dependent on others we ne'er will be
> So long as we're able to spin."

Impact on Daily Life

In Lowell and elsewhere, mill owners mostly hired women and children. They did this because they could pay women and children half of what they would have had to pay men.

Child labor

Boys and girls as young as seven years of age worked in factories. Small children were especially useful in textile mills because they could squeeze around the large machines to change spindles. "I can see myself now," recalled a woman who had worked in a mill as a child, "carrying in front of me a [spindle] bigger than I was."

Today, most Americans look upon child labor as cruel. Yet in the 1800s, farm children also worked hard from an early age. Most people did not see much difference between children working in a factory or on a farm. Often, a child's wages were needed to help support the family.

Long hours

Working hours in the mills were long—12 hours a day, 6 days a week. True, farmers also put in long hours. However, farmers worked shorter hours in winter. Mill workers, by contrast, worked nearly the same hours all year round.

In the early 1800s, conditions in American mills were generally much better than in most factories in Europe. As industries grew, however, competition increased and employers took less interest in the welfare of their workers. In later chapters, you will read how working conditions grew worse.

Viewing History ANSWER

The label prominently names the company that manufactured the goods; it shows a clean and productive factory setting.

★ Background ★ Historiography

Digging up history Stephen Mrozowski, et al., show how historians use archaeology to bring history to light in *Living on the Boott: Historical Archaeology at the Boott Boardinghouses, Lowell, Massachusetts.* Artifacts reveal rich details about the lives of Lowell workers.

From the Archives of American Heritage®

Hand sewing only An invention that would have been helpful to the textile industry was the sewing machine, but none was available. Efficient sewing machines had been invented but not come into use because of the opposition of hand sewers. Finally, in 1846, Elias Howe received a patent for his "Improvement in Sewing Machines."

Source: Frederic D. Schwarz, "The Time Machine," *American Heritage* magazine, September 1996.

ANSWERS

1. (a) Possible answer: More people worked in factories. **(b)** Possible answers: We can instantly communicate with people around the world; records are kept more quickly and easily. **2.** Possible answers: There will be more contact since we can quickly communicate with people, even in distant places; people will spend more time alone with their computers.

★Activity

Guided Instruction

Have students brainstorm for all the places that use computers, such as schools, doctors' offices, and stores. The webs should tell specific things computers do, such as "prints out report cards" and "prepares daily newspapers." Select a few computer tasks from the webs and have students debate whether computers have a positive or negative effect.

ASSESSMENT See the rubrics in the Alternative Assessment booklet in the Teaching Resources.

CAPTION ANSWER

that vast changes have taken place since the previous generation in the types of things people need to learn

Why Study History?

Because Technology Continues to Change Our Lives

Historical Background

Inventors like James Hargreaves and Richard Arkwright were not trying to change the world. They just wanted a better way to spin thread. (See page 294.) In the end, though, the Industrial Revolution changed forever how people worked, where they lived, and even how they spent their leisure time. Later inventions, such as the telephone and the automobile, have also transformed the world we live in.

Connections to Today

Not long before you were born, another revolution in technology began: the computer revolution. The earliest computers were not the kind you could have in your bedroom. One early model weighed 30 tons and filled an entire room!

Slowly, computers got smaller and spread out—to schools, businesses, hospitals, arcades, homes. Computers can help keep records, diagnose illnesses, or take people into outer space.

Connections to You

You already know some of the advantages of computers. You can research a report online and revise it on screen. You can enjoy a video game or create your own greeting cards. You can chat with people living in Sweden or Korea or Egypt.

Not every change is positive, though. Sitting at a computer screen for hours may cause severe headaches or hand injuries.

Some critics even fear that computers may lead to isolation. People can work, shop, and even make friends without leaving their homes. You may spend more time chatting with someone halfway around the world than going bowling with friends in your own neighborhood.

1. **Comprehension** **(a)** Name one result of the Industrial Revolution. **(b)** Name two results of the computer revolution.
2. **Critical Thinking** Do you think computers will lead to greater or less contact between people? Explain.

Making a Concept Web Make a concept web to show some of the ways that computers affect you. Then, review your web and decide whether each effect is positive, negative, or both.

What point is this cartoon making about the impact of computers?

Fast Facts

★ Humans used bone needles to sew animal skins with strips of sinew or leather by about 20,000 B.C.

★ An Englishman, William Lee, invented a knitting machine in 1589, but hand-knitters protested and prevented its use.

★ The recent presidential task force on "Connecting K–12 Schools to the Information Superhighway" estimates that 60 percent of the nation's jobs will require computer skills in the year 2000.

Bibliography

To read more about this topic:

1. *The Industrial Revolution,* Andrew Langley (Viking, 1994). Well-illustrated details of the English beginnings.

2. *Smithsonian Visual Timeline of Inventions,* Richard Platt (DK Publishing, 1994). Features more than 400 inventions.

3. Internet. Web site—US Patent and Trademark Office, including the PTO museum. (www.uspto.gov)

RESOURCE DIRECTORY

Teaching Resources
Why Study History?
• Technology Continues to Change Our Lives, pp. 43–46

Changes in home life

The Industrial Revolution had a great impact on home life. On farms or in home workshops, families worked together as a unit. As the factory system spread, more family members left the home to earn a living.

These changes affected ideas about the role of women. In poorer families, women often had to go out to work. In wealthier families, husbands supported the family while women stayed at home. For many husbands, having a wife who stayed at home became a sign of a success.

Interchangeable Parts

Manufacturers benefited from the pioneering work of American inventor **Eli Whitney**. Earlier, skilled workers made goods by hand. For example, a gunsmith spent days making the barrel, stock, and trigger for a single musket. Because the parts were handmade, each musket differed a bit from the next. If a part broke, a gunsmith had to fashion a new part to fit that gun.

Whitney wanted to speed up gunmaking by having machines manufacture each part. Machine-made parts would all be alike—for example, one trigger would be identical to another. **Interchangeable parts** would save time and money.

Because the government bought many guns, Whitney went to Washington, D.C., to demonstrate his method. At first, officials laughed at his plan. Whitney paid them no attention. Carefully, he sorted parts for 10 muskets into separate piles. He then asked an official to choose one part from each pile. In minutes, the first musket was assembled. Whitney repeated the process until 10 muskets were complete.

The idea of interchangeable parts spread rapidly. Inventors designed machines to produce interchangeable parts for clocks, locks, and many other goods. With such machines, small workshops grew into factories.

Growing Cities

Since colonial times, cities played an important role in American life. The vast majority of people lived in rural areas. However, farmers often sent crops to cities for sale or shipment. Cities were also centers of finance and manufacturing.

During the Industrial Revolution, many people left farms to work in factories. Older

Cause and Effect

Causes

- British ideas of a spinning mill and powerloom reach the United States
- War of 1812 prompts Americans to make their own goods
- Eli Whitney introduces the idea of interchangeable parts

The Industrial Revolution in the United States

Effects

- Factory system spreads
- Young women and children from nearby farms work in mills
- Growing cities face problems of fire, sewage, garbage, and disease

Effects Today

- United States becomes leader in industrialized world
- Oil is a highly valued natural resource

Graphic Organizer Skills

The Industrial Revolution brought with it many immediate and long-term changes.

1. **Comprehension** What inventions and ideas contributed to the spread of the Industrial Revolution?
2. **Critical Thinking** Do you think the impact of the Industrial Revolution was positive or negative? Give reasons.

Economics $

★ Customized Instruction ★
Kinesthetic Learners

Making models two ways Ask kinesthetic learners to make a paper teaching-clock—a cardboard circle with two moveable hands. Provide them with poster board, construction paper, markers, compasses, scissors, and string. Ask them to time how long they spend on the task. Then give them "interchangeable parts"—paper plates with the hours marked, brads, and pre-cut hands. Ask them to assemble as many clocks as they can in the time it took them to make their original clock. Have students discuss how they felt about making the clocks both ways and ask the class to draw some conclusions about productivity and job satisfaction. ELL

Reading Actively 

During Reading Ask students to consider why the concept of interchangeable parts made huge factories possible.

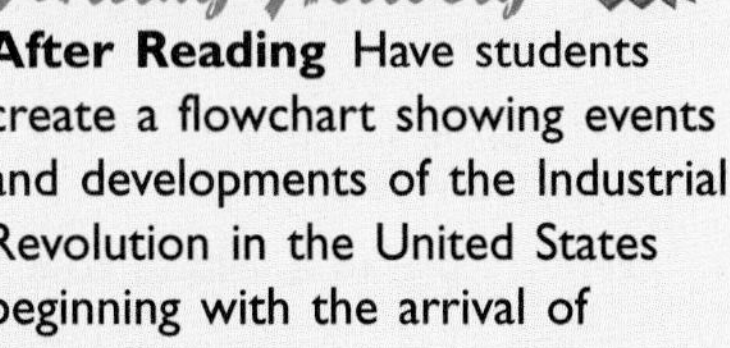

ANSWERS **1.** List will include the spinning mill, the powerloom, and interchangeable parts. **2.** Students should support their opinions with examples from the chart.

Writing Actively

After Reading Have students create a flowchart showing events and developments of the Industrial Revolution in the United States beginning with the arrival of Samuel Slater and ending with the growth of cities.

★ Section 1 Review ★

ANSWERS

1. **(a)** p. 294, **(b)** p. 296, **(c)** p. 296, **(d)** p. 296, **(e)** p. 296, **(f)** p. 296, **(g)** p. 299

2. **(a)** p. 294, **(b)** p. 296, **(c)** p. 296, **(d)** p. 299, **(e)** p. 300

3. Possible answers: The economy shifted from farming to manufacturing; much manufacturing shifted from homes to factories; cities grew.

4. Samuel Slater memorized the design for British machines and started a mill in Rhode Island with Moses Brown.

5. Working hours were 12 hours a day, 6 days a week.

6. Inventors played a critical role by creating new machines. Capitalists were necessary to provide the funds.

7. People moved from farms to work in factories. New cities grew up around some factories, while older cities grew in population.

Activity

Guided Instruction
Working with the class, list features of Lowell factory life on the chalkboard. Have students use the list as an outline to write their letters. They should contrast life at the mills with life on the farm.

ASSESSMENT See the rubrics in the Alternative Assessment booklet in the Teaching Resources.

RESOURCE DIRECTORY

Teaching Resources
Lesson Planner, p. 46
Unit 3/Chapter 11
- Biography Flashcard: P. T. Barnum, p. 28
- Section 1 Quiz, p. 29

cities expanded rapidly, while new cities sprang up around factories. This movement of the population from farms to cities is called **urbanization**.

Urbanization was a steady but gradual process. In 1800, only 6 percent of the nation's population lived in urban areas. By 1850, the number had risen to 15 percent. Not until 1920 did more Americans live in cities than on farms.

By today's standards, these early cities were small. A person could walk from one end of any American city to the other in 30 minutes. Buildings were only a few stories tall. As the factory system spread, the nation's cities grew.

Hazards

Growing cities had many problems. Dirt and gravel streets turned into mudholes when it rained. Cities had no sewers, and people threw garbage into the streets. A visitor to New York reported:

> "The streets are filthy, and the stranger is not a little surprised to meet the hogs walking about in them, for the purpose of devouring the vegetables and trash thrown into the gutter."

In these dirty, crowded conditions, disease spread easily. Epidemics of yellow fever or cholera (KAHL er uh) raged through cities, killing hundreds.

Fire posed another threat to safety. If a sooty chimney caught fire, the flames quickly spread from one wooden house to the next. Rival volunteer companies often competed to get to a blaze first. Sometimes, they fought each other instead of the fire!

Attractions

Cities had attractions, too. Theaters, museums, and circuses created an air of excitement. In New York City, P. T. Barnum exhibited rare animals at his American Museum.

In rural areas, people depended on door-to-door peddlers for ready-made goods. In cities, people could shop in fine stores that sold the latest fashions from Europe. Some offered modern "ready-to-wear" clothing. One store in New York City advertised that "gentlemen can rely upon being as well fitted from the shelves as if their measures were taken."

Most women continued to sew their own clothes. However, they enjoyed visiting hat shops, china shops, shoe stores, and "fancy-goods" stores.

★ Section 1 Review ★

Recall

1. **Identify** **(a)** Industrial Revolution, **(b)** Samuel Slater, **(c)** Moses Brown, **(d)** Francis Cabot Lowell, **(e)** Boston Associates, **(f)** "Lowell girls," **(g)** Eli Whitney.
2. **Define** **(a)** spinning jenny, **(b)** capitalist, **(c)** factory system, **(d)** interchangeable parts, **(e)** urbanization.

Comprehension

3. Describe three ways the Industrial Revolution changed life.
4. How did industry move from Britain to the United States?
5. What were conditions like in the Lowell mills?

Critical Thinking and Writing

6. **Drawing Conclusions** Why were both inventors and capitalists needed to bring about the Industrial Revolution?
7. **Understanding Causes and Effects** How did the building of factories encourage the growth of cities?

Activity **Writing a Letter** The time is 160 years ago. You are the same age you are now, but instead of being in school, you are working in the Lowell mills. Write a letter home describing how you feel about working in a factory to help support your family.

Moving Westward

As You Read

Explore These Questions
- How did settlers travel westward in the early 1800s?
- What steps did Americans take to improve roads?
- How did steamboats and canals affect transportation?

Define
- turnpike
- corduroy road
- canal

Identify
- Lancaster Turnpike
- National Road
- John Fitch
- Robert Fulton
- *Clermont*
- Henry Shreve
- Erie Canal
- DeWitt Clinton

An Irish visitor to the United States described a stagecoach trip through Maryland:

> "The driver frequently had to call to the passengers in the stage, to lean out of the carriage first at one side, then at the other, to prevent it from oversetting in the deep ruts with which the road abounds: 'Now gentlemen, to the right,' . . . 'Now gentlemen, to the left,' and so on."

In the 1790s, travel was as difficult as it had been in colonial times. Most roads were mud tracks. River travel could be difficult, too, when boats had to push their way upstream against the current. As the young nation grew westward, Americans saw the need to improve transportation.

To the Mississippi

Settlers had been moving steadily westward since the 1600s. By the early 1800s, "the West" referred to the land between the Appalachians and the Mississippi.

In the early 1800s, the stream of pioneers turned into a flood. By 1820, so many people had moved west that the population in some of the original 13 states had actually declined!

Western routes

Settlers took a number of routes west. One well-traveled path was the Great Wagon Road across Pennsylvania. It dated back to colonial days. Some settlers continued south and west along the trail opened by Daniel Boone before the Revolution. Known as the Wilderness Road, it led through the Cumberland Gap into Kentucky. (See the map on page 303.)

Other settlers pushed west to Pittsburgh. There, they loaded their animals and wagons onto flatboats and journeyed down the Ohio River into Indiana, Kentucky, and Illinois. Flatboats were well suited to the shallow waters of the Ohio. Even when carrying heavy cargoes, these raftlike barges rode high in the water.

Pioneers from Georgia and South Carolina followed other trails west to Alabama and Mississippi. Enslaved African Americans

Many settlers headed west in covered wagons, such as this Conestoga wagon.

Section 2
Moving Westward

LESSON PLAN

Objectives

★ Describe how settlers traveled westward in the early 1800s.
★ List the steps taken by Americans to improve roads.
★ Explain how steamboats and canals affected transportation.

1 Engage

Warm Up Ask students to list as many methods of transportation as they can in one minute. Then ask how many of these methods students have actually used. Explain that they will be reading about the origins of some of these types of transportation.

Activating Prior Knowledge Ask students to think about why factory owners and workers would support a strong transportation system for the United States. *(to help get goods to market)*

Reading Actively

Before Reading As they read, ask students to turn each of the subheads in the section into a question and then to look for the answer. For example, students might make the subhead "Better Roads" into the questions "How did Americans make better roads?" or "Why did Americans need better roads?"

Technology

Videodiscs/Videotapes
Prentice Hall United States History Video Collection™, Vol. 6, Ch. 22, "The Move West," 4 mins *(average)* ELL

Chapter 22

AmericanHeritage® History of the United States CD-ROM
- History Makers: Daniel Boone *(average)*

★ *Background* ★

Turning Points

New pathways for prosperity In the early 1800s, the South seemed to be the economic center of the country. The Ohio and Mississippi rivers carried goods from the West to New Orleans. From there, goods were shipped to Europe. By the 1820s, new east-west roads had shifted both the transport pattern and economic center to the north and east.

2 Explore

Ask students to read the section. When they have finished, ask them to summarize the main points about roads, steamboats, and canals. Then ask them why they think transportation became such an important issue for the United States.

3 Teach

Have students work in three groups—one group representing a steamboat company, one representing a canal company, and a third representing a road-building company. Have each group prepare a presentation for the governor of an eastern state in 1820, in which it asks for funds for its transportation project. Presentations should explain why the projects will make it easier for people of the state to ship goods. Students might include maps and other visuals with their presentations.

4 Assess

To close the lesson, have students complete the section review. As an alternative, have students create a graphic organizer that shows how new inventions and major engineering projects changed the pattern of transportation in the United States by the 1820s.

★ ★ ★ ★ ★ ★ ★ ★ ★ ★ ★ ★ ★ ★ ★ ★ ★

ANSWER

The road is steep and rough; one man was being jostled so much, he dropped his hat out the window.

RESOURCE DIRECTORY

Teaching Resources
Unit 3/Chapter 11
- Practice Your Skills: Analyzing a Primary Source, p. 24
- Map Mystery: The National Road, p. 26

Transparencies
Fine Art
- Fur Traders Descending the Missouri, p. D-35

A Need for Better Roads

This painting, by a visitor from Russia, shows a stagecoach on its run between Philadelphia, Pennsylvania, and Trenton, New Jersey. Passengers traveling on rocky, muddy, unpaved roads could expect to be "crushed, shaken, thrown about... and bumped." ★ **What details in this painting suggest that these passengers were having a rough ride?**

helped to carve plantations in the rich, fertile soil of these territories.

People from New England, New York, and Pennsylvania pushed into the Northwest Territory. Some settlers traveled west from Albany, New York, along the Mohawk River and across the Appalachians. Some settlers then followed Indian trails around Lake Erie. Others sailed across the lake into Ohio.

New states

Before long, some western territories had populations large enough to apply for statehood. Between 1792 and 1819, eight states joined the Union: Kentucky (1792), Tennessee (1796), Ohio (1803), Louisiana (1812), Indiana (1816), Mississippi (1817), Illinois (1818), and Alabama (1819).

Better Roads

Settlers faced a difficult journey. Many roads were narrow trails, barely wide enough for a single wagon. One pioneer wrote of "rotten banks down which horses plunged" and streams that "almost drowned them." Tree stumps stuck up through the road and often broke the axles on the wagons of careless travelers. The nation badly needed better roads.

Turnpikes and bridges

In the United States, as in Europe, private companies built gravel and stone roads. To pay for these roads, the companies collected tolls from travelers. At various points along the road, a pike, or pole, blocked the road. After a wagon driver paid a toll, the pike keeper turned the pole aside to let the wagon pass. As a result, these toll roads were called **turnpikes.**

Probably the best road in the United States was the **Lancaster Turnpike**. Built in the 1790s by a private company, the road linked Philadelphia and Lancaster, Pennsylvania. Because the road was set on a bed of gravel, water drained off quickly. It was topped with smooth, flat stones.

In swampy areas, roads were made of logs. These roads were known as **corduroy roads** because the lines of logs looked like corduroy cloth. Corduroy roads kept wagons from sinking into the mud, but they made for a bumpy ride.

Bridges carried travelers across streams and rivers. Stone bridges were costly to build, but wooden ones rotted quickly. A clever Massachusetts carpenter designed a wooden bridge with a roof to protect it from the weather. Covered bridges lasted much longer than open ones.

★ Customized Instruction ★

Visual Learners

Making a map Ask a small group of visual learners to make a poster-sized map that shows some of the important developments discussed in this section. Students should begin with a map of the eastern United States from the Atlantic Ocean to the Mississippi River. Suggest they look over the text and text maps for help in finding information for their maps. Ask them to label the states that existed in 1819. Students should label the Mississippi, Ohio, Potomac, Wabash, Illinois, and Hudson rivers, and the individual Great Lakes. Then students can add transportation features, including major roads and canals. Tell students to plan their map key carefully to avoid running out of space. ELL

The National Road

Some states set aside money to build or improve roads. In 1806, for the first time, Congress approved funds for a national road-building project. The **National Road** was to run from Cumberland, Maryland, to Wheeling, in western Virginia.

Work on the National Road began in 1811 and was completed in 1818. Later, the road was extended into Illinois. As each new section of road was built, settlers eagerly used it to drive their wagons west.

Steam Transport

Whenever possible, travelers and freight haulers used river transportation. Floating downstream on a flatboat was both faster and more comfortable than bumping along rutted roads. It also cost less.

Yet, river travel had its own problems. Moving upstream was difficult. People used paddles or long poles to push boats against the current. Sometimes, they hauled boats from the shore with ropes. Both methods were slow. A boat could travel downstream from Pittsburgh to New Orleans in about six weeks. The return trip upstream took at least 17 weeks!

Fitch and Fulton

A new invention, the steam engine, improved river travel. **John Fitch** improved on steam engines that had been built in Britain.

Early Roads West

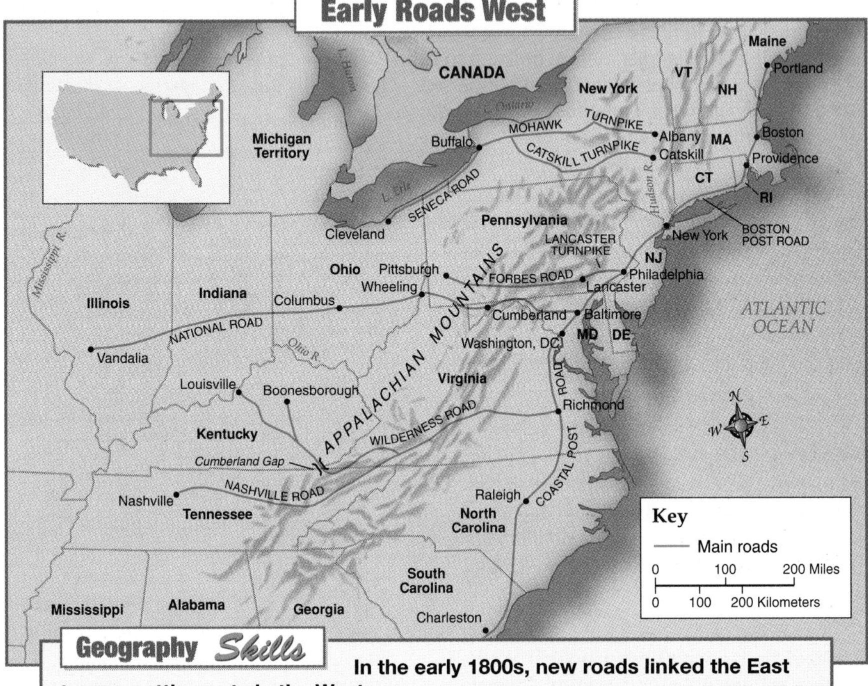

Geography *Skills* **In the early 1800s, new roads linked the East to new settlements in the West.**

1. **Location** On the map, locate: **(a)** Appalachian Mountains, **(b)** Cumberland Gap, **(c)** Wilderness Road, **(d)** Lancaster Turnpike, **(e)** National Road.
2. **Movement** What major roads would settlers use to travel from Boston, Massachussetts, to Nashville, Tennessee?
3. **Critical Thinking** Based on this map, what effect do you think roadbuilding had on cities like Philadelphia, Baltimore, and Richmond?

Geography *Skills*

ANSWERS **1.** Review locations with students. **2.** Boston Post Road, Coastal Post Road, Wilderness Road, Nashville Road **3.** All of these cities were meeting points for several roads. Road building probably helped these cities grow, as travelers and goods passed through them on their way to and from the West.

★ *Background* ★

Did You Know?

Drive the National Road Two highways, U.S. 40 and I-70, follow the route of the National Road from Cumberland, Maryland, to Wheeling, West Virginia, and Columbus, Ohio. The original road had a stone base and a gravel top—and stumps. In Indiana, it was legal to leave stumps as high as 15 inches above the roadbed in public roads.

From the Archives of American Heritage®

Americans invent the grand hotel In the early 1800s, travelers spent the night in inns, where they often had to share rooms with strangers. A new era for travelers began in 1829, with the opening of Tremont House in Boston, one of the first buildings ever built specifically as a hotel. It had private guest rooms with doors that locked.

Source: J. M. Fenster, "Palaces of the People," *American Heritage* magazine, Special Travel Issue, April 1994.

PRACTICE the Skill
ANSWERS

1. It is the original diary of a woman's impressions at the time.

2. (a) The ride was very bumpy; there were young ladies on the stagecoach. **(b)** They passed only a few cottages and farmhouses; some farms had broken gates.

3. Possible answers: Her discomfort and pride in her own nationality may have caused her to dislike the other passengers.

4. It is reliable in the sense that she was an eyewitness; however, she presents the information in a slanted way.

APPLY the Skill
Guided Instruction

Suggest students use a newscast or magazine article for the activity. They should note information about the person being interviewed. As they listen or read, they should jot down facts presented by the speaker. Have students work in pairs to decide whether the eyewitness is a reliable source of information.

ASSESSMENT See the rubrics in the Alternative Assessment booklet in the Teaching Resources.

RESOURCE DIRECTORY

Teaching Resources
Unit 3/Chapter 11
- Critical Thinking and Writing: Analyzing Visual Information, p. 25

Interdisciplinary Connections
- Main Idea: The Erie Canal, p. 66

Critical Thinking | Managing Information | Communication | Maps, Charts, and Graphs

Analyzing a Primary Source

How Will I Use This Skill ?

A **primary source** is firsthand information about people and events. Historians use primary sources to learn about the past. You, too, use primary sources—when you watch an interview on television, or listen to two friends tell their sides of something that happened. Learning to analyze primary sources helps you determine the reliability of the information that you get.

LEARN the Skill

1. Identify the source of the account. Decide if he or she has firsthand knowledge of the event.
2. Determine which words indicate facts. Are there enough facts to make the speaker reliable?
3. Recognize how emotions, points of view, and opinions affect the telling of the story.
4. Judge how reliable the source is.

PRACTICE the Skill

Fanny Kemble, an English actress, visited the United States in the early 1800s. In her journal, she described a stagecoach ride with her father and some Americans. Read the excerpt, then answer the following questions:

1. Explain why this journal is a primary source.
2. (a) What facts does Kemble include about stagecoach travel? (b) What facts does she include about American rural life?
3. What effect do you think Kemble's nationality and her discomfort may have had on her account?
4. Would you consider this journal a reliable source of information? Explain.

"Bones of me! what a road! Even my father's solid proportions…were jerked up to the roof and down again every three minutes. Our companions…laughed and talked [constantly], the young ladies, at the very top of their voices, and with the national nasal twang….The few cottages and farm-houses which we passed reminded me of similar dwellings in France and Ireland; yet the peasantry here have not the same excuse for disorder and [ruin] as either the Irish or French….The farms had the same desolate, untidy, untended look; the gates broken, the fences carelessly put up."

Excerpt from Journal by Frances Anne Kemble Butler

APPLY the Skill

Watch or read an interview given by an eyewitness to an event. Using the steps above, decide whether you think the interview is a reliable source of information.

★ *Background* ★

Viewpoints

Tocqueville weighs in Fanny Kemble was not the only European who made unflattering observations about country life in the United States. The French traveler Alexis de Tocqueville said, "The country-dwelling Americans spend half their lives cutting trees, and their children learn already at an early age to use the axe against the trees, their enemies."

American Heritage MAGAZINE

HISTORY HAPPENED HERE

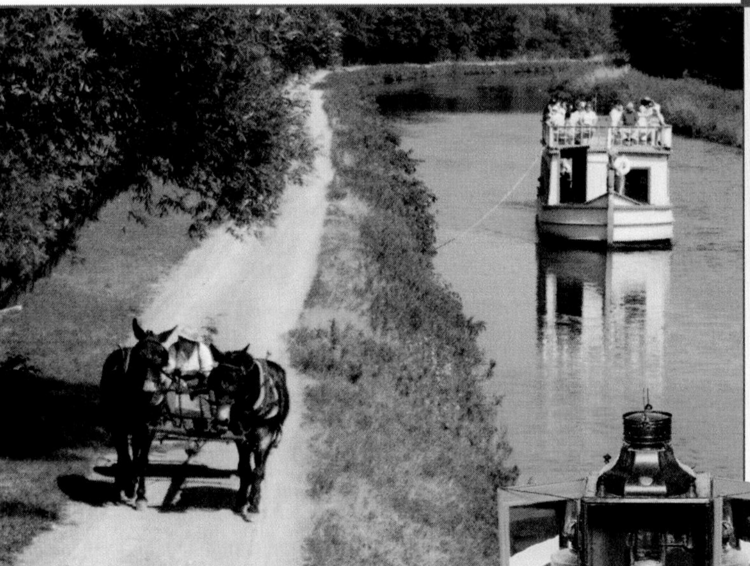

The Erie Canal

The opening of the Erie Canal in 1825 launched an age of canal building. Today, at the Erie Canal Village in Rome, New York, you can relive life along the old Erie Canal. Here, passengers ride atop a canal boat, pulled along by a team of mules, just as they did 150 years ago. Riding up top could be risky, though. When the boatmen yelled "Low bridge!" passengers who did not duck could bump their heads.

★ ***To learn more about this historic site, write:*** *Erie Canal Village, 5789 New London Road, Rome, NY 13440.*

Canal boat lantern

In 1787, he showed members of the Constitutional Convention how a steam engine could power a boat. He then opened a ferry service on the Delaware River. However, few people used the ferry, and Fitch went out of business.

Inventor **Robert Fulton** may have seen Fitch's steamboat in Philadelphia. In 1807, Fulton launched his own steamboat, the ***Clermont,*** on the Hudson River. On its first run, the *Clermont* carried passengers from New York City to Albany and back. The 300-mile (480-km) trip took just 62 hours—a record at the time.

The age of steamboats

Fulton's success ushered in the age of steamboats. Soon, steamboats were ferrying passengers up and down the Atlantic coast. More important, they revolutionized travel in the West. Besides carrying people, steamboats on the Mississippi, Ohio, and Missouri rivers gave farmers and merchants a cheap means of moving goods.

Because western rivers were shallow, **Henry Shreve** designed a flat-bottomed steamboat. It could carry heavy loads without getting stuck on sandbars.

Still, steamboat travel could be dangerous. Sparks from smokestacks could cause fires. As steamboat captains raced each other along the river, high-pressure boilers sometimes exploded. Between 1811 and 1851, 44 steamboats collided, 166 burned, and more than 200 exploded.

The Canal Boom

Steamboats and improved roads did not help western farmers get their goods directly to markets in the East. To meet this need, Americans dug canals. A **canal** is an artificial channel filled with water that allows boats to cross a stretch of land.

American Heritage MAGAZINE

The Erie Canal To learn more about taking a trip on a mule-drawn packet boat on the Erie Canal, go to www.5a.com/applegrove/missapplegrove.html.

Reading Actively

During Reading As students read, ask them to complete a chart entitled "Improvements in Transportation." The columns should have the headings "Roads," "Steamboats," and "Canals." The rows should be labeled "Dates," "Important Places," and "Important People." Have students leave plenty of room for entries in each block.

★ *Background* ★

Linking Past and Present

Songs of travel Many of our favorite folk songs date from the early 1800s and deal with traveling, moving west, and building roads and canals. Ask students to find tapes or CDs of songs, such as "Turkey in the Straw" and "The Erie Canal," and play them for the class. Ask students if they can think of popular songs of today about traveling. T

Chapter 11 ★ 305

Writing Actively

After Reading Ask students to write a journal entry or a short story featuring a trip on the Erie Canal in the year 1830. Students might do research to find pictures of some of the towns along the canal. They could include descriptions of these towns in their writing.

Geography Skills

ANSWERS **1.** Review locations with students. **2.** Lake Michigan and the Illinois River **3.** Wabash and Erie Canal to Lake Erie; Lake Erie to Erie Canal; Erie Canal to Hudson River; Hudson River to New York City

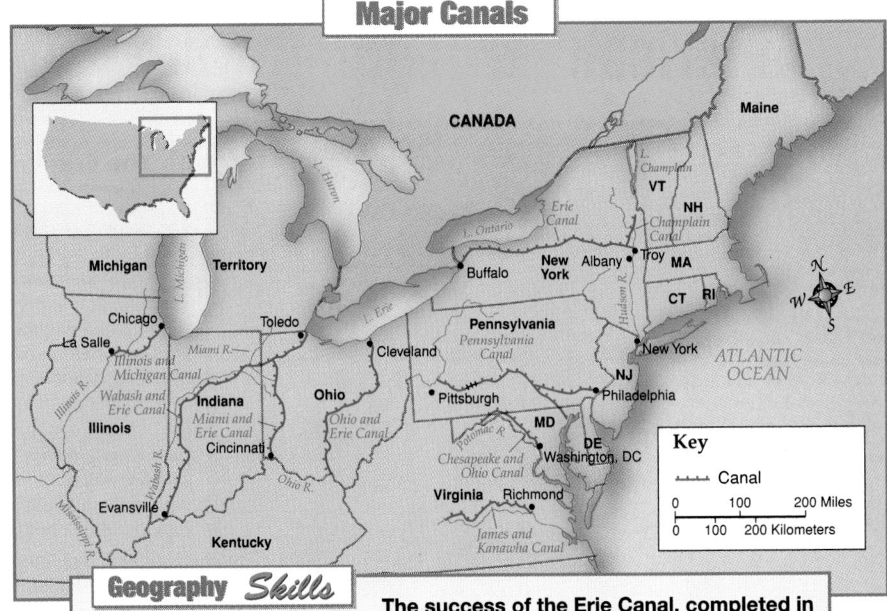

Geography Skills

The success of the Erie Canal, completed in 1825, set off an age of canal building.

1. **Location** On the map, locate: **(a)** New York City, **(b)** Troy, **(c)** Buffalo, **(d)** Lake Erie, **(e)** Erie Canal.
2. **Movement** What two bodies of water were linked by the Illinois and Michigan Canal?
3. **Critical Thinking** Use the map to describe an all-water route from Evansville, Indiana, to New York City.

The earliest American canals were no more than a few miles long. Some provided routes around waterfalls on a river. Other canals linked a river to a nearby lake. By the early 1800s, however, Americans were building longer canals.

Building the Erie Canal

Some New Yorkers had a bold idea. They wanted to build a canal linking the Great Lakes with the Mohawk and Hudson rivers. The **Erie Canal** would let western farmers ship their goods to the port of New York. It would also bring business to towns along the route.

To many people, the idea of such a canal seemed farfetched. When Thomas Jefferson heard of the plan, he exclaimed:

> "Why, sir, you talk of making a canal 350 miles through the wilderness—it is little short of madness to think of it at this day!"

New York governor **DeWitt Clinton** ignored such criticism. He persuaded state lawmakers to provide money for the Erie Canal. Scoffers referred to the project as "Clinton's Ditch."

Work on the Erie Canal began in 1817. At first, workers dug the waterway by hand. To speed up progress, inventors developed new equipment. One machine, a stump-puller, could pull out nearly 40 tree stumps a day. In two places, workers had to find ways to build stone bridges to carry the canal over other rivers along the way.

Resource Directory

Teaching Resources
Unit 3/Chapter 11
- Section 2 Quiz, p. 30

Interdisciplinary Connections
- Main Idea: The Erie Canal, pp. 61–66

Transparencies
Interdisciplinary Connections
- Erie Canal, p. B-51

★ Activity ★

Linking Past and Present

Planning a trip Ask small groups to decide how they would transport each of the following products or people from Columbus, Ohio, to New York City in 1830: cattle, fresh cabbages, hogs, lumber, grain, three children. How would they transport the same products or people today?

★ Activity ★

Connections With Economics

Exploring transportation issues Ask students to look for newspaper articles about transportation issues in their community, such as lack of parking areas or the need for an improved airport. Discuss why transportation is such an important issue to many groups of people, including workers and business people.

An instant success

By 1825, the immense job was finished. On opening day of the Erie Canal, a cannon fired a volley in Buffalo, New York. When the sound got to the next town along the route, it, too, fired a cannon. Town after town fired their cannons—all the way to New York City. The thunderous salute took 80 minutes to complete.

The Erie Canal was an instant success. It reduced travel time. The cost of shipping goods dropped to about 1/20 of what it was before the canal was built. The canal also helped to make New York City a center of commerce.

The success of the Erie Canal led other states to build canals. (See the map on the opposite page.) These canals created vital economic links between western farms and eastern cities.

Transportation Builds Prosperity

In 1831, a young Frenchman, Alexis de Tocqueville (TOHK vihl), made a nine-month tour of the United States. In his writings, Tocqueville described what he admired about the young nation. One of the things that impressed him most was the American transportation system.

"Of all the countries in the world," Tocqueville wrote, "America is that in which the spread of ideas and of human industry is most continual and most rapid." Tocqueville was amazed by "immense canals" and roads built in the middle of the wilderness. He also praised the American postal system:

> "In America one of the first things done in a new state is to make the post go there. In the forests of Michigan there is no cabin so isolated, no valley so wild but that letters and newspapers arrive at least once a week."

Tocqueville noted that Americans could easily ship goods from the western frontier to any part of the country. (By contrast, in his native France—a much smaller country—many large towns could not be reached by road at all!) Faster, easier transportation thus contributed to the growing prosperity of the United States.

★ Section 2 Review ★

Recall

1. **Locate** (a) Kentucky, (b) Tennessee, (c) Ohio, (d) Louisiana, (e) Indiana, (f) Mississippi, (g) Illinois, (h) Alabama.
2. **Identify** (a) Lancaster Turnpike, (b) National Road, (c) John Fitch, (d) Robert Fulton, (e) *Clermont,* (f) Henry Shreve, (g) Erie Canal, (h) DeWitt Clinton.
3. **Define** (a) turnpike, (b) corduroy road, (c) canal.

Comprehension

4. What means of transportation did settlers take to the West in the early 1800s?
5. (a) Why did the nation need better transportation in the early 1800s? (b) Describe two ways that travel improved.

Critical Thinking and Writing

6. **Linking Past and Present** Today, airplanes provide a faster means of travel than land transportation. Why do you think roads are still important to the nation?
7. **Identifying Alternatives** Examine the maps in this section. Then, describe two alternate ways a farmer might have shipped a cargo of grain from Cleveland, Ohio, to New York City.

Activity **Designing a Monument** You have been asked to design a monument honoring the two-hundredth anniversary of the Erie Canal. Draw a rough sketch of the monument, showing what design you would use. You may also include an inscription describing the importance of the canal.

★ Section 2 Review ★

ANSWERS

1. See maps, pp. 303, 306.
2. **(a)** p. 302, **(b)** p. 303, **(c)** p. 303, **(d)** p. 305, **(e)** p. 305, **(f)** p. 305, **(g)** p. 306, **(h)** p. 306
3. **(a)** p. 302, **(b)** p. 302, **(c)** p. 305
4. riverboats, wagons, and stagecoaches
5. **(a)** As more settlers moved west, the nation needed better transportation to move people and goods over long distances. **(b)** Possible answers: Steamboats made river travel faster; canals connected rivers and lakes.
6. Possible answer: Roads may be cheaper or more convenient to use.
7. by wagon on the Seneca Road and the Catskill Turnpike, then down the Hudson River by boat; by boat on Lake Erie, the Erie Canal, and the Hudson River

Activity

Guided Instruction
Suggest that students list the ways in which the canal improved daily life. Their design might symbolize one or more of these improvements. Some students may wish to go beyond the rough drawing stage to create a scale model of the monument.

ASSESSMENT See the rubrics in the Alternative Assessment booklet in the Teaching Resources.

★ *Background* ★

Recent Scholarship

A market revolution The Industrial Revolution led to a market revolution, an idea that historians have stressed in recent years. With improved transportation, textile mills could ship their cloth to towns and cities across the nation. Farmers could ship fruits, vegetables, and grains to hungry city residents. Southern planters could send their cotton to factories in Lowell and elsewhere. In his 1991 book *The Market Revolution,* Charles Sellers describes this revolution in markets.

Section 3

Building National Unity

LESSON PLAN

Objectives

★ Explain how Congress tried to strengthen the national economy.
★ Describe the goals of Henry Clay's American System.
★ Explain how the Supreme Court strengthened national unity.

1 Engage

Warm Up Ask students if they think the United States is a unified country today. Discuss the types of evidence they could use to support an answer to the question. *(news stories, people's experiences traveling to other parts of the country)*

Activating Prior Knowledge Ask students to describe the bitter conflicts between the Republicans and Federalists during the elections and administrations of John Adams and Thomas Jefferson.

Reading Actively

Before Reading Have students read the questions under Explore These Questions. As they read, have them jot down notes to help answer the questions.

RESOURCE DIRECTORY

Teaching Resources
Lesson Planner, p. 47
Document-Based Discovery
• Nationalism, pp. 10–13

Building National Unity

Explore These Questions

- How did Congress try to strengthen the national economy?
- What were the goals of Henry Clay's American System?
- How did the Supreme Court strengthen national unity?

Define

- dumping
- sectionalism
- interstate commerce

Identify

- James Monroe
- John C. Calhoun
- Daniel Webster
- Henry Clay
- American System
- *McCulloch* v. *Maryland*
- *Gibbon* v. *Ogden*

After his visit to the United States, Alexis de Tocqueville described what he saw as the character of the American people. He wrote:

> "The American . . . is less afraid than any other inhabitant of the globe to risk what he has gained in the hope of a better future. . . . There is not a country in the world where man more confidently takes charge of the future, or where he feels with more pride that he can fashion the universe to please himself."

Tocqueville echoed the confidence Americans felt in themselves. After the War of 1812, the country grew rapidly. New lands opened to settlers with improved transportation. New industries appeared. In Congress, a new generation of political leaders sought to direct this expansion.

An Era of Good Feelings

In 1816, the Republican candidate for President, **James Monroe**, easily defeated the Federalist, Rufus King. Once in office, Monroe spoke of creating a new sense of national unity.

Monroe was the last of three Presidents in a row to come from Virginia. He was also the last Revolutionary War officer to become President.

In 1817, Monroe made a goodwill tour of the country. Not since George Washington had a President made such a tour. In Boston, crowds cheered Monroe. Boston newspapers expressed surprise at this warm welcome for a Republican from Virginia. After all, Boston had been a Federalist stronghold. One newspaper wrote that the United States was entering an "Era of Good Feelings."

By the time Monroe ran for a second term in 1820, no candidate opposed him. The Federalist party had disappeared.

Three Sectional Leaders

While conflict between political parties declined, disputes between different sections of the nation sharpened. In Congress, three ambitious young men took center stage. All three played key roles in Congress for more than 30 years, as well as serving in other offices. Each represented a different section of the country.

Calhoun of the South

John C. Calhoun spoke for the South. He had grown up on a frontier farm in South Carolina. Later, he went to Yale College in Connecticut. Calhoun's immense energy and striking features earned him the nickname "young Hercules." His intense way of speaking sometimes made people uncomfortable in his presence.

Calhoun had supported the War of 1812. Like many southerners, though, he generally opposed policies that would strengthen the power of the federal government.

Skills FOR LIFE MINI LESSON

COMMUNICATION Understanding Points of View

1. Introduce the skill of understanding points of view by explaining to students that each person has a particular way of looking at issues. A person's point of view is shaped by his or her experiences, education, family, friends, and times.

2. Help students practice the skill by considering the points of view of Calhoun, Webster, and Clay. Ask students to explore how each politician's region of the country affected his point of view on the issues.

3. Help students apply the skill by telling how their own backgrounds affect their point of view on a current issue of concern in their community, such as a school election or plans for a local park.

Webster of the North

Daniel Webster of New Hampshire was perhaps the most skillful public speaker of his time. With eyes flashing and shoulders thrown back, Webster was an impressive sight when he stood up to speak in Congress. An observer described him as a "great cannon loaded to the lips."

Like many New Englanders, Webster had opposed the War of 1812. He even refused to vote for taxes to pay for the war effort. After the war, he wanted the federal government to take a larger role in building the nation's economy.

Clay of the West

Henry Clay spoke for the West. You have already met Clay as a leader of the War Hawks who pushed for war against Britain in 1812.

Clay was born in Virginia. When he was 20, he traveled across the Cumberland Gap into Kentucky. As a young lawyer, he was once fined for brawling with an opponent. Usually, however, he charmed both friends and rivals. Supporters called him "Gallant Harry of the West." Like Webster, Clay strongly favored a more active role for the central government.

A New National Bank

After the War of 1812, leaders like Calhoun, Webster, and Clay had to deal with the nation's economic weakness. The problem was due in part to the lack of a national bank.

The charter for the Bank of the United States ran out in 1811. Without the Bank to lend money and regulate the nation's money supply, the economy suffered. State banks made loans and issued money. Often, they put too much money into circulation. With so much money available to spend, prices rose rapidly.

In the nation's early years, Republicans like Jefferson and Madison had opposed a national bank. By 1816, however, many Republicans believed that a bank was needed. They supported a law to charter the second Bank of the United States. By lending money and restoring order to the nation's money supply, the Bank helped American businesses grow.

Protection From Foreign Competition

Another economic problem facing the nation was foreign competition, especially from

Viewing History **Three Sectional Leaders**

Henry Clay, left, was the first major political leader to emerge from the new states of the West. Along with Daniel Webster and John C. Calhoun, below, Clay played a major role in government for more than 30 years. ★ **What role did sectional politics play in the rise of Webster, Calhoun, and Clay?**

CLAY

★ Activity ★

Connections With Arts

Making comparisons Have students read Stephen Vincent Benêt's short story "The Devil and Daniel Webster." Then have them compare the fictional character in the short story to the politician as he is described here. T

2 Explore

Ask students to read the section. When they have finished, ask them to describe the major goals of three of the great leaders of the time: Calhoun, Webster, and Clay.

3 Teach

Divide the class into three groups—one to represent each of these areas of the country in about 1820—the North, the South, and the West. Have each group prepare a class presentation in support of the region's political views on the Tariff of 1816.

4 Assess

To close the lesson, have students complete the section review. As an alternative, have students make a chart showing the growing differences among these three regions of the country: North, South, and West.

★ ★ ★ ★ ★ ★ ★ ★ ★ ★ ★ ★ ★ ★ ★ ★ ★ ★ ★

ANSWER

The interests of the different sections were often in conflict in the early 1800s. Webster, Calhoun, and Clay rose to prominence because each spoke for the interests of one of the sections.

Technology

AmericanHeritage® History of the United States CD-ROM
- Presidents: James Monroe (*average*)

Chart *Skills*

ANSWERS 1. $500; $625
2. Southerners objected because the tariff raised the price of British goods, which they bought.

Writing Actively

After Reading Have students choose *McCulloch* v. *Maryland* or *Gibbon* v. *Ogden*. Ask them to write a sentence or two explaining the main point of the Court's decision.

Effect of a Protective Tariff

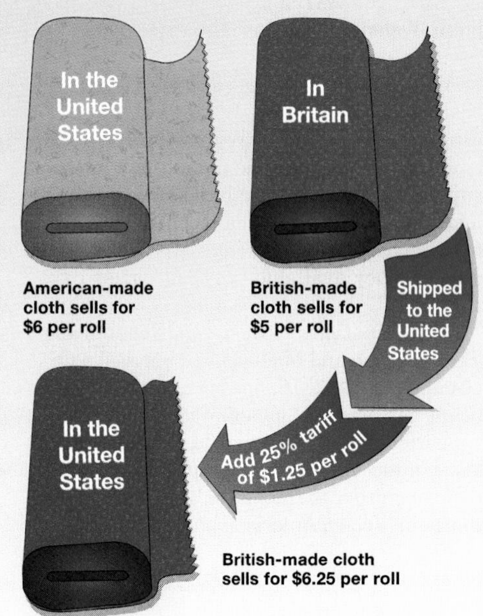

In the United States
In Britain
American-made cloth sells for $6 per roll
British-made cloth sells for $5 per roll
Shipped to the United States
Add 25% tariff of $1.25 per roll
In the United States
British-made cloth sells for $6.25 per roll

Chart *Skills* **In 1816, Congress passed a protective tariff to help American factory owners.**

1. **Comprehension** According to this chart, how much would 100 rolls of British cloth cost before the tariff? How much would they cost after the tariff?
2. **Critical Thinking** Why did southerners object to the tariff?

Economics $

Britain. In the early 1800s, the Embargo Act and then the War of 1812 kept most British goods out of the United States. In response, ambitious American business leaders like Francis Cabot Lowell set up their own mills and factories.

A flood of British goods

In 1815, British goods again poured into the United States. The British could make and sell goods more cheaply than Americans. Most British factories and machines were older and had already been paid for. By contrast, Americans still had to pay for building their new factories.

Sometimes, British manufacturers sold cloth in the United States for less than it cost to make. The practice of selling goods in another country at very low prices is today called **dumping.** Through dumping, British manufacturers hoped to put American rivals out of business.

Congress passes a protective tariff

Dumping caused dozens of New England businesses to fail. Angry owners asked Congress to place a protective tariff on all goods imported from Europe. As you recall, the purpose of a protective tariff is to protect a country's industries from foreign competition.

Congress responded by passing the Tariff of 1816. It greatly raised tariffs on imports. This increase made imported goods far more expensive than similar American-made goods. In 1818 and 1824, Congress passed even higher tariffs.

Higher tariffs led to angry protests, especially from southerners. Southerners had built few factories. As a result, they did not benefit from the tariff. Also, southerners bought many British goods. The new tariff drove up the price of British-made goods. Southerners complained that the tariff made northern manufacturers rich at the expense of the South.

Clay's American System

The bitter dispute over tariffs reflected the growth of sectionalism. **Sectionalism** is loyalty to one's state or section rather than to the nation as a whole. Americans identified themselves as southerners, northerners, or westerners. In Congress, representatives from different sections often clashed.

Henry Clay wanted to promote economic growth for all sections. He set out a program that became known as the **American System.** It called for high tariffs on imports, which would help northern factories. With wealth from industry, northerners would buy farm products from the West and the South. High tariffs would also reduce American dependence on foreign goods. Clay argued:

★ *Customized Instruction* ★

Auditory Learners

Conducting a dialogue After students have read the material on pp. 309–310 about the protective tariff, make sure the class understands the meaning of the word *tariff* and the effect of the Tariff of 1816 on the price of goods imported from Europe. Then ask students to take the roles of a farmer from Kentucky, the owner of two merchant ships from Boston, a worker in a textile mill in Rhode Island, and a plantation owner from South Carolina. Ask the students to conduct a conversation in which they explain how the tariff will affect each of them. Remind students to remain polite at all times.

Resource Directory

Teaching Resources
Unit 3/Chapter 11
• Section 3 Quiz, p. 31

310 ★ Chapter 11

“Every nation should . . . be able to feed and clothe and defend itself. If it rely upon a foreign supply that may be cut off . . . it cannot be independent.”

Clay also urged Congress to use money from tariffs to build roads, bridges, and canals. A better transportation system, he believed, would make it easier and cheaper for farmers in the West and the South to ship goods to city markets.

Clay's American System never went fully into effect. Tariffs did remain high. However, Congress spent little on internal improvements. Southerners in particular disliked Clay's plan. The South had many fine rivers to transport goods. Many southerners opposed paying for roads and canals that brought them no direct benefits.

The Supreme Court Expands Federal Power

Under Chief Justice John Marshall, the Supreme Court strengthened the power of the federal government to promote economic growth. After Congress chartered the second Bank of the United States, Maryland tried to tax the bank in order to drive it out of the state. James McCulloch, the bank cashier, refused to pay the tax.

In the case of ***McCulloch* v. *Maryland*** (1819), the Court ruled that states had no right to interfere with federal institutions within their borders. "The power to tax involves the power to destroy," warned Marshall. The ruling strengthened federal power. It also allowed the National Bank to continue, which helped the economy to expand.

In another case, ***Gibbon* v. *Ogden*** (1824), the Supreme Court upheld the power of the federal government to regulate commerce. The Court struck down a New York law that tried to control steamboat travel between New York and New Jersey. The Court ruled that a state could only regulate trade within its own borders. Only the federal government had the power to regulate **interstate commerce,** or trade between different states. This decision helped the national economy by making it easier for the government to regulate trade.

★ Section 3 Review ★

Recall

1. **Identify** (a) James Monroe, (b) John C. Calhoun, (c) Daniel Webster, (d) Henry Clay, (e) American System, (f) *McCulloch* v. *Maryland*, (g) *Gibbon* v. *Ogden*.
2. **Define** (a) dumping, (b) sectionalism, (c) interstate commerce.

Comprehension

3. How did Congress try to solve each of the following problems: (a) the money supply, (b) foreign competition?
4. Describe Clay's program to promote economic growth.
5. Describe one way the Supreme Court upheld the authority of the federal government.

Critical Thinking and Writing

6. **Analyzing a Primary Source** In 1816, a member of Congress said, "I will buy where I can get [manufactured goods] cheapest. . . . It is unjust to aggravate the burdens of the people for the purpose of favoring the manufacturers." Do you think this speaker favored or opposed the Tariff of 1816? Explain.
7. **Drawing Conclusions** Based on your reading, do you think sectional differences were a serious threat to national unity? Give examples to support your conclusion.

Activity **Conducting an Interview** You are a political reporter assigned to interview a Congressional leader around 1820. Choose either Clay, Calhoun, or Webster. List three or four questions you would ask about the issues facing the nation.

★ Section 3 Review ★

ANSWERS

1. (a) p. 308, **(b)** p. 308, **(c)** p. 309, **(d)** p. 309, **(e)** p. 310, **(f)** p. 311, **(g)** p. 311

2. (a) p. 310, **(b)** p. 310, **(c)** p. 311

3. (a) It passed a law to charter the second Bank of the United States. **(b)** It passed the Tariff of 1816, which made imported goods more expensive.

4. Clay's American System called for high tariffs on imports and government support for improved transportation.

5. Possible answer: In *Gibbon* v. *Ogden,* the Supreme Court ruled that only the federal government could regulate trade between states.

6. The speaker opposed the tariff because he felt people should be able to buy at the cheapest price.

7. Possible answer: Sectional differences threatened national unity. Conflict over the tariff prevented the passage of most of Clay's American System.

Activity

Guided Instruction
Students should explore sectional competition in at least two of their questions. Students having difficulty may review the information in the textbook.

ASSESSMENT See the rubrics in the Alternative Assessment booklet in the Teaching Resources.

★ *Background* ★
Did You Know?

Henry Clay's career

- Served in the House of Representatives almost continuously for 14 years
- Spent 10 years in the Senate
- Served as Secretary of State under John Quincy Adams
- Ran for President and lost three times (1824: the House of Representatives chose John Adams; 1832: lost to Andrew Jackson; 1844: lost to James K. Polk)

Technology

AmericanHeritage® History of the United States CD-ROM

- History Makers: Henry Clay (average)

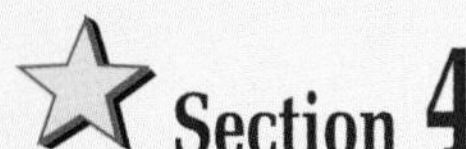

Section 4

Latin America and the United States

★ ★ ★ ★ ★ ★ ★ ★ ★ ★ ★ ★ ★ ★ ★ ★ ★

LESSON PLAN

Objectives

★ Describe how Latin American nations won independence.

★ Explain how the United States gained Florida.

★ State the purpose of the Monroe Doctrine.

1 Engage

Warm Up Ask students to list as many Latin American countries as they can.

Activating Prior Knowledge Ask students which European languages are spoken in South American countries and why.

Reading Actively

Before Reading Have students turn the main headings in the section into the main topics of an outline. Then, as they read, students should record two or three important subtopics for each main topic.

2 Explore

Ask students to read the section. For a homework assignment, ask students to find some additional biographical information on Miguel Hidalgo, José Morelos, Simón Bolívar, or José de San Martín. Write

RESOURCE DIRECTORY

Teaching Resources
Lesson Planner, p. 48

Latin America and the United States

Explore These Questions

- How did Latin American nations win independence?
- How did the United States gain Florida?
- What was the purpose of the Monroe Doctrine?

Define

- creole
- intervention

Identify

- Miguel Hidalgo
- Simón Bolívar
- José de San Martín
- "black Seminoles"
- John Quincy Adams
- Adams-Onís Treaty
- Monroe Doctrine

On a quiet Sunday in September 1810, the church bell rang in the Mexican village of Dolores. In the square, people found their priest, **Miguel Hidalgo** (mee GEHL ee DAHL goh), making a stirring speech. No one knows the exact words, but Mexicans remembered and passed along his message:

> ❝ My children. . . . Will you be free? Will you recover the lands stolen 300 years ago from your forefathers by the hated Spaniards? We must act at once! ❞

Thousands of Mexicans rallied to Father Hidalgo's call for freedom.

South of the United States, Spanish colonies in Latin America* fought wars for independence in the early 1800s. As new nations emerged, President Monroe formed a bold new foreign policy.

Revolution in Latin America

By 1810, many people in Spain's American colonies were eager for independence. They had many reasons for discontent. Most people, even wealthy creoles, had little or no say in government. **Creoles** were people born in Latin America to Spanish parents. Harsh laws ruled Indians and the poor. The French and American revolutions inspired colonists to seek self-rule.

Mexican independence

As you read, Miguel Hidalgo sounded the call for Mexican independence. Rebel forces won control of several provinces before Father Hidalgo was captured. In 1811, he was executed.

Another priest, José Morelos (hoh ZAY moh RAY lohs), took up the fight. Because he called for a program to give land to peasants, wealthy creoles opposed him. Before long, Morelos, too, was captured and killed by the Spanish.

Slowly, creoles began to support the revolution. In 1821, creole forces won control of Mexico. A few years later, Mexico became a republic with its own constitution.

The Liberator

In South America, too, a series of revolutions freed colonies from Spanish rule. The best-known revolutionary leader was **Simón Bolívar** (see MOHN boh LEE vahr). He became known as the Liberator for his role in the Latin American wars of independence.

Bolívar came from a wealthy creole family in Venezuela. As a young man, he took up the cause of Venezuelan independence. Bolívar promised, "I will never allow my hands to be idle, nor my soul to rest until I have broken the shackles which chain us to Spain."

Bolívar rose to become a leader of the rebel forces. In a bold move, he led an army

*Latin America refers to the region of the Western Hemisphere where Latin-based languages such as Spanish, French, and Portuguese are spoken. It includes Mexico, Central and South America, and the West Indies.

312 ★ Chapter 11

★ *Customized Instruction* ★

English Language Learners

Creating a classroom reference Ask English language learners of Latin American background to prepare a briefing paper about their country of ancestry. The briefing paper should include a map of the country; a picture of the country's flag; information about the main events in its history, including how it gained independence; and information about the country's culture and economy. The briefing paper should have a title page with the name of the country and the name of the student who prepared the paper. For ease of use, it should have a table of contents. Inform other students when the briefing paper is available. (*challenging*) ELL

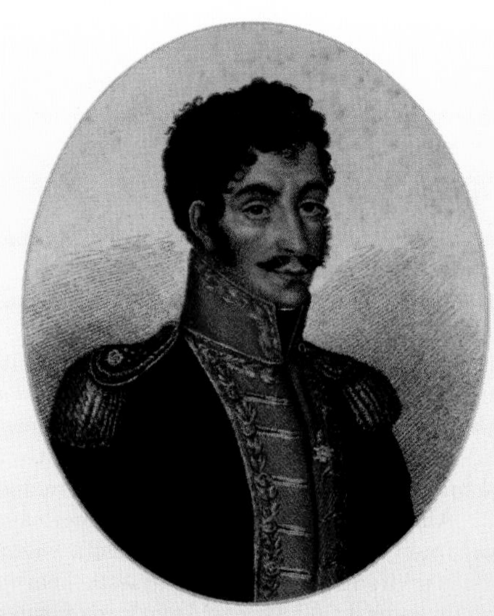

Biography **Simón Bolívar**

As a young man, Simón Bolívar enjoyed a life of wealth and privilege. He studied the republican form of government of the United States. He also admired the military genius of Napoleon. Later, Bolívar's democratic ideals and military skills helped him free several South American nations from Spanish rule.

★ **Which nations did Bolívar help to liberate?**

Crown given to Bolívar by South American Indians ➤

from Venezuela over the high Andes Mountains into Colombia. There, Bolívar took the Spanish forces by surprise and defeated them in 1819.

Soon after, Bolívar became president of the independent Republic of Great Colombia. It included the present-day nations of Venezuela, Colombia, Ecuador, and Panama.

Other new nations

Other independent nations emerged in Latin America. **José de San Martín** (san mahr TEEN) led Argentina to freedom in 1816. He then helped the people of Chile, Peru, and Ecuador win independence.

In 1821, the peoples of Central America declared independence from Spain. Two years later, they formed the United Provinces of Central America. It included the present-day nations of Nicaragua, Costa Rica, El Salvador, Honduras, and Guatemala. By 1825, Spain had lost all its colonies in Latin America except Puerto Rico and Cuba.

The Portuguese colony of Brazil won independence peacefully. Prince Pedro, son of the Portuguese king, ruled the colony. The king advised his son, "If Brazil demands independence, proclaim it yourself and put the crown on your own head." In 1822, Pedro became emperor of the new independent nation of Brazil.

The New Republics

Spain's former colonies modeled their constitutions on that of the United States. Yet their experience after independence was very different from that of their neighbor to the north.

Unlike the people of the 13 British colonies, the peoples of Latin America did not unite into a single country. In part, geography made unity difficult. Latin America covered a much larger area than the English colonies. Mountains like the high, rugged Andes acted as a barrier to travel and communication.

The new republics had a hard time setting up stable governments. Under Spanish rule, the colonists had little or no experience in self-government. Economic problems and deep divisions between social classes increased discontent. Powerful leaders took advantage of the turmoil to seize control. As a result, the new nations were often unable to achieve democratic rule.

Connections With Civics

Like the United States, new Latin American nations created national flags. Venezuela's flag of yellow, blue, and red symbolized the gold of the Americas separated from Spain by the blue ocean. Argentina's blue-white-blue flag was the same flag flown by pirates who attacked Spanish ports and ships along the coasts of South and Central America.

the names of the four freedom fighters on the chalkboard and have students add new pieces of information under each name.

3 Teach

After students have read the section, ask for a volunteer to read the excerpt from the Monroe Doctrine at the end of the section. Ask students to describe the events that led President Monroe to issue this foreign policy statement. What position did the United States promise to maintain toward European nations and colonies according to the Monroe Doctrine? How did the Monroe Doctrine want European nations to act in regard to the Americas?

4 Assess

To close the lesson, have students complete the section review. As an alternative, ask students to write a short essay or draw a political cartoon that supports or refutes this statement: "The Monroe Doctrine could not be enforced."

ANSWER

Venezuela, Colombia, Ecuador, and Panama

★ *Activity* ★

Connections With the World

Comparing Bolívar and Washington

Simón Bolívar, sometimes called the "George Washington of South America," was so highly regarded that the nation of Bolivia was named in his honor. Have students find out more about his career and then prepare brief reports comparing the achievements of the two leaders. (*challenging*)

Writing Actively

After Reading Ask students to write a news story about one of the following events: the destruction of Fort Apalachicola, the acceptance of the Adams-Onís Treaty, or Monroe's speech announcing the policy later called the Monroe Doctrine. Remind students to write objectively and to include the five w's: *who, what, where, when,* and *why.*

Geography *Skills*

ANSWERS **1.** Review locations with students. **2.** Cuba, Puerto Rico, British Honduras, British Guiana, Dutch Guiana, French Guiana **3.** Guatemala, Belize, El Salvador, Honduras, Nicaragua, Costa Rica

New Nations in Latin America

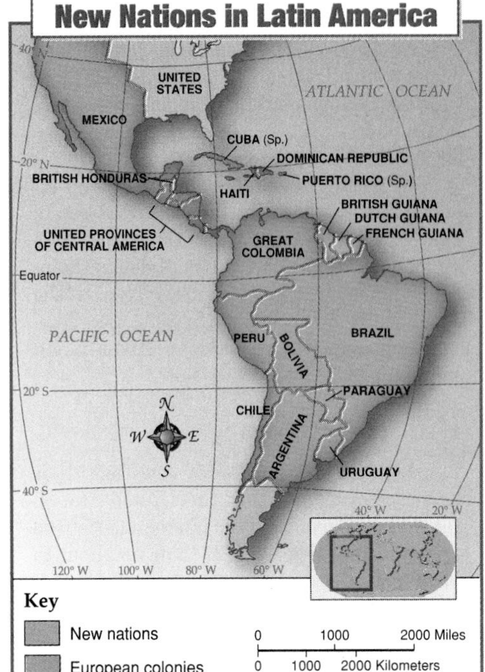

Key

New nations

European colonies

0 1000 2000 Miles

0 1000 2000 Kilometers

Geography *Skills* **Wars of independence led to the creation of many new countries in Latin America.**

1. **Location** On the map, locate: **(a)** Mexico, **(b)** Great Colombia, **(c)** United Provinces of Central America, **(d)** Brazil, **(e)** Argentina, **(f)** Chile, **(g)** Bolivia.
2. **Region** What parts of Latin America remained European colonies?
3. **Critical Thinking** Use the world map in the Reference Section to identify the modern nations that were eventually carved out of the United Provinces of Central America.

The United States Gains Florida

Spain lost another one of its colonies, Florida—not to independence, but to the United States. Many Americans wanted to gain possession of Florida. As early as 1810, President Madison tried to claim West Florida for the United States.

Concern over Florida grew, especially among Southerners. Creek and Seminole Indians in Florida sometimes raided settlements in Georgia. Also, Florida was a refuge for many enslaved African Americans.

"Black Seminoles"

Since the 1700s, Spanish officials had protected slaves who fled from plantations in Georgia and South Carolina. Seminole Indians allowed African Americans to live near their villages. In return, these **"black Seminoles"** gave the Indians a share of the crops they raised every year. The black Seminoles adopted many Indian customs. In addition, some African Americans married Seminoles.

After the War of 1812, African Americans occupied a fort on the Apalachicola River. They invited runaway slaves to settle nearby. Soon, some 1,000 African Americans farmed on the banks of the Apalachicola, protected by the "Negro Fort."

American gunboats attack

General Andrew Jackson demanded that Spain demolish the Negro Fort. The Spanish governor refused. In 1816, Jackson's gunboats invaded Spanish territory and sailed up the Apalachicola.

Inside the Negro Fort, a force of free African Americans waited, cannons ready. They knew that the Americans had come to return them to slavery. After a spirited fight, the gunboats destroyed the fort. Black settlers along the Apalachicola were forced to flee. Many joined nearby Seminoles. Together, they continued to resist American raids into Florida.

Spain gives up Florida

In 1818, Jackson headed to Florida again with a force of over 3,000 soldiers. Spain protested, but it was busy fighting rebels in Latin America. It could not risk war with the United States.

In the end, Spain agreed to peace talks. Secretary of State **John Quincy Adams** worked out a treaty with Spain. In it, Spain agreed to give Florida to the United States in exchange for $5 million. The **Adams-Onís Treaty** took effect in 1821.

RESOURCE DIRECTORY

Teaching Resources
Unit 3/Chapter 11
- Vocabulary Builder, p. 23
- Connecting History and Literature: Letter From an American Farmer, p. 27
- Section 4 Quiz, p. 32

Chapter Tests, Ch. 11, pp. 61–66

★ *Background* ★

Our Diverse Nation

Seminoles undefeated
- The Seminoles continued to fight American soldiers until 1842, when the government withdrew its forces.
- By 1842, about 4,000 Seminoles had been removed to the Indian Territory, in present-day Oklahoma.
- About 1,500 federal soldiers had been killed, and the government had spent about $20 million.
- A few hundred Seminoles remained deep in the Everglades. Their descendants still live in Florida today.

The Monroe Doctrine

Americans cheered as Latin American nations won independence. The actions of European powers, however, worried American officials. Prussia, France, Russia, and Austria seemed ready to help Spain regain its colonies in Latin America. In addition, Russia claimed lands on the Pacific coast of North America.

The British, too, were concerned about European nations meddling in the Western Hemisphere. They suggested issuing a joint statement with the United States. It would guarantee the freedom of the new nations.

Monroe decided to act independently of Britain. In a message to Congress in 1823, he made a bold foreign policy statement, known as the **Monroe Doctrine.** Monroe declared that the United States would not interfere in the affairs of European nations or colonies. At the same time, he warned European nations not to interfere with newly independent nations of Latin America:

> "The American continents . . . are henceforth not to be considered as subjects for future colonization by any European powers. . . . We should consider any attempt on their part to extend their system to any portion of this hemisphere as dangerous to our peace and safety."

The Monroe Doctrine also stated that the United States would oppose any attempt to build new colonies in the Americas. Monroe's message showed that the United States was determined to keep European powers out of the Western Hemisphere.

The United States did not have the military power to enforce the Monroe Doctrine. Britain, however, supported the statement. With its strong navy, it could stop Europeans from interfering in the Americas.

As the United States became stronger, the Monroe Doctrine grew in importance. On several occasions, the United States successfully challenged European **intervention,** or direct involvement, in Latin America. In the early 1900s, Presidents also used the Monroe Doctrine to justify sending troops to Caribbean nations. Thus, Monroe's bold statement helped shape United States foreign policy for more than 100 years.

★ Section 4 Review ★

Recall

1. **Locate** (a) Mexico, (b) Great Colombia, (c) Argentina, (d) United Provinces of Central America, (e) Brazil.
2. **Identify** (a) Miguel Hidalgo, (b) Simón Bolívar, (c) José de San Martín, (d) "black Seminoles," (e) John Quincy Adams, (f) Adams-Onís Treaty, (g) Monroe Doctrine.
3. **Define** (a) creole, (b) intervention.

Comprehension

4. (a) Why did Latin American nations seek independence in the early 1800s? (b) What problems did the new republics face?
5. Why did many Americans want to gain control of Florida?
6. Why did President Monroe issue the Monroe Doctrine?

Critical Thinking and Writing

7. **Making Inferences** How do you think the defenders of the Negro Fort in Florida might have inspired enslaved African Americans in the United States?
8. **Predicting Consequences** What do you think might have happened if Spain had sent an army to regain control of Mexico in the late 1820s?

Activity **Designing a Poster** Your school is participating in a "Know Your Neighbors" fair. The goal is to promote friendly relations with Latin American nations. Design a poster honoring how one neighboring nation gained independence.

★ Section 4 Review ★

ANSWERS

1. See map, p. 314.
2. (a) p. 312, (b) p. 312, (c) p. 313, (d) p. 314, (e) p. 314, (f) p. 314, (g) p. 315
3. (a) p. 312, (b) p. 315
4. (a) People had little say in government; the poor and Indians were oppressed; revolutions inspired change. (b) The people had little experience in self-government. Economic problems increased discontent. Powerful leaders took advantage of these problems and seized control.
5. Indians there were raiding settlements in Georgia. Spanish officials protected runaway slaves.
6. to keep European powers from interfering in the Americas
7. Possible answer: They might have inspired slaves to revolt.
8. Possible answer: The U.S. might have tried to defend Mexico.

Guided Instruction
Have students draw names of Latin American countries. Encourage them to stress positive features of their chosen nation's push for independence. Display the posters.

ASSESSMENT See the rubrics in the Alternative Assessment booklet in the Teaching Resources.

Technology

Videodiscs/Videotapes
Prentice Hall United States History Video Collection™, Vol. 6, Ch. 16, "Expansion and the Monroe Doctrine," 1:30 mins (*average*) ELL

Chapter 16

CD-ROM
Test Bank CD-ROM, Ch. 11
Interactive Student Tutorial

★ Background ★
Did You Know?

Fear and loathing and the League of Nations Americans guard their independence very jealously. One reason that some Americans opposed the League of Nations after World War I was the fear that the charter of the League would invalidate the Monroe Doctrine, allowing European nations to interfere in the Western Hemisphere.

Chapter 11

Review and Activities

Reviewing the Chapter

Define These Terms

1. b **2.** d **3.** e **4.** a **5.** c

Explore the Main Ideas

1. The factory system brought workers and machinery together in one location for the production of goods.

2. River travel was faster, cheaper, and more comfortable than travel by road.

3. John C. Calhoun represented the South. Daniel Webster represented the North. Henry Clay represented the West.

4. Factory owners, angered by the failure of dozens of New England businesses, asked Congress for the tariff to protect American goods against British dumping.

5. Monroe declared the United States would not interfere in Europe or in European colonies. At the same time, he warned that Europe should not interfere in Latin America.

Geography Activity

1. F **2.** B **3.** E **4.** C **5.** D **6.** A

Interaction Workers had to dig long distances through land covered with trees. In two places, the canal had to cross over rivers.

Critical Thinking and Writing

1. (a) The War of 1812 began before the formation of the Boston Associates. **(b)** American manufacturers like the Boston Associates were given a boost by the British blockade during the war.

2. Possible answer: Cities today have many of the same problems, such as overcrowding, poor housing, and violence. However, today most cities have better sanitation, roads, and fire protection.

3. Disputes among the different sections of the nation grew sharper. For example, Clay's American System was never put into effect because of southern protests. This suggests that the Era of Good Feelings would give way to sectional conflict.

4. Answers will vary, but students should recognize that the goal of Clay's American System was the benefit of the entire country, not just particular regions.

Using Primary Sources

(a) The workers seemed healthy and content with their work. **(b)** Possible answer: Americans from nonindustrialized regions might want to know if factories and mills would help or hurt their lives.

Chapter 11 Review and Activities

★ Sum It Up ★

Section 1 The Industrial Revolution

- The Industrial Revolution spread to the United States from Britain in the late 1700s.
- Though factory work was hard, many people moved from farms to work in factories in cities and towns.

Section 2 Moving Westward

- Westward movement was so heavy that eight new states joined the nation between 1789 and 1819.
- Improved roads, steamboats, and canals reduced travel time and lowered the cost of moving goods and people.

Section 3 Building National Unity

- As disputes between different sections of the nation grew more intense, great sectional leaders emerged.
- Political leaders tried to use their power to make the United States stronger economically.

Section 4 Latin America and the United States

- In the early 1800s, almost all of Spain's Latin American colonies won their independence.
- The Monroe Doctrine stated that the United States would oppose European efforts to create new colonies in the Western Hemisphere.

For additional review of the major ideas of Chapter 11, see ***Guide to the Essentials of American History*** or ***Interactive Student Tutorial CD-ROM,*** which contains interactive review activities, graphic organizers, and practice tests.

Reviewing the Chapter

Define These Terms

Match each term with the correct definition.

Column 1	Column 2
1. capitalist	**a.** channel that allows boats to cross a stretch of land
2. urbanization	**b.** person who invests in a business to make a profit
3. turnpike	**c.** practice of selling goods in another country at low prices
4. canal	**d.** movement of populations from farms to cities
5. dumping	**e.** toll road

Explore the Main Ideas

1. Describe the factory system.
2. Why was river travel better than travel by road?
3. Identify the great leader who spoke for each of the three sections of the United States.
4. Why did Congress pass the Tariff of 1816?
5. What two important points did Monroe make in the Monroe Doctrine?

Geography Activity

Match the letters on the map with the following places: **1.** Wheeling, Virginia, **2.** New York City, **3.** Cumberland Gap, **4.** Lancaster Turnpike, **5.** National Road, **6.** Erie Canal. **Interaction** What obstacles did Americans overcome in building the Erie Canal?

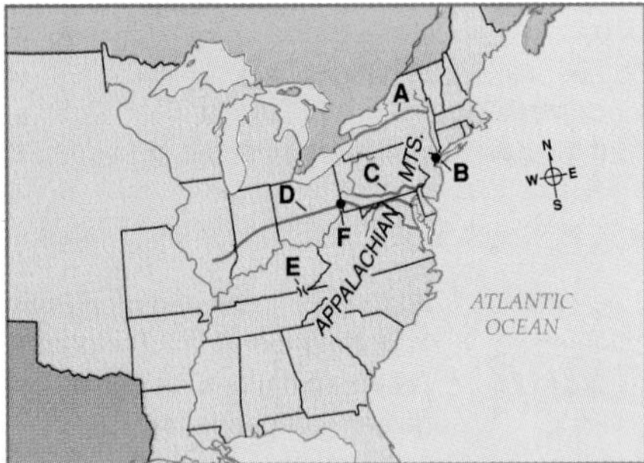

Critical Thinking and Writing

1. **Understanding Chronology** **(a)** Did the War of 1812 begin before or after the formation of the Boston Associates? **(b)** How were these two events linked?
2. **Linking Past and Present** Do cities today have the same kinds of problems as cities in the early 1800s? Explain.
3. **Evaluating Information** What information do you have that suggests that "The Era of Good Feelings" did not last?
4. Exploring Unit Themes **Nationalism** Henry Clay has been called the "most nationalistic" of the great congressional leaders. What facts support this opinion?

Using Primary Sources

Davy Crockett was a Tennessee settler who became a representative in Congress. He toured the city of Lowell in 1834 and gave this description:

> "The dinner bells were ringing, and the folks pouring out of the [work] houses like bees out of a gum [tree]. I looked at them as they passed, all well dressed, lively, genteel in their appearance. . . . I went in among the young girls, and talked with many of them. No one expressed herself as tired of her employment, or oppressed with work: all talked well, and looked healthy."

Source: *An Account of Col. Crockett's Tour to the North and Down East,* Davy Crockett, 1835.

Recognizing Points of View **(a)** What was the condition of the workers at Lowell, according to Crockett? **(b)** Why do you think a representative from Tennessee would have been interested in conditions at mills in Massachusetts?

ACTIVITY BANK

Interdisciplinary Activity

Exploring the Arts With a partner, create a skit, dance, or song about the difficulties of travel in the early 1800s.

Career Skills Activity

Engineers Draw a diagram or prepare a demonstration to show how early factories harnessed the force of water to create power to run machines.

Citizenship Activity

Understanding Regional Politics Sectional politics is still an issue in the United States. Prepare a report in which you describe the needs of your own region. Consider such questions as: Does your region have special resource or energy needs? How do the needs of your region compare with the needs of other regions? What policies would benefit your region?

Internet Activity

Use the Internet to find sites dealing with the National Road, now called Route 40. Using your Web research, create a tourist map of the road showing the towns it passes through, nearby hotels and restaurants, and historic or interesting information about it.

Take one of the following roles: a young woman working at the Lowell mills; a mayor of a frontier town; a settler living in the New York wilderness near the route of the Erie Canal; a black Seminole in Florida. In your EYEWITNESS JOURNAL, record three events that affected your life between 1800 and 1825.

★ 317

ACTIVITY BANK

ASSESSMENT To assess the activities on this page, see the rubrics in the Alternative Assessment booklet in the Teaching Resources. You might want to share the rubrics with your students before they begin work.

Interdisciplinary Activity

1. Students might begin by reviewing the chapter pictures showing steam boats, covered wagons, stagecoaches, and canal boats.
2. Remind students that they should base their work on facts. Encourage them to do outside research.
3. Schedule a class or extra period for students to present their work.

Career Skills Activity

1. Direct students to use encyclopedias, books on the history of technology, or visits to museums or historic sites to gain information about early factories.
2. The complexity of the demonstrations should depend upon student ability and interest. Allow for a wide range of student projects, but stress accuracy and comprehensibility as goals.
3. Display diagrams in the class or common areas of the school; schedule portions of class periods for demonstrations.

Citizenship Activity

1. Work with students in class to make sure they understand their region of the nation. For example, students living in a large city may not be aware that they are part of a smaller Congressional district. Students may wish to contact their representative for information on their region's special needs.
2. Students should present their reports orally or in written form.

EYEWITNESS Journal

1. Suggest students begin by reviewing the chapter to find events that might have affected the person they chose, then list likely personal events (such as the day the Lowell girl began her new job).
2. Journal entries should be based on fact, but may include creative elements.
3. Ask students to read their journal entries aloud if class time permits.

Internet Activity

1. Have students go to www.phschool.com, which contains updated information on a variety of topics.
2. One site you may find useful for this activity is National Road/U.S. Route 40 Home Page at users.aol.com/usroute40/.
3. Given the changing nature of the Internet, you may wish to preview this site before directing students to it.

History Through Literature

Rip Van Winkle

by Washington Irving

Author Note

Washington Irving Born in 1783, Irving was one of the 11 children of a wealthy merchant. He started out as a lawyer, but turned to writing in 1809. Later, he joined his family's company in Europe, but when it failed, he returned to writing. In 1820, a book of short stories and essays, including "Rip Van Winkle" and "The Legend of Sleepy Hollow," won him great acclaim abroad. He later served as a diplomat in Spain and completed a five-volume biography of George Washington shortly before he died in New York in 1859.

Build Vocabulary

Have students look up and discuss *yore, assemblage, incomprehensible, metamorphosed, buff, disputatious, tranquillity, haranguing,* and *vehemently* before they read. Ask: "Which words suggest that Rip is confused? Which suggest an unpleasant contrast to the tranquillity Rip expects to find in the village?"

Prereading Focus

Have students reread Section 3 in Chapter 7 to review what they have learned about the first political parties.

Connect Your Experience

Ask students to describe how it feels to be part of a conversation that you do not understand.

Purpose-Setting Question

Ask: "Suppose that you contracted a rare illness and slept for 20 years. How do you think your community would change while you slept?"

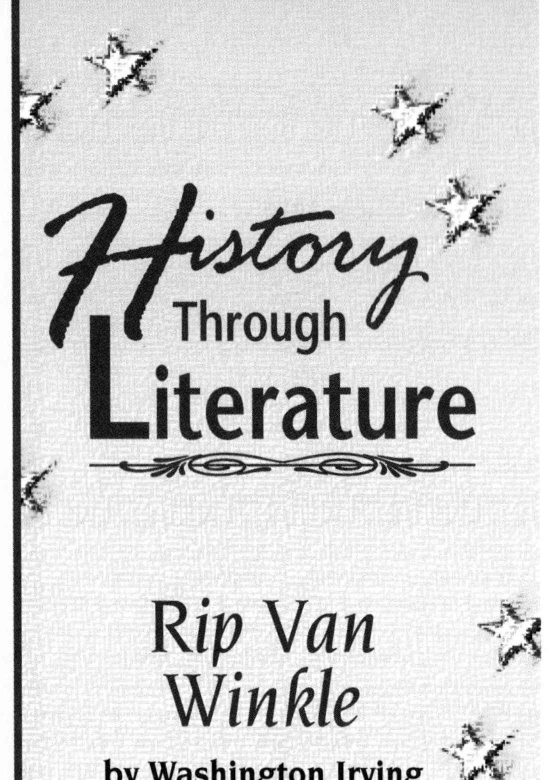

Introduction

Washington Irving (1783–1859) was the first American to make a living as a popular writer. "Rip Van Winkle" is Irving's best-loved tale. The story is a humorous fantasy about a lazy farmer in a small New York village. One night in the early 1770s, Rip Van Winkle wanders up into the Catskill Mountains, falls asleep—and does not wake up for 20 years! In the selection below, Rip returns to his old village after his long nap.

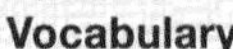

Vocabulary

Before you read the selection, find the meaning of these words in a dictionary: **yore, assemblage, incomprehensible, metamorphosed, buff, disputatious, tranquillity, haranguing, vehemently.**

He had now entered the skirts of the village. A troop of strange children ran at his heels, hooting after him and pointing at his gray beard. The dogs, too, not one of which he recognized for an old acquaintance, barked at him as he passed. The very village was altered; it was larger and more populous. There were rows of houses which he had never seen before, and those which had been his familiar haunts had disappeared. . . .

He now hurried forth and hastened to his old retreat, the village inn—but it too was gone. A large, rickety, wooden building stood in its place, with great gaping windows, some of them broken and mended with old hats and petticoats, and over the door was painted, "the Union Hotel, by Jonathan Doolittle." Instead of the great tree that used to shelter the quiet little Dutch town of yore, there now was reared a tall, naked pole, with something on the top that looked like a red nightcap,* and from it was fluttering a flag, on which was a singular assemblage of stars and stripes—all this was strange and incomprehensible. He recognized on the sign, however, the ruby face of King George . . . but even this was singularly metamorphosed. The red coat was changed for one of blue and buff, a sword was held in the hand instead of a scepter, the head was decorated with a cocked hat, and underneath was painted in large characters, GENERAL WASHINGTON.

There was, as usual, a crowd of folk about the door, but none that Rip recollected. The very character of the people seemed changed. There was a busy, bustling, disputatious tone about it, instead of the accustomed . . . drowsy tranquillity. He looked in vain for the sage Nicholas Vedder, with his broad face, double chin, and fair long pipe . . . or Van Bummel, the schoolmaster, doling forth the contents of an ancient newspaper. In place of these, a lean . . . fellow, with his pockets full of handbills, was haranguing vehemently about rights of citizens—elections—members of congress—liberty—Bunker's Hill—heroes of seventy-six—and other words, which were [strange] to the bewildered Van Winkle.

*"Liberty poles" and "liberty caps" were popular symbols of both the American and French revolutions.

Critical Reading

1. What had replaced the large tree outside the village inn? *(a liberty pole)*
2. What are the people at the hotel discussing? *(politics)*
3. Why did Rip Van Winkle tell the villagers he was a loyal subject of the king? *(It was an unsuccessful attempt to stop their questions and calm them down; it didn't work)*

Background for Understanding

The story of Rip Van Winkle begins when the henpecked, lazy Rip wanders into the Catskill Mountains to hide from his nagging wife. There he meets a group of strange, silent men, dressed in old-fashioned Dutch clothes. Rip drinks with them and watches them bowl. He falls asleep and when he awakens and returns to his home, he learns that 20 years have passed. Despite his confusion, Rip eventually finds a happy home with his daughter.

Viewing HISTORY **Rip Van Winkle Comes Home**

Painter John Quidor was a personal friend of Washington Irving. His painting, Return of Rip Van Winkle *(detail), shows Rip coming home to his village. Rip's long white beard and tattered clothing show the effects of his 20-year nap.*
★ **Identify two objects in this picture that confused Rip when he returned home. Why were they unfamiliar to him?**

The appearance of Rip, with his long, grizzled beard . . . and an army of women and children at his heels, soon attracted the attention of the tavern politicians. They crowded around him, eyeing him from head to foot with great curiosity. The orator bustled up to him and, drawing him partly aside, inquired "on which side he voted?" Rip stared in vacant stupidity. Another short but busy little fellow pulled him by the arm and, rising on tiptoe, inquired in his ear, "whether he was Federal or Democrat?" Rip was equally at a loss to comprehend the question. . . . "Alas! Gentlemen," cried Rip, somewhat dismayed, "I am a poor, quiet man, a native of this place, and a loyal subject of the king, God bless him!"

Here a general shout burst from the bystanders. "A tory! A tory! A spy! A refugee! Hustle him! Away with him!" It was with great difficulty that [a] self-important man in [a] cocked hat restored order; and . . . demanded again of the unknown culprit what he came there for and whom he was seeking. The poor man humbly assured him that he meant no harm, but merely came there in search of some of his neighbors, who used to keep about the tavern.

"Well—who are they? Name them."

Rip bethought himself a moment, and inquired . . . "Where's Brom Dutcher?"

"Oh, he went off to the army at the beginning of the war; some say he was killed at the storming of Stony Point—others say he was drowned in a squall at the foot of Antony's Nose. I don't know—he never came back again."

"Where's Van Bummel, the schoolmaster?"

"He went off to the wars, too, was a great militia general, and is now in congress."

Rip's heart died away at hearing of these sad changes in his home and friends, and finding himself thus alone in the world. Every answer puzzled him, too, by treating of such enormous lapses of time and of matter which he could not understand: war—congress—Stony Point. He had no courage to ask after any more friends, but cried out in despair, "Does nobody here know Rip Van Winkle?"

Analyzing Literature

1. Describe three changes Rip Van Winkle sees when he returns to his village.
2. Why does Rip get into trouble with the men gathered outside the tavern?
3. **Critical Thinking Making Inferences** According to the story, the very nature of the people seemed different to Rip. **(a)** How does Rip think the people changed? **(b)** What do you think may have caused this change?

ANSWER

Possible answer: The picture of George Washington on the hotel sign and the stars and stripes on the flag were unfamiliar to him because he had slept through the American Revolution.

Analyzing Literature

ANSWERS

1. Possible answers: Rip notices that the village is larger; he does not recognize the dogs or the children; the inn has been replaced by a hotel; the large tree is now a liberty pole; the sign bears the face of a man called General Washington instead of that of the king; his friends are gone.
2. Rip calls himself a subject of the king; the Americans get angry.
3. (a) He notices that the people are more argumentative, busier, and faster-moving than he remembers. **(b)** Possible answer: The task of building a new country has energized the people. Democracy has made the people more apt to argue than previously.

Teaching Alternatives

Team Teaching: Language Arts

You might work with a language arts teacher to present a lesson about characterization techniques. Ask students to note carefully how much Irving directly tells the reader about Rip and how much the reader learns from what Rip does and says. Discuss with students the literary advantages and limitations of each approach.

Connections With Arts

John Quidor (1801–1881) produced a number of paintings based on the stories of Washington Irving. Quidor was not a realist, and his fanciful distortions and exaggerations of people and things are often humorous, weird, and sometimes horrifying. Although he was praised by one critic as "an original genius," Quidor never enjoyed much success as an artist. For a livelihood, he painted signs and the panels of fire engines.

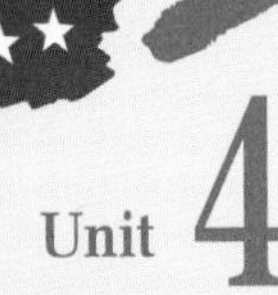

Unit 4

The Nation Expands

Thematic Overview

Between 1820 and 1860, the United States expanded in many ways. The nation expanded its territory until it stretched from coast to coast. Democracy grew as more and more citizens gained the right to vote. The nation's economy also grew.

Chapter 10 discusses the ways that democratic reforms brought the vote to more, but not all, Americans. (See pp. 250–271.) **Chapter 11** shows how the United States came to span the continent. (See pp. 272–299.) **Chapter 12** examines the expanding economy, with booming industry in the North and soaring cotton production in the South. (See pp. 300–323.) **Chapter 13** portrays one of the great eras of change in the United States, as reformers fought slavery and other social ills. (See pp. 324–345.)

Viewing UNIT THEMES ANSWER

Possible answers: tiring, difficult, exhausting, exciting. For more information on the artist, see the Background Art Note at the bottom of this page.

RESOURCE DIRECTORY

Teaching Resources
Document-Based Discovery
• Expansion, pp. 14–17

Unit 4

The Nation Expands

What's Ahead

Viewing UNIT THEMES **Wagon Trains to the West**

William Henry Jackson, who later became a famous photographer, painted this dramatic scene. It shows long lines of wagons carrying settlers westward across Nebraska toward Oregon. In the mid-1800s, wagon trains like this carried thousands of American families from the East to newly acquired territories in the West. ★ **Based on this painting, jot down four words or phrases that you would use to describe a journey to the West by wagon train.**

★ *Background* ★

Art Note

Wagon Trains to the West William Henry Jackson (1843–1942) was a photographer and painter devoted to preserving the heritage of the American West through images. After serving in the Union Army during the Civil War, he moved west and began photographing the people, places, and landscape of the American West. While an official photographer with a U.S. geographic expedition, he took photographs of what is now Yellowstone National Park. In fact, his photographs helped bring about the establishment of the park by convincing the public that the area should be preserved.

Unit Theme Expansion

From 1820 to 1860, the United States grew in several ways. The most dramatic growth was in the size of the nation. It gained vast western territories, including California, Texas, Oregon, and New Mexico. For the first time, an American could travel by land from the Atlantic Ocean to the Pacific without leaving the country.

How did people of the time feel about westward expansion? They can tell you in their own words.

Viewpoints on Westward Expansion

"Our population is rolling toward the shores of the Pacific.... It will soon... reach the Rocky Mountains and be ready to pour into the Oregon territory."

John C. Calhoun, South Carolina senator (1843)

"We traveled till 11 o'clock with the hope of finding water for the weary cattle. The sun was excessively oppressive."

Susan Shelby Magoffin, New Mexico pioneer (1846)

"The white man comes and cuts down the trees, building houses and fences and the buffaloes get frightened and leave and never come back, and the Indians are left to starve."

Muguara, Chief of the Penateka Comanche Indians (1840s)

Activity **Writing to Learn** Thousands of families left their homes in the East to make the long journey westward. What if your family was thinking of moving to another part of the country? List what you might gain by moving. Then, make another list of what you might lose. Use your lists to decide whether you want to move.

★ Background ★

Historians Debate

Images of the West To Frederick Jackson Turner in 1893, the existence of "free land" on the western frontier shaped America's development, fostering individualism, self-reliance, and the democratic spirit. Later historians revealed flaws in Turner's thesis. Still the frontier did have an impact, and its images survive in symbols of pioneers, cowhands, log cabins, and gunslingers.

Every generation of historians, however, reinterprets the past in the light of the present. Today, a new school of western historians has emerged. Among its proponents is Patricia Nelson Limerick, who argues that settling the West had more to do with lawyers and land titles than with cowhands and gunslingers.

Viewpoints on Westward Expansion

★ John C. Calhoun had great pride in his country and its limitless potential. Ironically, his political career was beset by the problems arising from the differences between North and South.

★ Susan Shelby Magoffin was an early pioneer on the Santa Fe Trail. She kept a diary of her hard journey towards what she hoped would be a better life.

★ Muguara and his people took action against the threat posed by white settlers. They kidnapped some settlers in hopes of obtaining concessions. Muguara was killed in battle soon after making this speech.

CRITICAL THINKING "The continent of North America [is] our proper dominion," predicted John Quincy Adams. Choose one speaker from this page and describe how he or she would have responded to Adams's prediction.

Guided Instruction
You might ask students who have moved recently to share their experiences with the class. Then suggest students work in pairs or small groups to create their lists. Each group can report their conclusions to the class.

ASSESSMENT See the rubrics in the Alternative Assessment booklet in the Teaching Resources.

Technology

AmericanHeritage® History of the United States CD-ROM
Access the Time Tour "An Expanding Nation" to accompany Unit 4.

Chapter 12 Manager

SECTION OBJECTIVES	TEACHING RESOURCES	ADDITIONAL RESOURC
1 A New Era in Politics (pp. 324–328) **Objectives** 1. Explain why John Quincy Adams was an unpopular President. 2. Describe how voting rights changed in the 1820s and 1830s. 3. Describe how political parties became more democratic.	**Lesson Planner,** p. 49 (average) .... **.45 mins.** **Unit 4/Chapter 12** • Map Mystery: Comparing Two Elections, p. 5 (challenging) .... **.30 mins.** • Section 1 Quiz, p. 8 (average) .... **.15 mins.** **Interdisciplinary Connections** • Main Idea: A Struggle for Democracy, pp. 68, 71 (average) .... **.20 mins.**	**Customized Reader** • On the Campaign Trail in Indiana, article IVB-12 (average)
2 Jackson in the White House (pp. 329–332) **Objectives** 1. Identify the qualities that helped Andrew Jackson succeed. 2. Explain why President Jackson replaced many officeholders. 3. Explain why Jackson fought against the Bank of the United States.	**Lesson Planner,** p. 50 (average) .... **.45 mins.** **Unit 4/Chapter 12** • Critical Thinking and Writing: Interpreting a Political Cartoon, p. 4 (average) .... **.30 mins.** • Section 2 Quiz, p. 9 (average) .... **.15 mins.**	**Voices of Freedom** • A Mother Advises a Future Presi p. 90 (average)
3 Struggles Over States' Rights (pp. 333–337) **Objectives** 1. Explain how John C. Calhoun and Daniel Webster disagreed on states' rights. 2. Describe how Jackson dealt with the Nullification Crisis. 3. Explain why Native Americans of the Southeast had to leave their lands.	**Lesson Planner,** p. 51 (average) .... **.45 mins.** **Unit 4/Chapter 12** • Practice Your Skills: Reaching a Compromise, p. 3 (challenging) .... **.30 mins.** • Biography Flashcard: Osceola, p. 7 (average) .... **.30 mins.** • Section 3 Quiz, p. 10 (average) .... **.15 mins.** **Interdisciplinary Connections** • Main Idea: A Struggle for Democracy, pp. 69, 70, 72 (average) .... **20 mins.**	**Voices of Freedom** • Webster's Defense of National Supremacy, pp. 91–92 (average) • Jackson Warns the Seminoles, pp. 93–94 (average) **Historical Outline Map Book** • Indian Removal, 1830–1842, p. 37 (average)
4 The Presidency After Jackson (pp. 338–341) **Objectives** 1. Describe the nation's economic problems during Van Buren's presidency. 2. Describe the Whig and Democratic presidential campaigns of 1840. 3. Explain why John Tyler had little success as President.	**Lesson Planner,** p. 52 (average) .... **60 mins.** **Unit 4/Chapter 12** • Connecting History and Literature: Johnny Appleseed, p. 6 (average) .... **.30 mins.** • Section 4 Quiz, p. 11 (average) .... **.15 mins.** **Chapter Tests,** pp. 67–72 (average) .... **.45 mins.** **Why Study History?** • You Will Choose Our Nation's Leaders, pp. 47–50 (average) .... **.90 mins.**	**Voices of Freedom** • A Campaign Song, pp. 94–95 (average)

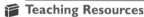

Assessment Options

Teaching Resources
- Alternative Assessment booklet
- Section Quizzes, Unit 4, Chapter 12, pp. 8–11
- Chapter Tests, Chapter 12, pp. 67–72
- Test Bank CD-ROM

Student Performance Pack
- Guide to the Essentials of American History, Chapter 12 Test, p. 70
- Standardized Test Prep Handbook
- Interactive Student Tutorial CD-ROM

Interdisciplinary Connections

Teaching Resources
- Map Mystery, Unit 4, Chapter 12, p. 5
- Connecting History and Literature, Unit 4, Chapter 12, p. 6
- Interdisciplinary Connections, pp. 67–72

Voices of Freedom, pp. 90–95

Customized Reader, article IVB-12

Historical Outline Map Book, p. 37

BLOCK SCHEDULING
Activities with this icon will help you meet your Block Scheduling needs.

ENGLISH LANGUAGE LEARNERS
Activities with this icon are suitable for English Language Learners.

TEAM TEACHING
Activities and Background Notes with this icon present starting points for Team Teaching.

Technology

AmericanHeritage® History of the United States CD-ROM
- Time Tour: The Jackson Era (1824–1840) in An Expanding Nation
- Presidents: John Quincy Adams, Andrew Jackson, Martin Van Buren, William Henry Harrison, John Tyler
- Arts and Entertainment: Books
- History Makers: Sequoyah
- Virtual Buildings: Log Cabin

Interactive Student Tutorial CD-ROM

Test Bank CD-ROM

Color Transparencies
- Civil Rights, p. B-53
- Jackson, Man of the People, p. G-17

Guided Reading Audiotapes
(English/Spanish), side 5

Resource Pro® CD-ROM

Prentice Hall United States History Video Collection™
(Spanish track available on disc version.) Vol. 7, Chs. 10, 13

Prentice Hall Home Page
www.phschool.com

Student Performance Pack

Guide to the Essentials of American History
- Ch. 12, pp. 66–70
  (Available in English and Spanish)

Guided Reading Audiotapes (English/Spanish), side 5

Standardized Test Prep Handbook

Interactive Student Tutorial CD-ROM

Teachers' Bibliography

Don't miss the special American Heritage® teaching notes found in this chapter.

Contact Teachers' Curriculum Institute to learn more about History Alive!® resources on democracy in the Age of Jackson: Manifest Destiny in a Growing Nation, Section 4, "Through the Eyes of Native Americans."

Explore your library to find these issues related to Chapter 12: *Andrew Jackson,* October 1991; *Cherokee Indians,* May 1984.

Prentice Hall Web Site You can access a structured, on-line environment that allows you to preview curriculum-related resources and receive updated information on groundbreaking events from around the nation and the world. (www.phschool.com)

Chapter 12

Democracy in the Age of Jackson 1824–1840

Introducing the Chapter

Have students preview the main ideas of this chapter by looking over the visuals. Suggest they look for illustrations that present aspects of democracy at work.

Using the Time Line To reinforce student understanding of the sequence of events in this chapter, ask students to look at the time line on these pages. Ask questions such as these: **(1)** When was Andrew Jackson first elected President? *(1828)* **(2)** Which Americans could vote in that election? *(most white men)* **(3)** Name one voting reform that occurred in Europe during this period. (e.g., *universal male suffrage in Switzerland)*

Ask students to calculate the first presidential election in which they will be 18 years old—old enough to vote. (Presidential elections will be held in 2000, 2004, 2008, 2012.) Tell students that in the 1800s, greater numbers of Americans were able to vote than ever before, and politicians worked hard to win votes.

For additional *Why Study History?* support, see p. 340.

Chapter 12

Democracy in the Age of Jackson 1824–1840

What's Ahead

In this chapter, you will learn that the Age of Jackson was a time of expanding democracy and political conflict. As more and more white males gained the right to vote, two political parties, the Whigs and Democrats, competed for their support. Nominating conventions and heated election campaigns became part of American politics. Not all, however, shared in democracy's growth. Women, Native Americans, African Americans, and others had to wait for political and social equality.

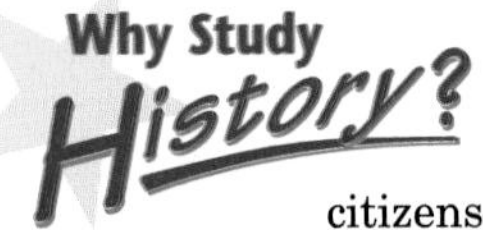

Soon, you will have a right and a responsibility of all American citizens—voting. Learning more about how politics worked in past elections may help you make wise voting decisions in the future. To learn more about politics and your right to vote, see this chapter's *Why Study History?* feature, "You Will Choose Our Nation's Leaders."

American Events

- **1820s** Right to vote extended to most white men
- **1828** Andrew Jackson is elected President
- **1830** Indian Removal Act forces Native Americans to move west of the Mississippi

1824 | 1826 | 1828 | 1830 | 1832

World Events

- **1824 World Event** Simón Bolívar becomes president of Peru
- **1829 World Event** Swiss adopt universal male suffrage

Viewing History: Election Day

The Age of Jackson was a time of expanding democracy. During the 1820s and 1830s, more and more Americans gained the right to vote. In his painting County Election, *George Caleb Bingham shows that Election Day was a time for voting, socializing, and celebrating.* ★ **How does this painting suggest that women were not allowed to participate fully in American democracy?**

1832 President Jackson vetoes charter of the Bank of the United States

1835 Seminole War begins

1840 William Henry Harrison is elected President

1832 | 1834 | 1836 | 1838 | 1840

1832 World Event Reform Act doubles number of eligible voters in Britain

1837 World Event Canadian colonists revolt, demanding democratic reform

★ *Background* ★
Art Note

Election Day In Bingham's painting *County Election,* the man in the red shirt is being sworn in as a voter. Bingham himself ran for the Missouri State Legislature several times and was elected in 1848. Bingham painted his political rival as the smiling candidate tipping his hat; Bingham himself is sitting on the step sketching. T

Documents and Literature

On pp. 563–565, you will find two readings to enrich this chapter:

1. Historical Document "Against Nullification," an excerpt from Daniel Webster's famous speech opposing nullification. (Use with Section 3.)

2. Eyewitness Account "The Cherokee Removal," an account by a missionary who accompanied the Cherokees on their march west. (Use with Section 3.)

Writing Actively

Responding to Art Ask students to write two or three paragraphs comparing the county election portrayed in the painting on this page to a contemporary local election. Students might mention the place and method of voting, the types of people voting, and the use of placards, posters, and buttons.

Viewing History ANSWER

There are no women waiting to vote.

Technology

Videodiscs/Videotapes

Show the *Prentice Hall United States History Video Collection*™ segments for this chapter. The videodisc version has a Spanish track. Press audio until you get the left channel for English or the right channel for Spanish, or use the bar codes in the Guidebook.

American Heritage® History of the United States CD-ROM

- Time Tour: The Jackson Era (1824–1840) in An Expanding Nation (*average*)

Section 1

A New Era in Politics

★ ★ ★ ★ ★ ★ ★ ★ ★ ★ ★ ★ ★ ★ ★ ★ ★

LESSON PLAN

Objectives

★ Explain why John Quincy Adams was an unpopular President.
★ Describe how voting rights changed in the 1820s and 1830s.
★ Describe how political parties became more democratic.

1 Engage

Warm Up Ask students to recall the last time they voted—in a class election, perhaps. How was the voting conducted?

Activating Prior Knowledge Challenge students to list the first five Presidents of the United States: Washington, John Adams, Jefferson, Madison, Monroe.

Reading Actively

Before Reading Have students reread the section title and turn it into a question. As they read the section, students should jot down notes to answer the question.

2 Explore

Ask students to read the section. For a homework assignment, ask students to make a simple chart showing the candidates and victors in the presidential elections of 1824 and 1828.

RESOURCE DIRECTORY

Teaching Resources
Lesson Planner, p. 49
Unit 4/Chapter 12
• Map Mystery: Comparing Two Elections, p. 5
Interdisciplinary Connections
• Main Idea: A Struggle for Democracy, p. 71

1 A New Era in Politics

As You Read

Explore These Questions
- Why was John Quincy Adams an unpopular President?
- How did voting rights change in the 1820s and 1830s?
- How did political parties become more democratic?

Define
- majority
- suffrage
- caucus
- nominating convention

Identify
- John Quincy Adams
- Whigs
- Democrats
- Alexis de Tocqueville

SETTING the Scene Harry Ward, a New England teacher, made a visit to Cincinnati, Ohio, during the 1824 presidential election campaign. Writing to a friend, he described how Ohioans felt about Andrew Jackson, who was running for President. "Strange! Wild! Infatuated! All for Jackson!" he observed.

On election day, more people voted for Andrew Jackson than for any of the other candidates. Oddly enough, Jackson did not become President that year.

The Disputed Election of 1824

There were four candidates for President in 1824. All four were members of the old Republican party. However, each had support in different parts of the country. **John Quincy Adams** was strong in New England. Henry Clay and Andrew Jackson had support in the West. William Crawford was favored in the South but became too ill to campaign.

The candidates

John Quincy Adams of Massachusetts was the son of Abigail and John Adams, the second President. The younger Adams was a graduate of Harvard University. He had served as Secretary of State and had helped end the War of 1812. People admired Adams for his intelligence and high morals. Adams, however, was uncomfortable campaigning among the common people.

Henry Clay, by contrast, was charming. A Kentuckian, Clay was a shrewd politician who had become Speaker of the House of Representatives. In Congress, Clay was a skillful negotiator. He worked out several important compromises. Despite his abilities, Clay was less popular than the other candidate from the West, Andrew Jackson.

Most Americans knew Andrew Jackson for his military victories in the War of 1812. He was the "Hero of New Orleans." Though he was a landowner and a slave owner, many saw him as a man of the people. Jackson was born in a log cabin and his parents were poor farmers. He was admired by small farmers and others who felt left out of the growing economy in the United States.

The "corrupt bargain"

No clear winner emerged from the election of 1824. Jackson won the popular vote, but no candidate won a **majority,** or more than half, of the electoral votes. As a result, the House of Representatives had to choose the President from among the top three candidates. Because he finished fourth, Clay was out of the running. As Speaker of the House, though, he was able to influence the results.

Clay urged members of the House to vote for Adams. After Adams became President, he made Clay his Secretary of State. Jackson and his backers were furious. They accused Adams and Clay of making a "corrupt bar-

★ Activity ★
Cooperative Learning

Reenacting a campaign Have students work in small groups to reenact parts of the campaign of 1824. Groups should choose a candidate to support. They should assign researchers, artists, writers, and speechmakers to do research about the campaign, create posters and handbills, and write and deliver a speech supporting the candidate. *(challenging)* ELL

From the Archives of American Heritage®

Adams's doubts about running At first, John Quincy Adams had rejected the idea of running for President. In 1821, he said, "If that office is to be the prize of cabal and intrigue, or purchasing newspapers, bribing by appointments, or bargaining for foreign missions, I have no ticket in that lottery."

Source: Peter Andrews, "The Press," *American Heritage* magazine, October 1994.

gain" and stealing the election from Jackson. As Jackson was riding home to Tennessee, he met an old friend. "Well, General," said the friend, "we did all we could for you here, but the rascals at Washington cheated you out of it."

"Indeed, my old friend," replied Jackson, "there was *cheating* and *corruption,* and *bribery,* too." In fact, such charges were not true. The election had been decided as the Constitution stated. Still, the anger of Jackson and his supporters seriously hampered President Adams's efforts to unify the nation.

An Unpopular President

Adams knew that the election had angered many Americans. To "bring the whole people together," he pushed for a program of economic growth through internal improvements. His plan backfired, however, and opposition to him grew.

Promoting economic growth

Similar to Alexander Hamilton and Henry Clay, Adams thought that the federal government should promote economic growth. He called for the government to pay for new roads and canals. These internal improvements would help farmers to transport goods to market.

Adams also favored projects to promote the arts and the sciences, as governments in Europe did. He suggested building a national university and an observatory from which astronomers could study the stars.

Most Americans objected to spending money on such programs. They feared that the federal government would become too powerful. Congress approved money for a national road and some canals, but turned down most of Adams's other programs.

A bitter campaign

In 1828, Adams faced an uphill battle for reelection. This time, Andrew Jackson was Adams's only opponent.

The campaign was a bitter contest. Jackson supporters renewed charges that Adams had made a "corrupt bargain" after the 1824 election. They attacked Adams as an aristocrat, or member of the upper class. Adams supporters replied with similar attacks. They called Jackson a dangerous "military chieftain." If Jackson became President, they warned, he could become a dictator like Napoleon Bonaparte of France.

Jackson won the election easily. His supporters cheered the outcome as a victory for common people. By common people, they meant farmers in the West and South and city workers in the East.

Election of 1828

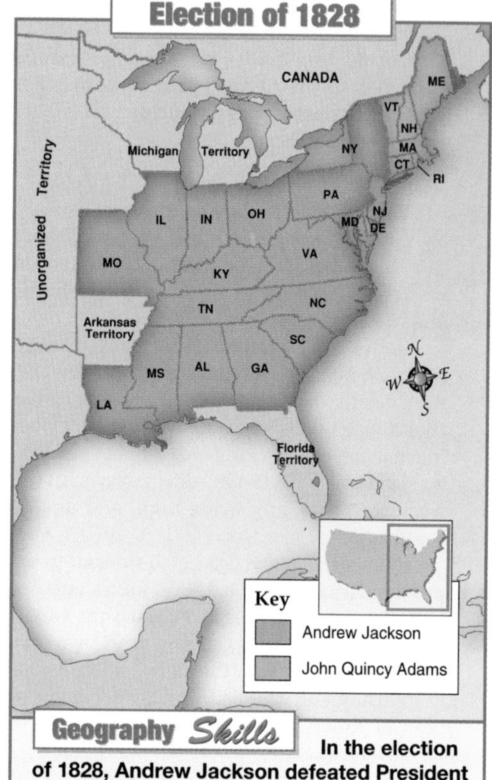

Geography *Skills* **In the election of 1828, Andrew Jackson defeated President John Quincy Adams.**

1. **Location** On the map, locate: **(a)** Massachusetts, **(b)** Kentucky, **(c)** Tennessee.
2. **Place** In which section of the country did Adams have the most support?
3. **Critical Thinking** Which of the two candidates would probably have won Florida and Arkansas if they had been states in 1828? Explain.

3 Teach

Have students label each of the following statements as fact or opinion. Ask students to give supporting evidence for each fact and tell why they agree or disagree with each opinion. **(a)** The 1824 election was decided by a "corrupt bargain." **(b)** The 1828 election was filled with personal attacks and name-calling. **(c)** Andrew Jackson's election in 1828 was a victory for the common people. **(d)** Nominating conventions were a fairer way of choosing candidates than caucuses.

4 Assess

To close the lesson, have students complete the section review. As an alternative, have students list the three or four most important facts from the section. Discuss students' points to create a class list.

★ ★ ★ ★ ★ ★ ★ ★ ★ ★ ★ ★ ★ ★ ★ ★ ★ ★ ★

Geography *Skills*

ANSWERS **1.** Review locations with students. **2.** in the New England states **3.** Jackson would probably have won because he had the support of the southern and western states.

★ *Background* ★

Turning Points

The House decides On February 9, 1825, the House of Representatives cast its votes for President. Each state had one vote. Adams won on the first ballot:

- John Quincy Adams, 13
- Andrew Jackson, 7
- William Crawford, 4

Technology

AmericanHeritage® History of the United States CD-ROM

- Presidents: John Quincy Adams (*average*)

Viewing History ANSWER

Possible answer: Without the right to vote, women might try to influence the views of their adult sons and husbands, who could vote.

Reading Actively

During Reading After students read the subsection More Voters, have them write one or two sentences telling how the subsection supports the idea that the 1820s and 1830s were a new era in politics.

RESOURCE DIRECTORY

Transparencies
Interdisciplinary Connections
• Civil Rights, p. B-53

More Voters

During the 1820s, more people gained **suffrage,** or the right to vote. Others, however, were denied full participation in the growing democracy.

Expanding suffrage

The United States was growing rapidly. New states were joining the Union and there were many new voters. Many of them lived in western states between the Appalachians and the Mississippi.

In the West, many frontier people began life poor, but prospered through hard work. As a result, westerners commonly believed that it was possible to achieve success by being honest and working hard. This democratic spirit was reflected in suffrage laws. In the western states, any white man over age 21 could vote.

Reformers in the East also worked to expand suffrage. By the 1830s, most eastern states dropped the requirement that voters own land. In this way, many craftsworkers and shopkeepers won the right to vote.

Throughout the country, growing numbers of Americans exercised their right to vote. Before 1828, the turnout of eligible voters was never more than 27 percent. That low percentage rose to nearly 58 percent in the election of 1828. By 1840, voter turnout was nearly 80 percent.

Limits on suffrage

Despite the growing democratic spirit, many Americans did not have the right to vote. They included women, Native Americans, and most African Americans. Slaves had no political rights.

In fact, as more white men were winning suffrage, free African Americans were losing it. In the early years of the nation, most northern states had allowed free African American men to vote. In the 1820s, many of these states took away that right. By 1830, only a few New England states permitted African American men to vote on equal terms with white men. In New York, African American men had to own property in order to vote. White men did not.

New Political Practices

By 1820, the disappearance of the Federalist party temporarily ended party differences. In the 1830s, new political parties took shape. They grew out of the conflict between John Quincy Adams and Andrew Jackson.

Two new parties

People who supported Adams and his programs for national growth called themselves National Republicans. In 1834, they became known as **Whigs.** Whigs wanted the federal government to spur the economy. Whigs included eastern business people, some south-

Viewing History **Limits on Suffrage**

The watercolor painting Two Women *by Eunice Pinney shows two women engaged in conversation. During the Age of Jackson, women could not vote in a single state. Most men of the time thought that women should take care of household responsibilities.*

★ **How do you think women were able to influence the outcome of elections?**

★ Customized Instruction ★
Extroverted Learners

A panel on voting rights Review the expansion or restriction of voting rights by forming a panel to simulate a meeting in 1830 of representatives of various groups. Students in the panel will enact the roles of the governor of a western state; an African American man who owns a house and his own livery stable in New York City; a male factory worker who rents his house, owns no land, and lives in an eastern state that requires land ownership for voting; and a widow in Pennsylvania who runs a large farm. The rest of the class may submit questions about suffrage to the panel either orally or in writing. (*average*)

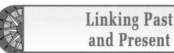

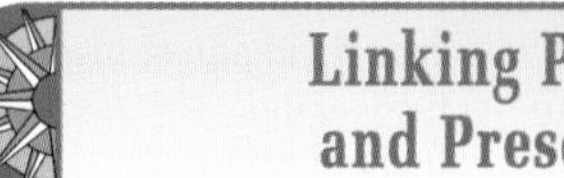
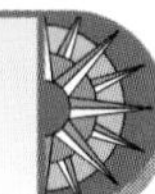

Linking Past and Present

Past

Present

The People and the Presidency

In 1829, President Jackson held a party at the White House to celebrate his inauguration. Cheerful guests helped themselves to slices of a huge cheese. Today, Presidents invite Americans into their home for tours or special events. One example is the Easter egg roll, held each year on the White House lawn. ★ **Why did some people criticize Jackson for opening the White House to the common people?**

ern planters, and former Federalists. Jackson and his supporters called themselves **Democrats.** Today's Democratic party traces its roots to Andrew Jackson's time. Democrats included frontier farmers, as well as factory workers in the East.

New ways to choose candidates

The two new political parties developed more democratic ways to choose candidates for President. In the past, powerful members of each party held a **caucus,** or private meeting. There, they chose their candidate. Critics called the caucus system undemocratic because only a few powerful people were able to take part in it.

In the 1830s, each party began to hold a **nominating convention,** where delegates from all the states chose the party's candidate for President. Nominating conventions gave people a more direct voice in choosing future leaders. Party leaders might still dominate a particular convention, but the nominating process was becoming subject to the will of the people. Today, the major political parties still hold conventions.

Growing Spirit of Equality

The spirit of democracy affected American ideas about social classes. Most Americans did not feel that the rich deserved special respect. "Does a man become wiser, stronger or more virtuous and patriotic because he has a fine house?" asked a Democrat.

Wealthy European visitors to the United States were surprised that American servants expected to be treated as equals. Others were amazed that butlers and maids refused to be summoned with bells, as in Europe. **Alexis de Tocqueville** (tohk VEEL), a visitor from France, became especially well known for his observations on American democracy.

★ *Background* ★

Turning Points

Democracy is contagious The idea of democracy was gaining ground elsewhere. In 1829, Great Britain passed the Catholic Emancipation Act, allowing British Catholics most civil rights, including freedom of worship. Daniel O'Connell, an Irish landowner and lawyer, was instrumental in its passage.

Linking Past and Present

ANSWER

They felt he was demeaning and dishonoring the office of the President.

Writing Actively

After Reading Have students create a crossword puzzle using key terms, names, and ideas from this section. You may want to have them complete each other's puzzles.

Technology

Videodiscs/Videotapes

Prentice Hall United States History Video Collection™, Vol. 7, Ch. 10, "New Day Dawning," 2 mins (average) ELL

Chapter 10

Prentice Hall United States History Video Collection™, Vol. 7, Ch. 13, "The Age of Jackson," 6:10 mins (average) ELL

Chapter 13

★ Section 1 Review ★

ANSWERS

1. See map, p. 325.

2. (a) p. 324, **(b)** p. 326, **(c)** p. 327, **(d)** p. 327

3. (a) p. 324, **(b)** p. 326, **(c)** p. 327, **(d)** p. 327

4. They opposed his economic policy. Jackson supporters attacked the aristocratic Adams for making a "corrupt bargain" in 1824.

5. (a) There were new voters in the new states. All white men over the age of 21 could vote in western states. Men in eastern states no longer had to own land to vote. **(b)** women, Native Americans, and most African Americans

6. Caucuses permitted few people to participate, but conventions included delegates from all states, so more people had a say.

7. The House would pick the President from the three candidates with the most votes in the election.

8. Answers will vary but should be supported by logical arguments.

Activity

Guided Instruction
Choose issues that will be important in an upcoming election. Have students brainstorm ways their advertisements can address these issues. Students should create and then write and perform 30-second interviews, jingles, or parodies of current ads.

Resource Directory

Teaching Resources
Lesson Planner, p. 50
Unit 4/Chapter 12
• Section 1 Quiz, p. 8
Interdisciplinary Connections
• Main Idea: A Struggle for Democracy, p. 68

Alexis de Tocqueville

In 1831, Alexis de Tocqueville arrived in the United States. The French government had sent him to study the American prison system. Over a period of several months, Tocqueville toured much of the United States. He observed much more than prisons. He observed a society that was becoming more and more democratic.

After his return to France, Tocqueville recorded his experiences and observations in a book titled *Democracy in America.* In it, he admired the American democratic spirit and its goals of equality and freedom.

> "Although the revolution that is taking place in the social condition, laws, ideas, and feelings of men is still far from coming to an end, yet its results are already incomparably greater than anything which has taken place in the world before."

Jacksonian democracy

Andrew Jackson's inauguration in 1829 reflected the spirit of Jacksonian democracy. As Jackson traveled to Washington, large crowds cheered him along the way. For the first time, thousands of ordinary people flooded the capital to watch the President take the oath of office.

After Jackson was sworn in, the crowd followed the new President to a reception at the White House. The appearance and behavior of the "common people" shocked an onlooker:

> "A rabble, a mob, of boys, negros, women, children, scrambling, fighting, romping. What a pity, what a pity! No arrangements had been made, no police officers on duty, and the whole house had been [filled] by the rabble mob."

The President, he continued, was "almost suffocated and torn to pieces by the people in their eagerness to shake hands."

Jackson's critics said the scene showed that "King Mob" was ruling the nation. Amos Kendall, a loyal Jackson supporter, viewed the inauguration celebration in a more positive way: "It was a proud day for the people. General Jackson is *their own* President."

★ Section 1 Review ★

Recall

1. **Locate** **(a)** Massachusetts, **(b)** Kentucky, **(c)** Tennessee.
2. **Identify** **(a)** John Quincy Adams, **(b)** Whigs, **(c)** Democrats, **(d)** Alexis de Tocqueville.
3. **Define** **(a)** majority, **(b)** suffrage, **(c)** caucus, **(d)** nominating convention.

Comprehension

4. Why did voters not reelect John Quincy Adams to the Presidency in 1828?
5. **(a)** How did suffrage expand in the 1820s and 1830s? **(b)** What Americans were denied suffrage?
6. How were nominating conventions more democratic than the caucus system?

Critical Thinking and Writing

7. **Applying Information** Based on what you learned about the election of 1824, if no candidate won a majority of electoral votes in the next presidential election, how would the President be chosen?
8. **Defending a Position** Do you agree or disagree with John Quincy Adams's position that the government should spend money to support the arts and sciences? Explain the reasons for your position.

Activity **Writing an Advertisement** Suffrage has expanded greatly since the Age of Jackson. Still, many Americans do not exercise their right to vote. Write a radio or television advertisement urging people to get out and vote next Election Day.

Skills for LIFE MINI LESSON

CRITICAL THINKING **Reading Actively**

1. Introduce the skill of reading actively by informing students that they can be active readers by asking themselves questions as they read.

2. Help students practice the skill by having them read the headings on p. 330. Suggest they turn each heading into a question that they might ask themselves as they read—for instance, "What was the spoils system?" or "Who was rewarded for victory?"

3. Help students apply this skill by directing them to choose two other pages of text and then to write questions they might ask themselves while reading the pages. (basic) ELL

Jackson in the White House

As You Read

Explore These Questions
- What qualities helped Jackson succeed?
- Why did Jackson replace many office-holders?
- Why did Jackson fight against the Bank of the United States?

Define
- spoils system
- pet bank

Identify
- Old Hickory
- kitchen cabinet
- Nicholas Biddle

Setting the Scene During the 1828 election campaign, many stories about Andrew Jackson spread. Like the one that follows, they often showed Jackson's courage and determination.

Years before he ran for President, Jackson was a judge in Tennessee. One day, a disorderly lawbreaker, Russell Bean, refused to appear before the court. The story tells how Jackson strutted out of the courthouse. "Surrender, you infernal villain," he roared, "or I'll blow you through." Bean looked into Jackson's blazing eyes and quietly surrendered. The iron will that made Russell Bean surrender also made Jackson a powerful President.

Andrew Jackson

Like many who admired him, Jackson was born in a log cabin on the frontier. His parents had left Ireland to settle on the Carolina frontier. Both died before Jackson was 15. Young Andrew had to grow up quickly.

A young Andrew Jackson

A tough fighter

Like many other boys who grew up on the frontier, young Andrew Jackson was a determined fighter. Even though he had a slight build, he was strong and determined. A friend who wrestled with him recalled, "I could throw him three times out of four, but he would never stay throwed."

Jackson showed his toughness during the American Revolution. At age 13, he joined the Patriots but was captured by the British. When a British officer ordered the young prisoner to clean his boots, Jackson refused. The officer took a sword and slashed the boy's hand and face. The memory of that attack stayed with Jackson for the rest of his life.

A self-made man

After the Revolution, Jackson studied law in North Carolina. Later, he moved to Tennessee and set up a successful law practice. He became very wealthy by buying and selling land in Georgia and Alabama. While still in his twenties, he was elected to Congress.

Jackson won national fame for his achievements during the War of 1812. He commanded the American forces to a major victory over the British at the Battle of New Orleans. He also defeated the Creek Indians and forced them to give up vast amounts of land in Georgia and Alabama.

Section 2
Jackson in the White House

LESSON PLAN

Objectives

★ Identify the qualities that helped Andrew Jackson succeed.
★ Explain why President Jackson replaced many officeholders.
★ Explain why Jackson fought against the Bank of the United States.

1 Engage

Warm Up Read students the following lines from the poem "The Statue of Andrew Jackson" by Vachel Lindsay. Then ask them to compare the Jackson of the poem to contemporary leaders:

Andrew Jackson was eight feet tall.
His arm was a hickory limb and a maul.
His sword was so long he dragged it on the ground.
Every friend was an equal.
Every foe was a hound. . . .

Activating Prior Knowledge Remind students that Jackson won a stunning victory in the election of 1828 and that the common people expected great things from his administration.

Reading Actively

Before Reading Have students lists the qualities they think a good president should have. As they read, students should rate Jackson, based on the qualities they named.

Technology

AmericanHeritage® History of the United States CD-ROM
- Presidents: Andrew Jackson (*average*)

★ *Background* ★

Did You Know?

No man of letters Although Andrew Jackson often wrote and spoke with great clarity and power, he was not a scholar. He
- received little education.
- had trouble with spelling and grammar.
- knew little history or political science.
- knew almost no mathematics or science.

2 Explore

Ask students to read the section. When they have finished, ask them to write one statement about Jackson's accomplishments and one statement about his mistakes.

3 Teach

Hold a classroom debate on the pros and cons of the spoils system. Have one group of students prepare arguments in favor of the system and another group prepare arguments against it. Appoint a student moderator. Ask class members to decide why they would or would not support legislation to outlaw the spoils system.

4 Assess

To close the lesson, have students complete the section review. As an alternative, ask students to write a short essay explaining whether or not Andrew Jackson deserved the nickname that his critics gave him: "King Andrew."

★ ★ ★ ★ ★ ★ ★ ★ ★ ★ ★ ★ ★ ★ ★ ★ ★

Graphic Organizer *Skills*

ANSWERS **1.** Jackson had been both a senator and a judge.
2. It taught him how to be an effective leader of great numbers of people.

A man of many qualities

Andrew Jackson was a man of many qualities. He had led a violent and adventurous life. He was no stranger to brawls, gambling, and duels. He was quick to lose his temper and he dealt with his enemies harshly.

Jackson's supporters admired his ability to inspire and lead others. They considered him a man of his word and a champion of the common people. The soldiers who served under Jackson called him **Old Hickory.** To them, he was as tough as the wood of a hickory tree.

To the Creek Indians, however, Jackson was an enemy who showed no mercy. After defeating them, Jackson had threatened to kill their leaders if they did not give up lands that earlier treaties had guaranteed them. As a result, the Creeks had no affection for Jackson. Their name for him was Sharp Knife.

The Spoils System

In 1828, President Jackson knew that Americans wanted change. "The people expected reform," he said. "This was the cry from Maine to Louisiana."

Reward for victory

After taking office, Jackson fired many government employees. He replaced them with his own supporters. Most other Presidents had done the same, but Jackson did it on a larger scale.

Critics accused Jackson of rewarding Democrats who had helped elect him instead of choosing qualified men. Jackson replied that he was serving democracy by letting more citizens take part in government. He felt that ordinary Americans could fill government jobs. "The duties of all public officers are . . . so plain and simple that men of intelligence may readily qualify themselves for their performance," he said.

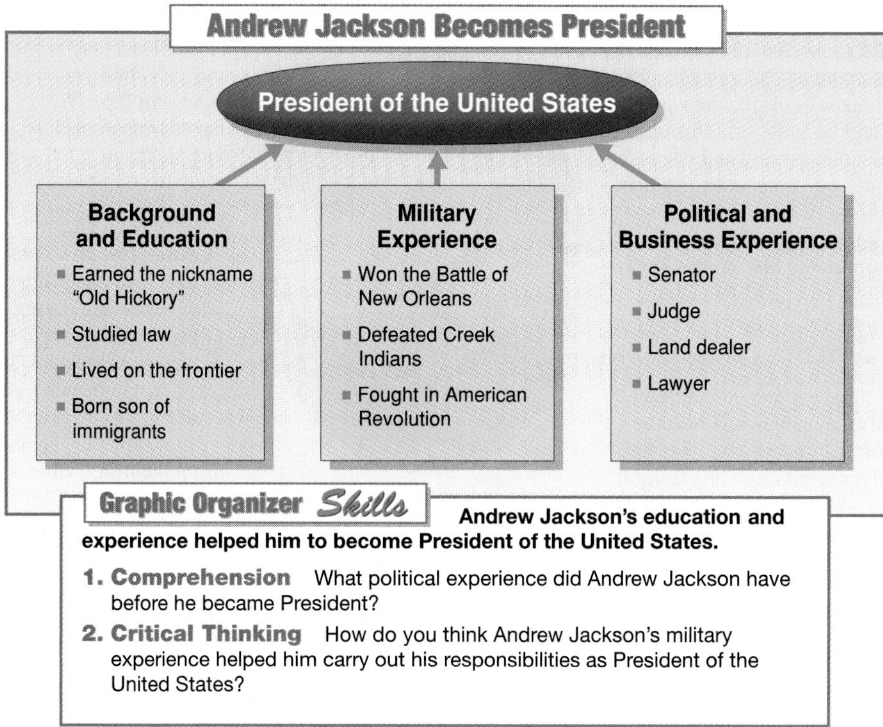

Andrew Jackson Becomes President
President of the United States
Background and Education
Earned the nickname "Old Hickory"
Studied law
Lived on the frontier
Born son of immigrants
Military Experience
Won the Battle of New Orleans
Defeated Creek Indians
Fought in American Revolution
Political and Business Experience
Senator
Judge
Land dealer
Lawyer

Graphic Organizer *Skills* **Andrew Jackson's education and experience helped him to become President of the United States.**

1. **Comprehension** What political experience did Andrew Jackson have before he became President?
2. **Critical Thinking** How do you think Andrew Jackson's military experience helped him carry out his responsibilities as President of the United States?

★ *Background* ★

Did You Know?

Temper, temper! Andrew Jackson's temper was legendary. He may have used this to his own advantage. In *The Life of Andrew Jackson,* biographer Robert T. Remini writes, "Young Andrew could flood a room with bloodcurdling oaths that frightened his listeners half to death. Indeed, he was so good at terrorizing those around him by his language and actions that throughout his life he frequently exploded in rage to scare his victims into doing what he wanted, even though his rage was completely feigned."

A Kitchen Cabinet Dispute

President Jackson often asked for advice from an unofficial group of advisers. This cartoon presents one artist's view of Jackson's "kitchen cabinet." ★ **What was the cartoonist's opinion of the kitchen cabinet? Explain.**

A Jackson supporter explained the system another way. "To the victor belong the spoils," he declared. Spoils are profits or benefits. From then on, the practice of rewarding supporters with government jobs became known as the **spoils system.**

The kitchen cabinet

Jackson rewarded a number of his supporters with Cabinet jobs. Only Secretary of State Martin Van Buren was truly qualified for his position.

As a result, Jackson seldom met with his official Cabinet. Instead, he relied on a group of unofficial advisers. They included Democratic leaders and newspaper editors. These men had a good sense of the nation's mood. Because Jackson met with them in the White House kitchen, the group became known as the **kitchen cabinet.**

The Bank War

President Jackson waged war on the Bank of the United States. Like many westerners, he thought that it was too powerful.

Mr. Biddle's bank

From the first, the Bank of the United States had been a subject of dispute. (See page 247.) The Bank had great power because it controlled loans made by state banks. When the Bank's directors thought that state banks were making too many loans, they limited the amount these banks could lend. The cutbacks angered farmers and merchants who borrowed money to buy land or finance new businesses.

President Jackson and other leading Democrats saw the Bank as undemocratic. Although Congress had created the Bank, it was run by private bankers. Jackson condemned these men as agents of "special privilege" who grew rich with public funds. He especially disliked **Nicholas Biddle,** president of the Bank since 1823.

Biddle came from a wealthy Philadelphia family. He was well qualified to run the bank, but he was also arrogant and vain. Jackson felt that Biddle used the Bank to benefit only the rich. He also resented Biddle's influence over certain members of Congress.

$ Connections With Economics

Today, the Federal Reserve Board supervises a national system of banks and has much influence over the economy. It can tighten the money supply and reduce inflation by raising interest rates. By lowering interest rates on loans, it can encourage economic growth.

ANSWER

Possible answer: The cartoonist probably opposed the kitchen cabinet since the cartoon shows the advisers arguing and fighting.

Reading Actively

During Reading Tell students to look for differences between Jackson's official cabinet and his kitchen cabinet as they read.

Writing Actively

After Reading Have students review their list of qualities of a good president. Ask them to write a paragraph in which they evaluate President Jackson in terms of those qualities.

★ Background ★

Viewpoints

Reason or rage? Views on Jackson's adamant position against the Bank of the United States differ widely. Of Jackson's veto message, Daniel Webster said it "manifestly seeks to inflame the poor against the rich. . . . " Historian Arthur M. Schlesinger, Jr., however, notes that "[e]ven advocates of the Bank conceded that [its] charter bestowed too much power."

★ Section 2 Review ★

ANSWERS

1. (a) p. 330, **(b)** p. 331, **(c)** p. 331

2. (a) p. 331, **(b)** p. 332

3. Possible answer: Education: It prepared him for dealing with Congress and the Supreme Court. Military experience: It made him a tough and determined leader.

4. because it gave jobs to those who helped elect Jackson, not to people who were qualified for the job

5. The Bank could limit the amount of money that state banks lent to farmers and merchants.

6. The official cabinet was filled with unqualified people; to gain sound advice, Jackson created the kitchen cabinet.

7. Possible answer: They considered him dangerous, someone who would hurt those who opposed him.

Activity

Guided Instruction

You might wish to have students work in groups. Suggest that they start the project by describing the setting, characters, and plot of their dramas. Ask students to consider resolutions that don't lead to the closing of the Bank of the United States. Have volunteers perform their television dramas.

Resource Directory

Teaching Resources
Lesson Planner, p. 51
Unit 4/Chapter 12
- Critical Thinking and Writing: Interpreting a Political Cartoon, p. 4
- Section 2 Quiz, p. 9

Transparencies
Political Cartoons
- Jackson, Man of the People, p. G-17

The war begins

Biddle and other Whigs worried that the President might try to destroy the Bank. Two Whig senators, Henry Clay and Daniel Webster, thought of a way to save the Bank and defeat Jackson at the same time.

The Bank's charter was not due for renewal by Congress until 1836. However, Clay and Webster wanted to make the Bank an issue in the 1832 election. They persuaded Biddle to apply for renewal early.

The Whigs believed that most Americans supported the Bank of the United States. If Jackson vetoed the bill to renew the charter, they felt sure that he would anger voters and lose the election. Clay pushed the charter renewal bill through Congress in 1832. Jackson was sick in bed when he heard that Congress had renewed the Bank's charter. "The Bank . . . is trying to kill me," Jackson fumed, "but I will kill it!"

Jackson's veto

In an angry message to Congress, Jackson vetoed the Bank bill. He gave two reasons for his veto. First, he declared the Bank unconstitutional, even though the Supreme Court had ruled in the Bank's favor. Jackson believed that only states, not the federal government, had the right to charter banks. Second, Jackson felt that the Bank helped aristocrats at the expense of the common people. He warned:

> "When the laws undertake . . . to make the rich richer and the potent more powerful, the humble members of society—the farmers, mechanics, and laborers— . . . have a right to complain of the injustice of their government."

As planned, the Whigs made the Bank a major issue in the election of 1832. They chose Henry Clay as their candidate to run against Andrew Jackson. When the votes were counted, Jackson won a stunning election victory. The common people had supported Jackson and rejected the Bank of the United States.

The Bank closes

Without a new charter, the Bank would have to close in 1836. Jackson refused to wait. He ordered Secretary of the Treasury Roger Taney to stop putting government money in the Bank. Instead, Taney deposited federal money in state banks. They became known as **pet banks** because Taney and his friends controlled many of them.

The loss of federal money crippled the Bank of the United States. Its closing in 1836 contributed to an economic crisis.

★ Section 2 Review ★

Recall

1. **Identify** (a) Old Hickory, (b) kitchen cabinet, (c) Nicholas Biddle.
2. **Define** (a) spoils system, (b) pet bank.

Comprehension

3. How did Andrew Jackson's education and experience help prepare him for the Presidency of the United States?
4. Why did critics object to the spoils system?
5. Why did many farmers and merchants dislike the Bank of the United States?

Critical Thinking and Writing

6. **Understanding Causes and Effects** How did the spoils system lead to the creation of the kitchen cabinet?
7. **Analyzing Information** What do you think the Creeks were saying about Jackson when they called him Sharp Knife?

Activity **Writing a Script** Write the script for a television drama in which Andrew Jackson and Nicholas Biddle discuss the Bank of the United States and pet banks.

★ Activity ★
Connections With Arts

Creating political cartoons Have students create political cartoons supporting or opposing Andrew Jackson's veto of the Bank bill. Suggest that students study the cartoon on p. 331 and other cartoons in library references for ideas about portraying Jackson. Tell students that their cartoons should express an opinion on whether Jackson's veto was a correct use of his power to check Congress. Each student should display his or her cartoon, and the display should offer a brief explanation of the cartoon's characters, symbols, and meaning. (*average*)

Struggles Over States' Rights

As You Read

Explore These Questions
- How did John C. Calhoun and Daniel Webster disagree on states' rights?
- How did Jackson deal with the Nullification Crisis?
- Why did Native Americans of the Southeast have to leave their lands?

Define
- nullification
- states' rights
- secede

Identify
- Tariff of Abominations
- Nullification Crisis
- Sequoyah
- Indian Removal Act
- Trail of Tears
- Osceola
- Seminole War

Setting the Scene As President, Andrew Jackson had to deal with a tariff crisis that threatened to split the nation. He also played a major role in deciding the future of many Native Americans. At the heart of both cases was a question that challenged the nation. Did states or the federal government have greater authority?

A Crisis Over Tariffs

In 1828, Congress passed the highest tariff in the nation's history. Southerners called it the **Tariff of Abominations.** An abomination is something that is hated.

Just like earlier tariffs, the new law protected manufacturers from foreign competition. Most manufacturers lived in the North. Southern planters, however, were hurt by the tariff. They sold their cotton in Europe and bought European goods in return. The high tariff meant that southerners had to pay more for these imports.

Calhoun vs. Webster

A leader in the South's fight against the tariff was Vice President John C. Calhoun. He used an argument that Thomas Jefferson had made in the Kentucky and Virginia resolutions. (See page 260.) Like Jefferson, Calhoun claimed that a state had the right to nullify, or cancel, a federal law that it considered to be unconstitutional. This idea is called **nullification.**

Calhoun supported **states' rights,** the right of states to limit the power of the federal government. He argued that the states had final authority because the states had created the national government.

Daniel Webster disagreed. In 1830, he made a speech in the Senate attacking the idea of nullification. The Constitution, he said, united the American people, not just the states. If states had the right to nullify federal laws, the nation would fall apart. Webster ended his speech with stirring words: "Liberty and Union, now and forever, one and inseparable."

A tariff collector used this stencil to mark goods.

Calhoun resigns

Southerners and westerners strongly supported states' rights. They expected Jackson, who had been born in the South and lived in the West, to support their view.

The President's position soon became clear. Jackson and Calhoun attended a political dinner in 1830. Several guests made toasts in favor of states' rights. Finally, Jackson rose. The room fell silent. Old Hickory

From the Archives of American Heritage®

No shortage of breath Daniel Webster's speech on the Senate floor attacking nullification was part of a debate with Senator Robert Hayne of South Carolina. Webster's speech, which began in a conversational tone and gradually built in intensity, lasted for two days!

Source: Ralph K. Andrist, ed., *The American Heritage® History of the Making of the Nation,* 1968.

Section 3
Struggles Over States' Rights

LESSON PLAN

Objectives

★ Explain how Calhoun and Webster disagreed on states' rights.
★ Describe how Jackson dealt with the Nullification Crisis.
★ Explain why Native Americans of the Southeast had to leave their lands.

1 Engage

Warm Up Write the words *states* and *federal government* on the chalkboard. Ask students which one has the greater power.

Activating Prior Knowledge Ask students: "Which part of the country was the most industrialized in the 1830s?" "Which might oppose taxes that benefit industry?"

Reading Actively

Before Reading As they read, have students look for cause-and-effect relationships among events.

2 Explore

Ask students to read the section. For homework, have them check the media for reports on issues such as health care or welfare reform, where the roles of federal and state governments conflict. Ask them to compare the federal/state balance of power today and in 1830.

(LESSON PLAN continues on p. 335)

Skills FOR LIFE

PRACTICE the Skill
ANSWERS

1. Northern manufacturers favored the tariff because it protected them; they opposed efforts, like nullification, that threatened it. Planters in the South were harmed by the tariff, wanted it ended, and supported the Nullification Act.

2. Jackson threatened to use the army to enforce the tariff; South Carolina passed the Nullification Act and threatened to secede.

3. Jackson supported a lower tariff, one less painful to the South. South Carolina repealed the Nullification Act and agreed to the new tariff.

4. Have students include information from the section. How would the tariff or Nullification Act affect them?

APPLY the Skill
Guided Instruction

Partners should specify the dispute, suggesting such issues as wages, hours, or working conditions. Each student should come to the negotiations with two lists: "What I want"; "What I am willing to give up." (Items may not end up in the final agreement.) After an acceptable agreement is reached, students should compare their initial lists with the final compromise.

Skills FOR LIFE

Critical Thinking | Managing Information | **Communication** | Maps, Charts, and Graphs

Reaching a Compromise

How Will I Use This Skill?
When individuals or groups disagree, they can solve the problem and avoid conflict by reaching a compromise. In a compromise, the opposing sides give up some of their demands in order to forge an agreement that both can accept. Knowing how to reach a compromise will help you settle disagreements, solve problems, and get along with others.

A compromise is often sealed by a handshake.

LEARN the Skill
You can reach a compromise by following these four steps:

1. Understand the positions of the opposing sides.
2. Recognize the probable effects of not reaching compromise.
3. Determine what each side might give up or concede in order to reach an agreement.
4. Negotiate a deal by discussing the conflicting issues and offering possible concessions. Compromise is reached when an agreement is acceptable to both sides.

PRACTICE the Skill
Using the steps above, review the compromise concerning the Tariff of Abominations and the Nullification Crisis in this section.

1. Explain the positions of northern manufacturers and southern planters on the two issues.
2. What did each side threaten to do if a compromise was not reached?
3. What did each side give up in order to reach an agreement?
4. With a partner, reenact a negotiation as it might have occurred between representatives of the North and South.

APPLY the Skill
Working with a partner, role-play a dispute that might occur today between an employer and an employee. Identify various issues that they might disagree on. Then, apply what you have learned in order to reach a compromise.

★ Customized Instruction ★
English Language Learners

Preparing an oral response Pair students who are learning English with students who are fluent in English. Ask students to work together to prepare an oral response to the federal government's plan to persuade or force the Southeast Indian nations to move to lands beyond the Mississippi. Students should include their personal feelings, based on their cultural backgrounds and experiences. Students should then prepare a joint response to be given by the ELL student. Student partners should rehearse the presentation, with the student who is fluent in English acting as pronunciation coach. Each oral response should take no more than five minutes. (challenging)

RESOURCE DIRECTORY

Teaching Resources
Unit 4/Chapter 12
- Practice Your Skills: Reaching a Compromise, p. 3

raised his glass, looked straight at the Vice President, and proclaimed, "Our Federal Union—it must be preserved!"

The drama continued. Calhoun raised his glass and answered the President's challenge: "The Union—next to our liberty, most dear." To him, the liberty of a state was more important than the Union.

Because Calhoun strongly disagreed with Jackson, he resigned from the office of Vice President. He was then elected senator from South Carolina. The debate over states' rights would rage for years.

The Nullification Crisis

Anger against the tariff increased in the South. In 1832, Congress passed a new tariff that lowered the rate slightly. South Carolina was not satisfied. It passed the Nullification Act, declaring the new tariff illegal. It also threatened to **secede,** or withdraw, from the Union if challenged.

Jackson was furious. He knew that nullification could lead to civil war. In private, he raged:

> "If one drop of blood be shed there in defiance of the laws of the United States, I will hang the first man of them I can get my hands on to the first tree I can find."

Publicly the President supported a lower compromise tariff proposed by Henry Clay. Jackson also asked Congress to pass the Force Bill. It allowed him to use the army, if necessary, to enforce the tariff.

Faced with Jackson's firm stand, no other state chose to support South Carolina. Calhoun supported the compromise tariff that Clay had proposed. South Carolina repealed the Nullification Act and the **Nullification Crisis** passed. However, sectional tensions between the North and South would increase in the years ahead.

Tragedy for Native Americans

Jackson took a firm stand on another key issue. It affected the fate of Native Americans. Since the early colonial era, white settlers had forced Native Americans off their land. Indian leaders like Pontiac and Tecumseh had failed to stop the invasion of white settlers.

Biography **Sequoyah**

Sequoyah adapted Greek, Hebrew, and English letters to create the 86 symbols of his Cherokee alphabet. The Cherokees used Sequoyah's alphabet to write a constitution. ★ **Why would the lack of a written language be a disadvantage to a society?**

Indian nations in the Southeast

The Creek, Choctaw, Chickasaw, Cherokee, and Seminole nations lived in the Southeast. Many hoped to live in peace with their white neighbors. Their fertile land, however, was ideal for growing cotton. Settlers wanted the land for themselves.

Like earlier Presidents, Jackson sided with the white settlers. At his urging, the government set aside lands beyond the Mississippi River and then persuaded or forced Indians to move there. Jackson believed that this policy would provide land for white settlers as well as protect Native Americans from destruction.

Few Indians wanted to move. Some, like the Cherokee nation, had adopted customs of

3 Teach

As students read about the actions of President Jackson, write the following topics on the chalkboard: Calhoun's advocacy of states' rights; Nullification Crisis; Supreme Court decision in favor of the Cherokees over the state of Georgia; and Indian Removal Act. Ask students to grade Jackson's actions in each situation from A to F. Have volunteers explain their grades.

4 Assess

To close the lesson, have students complete the section review. As an alternative, ask students to write a letter from a citizen who lived in the 1830s, giving a personal reaction to Jackson's stand on the Nullification Crisis or the Indian Removal Act.

★ ★ ★ ★ ★ ★ ★ ★ ★ ★ ★ ★ ★ ★ ★ ★ ★ ★ ★ ★

Biography ANSWER

Without a written language, it would be difficult for a society to deal effectively with other societies. It might be difficult to keep track of events and decisions over a period of time.

Reading Actively

During Reading Point out Jackson's angry words quoted on this page. He made this statement in private. Have students reword his statement as he might have made it in public, so that it expresses the same idea but does not reveal his anger.

★ Background ★ Recent Scholarship

Who paid for national expansion? In his 1997 book *American Frontiers: Cultural Encounters and Continental Conquest,* Gregory H. Nobles looks closely at the complex interactions among peoples on the American frontier as he traces the nation's history of territorial expansion. He calls Jackson the most "anti-Indian leader of the nation."

Technology

AmericanHeritage® History of the United States CD-ROM

- Arts and Entertainment: Books (average)
- History Makers: Sequoyah (average)

Geography Skills

ANSWERS **1.** Review locations with students. **2.** Seminole, Choctaw, Creek, Cherokee, Chickasaw **3.** Possible answer: They believed that Indian Territory was a vast desert and thus worthless.

Writing Actively

After Reading Have students create a cause-and-effect chart about the removal of Native Americans to Indian Territory.

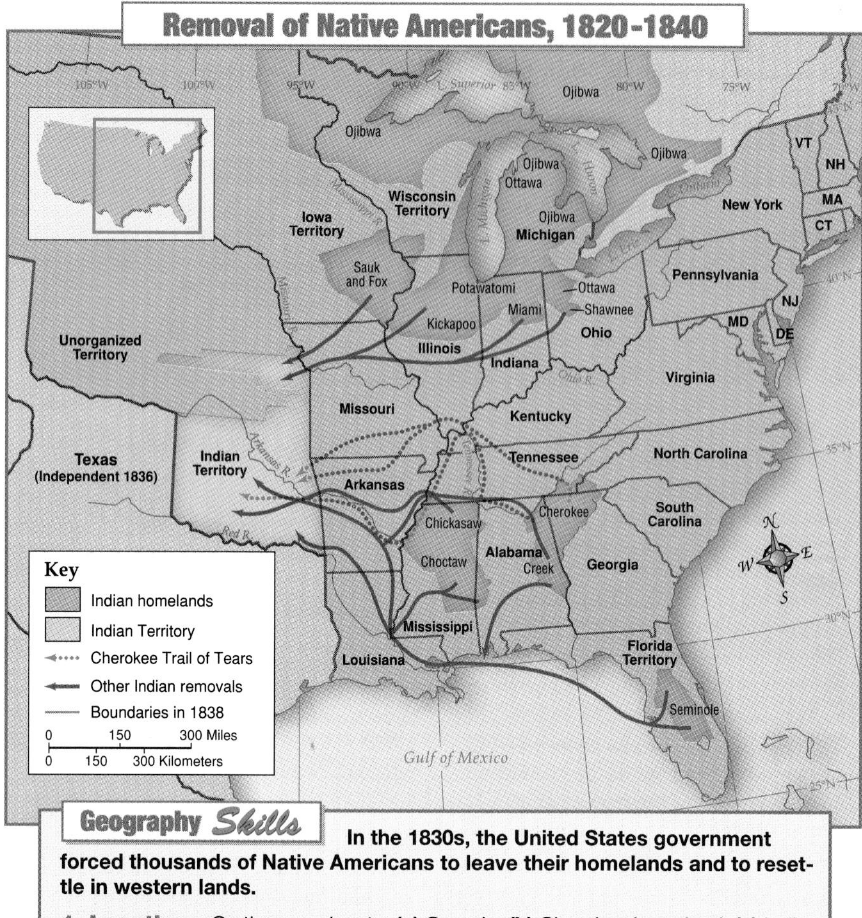

Geography Skills **In the 1830s, the United States government forced thousands of Native Americans to leave their homelands and to resettle in western lands.**

1. **Location** On the map, locate: **(a)** Georgia, **(b)** Cherokee homeland, **(c)** Indian Territory, **(d)** Seminole homeland.
2. **Movement** What five southeastern nations moved to Indian Territory?
3. **Critical Thinking** Why were many Americans willing to give Native Americans lands west of the Mississippi?

white settlers. The Cherokees lived in farming villages. They had a constitution that set up a republican form of government.

In 1821, **Sequoyah** (sih KWOI uh) created a written alphabet for his people. Using Sequoyah's letters, Cherokee children learned to read and write. The Cherokees also published a newspaper.

A legal battle

In 1828, Georgia claimed the right to make laws for the Cherokee nation. The Cherokees went to court to defend their rights. They pointed to treaties with the federal government that protected their rights and property. The Cherokee case reached the Supreme Court. In the 1832 case of *Worcester v. Georgia,* Chief Justice John Marshall ruled in favor of the Cherokees. The Court declared Georgia's action unconstitutional and stated that Native Americans were protected by the United States Constitution.

However, President Jackson refused to enforce the Court's decision. In the Nullifica-

★ Background ★
Our Diverse Nation

A cold shoulder Even the eloquent appeal of 23 Cherokee leaders and 15 white supporters, published on July 17, 1830, failed to turn the tide. The Indian Removal Act became law anyway. In 1838, as the appeal predicted, the Cherokees were "cruelly robbed of their country, in violation of the most solemn compacts, which it is possible for communities to form with each other."

RESOURCE DIRECTORY

Teaching Resources
Unit 4/Chapter 12
- Biography Flashcard: Osceola, p. 7
- Section 3 Quiz, p. 10

Interdisciplinary Connections
- Main Idea: A Struggle for Democracy, pp. 69, 70, 72

tion Crisis, Jackson defended the power of the federal government. In the Cherokee case, he backed states' rights. He said that the federal government could not stop Georgia from extending its authority over Cherokee lands. "John Marshall has made his decision," Jackson reportedly said. "Now let him enforce it."

Forced to Leave

In 1830, Jackson supporters in Congress pushed through the **Indian Removal Act.** It forced many Native Americans to move west of the Mississippi. Whites did not mind turning this land over to Indians because they thought the region was a vast desert. During the 1830s, thousands of southeastern Indians were driven from their homes and forced to march to Indian Territory, west of the Mississippi.

A tragic march

In 1838, the United States Army drove more than 15,000 Cherokees westward to a land they had never seen. The Cherokees trekked hundreds of miles over a period of several months. They had little food or shelter. Thousands perished during the march, mostly children and the elderly. In all, about one fourth of the Indians died.

The Cherokees' long, sorrowful journey west became known as the **Trail of Tears.** An eyewitness described the suffering:

> "The Cherokees are nearly all prisoners. They had been dragged from their homes and encamped at the forts and military places, all over the nation. In Georgia especially, multitudes were allowed no time to take anything with them except the clothes they had on."

The Seminoles resist

In Florida, the Seminole Indians resisted removal. Led by Chief **Osceola** (ahs ee OH luh), they fought the United States Army. The **Seminole War** lasted from 1835 to 1842. It was the costliest war waged by the government to gain Indian lands. More than 1,500 soldiers died in the war and about 20 million dollars were spent in the war effort.

In the end, the Seminoles were defeated. The government forced the Seminole leaders and most of their people to leave Florida. By 1844, only a few thousand Native Americans remained east of the Mississippi River.

★ Section 3 Review ★

Recall

1. **Locate** **(a)** South Carolina, **(b)** Georgia, **(c)** Cherokee homeland, **(d)** Indian Territory, **(e)** Seminole homeland.
2. **Identify** **(a)** Tariff of Abominations, **(b)** Nullification Crisis, **(c)** Sequoyah, **(d)** Indian Removal Act, **(e)** Trail of Tears, **(f)** Osceola, **(g)** Seminole War.
3. **Define** **(a)** nullification, **(b)** states' rights, **(c)** secede.

Comprehension

4. Why did northerners and southerners disagree on the tariff issue?
5. How did Andrew Jackson respond to South Carolina's Nullification Act?
6. Why did Jackson support the policy of using force to move Native Americans beyond the Mississippi River?

Critical Thinking and Writing

7. **Forecasting** What do you think might have happened if other southern states supported South Carolina in the Nullification Crisis?
8. **Drawing Conclusions** Why do you think Andrew Jackson supported states' rights in the Cherokee case but not in the Nullification Crisis?

★ ★

Activity **Writing a Protest Letter** You are a Cherokee on the Trail of Tears. Write a protest letter to President Jackson explaining why you consider his policy of Indian removal to be unjust.

Internet Activity

For more information about the Cherokees in Georgia, have students visit the Trail of Tears Web site: www.ngeorgia.com/history/nghisttt.shtml. Ask students to prepare a one-minute oral report on one of the historical figures from this period, such as John Ross or the Cherokee Rose. Because of the changing nature of the Internet, you may want to preview this site. (*average*)

★ Section 3 Review ★

ANSWERS

1. See map, p. 336.

2. **(a)** p. 333, **(b)** p. 335, **(c)** p. 336, **(d)** p. 337, **(e)** p. 337, **(f)** p. 337, **(g)** p. 337

3. **(a)** p. 333, **(b)** p. 333, **(c)** p. 335

4. Northern manufacturers liked the tariff; it protected them from foreign competition. Many southerners, who traded cotton for European goods, disliked it; it made foreign goods more expensive.

5. He supported a lower compromise tariff. He also asked Congress to pass the Force Bill, so he could use the army to enforce the tariff.

6. He believed it would provide land for white settlers and protect Indians from destruction.

7. Possible answer: Civil war might have occurred.

8. Possible answer: The Cherokee case: because he supported white settlers and did not see the case as a threat to the Union. The Nullification Crisis: because he saw nullification as such a threat.

Guided Instruction
Review the parts and structure of a protest letter, which can include facts and emotional appeals. Have student partners share letters and then respond as Jackson.

ASSESSMENT See the rubrics in the Alternative Assessment booklet in the Teaching Resources.

Section 4

The Presidency After Jackson

LESSON PLAN

Objectives

★ Describe the nation's economic problems during Van Buren's presidency.

★ Describe the Whig and Democratic presidential campaigns of 1840.

★ Explain why John Tyler had little success as President.

1 Engage

Warm Up Ask students to brainstorm about the phrase *hard times*. Discuss how people feel about elected officials during hard times.

Activating Prior Knowledge Ask students whether it is easier for elected officials to win reelection than to be elected for the first time. What are some of the factors that could make one situation less challenging than the other?

Reading Actively

Before Reading Read the questions under Explore These Questions. As you read, jot down notes to help you answer each question.

2 Explore

Ask students to read the section. For a homework assignment, ask them to write three questions to be addressed to one of the candidates of the election of 1840.

RESOURCE DIRECTORY

Teaching Resources
Lesson Planner, p. 52

The Presidency After Jackson

As You Read

Explore These Questions

- What economic problems did Martin Van Buren face?
- How did Whigs and Democrats compete for the Presidency in 1840?
- Why did John Tyler have little success as President?

Define

- speculator
- depression
- laissez faire
- mudslinging

Identify

- Martin Van Buren
- Panic of 1837
- William Henry Harrison
- John Tyler

SETTING the Scene Andrew Jackson retired from office after two terms. Americans then elected **Martin Van Buren** to the Presidency. Van Buren had served as Vice President during Jackson's second term.

As Van Buren took the oath of office in March 1837, Jackson stood at his side. Onlookers watched the outgoing President, not Van Buren. As Old Hickory left the platform, a rousing cheer rose from the crowd. In that moment, the people expressed their loyalty and respect for Andrew Jackson, the "Hero of New Orleans."

Van Buren and Hard Times

Martin Van Buren was very different from Andrew Jackson. He was a politician, not a war hero. Davy Crockett, a Congressman from Tennessee, once described Van Buren as "an artful, cunning, intriguing, selfish, speculating lawyer." As President, however, Van Buren needed more than sharp political instincts.

The Panic of 1837

Two months after taking office, Van Buren faced the worst economic crisis the nation had known. It was called the **Panic of 1837.** The panic had several causes. During the 1830s, the government sold millions of acres of public land in the West. Farmers bought some land, but **speculators** bought even more, hoping that their risky investment would earn them huge profits. To pay for the land, speculators borrowed money from state banks. After the Bank of the United States closed, the state banks could lend money without limit.

To meet the demand for loans, state banks printed more and more paper money. Often, the paper money was not backed by gold or silver. Paper money had value only if people trusted the banks that issued it.

Before leaving office, Jackson had grown alarmed at the wild speculation in land. To slow it down, he ordered that anyone buying public land had to pay for it with gold or silver. Speculators and others rushed to state banks to exchange their paper money for gold and silver. Many banks did not have enough gold and silver and had to close.

Economic depression

The panic worsened when cotton prices went down because of an oversupply. Cotton planters often borrowed money, which they repaid when they sold their crop. Low cotton prices meant that planters could not repay their loans. As a result, more banks failed.

The nation plunged into a deep economic **depression,** a period when business declines and many people lose their jobs. The depression lasted three years. In the worst days, 90 percent of the nation's factories were

★ *Customized Instruction* ★

Introverted Learners

A campaign reporter Ask students to prepare a series of short newspaper articles following the events of the campaign of 1840. Students may supplement articles with visuals. Each student should prepare three of the following:

- A feature on Van Buren's response to the Panic of 1837 (This article might include interviews with voters.)
- Interviews and sketches of Van Buren and Harrison
- An account of the voting
- An account of Harrison's death and Tyler's succession

closed. Thousands of people were out of work. In some cities, hungry crowds broke into warehouses and stole food.

Van Buren's response

It was easy for people to blame President Van Buren for the country's economic depression. Van Buren took little action because he believed in laissez faire—the idea that government should play as small a role as possible in the nation's economic affairs. "The less the government interferes with private pursuits," he said, "the better for the general prosperity."

Van Buren's limited actions did little to help the economy. He tried to set up a more stable banking system. He also cut back on government expenses. For example, when he entertained visitors at the White House, they were served simple dinners. Still, the depression wore on. As a result, criticism of Van Buren increased.

Campaigns of 1840

Even though Van Buren had lost support, the Democrats chose him to run for reelection in 1840. The Whigs, learning from the Democrats, chose a candidate who would appeal to the common people. He was **William Henry Harrison** of Ohio. Harrison was known as the hero of the Battle of Tippecanoe. (See page 281.) To run for Vice President, the Whigs chose John Tyler.

Log cabin campaign

Most Americans knew very little about Harrison's stand on the issues. To appeal to voters, the Whigs focused on his war record. "Tippecanoe and Tyler too" became their campaign slogan.

The Whigs created an image for Harrison as a "man of the people." They presented him as a humble farmer who had been born in a log cabin. Harrison was actually a wealthy, educated man who lived in a large mansion. Still, the Whigs made the log cabin their campaign symbol. In a typical Whig cartoon, Harrison stands outside a log cabin, greeting Van Buren and his aides:

> "Gentlemen, . . . If you will accept the [simple food] of a log cabin, with a western farmer's cheer, you are welcome. I have no champagne but can give you a mug of good cider, with some ham and eggs, and good clean beds. I am a plain backwoodsman. I have cleared some land, killed some Indians, and made the Red Coats fly in my time."

A new sort of politics

The campaigns of 1840 reflected a new sort of politics. Harrison traveled across the land, making speeches and greeting voters. Both parties competed for votes with rallies, banquets, and entertainment. Ordinary citizens participated by giving speeches and singing campaign songs like this one:

> "The times are bad, and want
> curing;
> They are getting past all enduring:
> So let's turn out Martin Van Buren
> And put in old Tippecanoe!"

Viewing History **Log Cabin Campaign**

Harrison's log cabin symbol swept the nation in 1840. Marchers in parades often carried miniature cabins such as the one shown here. The cabin was attached to a pole and raised aloft for all to see. ★ **Why was the log cabin image appealing to many voters?**

3 Teach

Tell the class members that they will analyze the presidential campaign of 1840 as if they were working for a large national newsmagazine. Groups of students will prepare one of the following articles or visuals:

- An overview of the Van Buren presidency
- A feature on the Panic of 1837
- A description of the Whig campaign
- An overview of the Harrison/Tyler presidency
- Visuals—charts, maps, and cartoons—to support the articles

4 Assess

To close the lesson, have students complete the section review. As an alternative, ask students to make a speech supporting Van Buren or William Henry Harrison. Students might also answer some of the questions prepared for Explore These Questions at the beginning of this lesson.

ANSWER

The log cabin image represented the common people. Many voters identified with that image.

Writing Actively

After Reading Have students devise a campaign slogan for Van Buren's campaign.

★ *Background* ★

Did You Know?

Keep the ball rolling The expression "keep the ball rolling" originated in the campaign of 1840. The Whigs made "Harrison balls" from twine, paper, leather, or tin. When the balls were 10 or 12 feet in diameter, Whigs rolled them through the streets from town to town while singing campaign songs.

Technology

AmericanHeritage® History of the United States CD-ROM

- Presidents: Martin Van Buren, William Henry Harrison (*average*)
- Virtual Buildings: Log Cabin (*average*)

Why Study *History?*

ANSWERS

1. (a) Whigs held parades, gave out free cider, chanted slogans, and engaged in name-calling. **(b)** Advertising helps voters become familiar with a candidate. It may inform them about what the candidate's positions are and also may try to show his or her opponent in a negative light.

2. You can research the accomplishments of the candidate based on earlier speeches and voting records.

★*Activity*

Guided Instruction

Have students brainstorm possible interview questions, such as: "How did you learn about the candidates?" and "What was more important—a candidate's past record or current statements?" Remind students that it is not necessary to find out who their interview subject voted for. Ask students to compare their conclusions with one another.

ASSESSMENT See the rubrics in the Alternative Assessment booklet in the Teaching Resources.

Why Study *History?*

Because You Will Choose Our Nation's Leaders

Historical Background

In the political campaigns of 1840, Democrats and Whigs showed little concern for the key issues of the day. Instead, they organized parades, chanted slogans, offered free cider, and participated in name-calling. Candidates also used newspapers, posters, and even whisky jugs to carry their political messages. In 1840, the Whigs' log cabin campaign was a success and William Henry Harrison was elected President. (See page 339.)

Connections to Today

When election day draws near today, politicians flood the radio, television, Internet, and various other media with campaign sound bites. Like politicians of the 1840s, some candidates try to avoid the issues. Some candidates may even use questionable or inappropriate campaign tactics to win votes.

Responsible voters are familiar with the workings of political campaigns. They make their voting decisions based on a clear understanding of the candidates' past performance and stand on the issues. They want to vote for the most qualified candidate. Other voters, however, may be swayed more by clever campaign tactics and political advertisements.

Connections to You

Right now, you may participate in school elections. In a few years, you will have the right and responsibility of voting for our nation's leaders. You will help to choose leaders of your nation, state, and community. Politicians of today, like those of the 1840s, will sometimes use aggressive campaign tactics to try to win your vote. Learning about politics during the Age of Jackson and during other eras of American history can help you to become a knowledgeable and responsible voter.

1. Comprehension

(a) What campaign tactics did the Whigs use in the election of 1840?

(b) What role does advertising play in political campaigns today?

2. Critical Thinking

How can you learn more about a candidate's past performance and stand on major issues?

Interviewing Write several questions to help you learn how people make their voting decisions. Then, use your questions to interview people you know who voted in a recent election. Keep a written or taped record of their responses. What conclusions can you draw from your interviews?

Resource Directory

Teaching Resources

Unit 4/Chapter 12
- Connecting History and Literature: Johnny Appleseed, p. 6
- Section 4 Quiz, p. 11

Chapter Tests, pp. 67–72

Why Study History?
- You Will Choose Our Nation's Leaders, pp. 47–50

Fast Facts

★ The first political consulting firm managed campaigns in California as early as 1933.

★ Political professionals use a trade magazine called *Campaigns and Elections* to find information about new campaign methods.

★ Dwight Eisenhower's famous "I Like Ike" slogan helped him win the presidency in 1952. At the beginning of the 1956 campaign, he resurrected the slogan, changing it to "Now—Do You Like Ike?"

Bibliography

To read more about this topic:

1. *Hail to the Candidate: Presidential Campaigns from Banners to Broadcasts,* Keith Melder (Smithsonian, 1992). Fascinating illustrated history.

2. *Presidential Campaigns,* Paul F. Boller, Jr. (Oxford, 1984). Light-hearted but accurate campaign history.

3. Internet. Web site—League of Women Voters (www.lwv.org). Political information, encouraging the active participation of citizens.

Along the campaign trail, Whigs organized colorful parades in both small towns and big cities. At every stop, they served plenty of free cider. The log cabin symbol appeared on banners, quilts, and even packages of shaving soap.

Name-calling, half-truths, and lies

In their campaigns, both Whigs and Democrats engaged in **mudslinging,** or the use of insults to attack an opponent's reputation. They used name-calling, half-truths, and lies to win votes.

The Whigs attacked the President. One newspaper falsely reported that Van Buren spent thousands of dollars to install a bathtub in the White House. They blamed "Martin Van Ruin" for the depression. Daniel Webster charged that the Democrats had replaced "Old Hickory" Jackson with "Slippery Elm" Van Buren.

The Democrats responded with their own attacks and name-calling. They revealed that "Granny Harrison, the Petticoat General," had resigned from the army before the War of 1812 ended. They accused "General Mum" of not speaking on the issues. "Should Harrison be elected?" they asked voters. "Read his name spelled backwards," they advised. "No sirrah."

Whigs in the White House

Harrison won the election of 1840 easily. As a result, a Whig was in the White House for the first time in 12 years. "We have taught them how to conquer us!" complained one Democrat.

The Whigs had a clear-cut program. They wanted to create a new Bank of the United States and improve roads and canals. Also, they wanted a high tariff.

However, Whig hopes soon crashed. Just weeks after taking office, President Harrison died of pneumonia. **John Tyler** became the first Vice President to succeed a President who died in office.

President Tyler failed to live up to Whig expectations. A former Democrat, he opposed some Whig plans for developing the economy. When the Whigs in Congress passed a bill to recharter the Bank of the United States, Tyler vetoed it.

In response, most of Tyler's Cabinet resigned and the Whigs threw Tyler out of their party. Democrats welcomed the squabbling. "Tyler is heartily despised by everyone," reported an observer. "He has no influence at all." With few friends in either the Whig or Democratic party, Tyler could do little during his term in office.

★ Section 4 Review ★

Recall

1. **Identify** **(a)** Martin Van Buren, **(b)** Panic of 1837, **(c)** William Henry Harrison, **(d)** John Tyler.
2. **Define** **(a)** speculator, **(b)** depression, **(c)** laissez faire, **(d)** mudslinging.

Comprehension

3. Describe the economic depression that occurred after the Panic of 1837.
4. Describe some of the campaign tactics Democrats and Whigs used in the election of 1840.
5. Why did the Whigs throw President Tyler out of their party?

Critical Thinking and Writing

6. **Solving Problems** What do you think President Van Buren could have done to ease the economic crisis of the 1830s?
7. **Comparing** How do campaign tactics of today compare with those of 1840?

Activity **Researching** If you had money in a bank that failed today, would you lose your money just as people did in the 1830s? To find the answer, conduct research on the Federal Deposit Insurance Corporation, also known as the FDIC.

★ Section 4 Review ★

ANSWERS

1. **(a)** p. 338, **(b)** p. 338, **(c)** p. 339, **(d)** p. 341

2. **(a)** p. 338, **(b)** p. 338, **(c)** p. 339, **(d)** p. 341

3. The depression lasted 3 years. Most factories closed and many were jobless.

4. The Whigs called the President "Martin Van Ruin" and other insulting names to reduce voter support for Van Buren. The Democrats called Harrison "General Mum" for not speaking out on the issues.

5. Tyler did not support their economic program.

6. Possible answer: He might have used government money to put the jobless to work and to feed the hungry.

7. Possible answer: They are similar since candidates still call each other names and try to avoid talking about the issues.

Activity

Guided Instruction
Have students list their sources. Once the research is done, assess students' understanding by asking questions, such as: "When was the FDIC established?" and "Are there any limits to FDIC coverage?"

ASSESSMENT See the rubrics in the Alternative Assessment booklet in the Teaching Resources.

★ *Activity* ★
Community Involvement

Supporting the vote Ask students to find out about the various groups in their community that encourage voter registration and help voters get to the polls on election day. Students should include a description of the tasks that teenagers can perform to assist these groups. (*average*)

Technology

AmericanHeritage® History of the United States CD-ROM
• Presidents: John Tyler (*average*)

CD-ROM
Test Bank CD-ROM, Ch. 12
Interactive Student Tutorial

Chapter 12

Review and Activities

Reviewing the Chapter

Define These Terms

1. b **2.** a **3.** d **4.** c **5.** e

Explore the Main Ideas

1. Suffrage had recently been extended to all white men in the West. Reforms in the East extended the vote to men without property. New states created new voters.

2. (a) Biddle was the director of the Bank and responded to Webster and Clay's urging to apply for a renewal of the Bank early in order to make it a campaign issue. **(b)** Clay supported the Bank and tried to use the issue to prevent Jackson's reelection in 1832. **(c)** Jackson opposed the Bank. He vetoed its renewal bill.

3. The tariff mainly affected agricultural states like South Carolina because they traded their cotton for European goods, which were made very expensive by the tariff.

4. He supported white settlers, who wanted to grow cotton on Indian land; he forced Indians to move West.

5. State banks closed when they could not stand behind their loans to speculators. People then rushed to other banks to withdraw their money, further damaging the banking system. More bank failures followed when cotton prices fell and planters could not repay the loans they took at the beginning of the planting season.

Geography Activity

1. F **2.** D **3.** C **4.** B **5.** A **6.** E

Place The settlers wanted the land for themselves because it was fertile and ideal for growing cotton.

Critical Thinking and Writing

1. Sample answer: Adams's plans might have created more wealth. With a strong federal Bank, which he and his followers supported, a crisis like the Panic of 1837 might have been lessened or avoided.

2. Jackson becomes President, the Cherokees are ordered off their land, the Seminole War begins.

3. Sample answer: Politicians today often use negative advertising to disparage their opponents. However, it is now harder to tell outright lies about an opponent.

4. Sample answer: Suffrage was gradually extended until all white males could vote. Jackson also opened up government employment to ordinary people.

Using Primary Sources

(a) He was sending a large military force to help them. **(b)** They resented him. He threatened to use force against them if they did not obey the order to move.

Chapter 12 Review and Activities

★ Sum It Up ★

Section 1 A New Era in Politics

- The 1828 election of Andrew Jackson for President was seen as a victory for the common people.
- In the 1820s, democracy expanded as more and more white males gained the right to vote.
- Women and African Americans did not share in the growth of democracy.

Section 2 Jackson in the White House

- Jackson rewarded his supporters with government jobs and relied on the advice of his unofficial kitchen cabinet.
- Jackson fought against the national bank, which he saw as a tool of the wealthy.

Section 3 Struggles Over States' Rights

- In his second term, Jackson used compromise and strong leadership to end a crisis over tariffs and states' rights.
- Jackson's Indian removal policy forced thousands of Native Americans to leave their homelands and move west.

Section 4 The Presidency After Jackson

- The Panic of 1837 brought an economic depression that caused President Van Buren to lose popular support.
- In 1840, Whigs used new political campaign tactics to get William Henry Harrison elected President.

For additional review of the major ideas of Chapter 12, see ***Guide to the Essentials of American History*** or ***Interactive Student Tutorial CD-ROM,*** which contains interactive review activities, graphic organizers, and practice tests.

Reviewing the Chapter

Define These Terms

Match each term with the correct definition.

Column 1	Column 2
1. suffrage	**a.** private meeting to choose candidates
2. caucus	**b.** right to vote
3. nominating convention	**c.** practice of rewarding supporters with government jobs
4. spoils system	**d.** meeting where state delegates choose candidates
5. kitchen cabinet	**e.** Jackson's group of unofficial advisers

Explore the Main Ideas

1. Why were there more voters in 1828 than in 1824?
2. What role did each of the following play in the struggle over the Bank: **(a)** Nicholas Biddle, **(b)** Henry Clay, **(c)** Andrew Jackson.
3. Why did South Carolina want to nullify the tariffs of 1828 and 1832?
4. Describe President Jackson's Indian removal policy.
5. What were the causes of the Panic of 1837?

Geography Activity

Match the letters on the map with the following places: **1.** Indian Territory, **2.** Chickasaw, **3.** Choctaw, **4.** Creek, **5.** Cherokee, **6.** Seminole. **Place** Why did settlers want Cherokee lands in the Southeast?

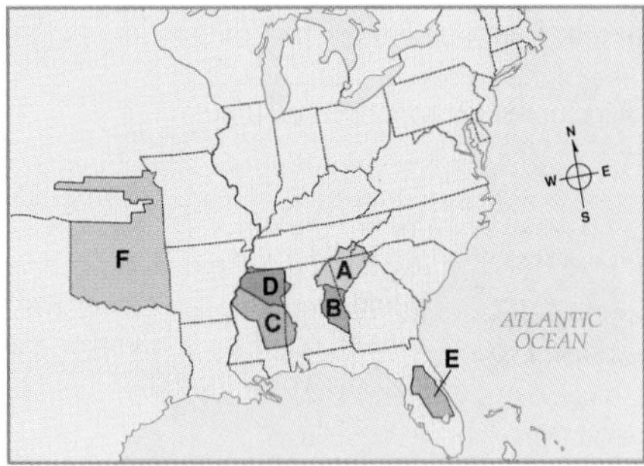

Critical Thinking and Writing

1. **Defending a Position** Do you think more Americans should have supported John Quincy Adams's plans to promote economic growth? Why or why not?
2. **Understanding Chronology** Place these events in chronological order: **(a)** Jackson becomes President, **(b)** the Cherokees are ordered off their land, **(c)** the Seminole War begins.
3. **Linking Past and Present** How are today's political tactics similar to those of the Jackson era? How are the tactics different?
4. Exploring Unit Themes **Expansion** We often think of the Age of Jackson as a time of expanding democracy. In what ways did American democracy expand during the Age of Jackson?

Using Primary Sources

President Jackson wanted to move all Native Americans west of the Mississippi River. In 1835, when it seemed that the Seminoles would resist, Jackson wrote a forceful letter to them.

> "My Children—
>
> I am sorry to have heard that you have been listening to bad counsel. . . . I have ordered a large military force to be sent among you. . . . If you listen to the voice of friendship and truth, you will go quietly and voluntarily. But should you listen to the bad birds that are always flying about you and refuse to move, I have then directed the commanding officer to remove you by force. This will be done. I pray the Great Spirit, therefore, to incline you to do what is right.
>
> Your friend,
>
> A. Jackson"

Source: "President Andrew Jackson's Letter to the Seminoles" in *History of the Indian Wars,* ed. Henry Trumbull, 1841.

Recognizing Points of View (a) How did President Jackson suggest that he was a friend of the Seminoles? **(b)** How do you think the Seminoles felt about Jackson after reading this letter?

Activity Bank

Interdisciplinary Activity

Exploring Economics Review the Tariff of Abominations. Then do research to learn about the North American Free Trade Agreement of the 1990s. In an oral report, explain the differences between these two national economic policies.

Career Skills Activity

Artists Select an issue or incident related to Andrew Jackson's presidency. Then create a political cartoon based on your selection. Remember that political cartoonists represent a point of view by using various symbols. Be prepared to explain your cartoon and its symbolism.

Citizenship Activity

Running a Food Drive Thousands of Cherokees died of starvation on the Trail of Tears. Today, in many communities, some people do not have enough food to eat. Form a student group to plan and run a food drive. Work with a charitable organization to deliver food to those in need.

Internet Activity

Search the Internet to find sites dealing with Cherokee culture and history. Continue exploring until you find Cherokee viewpoints on the Indian Removal and the Trail of Tears. Use the Cherokee viewpoints to write a poem about how people suffered on the Trail of Tears.

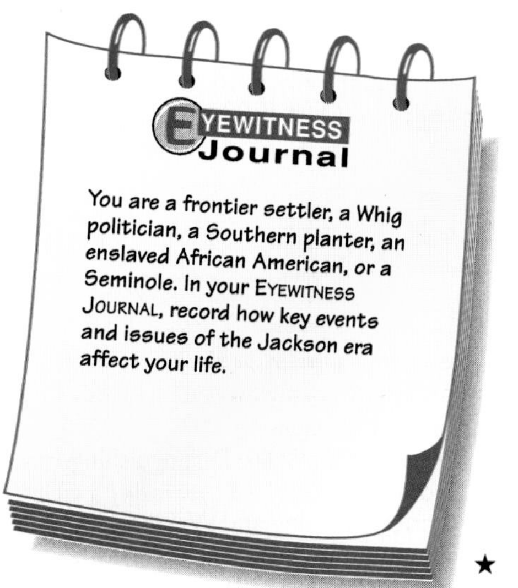

★ 343

Activity Bank

ASSESSMENT To assess the activities on this page, see the rubrics in the Alternative Assessment booklet in the Teaching Resources. You might want to share the rubrics with your students before they begin work.

Interdisciplinary Activity

1. Direct students to a library or on-line periodical index to survey information on the North American Free Trade Agreement (NAFTA).

2. Ask students to think about these questions as they research NAFTA: "Were any particular regions of the nation against NAFTA?" and "Were any particular groups of the nation (labor unions, corporations) especially for or against NAFTA?"

3. If you wish, students can present their findings in a mock Congressional committee hearing.

Career Skills Activity

1. Suggest such topics as the National Bank, the spoils system, nullification, and the Cherokee removal.

2. Remind students that they can clarify the symbols of their cartoon by using a few carefully selected labels in the cartoon itself.

3. When the cartoons are completed, have the class view and discuss the work.

Citizenship Activity

1. Tell students that the first step in planning a food drive will be contacting an organization to distribute the collected food. An area food pantry would be ideal.

2. Have students obtain from the distributor a list of preferred foods. For example, canned foods store well.

3. Students can canvass the community for donations or advertise central collection points at a supermarket or mall.

Eyewitness Journal

1. Students should reread their text and note how their characters would have been affected by events.
2. Students should also consider the impact on their characters of having to support a family.
3. Students could work together to prepare skits that dramatize the historical events from various points of view.

Internet Activity

1. Have students go to www.phschool.com, which contains updated information on a variety of topics.
2. Another site you may find useful is The Trail of Tears at www.ngeorgia.com/history/nghisttt.shtml.
3. Given the changing nature of the Internet, you may wish to preview this site before directing students to it.

Chapter 13 Manager

SECTION OBJECTIVES	TEACHING RESOURCES	ADDITIONAL RESOURC
1 Oregon Country (pp. 346–350) **Objectives** 1. Explain how rival claims to Oregon Country developed. 2. Explain how fur trappers and missionaries helped open up the Far West. 3. Identify the hardships that settlers faced.	**Lesson Planner,** p. 53 (average) . . . . .90 mins. **Unit 4/Chapter 13** • Section 1 Quiz, p. 18 (average) . . . . .15 mins.	**Historical Outline Map Book** • Trails to the West, p. 40 (average • Oregon Country, p. 38 (challengin **Customized Reader** • A Woman Missionary in Oregon Territory, article IVA-15 (basic) **Interdisciplinary Explorations** • Wagons West: Exploring the Oregon Trail (challenging)
2 Texas Wins Independence (pp. 351–355) **Objectives** 1. Explain why many Americans settled in Texas. 2. Describe how Texas became an independent nation. 3. Identify the challenges faced by the new Republic of Texas.	**Lesson Planner,** p. 54 (average) . . . . .90 mins. **Unit 4/Chapter 13** • Biography Flashcard: Stephen F. Austin, p. 17 (average) . . . . .30 mins. • Section 2 Quiz, p. 19 (average) . . . . .15 mins. **Why Study History?** • History Is All Around You, pp. 51–54 (average) . . . . .90 mins.	**Historical Outline Map Book** • Independence for Texas, p. 39 (average) **Customized Reader** • Tejanos' Petition to the Mexican Government, article IVA-12 (challenging) • A Mexican Account of the Alamo article IVA-8 (challenging)
3 California and the Southwest (pp. 356–359) **Objectives** 1. List the reasons the first white settlers came to New Mexico. 2. Describe what California life was like for Native Americans. 3. Explain why Americans wanted their nation to expand to the Pacific Ocean.	**Lesson Planner,** p. 55 (average) . . . . .90 mins. **Unit 4/Chapter 13** • Connecting History and Literature: A Frontier Lady, p. 16 (average) . . . . .30 mins. • Section 3 Quiz, p. 20 (average) . . . . .15 mins.	**Voices of Freedom** • America's Manifest Destiny, pp. 98–99 (average) **Customized Reader** • The Founding of San Diego: California's First Mission, article IIA-17 (average) • Life at San Gabriel Mission, article IIIA-15 (average) **Prentice Hall Literature Librar** • Literature of the American Southwest
4 War With Mexico (pp. 360–364) **Objectives** 1. Describe how the United States gained Oregon. 2. Identify the causes and results of the Mexican War. 3. Describe how cultures blended in the new United States territories.	**Lesson Planner,** p. 56 (average) . . . . .45 mins. **Unit 4/Chapter 13** • Practice Your Skills: Distinguishing Fact From Opinion, p. 13 (average) . . . . .20 mins. • Critical Thinking and Writing: Drawing Conclusions, p. 14 (average) . . . . .30 mins. • Section 4 Quiz, p. 21 (average) . . . . .15 mins. **Document-Based Discovery** • Expansion, pp. 14–17 (average) . . . . .90 mins.	**Voices of Freedom** • Black Opposition to the Mexican War, pp. 99–100 (average) **Historical Outline Map Book** • War With Mexico, 1846–1848, p. 41 (average) • Growth of the United States to 1853, p. 42 (average)
5 A Rush to the West (pp. 365–369) **Objectives** 1. Describe how the Mormons settled Utah. 2. Describe how the discovery of gold affected life in California. 3. Explain why California had a diverse population.	**Lesson Planner,** p. 57 (average) . . . . . . .90 mins. **Unit 4/Chapter 13** • Vocabulary Builder, p. 12 • Map Mystery: California Gold—and Growth, p. 15 (basic) . . . . .20 mins. • Section 5 Quiz, p. 22 (average) . . . . .15 mins. **Chapter Tests,** pp. 73–78 (average) . . . . .45 mins. **Interdisciplinary Connections** • Main Idea: The California Gold Rush, pp. 73–78 (average) . . . . .20 mins.	**Voices of Freedom** • Louise Clappe Strikes Gold, pp. 100–101 (average) **Customized Reader** • The Pioneer Chinese, article IVA-3 (average) • Discovering Gold at Sutter's Mill article IVB-9 (challenging) • A Mormon Village in the Early 1900s, article VIA-12 (challenging

Assessment Options

Teaching Resources
- Alternative Assessment booklet
- Section Quizzes, Unit 4, Chapter 13, pp. 18–22
- Chapter Tests, Chapter 13, pp. 73–78
- Test Bank CD-ROM

Student Performance Pack
- Guide to the Essentials of American History, Chapter 13 Test, p. 76
- Standardized Test Prep Handbook
- Interactive Student Tutorial CD-ROM

Interdisciplinary Connections

Teaching Resources
- Map Mystery, Unit 4, Chapter 13, p. 15
- Connecting History and Literature, Unit 4, Chapter 13, p. 16
- Interdisciplinary Connections, pp. 73–78

Interdisciplinary Explorations
- Wagons West: Exploring the Oregon Trail

Voices of Freedom, pp. 98–101

Customized Reader, articles IIA-17, IIIA-15, IVA-3, IVA-8, IVA-12, IVA-15, IVB-9, VIA-12

Historical Outline Map Book, pp. 38–42

Prentice Hall Literature Library
- Literature of the American Southwest

BLOCK SCHEDULING
Activities with this icon will help you meet your Block Scheduling needs.

ENGLISH LANGUAGE LEARNERS
Activities with this icon are suitable for English Language Learners.

TEAM TEACHING
Activities and Background Notes with this icon present starting points for Team Teaching.

Technology

AmericanHeritage® History of the United States CD-ROM
- Time Tour: Westward Expansion in An Expanding Nation
- Presidents: James K. Polk
- History Makers: Sam Houston

Interactive Student Tutorial CD-ROM

Test Bank CD-ROM

Color Transparencies
- The United States and the World, 1820–1860, p. E-19
- Westward Movement, p. F-19
- Pacific Coast States, p. 1-81
- Dancing on the Veranda, p. D-39
- South Central States, p. 1-69
- Expansion of the United States, p. 1-25
- Forty-Niners, p. B-55

Guided Reading Audiotapes
(English/Spanish), side 5

Resource Pro® CD-ROM

Prentice Hall United States History Video Collection™
(Spanish track available on disc version.) Vol. 6, Chs. 28, 31, 34

Prentice Hall Home Page
www.phschool.com

Student Performance Pack

Guide to the Essentials of American History
- Ch. 13, pp. 71–76
(Available in English and Spanish)

Guided Reading Audiotapes (English/Spanish), side 5

Standardized Test Prep Handbook

Interactive Student Tutorial CD-ROM

Teachers' Bibliography

FROM THE ARCHIVES OF AmericanHeritage®

Don't miss the special American Heritage® teaching notes found in this chapter.

Contact Teachers' Curriculum Institute to learn more about History Alive!® resources on westward expansion. See History Alive!® unit: Manifest Destiny in a Growing Nation, Section 3, "Many Paths to the West."

Explore your library to find these issues related to Chapter 13: *California History,* May 1982; *Mountain Men,* February 1991.

Prentice Hall Web Site You can access a structured, on-line environment that allows you to preview curriculum-related resources and receive updated information on groundbreaking events from around the nation and the world. (www.phschool.com)

Chapter 13

Westward Expansion
1820–1860

Introducing the Chapter

Have students preview the main ideas of this chapter by looking over the visuals. Suggest they look for features of western landscape or architecture. They can compare and contrast them with the landscape and architecture in your area.

Using the Time Line To provide students with practice in using the time line to understand chronology, ask questions such as these: **(1)** Did Santa Anna come to power before or after Oregon was admitted to the Union? *(before)* **(2)** What happened in Texas before Britain recognized the region as separate from Mexico? *(The Republic of Texas was formed.)* **(3)** What event took place the year after James K. Polk became President of the United States? *(Americans in northern California declared independence from Mexico.)* **(4)** About how long after the first white American traders arrived in New Mexico was Oregon admitted to the Union? *(about 38 years)*

Ask students to recall a visit they have made to a historic site, either in the local area or elsewhere. Have volunteers describe the sites they visited, including what insight on the past they gained by being able to see actual relics from history.

For additional *Why Study History?* support, see p. 353.

Chapter 13 Westward Expansion
1820–1860

What's Ahead

By the mid-1800s, Americans began to dream of extending their territory to the Pacific Ocean. In this chapter, you will see how that dream came true.

First, the United States secured the Pacific Northwest by signing a treaty with Britain. Next, after American settlers declared independence from Mexico, the United States brought Texas into the Union. Americans then won California and the Southwest by fighting a war with Mexico. As settlers poured into the Southwest, a new culture developed that blended American, Mexican, and Indian cultures.

Why Study History? Every year, millions of Americans visit historic memorials, from battlefields to the homes of famous people. To many Texans, for example, the best-loved historic site is a San Antonio mission called the Alamo. Why do so many Americans work to preserve the places where history happened? To explore this question, see this chapter's *Why Study History?* feature, "History Is All Around You."

American Events

1821 First white American traders arrive in Santa Fe, New Mexico

1836 Republic of Texas is formed

1820 | 1825 | 1830 | 1835 | 1840

World Events

1833 World Event
Santa Anna comes to power in Mexico

West side Main Plaza San Antonio Texas 1849 WGM Samuel

Viewing History **A Growing Texas City**

This painting by William G. Samuel shows a street in San Antonio, Texas, in 1849. Texas had joined the Union a few years before, after winning independence from Mexico. In the mid-1800s, the United States gained vast western territories, including Texas, California, Oregon, and New Mexico. As a result, the nation stretched from the Atlantic Ocean to the Pacific. ★ **How does this painting show the Mexican roots of the Southwest?**

1845 James K. Polk becomes President

1846 Americans in northern California declare independence from Mexico

1859 Oregon is admitted to the Union

1840 | 1845 | 1850 | 1855 | 1860

1840 World Event
Britain recognizes Texas as an independent nation

1854 World Event
Japan and United States sign trade agreement

★ 345

★ Background ★
Art Note

A Growing Texas City The San Fernando Cathedral and the large house of José Cassiano, a Mexican supporter of Texas in the revolution, are prominent in William G. Samuel's painting of San Antonio. Behind the cathedral, the American flag flies in the Military Plaza. Samuel was an amateur painter who later became a city marshal.

Documents and Literature

On pp. 566–569, you will find two readings to enrich this chapter:

1. Literature "Death Comes for the Archbishop," an excerpt from Willa Cather's novel set in the American Southwest during the 1850s. (Use with Section 3.)

2. Eyewitness Account "Trapped in the Sierra Nevada," an excerpt from the diary of one of the Donner party survivors. (Use with Section 1.)

Writing Actively

Responding to Art Have students examine the painting on this page and read the caption. Ask what year the painting shows. *(1849)* Then read students the following quotation from the diary of Sarah White Smith, a missionary who traveled west in 1838: "The soil I judge to be very fertile, but the people poor & indolent. The buildings look bad & the door yards converted into barn yards. I do not see what could induce any one to leave the refined society of New England for a residence among such a people, unless it be to do them good." Have students write a paragraph comparing the town Smith describes with the one shown in the painting. How do they account for the difference? *(Smith was biased.)*

Viewing History ANSWER

People are dressed in Mexican-style clothing. Buildings show the influence of Spanish architecture.

Technology

Videodiscs/Videotapes
Show the *Prentice Hall United States History Video Collection*™ segments for this chapter. The videodisc version has a Spanish track. Press audio until you get the left channel for English or the right channel for Spanish, or use the bar codes in the Guidebook.

AmericanHeritage® History of the United States CD-ROM
- Time Tour: Westward Expansion in An Expanding Nation *(average)*

Section 1 Oregon Country

LESSON PLAN

Objectives

★ Explain how rival claims to Oregon Country developed.
★ Explain how fur trappers and missionaries helped open up the Far West.
★ Identify the hardships that settlers faced.

1 Engage

Warm Up Ask students what they would think if they saw a person on the street wearing an outfit made of animal hides and porcupine quills. Tell them such people, the mountain men who helped to open up the Far West, were seen often in the early 1800s.

Activating Prior Knowledge Write "pioneer" on the chalkboard. Then ask students either to describe their idea of a typical pioneer or to draw a picture of a pioneer.

Reading Actively

Before Reading Ask students to skim the section, looking at the illustrations and reading the headings, and then to write, in two or three sentences, what the section will be about. As they read, have them verify or correct their predictions.

2 Explore

Ask students to read the section and then to draw a rough outline of the U.S. on the chalkboard, one

RESOURCE DIRECTORY

Teaching Resources
Lesson Planner, p. 53

Transparencies
Time Lines
• The United States and the World, 1820–1860, p. E-19

Oregon Country

As You Read

Explore These Questions
- How did rival claims to Oregon Country develop?
- How did fur trappers and missionaries help open up the Far West?
- What hardships did settlers face?

Define
- mountain man
- rendezvous

Identify
- John Jacob Astor
- James Beckwourth
- Marie Dorion
- Marcus and Narcissa Whitman

SETTING the Scene In 1851, Horace Greeley, a New York newspaper editor, published an article titled "To Aspiring Young Men." In it, Greeley offered the following advice:

> "If you have no family or friends to aid you, . . . turn your face to the great West and there build up your home and fortune."

The public soon came to know Greeley's message as a simple, four-word phrase: "Go West, young man." His advice exactly suited the spirit of the times. Thousands of young men—and women—rallied to the cry "Westward Ho!"

The Lure of Oregon

By the 1820s, white settlers had occupied much of the land between the Appalachians and the Mississippi River. Families in search of good farmland continued to move west. Few, however, settled on the Great Plains between the Mississippi and the Rockies. Instead, they went onward to lands in the Far West.

Americans first heard about the area known as Oregon Country in the early 1800s. Oregon Country was the huge area beyond the Rocky Mountains. Today, this land includes Oregon, Washington, Idaho, and parts of Wyoming, Montana, and Canada.

The varied geography of Oregon Country attracted both farmers and trappers. Along the Pacific coast, the soil is fertile. Temperatures are mild all year round and rainfall is plentiful. Early white settlers found fine farmland in the Willamette River valley and the lowlands around Puget Sound.

Farther inland, dense forests covered a coastal mountain range. Beaver and other fur-bearing animals roamed these forests, as well as the Rocky Mountains on the eastern boundary. As a result, trappers flocked to Oregon Country.

Between the coastal mountains and the Rockies is a high plateau. This intermountain region is much drier than the coast and has some desert areas. This region of Oregon had little to attract early settlers.

Competing Claims

In the early 1800s, four countries had claims to Oregon. These countries were the United States, Great Britain, Spain, and Russia. Of course, several Native American groups had lived in Oregon for thousands of years. The land rightfully belonged to them. However, the United States and competing European nations gave little thought to Indian rights.

The United States based its claim to Oregon on several expeditions to the area. For example, Lewis and Clark had journeyed through the area in 1805 and 1806.

The British claim to Oregon dated back to a visit by the English explorer Sir Francis Drake in 1579. Also, Fort Vancouver, built by

★ *Customized Instruction* ★

English Language Learners

Working with consonant blends Students learning English often have difficulty with writing as well as with reading because of basic differences between languages. For example, the consonant blend /st/ does not exist in many Asian languages and does not occur in the final position in Spanish. These ELL students may omit the *t* when writing a word such as *forest* and instead may write *fores*. Have ELL students search the section for words with *-st* endings. They include *west, forest, outpost,* and *breakfast.* Then ask these students to use each word in a sentence. Have students exchange papers and check each other's sentences for spelling and logic. (*average*) ELL the British, was the only permanent outpost in Oregon Country.

In 1818, the United States and Britain reached an agreement. The two countries would occupy Oregon jointly. Citizens of each nation would have equal rights in Oregon. Spain and Russia had few settlers in the area and agreed to drop their claims.

Fur Trappers in the Far West

At first, the few Europeans or Americans who traveled to Oregon Country were mostly fur traders. Since furs could be sold at tremendous profits in China, merchants from New England stopped along the Oregon coast before crossing the Pacific. In fact, so many Yankee traders came to Oregon that, in some areas, the Indian name for a white man was "Boston."

Only a few hardy trappers actually settled in Oregon. These adventurous men hiked through Oregon's vast forests, trapping animals and living off the land. They were known as **mountain men.**

Mountain men won admiration as rugged individualists, people who follow their own independent course in life. Even their colorful appearance set them apart from ordinary society. They wore shirts and trousers made of animal hides and decorated with porcupine quills. Their hair reached to their shoulders. Pistols and tomahawks hung from their belts.

Lives filled with danger

Mountain men could make a small fortune trapping beaver in Rocky Mountain streams. They led dangerous lives, however. The long, cold mountain winters demanded special survival skills. In the thick forests, trappers had to be on the lookout for attacks by bears, wildcats, or other animals.

During the harsh winters, game was scarce. Facing starvation, trappers would eat almost anything. "I have held my hands in an anthill until they were covered with ants, then greedily licked them off," one mountain man recalled.

Trappers often spent winters in Native American villages. They learned many trapping skills from Indians. Many mountain men married Indian women who taught the newcomers how to find their way and survive in the mountains.

Relations with Native Americans were not always friendly, however. Indians, like the Blackfeet, sometimes attacked mountain men who trapped on Indian hunting grounds without permission.

Trading furs

During the fall and spring, mountain men tended their traps. Then in July, they

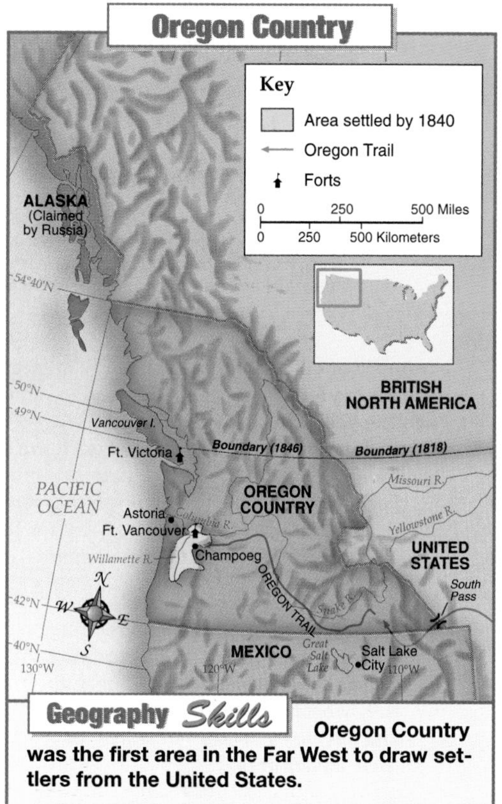

Geography *Skills* **Oregon Country was the first area in the Far West to draw settlers from the United States.**

1. **Location** On the map, locate: **(a)** Oregon Country, **(b)** British North America, **(c)** Willamette River, **(d)** Oregon Trail, **(e)** South Pass.
2. **Region** What line of latitude marked the northern boundary of Oregon Country?
3. **Critical Thinking** Why do you think the Oregon Trail often followed the course of a river?

with a road leading from east to west. Students should place the groups who headed west along the road in the order in which they went: mountain men, missionaries, farmers, other pioneers. Have students research one of the groups and write a brief summary of their findings.

3 Teach

Have students complete the following cause-and-effect statements: **(a)** Because the soil of Oregon Country is fertile, rainfall is plentiful, and the temperatures are mild, . . . **(b)** When fur-bearing animals grew scarce and beaver hats went out of style, . . . **(c)** When the glowing reports of the missionaries of Oregon Country reached Americans, . . .

4 Assess

To close the lesson, have students complete the section review; or have small groups create a short skit illustrating some aspect of the movement west. Give each group an opportunity to perform its skit for the class.

★ ★ ★ ★ ★ ★ ★ ★ ★ ★ ★ ★ ★ ★ ★ ★ ★

Geography *Skills*

ANSWERS **1.** Review map locations with students. **2.** 54°40'N **3.** Possible answers: Rivers provided water for pioneers and their livestock; because rivers west of the Rockies flowed west, they would keep pioneers going in the right direction; and rivers were one of the easiest means of travel at this time.

★ *Background* ★

Our Diverse Nation

Impostors! Native Americans taught the mountain men a biological trick for catching beavers. Beavers secrete a yellow oil called *castorum* from glands under their forelegs. Other beavers are attracted by the scent of the oil. Traps that mountain men baited with castorum lured countless beavers to their death.

During Reading Discuss with students the life of the fur trappers. Ask students to describe the relationship between trappers and Native Americans. Were their interactions generally peaceful or hostile? Have students give evidence from the reading material to support their answers.

Viewing History ANSWER

Trappers often spent winters in Native American villages. Indians taught them many trapping skills and survival methods.

Viewing History **The Fur Trade**

Alfred Miller painted this watercolor, Fort Laramie, *in 1837. Located in present-day Wyoming, Fort Laramie was originally built as a fur-trading post. Once a year, mountain men and Indian trappers gathered at trading posts like this one to sell their furs and have fun.* ★ **How did Native Americans help fur trappers?**

tramped out of the wilderness, ready to meet the fur traders. They headed to a place chosen the year before, called the **rendezvous** (RAHN day voo). Rendezvous is a French word meaning get-together.

For trappers, the first day of the rendezvous was a time to have fun. A visitor to one rendezvous captured the excitement:

> “[They] engaged in contests of skill at running, jumping, wrestling, shooting with the rifle, and running horses. . . . They sang, they laughed, they whooped; they tried to out-brag and out-lie each other in stories of their adventures.”

Soon, though, trappers and traders settled down to bargain. Because beaver hats were in demand in the East and in Europe, mountain men got a good price for their furs. Trading companies did even better. **John Jacob Astor,** a New Yorker, founded the American Fur Company. He made so much money in the fur trade that he became the richest man in the United States.

By the late 1830s, the fur trade was dying out. Trappers had killed so many beavers that the animals had grown scarce. Also, beaver hats went out of style. Even so, the mountain men's skills were still in demand. Some began leading settlers across the rugged trails into Oregon.

Exploring New Lands

In their search for furs, mountain men explored much new territory in the West. They followed Indian trails across the Rockies and through mountain passes. Later, they showed these trails to settlers moving west.

Jedediah Smith led white settlers across the Rockies through South Pass, in present-day Wyoming. Manuel Lisa, a Spanish American fur trader, led a trip up the Missouri River in 1807. He founded Fort Manuel, the first outpost on the upper Missouri.

James Beckwourth, an African American, headed west from Virginia to escape slavery. He was accepted as a chief by the Crow Indians. As a guide, Beckwourth discovered a mountain pass through the

★ *Background* ★

Viewpoints

A woman's view Martha Ann Morrison was 13 years old when she traveled west with her family in 1844. In her memoirs, she suggested that the western journey was harder on women than on men: "Some of the women I saw on the road went through a great deal of suffering and trial. I remember distinctly one girl my own age that died and was buried on the road. Her mother had a great deal of trouble and suffering. It strikes me as I think of it now that Mothers on the road had to undergo more trial and suffering than anybody else."

RESOURCE DIRECTORY

Transparencies
Cause and Effect
• Westward Movement, p. F-19
Geography and History
• Pacific Coast States, p. I-81

Sierra Nevadas that later became a major route to California.

At least one mountain "man" was a woman. **Marie Dorion,** an Iowa Indian, first went to Oregon with fur traders in 1811. She won fame for her survival skills.

Missionaries in Oregon

The first white Americans to build permanent homes in Oregon Country were missionaries. Among them were **Marcus and Narcissa Whitman**. The couple married in 1836 and set out for Oregon, where they planned to convert local Native Americans to Christianity.

The Whitmans built their mission near the Columbia River and began to work with Cayuse (KI oos) Indians. They set up a mission school. Soon, other missionaries and settlers joined the Whitmans. As more settlers arrived and took over Cayuse lands, conflicts arose. Even worse, the newcomers brought diseases that often killed the Indians.

In 1847, tragedy struck. An outbreak of measles among the settlers spread to the Cayuses. Many Cayuse children died. Blaming the settlers, a band of angry Indians attacked the mission, killing the Whitmans and 12 others.

Wagon Trains West

Despite the killing of the Whitmans, other bold pioneers set out on the long trek to Oregon. Missionaries sent back glowing reports about the land. Farmers back East marveled at tales of wheat that grew taller than a man and turnips five feet around. Stories like these touched off an outbreak of "Oregon fever."

Oregon fever spread quickly. Soon, pioneers clogged the trails west. Beginning in 1843, wagon trains left every spring for Oregon. They followed a route called the Oregon Trail. (See the map on page 347.)

Families planning to go west met at Independence, Missouri, in the early spring. When enough families had gathered, they formed a wagon train. Each group elected leaders to make decisions along the way.

The Oregon-bound pioneers hurried to leave Independence in May. Timing was important. Travelers had to reach Oregon by early October, before snow began to fall in the mountains. This meant that pioneers had to cover 2,000 miles (3,200 km) on foot in five months!

Life on the trail

Once on the trail, pioneer families woke to a bugle blast at dawn. Each person had a job to do. Young girls helped their mothers prepare breakfast. Men and boys harnessed the horses and oxen. By 6 A.M., the cry of "Wagons Ho!" rang out across the plains.

Biography **Narcissa Whitman**

Narcissa Prentiss married Marcus Whitman in 1836. They then set out on a seven-month journey to Oregon. When they finally reached the Columbia River valley, she wrote, "The beauty of this extensive valley at the hour of twilight was enchanting and [turned] my mind from the fatigue under which I was laboring."

★ **Why did Narcissa Whitman journey to Oregon?**

China trunk brought to Oregon by eastern pioneers ➤

Writing Actively

After Reading Have students look again at the chapter opening picture, or have them reread the description of pioneers or study the picture that they developed at the beginning of the lesson. Have them write a few sentences answering this question: "After reading to this point in the section, have your ideas changed about pioneers? Explain."

Biography

ANSWER

She and her husband were missionaries who went to Oregon to convert local Native Americans to Christianity.

★ *Background* ★

Recent Scholarship

Children moving west Emmy E. Werner's 1995 book *Pioneer Children on the Journey West* presents primary source materials that tell the stories of 120 pioneer children. A psychologist who has studied contemporary child survivors, Werner focuses on the children's own perceptions of their journeys—"their subjective experience of hardships along the way and how they managed to cope with them." Werner echoes the theme of most of the narratives: "human resilience in the face of great odds."

★ Section 1 Review ★

ANSWERS

1. See map, p. 347.

2. (a) p. 348, **(b)** p. 348, **(c)** p. 349, **(d)** p. 349

3. (a) p. 347, **(b)** p. 348

4. In 1818, both countries agreed to occupy Oregon jointly.

5. (a) for adventure and freedom; to trap animals for fur **(b)** Some mountain men led settlers into Oregon.

6. (a) because missionaries sent encouraging reports of open space and fertile soil **(b)** rain and snowstorms; sickness

7. Possible answers: **(a)** They were strongly independent and had survival skills, such as hunting and trapping. **(b)** Many successful people today are individualists.

8. When beaver hats were popular, mountain men got good prices for their furs. When the hats went out of style, their furs were not in demand—this is one reason fur trading died out.

Activity

Guided Instruction
Ask students to review the hardships faced by travelers. Have students conclude their letters by explaining why they wanted to go west and by reflecting on what they had gained and lost in going.

ASSESSMENT See the rubrics in the Alternative Assessment booklet in the Teaching Resources.

RESOURCE DIRECTORY

Teaching Resources
Lesson Planner, p. 54
Unit 4/Chapter 13
- Biography Flashcard: Stephen F. Austin, p. 17
- Section 1 Quiz, p. 18

Wagon trains stopped for a brief meal at noon. Then it was back on the trail until 6 or 7 P.M. At night, wagons were drawn up in a circle to keep the cattle from wandering.

Most pioneer families set out on the journey west with a lot of heavy gear. When it came time to cross rivers and scale mountains, however, many possessions were left behind to lighten the load. One traveler found the Oregon Trail littered with objects such as "blacksmiths' anvils, ploughs, large grindstones, baking ovens, kegs, barrels, harness [and] clothing."

The long trek west held many dangers. During spring rains, travelers risked their lives floating wagons across swollen rivers. In summer, they faced blistering heat on the treeless plains. Early snowstorms often blocked passes through the mountains.

The biggest threat was sickness. Cholera and other diseases could wipe out whole wagon trains. Because the travelers lived so close together, germs spread quickly.

Trading with Native Americans

As they moved west toward the Rockies, pioneers often saw Indians. The Indians seldom attacked the whites trespassing on their land. A guidebook published in 1845 warned that pioneers had more to fear from their own guns than from Indians: "We very frequently hear of emigrants being killed from the accidental discharge of firearms; but we very seldom hear of their being killed by Indians."

Many Native Americans traded with the wagon trains. Hungry pioneers were grateful for food the Indians sold. A traveler noted:

> "Whenever we camp near any Indian village, we are no sooner stopped than a whole crowd may be seen coming galloping into our camp. The [women] do all the swapping."

Oregon at last!

Despite the many hardships, more than 50,000 people reached Oregon between 1840 and 1860. Their wagon wheels cut so deeply into the plains that the ruts can still be seen today.

By the 1840s, Americans greatly outnumbered the British in parts of Oregon. As you have read, the two nations agreed to occupy Oregon jointly in 1818. Now, many Americans began to feel that Oregon should belong to the United States alone.

★ Section 1 Review ★

Recall

1. **Locate** (a) Oregon Country, (b) Willamette River, (c) South Pass, (d) Oregon Trail.
2. **Identify** (a) John Jacob Astor, (b) James Beckwourth, (c) Marie Dorion, (d) Marcus and Narcissa Whitman.
3. **Define** (a) mountain man, (b) rendezvous.

Comprehension

4. How did the United States and Britain settle their claims to Oregon Country?
5. (a) Why did mountain men first go to Oregon? (b) How did they contribute to later settlement?
6. (a) Why did settlers flock to Oregon after the 1840s? (b) Describe two difficulties along the way.

Critical Thinking and Writing

7. **Linking Past and Present** (a) What qualities helped the mountain men survive in the wilderness? (b) Do you think such qualities are still important today? Explain.
8. **Analyzing Ideas** Economists talk about the "law of supply and demand." It states that when people want a product that is hard to get, the price goes up. How does the Oregon fur trade illustrate the idea of supply and demand?

Activity **Writing a Letter to the Editor** You are one of the young people Horace Greeley told to "go West." You took his advice. Now, write him a letter and tell him what it was like traveling to the West!

★ Activity ★
Cooperative Learning

Creating a memorial Divide the class into groups. Tell students that state officials in Oregon have decided to create a memorial to the pioneers whose long journey west ended in Oregon Country. Each group is to act as the planning board for the proposed memorial and should choose a leader, designers, artists, and writers. The group must first decide on the type of memorial it will build—for example, a mural, a statue, or a garden. Next, each group should write a plan describing the memorial and how it honors the pioneers and the role of the state in the westward movement. A sketch or model of the proposed memorial should accompany each plan. (*average*) ELL

Texas Wins Independence

As You Read

Explore These Questions

- Why did many Americans settle in Texas?
- How did Texas become an independent nation?
- What challenges did the new Republic of Texas face?

Define

- siege
- annex

Identify

- Stephen Austin
- Antonio López de Santa Anna
- Tejanos
- Sam Houston
- Alamo
- William Travis
- Battle of San Jacinto
- Lone Star Republic

SETTING the Scene In late 1835, the word spread: Americans in Texas had rebelled against Mexico! Joseph Barnard, a young doctor, recalled:

> "I was at Chicago, Illinois, practicing medicine, when the news of the Texan revolt from Mexico reached our ears.... They were in arms for a cause that I had always been taught to consider sacred,... Republican principles and popular institutions."

Along with hundreds of other Americans, Dr. Barnard made his way to Texas. Their fight led to the creation of a new nation.

Americans in Mexican Texas

Since the early 1800s, American farmers, especially from the South, had looked eagerly at the vast region called Texas. At the time, Texas was part of the Spanish colony of Mexico.

At first, Spain refused to let Americans move into the region. Then in 1821, Spain gave Moses Austin a land grant in Texas. Austin died before he could set up a colony. His son Stephen took over the project.

Meanwhile, Mexico won its independence from Spain. The new nation let **Stephen Austin** lead settlers into Texas. Only about 4,000 Mexicans lived there. Mexico hoped that the Americans would help develop the area and control Indian attacks.

This seal from Mexican Texas shows an eagle, serpent, and cactus—symbols of Mexico.

Mexico gave each settler a large grant of land. In 1821, Austin and 300 families moved to Texas. Many of these newcomers were slaveowners who brought their slaves with them. Under Austin's leadership, the colony grew rapidly. By 1830, about 20,000 Americans had resettled in Texas.

Conflict With Mexico

In return for land, Austin and the original settlers agreed to become citizens of Mexico and worship in the Roman Catholic Church. However, later American settlers felt no loyalty to Mexico. They spoke only a few words of Spanish. Also, most of the Americans were Protestants. Conflict soon erupted with the Mexican government.

Mexico enforces its laws

In 1830, Mexico forbade any more Americans to move to Texas. Mexico feared that the Americans wanted to make Texas part of

★ Background ★

Did You Know?

Exodus to Texas By 1830, more than 20,000 white Americans had migrated to Texas. That number increased throughout the 1830s and 1840s. The letters "G.T.T." scrawled on the walls of abandoned cabins in the southern United States became a familiar sight. They stood for "Gone to Texas."

Section 2 Texas Wins Independence

LESSON PLAN

Objectives

★ Explain why many Americans settled in Texas.

★ Describe how Texas became an independent nation.

★ Identify the challenges faced by the new Republic of Texas.

1 Engage

Warm Up Ask students what would happen in a game that pitted 6 players against 18 players. Explain that these were the odds during one battle of the Texas war for independence.

Activating Prior Knowledge Ask which European country first sent explorers to the Southwest. Discuss Spanish influence in this region and remind students that Mexico fought for its independence from Spain.

Reading Actively

Before Reading Tell students they will be making a cause-and-effect chart, "Texas Declares Independence." As they read the section, they should identify information to be included on the chart.

2 Explore

Ask students to read the section. For homework, have them research Santa Anna and write a paragraph on why his rise to power spurred Texans to act against Mexico.

3 Teach

Have students create a vertical time line. The dates should run down the middle of the time line in 5-year increments—from 1820 to 1840. Down the left side of the time line, students should list key events from the section and the date on which they occurred. Down the right side of the time line, students should list key people associated with each event, if any.

4 Assess

To close the lesson, have students complete the section review. As an alternative, divide the class into two teams. Give each team 10 minutes to write several quiz questions about the section content. Then have the teams take turns asking each other the questions. For each correct answer, the team receives one of the letters in "TEXAS." For each wrong answer, it loses a letter. The first team to spell "TEXAS" wins.

★ ★ ★ ★ ★ ★ ★ ★ ★ ★ ★ ★ ★ ★ ★ ★ ★

Geography Skills

ANSWERS **1.** Review map locations with students. **2. (a)** at San Antonio **(b)** Texan forces swung north and east, while Mexican forces went south and east. They met and fought a battle at Gonzales. From there, Houston's forces and Mexican forces marched east, where they fought again at San Jacinto. **3.** The Republic of Texas is incorporated into the much larger Texas of today.

RESOURCE DIRECTORY

Teaching Resources
Why Study History?
- History Is All Around You, pp. 51–54

Transparencies
Fine Art
- Dancing on the Veranda, p. D-39

Independence for Texas

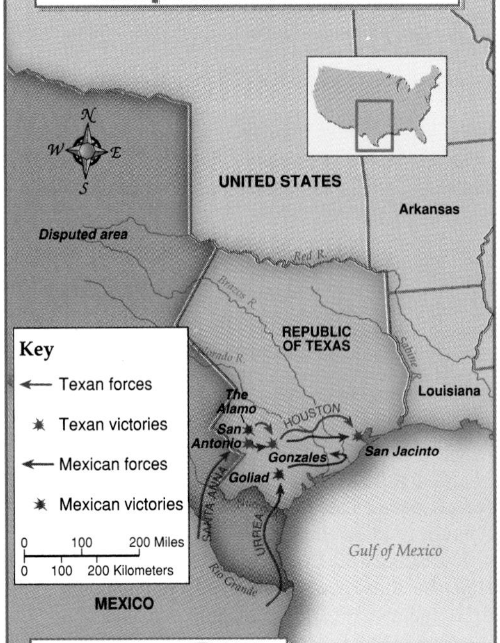

Geography Skills **After a brief but bloody war, Texas gained its independence from Mexico.**

1. **Location** On the map, locate: **(a)** Rio Grande, **(b)** Nueces River, **(c)** Gonzales, **(d)** San Antonio, **(e)** the Alamo, **(f)** Goliad, **(g)** San Jacinto.
2. **Movement** **(a)** Where did Santa Anna's army first fight the Texans? **(b)** Describe the movement of Mexican and Texan forces after the Alamo.
3. **Critical Thinking** Refer to the map of the United States in the Reference Section. How do the boundaries of the Republic of Texas compare with the boundaries of Texas?

the United States. Mexico had some reason for this fear. The United States had already tried twice to buy Texas.

Mexico also decided to make Texans obey Mexican laws that they had ignored for years. One was the law requiring Texans to worship in the Catholic Church. Another law banned slavery in Texas. Texans resented the laws and the Mexican troops who came north to enforce them.

In 1833, General **Antonio López de Santa Anna** came to power in Mexico. Two years later, he threw out the Mexican constitution. Rumors spread that Santa Anna intended to drive all Americans out of Texas.

Texans take action

Texans felt that the time had come for action. In this, they had the support of many **Tejanos** (teh HAH nohs), Mexicans who lived in Texas. Tejanos did not necessarily want independence from Mexico. However, they did want to be rid of Santa Anna, who ruled as a military dictator.

In October 1835, Texans in the town of Gonzales (gahn ZAH lehs) clashed with Mexican troops. The Texans forced the Mexicans to withdraw. Inspired by the victory, Stephen Austin vowed to "see Texas forever free from Mexican domination." Two months later, Texans stormed and took San Antonio. Determined to stamp out the rebellion, Santa Anna marched north with a large army.

While Santa Anna assembled his troops, Texans declared independence on March 2, 1836. They set up a new nation called the Republic of Texas and appointed **Sam Houston** commander of the army. Volunteers of many nationalities, as well as African Americans and Tejanos, joined the fight for Texan independence from Mexico.

Siege at the Alamo

By the time Santa Anna arrived in San Antonio, many of the Texans who had taken the city had drifted away. Fewer than 200 Texans remained as defenders.

In spite of the tremendous odds against them, the Texans refused to give up. Instead, they retired to an old Spanish mission called the **Alamo.**

Against tremendous odds

Texans who gathered in the Alamo in the winter of 1835–1836 were poorly equipped for a battle. Supplies of ammunition and medicine were low. Food consisted of some beef and corn, and access to water was limited. Worst of all, there were only about 150

★ Activity ★
Connections With Geography

Comparing size Have students use a U.S. map to trace the outline of the original 13 colonies on paper. Have them cut out the colonies, place them over Texas on the same map, and compare their sizes. How do students think its size might have affected American attitudes toward Texas in the 1830s? (*basic*) ELL

★ Background ★
Turning Points

Fateful decision The battle at the Alamo almost never happened. In 1836, realizing that the Alamo would be almost impossible to defend, Sam Houston ordered Jim Bowie to ride there and blow up the mission. Rather than follow orders, Bowie and his companions made the fateful—and fatal—decision to hold the fort against the attackers.

Why Study History?

Because History Is All Around You

Historical Background

Did you know that we almost lost the Alamo? After 1836, it was used as an army supply depot, a warehouse, and a general store. For a time, its neighbors included a beer garden and a meat market. In 1903, there was even talk that it might be turned into a hotel.

Then, the Daughters of the Republic of Texas stepped in. They urged the state government to save the Alamo from destruction. Adina De Zavala gained public attention by barricading herself inside the old mission. In 1905, the state of Texas entrusted the Alamo to the Daughters of the Republic.

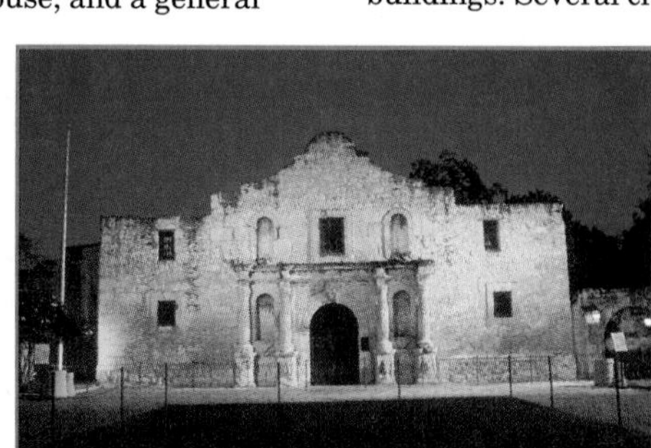

The Alamo

Connections to Today

Each year, thousands of tourists visit the Alamo. They walk the same ground where Texans fought for independence.

Throughout the nation, government and citizens work to save and restore important historic sites. Federal laws protect a variety of places, including ruins of Native American towns, homes of famous Americans, and even old factories. The National Trust for Historic Preservation, a nonprofit educational group, helps people to acquire and preserve historic properties.

Today, ordinary people are restoring and living in historic buildings. Some have transformed old train stations, schools, or factories into restaurants, shops, or apartment buildings. Several cities have revitalized old run-down neighborhoods and warehouse districts. These historic areas attract new businesses and residents.

Connections to You

History is all around you. It is there for you to visit and explore. Check out the *National Register of Historic Places* in your local library. It lists thousands of places and structures that have played a role in your nation's history. To find out how you can help preserve American history, contact your local historical society or the National Trust for Historic Preservation.

1. **Comprehension** What have ordinary citizens and local government done to save important historic sites?
2. **Critical Thinking** How can visiting an historic site be more interesting and informative than reading about it?

Visiting an Historic Site Visit a nearby historic site. In a brief presentation, explain the site's importance and describe how it has been preserved and restored.

Fast Facts

★ The National Register of Historic Places lists more than 66,000 historic places and areas in the United States.

★ In 1961, Jacqueline Kennedy, wife of President John F. Kennedy, formed a committee to restore the interior of the White House to reflect its historic significance. Private citizens donated the needed funds for the refurbishing.

★ In 1995, Texans began a major effort to preserve the Alamo church.

Bibliography

To read more about this topic:

1. *Historic Places of Early America*, David M. Brownstone (Atheneum, 1989). Tours 41 historic sites throughout North America.
2. *The Alamo in American History*, Roy Sorrels (Enslow, 1996). Describes events before, during, and after the battle.
3. **Internet.** An illustrated history of the Alamo: www.drtl.org/webchro1.html.

Why Study History?

ANSWERS

1. People are restoring historic buildings and turning them into homes, shops, and museums.

2. Possible answer: At historic sites, visitors can see—and sometimes touch—buildings and artifacts that make the related historic events more real and understandable.

Guided Instruction
Have students brainstorm for a list of historic sites in your vicinity. If a site has not been restored, students might describe plans and reasons for preserving a favorite place.

ASSESSMENT See the rubrics in the Alternative Assessment booklet in the Teaching Resources.

Reading Actively

During Reading Have students use what they know about the situation of the defenders of the Alamo—as well as all of the information available in the section to this point—to predict the outcome of the battle.

Technology

Videodiscs/Videotapes
Prentice Hall United States History Video Collection™, Vol. 6, Ch. 28, "The Southern Frontier," 2 mins (average) ELL

Chapter 28

AmericanHeritage® History of the United States CD-ROM
• History Makers: Sam Houston (average)

Viewing History ANSWER

It was the last battle of the war. Outnumbered Texans defeated the Mexicans. Santa Anna was captured and forced to sign a treaty granting Texas its independence.

Writing Actively

After Reading Have students complete their cause-and-effect charts, Texas Declares Independence, based on the information they identified while reading the section.

▲ Republic of Texas flag

Viewing History **Winning Texas Independence**

Sam Houston was wounded in the leg during the Battle of San Jacinto. Despite tremendous pain and a boot full of blood, Houston fought on to victory. This painting shows Houston accepting the surrender of Mexican commander Santa Anna.

★ **Why was San Jacinto a turning point in Texas history?**

Texans to defend the Alamo against 6,000 Mexican troops!

Young **William Travis** commanded the Texans inside the mission. Among the volunteers were the famous frontiersmen Jim Bowie and Davy Crockett. Several Tejano families, two Texan women, and two young male slaves were also present.

"Victory or Death!"

On February 23, 1836, Mexican troops began a siege of the Alamo. In a **siege**, enemy forces try to capture a city or fort, usually by surrounding and bombarding it. The Texan defenders fought bravely. Still, Travis knew that unless he received help, he and his troops were doomed. He sent a messenger through the Mexican lines with a letter addressed "to the People of Texas and all the Americans in the World":

> "The enemy have demanded a surrender. . . . I have answered the demand with a cannon shot and our flag still waves proudly from the walls.
>
> *I shall never surrender or retreat.*
>
> I call on you in the name of Liberty, of patriotism, and of everything dear to the American character to come to our aid with all dispatch. . . . *Victory or Death!*"

Travis also sent scouts to seek additional soldiers and provisions. About 40 men were able to sneak through enemy lines and join the fighters in the Alamo. However, no large force ever arrived.

For 12 days, the defenders held off Mexican bombardment. Then, at dawn on March 6, Mexican cannon fire broke through the Alamo walls. Thousands of Mexican soldiers poured into the mission. When the bodies were counted, 183 Texans and almost 1,500 Mexicans lay dead. The Texan survivors, including Davy Crockett, were executed.

Connections With Geography

Santa Anna crossed the Rio Grande on February 16, 1836, in the middle of a harsh Texas winter. Many of the army's cattle died from the brutal cold and inadequate grazing land. For the final thirty days before reaching the Alamo, soldiers ate only eight ounces of corn cake per day.

★ Background ★
Did You Know?

Warning message About 15 people, mostly women and children, were allowed to live when the Alamo was taken. Three Americans were among them: Susanna Dickinson, her 15-month-old baby, and William Travis's slave. Santa Anna sent these Americans to tell their tale to Sam Houston as a warning against further resistance.

Resource Directory

Unit 4/Chapter 13
- Section 2 Quiz, p. 19

Texan Independence

The fall of the Alamo set off cries for revenge. The fury of the Texans grew even stronger three weeks later, when Mexican forces killed several hundred Texan soldiers at Goliad after they had surrendered. Volunteers flooded into Sam Houston's army. Men from the United States also raced south to help the Texan cause.

On April 21, 1836, Houston decided that the moment had come to attack. Santa Anna was camped with his army near the San Jacinto (jah SEEN toh) River. With cries of "Remember the Alamo!" the Texans charged the surprised Mexicans.

The **Battle of San Jacinto** lasted only 18 minutes. Although they were outnumbered, Texans killed 630 Mexicans and captured 700 more. The following day, Texans captured Santa Anna himself. They forced the general to sign a treaty granting Texas its independence.

The Lone Star Republic

In battle, Texans had carried a flag with a single white star. After winning independence, they nicknamed their nation the **Lone Star Republic.** They drew up a constitution based on the Constitution of the United States and elected Sam Houston as their president.

The new country faced several problems. First, Mexico refused to accept the treaty signed by Santa Anna. Mexicans still claimed Texas as part of their country. Second, Texas was nearly bankrupt. Most Texans thought that the best way to solve both problems was for Texas to become part of the United States.

In the United States, Americans were divided about whether to **annex**, or add on, Texas. Most white southerners were in favor of the idea. Many northerners, however, were against it. At issue was slavery.

In the 1830s, antislavery feelings were growing in the North. Because many Texans owned slaves, northerners did not want to allow Texas to join the Union. President Andrew Jackson also worried that annexing Texas would lead to war with Mexico. As a result, Congress refused to annex Texas.

Over the next 10 years, the Lone Star Republic prospered under Houston's leadership. During the Panic of 1837, thousands of Americans moved to Texas to find land and start businesses. Settlers from Germany and Switzerland also swelled the population. By the 1840s, there were about 140,000 people in Texas, including many Mexicans and African Americans.

★ Section 2 Review ★

Recall

1. **Locate** (a) Mexico, (b) Gonzales, (c) Goliad, (d) Republic of Texas.
2. **Identify** (a) Stephen Austin, (b) Antonio López de Santa Anna, (c) Tejanos, (d) Sam Houston, (e) Alamo, (f) William Travis, (g) Battle of San Jacinto, (h) Lone Star Republic.
3. **Define** (a) siege, (b) annex.

Comprehension

4. Why did Mexico encourage Americans to move to Texas?
5. (a) Why did Texans seek independence from Mexico? (b) How did they finally achieve their goal?
6. Why did northerners and southerners disagree about annexing Texas?

Critical Thinking and Writing

7. **Drawing Conclusions** Why was the fall of the Alamo both a defeat and a victory for Texans?
8. **Solving Problems** Why do you think many Texans believed that annexation by the United States would help them solve their problems?

Activity **Writing an Appeal** You are trapped in the Alamo with the rebel Texans and Tejanos. Write an appeal to people in the United States to come help you—make it quick!

★ Section 2 Review ★

ANSWERS

1. See map, p. 352.
2. (a) p. 351, (b) p. 352, (c) p. 352, (d) p. 352, (e) p. 352, (f) p. 354, (g) p. 355, (h) p. 355
3. (a) p. 354, (b) p. 355
4. It hoped they would develop the area and control Indian attacks.
5. (a) They resented the ban on slavery, the law forcing them to worship as Catholics, and the Mexican troops who enforced the laws. (b) Following several clashes, Texans finally defeated the Mexicans at the Battle of San Jacinto.
6. Many Texans owned slaves, so southerners favored annexation; but many northerners opposed slavery, so they opposed annexation.
7. Defeat: They lost the battle. Victory: Inspired to continue the fight, they eventually won independence.
8. Possible answer: They knew they needed the support of the U.S. both to remain free of Mexico and to help them solve their financial woes.

Guided Instruction
Have students brainstorm themes of such a letter—the defenders' patriotism, the great odds against them. Tell students to include facts that tell readers *who, what, when, where, how,* and *why.*

ASSESSMENT See the rubrics in the Alternative Assessment booklet in the Teaching Resources.

★ Customized Instruction ★

Introverted Learners

Creating a help-wanted advertisement
Have introverted learners create a short help-wanted advertisement for people who are willing to join in the Texans' fight for independence. The advertisement should briefly describe the necessary qualifications and the potential rewards for becoming a soldier for the Republic of Texas. Students might include a map, drawing, or decorative border to give the advertisement some visual appeal. To make the activity more challenging, limit the advertisement copy to three or four lines. Post the finished advertisements on a class bulletin board. (*average*)

Section 3

California and the Southwest

LESSON PLAN

Objectives

★ List the reasons the first white settlers came to New Mexico.
★ Describe what California life was like for Native Americans.
★ Explain why Americans wanted their nation to expand to the Pacific Ocean.

1 Engage

Warm Up Write the terms *America* and *United States* on the chalkboard. Ask students if they are synonymous. Help students see that *America* defines an area larger than the United States.

Activating Prior Knowledge Give students 3 minutes to write down words that describe some aspect of California and the Southwest. Discuss the lists.

Reading Actively

Before Reading Have students look for information in the section on why the U.S. wanted to control California and the Southwest.

2 Explore

Have students read the section. Then explain that overland trails were not the only way to reach California. The first pioneers, white traders, came by boat and exchanged goods for products made on California's cattle ranches,

RESOURCE DIRECTORY

Teaching Resources
Lesson Planner, p. 55
Unit 4/Chapter 13
• Connecting History and Literature: A Frontier Lady, p. 16

California and the Southwest

As You Read

Explore These Questions
- What brought the first white settlers to New Mexico?
- What was life like for Native Americans in California?
- Why did Americans want to expand to the Pacific Ocean?

Identify
- New Mexico Territory
- William Becknell
- Santa Fe Trail
- Junípero Serra
- Manifest Destiny
- James K. Polk

SETTING the Scene In 1819, John Quincy Adams made a bold claim. The world, he said, would have to accept the fact that the United States would one day possess all of North America:

> "From the time we became an independent nation, it was as much a law of nature that this would become our claim as that the Mississippi should flow to the sea."

By the 1840s, many Americans agreed. They, too, believed that it was the mission of the United States to expand all the way to the Pacific Ocean. Americans began to look with interest to the vast, rich lands of California and the Southwest.

New Mexico Territory

The entire Southwest belonged to Mexico in the 1840s. This huge region was called **New Mexico Territory.** It included most of the present-day states of Arizona and New Mexico, all of Nevada and Utah, and parts of Colorado.

Much of the Southwest is hot and dry. In some areas, thick grasses grow. There are also desert and mountain areas. Before the Spanish arrived, Zuñi Indians irrigated and farmed the land. Other Native Americans, such as the Apaches, lived by hunting.

A Spanish explorer, Juan de Oñate, had claimed the territory of New Mexico for Spain in 1598. In the early 1600s, the Spanish built Santa Fe as the capital of the territory. Under the Spanish, Santa Fe grew into a busy trading town. However, Spain refused to let Americans settle in New Mexico. Only after Mexico won its independence in 1821 were Americans welcome in Santa Fe.

William Becknell, a merchant and adventurer, was the first American to head for Santa Fe. In 1821, Becknell led a group of traders from Franklin, Missouri, across the plains. When they reached Santa Fe, they found Mexicans eager to buy their cloth and other goods. Other Americans soon followed Becknell's route. It became known as the **Santa Fe Trail.** (See the map on page 366.)

Early Years in California

California, too, belonged to Mexico in the early 1840s. Spain had claimed the region 65 years before English colonists settled in Jamestown. In the years that followed, Spanish and Native American cultures shaped life in California.

Land and climate

California is a land of dramatic contrasts. Two tall mountain ranges slice through the region. One range hugs the coast. The other sits inland on the border of Nevada and Arizona. Between these two ranges is California's fertile Central Valley.

Northern California receives plenty of rain. In the south, though, water is scarce and much of the land is desert. California enjoys mild temperatures all year, except for areas high in the mountains.

★ *Activity* ★

Connections With Arts

Making a 3-D model Have students use a newspaper cut in strips and flour-and-water paste to create a three-dimensional map of California and the Southwest. Students may also create a model of a mission, using outside references for details. When finished, students can paint their models in appropriate colors. (*basic*) ELL T

★ *Background* ★

Did You Know?

Survival tale On Becknell's second trip to Santa Fe, his group blundered into the desert and ran out of water. Desperate, they drank blood from their mules. They were saved when they killed a stray buffalo and drank the liquids from its stomach. The strongest were then able to reach the Cimarron River and to return with water.

AmericanHeritage
M A G A Z I N E

HISTORY HAPPENED HERE

Mission San Juan Capistrano

In 1776, Father Junípero Serra founded Mission San Juan Capistrano in southern California. Today, you can still walk among its adobe walls, enjoy its peaceful gardens, and listen to its old bells. These mission bells told the priests and Native Americans who lived there when to wake up, when to eat, when to pray, when to work, and when to go to bed.

★ ***To learn more about this historic site, write:*** *Mission San Juan Capistrano, P.O. Box 697, San Juan Capistrano, CA 92693.*

◄ *Mission bells*

A string of missions

As you have read, Spanish soldiers and priests built the first European settlements in California. In 1769, Captain Gaspar de Portolá led a group of soldiers and missionaries up the Pacific coast. The chief missionary was Father **Junípero Serra** (hoo NEE peh roh SEHR rah). Father Serra built his first mission at San Diego. He went on to build eight others.

Eventually, there were 21 Spanish missions along the California coast. Each mission claimed the surrounding land and soon was able to take care of all its own needs. Spanish soldiers built forts near the missions. The missions supplied meat, grain, and other foods to the forts.

Mission life for Native Americans

California Indians lived in small, scattered groups rather than large, organized nations. As a result, they were not able to offer much organized resistance to soldiers who forced them to work for the missions.

Native Americans herded sheep and cattle and raised crops for the missions. In return, they lived at the missions and learned about the Roman Catholic religion. Many Spanish missionaries were truly concerned with converting the Indians to Christianity. However, mission life was hard. Thousands of Native Americans died from overwork and diseases.

Sometimes, Indians did resist mission life. Many were baptized as Christians but continued to follow their traditional beliefs. Others simply ran away. Still, most continued to live and labor at the missions.

After Mexico won its independence, conditions for Native Americans in California grew even worse. The new Mexican government offered mission land to ranchers. On some ranches, Indians faced cruel mistreatment. If they tried to run away, the ranchers hunted them down. An American observer reported that California Indians lived in a state "even more degrading, and more oppressive than that of our slaves in the South."

including tallow for candles and animal hides for shoes. Students can read more about California's past in Richard Henry Dana's classic *Two Years Before the Mast.*

3 Teach

Have students work in small groups to research one of these people: William Becknell, Father Junípero Serra, a California Indian, James K. Polk. Groups should use the section and additional research to prepare a 3-minute oral summary about the person's background, connection to the section content, and personal details.

4 Assess

To close the lesson, have students complete the section review. As an alternative, ask students to identify which term in the following sets does not belong. Then have students explain how the other three terms are related.
(a) California/valley/ocean/annex *(annex)*; **(b)** Spanish/New Mexico/Henry Clay/Santa Fe *(Henry Clay)*; **(c)** San Diego/Arizona/mission/Father Junípero Serra *(Arizona)*; **(d)** missions/merchant/Santa Fe Trail/William Becknell *(missions)*; **(e)** James K. Polk/national pride/expansion/Henry Clay *(Henry Clay)*

★ ★ ★ ★ ★ ★ ★ ★ ★ ★ ★ ★ ★ ★ ★ ★ ★ ★

AmericanHeritage
M A G A Z I N E

Mission San Juan Capistrano
To learn more about Mission San Juan Capistrano on the Internet, go to sanjuancapistrano.com/MissionSJC/.

Internet Activity

Tours on-line Have students explore the Internet for national, state, or local historic sites. They can use terms such as *historic site* and *memorial,* or they might go to the National Park Service home page (http://www.nps.gov) or the Historical Society page (http://www2.cybernex.net/~manty). Given the changing nature of the Internet, you may wish to preview this site. (*average*)

PRACTICE the Skill
ANSWERS

1. Facts: Southern California stretches from 21°N to 33°N latitude. It consists of mountains and deserts. Northern California has forests and lakes. They are facts because they can be measured and observed.

2. (a) "We . . . regard it as extremely desirable . . ." **(b)** "as sterile and hopelessly desolate" and "best portion of the province . . . one of the most beautiful regions on the face of the earth . . ."

3. Possible answer: He describes the wonderful environment of California and mentions the natural resources and great agricultural wealth. These qualities would make California a desirable addition to the United States.

APPLY the Skill
Guided Instruction

Be sure students can distinguish facts from opinions before beginning the activity. Have students consult editorials and reviews in newspapers. Ask students to describe facts that could be added to the article to back up any unsupported opinion.

ASSESSMENT See the rubrics in the Alternative Assessment booklet in the Teaching Resources.

RESOURCE DIRECTORY

Teaching Resources
Unit 4/Chapter 13
• Section 3 Quiz, p. 20

Skills FOR LIFE

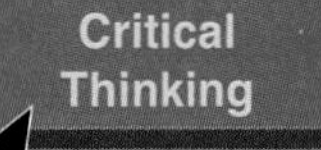

Managing Information | Communication | Maps, Charts, and Graphs

Distinguishing Fact From Opinion

How Will I Use This Skill?

A fact is a statement that can be observed or proven. An opinion is a judgment that reflects a person's beliefs or feelings. To get a true picture of events, even in everyday conversation, you must be able to distinguish between facts and personal opinions.

LEARN the Skill

To tell fact from opinion, follow these steps:

1. Identify facts. Look at each phrase or sentence and ask, "Can this be observed or proven?"
2. Identify words that express the writer's opinion. Some opinions are clearly indicated with phrases like "I think," or "In my opinion." Others are not so easy to identify. Watch for words that express or inspire emotion.
3. Decide whether the facts can support the writer's opinions. (Remember, this does not mean that you must *agree* with the opinion.)

PRACTICE the Skill

The excerpt to the right is from an 1846 newspaper article urging the United States to gain possession of California.

1. List three facts that are included in this article. What makes them facts?
2. (a) What words show that the first sentence is an opinion? (b) Identify two other opinions expressed in this excerpt.
3. How do the facts presented by the writer support his opinion about gaining California? Give two examples.

We do regard it as extremely desirable that California—a part, at least, of the province known by that name—should become the property of the United States. Lower California, embracing the long, narrow peninsula between the Gulf and the Pacific, stretching from the 21° to 33° latitude, a distance of about 800 miles, is universally represented by travelers as sterile and hopelessly desolate. It consists, indeed, of a chain of volcanic, treeless, barren mountains of rock, broken only by still more dreary plains of sand. It may well, therefore, be left to Mexico.

The remaining part of Upper California—that which lies nearest the Pacific coast—is not only by far the best portion of the province but one of the most beautiful regions on the face of the earth. Among the highlands which enclose this valley are vast forests filled with the loftiest and finest cedars and pines in the world, with every variety of soil, freshwater lakes, and every element of unbounded agricultural wealth, except a good climate.

Source:
Adapted from the *American Review*, January 1846.

APPLY the Skill

Choose an article in your local newspaper that includes opinions. Circle facts and underline opinions. Write a paragraph stating whether you think the facts in the article support the opinion.

These harsh conditions had a deadly effect. From 1770 to 1850, the Native American population of California declined from about 310,000 to 100,000.

Expansion: A Right and a Duty

As late as the mid-1840s, only about 700 people from the United States lived in California. Every year, however, more and more Americans began to look toward the West. The United States government even tried to buy California from Mexico several times. Officials were especially interested in gaining the fine ports at San Francisco and San Diego.

The nation's destiny

Many Americans saw the culture and the democratic government of the United States as the best in the world. They believed that the United States had the right and the duty to spread its rule all the way to the Pacific Ocean.

In the 1840s, a newspaper in New York coined a phrase for this belief. The phrase was **Manifest Destiny.** Manifest means clear or obvious. Destiny means something that is sure to happen. Americans who believed in Manifest Destiny thought that the United States was clearly meant to expand to the Pacific.

Manifest Destiny had another side, too. Many Americans believed that they were superior to Native Americans and Mexicans. For these Americans, racism justified taking over lands belonging to Indians and Mexicans.

Election of 1844

Manifest Destiny played an important part in the election of 1844. The Whigs nominated Henry Clay for President. Clay was a famous and respected national leader. The Democrats chose a little-known candidate, **James K. Polk**.

Voters soon came to know Polk as the candidate who favored expansion. Polk demanded that Texas and Oregon be added to the United States. Clay, on the other hand, opposed the annexation of Texas.

The Democrats made Oregon a special campaign issue. As you read, Britain and the United States held Oregon jointly. Polk demanded the whole region all the way to its northern border at latitude 54°40′N. "Fifty-four forty or fight!" became the Democrats' campaign cry. On election day, Americans showed their support for expansion by choosing Polk as President.

★ Section 3 Review ★

Recall

1. **Locate** **(a)** Sante Fe, **(b)** Santa Fe Trail, **(c)** California, **(d)** San Diego, **(e)** San Francisco.
2. **Identify** **(a)** New Mexico Territory, **(b)** William Becknell, **(c)** Santa Fe Trail, **(d)** Junípero Serra, **(e)** Manifest Destiny, **(f)** James K. Polk.

Comprehension

3. Describe how American settlers first went to New Mexico.
4. How did mission life affect Native Americans?
5. How did belief in Manifest Destiny affect the election of 1844?

Critical Thinking and Writing

6. **Making Inferences** How do you think missionaries justified forcing Indians to live and work on missions?
7. **Analyzing Ideas** "The irresistible army of [American settlers] has begun to pour down upon [California], armed with the plough and the rifle, and marking its trail with schools and colleges, courts and representative halls, mills and meetinghouses." What does this quotation show you about people's belief in the idea of Manifest Destiny?

Activity **Drawing a Political Cartoon** Draw a political cartoon from the point of view of Native Americans about conditions on California missions or ranches before 1845.

★ Section 3 Review ★

ANSWERS

1. See map, p. 366.
2. **(a)** p. 356, **(b)** p. 356, **(c)** p. 356, **(d)** p. 357, **(e)** p. 359, **(f)** p. 359
3. William Becknell led a group of traders from Missouri to trade with the Mexicans. Settlers soon began to use his route.
4. Forced to live and work on mission lands, they were cruelly treated and thousands died.
5. James Polk, who favored expansion, was elected.
6. Possible answer: They felt they were civilizing the Indians.
7. Possible answer: The speaker felt that Americans were bringing improvements to the lands annexed by the United States.

Guided Instruction
Ask students to think about the condition of Native Americans in Spanish California. Remind them to use symbols that are widely understood in their cartoons.

ASSESSMENT See the rubrics in the Alternative Assessment booklet in the Teaching Resources.

After Reading Have students write two or three sentences stating the main ideas of this section.

★ Background ★
Our Diverse Nation

Message lost The superior attitude inherent in the idea of Manifest Destiny caused many people great misery. In 1884, Helen Hunt Jackson published her novel *Ramona,* hoping to stimulate reform of the bad conditions under which many Mexican Americans and Indians were living in southern California. But most readers missed the message and focused on the novel's romantic images of a past era peopled with saintly Spanish missionaries, a kindly gentry, and contented Indians. As a result, the novel is credited with producing a romantic distortion of the era that was widely accepted as true. T

Technology

AmericanHeritage® History of the United States CD-ROM
- Presidents: James K. Polk (average)

Section 4
War With Mexico

LESSON PLAN

Objectives

★ Describe how the United States gained Oregon.
★ Identify the causes and results of the Mexican War.
★ Describe how cultures blended in the new United States territories.

1 Engage

Warm Up Have students find California, New Mexico, Utah, Nevada, Arizona, and Colorado on a map. Tell them that these present-day states all were gained through the Mexican War of 1846–1847.

Activating Prior Knowledge Have students suppose they are whites in Massachusetts in 1845. Ask: "Should the U.S. go to war with Mexico?" Explore other perspectives. Ask: "What if you were a slave or Native American?"

Reading Actively

Before Reading Have students turn the main section headings into the main topics of an outline. Have them record 2 or 3 subtopics for each main topic.

2 Explore

Ask students to read the section. Explain that opinion was divided—some opposed the Mexican War; others wanted to annex *all* of Mexico. Have students research public opinion on the war or the treaty and outline their findings.

RESOURCE DIRECTORY

Teaching Resources
Lesson Planner, p. 56
Document-Based Discovery
• Expansion, pp. 14–17

Transparencies
Geography and History
• South Central States, p. I-69

4 War With Mexico

As You Read

Explore These Questions
- How did the United States gain Oregon?
- What were the causes and results of the Mexican War?
- How did cultures blend in the new American territories?

Define
- cede

Identify
- Zachary Taylor
- Mexican War
- Winfield Scott
- Stephen Kearny
- Bear Flag Republic
- John C. Frémont
- Chapultepec
- Mexican Cession
- Gadsden Purchase

Setting the Scene American troops marched off to war with Mexico in 1846. Many Americans were eager to fight. Soldiers proudly sang new words to the popular tune "Yankee Doodle":

> "They attacked our men upon our land,
> And crossed our river too, sir.
> Now show them all with sword in hand
> What yankee boys can do, sir."

Not all Americans supported the war against Mexico. Some even accused President Polk of provoking the war himself in order to win Texas.

The bloody Mexican War lasted 20 months. In the end, it helped the United States achieve its dream of Manifest Destiny.

Dividing Oregon

James K. Polk took office in March 1845. Acting on his campaign promise, he moved to gain control of Oregon. War with Britain threatened.

Polk did not really want a war with Britain. In 1846, he agreed to a compromise. Oregon was divided at latitude 49°N. Britain got the lands north of the line, and the United States got the lands south of the line. The United States named its portion the Oregon Territory. Later, the states of Oregon (1859), Washington (1889), and Idaho (1890) were carved out of the Oregon Territory.

Annexing Texas

Texas proved a more dangerous problem. As you read, the United States at first refused to annex Texas. In 1844, Sam Houston, president of Texas, signed a treaty of annexation with the United States. The Senate again refused to ratify the treaty. Senators feared that annexing Texas would cause a war with Mexico.

Sam Houston would not give up. To persuade the Americans to annex Texas, he pretended that Texas might become an ally of Britain. Houston's trick worked. Americans did not want Europe's greatest power to gain a foothold on their western border. In 1845, Congress passed a joint resolution admitting Texas to the Union.

Sam Houston

★ Customized Instruction ★
Extroverted Learners

Teaching the class Allow extroverted students who are comfortable speaking before the class to prepare a 10-minute lesson on the section content. Encourage these students to do research in which they look for interesting information about California and the Southwest during the mid-1840s, as well as about the expansionist policies of the United States during this period. Students might prepare handouts for the class or draw maps or other illustrations on the chalkboard to support the lesson. Reserve about half the period to allow each of these students to present the lesson. *(challenging)*

Conflict With Mexico

The annexation of Texas made Mexicans furious. They had never accepted the independence of Texas. They also were concerned that the example set by Texas would encourage Americans in California and New Mexico to rebel.

At the same time, Americans resented Mexico. President Polk offered to pay Mexico $30 million for California and New Mexico. However, Mexico strongly opposed any further loss of territory and refused the offer. Many Americans felt that Mexico stood in the way of Manifest Destiny.

The war begins

A border dispute finally sparked war. The United States claimed that the southern border of Texas was the Rio Grande. Mexico argued that it was the Nueces (noo AY says) River, some 200 miles (320 km) to the north. Both nations claimed the land between the two rivers.

In January 1846, Polk ordered General **Zachary Taylor** to cross the Nueces River and set up posts in the disputed area along the Rio Grande. (See the map below.) Polk knew that the move might lead to war. In April 1846, Mexican troops crossed the Rio

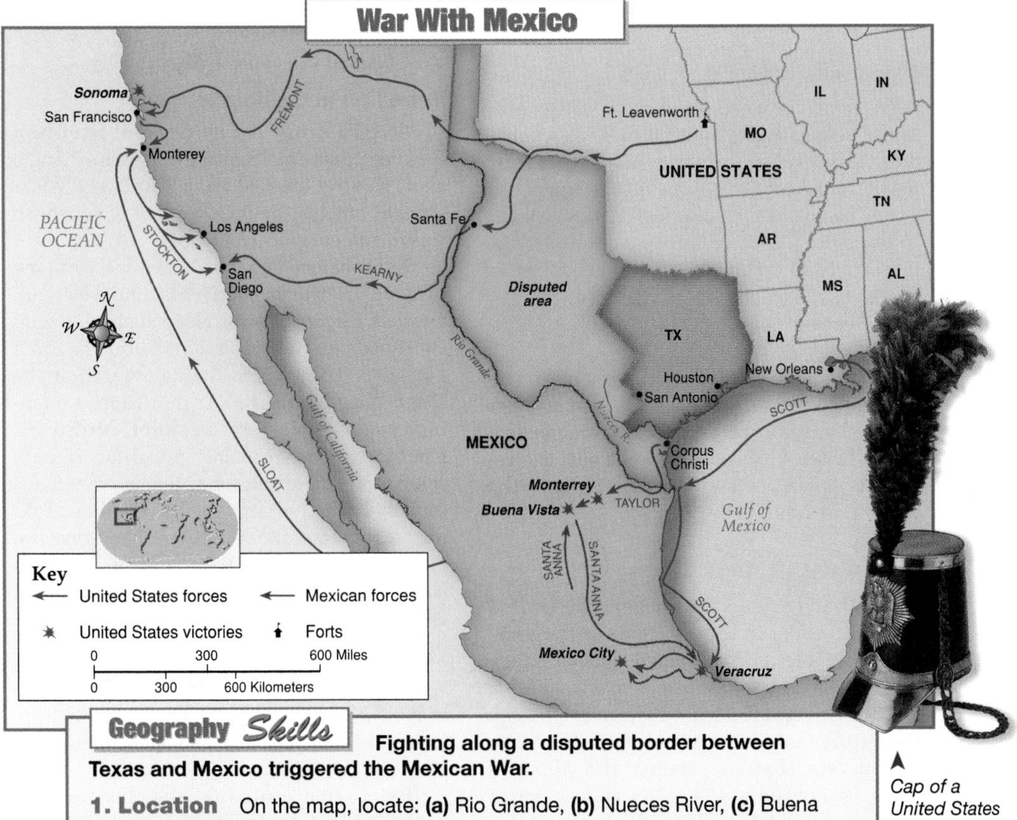

Geography Skills Fighting along a disputed border between Texas and Mexico triggered the Mexican War.

1. **Location** On the map, locate: **(a)** Rio Grande, **(b)** Nueces River, **(c)** Buena Vista, **(d)** Veracruz, **(e)** Mexico City.
2. **Movement** Describe the movements of each of the following American commanders: **(a)** Winfield Scott, **(b)** Stephen Kearny, **(c)** John Frémont.
3. **Critical Thinking** Based on the map, was sea power important to the United States in the Mexican War? Explain.

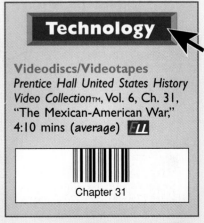

Cap of a United States soldier in the Mexican War

3 Teach

Students should prepare to hold a press conference on the Mexican War. Assign one student to each of these roles: President James K. Polk, Zachary Taylor, Winfield Scott, Stephen Kearny, John Frémont, a Mexican American, or an Indian. The rest of the class can be reporters. The reporters should prepare and ask questions about the events of the Mexican War; key figures should prepare to answer questions in character.

4 Assess

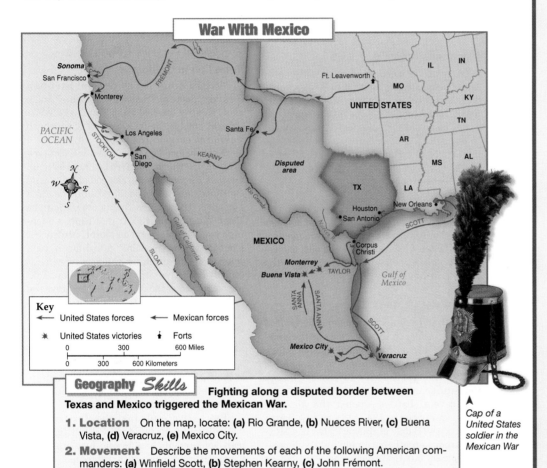

To close the lesson, have students complete the section review. As an alternative, have them write at least one statement to support these generalizations: **(a)** Annexing Texas was costly for the U.S. **(b)** Going to war with Mexico divided Americans. **(c)** U.S. forces waged a quick, successful war against Mexico.

Geography Skills

ANSWERS **1.** Review map locations. **2. (a)** Scott: from New Orleans, across the Gulf of Mexico to the Mexican coast; fought at Veracruz and then moved west toward Mexico City **(b)** Kearny: left Ft. Leavenworth, captured Santa Fe and marched to San Diego **(c)** Frémont: left Ft. Leavenworth, traveled west toward California and attacked San Francisco and Monterey **3.** Yes. Scott attacked Mexico and Sloat and Stockton attacked California by sea.

★ Activity ★
Connections With Geography

Redrawing the map Have students redraw the current map of the U.S. as if the entire area of Oregon Country had become U.S. territory. Ask students to research the major products of this area north of 49°N and to surmise how different the lifestyle of Americans in the northwestern U.S. would be today. (average) ELL T

Technology

Videodiscs/Videotapes
Prentice Hall United States History Video Collection™, Vol. 6, Ch. 31, "The Mexican-American War," 4:10 mins (average) ELL

Chapter 31

Reading Actively

During Reading Have students debate the question: "Who started the Mexican War?" They should use information from the reading to support their position.

Grande and fought briefly with the Americans. Soldiers on both sides were killed.

President Polk was already considering going to war with Mexico. When he heard about the fighting at the Rio Grande, he asked Congress to issue a declaration of war. Polk told Congress:

> "Mexico has passed the boundary of the United States, has invaded our territory, and shed American blood upon American soil."

Not everyone supported Polk's request. Abraham Lincoln, a young Whig Congressman, disputed Polk's claim that the fighting actually took place "upon American soil." Still, at Polk's urging, Congress declared war on Mexico.

Americans respond

Americans were divided over the war. Many people in the South and West wanted more land and so were eager to fight. Many northerners, however, opposed the war. They saw it as a southern plot to add slave states to the Union. "Fresh markets of human beings are to be established," claimed Charles Sumner, a Massachusetts opponent of slavery. "Further opportunities for this hateful traffic are to be opened."

Still, many Americans joined the war effort. Since the nation's standing army was small, thousands of volunteers were needed. When the call for recruits went out, the response was overwhelming, especially in the South and West.

Fighting in Mexico

As the **Mexican War** began, the United States attacked on several fronts at the same time. President Polk hoped this strategy would allow American forces to win a quick victory. General Zachary Taylor crossed the Rio Grande into northern Mexico. There, he won several battles against the Mexican army. In February 1847, Taylor met Santa Anna at the Battle of Buena Vista. The Mexican troops greatly outnumbered the American forces, but the Americans were better armed and led. After fierce fighting, Santa Anna retreated. A major in Taylor's army later recalled feeding wounded Mexican soldiers after the battle:

> "We collected the wounded, who were suffering awfully from hunger and thirst as well as their wounds, and sent them to hospitals in town.... When coffee and biscuit were placed before them, they showed even in their famished state some signs of surprise and gratitude. This was the greatest victory of all, a victory unstained by blood...."

Meanwhile, General **Winfield Scott** had landed another American army at the Mexican port of Veracruz. After a long battle, the Americans took the city. Scott then marched west toward the capital, Mexico City.

Rebellion in California

A third army, led by General **Stephen Kearny**, captured Santa Fe without firing a shot. Kearny hurried on to San Diego. After several battles, he took control of southern California early in 1847.

Even before hearing of the war, Americans in northern California had risen up against Mexican rule. The rebels declared California an independent republic on June 14, 1846. They called their new nation the **Bear Flag Republic.** At that time, a dashing young American explorer, **John C. Frémont,** was traveling in California on a scientific expedition for the army. Frémont quickly rushed to support the rebellion. Taking command of the rebel forces, he drove the Mexican governor's troops out of northern California. Frémont later joined forces with United States troops.

The final battle

By 1847, the United States controlled all of New Mexico and California. Meanwhile, General Scott had reached the outskirts of Mexico City.

Before they could take the Mexican capital, Scott's troops faced a fierce battle. Mexican soldiers made a heroic last stand at **Chapultepec** (chah POOL tuh pehk), a fort just outside Mexico City. Like the Texans who died at the Alamo, the Mexicans at Cha-

Resource Directory

Teaching Resources
Unit 4/Chapter 13
- Practice Your Skills: Distinguishing Fact From Opinion, p. 13
- Critical Thinking and Writing: Drawing Conclusions, p. 14

Transparencies
Geography and History
- Expansion of the United States, p. I-25

FROM THE ARCHIVES OF AmericanHeritage®

Lincoln on the right to rebel In Lincoln's speech against the Mexican War, he argued that if the people in the disputed land had wanted to end Mexico's rule, they did not need the U.S. to help them. They had the right to rebel, he said. Ironically, his words were later used against him by Confederate sympathizers.

Source: Frederic D. Schwarz, "The Time Machine," *American Heritage* magazine, December 1997.

★ Background ★

Turning Points

Training for the Civil War Many historians think of the battlefields of the Mexican War as training grounds for officers who would lead both sides during the Civil War of the 1860s. In addition, the fighting in Mexico laid the foundation for the important role that artillery would play in modern warfare.

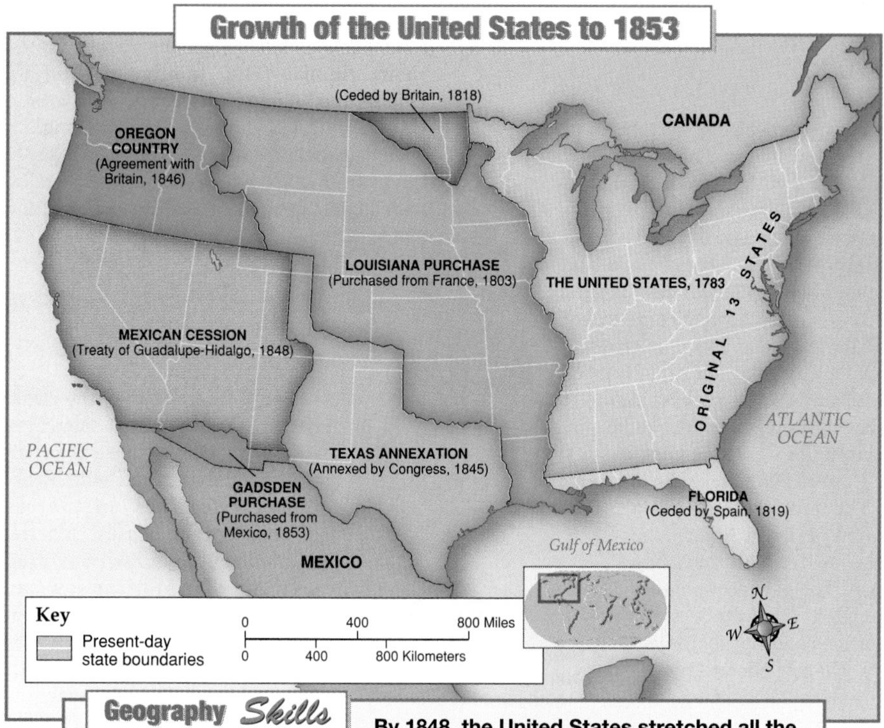

Geography Skills **By 1848, the United States stretched all the way from the Atlantic Ocean to the Pacific Ocean.**

1. **Location** On the map, locate: **(a)** Mexican Cession, **(b)** Gadsden Purchase, **(c)** Oregon Country.
2. **Region** Which of the territories shown on this map did the United States purchase from other nations?
3. **Critical Thinking** Refer to the map of the United States in the Reference Section. **(a)** Is your home state included on the map above? **(b)** If so, when and how did it become part of the United States?

pultepec fought to the last man. Today, Mexicans honor these young soldiers as heroes.

Achieving Manifest Destiny

With their capital in American hands, the Mexican government had no choice but to make peace. In 1848, Mexico signed the Treaty of Guadalupe-Hidalgo (gwah duh LOOP ay-ih DAHL goh). The treaty forced Mexico to **cede,** or give, all of California and New Mexico to the United States. These lands were called the **Mexican Cession.** (See the map above.)

In return, the United States paid Mexico $15 million. Americans also agreed to respect the rights of Spanish-speaking people in the Mexican Cession.

A few years after the end of the Mexican War, the United States completed its expansion across the continent. In 1853, it agreed to pay Mexico $10 million for a strip of land in present-day Arizona and New Mexico. The Americans needed this land to complete the building of a railroad. The land was called the **Gadsden Purchase.** The dream of Manifest Destiny was now complete.

Geography Skills

ANSWERS **1.** Review map locations with students. **2.** Louisiana Purchase from France, Gadsden Purchase from Mexico **3.** Answers will vary. Check students' answers with the map.

Writing Actively

After Reading Have students design a bumper sticker expressing a main idea about the expansion of the United States to the Pacific. The bumper sticker might be humorous or might imply a point of view about expansion.

Skills For LIFE MINI LESSON

MANAGING INFORMATION

Arranging and Understanding Events in Sequence

1. Teach the skill of arranging and understanding events in sequence by presenting these steps to students: Look for and list direct and indirect statements of time, and place events in order from first to last.

2. Have students practice the skill by looking through the section to find out when American and Mexican forces first clashed *(April 1846)* and when General Scott fought a battle in Mexico City *(early 1847)*.

3. Students can apply the skill by reviewing the section and preparing a sequential outline of the events both leading to the war and of the war itself.

★ Section 4 Review ★

ANSWERS

1. See map, p. 361.

2. (a) p. 361, **(b)** p. 362, **(c)** p. 362, **(d)** p. 362, **(e)** p. 362, **(f)** p. 362, **(g)** p. 362, **(h)** p. 363, **(i)** p. 363

3. p. 363

4. He agreed to divide Oregon.

5. (a) a border dispute **(b)** Mexico ceded California and New Mexico for $15 million.

6. (a) how to mine silver and irrigate the soil; Spanish and Indian words **(b)** a tradition of democracy

7. Answers will vary.

8. Possible answers: **(a)** He may have thought it would mean the expansion of slavery into new territory. **(b)** Other abolitionists might have agreed. Believers in Manifest Destiny may not have agreed.

Activity

Guided Instruction
Create a table on the chalkboard. Use the seven roles as headings across the top. Down the side, list three categories: "Attitude Toward the War," "Main Argument," and "Secondary Argument." Students can use the table to help them in their debate.

ASSESSMENT See the rubrics in the Alternative Assessment booklet in the Teaching Resources.

RESOURCE DIRECTORY

Teaching Resources
Lesson Planner, p. 57
Unit 4/Chapter 13
• Section 4 Quiz, p. 21

A Mix of Cultures in the Southwest

English-speaking settlers poured into the Southwest. They brought their own culture with them, including their ideas about democratic government. The newcomers also learned a great deal from the older residents of the region. Mexican Americans taught the newcomers how to mine silver and irrigate the soil for growing crops. Many Spanish and Native American words—such as stampede, buffalo, tortilla, soda, and tornado—became part of the English language.

The new settlers often treated Mexican Americans and Native Americans poorly. The earlier residents struggled to protect their traditions and rights. However, when Mexican Americans went to court to defend their property, judges rarely upheld their claims. The family of Mariano Guadalupe Vallejo (vah YAY hoh) had lived in California for decades before the English-speaking settlers arrived. Vallejo, a wealthy landowner, noted how some new settlers were able to gain control of much of the land:

> "In their dealings with the rancheros, [Americans] took advantage of laws which they understood, but which were new to the Spaniards."

Many Mexican homes in the Southwest contained religious statuettes like this one.

At the same time, Americans in the Southwest kept some Mexican laws. One of these laws said that a husband and wife owned property together. In the rest of the United States, married women could not own any property. Another Mexican law said that landowners could not cut off water to their neighbors. This law was important in the Southwest, where water was scarce.

★ Section 4 Review ★

Recall

1. **Locate** (a) Rio Grande, (b) Nueces River, (c) Buena Vista, (d) Veracruz, (e) Mexico City.
2. **Identify** (a) Zachary Taylor, (b) Mexican War, (c) Winfield Scott, (d) Stephen Kearny, (e) Bear Flag Republic, (f) John C. Frémont, (g) Chapultepec, (h) Mexican Cession, (i) Gadsden Purchase.
3. **Define** cede.

Comprehension

4. How did President Polk avoid war with Britain over Oregon?
5. (a) What event sparked the beginning of the Mexican War? (b) What were the final results of the war?
6. (a) Name two things that English-speaking settlers learned from Mexican Americans in the Southwest. (b) Name one tradition that settlers brought with them.

Critical Thinking and Writing

7. **Identifying Alternatives** Do you think the United States could have avoided going to war with Mexico in 1846? Explain.
8. **Recognizing Points of View** Frederick Douglass, an African American who fought to end slavery, wrote of the Mexican War that Americans "ought [to] blush and hang our heads for shame." (a) Why do you think Douglass opposed the war? (b) Who might have agreed with his statement? Who might have disagreed?

Activity **Roleplaying** With your classmates, choose among the following roles: a citizen of Mexico; a white American living in Texas; a Mexican living in Texas; an American Californian; a northerner; a southerner; President Polk. Hold a debate about whether the United States should go to war with Mexico.

★ *Customized Instruction* ★
English Language Learners

Researching word origins The Spanish-speaking people who lived in the Mexican Cession territory influenced American culture in many ways. Suggest that students learning English do a study of English words with Spanish and/or Native American origins. Have them create mini-dictionaries that list each word, its meaning, and origins. Dictionaries can be written or typed and bound using staples or brads. Encourage students to research and report on the following words: **Spanish:** alligator, arroyo, bonanza, breeze, canyon, cockroach, hoosegow, junta, machete, patio, plaza, savvy, vigilante. **Native American:** caribou, caucus, chipmunk, hickory, mackinaw, moose, opossum, pecan, persimmon, raccoon, skunk, squash, terrapin, toboggan, woodchuck. (*average*) ELL T

A Rush to the West

As You Read

Explore These Questions
- How did the Mormons settle Utah?
- How did the discovery of gold affect life in California?
- Why did California have a diverse population?

Define
- forty-niner
- vigilante

Identify
- Mormons
- Joseph Smith
- Brigham Young
- Sutter's Mill

SETTING the Scene In 1848, exciting news reached Toishan, a district in southern China. Mountains of gold had been discovered across the Pacific Ocean, in a place called California. It was there just for the digging!

The penalty for trying to leave China was harsh and sure—a swift beheading. Still, tens of thousands of Chinese risked the executioner's axe to cross the Pacific. Like other prospectors from Europe to Boston to South America, they were eager to join the California Gold Rush.

Gold was not the only thing that attracted settlers to the West in the mid-1800s. California, New Mexico, Oregon, and Texas were all now part of the United States. Restless pioneers, always eager to try something new, headed into these lands to build homes and a new way of life.

A Refuge for the Mormons

The largest group of settlers to move into the Mexican Cession were the **Mormons.** Mormons belonged to the Church of Jesus Christ of Latter-day Saints. The church was founded by **Joseph Smith** in 1830. Smith, a farmer who lived in upstate New York, attracted many followers.

Troubles with neighbors

Smith was an energetic and popular man. His teachings, however, angered many non-Mormons. For example, Mormons at first believed that property should be owned in common. Smith also said that a man could have more than one wife. Angry neighbors forced the Mormons to leave New York for Ohio. From Ohio, they were forced to move to Missouri, and from there to Illinois. In the 1840s, the Mormons built a community called Nauvoo on the banks of the Mississippi River in Illinois.

Before long, the Mormons again clashed with their neighbors. In 1844, an angry mob killed Joseph Smith. The Mormons chose **Brigham Young** as their new leader.

Brigham Young realized that the Mormons needed to find a home where they would be safe. He had read about a valley between the Rocky Mountains and the Great Salt Lake in Utah. Young decided that the isolated valley would make a good home for the Mormons.

A difficult journey

To move 15,000 men, women, and children from Illinois to Utah in the 1840s was an awesome challenge. Relying on religious faith and careful planning, Brigham Young achieved his goal.

In 1847, Young led an advance party into the Great Salt Lake valley. Wave after wave of Mormons followed. For the next few years, Mormon wagon trains struggled across the plains and over the Rockies to Utah. When they ran short of wagons and oxen, thousands made the long trip pulling their gear in handcarts.

★ Activity ★ Linking Past and Present

Reporting In the spring of 1997, thousands of people, most of them Mormons, embarked on a grueling reenactment of the great Mormon migration of 150 years before. Have students research this event and prepare a news broadcast about it. Suggest they include information on why people participated and how the reenactment differed from the original trip. *(average)* ELL T

Section 5 A Rush to the West

LESSON PLAN

Objectives

★ Describe how the Mormons settled Utah.
★ Describe how the discovery of gold affected life in California.
★ Explain why California had a diverse population.

1 Engage

Warm Up Ask students whether they can think of any event that would cause them to leave their homes and schools and suddenly rush to live in another place. Tell them that many people did just that in the mid-1800s.

Activating Prior Knowledge Ask students how religion and riches motivated Europeans in the 1500s. Then tell students that these same motives led people to move west in the mid-1800s.

Reading Actively

Before Reading Have students preview the words listed in Define and Identify. As they read, have them jot notes on the meaning of the word or term.

2 Explore

Ask students to read the section. For a homework assignment, have them research how the Mormon settlement in Utah affected the mix of peoples in 1850 and in 1896, when it became a state.

3 Teach

Draw a blank chart on the chalkboard with two columns: "Utah" and "California." Label four rows down the side: "Years of American Settlement," "Reasons for Settlement," "Problems Encountered," and "Year of Statehood." Help students complete the chart using information from the text. *(Utah: mid-1800s; religious; harsh climate; 1896. California: mid-1800s; gold; lawlessness and mistreatment of nonwhite groups; 1850)*

4 Assess

To close the lesson, have students complete the section review. As an alternative, have students work in pairs to create a board game dealing with the surge to the West. For example, the game could have an elaborate pathway leading west and ending in a beautiful Salt Lake City and in a pot of gold in California. Along the path, a player might have to go back three spaces for spending an unsuccessful week panning for gold.

★ ★ ★ ★ ★ ★ ★ ★ ★ ★ ★ ★ ★ ★ ★ ★ ★

Geography *Skills*

ANSWERS **1.** Review map locations with students. **2.** California Trail, Old Spanish Trail, Butterfield Overland Mail, Gila River Trail **3. (a)** Oregon Trail to the California Trail to Sutter's Fort **(b)** Rocky Mountains and Sierra Nevada **(c)** Ft. Laramie

Resource Directory

Teaching Resources
Unit 4/Chapter 13
- Map Mystery: California Gold—and Growth, p. 15

Interdisciplinary Connections
- Main Idea: The California Gold Rush, pp. 76–77

Transparencies
Interdisciplinary Connections
- Forty-Niners, p. B-55

Trails to the West

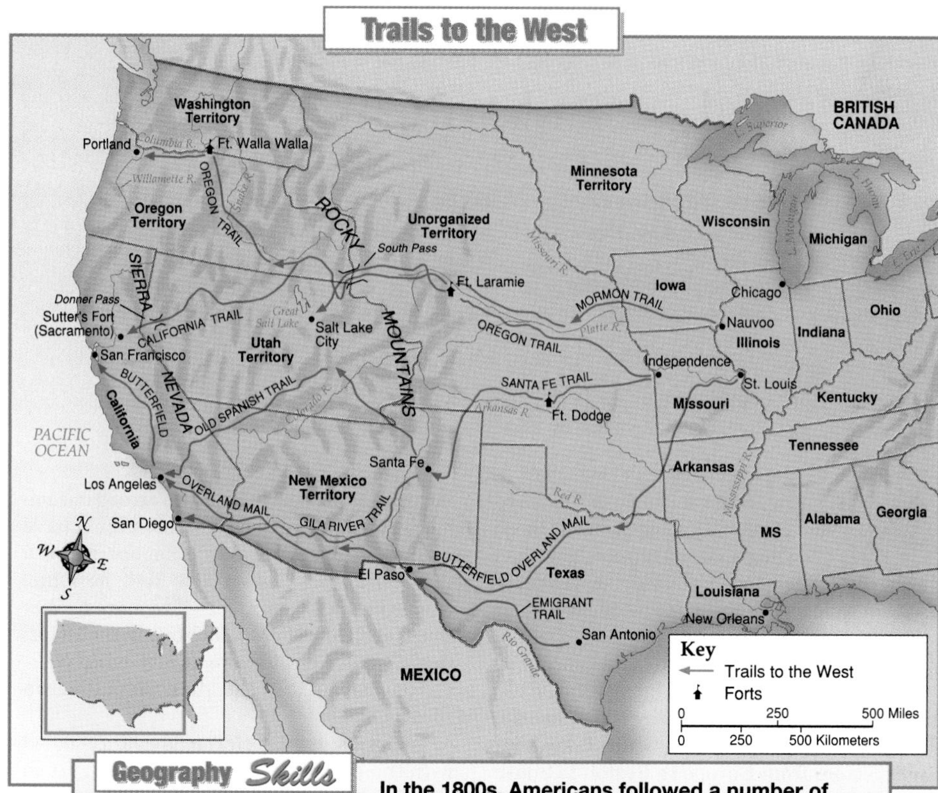

Geography *Skills* **In the 1800s, Americans followed a number of different trails to the West. Mountain passes allowed settlers to cross the Rockies and Sierra Nevada.**

1. **Location** On the map, locate: **(a)** Santa Fe, **(b)** Santa Fe Trail, **(c)** Sierra Nevada, **(d)** Rocky Mountains, **(e)** San Diego, **(f)** San Francisco, **(g)** Salt Lake City.
2. **Movement** Which trails ended in cities in California?
3. **Critical Thinking** **(a)** What would be the best route for a pioneer family to take from Independence, Missouri, to Sutter's Fort, California? **(b)** What mountains would they have to cross? **(c)** In which town might they seek shelter along the way?

Prospering in the desert

In Utah, the Mormons had to survive in a harsh desert climate. Still, Young was convinced that, for the Mormons, Utah was Zion, or the promised land:

> ❝We will raise our wheat, build our houses, fence our farms, plant our vineyards and orchards, and produce everything that will make our bodies comfortable and happy and in this manner we intend to build up Zion on the earth.❞

To meet his goals, Young planned an irrigation system to bring water to farms. He also drew up plans for a large city, called Salt Lake City, to be built in the desert.

The Mormon settlement in Utah grew quickly. Like other whites, Mormons took over thousands of acres of Native American land, usually paying nothing for it.

Congress recognized Brigham Young as governor of the Utah Territory in 1850. Trouble later broke out when non-Mormons moved to the area. In the end, peace was restored, and Utah became a state in 1896.

★ *Background* ★
Did You Know?

Saved by the gulls! Utah's state bird is the sea gull. The reason lies in history. In the late 1840s, Mormon farmers in north-central Utah were plagued by grasshoppers. Complete destruction of the crops seemed inevitable. Then flocks of sea gulls flew in from the Great Salt Lake, devouring the insects and saving the crops. T

★ *Background* ★
Recent Scholarship

Whose frontier? Richard White and Patricia Limerick explore the concept of frontier in their book *The Frontier in American Culture.* They point out that historians and the public often focus on the Anglo-American settlers' side of the frontier, ignoring the perspectives of Native Americans, Hispanic settlers, Mexican immigrants, and Asians.

California Gold Rush

While the Mormons trekked to Utah, thousands of other Americans were racing to California. These adventurous men and women all had a single objective: Gold!

Sutter's Mill

In 1848, John Sutter was building a sawmill on the American River, north of Sacramento, California. James Marshall was in charge of the job. On the morning of January 24, Marshall set out to inspect a ditch his crew was digging. He later told a friend what he saw that day:

> "It was a clear, cold morning; I shall never forget that morning. As I was taking my usual walk, . . . my eye was caught with the glimpse of something shining in the bottom of the ditch. There was about a foot of water running then. I reached my hand down and picked it up; it made my heart thump, for I was certain it was gold."

In a few days, word of the gold strike at **Sutter's Mill** spread to San Francisco. Carpenters threw down their saws. Bakers left bread in their ovens. Schools emptied as teachers and students joined the rush to the gold fields.

From San Francisco, the news spread across the United States and to the rest of the world. Thousands of Americans caught gold fever. People from Europe, China, Australia, and South America joined the rush as well. More than 80,000 people made the long journey to California in 1849. They became known as **forty-niners.**

In the gold fields

The first miners needed little skill. Because the gold was near the surface of the Earth, they could dig it out with knives. Later, the miners found a better way. They loaded sand and gravel from the riverbed into a washing pan. Then, they held the pan under water and swirled it gently. The water washed away lighter gravel, leaving the heavier gold in the pan. This process was known as "panning for gold."

Cause and Effect

Causes

- Oregon has fertile land
- Texas is ideal for raising cattle and growing cotton
- Many Americans believe in Manifest Destiny
- Mormons seek a safe home
- Gold is discovered in California

Westward Movement

Effects

- Texas wins war for independence
- United States annexes Texas
- Britain and United States divide Oregon
- United States defeats Mexico in war
- Cotton Kingdom spreads

Effects Today

- United States stretches from sea to sea
- California and Texas are the most populous states
- Mexican American culture enriches the United States

Graphic Organizer *Skills*

Westward movement increased at a tremendous rate in the mid-1800s.

1. **Comprehension** List two attractions that drew Americans to the West.
2. **Critical Thinking** According to this chart, was Manifest Destiny successful? Explain.

Economics $

Only a few miners actually struck it rich. Most went broke trying to make their fortunes. Still, although many miners left the gold fields, they stayed in California.

Reading Actively

During Reading Call students' attention to the "Effects Today" section of the cause-and-effect chart. Together have them brainstorm for other effects that could be added to the chart.

Graphic Organizer *Skills*

ANSWERS **1.** Possible answers: fertile land in Oregon and gold in California **2.** Yes. As a result of this idea, the United States stretches from sea to sea.

★ *Customized Instruction* ★

Kinesthetic Learners

Reenacting history Have kinesthetic learners do dramatic reenactments both of the discovery of gold at Sutter's Mill in California and of the spread of the news across the country. Students can work alone, in pairs, or in small groups. In addition to James Marshall's discovery, scenes might include a young man telling his family he is heading west to mine for gold, a traveler arriving in a town with the news, or a business person brainstorming on how to profit from the Gold Rush. Each scene should be no longer than 5 minutes. If possible, have a volunteer videotape the reenactments and use the tapes to help students review section content. (*average*)

Technology

Videodiscs/Videotapes

Prentice Hall United States History Video Collection™, Vol. 6, Ch. 34, "California Gold Rush," 1:30 min (*average*) ELL

Chapter 34

Writing Actively 

After Reading Ask students to write their own journal account about discovering gold in California. They should use information from the chapter to create a plausible character with unique hopes and dreams.

 Linking United States and the World

ANSWER

Possible answers: courage to deal with extremely harsh conditions, determination to work hard, dream of becoming very rich, willingness to take chances, and a sense of adventure

RESOURCE DIRECTORY

Teaching Resources
Unit 4/Chapter 13
- Vocabulary Builder, p. 12
- Section 5 Quiz, p. 22

Chapter Tests, pp. 73–78
Interdisciplinary Connections
- Main Idea: The California Gold Rush, pp. 73–75, 78

 Linking United States and the World 

China

From China to the Golden Mountain

Some 25,000 Chinese left their ordered society for the rough-and-tumble world of the California gold fields. Few struck it rich, but their knowledge of farming helped the territory prosper. At left, Chinese peasants tend a rice field. At right, Chinese miners work at a gold claim. ★ **What qualities did the Chinese and other forty-niners need to succeed?**

Women joined the gold rush. Some staked claims and mined for gold. Others took advantage of economic opportunities in the mining camps. Women ran boarding houses, took in laundry, sewed, and ran bakeries.

A new state

The Gold Rush changed life in California. Almost overnight, San Francisco grew from a sleepy town to a bustling city.

Greed led some forty-niners to become criminals. Murders and robberies plagued many mining camps. To fight crime, miners formed vigilance committees. **Vigilantes** (vihj uh LAN teez), self-appointed law enforcers, dealt out punishment even though they had no legal power to do so. Sometimes an accused criminal was lynched, that is, hanged without a legal trial.

Californians realized they needed a government to stop the lawlessness. In 1849, they drafted a state constitution. They then asked to be admitted to the Union. Their request caused an uproar in the United States. Americans wondered whether the new state would allow slavery. As you will read, after a heated debate, California was admitted to the Union in 1850 as a free state.

Connections With Arts

The California Gold Rush provided the background for the still-popular folk song "My Darling Clementine." The song begins: "In a canyon, in a cavern / Excavating for a mine / Lived a miner, forty-niner / And his daughter Clementine."

California's Unique Culture

Most mining camps in California included a mix of peoples. A visitor to a mining town might meet runaway slaves from the South, Native Americans, and New Englanders. There were also people from Hawaii, China, Peru, Chile, France, Germany, Italy, Ireland, and Australia.

FROM THE ARCHIVES OF AmericanHeritage®

"Oh, Susanna" Another popular song of the gold fields was "Oh, Susanna" by Stephen Foster. The song, which launched Foster's career, became the unofficial anthem of the Gold Rush. Soon it had become a worldwide hit. Americans reported hearing it sung in China, India, Central America, and many cities in Europe.

Source: Frederic D. Schwarz, "The Time Machine," *American Heritage* magazine, September 1997.

★ *Background* ★

Viewpoints

Hindsight is 20/20 Without a doubt, his descendants regretted this view expressed in forty-niner Alfred Jackson's diary: "Pard . . . has made up his mind to invest [his gold money] in San Francisco lots. He wants me to join him in the speculation and argues that some day it will be a big city. I haven't got much faith in it. . . . "

Most of the miners, however, were white Americans. During the wild days of the Gold Rush, they often ignored the rights of other Californians.

Mexican Americans and Indians

California included many Mexicans and Native Americans who had lived there long before the Gold Rush. In many instances, Mexican Americans lost land they had owned for generations. Still, they fought to preserve the customs of their people. José Carrillo (cah REE yoh) was from one of the oldest families in California. In part through his efforts, the state's first constitution was written in both Spanish and English.

Indians fared worst of all. Many Native Americans were driven off their lands and later died of starvation or diseases. Others were murdered. In 1850, about 100,000 Indians lived in California. By the 1870s, there were only 17,000 Indians left in the state.

Chinese Americans

Attracted by the tales of a "mountain of gold," thousands of Chinese began arriving in California in 1848. Because California needed workers, the Chinese were welcomed at first. When the Chinese staked claims in the gold fields, however, white miners often drove them off.

Discrimination against Chinese Americans and, later, other Asians would continue in California for many decades. Still, many Chinese Americans stayed in California and helped the state to grow. They farmed, irrigated, and reclaimed vast stretches of land.

African Americans

Free blacks, too, rushed to the California gold fields hoping to strike it rich. Some did become wealthy. By the 1850s, in fact, California had the richest African American population of any state. Yet African Americans were also denied certain rights. For example, California law denied blacks and other minorities the right to testify against whites in court. After a long struggle, blacks gained this right in 1863.

In spite of these problems, California thrived and grew. Settlers continued to arrive in the state. By 1860, it had 100,000 citizens. The mix of peoples in California gave it a unique culture.

★ Section 5 Review ★

Recall

1. **Locate** (a) Nauvoo, (b) Salt Lake City, (c) Sacramento, (d) San Francisco.
2. **Identify** (a) Mormons, (b) Joseph Smith, (c) Brigham Young, (d) Sutter's Mill.
3. **Define** (a) forty-niner, (b) vigilante.

Comprehension

4. Why did Brigham Young lead the Mormons to Utah?
5. Describe two effects of the Gold Rush on California.
6. Explain the problems that each of the following faced in California: (a) Mexican Americans, (b) Native Americans, (c) Chinese Americans, (d) African Americans.

Critical Thinking and Writing

7. **Comparing** Compare the settling of Utah with the settling of California. How were they similar? How were they different?
8. **Linking Past and Present** In the 1990s, almost 30 percent of immigrants to the United States settled in California. The largest group were from Asia. (a) Why do you think California still attracts many immigrants? (b) Why do so many Asian immigrants come to California?

Activity **Writing a Speech** There's trouble ahead! You and your friend went to California in the Gold Rush. Now, vigilantes are accusing your friend of a crime he didn't commit—stealing a horse. Write a speech in which you declare his innocence and call upon the vigilantes to wait until your friend can receive a legal trial.

★ Section 5 Review ★

ANSWERS

1. See map, p. 366.

2. (a)–(c) p. 365, **(d)** p. 367

3. (a) p. 367, **(b)** p. 368

4. The Mormons had to move often because their beliefs were unpopular. Young thought Utah was a safe place in which to settle.

5. Possible answers: San Francisco became a bustling city; California became a state.

6. (a) often lost family lands **(b)** driven off their lands; starvation, diseases **(c)** discrimination **(d)** denied certain rights

7. Possible answer: Both were settled by people looking for a better life, but California's population was more diverse.

8. Possible answers: **(a)** It is home to many ethnic groups, so immigrants can live close to people who share their language and traditions. **(b)** California is the U.S. mainland state closest to Asia.

Guided Instruction
Ask students to think about how frightening the situation would be. Have them consider the value of a legal system based on laws and not on individuals' whims. Perhaps organize a mock trial, with students arguing both sides of the case.

ASSESSMENT See the rubrics in the Alternative Assessment booklet in the Teaching Resources.

★ Activity ★

Community Involvement

Planning a culture fair The California of 1860 had a wide variety of ethnic groups. Find out what ethnic groups are represented in your community. Then plan a Celebrating Diversity Fair. The fair can showcase ethnic foods, music, and costumes as well as highlight the shared heritage found in your community's history. (*challenging*)

CD-ROM
Test Bank CD-ROM, Ch. 13
Interactive Student Tutorial

Chapter 13

Review and Activities

Reviewing the Chapter

Define These Terms

1. a **2.** d **3.** c **4.** b **5.** e

Explore the Main Ideas

1. The mountain men were rugged individualists with a colorful appearance. They lived dangerous lives trapping animals in the western wilderness.

2. The Texans captured Santa Anna and would not let him go until he had signed Texas over to them.

3. Spanish missionaries were the first settlers in California, eliminating native resistance and paving the way for further settlement.

4. American belief in Manifest Destiny and then the need for more territory helped cause it. The expansion of the United States across the continent was one result.

5. The groups that made up the culture of California included Native Americans, Chinese, Mexican Americans, African Americans, white Americans, and people from many other countries.

Geography Activity

1. B **2.** G **3.** E **4.** C **5.** A **6.** D **7.** F **Location** 49° N

Critical Thinking and Writing

1. Answers will vary.

2. (a) Battle of San Jacinto, Lone Star Republic, annexation of Texas, Mexican War, Treaty of Guadalupe-Hidalgo **(b)** The United States would have no good excuse for going to war with Mexico until it was defending Texas as its own territory.

3. (a) The immediate cause was a border dispute with Mexico over the Texas border. **(b)** the American desire for more territory as a part of Manifest Destiny and the Mexican refusal to sell California and New Mexico

4. (a) It held that the United States had the right and duty to expand across the continent. **(b)** It was achieved through conquest, settlement, and negotiation. **(c)** Belief in Manifest Destiny greatly enlarged and unified the young country. However, Americans' racist beliefs in their own superiority resulted in discrimination and violence against non-Americans.

Using Primary Sources

(a) Clay believed the annexation of Texas would lead to war with Mexico. **(b)** He thought war for territory was unjustified. **(c)** Possible answer: Houston might have argued that war was necessary to protect the freedom of Americans in Texas, which Mexico might try to take control of again.

Chapter 13 Review and Activities

★ Sum It Up ★

Section 1 Oregon Country

- The first white people to live in Oregon Country were hardy fur trappers.
- Settlers traveling by wagon train braved great dangers to reach Oregon Country.

Section 2 Texas Wins Independence

- Americans living in Texas, as well as Tejanos, rebelled against the Mexican government in 1835.
- After winning several battles, Texans set up an independent republic.

Section 3 California and the Southwest

- In the early years of white settlement, California was dotted with Spanish missions, forts, and ranches.
- In the 1840s, many Americans came to believe that the United States was destined to expand to the Pacific.

Section 4 War With Mexico

- The United States made Texas a part of the Union, and then went to war with Mexico in a border dispute.
- After defeating Mexico, the United States gained the Southwest and California.

Section 5 A Rush to the West

- Seeking religious freedom, the Mormons built a community in the Utah desert.
- A gold rush in California drew many newcomers to that region.

For additional review of the major ideas of Chapter 13, see ***Guide to the Essentials of American History*** or ***Interactive Student Tutorial CD-ROM,*** which contains interactive review activities, graphic organizers, and practice tests.

Reviewing the Chapter

Define These Terms

Match each term with the correct definition.

Column 1	Column 2
1. rendezvous	**a.** get-together for trappers
2. annex	**b.** person who joined the California Gold Rush
3. cede	**c.** to give something up
4. forty-niner	**d.** to add something on
5. vigilante	**e.** self-appointed law enforcer

Explore the Main Ideas

1. Describe the way of life of the mountain men in Oregon Country.
2. How did Texans force Santa Anna to grant them independence?
3. What role did the Catholic Church play in the settlement of California?
4. Describe one cause and one effect of the Mexican War.
5. Name the groups that made up the mixed culture of California in the mid-1800s.

Geography Activity

Match the letters on the map with the following places: **1.** Louisiana Purchase, **2.** Gadsden Purchase, **3.** Oregon Country, **4.** Florida, **5.** The United States in 1783, **6.** Texas Annexation, **7.** Mexican Cession. **Location** At what latitude did the United States and Britain agree to divide Oregon?

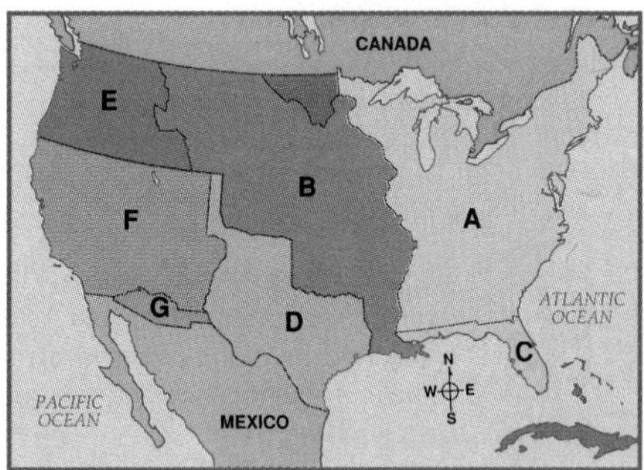

Critical Thinking and Writing

1. **Linking Past and Present** If you were Horace Greeley today, what advice would you give to young people seeking opportunity?
2. **Understanding Chronology** **(a)** List the following events in their correct order: Mexican War; annexation of Texas; founding of the Lone Star Republic; Battle of San Jacinto; Treaty of Guadalupe-Hidalgo. **(b)** Why was it unlikely that the United States would go to war with Mexico *before* Texas joined the Union?
3. **Understanding Causes and Effects** **(a)** What was the immediate cause of the war with Mexico? **(b)** Identify two long-range causes.
4. Exploring Unit Themes **Expansion** **(a)** Describe the idea of Manifest Destiny. **(b)** Explain how the nation achieved this goal. **(c)** What do you think were some of the positive and negative effects of Manifest Destiny?

Using Primary Sources

In a letter written in 1844, Henry Clay explained his thoughts about the annexation of Texas:

> “Annexation and war with Mexico are identical. Now, for one, I certainly am not willing to involve this country in a foreign war for the object of acquiring Texas. I know there are those who regard such a war… as a trifling affair, on account of the weakness of Mexico.… But I do not look upon it thus lightly. I regard all wars as great calamities, to be avoided, if possible, and honorable peace as the wisest and truest policy of this country.”

Source: *National Intelligencer*, April, 17, 1844.

Recognizing Points of View **(a)** What did Clay predict would happen if the United States annexed Texas? **(b)** Why did he oppose the idea? **(c)** How do you think Sam Houston would have responded to Clay's letter?

Activity Bank

Interdisciplinary Activity

Exploring Science Working with a partner, give a presentation on how a geologic feature of the West influenced history. For example, you might choose the Rio Grande, the Great Salt Lake, the Rocky Mountains, the Central Valley of California, or the gold in California.

Career Skills Activity

City Planner You are a city official of San Francisco in 1849. You know that thousands of people will be moving to your city over the next few years. Write a report in which you propose a plan for growth.

Citizenship Activity

Exploring Immigration Like Californians, most Americans today are immigrants or descended from immigrants. Do you know when any of your ancestors first came to this country? If so, prepare a chart tracing your ancestors back to the first people in your family to come to the United States.

Internet Activity

Use the Internet to find sites dealing with the early history of the Mormons. Take notes on what you find and use them to compose a two-paragraph report on early Mormon history.

You are a mountain man or a missionary in Oregon; an American or Tejano in Texas; an American or Mexican in California; a Mormon in Utah; or a forty-niner. In your EYEWITNESS JOURNAL, *describe your participation in whatever was, for you, the single most important event of the years 1820–1860.*

Activity Bank

ASSESSMENT To assess the activities on this page, see the rubrics in the Alternative Assessment booklet in the Teaching Resources. You might want to share the rubrics with your students before they begin work.

Interdisciplinary Activity

1. If possible, team teach with a geology or physical sciences teacher for this activity. Students may receive credit in both classes for the work they do. Even if this is not possible, your colleague may be able to give students advice on how to do research for the activity.

2. Ask students to use diagrams and maps in their presentations.

3. If you are conducting a joint activity with a physical sciences or geology class, students can give their presentations in a special joint class.

Career Skills Activity

1. Remind students that they should first consider the basic needs of all the new arrivals, including food, clean water, and housing.

2. Interested students can obtain a map of the San Francisco Bay area, trace its outlines, and create a city map showing their proposed streets.

3. You may wish to have critique sessions in which students first read their reports and then the rest of the class evaluates their proposals.

Citizenship Activity

1. Suggest to students that they talk to their parents, grandparents, or other relatives to gather information.

2. Show students how to map their ancestors by drawing a sample tree chart on the chalkboard.

3. You may wish to ask students to share the results of their research to reinforce the lesson that nearly all citizens are immigrants in one sense or another.

Eyewitness Journal

1. The event described by students should be a real historical event, not a personal one.
2. Students may present their journal material in the form of prose or poetry.
3. You may wish to take the opportunity to discuss the importance of individuals in history and give examples (Sam Houston, John Frémont).

Internet Activity

1. Have students go to www.phschool.com, which contains updated information on a variety of topics.
2. Another site you might find useful for this activity is Trail of Hope at www.pbs.org/trailofhope.
3. Given the changing nature of the Internet, you may wish to preview this site before directing students to it.

Chapter 14 Manager

SECTION OBJECTIVES	TEACHING RESOURCES	ADDITIONAL RESOURCE
1 Industry in the North (pp. 374–377) **Objectives** 1. Describe how new inventions changed manufacturing and farming in the North. 2. Explain how new means of communication and transportation benefited business. 3. Explain how steam power helped industry grow.	**Lesson Planner,** p. 58 (average) .... 45 mins. **Unit 4/Chapter 14** • Critical Thinking and Writing: Comparing Points of View, p. 25 (average) .... 30 mins. • Map Mystery: Early Manufacturing, p. 26 (challenging) .... 30 mins. • Section 1 Quiz, p. 29 (average) .... 15 mins.	**Voices of Freedom** • At Work on a Clipper, pp. 101–102 (average) **Historical Outline Map Book** • The Northern States, p. 43 (average) **Customized Reader** • Chicago in 1833, article IVB-18 (average)
2 Life in the North (pp. 378–382) **Objectives** 1. Identify the conditions that caused northern workers to organize. 2. Give reasons for European emigration to the United States in the mid-1800s. 3. Describe what life was like for African Americans in the North.	**Lesson Planner,** p. 59 (average) .... 90 mins. **Unit 4/Chapter 14** • Practice Your Skills: Teaching Others, p. 24 (challenging) .... 30 mins. • Section 2 Quiz, p. 30 (average) .... 15 mins. **Interdisciplinary Connections** • Main Idea: African American Contributions, p. 81 (average) .... 20 mins.	**Voices of Freedom** • Life in a Mill in 1832, pp. 102–103 (average) • A Violent Reaction to Foreign-Born Voters, pp. 103–104 (average) **Customized Reader** • A Swiss Family's Immigration to the United States, article IVA-13 (average)
3 Cotton Kingdom in the South (pp. 383–387) **Objectives** 1. Explain why cotton planters moved westward. 2. Describe how the cotton gin affected slavery in the South. 3. Give reasons why the South was less industrialized than the North.	**Lesson Planner,** p. 60 (average) .... 45 mins. **Unit 4/Chapter 14** • Connecting History and Literature: Go Down, Moses, p. 27 (average) .... 20 mins. • Section 3 Quiz, p. 31 (average) .... 15 mins. **Interdisciplinary Connections** • Main Idea: African American Contributions, p. 84 (average) .... 20 mins.	**Voices of Freedom** • Inventing the Cotton Gin, pp. 104–105 (average) **Historical Outline Map Book** • The Southern States, p. 44 (average) **Customized Reader** • A Ship's Captain Describes the Illegal African Slave Trade, article IVB-10 (average)
4 Life in the South (pp. 388–393) **Objectives** 1. Identify the five groups that made up southern society. 2. Describe the sufferings of African Americans under slavery. 3. Describe how African Americans struggled against slavery.	**Lesson Planner,** p. 61 (average) .... 90 mins. **Unit 4/Chapter 14** • Vocabulary Builder, p. 23 (basic) .... 15 mins. • Biography Flashcard: Ira F. Aldridge, p. 28 (average) .... 20 mins. • Section 4 Quiz, p. 32 (average) .... 15 mins. **Chapter Tests,** pp. 79–84 (average) .... 45 mins. **Why Study History?** • Music Is Part of Our Culture, pp. 55–58 (average) .... 90 mins. **Interdisciplinary Connections** • Main Idea: African American Contributions, pp. 80, 82, 83 (average) .... 20 mins.	**Customized Reader** • Traveling Through the Carolinas i 1828, article IVB-19 (challenging) • Life in Natchez, Mississippi, article IVA-19 (challenging) • African Americans Recall Their Lives as Slaves, article IVA-7 (average) • A Slave Auction, article IVB-11 (average) • A Cheerful View of Slavery, article IVB-13 (average) • Henry "Box" Brown Mails Himse to Freedom, article IVA-11 (basic) **Prentice Hall Literature Library** • Southern Writers

Assessment Options

Teaching Resources
- Alternative Assessment booklet
- Section Quizzes, Unit 4, Chapter 14, pp. 29–32
- Chapter Tests, Chapter 14, pp. 79–84
- Test Bank CD-ROM

Student Performance Pack
- Guide to the Essentials of American History, Chapter 14 Test, p. 81
- Standardized Test Prep Handbook
- Interactive Student Tutorial CD-ROM

Interdisciplinary Connections

Teaching Resources
- Map Mystery, Unit 4, Chapter 14, p. 26
- Connecting History and Literature, Unit 4, Chapter 14, p. 27
- Interdisciplinary Connections, pp. 79–84

Voices of Freedom, pp. 101–105

Customized Reader, articles IVA-7, IVA-11, IVA-13, IVA-19, IVB-10, IVB-11, IVB-13, IVB-18, IVB-19

Historical Outline Map Book, pp. 43–44

Prentice Hall Literature Library
- Southern Writers

BLOCK SCHEDULING
Activities with this icon will help you meet your Block Scheduling needs.

ENGLISH LANGUAGE LEARNERS
Activities with this icon are suitable for English Language Learners.

TEAM TEACHING
Activities and Background Notes with this icon present starting points for Team Teaching.

Technology

AmericanHeritage® History of the United States CD-ROM
- Time Tour: The Worlds of North and South (1820–1860) in An Expanding Nation

Interactive Student Tutorial CD-ROM

Test Bank CD-ROM

Color Transparencies
- Plow, p. H-37
- American Labor Force, p. B-57
- Cotton Gin, p. H-33

Guided Reading Audiotapes (English/Spanish), side 5

Listening to Music CD
- Swing Low, Sweet Chariot, track 7
- Go Down, Moses, track 8

Resource Pro® CD-ROM

Prentice Hall United States History Video Collection™ (Spanish track available on disc version.) Vol. 8, Chs. 7, 10, 13, 16

Prentice Hall Home Page www.phschool.com

Student Performance Pack

Guide to the Essentials of American History
- Ch. 14, pp. 77–81 (Available in English and Spanish)

Guided Reading Audiotapes (English/Spanish), side 5

Standardized Test Prep Handbook

Interactive Student Tutorial CD-ROM

Teachers' Bibliography

From the Archives of AmericanHeritage®

Don't miss the special American Heritage® teaching notes found in this chapter.

Contact Teachers' Curriculum Institute to learn more about History Alive!® resources on the differences between the North and South. See History Alive!® unit: The Civil War and Reconstruction, Section 1, "Contrasting North and South."

Explore your library to find these issues related to Chapter 14: *Irish Americans,* March 1994; *Anti-Slavery Movement,* February 1993.

Prentice Hall Web Site You can access a structured, on-line environment that allows you to preview curriculum-related resources and receive updated information on groundbreaking events from around the nation and the world. (www.phschool.com)

Chapter 14

The Worlds of North and South

1820–1860

Introducing the Chapter

Have students preview the main ideas of this chapter by looking over the visuals. Suggest they look for illustrations that allow them to compare and contrast the North and the South.

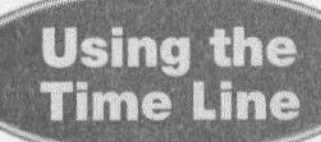

To reinforce student understanding of the sequence of events in this chapter, ask students to look at the time line on these pages. Ask questions such as these: **(1)** When did unions first begin? *(in the 1820s)* **(2)** Which development came first—the spread of slavery in the South or the cotton boom? *(cotton boom)* **(3)** What world event had an effect on increased immigration in the 1850s? *(revolutions in Germany)*

Ask students to think of examples of currently popular music that have origins in American musical traditions, such as the blues, or in the musical traditions of other cultures. Encourage students to discuss specific tunes or songs that contain various influences.

For additional *Why Study History?* support, see p. 391.

Chapter 14

The Worlds of North and South 1820–1860

What's Ahead

As the 1800s progressed, the North and the South continued to develop differently. In many ways, the two regions were like separate worlds. The North based its economy largely on industry. The South, meanwhile, developed an agricultural system that relied primarily on cotton. The industry of the North depended on paid workers. These workers struggled to make a living and endured hard working conditions. Still, they were free. In contrast, cotton production in the South depended on the labor of enslaved African Americans. These enslaved people had no rights or freedoms.

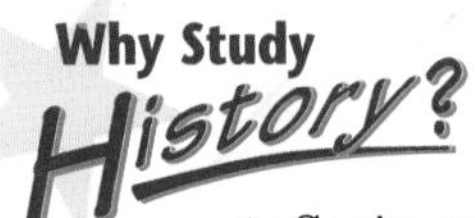

In the mid-1800s, many Americans could trace their roots to one of the British Isles, to Spain, or to a particular region of Africa. New immigrants were arriving from Germany, Ireland, and other European nations. Americans of all backgrounds were proud of their rich heritage. To learn about cultural influences that helped to shape several styles of American music, see this chapter's *Why Study History?* feature, "Music Is Part of Our Culture."

American Events

1820s Skilled workers begin to organize unions

1830s Railroads allow goods to be shipped quickly and cheaply

1820 | 1825 | 1830 | 1835 | 1840

World Events

1829 World Event Steam-powered locomotive travels 30 miles per hour in England

Different Worlds

By the mid-1800s, the North and South had different economies. The North developed a variety of industries based on the labor of free workers. The South depended largely on agriculture and the labor of enslaved African Americans. A typical southern scene appears in William Aiken Walker's painting Plantation Economy in the Old South, *shown above.* ★ **What other economic differences between North and South do the pictures above suggest?**

1840s Cotton boom in South leads to spread of slavery

1844 Morse receives patent for telegraph

1850s Millions of Irish and German immigrants settle in the United States

1840 — 1845 — 1850 — 1855 — 1860

1840 World Event World Anti-Slavery Convention held in Great Britain

1848 World Event Revolutions in Germany

Writing Actively

Responding to Art Ask students to study the two pictures on this page. Then ask them to write a brief article for a northern newspaper in which a group of northern workers from the factory describe their reactions to a visit to the plantation shown in the Walker painting. How do the workers think plantation life compares to their own?

Viewing History ANSWER

Possible answer: Railroad transportation was more developed in the North than in the South.

★ Background ★

Art Note

Different Worlds The images on this page highlight the contrasts between the North and the South. Even the media used suggest the regional differences. *Fast Freight When America Was Young* is a lithograph—a print whose original image is designed to produce multiple copies. William Walker's portrayal of a cotton plantation was painted in oil on canvas. T

Documents and Literature

On pp. 570–573, you will find two readings to enrich this chapter:

1. Eyewitness Account "Three Views of Irish Immigration," excerpts from letters by Irish immigrants to their families back home. (Use with Section 2.)

2. Literature "The Fires of Jubilee," a dramatic account of how the white community reacted to Nat Turner's rebellion. (Use with Section 4.)

Technology

Videodiscs/Videotapes
Show the *Prentice Hall United States History Video Collection*™ segments for this chapter. The videodisc version has a Spanish track. Press audio until you get the left channel for English or the right channel for Spanish, or use the bar codes in the Guidebook.

AmericanHeritage® History of the United States CD-ROM
- Time Tour: The Worlds of North and South (1820–1860) in An Expanding Nation (*average*)

Section 1

Industry in the North

LESSON PLAN

Objectives

★ Describe how new inventions changed manufacturing and farming in the North.

★ Explain how new means of communication and transportation benefited business.

★ Explain how steam power helped industry grow.

1 Engage

Warm Up Ask students to list all the different machines they use in a day, including household appliances, computers, cars, and specialized equipment at school.

Activating Prior Knowledge Ask students if the United States was an industrial nation in 1800. When do students think the United States first started to become a nation of industry rather than a nation of farms?

Reading Actively

Before Reading Have students read to construct a concept map about new inventions discussed in this section.

RESOURCE DIRECTORY

Teaching Resources
Lesson Planner, p. 58
Unit 4/Chapter 14
- Map Mystery: Early Manufacturing, p. 26

Transparencies
Exploring Technology
- Plow, p. H-37

Industry in the North

As You Read

Explore These Questions
- How did new inventions change manufacturing and farming in the North?
- How did new means of communication and transportation benefit business?
- How did steam power help industry grow?

Define
- telegraph
- locomotive
- clipper ship

Identify
- Elias Howe
- John Deere
- Cyrus McCormick
- Samuel F. B. Morse
- John Griffiths

Elias Howe sewing machine

SETTING the Scene In 1834, a young French engineer, Michel Chevalier, toured the North. He was most impressed by the burst of industry there—the textile factories, shipyards, and iron mills. He wrote:

> "Everywhere is heard the noise of hammers, of spindles, of bells calling the hands to their work, or dismissing them from their tasks.... It is the peaceful hum of an industrious population, whose movements are regulated like clockwork."

Northern industry grew steadily in the mid-1800s. Most northerners still lived on farms. However, more and more of the northern economy centered on manufacturing and trade.

New Machines

The 1800s brought a flood of new inventions in the North. "In Massachusetts and Connecticut," a European visitor exclaimed, "there is not a laborer who has not invented a machine or a tool."

In 1846, **Elias Howe** patented a sewing machine. A few years later, Isaac Singer improved on Howe's machine. Soon, clothing makers bought hundreds of the new sewing machines. Workers could now make dozens of shirts in the time it took a tailor to sew one by hand.

Some new inventions made work easier for farmers. **John Deere** invented a lightweight steel plow. Earlier plows made of heavy iron or wood had to be pulled by slow-moving oxen. A horse could pull a steel plow through a field more quickly.

In 1847, **Cyrus McCormick** opened a factory in Chicago that produced mechanical reapers. The reaper was a horse-drawn machine that mowed wheat and other grains. McCormick's reaper could do the work of five people using hand tools.

The reaper and the steel plow helped farmers raise more grain with fewer hands. As a result, thousands of farm workers left the countryside. Some went west to start farms of their own. Others found jobs in new factories in northern cities.

Connections With Economics

Cyrus McCormick used a new business practice to help struggling farmers buy a reaper. He let farmers put some money down and pay the rest in installments. This practice is known as the installment plan or buying on credit.

★ *Customized Instruction* ★

English Language Learners

Industrial dictionary Visual images of unfamiliar words and objects may help ELL students grasp difficult concepts. For the inventions mentioned in this section, have ELL students start a picture dictionary of the inventions and the industries and words connected with them. Inventions include *sewing machine, steel plow, reaper, telegraph, steam-powered locomotive engine,* and *clipper ships.* Students may use the descriptions and context clues in the section as well as dictionaries and other reference books for definitions. Students may draw or photocopy illustrations. By illustrating these words, students will gain a better understanding of their meaning and will create a reference that can become part of the classroom library. (*average*) ELL

The Telegraph

In 1844, **Samuel F. B. Morse** received a patent for a "talking wire," or telegraph. The **telegraph** was a device that sent electrical signals along a wire. The signals were based on a code of dots, dashes, and spaces. Later, this system of dots and dashes became known as the Morse code.

Congress gave Morse funds to run wire from Washington, D.C., to Baltimore. On May 24, 1844, Morse set up his telegraph in the Supreme Court chamber in Washington. As a crowd of onlookers watched, Morse tapped out a short message: "What hath God wrought!" A few seconds later, the operator in Baltimore tapped back the same message. The telegraph worked!

Morse's invention was an instant success. Telegraph companies sprang up everywhere. Thousands of miles of wire soon stretched across the country. As a result of the telegraph, news could now travel long distances in a matter of minutes.

The telegraph helped many businesses to thrive. Merchants and farmers could have quick access to information about supply, demand, and prices of goods in different areas of the country. For example, western farmers might learn of a wheat shortage in New York and ship their grain east to meet the demand.

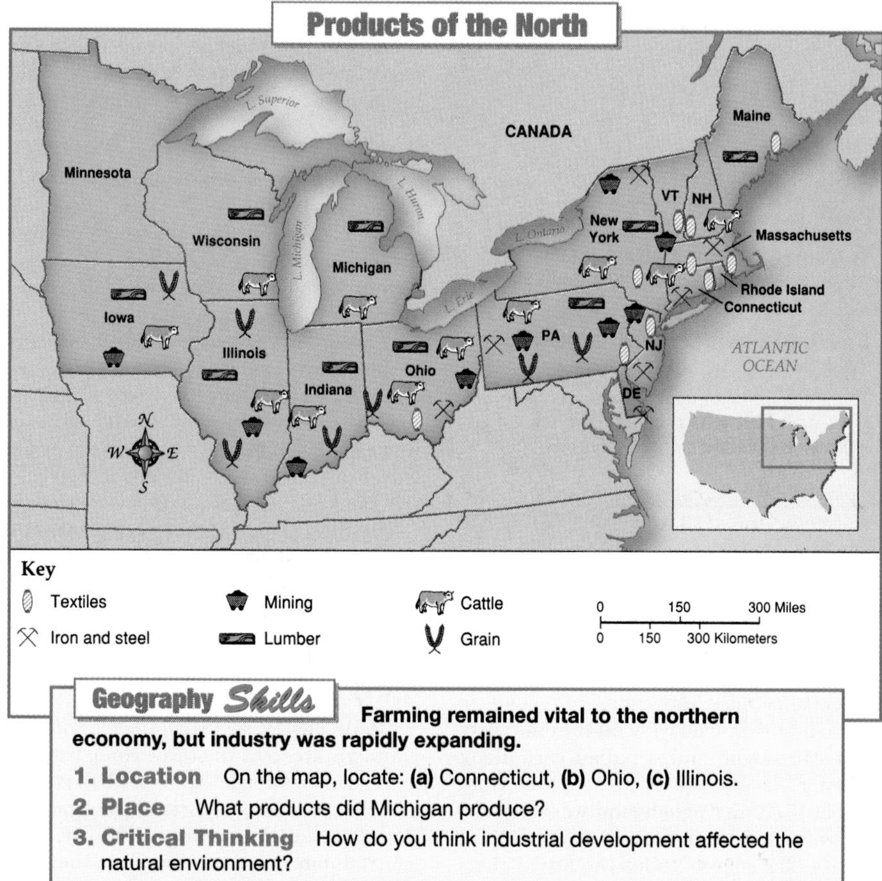

Geography Skills **Farming remained vital to the northern economy, but industry was rapidly expanding.**

1. **Location** On the map, locate: **(a)** Connecticut, **(b)** Ohio, **(c)** Illinois.
2. **Place** What products did Michigan produce?
3. **Critical Thinking** How do you think industrial development affected the natural environment?

2 Explore

Ask students to read the section and then summarize the main points. Point out to students that the text notes several ways that changes in industry affected life on the nation's farms. For a homework assignment, ask students to list these changes or write a short essay describing them.

3 Teach

Pair students and have partners role-play an interview with an inventor from this section. Have the interviewer ask the inventor for a description of the noted invention, of how it works, and of the ways in which it will revolutionize American life. You might videotape the interviews and play selected interviews for the class.

4 Assess

To close the lesson, have students complete the section review. As an alternative, ask students to write a brief essay in which they describe their choice for the most revolutionary invention described in the section.

★ ★ ★ ★ ★ ★ ★ ★ ★ ★ ★ ★ ★ ★ ★ ★ ★

Geography Skills

ANSWERS **1.** Review locations with students. **2.** lumber and cattle **3.** Possible answer: It led to the use of more natural resources, such as minerals and fuels.

★ Background ★
Linking Past and Present

John Deere Corporation The Deere Corporation has its headquarters in Moline, Illinois, where John Deere moved his operations in 1848 to make use of the Mississippi River for transportation and water power. In 1996, the company made its single largest agricultural sale, selling $187 million worth of combines to Ukraine.

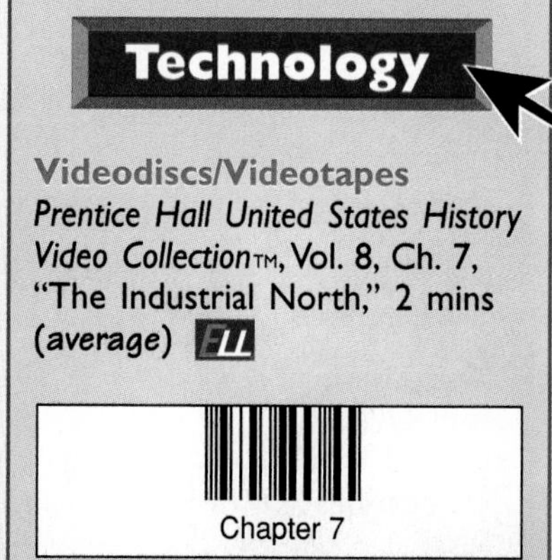

Graph *Skills*

ANSWERS **1.** Approximately 11,000–12,000 miles of track were laid.
2. Possible answer: Iron was used for the rails and locomotives. Wood was used for the railroad ties and train cars. Coal was used to fuel the locomotives.

Reading Actively

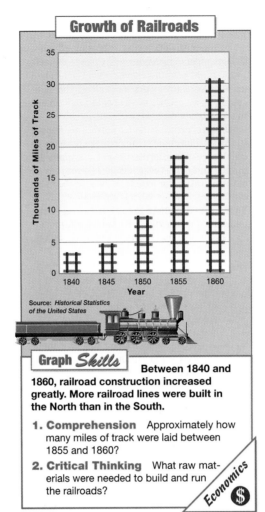

During Reading Ask students to note the problems faced by early railroad builders and the advances that improved railroad safety. Discuss with students how new products or technologies might threaten established industries today. For example, ask students which industries might oppose the widespread use of electric-powered cars.

Writing Actively

After Reading Have students complete the concept maps that they started at the beginning of the section. Then ask them to write a generalization based on their map.

RESOURCE DIRECTORY

Teaching Resources
Unit 4/Chapter 14
- Critical Thinking and Writing: Comparing Points of View, p. 25
- Section 1 Quiz, p. 29

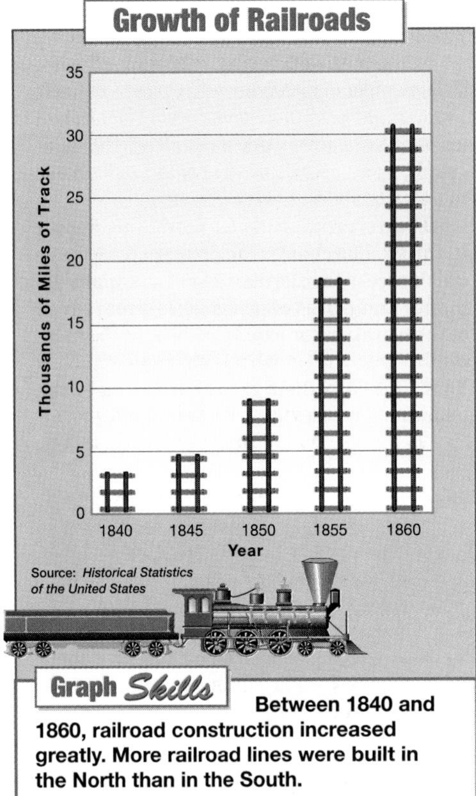

Graph *Skills* **Between 1840 and 1860, railroad construction increased greatly. More railroad lines were built in the North than in the South.**

1. **Comprehension** Approximately how many miles of track were laid between 1855 and 1860?
2. **Critical Thinking** What raw materials were needed to build and run the railroads?

Economics $

The First Railroads

Improved transportation also boosted the economy. Americans continued to build new roads and canals. The greatest change, however, came with the railroads.

The first railroads were built in the early 1800s. Horses or mules pulled cars along wooden rails covered with strips of iron. Then, in 1829, an English family developed a steam-powered **locomotive** engine to pull rail cars. The engine, called the *Rocket,* barreled along at 30 miles (48 km) per hour.

Early difficulties

In the United States, there was some initial opposition to railroads. Farmers did not want railroads running through their fields. Teamsters who moved freight on horse-drawn wagons feared that they would lose their jobs. Likewise, people who invested in canals worried that competition from the railroads might cause them to lose their investments. Some states protected the canals by placing limits on railroads. One such limit was that railroads could carry freight only when canals were frozen.

Another problem for the railroads was concern over reliability and safety. Early steam locomotives often broke down. Soft roadbeds and weak bridges contributed to accidents. Locomotives were extremely noisy and belched thick black smoke from their smokestacks. Hot embers from smokestacks sometimes burned holes in passengers' clothing or set nearby buildings on fire.

A railroad boom

Despite these problems, promoters believed in the future of train travel. One boasted that the railroads were "unrivaled for speed, cleanliness, civility of officers and servants, and admirable accommodations of every kind."

Gradually, railroad builders overcame problems and removed obstacles. Engineers learned to build sturdier bridges and solid roadbeds. They replaced wooden rails with iron rails. Such improvements made railroad travel safer and faster. Meanwhile, legal restrictions on railroad building were removed.

By the 1850s, railroads crisscrossed the nation. The major lines were concentrated in the North and West. New York, Chicago, and Cincinnati became major rail centers. The South had much less track than the North.

Yankee Clippers

Railroads increased commerce within the United States. At the same time, trade also increased between the United States and other nations. At seaports in the Northeast, captains loaded their ships with cotton, fur, wheat, lumber, and tobacco. Then they sailed to the four corners of the world.

★ *Activity* ★

Cooperative Learning

Debating about railroads Divide the class into groups of eight; then assign half of each large group the pro position on the subject of railroads in the early and mid-1800s. Have the balance of each group take the con position and instruct each subgroup to brainstorm about arguments for or against railroads, as assigned. Encourage students to be creative in their arguments, particularly those taking a position against the railroads since, historically, they lost. Have students stage a debate between the subgroups of each group. Ask the class to rate each debate on the strength of the arguments presented. (*average*)

Speed was the key to successful trade at sea. In 1845, an American named **John Griffiths** launched the *Rainbow,* the first of the **clipper ships.** These sleek vessels had tall masts and huge sails that caught every gust of wind. Their narrow hulls clipped swiftly through the water.

In the 1840s, American clipper ships broke every speed record. One clipper sped from New York to Hong Kong in 81 days, flying past older ships that took five months to reach China. The speed of the clippers helped the United States win a large share of the world's sea trade in the 1840s and 1850s.

The golden age of the clipper ship was brief. In the 1850s, Britain launched the first oceangoing iron steamships. These sturdy vessels carried more cargo and traveled even faster than clippers.

The Northern Economy Expands

By the 1830s, factories began to use steam power instead of water power. Machines that were driven by steam were powerful and cheap to run. Also, factories that used steam power could be built almost anywhere, not just along the banks of swift-flowing rivers. As a result, American industry expanded rapidly.

At the same time, new machines made it possible to produce more goods at a lower cost. These more affordable goods attracted eager buyers. Families no longer had to make clothing and other goods in their homes. Instead, they could buy factory-made products.

Railroads allowed factory owners to transport large amounts of raw materials and finished goods cheaply and quickly. Also, as railroads stretched across the nation, they linked distant towns with cities and factories. These towns became new markets for factory goods.

The growth of railroads also affected northern farming. Railroads brought cheap grain and other foods from the West to New England. New England farmers could not compete with this new source of cheap foods. Many left their farms to find new jobs as factory workers, store clerks, and sailors. More and more, New Englanders turned to manufacturing and trade.

★ Section 1 Review ★

Recall

1. **Identify** **(a)** Elias Howe, **(b)** John Deere, **(c)** Cyrus McCormick, **(d)** Samuel F. B. Morse, **(e)** John Griffiths.
2. **Define** **(a)** telegraph, **(b)** locomotive, **(c)** clipper ship.

Comprehension

3. What new inventions made work easier for farmers?
4. Explain how each of the following helped industry grow: **(a)** telegraph, **(b)** railroads, **(c)** clipper ships.
5. How did steam power and new machines change northern industry?

Critical Thinking and Writing

6. **Linking Past and Present** What technology of today helps businesses in the same way that the telegraph helped businesses in the 1800s?
7. **Understanding Causes and Effects** How did the building of railroads cause many New Englanders to abandon farming?

Activity **Creating an Advertisement** It is the mid-1800s and you are working at an advertising agency. Create an advertisement poster urging people to buy or use one of the new inventions of the period. Use both words and pictures to make your advertisement persuasive.

★ Section 1 Review ★

ANSWERS

1. (a) p. 374, **(b)** p. 374, **(c)** p. 374, **(d)** p. 375, **(e)** p. 377

2. (a) p. 375, **(b)** p. 376, **(c)** p. 377

3. the steel plow and the reaper

4. (a) Businesspeople could learn instantly about supply, demand, and prices in different areas. **(b)** Factory owners could ship raw materials and finished goods cheaply and quickly. **(c)** The fast ships helped the U.S. win a large share of world trade.

5. The new machines were powerful and cheap to run; factories could be built almost anywhere; goods could be produced at low cost.

6. Cellular telephones, the Internet, television, and satellites help businesses gain and spread information.

7. Railroads brought cheap produce from the West. Unable to compete, New England farmers turned to industry and trade.

Activity

Guided Instruction
Suggest that students list the inventions discussed in the chapter and then choose the one they wish to advertise. Remind them that advertisements are meant to be persuasive and often include a catchy slogan or symbol. You might display the ads around the room.

ASSESSMENT See the rubrics in the Alternative Assessment booklet in the Teaching Resources.

★ Background ★
Recent Scholarship

Black Jacks Jeffrey Bolster's work, *Black Jacks: African American Seamen in the Age of Sail,* notes that about 20 percent of American sailors in the early 1800s were black. Bolster describes the unique contribution of black sailors to African American culture. Sailors carried the news of the day and new ideas and customs from one place to another.

FROM THE ARCHIVES OF American Heritage®

Tom Thumb The first locomotive built in the United States was the *Tom Thumb,* which was built by Peter Cooper. On its first run in 1830, it carried 42 passengers at a speed of up to 18 miles an hour. Some critics thought that such speeds could addle the brain. To disprove this, some of the passengers spent time on the trip writing coherent sentences.

Source: John Steele Gordon, "The Business of America," *American Heritage* magazine, October 1996.

Section 2

Life in the North

LESSON PLAN

Objectives

★ Identify the conditions that caused northern workers to organize.

★ Give reasons for European emigration to the United States in the mid-1800s.

★ Describe what life was like for African Americans in the North.

1 Engage

Warm Up Ask students to list some words to describe the ideal working conditions—the conditions for the job they would like to have someday. Then read aloud the Setting the Scene material on this page. Ask students to list some words to describe the working conditions Alzina Parsons endured.

Activating Prior Knowledge Remind students that early textile mills of New England employed many young women from New England farms. Their working conditions were generally good. The "mill girls" lived in chaperoned boarding houses and worked in the factories for a few years before returning home. Have students discuss how factory conditions changed by the mid-1800s, and ask them to suggest possible reasons for the changes.

RESOURCE DIRECTORY

Teaching Resources
Lesson Planner, p. 59

Transparencies
Interdisciplinary Connections
• American Labor Force, p. B-57

2 Life in the North

As You Read

Explore These Questions

- What conditions caused northern workers to organize?
- Why did many Europeans move to the United States in the mid-1800s?
- What was life like for African Americans in the North?

Define

- artisan
- trade union
- strike
- famine
- nativist
- discrimination

Identify

- Sarah Bagley
- Know-Nothing party
- Henry Boyd
- Macon Allen
- John Russworm

SETTING the Scene Alzina Parsons never forgot her thirteenth birthday. The day began as usual, with work in the local spinning mill. Suddenly, Alzina cried out. She had caught her hand in the spinning machine, badly mangling her fingers. The foreman summoned the factory doctor. He cut off one of the injured fingers and sent the girl back to work.

In the early 1800s, such an incident probably would not have happened. Factory work was hard, but mill owners treated workers like human beings. By the 1840s, however, there was an oversupply of workers. Many factory owners now treated workers like machines.

Factory Conditions Worsen

Factories of the 1840s and 1850s were very different from the mills of the early 1800s. The factories were larger, and they used steam-powered machines. More laborers worked longer hours for lower wages. Workers lived in dark, dingy houses in the shadow of the factory.

Families in factories

As the need for workers increased, entire families labored in factories. In some cases, a family agreed to work for one year. If even one family member broke the contract, the entire family might be fired.

The factory day began when a whistle sounded at 4 A.M. Father, mother, and children dressed in the dark and headed off to work. At 7:30 A.M. and at noon, the whistle sounded again to announce breakfast and lunch breaks. The workday did not end until 7:30 P.M., when a final whistle sent the workers home.

Hazards at work

During their long day, factory workers faced discomfort and danger. Few factories had windows or heating systems. In summer, the heat and humidity inside the factory were stifling. In winter, the extreme cold chilled workers' bones and contributed to frequent sickness.

Factory machines had no safety devices, and accidents were common. Owners ignored the hazards. There were no laws regulating factory conditions. Injured workers often lost their jobs.

In 1855, a visitor to a textile mill in Fall River, Massachusetts, asked the manager of the mill how he treated his workers. In his reply, the manager was harsh but honest. He described his feelings about the workers.

> "I regard people just as I regard my machinery. So long as they can do my work for what I choose to pay them, I keep them, getting out of them all I can."

378 ★ Chapter 14

★ Customized Instruction ★

Visual Learners

Concept maps As they read this section, have individual students create concept maps to support each of the following generalizations about life in the mid-1800s: **(a)** Factory workers led difficult lives. **(b)** Workers faced opposition when they tried to organize. **(c)** Many Europeans considered the United States to be a land of freedom and opportunity. **(d)** Immigrants and free African Americans faced prejudice. Remind students to put the generalization in a circle in the center of their paper. They should write related facts in circles that connect to the center circle (and perhaps to one another). Combine concept maps into sets that cover the four generalizations. Make the sets available to the class as an aid to the section review. (*basic*)

Workers Join Together

Poor working conditions and low wages led workers to organize. The first to do so were **artisans.** Artisans are workers who have learned a trade, such as carpentry or shoemaking.

Trade unions and strikes

In the 1820s and 1830s, artisans in each trade united to form **trade unions**. The unions called for a shorter workday, higher wages, and better working conditions. Sometimes, unions went on strike to gain their demands. In a **strike**, union workers refuse to do their jobs.

At the time, strikes were illegal in many parts of the United States. Strikers faced fines or jail sentences. Employers often fired strike leaders.

Progress for artisans

Slowly, however, workers made progress. In 1840, President Van Buren approved a 10-hour workday for government employees. Other workers pressed their demands until they won the same hours as government workers. Workers celebrated another victory in 1842 when a Massachusetts court declared that they had the right to strike.

Artisans won better pay because factory owners needed their skills. Unskilled workers, however, were unable to bargain for better wages. Unskilled workers held jobs that required little or no training. Because these workers were easy to replace, employers did not listen to their demands.

Women Workers Organize

The success of trade unions encouraged other workers to organize. Workers in New England textile mills especially were eager to protest cuts in wages and unfair work rules. Many of these workers were women.

Women workers faced special problems. First, they had always earned less money than men did. Second, most union leaders did not want women in their ranks. Like many people at the time, they believed that women should not work outside the home. In fact, the goal of many unions was to raise men's wages so that their wives could leave their factory jobs.

Viewing HISTORY **Working in a Factory**

Factory employees faced crowded and dangerous working conditions. Many were injured on the job. The workers in this scene are making McCormick reapers. ★ **What kinds of accidents could occur in a factory such as this?**

▼ *A worker's lunch pail*

Reading Actively

Before Reading Have students read the questions under Explore These Questions. As they read, they should jot down notes to help them answer each question.

2 Explore

Ask students to scan the section and look at the illustrations. When they have finished, ask them to list the groups of people about whom they will read in the section. *(men workers, women workers, immigrants, African Americans)*

3 Teach

Ask students to draft statements by each of the following groups, describing their views of life in the North in the mid-1800s: skilled workers, unskilled workers, women workers, factory owners, Irish immigrants, German immigrants, nativists, and African Americans. Use volunteers' statements as a springboard for class discussion.

4 Assess

To close the lesson, have students complete the section review. As an alternative, ask students to turn each of the subheads in the section into a question, then to trade and answer the questions.

Viewing HISTORY ANSWER

Possible answer: A worker's hands could be injured by the rapidly moving belts and gears. A worker could trip and fall over the piles of machine parts.

★ *Background* ★

Our Diverse Nation

A sole machine By the 1830s, shoes were made in small factories rather than in shoemakers' shops. In the factories, artisans each performed only part of the process, such as tacking on heels. Later in the century, African American Jan Matzeliger invented a machine that attached soles to shoes. This increased worker productivity by about 500 percent. T

PRACTICE the Skill ANSWERS

Assess each step of the teaching process. Be sure the teaching plan has an appropriate amount of content. Offer suggestions if students want to revise their lessons and teach them again.

APPLY the Skill

Guided Instruction

Students will find the activity most meaningful if they can choose the skills they teach and learn. Help students choose appropriate teaching situations. You may want to have pairs of students teach each other. One may offer to teach an academic concept; the other may teach a game or magic trick. Check that students have complete teaching plans.

ASSESSMENT See the rubrics in the Alternative Assessment booklet in the Teaching Resources.

RESOURCE DIRECTORY

Teaching Resources
Unit 4/Chapter 14
- Practice Your Skills: Teaching Others, p. 24

Skills FOR LIFE

Critical Thinking | Managing Information | **Communication** | Maps, Charts, and Graphs

Teaching Others

How Will I Use This Skill?

You already use it. You may teach others how to do school work, how to make something, how to play a sport, or how to use a computer program. In the future, you may teach job skills to co-workers. If you become a parent, you will teach your child. We are all teachers.

LEARN the Skill

You can teach others by following these four steps:

1. Make sure you know the material you will teach.
2. Prepare a teaching plan that is interesting, informative, and at the proper level of difficulty.
3. Present your lesson. Encourage your students to participate and to ask questions.
4. Check that your students have learned the material and reteach if necessary.

PRACTICE the Skill

Using the steps above, teach some classmates about the immigrants who came to the United States in the mid-1800s.

1. Study and take notes on the material in this section under the heading Millions of New Americans.

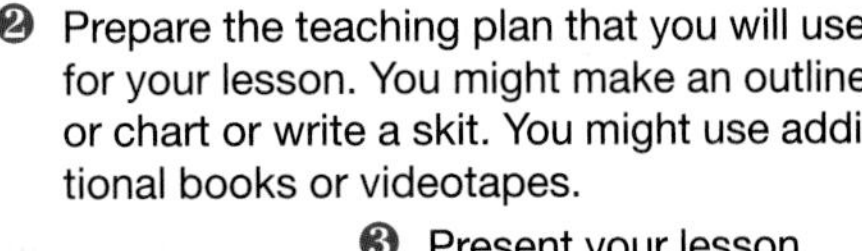

2. Prepare the teaching plan that you will use for your lesson. You might make an outline or chart or write a skit. You might use additional books or videotapes.
3. Present your lesson. Keep your students involved! Ask interesting questions and encourage your students to participate.
4. Provide a quiz or activity to check for student understanding. If your students did not learn the lesson well enough, use a different method and try again.

Teaching and learning

APPLY the Skill

You can apply this skill by volunteering to tutor a classmate or younger student who is having difficulty with reading, mathematics, or another school subject. You might also teach a friend about a hobby or game that interests you.

★ Background ★

Turning Points

A woman's voice Sarah Bagley campaigned tirelessly for workers' rights as factory conditions worsened and as employers' demands increased. Undaunted by social taboos against public statements by women, she gave speeches and wrote articles voicing workers' discontent. Bagley founded the Lowell Female Labor Reform Association (LFLRA) in 1845 and served as its first president. Her clear message was stated in an article in the first of the *Factory Tracts* that LFLRA published: "We will show those drivelling cotton lords . . . that our rights cannot be trampled upon with impunity."

Despite these problems, women workers organized. They staged several strikes at Lowell, Massachusetts, in the 1830s. In the 1840s, **Sarah Bagley** organized the Lowell Female Labor Reform Association. The group petitioned the state legislature for a 10-hour workday.

Millions of New Americans

By the late 1840s, many factory workers in the North were immigrants. An immigrant is a person who enters a new country in order to settle there. In the 1840s and 1850s, about 4 million immigrants arrived in the United States.

From Ireland and Germany

In the 1840s, a disease destroyed the potato crop across Europe. The loss of the crop caused a **famine**, or severe food shortage, especially in Ireland. Between 1845 and 1860, over 1.5 million Irish fled to the United States.

Most Irish immigrants were too poor to buy farmland. They settled in the cities where their ships landed. In New York and Boston, thousands of Irish crowded into poor neighborhoods.

In the 1850s, nearly one million German immigrants arrived in the United States. In 1848, revolutions had broken out in several parts of Germany. The rebels fought for democratic reforms. When the revolts failed, thousands had to flee.

Many other German immigrants came to the United States simply to make a better life for themselves.

Enriching the nation

Immigrants supplied much of the labor that helped the nation's economy to grow. Many Irish immigrants worked in northern factories because they did not have enough money to buy farmland. Other Irish workers helped build the canals and railroads that were crisscrossing the nation.

Immigrants from Germany often had enough money to move west and buy good farmland. Many of them were artisans and merchants. Towns of the Midwest often had German grocers, butchers, and bakers.

A Reaction Against Immigrants

Not everyone welcomed the flood of immigrants. One group of Americans, called **nativists**, wanted to preserve the country for native-born, white citizens. Using the slogan "Americans must rule America," they called for laws to limit immigration. They also wanted to keep immigrants from voting until they had lived in the United States for 21 years. At the time, newcomers could vote after only 5 years in the country.

Some nativists protested that newcomers "stole" jobs from native-born Americans by working for lower pay. Others blamed immigrants for crime in the growing cities. Still others mistrusted Irish and German newcomers because many of them were Catholics. Until the 1840s, the majority of immigrants from Europe were Protestants.

In the 1850s, nativists formed a new political party. It was known as the **Know-Nothing party** because members answered, "I know nothing," when asked about the party. Many meetings and rituals of the party were kept secret. In 1856, the Know-Nothing candidate for President won 21 percent of the popular vote. Soon after, however, the party died out. Still, many Americans continued to blame the nation's problems on immigrants.

African Americans in the North

During the nation's early years, slavery was legal in the North. By the early 1800s, however, all the northern states had outlawed slavery. As a result, thousands of free African Americans lived in the North.

Denied equal rights

Free African Americans in the North faced discrimination. **Discrimination** is a policy or an attitude that denies equal rights to certain groups of people. As one writer pointed out, African Americans were denied "the ballot-box, the jury box, the halls of the legislature, the army, the public lands, the school, and the church."

Writing Actively

After Reading Have students refer to the notes they jotted down while reading the section. Ask them to write one or two sentences to answer each question under Explore These Questions at the beginning of the section.

★ Background ★
Recent Scholarship

The Irish domestics More Irish women became domestic servants in the United States than did women from other countries. In part, this was because most Irish women immigrants were unmarried and unattached to families. In his book *A Different Mirror,* Ronald Takaki discusses the results of Irish competition with Chinese and African American workers.

From the Archives of American Heritage®

American export—potato blight The potato had made its way to Ireland from the Americas through the Columbian Exchange in the 1500s. The fungus that brought on the terrible famine also originated in the Americas. The cause of the blight, a spore-spreading fungus, was first spotted in the eastern U.S. in 1843.

Source: Peter Quinn, "The Tragedy of Bridget Such-a-One," *American Heritage* magazine, December 1997.

★ Section 2 Review ★

ANSWERS

1. (a)–(b) p. 381, **(c)–(e)** p. 382

2. (a)–(c) p. 379, **(d)–(f)** p. 381

3. The work was dangerous; hours were longer; pay was lower.

4. Irish fled famine in Ireland. Failed revolutions led to German migration. Both sought better lives.

5. Free African Americans were denied equal rights and decent jobs.

6. Factory owners, because strikes would reduce their profits

7. Organizer should include: fear of immigrants (criminals; replacement workers); prejudice against Catholics

Activity

Guided Instruction
Remind students to be persuasive, to cite facts and use emotional appeals based on those facts (e.g., "Lowell women work 72 hours a week. Do you want your daughter to work that much?"). Students might find out about conditions at an area factory and compare them to those in the Lowell mills.

ASSESSMENT See the rubrics in the Alternative Assessment booklet in the Teaching Resources.

ANSWER

Possible answer: discrimination; resistance to his ideas on education

RESOURCE DIRECTORY

Teaching Resources
Lesson Planner, p. 60
Unit 4/Chapter 14
• Section 2 Quiz, p. 30
Interdisciplinary Connections
• Main Idea: African American Contributions, p. 81

Biography **John Jones**

In the 1840s, John Jones ran a profitable tailoring business in Chicago. He helped runaway slaves and opposed Illinois laws that discriminated against African Americans. In the 1870s, he would help to integrate Chicago's public schools.
★ **What obstacles did Jones probably have to overcome?**

Even skilled African Americans had trouble finding good jobs. One black carpenter was turned away by every furniture maker in Cincinnati. At last, a shop owner hired him. However, when he entered the shop, the other carpenters dropped their tools. Either he must leave or they would, they declared. Similar experiences occurred throughout the North.

Some success

Despite the obstacles in their way, some African Americans achieved notable success in business. William Whipper grew wealthy as the owner of a lumber yard in Pennsylvania. He devoted much of his time and money to help bring an end to slavery. **Henry Boyd** operated a profitable furniture company in Cincinnati.

African Americans made strides in other areas as well. Henry Blair invented a corn planter and a cotton seed planter. In 1845, **Macon Allen** became the first African American licensed to practice law in the United States. After graduating from Bowdoin College in Maine, **John Russworm** became one of the editors of *Freedom's Journal*, the first African American newspaper.

★ Section 2 Review ★

Recall

1. **Identify** **(a)** Sarah Bagley, **(b)** Know-Nothing party, **(c)** Henry Boyd, **(d)** Macon Allen, **(e)** John Russworm.
2. **Define** **(a)** artisan, **(b)** trade union, **(c)** strike, **(d)** famine, **(e)** nativist, **(f)** discrimination.

Comprehension

3. How did working conditions in factories worsen in the 1840s and 1850s?
4. In the mid-1800s, why did so many immigrants to the United States come from Ireland and Germany?
5. How did discrimination affect free African Americans in the North?

Critical Thinking and Writing

6. **Making Inferences** Who do you think were the strongest supporters of laws that made strikes illegal? Explain.
7. **Recognizing Points of View** Make a graphic organizer that identifies the reasons for the nativist point of view.

Activity **Writing a Petition** You are a female mill worker of the 1840s. You are unhappy about the harsh working conditions in the mills. Write a petition to the state legislature listing your complaints and asking for better working conditions.

Cotton Kingdom in the South

As You Read

Explore These Questions

- Why did cotton planters begin to move westward?
- How did the cotton gin affect slavery in the South?
- Why did the South have less industry than the North?

Identify

- Eli Whitney
- Cotton Kingdom
- William Gregg

Cotton gin

SETTING the Scene In 1827, an Englishman, Basil Hall, traveled through much of the South aboard a riverboat. He complained that the southerners he met were interested in only one thing—cotton:

> "All day and almost all night long, the captain, pilot, crew and passengers were talking of nothing else; and sometimes our ears were so wearied with the sound of cotton! cotton! cotton! that we gladly hailed fresh . . . company in hopes of some change—but alas! . . . 'What's cotton at?' was the first eager inquiry."

Cotton became even more important to the South in the years after Hall's visit. Even though southerners grew other crops, cotton was the region's leading export. Cotton plantations—and the slave system on which they depended—shaped the way of life in the South.

Cotton Gin, Cotton Boom

The Industrial Revolution greatly increased the demand for southern cotton. Textile mills in the North and in Britain needed more and more cotton to make cloth. At first, southern planters could not meet the demand. They could grow plenty of cotton because the South's soil and climate were ideal. However, removing the seeds from the cotton by hand was a slow process. Planters needed a better way to clean cotton.

Eli Whitney's invention

In 1793, **Eli Whitney**, a young Connecticut schoolteacher, was traveling to Georgia. He was going to be a tutor on a plantation. When Whitney learned of the planters' problem, he decided to build a machine to clean cotton.

In only 10 days, Whitney came up with a model. His cotton engine, or gin, had two rollers with thin wire teeth. When cotton was swept between the rollers, the teeth separated the seeds from the fibers. (See Linking History and Technology on page 384.)

The cotton gin was simple, but its effects were enormous. A worker using a gin could do the work of 50 people cleaning cotton by hand. Because of the gin, planters could now grow cotton at a huge profit.

Connections With Science

Technology thieves stole Eli Whitney's first cotton gin. Before Whitney could build another, someone filed a patent for a machine that copied his invention. To receive the profits that were due to him, Whitney went to court. He filed more than 50 lawsuits.

Section 3 Cotton Kingdom in the South

LESSON PLAN

Objectives

★ Explain why cotton planters moved westward.
★ Describe how the cotton gin affected slavery in the South.
★ Give reasons why the South was less industrialized than the North.

1 Engage

Warm Up Ask students if they have any clothes made of cotton. Ask what qualities of cotton make it such a popular fabric for clothes.

Activating Prior Knowledge Remind students that many factories in the North were textile factories. They made thread and cloth from cotton. Ask students where the cotton used in the factories was grown.

Reading Actively

Before Reading As they read the section, have students note short-term and long-term effects of the invention of the cotton gin. They can use the information to create an Effects chart.

★ Activity ★

Connections With Economics

Finding supporting evidence Explain that in the 1830s and 1840s, New Orleans was the nation's busiest port. But by the 1850s, New York was busier. Ask students to search the chapter for causes for this change. (*Answers: South's dependence on cotton, rise of railroads, and North's increased industry and manufacturing*) (*average*) T

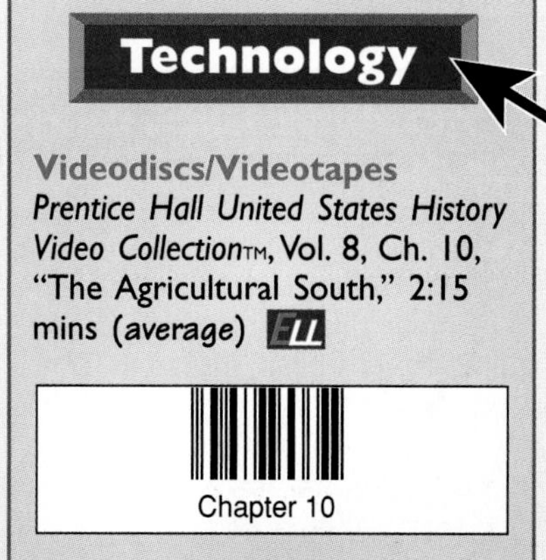

Technology

Videodiscs/Videotapes

Prentice Hall United States History Video Collection™, Vol. 8, Ch. 10, "The Agricultural South," 2:15 mins (*average*) ELL

Chapter 10

2 Explore

Ask students to skim the section. Ask them to make a generalization about the relationship between cotton and slavery. Then ask them to read the section carefully, looking for evidence to support or refute their generalization.

3 Teach

Tell students that in 1858, South Carolina Senator James Henry said, "Cotton is king. You dare not make war on cotton!" Ask students to list ways that economic dependence on cotton helped the South and ways that this dependence harmed the South. Students may present this information in chart form.

4 Assess

To close the lesson, have students complete the section review. As an alternative, ask students to take the role of a southern plantation worker and to write a journal entry describing how the use of Whitney's new cotton gin has affected life on the plantation.

★ ★ ★ ★ ★ ★ ★ ★ ★ ★ ★ ★ ★ ★ ★ ★ ★

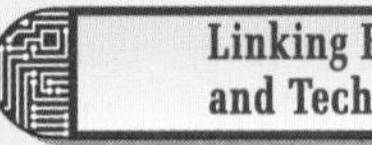

ANSWER

The cotton seeds were too large to pass through the narrow slots of the machine. The seeds fell to the bottom of the gin.

RESOURCE DIRECTORY

Teaching Resources
Unit 4/Chapter 14
- Connecting History and Literature: Go Down, Moses, p. 27

Transparencies
Exploring Technology
- Cotton Gin, p. H-33

Linking History and Technology

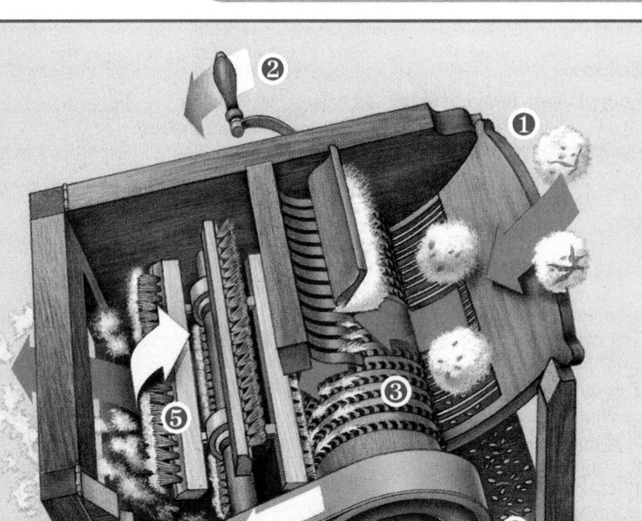

❶ *Cotton bolls, made up of fiber and seeds, are fed into the cotton gin. The red arrows show the path of the cotton through the gin.*

❷ *As the handle is turned, the cylinder and brushes rotate.*

❸ *Wire teeth catch the cotton bolls and pull them through narrow wire slots.*

❹ *The seeds are too large to pass through the slots. They fall to the bottom of the gin.*

❺ *Rotating brushes pull cleaned cotton fiber from the wire teeth and sweep it out of the gin.*

The Cotton Gin

The cotton gin separated unwanted seeds from cotton fiber. With the help of a gin, a worker was able to process as much as 50 pounds of cotton in a single day. As a result, cotton production became a very profitable business.
★ **How did the gin separate the seeds from the fiber?**

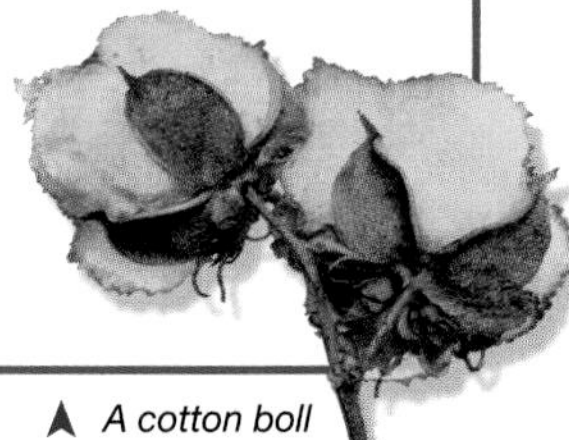

▲ *A cotton boll*

Cotton Kingdom and slavery

The cotton gin led to a boom in cotton production. In 1792, planters grew only 6,000 bales of cotton a year. By 1850, the figure was over 2 million bales.

Planters soon learned that soil wore out if planted with cotton year after year. They needed new land to cultivate. After the War of 1812, cotton planters began to move west.

By the 1850s, there were cotton plantations extending in a wide band from South Carolina through Alabama and Mississippi to Texas. (See the map on page 386.) This area of the South became known as the **Cotton Kingdom**.

Tragically, as the Cotton Kingdom spread, so did slavery. Even though cotton could now be cleaned by machine, it still had to be planted and picked by hand. The result was a cruel cycle. The work of slaves brought profits to planters. Planters used the profits to buy more land and more slaves.

Skills For LIFE MINI LESSON

COMMUNICATION Giving Directions

1. Introduce the skill of giving directions by pointing out the diagram of the cotton gin above. The labels beside the drawing explain how the gin works. It breaks down the process of separating the cotton fibers from the seeds into its individual steps.

2. Help students practice the skill by telling them to select an item that they use frequently and that is somewhat complicated to operate. Some examples include a VCR, a two-track tape player, a microwave, and a computer. Ask students to sketch the item and provide directions for its use.

3. Help students apply the skill by using their sketches and directions to "teach" classmates how to use the item. T

An Agricultural Economy

Cotton was the South's most profitable cash crop. However, the best conditions for growing cotton could be found mostly in the southernmost portion of the South. In other areas of the South, rice, sugar cane, and tobacco were major crops. In addition, Southerners raised much of the nation's livestock.

Rice was an important crop along the coasts of South Carolina and Georgia. Sugar cane was important in Louisiana and Texas. Growing rice and sugar cane required expensive irrigation and drainage systems. Cane growers also needed costly machinery to grind their harvest. Small-scale farmers could not afford such expensive equipment, however. As a result, the plantation system dominated areas of sugar and rice production just as it did areas of cotton production.

Tobacco had been an export of the South since 1619, and it continued to be planted in Virginia, North Carolina, and Kentucky. However, in the early 1800s, the large tobacco plantations of colonial days had given way to small tobacco farms. On these farms, a few field hands tended five or six acres of tobacco.

In addition to the major cash crops of cotton, rice, sugar, and tobacco, the South also led the nation in livestock production. Southern livestock owners profited from hogs, oxen, horses, mules, and beef cattle. Much of this livestock was raised in areas that were unsuitable for growing crops, such as the pine woods of North Carolina.

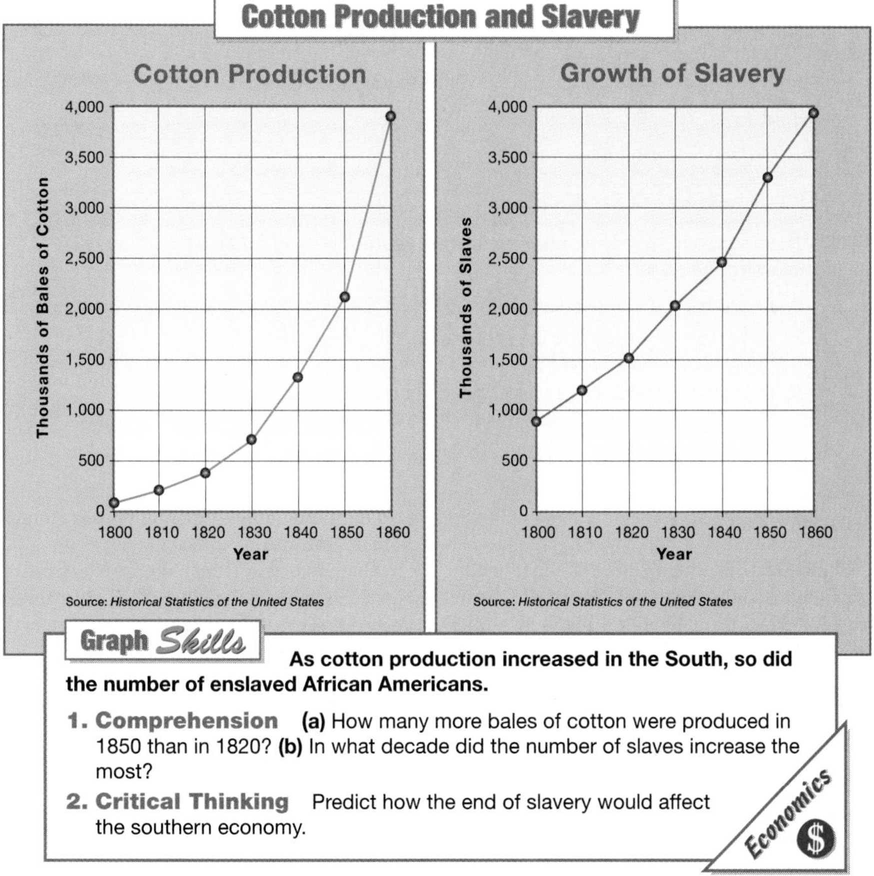

Graph Skills **As cotton production increased in the South, so did the number of enslaved African Americans.**

1. **Comprehension** **(a)** How many more bales of cotton were produced in 1850 than in 1820? **(b)** In what decade did the number of slaves increase the most?
2. **Critical Thinking** Predict how the end of slavery would affect the southern economy.

Reading Actively

During Reading Ask students to list the crops other than cotton that were grown in the South. Which of these crops were grown on large plantations?

Graph Skills

ANSWERS **1. (a)** Approximately 1,700,000 more bales of cotton were produced in 1850 than in 1820. **(b)** the 1840s **2.** Possible answer: Cotton production might decrease. Planters would have to pay workers, which would reduce profits. Formerly enslaved African Americans might have difficulty finding decent jobs.

★ Background ★
Our Diverse Nation

To be enslaved In the 1840s and 1850s, slave narratives were very popular in the United States. Perhaps the greatest and most influential was *My Bondage and My Freedom*, the autobiography of Frederick Douglass, published in 1855. It not only recounts Douglass's years in slavery but discusses what slavery meant in the minds of both African Americans and whites.

★ Background ★
Recent Scholarship

Illegal slave trade The slave trade, ended by law in 1807, continued to some degree for about 50 years. In his recent book *The Slave Trade*, Hugh Thomas describes some of the common routes for smuggling enslaved Africans into the United States. In addition, Thomas describes how U.S. shippers exported enslaved Africans to Cuba and other Spanish colonies.

Geography *Skills*

ANSWERS **1.** Review locations with students. **2.** Cotton production moved west into Georgia, Alabama, Mississippi, Louisiana, and Texas. **3. (a)** tobacco **(b)** Virginia's soil and climate were more suited to growing tobacco than to growing cotton.

Writing Actively

After Reading Ask students to write an editorial for a southern newspaper encouraging the growth of industry. The editorials should compare the industrial North to the agricultural South in the mid-1800s. Tell students to review Section 1 of this chapter for information about the industry of the North.

ANSWER Possible answer to caption, p. 387: The climate and fertile soil made investments in land and slaves more appealing to investors than investments in factories.

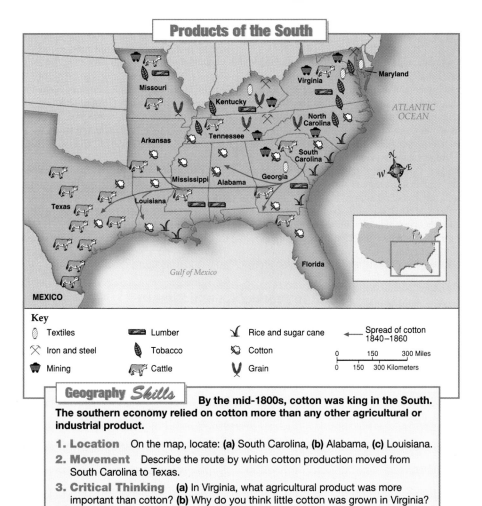

Products of the South

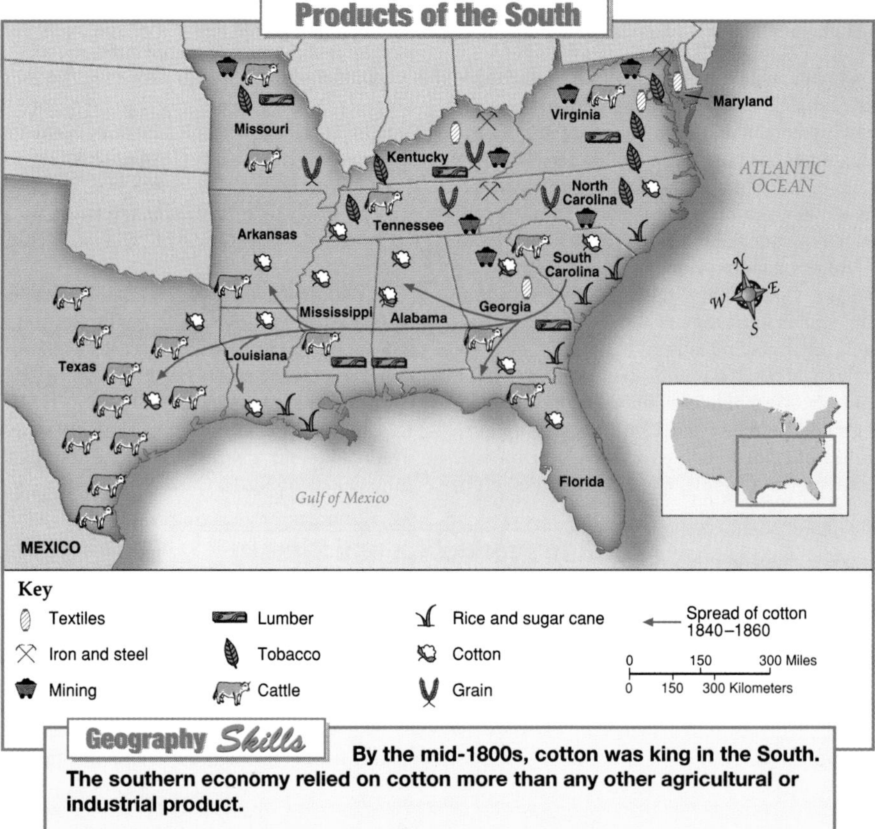

Geography *Skills*

By the mid-1800s, cotton was king in the South. The southern economy relied on cotton more than any other agricultural or industrial product.

1. **Location** On the map, locate: **(a)** South Carolina, **(b)** Alabama, **(c)** Louisiana.
2. **Movement** Describe the route by which cotton production moved from South Carolina to Texas.
3. **Critical Thinking** **(a)** In Virginia, what agricultural product was more important than cotton? **(b)** Why do you think little cotton was grown in Virginia?

Limited Industry

Some southerners wanted to encourage the growth of industry in the South. **William Gregg**, for example, modeled his cotton mill in South Carolina on the mills in Lowell, Massachusetts. Gregg built houses and gardens for his workers and schools for their children.

The South also developed a few other successful industries. In Richmond, Virginia, for example, the Tredegar Iron Works turned out railroad equipment, machinery, tools, and cannons. Flour milling was another important southern industry.

Even so, the South lagged behind the North in manufacturing. Rich planters invested their money in land and slaves rather than in factories.

Also, slavery reduced the need for southern industry. In the North, most people had enough money to buy factory goods. In the South, however, millions of slaves could not buy anything. As a result, the demand for goods in the South was not as great as in the North. This hurt southern industry.

★ *Customized Instruction* ★

Kinesthetic Learners

Panel discussion Direct some students to assume the following roles for a panel discussion: Eli Whitney, William Gregg, plantation owners in South Carolina, small farmers in Kentucky, landowners in Mississippi, enslaved African Americans in Virginia and on a new plantation in Louisiana. Other students should take the roles of reporters asking questions of the panelists. Each reporter should have a specialty, such as business/economics, agriculture, or politics. Assign one student to act as the moderator. Through introductory statements and questions and answers, panelists should explain their views about the future of the South. (*challenging*)

RESOURCE DIRECTORY

Teaching Resources
Unit 4/Chapter 14
- Section 3 Quiz, p. 31

Interdisciplinary Connections
- Main Idea: African American Contributions, p. 84

Viewing HISTORY **Economically Dependent**

Many southerners ordered goods from northern and European manufacturers. This advertisement appeared in the mail-order catalog of a store located in Milledgeville, Illinois. ★ **Why were there so few factories in the South?**

Economically Dependent

With little industry of its own, the South came to depend more and more on the North and on Europe. Southern planters often borrowed money from northern banks in order to expand their plantations. They also purchased much of their furniture, farm tools, and machines from northern or European factories.

Many southerners resented this situation. One southerner described a burial to show how the South depended on the North for many goods in the 1850s:

> “The grave was dug through solid marble, but the marble headstone came from Vermont. It was in a pine wilderness but the pine coffin came from Cincinnati. An iron mountain overshadowed it but the coffin nails and the screws and the shovel came from Pittsburgh. . . . A hickory grove grew nearby, but the pick and shovel handles came from New York. . . . That country, so rich in underdeveloped resources, furnished nothing for the funeral except the corpse and the hole in the ground.”

Still, most southerners were proud of the booming cotton industry in their region. As long as cotton remained king, southerners believed, they could look to the future with confidence.

★ Section 3 Review ★

Recall

1. **Locate** **(a)** South Carolina, **(b)** Alabama, **(c)** Mississippi, **(d)** Texas.
2. **Identify** **(a)** Eli Whitney, **(b)** Cotton Kingdom, **(c)** William Gregg.

Comprehension

3. Why did the Cotton Kingdom spread westward?
4. How did the cotton gin cause slavery to expand in the South?
5. Why did the South not develop as much industry as the North?

Critical Thinking and Writing

6. **Predicting Consequences** How might the southern economy have developed differently if the cotton gin had never been invented?
7. **Analyzing Primary Sources** Review the quotation that appears at the end of the section. Is the southerner praising or criticizing the economy of the South? Explain.

Activity **Linking Past and Present** The cotton gin had a major impact on the South's way of life. In a chart, list some modern inventions, describe what they do, and explain how they are changing the way you live today.

Internet Activity

What's the big deal about cotton? Direct students to the Web site maintained by Cotton Incorporated (www.cottoninc.com). Students can learn how T-shirts were named, what makes cotton wrinkle, and where cotton is grown today. Given the changing nature of the Internet, you may wish to preview the site before directing students to it. (*basic*)

★ Section 3 Review ★

ANSWERS

1. See map, p. 386.
2. **(a)** p. 383, **(b)** p. 384, **(c)** p. 386
3. Growing cotton on the same land year after year exhausted the soil. Planters sought new, fertile land in the West.
4. Because of the gin, planters could grow cotton at a huge profit. Cotton plantations spread across the South. Planters needed more slaves to work the plantations.
5. Planters invested in land and slaves, not factories. Because millions of slaves had no money, demand for factory goods in the South was less than in the North.
6. Possible answers: The number of slaves might not have increased as much. The southern economy might have developed more industry.
7. The southerner is criticizing the South for not using its natural resources to produce more.

Activity

Guided Instruction
Have students brainstorm the list of modern inventions. Each student might then describe one or two inventions and explain their impact on life today. Interested students could convert the ideas into a chart or other graphic organizer.

ASSESSMENT See the rubrics in the Alternative Assessment booklet in the Teaching Resources.

Section 4
Life in the South

LESSON PLAN

Objectives

★ Identify the five groups that made up southern society.
★ Describe the sufferings of African Americans under slavery.
★ Describe how African Americans struggled against slavery.

1 Engage

Warm Up Ask students to write as many phrases as they can that they associate with the idea of "freedom."

Activating Prior Knowledge Ask students how slavery began in the United States and why it existed in the South but not in the North in the mid-1800s.

Reading Actively
Before Reading Have students turn the main headings in the section into the main topics of an outline. Then, as they read, have them record two or three important subtopics for each main topic.

2 Explore

Ask students to read the section. For a homework assignment, ask them to write one or two sentences about each of the five groups of southern society.

RESOURCE DIRECTORY

Teaching Resources
Lesson Planner, p. 61
Unit 4/Chapter 14
• Biography Flashcard: Ira F. Aldridge, p. 28

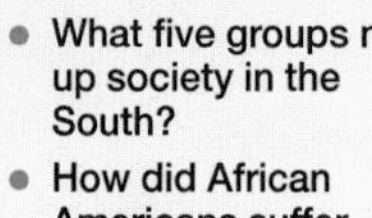

Life in the South

As You Read

Explore These Questions
- What five groups made up society in the South?
- How did African Americans suffer under slavery?
- How did African Americans struggle against slavery?

Define
- slave code
- extended family

Identify
- "cottonocracy"
- Norbert Rillieux
- Henry Blair
- Denmark Vesey
- Nat Turner

Setting the Scene

"I was born in 1844.... First [thing] I remember was my ma and us [children] being sold off the [auction] block to Mistress Payne. When I was... too little to work in the field, I stayed at the big house most of the time and helped Mistress Payne feed the chickens, make scarecrows to keep the hawks away and put wood on the fires. After I got big enough to hoe, I went to the field same as the other[s]."

In this excerpt, Jack Payne recalls his life as an enslaved person in Texas. Payne was only one of millions of African Americans throughout the South who suffered the anguish of slavery. Toiling from dawn till dusk, they had neither freedom nor rights.

White Southerners

The Old South is often pictured as a land of vast plantations worked by hundreds of slaves. Such grand estates did exist in the South. However, most white southerners were not rich planters. In fact, most whites owned no slaves at all.

The "cottonocracy"

A planter was someone who owned at least 20 slaves. In 1860, only one white southerner in 30 belonged to a planter family. An even smaller number—less than 1 percent—owned 50 or more slaves. These wealthy families were called the **"cottonocracy"** because they made huge amounts of money from cotton. Though few in number, their views and way of life dominated the South.

The richest planters built elegant homes and filled them with expensive furniture from Europe. They entertained lavishly. They tried to dress and behave like European nobility.

Planters had responsibilities, too. Because of their wealth and influence, many planters became political leaders. They devoted many hours to local, state, and national politics. Planters hired overseers to run day-to-day affairs on their plantations and to manage the work of slaves.

Small farmers

About 75 percent of southern whites were small farmers. These "plain folk" owned the

Connections With Arts

In later years, both literature and film gave a false view of plantation life. Writers and film producers focused on the "gentility" of the planters and largely ignored the injustices of slavery. The most successful of these fictional works is the 1939 film *Gone With the Wind.* Based on Margaret Mitchell's novel, the film won 10 Academy Awards, including Best Picture.

★ Customized Instruction ★
Introverted Learners

A southern biography Ask introverted learners to read a biography of an important African American from this period, such as Frederick Douglass, Denmark Vesey, or Nat Turner. Students may write or record a summary of the major events in the biography. Ask students to pick out one short quotation from the biography that they think is especially meaningful or interesting. As an alternative, introverted learners might write a fictional biographical sketch of a slave's life in the 1840s or 1850s. Ask students to include as many details as they can, such as work assignments, living conditions, family, and knowledge of the outside world. Students may present their work in a written report or in a storyboard format. (*average*) T

AmericanHeritage
M A G A Z I N E

Rosedown Plantation

Rosedown Plantation, built in 1835, is located in St. Francisville, Louisiana. It was owned by the wealthy cotton planter, Daniel Turnbull, and his wife Martha. The Turnbulls filled their mansion with beautiful furniture and art from Europe. They surrounded their home with avenues of trees and formal gardens. Today, visitors can tour Rosedown, its gardens, and its many outbuildings. You can even stay overnight and recall the luxurious lifestyle of the southern aristocracy.

★ ***To learn more about this historic site, write:*** *Rosedown Plantation, 12501 Highway 10, St. Francisville, LA 70775.*

Original bedroom furniture at Rosedown

land they farmed. They might also own one or two slaves. Unlike planters, plain folk worked with their slaves in the fields.

Among small farmers, helping each other was an important duty. "People who lived miles apart counted themselves as neighbors," wrote a farmer in Mississippi. "And in case of sorrow or sickness, there was no limit to the service neighbors provided."

Poor whites

Lower on the social ladder was a small group of poor whites. They did not own the land they farmed. Instead, they rented it, often paying the owner with part of their crop. Many barely made a living.

Poor whites often lived in the hilly, wooded areas of the South. They planted crops such as corn, potatoes, and other vegetables. They also herded cattle and pigs. Poor whites had hard lives, but they enjoyed rights denied to all African Americans, enslaved or free.

African American Southerners

Both free and enslaved African Americans lived in the South. Although free under the law, free African Americans faced harsh discrimination. Enslaved African Americans had no rights at all.

Free African Americans

Most free African Americans were descendants of slaves freed during and after the American Revolution. Others had bought their freedom. In 1860, over 200,000 free blacks lived in the South. Most lived in Maryland and Delaware, where slavery was

3 Teach

Divide the class into five teams. Assign each team one of the five groups of southern society. Tell each team to prepare a presentation to the class in which the team members summarize the key characteristics, rights, duties, and contributions of their group. Presentations may be reports, posters, dialogues, or panel discussions.

4 Assess

To close the lesson, have students complete the section review. As an alternative, ask students to make a speech or write a statement describing what they consider the most terrible aspect of the slave system.

AmericanHeritage
M A G A Z I N E

Rosedown Plantation To learn more about Rosedown Plantation on the Internet, go to cimarron.net/usa/la/rosedown.html.

★ *Background* ★

Did You Know?

The newly rich Davises Jefferson Davis, who became the President of the Confederacy, was born in Kentucky into a poor farm family. Jefferson's brother Joseph moved to Mississippi and became a successful planter. Joseph sent Jefferson to West Point and provided him with a large plantation of his own.

Technology

Videodiscs/Videotapes
Prentice Hall United States History Video Collection™, Vol. 8, Ch. 13, "The Slave South," 3:15 mins (average) ELL

Chapter 13

Graphic Organizer Skills

ANSWERS **1.** whites who owned no slaves **2.** Possible answer: They had much respect for the planters and their way of life. Poor white southerners might have feared that the end of slavery would mean that they would have to compete for jobs with free African Americans.

Reading Actively

During Reading Ask students why they think slave owners were afraid of free African Americans and of enslaved African Americans. How did slave owners express their fears? *(They were afraid of slave uprisings, and they were afraid of having their slaves run away. They expressed their fears in laws to restrict the movement of African Americans, both free and enslaved.)*

Southern Society in 1860

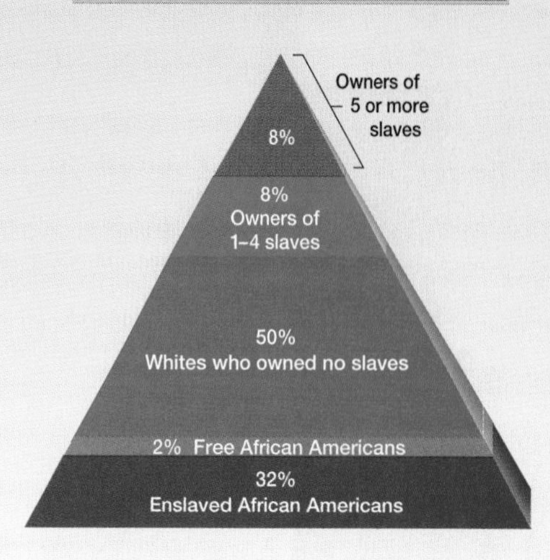

Source: *Historical Statistics of the United States*

Graphic Organizer Skills

This social pyramid represents the structure of southern society in 1860. At the top were wealthy and powerful planters. At the bottom were millions of enslaved African Americans.

1. **Comprehension** Which group in southern society was most numerous?
2. **Critical Thinking** Many white southerners owned no slaves but still supported the institution of slavery. Why do you think they did so?

in decline. Others lived in cities such as New Orleans, Richmond, and Charleston.

Slave owners did not like free African Americans living in the South. They feared that free African Americans set a bad example, encouraging slaves to rebel. Also, slave owners justified slavery by claiming that African Americans could not take care of themselves. Free African American workers proved this idea wrong.

To discourage free African Americans, southern states passed laws that made life even harder for them. Free African Americans were not allowed to vote or travel. In some southern states, they either had to move out of the state or allow themselves to be enslaved.

Despite these limits, free African Americans made valuable contributions to southern life. For example, **Norbert Rillieux** (RIHL yoo) invented a machine that revolutionized the way sugar was made. Another inventor, **Henry Blair,** patented a seed planter.

Enslaved African Americans

By 1860, enslaved African Americans made up one third of the South's population. Most worked as field hands on cotton plantations. Both men and women cleared new land and planted and harvested crops. Children helped by pulling weeds, collecting wood, and carrying water to the field hands. By the time they were teenagers, they too worked between 12 and 14 hours a day.

On large plantations, some African Americans became skilled workers, such as carpenters and blacksmiths. A few worked in cities and lived almost as if they were free. Their earnings, however, belonged to their owners.

Life Without Freedom

The life of enslaved African Americans was determined by strict laws and the practices of individual slave owners. Conditions varied from plantation to plantation. Some owners made sure their slaves had clean cabins, decent food, and warm clothes. Other planters spent as little as possible on their slaves.

Slave codes

Southern states passed laws known as **slave codes** to keep slaves from either running away or rebelling. Under the codes, enslaved African Americans were forbidden to gather in groups of more than three. They could not leave their owner's land without a written pass. They were not allowed to own guns.

Slave codes also made it a crime for slaves to learn how to read and write. Owners hoped that this law would make it hard for African Americans to escape slavery. They reasoned that uneducated runaway slaves would not be able to use maps or read train schedules. They would not be able to find their way north.

Resource Directory

Teaching Resources
Why Study History?
- Music Is Part of Our Culture, pp. 55–58

Interdisciplinary Connections
- Main Idea: African American Contributions, pp. 82, 83

★ Background ★
Did You Know?

New York witch hunt Fear of slave revolts affected both the North and South long before the mid-1800s. In 1741, Mary Burton, an indentured servant in New York City, claimed that slaves had set a series of fires. Over time Burton's story grew to include a slave plot to burn the city and slaughter its citizens. The resulting panic led to the hanging of 31 slaves.

Why Study History?

Because Music Is Part of Our Culture

Historical Background

From the colonial era on, southerners of diverse backgrounds shared their music with one another. As a result, a variety of rich musical traditions developed in the American South.

African Americans built on the musical heritage of their ancestral homelands. One common technique was the "call and response" in which a soloist sang a line and the group responded. African American music stressed varied rhythms and improvisation, the spontaneous creation of new lyrics and melodies. In the 1800s, these qualities were typical of African American work songs, religious songs, and folk songs.

The early musical traditions of most white southerners were rooted in the tunes and melodies of the British Isles. German, Mexican, Cajun, and other traditions also enriched Southern folk music. The sounds of fiddles and banjos often celebrated house raisings, harvest feasts, and other major events.

Connections to Today

Several American music styles of today are firmly rooted in the South. Blues, jazz, and gospel music emerged from the traditions of African American southerners. Country music and rock-and-roll developed from the folk music of both white and black southerners. In fact, most early rock performers of the 1950s came from the South.

Connections to You

The sounds of jazz, country, and rock are all around you. The next time you pop in your favorite CD, consider the roots of the music you hear. When you watch a television show, note its theme music. When you go to the movies, listen to the soundtrack. You will discover that American music owes much to the rich and diverse traditions of the American South.

▲ Gospel singers

▲ Country music singer

1. **Comprehension** What music styles of today can be traced to traditions in the American South?
2. **Critical Thinking** Why do you think jazz and blues music developed in the South rather than in the North?

★Activity **Planning a Documentary** Research the history of a music style discussed here. Then, outline a television documentary on that style. List the topics and pictures that will appear in your documentary.

ANSWERS

1. blues, jazz, gospel music, country, and rock-and-roll **2.** Possible answer: Jazz and blues grew out of African American musical tradition and were expressions of American life in the South.

Guided Instruction

Direct students to books and articles about their subjects. Review outlining skills. Remind students that each section of the outline should cover one aspect of the topic.

ASSESSMENT See the rubrics in the Alternative Assessment booklet in the Teaching Resources.

Fast Facts

★ Blues music is easily recognizable because of its common structures and harmonies. Pieces often differ only in key.

★ By the 1850s, all southern cities had military bands that played at military events and parades. Some bands were composed entirely of African American musicians.

★ Some historians believe that jazz began with the drum rhythms in Congo Square in New Orleans, where African slaves gathered in their free time to play drums and dance.

Bibliography

To read more about this topic:

1. *The First Book of Jazz,* Langston Hughes (Ecco Press, 1997). Classic history of jazz.

2. *Gonna Sing My Head Off! American Folk Songs Arranged for Children,* Kathleen Krull (Knopf, 1992). Presents 62 familiar songs in interesting, easy arrangements.

3. Internet. Historical and contemporary information about jazz (www.jazzonln.com).

Technology

Listening to Music CD

- Swing Low, Sweet Chariot, track 7 *(average)*
- Go Down, Moses, track 8 *(average)*

Viewing History ANSWER

Possible answer: Religion helped to unite the African American community. Faith in God and the teachings of the Bible gave enslaved people hope for a better life in the future.

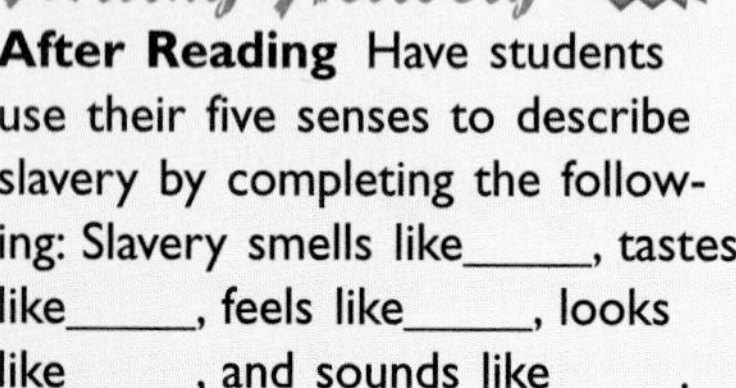

Writing Actively

After Reading Have students use their five senses to describe slavery by completing the following: Slavery smells like_____, tastes like_____, feels like_____, looks like_____, and sounds like_____.

Viewing History **African American Community**

The painting Plantation Burial *by John Antrobus is unusual for providing a realistic portrait of life on a southern plantation. The central figures are African Americans. To the left, a white couple keeps a respectful distance from the religious ceremony.* ★ **What role did religion play in the life of enslaved African Americans?**

Some laws were meant to protect slaves, but only from the worst forms of abuse. However, enslaved African Americans did not have the right to testify in court. As a result, they were not able to bring charges against owners who abused them.

Enslaved African Americans had only one real protection against mistreatment. Owners looked on their slaves as valuable property. Most slave owners wanted to keep this human property healthy and productive.

Hard work

Even the kindest owners insisted that their slaves work long, hard days. Slaves worked from "can see to can't see," or from dawn to dusk, up to 16 hours a day. Frederick Douglass, who escaped slavery, recalled his life under one harsh master:

> "We were worked in all weathers. It was never too hot or too cold; it could never rain, blow, hail, or snow too hard for us to work in the field. Work, work, work.... The longest days were too short for him and the shortest nights too long for him."

Some owners and overseers whipped slaves to get a full day's work. However, the worst part of slavery was not the beatings. It was the complete loss of freedom.

Family life

It was hard for enslaved African Americans to keep their families together. Southern laws did not recognize slave marriages or slave families. As a result, owners could sell a husband and wife to different buyers. Children were often taken from their parents and sold.

On large plantations, many enslaved families did manage to stay together. For those African Americans, the family was a

★ *Background* ★

Linking Past and Present

Amistad In 1997, a film by director Steven Spielberg was released entitled *Amistad.* It is based on the true story of 53 Africans who revolted on board their Cuban slave ship on the evening of July 1, 1839. Two Cubans remaining on board sailed the ship into United States waters. The United States Navy apprehended the *Amistad*; the Africans, who spoke no English, were imprisoned and tried for murder and conspiracy. The Supreme Court declared the Africans of the *Amistad* free, largely thanks to the efforts of former President John Quincy Adams. Spielberg said of making the film, "I felt very much that I was telling everybody's story—a story that people of all races and nationalities should know."

RESOURCE DIRECTORY

Teaching Resources
Unit 4/Chapter 14
- Vocabulary Builder, p. 23
- Section 4 Quiz, p. 32

Chapter Tests, pp. 79–84
Interdisciplinary Connections
- Main Idea: African American Contributions, p. 80

source of strength, pride, and love. Grandparents, parents, children, aunts, uncles, and cousins formed a close-knit group. This idea of an **extended family** had its roots in Africa.

Enslaved African Americans preserved other traditions as well. Parents taught their children traditional African stories and songs. They used folk tales to pass on African history and moral beliefs.

Religion offers hope

By the 1800s, many enslaved African Americans were devout Christians. Planters often allowed white ministers to preach to their slaves. African Americans also had their own preachers and beliefs.

Religion helped African Americans cope with the harshness of slave life. Bible stories about how the ancient Hebrews had escaped from slavery inspired many spiritual songs. As they worked in the fields, slaves sang about a coming day of freedom. One spiritual, "Go Down, Moses," includes these lines:

> "We need not always weep and
> moan,
> Let my people go.
> And wear these slavery chains
> forlorn,
> Let my people go."

Resistance Against Slavery

Enslaved African Americans struck back against the system that denied them both freedom and wages. Some broke tools, destroyed crops, and stole food.

Many enslaved African Americans tried to escape to the North. Because the journey was long and dangerous, very few made it to freedom. Every county had slave patrols and sheriffs ready to question an unknown black person.

A few African Americans used violence to resist the brutal slave system. **Denmark Vesey**, a free African American, planned a revolt in 1822. Vesey was betrayed before the revolt began. He and 35 other people were executed.

In 1831, an African American preacher named **Nat Turner** led a major revolt. Turner led his followers through Virginia, killing more than 57 whites. Terrified whites hunted the countryside for Turner. They killed many innocent African Americans before catching and hanging him.

Nat Turner's revolt increased southern fears of an uprising of enslaved African Americans. Revolts were rare, however. Since whites were cautious and well armed, a revolt by African Americans had almost no chance of success.

★ Section 4 Review ★

Recall

1. **Identify** (a) "cottonocracy," (b) Norbert Rillieux, (c) Henry Blair, (d) Denmark Vesey, (e) Nat Turner.
2. **Define** (a) slave code, (b) extended family.

Comprehension

3. How did the "cottonocracy" dominate economics and politics in the South?
4. Describe three ways that African Americans suffered under slavery.
5. How did African Americans struggle against the slave system?

Critical Thinking and Writing

6. **Applying Information** How were successful free African Americans a threat to the slave system?
7. **Making Decisions** If you had been an enslaved African American, would you have decided to live under slavery, to try to escape, or to rebel? Explain the reasons for your decision.

Activity **Writing a Speech** You are an enslaved African American living in the South in the 1850s. Write a speech encouraging people to resist slavery and explaining ways in which they can do it.

★ Activity ★

Connections With Arts

Exploring African American culture Ask students to research various forms of African culture preserved by enslaved African Americans. Ask students to find audiotapes or CDs of spirituals that they can share with the class. Other students might prepare a reading of an African American folk tale. Some students might demonstrate African American crafts and recipes to the class. (*average*) ELL T

★ Section 4 Review ★

ANSWERS

1. (a) p. 388, **(b)** p. 390, **(c)** p. 390, **(d)** p. 393, **(e)** p. 393

2. (a) p. 390, **(b)** p. 393

3. It was the wealthiest group. Its members were prominent in local, state, and national politics.

4. Possible answer: Enslaved African Americans were forced to work without pay. Families were broken up. Slaves were denied an education.

5. Some destroyed or stole the planters' property; some escaped. A few engaged in violent revolts.

6. They disproved the idea that African Americans could not care for themselves. This idea was used to justify slavery.

7. Answers will vary.

Guided Instruction
Have students review the passage that describes ways in which enslaved people resisted. Encourage students to empathize with the situation of a slave. Their speeches should appeal to the need for freedom and the desire to resist oppression. Re-create a secret meeting of enslaved people and have students take turns giving their speeches.

ASSESSMENT See the rubrics in the Alternative Assessment booklet in the Teaching Resources.

Technology

Videodiscs/Videotapes
Prentice Hall United States History Video Collection™, Vol. 8, Ch. 16, "Slave Life and Revolt," 2:15 mins (*average*) ELL

Chapter 16

CD-ROM
Test Bank CD-ROM, Ch. 14
Interactive Student Tutorial

Chapter 14

Review and Activities

Reviewing the Chapter

Define These Terms

1. b **2.** d **3.** a **4.** c

Explore the Main Ideas

1. Possible answers include: the telegraph, the use of machines, railroads, and the use of steam power.

2. (a) Workers organized to fight for better working conditions and higher wages. **(b)** Famine in Ireland and political unrest in Germany prompted millions to migrate to the U.S.

3. The cotton gin enormously increased production, but it led both to an expansion of slavery and to Southern dependence on the North and Europe for nearly all of its manufactured items.

4. Possible answers: Slaves resisted by escaping and organizing revolts.

5. The North had a diverse economy, while the South was almost completely dependent on cotton; slaves were used as labor in the South, while northern workers were paid.

Graph Activity

1. 1847 **2.** about 225,000 **Critical Thinking** Some people feared that immigrants would take jobs from native-born Americans and that immigrants caused crime in cities. Some mistrusted Irish immigrants because they were Catholic.

Critical Thinking and Writing

1. Famine breaks out in Ireland; over 1.5 million Irish enter the United States; the Know-Nothing party forms. **2.** Answers will vary but should be based on information in the chapter. **3.** Possible answer: Industry, because manufacturing new goods helps a country develop.

4. (a) The demand for cotton and the wearing out of the soil at existing plantations caused the movement west. **(b)** The North outlawed slavery and industrialized, while the South's economy remained agricultural and was based on slave labor.

Using Primary Sources

(a) He describes its inadequate space and lack of protection from the elements. **(b)** He dreads the beginning of each day because he must rush to work or risk being flogged.

Chapter 14 Review and Activities

★ Sum It Up ★

Section 1 Industry in the North

- During the mid-1800s, new inventions helped industry grow in the North.
- Railroads linked the Northeast with Chicago and other midwestern cities.
- With produce coming in from western farms, agriculture declined in the Northeast.

Section 2 Life in the North

- Northern factory workers endured long hours, dangerous conditions, and low pay.
- As millions of immigrants arrived in the United States, nativist fears grew.
- Free African Americans faced discrimination. Still, some became very successful.

Section 3 Cotton Kingdom in the South

- Due to the invention of the cotton gin, growing cotton became very profitable.
- As the Cotton Kingdom spread from the Atlantic coast to Texas, so did slavery.
- As planters invested in land and slaves, the South developed an agricultural economy rather than an industrial one.

Section 4 Life in the South

- Southern society consisted of rich planters, small farmers, poor whites, and free and enslaved African Americans.
- Enslaved people lacked freedoms and rights and were forced to work for no pay.
- Some enslaved African Americans resisted slavery by rebelling or running away.

For additional review of the major ideas of Chapter 14, see ***Guide to the Essentials of American History*** or ***Interactive Student Tutorial CD-ROM,*** which contains interactive review activities, graphic organizers, and practice tests.

Reviewing the Chapter

Define These Terms

Match each term with the correct definition.

Column 1	Column 2
1. clipper	**a.** a policy or attitude that denies equal rights to certain groups
2. nativist	**b.** a swift ship with tall masts, huge sails, and a narrow hull
3. discrimination	**c.** a person who has learned a trade
4. skilled worker	**d.** someone who favors native-born citizens

Explore the Main Ideas

1. Describe three developments that caused the North's economy to expand.
2. **(a)** Why did workers form unions in the early and mid-1800s? **(b)** Describe two reasons for immigration to the United States in the 1840s and 1850s.
3. How did the cotton gin change life in the South?
4. Describe two ways that slaves resisted slavery.
5. What were two key differences between the North's economy and the South's economy?

Graph Activity

Use the graph below to answer the following questions: **1.** In what year did Irish immigration to the United States double? **2.** How many Irish immigrants came to the United States in 1851? **Critical Thinking** Why did increasing immigration alarm some Americans?

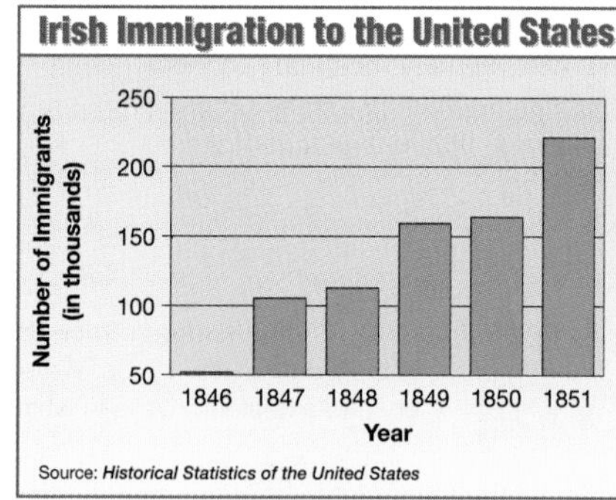

Critical Thinking and Writing

1. **Using Chronology** Place these events in chronological order: **(a)** over 1.5 million Irish enter the United States, **(b)** the Know-Nothing party forms, **(c)** famine breaks out in Ireland.
2. **Ranking** In your opinion, what two inventions had the greatest impact on American life in the early and mid-1800s? Explain.
3. **Making Decisions** If you were directing a nation's economy, would you develop agriculture more than industry or industry more than agriculture? Explain.
4. Exploring Unit Themes **Expansion** **(a)** Why did slavery spread west during the early 1800s? **(b)** How did economic differences between the North and South grow?

Using Primary Sources

Solomon Northrup was a free African American until he was kidnapped and sold as a slave in 1845. For the next twelve years, he worked on a cotton plantation in Louisiana. Below, he describes the start of a typical workday.

> "[My bed] . . . was a plank twelve inches wide and ten feet long. My pillow was a stick of wood. The bedding was a coarse blanket. . . . The cabin is constructed of logs, without floor or window. . . . In stormy weather, the rain drives through [spaces between the logs]. . . . An hour before daylight the horn is blown. Then the slaves arouse, prepare their breakfast . . . and hurry to the field again. It is an offense invariably followed by a flogging, to be found at the quarters after daybreak."

Source: *Twelve Years a Slave* by Solomon Northrup, 1853.

Recognizing Points of View **(a)** How does Northrup show his home to be uncomfortable? **(b)** How does he feel about the start of each day? Explain.

Activity Bank

Interdisciplinary Activity

Exploring Science It is fairly easy to make a telegraph. In your school or local library, find a science book with information on how to build one. Working with other students, create your own telegraph and transmit a message using Morse code.

Career Skills Activity

Musicians Learn a spiritual sung by enslaved people in the South in the 1800s. Possible songs are "Go Down, Moses," "Deep River," and "Swing Low, Sweet Chariot." Perform the spiritual for the class and then explain the meaning of the song.

Citizenship Activity

Protecting Religious Freedom Nativists of the mid-1800s discriminated against Catholics even though Americans are guaranteed religious freedom. Create a poster encouraging citizens to respect the religious beliefs of all Americans.

Internet Activity

Use the Internet to find primary sources on enslaved African Americans in the 1800s. Use the information you find to write a short story about a typical day in the life of an enslaved African American.

Eyewitness Journal
In the early 1800s, you are a northern manufacturer or farmer, or a southern planter or enslaved person. In your EYEWITNESS JOURNAL, describe how new inventions are changing your life.

Activity Bank

ASSESSMENT To assess the activities on this page, see the rubrics in the Alternative Assessment booklet in the Teaching Resources. You might want to share the rubrics with your students before they begin work.

Interdisciplinary Activity

1. Students can make their own telegraph keys or purchase them from electronic supply stores. Wire can be obtained in a hardware store. The Morse code can be found in many reference books.

2. Ask students to transmit the same message that Morse used or hold a contest to decide on an appropriate first message.

3. Once you are sure the telegraph is operating, you may wish to have students demonstrate its workings in science class.

Career Skills Activity

1. Ask students to try to make their performances capture the mood and sentiment of the lyrics.

2. Reassure students that their effort—and not their musical ability—will be evaluated.

3. When the performance and explanation are completed, discuss with students the ways in which they can empathize with the feelings expressed in the song.

Citizenship Activity

1. Refer students to the First Amendment of the Constitution in the Reference Section at the end of their textbook. Read and explain to them the text of the amendment. Encourage them to incorporate the text, or part of it, into their posters.

2. Display student posters in a public place, if possible.

Eyewitness Journal

1. Have students write down the inventions that would have most affected the character they selected.
2. Students can conclude by explaining how their character feels about the new technology.
3. Have a discussion, based on students' journals, on the changes brought about by technology during this time.

Internet Activity

1. Have students go to www.phschool.com, which contains updated information on a variety of topics.
2. Another site you might find useful for this activity is Documenting the American South: Narratives on Slavery at sunsite.unc.edu/docsouth/narratives.html.
3. Given the changing nature of the Internet, you may wish to preview this site.

Chapter 15 Manager

SECTION OBJECTIVES	TEACHING RESOURCES	ADDITIONAL RESOURCE
1 The Spirit of Reform (pp. 398–402) **Objectives** 1. Identify the political and religious roots of reform. 2. Describe the goals social reformers pursued. 3. Explain how Americans improved public education in the mid-1800s.	**Lesson Planner,** p. 62 (average) . . . . **.90 mins.** **Unit 4/Chapter 15** • Biography Flashcard: Prudence Crandell, p. 38 (average) . . . . **.20 mins.** • Section 1 Quiz, p. 39 (average) . . . . **.15 mins.** **Why Study History?** • The Fight Against Alcohol Abuse Continues, pp. 59–62 (challenging) . . . . . **.90 mins.** **Interdisciplinary Connections** • Main Idea: Reform, pp. 86, 87, 89 (average) . . . . **.20 mins.**	**Customized Reader** • An Appeal to Improve Care for the Mentally Ill, article IVA-9 (basic) • A Plea for Humane Treatment of the Sick and Poor, article IVA-18 (basic)
2 The Fight Against Slavery (pp. 403–407) **Objectives** 1. Identify the actions taken by reformers to end slavery. 2. Describe how the underground railroad operated. 3. Explain how Americans reacted to the antislavery movement.	**Lesson Planner,** p. 63 (average) . . . . **.60 mins.** **Unit 4/Chapter 15** • Practice Your Skills: Analyzing Visual Evidence, p. 34 (challenging) . . . . **.30 mins.** • Critical Thinking and Writing: Making Decisions, p. 35 (average) . . . . **.30 mins.** • Map Mystery: Escape to Freedom—But Where? p. 36 (average) . . . . **.30 mins.** • Connecting History and Literature: Harriet Tubman: Conductor of the Underground Railroad, p. 37 (average) . . . . **.20 mins.** • Section 2 Quiz, p. 40 (average) . . . . **.15 mins.** **Interdisciplinary Connections** • Main Idea: Reform, p. 88 (average) . . . . . . **.20 mins.**	**Voices of Freedom** • A Daring Escape to Freedom, pp. 106–107 (average) • The Case for Slavery, p. 108 (average) **Customized Reader** • Opposing Views of the African Colonization Movement, article IIIA-12 (challenging) • A "Conductor" on the Underground Railroad, article IVA-10 (basic)
3 Struggle for Women's Rights (pp. 408–411) **Objectives** 1. Describe the rights that women lacked in the early 1800s. 2. Identify the goals of the Seneca Falls Convention. 3. Explain how opportunities for women improved in the mid-1800s.	**Lesson Planner,** p. 64 (average) . . . . **.45 mins.** **Unit 4/Chapter 15** • Section 3 Quiz, p. 41 (average) . . . . **.15 mins.** **Interdisciplinary Connections** • Main Idea: Reform, p. 90 (basic) . . . . **.20 mins.**	**Voices of Freedom** • A New Approach to Raising Girls, p. 109 (average) **Customized Reader** • Two Letters, article IVA-4 (challenging) • New York's First African-Americar Woman Doctor, article VA-1 (average) **History Alive!® Activity Pack** • How Far Have We Come Since Seneca Falls?
4 American Literature and Art (pp. 412–415) **Objectives** 1. Identify themes explored by American novelists and poets. 2. Describe the ideas expressed by Emerson and Thoreau. 3. Explain how American painters created their own styles.	**Lesson Planner,** p. 65 (average) . . . . **.60 mins.** **Unit 4/Chapter 15** • Vocabulary Builder, p. 33 (basic) . . . . **.10 mins.** • Section 4 Quiz, p. 42 (average) . . . . **.15 mins.** **Chapter Tests,** pp. 85–90 (average) . . . . . . **.45 mins.**	**Voices of Freedom** • A Plea for Simplicity, p. 111 (average)

Assessment Options

Teaching Resources
- Alternative Assessment booklet
- Section Quizzes, Unit 4, Chapter 15, pp. 39–42
- Chapter Tests, Chapter 15, pp. 85–90
- Test Bank CD-ROM

Student Performance Pack
- Guide to the Essentials of American History, Chapter 15 Test, p. 86
- Standardized Test Prep Handbook
- Interactive Student Tutorial CD-ROM

Interdisciplinary Connections

Teaching Resources
- Map Mystery, Unit 4, Chapter 15, p. 36
- Connecting History and Literature, Unit 4, Chapter 15, p. 37
- Interdisciplinary Connections, pp. 85–90

Voices of Freedom, pp. 106–109, 111

Customized Reader, articles IIIA-12, IVA-4, IVA-9, IVA-10, IVA-18, VA-1

Technology

AmericanHeritage® History of the United States CD-ROM
- Time Tour: A Reforming Age (1820–1860) in An Expanding Nation
- History Makers: Frederick Douglass, Harriet Tubman, Elizabeth Cady Stanton, Emily Dickinson

Interactive Student Tutorial CD-ROM

Test Bank CD-ROM

Color Transparencies
- Bloomers, p. B-59
- Landscape, p. D-33

Guided Reading Audiotapes (English/Spanish), side 6

Listening to Music CD
- "Bonnets of Blue," from *New Cotillions*
- "Northfield," from *The Carmina Sacra*
- "Swing Low, Sweet Chariot"
- "Go Down, Moses"

Resource Pro® CD-ROM

Prentice Hall United States History Video Collection™ (Spanish track available on disc version.) Vol. 7, Chs. 16, 19, 25; Vol. 8, Chs. 19, 22

Prentice Hall Home Page
www.phschool.com

Student Performance Pack

Guide to the Essentials of American History
- Ch. 15, pp. 82–86 (Available in English and Spanish)

Guided Reading Audiotapes (English/Spanish), side 6

Standardized Test Prep Handbook

Interactive Student Tutorial CD-ROM

BLOCK SCHEDULING
Activities with this icon will help you meet your Block Scheduling needs.

ENGLISH LANGUAGE LEARNERS
Activities with this icon are suitable for English Language Learners.

TEAM TEACHING
Activities and Background Notes with this icon present starting points for Team Teaching.

Teachers' Bibliography

Don't miss the special American Heritage® teaching notes found in this chapter.

HISTORY ALIVE!®

Contact Teachers' Curriculum Institute to learn more about History Alive!® resources on the age of reform. See History Alive!® unit: Manifest Destiny in a Growing Nation, Section 5, "A Case Study of Reform: Women's Rights."

Explore your library to find these issues related to Chapter 15: *Transcendentalists,* June 1987; *Harriet Tubman,* February 1982.

Prentice Hall Web Site You can access a structured, on-line environment that allows you to preview curriculum-related resources and receive updated information on groundbreaking events from around the nation and the world. (www.phschool.com)

Chapter 15

An Era of Reform
1820–1860

Introducing the Chapter

Have students preview the main ideas of this chapter by looking over the visuals. Suggest they look for evidence that Americans were involved in many types of reform during the mid-1800s.

Using the Time Line To reinforce student understanding of the sequence of events in this chapter, ask students to look at the time line on these pages. Ask questions such as these: **(1)** Approximately how many years does the time line cover? *(1820–1860; 40 years)* **(2)** Did the first women's college in Great Britain open before or after Horace Mann began educational reforms in Massachusetts? *(after)* **(3)** In what year was the Women's Rights Convention at Seneca Falls? *(1848)* **(4)** Which book was published first: *A Christmas Carol* or *The Last of the Mohicans*? *(The Last of the Mohicans)*

Ask students to think of the most important social problems facing the United States today and to describe what people are doing to solve them. Have students name some present-day attempts at reform, such as campaigns to discourage teens from smoking cigarettes.

For additional *Why Study History?* support, see p. 400.

Chapter 15

An Era of Reform
1820–1860

What's Ahead

Section 1 The Spirit of Reform

Section 2 The Fight Against Slavery

Section 3 Struggle for Women's Rights

Section 4 American Literature and Art

In the mid-1800s, dedicated reformers sought to better American society. Many of these reformers acted out of political ideals. They wanted the nation to live up to its promise of "liberty and equality for all." Religious feeling also spurred many reformers.

Reform took many directions. Two of the most sweeping goals were equal rights for women and the abolition of slavery. Reformers often faced opposition, criticism, and even threats. Yet, they continued to struggle and slowly gained support. In this chapter, you will read about the individuals who contributed to this era of reform.

Why Study History? Today, as in the 1800s, the reforming impulse is strong in the United States. Americans still work to correct many types of social problems. To learn more about one reform movement that has attracted many Americans, young and old, see the *Why Study History?* feature, "The Fight Against Alcohol Abuse Continues," in this chapter.

American Events

1826 James Fenimore Cooper publishes *The Last of the Mohicans*

1831 William Lloyd Garrison begins antislavery newspaper

1837 Horace Mann begins educational reforms in Massachusetts

1820 | 1825 | 1830 | 1835 | 1840

World Events

1822 World Event Liberia is established in Western Africa

1837 World Event First kindergarten opens in Germany

★ Background ★

Turning Points

Changing communities A change in the nature of community in the U.S. led to the need for reform institutions. In cities, the gap between rich and poor grew very wide. City dwellers often did not know their neighbors. Even in rural areas, the company of strangers became more common as Americans became more mobile. Life was becoming less personal.

Viewing History **Spirit of Religion**

This painted tray honors Lemuel Haynes, a famous African American preacher. From the nation's earliest years, religion was a powerful influence in the United States. In the early 1800s, a religious revival movement fed a new spirit of reform. ★ **Why would religious feelings lead some people to try to find ways to improve society?**

1848 Women's Rights Convention is held at Seneca Falls

1851 Maine bans the sale of alcohol

1840 | 1845 | 1850 | 1855 | 1860

1843 World Event Charles Dickens publishes *A Christmas Carol*

1848 World Event First women's college in Great Britain opens

★ 397

★ Background ★

Art Note

Spirit of Religion The papier-mâché tray above is a fine example of folk art. Folk art is usually characterized by simplified drawing, arbitrary use of color, and an emphasis on repeated patterns. Often, the artist ignores the rules of perspective and proportion; thus, folk art does not imitate reality. Folk artists of the mid-1800s frequently decorated useful objects. T

Documents and Literature

On pp. 574–577, you will find two readings to enrich this chapter:

1. Eyewitness Account "Education of a Slave," an excerpt from Frederick Douglass's autobiography. (Use with Section 2.)

2. Historical Document "Declaration of Sentiments," excerpts from the women's rights declaration adopted at the Seneca Falls Convention. (Use with Section 3.)

Writing Actively 

Responding to Art Art historians do not know whether the painter of the scene in which Reverend Haynes is preaching was a member of his congregation or someone who had heard about his achievements and was moved to commemorate them. Have students write a short letter from the painter; tell them that this letter will accompany the tray, which will be given as a gift to a dear friend. In the letter, the students will tell why they painted the church scene and what they hoped to capture in their painting.

Viewing History ANSWER

Possible answer: Many felt that as they tried to improve themselves and become better people, they should also try to end wrongdoing and corruption in society.

Technology

Videodiscs/Videotapes

Show the *Prentice Hall United States History Video Collection*™ segments for this chapter. The videodisc version has a Spanish track. Press audio until you get the left channel for English or the right channel for Spanish, or use the bar codes in the Guidebook.

AmericanHeritage® History of the United States CD-ROM

- Time Tour: A Reforming Age (1820–1860) in An Expanding Nation (*average*)

Section 1 The Spirit of Reform

LESSON PLAN

Objectives

★ Identify the political and religious roots of reform.
★ Describe the goals social reformers pursued.
★ Explain how Americans improved public education in the mid-1800s.

1 Engage

Warm Up Ask students if they ever made a New Year's resolution. Ask why people make resolutions to improve, or reform, themselves.

Activating Prior Knowledge Ask the class to make two concept webs that describe the economy and society of the North and of the South in the early to mid-1800s. Record their ideas on large webs on the chalkboard.

Reading Actively

Before Reading Before they read the section, have students turn the red headings into the main topics of an outline. Then, as they read, have them record 2–3 important subtopics for each main topic.

2 Explore

Ask students to read the section. For a homework assignment, have them rank the reform movements discussed in the section (help for the mentally ill, prison reform, temperance, education) in order of

RESOURCE DIRECTORY

Teaching Resources
Lesson Planner, p. 62
Unit 4/Chapter 15
• Biography Flashcard: Prudence Crandall, p. 38

1 The Spirit of Reform

As You Read

Explore These Questions
- What were the political and religious roots of reform?
- What goals did social reformers pursue?
- How did Americans improve public education in the mid-1800s?

Define
- social reform
- predestination
- revival
- penal system
- temperance movement

Identify
- Second Great Awakening
- Charles Grandison Finney
- Dorothea Dix
- Horace Mann
- Prudence Crandall
- Thomas Gallaudet
- Samuel Gridley Howe
- Laura Bridgman

SETTING the Scene In 1840, New England philosopher Ralph Waldo Emerson wrote about Americans' growing passion for improving society:

> "We are all a little wild here with numberless projects for social reform. But what is man born for but to be a Reformer... a restorer of truth and good?"

Many idealistic Americans shared Emerson's beliefs. Between 1820 and 1860, a wide variety of reform movements sprang up to cure the nation's ills.

The Reforming Impulse

Social reform is an organized attempt to improve what is unjust or imperfect in society. The reforming impulse had both political and religious roots. The political roots went back to the ideals of liberty and equality expressed in the Declaration of Independence. The religious reform involved new teachings about salvation and the individual.

Political ideals

The election of Andrew Jackson in 1828 unleashed a wave of democratic change in the nation. More people could vote and take part in government than ever before.

Still, some critics argued that "Jacksonian democracy" was far from democratic. Many said that a true democracy would not allow slavery. Others questioned why women had fewer rights than men. Reformers hoped that by changing such injustices, they might move the nation closer to its political ideals.

A new religious movement

Many early American Protestants believed that God decided in advance which people would gain salvation in heaven. This idea is known as **predestination.** Belief in predestination led many people to think that society could not be changed. In fact, they felt it was sinful to want to improve the world.

In the early 1800s, a dynamic religious movement, known as the **Second Great Awakening,** swept the nation. Its leaders stressed free will rather than predestination. They taught that individuals could choose by their own actions to save their own souls.

Throughout the nation, preachers held huge outdoor meetings. The goal of these **revivals** was to stir religious feelings. Revivals often lasted for days and attracted thousands of people. A witness described the excitement of a revival in Kentucky:

> "The vast sea of human beings seemed to be agitated as if by storm. I counted seven ministers all preaching at once.... Some of the people were singing, others praying, some crying for mercy."

Deeply affected, converts vowed to reform their lives.

★ *Customized Instruction* ★

Extroverted Learners

Writing public service announcements List some reform issues of the mid-1800s on the chalkboard. Have students brainstorm a list of current reform issues, and then have them list the issues on the chalkboard. Tell students to find issues common to both lists; then divide the class into groups and tell each group to select one of the common issues. Have each group write two public service radio announcements about the issue. One should appeal to people of the mid-1800s (although they did not have radio). The second should appeal to a modern audience. Both announcements should provide information about why the issue is important and what listeners can do to help. Volunteers from each group should present the announcements to the class. (*average*) T

One of the leaders of the Second Great Awakening was a Presbyterian minister named **Charles Grandison Finney.** A powerful speaker, Finney wrote articles giving tips on effective preaching. He also taught that individual salvation was the first step toward improving society. He told followers that their goal was "the complete reformation of the whole world." Through teachings like these, the Second Great Awakening encouraged the growing spirit of reform.

Helping the Mentally Ill

Some reformers turned their attention to what one minister called the "outsiders" in society—criminals and the mentally ill. One of the most vigorous of these reformers was a Boston schoolteacher named **Dorothea Dix.**

One day in 1841, Dix visited a jail for women near Boston. She was shocked to discover that some of the prisoners had committed no crime. These women were in jail because they were mentally ill.

The jailer locked the mentally ill prisoners in small, dark, unheated cells. The women were half frozen. Dix demanded to know why these women were treated so cruelly. The jailer replied that "lunatics" did not feel the cold.

That moment changed Dix's life forever. During the next 18 months, Dix visited every jail, poorhouse, and hospital in Massachusetts. Her report shocked state legislators:

> "I proceed, gentlemen, briefly to call your attention to the present state of Insane Persons confined . . . in cages, closets, cellars, stalls, pens! Chained, naked, beaten with rods, and lashed into obedience."

Eventually, legislators agreed to fund a new mental hospital. Dix then went on to inspect jails in states as far away as Louisiana and Illinois. In nearly every state, her reports persuaded legislatures to treat the mentally ill as patients, not criminals.

Reforming Prisons

Dix also joined others in trying to reform the **penal system,** or system of prisons. Prisons were at the time fairly new to the United States. In colonial days, states generally imposed the death penalty for serious offenses. People who committed minor offenses received some form of physical punishment, such as a public whipping.

In the early 1800s, imprisonment gradually replaced physical punishment. In the early prisons, men, women, and children were often crammed together in cold, damp rooms. When food supplies were low, prisoners might go hungry—unless they had money to buy meals from jailers. Some jailers even made extra money selling rum to prisoners.

Five out of six people in northern jails were in jail because they could not pay their debts. While behind bars, debtors had no way to earn money to pay back their debts.

Biography **Dorothea Dix**

Dorothea Dix was shocked by the sight of "harmless lunatics" shackled in dark cells. When she was told that "nothing" could be done, Dix replied, "I know no such word." Largely through her efforts, more than 15 states established special hospitals for the care of the mentally ill by 1860. ★ **How did Dix go about achieving reform?**

importance to society. Ask students to be prepared to explain their rankings.

3 Teach

Write the following headings on the chalkboard: "Reform Effort," "Leader(s)," and "Successes." Ask students to write the appropriate information under the headings for each of the following reform efforts: help for the mentally ill, prison reform, temperance, and education. Students should copy the completed chart for review.

4 Assess

To close the lesson, have students complete the section review. As an alternative, have students work in pairs to create and then answer a series of *who, what, where, when, how,* and *why* questions about the reform movements discussed in this section.

★ ★ ★ ★ ★ ★ ★ ★ ★ ★ ★ ★ ★ ★ ★ ★ ★ ★

Biography

ANSWER

She reported on the horrible situation in mental institutions and prisons, which persuaded legislators to improve conditions.

★ Background ★

Did You Know?

Inspiring reform Charles Grandison Finney, a brilliant preacher, was the first person to allow women to pray aloud, a practice banned in many Christian churches of the time. Finney also inspired William Miller, who founded the Millerites. This adventist group predicted that the world would end in 1843 or 1844, and it preached reform while there was yet time.

Technology

Videodiscs/Videotapes

Prentice Hall United States History Video Collection™, Vol. 7, Ch. 25, "Cages, Closets, and Cellars," 2:05 mins (*average*) ELL

Chapter 25

Prentice Hall United States History Video Collection™, Vol. 7, Ch. 16, "Awake My Soul," 2:35 mins (*average*) ELL

Chapter 16

Why Study *History?*

ANSWERS

1. The Eighteenth Amendment banned the production and sale of alcohol. The Twenty-first Amendment repealed the Eighteenth.

2. Possible answers: to seem "cool"; because they believe they can handle it

 Activity

Guided Instruction

Suggest that students begin by deciding who their target audience is (for example, teenagers, preteens, adults). Then they can brainstorm ways to effectively reach that audience. Remind them that images as well as words can give weight to their message.

Why Study *History?*

Because the Fight Against Alcohol Abuse Continues

Historical Background

Americans in the early 1800s consumed more alcohol per person than at any other time in American history. Some American reformers grew concerned about the impact of alcohol on society. The temperance movement that began in the 1820s hoped to end alcohol abuse.

In the late 1800s, the temperance movement grew. Groups like the Women's Christian Temperance Union attracted many followers. Finally, in 1919, the states ratified the Eighteenth Amendment, prohibiting the production and sale of alcoholic drinks. However, law enforcement officials found it nearly impossible to enforce Prohibition. It was repealed in 1933 by the Twenty-first Amendment.

Connections to Today

Reformers now focus on the problems of underage and excessive drinking. Today, the legal drinking age in every state is 21 years. A variety of organizations and programs exist to help people who suffer from alcoholism. Still, as many as 40 million Americans are problem drinkers—people whose drinking causes harm to themselves or their family and friends.

One of the most destructive forms of alcohol abuse is drinking and driving. In the early 1990s, more than 25,000 Americans died each year in accidents involving drunk drivers. Young people were often the victims. In fact, alcohol-related accidents were the number-one killer of teenagers.

Students organize to warn about the dangers of alcohol.

Connections to You

If you or someone you know has a problem with alcohol, there are several things you can do. You can seek support from your parents or other family members. You can get information from school counselors or a family physician. Also, your school may participate in the Students Against Drunk Driving (SADD) program. Students who belong to SADD promise to call their parents if they cannot get a safe ride with a sober driver.

1. **Comprehension** Name and describe the two constitutional amendments related to the use of alcohol in the United States.
2. **Critical Thinking** Why do you think some people make the irresponsible decision to drink and drive?

 **Making a Poster** Construct a poster that warns people about the dangers of underage drinking, excessive drinking, or drinking and driving.

Fast Facts

★ In 1984, Congress passed legislation to prod states to raise the minimum drinking age to 21. All states did so by 1988.

★ *Time Magazine* reported in 1997 that America's 12 million college students drink 4 billion cans of beer per year. Excessive drinking on campuses caused at least six deaths in 1997.

★ SADD was founded in 1981 in Wayland, Massachusetts, and has spread to all 50 states, Canada, and New Zealand.

Bibliography

To read more about this topic:

1. "Knowing When to Say When," Michelle Heller, *Hispanic* (October 1993). Special on-campus report.

2. "Teens Take a Stand Against Tobacco," *Current Health* (February 1997). Another teen reform movement.

3. Internet. The SADD Contract for Life at: www.albany.edu/counseling_center/sadd.html.

RESOURCE DIRECTORY

Teaching Resources

Why Study History?

- The Fight Against Alcohol Abuse Continues, pp. 59–62

Interdisciplinary Connections

- Main Idea: Reform, pp. 87, 89

As a result, many debtors remained in prison for years.

Dorothea Dix and others called for changes in the penal system. Some states built prisons with only one or two inmates to a cell. Cruel punishments were banned, and people convicted of minor crimes received shorter sentences. Slowly, states stopped treating debtors as criminals.

Pages from McGuffey's First Eclectic Reader

Mug to reward good performance

Battling "Demon Rum"

Alcohol abuse was widespread in the early 1800s. At political rallies, weddings, and funerals, men, women, and sometimes even children drank heavily. Men could buy whiskey in candy stores or barber shops as easily as at taverns.

During the late 1820s, reformers began the **temperance movement,** a campaign against alcohol abuse. Women often took a leading role in the temperance movement. They knew that "demon rum" could lead to wife beating, child abuse, and the breakup of families.

Some temperance groups urged people to drink less. Others sought to wipe out all drinking of alcohol. They won a major victory in the 1850s, when Maine banned the sale of alcohol. Eight other states passed "Maine laws." Although most states later repealed the laws, temperance crusaders pressed on. They gained new strength in the late 1800s.

Viewing History — A Better Education

The painting Homework *by Winslow Homer shows an elementary school student of the mid-1800s. This boy may be reading a lesson from one of William McGuffey's* Eclectic Readers. *First published in 1836, McGuffey's popular textbooks used rhymes and stories to teach spelling, grammar, and good behavior.* ★ **What methods are used today to teach children to read?**

Improving Education

In 1816, Thomas Jefferson wrote, "If a nation expects to be ignorant and free, it expects what never was and never will be." He knew that a republic needed educated citizens. As more men won the right to vote, reformers acted to improve education.

Before the 1820s, few American children attended school. Public schools were rare. Those that did exist were usually old and run-down. Teachers were poorly trained and ill paid. Students of all ages crowded together in a single room.

Growth of public schools

New York State took the lead in improving public education. In the 1820s, the state ordered every town to build a grade school. Before long, other northern states required towns to support public schools.

Connections With Economics

The temperance movement got a lot of support from factory owners. They thought workers would be more productive if they did not drink. Today, many businesses pay for programs to combat alcohol and drug abuse among their employees. In what ways do you think drug or alcohol abuse can hurt the economy?

Viewing History ANSWER

Possible answers: textbooks, readers, educational television shows like *Sesame Street,* and CD-ROMs

Writing Actively

After Reading Have students complete this structured paragraph about the temperance movement: Alcohol abuse was widespread because ________. Therefore, reformers tried to ________. As a result, ________________.

★ Background ★

Did You Know?

Helping the helpless Children's Aid Society founded by Charles Loring Brace in 1853

- Sent poor, homeless city children to live with farm families
- By 1857, placed nearly 600 children with farm families in the West
- Eventually sent about 100,000 children to new homes

Helping animals American Society for the Prevention of Cruelty to Animals (ASPCA) founded by Henry Bergh in 1866

- Law passed by New York State in 1866 making cruelty to animals a crime
- Used first ambulance for horses in 1867 (two years later, Bellevue Hospital began using ambulances for human beings)

Technology

Videodiscs/Videotapes

Prentice Hall United States History Video Collection™, Vol. 7, Ch. 19, "Demon Rum," 3:05 mins (average) ELL

Chapter 19

★ Section 1 Review ★

ANSWERS

1. (a) p. 398, **(b)** p. 399, **(c)** p. 399, **(d)** p. 402, **(e)** p. 402, **(f)** p. 402, **(g)** p. 402, **(h)** p. 402

2. (a) p. 398, **(b)** p. 398, **(c)** p. 398, **(d)** p. 399, **(e)** p. 401

3. Americans wanted to move the nation closer to its democratic ideals. The Second Great Awakening encouraged the notion that society could be improved.

4. (a) to end conditions such as overcrowding and to ban cruel punishments **(b)** to end alcohol abuse

5. Public schools were set up, new schools were built, the school year was extended, pay for teachers was increased, and colleges were opened to train teachers.

6. Answers will vary.

7. Prejudices would be reinforced.

Activity

Guided Instruction
Have students consider how people they know might react to spending more tax dollars on prisoners. Have them use those reactions in their dialogues with Dix. Students should review the text for Dix's opinions before starting the activity. Choose two or three pairs of students and ask them to present their arguments to the class.

ASSESSMENT See the rubrics in the Alternative Assessment booklet in the Teaching Resources.

RESOURCE DIRECTORY

Teaching Resources
Lesson Planner, p. 63
Unit 4/Chapter 15
• Section 1 Quiz, p. 39
Interdisciplinary Connections
• Main Idea: Reform, p. 86

In Massachusetts, **Horace Mann** led the fight for better schools. Mann became head of the state board of education in 1837. He hounded legislators to provide more money for education. Under his leadership, Massachusetts built new schools, extended the school year, and raised teacher pay. The state also opened three colleges to train teachers.

Reformers in other states urged their legislatures to follow the lead of Massachusetts and New York. By the 1850s, most northern states had set up free tax-supported elementary schools. Schools in the South improved more slowly. In both the North and South, schooling usually ended in the eighth grade. There were few public high schools.

Education for African Americans

In most areas, African Americans had little chance to attend school. A few cities, like Boston and New York, set up separate schools for black students. However, these schools received less money than schools for white students did.

Some attempts to educate African Americans met with great hostility. In the 1830s, **Prudence Crandall,** a Connecticut Quaker, began a school for African American girls. The community was outraged. Crandall continued to teach even when rocks crashed through the classroom window. She was jailed three times. Finally, a band of men broke in one night and destroyed the school.

Despite such obstacles, some free African Americans attended private colleges such as Harvard, Dartmouth, and Oberlin. In the 1850s, several colleges for African Americans opened in the North. The first was Lincoln University, in Pennsylvania.

Meeting special needs

Some reformers took steps to improve education for people with disabilities. In 1817, **Thomas Gallaudet** (gal uh DEHT) set up a school for the deaf in Hartford, Connecticut.

A few years later, **Samuel Gridley Howe** became director of the first American school for blind students. Howe created a system of raised letters that allowed blind students to read with their fingers. One of Howe's pupils, **Laura Bridgman,** was the first deaf and blind student to receive a formal education. She later assisted Howe in teaching other blind students.

★ Section 1 Review ★

Recall

1. **Identify** **(a)** Second Great Awakening, **(b)** Charles Grandison Finney, **(c)** Dorothea Dix, **(d)** Horace Mann, **(e)** Prudence Crandall, **(f)** Thomas Gallaudet, **(g)** Samuel Gridley Howe, **(h)** Laura Bridgman.
2. **Define** **(a)** social reform, **(b)** predestination, **(c)** revival, **(d)** penal system, **(e)** temperance movement.

Comprehension

3. Describe two reasons the reforming spirit grew in the mid-1800s.
4. What were the goals of **(a)** prison reformers, and **(b)** leaders of the temperance movement?
5. What improvements were made in public education after the 1820s?

Critical Thinking and Writing

6. **Linking Past and Present** Do churches and religious leaders still take an active role in promoting social reform today? Give examples.
7. **Understanding Causes and Effects** How would lack of educational opportunities for African Americans contribute to prejudice against them?

Activity **Acting a Scene** The year is 1843. You are a legislator. You are unwilling to raise taxes to improve conditions for prisoners while tax money is needed to improve conditions for law-abiding citizens. With a partner, act out a scene between you and Dorothea Dix. For each argument for prison reform given by Dix, present an opposing argument.

402 ★ Chapter 15

★ *Customized Instruction* ★

English Language Learners

Finding word relations ELL students will benefit from a close look at word relations; for example, they may not realize that the word *abolish* is related to the words *abolition* and *abolitionist* or that the word *debt* is related to the word *debtor*. Discuss relations among the following words from the chapter: *colony/colonization*; *liberty/Liberia/liberator*; *educate/education*; *crime/criminal*; *slave/slavery*; *equal/inequality/equality*. Ask students to use each form of these words in a sentence. Pair students and ask them to look for related words as they read the chapter. They should list the words in groups and be prepared to use each form of the word in a sentence. (*average*) ELL

The Fight Against Slavery

As You Read

Explore These Questions
- How did reformers try to end slavery?
- How did the underground railroad work?
- How did Americans react to the antislavery movement?

Define
- abolitionist
- underground railroad

Identify
- American Colonization Society
- David Walker
- Maria Stewart
- Frederick Douglass
- William Lloyd Garrison
- Angelina and Sarah Grimké
- Harriet Tubman

This medallion was a popular emblem of the antislavery movement.

SETTING the Scene In 1848, a group of reformers met to listen to a minister named Henry Highland Garnet. Garnet had once escaped slavery himself. He told the crowd:

> ❝America is my home, my country. . . . I mourn because the accursed shade of slavery rest[s] upon it. I love my country's flag, and I hope that soon it will be cleansed of its stains, and be hailed by all nations as the emblem of freedom and independence.❞

A growing number of Americans—black and white—spoke out against slavery. Only by ending slavery, they believed, could the United States become truly democratic.

Roots of the Antislavery Movement

In the Declaration of Independence, Thomas Jefferson wrote that "all men are created equal." Yet, many white Americans, including Jefferson, did not think the statement applied to enslaved African Americans. In the 1800s, many reformers disagreed.

Religious beliefs led some Americans to speak out against slavery. Since colonial times, Quakers had said that it was a sin for one human being to own another. They preached that all men and women were equal in the eyes of God. Later, ministers like Charles Grandison Finney called on other Christians to join a crusade to stamp out slavery.

In the North, slavery came to an early end. By 1804, all states from Pennsylvania to New England had promised to free their slaves. Still, there were only 50,000 slaves in the North in 1800, compared to nearly one million in the South.

A Colony in Africa

Some Americans proposed to end slavery by setting up an independent colony in Africa for freed slaves. Supporters of colonization founded the **American Colonization Society** in 1817. Five years later, President Monroe helped the society found the nation of Liberia in western Africa. The name Liberia comes from the Latin word for free.

Many white southerners supported the colonization movement because it did not call for an end to slavery. The society promised to pay slave owners who freed their slaves.

Some African Americans also favored colonization. They felt they would never have equal rights in the United States. Most African Americans, however, opposed the movement. Nearly all, enslaved or free, were born in the United States. They wanted to stay in their homeland. In the end, only a few thousand Americans settled in Liberia.

★ Background ★

Linking Past and Present

The Republic of Liberia Former slaves from the U.S. who settled in what is now Liberia did not allow local people to participate in the government. Many conflicts have since resulted. Native Liberians overthrew an American-descended president in 1980. Civil war raged from 1990 to 1995, leaving the Americo-Liberians again in control of the country.

Section 2

The Fight Against Slavery

LESSON PLAN

Objectives

★ Identify the actions taken by reformers to end slavery.
★ Describe how the underground railroad operated.
★ Explain how Americans reacted to the antislavery movement.

1 Engage

Warm Up Ask students to consider what actions or risks they might be willing to take to correct a situation that they considered to be unjust.

Activating Prior Knowledge Remind students that the invention of the cotton gin in 1793 made cotton a very profitable crop—as long as slaves were available to work the cotton fields. Have students discuss how profitable the cotton crop might have been without slavery.

Reading Actively

Before Reading Have students read the questions under Explore These Questions. As they read,

Technology

Videodiscs/Videotapes
Prentice Hall United States History Video Collection™, Vol. 8, Ch. 19, "The Abolition Movement," 4 mins (average) ELL

Chapter 19

Prentice Hall United States History Video Collection™, Vol. 8, Ch. 22, "The Argument for Slavery," 2:10 mins (average) ELL

Chapter 22

have them jot down notes to help answer each question.

2 Explore

Ask students to scan the section and look at the illustrations and headings. When they have finished, ask them to identify some of the people who favored abolition.

3 Teach

As students read the section, direct their attention to the following concepts: colonization, gradual abolition, and immediate abolition. Ask students to explain the differences between these three approaches to ending slavery. Then have students work in small groups to prepare a panel discussion among supporters of each approach, explaining how the group would end slavery.

4 Assess

To close the lesson, have students complete the section review. As an alternative, ask students to write a speech for David Walker or Frederick Douglass explaining his beliefs about the need for the abolition of slavery.

★ ★ ★ ★ ★ ★ ★ ★ ★ ★ ★ ★ ★ ★ ★ ★ ★

Biography

ANSWER

Garrison published an antislavery newspaper, *The Liberator*, to spread his message.

Biography **William Lloyd Garrison**

To William Lloyd Garrison, slavery was a disease that threatened the whole nation. He once even burned a copy of the Constitution because the document permitted slavery. Garrison refused to back down even after a mob in Boston almost killed him. ★ **How did Garrison spread his antislavery message?**

▲ Garrison's vow

A Call to End Slavery

Supporters of colonization did not attack slavery directly. Another group of Americans, known as **abolitionists,** wanted to end slavery in the United States completely.

Some abolitionists favored a gradual end to slavery. They expected slavery to die out if it were kept out of the western territories. Other abolitionists demanded that slavery end everywhere, at once.

African American abolitionists

African Americans played an important part in the abolitionist movement. Some tried to end slavery through lawsuits and petitions. James Forten and other wealthy African Americans gave generously to antislavery efforts. In the 1820s, Samuel Cornish and John Russwurm set up an abolitionist newspaper, *Freedom's Journal.* They hoped to turn public opinion against slavery by printing stories about the brutal treatment of enslaved African Americans.

David Walker called for stronger measures. In 1829, he published *Appeal to the Colored Citizens of the World.* He encouraged enslaved African Americans to free themselves by any means necessary. Walker's friend **Maria Stewart** also spoke out against slavery. Stewart was the first American woman to make public political speeches.

Douglass speaks out

The best known African American abolitionist was **Frederick Douglass.** Douglass was born into slavery in Maryland. As a child, he defied the slave codes and taught himself to read.

In 1838, Douglass escaped and made his way to Boston. One day at an antislavery meeting, he felt a powerful urge to speak. Rising to his feet, he talked about the sorrows of slavery and the meaning of freedom. The audience was moved to tears. Soon, Douglass was lecturing across the United States and Britain. In 1847, he began publishing an antislavery newspaper, the *North Star.*

Garrison and *The Liberator*

The most outspoken white abolitionist was a fiery, young man named **William Lloyd Garrison.** Garrison launched his antislavery paper, *The Liberator,* in 1831. In it, he proclaimed that slavery was an evil to be ended immediately. On the very first page of the first issue, Garrison revealed his commitment:

> "I will be as harsh as truth, and as uncompromising as justice . . . I am in earnest . . . I will not excuse—I will not retreat a single inch—and I WILL BE HEARD."

★ *Background* ★

Recent Scholarship

Free blacks on abolition In his 1997 book *Black Movements in America,* Cedric Robinson, an historian and political scientist, suggests that free blacks of the middle class were likely to support nonviolent abolition. They hoped that "ending slavery would secure their own rights, ensure their personal security, and add dignity to their claims."

Until the 1850s, few free blacks favored radical proposals such as slave revolts. However, the passage of the Fugitive Slave Law of 1850, the unsuccessful attempts to win black suffrage, and the Dred Scott decision in 1857 radicalized many blacks. According to Robinson, many free blacks then actively supported the concept of separate black nations and an insurrection of slaves.

RESOURCE DIRECTORY

Teaching Resources
Unit 4/Chapter 15
- Critical Thinking and Writing: Making Decisions, p. 35
- Map Mystery: Escape to Freedom—but Where? p. 36

Interdisciplinary Connections
- Main Idea: Reform, p. 88

A year later, Garrison helped to found the New England Anti-Slavery Society. Members included Theodore Weld, a young minister connected with Charles Grandison Finney. Weld brought the energy of a religious revival to antislavery meetings.

The Grimké sisters

Women also played an important role in the abolitionist cause. **Angelina and Sarah Grimké** were the daughters of a wealthy slaveholder in South Carolina. They came to hate slavery and moved to Philadelphia to work for abolition. Their lectures drew large crowds.

Some people, including other abolitionists, objected to women speaking out in public. Sarah Grimké replied that "whatsoever it is morally right for a man to do, it is morally right for a woman to do." As you will see, this belief led the Grimkés and others to crusade for women's rights.

The Underground Railroad

Some abolitionists, black and white, risked prison and death to help African Americans escape slavery. These bold men and women formed the **underground railroad.** It was not a real railroad, but a network of abolitionists who secretly helped slaves reach freedom in the North or Canada.

"Conductors" guided runaways to "stations" where they could spend the night. Some stations were homes of abolitionists. Others were churches, or even caves. Conductors sometimes hid runaways under loads of hay in wagons with false bottoms.

One daring conductor, **Harriet Tubman,** had escaped slavery herself. Risking her freedom and her life, Tubman returned to the South 19 times. She led more than 300 slaves, including her parents, to freedom.

Admirers called Tubman the "Black Moses," after the ancient Hebrew leader who

Viewing History **Conductor on the Underground Railroad**

"There was one of two things I had a right to," declared Harriet Tubman, "liberty or death. If I could not have the one, I would have the other." After escaping slavery, Tubman became a fearless conductor on the underground railroad. Here, Tubman (left) poses with some of the hundreds of people she led to freedom.

★ **Why was Tubman called the "Black Moses"?**

After Reading After students finish reading the section, ask them to list the techniques used by abolitionists to bring about the end of slavery.

Viewing History ANSWER

She was named after the ancient Hebrew leader Moses, who led his people, the Israelites, from slavery to freedom. Tubman led her own people, who were likewise slaves, to freedom on the underground railroad.

FROM THE ARCHIVES OF AmericanHeritage®

Underground railroad station An important stop on the underground railroad was Rev. John Rankin's home, located on a bluff above the Ohio River. He placed a lantern in a bedroom window to light the way for slaves escaping from Kentucky. Rankin may have helped as many as 2,000 fugitives escape to freedom. The house has been restored and can be visited today.

Source: George Cantor, "Touring the Black Past," *American Legacy*, February/March 1995.

★ *Activity* ★

Connections With Music

Celebrated in music The popular spiritual "Go Down, Moses" became associated with Harriet Tubman, the famous underground railroad conductor. Have students find the song's words and work out possible symbolic meanings. For example, what might "Egypt" represent? *(slaveholding states)* The class can practice singing the spiritual. (*average*) T

Technology

AmericanHeritage® History of the United States CD-ROM

- History Makers: Frederick Douglass, Harriet Tubman (*average*)

Listening to Music CD
The American Experience

- "Swing Low, Sweet Chariot"
- "Go Down, Moses"

PRACTICE the Skill

ANSWERS

1. Possible answers: **(a)** on a road along the underground railroad **(b)** the white woman: a conductor; the man: an escaping slave **(c)** With the help of the conductor, slaves are getting out of the wagon and trying to get to a safe hideout.

2. (a) a stick; that he is old or blind **(b)** that she is concerned for the man **(c)** The escaping slaves probably traveled by wagon.

3. Possible answer: Yes; the conductors look sympathetic; the scene shows a whole family being rescued.

4. Possible answer: Since the artist seems to have favored the underground railroad, he or she probably included only details that supported that favorable view.

APPLY the Skill

Guided Instruction

Provide newspapers and news magazines. Ask: "What is the subject of this photo?" "What is your emotional reaction to it?" "What details might have affected your reaction?" and "Would you have a different reaction if the person were doing something else?"

ASSESSMENT See the rubrics in the Alternative Assessment booklet in the Teaching Resources.

RESOURCE DIRECTORY

Teaching Resources
Unit 4/Chapter 15

- Practice Your Skills: Analyzing Visual Information, p. 34
- Connecting History and Literature: Harriet Tubman: Conductor of the Underground Railroad, p. 37
- Section 2 Quiz, p. 40

Skills FOR LIFE

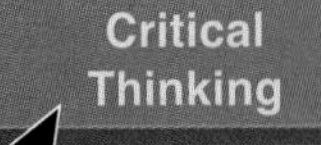

Critical Thinking | Managing Information | Communication | Maps, Charts, and Graphs

Analyzing Visual Evidence

How Will I Use This Skill?

Today, newspapers and television present us with a world full of images. A photograph of a bombing victim or a sketch of a courtroom can have a powerful impact. Still, artists and photographers can be influenced by their own viewpoints. We must analyze visual evidence to determine the reliability of what we see.

LEARN the Skill

1. Identify the subject matter of the drawing, painting, or photograph.
2. Note the details of the picture. Pay attention to facial expressions, actions, objects, and clothing.
3. What is the artist's point of view? How does the artist use details to stir sympathy or anger?
4. Determine the reliability of the visual evidence. Is it an accurate picture of what is shown? What may have been left out?

PRACTICE the Skill

The painting at right depicts a scene of the underground railroad. Look at the picture and answer the following questions.

1. (a) Where do you think this scene is taking place? (b) Who are the two people in the center of the picture? (c) Describe what is happening in this scene.
2. (a) What is the man holding in his right hand? What does this tell you about him? (b) What does the expression on the woman's face tell you about her? (c) Why is there a hay wagon in the background?
3. Do you think the artist was sympathetic toward the underground railroad? How can you tell?
4. Based on your reading, do you think this picture is reliable? Explain.

APPLY the Skill

Analyze a news photograph that had an emotional impact on you. List the details of the photograph that added to the emotional effect.

★ Customized Instruction ★

Kinesthetic Learners

An abolitionist newspaper Divide the class into two groups, and have each one produce its own antislavery newspaper. First, have each group form a newspaper staff that has editors, writers, artists, and designers. Each group should work to prepare articles about the history of slavery in the United States, first-hand accounts of slave life, successes of the underground railroad, or attacks upon abolitionists. Writers may produce editorials, letters, or articles from the viewpoints of abolitionists mentioned in this section. Artists and designers should prepare a layout, political cartoons about abolition, line drawings, and other graphics. Each article should have a headline and a byline. (*average*) led the Israelites out of slavery in Egypt. Slave owners offered a $40,000 reward for Tubman's capture.

Reaction in the North

Abolitionists like Douglass and Garrison made enemies in both the North and the South. Northern mill owners, bankers, and merchants depended on cotton from the South. They saw attacks on slavery as a threat to their livelihood. Some northern workers also opposed abolition. They feared that African Americans might come north and take their jobs by working for low pay.

In New York and other northern cities, mobs sometimes broke up antislavery meetings or attacked homes of abolitionists. At times, the attacks backfired and won support for the abolitionists. One night, a Boston mob dragged William Lloyd Garrison through the streets at the end of a rope. A witness wrote, "I am an abolitionist from this very moment."

Reaction in the South

Not all white southerners favored slavery. Some bravely spoke out against it. Others, such as the Grimké sisters, moved north rather than live in a slaveholding state.

Most white southerners, however, were disturbed by the growing abolitionist movement. They accused abolitionists of preaching violence. Many southerners blamed Nat Turner's revolt on William Lloyd Garrison. (See page 383.) Garrison had founded *The Liberator* in 1831, only a few months before Turner's rebellion. David Walker's call for a slave revolt seemed to confirm the worst fears of southerners.

Many slave owners reacted to the abolitionist crusade by defending slavery even more. One slave owner wrote that if slaves were treated well, they would "love their master and serve him . . . faithfully." Other owners argued that slaves were better off than northern workers who labored long hours in dusty, airless factories.

Even some southerners who owned no slaves defended slavery. To them, slavery was essential to the southern economy. Many southerners believed northern support for the antislavery movement was greater than it really was. They began to fear that northerners wanted to destroy their way of life.

★ Section 2 Review ★

Recall

1. **Locate** Liberia.
2. **Identify** **(a)** American Colonization Society, **(b)** David Walker, **(c)** Maria Stewart, **(d)** Frederick Douglass, **(e)** William Lloyd Garrison, **(f)** Angelina and Sarah Grimké, **(g)** Harriet Tubman.
3. **Define** **(a)** abolitionist, **(b)** underground railroad.

Comprehension

4. Choose two abolitionists. Describe how each contributed to the antislavery movement.
5. **(a)** Why did some northerners oppose abolition? **(b)** Describe two effects of the abolitionist movement in the South.

Critical Thinking and Writing

6. **Drawing Conclusions** Why do you think slavery ended more easily in the North than in the South?
7. **Defending a Position** **(a)** Why do you think some abolitionists favored a gradual end to slavery? **(b)** How do you think William Lloyd Garrison or Frederick Douglass would have replied?

Activity **Writing a Letter** You are a conductor on the underground railroad. You have a cousin in New Jersey whom you need to hide runaway slaves. Write a letter to the cousin describing who will be coming, what signals they will use to gain entry, and how they can be helped. (You might want to disguise your message in case it gets into the wrong hands.)

★ Section 2 Review ★

ANSWERS

1. See Geographic Atlas map in the Reference Section.

2. (a) p. 403, **(b)–(e)** p. 404, **(f)–(g)** p. 405

3. (a) p. 404, **(b)** p. 405

4. Possible answer: Douglass lectured and published the antislavery *North Star*. Garrison put out *The Liberator* and founded the New England Anti-Slavery Society.

5. (a) Many northerners depended indirectly on cotton; northern workers thought freed slaves would take their jobs. **(b)** It caused some southerners to defend slavery even more; some southerners feared it would lead to violence.

6. The North's economy could produce profits without the cheap labor that agriculture required.

7. (a) Realizing that slavery's abrupt end would hurt the economy, some wanted to lessen the impact. **(b)** They would have replied that there was no justification for permitting slavery for even another day.

Activity

Guided Instruction
Ask students to consider carefully what escaping slaves might need: food, water, and help in reaching the next railroad station. If you wish, have students create a binder with all their responses.

ASSESSMENT See the rubrics in the Alternative Assessment booklet in the Teaching Resources.

Internet Activity

The underground railroad In May 1996, historian Anthony Cohen traced on foot an underground railroad route from Montgomery City, Maryland, to Ontario, Canada. Direct students to Cohen's Web site at www.ugrr.org/walk.html to read reports of his journey. You may also wish to have students chart Cohen's progress on a map. Given the changing nature of the Internet, you may wish to preview this site before directing students to it. (*basic*)

Section 3 Struggle for Women's Rights

LESSON PLAN

Objectives

★ Describe the rights that women lacked in the early 1800s.
★ Identify the goals of the Seneca Falls Convention.
★ Explain how opportunities for women improved in the mid-1800s.

1 Engage

Warm Up Ask students to list some occupations open to women today that would probably have shocked people in the 1800s.

Activating Prior Knowledge Remind students that many women were active in many different reform movements, including abolition. Remind them, too, that women could not vote. They lacked many rights taken for granted today.

Reading Actively

Before Reading Have students read the Sojourner Truth quotation on this page. Ask them to explain the main idea of her speech. Ask them to write two or three sentences predicting the types of reforms Truth would favor.

2 Explore

Ask students to read the section. When they have finished, ask them to summarize the main points

RESOURCE DIRECTORY

Teaching Resources
Lesson Planner, p. 64
Interdisciplinary Connections
• Main Idea: Reform, p. 90

Transparencies
Interdisciplinary Connections
• Bloomers, p. B-59

Struggle for Women's Rights

As You Read

Explore These Questions
- What rights did women lack in the early 1800s?
- What were the goals of the Seneca Falls Convention?
- How did opportunities for women improve in the mid-1800s?

Define
- women's rights movement

Identify
- Sojourner Truth
- Lucretia Mott
- Elizabeth Cady Stanton
- Seneca Falls Convention
- Susan B. Anthony
- Emma Willard
- Mary Lyon
- Elizabeth Blackwell

Setting the Scene As you have read, Sarah and Angelina Grimké became powerful speakers against slavery. However, the boldness of their activities shocked many people. Some New England ministers even scolded the sisters in a newspaper. "When [a woman] assumes the place and tone of a man as a public reformer," they wrote, "her character becomes unnatural."

Unmoved by such criticism, Angelina Grimké asked, "What then can woman do for the slave, when she herself is under the feet of man and shamed into silence?" More determined than ever, the Grimkés continued their crusade. Now, however, they had a second topic to lecture about—women's rights.

Seeking Equal Rights

Women had few political or legal rights in the mid-1800s. They could not vote or hold office. When a woman married, her husband became owner of all her property. If a woman worked outside the home, her wages belonged to her husband. A husband also had the right to hit his wife as long as he did not seriously injure her.

Many women, like the Grimkés, had joined the abolitionist movement. As these women worked to end slavery, they became aware that they lacked full social and political rights themselves. Both black and white abolitionists joined the struggle for women's rights.

Truth speaks out

One of the most effective women's rights leaders was born into slavery in New York. Her original name was Isabella Baumfree. After gaining her freedom, she came to believe that God wanted her to crusade against slavery. Vowing to sojourn, or travel, across the land speaking the truth, Baumfree took the name **Sojourner Truth.**

Truth was a spellbinding speaker. Her exact words were rarely written down. However, her powerful message spread by word of mouth. According to one witness, Truth ridiculed the idea that women were inferior to men by nature:

> "I have as much muscle as any man, and can do as much work as any man. I have plowed and reaped and husked and chopped and mowed, and can any man do more than that?"

Connections With Science

In the mid-1800s, women wore tightly laced corsets to make the waist as tiny as possible. Doctors warned that these "tightlacers" caused fainting, squeezed the internal organs, and could even crush the rib cage. Instead, reformers supported a looser, trouserlike garment known as bloomers.

★ Background ★
Recent Scholarship

Sojourner Truth Nell Irvin Painter's recent biography, *Sojourner Truth: A Life, A Symbol*, acknowledges Truth's current status as the symbol of the "Strong Black Woman." Truth's frequently quoted question ("Ar'n't I a woman?") has inspired many women. However, Painter finds that Truth may not have asked that question in those words. The words were an invention of Frances Dana Gage, who printed an account of Truth's speech at an 1851 meeting in Akron, Ohio. Gage's dramatic version—with the repeated question, "Ar'n't I a woman?"—differs from the account of another eyewitness. In addition, according to Gage's version, Truth speaks in a heavy southern dialect. In fact, Truth probably spoke with traces of the Dutch language she learned as a child.

Mott and Stanton

Other abolitionists also turned to the cause of women's rights. The two most influential were Lucretia Mott and Elizabeth Cady Stanton.

Lucretia Mott was a Quaker and the mother of five children. A quiet speaker, she won the respect of many listeners with her persuasive logic. Mott also used her organizing skills to set up petition drives across the North.

Elizabeth Cady Stanton was the daughter of a New York judge. As a child, she was an excellent student as well as an athlete. However, her father gave his gifted daughter little encouragement. Stanton later remarked that her "father would have felt a proper pride had I been a man." In addition, clerks in her father's law office used to tease her by reading laws that denied basic rights to women. Such experiences made her a lifelong foe of inequality.

In 1840, Stanton and Mott joined a group of Americans at a World Antislavery Convention in London. However, convention officials refused to let women take an active part in the proceedings. Female delegates were even forced to sit behind a curtain, hidden from view. After returning home, Mott and Stanton took up the cause of women's rights with new energy.

A Historic Meeting

While they were still in London, Mott and Stanton decided to hold a convention to draw attention to the problems women faced. "The men... had [shown] a great need for some education on that question," Stanton later recalled.

Eight years later, in 1848, in Seneca Falls, New York, the meeting finally took place. About 200 women and 40 men attended the **Seneca Falls Convention.**

Biography **Elizabeth Cady Stanton and Sojourner Truth**

Elizabeth Cady Stanton (left) was born into a well-to-do, middle-class family and raised her own children in comfort. Sojourner Truth (right) was born into slavery and saw at least one of her children sold. Despite their vastly different backgrounds, the two women became allies in the fight for women's rights. ★ **Both Truth and Stanton were abolitionists. How was abolition linked to the movement for women's rights?**

about women's work for equal rights. Ask them which of the women leaders they found most interesting.

3 Teach

Have the class create a time line entitled "United States Women's History, 1800–1860." The students in the class should divide the time line into 5-year intervals. Ask students to plot on the time line the key events from the text. Next, have them research some additional achievements by American women, and have them place these achievements along the line. Students can briefly explain the importance of each entry. To research, they might use references such as *Notable American Women.*

4 Assess

To close the lesson, have students complete the section review. As an alternative, ask students to write a letter from a woman at the Seneca Falls Convention to her sister, in which she describes the convention and explains why women's rights are important.

★ ★ ★ ★ ★ ★ ★ ★ ★ ★ ★ ★ ★ ★ ★ ★ ★

Biography

ANSWER

Both abolitionists and women's advocates abhorred injustice and inequality, and some activists, like Stanton and Truth, fought for both causes.

Internet Activity

Encyclopedia of Women's History

This site, at www.teleport.com/~megaines/women.html, is written by and for students. Have students read about the women cited in this section; tell them that entries were created by students. They can write their own entries, following the site's instructions. Given the changing nature of the Internet, you may wish to preview this site.

Technology

AmericanHeritage® History of the United States CD-ROM

- History Makers: Elizabeth Cady Stanton (*average*)

Graphic Organizer *Skills*

ANSWERS **1.** Possible answers: improved treatment of mentally ill people, prison reform, temperance, improvements in education
2. Possible answer: They all had the goal of improving people's lives.

Writing Actively

After Reading Have students read the material on these pages, and then ask them to list the rights that women of the mid-1800s sought and the new opportunities that opened to them. Have them compare the list to the predictions they made before reading the section.

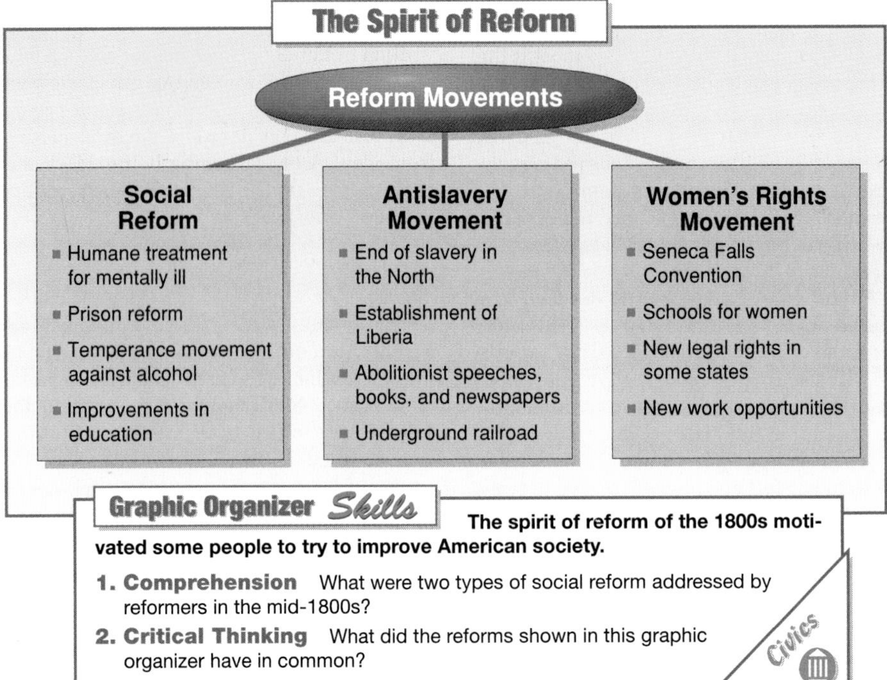

The Spirit of Reform
Reform Movements
Social Reform
Humane treatment for mentally ill
Prison reform
Temperance movement against alcohol
Improvements in education
Antislavery Movement
End of slavery in the North
Establishment of Liberia
Abolitionist speeches, books, and newspapers
Underground railroad
Women's Rights Movement
Seneca Falls Convention
Schools for women
New legal rights in some states
New work opportunities
Civics

Graphic Organizer *Skills* **The spirit of reform of the 1800s motivated some people to try to improve American society.**

1. **Comprehension** What were two types of social reform addressed by reformers in the mid-1800s?
2. **Critical Thinking** What did the reforms shown in this graphic organizer have in common?

"Women are created equal"

At the meeting, leaders of the women's rights movement presented a Declaration of Sentiments. Modeled on the Declaration of Independence, it proclaimed, "We hold these truths to be self-evident: that all men and women are created equal."

The women and men at Seneca Falls voted for resolutions that demanded equality for women at work, at school, and in church. Only one resolution met any opposition at the convention. It demanded that women be allowed to vote. Even the bold women at Seneca Falls hesitated to take this step. In the end, the resolution narrowly passed.

A long struggle

The Seneca Falls Convention marked the start of an organized campaign for equal rights, or **women's rights movement.** Other leaders took up the struggle. **Susan B. Anthony** built a close-working partnership with Elizabeth Cady Stanton. While Stanton usually had to stay at home with her seven children, Anthony was free to travel across the country. Anthony was a tireless speaker. Even when audiences heckled her and threw eggs, she always finished her speech.

In the years after 1848, women worked for change in many areas. They won additional legal rights in some states. For example, New York passed laws allowing married women to keep their own property and wages. Still, many men and women opposed the women's rights movement. The struggle for equal rights would last many years.

New Opportunities

In the early 1800s, women from poor families had little hope of learning even to read. Middle-class girls who went to school learned dancing and drawing rather than science or mathematics. After all, people argued, women were expected to care for their families. Why did they need an education?

★ *Customized Instruction* ★

Visual Learners

A museum exhibit Have visual learners plan a museum exhibit about the women's rights movement of the 1800s. First have students list the events and people that they think should be included. Then have them brainstorm specific items that they would include to illustrate specific events and to represent the contributions of specific people. If students have trouble getting started, ask them to brainstorm a list of the kind of items they have seen at historical or natural history museums: dioramas, photographs, artifacts, drawings, time lines, and documents. Give the group a large sheet of poster paper on which to draw both a floor plan of its exhibit and sketches of the items it would like to include. (*average*) ELL T

Resource Directory

Teaching Resources
Unit 4/Chapter 15
- Section 3 Quiz, p. 41

The women at Seneca Falls believed that education was a key to equality. Elizabeth Cady Stanton said:

> "The girl must be allowed to romp and play, climb, skate, and swim. Her clothes must be more like those of the boy—strong, loose-fitting garments, thick boots. . . . Like the boy, she must be taught to look forward to a life of self-dependence and to prepare herself early for some trade profession."

The American Medical Women's Association gives this annual medal in honor of Elizabeth Blackwell.

Schools for women

Reformers worked to improve education for women. **Emma Willard** opened a high school for girls in Troy, New York. Here, young women studied "men's" subjects, such as mathematics and physics.

Mary Lyon opened Mount Holyoke Female Seminary in Massachusetts in 1837. She did not call the school a college because many people thought it was wrong for women to attend college. In fact, Mount Holyoke was the first women's college in the United States.

New careers

At about this time, a few men's colleges began to admit women. As their education improved, women found jobs teaching, especially in grade schools.

A few women entered fields such as medicine. **Elizabeth Blackwell** attended medical school at Geneva College in New York. To the surprise of school officials, she graduated first in her class. Women had provided medical care since colonial times, but Blackwell was the first woman in the United States to earn a medical degree. She later set up the nation's first medical school for women.

Women made their mark in other fields as well. Maria Mitchell became a noted astronomer. In the 1850s, Antoinette Blackwell was the first American woman to be ordained as a minister. She also campaigned for abolitionism, temperance, and women's right to vote.

★ Section 3 Review ★

Recall

1. **Identify** **(a)** Sojourner Truth, **(b)** Lucretia Mott, **(c)** Elizabeth Cady Stanton, **(d)** Seneca Falls Convention, **(e)** Susan B. Anthony, **(f)** Emma Willard, **(g)** Mary Lyon, **(h)** Elizabeth Blackwell.
2. **Define** women's rights movement.

Comprehension

3. Describe three ways that laws discriminated against women in the early 1800s.
4. What resolutions did the delegates at Seneca Falls make?
5. **(a)** What type of education did most women receive in the mid-1800s? **(b)** How did reformers change women's education?

Critical Thinking and Writing

6. **Understanding Causes and Effects** How was the women's rights movement a long-term effect of the antislavery movement?
7. **Predicting Consequences** How do you think the growth of educational opportunities affected the future of the women's rights movement?

History AND YOU **Activity** **Designing a T-shirt** It is four weeks before the Seneca Falls Convention. You have been asked to create a T-shirt for all the attendees. Draw a clever and attractive design that expresses the feelings and demands of the women's rights movement.

★ Section 3 Review ★

ANSWERS

1. (a) p. 408, **(b)–(d)** p. 409, **(e)** p. 410, **(f)–(h)** p. 411

2. p. 410

3. could not vote or hold office; property and wages belonged to her husband; could be beaten by her husband

4. equality for women at work, at school, in church, and in voting

5. (a) Many poor women were not taught to read or write. Middle-class women learned dancing and drawing, not math or science. **(b)** They opened opportunities for women to study all subjects, including math and physics.

6. Women active in the antislavery movement realized how limited their rights were.

7. Education helped women become more effective leaders and made them eager to remove barriers to equality.

Activity

Guided Instruction
Suggest that the shirts contain *who, what, when,* and *where* information about the convention. Ask students to design a logo for the conference. They can use computer software and iron-on transfers to create real T-shirts.

ASSESSMENT See the rubrics in the Alternative Assessment booklet in the Teaching Resources.

Skills for LIFE MINI LESSON

CRITICAL THINKING Recognizing Stereotypes

1. Introduce the skill by writing this definition of *stereotypes* on the chalkboard: "an oversimplified opinion, concept, or idea that is usually acquired secondhand or indirectly."

2. Have students practice the skill by thinking about the stereotypes suggested by this children's rhyme: "Sugar and spice and everything nice, that's what little girls are made of." How does it stereotype girls? What does it associate them with? *(cooking and homemaking)*

3. Help students apply this skill by finding stereotypes common in the mid-1800s about women, as noted in this section. *(Women do not need education; some academic subjects are not appropriate for girls; women are not suited for some professions.)*

Section 4
American Literature and Art

LESSON PLAN

Objectives

★ Identify themes explored by American novelists and poets.
★ Describe the ideas expressed by Emerson and Thoreau.
★ Explain how American painters created their own styles.

1 Engage

Warm Up Ask students to describe what they would write about or what they would paint to create a work that people would recognize as "American."

Activating Prior Knowledge Ask students to see how many of the following categories they can match with the name of an American artist: painter, novelist, poet, playwright, and composer. Invite students to share anything they know about the artists they name.

Reading Actively

Before Reading Have students note the statement on this page that in 1820, ". . . American writers and artists were breaking free of European traditions." Ask students to find evidence to support this statement as they read the section.

2 Explore

Ask students to read the section. For a homework assignment, have

RESOURCE DIRECTORY

Teaching Resources
Lesson Planner, p. 65

American Literature and Art

As You Read

Explore These Questions
- What themes did American novelists and poets explore?
- What ideas did Emerson and Thoreau express?
- How did American painters create their own styles?

Define
- transcendentalism

Identify
- Washington Irving
- James Fenimore Cooper
- Ralph Waldo Emerson
- Henry David Thoreau
- Walt Whitman
- Emily Dickinson
- Hudson River School

In 1820, a Scottish minister named Sydney Smith blasted what he saw as a lack of culture in the United States:

> "In the four quarters of the globe, who reads an American book? Or goes to an American play? Or looks at an American picture or statue? What does the world yet owe to Americans?"

Even as Smith wrote these words, American writers and artists were breaking free of European traditions. These men and women created a voice and a vision that were truly American.

American Storytellers

Until the early 1800s, most American writers depended on Europe for their ideas and inspiration. In the 1820s, however, a new crop of writers began to write stories with American themes.

Two early writers

One of the most popular American writers was **Washington Irving,** a New Yorker. Irving first became known for *The Sketch Book,* a collection of tales published in 1820. Two of the best-loved tales are "Rip Van Winkle" and "The Legend of Sleepy Hollow." (See page 318.)

Irving's stories gave Americans a sense of the richness of their past. His appeal went beyond the United States, however. Irving was the first American writer to also enjoy fame in Europe.

James Fenimore Cooper also published novels set in the past. In *The Deerslayer* and *The Last of the Mohicans,* Cooper created the character Natty Bumppo, a heroic model of a strong, silent, solitary frontiersman. The novels also gave an idealized view of relations between whites and Native Americans on the frontier. The stories were so exciting, however, that few readers cared if they were true to life.

Later writers

Nathaniel Hawthorne drew on the history of Puritan New England to create his novels and short stories. Hawthorne was fascinated by Puritan notions of sin and guilt. His best-known novel, *The Scarlet Letter,* was published in 1850.

In 1851, Herman Melville published *Moby-Dick.* The novel tells the story of Ahab, the crazed captain of a whaling ship. Ahab vows revenge against the white whale that years earlier bit off his leg. *Moby-Dick* had only limited success when it was first published. Today, however, critics rank it among the finest American novels.

Edgar Allan Poe became famous for his many tales of horror. His short story "The Tell-Tale Heart" tells of a murderer, driven mad by guilt, who imagines he can hear his victim's heartbeat. Poe is also called the "father of the detective story" for his mystery

★ *Background* ★

Our Diverse Nation

African American writers William Wells Brown was the son of a slave mother and a slaveholder. In the first chapter of his novel *Clotel,* a slave once owned by Thomas Jefferson and the two daughters she bore to him are sold at auction. The book was published as written in London in 1853. In the version published in the United States in 1864, the character of Jefferson was replaced by a southern senator. The original version of *Clotel* was not published in the United States until 1969.

Harriet Wilson's novel *Our Nig* was published in 1859, making it the first novel by an African American printed in the United States. The novel tells the story of an abandoned mulatto girl who grows up in a white northern household. T stories, such as "The Murders in the Rue Morgue."

William Wells Brown published *Clotel,* a novel about slave life, in 1853. Brown was the first African American to earn his living as a writer.

Women writers

Many best-selling novels of the period were written by women. Some novels told about young women who gained wealth and happiness through honesty and self-sacrifice. Others showed the hardships faced by widows and orphans.

Few of these novels are read today. However, writers like Catherine Sedgwick and Fanny Fern earned far more than Hawthorne or Melville. Hawthorne complained about the success of a "mob of scribbling women."

The "Inner Light"

In New England, a small group of writers and thinkers, known as Transcendentalists, emerged. **Transcendentalism** was the belief that the most important truths in life transcended, or went beyond, human reason. Transcendentalists stressed emotions over reason. They believed that each individual had control over his or her life. This belief influenced many transcendentalists to support social reform.

One Transcendentalist, Margaret Fuller, wrote *Woman in the Nineteenth Century.* The book strongly influenced the movement for women's rights.

Emerson

The leading Transcendentalist was **Ralph Waldo Emerson.** Emerson was the most popular essayist and lecturer of his day. Audiences flocked to hear him talk on subjects such as self-reliance and character. Emerson believed that the human spirit was reflected in nature. Civilization might provide material wealth, he said, but nature held higher values that came from God.

Linking Past and Present

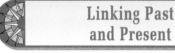

Past

Present

An Enduring American Tale

In 1826, James Fenimore Cooper's frontier tale The Last of the Mohicans *(left) was a best-seller. In 1992, a film version of Cooper's novel (right) was one of the year's most popular movies. The works of other early American writers, such as Hawthorne and Melville, have also been turned into movies or television miniseries.* ★ **Why do you think modern audiences would still enjoy a movie version of *The Last of the Mohicans?***

them write one paragraph summarizing what they read regarding the development of an American style in literature and painting. Then ask them to explain which writer or painter they most enjoyed reading about.

3 Teach

As students read the section, have them complete a chart entitled "American Writers and Artists." Write the following headings for two columns across the chalkboard: "Major Work" and "Identifying Characteristics." Down the left column, write the following headings: "Early Writers," "Later Writers," "Women Writers," "Transcendentalists," "Poets," and "Painters." Ask students to add information to the chart as they read.

4 Assess

To close the lesson, have students complete the section review. As an alternative, ask students to select one of the writers or artists discussed in the section and to explain what makes his or her work "American."

★ ★ ★ ★ ★ ★ ★ ★ ★ ★ ★ ★ ★ ★ ★ ★ ★

Linking Past and Present

ANSWER

Possible answer: The exciting stories and heroic characters are still of interest to modern audiences.

★ *Activity* ★

Cooperative Learning

Making a book jacket Ask students to work in groups to design a book jacket for a book mentioned on these pages. Jackets should include information about the book's contents and about the author; the design should attract readers. Provide examples of published book covers. Direct students to consult the *Reader's Encyclopedia* and other references. (*average*) ELL

Technology

Listening to Music CD

- "Bonnets of Blue," from *New Cotillions,* side 3 (*basic*)
- "Northfield," from *The Carmina Sacra,* side 4 (*basic*)

Viewing History ANSWER

Possible answers: anxiety over an approaching storm, one with a darkening sky; the quiet and peacefulness of the wide-open forest; awe at the immense size of the valley and falls (compared to the size of the person on the rock)

Reading Actively

During Reading Have students read about the work of Henry David Thoreau, and then ask them questions such as these: "Do you know any person who 'hears a different drummer'?" "What are some potential costs of maintaining a strong individuality?" and "What can a person gain by being true to his or her own beliefs and feelings?"

Writing Actively

After Reading Have students choose a work of art by an American artist found in an earlier chapter. Then have them use their own observations and their reading of this section to write a paragraph comparing the earlier painting to the one on this page. T

Viewing History: The Hudson River School

Thomas Cole wrote that "it is of the greatest importance for a painter always to have his mind upon Nature." In paintings like Kaaterskill Falls, *left, Cole captured the beauty and power of New York's Hudson River valley.*
★ **What kinds of emotion might a painting like this stir?**

In his essays and lectures, Emerson stressed the importance of the individual. Each person, Emerson said, has an "inner light." He urged people to use this inner light to guide their lives and improve society.

Thoreau

Henry David Thoreau (thuh ROW), Emerson's friend and neighbor, believed that the growth of industry and the rise of cities were ruining the nation. He urged people to live as simply as possible. In *Walden,* his best-known work, Thoreau describes spending a year alone in a cabin on Walden Pond in Massachusetts.

Like Emerson, Thoreau believed that each individual must decide what is right or wrong. He wrote:

> "If a man does not keep pace with his companions, perhaps it is because he hears a different drummer. Let him step to the music he hears."

Thoreau's "different drummer" told him that slavery was wrong. He was a fierce abolitionist and served as a conductor on the underground railroad.

Poetic Voices

Henry Wadsworth Longfellow was the favorite poet of Americans in the mid-1800s. Longfellow based many poems on events from the past. "Paul Revere's Ride" honored the Revolutionary War hero. "The Song of Hiawatha" idealized Native American life.

Other poets spoke out on social issues. John Greenleaf Whittier, a Quaker from Massachusetts, and Frances Watkins Harper, an African American woman from Maryland, used their pens to make readers aware of the evils of slavery.

Walt Whitman published only one book of poems, *Leaves of Grass.* However, he added to it over a period of 27 years. Whitman had great faith in the common people. His poetry celebrated democracy and the diverse people who made the nation great. He wrote proudly of being part of a "Nation of many nations":

Connections With Civics

In his essay *Civil Disobedience,* Thoreau argued that people had a right to disobey unjust laws if their consciences demanded it. He once went to jail for refusing to pay taxes to support the Mexican War, which he felt promoted slavery. Thoreau's ideas on nonviolent protest later influenced Mohandas Gandhi and Martin Luther King, Jr.

★ Customized Instruction ★
Extroverted Learners

A reading by the author Ask extroverted learners to research the life of one of the writers mentioned in the section. Then have these students prepare to read to the class some of the writer's work. For novelists, ask students to find a short, dramatic scene. For poets, ask students to select several short poems or several meaningful passages from a longer work. On the day of the readings, ask students to assume the role of the writer. (You may wish to have students come in costume.) They should introduce themselves, tell something about their lives, and then introduce the work from which they will read. Ask students to give enough information to enable the class to understand what is being read. (*average*) T

Resource Directory

Teaching Resources
Unit 4/Chapter 15
- Vocabulary Builder, p. 33
- Section 4 Quiz, p. 42

Chapter Tests, pp. 85–90

Transparencies
Fine Art
- Landscape, p. D-33

"A Southerner soon as a
Northerner...
At home on the hills of Vermont or
in the woods of Maine, or the
Texan ranch,
Comrade of Californians, comrade of
free North-Westerners....
Of every hue and caste am I, of
every rank and religion,
A farmer, mechanic, artist, gentle-
man, sailor, quaker,
Prisoner, fancy-man, rowdy, lawyer,
physician, priest."

Today, critics consider **Emily Dickinson** one of the nation's greatest poets. Yet, only seven of her more than 1,700 poems were published in her lifetime. A shy woman who rarely left her home, Dickinson called her poetry "my letter to the world / That never wrote to me."

American Painters

Before the 1800s, most American painters studied in Europe. In 1772, Benjamin West of Philadelphia was appointed historical painter to King George III. Many American painters journeyed to London to study with West, including Charles Willson Peale and Gilbert Stuart. Both Peale and Stuart painted famous portraits of George Washington.

By the mid-1800s, American artists began to develop their own style. The first group to do so became known as the **Hudson River School** because they painted landscapes of New York's Hudson River region. Two of the best-known painters of the Hudson River School were Thomas Cole and Asher B. Durand. African American artist Robert S. Duncanson also reflected the style of the Hudson River School.

Other American artists painted scenes of hardworking country people. George Caleb Bingham was inspired by his native Missouri. His paintings show frontier life along the rivers that feed the great Mississippi.

Several painters tried to capture the culture of Native Americans on canvas. George Catlin and Alfred Jacob Miller traveled to the Far West. Their paintings record the daily life of Indians on the Great Plains and in the Rockies.

★ Section 4 Review ★

Recall

1. **Identify** **(a)** Washington Irving, **(b)** James Fenimore Cooper, **(c)** Ralph Waldo Emerson, **(d)** Henry David Thoreau, **(e)** Walt Whitman, **(f)** Emily Dickinson, **(g)** Hudson River School.
2. **Define** Transcendentalism.

Comprehension

3. Describe the subjects explored by each of the following writers: **(a)** Nathaniel Hawthorne, **(b)** Edgar Allan Poe, **(c)** William Wells Brown, **(d)** Henry Wadsworth Longfellow.
4. What did Emerson and Thoreau think about the importance of the individual?
5. **(a)** Where did early American painters get their inspiration? **(b)** How did this situation change in the mid-1800s?

Critical Thinking and Writing

6. **Drawing Conclusions** Why do you think writers and artists did not develop a unique American style until the mid-1800s?
7. **Linking Past and Present** **(a)** What do you think Walt Whitman meant when he called the United States a "Nation of many nations"? **(b)** Do you think these words can still be used to describe the nation today? Explain.

Activity **Creating a Chart** Henry David Thoreau is returning to look at today's society. He will spend a week in your community. Make a two-column chart. In the left column, list things, places, and activities he will probably criticize. On the right, list things, places, and activities he will appreciate.

★ Section 4 Review ★

ANSWERS

1. **(a)** p. 412, **(b)** p. 412, **(c)** p. 413, **(d)–(e)** p. 414, **(f)–(g)** p. 415

2. p. 413

3. **(a)** Puritanism **(b)** horror, mystery **(c)** slavery **(d)** the American past

4. Emerson: Each individual's "inner light" should guide him or her. Thoreau: The individual alone must decide what is right or wrong.

5. **(a)** from Europe **(b)** American artists developed their own style and painted American subjects.

6. It took the young nation time to develop its identity.

7. **(a)** that the U.S. was composed of different regions, cultures, and people but all were united by the democratic ideal. **(b)** Possible answer: Yes, because of our diverse, multicultural society.

Activity

Guided Instruction

Remind students that Thoreau wanted to simplify life and opposed the expansion of cities and unnecessary industries. Ask them to target areas of overly complicated lifestyles in the left column and to feature aspects of a simple, low-technology lifestyle in the right column.

ASSESSMENT See the rubrics in the Alternative Assessment booklet in the Teaching Resources.

FROM THE ARCHIVES OF American Heritage®

American symphony orchestra The first significant orchestra in the United States, today's New York Philharmonic, performed its first concert in 1842. Made up of 63 musicians, the orchestra performed Beethoven's Fifth Symphony, as well as several shorter works.

Source: Nathan Ward, "The Time Machine," *American Heritage* magazine, December 1992.

★ Activity ★

Connections With Arts

Planning a painting Remind students that the American painters discussed in this section painted landscapes, scenes of country people along the Mississippi and other rivers, as well as illustrations of the culture of the Native Americans. Ask students to decide what they would paint to illustrate American life today. Then ask them to execute their ideas. (*average*) T

Technology

American Heritage® History of the United States CD-ROM
- History Makers: Emily Dickinson (*average*)

CD-ROM
Test Bank CD-ROM, Ch. 15
Interactive Student Tutorial

Chapter 15

Review and Activities

Reviewing the Chapter

Define These Terms

1. e **2.** c **3.** d **4.** b **5.** a

Explore the Main Ideas

1. One was to stir up religious feeling; another was to reform society.

2. Dix worked to have mentally ill people treated as patients, not prisoners. She also tried to improve conditions in prisons.

3. Like Moses, who led the Israelites out of Egypt, she led a great number of people out of slavery.

4. They believed education was the key to equality.

5. James Fenimore Cooper and Nathaniel Hawthorne

Graph Activity

1. 2 million; about 5.5 million

2. more than 3 million

Critical Thinking Possible answer: A number of states increased the number of free public schools and improved teacher training.

Critical Thinking and Writing

1. (a) Reformers in the 1800s published newspapers, organized public meetings, and gave speeches. **(b)** People today use very similar methods, and they also try to get press coverage in media such as radio and television.

2. (a) from the Declaration of Independence **(b)** He wanted to show that the United States was not living up to its own ideals.

3. Answers will vary, but students should be able to support their ranking with logical reasons.

4. Westward expansion increased concerns about slavery because as territories became states, the question of whether slavery should be permitted in them had to be answered.

Chapter 15

Review and Activities

★ Sum It Up ★

Section 1 The Spirit of Reform

- Political and religious ideals encouraged a spirit of reform.
- Reformers worked for many goals, including temperance, improved education, and better treatment for the mentally ill.

Section 2 The Fight Against Slavery

- Abolitionists fought to end slavery in many ways, including publishing newspapers, lecturing, and helping runaway slaves escape on the underground railroad.
- Slavery was defended by northerners who depended on cotton for their livelihood and by Southerners who felt their economy depended on slavery.

Section 3 Struggle for Women's Rights

- Many women joined the struggle for women's rights after fighting for abolition of slavery.
- The Seneca Falls Convention in 1848 marked the beginning of an organized women's rights movement.

Section 4 American Literature and Art

- In the 1820s, American writers began to explore American themes in their stories and poems.
- American artists gradually broke away from European models and developed their own styles.

For additional review of the major ideas of Chapter 15, see ***Guide to the Essentials of American History*** or ***Interactive Student Tutorial CD-ROM,*** which contains interactive review activities, graphic organizers, and practice tests.

Reviewing the Chapter

Define These Terms

Match each term with the correct definition.

Column 1	Column 2
1. revival	a. system of prisons
2. temperance movement	b. network of people who helped runaway slaves reach freedom
3. abolitionist	c. campaign against drinking
4. underground railroad	d. person who wanted to end slavery
5. penal system	e. huge outdoor religious meeting

Explore the Main Ideas

1. What were two goals of the Second Great Awakening?
2. What goals did Dorothea Dix pursue?
3. Why was Harriet Tubman called the "Black Moses"?
4. Why did supporters of the women's rights movement seek better education for women?
5. Name two writers in the 1800s who wrote about American experiences.

Graph Activity

Look at the graph below and answer the following questions: **1.** About how many students were enrolled in American schools in 1840? In 1860? **2.** How much did school enrollment increase between 1850 and 1870? **Critical Thinking** Based on what you have read, why did school enrollment increase steadily in the mid-1800s?

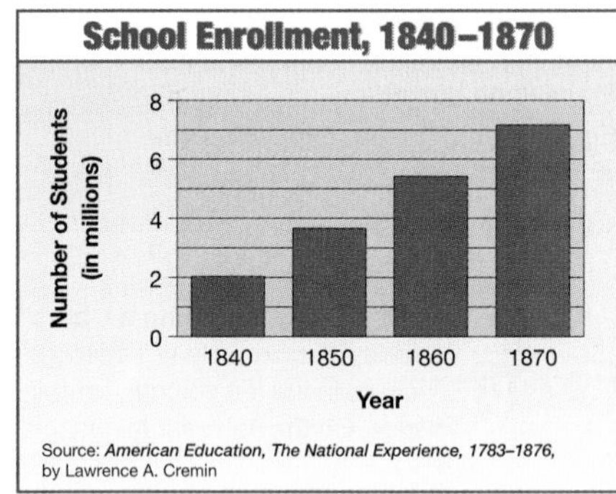

Using Primary Sources

(a) The "fighting" words in Douglass's speech are "murderous," "bleeding," and "doleful." **(b)** Douglass meant that Americans may boast that the United States is a republican state, one ruled by the people, but, in fact, many of its people—those who were enslaved—had no say in its government. **(c)** Douglass had escaped from slavery. He knew what slavery was like and could describe it truthfully and vividly.

Critical Thinking and Writing

1. **Linking Past and Present** **(a)** How did reformers in the 1800s try to gain public support? **(b)** What methods do people use to win public support today?
2. **Analyzing Ideas** In his *Appeal to the Colored Citizens of the World,* David Walker wrote that "all men are created equal; that they are endowed by their Creator with certain inalienable rights." **(a)** From which document did Walker borrow this idea? **(b)** What point do you think he was making by including these words?
3. **Ranking** In the mid-1800s, women like Sojourner Truth, the Grimké sisters, Lucretia Mott, and Elizabeth Cady Stanton organized to fight for abolition and women's rights. Make a list of the demands of these women. Then rank the demands from most important to least important. Give reasons for this ranking.
4. Exploring Unit Themes **Expansion** How do you think westward expansion increased concerns about slavery?

Using Primary Sources

Frederick Douglass denounced the slave trade in the South:

> "Fellow citizens, this murderous traffic is, today, in active operation in this boasted republic. I see the bleeding footsteps; I hear the doleful wail of [chained] humanity on the way to the slave markets where the victims are to be sold like horse, sheep, and swine.... My soul sickens at the sight."

Source: Frederick Douglass, speech to New York abolitionist society, 1852.

Recognizing Points of View **(a)** What words did Douglass use to stir up anger against the slave trade? **(b)** What did he mean when he called the United States a "boasted republic"? **(c)** How did Douglass's background make him an effective speaker on the subject of slavery?

Activity Bank

Interdisciplinary Activity

Exploring the Arts Do research on one of the American painters discussed in this chapter. Then, prepare a guidebook for a museum exhibit of that painter's work. Include a brief biographical note and descriptions of two or three paintings.

Career Skills Activity

Musicians Write and perform a marching song to be used at one of the following events: a temperance rally; an abolitionist meeting; the Seneca Falls Convention. You may work alone or with a group.

Citizenship Activity

Creating a Campaign Today, as in the past, communities are concerned with making sure all students get a good education. Plan a campaign designed to encourage students to stay in school. Your campaign may include posters, speeches, or other public events.

Internet Activity

Use the Internet to find information on any five of the following women: Antoinette Blackwell, Emily Blackwell, Amelia Bloomer, Myra Bradwell, Margaret Fuller, Matilda Joslyn Gage, Maria Mitchell, Lucy Stone. Write a one-sentence summary of the contribution each woman made to the women's rights movement.

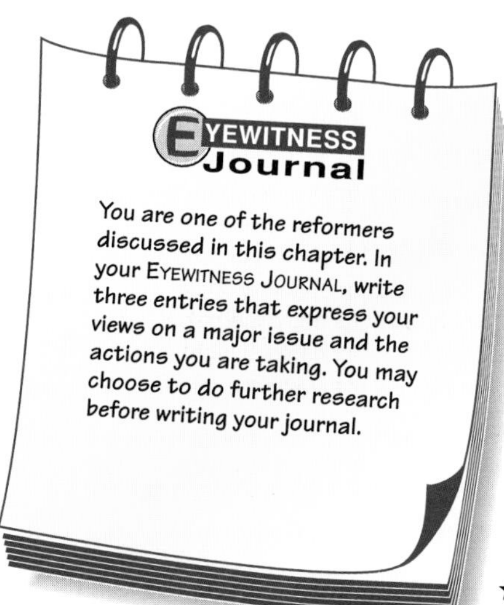

Eyewitness Journal
You are one of the reformers discussed in this chapter. In your Eyewitness Journal, write three entries that express your views on a major issue and the actions you are taking. You may choose to do further research before writing your journal.

Activity Bank

ASSESSMENT To assess the activities on this page, see the rubrics in the Alternative Assessment booklet in the Teaching Resources. You might want to share the rubrics with your students before they begin work.

Interdisciplinary Activity

1. If possible, supply students with a guidebook or catalog from a gallery exhibit as a model.

2. Ask students to consult a book-length study if at all possible.

3. Remind students to situate their painter within the larger context of the artistic search for a uniquely American style and subject matter.

Career Skills Activity

1. You may wish to play a classic demonstration song as an example for students (e.g., "We Shall Overcome"). Encourage them to try to inspire and energize marchers with their song.

2. Hold a performance period for students to share their work.

3. Ask students if any of their songs could be applied to current issues. Point out parallels between past and present issues, such as the temperance-like crusade against drug use and the continuing fight by women's organizations for equal rights.

Citizenship Activity

1. You may wish to begin the activity by having a member of the administration or a former dropout give a presentation on the value of staying in school.

2. As a pre-exercise, ask students to make a chart listing the benefits of staying in school versus the disadvantages of dropping out.

3. You may wish to have students investigate ongoing education campaigns in their community for ideas.

Eyewitness Journal

1. Suggest that the entries could describe a trip to a place that a reformer might have been to, such as a factory or plantation.
2. Ask students to enrich their journals with dialogue between the reformer and opponents.
3. Ask for student volunteers to share their work.

Internet Activity

1. Have students go to www.phschool.com, which contains updated information on a variety of topics.
2. Another site you may find useful for this activity is the Women's International Center and its Women's History in America page at www.wic.org/misc/history.
3. Given the changing nature of the Internet, you may wish to preview this site.

Nightjohn

by Gary Paulsen

Author Note

Gary Paulsen A well-known and prolific author of children's books, Gary Paulsen has won three Newbery Awards. His works of fiction and nonfiction deal with such diverse subjects as the Vietnam War, tracking and hunting, and dogsled racing. In addition to giving public readings and performances, Paulsen is involved in a variety of activities and is active in civic causes.

Build Vocabulary

The vocabulary in this selection is not particularly difficult. Some students, however, might be unfamiliar with the use of dialect. Have them point out words or phrases that are examples of dialect.

Prereading Focus

You might have students reread Section 4 in Chapter 12 to review what they have learned about slave codes that make it a crime for a slave to learn how to read or write.

Connect Your Experience

Ask whether students are familiar with the phrase "Knowledge is power." Have a volunteer explain what it means. Then ask students whether or not they agree with the idea expressed in that phrase.

Purpose-Setting Question

Ask: "Imagine that you are a slave who has been forbidden to learn to read or write. How would you respond if someone offered to teach you?"

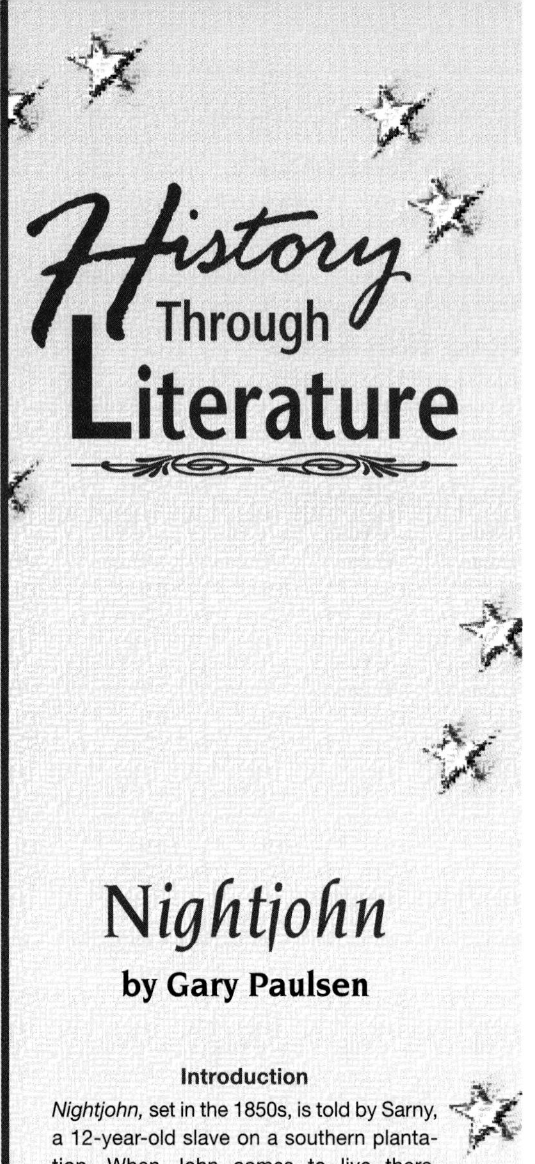

Nightjohn

by Gary Paulsen

Introduction

Nightjohn, set in the 1850s, is told by Sarny, a 12-year-old slave on a southern plantation. When John comes to live there, Sarny's life is changed forever. John had escaped to the North. Yet, he came back—to teach others to read. As this excerpt begins, Sarny is talking to John late at night in the slave quarters. She is deciding whether to let John teach her some letters.

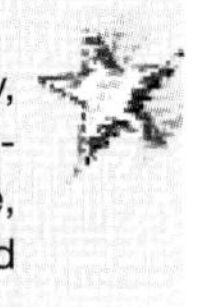

I knew about reading. It was something that the people in the white house did from paper. They could read words on paper. But we weren't allowed to be reading. We weren't allowed to understand or read nothing but once I saw some funny lines on the side of a feed sack. It said:

100 lbs.

I wrote them down in the dirt with a stick and mammy gave me a smack on the back of the head that like to drove me into the ground.

"Don't you take to that, take to writing," she said.

"I wasn't doing it. I was just copying something I saw on a feed sack."

"Don't. They catch you doing that and they'll think you're learning to read. You learn to read and they'll whip you.... Or cut your thumb off. Stay away from writing and reading."

So I did. But I remembered how it had looked, the drawings on the sack and in the dirt, and it still puzzled me....

[Sarny then speaks to John.]

"You saying you can read?"

He nodded.

"I give you something to read, you can read it? Just like that?"

"I can."...

"Way it works," he said, "is you got to learn all the letters and numbers before you can learn to read. You got to learn the alphabet."

"Alphabet?"

He nodded. "There be lots of letters, and each one means something different. You got to learn each one."

...Then he made a drawing with his thumb.

A

"Tonight we just do *A*." He sat back on his heels and pointed. "There it be."...

"What does it mean?"

"It means *A*—just like I said. It's the first letter in the alphabet. And when you see it you make a sound like this: *ayyy,* or *ahhhh.*"

Critical Reading

1. When Sarny wrote "100 lbs." in the dirt, how did her mother react? Why? *(She hit her in the head. She was fearful of what the owners would do if they saw Sarny writing anything.)*

2. Why did John laugh when Sarny said reading was not "hard at all"? *(because all she had learned was the very first letter, but she thought she knew all about reading)*

3. Why do you think Sarny was not able to sleep? *(Possible answer: She had been introduced to a whole new world. She was excited about what reading could mean for her.)*

Background for Understanding

In his autobiography, the African American abolitionist Frederick Douglass recalled an experience he had as a young child. A woman in whose home Douglass was a slave had begun to teach him to read. When her husband found out, he forbade the lessons. The man's reaction profoundly affected Douglass. He began to understand that knowledge is power. As long as slaveowners kept knowledge away from their slaves, they kept those slaves under their control.

Viewing History **Learning to Read—In Secret**

This illustration from the novel Nightjohn *shows John teaching Sarny to read. By the mid-1800s, many southern states had made it illegal for enslaved African Americans to learn to read and write. Yet many slaves risked severe punishment to learn anyway.*

★ **Why do you think enslaved African Americans valued education so highly?**

"That's reading? To make that sound?" He nodded. "When you see that letter on paper or a sack or in the dirt you make one of those sounds. That's reading."

"Well, that ain't hard at all."

He laughed. That same low roll. Made me think of thunder long ways off, moving in a summer sky. "There's more to it. Other letters. But that's it."

"Why they be cutting our thumbs off if we learn to read—if that's all it is?"

"'Cause to know things, for us to know things, is bad for them. We get to wanting and when we get to wanting it's bad for them. They thinks we want what they got.... That's why they don't want us reading." He sighed. "I got to rest now. They run me ten miles in a day and worked me into the ground. I need some sleep."

He moved back to the corner and settled down and I curled up to mammy in amongst the young ones again.

A, I thought, *ayyy, ahhhh.* There it is. I be reading.

"Hey there in the corner," I whispered.

"What?"

"What's your name?"

"I be John."

"I be Sarny."

"Go to sleep, Sarny."

But I didn't. I snuggled into mammy and pulled a couple of the young ones in for heat and kept my eyes open so I wouldn't sleep and thought:

A.

Analyzing Literature

1. Why did Sarny's mother tell her to stay away from reading and writing?
2. According to John, why did the slave owners want to keep the slaves from learning to read and write?
3. **Critical Thinking** **Making Inferences** Based on this excerpt, what are some of John's qualities? How can you tell?

ANSWER

Possible answers: An education would open up new worlds to them; it would give them power.

Analyzing Literature

ANSWERS

1. Slaves were punished if they were discovered reading or writing. Sarny's mother warned her that they would whip her or cut her thumbs off.

2. He explained that when slaves know things, it's bad for the owners. Once slaves knew things, they would begin to want things—perhaps wanting what the owners have.

3. Possible answer: John is intelligent, perceptive, helpful, hard-working, and able to find humor in difficult situations. John's answers to Sarny's questions show his intelligence, humor, and willingness to help.

Teaching Alternatives

Team Teaching: Language Arts

You might work with a language arts teacher to present a brief lesson about historical narratives. Ask students to find details in *Nightjohn* that had to be historically accurate. Ask: "What information can be fictional?" Class discussion could focus on the difficulties involved in writing historical narratives.

Connections With Arts

This cover illustration for *Nightjohn* was done by Jerry Pinkney, who has created award-winning artwork for many children's books. Pinkney won the Caldecott Honor Medal for *The Talking Eggs* and *Mirandy and Brother Wind*. In addition to book illustrations, Pinkney has created works for such clients as RCA Records and *National Geographic*. He also designed 11 postage stamps for the U.S. Postal Service's Black Heritage series.

Unit 5

Division and Reunion

Thematic Overview

By 1850, bitter sectional divisions were emerging—North vs. South, East vs. West. Divisions between northerners and southerners grew increasingly hostile as their economies and views on slavery diverged.

Chapter 14 describes escalating differences between North and South. (See pp. 350–373.) **Chapter 15** tells the story of the Civil War. (See pp. 374–403.) **Chapter 16** discusses the process of rebuilding the South and the dramatic changes that occurred there after the war. (See pp. 404–425.)

ANSWER

Possible answers: The economy of the North was based on industry, while that of the South was based on agriculture; slavery was illegal in the North but widespread in the South, where it formed the backbone of the economy. For more information on Winslow Homer's portrayal of Union and Confederate soldiers, see the Background Art Note at the bottom of this page.

RESOURCE DIRECTORY

Teaching Resources
Document-Based Discovery
• Sectionalism, pp. 18–21

Unit 5

Division and Reunion

What's Ahead

Viewing UNIT THEMES **War Divides the Nation**

In 1861, conflict between the North and the South erupted into war. Winslow Homer, one of the country's greatest artists, painted Prisoners From the Front. *It shows a northern officer (right) inspecting captured southern troops (left). The opposing soldiers look on each other with pride and hostility.* ★ **Based on what you have learned in earlier units, identify two differences between the North and South.**

★ *Background* ★

Art Note

War Divides the Nation Winslow Homer's *Prisoners From the Front* depicts the historic capture of a Confederate division and two generals by the Union General Francis Channing Barlow in 1864. Homer's northern biases are apparent in his portrayal of the captured soldiers. The Union officer appears dignified and strong while each of the three Confederate soldiers is portrayed as reckless, bewildered, or ignorant. Compare this treatment of Union and Confederate soldiers with that in the picture titled "The Faces of War" on p. 392.

Unit Theme Sectionalism

Sectionalism is loyalty to a state or region rather than to the country as a whole. From colonial days, Americans felt strong loyalties to the regions where they lived. By the mid-1800s, several issues increased sectional differences between the North and South. The most dramatic of these issues was slavery. Extreme sectionalism eventually led to war.

How did people of the time feel about sectional divisions? They can tell you in their own words.

Viewpoints on Sectional Divisions

"We have always been taught to look upon the people of New England as a selfish, cunning set of fellows."

Davy Crockett, Tennessee member of Congress (1835)

"I have heard something said about allegiance to the South. I know no South, no North, no East, no West, to which I owe any allegiance.... The Union, sir, is my country."

Henry Clay, senator from Kentucky (1848)

"Union! I can more easily conceive of the Lion and Lambs lying down together, than of a union of the North and South."

Sarah Chase, Massachusetts teacher in the South (1866)

Activity Writing to Learn Today, the United States is often divided into these geographic regions: the Northeast; the Midatlantic; the Southeast; the Midwest; the Rocky Mountain states; the Southwest; the Pacific Coast states. List three features, other than location, that make the region you live in special. Then, write a paragraph explaining whether you feel more loyal to your region or to the United States as a whole.

★ Background ★ Historians Debate

Debate over Reconstruction Historians have studied all aspects of the Civil War era from early sectional struggles to the aftermath of emancipation. From the 1870s to the 1950s, historians such as Claude G. Bowers, imbued with the prevailing racial views, saw Reconstruction as the punishment imposed by radical Republicans determined to force black equality on the defeated South.

The civil rights movement of the 1950s and 1960s led historians to reexamine that view and develop a new, more balanced interpretation. To noted historian Eric Foner, author of *Reconstruction: America's Unfinished Revolution, 1863–1877*, Reconstruction was "not radical enough" because it left freedmen without the economic means to succeed in the postwar South.

Viewpoints on Sectional Divisions

★ Davy Crockett, self-educated frontiersman and politician, died at the Alamo during the Texas war for independence.

★ Henry Clay earned the nickname "The Great Compromiser" for working to resolve North-South tensions over the spread of slavery.

★ Sarah Chase traveled to the South during the Civil War to teach and care for African Americans held in displaced persons camps there.

CRITICAL THINKING Each of these speakers had a unique insight into the impact of sectionalism on the United States. Refer students to the southerner's statement about a burial in Chapter 12, p. 315. Ask them how Crockett, Clay, and Chase would each have viewed this situation.

Guided Instruction
Have students identify and locate the region in which they live. Encourage students to think about special features of their region, such as climate, terrain, economic activities, traditions and history, and lifestyles.

ASSESSMENT See the rubrics in the Alternative Assessment booklet in the Teaching Resources.

Technology

AmericanHeritage® History of the United States CD-ROM
Access the Time Tour "The Nation Torn Apart" to accompany Unit 5.

Chapter 16 Manager

SECTION OBJECTIVES	TEACHING RESOURCES	ADDITIONAL RESOURCES
1 The Slavery Issue in the West (pp. 424–429) **Objectives** 1. Describe the various views on slavery in the West. 2. Identify the goal of the Free Soil party. 3. Describe the results of the Compromise of 1850.	**Lesson Planner,** p. 66 (average) . . . . .60 mins. **Unit 5/Chapter 16** • Critical Thinking and Writing: Drawing Conclusions, p. 4 (average) . . . . .30 mins. • Section 1 Quiz, p. 8 (average) . . . . .15 mins. **Interdisciplinary Connections** • Main Idea: The Debate Over Slavery, pp. 92, 94, 96 (average) . . . . .20 mins.	**Voices of Freedom** • A Question of Slavery in the West, p. 112 (average) • How Can the Union be Saved? pp. 113–114 (average) • A Plea to Preserve the Union, pp. 114–115 (average) **Customized Reader** • Description of a Southern Slave Catcher, article IVB-4 (average) **Historical Outline Map Book** • The Missouri Compromise, 182[0] p. 45 (average) • The Compromise of 1850, p. 46 (average)
2 The Crisis Turns Violent (pp. 430–434) **Objectives** 1. Describe how *Uncle Tom's Cabin* affected attitudes toward slavery. 2. Explain why a civil war broke out in Kansas. 3. Describe how the Dred Scott decision divided the nation.	**Lesson Planner,** p. 67 (average) . . . . .45 mins. **Unit 5/Chapter 16** • Connecting History and Literature: My Bondage and My Freedom, p. 6 (average) . . . . .20 mins. • Section 2 Quiz, p. 9 (average) . . . . .15 mins. **Interdisciplinary Connections** • Main Idea: The Debate Over Slavery, pp. 93, 95 (average) . . . . .20 mins.	**Voices of Freedom** • The Suffering of Uncle Tom, pp. 115–116 (average) • The Dred Scott Decision: A Black View, p. 117 (average) **Customized Reader** • Editorials About Brooks' Beating of Sumner, article IVB-16 (average) • The Destruction of Lawrence, Kansas, article IVB-17 (average) **Historical Outline Map Book** • Kansas-Nebraska Act, 1854, p. 47 (average)
3 A New Party Challenges Slavery (pp. 435–438) **Objectives** 1. Explain why the Republican party came into being in the mid-1850s. 2. Outline Abraham Lincoln's views on slavery. 3. Describe the different reactions of northerners and southerners to the raid on Harpers Ferry.	**Lesson Planner,** p. 68 (average) . . . . .90 mins. **Unit 5/Chapter 16** • Biography Flashcard: Carl Schurz, p. 7 (average) . . . . .20 mins. • Section 3 Quiz, p. 10 (average) . . . . .15 mins. **Why Study History?** • Heroes of the Past Can Be Models for Today, pp. 63–66 (average) . . . . .90 mins.	**Voices of Freedom** • Singing the Praises of John Brown, pp. 117–118 (average)
4 The Nation Splits in Two (pp. 439–443) **Objectives** 1. Explain why Abraham Lincoln was able to win the election of 1860. 2. Describe how the South reacted to Lincoln's election victory. 3. Identify the events that led to the outbreak of the Civil War.	**Lesson Planner,** p. 69 (average) . . . . .60 mins. **Unit 5/Chapter 16** • Vocabulary Builder, p. 2 (basic) . . . . .10 mins. • Practice Your Skills: Comparing Points of View, p. 3 (challenging) . . . . .30 mins. • Map Mystery: The Decision to Secede, p. 5 (challenging) . . . . .30 mins. • Section 4 Quiz, p. 11 (average) . . . . .15 mins. **Chapter Tests,** pp. 91–96 (average) . . . . .45 mins.	**History Alive!® Activity Pack** • A Press Conference on the Eve of the Civil War

Assessment Options

Teaching Resources
- Alternative Assessment booklet
- Section Quizzes, Unit 5, Chapter 16, pp. 8–11
- Chapter Tests, Chapter 16, pp. 91–96
- Test Bank CD-ROM

Student Performance Pack
- Guide to the Essentials of American History, Chapter 16 Test, p. 91
- Standardized Test Prep Handbook
- Interactive Student Tutorial CD-ROM

Interdisciplinary Connections

Teaching Resources
- Map Mystery, Unit 5, Chapter 16, p. 5
- Connecting History and Literature, Unit 5, Chapter 16, p. 6
- Interdisciplinary Connections, pp. 91–96

Voices of Freedom, pp. 112–118

Customized Reader, articles IVB-4, IVB-16, IVB-17

Historical Outline Map Book, pp. 45–47

BLOCK SCHEDULING
Activities with this icon will help you meet your Block Scheduling needs.

ENGLISH LANGUAGE LEARNERS
Activities with this icon are suitable for English Language Learners.

TEAM TEACHING
Activities and Background Notes with this icon present starting points for Team Teaching.

Technology

AmericanHeritage® History of the United States CD-ROM
- Time Tour: The Road to Civil War (1820–1861) in The Nation Torn Apart
- Presidents: Zachary Taylor, Millard Fillmore, Franklin Pierce, James Buchanan, Abraham Lincoln
- History Makers: Harriet Beecher Stowe
- Face the Issues: Fugitive Slave Law

Interactive Student Tutorial CD-ROM

Test Bank CD-ROM

Color Transparencies
- Missouri Compromise, p. B-61
- North Central States, p. I-73

Guided Reading Audiotapes (English/Spanish), side 6

Resource Pro® CD-ROM

Prentice Hall United States History Video Collection™ (Spanish track available on disc version.) Vol. 8, Chs. 25, 28, 31, 34; Vol. 9, Ch. 7

Prentice Hall Home Page
www.phschool.com

Student Performance Pack

Guide to the Essentials of American History
- Ch. 16, pp. 87–91 (Available in English and Spanish)

Guided Reading Audiotapes (English/Spanish), side 6

Standardized Test Prep Handbook

Interactive Student Tutorial CD-ROM

Teachers' Bibliography

FROM THE ARCHIVES OF AmericanHeritage®

Don't miss the special American Heritage® teaching notes found in this chapter.

Contact Teachers' Curriculum Institute to learn more about History Alive!® resources on the growing tension between North and South. See History Alive!® unit: The Civil War and Reconstruction, Section 2, "The Coming of the Civil War."

Explore your library to find these issues related to Chapter 16: *Abraham Lincoln,* May 1994; *Frederick Douglass,* February 1989.

Prentice Hall Web Site You can access a structured, on-line environment that allows you to preview curriculum-related resources and receive updated information on groundbreaking events from around the nation and the world. (www.phschool.com)

Chapter 16

A Dividing Nation
1820–1861

Introducing the Chapter

Have students preview the main ideas of this chapter by looking over the visuals. Suggest they look for evidence of the growing sectional tension of the pre-Civil War era.

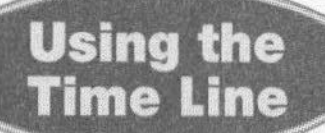

To provide students with practice in using the time line, ask questions such as these: **(1)** What is the connection between the American event shown in 1820 and that shown in 1857? *(Both deal with the issue of slavery in the territories.)* **(2)** What event happened in Mexico the same year that the United States Supreme Court ruled on slavery in the territories? *(Mexico adopted a new constitution that prohibited slavery.)* **(3)** In what year did Abraham Lincoln become President? *(1861)* **(4)** When was slavery abolished in the British empire? *(1833)*

Ask students to name people whom they consider to be heroes. The people may be living or deceased, and they may be sports figures, political figures, or even relatives or community figures. Then ask them to consider what qualities make these people special. On the chalkboard, write a list of the qualities that were suggested by students. Then have students record the list for reference when they read about Abraham Lincoln later in the chapter.

For additional *Why Study History?* support, see p. 437.

Chapter 16

A Dividing Nation
1820–1861

What's Ahead

Between 1820 and 1861, the nation grew increasingly divided as it struggled to answer difficult questions concerning slavery. Should slavery be allowed to spread to the West? Should slavery be abolished throughout the nation? For a time, northerners and southerners settled their differences through compromises. Gradually, however, violence became more and more common. In 1860, voters elected Abraham Lincoln, a member of the antislavery Republican party, to be the next President of the United States. In response, southern states withdrew from the Union. The North and the South then prepared for war.

Why Study History?

Many consider Abraham Lincoln to be one of the greatest leaders in American history. Some call him an American hero. Frequently, therefore, he is held as a role model for others to imitate. Could Lincoln be a role model for you? To answer this question, see this chapter's *Why Study History?* feature, "Heroes of the Past Can Be Models for Today."

American Events

1820 Missouri Compromise allows slavery in some western territories

1850 Fugitive Slave Law requires citizens to help catch runaway slaves

1852 *Uncle Tom's Cabin* increases support for abolitionism

1820 | 1848 | 1850 | 1852 | 1854

World Events

1833 World Event Slavery is abolished in British empire

1850 World Event Taiping Rebellion begins civil war in China

Writing Actively

Responding to Art Have students first examine the painting on this page and then read the caption. Then ask them to write a short descriptive paragraph in which they detail what they think is taking place in the painting. What is the mood of the painting? What emotions do the people appear to be experiencing? To make their writing more realistic, students may choose to assign names to the characters in the painting.

Viewing History **From Slavery to Freedom**

In the painting On to Liberty *by Theodor Kaufmann, fugitive slave families try to reach the North and freedom. In the 1850s, many northerners protested against a law requiring all citizens to help return runaway slaves. Disagreement over slavery heightened the growing division between North and South.* ★ **How do you think enslaved African Americans felt as they tried to escape to the North?**

Viewing History ANSWER

Possible answers: They feared being caught. They welcomed the possibility of attaining freedom. They worried about how they would make a living in the North.

1854 Kansas-Nebraska Act leads to violence

1857 Supreme Court says Congress cannot outlaw slavery in territories

1861 Abraham Lincoln becomes President

1854 | 1856 | 1858 | 1860 | 1862

1857 World Event New constitution in Mexico prohibits slavery

★ 423

★ Background ★
Art Note

From Slavery to Freedom Theodor Kaufmann painted this dramatic picture, *On to Liberty*, in 1867. He shows frightened escapees headed for free territory, symbolized by the light in the distance. Kaufmann served with the Union forces in the Civil War. His works include the historical paintings *Farragut in the Rigging* and *Genl. Sherman at the Watchfire*. T

Documents and Literature

On pp. 578–581, you will find two readings to enrich this chapter:

1. Literature "Caleb's Choice," an excerpt from a novel that shows the conflicting feelings about the Fugitive Slave Law. (Use with Section 1.)

2. Eyewitness Account "Two Views of the War in Kansas," letters expressing northern and southern views of the fighting in Kansas. (Use with Section 2.)

Technology

Videodiscs/Videotapes

Show the *Prentice Hall United States History Video Collection*™ segments for this chapter. The videodisc version has a Spanish track. Press audio until you get the left channel for English or the right channel for Spanish, or use the bar codes in the Guidebook.

AmericanHeritage® History of the United States CD-ROM

- Time Tour: The Road to Civil War (1820–1861) in The Nation Torn Apart (*average*)

Section 1

The Slavery Issue in the West

LESSON PLAN

Objectives

★ Describe the various views on slavery in the West.

★ Identify the goal of the Free Soil party.

★ Describe the results of the Compromise of 1850.

1 Engage

Warm Up Point out to students that many southerners depended on the labor of slaves. Then ask them why they think so many people felt so strongly about the slavery issue.

Activating Prior Knowledge Ask students to draw a graphic organizer with the words *Slavery in the West* in the center. Around the outside, students should list groups with some stake in whether the West permitted slavery; then they should indicate each group's position.

Reading Actively

Before Reading Direct students' attention to the first question under Explore These Questions. As they read, have them identify various views about slavery in the West.

RESOURCE DIRECTORY

Teaching Resources
Lesson Planner, p. 66
Unit 5/Chapter 16
- Critical Thinking and Writing: Drawing Conclusions, p. 4

Interdisciplinary Connections
- Main Idea: The Debate Over Slavery, p. 94

Transparencies
Interdisciplinary Connections
- Missouri Compromise, p. B-61

The Slavery Issue in the West

As You Read

Explore These Questions
- What were the various views on slavery in the West?
- What was the goal of the Free Soil party?
- What were the results of the Compromise of 1850?

Define
- sectionalism
- popular sovereignty
- secede
- fugitive
- civil war

Identify
- Missouri Compromise
- Wilmot Proviso
- Free Soil party
- Zachary Taylor
- Stephen Douglas
- Compromise of 1850
- Fugitive Slave Law of 1850

SETTING the Scene In 1820, Thomas Jefferson was in his seventies. The former President had vowed "never to write, talk, or even think of politics." Still, he voiced alarm when he heard about a fierce debate going on in Congress:

> ❝ In the gloomiest moment of the revolutionary war, I never had any [fears] equal to what I feel from this source.... We have a wolf by the ears, and we can neither hold him nor safely let him go. ❞

Jefferson feared that the "wolf," or the issue of slavery, would tear the North and South apart. He was correct. As settlers continued to move west, tension over slavery worsened. Again and again, Congress faced an agonizing decision. Should it prohibit slavery in the territories and later admit them to the Union as free states? Or should it permit slavery in the territories and later admit them as slave states?

The Missouri Compromise

When Missouri asked to join the Union as a slave state, a crisis erupted. The admission of Missouri would upset the balance of power in the Senate. In 1819, there were 11 free states and 11 slave states. (See the graph on page 427.) Missouri's admission would give the South a majority in the Senate. Determined not to lose power, northerners opposed letting Missouri enter as a slave state.

The argument over Missouri lasted many months. Finally, Senator Henry Clay proposed a compromise. During the long debate, Maine had also applied for statehood. Clay suggested admitting Missouri as a slave state and Maine as a free state. His plan, called the **Missouri Compromise,** kept the number of slave and free states equal.

As part of the Missouri Compromise, Congress drew an imaginary line across the southern border of Missouri at latitude 36° 30′ N. Slavery was permitted in the part of the Louisiana Purchase south of that line. It was banned north of the line. The only exception to this was Missouri. (See the map on page 431.)

New Western Lands

The Missouri Compromise applied only to the Louisiana Purchase. In 1848, the Mexican War added a vast stretch of western land to the United States. (See the map on page 363.) Once again, the question of slavery in the territories arose.

The Wilmot Proviso

Many northerners feared that the South would extend slavery into the West. David Wilmot, a Congressman from Pennsylvania, called for a law to ban slavery in any lands won from Mexico. Southern leaders angrily opposed the **Wilmot Proviso.** They said that Congress had no right to ban slavery in the western territories.

★ ***Background*** ★

Did You Know?

A lot of bunk Most members of Congress wanted to speak in the Missouri Compromise debate. Speeches were so dull that when Felix Walker of North Carolina asked to speak, his request was refused. Walker demanded the right to "make a speech for Buncombe [County]." The phrase "speaking for Buncombe" was later shortened to "bunkum," and finally "bunk."

★ ***Activity*** ★

Connections With Civics

Understanding the legislative process The Wilmot Proviso was the first important rider to a congressional bill. Have students find out the importance of riders in our congressional process. Ask students to research and report on an important or controversial rider to a recent congressional bill. (*challenging*) T

Linking United States and the World

United States

Russia

Forced Labor

In the painting at left, enslaved African Americans await the results of a slave auction. At the same time in Russia, millions of workers were serfs. Serfs were bound to the land and had to work for wealthy nobles. One Russian observer sadly reported "of men and women torn from their families and their villages, and sold . . . of children taken from their parents and sold to cruel masters." ★ **How was slavery in the United States similar to serfdom in Russia?**

In 1846, the House passed the Wilmot Proviso, but the Senate defeated it. As a result, Americans continued to argue about slavery in the West even while their army fought in Mexico.

Opposing views

The Mexican War strengthened feelings of **sectionalism** in the North and South. Sectionalism is loyalty to a state or section, rather than to the country as a whole. Many southerners were united by their support for slavery. They saw the North as a growing threat to their way of life. Many northerners saw the South as a foreign country, where American rights and liberties did not exist.

As the debate over slavery heated up, people found it hard not to take sides. Northern abolitionists demanded that slavery be banned throughout the country. They insisted that slavery was morally wrong. By the late 1840s, many northerners agreed.

Southern slaveholders thought that slavery should be allowed in any territory. They also demanded that slaves who escaped to the North be returned to them. Even white southerners who did not own slaves generally agreed with these ideas.

Between these two extreme views were more moderate positions. Some moderates argued that the Missouri Compromise line should be extended across the Mexican Cession to the Pacific Ocean. Any new state north of the line would be a free state. Any new state south of the line could allow slavery.

$ Connections With Economics

In response to the Wilmot Proviso, some southern states proposed cutting off all trade with the North. Another economic threat was that southerners would stop payments on debts owed to northern banks and businesses.

★ *Background* ★

Recent Scholarship

Displacing a giant In his 1996 book *Arguing About Slavery,* William Lee Miller suggests that the elimination of slavery seemed impossible for many years, not least because of the huge monetary interests involved. He compares the situation to the stamina of today's tobacco industry, a smaller and considerably less powerful institution than slavery was in its time.

2 Explore

Review with students how the balance of free and slave states in the West became a divisive issue. Then ask them to research one of these topics: Missouri Compromise, Wilmot Proviso, Free Soil party, Fugitive Slave Law of 1850.

3 Teach

Tell students to rewrite the following incorrect statements to make them correct. **(a)** Fearing competition with northern industries, northerners opposed admitting Missouri to the Union. **(b)** The Free Soil party wanted tax-free land for farmers. **(c)** Senator John C. Calhoun said the Union must be preserved at any cost. **(d)** Under the Compromise of 1850, New Mexico and Utah became free states.

4 Assess

To close the lesson, have students complete the section review. Or have them work in small groups to stage informal discussions about the Compromise of 1850, supposing they are in the North or South at the time of the compromise. Ask them how and when Americans discuss politics today.

Linking United States and the World

ANSWER

Possible answer: In both, people were unfree, poor, mistreated, and tied to the land.

Other moderates supported the idea of popular sovereignty, or control by the people. In other words, voters in a new territory would decide for themselves whether or not to allow slavery in the territory. Slaves, of course, could not vote.

The Free Soil Party

The debate over slavery led to the birth of a new political party. By 1848, many northerners in both the Democratic party and the Whig party opposed the spread of slavery. However, the leaders of both parties refused to take a stand on the question. They did not want to give up their chance of winning votes in the South. Some also feared that the slavery issue would split the nation.

In 1848, antislavery members of both parties met in Buffalo, New York. There, they founded the **Free Soil party.** Their slogan was "Free soil, free speech, free labor, and free men." The main goal of the Free Soil party was to keep slavery out of the western territories. Only a few Free Soilers were abolitionists who wanted to end slavery in the South.

In the 1848 presidential campaign, Free Soilers named former President Martin Van Buren as their candidate. Democrats chose Lewis Cass of Michigan. The Whigs selected **Zachary Taylor,** a hero of the Mexican War.

For the first time, slavery was an important election issue. Van Buren called for a ban on slavery in the Mexican Cession. Cass supported popular sovereignty. Because Taylor was a slave owner from Louisiana, many southern voters assumed that he supported slavery.

Zachary Taylor won the election, but Van Buren took 10 percent of the popular vote. Thirteen other Free Soil candidates won seats in Congress. The success of the new Free Soil party showed that slavery had become a national issue.

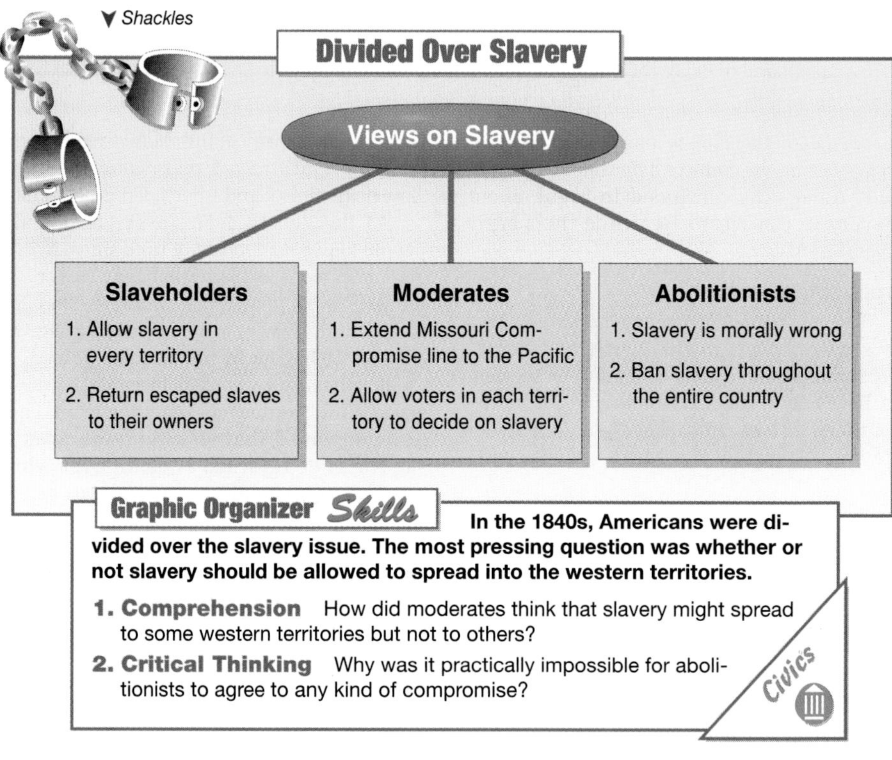
▼ Shackles
Divided Over Slavery
Views on Slavery
Slaveholders
1. Allow slavery in every territory
2. Return escaped slaves to their owners
Moderates
1. Extend Missouri Compromise line to the Pacific
2. Allow voters in each territory to decide on slavery
Abolitionists
1. Slavery is morally wrong
2. Ban slavery throughout the entire country
Civics

Graphic Organizer Skills **In the 1840s, Americans were divided over the slavery issue. The most pressing question was whether or not slavery should be allowed to spread into the western territories.**

1. **Comprehension** How did moderates think that slavery might spread to some western territories but not to others?
2. **Critical Thinking** Why was it practically impossible for abolitionists to agree to any kind of compromise?

Graphic Organizer Skills

ANSWERS **1.** Extension of the Missouri Compromise line would allow slavery in southern territories but not in northern territories. Popular sovereignty would permit some territories to allow slavery and others to forbid it, depending on the outcome of popular votes held in the territories. **2.** Many abolitionists refused to compromise because they said slavery was immoral. They were unwilling to compromise on morality.

Resource Directory

Teaching Resources
Interdisciplinary Connections
• Main Idea: The Debate Over Slavery, p. 92

★ Customized Instruction ★
Kinesthetic Learners

Producing a news program Divide the class into groups, and then ask students to suppose that they are part of a production team for a national news program. Have students use the information in Section 1 to plan a program that would be informative in the mid-1800s, dealing with the many issues surrounding the debate over slavery. Students must choose whom they would ask to be guests on the show and what they would ask each guest. They should also write a summary of the different political, economic, and moral positions that people took on the issue of slavery, in order to provide the anchor with information he or she might need for the broadcast. Encourage each group to present its news program. (*challenging*)

Need for a New Compromise

For a time after the Missouri Compromise, both slave and free states entered the Union peacefully. However, when California requested admission to the Union as a free state in 1850, the balance of power in the Senate was once again threatened. (See the graph to the right.)

California's impact

In 1849, there were 15 slave states and 15 free states in the nation. If California entered the union as a free state, the balance of power would be broken. Furthermore, it seemed quite possible that Oregon, Utah, and New Mexico might also join the Union as free states.

Many Southerners feared that the South would be hopelessly outvoted in the Senate. Some even suggested that southern states might want to **secede,** or remove themselves, from the United States. Northern congressmen, meanwhile, argued that California should enter the Union as a free state because most of the territory lay north of the Missouri Compromise line.

As Congress tried to reach a new compromise, tempers raged. One frightening incident involved Senators Thomas Hart Benton of Missouri and Henry Foote of Mississippi. Benton supported California's entry as a free state even though he himself was a slave owner. He denounced Foote for opposing California's admission. In response, Foote rose angrily from his seat and aimed a pistol at Benton. As other senators watched in horror, Benton roared, "Let him fire. Stand out of the way and let the assassin fire!"

No blood was shed in the Senate that day. However, it was clear that the nation faced a crisis. Many in Congress looked to Senator Henry Clay for a solution.

Chart Skills **Both the North and the South were determined to maintain the delicate balance in the Senate between slave and free states.**

1. **Comprehension** **(a)** How many of the original 13 states were free states? **(b)** How many of them were slave states?
2. **Critical Thinking** How did the balance of power in the Senate change in 1850?

Civics

Clay vs. Calhoun

Clay had won the nickname "the Great Compromiser" for working out the Missouri Compromise. Now, nearly 30 years later, the 73-year-old Clay was frail and ill. Still, he pleaded for the North and South to reach an agreement. If they failed to do so, Clay warned, the nation could break apart.

Senator John C. Calhoun of South Carolina prepared the South's reply to Clay. Calhoun was dying of tuberculosis and could not speak loudly enough to address the Senate. He stared defiantly at his northern foes while Senator James Mason of Virginia read his speech.

Reading Actively

During Reading After students have read about the turmoil that surrounded California's request to enter the Union, have them write two or three sentences in response to this question: "Why were people so concerned about the balance of power in Congress?"

Chart *Skills*

ANSWERS **1. (a)** seven **(b)** six **2.** The admission of California gave free states more power. There were now 16 free states and only 15 slave states. In other words, 32 senators represented free states and only 30 senators represented slave states.

★ *Background* ★
Did You Know?

Guns at the ready Senator Benton was not the only one to be concerned about the use of firearms in Congress. Tensions were so great at this time that members of both proslavery and antislavery views often carried concealed pistols and knives, especially when debates were going on. One senator commented that the only congressmen who were not carrying a knife and a revolver were those who were carrying two revolvers. Indiana Senator William S. Holman recalls that, once, when a congressman's hidden pistol accidentally fired, "there were [instantly] thirty or forty pistols in the air, and the scene looked more like a . . . barroom, than the Congress of the United States."

Technology

Videodiscs/Videotapes
Prentice Hall United States History Video Collection™, Vol. 8, Ch. 25, "Liberty and the Constitution," 1:50 min (*average*) ELL

Chapter 25

AmericanHeritage® History of the United States CD-ROM
- Presidents: Zachary Taylor (*average*)

ANSWER

Possible answers: Some students might say that, legally, the court had to uphold the Fugitive Slave Law of 1850. Others might argue that the court should not have enforced an unjust law.

Writing Actively

After Reading After students have read about the Compromise of 1850, have them create a graphic organizer showing the effects of the compromise.

Protest!

In 1854, a Boston court ordered that fugitive slaves Anthony Burns and Thomas Sims be returned to their owners in the South. Public outcry against the decision was so great that United States marines and artillery were sent into Boston. Angry protesters lined the streets as the two were led to the ship that would return them to slavery.

★ **Do you think the court made the right decision in this case? Explain.**

Calhoun refused to compromise. He insisted that slavery be allowed in the western territories. Calhoun also demanded that **fugitive**, or runaway, slaves be returned to their owners in the South. He wanted northerners to admit that southern slaveholders had the right to reclaim their "property."

If the North would not agree to the South's demands, Calhoun told the Senate, "let the states . . . agree to part in peace. If you are unwilling that we should part in peace, tell us so, and we shall know what to do." Everyone knew what Calhoun meant. If an agreement could not be reached, the South would secede from the Union.

Webster calls for unity

Daniel Webster of Massachusetts spoke next. He supported Clay's plea to save the Union. Webster stated his position clearly:

> ❝ I speak today not as a Massachusetts man, nor as a northern man, but as an American. . . . I speak today for the preservation of the Union. . . . There can be no such thing as a peaceable secession. Peaceable secession is an utter impossibility. ❞

Webster feared that the states could not separate without a **civil war.** A civil war is a war between people of the same country.

Like many northerners, Webster viewed slavery as evil. Disunion, however, he believed was worse. To save the Union, Webster was willing to compromise with the South. He would support its demand that northerners be required to return fugitive slaves.

Compromise of 1850

In 1850, as the debate raged, Calhoun died. His last words reportedly were "The South! The South! God knows what will become of her!" President Taylor also died in 1850. The new President was Millard Fillmore. Unlike Taylor, he supported Clay's compromise plan. An agreement finally seemed possible.

Henry Clay gave more than 70 speeches in favor of a compromise. At last, however, he became too sick to continue. **Stephen Douglas,** an energetic senator from Illinois, took up the fight for him. Douglas tirelessly guided each part of Clay's plan, called the **Compromise of 1850,** through Congress.

The Compromise of 1850 had five parts. First, it allowed California to enter the Union as a free state. Second, it divided the rest of the Mexican Cession into the territo-

★ *Activity* ★

Cooperative Learning

Creating a book of quotations Divide the class into small groups. Assign each group one of the important people discussed in the section. Then ask students to do library research to find quotations from that person. Students should choose quotations that they feel are significant to the section content. After each group gathers three to six quotations, the groups should work together to create a book of quotations on the issue of slavery in the United States in the mid-1800s. The books can be typeset and illustrated on the computer, or students can do the work by hand. (*average*) ELL T

RESOURCE DIRECTORY

Teaching Resources
Unit 5/Chapter 16
- Section 1 Quiz, p. 8

Interdisciplinary Connections
- Main Idea: The Debate Over Slavery, p. 96

ries of New Mexico and Utah. Voters in each would decide the slavery question according to popular sovereignty. Third, it ended the slave trade in Washington, D.C., the nation's capital. Congress, however, declared that it had no power to ban slave trade between slave states. Fourth, it included a strict fugitive slave law. Fifth, it settled a border dispute between Texas and New Mexico.

Fugitive Slave Law of 1850

Most northerners had ignored the Fugitive Slave Law of 1793. As a result, fugitive slaves often lived as free citizens in northern cities. The **Fugitive Slave Law of 1850** was harder to ignore. It required all citizens to help catch runaway slaves. People who let fugitives escape could be fined $1,000 and jailed for six months.

The new law also set up special courts to handle the cases of runaways. Judges received $10 for sending an accused runaway to the South. They received only $5 for setting someone free. Lured by the extra money, some judges sent African Americans to the South whether or not they were runaways.

The Fugitive Slave Law enraged antislavery northerners. By forcing them to catch runaways, the law made northerners feel they were part of the slave system. In several northern cities, crowds tried to rescue fugitive slaves from their captors.

Martin R. Delany, an African American newspaper editor, spoke for many northerners, black and white:

> "My house is my castle.... If any man approaches that house in search of a slave—I care not who he may be, whether constable or sheriff, magistrate or even judge of the Supreme Court... if he crosses the threshold of my door, and I do not lay him a lifeless corpse at my feet, I hope the grave may refuse my body a resting place."

The North and South had reached a compromise. Still, tensions remained because neither side got everything that it wanted. The new Fugitive Slave Law was especially hard for northerners to accept. Each time the law was enforced, it convinced more northerners that slavery was evil.

★ Section 1 Review ★

Recall

1. **Locate** (a) Missouri, (b) Maine, (c) Missouri Compromise Line, (d) California, (e) New Mexico Territory, (f) Utah Territory.
2. **Identify** (a) Missouri Compromise, (b) Wilmot Proviso, (c) Free Soil party, (d) Zachary Taylor, (e) Stephen Douglas, (f) Compromise of 1850, (g) Fugitive Slave Law of 1850.
3. **Define** (a) sectionalism, (b) popular sovereignty, (c) secede, (d) fugitive, (e) civil war.

Comprehension

4. Describe three different views on the issue of slavery in the West.
5. Why did some people leave the Whig and Democratic parties and create the Free Soil party?
6. Explain the five parts of the Compromise of 1850.

Critical Thinking and Writing

7. **Analyzing Ideas** Why might the goals of the Free Soil party have pleased some northerners but not others?
8. **Analyzing Visual Evidence** Based on your understanding of the painting on page 356, how did the Compromise of 1850 create new conflict over the slavery issue?

Activity **Making a Decision** You are a northerner of the 1850s. There is a knock at your door. It's a fugitive slave! Will you help the runaway or will you turn the person in to the authorities? Write a brief statement explaining the reasons for your decision.

★ Section 1 Review ★

ANSWERS

1. See map, p. 431.
2. **(a)–(b)** p. 424, **(c)–(d)** p. 426, **(e)–(f)** p. 428, **(g)** p. 429
3. **(a)** p. 425, **(b)** p. 426, **(c)** p. 427, **(d)** p. 428, **(e)** p. 428
4. Abolitionists: slavery's end; southerners: allow slavery in new territories; moderates: allow it in some territories, not others
5. because both refused to reject the spread of slavery
6. made California a free state; let popular sovereignty settle the slavery issue in New Mexico/Utah; ended slave trade in Washington, D.C.; enacted fugitive slave law; settled Texas/New Mexico border dispute
7. By accepting slavery in the South, Free Soilers displeased abolitionists; by opposing its spread, they pleased some northerners.
8. Requiring the return of fugitive slaves brought everyone into the slave system, increasing North–South conflict.

Guided Instruction

Have students reread the subsection Fugitive Slave Law of 1850. Student statements should reflect pressures for and against helping the runaway.

ASSESSMENT See the rubrics in the Alternative Assessment booklet in the Teaching Resources.

★ Background ★
Turning Points

An aggressive act Historians have suggested that the Fugitive Slave Law of 1850 can be seen as an aggressive act on the part of the South, one designed more to provoke northerners than to recapture runaway slaves. By this interpretation, it was one of the first concrete moves taken by either side toward civil war.

From the Archives of AmericanHeritage®

Civil disobedience Henry David Thoreau's 1849 essay "On the Duty of Civil Disobedience" states that prison may be "the only house in a slave State in which a free man can abide with honor." Though Thoreau himself was more of a theorist, others acted on his ideas by disobeying laws they felt were unjust, such as the Fugitive Slave Law.

Source: Bernard Schwartz, *The American Heritage® History of the Law in America,* 1974.

Technology

AmericanHeritage® History of the United States CD-ROM

- Face the Issues: Fugitive Slave Law (challenging)
- Presidents: Millard Fillmore (average)

Section 2

The Crisis Turns Violent

LESSON PLAN

Objectives

★ Describe how *Uncle Tom's Cabin* affected attitudes toward slavery.

★ Explain why a civil war broke out in Kansas.

★ Describe how the Dred Scott decision divided the nation.

1 Engage

Warm Up Tell students that a book, an act of Congress, and a Supreme Court ruling moved the U.S. toward civil war. Then have them guess about the situations surrounding these three things.

Activating Prior Knowledge Have students form small groups to discuss how a current event, such as an act of Congress, might affect them today (e.g., a law raising the U.S. driving age to 21).

Reading Actively

Before Reading On the chalkboard, write "*Uncle Tom's Cabin,*" "Kansas-Nebraska Act," "Dred Scott decision." As they read, students will write cause-and-effect comments for each item—as a cause, effect, or both.

2 Explore

After reading the section, students should summarize how *Uncle Tom's*

RESOURCE DIRECTORY

Teaching Resources
Lesson Planner, p. 67
Unit 5/Chapter 16
- Connecting History and Literature: My Bondage and My Freedom, p. 6

Interdisciplinary Connections
- Main Idea: The Debate Over Slavery, p. 95

Transparencies
Geography and History
- North Central States, p. I-73

The Crisis Turns Violent

As You Read

Explore These Questions
- How did *Uncle Tom's Cabin* affect attitudes toward slavery?
- Why did a civil war break out in Kansas?
- How did the Dred Scott decision divide the nation?

Define
- repeal
- guerrilla warfare
- lawsuit

Identify
- Harriet Beecher Stowe
- *Uncle Tom's Cabin*
- Kansas-Nebraska Act
- Franklin Pierce
- Border Ruffians
- John Brown
- Bleeding Kansas
- Charles Sumner
- Dred Scott decision

SETTING the Scene In the mid-1850s, proslavery and antislavery forces battled for control of the territory of Kansas. An observer described election day in one Kansas district in 1855:

> ❝ On the morning of the election, before the polls were opened, some 300 or 400 Missourians and others were collected in the yard . . . where the election was to be held, armed with bowie-knives, revolvers, and clubs. They said they came to vote, and whip the . . . Yankees, and would vote without being sworn. Some said they came to have a fight, and wanted one. ❞

Hearing of events in Kansas, Abraham Lincoln, then a young lawyer in Illinois, predicted that "the contest will come to blows, and bloodshed." Once again, the issue of slavery in the territories divided the nation.

An Antislavery Bestseller

An event in 1852 added to the growing antislavery mood of the North. That year, **Harriet Beecher Stowe** published a novel called ***Uncle Tom's Cabin.*** Stowe wrote the novel to show the evils of slavery and the injustice of the Fugitive Slave Law. She had originally published the story as a serial in an abolitionist newspaper.

A powerful story

Stowe told the story of Uncle Tom, an enslaved African American noted for his kindness and his devotion to his religion. Tom is bought by Simon Legree, a cruel planter who treats his slaves brutally. In the end, Uncle Tom refuses to obey Legree's order to whip another slave. Legree then whips Uncle Tom to death.

Uncle Tom's Cabin had wide appeal in the North. The first 5,000 copies that were printed sold out in two days. In its first year, Stowe's novel sold 300,000 copies. The book was also published in many different languages. Soon, a play based on the novel appeared in cities not only in the North but around the world.

Nationwide reaction

Although *Uncle Tom's Cabin* was popular in the North, southerners objected to the book. They claimed that it did not give a true picture of slave life. Indeed, Stowe had seen little of slavery firsthand.

Even so, the book helped to change the way northerners felt about slavery. No longer could they ignore slavery as a political problem for Congress to settle. They now saw the slavery issue as a moral problem facing every American. For this reason, *Uncle Tom's Cabin* was one of the most important books in American history.

★ Customized Instruction ★

English Language Learners

Reinforcing information Have English language learners work together to create an audiotape of the section. First, have students practice reading the section aloud to one another. As they read, have them note words or phrases that they find difficult to pronounce or whose meaning is unclear to them. Meet with the students to review these terms and phrases until they begin to feel confident with them. Then students can take turns reading the section aloud into a tape recorder. At the end of the recording, have students describe the main ideas of the section. The audiotape can be used by the entire class as a tool for review. (basic) ELL

Kansas-Nebraska Act

Americans had hoped that the Compromise of 1850 would end debate over slavery in the West. In 1854, however, the issue of slavery in the territories surfaced yet again.

In January 1854, Senator Stephen Douglas introduced a bill to set up a government for the Nebraska Territory. This territory stretched from Texas north to Canada, and from Missouri west to the Rockies.

Douglas knew that white southerners did not want to add another free state to the Union. He proposed that the Nebraska Territory be divided into two territories, Kansas and Nebraska. (See the map below.) The settlers living in each territory would decide the issue of slavery by popular sovereignty. Douglas's bill was known as the **Kansas-Nebraska Act.**

Support for the act

The Kansas-Nebraska Act seemed fair to many people. After all, the Compromise of 1850 had applied popular sovereignty in New Mexico and Utah.

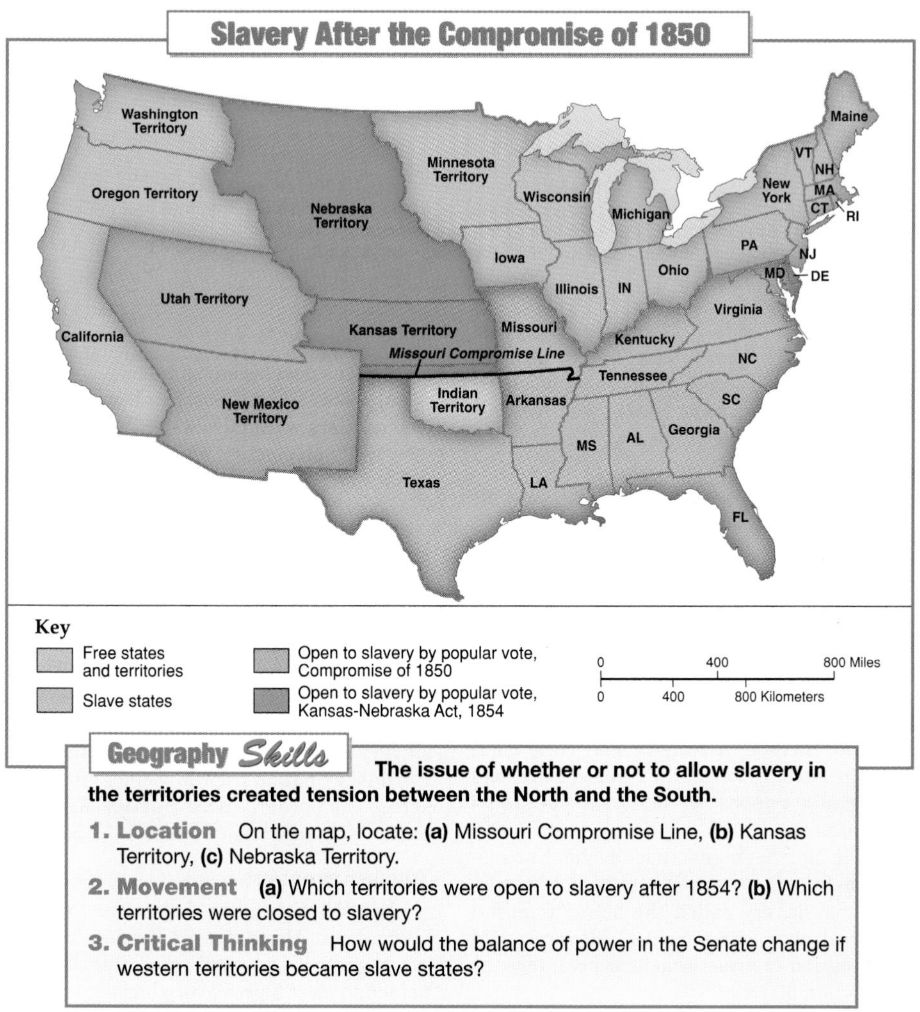

Geography Skills **The issue of whether or not to allow slavery in the territories created tension between the North and the South.**

1. **Location** On the map, locate: **(a)** Missouri Compromise Line, **(b)** Kansas Territory, **(c)** Nebraska Territory.
2. **Movement** **(a)** Which territories were open to slavery after 1854? **(b)** Which territories were closed to slavery?
3. **Critical Thinking** How would the balance of power in the Senate change if western territories became slave states?

Cabin, the Kansas-Nebraska Act, and the Dred Scott decision influenced the slavery debate.

3 Teach

Students should supply at least two supporting details for each of these main ideas: **(a)** *Uncle Tom's Cabin* fueled the antislavery feeling in the North. **(b)** The Kansas-Nebraska Act divided Nebraska into two territories. **(c)** Pro- and antislavery forces sent settlers to take control of Kansas. **(d)** The Kansas conflict led to violence in the Senate. **(e)** Americans hoped that the Dred Scott decision would end the slavery debate for good.

4 Assess

To close the lesson, have students complete the section review. Or have them work in groups to prepare front pages of Atlanta and Boston papers announcing: publication of *Uncle Tom's Cabin,* passage of the Kansas-Nebraska Act, violence in Kansas, or the Dred Scott decision. Students should include editorials and drawings as well as interviews, headlines, and news accounts.

★ ★ ★ ★ ★ ★ ★ ★ ★ ★ ★ ★ ★ ★ ★ ★ ★ ★

Geography Skills

ANSWERS **1.** Review locations with students. **2. (a)** Nebraska, Kansas, Utah, New Mexico **(b)** Washington, Oregon, Minnesota **3.** Slave states would outnumber free states, tipping the balance of power to the South.

★ Activity ★
Connections With the World

Researching emancipation In 1833, slavery was abolished throughout the British Empire. Most Latin American nations abolished slavery before the United States did: Mexico—1829, Colombia—1851, and Argentina—1853. Have students research and report on emancipation in one of these countries. (*average*)

Technology

AmericanHeritage® History of the United States CD-ROM
- History Makers: Harriet Beecher Stowe (*average*)

During Reading Ask students to explain in their own words why some people supported the Kansas-Nebraska Act while others thought it unfair.

Viewing HISTORY ANSWER

The Kansas-Nebraska Act left it to the people of Kansas to decide whether slavery would be allowed in the territory. People from both sides went to Kansas hoping to influence the vote.

Abolitionist's saber

Viewing HISTORY Bleeding Kansas

In 1856, a bloody civil war broke out in Kansas. Proslavery and antislavery forces fought for control of the territory. The battle depicted here took place at Hickory Point, 25 miles north of Lawrence. ★ **How was the violence in Kansas related to the Kansas-Nebraska Act?**

Southern leaders especially supported the Kansas-Nebraska Act. They were sure that slave owners from neighboring Missouri would move across the border into Kansas. In time, they hoped, Kansas would become a slave state.

President **Franklin Pierce,** a Democrat elected in 1852, also supported the bill. With the President's help, Douglas pushed the Kansas-Nebraska Act through Congress. He did not realize it at the time, but he had lit a fire under a powder keg.

Northern outrage

Other people were unhappy with the new law. The Missouri Compromise had already banned slavery in Kansas and Nebraska, they insisted. In effect, the Kansas-Nebraska Act would **repeal,** or undo, the Missouri Compromise.

The northern reaction to the Kansas-Nebraska Act was swift and angry. Opponents of slavery called the act a "criminal betrayal of precious rights." Slavery could now spread to areas that had been free for more than 30 years.

Bleeding Kansas

Kansas now became a testing ground for popular sovereignty. Stephen Douglas hoped that settlers would decide the slavery issue peacefully on election day. Instead, proslavery and antislavery forces sent settlers to Kansas to fight for control of the territory.

Most of the new arrivals were farmers from neighboring states. Their main interest in moving to Kansas was to acquire cheap land. Few of these settlers owned slaves. At the same time, abolitionists brought in more than 1,000 settlers from New England.

Proslavery settlers moved into Kansas as well. They wanted to make sure that antislavery forces did not overrun the territory. Proslavery bands from Missouri often rode across the border. These **Border Ruffians** battled the antislavery forces in Kansas.

Two governments

In 1855, Kansas held elections to choose lawmakers. Hundreds of Border Ruffians crossed into Kansas and voted illegally. They helped to elect a proslavery legislature.

★ *Background* ★

Religion and Ethics

From the pulpit Henry Ward Beecher, the brother of Harriet Beecher Stowe, was a well-known pastor in Brooklyn, New York, who frequently denounced slavery. When settlers began flooding into Kansas, he declared that rifles would do more against slavery in Kansas than Bibles. From then on, rifles sent to antislavery settlers in Kansas were called "Beecher's Bibles."

★ *Background* ★

Recent Scholarship

Point of no return Noted historian Kenneth Stampp writes in his book *America in 1857: A Nation on the Brink* that "1857 was probably . . . when the North and South reached the political point of no return—when it became well nigh impossible to head off a violent resolution of the differences between them." The book considers how that volatile point was reached.

RESOURCE DIRECTORY

Teaching Resources
Interdisciplinary Connections
• Main Idea: The Debate Over Slavery, p. 93

The new legislature quickly passed laws to support slavery. One law said that people could be put to death for helping slaves escape. Another made speaking out against slavery a crime punishable by two years of hard labor.

Antislavery settlers refused to accept these laws. They elected their own governor and legislature. With two rival governments, Kansas was in chaos. Armed gangs roamed the land looking for trouble.

A bloody battleground

In 1856, a band of proslavery men raided the town of Lawrence, an antislavery stronghold. The attackers destroyed homes and smashed the press of a Free Soil newspaper.

John Brown, an abolitionist, decided to strike back. Brown had moved to Kansas to help make it a free state. He claimed that God had sent him to punish supporters of slavery.

Brown rode with his four sons and two other men to the town of Pottawatomie (paht uh WAHT uh mee) Creek. In the middle of the night, they dragged five proslavery settlers from their beds and murdered them.

The killings at Pottawatomie Creek led to more violence. Both sides fought fiercely and engaged in **guerrilla warfare,** or the use of hit-and-run tactics. By late 1856, more than 200 people had been killed. Newspapers called the territory **Bleeding Kansas.**

Violence in the Senate

Even before John Brown's attack, the battle over Kansas had spilled into the Senate. **Charles Sumner** of Massachusetts was the leading abolitionist senator. In one speech, the sharp-tongued Sumner denounced the proslavery legislature of Kansas. He then viciously criticized his southern foes, singling out Andrew Butler, an elderly senator from South Carolina.

Butler was not in the Senate on the day Sumner spoke. A few days later, however, Butler's nephew, Congressman Preston Brooks, marched into the Senate chamber. Using a heavy cane, Brooks beat Sumner until he fell down, bloody and unconscious, to the floor.

Many southerners felt that Sumner got what he deserved for his verbal abuse of another senator. Hundreds of people sent canes to Brooks to show their support. To northerners, however, the brutal act was just more evidence that slavery led to violence.

The Dred Scott Case

With Congress in an uproar, many Americans looked to the Supreme Court to settle the slavery issue and restore peace. In 1857, the Court ruled on a case involving a slave named Dred Scott. Instead of bringing harmony, however, the Court's decision further divided North and South.

Dred Scott had lived for many years in Missouri. Later, he moved with his owner to Illinois and then to the Wisconsin Territory,

Biography **Dred Scott**

Dred Scott filed a lawsuit for his freedom. He argued that he should be a free man because he had lived in a free territory. The Supreme Court, however, ruled that he had no right to sue because he was property and not a citizen. After the decision, Scott's new owner granted freedom to Scott and his family. Just one year later, Scott died of consumption. ★ **How did the Dred Scott decision overturn the Missouri Compromise?**

Writing Actively 

After Reading Ask students to choose one key event in this section. Have them write a telegram (25 words maximum) telling about the event from the point of view of an eyewitness.

Biography

ANSWER

The Supreme Court said that the Missouri Compromise was unconstitutional because it had forbidden slavery in some territories. The Court said that Congress did not have the power to outlaw slavery in any territory.

★ Background ★

Viewpoints

Outrageous attack or just desserts? The morning after the attack on Sumner, Senator Henry Wilson of Massachusetts addressed his colleagues. He said, "... to assail a member of the Senate ... 'for words spoken in debate,' is a grave offense not only against the rights of the senator but the constitutional privileges of this house; but ... to come into this chamber and assault a member in his seat until he falls exhausted and senseless on this floor, is an offense requiring the prompt and decisive action of the Senate." Conversely, the *Richmond Whig* had this comment: "The only regret we feel is, that Mr. Brooks did not employ a horsewhip or cowhide upon [Sumner's] slanderous back, instead of a cane."

Technology

Videodiscs/Videotapes

Prentice Hall United States History Video Collection™, Vol. 8, Ch. 28, "Slavery and the Western Territories," 3 mins (*average*) ELL

Chapter 28

Prentice Hall United States History Video Collection™, Vol. 8, Ch. 31, "Dred Scott *v.* John F. A. Sandford," 3:45 mins (*average*) ELL

Chapter 31

AmericanHeritage® History of the United States CD-ROM

- Presidents: Franklin Pierce (*average*)

★ Section 2 Review ★

ANSWERS

1. See map, p. 431.

2. (a) p. 432, **(b)** p. 433, **(c)** p. 434

3. (a)–(b) p. 430, **(c)** p. 431, **(d)–(e)** p. 432, **(f)–(h)** p. 433, **(i)** p. 434

4. (a) as an unjust system in which kindly slaves were brutally treated by owners **(b)** It made northerners see slavery as a moral problem facing every American.

5. It led pro- and antislavery forces to battle for control of the territory.

6. (a) pleased, because it recognized slaves as property and kept Congress from banning slavery in any territory **(b)** angry; but some felt that the decision would help the abolitionist movement **(c)** shocked, because they had hoped slavery would die out, not spread

7. (a) that the people in the West would decide the issue **(b)** Possible answers: Agree: The issue would not be decided in Congress. Disagree: It would be decided by civil war, not westerners.

8. Both opposed slavery; Stowe was nonviolent, Brown was violent.

Activity

Guided Instruction
Review the decision before students begin to write.

ASSESSMENT See the rubrics in the Alternative Assessment booklet in the Teaching Resources.

RESOURCE DIRECTORY

Teaching Resources
Lesson Planner, p. 68
Unit 5/Chapter 16
• Section 2 Quiz, p. 9

where slavery was not allowed. After they returned to Missouri, Scott's owner died. Antislavery lawyers helped Scott to file a **lawsuit,** a legal case brought by a person or group against another to settle a dispute between them. Scott's lawyers argued that since Scott had lived in a free territory, he was a free man.

The Supreme Court's decision

In time, the case reached the Supreme Court. The Court's decision startled Americans who opposed slavery. The Court ruled that Scott could not file a lawsuit because, as an enslaved person, he was not a citizen. Also, the Court clearly stated that slaves were property.

The Court's ruling did not stop there. Instead, the Justices went on to make a sweeping decision about the larger issue of slavery in the territories. According to the Court, Congress did not have the power to outlaw slavery in any territory. The Court's ruling meant that the Missouri Compromise was unconstitutional.

The nation reacts

White southerners rejoiced at the **Dred Scott decision.** It meant that slavery was legal in all the territories. This was just what white southerners had been demanding for years.

African Americans responded angrily to the Dred Scott decision. In the North, many held public meetings to condemn the ruling. At a meeting in Philadelphia, a speaker hoped that the Dred Scott decision would lead more whites to "join with us in our efforts to recover the long lost boon of freedom."

White northerners were also shocked by the ruling. Many had hoped that slavery would eventually die out if it were restricted to the South. Now, however, slavery could spread throughout the West. Even northerners who disliked abolitionists felt that the Dred Scott ruling was wrong. A newspaper in Cincinnati declared, "We are now one great . . . slaveholding community." In New England, another newspaper asked, "Where will it all end?"

★ Section 2 Review ★

Recall

1. **Locate** (a) Kansas Territory, (b) Nebraska Territory.
2. **Define** (a) repeal, (b) guerrilla warfare, (c) lawsuit.
3. **Identify** (a) Harriet Beecher Stowe, (b) *Uncle Tom's Cabin,* (c) Kansas-Nebraska Act, (d) Franklin Pierce, (e) Border Ruffians, (f) John Brown, (g) Bleeding Kansas, (h) Charles Sumner, (i) Dred Scott decision.

Comprehension

4. (a) How did *Uncle Tom's Cabin* portray slavery? (b) How did the book affect people's attitudes toward slavery?
5. How did the Kansas-Nebraska Act lead to violence in Kansas?
6. Explain how each of the following reacted to the Dred Scott decision: (a) white southerners, (b) African Americans, (c) white northerners.

Critical Thinking and Writing

7. **Analyzing Primary Sources** After the Kansas-Nebraska Act was passed, Stephen Douglas stated, "The struggle for freedom was forever banished from the halls of Congress to the western plains." (a) What did Douglas mean? (b) Do you agree or disagree with his statement? Explain.
8. **Comparing** Compare Harriet Beecher Stowe's and John Brown's contributions to the abolitionist movement.

Activity **Writing a Protest Letter** You are outraged by the Dred Scott decision! Write a protest letter to the justices of the Supreme Court explaining why you think their decision in this case was wrong.

★ Background ★
Our Diverse Nation

The trials of Mr. Scott While his case was being tried in Missouri, Dred Scot remained under the authority of the sheriff of St. Louis. The sheriff hired Scott out for five dollars a month. After the Court decision, Scott was sold, and his new owner freed him. He then worked as a porter at Barnum's Hotel in St. Louis. Scott died from tuberculosis in 1858.

★ Activity ★
Connections With Civics

Staging a talk show Have students stage a talk show featuring several justices who participated in the Dred Scott decision. One or more students should pose as the talk show host(s). Students should prepare questions for the justices that relate to the Court's decision in the case. Justices should be prepared to respond to such questions. (*average*) T

A New Party Challenges Slavery

As You Read

Explore These Questions

- Why did the Republican party come into being in the mid-1850s?
- What were Abraham Lincoln's views on slavery?
- How did northerners and southerners respond differently to the raid on Harpers Ferry?

Define

- arsenal
- martyr

Identify

- Republican party
- John C. Frémont
- James Buchanan
- Abraham Lincoln

SETTING the Scene In the mid-1850s, people who opposed slavery in the territories needed a new political voice. Neither Whigs nor Democrats would take a strong stand against slavery. "We have submitted to slavery long enough," an Ohio Democrat declared.

Free Soilers, northern Democrats, and antislavery Whigs met in towns and cities across the North. In 1854, a group gathered in Michigan to form the **Republican party.** The new party grew quickly. By 1856, it was ready to challenge the older parties for power.

The Republican Party

In the 1850s, the main goal of the Republican party was to keep slavery out of the western territories. A few Republicans were abolitionists. They hoped to end slavery in the South as well. Most Republicans, however, wanted only to stop the spread of slavery.

In 1856, Republicans selected **John C. Frémont** to run for President. Frémont was a frontiersman who had fought for California's independence. (See page 362.) He had little political experience, but he opposed the spread of slavery.

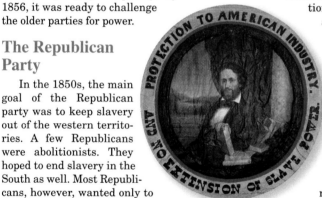

Frémont's main opponent was Democrat **James Buchanan** of Pennsylvania. He had served as a senator and as Secretary of State. Many Democrats considered Buchanan to be a "compromise" candidate because he was a "northern man with southern principles." They hoped that he would attract voters in both the North and the South.

Buchanan won the election with support from a large majority of southerners and many northerners. Still, the Republicans made a strong showing in the election. Without the support of a single southern state, Frémont won one third of the popular vote. Southerners worried that their influence in the national government was fading.

Abe Lincoln of Illinois

The next test for the Republican party came in 1858 in the state of Illinois. **Abraham Lincoln,** a Republican, challenged Democrat Stephen Douglas for his seat in the Senate. The election captured the attention of the whole nation. The race was important because most Americans thought that Douglas would run for President in 1860.

PROTECTION TO AMERICAN INDUSTRY, AND NO EXTENSION OF SLAVE POWER.

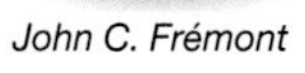

John C. Frémont

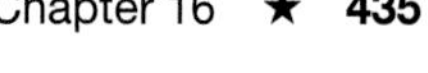

Section 3

A New Party Challenges Slavery

LESSON PLAN

Objectives

★ Explain why the Republican party came into being in the mid-1850s.

★ Outline Abraham Lincoln's views on slavery.

★ Describe the different reactions of northerners and southerners to the raid on Harpers Ferry.

1 Engage

Warm Up Have students list things they think of when they hear the name Abraham Lincoln (e.g., the face on a penny, honesty, and so on). Have them add to their lists as they read.

Activating Prior Knowledge Point out to students that some election outcomes have greater historical impact than others. Have students think of elections they have learned about that had a large impact on history *(e.g., 1800, Thomas Jefferson, end of Federalist era; 1828, Andrew Jackson, a new democracy).*

Reading Actively

Before Reading Have students note the statement on this page: ". . . the main goal of the Republican party was to keep slavery out of the western territories." Ask students to find evidence to support this statement as they read the section.

Technology

AmericanHeritage® History of the United States CD-ROM

- Presidents: James Buchanan *(average)*

★ Background ★

Turning Points

Won by the minority Buchanan's two rivals together actually had more popular votes than he did. If only 27 of his electoral votes had gone to Frémont, the election would have moved to the House. In that case, Frémont might have won, and the Civil War might have started five years earlier, since most southern states had threatened to secede if Frémont won the election.

2 Explore

Ask students to read the section. Then explain that Lincoln challenged Douglas to the debates in order to increase his visibility; unlike Douglas, he was not a national figure. The popular debates helped Lincoln to achieve his aim.

3 Teach

Have students read selections from one of the many Lincoln biographies. Then ask them to select one fact or anecdote from the book about his life to report to the class. Have a recorder note down each reported item; use the information to create a bulletin board display or a display in a showcase for the entire school.

4 Assess

To close the lesson, have students complete the section review. As an alternative, ask students to write an essay in which they compare the Lincoln-Douglas debates with the ways that politicians campaign for office today.

★ ★ ★ ★ ★ ★ ★ ★ ★ ★ ★ ★ ★ ★ ★ ★ ★

During Reading Have students review the subsection under the heading Just Folks. Ask them to explain in their own words Lincoln's reply to the confused listener.

Viewing History **ANSWER**

Slavery was the most important issue.

RESOURCE DIRECTORY

Teaching Resources
Unit 5/Chapter 16
- Biography Flashcard: Carl Schurz, p. 7

Why Study History?
- Heroes of the Past Can Be Models for Today, pp. 63–66

The Lincoln-Douglas Debates

In this painting, Stephen Douglas sits to Lincoln's right during a debate held at Charleston, Illinois, in September 1858. Thousands of people attended the Lincoln-Douglas debates. ★ **What was the most important issue discussed in the debates?**

A self-starter from Kentucky

Abraham Lincoln was born in the backcountry of Kentucky. Like many frontier people, his parents moved often to find better land. The family lived in Indiana and later in Illinois. As a child, Lincoln spent only a year in school. Still, he taught himself to read and spent many hours reading by firelight.

After Lincoln left home, he opened a store in Illinois. There, he studied law on his own and launched a career in politics. After spending eight years in the state legislature, Lincoln served one term in Congress. Bitterly opposed to the Kansas-Nebraska Act, he decided to run for the Senate in 1858.

"Just folks"

When the race began, Lincoln was not a national figure. Still, people in Illinois knew him well and liked him. To them, he was "just folks"—someone who enjoyed picnics, wrestling contests, and all their other favorite pastimes.

People also admired his honesty and wit. His plainspoken manner made him a good speaker. Even so, a listener once complained that he could not understand one of Lincoln's speeches. "There are always some fleas a dog can't reach" was Lincoln's reply.

Lincoln-Douglas Debates

During the Senate campaign, Lincoln challenged Douglas to a series of debates. Douglas was not eager to accept, but he did. During the campaign, the two debated seven times. Slavery was the important issue.

Views on slavery

Douglas wanted to settle the slavery question by popular sovereignty. He disliked slavery, but he thought that people in the territories should be able to vote "down or up" for it.

Lincoln, like nearly all whites of his day, did not believe in "perfect equality" between blacks and whites. He did, however, believe that slavery was a "moral, social, and political wrong." He believed that blacks were entitled to the rights named in the Declaration of Independence—"life, liberty, and the pursuit of happiness."

Since slavery was wrong, said Lincoln, Douglas and other Americans should not treat it as an unimportant question to be voted "down or up." Lincoln was totally opposed to slavery in the territories. Still, he was not an abolitionist. He had no wish to interfere with slavery in the states where it already existed.

Lincoln believed that the nation could not survive if it remained divided by slavery. On June 16, 1858, Lincoln spoke in a crowded hall in Springfield, Illinois:

> ❝A house divided against itself cannot stand. I believe this government cannot endure permanently half slave and half free. I do not expect the Union to be dissolved—I do not expect the house to fall—but I do expect it will cease to be divided. It will become all one thing, or all the other.❞

436 ★ Chapter 16

★ *Customized Instruction* ★

Kinesthetic Learners

Recreating history Have students use a source such as *The Lincoln-Douglas Debates of 1858*, edited by R. W. Johannsen. Ask them to select passages from the speeches given by Lincoln and Douglas during the debates. After allowing sufficient time to practice, have them re-create this part of United States history by performing dramatic presentations of the passages to the class. Students can dress the part, if they wish, and they can offer the audience some background information on their characters before their performances. After the reenactments, students can ask the "Lincolns" and "Douglases" questions to check their own understanding. (*average*)

Why Study History?

Because Heroes of the Past Can Be Models for Today

Historical Background

Many consider Abraham Lincoln one of the truly heroic figures in American history. Through education and hard work, "Honest Abe" rose from humble beginnings to national leadership. As President, he would lead the nation through the horrors of a civil war and help bring an end to slavery.

Lincoln Memorial

Connections to Today

Today, we still honor Lincoln. Each year, we remember him on Presidents' Day. His image is on the money we use every day. In addition, thousands of people show their respect by visiting the Lincoln Memorial in Washington, D.C.

Admirers of Lincoln consider him a model for others to imitate. They point to his easygoing manner, keen wit, high sense of morality, and ability to make wise decisions in tough situations.

Connections to You

Do you think Lincoln is an American hero? Should you look to him as a role model? To help you decide, read the following excerpts from Lincoln's conversations, speeches, and writings.

"I have no other [ambition] so great as that of being truly esteemed of my fellow men, by rendering myself worthy of their esteem."—June 13, 1836

"The better part of one's life consists in his friendships." —May 19, 1849

"Let us have faith that Right makes Might, and in that faith, let us to the end, dare to do our duty." —February 27, 1860

"I want every man to have a chance—and I believe a black man is entitled to it—in which he can better his condition."—March 6, 1860

"The people's will, constitutionally expressed, is the ultimate law for all."—October 19, 1864

"Whenever I hear anyone arguing for slavery, I feel a strong impulse to see it tried on him personally." —March 17, 1865

1. Comprehension How do Americans show their respect for Abraham Lincoln today?

2. Critical Thinking **(a)** Which quotation deals most directly with the idea of racial equality? **(b)** What was Lincoln's position on equality?

★Activity **Writing an Essay** Do you consider Lincoln an American hero and role model? Develop your answer in a brief essay, using the quotations above to describe some of Lincoln's ideas and values.

ANSWERS

1. by recognizing him on Presidents' Day; by visiting the Lincoln Memorial in Washington, D.C.

2. (a) the quotation from March 6, 1860 **(b)** that every person should have an equal opportunity to improve his or her situation

★Activity

Guided Instruction

Encourage students to decide whether or not they consider Lincoln to be a role model. Then have them reread each quotation, noting whether it supports their view. They might make a concept web or outline before beginning to write the essay. Remind students to revise the draft for spelling, grammar, and punctuation.

ASSESSMENT See the rubrics in the Alternative Assessment booklet in the Teaching Resources.

Writing Actively

After Reading Have students review the section to find one fact about Abraham Lincoln that surprised them. Ask them to write a few sentences presenting the fact and explaining why it surprised them.

Fast Facts

★ The statue of Lincoln in the Lincoln Memorial is 19 feet high and sits on an 11-foot-high base. It weighs 175 tons.

★ In 1876, grave robbers almost took Lincoln's body from its crypt in Springfield, Illinois, but they were captured. They had planned to ransom the body.

★ Lincoln is consistently seen as the greatest President. In 1996, the noted Schlesinger survey of respected historians again found him at the very top.

Bibliography

To read more about this topic:

1. *A Memorial for Mr. Lincoln*, Brent Ashabranner (Putnam, 1992). Detailed history of the Lincoln Memorial.

2. *Lincoln: A Photobiography*, Russell Freedman (Clarion Books, 1987). Lincoln's life in text and photographs.

3. Internet. Abraham Lincoln on-line at www.netins.net/showcase/creative/lincoln.html. A clearinghouse of information about the President.

★ Section 3 Review ★

ANSWERS

1. (a)–(d) p. 435

2. (a) p. 438, **(b)** p. 438

3. to keep slavery out of the territories

4. Lincoln felt that as a moral wrong, slavery should not be extended to the territories. He believed the nation could not survive if slavery divided it. Douglas believed the people in each territory should decide the slavery question.

5. (a) Northerners praised Brown as a freedom fighter and mourned his death. **(b)** Southerners saw him as an insane person who threatened their way of life.

6. Lincoln was admired as down-to-earth, honest, and witty.

7. Possible answer: Yes, because many northerners came to see it as a terrible wrong that went against the American principle that all people are equal.

Activity

Guided Instruction

Point out to students that headlines both sum up a story and grab the reader's attention. Provide examples from recent newspapers to illustrate this point. Extend the exercise by having students write articles about the events mentioned in their headlines.

ASSESSMENT See the rubrics in the Alternative Assessment booklet in the Teaching Resources.

RESOURCE DIRECTORY

Teaching Resources
Lesson Planner, p. 69
Unit 5/Chapter 16
• Section 3 Quiz, p. 10

A leader emerges

Week after week, both men spoke nearly every day to large crowds. Newspapers reprinted their campaign speeches. The more northerners read Lincoln's speeches, the more they thought about the injustice of slavery.

In the end, Douglas won the election by a slim margin. However, Lincoln was a winner, too. He was now known throughout the country. Two years later, the two rivals would again meet face to face—both seeking the office of President.

John Brown's Raid

In the meantime, more bloodshed pushed the North and South farther apart. In 1859, John Brown carried his antislavery campaign from Kansas to the East. He led a group of followers, including five African Americans, to Harpers Ferry, Virginia.

There, Brown planned to raid a federal **arsenal,** or gun warehouse. He thought that enslaved African Americans would flock to him at the arsenal. He would then give them weapons and lead them in a revolt.

Sentenced to death

Brown quickly gained control of the arsenal. No slave uprising took place, however. Instead, troops led by Robert E. Lee killed 10 of the raiders and captured Brown.

Most people, in both the North and the South, thought that Brown's plan to lead a slave revolt was insane. After all, there were not many enslaved African Americans in Harpers Ferry. At his trial, however, Brown seemed perfectly sane. He sat quietly as the court found him guilty of murder and treason and sentenced him to death.

Hero or villain?

Brown became a hero to many northerners. Some considered him a **martyr** because he was willing to give up his life for his beliefs. On the morning he was hanged, church bells rang solemnly throughout the North. In years to come, New Englanders would sing a popular song: "John Brown's body lies a mold'ring in the grave, but his soul is marching on."

To white southerners, the northern response to John Brown's death was outrageous. People were singing the praises of a man who had tried to lead a slave revolt! Many southerners became convinced that the North wanted to destroy slavery—and the South along with it. The nation was poised for a violent clash.

★ Section 3 Review ★

Recall

1. **Identify** **(a)** Republican party, **(b)** John C. Frémont, **(c)** James Buchanan, **(d)** Abraham Lincoln.
2. **Define** **(a)** arsenal, **(b)** martyr.

Comprehension

3. What was the main goal of the Republican party?
4. How did Abraham Lincoln's opinions on slavery differ from those of Stephen Douglas?
5. **(a)** How did Northerners respond to John Brown's execution? **(b)** How did Southerners respond?

Critical Thinking and Writing

6. **Identifying Main Ideas** Reread the subsection on page 436 called Just folks. State the main idea of this subsection.
7. **Analyzing Ideas** Lincoln said the nation could not "endure permanently half slave and half free." Do you agree that slavery was too great an issue to allow differences among the states? Explain.

Activity **Writing Headlines** You are a journalist in the 1850s. Choose three events discussed in Section 3. Write two headlines for each event—one for a northern newspaper, the other for a southern newspaper.

438 ★ Chapter 16

FROM THE ARCHIVES OF AmericanHeritage®

Brown's supporters Brown received much of his financial support from the so-called Secret Six. The group consisted of two Protestant ministers; two wealthy philanthropists; a teacher; and a doctor best known for his work with the blind. The group hoped to provoke a civil war that would bring about the end of slavery.

Source: Geoffrey C. Ward, "Terror, Practical and Impractical," *American Heritage* magazine, September 1995.

The Nation Splits in Two

As You Read

Explore These Questions

- Why was Abraham Lincoln able to win the election of 1860?
- How did the South react to Lincoln's election victory?
- What events led to the outbreak of the Civil War?

Identify

- John Breckinridge
- John Bell
- John Crittenden
- Confederate States of America
- Jefferson Davis
- Fort Sumter

SETTING the Scene In May 1860, thousands of people swarmed into Chicago for the Republican national convention. They filled the city's 42 hotels. When beds ran out, they slept on billiard tables. All were there to find out one thing. Who would win the Republican nomination for President—William Seward of New York or Abraham Lincoln of Illinois?

On the third day of the convention, a delegate rushed to the roof of the hall. There, a man stood waiting next to a cannon. "Fire the salute," ordered the delegate. "Old Abe is nominated!"

As the cannon fired, crowds surrounding the hall burst into cheers. Amid the celebration, a delegate from Kentucky struck a somber note. "Gentlemen, we are on the brink of a great civil war."

The Election of 1860

The Democrats held their convention in Charleston, South Carolina. Southerners wanted the party to support slavery in the territories. However, Northern Democrats refused to do so.

In the end, the party split in two. Northern Democrats chose Stephen Douglas to run for President. Southern Democrats picked **John Breckinridge** of Kentucky.

Some Americans tried to heal the split between North and South by forming a new party. The Constitutional Union party chose **John Bell** of Tennessee, a Whig, to run for President. Bell was a moderate who wanted to keep the Union together. He got support only in a few southern states that were still trying to find a compromise.

Republican campaign banner

Senator Douglas was sure that Lincoln would win the election. However, he believed that Democrats "must try to save the Union." He pleaded with southern voters to stay with the Union, no matter who was elected.

When the votes were counted, Lincoln had carried the North and won the election. Southern votes did not affect the outcome at all. Lincoln's name was not even on the ballot in 10 southern states. Northerners outnumbered southerners and outvoted them.

The Union Is Broken

Lincoln's election brought a strong reaction in the South. A South Carolina woman described how the news was received:

> "The excitement was very great. Everybody was talking at the same time. One... more moved than the others, stood up saying...'The die is cast—No more vain regrets—Sad forebodings are useless. The stake is life or death—'...No doubt of it."

Section 4 The Nation Splits in Two

LESSON PLAN

Objectives

★ Explain why Abraham Lincoln was able to win the election of 1860.

★ Describe how the South reacted to Lincoln's election victory.

★ Identify the events that led to the outbreak of the Civil War.

1 Engage

Warm Up Write the term "civil war" on the chalkboard and ask students: "In what ways is a civil war different from other wars?" and "Why might a civil war be considered the most tragic kind of war?"

Activating Prior Knowledge Have students form small groups to discuss the idea of civil war, focusing on modern civil wars such as the ones in the Balkans or Rwanda.

Reading Actively

Before Reading Direct students to the third question under Explore These Questions. As they read, have them list, in order, the events leading to the Civil War.

2 Explore

Ask students to read the section. For homework, ask them to research the reactions of ordinary people in the North and South when the first states seceded.

★ *Background* ★

Did You Know?

Beyond slavery Historian Avery Craven notes that voters had a wide variety of reasons for electing Lincoln:

- Immigrants were motivated by their interest in homesteads.
- Pennsylvanians liked Lincoln's stand on tariffs.
- Others voted Republican to voice their disapproval of Buchanan and the Democrats.

Technology

AmericanHeritage® History of the United States CD-ROM

- Presidents: Abraham Lincoln (*average*)

3 Teach

Prepare and fold slips of paper with the names of the people mentioned in the section (William Seward, John Crittenden, Abraham Lincoln, Stephen Douglas, John Breckinridge, John Bell, Jefferson Davis, Robert Anderson). Ask each student to draw a slip and note the name without revealing it to anyone else. Have students work in pairs, asking "yes or no" questions until each determines which name the other drew.

4 Assess

To close the lesson, have students complete the section review. As an alternative, have students write diary entries from one of these perspectives: the son or daughter of a South Carolina planter, a northern abolitionist, a slave who had learned how to read and write in secret. Entries should discuss the election of Lincoln, the secession of South Carolina, the formation of the Confederacy, and/or the attack on Fort Sumter.

★ ★ ★ ★ ★ ★ ★ ★ ★ ★ ★ ★ ★ ★ ★ ★ ★

Geography *Skills*

ANSWERS **1.** Review locations with students. **2. (a)** Republican party **(b)** Southern Democrat **3.** Since all of Lincoln's votes came from the North and West and since the South voted as a bloc against him, his chances of leading a united nation were much weakened.

Resource Directory

Teaching Resources
Unit 5/Chapter 16

- Practice Your Skills: Comparing Points of View, p. 3
- Map Mystery: The Decision to Secede, p. 5

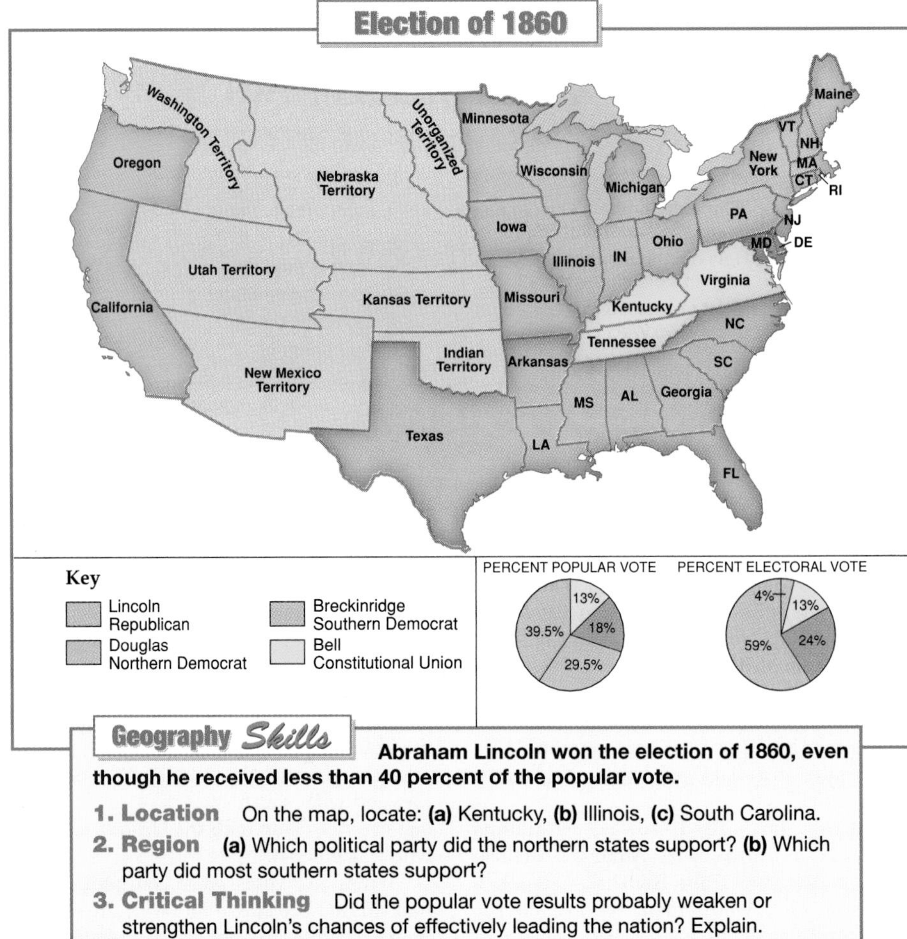

Geography *Skills*

Abraham Lincoln won the election of 1860, even though he received less than 40 percent of the popular vote.

1. **Location** On the map, locate: **(a)** Kentucky, **(b)** Illinois, **(c)** South Carolina.
2. **Region** **(a)** Which political party did the northern states support? **(b)** Which party did most southern states support?
3. **Critical Thinking** Did the popular vote results probably weaken or strengthen Lincoln's chances of effectively leading the nation? Explain.

To many southerners, Lincoln's election meant that the South no longer had a voice in national government. They believed that the President and Congress were now set against their interests—especially slavery. Even before the election, South Carolina's governor had written to other southern governors. If Lincoln won, he wrote, it would be their duty to leave the Union.

Secession

Senator **John Crittenden** of Kentucky made a last effort to save the Union. In December 1860, he introduced a bill to extend the Missouri Compromise line to the Pacific. He also suggested adding an "unamendable" amendment to the Constitution to forever guarantee the right to hold slaves in states south of the compromise line.

The compromise bill received little support. Slavery in the West was no longer the issue. Many southerners believed that the North had put an abolitionist in the White House. They felt that secession was their only choice. Most Republicans also refused to compromise. They were unwilling to surrender what they had won in the national election.

Skills for LIFE MINI LESSON

MAPS, CHARTS, AND GRAPHS

Reading an Election Map

1. Teach the skill by pointing out to students that the purpose of an election map is to show how votes were distributed geographically among candidates. Explain that an election map is color-coded to show which states voted for each candidate.

2. Help students practice the skill by looking at the map above and identifying which candidate the westernmost states (Oregon and California) supported. *(Lincoln)*

3. Have students apply the skill by answering this question: "How would you describe the major geographic distribution of votes in the election of 1860?" *(Northern states voted for Lincoln, southern states for Breckinridge)*

Critical Thinking | Managing Information | Communication | Maps, Charts, and Graphs

Comparing Points of View

How Will I Use This Skill?

When two or more people describe the same event, their descriptions of the event often differ. That is because each person's point of view is subjective, or influenced by personal experiences and feelings. By comparing different sources, you can learn objective information, or facts, as well as subjective points of view regarding those facts.

Bullying the Free States

November 19, 1860
The New York Tribune

Abraham Lincoln has been designated for next President of this Republic by the popular vote of nearly every Free State, and the ruling politicians of the Slave States are not pleased with the selection. We can fancy their feelings, as we felt much the same when they put a most undesired President upon us four years ago. Moreover, we...advise them to do as we did—Bear it with fortitude, and hope to do better next time.

Devotion to the Union Is Treason to the South

November 19, 1860
Oxford Mississippi Mercury

We have at last reached that point in our history when it is necessary for the South to withdraw from the Union....

[A] powerful sectional majority are now about to seize upon the Government...to destroy the institution of Slavery....We cannot stand still and quietly see the Government pass into the hands of such an infamous crew.

South Carolina,...Georgia, Mississippi, Alabama, Louisiana, Texas, and Arkansas, will soon be united as brothers to defend each other from the inroads of the fanatics of the North.

LEARN the Skill

You can compare points of view by following the steps below.

1. Identify the author of each source. Consider how each report might be affected by the author's point of view.
2. Find objective information common to two or more sources.
3. Identify subjective statements that reflect the author's point of view.
4. Draw conclusions about the historical event and different points of view on it.

PRACTICE the Skill

The newspaper articles above give different viewpoints on Abraham Lincoln's victory in the election of 1860. Compare the two viewpoints by answering the following questions.

1. (a) Which source is a southern newspaper? (b) Which source is a northern newspaper? (c) Why would you expect the two to have different opinions about Lincoln?
2. What factual information do you find in both articles?
3. How do the two articles describe the election result differently?
4. (a) Why did the election cause conflict between North and South? (b) What did the *Tribune* think the South should do? (c) What did the *Mercury* recommend?

APPLY the Skill

In two or more newspapers or news magazines, find different points of view on some issue or event. Use the steps you have learned to compare the various viewpoints.

★ Activity ★

Connections With Science and Technology

Understanding communications When South Carolina seceded in 1860, there were no televisions, telephones, radios, fax machines, or e-mail by which to spread the word. Have students research the methods of communication available at the time. Then have them use that information to create an illustrated glossary that helps explain some of the ways that news traveled. (*average*) T

PRACTICE the Skill

ANSWERS

1. (a) *Oxford Mississippi Mercury* **(b)** *The New York Tribune* **(c)** Most northern states voted for Lincoln; most southerners feared that Lincoln's election would lead to the end of their way of life.

2. Politicians in the slave states are unhappy about the election's outcome.

3. The northern newspaper said Lincoln had the vote of nearly every free state. The southern newspaper called this a "powerful sectional majority."

4. (a) Southerners feared Lincoln would destroy slavery. **(b)** bear with the election results and hope to do better next time **(c)** withdraw from the Union

APPLY the Skill

Guided Instruction

You might want to distribute newspapers and magazines and have students make a list of current issues. Then have each student search for different points of view on one issue. Ask students to identify experiences of each author that might affect the points of view in the articles.

ASSESSMENT See the rubrics in the Alternative Assessment booklet in the Teaching Resources.

Technology

Videodiscs/Videotapes

Prentice Hall United States History Video Collection™, Vol. 8, Ch. 34, "A House Divided," 2:10 mins (*average*) ELL

Chapter 34

AmericanHeritage
MAGAZINE

Fort Sumter To learn more about Fort Sumter on the Internet, go to www.nps.gov/fosu.

Writing Actively

After Reading Have students use their list of events leading to the Civil War to make an annotated time line of the 1860–1861 period.

RESOURCE DIRECTORY

Teaching Resources
Unit 5/Chapter 16
- Vocabulary Builder, p. 2
- Section 4 Quiz, p. 11

Chapter Tests, pp. 91–96

AmericanHeritage
MAGAZINE

HISTORY HAPPENED HERE

◄ Union flag from Fort Sumter

Fort Sumter

The Civil War began in 1861 when Confederate forces bombarded and captured Fort Sumter in Charleston Harbor, South Carolina. Later in the war, Union gunships reduced Sumter to rubble. The fort was rebuilt, and it remained part of the seacoast defenses until 1947. Today, Fort Sumter is a national monument. Tour boats to the fort leave regularly from downtown Charleston.

★ ***To learn more about this historic site, write:*** *Fort Sumter National Monument, Sullivan's Island, SC 29482.*

The first state to secede was South Carolina. On December 20, 1860, delegates to a convention in Charleston voted for secession. "The state of South Carolina has resumed her position among the nations of the world," the delegates proudly declared. By late February, 1861, Alabama, Florida, Georgia, Louisiana, Mississippi, and Texas had seceded.

The Confederacy

The seven states that had seceded held a convention in Montgomery, Alabama. There, the southern states formed a new nation, the **Confederate States of America.** To lead the new country, they named **Jefferson Davis** of Mississippi as the first president of the Confederacy.

Most southerners believed that they had every right to secede. After all, the Declaration of Independence said that "it is the right of the people to alter or to abolish" a government that denies the rights of its citizens. Lincoln, they believed, would deny white southerners their right to own slaves.

Lincoln Speaks to the Nation

When Abraham Lincoln took office on March 4, 1861, he faced a national crisis. Crowds gathered in Washington, D.C., to hear him take the presidential oath of office. In his Inaugural Address, the new President assured Americans of both the North and the South that he had two goals. He hoped to maintain the Union and avoid war.

On the first goal, preserving the Union, Lincoln would not compromise. Secession of states from the Union, he said, was unconstitutional. Lincoln believed that his duty as

Connections With Civics

Texas voters chose secession, but Governor Sam Houston refused to swear allegiance to the new Confederacy. He was replaced by a new governor. Houston sadly warned his fellow Texans that the North would "move with the steady momentum and perseverance of a mighty avalanche; and...overwhelm the South."

★ ***Background*** ★

Did You Know?

Long road to Montgomery Jefferson Davis took the oath of office as President of the Confederate States of America in Montgomery, Alabama. Although his plantation was only 285 miles from Montgomery, Davis had to travel 600 miles by rail to get there. Such was the state of transportation in the South at the time of the Civil War.

Internet Activity

Exploring Fort Sumter Have students read about Fort Sumter at the Charleston County Public Library at http://www.ccpl.org/ccl/sumtertour.html. Ask them: "How many Union commanders tried to retake the fort?" "When did it become a national monument?" Given the changing nature of the Internet, you may wish to preview this site. (*average*)

442 ★ Chapter 16

President was clear. He would take strong action to preserve national union.

> “In view of the Constitution and the law, the Union is unbroken;... I will take care... that the laws of the Union be faithfully executed in all the States.”

At the same time, however, Lincoln tried to reassure the South. He promised that there would not be war with the South unless southern states started it:

> “We are not enemies, but friends. We must not be enemies. Though passion may have strained, it must not break our bonds of affection.”

Civil War

The Confederacy, however, had already started seizing federal forts in the South. It felt that the forts were a threat because the United States was now a “foreign power.”

Lincoln's difficult decision

President Lincoln faced a difficult decision. Should he let the Confederates take over federal property? If he did, he would seem to be admitting that states had the right to leave the Union. On the other hand, if he sent troops to hold the forts, he might start a civil war. He might also lose the support of the eight slave states that had not seceded from the Union.

In April, the Confederacy forced Lincoln to make up his mind. By then, Confederate troops controlled nearly all forts, post offices, and other federal buildings in the South. The Union held only three forts off the Florida coast and Fort Sumter in South Carolina. **Fort Sumter** was important to the Confederacy because it guarded Charleston Harbor.

Bombardment of Fort Sumter

President Lincoln learned that food supplies at Fort Sumter were running low. He notified the governor of South Carolina that he was going to ship food to the fort. Lincoln promised not to send troops or weapons.

The Confederates could not leave the fort in Union hands, however. On April 11, 1861, they asked for Fort Sumter's surrender.

Major Robert Anderson, the Union commander, refused to give in. Confederate guns then opened fire. Anderson and his troops quickly ran out of ammunition. On April 13, Anderson surrendered the fort.

When Confederate troops shelled Fort Sumter, people in Charleston had gathered on their rooftops to watch. To many, it was like a fireworks display. No one knew that the fireworks marked the beginning of a civil war that would last four terrible years.

★ Section 4 Review ★

Recall

1. **Identify** (a) John Breckinridge, (b) John Bell, (c) John Crittenden, (d) Confederate States of America, (e) Jefferson Davis, (f) Fort Sumter.

Comprehension

2. Why were there two Democratic candidates for President in 1860?
3. Why did many southerners feel that secession was necessary after Lincoln won the Presidency in 1860?
4. How did the Civil War begin at Fort Sumter in 1861?

Critical Thinking and Writing

5. **Making Inferences** How do you think the split in the Democratic party helped Lincoln win the election of 1860?
6. **Solving Problems** Write a compromise plan that tries to save the Union in 1861. Your plan should offer advantages to both the North and the South.

Activity **Writing Slogans** You are a famous political campaign manager of the mid-1800s. Write a campaign slogan for each of the four candidates in the presidential election of 1860.

★ Customized Instruction ★

Visual Learners

Creating study aids Have students work in small groups to create flashcards or puzzles to use as section study aids. Flashcards should show large pictures or single-word clues to events in the section. On the back of the flashcard should be the correct identification of the picture or word. Puzzles should be made of heavy cardboard on which students draw graphic organizers. Then, students should cut the cardboard into irregularly shaped pieces. The graphic organizers should show the sequence of events leading to the start of the Civil War, beginning with “Lincoln elected President (1860).” When finished, groups can trade puzzles and sets of flashcards and use them to review section content. (basic) ELL

★ Section 4 Review ★

ANSWERS

1. (a) p. 439, **(b)** p. 439, **(c)** p. 440, **(d)** p. 442, **(e)** p. 442, **(f)** p. 443

2. Northern and southern Democrats split over slavery and nominated two different candidates.

3. They thought the newly elected president was an abolitionist who would make compromise impossible.

4. The fighting began when the Union commander of Fort Sumter, a fort in southern territory still controlled by the North, refused to surrender to the Confederacy.

5. With the Democrats split between two candidates, Lincoln won far more votes than either of his Democratic opponents.

6. Answers will vary but should take into account the needs of both the North and the South.

Guided Instruction
Remind students that such slogans are short and to the point, yet they capture something essential and important about a candidate. Before writing, students should reread the relevant text and jot down the basic goal of each man.

ASSESSMENT See the rubrics in the Alternative Assessment booklet in the Teaching Resources.

Technology

Videodiscs/Videotapes
Prentice Hall United States History Video Collection™, Vol. 9, Ch. 7, “1861 Crisis at Sumter,” 1:50 min (*average*) ELL

CD-ROM
Test Bank CD-ROM, Ch. 16
Interactive Student Tutorial

Chapter 16

Review and Activities

Reviewing the Chapter

Define These Terms

1. e **2.** b **3.** d **4.** c **5.** a

Explore the Main Ideas

1. Possible answers: California was allowed to enter the Union as a free state; the rest of the Mexican Cession was divided into territories in which voters would decide the slavery question; the slave trade was ended in Washington, D.C.; a fugitive slave law was passed; a border dispute between Texas and New Mexico was settled.

2. Pro- and antislavery forces battled over whether Kansas would be a slave or free state.

3. It made the Missouri Compromise unconstitutional.

4. Free Soilers, northern Democrats, and antislavery Whigs

5. South Carolina seceded when Lincoln was elected President because people thought he was set against the state's interests.

Geography Activity

1. F **2.** G **3.** A **4.** E **5.** D **6.** C **7.** B **Region** California

Critical Thinking and Writing

1. Compromise of 1850; the Kansas-Nebraska Act; Dred Scott decision; Lincoln becomes President

2. (a) The split was caused by the Democratic party's inability to come to a single position on slavery. **(b)** The split weakened the Democrats, who ran not only against Lincoln but also against each other.

Chapter 16 Review and Activities

★ Sum It Up ★

Section 1 The Slavery Issue in the West

- Americans disagreed on whether slavery should be allowed in the western territories.
- The new Free Soil party wanted to limit the spread of slavery.
- The Compromise of 1850 settled the issue for a time, but the new Fugitive Slave Law angered many.

Section 2 The Crisis Turns Violent

- The novel *Uncle Tom's Cabin* turned many northerners against slavery.
- After the Kansas-Nebraska Act of 1854, proslavery and antislavery settlers battled for control of Kansas.
- In the Dred Scott case, the Supreme Court ruled that Congress could not outlaw slavery in any territory.

Section 3 A New Party Challenges Slavery

- The Republican party wanted to keep slavery out of the western territories.
- Abraham Lincoln emerged as a leader of the Republican party.
- John Brown's raid on Harpers Ferry brought the nation to the brink of war.

Section 4 The Nation Splits in Two

- Abraham Lincoln won the presidential election of 1860.
- Southern states seceded from the Union and formed a new nation.
- A civil war broke out between the North and the South.

For additional review of the major ideas of Chapter 16, see ***Guide to the Essentials of American History*** or ***Interactive Student Tutorial CD-ROM,*** which contains interactive review activities, graphic organizers, and practice tests.

Reviewing the Chapter

Define These Terms

Match each term with the correct definition.

Column 1	Column 2
1. sectionalism	**a.** a law to ban slavery in any lands won from Mexico
2. fugitive	**b.** a runaway
3. civil war	**c.** a gun warehouse
4. arsenal	**d.** a war between people of the same country
5. Wilmot Proviso	**e.** loyalty to a part of a nation rather than the whole

Explore the Main Ideas

1. What were the four parts of the Compromise of 1850?
2. Why was Kansas referred to as Bleeding Kansas in the 1850s?
3. What effect did the Dred Scott decision have on the Missouri Compromise?
4. What groups combined to form the new Republican party?
5. Why did South Carolina secede from the Union in 1860?

Geography Activity

Match the letters on the map with the following places: **1.** Missouri, **2.** Maine, **3.** California, **4.** Kansas Territory, **5.** Nebraska Territory, **6.** New Mexico Territory, **7.** Utah Territory. **Region** Which area listed above was admitted to the Union as a free state in 1850?

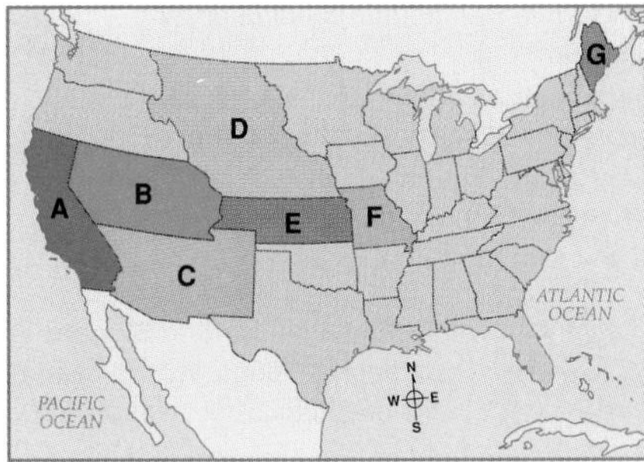

3. Possible answer: They could have continued to negotiate and work for compromise, hoping that the next national election would be more in their favor.

4. Holding the convention in the West helped persuade western voters that the Republican candidate represented them.

Using Primary Sources

(a) No, he thought people could not be forced to accept the Union if they did not want to and that there was no point in fighting the South. **(b)** Possible answer: Agree: As the southerners argued, the Constitution is a social contract that can and should be rejected if it no longer serves the purpose for which it was created. Disagree: As the outcome of the war shows, southerners were forced to accept the Union, and they still live under it to this day.

Critical Thinking and Writing

1. **Understanding Chronology** Place the following events in chronological order: **(a)** Kansas-Nebraska Act, **(b)** Compromise of 1850, **(c)** Lincoln becomes President, **(d)** Dred Scott decision.
2. **Understanding Cause and Effect** **(a)** What caused the Democratic party to split in 1860? **(b)** How did the split affect the election of 1860?
3. **Identifying Alternatives** Describe one alternative to secession that the slave states could have chosen.
4. Exploring Unit Themes **Sectionalism** The 1860 Republican convention was held in Illinois, then considered a western state. How did this help bring victory for Lincoln in the national election?

Using Primary Sources

In 1860, Abraham Lincoln was elected to succeed James Buchanan as President. As his term of office came to an end, President Buchanan offered his thoughts on the possibility of secession and civil war:

> “Our Union rests upon public opinion, and can never be cemented by the blood of its citizens shed in civil war. If it cannot live in the affections of the people, it must one day perish. Congress may possess many means of preserving it by [compromise], but the sword was not placed in their hand to preserve it by force.”

Source: *The Rise and Fall of the Confederate Government* by Jefferson Davis, 1881.

Recognizing Points of View **(a)** Was Buchanan in favor of a war to prevent southern states from leaving the Union? Explain. **(b)** Do you agree or disagree with Buchanan? Defend your position.

Activity Bank

Interdisciplinary Activity

Exploring the Arts In a painting, drawing, collage, sculpture, or other form of art, express the reaction of the North or the South to one event described in this chapter. Display your work to the class. Ask other students to identify the event and point of view that your art work reflects.

Career Skills Activity

Lawyer Choose the role of prosecutor or defense lawyer at the trial of John Brown. Depending on the role you have chosen, write a speech declaring Brown to be either guilty or not guilty. Present your speech to the class and ask them to reach a verdict.

Citizenship Activity

Reaching a Compromise Find an issue in your community that is the subject of heated debate between two groups. Then brainstorm solutions to the problem that will offer something to both sides. Type up your suggestions and offer them to a neutral party who might be able to mediate between the two groups.

Internet Activity

Use the Internet to find sites dealing with Abraham Lincoln. Use your research to write a biography or a character sketch. Use as many quotations as possible. Make a bibliography by writing down the title, author, and address of each Web site that you use.

You are an African American or white American living in the North or the South between 1820 and 1861. In your Eyewitness Journal, *describe your reaction to the important events of these years: 1820, 1850, 1859, 1860, 1861.*

★ 445

Activity Bank

ASSESSMENT To assess the activities on this page, see the rubrics in the Alternative Assessment booklet in the Teaching Resources. You might want to share the rubrics with your students before they begin work.

Interdisciplinary Activity

1. Stress that the work will be judged not on the basis of its artistic merit but on how well it represents the concerns of the people of the United States at the time.

2. Act as a referee to ensure that conjecture about the works of art does not give away too much, thus spoiling the activity. You may wish to have students make their guesses by secret ballot and discuss them afterward.

Career Skills Activity

1. Explain to students the difference between a defense lawyer and a prosecutor.

2. Tell students that Brown was tried for treason not against the United States but against the state of Virginia. This may make a difference in the way they make their arguments.

Citizenship Activity

1. If you wish, you can make the exercise into a class activity. As the students brainstorm, you can jot their ideas down on the chalkboard. Students can later transfer ideas from the chalkboard to a word processor.

2. Oversee the activity carefully to ensure that students do not offend either party. Instead, they should offer their help as friendly, neutral onlookers.

Eyewitness Journal

1. Make sure students can identify the great events of the years listed: 1820 *(Missouri Compromise)*, 1850 *(Compromise of 1850)*, 1859 *(John Brown's raid)*, 1860 *(Lincoln's election; secession of South Carolina)*, 1861 *(secession of other southern states)*.
2. Encourage students to think about their chosen point of view. What would make it different from the others?

Internet Activity

1. Have students go to www.phschool.com, which contains updated information on a variety of topics.
2. Another site you may find useful for this activity is the White House site on Abraham Lincoln at www.whitehouse.gov/WH/glimpse/presidents/html/al16.html.
3. Given the changing nature of the Internet, you may wish to preview this site.

Chapter 17 Manager

SECTION OBJECTIVES	TEACHING RESOURCES	ADDITIONAL RESOURC
1 The Conflict Takes Shape (pp. 448–452) **Objectives** 1. Identify the strengths and weaknesses of the Confederacy. 2. Identify the strengths and weaknesses of the Union. 3. Describe the special qualities of Presidents Lincoln and Davis.	**Lesson Planner,** p. 70 (average) . . . . .90 mins. **Unit 5/Chapter 17** • Section 1 Quiz, p. 18 (average) . . . . .15 mins.	**Voices of Freedom** • The Bonnie Blue Flag, pp. 119–12 (average) • Encouraging Union Soldiers, pp. 120–121 (average) **Literature Library** • Red Badge of Courage (challeng
2 A Long, Difficult Struggle (pp. 453–458) **Objectives** 1. Describe the military plans of each side. 2. Name the military goals that the Union achieved. 3. Explain why the Union failed to win major battles in the East.	**Lesson Planner,** p. 71 (average) . . . . .60 mins. **Unit 5/Chapter 17** • Section 2 Quiz, p. 19 (average) . . . . .15 mins.	**Customized Reader** • Letter from a Union Soldier at Vicksburg, article VB-5 (average) **Historical Outline Map Book** • Major Battles of the Civil War, p. (average) • The Civil War in the East, p. 51 (average) • Union Advances, p. 52 (average)
3 A Promise of Freedom (pp. 459–462) **Objectives** 1. Explain why Lincoln issued the Emancipation Proclamation. 2. Identify the effects of the Proclamation. 3. Describe the contributions of African Americans to the Union war effort.	**Lesson Planner,** p. 72 (average) . . . . . . .90 mins. **Unit 5/Chapter 17** • Map Mystery: African Americans Join the War, p. 15 (challenging) . . . . .30 mins. • Connecting History and Literature, p. 16 (average) .20 mins. • Biography Flashcard: William H. Carney, p. 17 (average) .15 mins. • Section 3 Quiz, p. 20 (average) . . . . .15 mins. **Interdisciplinary Connections** • Main Idea: The War Up Close, p. 98 (average) . . . . .20 mins.	
4 Hardships of War (pp. 463–467) **Objectives** 1. Describe what life was like for soldiers in the Civil War. 2. Explain how women contributed to the war effort. 3. Identify the problems each side faced during the war.	**Lesson Planner,** p. 73 (average) . . . . .45 mins. **Unit 5/Chapter 17** • Section 4 Quiz, p. 21 (average) . . . . .15 mins. **Why Study History?** • One Person Can Make a Difference, pp. 67–70 (average) . . . . .90 mins. **Interdisciplinary Connections** • Main Idea: The War Up Close, pp. 99, 101, 102 (average) . . . . .20 mins.	**Voices of Freedom** • A Southern Woman Takes Over at Home, p. 124 (average) **Customized Reader** • Journal of a Union Soldier in Andersonville, article VB-8 (aver
5 The War Ends (pp. 468–473) **Objectives** 1. Explain the significance of the Union victories at Vicksburg and Gettysburg. 2. Describe the ideals expressed by Lincoln in the Gettysburg Address. 3. Explain how Union generals used a new type of war to defeat the Confederacy.	**Lesson Planner,** p. 74 (average) . . . . . . .60 mins. **Unit 5/Chapter 17** • Vocabulary Builder, p. 12 (basic) . . . . .10 mins. • Critical Thinking and Writing: Understanding Causes and Effects, p. 14 (basic) . . . . .20 mins. • Section 5 Quiz, p. 22 (average) . . . . .15 mins. **Chapter Tests,** pp. 97–102 (average) . . . .45 mins. **Interdisciplinary Connections** • Main Idea: The War Up Close, p. 100 (average) . . . . .20 mins.	**Voices of Freedom** • Lee Takes Pity on a Union Soldi pp. 121–122 (average) • Lee and Grant Meet at Appoma p. 125 (average) **Historical Outline Map Book** • Union Advances, p. 52 (average)

Assessment Options

Teaching Resources
- Alternative Assessment booklet
- Section Quizzes, Unit 5, Chapter 17, pp. 18–22
- Chapter Tests, Chapter 17, pp. 97–102
- Test Bank CD-ROM

Student Performance Pack
- Guide to the Essentials of American History, Chapter 17 Test, p. 97
- Standardized Test Prep Handbook
- Interactive Student Tutorial CD-ROM

Interdisciplinary Connections

Teaching Resources
- Map Mystery, Unit 5, Chapter 17, p. 15
- Connecting History and Literature, Unit 5, Chapter 17, p. 16
- Interdisciplinary Connections, pp. 97–102

Voices of Freedom, pp. 119–125

Customized Reader, articles VB-5, VB-8

Historical Outline Map Book, pp. 50–52

Prentice Hall Literature Library
- Red Badge of Courage

Technology

AmericanHeritage® History of the United States CD-ROM
- Time Tour: Torn by War (1861–1865)
- History Makers: Robert E. Lee, Clara Barton

Interactive Student Tutorial CD-ROM

Test Bank CD-ROM

Color Transparencies
- The Civil War, p. F-21
- Slavery and the Civil War, p. I-31
- Ironclad Ship, p. H-43
- Civil War Medical Treatment, p. B-63

Guided Reading Audiotapes (English/Spanish), side 6

Listening to Literature Audiocassettes: The American Experience
- The Gettysburg Address, side 5

Listening to Music CD
- Willie Has Gone to War

Resource Pro® CD-ROM

Prentice Hall United States History Video Collection™ (Spanish track available on disc version.) Vol. 9, Chs. 10, 13, 16, 19, 22, 25, 28, 31, 34

Prentice Hall Home Page www.phschool.com

Student Performance Pack

Guide to the Essentials of American History
- Ch. 17, pp. 92–97 (Available in English and Spanish)

Guided Reading Audiotapes (English/Spanish), side 6

Standardized Test Prep Handbook

Interactive Student Tutorial CD-ROM

BLOCK SCHEDULING Activities with this icon will help you meet your Block Scheduling needs.

ENGLISH LANGUAGE LEARNERS Activities with this icon are suitable for English Language Learners.

TEAM TEACHING Activities and Background Notes with this icon present starting points for Team Teaching.

Teachers' Bibliography

From the Archives of AmericanHeritage®

Don't miss the special American Heritage® teaching notes found in this chapter.

Contact Teachers' Curriculum Institute to learn more about History Alive!® resources on the war between the North and South. See History Alive!® unit: The Civil War and Reconstruction, Section 3, "A Family Divided: Fighting the Civil War."

Explore your library to find these issues related to Chapter 17: *Robert E. Lee,* September 1993; *The Battle of Gettysburg,* July 1988; *Civil War Highlights,* April 1981.

Prentice Hall Web Site You can access a structured, on-line environment that allows you to preview curriculum-related resources and receive updated information on groundbreaking events from around the nation and the world. (www.phschool.com)

Chapter 17

The Civil War

1861–1865

Introducing the Chapter

Have students preview the main ideas of this chapter by looking over the visuals. Suggest they look for examples that show the ordinary soldier's life and women's contributions to the war effort.

Using the Time Line To help students understand the sequence of events in this chapter, ask students questions such as these: **(1)** What years does the time line cover? *(1861–1865)* **(2)** What event marked the beginning of the Civil War? *(attack on Fort Sumter; 1861)* **(3)** What world event took place the year that the Battle of Gettysburg was fought? *(first Red Cross societies were set up in Europe)*

Ask students to recall a time when one person made a difference in their lives or a time when they made a difference in someone else's life. Volunteers may want to relate what the particular situations were and why they proved to be significant. Tell students that during the Civil War, many people gave generously of themselves and, in many cases, risked their lives to help others.

For additional *Why Study History?* support, see p. 465.

Chapter 17

The Civil War

1861–1865

For more than four years, Americans fought Americans in the Civil War. The South wanted to exist as an independent nation. The North wanted to force the South back into the Union. The war was also linked closely to the question of slavery. President Lincoln made this clear when he issued the Emancipation Proclamation.

Throughout the North and the South, both soldiers and civilians experienced much suffering. The Union's armies struggled in the early years of the war. However, the North's superior resources wore heavily on the South. By the end of 1863, the South was in retreat. In 1865, the South surrendered and the Civil War came to an end.

Why Study History? During the Civil War, millions of northerners and southerners served their nation well. Their efforts, as both soldiers and civilians, affected the course of the war. To see an example of how one person can affect the course of history, see this chapter's *Why Study History?* feature, "One Person Can Make a Difference." The feature focuses on the achievements of Clara Barton.

American Events

- **1861** Civil War begins with attack on Fort Sumter
- **1862** Union gunboats capture New Orleans and Memphis
- **1863** Abraham Lincoln issues Emancipation Proclamation

1861 — 1862 — 1863

World Events

- **1861 World Event** Russian czar frees serfs
- **1862 World Event** Britain refuses to recognize the Confederacy

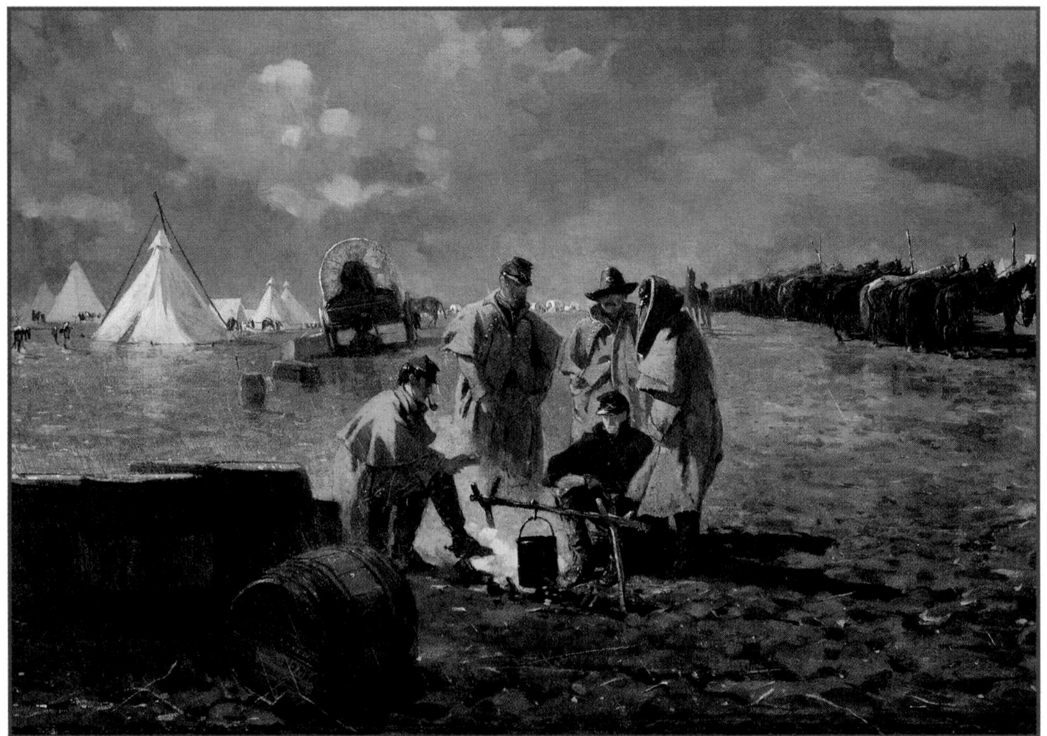

Viewing History **The Soldiers of the Civil War**

In A Rainy Day in Camp *by Winslow Homer, Civil War soldiers find time to gather around a campfire. It is estimated that more than 2,500,000 men served as soldiers in the Civil War. Over 600,000 of them died—more than in any other American war.* ★ **What emotions do you think soldiers felt on the eve of a battle? Explain.**

1863 Battle of Gettysburg ends Confederate drive into the North

1864 General Grant becomes commander of Union army

1865 General Lee surrenders at Appomattox Courthouse

1863 | 1864 | 1865

1863 World Event First Red Cross societies established in Europe

★ Background ★
Art Note

The Soldiers of the Civil War Winslow Homer (1836–1910) began his career making designs for wood engravings published in *Harper's Weekly.* During the Civil War, he went to the front to sketch troops. Homer avoided the more gruesome scenes, filling his notebooks with sketches of sharpshooters, skirmishes, and soldiers drilling and whiling away the long waits in camp. T

Documents and Literature

On pp. 582–584, you will find two readings to enrich this chapter:

1. Eyewitness Account "A Nurse in the Civil War," an excerpt from Louisa May Alcott's *Hospital Sketches,* about her experiences as a Union nurse. (Use with Section 4.)

2. Historical Document "The Gettysburg Address," Abraham Lincoln's stirring speech. (Use with Section 5.)

Writing Actively 

Responding to Art Ask students to look closely at the soldiers in Winslow Homer's painting, *A Rainy Day at Camp*. (It is also available in the *Color Transparencies,* p. D-41.) Ask them to think about what the soldiers do when they are not fighting. Then have them list hardships, other than battles, that Civil War soldiers had to endure. Ask students to be as specific as possible.

Viewing History ANSWER

Answers may vary. Students may discuss feelings such as fear, excitement, pride, nervousness, anxiety, homesickness.

Technology

Videodiscs/Videotapes
Show the *Prentice Hall United States History Video Collection*™ segments for this chapter. The videodisc version has a Spanish track. Press audio until you get the left channel for English or the right channel for Spanish, or use the bar codes in the Guidebook.

AmericanHeritage® History of the United States CD-ROM
- Time Tour: Torn by War (1861–1865) in The Nation Torn Apart (*average*)

Section 1 The Conflict Takes Shape

LESSON PLAN

Objectives

★ Identify the strengths and weaknesses of the Confederacy.

★ Identify the strengths and weaknesses of the Union.

★ Describe the special qualities possessed by Presidents Abraham Lincoln and Jefferson Davis.

1 Engage

Warm Up Ask students to list differences between northern and southern states today. They can start by thinking about weather, lifestyles, and food.

Activating Prior Knowledge Write the words "North" and "South" on the chalkboard. Then ask students to randomly list distinguishing traits of each region's states in 1861. Suggest that they consider transportation, industry, population, geography, food supply, and political opinions.

Reading Actively

Before Reading Suggest that students jot down notes while reading the section in order to help them answer the questions under Explore These Questions. They can then use these notes to write the answers to the Comprehension questions in the section review.

RESOURCE DIRECTORY

Teaching Resources
Lesson Planner, p. 70

Transparencies
Cause and Effect
• The Civil War, p. F-21

The Conflict Takes Shape

As You Read

Explore These Questions

- What strengths and weaknesses did the Confederacy have?
- What strengths and weaknesses did the Union have?
- What special qualities did Presidents Abraham Lincoln and Jefferson Davis possess?

Define

- racism
- martial law

Identify

- border states
- Robert E. Lee

Confederate canteen

SETTING the Scene In April 1861, President Abraham Lincoln called for 75,000 volunteers to serve as soldiers for 90 days in a campaign against the South. The response was overwhelming. Throughout the North, crowds cheered the Stars and Stripes and booed the southern "traitors."

Southerners were just as enthusiastic for the war. They rallied to the Stars and Bars, as they called the new Confederate flag. Volunteers flooded into the Confederate army.

With flags held high, both northerners and southerners marched off to war. Most felt certain that a single, gallant battle would bring a quick end to the conflict. Few suspected that the Civil War would last four terrible years and be the most destructive war in the nation's history.

A Nation Divided

As the war began, each side was convinced that its cause was just. Southerners believed that they had the right to leave the Union. In fact, they called the conflict the War for Southern Independence. Southerners wanted independence so that they could keep their traditional way of life—including the institution of slavery.

Northerners, meanwhile, believed that they had to fight to save the Union. At the outset of the war, abolishing slavery was not an official goal of the North. In fact, many northerners, guided by feelings of racism, approved of slavery. **Racism** is the belief that one race is superior to another.

In April 1861, eight slave states were still in the Union. They had to make the difficult decision of which side to join. Virginia,* North Carolina, Tennessee, and Arkansas joined the Confederacy. The four **border states** of Delaware, Kentucky, Missouri, and Maryland remained in the Union. (See the map on page 449.)

Still, some citizens of the border states supported the South. For example, in April 1861, pro-Confederate mobs attacked Union troops in Baltimore, Maryland. In response, President Lincoln declared **martial law,** or rule by the army instead of the elected government. Many people who sided with the South were arrested.

Strengths and Weaknesses

Both sides in the conflict had strengths and weaknesses as the war began. The South had the strong advantage of fighting a defensive war. It was up to the North to go on the offensive, to attack and defeat the South. If the North did not move its forces into the South, the Confederacy would remain a separate country.

*Many people in western Virginia supported the Union. When Virginia seceded, westerners formed their own government. West Virginia became a state of the Union in 1863.

★ Background ★

Did You Know?

Amateur armies In 1861, the entire U.S. army consisted of 16,000 men, most scattered in 79 frontier outposts west of the Mississippi. Thus, the burden of fighting the war was carried by volunteers. The earliest regiments arrived clad in colorful uniforms representing not the North or South but the colors of their state or state militias. The earliest Union forces that gathered in Washington looked more like a circus on parade than an army. Volunteers at the beginning of the war received little training; many learned how to fight on the battlefield itself.

The South

Southerners believed that they were fighting a war for independence, similar to the American Revolution. Defending their homeland and their way of life gave them a strong reason to fight bravely. "Our men must prevail in combat," one Confederate said, "or they will lose their property, country, freedom—in short, everything."

Also, many southerners had skills that made them good soldiers. Hunting was an important part of southern life. From an early age, boys learned to ride horses and use guns. Wealthy young men often went to military school. Before the Civil War, many of the best officers in the United States Army were from the South.

The South, however, had serious economic weaknesses. (See the chart on page 450.) It had few factories to produce weapons and other vital supplies. It also had few railroads to move troops and supplies. The railroads that it did have often did not connect to one another. The South also had political problems. The Confederate constitution favored states' rights and limited the authority

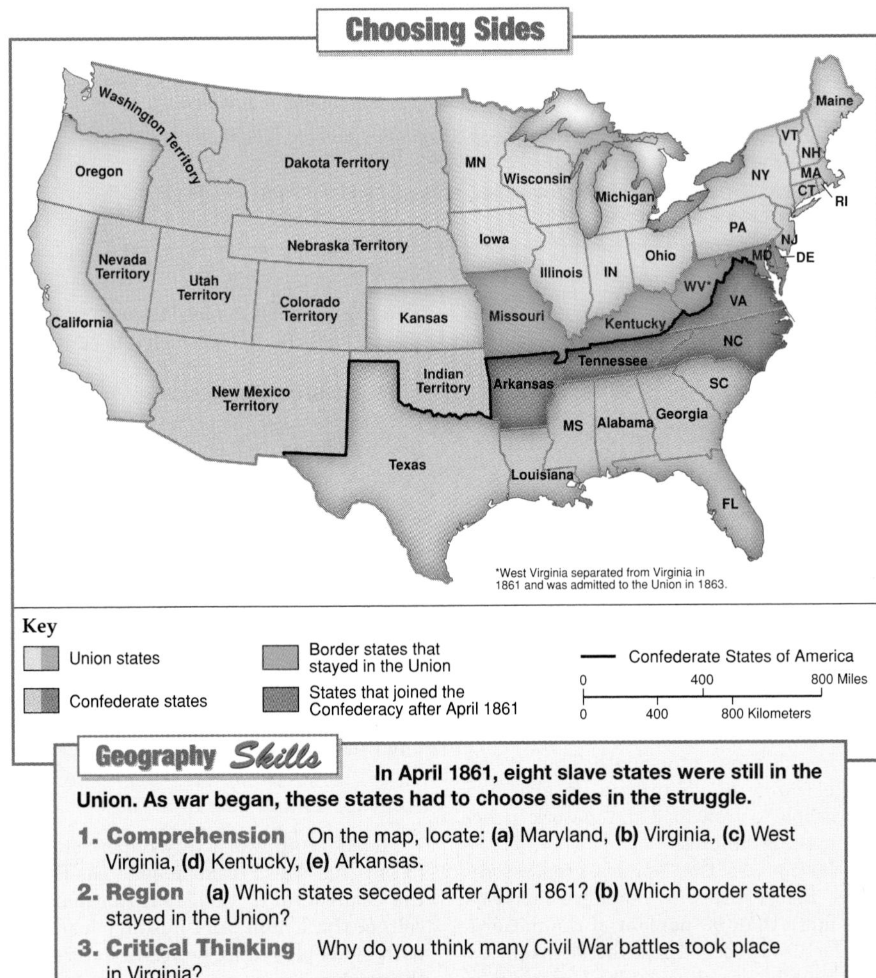

Geography *Skills* **In April 1861, eight slave states were still in the Union. As war began, these states had to choose sides in the struggle.**

1. **Comprehension** On the map, locate: **(a)** Maryland, **(b)** Virginia, **(c)** West Virginia, **(d)** Kentucky, **(e)** Arkansas.
2. **Region** **(a)** Which states seceded after April 1861? **(b)** Which border states stayed in the Union?
3. **Critical Thinking** Why do you think many Civil War battles took place in Virginia?

2 Explore

Ask students to read the section. For a homework assignment, ask them to check the Internet for information about recent civil wars (e.g., the conflict in the former Yugoslavia). Ask them to summarize the information they find.

3 Teach

Divide the class into small groups and ask each group to summarize the strengths and weaknesses of the North and South as war began. Have groups pick one region and write a flyer encouraging young men to join its cause. Flyers should consider the audience, reasons for fighting, the consequences if the war is lost. A member of each group should present the flyer to the class for discussion.

4 Assess

To close the lesson, have students complete the section review; or ask them to write an essay comparing and contrasting the readiness of the North and South for war.

★ ★ ★ ★ ★ ★ ★ ★ ★ ★ ★ ★ ★ ★ ★ ★ ★

Geography *Skills*

ANSWERS **1.** Review locations with students. **2. (a)** Virginia, North Carolina, Tennessee, Arkansas **(b)** Delaware, Maryland, West Virginia, Missouri, and Kentucky **3.** Virginia was just across the Potomac River from Washington, D.C. The Confederate capital was located at Richmond, Virginia.

★ *Activity* ★

Linking Past and Present

Understanding federalism The question of states' rights and the role of the federal government was a key issue in the Civil War era. Opinions differ even today. Ask students to research and discuss in class recent examples of this continuing debate—for example, proposals for a federal health insurance program or federal regulation of business and education. *(challenging)* T

Technology

Videodiscs/Videotapes

Prentice Hall United States History Video Collection™, Vol. 9, Ch. 10, "Rush to Arms," 3:25 mins *(average)*

Chapter 10

Chart *Skills*

ANSWERS **1. (a)** The North had 105,835 acres; the South had 56,832 acres. **(b)** 15 percent **2. (a)** the North **(b)** This enabled the North to move troops and supplies more rapidly than the South could.

Reading Actively

During Reading Have students note the statement on this page: "Industry was the North's greatest resource." Ask students to find evidence to support this statement as they read the section.

RESOURCE DIRECTORY

Transparencies
Geography and History
• Slavery and the Civil War, p. I-31

Resources of the North and South, 1861

Resources	North		South	
	Number	Percent of Total	Number	Percent of Total
Farmland	105,835 acres	65%	56,832 acres	35%
Railroad Track	21,847 miles	71%	8,947 miles	29%
Value of Manufactured Goods	$1,794,417,000	92%	$155,552,000	8%
Factories	119,500	85%	20,600	15%
Workers in Industry	1,198,000	92%	111,000	8%
Population	22,340,000	63%	9,103,000 (3,954,000 slaves)	37%

Source: *Historical Statistics of the United States*

Chart *Skills* **As the Civil War began, the North enjoyed a number of economic advantages over the South. These advantages affected the war's outcome.**

1. **Comprehension** **(a)** How many acres of farmland did each side have? **(b)** What percentage of the nation's factories did the South have?
2. **Critical Thinking** **(a)** Which side had more railroad track? **(b)** How do you think this advantage affected the war?

Economics $

of the central government. As a result, it was often difficult for the Confederate government to get things done. On one occasion, for example, the governor of Georgia insisted that only Georgia officers be in command of Georgia troops.

Finally, the South had a small population. Only about 9 million people lived in the Confederacy, compared with 22 million in the Union. More than one third of the southern population were enslaved African Americans. As a result, the South did not have enough people to serve as soldiers and to support the war effort.

The North

The North had almost four times as many free citizens as the South. Thus, it had a large source of volunteers. It also had many people to grow food and to work in factories making supplies.

Industry was the North's greatest resource. Before the war, northern factories made more than 90 percent of the nation's manufactured goods. These factories quickly began making supplies for the Union army. The North also had more than 70 percent of the nation's rail lines, which it used to transport both troops and supplies.

The North also benefited from a strong navy and a large fleet of trading ships. With few warships and only a small merchant fleet, the South was unable to compete with the North at sea.

Despite these advantages, the North faced a difficult military challenge. To bring the South back into the Union, northern soldiers had to conquer a huge area. Instead of defending their homes, they were invading unfamiliar land. As Union armies invaded the South, their lines of supply would be much longer than those of the Confederates and thus more open to attack.

Wartime Leaders

Leadership was a very important factor in the Civil War. President Jefferson Davis of the Confederacy, President Abraham Lincoln of the Union, and military leaders on both sides played key roles in determining the war's outcome.

★ *Customized Instruction* ★

Introverted Learners

A losing proposition? If, as the chart on this page indicates, the North had clear advantages in terms of industry, transportation, and population, why did southerners believe they could win the war? Ask introverted learners to research this question. You might suggest they start by considering one or more of the following: southern food supply, cotton production (and British dependence on this cotton), the South's military strategy (defensive), its morale level and enthusiasm for the war, its military talent, and the ability of its civilian population to adapt to a soldier's life. Students might want to summarize the results of their research in a graphic organizer and display it for the class. (*average*)

Critical Thinking | Managing Information | Communication | Maps, Charts, and Graphs

Keeping Files

How Will I Use This Skill ?

A file system is a method for organizing and storing information, usually in a cabinet or on a computer disk. By keeping files, you can save and retrieve information quickly and easily. In school, this skill is useful for research projects. At home, a file system can help organize recipes, coupons, or documents and bills. Finally, you will probably use a file system in your future job or career.

Recipe file

LEARN the Skill

1. Set up and name various file sections. For example, a recipe file would need separate sections for appetizers, entrees, and desserts.
2. Create and label file folders for each section of the file. For example, a dessert section of a recipe file might need one folder for pies and another for cakes.
3. Create or collect the information or material that will be filed.
4. File the informtion or material in the appropriate folders.

PRACTICE the Skill

Read the subsection titled Strengths and Weaknesses on pages 448–450. Use the following steps to file information on the North and South.

1. Create a file system with two sections. Label one section The South. What should you label the other section?
2. For each of the two sections, create a file folder labeled Economy. Create and name two other file folders for each section. (You will have a total of six folders.)
3. For each of the two sections, record two or three facts to go into the Economy file folders. Write each fact on a separate sheet of paper. Place each sheet of paper in the appropriate folder.
4. In the same way, record and file other facts about the North and South.

APPLY the Skill

Create a file system for discount grocery coupons. You might start by making a section for dairy products that includes a folder for yogurt, another for cheese, and a third for butter. Offer your completed file system to someone who uses discount coupons.

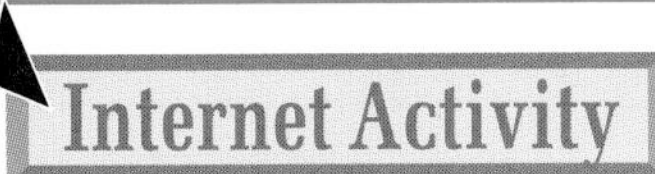

Researching the Civil War The Internet has extensive material on the Civil War. Have students explore The American Civil War Homepage at sunsite.utk.edu/civil-war/ and prepare a bibliography of Internet sites by subject area, using categories such as battles, notable events, and biographies. Given the changing nature of the Internet, you may wish to preview sites. (*basic*)

PRACTICE the Skill

ANSWERS

1. the North
2. Possible answers: military factors; population
3. Possible answers: The South: few factories to produce goods; few railroads to move troops and supplies. The North: produced 90 percent of the nation's manufactured goods; had more than 70 percent of its rail lines.
4. Students can file facts from the text and from the chart on p. 450 and create more folders if necessary.

APPLY the Skill

Guided Instruction

Students might use the same organization as the local supermarket's aisles, in which each aisle is seen as a file section. For example, the frozen foods section might have three folders: frozen vegetables, desserts, and juices.

ASSESSMENT See the rubrics in the Alternative Assessment booklet in the Teaching Resources.

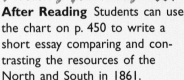

Writing Actively

After Reading Students can use the chart on p. 450 to write a short essay comparing and contrasting the resources of the North and South in 1861.

★ Section 1 Review ★

ANSWERS

1. See map, p. 449.

2. (a) p. 448, **(b)** p. 452

3. (a) p. 448, **(b)** p. 448

4. Possible answer: fighting defensively; better military leaders

5. Possible answer: a larger population and therefore more potential soldiers; more industry

6. (a) Lincoln: patient, strong; no military experience **(b)** Davis: honest, courageous; disliked delegating

7. Possible answer: For: Its economy would suffer less; if slavery were abolished, slave owners would be more likely to receive some payment from the government. Against: It would be betraying the South.

8. (a) that the North had no right to force laws on the South **(b)** because many in the North wanted the nation to stay united and wanted to end slavery

Activity

Guided Instruction

Tell students they can refuse or accept the offer, but they should draw a parallel between their situation and Lee's. They can also note how the two situations differ.

ASSESSMENT See the rubrics in the Alternative Assessment booklet in the Teaching Resources.

RESOURCE DIRECTORY

Teaching Resources
Lesson Planner, p. 71
Unit 5/Chapter 17
• Section 1 Quiz, p. 18

President Jefferson Davis

Many people thought Davis was a stronger leader than Lincoln. Davis had attended the United States Military Academy at West Point. He had served as an officer in the Mexican War. Later, he served as Secretary of War. He was widely respected for his honesty and courage.

Davis, however, did not like to turn over to others the details of military planning. When he made a decision, according to his wife, he "could not understand any other man coming to a different conclusion." As a result, Davis spent much time arguing with his advisers.

President Abraham Lincoln

At first, some northerners had doubts about Abraham Lincoln's ability to lead. He had little experience in national politics or military matters. In time, however, Lincoln proved to be a patient but strong leader and a fine war planner.

Day by day, Lincoln gained the respect of those around him. Many especially liked his sense of humor. They noted that Lincoln even accepted criticism with a smile. When Secretary of War Edwin Stanton called Lincoln a fool, Lincoln commented, "Did Stanton say I was a fool? Then I must be one, for Stanton is generally right and he always says what he means."

Military leaders

As the war began, army officers in the South had to make a choice. They could stay in the Union army and fight against their home states, or they could join the Confederate forces.

Robert E. Lee faced this dilemma when his home state of Virginia seceded. President Lincoln asked Lee to command the Union army. Lee refused. He explained in a letter to a friend:

> "I cannot raise my hand against my birthplace, my home, my children. I should like, above all things, that our difficulties might be peaceably arranged. . . . What ever may be the result of the contest, I foresee that the country will have to pass through a terrible ordeal."

Later, **Robert E. Lee** became commander of the Confederate army. In fact, many of the best officers served for the Confederacy. As a result, President Lincoln had trouble finding generals to match those of the South.

★ Section 1 Review ★

Recall

1. **Locate** **(a)** West Virginia, **(b)** Delaware, **(c)** Kentucky, **(d)** Missouri, **(e)** Maryland.
2. **Identify** **(a)** border states, **(b)** Robert E. Lee.
3. **Define** **(a)** racism, **(b)** martial law.

Comprehension

4. Describe two advantages that the South had over the North at the start of the Civil War.
5. Describe two advantages that the North had over the South at the start of the Civil War.
6. Explain one strength and one weakness of each of the following leaders: **(a)** President Abraham Lincoln, **(b)** President Jefferson Davis.

Critical Thinking and Writing

7. **Identifying Alternatives** List arguments for and against a border state's staying in the Union in 1861.
8. **Analyzing Ideas** Jefferson Davis said this of the Confederacy: "All we ask is to be left alone." **(a)** What do you think Davis meant? **(b)** Why was the Union unwilling to agree to Davis's wish?

Activity **Making a Decision** You are the captain of your hometown school basketball team. A rival school's coach has offered you a scholarship if you will play for them. Write the coach a letter informing him of your decision and the reasons for your decision. As you write your letter, keep in mind Robert E. Lee's difficult choice at the start of the Civil War.

★ Background ★

Viewpoints

A matter of outlook Although Abraham Lincoln and Jefferson Davis never met, the two men faced similar challenges. Neither man was a popular leader. Both men received criticism for the way they handled military affairs; both had a difficult time dealing with their generals. Lincoln and Davis had known personal tragedy and loss before the war and each would lose a son, as well as many friends, during the course of the war. There were telling differences, however, in their personal outlook and style. Davis had nothing resembling Lincoln's sense of humor and lacked the ability to work with people with whom he disagreed. To Lincoln it was more important to win the war than win an argument; to Davis it was often more important to win the argument.

A Long, Difficult Struggle

As You Read

Explore These Questions

- What were the military plans of each side?
- Which of its military goals did the Union achieve?
- Why did the Union fail to win major battles in the East?

Identify

- Stonewall Jackson
- Battle of Bull Run
- George McClellan
- *Merrimack*
- *Monitor*
- Battle of Antietam
- Battle of Fredericksburg
- Battle of Chancellorsville
- Ulysses S. Grant
- Battle of Shiloh

Union infantry drum

SETTING the Scene In the summer of 1861, the armies of the North and the South marched off to war with flags flying and crowds cheering. Each side expected a quick victory. However, the reality of war soon shattered this dream. Abner Small, a volunteer from Maine, described a scene that would be repeated again and again:

> "I saw... the dead and hurt men lying limp on the ground. From somewhere across the field a battery [heavy guns] pounded us. We wavered, and rallied, and fired blindly; and men fell writhing."

It soon became clear that there would be no quick, easy end to the war. Leaders on both sides began to plan for a long, difficult struggle.

Strategies for Victory

The North and South had different strategies for victory. The Union planned to use its naval power to cripple the South's economy. At the same time, Union armies would invade southern territory. The South, meanwhile, planned to defend itself until the North lost the will to fight.

Union plans

First, the Union planned to use its navy to blockade southern ports. This would cut off the South's supply of manufactured goods by halting its trade with Europe.

In the East, Union generals wanted to seize Richmond, Virginia, the Confederate capital. They thought that they might end the war quickly by capturing the Confederate government.

In the West, the Union planned to seize control of the Mississippi River. This would prevent the South from using the river to supply its troops. It would also separate Arkansas, Texas, and Louisiana from the rest of the Confederacy.

Confederate plans

The South's strategy was simpler: The Confederate army would fight a defensive war until northerners tired of the fighting. If the war became unpopular in the North, President Lincoln would have to stop the war and recognize the South's independence.

The Confederacy counted on European money and supplies to help fight the war. Southern cotton was important to the textile mills of England and other countries. Southerners were confident that Europeans would quickly recognize the Confederacy as an

★ Section 2

A Long, Difficult Struggle

LESSON PLAN

Objectives

★ Describe the military plans of each side.

★ Name the military goals that the Union achieved.

★ Explain why the Union failed to win major battles in the East.

1 Engage

Warm Up Ask students to list any local events, monuments, or reenactments connected with the Civil War. To this list, they may also add books, television programs, or films on the subject with which they are familiar.

Activating Prior Knowledge Ask students to form small groups and devise a group description of the differences between an offensive and defensive strategy. Suggest that they think about differences between offensive and defensive strategies in sports such as football, basketball, or tennis.

Reading Actively

Before Reading Ask students to skim the section, looking at the illustrations and reading the headings. Ask them to write two or three sentences predicting what the section will be about. As they read, have students verify or correct their predictions.

★ *Activity* ★

Connections With Mathematics

Counting troops In the Union Army: 10 companies = 1 regiment; 4 regiments = 1 brigade; 4 brigades = 1 division; 1–2 divisions = one army corps. On paper, a regiment had about 1,000 troops. Ask: How many soldiers were in a company? *(100)* Brigade? *(4,000)* Division? *(16,000)* Corps of 2 divisions? *(32,000)* (*basic*) T

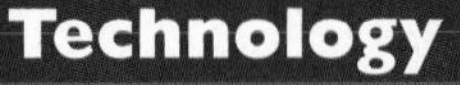

Technology

AmericanHeritage® History of the United States CD-ROM

- History Makers: Robert E. Lee (*average*)

2 Explore

Ask students to read the section. For a homework assignment, ask students to summarize the strategy each side used to win the war. Remind students that a strategy has to do with an overall plan for winning.

3 Teach

Divide the class into several small groups. Assign each group one of the battles discussed in the text and have each group prepare an account of its assigned battle from the viewpoint of a Union soldier, a Confederate soldier, or a reporter. After the groups present their accounts, have students summarize the importance of each battle.

4 Assess

To close the lesson, have students complete the section review. As an alternative, ask students to write an essay discussing what either side might have done to bring about a quicker end to the war.

★ ★ ★ ★ ★ ★ ★ ★ ★ ★ ★ ★ ★ ★ ★ ★ ★

Geography *Skills*

ANSWERS **1.** Review locations with students. **2.** General McClellan left Washington, D.C., by water to the mouth of the James River. He marched northwest toward Richmond. Before reaching it, he had to retreat back to the coast. **3.** Possible answer: Richmond was too far north. This made it easy for Union forces to constantly threaten the Confederate capital.

The Civil War in the East, 1861–1863

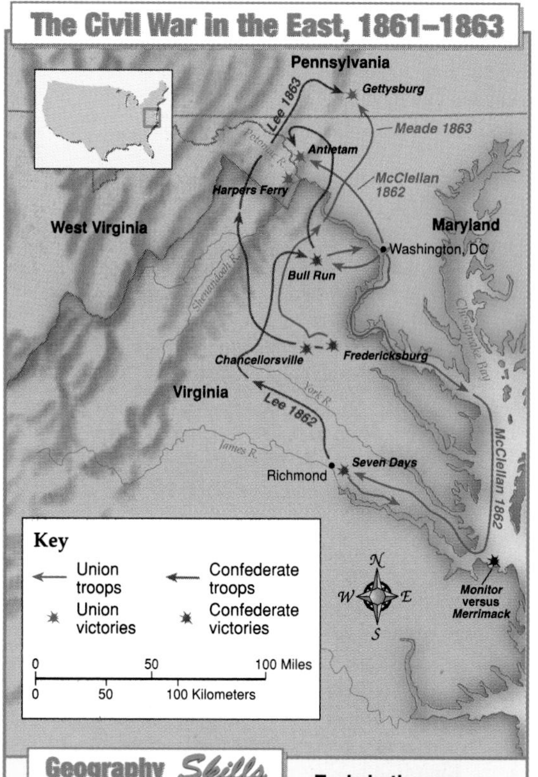

Geography *Skills* **Early in the war, Union armies were unsuccessful in their attempt to capture Richmond, the Confederate capital.**

1. **Location** On the map, locate: **(a)** Washington, DC, **(b)** Richmond, **(c)** Bull Run, **(d)** Chancellorsville, **(e)** Potomac River.
2. **Movement** Describe the route that General McClellan took when he tried to capture Richmond in 1862.
3. **Critical Thinking** Do you think the Confederacy made a wise decision in locating its capital at Richmond? Explain.

independent nation and continue to buy southern cotton for their factories.

Forward to Richmond!

"Forward to Richmond! Forward to Richmond!" Every day for more than a month, the influential *New York Tribune* blazed this "Nation's War Cry" across its front page. Responding to popular pressure for a quick victory, President Lincoln ordered the attack.

Battle of Bull Run

In July 1861, Union troops set out from Washington, D.C., for Richmond, about 100 miles (160 km) away. They met with Confederate soldiers soon after they left. The battle that followed took place near a small stream called Bull Run, in Virginia.

July 21, 1861, was a lovely summer day. Hundreds of Washingtonians rode out to watch their army crush the Confederates. Many carried picnic baskets. In a holiday mood, they spread out on a grassy hilltop overlooking Bull Run and awaited the battle.

The spectators, however, were shocked. Southern troops did not turn and run as expected. Inspired by the example of General Thomas Jackson, they held their ground. A Confederate officer remarked that Jackson stood his ground "like a stone wall." From that day on, the general was known as **"Stonewall" Jackson.**

In the end, it was Union troops who panicked and ran. A congressman who witnessed the retreat reported,

> "Off they went... across fields, toward the woods, anywhere, everywhere, to escape.... To enable them better to run, they threw away their blankets, knapsacks, canteens, and finally muskets, cartridge-boxes, and everything else."

The Confederates did not pursue the fleeing Union army. Had they done so, they might even have captured Washington, D.C. Instead, they remained behind to gather the gear thrown away by the Union troops.

The **Battle of Bull Run** showed both the Union and the Confederacy that their soldiers needed training. It also showed that the war would be long and bloody.

Caution, delay, and retreat

After the shocking disaster at Bull Run, President Lincoln appointed General **George McClellan** as commander of the Union army of the East, known as the Army of the Potomac. McClellan, a superb

★ *Background* ★

Turning Points

A moment's hesitation Uniforms were a cause of much confusion during the Battle of Bull Run. For 2 hours, the Union soldiers had steadily pushed the Confederates back toward and up the slopes of Henry House Hill (named for the home of Judith Henry, a bedridden widow). Two Union artillery batteries were blasting gaps in the Confederate lines when a blueclad regiment emerged from the woods. Thinking the regiment was infantry support it had requested, Union soldiers stopped firing. The regiment, which turned out to be Confederate, leveled muskets, fired, and wiped out the Union guns. From that point on in the battle, the tide shifted to the Confederates.

Biography

Robert E. Lee and Stonewall Jackson

Robert E. Lee (left) was perhaps the greatest general of the Civil War. Earlier, he had served admirably in the Mexican War and as superintendent of the United States Military Academy. Stonewall Jackson (right) was one of Lee's most skillful generals. Jackson's clever tactics and swift troop movements contributed to many victories.
★ **How did Jackson earn the nickname of "Stonewall" Jackson?**

organizer, transformed inexperienced recruits into an army of trained soldiers prepared for battle.

McClellan, however, was very cautious. He delayed leading his troops into battle. Newspapers reported "all quiet along the Potomac" so often that the phrase became a national joke. Finally, President Lincoln lost patience. "If McClellan is not using the army," the President snapped, "I should like to borrow it."

Finally, in March 1862, McClellan was ready to move. He and most of his troops left Washington by steamboat and sailed down the Potomac River for Richmond. The rest of the army stayed in Washington.

Landing south of Richmond, McClellan began inching slowly toward the Confederate capital. General Robert E. Lee launched a series of brilliant counterattacks. Lee also sent General Stonewall Jackson north to threaten Washington. Lincoln was thus prevented from sending the rest of the Union army to help McClellan. Cautious as usual, McClellan abandoned the attack and retreated. Once again, there was a lull in the war in the East.

Naval Action

Early in the war, Union ships blockaded southern ports. At first, some small, fast ships slipped through the blockade. These "blockade runners" brought everything from matches to guns into the Confederacy.

In time, however, the blockade became more effective. Trade through southern ports dropped by more than 90 percent. The South desperately needed a way to break the Union blockade. One method it tried was the ironclad ship.

At the start of the war, the Union abandoned a warship named the ***Merrimack*** near Portsmouth, Virginia. Confederates covered the ship with iron plates 4 inches (10.2 cm) thick and sent it into battle against the Union navy. On March 8, 1862, the *Merrimack* sank one Union ship, drove another aground, and forced a third to surrender. The Union vessels' cannonballs bounced harmlessly off the *Merrimack's* metal skin.

The Union countered with its own ironclads. One of these, the ***Monitor,*** battled the *Merrimack* in the waters off Hampton Roads, Virginia. The Confederate ship had more firepower, but the *Monitor* maneuvered more easily. In the end, neither ship seriously damaged the other, and both withdrew.

Ironclad ships changed naval warfare. Both sides rushed to build more of them. However, the South never mounted a serious attack against the Union navy. The Union blockade held throughout the war.

Biography

ANSWER

Jackson earned his nickname at the Battle of Bull Run, where he stood his ground "like a stone wall."

Reading Actively

During Reading Have students prepare a graphic organizer comparing and contrasting the military strategies of generals George McClellan and Robert E. Lee.

★ Background ★

Viewpoints

Caution or cowardice? After the Union's initial disasters, volunteers flooded the capital, numbering almost 200,000 by midwinter. Politicians and journalists were unhappy with McClellan, who appeared to be doing little more than overseeing parades. Reporters used the phrase "all quiet along the Potomac" as derisive shorthand for McClellan's reluctance to begin the fight.

★ Activity ★

Linking Past and Present

Investigating today's navy Ask students to work in small groups to investigate technological advances in modern naval vessels. Suggest that each group pick three particularly significant advances and present this information to the rest of the class. Students may wish to use slides, photos, drawings, and other illustrations during their oral presentations. (*average*)

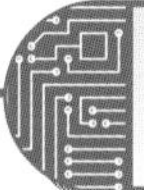
Linking History and Technology
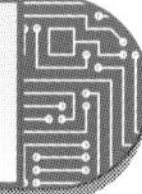

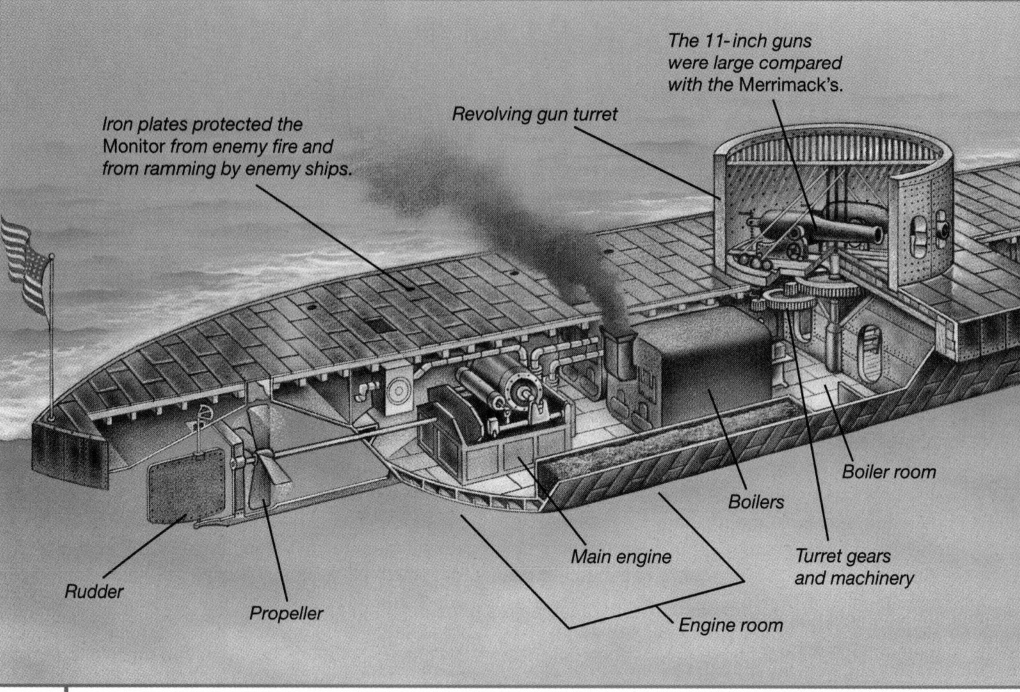
The 11-inch guns were large compared with the Merrimack's.
Revolving gun turret
Iron plates protected the Monitor from enemy fire and from ramming by enemy ships.
Boiler room
Boilers
Main engine
Turret gears and machinery
Rudder
Propeller
Engine room

Antietam

In September 1862, General Lee took the offensive and marched his troops north into Maryland. He believed that a southern victory on northern soil would be a great blow to northern morale.

Luck was against Lee, however. A Confederate messenger lost Lee's battle plans. Two Union soldiers found them and turned them over to General McClellan.

Even with Lee's battle plan before him, however, McClellan was slow to act. After waiting a few days, he finally attacked Lee's main force at Antietam (an TEE tuhm) on September 17. In the day-long battle that followed, more than 23,000 Union and Confederate soldiers were killed or wounded.

On the night of September 18, Lee ordered his troops to slip back into Virginia. The Confederates breathed a sigh of relief when they saw that McClellan was not pursuing them.

Neither side was a clear winner at the **Battle of Antietam.** The North was able to claim victory, though, because Lee had ordered his forces to withdraw. As a result, northern morale increased. Still, President Lincoln was keenly disappointed. The Union army had suffered huge numbers of dead and wounded. Furthermore, General McClellan had failed to follow up his victory by pursuing

★ *Customized Instruction* ★

Visual Learners

Outfitting the troops Suggest that visual learners research the kinds of equipment that Union and Confederate soldiers typically carried. Have them draw a picture of a representative soldier from each side and label the items they carried. Use the pictures as an exhibit on which to center a class discussion. For instance, you may want to ask students to think about how the differences in Union and Confederate equipment illustrate the differences between the regions. *(Students might find that items such as rations, clothing, and weapons were poorer in quality, or more widely varied in type, among Union or Confederate soldiers. They might find that a wider variation in equipment reflected southern resistance to Confederate federal authority.)* (average) ELL

RESOURCE DIRECTORY

Transparencies
Exploring Technology
• Ironclad Ship, p. H-43

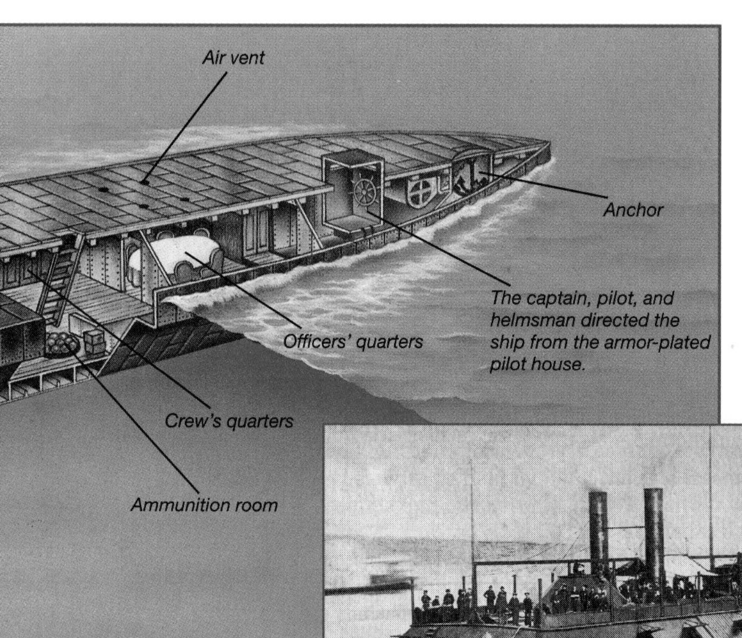
Air vent
Anchor
The captain, pilot, and helmsman directed the ship from the armor-plated pilot house.
Officers' quarters
Crew's quarters
Ammunition room

Ironclad Warship

The Monitor, *the first Union ironclad ship, looked like a "tin can on a raft." Its most unusual feature was the revolving gun turret, which made it possible to fire at the enemy from any angle without having to turn the ship around. The Union added more ironclads to its fleet, such as the one in the photograph below.* ★ **How did the Union navy hurt the Confederate economy?**

the Confederates. In November, Lincoln appointed General Ambrose Burnside to replace McClellan as commander of the Army of the Potomac.

Confederate Victories

Two stunning victories for the Confederacy came in late 1862 and 1863. (See the map on page 454.) General Robert E. Lee won by outsmarting the Union generals who fought against him.

Fredericksburg

In December 1862, Union forces set out once again toward Richmond. This time, they were led by General Ambrose Burnside.

Meeting Lee's army outside Fredericksburg, Virginia, Burnside ordered his troops to attack. Lee pulled back and left the town to Burnside. The Confederates dug in at the crest of a treeless hill above Fredericksburg. There, in a strong defensive position, they waited for the Union attack.

As the Union soldiers advanced, Confederate guns mowed them down by the thousands. Six times Burnside ordered his men to charge. Six times the rebels drove them back. "We forgot they were fighting us," one southerner wrote, "and cheer after cheer at their fearlessness went up along our lines." The **Battle of Fredericksburg** was one of the Union's worst defeats.

Linking History and Technology

ANSWER

The Union navy prevented Confederate trade with European nations by maintaining a blockade of southern ports.

Writing Actively

After Reading Ask students to consult their updated predictions about the contents of the section and write two or three main ideas that summarize the section. Have them compare their main ideas with those listed for Section 2 in Sum It Up at the end of the chapter.

★ *Background* ★

Did You Know?

Another lackluster leader General Ambrose Burnside's most lasting legacy may be the word "sideburns," which was first used to describe his muttonchop whiskers. Burnside, who replaced McClellan as head of the Army of the Potomac, had twice refused the job because he felt inadequate for it. His assessment of himself proved valid; his talents did not lie with military tactics.

FROM THE ARCHIVES OF **AmericanHeritage®**

Navy on the rivers A different type of vessel, known as a tinclad, patrolled the rivers and shallow tributaries of the West, gathering information and sparring with Confederate guerrillas. The tinclads, specially designed for river travel, numbered more than 70 by the war's end.

Source: Richard W. Kaeuper, "The Forgotten Triumph of the *Paw Paw*," *American Heritage* magazine, October 1995.

Technology

Videodiscs/Videotapes

Prentice Hall United States History Video Collection™, Vol. 9, Ch. 13, "The Harsh Face of War," 2:20 mins (*average*) ELL

Chapter 13

★ Section 2 Review ★

ANSWERS

1. See maps, pp. 454, 470.

2. (a)–(c) p. 454, **(d)–(e)** p. 455, **(f)** p. 456, **(g)** p. 457, **(h)–(j)** p. 458

3. (a) to blockade southern ports; capture Richmond, the Confederate capital; and seize control of the Mississippi River **(b)** It blockaded southern ports early in the war.

4. McClellan was overly cautious and did not attack aggressively. He missed many opportunities to defeat the Confederacy in battle.

5. The Union controlled both ends of the Mississippi, so the river was lost as a supply line.

6. that Jackson was one of the South's most gifted generals and that his loss was a great blow to the South

7. Possible answer: Iron plates protected these ships from enemy fire and from ramming by enemy ships.

Activity

Guided Instruction

On their maps, suggest that students use color or another device to differentiate the three parts of the Union's plan. They might also highlight the natural features and major geographic features that its army could exploit.

ASSESSMENT See the rubrics in the Alternative Assessment booklet in the Teaching Resources.

RESOURCE DIRECTORY

Teaching Resources
Lesson Planner, p. 72
Unit 5/Chapter 17
• Section 2 Quiz, p. 19

Chancellorsville

In May 1863, Lee, aided by Stonewall Jackson, again outwitted the Union army. This time, the battle took place on thickly wooded ground near Chancellorsville, Virginia. Lee and Jackson defeated the Union troops in three days.

Although the South won the **Battle of Chancellorsville,** it paid a high price for the victory. At the end of one day, nervous Confederate sentries fired at what they thought was an approaching Union soldier. The "Union soldier" was General Stonewall Jackson. Jackson died as a result of his injuries several days later.

The War in the West

While Union forces struggled in the East, those in the West met with success. As you have read, the Union strategy was to seize control of the Mississippi River. General **Ulysses S. Grant** began moving toward that goal. (See the map on page 470.) In February 1862, Grant attacked and captured Fort Henry and Fort Donelson in Tennessee. These Confederate forts guarded two important tributaries of the Mississippi.

Grant now pushed south to Shiloh, a village on the Tennessee River. At Shiloh, on April 6, he was surprised by Confederate forces. The Confederates won the first day of the **Battle of Shiloh.** They drove the Union troops back toward the river.

Grant now showed the toughness and determination that would enable him to win many battles in the future. "Retreat?" he replied to his doubting officers after that first day. "No. I propose to attack at daylight and whip them."

With the aid of reinforcements, Grant was able to win his victory and beat back the Confederates. However, the Battle of Shiloh was one of the bloodiest encounters of the Civil War. More Americans were killed or wounded at Shiloh than in the American Revolution, the War of 1812, and the Mexican War combined.

While Grant was fighting at Shiloh, the Union navy moved to gain control of the Mississippi River. In April 1862, Union gunboats captured New Orleans. Other ships seized Memphis, Tennessee. By capturing these two cities, the Union controlled both ends of the Mississippi. No longer could the South use the river as a supply line.

★ Section 2 Review ★

Recall

1. **Locate** **(a)** Richmond, **(b)** Washington, D.C., **(c)** Potomac River, **(d)** Fort Henry, **(e)** Fort Donelson, **(f)** New Orleans, **(g)** Memphis.
2. **Identify** **(a)** Stonewall Jackson, **(b)** Battle of Bull Run, **(c)** George McClellan, **(d)** *Merrimack,* **(e)** *Monitor,* **(f)** Battle of Antietam, **(g)** Battle of Fredericksburg, **(h)** Battle of Chancellorsville, **(i)** Ulysses S. Grant, **(j)** Battle of Shiloh.

Comprehension

3. **(a)** Describe the North's three-part plan for defeating the South. **(b)** Which part of the plan did the North achieve first?
4. Why was President Lincoln unhappy with General McClellan's performance as commander of the Union armies?
5. How did the loss of New Orleans and Memphis affect the South?

Critical Thinking and Writing

6. **Analyzing Primary Sources** In response to Stonewall Jackson's death, General Lee said, "I have lost my right arm." What did Lee mean by this statement?
7. **Analyzing Visual Evidence** Study the ironclad ships on pages 456-457. Explain how such ships were superior to wooden sailing ships.

Activity **Making a Map** You are the chief cartographer for the Union army. Your assignment is to make a map illustrating the Union's three-part plan for defeating the South.

A Promise of Freedom

As You Read

Explore These Questions
- Why did Lincoln issue the Emancipation Proclamation?
- What were the effects of the Proclamation?
- How did African Americans contribute to the Union war effort?

Define
- emancipate
- discrimination

Identify
- Emancipation Proclamation
- 54th Massachusetts Regiment
- Fort Wagner

Antislavery potholders

Setting the Scene At first, the Civil War was not a war against slavery. Yet wherever Union troops went, enslaved African Americans eagerly rushed to them, expecting to be freed. Most were sorely disappointed. Union officers often held these runaways until their masters arrived to take them back to slavery.

Some northerners began to raise questions. Was slavery not the root of the conflict between North and South? Were tens of thousands of men dying so that a slaveholding South would come back into the Union? Questions like these led Northerners to wonder what the real aim of the war should be.

Lincoln Was Cautious

The Civil War began as a war to restore the Union, not to end the institution of slavery. President Lincoln made this clear in the following statement.

> "If I could save the Union without freeing any slave, I would do it; and if I could save it by freeing all the slaves, I would do it; and if I could do it by freeing some and leaving others alone, I would also do that."

Lincoln had a reason for handling the slavery issue cautiously. As you have read, four slave states remained in the Union. The President did not want to do anything that might cause these states to shift their loyalty to the Confederacy. The resources of the border states might allow the South to turn the tide of the war.

The Emancipation Proclamation

By mid-1862, however, Lincoln came to believe that he could save the Union only by broadening the goals of the war. He decided to **emancipate,** or free, enslaved African Americans living in the Confederacy. In the four loyal slave states, however, slaves would not be freed. Nor would slaves be freed in Confederate lands that had already been captured by the Union, such as the city of New Orleans.

Motives and timing

Lincoln had practical reasons for his emancipation plan. At the start of the Civil War, more than 3 million enslaved people labored for the Confederacy. They helped grow the food that fed Confederate soldiers. They also worked in iron and lead mines that were vital to the South's war effort. Some served as nurses and cooks for the army. Lincoln knew that emancipation would weaken the Confederacy's ability to carry on the war.

However, Lincoln did not want to anger slave owners in the Union. Also, he knew that many northerners opposed freedom for

Section 3
A Promise of Freedom

LESSON PLAN

Objectives

★ Explain why Lincoln issued the Emancipation Proclamation.
★ Identify the effects of the Proclamation.
★ Describe the contributions of African Americans to the Union war effort.

1 Engage

Warm Up Ask: "When was the U.S. Army integrated?" *(under President Truman in 1948)* Have students jot down the answer if they know it or have them guess if they don't before you mention the date.

Activating Prior Knowledge Ask students to recall from their reading in the text when slavery ended in the North. *(1804)* Then ask them to recall why it was easier to end slavery in the North than in the South. *(Slavery in the South was closely tied to the southern economy.)*

Reading Actively

Before Reading Ask students to turn the title of this section into a question. As they read the section, have students jot down notes to help them answer the question.

★ *Background* ★

Did You Know?

The world supports freedom The tide of the world's opinion was clearly turning on the issue of slavery. After the Emancipation Proclamation was issued, English workers refused to build ships for the Confederacy and the czar of Russia sent warships to New York and San Francisco to show support for the Union.

Technology
Videodiscs/Videotapes
Prentice Hall United States History Video Collection™, Vol. 9, Ch. 28, "Western Front," 2 mins (average) ELL
Chapter 28

2 Explore

Ask students to read the section. For a homework assignment, ask students to investigate either at the library or on the Internet examples of African Americans who have distinguished themselves by service in the armed forces. Ask them to summarize the information they find.

3 Teach

Review the provisions of the Emancipation Proclamation with the class. If possible, obtain a copy of the document and read portions to the class. Then ask students to assess how each of the following people might have reacted to news of the Proclamation: **(a)** a slave in Georgia, **(b)** a slave in Maryland, **(c)** a slaveowner in each of these states, **(d)** a free African American in Pennsylvania, **(e)** an abolitionist in Boston, **(f)** a Union soldier, and **(g)** a Confederate soldier.

4 Assess

To close the lesson, have students complete the section review. As an alternative, ask students to prepare a skit in which a young African American explains why he wants to enlist in the Union army in 1862.

★ ★ ★ ★ ★ ★ ★ ★ ★ ★ ★ ★ ★ ★ ★ ★ ★

Viewing History ANSWER

Lincoln is surrounded by flags and the American eagle, symbols that stir feelings of patriotism for the Union. The twin icons of justice and liberty help to illustrate the contents of the Emancipation Proclamation.

RESOURCE DIRECTORY

Teaching Resources
Unit 5/Chapter 17

- Connecting History and Literature: Speech about the Emancipation Proclamation, p. 16
- Biography Flashcard: William H. Carney, p. 17

Interdisciplinary Connections

- Main Idea: The War Up Close, p. 98

Viewing History: The Emancipation Proclamation

The Emancipation Proclamation meant that Union troops were now fighting to end slavery. Lincoln's action, however, did not please all northerners. Opposition to the preliminary proclamation contributed to Republican party losses in the Congressional elections of 1862.

★ **How does this poster make use of symbolism?**

enslaved African Americans. Lincoln therefore hoped to introduce the idea of emancipation slowly, by limiting it to territory controlled by the Confederacy.

The President had another very important motive, too. As you read in Chapter 16, Lincoln believed that slavery was wrong. When he felt that he could act to free slaves without threatening the Union, he did so.

Lincoln was concerned about the timing of his announcement. The war was not going well for the Union. He did not want Americans to think he was freeing slaves as a desperate effort to save a losing cause. He waited for a victory to announce his plan.

Freedom proclaimed

On September 22, 1862, five days after the Union victory at Antietam, Lincoln issued a preliminary proclamation. It warned that on January 1, 1863, anyone held as a slave in a state still in rebellion against the United States would be emancipated.

Then, on January 1, 1863, Lincoln issued the formal Emancipation Proclamation. The **Emancipation Proclamation** declared:

> “On the 1st day of January, in the year of our Lord 1863, all persons held as slaves within any state or... part of a state [whose] people... shall then be in rebellion against the United States, shall be then, thenceforward, and forever free.”

Impact of the Proclamation

Because the rebelling states were not under Union control, no slaves actually gained their freedom on January 1, 1863. Nevertheless, as a result of the Emancipation Proclamation, the purpose of the war changed. Now, Union troops were fighting to end slavery as well as to save the Union.

The opponents of slavery greeted the proclamation with joy. In Boston, African American abolitionist Frederick Douglass witnessed one of the many emotional celebrations that took place:

> “The effect of this announcement was startling... and the scene was wild and grand.... My old friend Rue, a Negro preacher,... expressed the heartfelt emotion of the hour, when he led all voices in the anthem, ‘Sound the loud timbrel o'er Egypt's dark sea, Jehovah hath triumphed, his people are free!’”

Connections With Arts

Many northerners greeted the Emancipation Proclamation with music and song. At Boston's Music Hall, people celebrated with performances of Mendelssohn's *Hymn of Praise,* and Handel's *Hallelujah Chorus*.

★ Background ★ Did You Know?

No second thoughts President Lincoln had spent three hours shaking hands with people at a White House reception. He went to sign the Emancipation Proclamation concerned that his tired hand might shake, giving a false impression that he was somehow hesitant. “I have never in my life felt more certain that I was doing right,” he told Secretary of State William H. Seward.

★ Background ★ Recent Scholarship

In their own words *Free at Last,* edited by Ira Berlin, and *Families and Freedom,* edited by Ira Berlin and Leslie S. Rowland, provide a wealth of information concerning the history of enslaved African Americans and their struggle for freedom. These firsthand accounts provide dramatic and moving testimony to this important part of the Civil War story.

The Proclamation won the Union the sympathy of people in Europe, especially workers. As a result, it became less likely that Britain or any other European country would come to the aid of the South.

African Americans Help

When the war began, thousands of free blacks volunteered to fight for the Union. At first, federal law forbade African Americans to serve as soldiers. When Congress repealed that law in 1862, however, both free African Americans and escaped slaves enlisted in the Union army.

In the Union army

The army assigned these volunteers to all-black units, commanded by white officers. At first, the black troops served only as laborers. They performed noncombat duties such as building roads and guarding supplies. Black troops received only half the pay of white soldiers.

African American soldiers protested against this policy of discrimination that denied them the same rights and treatment as other soldiers. Gradually, conditions changed. By 1863, African American troops were fighting in major battles against the Confederates. In 1864, the United States War Department announced that all soldiers would receive equal pay. By the end of the war, about 200,000 African Americans had fought for the Union. Nearly 40,000 lost their lives.

Acts of bravery

One of the most famous African American units in the Union army was the **54th Massachusetts Regiment.** The 54th accepted African Americans from all across the

Viewing HISTORY **Assault on Fort Wagner**

In this painting by Tom Lovell, African American soldiers of the 54th Massachussetts Regiment charge against Confederate troops at Fort Wagner. Nearly half the regiment died in the failed attack, including the regiment's commander, Colonel Robert Gould Shaw. ★ **Why do you think the Union army was reluctant to appoint African American officers?**

Reading Actively

During Reading Ask students to prepare a map or graphic organizer that shows the states in which the Emancipation Proclamation freed slaves and the states in which slavery remained intact.

Writing Actively

After Reading Have students write a summary of the ways in which African Americans throughout the country contributed to the Union war effort.

Viewing HISTORY ANSWER

Possible answer: Like many other white Americans of the time, Union army commanders had certain prejudices about African Americans. Army officials were not confident in the ability of African Americans to lead and command troops.

★ *Activity* ★

Cooperative Learning

Preparing a presentation Divide the class into small groups. Have each group research one of the following people and prepare a presentation about his or her contributions to the war effort: Mary Elizabeth Bowser (house servant in the Confederate White House), Robert Smalls (wheelman on the Confederate steamer *Planter*), Susie King Taylor (cared for the wounded in South Carolina), and Colonel Robert Gould Shaw (leader of the 54th Massachusetts Regiment). Encourage groups to assign a role to each student—notetaker, writer, editor, and so on. Afterward, have students evaluate the success of their cooperative group. (*average*)

Technology

Videodiscs/Videotapes

Prentice Hall United States History Video Collection™, Vol. 9, Ch. 16, "Oh, Freedom!" 5 mins (average) ELL

Chapter 16

★ Section 3 Review ★

ANSWERS

1. (a) p. 460, **(b)** p. 461, **(c)** p. 462

2. (a) p. 459, **(b)** p. 461

3. (a) He did not want to force the border states to join the Confederacy. **(b)** He believed it would weaken the Confederacy militarily, and he also believed that slavery was wrong.

4. Because the slave states were not under Union control, no slaves were actually freed.

5. (a) Their heroism and heavy losses in the attack won them the public's respect. **(b)** by slowing down their work or refusing to work at all

6. that northerners were still prejudiced and believed that blacks should be separated from whites

7. (a) that blacks should be allowed to perform combat duties and fight alongside whites **(b)** Yes, the Union government eventually let African American soldiers fight and gave them equal pay.

Activity

Guided Instruction
Encourage students to be creative, using free verse or structured, rhymed verse. Poems might reflect emotions, as well as facts.

ASSESSMENT See the rubrics in the Alternative Assessment booklet in the Teaching Resources.

North. Frederick Douglass helped recruit troops for the regiment, and two of his sons served in it.

On July 18, 1863, the 54th Massachusetts Regiment led an attack on **Fort Wagner** near Charleston. Under heavy fire, troops fought their way into the fort before being forced to withdraw. In the desperate fighting, almost half the regiment, including its young commander, Robert Shaw, were killed.

The courage of the 54th Massachusetts and other regiments helped to win respect for African American soldiers. Sergeant William Carney of the 54th Massachusetts was awarded the Congressional Medal of Honor for acts of bravery. He was the first of 16 African American soldiers to be so honored during the Civil War. In a letter to President Lincoln, Secretary of War Stanton praised African American soldiers.

> "[They] have proved themselves among the bravest of the brave, performing deeds of daring and shedding their blood with a heroism unsurpassed by soldiers of any race."

Behind Confederate lines

In the South, despite the Emancipation Proclamation, African Americans still had to work as slaves on plantations. However, many enslaved African Americans slowed down their work. Others refused to work at all or to submit to punishment. In so doing, they knew they were helping to weaken the South's war effort. They knew that when victorious Union troops arrived in their area, they would be free.

Throughout the South, thousands of enslaved African Americans also took direct action to free themselves. Whenever a Union army appeared in an area, the slaves from all around would flee their former masters. They crossed over to the Union lines and to freedom. By the end of the war, about one fourth of the enslaved population in the South had escaped to freedom.

The former slaves helped Union armies achieve victory in a variety of ways. They used their knowledge of the local terrain to serve as guides and spies. Many more enlisted in African American regiments of the Union army.

★ Section 3 Review ★

Recall

1. **Identify** (a) Emancipation Proclamation, (b) 54th Massachusetts Regiment, (c) Fort Wagner.
2. **Define** (a) emancipate, (b) discrimination.

Comprehension

3. (a) Why was President Lincoln cautious about making emancipation a goal of the war? (b) Why did he finally decide to issue the Emancipation Proclamation?
4. Why were no slaves actually freed when the Proclamation was issued?
5. (a) How did the 54th Massachussetts Regiment's attack on Fort Wagner affect public opinion about enslaved African American soldiers? (b) How did African Americans help to weaken the Confederacy?

Critical Thinking and Writing

6. **Drawing Conclusions** What did the Union army's policy toward all-black regiments reveal about northern attitudes toward African Americans? Explain.
7. **Analyzing Primary Sources** In 1861, Frederick Douglass said, "This is no time to fight with one hand when both hands are needed. This is no time to fight with only your white hand, and allow your black hand to remain tied!" (a) What did Douglass mean by this statement? (b) Did the United States Congress agree with Douglass? Explain.

Activity **Writing a Poem** A monument is being built to honor the courageous African American soldiers of the Civil War. Write a poem to be engraved on the monument, mentioning some of the facts you have learned in this section.

★ Customized Instruction ★
Extroverted Learners

Portraying a character from historical fiction Ask extroverted students to read *Which Way Freedom* by Joyce Hansen, or *Corey* by Jane Miner. Explain to students that both books deal with the lives of African Americans during the Civil War. *Which Way Freedom* tells the story of the runaway slave Obi, who fights with a black regiment of Union soldiers. *Corey* describes the life of a house slave whose freedom comes when General Sherman's troops destroy the North Carolina plantation where she lives. Ask volunteers to play the parts of Obi and Corey. Each student should briefly describe the life of his or her character and then act out a scene from the book. Students may enlist the aid of classmates to play supporting roles. (challenging) T

RESOURCE DIRECTORY

Teaching Resources
Lesson Planner, p. 73
Unit 5/Chapter 17
- Map Mystery: African Americans Join the War, p. 15
- Section 3 Quiz, p. 20

Interdisciplinary Connections
- Main Idea: The War Up Close, p. 101

Hardships of War

As You Read

Explore These Questions
- What was life like for soldiers in the Civil War?
- How did women contribute to the war effort?
- What problems did each side face during the war?

Define
- civilians
- draft
- habeas corpus
- income tax
- inflation
- profiteer

Identify
- Copperheads
- Loreta Janeta Velazquez
- Rose Greenhow
- Dorothea Dix
- Clara Barton
- Sojourner Truth
- Sally Tompkins

Setting the Scene The Civil War caused hardships not only for soldiers but for people at home as well. Southerners, especially, suffered from the war, because most of the fighting took place in the South.

On both sides, **civilians,** or people who were not in the army, worked on farms and labored in factories to support the war effort. They used their mules to move troops and supplies. They tended the wounded. As their hardships increased, so did opposition to the war.

The Hard Life of Soldiers

On both sides, most soldiers were under age 21. However, war quickly turned gentle boys into tough men. Soldiers drilled and marched for long hours. They slept on the ground even in rain and snow. In combat, boys of 18 learned to stand firm as cannon blasts shook the earth and bullets whizzed past their ears.

New technology added to the horror of war. Cone-shaped bullets, which made rifles twice as accurate, replaced round musket balls. New cannons could hurl exploding shells several miles. The new weapons had deadly results. In most battles, one fourth or more of the soldiers were killed or wounded.

Sick and wounded soldiers faced other horrors. Medical care on the battlefield was crude. Surgeons routinely cut off injured arms and legs. Minor wounds often became infected. With no medicines to fight infection, thousands of wounded died. Diseases like pneumonia and malaria killed more men than guns or cannons did.

Confederate cap

Union cap

On both sides, prisoners of war faced horrifying conditions. At Andersonville, a prison camp in Georgia, more than one Union prisoner out of three died of disease or starvation. One prisoner wrote:

> "There is no such thing as delicacy here.... In the middle of last night I was awakened by being kicked by a dying man. He was soon dead. I got up and moved the body off a few feet, and went to sleep to dream of the hideous sights."

Discontent in the North

Some northerners opposed using force to keep the South in the Union. Supporters of the war called these people **Copperheads,** after the poisonous snake. Other northerners supported the war but opposed the way Lincoln was conducting it. In some northern cities, this opposition led to riots.

From the Archives of American Heritage®

Medical help? Injured Civil War soldiers could have benefited from modern medicine; but knowledge was less advanced at the time. Surgeons, for example, thought that pus at the site of a wound was a good sign; they called it "laudable pus." In fact, pus generally indicated bacterial infection that in time would kill the soldier.

Source: Bruce Catton, *The American Heritage® Picture History of the Civil War,* 1960.

Section 4 Hardships of War

LESSON PLAN

Objectives

★ Describe what life was like for soldiers in the Civil War.

★ Explain how women contributed to the war effort.

★ Identify the problems each side faced during the war.

1 Engage

Warm Up Create two columns on the chalkboard that are headed "Life in Combat" and "Life at Home." Have students list possible details about daily life in each environment during the Civil War.

Activating Prior Knowledge Remind students that many soldiers on both sides in the Civil War were teenagers. Ask students, "How do you think you would feel if you were asked to fight in a war at the age of 17 or 18?" "How do you think your family and friends would react?" and "Under what conditions might you be willing to volunteer?"

Reading Actively

Before Reading Ask students to skim the section, looking at the illustrations and reading the headings. Have them write two or three sentences predicting what the section will be about. As they read, have students verify or correct their predictions.

Technology

Listening to Music CD
- Willie Has Gone to War (average)

2 Explore

Ask students to read the section. For a homework assignment, have students make a chart with the following headings: "Soldiers," "the North," "the South," and "Women." Under each heading, ask students to list specific hardships.

3 Teach

Review Lincoln's reactions to the draft riots in the North as described on this page. Then have the class debate the following resolution: "Lincoln's suspension of protesters' civil liberties was in the best interests of the Union." After debate, have the students use their notes to discuss what, if any, limits should be placed on civilian protest during time of war.

4 Assess

To close the lesson, have students complete the section review. As an alternative, ask students to create an outline or concept map about the hardships endured by men and women during the Civil War.

ANSWER

Desertion rates were high on both sides because soldiers feared dying and suffering for causes they did not volunteer to support. Therefore, many draftees on both sides did not want to fight.

RESOURCE DIRECTORY

Teaching Resources
Why Study History?
- One Person Can Make a Difference, pp. 67–70

Viewing History: The Faces of War

Confederate soldiers wore gray uniforms and were sometimes called Johnny Rebs. Union soldiers wore blue and were called Billy Yanks. During the Civil War, about 1 of every 10 soldiers deserted from service. ★ **Why do you think desertion rates were high in both armies?**

The draft law

As the war dragged on, public support dwindled. Soon, not enough men were volunteering to serve in the Union army. The government took action.

In 1863, Congress passed a **draft** law. It required all able-bodied males between the ages of 20 and 45 to serve in the military if they were called.

Under the law, a man could avoid the draft by paying the government $300 or by hiring someone to serve in his place. This angered many people. They began to see the Civil War as "a rich man's war and a poor man's fight."

Riots in the cities

Opposition to the draft law led to riots in several northern cities. The draft law had gone into effect soon after Lincoln issued the Emancipation Proclamation. As a result, some northerners believed that they were being forced to fight to end slavery. This idea angered some white workers, especially recent immigrants in the cities. Like many other northerners, some of these immigrants held racist beliefs. They also feared that free African Americans would be employed at jobs that they needed, too.

The worst riot took place in New York City during July 1863. For four days, white workers attacked free blacks. Rioters also attacked rich New Yorkers who had paid to avoid serving in the army. At least 74 people were killed during the riot.

President Lincoln moved to stop the riots and other "disloyal practices." Several times, he denied **habeas corpus** (HAY bee uhs KOR puhs), the right to have charges filed or a hearing before being jailed. Lincoln defended his actions by saying that the Constitution gave him the right to deny people their rights "when in the cases of rebellion or invasion, the public safety may require it."

Problems in the South

President Davis, meanwhile, struggled to create a strong federal government for the Confederacy. Many southerners were strong supporters of states' rights. They resisted paying taxes to a central government. At one point, Georgia threatened to secede from the Confederacy!

Like the North, the South had to pass a draft law to fill its army. However, men who owned or supervised more than 20 slaves did not have to serve in the army. Southern farmers who owned few or no slaves resented this law.

Near war's end, the South no longer had enough white men to fill the ranks. Robert E. Lee urged that enslaved African Americans be allowed to serve as soldiers. Desperate, the Confederate congress finally agreed. However, the war ended before any enslaved people put on Confederate uniforms.

★ *Activity* ★

Connections With Economics

Probing causes To help students understand more fully the causes of the New York City draft riots, suggest that they explore the following: the bounty system *(payment for voluntarily joining the army)*; bounty jumpers *(men who enlisted, collected their bounty, deserted, and then reenlisted in another locality)*; draft lotteries *(random drawings of names for those to be called into army service)*; draft substitution *(men who were drafted could pay a substitute to go to war in their place)*; the meaning of the slogan "a rich man's war and a poor man's fight"; the political and economic conditions in New York City that contributed to the riot; and who or what the rioters attacked and why. *(average)* T

Why Study History?

Because One Person Can Make a Difference

Historical Background

In the early days of the Civil War, Clara Barton and other women provided medical care to wounded soldiers. However, the government required women to stay far from battle. As a result, many soldiers received treatment too late and died of their wounds. Barton therefore sought permission to work directly on the fields of battle.

After some initial refusals, the government gave in. Through the remainder of the war, Clara Barton served as a battlefield nurse. Because of her courageous efforts, she became known as the "Angel of the Battlefield."

Connections to Today

After the Civil War, Barton continued to make a difference. In Europe, she worked with the International Red Cross, an organization that aided victims of war. In 1881, after returning to the United States, she founded the American Red Cross. This new organization served both victims of war and victims of natural disaster.

Today, disaster relief remains a primary service of the Red Cross. The Red Cross helps people recover from natural disasters such as fires, floods, and hurricanes. It provides victims with medical assistance, food, clothing, and shelter.

The American Red Cross provides other services as well. It helps homeless people and seniors in need. It supervises donations of blood and other organs. It also provides instruction in a variety of safety programs.

Connections to You

Like Clara Barton, you too can make a difference. You can learn about first aid and safety procedures in a Red Cross educational course. Courses include first aid, water safety, fire prevention, and even babysitting. Some local Red Cross chapters invite teens to serve as volunteers. You might also organize or participate in a drive to help raise funds for the Red Cross. Red Cross disaster relief services are provided free of charge because of contributions made by caring Americans.

▲ *Clara Barton*

▲ *Red Cross book*

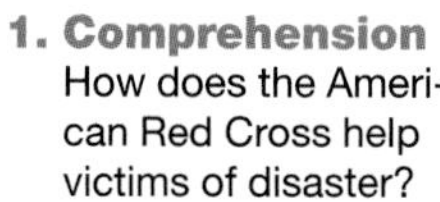

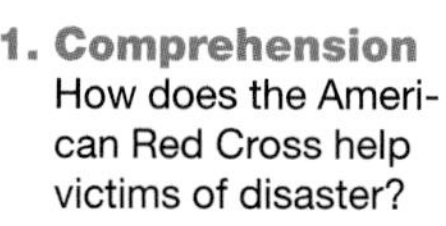

1. **Comprehension** How does the American Red Cross help victims of disaster?
2. **Critical Thinking** At the start of the Civil War, why do you think government officials allowed men, but not women, to aid wounded soldiers on the field of battle?

Making an Advertisement Create an advertisement that seeks public support for the Red Cross by informing people about the many services the Red Cross provides.

Why Study History?

ANSWERS

1. It provides medical assistance, food, clothing, and shelter. **2.** Possible answer: They thought that women couldn't do the job and that women needed to be protected from the horrors of war.

★Activity

Guided Instruction

You might have the class compile a list of visual images that could be used to illustrate the services of the Red Cross. Then discuss which images would be most compelling in an advertisement. If possible, contact the Red Cross in your area for more information and samples of its advertisements.

ASSESSMENT See the rubrics in the Alternative Assessment booklet in the Teaching Resources.

Fast Facts

★ Even Harvard Medical School did not own a microscope or a stethoscope until 1868—four years after the Civil War ended.

★ Clara Barton believed that if nursing on the battlefield seemed "rough and unseemly for a *woman*," fighting wars was equally "rough and unseemly for *men*."

★ Louisa May Alcott, author of *Little Women*, once served as a Union nurse herself. Her first book, *Hospital Sketches*, was based on these experiences.

Bibliography

To read more about this topic:

1. *Bonnet Brigades*, Mary E. Massey (Knopf, 1966). Women's Civil War contributions.

2. *Microbes and Minie Balls: An Annotated Bibliography of Civil War Medicine*, Frank R. Freemon (Fairleigh Dickinson University Press, 1993).

3. Internet. The National Women's History Project. Extensive biographical and historical information: www.nwhp.org.

Technology

Videodiscs/Videotapes

Prentice Hall United States History Video Collection™, Vol. 9, Ch. 22, "Angels of the Battlefield," 2:45 mins (*average*) ELL

Chapter 22

American Heritage® History of the United States CD-ROM

• History Makers: Clara Barton (*average*)

ANSWER

Many women raised money to help supply troops and some even fought in the war or acted as spies.

Writing Actively

After Reading Ask students to write a paragraph summarizing the contributions of women to the war effort.

Viewing History **Nursing the Wounded**

In this Civil War scene, painted by Allyn Cox in 1974, women are nursing the wounded in the rotunda of the Capitol building. During the war, many public buildings served as temporary hospitals. The painting decorates a corridor of the Capitol today.

★ **How else did women help in the war effort?**

The Northern Economy

The Civil War cost far more than any earlier war. The Union had to use several strategies to raise money. In some ways, though, war helped the North's economy.

Taxation and inflation

In 1861, to pay for the war, Congress established the nation's first **income tax** on people's earnings. In addition, the Union issued bonds worth millions of dollars. Still, taxes and bonds did not raise enough money. To get the funds it needed, the North printed more than $400 million in paper money.

As the money supply increased, each dollar was worth less. In response, businesses charged more for their goods. The North was experiencing **inflation,** a rise in prices and a decrease in the value of money. During the war, prices for goods nearly doubled in the North.

Economic benefits

In some ways, the war helped the North's economy. Because many farmers went off to fight, more machines were used to plant and harvest crops. As a result, farm production actually went up during the war.

The wartime demand for clothing, shoes, guns, and other goods helped many northern industries. Some manufacturers made fortunes by profiteering. **Profiteers** charged excessive prices for goods the government desperately needed for the war.

The Southern Economy

For the South, war brought economic ruin. The South had to struggle with the cost of the war, the loss of the cotton trade, and severe shortages brought on by the Union blockade.

The economy suffers

To raise money, the Confederacy imposed an income tax and a tax-in-kind. The tax-in-kind required farmers to turn over one tenth of their crops to the government. The government took crops because it knew that southern farmers had little money.

Like the North, the South printed paper money. It printed so much, in fact, that wild inflation set in. By 1865, one Confederate dollar was worth only two cents in gold.

The war did serious damage to the cotton trade, the South's main source of income. Early in the war, President Davis halted cotton shipments to Britain. He hoped that Britain would side with the South in order to get cotton. The tactic backfired. Britain simply bought more cotton from Egypt and

$ Connections With Economics

As inflation in the South worsened, it became more and more difficult to feed and clothe a family. Near the end of the war, a barrel of flour cost $1,000 and a pair of shoes cost $400.

RESOURCE DIRECTORY

Teaching Resources
Unit 5/Chapter 17
- Section 4 Quiz, p. 21

Interdisciplinary Connections
- Main Idea: The War Up Close, pp. 99, 102

Transparencies
Interdisciplinary Connections
- Civil War Medical Treatment, p. B-63

★ **Background** ★

Recent Scholarship

Where to find it *The American Civil War: A Handbook of Literature and Research*, edited by Steven E. Woodworth (Westport, CT: Greenwood Press, 1996), provides a comprehensive survey and analysis of Civil War research and literature. It includes more than 40 essays, each by a specialist in a particular subfield of Civil War history.

India. Davis succeeded only in cutting the South's income.

Effects of the blockade

The Union blockade created severe shortages in the South. Confederate armies sometimes had to wait weeks for supplies of food and clothing. Guns and ammunition were also in short supply. With few factories of its own, the South bought many of its weapons in Europe. However, the blockade cut off most deliveries from Europe.

For civilians, the blockade brought food shortages. Even the wealthy went hungry. "I had a little piece of bread and a little molasses today for my dinner," wrote plantation mistress Mary Chesnut in her diary. By 1865, there was widespread famine in the Confederacy.

Women at War

Women of both the North and South played vital roles during the war. As men left for the battlefields, women took jobs in industry, in teaching, and on farms.

Women and the military

Women's aid societies helped supply the troops with food, bedding, clothing, and medicine. Throughout the North, women held fairs and other fund-raising events to pay for the supplies. They succeeded in raising millions of dollars.

A few women disguised themselves so they could serve as soldiers. **Loreta Janeta Velazquez,** for example, fought for the South at Bull Run and Shiloh. Other women worked as spies. **Rose Greenhow** gathered information for the South while entertaining Union leaders in her Washington, D.C., home. She was caught, convicted of treason, and exiled.

Nursing the wounded

Women on both sides worked as nurses. Doctors were unwilling at first to permit even trained nurses to work in military hospitals. When wounded men began to swamp army hospitals, however, this attitude soon changed.

Dorothea Dix, famous for her work reforming prisons and mental hospitals, became superintendent of nurses for the Union army. **Clara Barton** earned fame as a Civil War nurse. She later founded the American Red Cross. **Sojourner Truth,** the African American antislavery leader, worked in Union hospitals and in camps for freed slaves. In the South, **Sally Tompkins** set up a hospital in Richmond, Virginia.

★ Section 4 Review ★

Recall

1. **Identify** (a) Copperheads, (b) Loreta Janeta Velazquez, (c) Rose Greenhow, (d) Dorothea Dix, (e) Clara Barton, (f) Sojourner Truth, (g) Sally Tompkins.
2. **Define** (a) civilians, (b) draft, (c) habeas corpus, (d) income tax, (e) inflation, (f) profiteer.

Comprehension

3. Describe three hardships faced by soldiers during the Civil War.
4. Describe three ways women contributed to the war effort.
5. How did the Union blockade affect the South?

Critical Thinking and Writing

6. **Linking Past and Present** (a) What advances in technology made Civil War battles deadly? (b) In what ways would a war today be even more deadly?
7. **Defending a Position** What facts support the charge that the Civil War was "a rich man's war and a poor man's fight"?

Activity **Making a Chart** You are the graphic illustrator for an economics magazine. Create a flowchart or cause-and-effect chart to illustrate how the high cost of the Civil War led to high inflation.

★ Section 4 Review ★

ANSWERS

1. (a) p. 463, (b)–(g) p. 467
2. (a) p. 463, (b) p. 464, (c) p. 464, (d) p. 466, (e) p. 466, (f) p. 466
3. Possible answer: long hours drilling and marching; living outdoors in all weather; combat
4. They took over the jobs held by men who went to fight; they served as soldiers and spies; and they nursed the wounded.
5. It created severe shortages (of food, weapons, and industrial goods such as railroad equipment) for both soldiers and civilians.
6. (a) cone-shaped bullets and new cannons (b) Possible answer: War today can cause much greater destruction because of inventions like nuclear and chemical weapons, planes, and tanks.
7. Possible answer: Rich men could pay to escape military service. The poor could not afford to do this, so they made up most of the army.

Activity

Guided Instruction

Have students review the information on the northern and southern economies. Their charts should show why costs rose, why goods were hard to come by, and how shortages led to inflation.

ASSESSMENT See the rubrics in the Alternative Assessment booklet in the Teaching Resources.

★ *Customized Instruction* ★

English Language Learners

Student-teacher journals Use the following strategy to improve communications with English language learners who are reluctant to speak up in class. Provide notebooks to these students and explain that the notebook is a student-teacher journal. In this notebook you and the student will write to each other about the Civil War. Explain to students that they can write about things they don't understand, questions they might have, or relevant personal experiences. Include one or two questions for a student response in the journal. If possible, exchange the journal every other day so that the student is continually communicating with you. (*average*) ELL

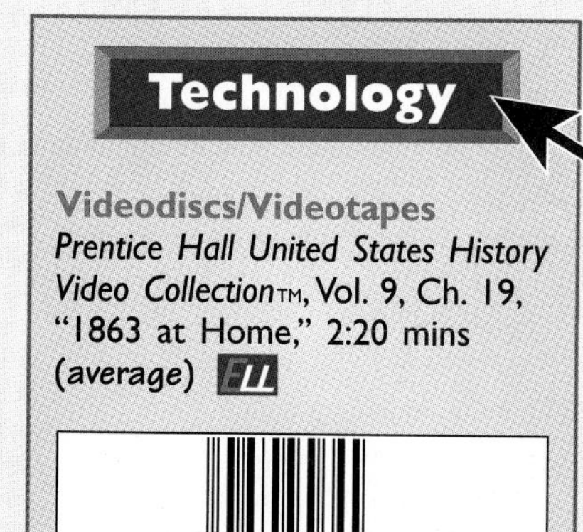

Technology

Videodiscs/Videotapes

Prentice Hall United States History Video Collection™, Vol. 9, Ch. 19, "1863 at Home," 2:20 mins (*average*) ELL

Chapter 19

Section 5

The War Ends

LESSON PLAN

Objectives

★ Explain the significance of the Union victories at Vicksburg and Gettysburg.

★ Describe the ideals expressed by Lincoln in the Gettysburg Address.

★ Explain how Union generals used a new type of war to defeat the Confederacy.

1 Engage

Warm Up Ask students to explain what they think the phrase "government of the people, by the people, for the people" means.

Activating Prior Knowledge The Civil War is often described as a major turning point in American history. Ask students to think about what the phrase "turning point" means. Suggest that they think of times in their own lives when they reached a turning point.

Reading Actively

Before Reading Tell students to read the questions under Explore These Questions. As they read, have them jot down notes to help them answer the questions. At the end of the section, tell students to use their notes to help them write the answers to the Comprehension questions in the section review.

RESOURCE DIRECTORY

Teaching Resources
Lesson Planner, p. 74
Interdisciplinary Connections
• Main Idea: The War Up Close, p. 100

The War Ends

As You Read

Explore These Questions
- What was the significance of the Union victories at Vicksburg and Gettysburg?
- What ideals did Lincoln express in the Gettysburg Address?
- How did Union generals use a new type of war to defeat the Confederacy?

Define
- siege
- total war

Identify
- Battle of Gettysburg
- Gettysburg Address
- Ulysses S. Grant
- Philip Sheridan
- William Tecumseh Sherman

SETTING the Scene As you have read, Confederate armies won major battles at Fredericksburg in December 1862 and at Chancellorsville in May 1863. These were gloomy days for the North.

Then, in July 1863, the tide of war turned against the South. In the West, the Union extended its control of the Mississippi River and cut the South in two. At the Battle of Gettysburg, in Pennsylvania, both Union and Confederate forces suffered terrible losses. However, as President Davis later explained, "Theirs could be repaired, ours could not."

The following year, President Lincoln would appoint Ulysses S. Grant commander in chief of the Union army. In Grant, Lincoln had found the general who could lead the Union to victory.

The Fall of Vicksburg

After capturing New Orleans and Memphis, the Union controlled both ends of the Mississippi River. Still, the North could not safely use the river because Confederates held Vicksburg, Mississippi. Vicksburg sat on a cliff high above the river. Cannons there could shell boats traveling between New Orleans and Memphis.

Early in 1863, Grant's forces tried again and again to seize Vicksburg. The Confederates held out bravely. At last, Grant devised a brilliant plan. Marching his troops inland, he launched a surprise attack on Jackson, Mississippi. Then, he turned west and attacked Vicksburg from the rear. (See the map on page 470.)

For over six weeks, Grant's forces lay siege to Vicksburg. A **siege** is a military blockade of an enemy town or position in order to force it to surrender. Day after day, the Union soldiers pushed their lines closer to the town. Union artillery and gunboats on the Mississippi bombarded the besieged soldiers and inhabitants. As their food supplies ran out, the southerners began to use mules and rats as food. Finally, on July 4, 1863, the Confederates surrendered Vicksburg.

On July 9, Union forces also captured Port Hudson, Louisiana. The entire Mississippi was now under Union control. The Confederacy was split into two parts. Texas, Arkansas, and Louisiana were cut off from the rest of the Confederacy.

Union Victory at Gettysburg

In the East, after his victory at Chancellorsville, General Lee moved his army north into Pennsylvania. He hoped to take the Yankees by surprise. If he was successful, Lee planned to then swing south and capture Washington, D.C.

★ *Customized Instruction* ★

Kinesthetic Learners

Making a model Ask kinesthetic learners to prepare a model that could have been used as part of a report to General Lee before the battle of Gettysburg. Tell students to begin by researching the geography of Gettysburg. Remind them that their model should show main roads, bodies of water, hills, valleys, and major towns in the area. Tell them to include a notation of scale and direction in their model. Students may use clay, papier-mâché, and other craft materials to give their model appropriate, three-dimensional detail. Finally, ask them to write a short report explaining the key points on the model and giving suggestions for winning the coming battle. (*challenging*) T

AmericanHeritage MAGAZINE

HISTORY HAPPENED HERE

◀ Ohio regiment monument

Vicksburg National Military Park

You can learn about the siege of Vicksburg, Mississippi, by touring the actual battle site. The park includes a museum, miles of defensive earthworks, and more than 125 cannons. You can even walk the deck of a Union ironclad gunboat, raised from the Mississippi River in the 1960s. Throughout the park, numerous monuments honor the soldiers who fought and died for control of this small Mississippi River town.

★ ***To learn more about this historic site, write:*** *Vicksburg National Military Park, 3201 Clay Street, Vicksburg, MS 39180.*

On June 30, 1863, a Union force under General George C. Meade met part of Lee's army at the small town of Gettysburg, Pennsylvania. Both sides quickly sent in reinforcements. The three-day Battle of Gettysburg that followed was one of the most important battles of the Civil War.

At the start of the battle, the Confederates drove the Union forces out of Gettysburg. The Yankees took up strong positions on Cemetery Ridge, overlooking the town. On July 2, a Confederate attack failed with heavy casualties. Nevertheless, Lee decided to launch another attack. On July 3, he ordered General George Pickett to lead 15,000 men in a daring charge against the center of the Union line. To reach the Yankees, Pickett's men had to cross an open field and run up a steep slope.

Pickett gave the order to charge and the Union guns opened fire. Row after row of soldiers fell to the ground, bleeding. Still, the Confederate troops continued to rush forward against a rain of bullets and shells. Few were able to reach the Union lines. A Union soldier described the fighting at the crest of the ridge:

> "Men fire into each other's faces not five feet apart. There are bayonet thrusts, saber strokes, pistol shots, men going down on their hands and knees... gulping blood, falling, legless, armless, headless."

Pickett's charge failed. As the survivors limped back, Lee rode among them. "It's all my fault," he admitted humbly. Lee had no choice but to retreat. After their defeat at the **Battle of Gettysburg,** the Confederates would never again invade the North.

The Union victories at Vicksburg and Gettysburg marked the turning point of the Civil War. On July 4, 1863, northerners had good reason to celebrate.

2 Explore

Ask students to read the section. For a homework assignment, ask students to create concept maps to explain the importance of the Battles at Vicksburg and Gettysburg.

3 Teach

With the class, create a chart of major battles of the Civil War. Label the columns "Battle," "Date," "Location," "Outcome," and "Importance." Have students skim Section 2 for additional battles to be included in the chart. Suggest that students keep copies of the chart for future reference and review.

4 Assess

To close the lesson, have students complete the section review. As an alternative, ask students to choose a person mentioned in the section and take turns with a partner asking "yes or no" questions until each can discover the other's identity.

AmericanHeritage MAGAZINE

Vicksburg National Military Park To learn more about Vicksburg National Military Park on the Internet, go to www.americanparks.com/parklist/nsvicks.htm

★ *Background* ★

Turning Points

Importance of Gettysburg and Vicksburg Gettysburg and Vicksburg proved to be crucial turning points: Never again would Confederate troops try to invade the North. Lee lost more than a third of his army at Gettysburg. Vicksburg surrendered on July 4, 1863, and the city did not officially celebrate Independence Day again until 1945, at the end of the World War II.

Technology

Videodiscs/Videotapes
Prentice Hall United States History Video Collection™, Vol. 9, Ch. 25, "Gettysburg," 3:10 mins (average) ELL

Chapter 25

Geography Skills

ANSWERS **1.** Review locations with students. **2.** Arkansas, Texas, and Louisiana **3.** Because most of the fighting took place in the South, more southern property was damaged or destroyed than northern property.

Reading Actively

During Reading Suggest that students turn the head The Union Wages Total War into a question. *(for example, How did the Union wage total war?)* Tell students to jot down answers to this question as they read.

The Gettysburg Address

The Battle of Gettysburg left more than 40,000 dead or wounded. When the soldiers who died there were buried, their graves stretched as far as the eye could see. On November 19, 1863, northerners held a ceremony to dedicate this cemetery.

President Lincoln attended the ceremony, but he was not the main speaker. At the time, his popularity was quite low. Lincoln sat with his hands folded as another speaker talked for two hours. When it was his turn, the President rose and spoke for about three minutes.

In his **Gettysburg Address,** Lincoln said that the Civil War was a test of whether or not a democratic nation could survive. He reminded Americans that their nation was founded on the belief that "all men are created equal." Looking out at the thousands of graves, Lincoln told the audience:

> "We here highly resolve that these dead shall not have died in vain—that this nation, under God, shall have a new birth of freedom—and that government of the people, by the people, for the people, shall not perish from the earth."

Geography Skills As the Civil War dragged on, Union armies advanced deeper and deeper into the South. General Sherman marched his troops through Georgia and the Carolinas.

1. **Location** On the map, locate: **(a)** Vicksburg, **(b)** Atlanta, **(c)** Savannah.
2. **Place** What three Confederate states were cut off from the rest of the Confederacy after Union forces gained control of the Mississippi River?
3. **Critical Thinking** Based on the map, why would the South be hurt more than the North—no matter who won the war?

Skills For Life MINI LESSON

MAPS, CHARTS, AND GRAPHS Using a Special Purpose Map

1. Introduce the skill of using a special purpose map by having students study the map (and key) on this page; then discuss how it adds to the text information. Point out that the map visually shows the progress of the war and the areas of the South affected by it.

2. Help students practice the skill by having them compare the events along the Mississippi River in 1862 and 1863, according to this map, with events in the same time period in the East, according to the Section 2 map.

3. Help students apply the skill by asking them to use the map on p. 472 to explain when and where the final battles of the Civil War occurred, and who was leading each force.

Resource Directory

Teaching Resources
Unit 5/Chapter 17
- Critical Thinking and Writing: Understanding Causes and Effects, p. 14

Few people listened to Lincoln that day. Newspapers gave his speech little attention. Later generations, however, have honored Lincoln's brief address as a profound statement of American ideals.

The Union Wages Total War

For three years, Lincoln had searched for a general who could lead the Union to victory. More and more, he thought of **Ulysses S. Grant.** After capturing Vicksburg, Grant continued to win battles in the West. In 1864, Lincoln appointed him commander of the Union forces.

Some questioned the choice, but President Lincoln felt that "Unconditional Surrender" Grant was the general who would lead the Union to victory. "I can't spare this man," Lincoln said. "He fights."

Grant and other Union generals began to wage **total war** against the South. In total war, civilians as well as soldiers are affected. The Union army waged total war by destroying food and equipment that might be useful to the enemy. Civilians in the South suffered the same hardships as soldiers.

Sheridan in the Shenandoah

Grant had a plan for ending the war. He wanted to destroy the South's ability to fight. Grant sent General **Philip Sheridan** and his cavalry into the rich farmland of Virginia's Shenandoah Valley. He instructed Sheridan:

> "Leave nothing to invite the enemy to return. Destroy whatever cannot be consumed. Let the valley be left so that crows flying over it will have to carry their rations along with them."

Sheridan obeyed. In the summer and fall of 1864, he marched through the valley, destroying farms and livestock.

Sherman's march to the sea

Grant also ordered General **William Tecumseh Sherman** to capture Atlanta, Georgia, and then march to the Atlantic coast. Like Sheridan, Sherman had orders to destroy everything useful to the South.

Cause and Effect

Causes

- Issue of slavery in the territories divides the North and South
- Abolitionists want slavery to end
- South fears it will lose power in the national government
- Southern states secede after Lincoln's election
- Confederates bombard Fort Sumter

The Civil War

Effects

- Lincoln issues the Emancipation Proclamation
- Northern economy booms
- South loses its cotton trade with Britain
- Total war destroys the South's economy
- Hundreds of thousands of Americans killed

Effects Today

- Sectionalism is less of a force in American life and politics
- African Americans have equal protection under the Constitution
- Millions of Americans visit Civil War battlefields each year

Graphic Organizer *Skills*

The Civil War was a major turning point in the history of the United States.

1. **Comprehension** How did the war affect the northern and southern economies differently?
2. **Critical Thinking** Describe another cause or effect that could be added to this chart.

Graphic Organizer *Skills*

ANSWERS **1.** The northern economy boomed. The South lost its cotton trade with Britain, and total war destroyed the South's economy. **2.** Possible answers: Another cause was that the North and South disagreed about tariffs and other economic issues. Another effect was that millions of freed African Americans had to find a way to make a living.

★ *Background* ★
Linking Past and Present

Visiting history The casualties at the Battle of Gettysburg included 23,000 out of 88,000 Union troops and more than 20,000 out of 75,000 Confederate troops. The battle site is today one of ten designated national military parks in the United States. Visitors can tour the battlefield and see where various events occurred, as well as the site of Lincoln's address.

Technology

Videodiscs/Videotapes
Prentice Hall United States History Video Collection™, Vol. 9, Ch. 31, "Toward Union Victory," 2:30 mins (*average*) ELL

Chapter 31

Listening to Literature Audiocassettes
The American Experience
- The Gettysburg Address, side 5 (*average*) ELL

Geography *Skills*

ANSWERS **1.** Review locations with students. **2.** Petersburg, Virginia **3.** Spotsylvania. The arrows show that Grant and Lee moved their armies to Cold Harbor after the battle at Spotsylvania.

Writing Actively

After Reading Ask students to use the cause-and-effect chart on p. 471 as the basis for writing an essay summarizing the effects of the Civil War.

Sherman's troops captured Atlanta in September 1864. They burned the city in November. Then Sherman began his "march to the sea."

Sherman's troops ripped up railroad tracks, built bonfires from the ties, then heated and twisted the rails. They killed livestock and tore up fields. They burned barns, homes, and factories.

Lincoln Is Reelected

In 1864, Lincoln ran for reelection. At first, his defeat seemed, in his own words, "extremely probable." Before the capture of Atlanta, Union chances for victory looked bleak. Lincoln knew that many northerners were unhappy with his handling of the war. He thought that this might cost him the election.

The Democrats nominated General George McClellan to oppose Lincoln. Although he had commanded the Union army, McClellan was more willing than Lincoln to compromise with the South. If peace could be achieved, he was ready to restore slavery.

When Sherman took Atlanta in September, the North rallied around Lincoln. Sheridan's smashing victories in the Shenandoah Valley in October further increased Lincoln's popular support. In the election in November, the vote was close, but Lincoln remained President.

In his second Inaugural Address, Lincoln looked forward to the coming of peace:

> ❝With malice toward none, with charity for all . . . let us strive . . . to bind up the nation's wounds . . . to do all which may achieve a just and a lasting peace among ourselves and with all nations.❞

The Final Battles

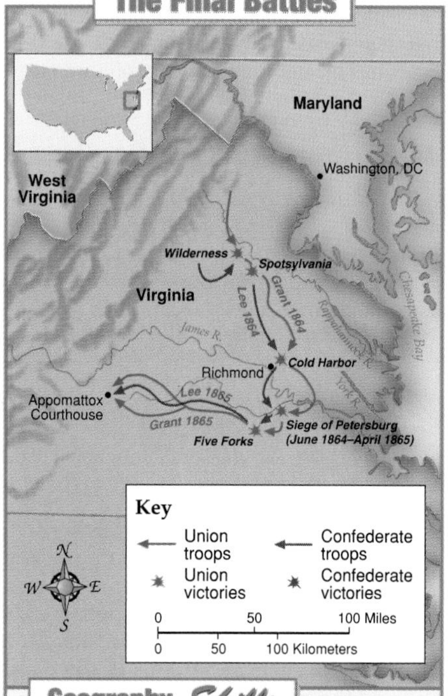

Geography *Skills* **The final battles of the Civil War pitted Grant against Lee in Virginia. Finally, on April 9, 1865, Lee surrendered at Appomattox Courthouse.**

1. **Location** On the map, locate: **(a)** Richmond, **(b)** Petersburg, **(c)** Appomattox Courthouse.
2. **Place** Where did Grant hold Lee under siege for nine months?
3. **Critical Thinking** Which battle took place first: Cold Harbor or Spotsylvania? Explain.

The War Ends

Grant had begun a drive to capture Richmond in May 1864. Throughout the spring and summer, he and Lee fought a series of costly battles.

Northerners read with horror that Grant had lost 60,000 dead and wounded in a single month at the battles of the Wilderness, Spotsylvania, and Cold Harbor. Still, Grant pressed on. He knew that the Union could replace men and supplies. The South could not.

Lee dug in at Petersburg, near Richmond. Here, Grant kept Lee under siege for nine months. At last, with a fresh supply of troops, Grant took Petersburg on April 2, 1865. The same day, Richmond fell.

★ *Activity* ★
Cooperative Learning

Who's Who Brainstorm with the class to compile a list of important figures from the Civil War. Then divide the class into teams of three or four students and have each team prepare several profiles for a Who's Who in the Civil War to be used for class reference. Divide the list of important figures randomly among the teams and ask members to begin profiles based on information in this chapter. If possible, work with the school librarian to allow additional research during a class period. After the teams have completed their profiles, have them alphabetize their entries and organize them in book form. Make copies of the completed works and distribute one to each student. (*average*) T

Resource Directory

Teaching Resources
Unit 5/Chapter 17
- Vocabulary Builder, p. 12
- Section 5 Quiz, p. 22

Chapter Tests, pp. 97–102

General Lee surrenders to General Grant at Appomattox Courthouse.

Lee and his army withdrew to a small Virginia town called Appomattox Courthouse. There, a week later, they were trapped by Union troops. Lee knew that his men would be slaughtered if he kept fighting. On April 9, 1865, Lee surrendered.

At Appomattox Courthouse, Grant offered generous terms of surrender to the defeated Confederate army. Soldiers were required to turn over their rifles, but officers were allowed to keep their pistols. Soldiers who had horses could keep them. Grant knew that southerners would need the animals for spring plowing.

As the Confederates surrendered, Union soldiers began to cheer. Grant ordered them to be silent. "The war is over," he said. "The rebels are our countrymen again."

Effects of the War

More than 360,000 Union soldiers and 250,000 Confederate soldiers lost their lives in the Civil War. No war has ever resulted in more American deaths. As a result, feelings of bitterness remained among both northerners and southerners.

Southerners had special reasons to view the North with resentment. They had lost their struggle for independence. Their way of life had been forcibly changed. Union armies had destroyed much of their land. In addition, many southerners feared that the North would seek revenge against the South after the war.

Finally, the Civil War was a major turning point in American history. The Union was secure. States' rights had suffered a terrible blow. As a result, the power of the federal government grew. The war also brought freedom to millions of African Americans. Still, a long and difficult struggle for equality lay ahead.

★ Section 5 Review ★

Recall

1. **Locate** **(a)** Vicksburg, **(b)** Port Hudson, **(c)** Gettysburg, **(d)** Atlanta, **(e)** Petersburg, **(f)** Appomattox Courthouse.
2. **Identify** **(a)** Battle of Gettysburg, **(b)** Gettysburg Address, **(c)** Ulysses S. Grant, **(d)** Philip Sheridan, **(e)** William Tecumseh Sherman.
3. **Define** **(a)** siege, **(b)** total war.

Comprehension

4. Why did the Union victories at Vicksburg and Gettysburg mark a turning point in the war?
5. What ideals did Lincoln express in his Gettysburg Address and Second Inaugural Address?
6. How did Sheridan and Sherman use total war to destroy the South's ability to fight?

Critical Thinking and Writing

7. **Predicting Consequences** If Sherman and Sheridan had not won victories just before the election of 1864, how might the election and the war have turned out differently?
8. **Defending a Position** Some people have condemned Grant's decision to wage total war. Do you agree or disagree with this position? Explain.

Activity **Writing a Speech** It is a sad day for the South. You are a member of the Confederate Congress and you have just heard of Lee's surrender. Write a speech in which you reflect on the hardships of the war and offer hope for the future.

★ Section 5 Review ★

ANSWERS

1. See maps, pp. 454, 470, and 472.

2. **(a)** p. 469, **(b)** p. 470, **(c)** p. 471, **(d)** p. 471, **(e)** p. 471

3. **(a)** p. 468, **(b)** p. 471

4. Vicksburg: The North took full control of the Mississippi. Gettysburg: The South would never again invade the North, and the war would now be fought in the South.

5. freedom, equality, justice, faith in American democracy

6. They left the South without the food and equipment it needed.

7. McClellan, who sought compromise with the South, might have won. Slavery could have continued; the U.S. might have stayed divided.

8. Agree: Total war made civilians suffer and starve. Disagree: It ended the war more quickly, thus reducing bloodshed and suffering.

Activity

Guided Instruction
Suggest that students consider what southerners wanted from the war (e.g., independence). They may wish to think about the South's economy without slavery.

ASSESSMENT See the rubrics in the Alternative Assessment booklet in the Teaching Resources.

★ Background ★
Recent Scholarship

Lincoln biography David Herbert Donald's biography *Lincoln* (New York: Simon & Schuster, 1992) is a richly detailed account of the man who steered the Union to victory in the Civil War. The book provides a wealth of information on a brilliant and complex leader and the times in which he lived.

Technology

Videodiscs/Videotapes
Prentice Hall United States History Video Collection™, Vol. 9, Ch. 34, "1865 Conclusion at Appomattox," 2 mins (*average*) ELL

Chapter 34

CD-ROM
Test Bank CD-ROM, Ch. 17
Interactive Student Tutorial

Chapter 17

Review and Activities

Reviewing the Chapter

Define These Terms

1. b **2.** a **3.** e **4.** c **5.** d

Explore the Main Ideas

1. The Union had a larger population, more soldiers, and more industry.

2. The South had better leaders and the advantage of having only to defend itself.

3. The Emancipation Proclamation gave the North's war effort the new moral goal of freeing the slaves, gave slaves in the South hope, and reduced the possibility that Europeans might come to the South's aid.

4. Women acted as spies and nurses and took over the jobs of men who went to fight in the war.

5. Total war devastated the South's economy and caused civilians to suffer the same hardships as soldiers.

Chart Activity

1. 27 **2.** 122 **3.** Crude medical care and shortage of medicines allowed diseases to spread through the camps.

Critical Thinking and Writing

1. (a) Battle of Bull Run **(b)** Emancipation Proclamation **(c)** fall of Vicksburg

2. Possible answers: If the war were not popular, the public would react with outrage and call for the general to be dismissed. If the majority of the people believed the war was fought for a good cause, the public might be willing to accept these tremendous losses.

3. African Americans might have decided to volunteer because they would be helping bring an end to slavery sooner or, if they were former slaves, to get revenge. They might have decided not to volunteer because the war was not yet being fought to free the slaves or because the army was discriminatory.

4. Possible answer: Yes, over 60 years of sectional differences had proved that sectionalism ran too deep to be quickly rooted out and eliminated.

Using Primary Sources

(a) They wept because they would have preferred to go on fighting and possibly die rather than surrender. **(b)** Possible answer: He is proud because their desire to keep fighting showed their strong loyalty to the South. **(c)** They deeply resented the North's occupation and never truly surrendered in their hearts.

Chapter 17

Review and Activities

★ Sum It Up ★

Section 1 The Conflict Takes Shape

- The Union's advantages included a greater population and superior industrial resources.
- The Confederacy's advantages included better military leaders and its position of defending the homeland.

Section 2 A Long, Difficult Struggle

- The Union navy blockaded southern ports. Union armies tried to take Richmond and the Mississippi Valley.
- The Confederates won major battles in the East. Union armies were more successful in the West.

Section 3 A Promise of Freedom

- The Emancipation Proclamation made the end of slavery a goal of the war.
- African Americans worked, fought, and died in the effort to preserve the Union and end slavery.

Section 4 Hardships of War

- Both men and women suffered hardships in their efforts to win the war.
- During the war, the Union and Confederacy both struggled with political and economic problems.

Section 5 The War Ends

- The North waged total war deep into the South, disrupting civilian lives and inflicting great losses.
- Lee surrendered his army at Appomattox Courthouse, Virginia, on April 9, 1865.

For additional review of the major ideas of Chapter 17, see ***Guide to the Essentials of American History*** or ***Interactive Student Tutorial CD-ROM,*** which contains interactive review activities, graphic organizers, and practice tests.

Reviewing the Chapter

Define These Terms

Match each term with the correct definition.

Column 1

1. emancipate
2. martial law
3. draft
4. profiteers
5. inflation

Column 2

a. rule by the army
b. set free
c. people who overcharge for desperately needed goods
d. a rise in prices
e. a law requiring people to serve in the military

Explore the Main Ideas

1. What advantages did the United States have over the Confederate States?
2. Why were Confederate armies in the East often victorious in the early years of the war?
3. What were the results of the Emancipation Proclamation?
4. How did women support the war effort?
5. Explain how total war affected the South.

Chart Activity

Use the chart below to answer the following questions: **1.** How many members of Company D were captured and imprisoned by the Union? **2.** How many soldiers were in Company D at the start of the war? **Critical Thinking** Why do you think so many soldiers died from disease?

Seventh Virginia Infantry, Company D

Original members	122
Killed in battle or died of wounds	17
Died of disease	14
Discharged	29
Transferred	6
Prisoners of war	27
On leave, hospitalized, or at home	8
Deserted	12
Surrendered at Appomattox	9

Source: David E. Johnston, *The Story of a Confederate Boy in the Civil War*

Critical Thinking and Writing

1. **Understanding Chronology** For each pair of events that follow, select the event that happened first: **(a)** Battle of Bull Run, Battle of Gettysburg; **(b)** fall of Richmond, Emancipation Proclamation; **(c)** Sherman's march to the sea, fall of Vicksburg.
2. **Linking Past and Present** How do you think Americans would react today if a general lost 60,000 soldiers in one month as General Grant once did? Explain your answer.
3. **Identifying Alternatives** Should African American men have volunteered to serve in the Union army in 1862? Explain two reasons for volunteering and two reasons for not volunteering.
4. **Exploring Unit Themes** **Sectionalism** Do you think sectional differences and conflicts continued even after the end of the Civil War? Explain the reasons for your answer.

Using Primary Sources

Confederate General John B. Gordon described how his troops felt at Appomattox Courthouse as General Lee was about to surrender:

> "The men cried like children. Worn, starved, and bleeding as they were, they had rather have died than have surrendered.... But I could not permit it.... That these men should have wept at surrendering so unequal a fight, at being taken out of this constant [bloodshed] and storm, at being sent back to their families ... was [proof of bravery] and patriotism that might set an example."

Source: *Reminiscences of the Civil War* by John B. Gordon, 1903.

Recognizing Points of View **(a)** Why did General Gordon's troops cry? **(b)** How did Gordon feel about the behavior of the soldiers? **(c)** How do you think Confederate veterans felt about northern soldiers occupying southern lands after the war?

Activity Bank

Interdisciplinary Activity

Exploring Science Research and prepare a report on medical care during the Civil War. Include information on battlefield hospitals, common diseases, and people who cared for the sick and wounded.

Career Skills Activity

Cartographer Choose a Civil War battle and make a map showing the positions and movements of troops in the battle. Do research to find the information you need.

Citizenship Activity

Writing a Speech In the late 1860s, Memorial Day emerged as a day to honor soldiers who had died in the Civil War. Today, the holiday honors those whose lives were sacrificed in all American wars. Write a brief speech explaining why it is important to honor those who have died in American wars.

Internet Activity

On the Internet, find sites dealing with the Civil War. Choose a specific Civil War topic and prepare a five-minute presentation to give to the class. Possible topics include: a specific battle, a particular military or political leader, or the poetry and music of the Civil War.

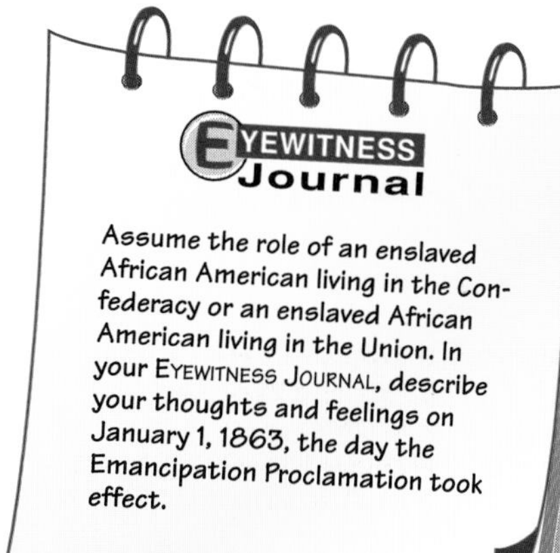

EYEWITNESS Journal
Assume the role of an enslaved African American living in the Confederacy or an enslaved African American living in the Union. In your EYEWITNESS JOURNAL, describe your thoughts and feelings on January 1, 1863, the day the Emancipation Proclamation took effect.

Activity Bank

ASSESSMENT To assess the activities on this page, see the rubrics in the Alternative Assessment booklet in the Teaching Resources. You might want to share the rubrics with your students before they begin work.

Interdisciplinary Activity

1. Reports should include explanations of the symptoms and effects of malaria, dysentery, and typhoid and describe how these diseases should best be treated.

2. Students might highlight the contributions of such individuals as Clara Barton, Dorothea Dix, Sally Tompkins, and Sojourner Truth in improving medical care.

3. Extend the activity by having students compare Civil War's medical knowledge to today's.

Career Skills Activity

1. Point out to students that there were many important battles of the Civil War that the text is not able to cover. Students can consult histories of the Civil War to find out more about these battles.

2. Single-volume histories of the individual battles are good sources of information. For example, Gettysburg has been the subject of many history books that are illustrated with detailed maps.

3. Students can compile their maps into an atlas of major civil war battles.

Citizenship Activity

1. Students might begin by considering what privileges they might not have today if these soldiers had not given their lives fighting for their country.

2. You may wish to make the activity a contest. Get a panel of student judges to choose the most compelling speech from those submitted. If possible, you can invite other classes and schools to submit their entries.

Eyewitness Journal

1. Have students use the index to review the material on slavery in their text.
2. Remind students that although the Proclamation went into effect the day it was issued, no slaves were actually freed then. Slaves were gradually freed as Union troops took control of southern states.
3. Students should also consider the uncertainties freedom might bring.

Internet Activity

1. Have students go to www.phschool.com, which contains updated information on a variety of topics.
2. Another site you may find useful for this activity is the United States Civil War page at www.uscivilwar.com/uscwhp2.cfm.
3. Given the changing nature of the Internet, you may wish to preview this site before directing students to it.

Chapter 18 Manager

SECTION OBJECTIVES	TEACHING RESOURCES	ADDITIONAL RESOURC
1 First Steps to Reunion (pp. 478–481) **Objectives** 1. Describe the hardships the South faced after the Civil War. 2. Outline President Lincoln's plan for reuniting the nation. 3. Explain why Congress opposed President Johnson's Reconstruction plan.	**Lesson Planner,** p. 75 (*average*) .... 45 mins. **Unit 5/Chapter 18** • Connecting History and Literature: "O Captain! My Captain!" p. 27 (*average*) .... 20 mins. • Section 1 Quiz, p. 29 (*average*) .... 15 mins. **Interdisciplinary Connections** • Main Idea: Reconstruction, pp. 105, 107 (*average*) .... 20 mins. **Document-Based Discovery** • Sectionalism, pp. 18–21 (*average*) .... 90 mins.	**Voices of Freedom** • A Planter Faces the Future, pp. 126–127 (*average*)
2 Radical Reconstruction (pp. 482–485) **Objectives** 1. Describe the goals of the Radical Republicans. 2. Explain why Congress tried to remove President Johnson from office. 3. Outline the provisions of the Fourteenth and Fifteenth Amendments.	**Lesson Planner,** p. 76 (*average*) .... 90 mins. **Unit 5/Chapter 18** • Section 2 Quiz, p. 30 (*average*) .... 15 mins. **Interdisciplinary Connections** • Main Idea: Reconstruction, pp. 104, 106 (*average*) .... 20 mins.	**Voices of Freedom** • From the Black Codes, pp. 127–128 (*average*) **Customized Reader** • Resolutions of the Illinois Convention of Colored Men, article VA-14 (*average*)
3 Changes in the South (pp. 486–490) **Objectives** 1. List the groups that dominated southern politics during Reconstruction. 2. Summarize the steps taken by Reconstruction governments to rebuild the South. 3. Explain why many southerners sank into a cycle of poverty.	**Lesson Planner,** p. 77 (*average*) .... 60 mins. **Unit 5/Chapter 18** • Practice Your Skills: Interpreting a Political Cartoon, p. 24 (*challenging*) .... 20 mins. • Critical Thinking and Writing: Identifying Alternatives, p. 25 (*average*) .... 20 mins. • Biography Flashcard: Josephine White Griffing, p. 28 (*average*) .... 20 mins. • Section 3 Quiz, p. 31 (*average*) .... 15 mins. **Interdisciplinary Connections** • Main Idea: Reconstruction, p. 108 (*average*) .... 20 mins.	**Voices of Freedom** • A Former Slave on Reconstructi[on], pp. 128–129 (*average*)
4 Reconstruction Ends (pp. 491–495) **Objectives** 1. Explain why Reconstruction ended. 2. Describe how the southern economy expanded after Reconstruction. 3. Discuss how African Americans in the South lost rights.	**Lesson Planner,** p. 78 (*average*) .... 45 mins. **Unit 5/Chapter 18** • Vocabulary Builder, p. 23 (*basic*) .... 10 mins. • Map Mystery: Voting Patterns in Reconstruction, p. 26 (*average*) .... 20 mins. • Section 4 Quiz, p. 32 (*average*) .... 15 mins. **Why Study History?** • Tolerance Begins With You, pp. 71–74 (*average*) .... 90 mins. **Chapter Tests,** pp. 103–108 (*average*) .... 45 mins.	**Voices of Freedom** • Winning and Losing the Right to Vote, p. 129 (*average*) **Historical Outline Map Book** • Election of 1876, p. 54 (*average*)

Assessment Options

Teaching Resources
- Alternative Assessment booklet
- Section Quizzes, Unit 5, Chapter 18, pp. 29–32
- Chapter Tests, Chapter 18, pp. 103–108
- Test Bank CD-ROM

Student Performance Pack
- Guide to the Essentials of American History, Chapter 18 Test, p. 102
- Standardized Test Prep Handbook
- Interactive Student Tutorial CD-ROM

Interdisciplinary Connections

Teaching Resources
- Map Mystery, Unit 5, Chapter 18, p. 26
- Connecting History and Literature, Unit 5, Chapter 18, p. 27
- Interdisciplinary Connections, pp. 103–108

Voices of Freedom, pp. 126–129

Customized Reader, article VA-14

Historical Outline Map Book, p. 54

Technology

AmericanHeritage® History of the United States CD-ROM
- Time Tour: Rebuilding the Nation (1864–1877) in The Nation Torn Apart
- Presidents: Andrew Johnson, Ulysses S. Grant, Rutherford B. Hayes
- History Makers: Hiram Revels

Interactive Student Tutorial CD-ROM

Test Bank CD-ROM

Color Transparencies
- Andrew Johnson Mends the Union, p. G-19
- Dr. George Washington Carver, p. B-65

Guided Reading Audiotapes
(English/Spanish), side 7

Resource Pro® CD-ROM

Prentice Hall United States History Video Collection™
(Spanish track available on disc version.) Vol. 10, Chs. 7, 10, 16, 22, 25, 28, 31

Prentice Hall Home Page
www.phschool.com

Student Performance Pack

Guide to the Essentials of American History
- Ch. 18, pp. 98–102
  (Available in English and Spanish)

Guided Reading Audiotapes (English/Spanish), side 7

Standardized Test Prep Handbook

Interactive Student Tutorial CD-ROM

BLOCK SCHEDULING
Activities with this icon will help you meet your Block Scheduling needs.

ENGLISH LANGUAGE LEARNERS
Activities with this icon are suitable for English Language Learners.

TEAM TEACHING
Activities and Background Notes with this icon present starting points for Team Teaching.

Teachers' Bibliography

From the Archives of AmericanHeritage®

Don't miss the special American Heritage® teaching notes found in this chapter.

Contact Teachers' Curriculum Institute to learn more about History Alive!® resources on the Reconstruction era. See History Alive!® unit: The Civil War and Reconstruction, Section 4, "Reconstructing the Union."

Explore your library to find these issues related to Chapter 18: *The Civil War: Reconstruction,* May 1987; *Ulysses S. Grant,* October 1995.

Prentice Hall Web Site You can access a structured, on-line environment that allows you to preview curriculum-related resources and receive updated information on groundbreaking events from around the nation and the world. (www.phschool.com)

Chapter 18

The Reconstruction Era
1864–1877

Introducing the Chapter

Have students preview the main ideas of this chapter by looking over the visuals. Suggest they look for clues that reveal what life was like for African Americans following the Civil War.

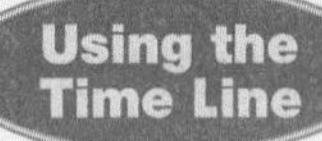

To provide students with practice in using the time line, ask questions such as these: **(1)** In what year did African American men win the vote? *(1870)* **(2)** What happened in Italy that same year? *(Italy was unified.)* **(3)** What happened in the United States the year that the Dominion of Canada was formed? *(The Reconstruction Act imposed strict measures on the South.)* **(4)** Did Congress pardon former Confederate officials before or after the House voted to impeach President Johnson? *(after)*

Ask students to define the term *prejudice.* Then ask this question: "What do you think is the root of prejudice?" Hold a class discussion about the reasons behind most prejudice (e.g., upbringing, lack of personal experience, misconceptions).

For additional *Why Study History?* support, see p. 494.

Chapter 18

The Reconstruction Era
1864–1877

What's Ahead

After the Civil War, rebuilding the ruined South was a tremendous job. Just as troubling was the task of bringing the former Confederate states back into the Union. Should southerners who had fought against the United States government be welcomed back or treated harshly? How could the nation protect the newly won rights of freed African Americans?

During a period called Reconstruction, North and South slowly reunited. At the same time, the economy of the South slowly recovered, and African Americans in the South gained several important rights and freedoms. However, in the years following Reconstruction, many of these rights were lost.

Why Study History?

During Reconstruction and after, many African Americans became victims of violence. Groups like the Ku Klux Klan used terror to prevent black citizens from voting. Today, Americans continue to battle "hate crimes" and encourage tolerance, or acceptance of all people. To focus on this connection, see the *Why Study History?* feature in this chapter, "Tolerance Begins With You."

American Events

- **1865** Abraham Lincoln is assassinated
- **1867** Reconstruction Act imposes strict measures on southern states
- **1868** House of Representatives votes to impeach President Johnson

1864 | 1866 | 1868 | 187

World Events

- **1864 World Event** Maximillian becomes Emperor of Mexico
- **1867 World Event** Dominion of Canada is formed

Viewing HISTORY **Reunion Begins**

This painting by Dennis Malone Carter shows Abraham Lincoln arriving in Richmond, Virginia. The President visited the captured Confederate capital during the final days of the Civil War. The painting shows Lincoln receiving a hero's welcome. In fact, though, many Richmond residents resented the visit by the leader of the victorious North. The reunion of the nation would not be easy. ★ **Predict two problems that the nation would face as the North and South reunited.**

1870 Fifteenth Amendment guarantees voting rights for African American men

1872 Congress pardons former Confederate officials

1877 Rutherford B. Hayes becomes President; Reconstruction ends

1870 | 1872 | 1874 | 1876

1870 World Event Italy is unified

1873 World Event Abolition of slave markets in Zanzibar

Writing Actively

Responding to Art Have students examine the painting on this page and read the caption. Then ask them to suppose that they are one of the African American characters in the painting. As that character, have students write a diary entry describing the exciting day when President Lincoln came to Richmond.

Viewing HISTORY ANSWER

Possible answer: The treatment of former slaves and rebuilding the South's economy would be problems for the reunited nation.

★ Background ★

Art Note

Reunion Begins Dennis Malone Carter attempted to rewrite history when he showed Lincoln as the conquering hero who was greeted by jubilant blacks and whites. In fact, a journalist who was an eyewitness to the scene later reported that the Confederates in the crowd turned away from Lincoln and his supporters "as if [they were] a disgusting sight."

Documents and Literature

On pp. 585–588, you will find two readings to enrich this chapter:

1. Eyewitness Account "A Southerner Looks to the Future," excerpts from a southern woman's diary describing life after the Civil War. (Use with Section 3.)

2. Literature "Out From This Place," an excerpt from a novel about freed slaves at the start of Reconstruction. (Use with Section 3.)

Technology

Videodiscs/Videotapes

Show the *Prentice Hall United States History Video Collection*™ segments for this chapter. The videodisc version has a Spanish track. Press audio until you get the left channel for English or the right channel for Spanish, or use the bar codes in the Guidebook.

AmericanHeritage® History of the United States CD-ROM

- Time Tour: Rebuilding the Nation (1864–1877) in The Nation Torn Apart (*average*)

Section 1 First Steps to Reunion

LESSON PLAN

Objectives

★ Describe the hardships the South faced after the Civil War.

★ Outline President Lincoln's plan for reuniting the nation.

★ Explain why Congress opposed President Johnson's Reconstruction plan.

1 Engage

Warm Up Ask students to explain the meaning of this passage from President Lincoln's second inaugural address: "With malice toward none; with charity for all." How do students think this relates to the period following the Civil War?

Activating Prior Knowledge Have students recall the differences between the North and South up to this time. Small groups of students should use this information to discuss what they think the reaction of the South will be to losing the war. Have them write down their predictions, for referring to after they have read the section.

Reading Actively

Before Reading Tell students to read the section title and to turn it into a question that they write at the top of a sheet of paper.

RESOURCE DIRECTORY

Teaching Resources
Lesson Planner, p. 75
Interdisciplinary Connections
• Main Idea: Reconstruction, p. 105

First Steps to Reunion

As You Read

Explore These Questions
- What hardships did the South face after the Civil War?
- What was President Lincoln's plan for reuniting the nation?
- Why did Congress oppose President Johnson's Reconstruction plan?

Define
- freedmen
- amnesty

Identify
- Reconstruction
- Ten Percent Plan
- Wade-Davis Bill
- Freedmen's Bureau
- John Wilkes Booth
- Andrew Johnson
- Thirteenth Amendment

SETTING the Scene At the end of the Civil War, the future looked bleak to many southerners. Susan Dabney Smedes described how her father, once a wealthy planter, coped with life after the war:

> "My father had come home to a house stripped of nearly every article of furniture and to a plantation stripped of the means of cultivating any but a small proportion of it. A few mules and one cow were all that were left of the stock.... When he was 70 years of age, he decided to grow a garden. He had never performed manual labor, but he now applied himself to learn to hoe as a way of supplying his family with vegetables."

The South faced staggering problems after the war. Southern cities and farmlands lay in ruins, and a whole way of life had ended. All southerners—rich and poor, black and white—faced a long, uphill struggle to rebuild their lives.

Postwar Problems

After four years of war, both northerners and southerners had to adjust to a changed world. The adjustment was far more difficult in the South.

The victorious North

Despite their victory, the North faced some economic problems after the Civil War. Some 800,000 returning Union soldiers needed jobs. Yet the government was canceling its war orders. Factories were laying off workers, not hiring them. Still, the North's economic disruption was only temporary. Boom times quickly returned.

The North lost more soldiers in the war than the South did. However, except for the battles of Gettysburg and Antietam, no fighting had taken place on northern soil. Northern farms and cities were hardly touched. One returning Union soldier remarked, "It seemed... as if I had been away only a day or two, and had just taken up... where I had left off."

The defeated South

Confederate soldiers had little chance of taking up where they left off. In some areas, every house, barn, and bridge had been destroyed. "The fine houses have fallen to decay or been burnt down," reported one witness, "the grounds neglected and grown over with weeds." Two thirds of the South's railroad tracks had been turned into twisted heaps of scrap. The cities of Columbia, Richmond, and Atlanta had been leveled.

The war wrecked the South's financial system. After the war, Confederate money was worthless. People who lent money to the Confederacy were never repaid. Many southern banks closed, and depositors lost their savings.

Southern society was changed forever by the war. No longer were there white owners

★ *Customized Instruction* ★

Extroverted Learners

Directing a multimedia presentation
Have interested students direct a multimedia presentation on one of the following topics: postwar problems in the North and South, the Freedmen's Bureau, Lincoln's assassination, or the conflict between Congress and President Johnson. Directors should work with a group of students to create a presentation that uses pictures, music, quotations, graphic organizers, overhead transparencies, and other media to explore their topic in depth. Directors are responsible for determining the focus of the presentation, assigning tasks to each member, overseeing rehearsals, and fine-tuning the project until it is ready to be presented to the class. (challenging) ELL T

and black slaves. Now, almost four million **freedmen**—men and women who had been slaves—lived in the South. Most had no land, no jobs, and no education. Under slavery, they had been forbidden to own property and to learn to read and write. What would become of them?

Early Plans for Reconstruction

Even before the war ended, President Lincoln worried about rebuilding the South. He wanted to make it fairly easy for southerners to rejoin the Union. The sooner the nation was reunited, Lincoln believed, the faster the South would be able to rebuild.

As early as 1863, Lincoln outlined a Reconstruction plan. **Reconstruction** refers to the rebuilding of the South after the Civil War. Under Lincoln's **Ten Percent Plan,** a southern state could form a new government after 10 percent of its voters swore an oath of loyalty to the United States. Once it was formed, the new government had to abolish slavery. Voters could then elect members of Congress and take part in the national government once again.

Lincoln's plan also offered **amnesty,** or a government pardon, to Confederates who swore loyalty to the Union. Amnesty would not apply to former leaders of the Confederacy, however.

Many Republicans in Congress felt that Lincoln's plan was too generous toward the South. In 1864, they passed the **Wade-Davis Bill,** a rival plan for Reconstruction. It required a majority of white men in each southern state to swear loyalty to the Union. It also denied the right to vote or hold office to anyone who had volunteered to fight for the Confederacy.

The Freedmen's Bureau

Lincoln refused to sign the Wade-Davis Bill because he felt it was too harsh. Congress and the President did agree on one proposal, however. One month before Lee

Linking Past and Present

Past

Present

Ruin and Revival

If you visit the city of Richmond, Virginia, today, you will see an attractive, modern city. You would not guess that, at one time, the city was largely in ruins. Rebuilding its cities and farms was one of the first tasks facing the South after the Civil War. ★ **Why was Richmond so badly damaged in the Civil War?**

As they read the section, have students jot down notes that will help them answer the question.

2 Explore

Ask students to read the section and then to research and report on the Freedmen's Bureau or the assassination of Lincoln.

3 Teach

Draw a three-column chart on the chalkboard and have students copy it into their notebooks. Tell them to use the chart to compare these three Reconstruction plans: those of Lincoln, congressional Republicans, and Andrew Johnson. Ask them these questions: "What did southerners have to do to regain voting rights under each plan? In order to hold office?"

4 Assess

To close the lesson, have students complete the section review; or have them work in pairs to compile a pollster's questionnaire that might have been used in the late 1800s to gauge the success of Reconstruction. Polls might focus on the work of the Freedmen's Bureau, various aspects of Johnson's plan for rebuilding the Union, and so on.

★ ★ ★ ★ ★ ★ ★ ★ ★ ★ ★ ★ ★ ★ ★ ★ ★

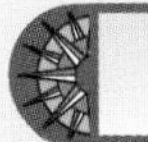

Linking Past and Present

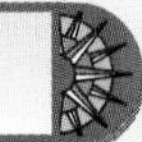

ANSWER

It had been the capital of the Confederacy, and several battles had been fought for control of the city.

★ *Background* ★

Viewpoints

Face-off An author of the Wade-Davis Bill, Ben Wade, at one point demanded that Lincoln fire General Grant. When Lincoln declined, Wade exploded, "This government is on the road to hell, sir, by reason of your obstinacy, and you are not a mile from there this minute!" Lincoln replied, "Senator, that is just about the distance from here to the Capitol, is it not?"

Technology

Videodiscs/Videotapes

Prentice Hall United States History Video Collection™, Vol. 10, Ch. 7, "Presidential Reconstruction," 5:50 mins (*average*) ELL

Chapter 7

Writing Actively

After Reading Have students write three or four main ideas for the section. Then have them read Sum It Up for this section at the end of the chapter. Ask students to compare their main ideas with those listed in Sum It Up.

Biography

ANSWER

Learning to read, write, and do arithmetic would help freedmen become independent and self-reliant. It was also a sign of their freedom, since they had been denied this right as slaves. Education would also increase their political and economic power.

RESOURCE DIRECTORY

Teaching Resources
Unit 5/Chapter 18
- Connecting History and Literature: "O Captain! My Captain!" p. 27
- Section 1 Quiz, p. 29

Interdisciplinary Connections
- Main Idea: Reconstruction, p. 107

Document-Based Discovery
- Sectionalism, pp. 18–21

Biography **Charlotte Forten**

Charlotte Forten came from a wealthy Philadelphia family. A strong abolitionist, she devoted her life to helping other African Americans improve their lives through education. When she was 25, she helped set up a school on the Sea Islands off South Carolina. Later, she helped recruit other teachers for the Freedmen's Bureau. ★ **Why do you think education was so important to freedmen?**

surrendered, Congress passed a bill creating the **Freedmen's Bureau.** Lincoln signed it.

The Freedmen's Bureau gave food and clothing to former slaves. It also tried to find jobs for freedmen. The bureau helped poor whites as well. It provided medical care for more than one million people. One former Confederate was amazed to see "a Government which was lately fighting us with fire, and sword, and shell, now generously feeding our poor and distressed."

One of the bureau's most important tasks was to set up schools for freed slaves in the South. By 1869, about 300,000 African Americans attended bureau schools. Most of the teachers were volunteers, often women, from the North.

Both old and young were eager to learn. Grandparents and grandchildren sat side by side in the classroom. One bureau agent in South Carolina observed that freedmen "will starve themselves, and go without clothes, in order to send their children to school." Charlotte Forten, an African American woman from Philadelphia, came south as a volunteer teacher. She wrote of her students:

> ❝ I never before saw children so eager to learn.... It is wonderful how a people who have been so long crushed to the earth... can have so great a desire for knowledge, and such a capacity for attaining it. ❞

The Freedmen's Bureau laid the foundation for the South's public school system. It set up more than 4,300 grade schools. It also created colleges for African American students, including Howard, Morehouse, and Fisk. Many graduates of these schools became teachers themselves. By the 1870s, African Americans were teaching in grade schools throughout the South.

Lincoln Is Assassinated

President Lincoln hoped to persuade Congress to accept his Reconstruction plan. However, he never got the chance.

On April 14, 1865, just five days after Lee's surrender, the President attended a play at Ford's Theater in Washington, D.C. As Lincoln watched the play, **John Wilkes Booth,** a popular actor from the South, crept into the President's box and shot Lincoln in the head. Within a few hours, the President was dead. Booth was later caught and killed in a barn outside the city.

Connections With Arts

Walt Whitman's famous poem "O Captain! My Captain!" expresses his grief at the death of Lincoln. It begins, "O Captain! my Captain! our fearful trip is done, / The ship has weather'd every rack, the prize we sought is won." You can find this and other Civil War poems in Whitman's collection *Leaves of Grass.*

★ *Activity* ★

Linking Past and Present

Researching a continuing saga Have students choose one of the colleges mentioned under the subhead The Freedmen's Bureau. Ask them to research and prepare a report on the history of that institution, its current mission, and the students who attend the college now. Suggest that students use the Internet as one source for information. (*basic*)

FROM THE ARCHIVES OF AmericanHeritage®

Family trade Edwin Booth, John Wilkes's older brother, was the nation's foremost Shakespearean actor. John was gaining respect as an actor before achieving infamy with the assassination of Lincoln. Perhaps not surprisingly, his interpretation of Hamlet was described by a fellow British actor as "insane [and] fiery."

Source: Arthur Nielsen, "The Time Machine," *American Heritage* magazine, November 1989.

The nation plunged into grief. Millions who had been celebrating the war's end now mourned Lincoln's death. "Now he belongs to the ages," commented Secretary of War Edwin Stanton.

A New President

Vice President **Andrew Johnson** became President when Lincoln died. Johnson had served as governor of Tennessee and had represented that state in Congress. When Tennessee seceded, Johnson had remained loyal to the Union.

At first, many Republicans in Congress were pleased when Johnson became President. They believed that he would support a strict Reconstruction plan. As it turned out, Johnson's plan was much milder than expected.

Playbill from Ford's Theater on the night Lincoln was shot

Johnson called for a majority of voters in each southern state to pledge loyalty to the United States. He also demanded that each state ratify the **Thirteenth Amendment,** which banned slavery throughout the nation. (As you have read, Lincoln's Emancipation Proclamation did not free slaves in states that remained loyal to the Union.) Congress had approved the Thirteenth Amendment in January 1865.

Rebellion in Congress

The southern states quickly met Johnson's conditions. As a result, the President approved their new state governments in late 1865. Voters in the South then elected representatives to Congress. Many of those elected had held office in the Confederacy. For example, Alexander Stephens, the former vice president of the Confederacy, was elected senator from Georgia.

Republicans in Congress were outraged. The men who had led the South out of the Union were being elected to the House and Senate. Also, no southern state allowed African Americans to vote.

When Congress met in December 1865, Republicans refused to let southern representatives take their seats. Instead, they set up a Joint Committee on Reconstruction to draw up a new plan for the South. The stage was set for a showdown between Congress and the President.

★ Section 1 Review ★

Recall

1. **Identify** **(a)** Reconstruction, **(b)** Ten Percent Plan, **(c)** Wade-Davis Bill, **(d)** Freedmen's Bureau, **(e)** John Wilkes Booth, **(f)** Andrew Johnson, **(g)** Thirteenth Amendment.
2. **Define** **(a)** freedmen, **(b)** amnesty.

Comprehension

3. Describe two problems the South faced after the Civil War.
4. **(a)** What was President Lincoln's Reconstruction plan? **(b)** How did it differ from the Wade-Davis Bill?
5. **(a)** What was President Johnson's plan for readmitting the former Confederate states to the Union? **(b)** How did Republicans in Congress react to Johnson's plan?

Critical Thinking and Writing

6. **Analyzing Information** The North lost more soldiers in the Civil War than the South did. Why was it easier for the North to recover from the war?
7. **Ranking** **(a)** What services did the Freedmen's Bureau provide? **(b)** Which do you think was most important? Explain.

Activity **Writing a Poem** President Lincoln has been shot! Taking the viewpoint of a northerner or southerner, write a poem about the death of Lincoln. If you like, you may set your poem to music.

★ Section 1 Review ★

ANSWERS

1. (a)–(c) p. 479, **(d)–(e)** p. 480, **(f)–(g)** p. 481

2. (a) p. 479, **(b)** p. 479

3. Cities and railroads were destroyed; 4 million freedmen had no land, jobs, or education.

4. (a) A state government could form if 10 percent of voters swore loyalty to the Union; once slavery was ended, voters could vote in national elections. **(b)** less harsh; Wade-Davis: majority of white men in a state had to swear loyalty; denied Confederate volunteers the right to vote or hold office

5. (a) a voting majority in each state to pledge loyalty; states to ratify the 13th Amendment **(b)** rejected it and southern representatives; created a new plan

6. North had not suffered physical destruction as South had; its economy was not dislocated by emancipation.

7. (a) basic necessities for freedmen and poor whites, schools for freed slaves **(b)** Possible answer: education, which enabled freedmen to become independent

Activity

Guided Instruction
Share with students Whitman's "Memories of President Lincoln."

ASSESSMENT See the rubrics in the Alternative Assessment booklet in the Teaching Resources.

★ Background ★

Did You Know?

History in words John Wilkes Booth broke his leg while escaping from Ford's Theater and went to the home of Dr. Samuel Mudd. Mudd, not knowing who Booth was, set the bone and was later imprisoned for conspiracy in Lincoln's murder. He was pardoned in 1869, but his name became synonymous with having a bad reputation: "Your name is mud (Mudd)."

Technology

AmericanHeritage® History of the United States CD-ROM
- Presidents: Andrew Johnson (*average*)

Section 2 Radical Reconstruction

LESSON PLAN

Objectives

★ Describe the goals of the Radical Republicans.

★ Explain why Congress tried to remove President Johnson from office.

★ Outline the provisions of the Fourteenth and Fifteenth Amendments.

1 Engage

Warm Up Ask students to define *radical* in their own words and to share names and/or images that they associate with the term.

Activating Prior Knowledge Ask students to recall the Republican position on slavery before the Civil War and then to hypothesize about the goals of Radical Republicans during Reconstruction.

Reading Actively

Before Reading In order to answer the questions in Explore These Questions, students should jot down notes as they read. They will then use these notes to write the answers to the Comprehension questions in the section review.

2 Explore

After students have read the section, ask volunteers to summarize the section, noting the following: In

RESOURCE DIRECTORY

Teaching Resources
Lesson Planner, p. 76
Interdisciplinary Connections
• Main Idea: Reconstruction, pp. 104, 106

Transparencies
Political Cartoons
• Andrew Johnson Mends the Union, p. G-19

Radical Reconstruction

As You Read

Explore These Questions

- What were the goals of the Radical Republicans?
- Why did Congress try to remove President Johnson from office?
- What were the Fourteenth and Fifteenth Amendments?

Define

- black codes
- radical
- impeach

Identify

- Radical Republicans
- Thaddeus Stevens
- Charles Sumner
- Fourteenth Amendment
- Radical Reconstruction
- Reconstruction Act
- Fifteenth Amendment

SETTING the Scene In the spring of 1866, disturbing reports trickled into Congress. In some southern cities, peddlers were openly selling Confederate flags. Throughout the South, people sang a new song, "I'm a good old rebel / And I don't want no pardon for anything I done."

These reports confirmed what many Republicans had suspected. "The rebellion has not ended," declared one angry Republican. "It has only changed its weapons!"

Black Codes

After the war, most southern states had promptly ratified the Thirteenth Amendment, which banned slavery. At the same time, however, Southern legislatures passed **black codes,** laws that severely limited the rights of freedmen.

Black codes forbade African Americans to vote, own guns, or serve on juries. In some states, African Americans were permitted to work only as servants or farm laborers. In others, the codes required freedmen to sign contracts for a year's work. Those without contracts could be arrested and sentenced to work on a plantation.

Black codes did give African Americans some rights they did not have before the Civil War. For example, the codes permitted African Americans to marry legally and to own some kinds of property. Still, the codes were clearly meant to keep freedmen from gaining political or economic power.

The North Reacts

Republicans were angered by the black codes, as well as by the election of former Confederate leaders to Congress. The Joint Committee on Reconstruction sent the President a report accusing the South of trying to "preserve slavery in its original form as much and as long as possible." When Johnson ignored the report, members of Congress vowed to take Reconstruction out of the President's hands.

Those who led the opposition to President Johnson were called **Radical Republicans,** or Radicals. A **radical** wants to make drastic changes in society. **Thaddeus Stevens** of Pennsylvania led the Radicals in the House. **Charles Sumner** of Massachusetts was the chief Radical Republican in the Senate.

Radicals had two main goals. First, they wanted to break the power of wealthy planters who had long ruled the South. Radicals blamed these "aristocrats" for the Civil War. Second, Radicals wanted to ensure that freedmen received the right to vote.

Radical Republicans did not control Congress. To accomplish their goals, they needed the support of moderate Republicans, the largest group in Congress. Moderates and Radicals disagreed on many issues. However, they shared a strong political motive for endorsing strict treatment of the South. Most southerners were Democrats. With southerners barred from Congress, Republicans easily controlled both houses.

482 ★ Chapter 18

★ *Background* ★

Recent Scholarship

Protesting black codes John David Smith reports in his 1996 book *Black Voices from Reconstruction* on a convention of South Carolina freedmen that was held in November 1865. These freedmen were no longer willing to accept meekly an inferior position in the society of those who had enslaved them. In their proceedings, they stated that "[N]ow that we are freemen . . . we have resolved to come forward, and, like MEN, speak and *act* for ourselves. . . . We ask for no special privileges or peculiar favors. We ask only for *even-handed Justice,* or for the removal of such . . . obstructions and disabilities as . . . legislators have seen fit to throw in our way, and heap upon us."

The President vs. Congress

The conflict between the President and Congress came to a head in 1866. In April, Congress passed the Civil Rights Act, giving citizenship to African Americans. Congress hoped to combat the black codes and secure basic rights for African Americans. When Johnson vetoed the bill, Congress overrode the veto.

The Fourteenth Amendment

Congressional Republicans worried that the Supreme Court might declare the Civil Rights Act unconstitutional. In the Dred Scott decision of 1857, the Court had ruled that African Americans were not citizens. Hoping to avoid a similar ruling, Republicans proposed the Fourteenth Amendment.

The **Fourteenth Amendment** granted citizenship to all persons born in the United States. This included nearly all African Americans. It also guaranteed all citizens "equal protection of the laws" and declared that no state could "deprive any person of life, liberty, or property without due process of law." This provision made it illegal for states to discriminate against an individual on unreasonable grounds, such as skin color.

The Fourteenth Amendment also provided that any state that denied African Americans the right to vote would have its representation in Congress reduced. Republicans believed that freedmen would be able to defend their rights if they could vote.

With the Fourteenth Amendment, Republicans hoped to secure basic political rights for African Americans in the South. In fact, the nation had far to go before all Americans achieved equality. Over the next 100 years, citizens would seek to obtain their rights by asking the courts to enforce the Fourteenth Amendment.

Election of 1866

President Johnson urged the former Confederate states to reject the Fourteenth Amendment. He also decided to make the amendment an issue in the November 1866 congressional elections. Traveling through the North, the President called on voters to reject the Radical Republicans.

FAMILY RECORD
BEFORE THE WAR AND SINCE THE WAR

Viewing History **New Rights for Freedmen**

Under the black codes, former slaves gained some new rights, such as the right to marry legally. Forms like this one helped freedmen keep their marriage and family records. ★ **Why were family records so valuable to freedmen?**

In many towns, audiences heckled the President. One heckler shouted that Johnson should hang Jefferson Davis. Losing his temper, Johnson yelled back, "Why not hang Thad Stevens?" Many northerners criticized Johnson for acting in an undignified manner.

In July, white mobs in New Orleans, Louisiana, killed 34 African Americans. This convinced many northerners that stronger measures were needed to protect freedmen.

In the end, the election results were a disaster for Johnson. Republicans won majorities in both houses of Congress. They also won every northern governorship and majorities in every northern state legislature.

The Radical Program

In 1867, Republicans in Congress prepared to take charge of Reconstruction. The period that followed is often called **Radical Reconstruction.** With huge majorities in

1866, Radical Republicans won a majority in Congress, championed a new Reconstruction policy that had a dramatic impact on the South, and brought impeachment charges against President Johnson.

3 Teach

Divide the class into 3 groups to conduct a debate on this resolution: "Resolved: that President Johnson should be impeached." Have each group assume one of the following roles: **(a)** Radical Republican senators for the resolution, **(b)** moderate Republican senators against it, or **(c)** moderators. Allow the groups time to prepare before offering their arguments. Moderators may ask questions and should decide which side was the most convincing.

4 Assess

To close the lesson, have students complete the section review; or have them write eight true/false questions about the section and then exchange papers and answer another student's questions. Review the questions and their answers as a class.

★ ★ ★ ★ ★ ★ ★ ★ ★ ★ ★ ★ ★ ★ ★ ★ ★

Viewing History ANSWER

They valued such records because they had not been allowed to have them as slaves. Southern laws did not recognize slave marriages before the Civil War, and this had made it hard for African Americans to keep their families together.

Internet Activity

Radical Republicans Have students go to the Smithsonian's Mathew Brady Gallery to learn more about Thaddeus Stevens: www.npg.si.edu/exh/brady/gallery/19gal.html. Ask them to note two new facts, then to seek other sites that mention Stevens or the Radical Republicans. Given the changing nature of the Internet, you may wish to preview sites. (*average*)

Technology

Videodiscs/Videotapes
Prentice Hall United States History Video Collection™, Vol. 10, Ch. 10, "Radical Reconstruction," 1:45 min (*average*) ELL

Writing Actively

After Reading Ask students to use the information in the chart on this page as the basis for a short essay on the various plans for Reconstruction that were proposed from 1863 to 1867.

Graphic Organizer Skills

ANSWERS **1.** Possible answers: **(a)** Both required a majority of white male voters to swear a loyalty oath. **(b)** Johnson's plan allowed former Confederate officials to vote and hold office, while the Wade-Davis bill did not. **2.** Possible answer: Since Lincoln wanted to make it fairly easy for southerners to rejoin the Union, he probably would not have supported the hard terms of the 1867 Reconstruction Act.

Resource Directory

Teaching Resources
Unit 5/Chapter 18
• Section 2 Quiz, p. 30

Rival Plans for Reconstruction

Plan	Ten Percent Plan	Wade-Davis Bill	Johnson Plan	Reconstruction Act
Proposed by	President Abraham Lincoln (1863)	Republicans in Congress (1864)	President Andrew Johnson (1865)	Radical Republicans (1867)
Conditions for former Confederate states to rejoin Union	▪ 10 percent of voters must swear loyalty to Union ▪ Must abolish slavery	▪ Majority of white men must swear loyalty ▪ Former Confederate volunteers cannot vote or hold office	▪ Majority of white men must swear loyalty ▪ Must ratify Thirteenth Amendment ▪ Former Confederate officials may vote and hold office	▪ Must disband state governments ▪ Must write new constitutions ▪ Must ratify Fourteenth Amendment ▪ African American men must be allowed to vote

Graphic Organizer Skills In the early years of Reconstruction, federal leaders debated several plans for readmitting southern states.

1. **Comprehension** **(a)** Identify one similarity between the Wade-Davis Bill and President Johnson's plan. **(b)** Identify one difference.
2. **Critical Thinking** If Lincoln had lived, do you think he would have supported the 1867 Reconstruction Act? Explain.

Civics

both the House and the Senate, Congress could easily override a presidential veto.

First Reconstruction Act

In March 1867, Congress passed the first **Reconstruction Act** over Johnson's veto. The Reconstruction Act threw out the southern state governments that had refused to ratify the Fourteenth Amendment—all the former Confederate states except Tennessee. The act also divided the South into five military districts under army control.

The Reconstruction Act required the former Confederate states to write new constitutions and to ratify the Fourteenth Amendment before rejoining the Union. Most important, the act stated that African Americans must be allowed to vote in all southern states.

Further Republican victories

Once the new constitutions were in place, the reconstructed states held elections to set up new state governments. To show their disgust with Radical Reconstruction policies, many white southerners stayed away from the polls. Freedmen, on the other hand, proudly turned out to exercise their new right to vote. As a result, Republicans gained control of all of the new southern state governments.

Congress passed several more Reconstruction acts. Each time, the Republicans easily overrode Johnson's veto.

Johnson Is Impeached

It was Johnson's duty, as President, to enforce the new Reconstruction laws. However, many Republicans feared he would not do so. Republicans in Congress decided to remove the President from office.

On February 24, 1868, the House of Representatives voted to impeach President Johnson. To **impeach** means to bring formal charges of wrongdoing against an elected

★ Customized Instruction ★
English Language Learners

Checking comprehension Make enough photocopies of the section so that each English language learner has one. As they read, have students underline key points in the section content. Review the points they have underlined to be sure they can pick out the main ideas in the section. Ask whether they have any questions about the meaning of the sentences they have underlined. Discuss their concerns until you are satisfied that they understand both the key points and the actual sentence structure and vocabulary. Then ask the students to use their underlined copy of the section to write a summary of the section. Distribute the summaries to the rest of the class as a tool for review. (average) ELL official. According to the Constitution, the House can impeach the President only for "high crimes and misdemeanors." The Senate tries the case. The President is removed from office only if found guilty by two thirds of the senators.

During Johnson's trial, it became clear that he was not guilty of high crimes and misdemeanors. Even Charles Sumner, the President's bitter foe, admitted that the charges were "political in character."

Despite intense pressure, seven Republican senators refused to vote for conviction. The Constitution, they believed, did not allow a President to be removed from office simply because he disagreed with Congress. In the end, the Senate vote was 35 for and 19 against impeachment—one vote short of the two-thirds majority needed to remove the President from office. Johnson served out the few remaining months of his term.

A New President

In 1868, Republicans nominated General Ulysses S. Grant as their candidate for President. Grant was the Union's greatest hero in the Civil War.

By election day, most of the southern states had rejoined the Union. As Congress demanded, the new southern governments allowed African Americans to vote. About 500,000 blacks went to the polls in the 1868 election. Nearly all cast their votes for Grant. He easily defeated his opponent, Horatio Seymour.

The Fifteenth Amendment

In 1869, Republicans in Congress proposed another amendment to the Constitution. The **Fifteenth Amendment** forbade any state to deny African Americans the right to vote because of their race.

Many Republicans had moral reasons for supporting the Fifteenth Amendment. They remembered the great sacrifices that were made by African American soldiers in the Civil War. They also felt it was wrong to let African Americans vote in the South but not in the North.

Some Republicans also supported the Fifteenth Amendment for political reasons. African American votes had brought Republicans victory in the South. If African Americans could also vote in the North, they would help Republicans to win elections there, too.

The Fifteenth Amendment was ratified in 1870. At last, all African American men over age 21 had the right to vote.

★ Section 2 Review ★

Recall

1. **Identify** (a) Radical Republicans, (b) Thaddeus Stevens, (c) Charles Sumner, (d) Fourteenth Amendment, (e) Radical Reconstruction, (f) Reconstruction Act, (g) Fifteenth Amendment.
2. **Define** (a) black codes, (b) radical, (c) impeach.

Comprehension

3. Describe the Reconstruction plan enacted by Congress in 1867.
4. (a) Why did Congress impeach President Johnson? (b) What was the result?
5. Describe the goals of: (a) the Fourteenth Amendment; (b) the Fifteenth Amendment.

Critical Thinking and Writing

6. **Defending a Position** (a) Compare Johnson's plan for Reconstruction with the Radical Reconstruction plan. (b) Which plan would you have supported? Defend your position.
7. **Analyzing Ideas** A senator who voted against the removal of President Johnson later said that he did not vote in favor of Johnson but in favor of the presidency. What do you think he meant?

Activity **Writing a Speech** Write a speech from the point of view of a radical or moderate Republican. Present your position on Reconstruction and give reasons for your opinion.

★ Section 2 Review ★

ANSWERS

1. (a)–(c) p. 482, **(d)–(e)** p. 483, **(f)** p. 484, **(g)** p. 485

2. (a) p. 482, **(b)** p. 482, **(c)** p. 484

3. It disbanded those southern state governments that rejected the 14th Amendment; created 5 southern military districts; made affected states write new constitutions, ratify the 14th Amendment, and extend the vote to black men.

4. (a) It feared he would not enforce its policies. **(b)** The Senate failed to impeach Johnson.

5. (a) 14th: basic political rights for African Americans **(b)** 15th: guaranteed voting rights for blacks

6. (a) Answers will vary, but all should note that Johnson's plan was less harsh. **(b)** Johnson's: restores the Union, and the country moves on; Radical Reconstructionists': ensures full rights for African Americans

7. that the impeachment effort had a political, not constitutional, basis; that voting for it would weaken the office and Constitution

Activity

Guided Instruction
Students should first create a chart comparing both positions. Remind them to include a topic sentence and conclusion.

ASSESSMENT See the rubrics in the Alternative Assessment booklet in the Teaching Resources.

FROM THE ARCHIVES OF AmericanHeritage®

Women vote In 1872, Susan B. Anthony, the women's rights activist, voted for Grant in the presidential election. As a result, she was tried and fined for violating federal electoral laws. In another case, the Supreme Court denied her argument that the 14th Amendment already granted women the right to vote.

Source: Frederic D. Schwarz, "The Time Machine," http://www.americanheritage.com/97/nov/timemachine/1872.htm#Anthony

★ Activity ★

Connections With Arts

Presenting a monologue Edmund Ross of Kansas was one of the senators who refused to vote for impeachment. His vote set off a firestorm of controversy and a House investigation into charges of corruption. Have students research his role in this historical drama and then present a monologue in Ross's voice on the reasons for his decision. *(average)* T

Technology

AmericanHeritage® History of the United States CD-ROM
- Presidents: Ulysses S. Grant *(average)*

Section 3

Changes in the South

LESSON PLAN

Objectives

★ List the groups that dominated southern politics during Reconstruction.

★ Summarize the steps taken by Reconstruction governments to rebuild the South.

★ Explain why many southerners sank into a cycle of poverty.

1 Engage

Warm Up Ask students to suppose that a smaller, younger child whom they have bullied in the past is now taller, stronger, and better coordinated than they are. How would the two of them react if they met each other now?

Activating Prior Knowledge Write on the chalkboard "Emancipation," "South Defeated," "14th Amendment," and "15th Amendment." Ask students: "How are these topics connected?" Then have them brainstorm about how white southerners might have reacted as political power shifted toward freedmen and Republicans during Reconstruction.

Reading Actively

Before Reading Ask students to look at section illustrations and headings and then write three sentences predicting what the section will discuss. They can check the predictions while reading.

RESOURCE DIRECTORY

Teaching Resources
Lesson Planner, p. 77
Unit 5/Chapter 18
• Biography Flashcard: Josephine White Griffing, p. 28

3 Changes in the South

As You Read

Explore These Questions
- What groups dominated southern politics during Reconstruction?
- What did Reconstruction governments do to rebuild the South?
- Why did many southerners sink into a cycle of poverty?

Define
- scalawag
- carpetbagger
- sharecropper

Identify
- Hiram Revels
- Blanche K. Bruce
- Conservatives
- Ku Klux Klan

SETTING the Scene By 1867, life in the South had changed dramatically. African Americans were free to work for themselves, to vote, and to run for office. In Alabama, a political convention of freedmen drew up this ringing declaration:

> ❝We claim exactly the same rights, privileges and immunities as are enjoyed by white men. We ask nothing more and will be content with nothing less.❞

Before the Civil War, a small group of rich planters controlled southern politics. During Reconstruction, however, new groups dominated state governments in the South. They tried to reshape southern politics. At the same time, others were taking strong action to reverse the gains made by African Americans.

New Forces in Southern Politics

The state governments created during Radical Reconstruction were different from any governments the South had known before. The old leaders had lost much of their influence. Three groups stepped in to replace them. These new groups were white southerners who supported the Republicans, northerners who moved south after the war, and African Americans.

Scalawags

Some white southerners supported the new Republican governments. Many were business people who had opposed secession in 1860. They wanted to forget the war and get on with rebuilding the South.

Many whites in the South felt that any southerner who helped the Republicans was a traitor. They called white southern Republicans **scalawags,** a word used for small, scruffy horses.

Carpetbaggers

Northerners who came south after the war were another important force. To white southerners, the new arrivals from the North were **carpetbaggers**—fortune hunters hoping to profit from the South's misery. Southerners claimed that these northerners were in such a hurry they had time only to fling a few clothes into cheap suitcases, or carpetbags.

To many southerners, the carpetbag became a hated symbol of Reconstruction.

In fact, northerners went south for a number of reasons. A few were fortune hunters who hoped to profit as the South was being rebuilt. Many more, however, were Union soldiers who had grown to love the South's rich land. Others, both white and

★ Background ★

Linking Past and Present

African Americans in government In 1966, Edward W. Brooke of Massachusetts became the first African American to be elected to the U.S. Senate since Reconstruction. Elected in 1992, Carol Moseley Braun of Illinois became the first African American woman senator. By 1995, 40 African Americans (a record number) were members of Congress.

Viewing HISTORY African Americans in Congress

During Reconstruction, several African Americans won election to Congress. Here, Robert Brown Elliott of South Carolina stands in the House of Representatives to argue for a civil rights bill. Words from his speech appear on the banner above. "What you give to one class, you must give to all. What you deny to one class, you shall deny to all." ★ **Summarize Elliott's main point in your own words.**

black, were teachers, ministers, and reformers who sincerely wanted to improve the lives of the freedmen.

African Americans

Freedmen and other African Americans were the third major new group in southern politics. Before the war, African Americans had no voice in southern government. During Reconstruction, they not only voted in large numbers, but they also ran for and were elected to public office in the South.

African Americans became sheriffs, mayors, and legislators in the new state and local governments. Between 1869 and 1880, 16 African Americans were elected to Congress.

Two African Americans, both representing Mississippi, served in the Senate. **Hiram Revels,** a clergyman and teacher, became the nation's first black senator in 1870. He completed the unfinished term of former Confederate president Jefferson Davis. In 1874, **Blanche K. Bruce** became the first African American to serve a full term in the Senate. Born into slavery, Bruce escaped to freedom when the Civil War began and later served as a country sheriff.

Freedmen had less political influence than many whites claimed, however. Only in South Carolina did African Americans win a majority in one house of the state legislature. No state elected a black governor.

Conservatives Resist

From the start, most prominent white southerners resisted Reconstruction. These **Conservatives** wanted the South to change as little as possible. They were willing to let African Americans vote and hold a few offices. Still, they were determined that real power would remain in the hands of whites.

A few wealthy planters tried to force African Americans back onto plantations. Many small farmers and laborers wanted the government to take action against the millions of freedmen who now competed with them for land and power.

Most of these white southerners were Democrats. They declared war on anyone who cooperated with the Republicans. "This is a white man's country," they cried, "and white men must govern it."

Spreading terror

White southerners formed secret societies to help them regain power. The most dangerous was the **Ku Klux Klan,** or KKK. The Klan worked to keep blacks and white Republicans out of office.

2 Explore

Ask students to read the section. Then discuss with them the challenges African Americans faced during Reconstruction. Ask students to respond to this statement: "It is remarkable that any African Americans at all served in public office during the 1800s."

3 Teach

Students should write 2 supporting facts for each of the following main ideas. **(a)** Three groups took control of state governments after the war. **(b)** Conservatives wanted to keep African Americans from gaining any real power. **(c)** Reconstruction governments tried to rebuild the South. **(d)** Many southerners were trapped in a cycle of poverty after the Civil War.

4 Assess

To close the lesson, have students complete the section review; or posing as one of the following southerners, they can write letters to the editor of a northern paper: a freedman newly elected to the state legislature, a scalawag, a small farmer. Letters should describe conditions in the South during Reconstruction and the writer's feelings about these conditions.

★ ★ ★ ★ ★ ★ ★ ★ ★ ★ ★ ★ ★ ★ ★ ★ ★ ★

ANSWER

Elliot wants all people to be treated equally.

★ *Background* ★

Our Diverse Nation

Defender of the downtrodden While a United States senator, Blanche K. Bruce was one of the few members of Congress to defend the rights of Native Americans against unfair federal laws. He said, "Our Indian policy and administration seem to me to have been inspired . . . by a stern selfishness." Bruce also campaigned against a measure to restrict Chinese immigration.

Technology

Videodiscs/Videotapes

Prentice Hall United States History Video Collection™, Vol. 10, Ch. 16, "The Fate of the Freedmen," 4:30 mins (*average*) ELL

AmericanHeritage® History of the United States CD-ROM

- History Makers: Hiram Revels (*average*)

Writing Actively

After Reading Ask students to write two or three main ideas for this section before reading the Sum It Up for the section at the end of the chapter. Then have them compare their main ideas with the main ideas of Sum It Up.

ANSWER

Possible answer: The two Klan actions shown are a lynching (execution) and the burning of a schoolhouse. It was worse than slavery because death (symbolized by a skull and crossbones) was now hanging over African Americans.

Viewing History — Spreading Terror

Wearing white hoods, the Ku Klux Klan used terror and violence to keep African Americans from voting. Famous cartoonist Thomas Nast attacked the Klan and other secret societies.

★ **Identify two Klan actions shown in the cartoon. Why do you think Nast labeled his cartoon "WORSE THAN SLAVERY"?**

Ku Klux Klan hood ➤

Dressed in white robes and hoods to hide their identity, Klansmen rode at night to the homes of African American voters, shouting threats and burning wooden crosses. When threats did not work, the Klan turned to violence. Klan members murdered hundreds of African Americans and their white allies.

Congress responds

Many moderate southerners condemned the violence of the Klan. Yet they could do little to stop the Klan's reign of terror. Freedmen turned to the federal government for help. In Kentucky, African American voters wrote to Congress:

> ❝We believe you are not familiar with the Ku Klux Klan's riding nightly over the country spreading terror wherever they go by robbing, whipping, and killing our people without provocation.❞

Congress tried to end Klan violence. In 1870, Congress made it a crime to use force to keep people from voting. As a result, Klan activities decreased. Yet the threat of violence lingered. Some African Americans continued to vote and hold office despite the risk. Many others were frightened away from the ballot box.

The Task of Rebuilding

Despite political problems, Reconstruction governments tried to rebuild the South. They built public schools for both black and white children. Many states gave women the right to own property. In addition, Reconstruction governments rebuilt railroads, telegraph lines, bridges, and roads. Between 1865 and 1879, the South put down 7,000 miles of railroad track.

Rebuilding cost money. Before the war, southerners paid very low taxes. Reconstruction governments raised taxes sharply. This created discontent among many southern whites.

Southerners were further angered by widespread corruption in the Reconstruction governments. One state legislature, for example, voted $1,000 to cover a member's bet on a horse race. Other items billed to the state included hams, perfume, and a coffin.

Corruption was not limited to the South. After the Civil War, dishonesty plagued northern governments as well. In fact, most southern officeholders served their states honestly.

A Cycle of Poverty

In the first months after the war, freedmen left the plantations on which they had

$ Connections With Economics

While the Ku Klux Klan carried out its program of violence, others used economic weapons to intimidate African Americans. Planters refused to rent land to blacks. Employers refused to hire them, and storekeepers denied them credit. What effect do you think such pressures had?

★ *Customized Instruction* ★

Introverted Learners

Compiling an annotated bibliography
Have students do library research to compile a list of books (both fiction and nonfiction), videos, and Internet Web sites that deal with the following topics that are discussed in this section: Reconstruction, the southern economy following the Civil War, and sharecropping. Ask students to annotate their bibliographies with a short description of each item. Then have them classify the entries into subject areas and identify the difficulty level of each work. When a student finishes the annotated bibliography, he or she should hand it out to the rest of the class members. They should then choose one of the items to view or read to further their understanding of the section. (challenging)

RESOURCE DIRECTORY

Teaching Resources
Unit 5/Chapter 18
- Practice Your Skills: Interpreting a Political Cartoon, p. 24
- Critical Thinking and Writing: Identifying Alternatives, p. 25

FOR LIFE

Critical Thinking | Managing Information | Communication | Maps, Charts, and Graphs

Interpreting a Political Cartoon

How Will I Use This Skill?

Almost every newspaper today includes political cartoons. Cartoonists comment on current events through both visual imagery and words. Their pictures often use symbols and exaggeration to make their point. Learning to analyze cartoons can help you better understand views on current issues.

LEARN the Skill

1. Identify the characters and symbols used in the cartoon. Remember that a symbol is an object that represents something beyond itself. The eagle, for example, is often used as a symbol for the United States.
2. Note details in the drawing. Are some details larger or smaller than normal? Are any facial features or actions in the cartoon exaggerated?
3. Analyze the relationship between the pictures and any words in the cartoon.
4. Identify the cartoonist's point of view. Try to identify policies or actions that the cartoonist wants readers to support.

PRACTICE the Skill

The cartoon on the right appeared in a northern newspaper in the 1870s. Use the steps above to analyze the cartoon.

1. The figure at the top of the cartoon is President Grant. Explain what these other symbols represent: (a) the woman; (b) the soldiers; (c) the carpetbag.
2. (a) Note the size of the details in this drawing. Are any larger than normal? Why? (b) What do Grant's facial expression and the position of his arms suggest about his attitude toward the South?
3. (a) What words are written on the paper sticking out of the carpetbag? What do they mean? (b) What is the woman doing? (c) Is her task easy or difficult?
4. (a) How do you think this cartoonist felt about Radical Reconstruction? Explain. (b) What policy do you think the cartoonist would want his readers to support?

APPLY the Skill

Find a current political cartoon in the editorial section of a newspaper. Using the skills you have learned in this section, write a paragraph explaining the cartoon.

★ Background ★
Did You Know?

Cowardice and hatred—dressed to kill The Ku Klux Klan was not a tiny, fringe group. In one southern state before 1868, Klansmen killed at least 1,000 people. Of the KKK, one former slave said, "Men you thought was your friends was Ku Kluxes, and you'd deal with them in the stores in the daytime, and at night they'd come out to your house and kill you."

★ Background ★
Recent Scholarship

The creative South Edward Ayer's *The Promise of the New South: Life After Reconstruction* examines the changing politics, economics, and race relations of the period. It gives new life to the times, however, with its focus on the fresh and passionate contributions of women, poor whites, and African Americans to American music, religion, and literature.

Skills FOR LIFE

PRACTICE the Skill ANSWERS

1. (a) the South **(b)** the Union army in the South **(c)** the North

2. (a) Larger: the carpetbag, which may represent the size of the North's role in the post-war South **(b)** Possible answer: that he favors harsh treatment of the South

3. (a) "Rule or Ruin." The South had to accept the North's rule or face ruin. **(b)** carrying the carpetbag **(c)** difficult; she is struggling.

4. Possible answers: **(a)** The cartoonist thought of it as a great burden on the South. **(b)** more lenient treatment toward the South that did not involve force

APPLY the Skill

Guided Instruction

Remind students that political cartoons in newspapers can cover local, state, national, or international issues. Suggest that their selection be on a familiar issue, one to which they can apply the skills taught in the lesson.

ASSESSMENT See the rubrics in the Alternative Assessment booklet in the Teaching Resources.

Technology

Videodiscs/Videotapes

Prentice Hall United States History Video Collection™, Vol. 10, Ch. 31, "Economic Reconstruction," 2:30 mins (*average*) ELL

Chapter 31

Vol. 10, Ch. 22, "The White Redeemers," 1 min (*average*) ELL

Chapter 22

★ Section 3 Review ★

ANSWERS

1. (a)–(d) p. 487

2. (a) p. 486, **(b)** p. 486, **(c)** p. 490

3. (a) Many held office in the South's new governments; a few won election to Congress. **(b)** Before the war, they could not vote and had no voice in government.

4. Possible answers: **(a)** They built public schools and rebuilt railroads and roads. **(b)** Taxes and corruption both increased.

5. Because they had no land, money, or credit, they farmed the land of large landowners, who gave them a share of the fall crop.

6. Possible answer: Since southern Conservatives believed that blacks were inferior, nothing blacks did would shake that belief.

7. (a) Possible answer: They often oppose them but may accept increases for some programs. **(b)** Answers may vary.

Activity

Guided Instruction
Before students create their own cartoons, have them review the elements and techniques of such cartoons. Give several examples from local papers; students can use these models as a guide. They can mount their efforts on large posterboard and display them.

ASSESSMENT See the rubrics in the Alternative Assessment booklet in the Teaching Resources.

RESOURCE DIRECTORY

Teaching Resources
Lesson Planner, p. 78
Unit 5/Chapter 18
• Section 3 Quiz, p. 31
Interdisciplinary Connections
• Main Idea: Reconstruction, p. 108

lived and worked. They found few opportunities, however.

"Nothing but freedom"

Some Radical Republicans talked about giving each freedman "40 acres and a mule." Thaddeus Stevens suggested breaking up big plantations and distributing the land. Most Americans opposed the plan, however. In the end, former slaves received—in the words of a freedman—"nothing but freedom."

Through hard work or good luck, some freedmen were able to become landowners. Most, however, had little choice but to return to where they had lived in slavery.

Sharecropping

Some large planters had held onto their land and wealth through the war. Now, they had land but no slaves to work it. During Reconstruction, many freedmen and poor whites went to work on the large plantations. These **sharecroppers** farmed the land, using seed, fertilizer, and tools provided by the planters. In return, the planters got a share of the crop at harvest time. Sharecroppers hoped to have their own land one day. Meanwhile, they were lucky to have enough food for themselves and their families.

Even farmers who owned land faced hard times. Each spring, the farmers received supplies on credit. In the fall, they had to repay what they had borrowed. Often, the harvest did not cover the debt. Unable to pay, many farmers lost their land and became sharecroppers themselves. Many southerners became locked in a cycle of poverty.

Sharecroppers growing cotton behind their cabin

★ Section 3 Review ★

Recall

1. **Identify** (a) Hiram Revels, (b) Blanche K. Bruce, (c) Conservatives, (d) Ku Klux Klan.
2. **Define** (a) scalawag, (b) carpetbagger, (c) sharecropper.

Comprehension

3. (a) What role did freedmen play in Reconstruction governments? (b) How was this different from the role of African Americans before the Civil War?
4. (a) What were two accomplishments of Reconstruction governments? (b) What were two problems?
5. Why did many freedmen and poor whites become sharecroppers?

Critical Thinking and Writing

6. **Understanding Causes and Effects** During Reconstruction, freedmen proved that, given the chance, they could do the same jobs as whites. Do you think this made southern Conservatives more willing or less willing to accept African Americans as equals? Explain.
7. **Linking Past and Present** Many southerners were angered by high taxes imposed by Reconstruction governments. (a) How do voters today feel about paying high taxes? (b) Do you think some services should be provided even if they require high taxes? Explain.

Activity **Drawing a Political Cartoon** Draw a political cartoon expressing your opinion about scalawags, carpetbaggers, the Ku Klux Klan, or another aspect of Reconstruction in the South.

★ Activity ★

Our Diverse Nation

Learning from oral history Explain that during the late 1800s, people interviewed former slaves to record their recollections of slave life. This technique is called oral history. Have students research some of these accounts for oral presentations before the class. One source of information is *Eyewitness: The Negro in American History* by William Loren Katz.

You might also suggest that several students discover more about the experiences of African American women during Reconstruction and share their findings with the class. Sources include passages from *Labor of Love, Labor of Sorrow* by Jacqueline Jones or *The Trouble They Seen: Black People Tell the Story of Reconstruction,* edited by Dorothy Sterling. (*average*)

Reconstruction Ends

As You Read

Explore These Questions
- Why did Reconstruction end?
- How did the southern economy expand after Reconstruction?
- How did African Americans in the South lose rights?

Define
- poll tax
- literacy test
- grandfather clause
- segregation
- lynching

Identify
- Rutherford B. Hayes
- Henry Grady
- James Duke
- Jim Crow laws
- *Plessy* v. *Ferguson*

SETTING the Scene In 1876, millions of Americans visited a great Centennial Exposition held in Philadelphia. The fair celebrated the first hundred years of the United States. Visitors gazed at the latest wonders of modern industry—the elevator, the telephone, a giant steam engine.

As Americans looked to the future, they lost interest in Reconstruction. By the late 1870s, white Conservatives had regained control of the South.

Radicals in Decline

By the 1870s, Radical Republicans were losing power in Congress. Many northerners grew weary of trying to reform the South. It was time to forget the Civil War, they believed, and let southerners run their own governments—even if that meant African Americans might lose their rights.

Republicans were also hurt by disclosure of widespread corruption in the government of President Grant. The President had appointed many friends to office. Some used their position to steal large sums of money from the government. Grant won reelection in 1872, but many northerners had lost faith in Republican leaders and their policies.

Congress reflected the new mood of the North. In May 1872, it passed the Amnesty Act, which restored the right to vote to nearly all white southerners. As expected, they voted solidly Democratic. At the same time, southern whites terrorized African Americans who tried to vote.

White Conservatives were firmly in control once more. One by one, the Republican governments in the South fell. By 1876, only three southern states—Louisiana, South Carolina, and Florida—were still controlled by Republicans.

Election of 1876

The end of Reconstruction came with the election of 1876. The Democrats nominated Samuel Tilden, governor of New York, for President. Tilden was known for fighting corruption. The Republican candidate was **Rutherford B. Hayes,** governor of Ohio. Like Tilden, Hayes vowed to fight dishonesty in government.

Tilden won 250,000 more popular votes than Hayes. However, Tilden had only 184 electoral votes—one vote short of the number needed to win. Twenty other votes were in dispute. The outcome of the election hung on these votes. All but one of the disputed votes came from Florida, Louisiana, and South Carolina—the three southern states still controlled by Republicans.

As inauguration day drew near, the nation still had no one to swear in as President. Congress set up a special commission to settle the crisis. A majority of the commission members were Republicans. The commission decided to give all the disputed electoral votes to Hayes.

Southern Democrats could have fought the election of Hayes. Hayes, however, had privately agreed to end Reconstruction. Once

Section 4
Reconstruction Ends

LESSON PLAN

Objectives
★ Explain why Reconstruction ended.
★ Describe how the southern economy expanded after Reconstruction.
★ Discuss how African Americans in the South lost rights.

1 Engage
Warm Up Tell students that historians still disagree about the success or failure of Reconstruction. Why do students think the question is so difficult to answer?

Activating Prior Knowledge Have students list the goals of Reconstruction and then indicate whether they were achieved.

Reading Actively **Before Reading** Ask students to turn the section title into a question and then take notes to help them answer it as they read.

2 Explore
Ask students to read the section. Then tell them that a financial panic swept the nation in the 1870s; it began with major fires in Boston and Chicago that hurt the insurance industry. The collapse of a prominent investment firm contributed to the panic. The

Technology

Videodiscs/Videotapes
Prentice Hall United States History Video Collection™, Vol. 10, Ch. 28, "The End of an Era," 1:50 min (*average*) ELL

Chapter 28

AmericanHeritage® History of the United States CD-ROM
- Presidents: Rutherford B. Hayes (*average*)

depression lasted 5 years and caused widespread unemployment and starvation. The crisis further weakened the North's commitment to Reconstruction.

3 Teach

Divide the class into small groups. Each group will create and name two southern characters: a white and an African American. They should create plausible personal histories for each character based on what they know about the Civil War and Reconstruction so far. Then have them write an outline for a movie script that would involve incidents and themes from the section.

4 Assess

To close the lesson, have students complete the section review; or have them give at least one cause for each of the following effects: "declining power of Radical Republicans in Congress," "loss of African American voting rights," "return of power to Democrats in the South," and "legal racial segregation."

* * * * * * * * * * * * * * * * * *

Geography Skills

ANSWERS **1.** Review locations with students. **2.** Tilden **3.** Possible answer: The map indicates that sectionalism was still strong after the Civil War. The vote is divided between North and South; Democrats won most of the southern vote and Republicans won most of the northern, midwestern, and western vote.

Resource Directory

Teaching Resources
Unit 5/Chapter 18
- Map Mystery: Voting Patterns in Reconstruction, p. 26

Transparencies
Interdisciplinary Connections
- Dr. George Washington Carver, p. B-65

in office, he removed all remaining federal troops from South Carolina, Louisiana, and Florida. Reconstruction was over.

Industry and the "New South"

During Reconstruction, the South made some progress toward rebuilding its economy. Cotton production, long the basis of the South's economy, slowly recovered. By 1880, planters were growing as much cotton as they had in 1860.

After Reconstruction, a new generation of southern leaders worked to expand the economy. **Henry Grady,** editor of the *Atlanta Constitution,* made stirring speeches calling for the growth of a "New South." Grady argued that the South should use its vast natural resources to build up its own industry, instead of depending on the North.

Agricultural industries

Southerners agreed that the best way to begin industrializing was to process the region's agricultural goods. Investors built textile mills to turn cotton into cloth. By 1880, the entire South was still producing fewer textiles than Massachusetts. In the next decade, though, more and more communities started building textile mills.

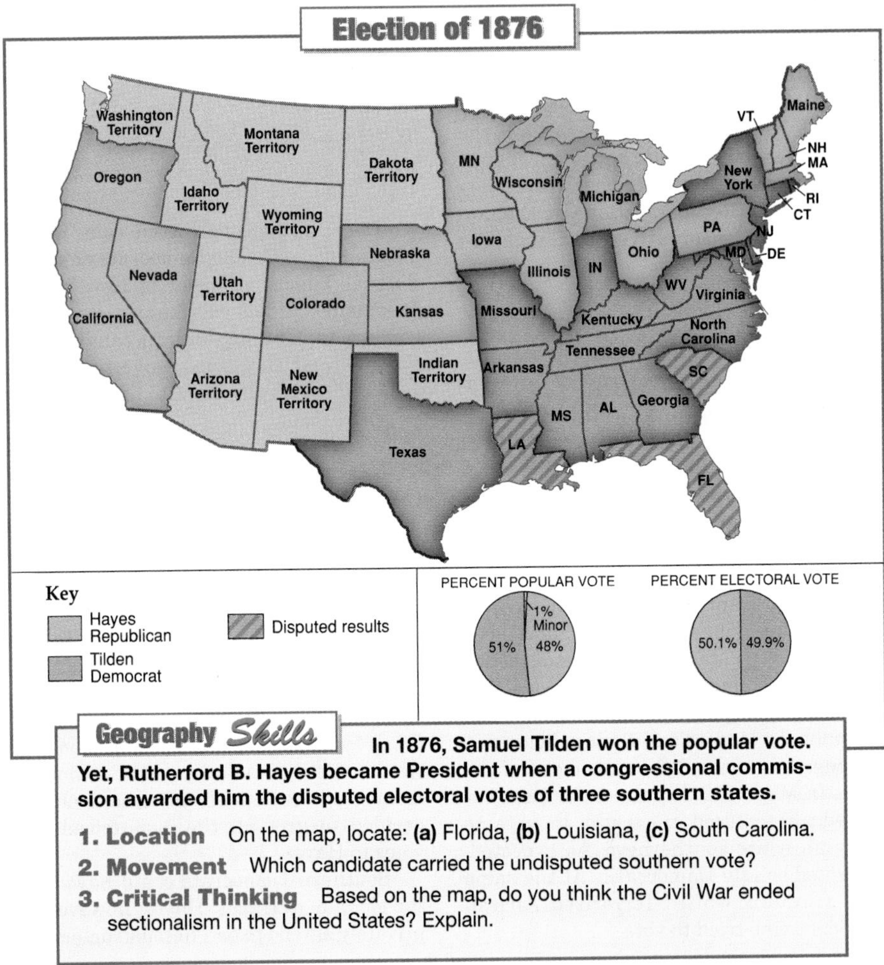

Geography Skills

In 1876, Samuel Tilden won the popular vote. Yet, Rutherford B. Hayes became President when a congressional commission awarded him the disputed electoral votes of three southern states.

1. **Location** On the map, locate: **(a)** Florida, **(b)** Louisiana, **(c)** South Carolina.
2. **Movement** Which candidate carried the undisputed southern vote?
3. **Critical Thinking** Based on the map, do you think the Civil War ended sectionalism in the United States? Explain.

Skills for Life Mini Lesson

CRITICAL THINKING Exploring Local History

1. You might introduce the skill of exploring local history by explaining that many sources, including the public library, local historical societies, elderly people in the community, and old newspapers, can provide interesting material. Point out to students that local historical material can complement and enrich the study of the history of the American nation.

2. Help students to practice the skill by providing photocopies of old local newspapers for them to study. Have them write a summary of the events reported in the papers for a given day.

3. Have students apply the skill by doing research at the local library or historical society on local events between 1864 and 1877 and sharing their findings with the class.

The tobacco industry also grew rapidly. In North Carolina, **James Duke** used new machinery to revolutionize production of tobacco products. In 1890, he bought out several competitors to form the American Tobacco Company. Duke eventually controlled 90 percent of the nation's tobacco industry.

New industries

The South also tapped its mineral resources. Local deposits of iron ore and coal, as well as low wages for workers, made steel production cheaper in Alabama than in Pennsylvania. Oil refineries developed in Louisiana and Texas. Other states became leading producers of coal, copper, granite, and marble.

By the 1890s, many northern forests had been cut down. The southern yellow pine was competing with the northwestern white pine as a lumber source. Some southern factories began to make cypress shingles and hardwood furniture.

A visitor from New England described what he found on a visit to the South in 1887:

> "We find a South wide awake with business, excited and even astonished at the development of its own immense resources in metals, marbles, coal, timber, fertilizers, eagerly laying lines of communication, rapidly opening mines, building furnaces, foundries, and all sorts of shops for utilizing the native riches."

By 1900, the South had developed a more balanced economy. Still, it failed to keep up with even more rapid growth in the North and the West.

Viewing History **Rise of the New South**

From Darkness to Light *by Grant Hamilton shows the New South rising from the ruins of war. Hamilton created this picture for one of several industrial expositions held in Atlanta, Georgia, in the late 1800s.* ★ **According to this picture, what products helped the southern economy grow?**

Restricting the Rights of African Americans

The years after Reconstruction brought prosperity to some southerners. For African Americans, though, the end of Reconstruction had tragic effects.

With the North out of southern affairs, white Conservatives tightened their grip on southern governments. Some groups continued to use violence to keep African Americans from voting. Southern states also found new ways to keep African Americans from exercising their rights.

Voting restrictions

In the 1880s, many southern states began passing new laws that restricted the right to vote. **Poll taxes** required voters to pay a fee each time they voted. As a result, poor freedmen could rarely afford to vote. **Literacy tests** required voters to read and explain a section of the Constitution. Since most freedmen had little education, such tests kept them away from the polls.

Many poor southern whites also could not pass the literacy test. To increase the number of eligible white voters, states passed **grandfather clauses.** If a voter's father or grandfather had been eligible to vote on January 1, 1867, the voter did not have to take

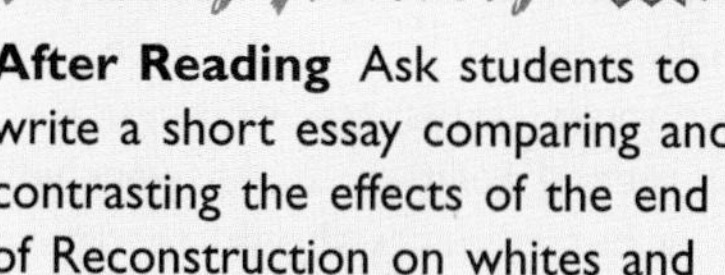

Reading Actively

During Reading Refer students to the map on the opposite page. As they read the section, ask them to take notes on how the disputed electoral votes were assigned in the election of 1876 and what impact the election results had in the South.

Writing Actively

After Reading Ask students to write a short essay comparing and contrasting the effects of the end of Reconstruction on whites and blacks in the South.

Viewing History ANSWER

cotton, pig iron, iron, tobacco, steel, and sugar

★ *Customized Instruction* ★

Auditory Learners

Recording a radio talk show After they read the section, have students form small groups to prepare and record a radio talk show that might have taken place in 1876 or 1877. Each group should include a host and several "experts" who are guests on the show. Possibilities include politicians commenting on the controversy surrounding the election of 1876, James Duke or another southern industrialist, and an African American state legislator. Talk shows can be scripted or impromptu, but questions from the host should focus on issues relevant to the section. Remind students that the more enthusiastic the talk show guests are, the more interesting the show will be for listeners. Students should tape-record their radio show and play it for the class. (*challenging*)

Technology

Videodiscs/Videotapes

Prentice Hall United States History Video Collection™, Vol. 10, Ch. 25, "The Persistence of Racism in the North," 1:15 min (*average*) ELL

Chapter 25

Why Study History?

ANSWERS

1. (a) They used violence and terror against African Americans, setting fire to homes, churches, and schools and even lynching people. **(b)** Students may mention discrimination based on religion, race, economic status, age, or physical or mental abilities. **2.** Answers will vary, but students should recognize that prejudice and discrimination are rooted in fear of and ignorance about those who are different. Prejudice and discrimination can result when people see others as representative of a group rather than as individuals.

★Activity

Guided Instruction

You might have students work in groups to create their posters. Group members might first work individually to list ways to promote tolerance. Then, as a group, the members can choose the three best ways and decide which one to illustrate in their poster. You may wish to display the finished posters in the classroom or elsewhere in the school.

ASSESSMENT See the rubrics in the Alternative Assessment booklet in the Teaching Resources.

Why Study History?

Because Tolerance Begins With You

Historical Background

During and after Reconstruction, hate groups like the Ku Klux Klan used violence and terror to keep African Americans from voting or holding any political office. Angry mobs set fire to African American homes, churches, and schools. They even lynched people. Often, these tactics worked. Yet many whites and African Americans continued to speak out against injustice.

Artist Jim Osborn created this painting to encourage respect and tolerance.

Connections to Today

Discrimination and hate crimes have not been limited to African Americans in the South in the 1800s. Almost every group in this nation has suffered the pain of senseless hatred. People feel the sting of prejudice for many reasons: religion, race, economic status, age, or physical or mental abilities.

Acts of prejudice continue today. In recent years, Jewish cemeteries have been vandalized. African American churches have been burned. Asian American stores have been covered in racist graffiti. Mexican American or Arab American businesses have been attacked. In some areas, police have set up special "hate crime" units to investigate actions such as these.

Connections to You

Tolerance begins with you. You can fight prejudice by respecting and appreciating people's differences. Everyone in your class has different talents and experiences. You can get to know your classmates for who they are, rather than on the basis of what you think you know about them. You will find that you have much in common with students who seem different.

Many schools provide opportunities for you to increase your ability to get along with others. Human relations clubs promote understanding of diverse groups. Peer-mediation programs can teach you how to deal with anger and conflict. By keeping an open mind and educating yourself, you can help end discrimination and prejudice.

1. **Comprehension** **(a)** What tactics did hate groups use against African Americans in the South? **(b)** Identify two kinds of discrimination some people face today.
2. **Critical Thinking** How do prejudice and discrimination begin?

Making a Poster Make a list of three things that you could do to promote tolerance. Create a poster illustrating one of them.

Resource Directory

Teaching Resources
Unit 5/Chapter 18
- Vocabulary Builder, p. 23
- Section 4 Quiz, p. 32

Chapter Tests, pp. 103–108
Why Study History?
- Tolerance Begins With You, pp. 71–74

Fast Facts

★ The Ku Klux Klan reemerged after World War I. By 1924, no longer limited to the South, it had 4–5 million members.

★ A 65-year-old mystery was solved in 1935 when a respected businessman died and left a confession admitting his role in the 1870 KKK execution of a state senator.

★ White women joined the Ku Klux Klan in record numbers during the 1920s—they made up half the membership in some states.

Bibliography

To read more about this topic:

1. *United They Hate: White Supremacist Groups in America,* Michael Kronenwetter (Walker & Co, 1992). Analyzes the motives and weaknesses of such groups.

2. *Social Justice: Opposing Viewpoints,* David Bender, ed. (Greenhaven Press, 1990). Debates on social issues (e.g., race, gender).

3. Internet. Resources for teachers for promoting equity and respect. (www.splcenter.org/teachingtolerance.html)

a literacy test. Since no African Americans in the South could vote before 1868, grandfather clauses were a way to ensure that only white men could vote.

Racial segregation

Southern blacks lost more than the right to vote. After 1877, segregation became the law of the South. **Segregation** means separating people of different races in public places. Southern states passed laws that separated blacks and whites in schools, restaurants, theaters, trains, streetcars, playgrounds, hospitals, and even cemeteries. **Jim Crow laws,** as they were known, trapped southern blacks in a hopeless situation. In 1885, the Louisiana novelist George Washington Cable described segregation as:

> "... a system of oppression so rank that nothing could make it seem small except the fact that [African Americans] had already been ground under it for a century and a half."

African Americans brought lawsuits to challenge segregation. In 1896, in the case of ***Plessy* v. *Ferguson*,** the Supreme Court ruled that segregation was legal so long as facilities for blacks and whites were equal. In fact, facilities were rarely equal. For example, southern states spent much less on schools for blacks than for whites.

Violence

When Reconstruction ended, groups like the Ku Klux Klan declined. However, violent acts against African Americans continued. During the 1890s, almost 200 Americans were lynched each year. **Lynching** is the illegal seizure and execution of someone by a mob. Four out of five lynchings took place in the South, and the majority of the victims were African American.

Some lynching victims were accused of crimes. Others were simply considered troublemakers. Victims—including some women and children—were hanged, shot, or burned to death, often after painful torture. Members of lynch mobs rarely faced punishment. By the late 1800s, some reformers began to speak out against lynching.

Results of Reconstruction

Reconstruction was a time of both success and failure. Southerners faced hard times. Still, the South gained a public education system and expanded its rail lines.

As a result of Reconstruction, all African Americans became citizens for the first time. These rights eroded after Reconstruction ended. However, the laws passed during Reconstruction, such as the Fourteenth Amendment, became the basis of the civil rights movement almost 100 years later.

★ Section 4 Review ★

Recall

1. **Identify** **(a)** Rutherford B. Hayes, **(b)** Henry Grady, **(c)** James Duke, **(d)** Jim Crow laws, **(e)** *Plessy* v. *Ferguson*.
2. **Define** **(a)** poll tax, **(b)** literacy test, **(c)** grandfather clause, **(d)** segregation, **(e)** lynching.

Comprehension

3. Why did Radical Republicans' power decline?
4. How did the economy of the South change?
5. Describe two ways that African Americans lost their rights after Reconstruction ended.

Critical Thinking and Writing

6. **Evaluating Information** Do you think that Reconstruction was successful? Explain.
7. **Predicting Consequences** How do you think *Plessy* v. *Ferguson* affected later efforts to achieve equality for African Americans?

Activity **Acting a Scene** With a partner, act out a scene of an African American man trying to vote in the South in the late 1880s. Begin by considering how you might feel if you knew that you had the right to vote, yet someone was able to prevent you from voting.

★ Section 4 Review ★

ANSWERS

1. **(a)** p. 491, **(b)** p. 492, **(c)** p. 493, **(d)** p. 495, **(e)** p. 495

2. **(a)–(c)** p. 493, **(d)–(e)** p. 495

3. Many northerners wanted to forget the Civil War and let the South run its own affairs; Republicans were hurt by corruption.

4. It became more balanced, with the regional processing of cotton and tobacco and the industrial use of regional metals and coal.

5. Voting rights were lost (e.g., poll taxes); segregation became law.

6. Possible answers: Successful: Blacks became citizens who could vote. Unsuccessful: Racism still exists.

7. Students should realize that the decision hurt blacks because it gave whites a legal excuse to deprive blacks of their rights.

Activity

Guided Instruction
Ask students to consider possible obstacles to voting (e.g., poll taxes). Students can use this outline: **(a)** thoughts when going to the polls; **(b)** talking with officials; **(c)** first problem; **(d)** solution; **(e)** second problem; **(f)** failed solution; **(g)** final thoughts.

ASSESSMENT See the rubrics in the Alternative Assessment booklet in the Teaching Resources.

★ *Activity* ★
Cooperative Learning

Creating scrapbooks Have students work together in small groups to prepare scrapbooks about Reconstruction in the South. Students should use cardboard for pages and then create drawings, cartoons, newspaper headlines, collages, and other "memorabilia" to glue into the scrapbook. Each item should have a short caption explaining the item's relevance to Reconstruction. The book should be divided into two sections: "Reconstruction: The Good" and "Reconstruction: The Bad." (*average*)  ELL

Technology

CD-ROM
Test Bank CD-ROM, Ch. 18
Interactive Student Tutorial

Chapter 18

Review and Activities

Reviewing the Chapter

Define These Terms

1. d **2.** a **3.** c **4.** b **5.** e

Explore the Main Ideas

1. The South was in ruins after the Civil War. In some areas, every structure had been destroyed. Two-thirds of the South's railroads had been destroyed, and the cities of Columbia, Richmond, and Atlanta had been leveled.

2. After the election of 1866, Republicans had overwhelming majorities in both the House and Senate, a situation which allowed them to push through their own measures by overriding Johnson's vetoes.

3. For political reasons: African Americans voting in the North could bring Republicans more political power. For moral reasons: Republicans remembered the sacrifices of African Americans in the war and also felt it was wrong to let them vote in the South but not in the North.

4. Cotton production recovered slowly. The southern economy also expanded in other areas, such as textile mills, tobacco, minerals, and forest-related industries.

5. They looked to the future, grew weary of trying to reform the South, and wanted to forget the Civil War.

6. Jim Crow laws segregated blacks from whites in public places.

Geography Activity

1. E **2.** D **3.** C **4.** A **5.** B

Region Florida, Louisiana, and South Carolina

Critical Thinking and Writing

1. (a) the Ten Percent Plan; the Wade-Davis Bill; the Reconstruction Acts; Jim Crow laws **(b)** He was assassinated just five days after Lee's surrender.

Chapter 18 Review and Activities

★ Sum It Up ★

Section 1 First Steps to Reunion

- After the Civil War, the South faced the task of repairing tremendous destruction.
- The Freedmen's Bureau helped newly freed African Americans learn to read, and provided food and clothing to the needy.
- Presidents Lincoln and Johnson recommended mild plans for Reconstruction, but Congress refused to accept either one.

Section 2 Radical Reconstruction

- Radical Republicans wanted to break the power of rich planters in the South and make sure that freedmen could vote.
- Congress tried and failed to remove President Johnson from office.
- Republicans proposed the Fourteenth and Fifteenth amendments to ensure the civil rights of African Americans.

Section 3 Changes in the South

- Southern Republicans, whites from the North, and freed African Americans played important roles in southern governments.
- Landless black and white sharecroppers became locked in a cycle of poverty.

Section 4 Reconstruction Ends

- Reconstruction ended after presidential candidate Rutherford B. Hayes made a private deal with southern politicians.
- After Reconstruction, a new industrial economy began to emerge in the South.
- Southern whites passed new laws to deny African Americans equal rights.

For additional review of the major ideas of Chapter 18, see ***Guide to the Essentials of American History*** or ***Interactive Student Tutorial CD-ROM,*** which contains interactive review activities, graphic organizers, and practice tests.

Reviewing the Chapter

Define These Terms

Match each term with the correct definition.

Column 1	Column 2
1. freedman	**a.** laws that severely limited the rights of freedmen
2. black codes	**b.** tax required before someone could vote
3. scalawag	**c.** white southern Republican
4. poll tax	**d.** former slave
5. segregation	**e.** separating people of different races in public places

Explore the Main Ideas

1. Describe the condition of the South after the war.
2. How did Republicans in Congress gain control of Reconstruction?
3. Give two reasons why Republicans supported the Fifteenth Amendment.
4. Describe the economic recovery of the South after the Civil War.
5. Why did most Americans lose interest in Reconstruction in the 1870s?
6. What was the purpose of Jim Crow laws?

Geography Activity

Match the letters on the map with the following places: **1.** South Carolina, **2.** Florida, **3.** Louisiana, **4.** Ohio, **5.** New York. **Region** Which southern states were under Republican control in 1876?

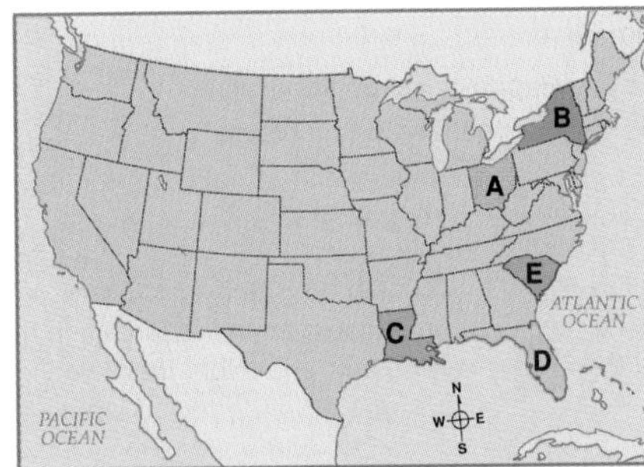

2. Answers should reflect an understanding of the sectional differences that continued after the Civil War (the South's lack of industry and the aftereffects of slavery), and answers should also propose ways of dealing with these issues.

3. Possible answer: They contradict American values, because they believe that whites are naturally superior and should actively restrict other groups' freedoms and opportunities.

4. Possible answer: The destruction of its infrastructure prevented the South from participating fully in the industrial growth of the postwar era.

Using Primary Sources

(a) The slaves rejoiced because they now had their freedom. **(b)** Their rejoicing ended because they began to understand the new burdens freedom would impose on them. **(c)** They had no experience of freedom in the outside world.

496 ★ Chapter 18

Critical Thinking and Writing

1. **Understanding Chronology** **(a)** Put the following in the order in which they were first proposed: the Reconstruction Acts; the Wade-Davis Bill; the Ten Percent Plan; Jim Crow laws. **(b)** Why did Lincoln have so little influence on Reconstruction?
2. Exploring Unit Themes **Sectionalism** Briefly state your own plan for repairing the bitter feelings between North and South.
3. **Analyzing Ideas** Most people call groups such as the Ku Klux Klan "un-American." Explain the reasons for this belief.
4. **Predicting Consequences** After the Civil War, the United States entered a period of industrial growth that made it the richest nation in the world. How do you think the South's experiences during Reconstruction affected its share in this industrial boom?

Using Primary Sources

Born into slavery, Booker T. Washington became a leading educator. Here, he describes one of the problems that came with emancipation:

> "Was it any wonder that within a few hours the wild rejoicing ceased and a feeling of deep gloom seemed to pervade the slave quarters? To some it seemed that, now that they were in actual possession of it, freedom was a more serious thing than they expected to find it. Some of the slaves were seventy or eighty years old; their best days were gone. They had no strength with which to earn a living in a strange place and among strange people, even if they had been sure where to find a new place of abode."

Source: *Up From Slavery,* Booker T. Washington, 1901.

Recognizing Points of View **(a)** What caused the "wild rejoicing" Washington mentions? **(b)** Why did the rejoicing end so quickly? **(c)** Why do you think many African Americans were unprepared for the realities of freedom?

Activity Bank

Interdisciplinary Activity

Connections With Arts Review the goals of the Freedmen's Bureau. Then create a poster advertising the Bureau's work and encouraging volunteers to participate.

Career Skills Activity

Playwrights and Actors Find out more about the events and issues leading up to the trial of President Andrew Johnson. Then prepare a skit in which you act out Johnson's trial in the United States Senate.

Citizenship Activity

Understanding the Constitution Study the text of the Fourteenth and Fifteenth amendments printed in the Reference Section. Create a graphic organizer for each amendment. Include the main ideas of each amendment and show how it affects the daily lives of Americans today. You may illustrate your work with original drawings or clippings.

Internet Activity

Use the Internet to find primary sources on Reconstruction. Then use the primary source to create a newspaper interview with the person who wrote the material you have found. Create questions that are answered by quotations taken from the primary source.

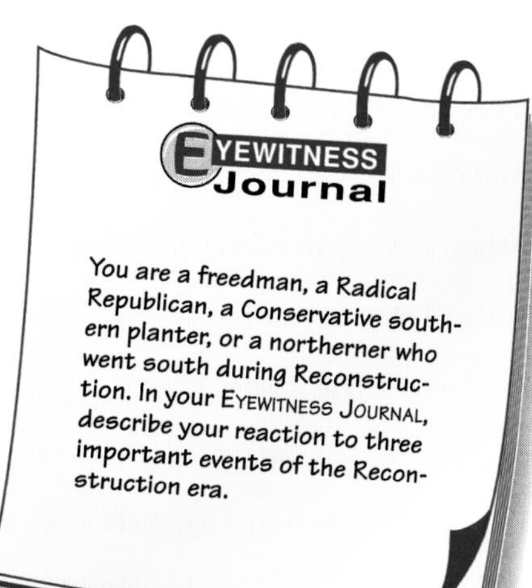

EYEWITNESS Journal
You are a freedman, a Radical Republican, a Conservative southern planter, or a northerner who went south during Reconstruction. In your EYEWITNESS JOURNAL, describe your reaction to three important events of the Reconstruction era.

Activity Bank

ASSESSMENT To assess the activities on this page, see the rubrics in the Alternative Assessment booklet in the Teaching Resources. You might want to share the rubrics with your students before they begin work.

Interdisciplinary Activity

1. Reassure students that they will not be evaluated on the basis of their artistic ability. Emphasize, however, that posters should capture the interest of prospective volunteers and accurately present the work of the Freedmen's Bureau.

2. You may wish to combine this activity with the Internet activity. Students can use the Internet to find information to make their posters more interesting and authentic.

Career Skills Activity

1. Encourage students to attempt to realistically portray what certain people might have said during the trial.

2. Ask students to try to express the personalities and opinions of the characters through movement, facial expression, and voice inflection.

3. If you feel the skit warrants it, invite other classes to a special repeat performance.

Citizenship Activity

1. Because the rights given by the amendments are ones we now take for granted, ask students to imagine situations that could occur today if these amendments were not in place.

2. When students begin to add artwork to their organizers, ask them to think of symbols that might reflect the main ideas of each amendment and its impact.

Eyewitness Journal

1. Ask students to reread Sections 1, 2, and 3 to review information on these points of view.

2. Point out to students that viewpoints might overlap and differ at the same time. Suggest they try to remain open-minded in their journals and to avoid stereotypes or simplification.

Internet Activity

1. Have students go to www.phschool.com, which contains updated information on a variety of topics.

2. Another site you may find useful for this activity is Andrew Johnson's biography at www.whitehouse.gov/WH/glimpse/presidents/html/aj17.html.

3. Given the changing nature of the Internet, you may wish to preview this site.

History Through Literature

The Red Badge of Courage

by Stephen Crane

Author Note

Stephen Crane Often called the first modern American writer, Stephen Crane (1871–1900) was a newspaper reporter, novelist, poet, and short-story writer. His works are known for their naturalism—for their objective and realistic presentation of characters and situations. *The Red Badge of Courage* (1895) is Crane's most popular novel.

Build Vocabulary

Have students look up and discuss *doggedly, shirking, monotonous, province, pickets, philosophical, reflectively, reproached, infantile,* and *assurance* before they read. Ask: "To what aspects of military life do words such as *doggedly* and *monotonous* apply? Why do you think a war story has so many words related to thought (such as *philosophical, reflectively,* and *assurance*)?"

Prereading Focus

You might have students reread Section 4 in Chapter 15 to review what they learned about life in the military during the Civil War.

Connect Your Experience

Have students list several Civil War military leaders. Ask: "What do you remember about each one?" and "How would you feel if you rarely saw your leaders in action?"

Purpose-Setting Question

If students have understood Unit 5, they realize the destructiveness of war. Ask: "If war can be so terrible, why do soldiers like Henry Fleming volunteer to fight?"

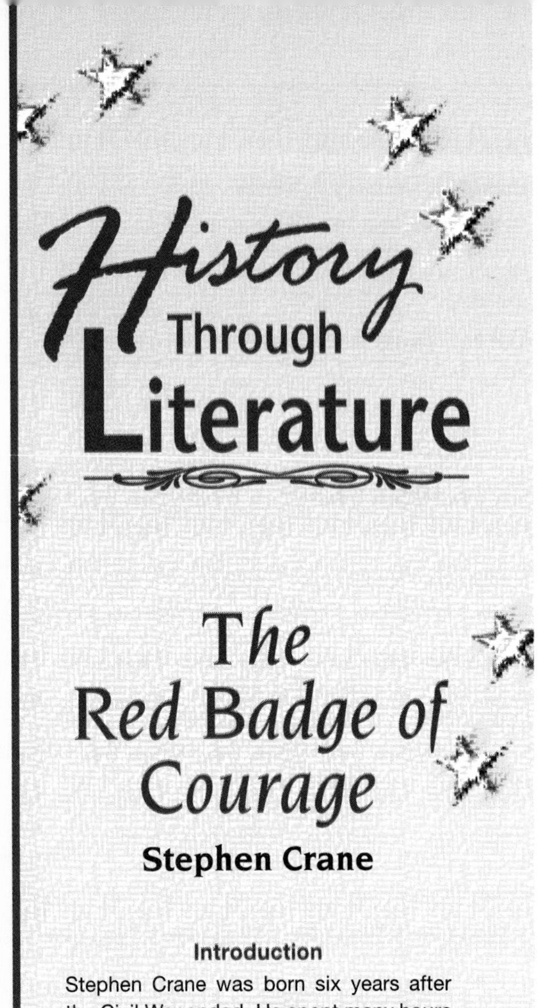

The Red Badge of Courage

Stephen Crane

Introduction

Stephen Crane was born six years after the Civil War ended. He spent many hours reading about the war and talking to veterans. In 1895, he published his great Civil War novel, *The Red Badge of Courage.* It tells the story of Henry Fleming, a young volunteer in the Union Army. The following passage describes Henry's departure from home and his early days in the army.

Vocabulary

Before you read the selection, find the meaning of these words in a dictionary: **doggedly, shirking, monotonous, province, pickets, philosophical, reflectively, reproached, infantile, assurance.**

When [Henry] had stood in the doorway with his soldier's clothes on his back, and with the light of excitement and expectancy in his eyes almost defeating the glow of regret for the home bonds, he had seen two tears leaving their trails on his mother's scarred cheeks.

Still, she had disappointed him by saying nothing whatever about returning with his shield or on it.* He had privately primed himself for a beautiful scene. He had prepared certain sentences which he thought could be used with touching effect. But her words destroyed his plans. She had doggedly peeled potatoes and addressed him as follows: "You watch out, Henry, an' take good care of yerself in this here fighting business—you watch out, an' take good care of yerself. Don't go a-thinkin' you can lick the hull rebel army at the start, because yeh can't. Yer jest one little feller amongst a hull lot of others, and yeh've got to keep quiet an' do what they tell yeh. I know how you are, Henry.

"I've knet yeh eight pair of socks, Henry, and I've put in all yer best shirts, because I want my boy to be jest as warm and com-f'able as anybody in the army. Whenever they get holes in 'em, I want yeh to send 'em rightaway back to me, so's I kin dern 'em.

"An' allus be careful an' choose yer comp'ny. There's lots of bad men in the army, Henry. The army makes 'em wild, and they like nothing better than the job of leading off a young feller like you, as ain't never been away from home much and has allus had a mother, an' a-learning 'em to drink and swear. Keep clear of them folks, Henry. . . .

"I don't know what else to tell yeh, Henry, excepting that yeh must never do no shirking, child, on my account. If so be a time comes when yeh have to be kilt or do a mean thing, why, Henry, don't think of anything 'cept what's right, because there's many a woman has to bear up 'ginst sech things these times, and the Lord'll take keer of us all.

"Don' forget about the socks and the shirts, child; and I've put a cup of blackberry jam with yer bundle, because I know yeh like it

* The Spartan people of ancient Greece carried home their dead warriors on their shields.

Critical Reading

1. What did Henry's mother say about Henry's possible death? *(that he shouldn't avoid it because it may cause her grief; that she and other women must bear such loss as best they can)*

2. Why was Henry embarrassed at his mother's farewell speech? *(He had wanted her to talk about the glory of war. Instead, she gave him instructions and practical advice.)*

3. What does the narrator mean by saying that Henry soon saw himself "merely as a part of a vast blue demonstration"? *(Possible answer: Henry had lost his individuality.)*

Background for Understanding

The monotony that Henry experienced in camp was not unusual. Soldiers often spent weeks waiting to go into battle. All that free time helped popularize the game of baseball.

When baseball was invented in the early 1800s, it was largely a New York pastime. During the Civil War, New Yorkers taught the game to Union soldiers. Soon it was played in both Union and Confederate camps. By the end of the war, people from around the country played baseball.

Viewing History: A Soldier Says Goodbye

This anonymous painting, Off to the Front, 1861, *is owned by the museum of the United States Military Academy at West Point, New York. It shows a young soldier saying goodbye to his family in the first year of the Civil War. Scenes like this were common in homes throughout the North and South.* ★ **Choose one of the people in this painting. What do you think are that person's thoughts and feelings?**

above all things. Good-by, Henry. Watch out, and be a good boy."

He had, of course, been impatient under the ordeal of this speech. It had not been quite what he expected, and he had borne it with an air of irritation. He departed feeling vague relief.

Still, when he had looked back from the gate, he had seen his mother kneeling among the potato parings. Her brown face, upraised, was stained with tears, and her spare form was quivering. He bowed his head and went on, feeling suddenly ashamed. . . .

After complicated journeyings with many pauses, there had come months of monotonous life in a camp. He had had the belief that real war was a series of death struggles with small time in between for sleep and meals; but since his regiment had come to the field the army had done little but sit still and try to keep warm. . . .

He had grown to regard himself merely as a part of a vast blue demonstration. His province was to look out, as far as he could, for his personal comfort. For recreation he could twiddle his thumbs and speculate on the thoughts which must agitate the minds of the generals. Also, he was drilled and drilled and reviewed, and drilled and drilled and reviewed.

The only foes he had seen were some pickets along the river bank. They were a suntanned, philosophical lot, who sometimes shot reflectively at the blue pickets. When reproached for this afterward, they usually expressed sorrow, and swore by their gods that the guns had exploded without their permission. The youth, on guard duty one night, conversed across the stream with one of them. He was a slightly ragged man, who spat skillfully between his shoes and possessed a great fund of bland and infantile assurance. The youth liked him personally.

"Yank," the other had informed him, "yer a right dum good feller." This sentiment, floating to him upon the still air, had made him temporarily regret war.

Analyzing Literature

1. What advice did Henry's mother give him?
2. How was a soldier's life different than what Henry expected?
3. **Making Generalizations** What does Henry's experience with the enemy picket suggest about the special problems of fighting a civil war?

Viewing History ANSWER

Possible answers: The soldier may be excited to be fighting for a cause he believes in, sad to be leaving his family, and fearful of being injured or killed in battle. The other family members may be sad to see him go, afraid for his safety, but proud that he is doing what they see as his duty.

Analyzing Literature

ANSWERS

1. She advised him to take care of himself and to remember that he was just one soldier in a large army. She warned him to stay away from "bad men" and to avoid shirking his responsibilities on her account. She encouraged him to send his mending home to her and to "be a good boy."

2. Henry had believed that a soldier's life consisted of "a series of death struggles," but he learned that most of a soldier's time was spent in camp—in pursuit of personal comfort and in monotonous military drills. Furthermore, his only recreation was to imagine what the generals were planning, rather than to daydream about his own glory on the battlefield.

3. Possible answer: Henry saw the Confederate picket as a human being and even "liked him personally." The picket expressed admiration for Henry as well. This exchange suggests that civil war pits against each other citizens who have much in common and who otherwise might very well be friends.

Teaching Alternatives

Team Teaching: Language Arts

You might work with a language arts teacher to present a brief lesson about the literary school known as naturalism. Point out that naturalistic writing may present a character whose values or ideals are challenged in difficult situations. Help students to see that even in this excerpt from *The Red Badge of Courage,* Henry Fleming reconsiders his views about the glory of warfare when he is faced with the routine of camp life and the humanity of the enemy.

Connections With Arts

Little is known about the painting *Off to the Front.* The work depicts the time when the armies of the North and South were marching off to war; yet the anonymous artist does not focus on the anticipation of battlefield glory. Rather, the painting conveys a sense of restrained sadness. This carefully rendered work of folk art could well have been painted by a resigned, unhappy sister or wife.

Epilogue

SECTION OBJECTIVES	TEACHING RESOURCES	ADDITIONAL RESOURC
1 A Diverse Nation (pp. 502–505) **Objectives** 1. Explain why immigrants have come to the United States from all parts of the world. 2. Describe how the growth of cities changed American culture. 3. Describe how advances in communication have transformed American life.	**Lesson Planner,** p. 88 (average) ....45 mins. p. 106 (challenging) ....90 mins. **Unit 8/Chapter 26** • Biography Flashcards: Carlos Bulosan, p. 18 (average) ....20 mins. **Unit 9/Chapter 29** • Connecting History and Literature: The Bird Perched for Flight, p. 17 (average) ....20 mins. **Unit 9/Chapter 30** • Map Mystery: Latinos: One Group or Many? p. 26 (average) ....20 mins. **Interdisciplinary Connections** • Main Idea: The Lure of the City, pp. 121–126 (average) ....100 mins.	**Voices of Freedom** • The Ethnic Map of New York, pp. 162–164 (average) **Customized Reader** • The Poetry of Chinese Immigrants at Angel Island, article VIA-16 (average) • The Debate Over Multiculturalism in Schools, article XA-3 (average) • A Hispanic Radio Personality, article XA-5 (average) **Interdisciplinary Explorations:** A Nation of Immigrants
2 A Changing Economy (pp. 506–509) **Objectives** 1. Describe how the growth of railroads changed the nation. 2. Describe new ways of doing business that developed in the late 1800s. 3. Explain how the United States is linked with other nations in today's global economy.	**Lesson Planner,** p. 82 (average) ....90 mins. **Unit 6/Chapter 17** • Biography Flashcards: Susette La Flesche, p. 7 (average) ....20 mins. **Unit 6/Chapter 18** • Map Mystery: From Competition to Combination, p. 16 (challenging) .....30 mins. **Unit 6/Chapter 18** • Connecting History and Literature: John Henry, p. 17 (average) ....30 mins. **Interdisciplinary Connections** • Main Idea: New Industries and New Inventions, pp. 115–120 (average) ....100 mins.	**Voices of Freedom** • Building the Union Pacific, pp. 135–136 (average) • Founding Standard Oil, pp. 148–149 (average) • Evelyn Finn Organizes a Union, pp. 238–239 (average) • A New Car, p. 216 (average) **Historical Outline Map Book** • Opening the West, p. 56 (averag **Customized Reader** • The Great Sit-Down Strike, article VIB-10 (average)
3 A Changing Government (pp. 510–514) **Objectives** 1. Explain how women and minorities won the full rights of citizenship. 2. Describe how the role of government increased as a result of the Great Depression. 3. Explain why some people want to limit the power of the government.	**Lesson Planner,** p. 124 (challenging) ....60 mins. p. 130 (average) ....90 mins. p. 110 (challenging) ....45 mins. **Unit 7/Chapter 20** • Biography Flashcards: Belva Ann Bennett Lockwood, p. 7 (average) ....20 mins. **Unit 8/Chapter 26** • Connecting History and Literature: Hard Times, p. 17 (average) ....20 mins. **Interdisciplinary Connections** • Main Idea: Working Together to Make a Difference, p. 171 (average) ....100 mins.	**Voices of Freedom** • Launching the NAACP, pp. 178–179 (average) • Suffragists on a Hunger Strike, pp. 189–190 (average) • When Was the New Deal? pp. 229–230 (average) • This Gentlemen in the White House, pp. 242–243 (average) • The Montgomery Boycott, pp. 286–288 (average) **Customized Reader** • Mexican Americans and the Depression, article VIIA-6 (averag
4 Becoming a World Power (pp. 515–519) **Objectives** 1. Explain why the United States became more involved in world affairs. 2. Describe the Cold War. 3. Describe the role the United States plays in the world today.	**Lesson Planner,** p. 113 (average) ......90 mins. p. 122 (average) ....90 mins. **Unit 7/Chapter 21** • Map Mystery: Why Hawaii? p. 16 (average) ....30 mins. **Unit 7/Chapter 22** • Biography Flashcards: Sergeant York, p. 27 (average) ....20 mins. **Unit 9/Chapter 28** • Connecting History and Literature: Hallelujah! p. 6 (average) ....20 mins. **Interdisciplinary Connections** • Main Idea: Facing the Future, pp. 175–180 (average) ....100 mins.	**Voices of Freedom** • The Roosevelt Corollary, p. 191 (average) • A "Sheet of Sun" at Hiroshima, pp. 267–269 (average) **Historical Outline Map Book** • The United States and the Caribbean, 1895–1917, p. 58 • Europe in World War I, p. 60 • Aggression in Europe, p. 64 • World War II in the Pacific, p. 66 **Customized Reader** • War Hero Recounts a Battle in Germany, article VIIB-1 (average • A Woman Journalist in Vietnam, article IXA-5 (average)

Assessment Options

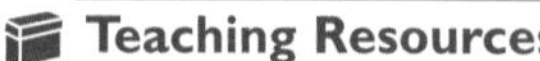
Teaching Resources
- Alternative Assessment booklet
- Test Bank CD-ROM

Student Performance Pack
- Guide to the Essentials of American History, pp. 138, 143, 149, 155, 160, 166
- Standardized Test Prep Handbook
- Interactive Student Tutorial CD-ROM

Interdisciplinary Connections

Teaching Resources
- Map Mystery, Unit 6, Chapter 20, p. 16; Unit 7, Chapter 23, p.16; Unit 8, Chapter 25, p. 5; Unit 9, Chapter 30, p.26
- Connecting History and Literature, Unit 6, Chapter 20, p. 17; Unit 8, Chapter 26, p.16; Unit 9, Chapter 28, p.6, Chapter 29, p.17
- Interdisciplinary Connections, pp. 115–120, 121–126, 171, 175–181
- Interdisciplinary Explorations: A Nation of Immigrants

Voices of Freedom, pp. 135–136, 148–149, 162–164, 170–171, 178–179, 189–191, 216, 229–230, 238–239, 242–243, 267–269, 286–288

Customized Reader, articles VIA-16, VIB-10, VIIA-6, VIIB-1, IXA-5, XA-3, XA-5

Historical Outline Map Book, pp. 56, 58, 60, 64, 66

BLOCK SCHEDULING
Activities with this icon will help you meet your Block Scheduling needs.

ENGLISH LANGUAGE LEARNERS
Activities with this icon are suitable for English Language Learners.

TEAM TEACHING
Activities and Background Notes with this icon present starting points for Team Teaching.

Technology

AmericanHeritage® History of the United States CD-ROM
- Time Tour: all units from "The Frontier West" to "Toward a New Century"
- Presidents: all Presidents from Rutherford B. Hayes to William J. Clinton
- Face the Issues: Women's Suffrage, *Brown* v. *Board of Education,* The Vietnam War
- History Makers: Thomas Edison, Henry Ford, Wilbur and Orville Wright, Louis Armstrong, Eleanor Roosevelt, Martin Luther King, Jr., Sandra Day O' Connor

Interactive Student Tutorial CD-ROM

Test Bank CD-ROM

Color Transparencies
- Immigration to the United States, 1840–1940, p. C-15
- Immigration to the United States, 1960–1990, p. C-23
- Languages Spoken in American Homes, p. C-35
- Battle of the Big Horns, p. D-57
- The United States and the World, 1933–1945, p. E-25
- Overseas Expansion, p. F-25
- America's Entry Into World War I, p. F-27
- End of the Cold War, p. F-33
- The Ford Assembly Line, p. H-57

Resource Pro® CD-ROM

Prentice Hall United States History Video Collection™ (Spanish track available on disc version.) Vol. 12, Ch. 7; Vol. 15, Ch. 10

Prentice Hall Home Page www.phschool.com

Student Performance Pack

Guide to the Essentials of American History
- Chs. 25–30, pp. 134–166 (Available in English and Spanish)

Standardized Test Prep Handbook

Interactive Student Tutorial CD-ROM

Teachers' Bibliography

Don't miss the special American Heritage® teaching notes found in this chapter.

Contact Teachers' Curriculum Institute to learn more about History Alive!® resources on the United States today. See History Alive!® units: The Rise of Industrial America; The United States Coming of Age: 1890–1920; The Roaring Twenties and the Great Depression; The United States in World War II; The Cold War; The Civil Rights Movement; and Contemporary American Society.

Explore your library to find these issues related to the Epilogue: *Martin Luther King, Jr., and the Civil Rights Movement,* February 1994; *Frontiers in Flight,* April 1994; *History of Labor,* October 1992; *Chinese Americans,* March 1991; *Entrepreneurs of the Past,* May 1989; *Hispanic Americans,* April 1989; *Television,* October 1989; *Radio,* October 1988; *Automobiles,* July 1987; *The Great Depression,* April 1994.

PRENTICE HALL School

Prentice Hall Web Site You can access a structured, on-line environment that allows you to preview curriculum-related resources and receive updated information on groundbreaking events from around the nation and the world. (www.phschool.com)

Epilogue

Linking Past to Present

1877–Present

Introducing the Epilogue

Have students preview the main ideas of the Epilogue by looking over the visuals. Suggest they look for people and trends that helped shape the nation we live in today.

Using the Time Line To provide students with practice in using the Time Line, ask questions such as these: **(1)** What twentieth-century wars does the time line name? *(World War I, World War II, and the Cold War)* **(2)** What conflict occurred in Korea in 1950? *(North Korea invaded South Korea.)* **(3)** How many years elapsed between the beginning of the Cold War and the breakup of the Soviet Union? *(about 46)* **(4)** How are the events listed for 1893 and 1965 related? *(Both concern voting rights.)* **(5)** What economic crisis occurred in 1929? *(the beginning of the Great Depression in the United States)*

Epilogue

Linking Past to Present

1877–Present

After the Civil War, the United States enjoyed tremendous growth. Technology and new business practices helped the economy to soar. Despite periods of hard times, the United States became the most prosperous nation in the world. In addition, by the 1940s, the United States was a world superpower.

The nation also saw tremendous social and political changes. Immigrants helped build a rich cultural diversity. African Americans waged a long struggle to win back their constitutional rights. Women won their right to vote, as well as greater opportunities in other areas. Reformers sought to put more power in the hands of voters. As a result, more Americans enjoy the rights of citizenship today than ever before.

Why Study History? You have learned a lot about American history this year. By studying our nation's past you can become an informed, responsible citizen. There are many other things you can learn from the past. As historian Gerda Lerner noted, "Human beings have always used history in order to find their direction toward the future: to repeat the past or depart from it."

American Events

- **1880s** Immigration from Southern and Eastern Europe increases
- **1913** Henry Ford introduces assembly line
- **1929** Great Depression begins

1875 — 1910 — 1945

World Events

- **1893 World Event** New Zealand gives vote to women
- **1914 World Event** World War I begins in Europe

★ *Background* ★

Linking Past to Present

Houses by mail Giant catalog companies sold not only clothing and shoes by mail, but even houses. In the early 1900s, more than 100,000 families bought homes by catalog from Sears, Roebuck. After ordering, a buyer got instructions and blueprints by mail, and lumber and other materials by rail. Today's realtors use phones, faxes, TVs, and the Internet, but not mail-order lumber.

Viewing History **A Land of Liberty**

Since the nation's beginning, millions of people have come to the United States seeking freedom and opportunity. One of these immigrants was the Taiwanese-born artist Tsing-fang Chen. In his 1986 painting Liberty States, *Chen uses familiar images to stress the continuing importance of liberty to the American nation.*
★ **What do the figures in the lower left and right corners represent?**

1945 World War II ends; Cold War begins

1965 Congress passes Voting Rights Act

1993 United States signs North American Free Trade Agreement

1945 | **1980** | **Present**

1950 World Event North Korean troops invade South Korea

1991 World Event Soviet Union breaks up

★ 501

Writing Actively

Responding to Art Give students a few moments to enjoy the painting shown on this page and read the caption. Then have them write a short poem or song lyrics that the artwork inspires. Model such opening lines as: *Liberty is like . . . , My country's freedoms are a rainbow of . . . ,* or *The United States shines like a beacon. . . .*

ANSWER

The Statue of Liberty

★ Background ★

Art Note

A Land of Liberty Speaking of his distinctive approach to art, Chen once said, "I belong to a new generation in civilization... which synthesizes a new society for everyone." Chen has had more than 70 one-person shows around the world. In 1986, he painted 100 studies of the Statue of Liberty as part of a one-hundredth birthday celebration for this American symbol.

Technology

Videodiscs/Videotapes
Show the *Prentice Hall United States History Video Collection*™ segments for this chapter. The videodisc version has a Spanish track. Press audio until you get the left channel for English or the right channel for Spanish, or use the bar codes in the Guidebook.

AmericanHeritage® History of the United States CD-ROM
- Time Tour: all units from The Frontier West through Toward a New Century

Section 1

A Diverse Nation

LESSON PLAN

Objectives

★ Explain why immigrants have come to the United States from all parts of the world.

★ Describe how the growth of cities changed American culture.

★ Describe how advances in communication have transformed American life.

1 Engage

Warm Up Play a recording of Neil Diamond's song "Coming to America." Ask students to share their thoughts about the song.

Activating Prior Knowledge Refer students to Chapter 14, Section 1—Industry in the North. Have students list the pre–Civil War innovations in communication and transportation. *(telegraph, railroads, clipper ships)*

Reading Actively

Before Reading Ask students to rewrite the major subheadings as questions, jotting down answers as they read.

RESOURCE DIRECTORY

Teaching Resources

Lesson Planner, p. 88

Unit 8/Chapter 26

- Biography Flashcards: Carlos Bulosan, p. 18

Unit 9/Chapter 30

- Map Mystery: Latinos: One Group or Many? p. 26

Transparencies

Our Multicultural Heritage

- Immigration to the United States, 1840–1940, p. C-15
- Immigration to the United States, 1960–1990, p. C-23
- Languages Spoken in American Homes, p. C-35

A Diverse Nation

As You Read

Explore These Questions

- Why have immigrants come to the United States from all parts of the world?
- How did the growth of cities change American culture?
- How have advances in communication transformed American life?

Define

- quota system
- illegal alien
- amnesty
- jazz

Identify

- Sunbelt
- Louis Armstrong
- Elvis Presley
- Neil Armstrong

SETTING the Scene In 1884, Rosa Cristoforo left her village in Italy to join her husband in "l'America." After two weeks on a cramped steamship, she finally caught sight of land:

> "America! The country where everyone could find work! Where wages were so high no one had to go hungry! Where all men were free and equal and where even the poor could own land! But now we were so near it seemed too much to believe."

Millions of immigrants flocked to the United States after the Civil War. Most came from Eastern and Southern Europe. Latin Americans and Asians came, too. All left homelands that offered them little hope for a better future. The United States, they heard, was a land of opportunity.

Today, as in the past, immigrants continue to add to the diversity of the United States. Such diversity has brought its share of challenges. At the same time, diversity has been a major source of pride and strength for Americans.

A Tide of Immigration

Between 1866 and 1915, more than 25 million immigrants entered the United States. Most of these "new immigrants" were far different from earlier groups.

"New immigrants"

Most early European immigrants were Protestants who came from Northern or Western Europe. The new immigrants, however, came from countries in Southern and Eastern Europe, such as Italy, Poland, or Russia. Many were Catholics. Others were Jews fleeing persecution in Eastern Europe. Besides Europeans, immigrants from Asia and Latin America also arrived.

The new immigrants endured great hardships to reach the United States. Spurred by dreams of a better life, they left their homes and families. Many suffered a long, rough voyage across the Atlantic or Pacific. On the return journey, cattle and cargo filled the same spaces that had held the immigrants.

Most European immigrants arrived at Ellis Island, near the Statue of Liberty in New York Harbor. After 1900, the city of Galveston, Texas, took many immigrants that Ellis Island could not handle. On the West Coast, immigrants from China, Japan, and Korea entered through San Francisco, California, as well as Seattle, Washington, and Oahu, Hawaii. From Mexico,

ENGLISH-CHINESE PHRASEOLOGY.

What goods have you for sale?

I have all kinds.

I want to get a pair of your best pants.

What do you ask for them?

Can you take less for them?

I can not, sir.

Phrase book for Chinese immigrants

★ *Customized Instruction* ★

English Language Learners

Developing speaking skills Have English language learners work in groups to master the boldfaced vocabulary terms and names in the section. Have them locate each term, find the context clues that help them understand its meaning, and take turns reading aloud the surrounding paragraphs. Then have group members give oral summaries for each of the subsections: A Tide of Immigration (including New immigrants, Facing discrimination, Recent newcomers), The Rise of Cities, A Rich Musical Heritage, Mass Communication, and Technology. Encourage students to prepare written notes to use when giving their oral summaries. *(average)* ELL families traveled north to El Paso and Laredo in Texas.

Facing discrimination

Like the Irish and Germans who arrived in the 1840s and 1850s, the new immigrants faced discrimination. Their religious beliefs, customs, and languages seemed strange to many Americans. Congress responded to anti-immigrant feeling by passing laws to restrict immigration. An 1882 law excluded Chinese immigrants. In the 1920s, another law set up a **quota system,** allowing only a set number of people from each country to enter the United States each year. The quota system favored immigrants from Northern Europe, especially Britain.

Despite the new restrictions, people from all over the world still dreamed of coming to the United States. They, too, wanted to share in the American dream of freedom and economic opportunity.

Recent newcomers

In 1965, Congress ended the quota system. In the years that followed, many immigrants arrived from Latin American nations, especially Mexico and Cuba. By 2000, Latin Americans were becoming the largest ethnic minority in the United States.

The number of immigrants from Asia rose sharply as well. Most were Filipinos, Chinese, and Koreans. During and after the Vietnam War, many Vietnamese and Cambodians also sought new homes in the United States. Today, Asian Americans are the nation's fastest-growing ethnic group.

In the 1980s, about 6 million immigrants entered the United States legally. Another 3 to 5 million were **illegal aliens,** people who enter the nation without permission. In 1986, Congress took steps to control illegal immigration. It did, however, grant an **amnesty,** or pardon, to illegal aliens who had arrived before 1982. Despite the legislation, illegal aliens continued to enter the country. In 1994, Congress passed a law that allowed local police to arrest illegal immigrants. It also nearly doubled the number of officials who patrol certain of the nation's borders.

At the same time, legal immigration has continued to rise. By 1995, legal immigrants were applying for Amercan citizenship in record numbers.

Each wave of immigrants has enriched American life. Over the years, immigrants have helped to build railroads, subways, and factories. They have worked on farms, built skyscrapers, and started new businesses. Their songs, stories, foods, and customs have helped to make American culture richer.

The Rise of Cities

The growth of cities also changed American life. At the end of Reconstruction, less

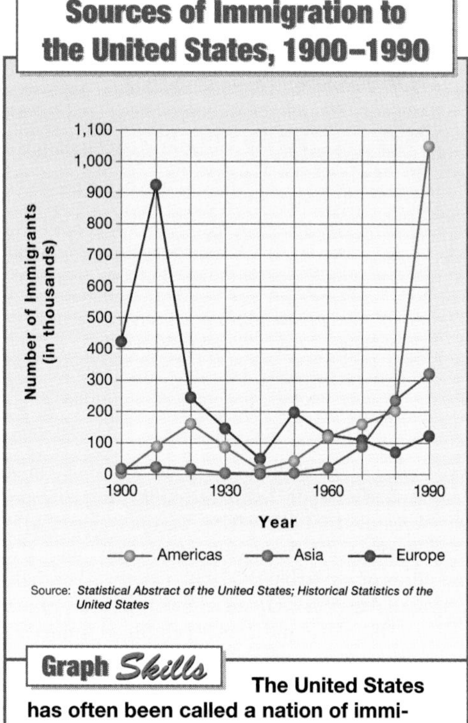

Graph Skills **The United States has often been called a nation of immigrants. Since 1900, patterns of immigration have shifted dramatically.**

1. **Comprehension** Where did the largest number of immigrants come from in 1900? In 1990?
2. **Critical Thinking** Why did the number of immigrants from Asia increase sharply after the 1960s?

2 Explore

Have students read the section. For homework, have them prepare a brief report on an ethnic background or country of origin from their own family history, focusing on special contributions that group has made to American culture.

3 Teach

Divide the class into five teams, assigning each team one of the major subsections in the section. Have each team prepare a panel discussion tracing post–Civil War changes in their assigned area of study. Tell them to use at least one original illustration in their discussion. After students have had time to prepare, ask teams to make their presentations in class.

4 Assess

To close the lesson, have students complete the section review. As an alternative, have them compose brief magazine feature articles describing **(a)** who Americans are, and **(b)** how they live today. Students should title their finished articles appropriately.

★ ★ ★ ★ ★ ★ ★ ★ ★ ★ ★ ★ ★ ★ ★ ★ ★

Graph Skills

ANSWERS **1.** Europe; Americas **2.** Wars and famines drove many Asians, such as Vietnam's "boat people," from their homes, and these immigrants resettled in other parts of the world, including the United States.

★ Background ★
Our Diverse Nation

An inventive Chinese American In the 1950s, An Wang patented a device that stored memory in computers. He also invented the first digital scoreboard for a sports stadium and pioneered in making word processors for offices. Wang had come to the United States in 1945. Before he died in 1990, Wang office systems were in use around the world.

Technology

Videodiscs/Videotapes
Prentice Hall United States History Video Collection™, Vol. 12, Ch. 7, "The New Immigration," 3:15 mins (*average*) LI

Chapter 7

Reading Actively

During Reading After students have read the subsection A Rich Musical Heritage, have them create a before-and-after graphic organizer depicting pre– and post–Civil War music, extending to the present.

Biography

ANSWER

Jazz arose in the South. It combined West African rhythms, African American songs, and European harmonies.

Writing Actively

After Reading Have students study the line graph on page 503 and write a short paragraph summarizing immigration patterns in the twentieth century.

Biography **Louis Armstrong**

Louis "Satchmo" Armstrong was one of the brilliant young musicians who helped create jazz. Armstrong learned to play the trumpet in a New Orleans orphanage. After coming to Chicago in 1922, he quickly became the most popular jazz musician of his day. Armstrong often experimented with a simple melody, allowing his listeners to hear many different sides of it. ★ **What were the origins of jazz?**

than one quarter of all Americans lived in cities. Between 1880 and 1900, the number of people living in cities doubled. By 1920, a majority of Americans made their homes in cities or suburbs. By 1990, nearly 80 percent of all Americans lived in metropolitan areas.

The move to the cities changed American culture. City newspapers printed more interesting—and sometimes more sensational—news stories. Huge department stores offered a wide range of goods. Subways and trolleys whisked people from one side of town to the other. Cities offered a wide variety of recreation, from theaters to professional sports.

During the 1970s and 1980s, older cities of the Northeast and Midwest lost population. Many people were moving to the **Sunbelt,** the states of the Southeast and Southwest. Many went in search of jobs. The sunny climate with mild winters also was an attraction. By 1990, the 30 fastest-growing urban areas in the nation were all in the South and the West.

A Rich Musical Heritage

The richness of American life has always been expressed in music. Since colonial times, folk songs have been popular. Some were the ballads of Irish and Scottish immigrants. Some were spirituals sung in slave quarters. Others were banjo tunes from the gold fields of California.

As the United States changed, so did its music. In the early 1900s, a new kind of music, called jazz, was heard in the South. **Jazz** combined West African rhythms, African American work songs and spirituals, and European harmonies. African American musicians like **Louis Armstrong** helped develop jazz into a unique American musical form that is still popular around the world.

In the 1950s, another sound swept the nation—rock 'n' roll. Artists like Chuck Berry, Little Richard, and Bill Haley used drums and electric guitars to create music with a strong, lively beat. **Elvis Presley** captured the attention of millions of young Americans. Across the nation, teenagers dressed like him, bought his records, and nicknamed him "the King."

Over the past 50 years, popular music has taken many forms. Americans of all ages and backgrounds have enjoyed country and western, rhythm and blues, heavy metal, new wave, jazz, and rap. Superstars like Pearl Jam, Garth Brooks, Queen Latifah, and Madonna have sold millions of recordings.

Mass Communication

Advances in communication have transformed American life since the late 1800s. Radio, motion pictures, and television all have brought Americans closer together.

During the 1920s, radio stations began to broadcast across the nation. They brought news, sports, and entertainment into American homes. Today, new media such as computers and television have replaced radio as the major information and entertainment

Resource Directory

Teaching Resources
Lesson Planner, p. 106
Unit 9/Chapter 29
- Connecting History and Literature: The Bird Perched for Flight, p. 17

Interdisciplinary Connections
- Main Idea: The Lure of the City, pp. 121–126

Transparencies
Fine Art
- Battle of the Big Horns, p. D-57

★ Background ★
Recent Scholarship

Hidden aristocracy The migration of poor African Americans from the rural South to northern cities is well-documented, but the presence of a small, well-educated, and self-aware "black aristocracy" in these cities is less well known. Willard B. Gatewood's *Aristocrats of Color* examines the lives, contributions, and goals of this elite group from 1880 to 1920.

From the Archives of American Heritage®

Rock 'n' roll pioneers Jackie Brenston's "Rocket 88" was quite possibly the first rock 'n' roll song. It was released by Phil and Leonard Chess on the Aristocrat label in 1951. The Chesses were two immigrant brothers who made records and sold them out of the back of their car on Chicago's Maxwell Street. Their records helped start a music revolution.

Source: Phil Patton, "Agents of Change," *American Heritage* magazine, December 1994.

source. Still, thanks to advanced technology, tiny radios the size of a credit card have become a standard feature of American life.

Motion pictures revolutionized American culture as well. The first movie theaters opened in the early 1900s. Until 1927, movies were silent—that is, they had no sound track. Audiences read subtitles to follow the plot. Today, movies feature not only sound but computer-generated special effects that both startle and scare.

Television became popular in the late 1940s. By the 1950s, millions of Americans were buying television sets. Today, almost every home has at least one TV, and television—for better or worse—has become a major influence in American life. In the 1980s, cable television greatly increased the number of television channels and the variety of programs available. Cable channels offer programs for country-and-western music fans, home shoppers, and comedy lovers. Channels like Univision (UNI), which broadcasts in Spanish, serve a variety of specific audiences.

Radio, movies, and television allow Americans to share experiences. They also help to shape public opinion. For example, many Americans make voting decisions after watching candidates debate on television.

Technology

In July 1969, American astronaut **Neil Armstrong** became the first person to walk on the moon. "That's one small step for a man, one giant leap for mankind," he declared as he stepped onto the moon's surface. The moon landing was only one example of advanced American technology following World War II. Much of this technological progress can be traced to development of the electronic computer.

The first electronic computers were built in the 1940s. Since then, the computer revolution has affected every aspect of American life. Businesses use computers to print documents or send bills. Students use computers to research and write papers. Without computers, our complex government could not function as efficiently.

Some people have expressed concern about the spread of computers. Computers keep records of nearly everything we do, from banking to visiting the doctor. People could abuse this information and threaten our privacy. Others, however, argue that computer technology has helped to spread information among diverse people and increased communication around the world.

★ Section 1 Review ★

Recall

1. **Identify** **(a)** Sunbelt, **(b)** Louis Armstrong, **(c)** Elvis Presley, **(d)** Neil Armstrong.
2. **Define** **(a)** quota system, **(b)** illegal alien, **(c)** amnesty, **(d)** jazz.

Comprehension

3. **(a)** How did Congress respond to anti-immigrant feeling in the 1920s? **(b)** What changes did Congress make in the immigration laws in 1965?
4. Describe the growth of cities from the time of Reconstruction to today.
5. What new forms of communication developed in the 1900s?

Critical Thinking and Writing

6. **Predicting Consequences** **(a)** Where did most immigrants come from in the late 1800s? **(b)** Where do most immigrants come from today? **(c)** How might this change affect the nation's culture in the future?
7. **Making Inferences** How do mass media such as movies and television bring Americans closer together?

Activity **Writing a Handbook** You are an immigrant to the United States, either 100 years ago or today. Write at least one page for a handbook for future immigrants from your country. Tell them what problems they should expect to have and how they can overcome those problems.

★ Activity ★
Linking Past and Present

Discussing and evaluating television
Divide the class into groups to discuss the portrayal of family life on television today. Have groups develop a consensus statement about whether or not TV family life is realistic and has any influence on American society. Let groups share their statements and have the class suggest criteria for judging such television programming. (*average*)

★ Section 1 Review ★

ANSWERS

1. (a)–(c) p. 504, **(d)** p. 505

2. (a)–(c) p. 503, **(d)** p. 504

3. (a) It cut back sharply the number of immigrants who were allowed to enter the U.S. and set up a quota system. **(b)** It did away with the quota system.

4. Between 1880 and 1900, the number of people living in cities doubled. By 1990, nearly 80 percent of all Americans lived in metropolitan areas.

5. Radio, movies, television, cable television, computers

6. (a) Eastern and Southern Europe **(b)** Latin America and Asia **(c)** Possible answer: Latin American and Asian cultural influences will increase.

7. People in all areas and of all backgrounds see the same programs and movies. This gives them a common body of knowledge that they can share.

Activity

Guided Instruction
Have students list the problems cited in the text, then brainstorm to infer others. Students can choose a particular country and then tailor the handbook to specific immigrant audiences.

ASSESSMENT See the rubrics in the Alternative Assessment booklet in the Teaching Resources.

Technology

AmericanHeritage® History of the United States CD-ROM
- History Makers: Louis Armstrong

Section 2
A Changing Economy

LESSON PLAN

Objectives

★ Describe how the growth of railroads changed the nation.
★ Describe new ways of doing business that developed in the late 1800s.
★ Explain how the United States is linked with other nations in today's global economy.

1 Engage

Warm Up Ask students to consider the major means of communication and transportation available to the average American at the end of Reconstruction.

Activating Prior Knowledge Write this sentence on the chalkboard: "It's a small world!" Have students discuss what the expression means, and how various methods of communication and transportation have contributed to this concept.

Reading Actively

Before Reading Ask students to skim the section, looking at the illustrations and reading the headings. Have them write two or three sentences predicting what they will learn about the changing economy. Ask students to verify or correct predictions as they read.

RESOURCE DIRECTORY

Teaching Resources
Lesson Planner, p. 82
Unit 6/Chapter 17
• Biography Flashcards: Susette La Flesche, p. 7
Unit 6/Chapter 18
• Connecting History and Literature: John Henry, p. 17

Transparencies
Exploring Technology
• The Ford Assembly Line, p. H-57

A Changing Economy

As You Read

Explore These Questions
- How did the growth of railroads change the nation?
- What new ways of doing business developed in the late 1800s?
- How is the United States linked with other nations in today's global economy?

Define
- transcontinental railroad
- reservation
- assembly line
- corporation
- stock
- monopoly
- conglomerate
- service industry
- trade deficit

Identify
- Thomas Alva Edison
- Henry Ford
- Orville and Wilbur Wright
- North American Free Trade Agreement

SETTING the Scene At the end of the Civil War, train travel usually meant discomfort and delay. Journeys were long, and passengers had no place to eat or sleep. Often, they had to wait for hours while workers fixed a derailed car or switched locomotives.

Within 20 years, American railroads had been transformed. In 1882, a British tourist boasted about his "scamper through America" on a train outfitted with luxurious sleeping cars and serving a breakfast of hot breads, eggs, sausage, oysters, and trout.

Most important, the improved railroads benefited business. Able to move goods cheaply and easily, they linked the distant sections of the nation and opened every corner to settlement and industry.

Growth of the Railroads

After 1865, railroads expanded quickly. Rail service became more efficient, and the cost of shipping freight by rail dropped sharply.

In 1869, workers completed the first railroad that stretched across the continent from coast to coast. In the next 25 years, four more **transcontinental railroads** spanned the nation. These railroads opened up the West to settlement by miners, cattle ranchers, and farmers.

As settlers moved into the Great Plains and the Far West, they clashed with Native Americans living there. In a series of wars, the United States Army defeated the Indians. The government forced Indians to move onto **reservations**—limited areas set aside for Native Americans. For Plains Indians, this marked the end of their traditional way of life.

The expanding rail system gave a giant boost to industry. Railroad construction created a huge demand for coal, iron, steel, and lumber. Also, the railroads opened up new markets in towns and villages across the nation. New businesses sprang up where rail lines crossed.

An Age of Invention

From 1860 to 1890, the United States patent office issued more than half a million patents for new inventions. These inventions helped industry to grow and become more efficient. They also made daily life easier for many Americans.

For industry, one of the most important innovations was a new way to make steel. The Bessemer process, as it was called, was developed in the 1850s. It enabled steelmakers to make high-grade steel much more cheaply than before. The new steel found many uses. Long-lasting steel rails replaced rust-prone iron rails on the nation's rail-

★ *Background* ★

Did You Know?

Domestic luxury Historian Daniel Boorstin notes that the French had built a "train impérial" for Napoleon III before George Pullman sent his luxury cars rolling, but "the sleeping-car luxury the French had prepared for their emperor, and that in Europe would be reserved for the rich, was destined from its American beginnings to attain a wider, more democratic reach."

Giving kudos for creativity Have students view MIT's Invention Dimension Web site (web.mit.edu/invent). Have students browse the site and select their own "Inventor of the Week." Then have them write a paragraph describing the inventor's work. Given the changing nature of the Internet, you may wish to preview this site before directing students to it. (*average*)

American Heritage MAGAZINE

HISTORY HAPPENED HERE

The Henry Ford Museum

Not far from his Detroit auto plant, Henry Ford built a place to display "every household article, every kind of vehicle, every sort of tool." Today, at the Henry Ford Museum, you can explore the world's largest transportation collection, from canoes to giant locomotives to classic cars. You can also see devices you might have had in your home 100 years ago.

★ ***To learn more about this historic site, write: Henry Ford Museum, P.O. Box 1970, Dearborn, MI 48121.***

Early American washing machine ➤

roads. Steel girders supported skyscrapers, or buildings of 20 stories or more. Many everyday items, such as nails, screws, needles, and pins, also began to be made of steel.

During the late 1800s, **Thomas Alva Edison** pioneered a new approach to invention. He set up the first modern research laboratory, where teams of experts worked together to develop inventions. Hundreds of new products came out of Edison's laboratory, including the phonograph, the motion picture camera, and the electric light bulb. Today, huge research laboratories run by American companies produce thousands of inventions every year.

Edison also developed the electric power plant. Soon, American streets, businesses, and homes were lit by electric lights.

A Transportation Revolution

In the 1900s, Americans were introduced to two new means of transportation—the automobile and the airplane. In time, the car and the plane transformed the world.

Automobiles

In 1900, only 4,000 "horseless carriages" chugged along the nation's dirt roads. Then, in 1913, automaker **Henry Ford** introduced the **assembly line.** In this method of production, workers are stationed in one place as products edge along on a moving belt. The assembly line made it possible for workers to put together many cars quickly and cheaply. Ford explained:

> ❝ The way to make automobiles is to make one automobile like another automobile . . . just as one pin is like another pin when it comes from a pin factory. ❞

Because of the assembly line, Ford could sell his cars at lower prices that more people could afford. By 1920, more than 9 million cars were on the roads. By the mid-1990s,

2 Explore

Ask students to read the section. For homework, have them do research and report on a late-nineteenth-century invention not mentioned in the text, and explain how that invention affected the American economy or way of life.

3 Teach

Divide the class into groups of four or five students. Assign each group one of the subsections of Section 2, and have each group write a generalization that summarizes the main idea of its subsection. Then write each group's statement on the chalkboard and have the rest of the class list facts that support the statement.

4 Assess

To close the lesson, have students complete the section review. As an alternative, ask students to write six incorrect sentences about the content of the section. Have students exchange statements with a partner and have each partner rewrite the other's incorrect statements to make them true.

★ ★ ★ ★ ★ ★ ★ ★ ★ ★ ★ ★ ★ ★ ★ ★ ★

American Heritage MAGAZINE

The Henry Ford Museum To learn more about the Henry Ford Museum on the Internet, go to www.hfmgv.org/index.html.

FROM THE ARCHIVES OF American Heritage®

Driving progress Cars really took off:

- 4000 cars were made in 1900; 187,000 were produced in 1910!
- The first gas station opened in 1905 in St. Louis, Missouri.
- The physical strength needed to crank-start the first cars kept most women off the road until the introduction of the electric starter in 1911.

Source: John Steele Gordon, "Engine of Liberation," *American Heritage* magazine, November 1996.

Technology

American Heritage® History of the United States CD-ROM

- History Makers: Thomas Edison, Henry Ford

Reading Actively

During Reading Have students read to find evidence to support this statement: During the late 1800s, businesses developed new ways to run more efficiently.

Writing Actively

After Reading Have students write a paragraph comparing and contrasting monopolies with conglomerates, including an explanation of why today conglomerates are common but monopolies are not.

Graph Skills

ANSWERS **1.** 1975–1980
2. shrink

RESOURCE DIRECTORY

Teaching Resources
Unit 6/Chapter 18
- Map Mystery: From Competition to Combination, p. 16

Interdisciplinary Connections
- Main Idea: New Industries and New Inventions, pp. 115–120

that number had skyrocketed to more than 140 million.

Airplanes

In 1903, two bicycle mechanics, **Orville and Wilbur Wright,** made the first successful airplane flight. The first passenger airline in the United States began service in 1914. Airplanes were also used during World War I (1914–1918).

After the war, planes moved more and more mail, freight, and passengers. During World War II (1939–1945), scientists developed jet engines. Today, jets traveling at hundreds of miles per hour carry goods and people to all parts of the world.

Foreign Trade, 1975–1995

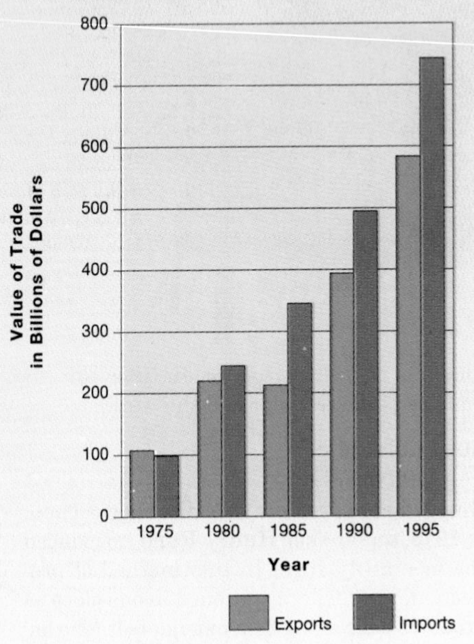

Source: U.S. Bureau of the Census

Graph Skills **In recent years, many Americans have become worried because the United States now imports more goods than it exports. Such a situation is called a trade deficit.**

1. **Comprehension** According to this graph, during what period did the United States develop a trade deficit?
2. **Critical Thinking** Between 1985 and 1990, did the trade deficit grow or shrink?

Economics

New Business Methods

Before the Civil War, most businesses were small. They usually sold their products in their own or neighboring villages or towns. After the war, increased demand for products caused businesses to grow.

Growth of corporations

During the late 1800s, businesses developed new ways to run more efficiently. Many businesses became **corporations,** or businesses owned by investors. A corporation sells **stock,** or shares in the business, to investors. The corporation can use the money invested by stockholders to build new factories or buy new machines.

Still, the rapid growth of industry caused problems. In many industries, companies became large enough to force almost all competitors out of business. A company that gains control over the business in a certain industry is known as a **monopoly.** Monopolies dominated steel, oil, and sugar production, as well as other industries.

Government regulation

Reformers in the early 1900s fought against the abuses of monopolies. They called for government regulation of industry. Many monopolies were broken up under Presidents Theodore Roosevelt, William Howard Taft, and Woodrow Wilson.

Today, government regulations are intended to prevent any company from gaining a monopoly. Still, many modern companies are far larger than the monopolies of the late 1800s. Often, a single corporation owns a large number of smaller companies in different fields. These giant corporations are known as **conglomerates.** A single conglomerate may own a bus company, a cosmetics company, a toy company, and a football team.

The Labor Force

The rise of large corporations changed the American workplace. Many factories were dangerous places to work. In steel

★ Background ★

Recent Scholarship

A new presidency Political scholar Michael P. Riccards calls Theodore Roosevelt the "first modern president." In *The Ferocious Engine of Democracy,* Riccards asserts that before Roosevelt, the presidency was little more than a "national clerkship." He credits Roosevelt with radically changing the office by making it "more of a populist, visible, and activist institution." T mills, for example, workers stood only inches away from vats of hissing, molten steel.

Unions gain strength

To protect themselves against poor working conditions and long hours, some workers joined together in labor unions. At first, labor unions faced opposition from both factory owners and the public. In the late 1800s, the police or the army often arrested strikers.

Slowly, however, unions won acceptance. In 1935, Congress passed a law making it legal for unions to bargain with factory owners. By 1940, there were 9 million union workers. Large labor unions became an accepted part of American business.

A shifting job market

Today, the workplace is changing once more. In some industries, computers direct the operation of labor-saving robots. Skilled workers program the computers and maintain the equipment. In other industries, workers face hazards from newly developed materials. Often, the long-range health effects of new products are not known for many years.

More people today are working in **service industries,** businesses in which workers provide a service rather than produce goods. Service industries range from banking and education to recreation and transportation.

Foreign Competition

In the 1900s, the United States developed a healthy foreign trade. It exported far more goods than it imported. By the 1980s, however, American industries faced greater competition from other countries in Asia and Europe. Foreign competition caused a trade deficit for the United States. A **trade deficit** occurs when a nation buys more goods and services from foreign countries than it sells to them.

American industries have taken steps to meet foreign competition. Many have improved their plants and products. Some have asked the government to limit foreign imports by imposing tariffs.

Today, industries across the world are linked in a global economy. Many nations have signed trade agreements that allow them to compete more fairly. In 1993, for example, the United States, Canada, and Mexico ratified the **North American Free Trade Agreement,** or NAFTA. NAFTA reduced or eliminated many tariffs among the three countries.

★ Section 2 Review ★

Recall

1. **Identify** **(a)** Thomas Alva Edison, **(b)** Henry Ford, **(c)** Orville and Wilbur Wright, **(d)** North American Free Trade Agreement.
2. **Define** **(a)** transcontinental railroad, **(b)** reservation, **(c)** assembly line, **(d)** corporation, **(e)** stock, **(f)** monopoly, **(g)** conglomerate, **(h)** service industry, **(i)** trade deficit.

Comprehension

3. List three ways that the railroads changed the United States.
4. **(a)** Why did businesses form corporations in the late 1800s? **(b)** What problems resulted?
5. What steps is the United States taking to meet foreign competition today?

Critical Thinking and Writing

6. **Ranking** List five inventions that you have read about in this section. Then, rank the inventions in order of importance. Explain your ranking.
7. **Making a Generalization** Make a generalization about a trend in American business or labor since the late 1800s. List two facts to support your generalization.

Activity **Playing a Role** Choose one of the inventions mentioned in this section. In a brief skit, play the role of a person seeing the invention for the first time.

★ Section 2 Review ★

ANSWERS

1. (a)–(b) p. 507, **(c)** p. 508, **(d)** p. 509

2. (a)–(b) p. 506, **(c)** p. 507, **(d)–(g)** p. 508, **(h)–(i)** p. 509

3. Railroads spurred the growth of industry, linked the nation, and opened every corner to settlement.

4. (a) Businesses could use money they raised by selling stock to build factories and buy machines. **(b)** In many industries, companies became monopolies.

5. American industries have improved their plants and products. The government has limited foreign imports by imposing tariffs. The U.S. has signed trade agreements to bring fair competition.

6. Answers include Bessemer steel, phonograph, motion picture, electric light bulb, automobile, airplane. Rankings will vary.

7. Possible answer: Generalization: American business has grown increasingly big since the late 1800s. Facts: Businesses began to form corporations in the late 1800s. Today, large conglomerates control many industries.

Guided Instruction
Before students begin, suggest they take a few minutes to imagine the reaction of someone who has never seen the invention.

ASSESSMENT See rubrics in Alternative Assessment booklet.

★ *Customized Instruction* ★

Extroverted Learners

Reporting on working conditions
Arrange extroverted learners into groups of three or four. Have most groups research labor practices in industry during the late 1800s and early 1900s, such as child labor, low wages and long hours, and health and safety hazards. Each of these groups should prepare an investigative report to present before a congressional committee. Have one group research the position of the owners in a labor-intensive industry. Those presenting investigative reports will call for the legalization of unions to help correct the abuses they have found. Those presenting owners' views will defend labor practices. Groups may take turns playing the role of congressional committee members, asking relevant questions of presenting groups. (*average*)

Technology

AmericanHeritage® History of the United States CD-ROM
- History Makers: Wilbur and Orville Wright

Section 3

A Changing Government

LESSON PLAN

Objectives

★ Explain how women and minorities won the full rights of citizenship.

★ Describe how the role of government increased as a result of the Great Depression.

★ Explain why some people want to limit the power of the government.

1 Engage

Warm Up Write this incomplete sentence on the chalkboard and have students complete it in their own way: "Because they have the right to vote, citizens of the United States are able to..."

Activating Prior Knowledge Ask students to recall what happened to the civil rights of African Americans when Reconstruction ended. Focus on the effects of *Plessy* v. *Ferguson*, 1896.

Reading Actively

Before Reading Have students rewrite the section title as a question, and look for answers as they read.

2 Explore

Ask students to read the section. For homework, have them find out about the 1954 Supreme Court decision *(Brown* v. *Board of Education)* outlawing school segregation:

RESOURCE DIRECTORY

Teaching Resources

Lesson Planner, pp. 124, 130

Interdisciplinary Connections

• Main Idea: Working Together to Make a Difference, p. 171

A Changing Government

As You Read

Explore These Questions
- How did women and minorities win the full rights of citizenship?
- How did the role of government increase as a result of the Great Depression?
- Why do some people want to limit the power of the government?

Define
- integration
- civil disobedience
- suffragist
- initiative
- referendum
- recall
- primary

Identify
- civil rights movement
- Martin Luther King, Jr.
- Voting Rights Act of 1965
- Nineteenth Amendment
- Sandra Day O'Connor
- Progressives
- Great Depression
- Franklin Roosevelt
- New Deal
- Ronald Reagan

Setting the Scene In 1916, President Woodrow Wilson was giving his annual State of the Union message to Congress. Suddenly, six women leaned over the balcony above and unrolled a yellow banner. Its bold letters read, "Mr. President, what will you do for woman suffrage?"

Wilson smiled faintly and continued his speech. A doorkeeper ran angrily up the aisle and pulled the banner down. Still, the women had made their point. Newspapers across the nation carried the story. Before long, Wilson gave his support to the campaign to give women the vote.

Woman suffrage was only one political issue that occupied the nation after the Civil War. From the late 1800s on, many citizens have worked to broaden rights for individuals and reform government in other ways.

Rights for All

Today, all American citizens over age 18 have the right to vote. In 1860, however, only white men age 21 or over could vote. For the nation's women and minorities, winning the full rights of citizenship has been a long, hard struggle.

Rights for African Americans

In 1870, the Fifteenth Amendment gave black men the right to vote. After Reconstruction, however, southern states passed laws that made it difficult or impossible for African Americans to vote. Also, as you read, Jim Crow laws segregated blacks and whites.

In the North, too, African Americans faced discrimination. Landlords in white neighborhoods refused to rent them homes. Hotels and restaurants would not serve them. Employers hired them for only the lowest-paying jobs.

Thousands of African Americans fought in World War I and World War II, serving in all-black regiments. Finally, in 1948, President Harry Truman ordered the **integration,** or bringing together, of blacks and whites in the military.

In the 1950s and 1960s, African Americans and their white supporters began new campaigns for equal treatment under the law. Their efforts became known as the **civil rights movement.** Civil rights workers won a major victory in 1954, when the Supreme Court outlawed segregation in schools.

A Baptist minister, **Martin Luther King, Jr.,** emerged as the main leader of the civil rights movement. He led his followers in acts of **civil disobedience,** or nonviolent protest and refusal to obey laws that are seen as unjust. King told his followers:

> "If we protest courageously, and yet with dignity and Christian love,

★ *Background* ★

Our Diverse Nation

Winning rights Two Supreme Court cases won some rights for Chinese Americans and laid the groundwork for later civil rights movements. In 1886, the Supreme Court ruled in *Yick Woo* v. *Hopkins* that a San Francisco ordinance targeting Chinese laundries was "illegal discrimination" under the 14th Amendment. Wong Kim Ark, an American-born son of Chinese immigrants, tested another part of the 14th Amendment. When Wong returned from a trip to China, San Francisco authorities tried to bar him from reentry under the Chinese Exclusion Act. Wong fought his case to the Supreme Court, and, in 1898, *Wong Kim Ark* v. *U.S.* became the first ruling to uphold the 14th Amendment's grant of citizenship to anyone born in the United States.

when the future history books are written, somebody will have to say, 'There lived a race of people, of black people, of people who had the moral courage to stand up for their rights.' ❞

In response to the civil rights movement, Congress passed laws to help end segregation and discrimination. The **Voting Rights Act of 1965** protected African Americans who registered to vote. In 1964, only 35 percent of African Americans in the South were registered. By the 1990s, about 7,500 African Americans held elected office in the United States. They included more than 330 mayors and 26 members of Congress.

Citizenship for Asian immigrants

From its earliest days, the United States welcomed immigrants from other lands and provided that they could become citizens after a certain number of years. A law passed in 1790, however, restricted the right of citizenship to "white" immigrants.

As a result of this law, Asian immigrants were denied full participation in American life. Unlike other immigrants, they could not become citizens and vote. In states that allowed only citizens to own property, Asian immigrants could not own farms, businesses, or even their own homes.

In the 1920s, Takao Ozawa, a Japanese immigrant who had lived in the United States more than 20 years, challenged the law. However, the Supreme Court ruled against him. Finally, in 1952, Congress allowed Asian immigrants to become citizens.

Women's rights

As you read, the Seneca Falls Convention in 1848 passed a resolution demanding suffrage for women. (See page 410.) During the late 1800s and early 1900s, **suffragists** campaigned to win women's right to vote. One

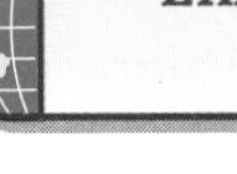

Linking United States and the World

India

United States

Civil Disobedience

Mohandas Gandhi (left) used nonviolent resistance to help free India from British rule. Gandhi and his followers refused to obey unjust laws. When arrested, they submitted peacefully. American civil rights leader Martin Luther King, Jr., adopted Gandhi's idea of civil disobedience. At right, King leads a peaceful protest march. ★ **Why do you think Gandhi and King were willing to be arrested?**

how the case was brought before the Court, what now-famous lawyer pleaded the case, and reactions to the decision.

3 Teach

On the chalkboard, create a four-column chart titled: Milestones in the Broadening of American Democracy. Head the columns: African Americans, Asian Americans, Women, Voters at Large. As you work through the section, have students enter appropriate data in each column. Close by discussing this question: Does a large and powerful federal government promote greater democracy or weaken it? Ask students to give reasons for their opinions.

4 Assess

To close the lesson, have students complete the section review. As an alternative, ask them to write five "Who/What am I?" questions on individual index cards or small pieces of paper. Students should write the correct answer on the back of each card. Students may draw on the Define and Identify lists at the opening of the section, and/or select items from the text. Collect completed cards and use them to conduct a rapid-fire question-and-answer session.

Linking United States and the World

ANSWER

Possible answer: They believed their cause was more important than their personal comfort.

★ Background ★
Did You Know?

Courage and determination One of the first black high school students in Little Rock, Arkansas, later recalled how white students harassed her: "We'd be showering in the gym and someone would turn your shower... scalding. You'd be walking out to the volleyball court and someone would break a bottle and trip you on the bottle. I have scars on my right knee from that."

Technology

AmericanHeritage® History of the United States CD-ROM

- History Makers: Martin Luther King, Jr.
- Face the Issues: *Brown* v. *Board of Education*

Viewing HISTORY ANSWER

Possible answer: Women wanted to show that fighting for their rights was a patriotic activity, parallel to the struggles for freedom of earlier Americans.

Reading Actively

During Reading After students have read the subsection A More Active Federal Government, have them create a graphic organizer comparing and contrasting the views of President Franklin D. Roosevelt and those of President Ronald Reagan.

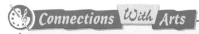

Window banner from 1915

Viewing HISTORY Women Demand the Vote

To win the vote, suffragists staged parades across the country. These women, along with their children, are marching down a New York City street in 1912.

★ **Why do you think these marchers carried American flags?**

suffragist told of her efforts during a train trip through Kansas:

> “About a dozen passengers were in the caboose . . . and we held a meeting and discussion which lasted about 45 minutes. Upon reaching Osborne at three o'clock I found about 100 people assembled for an auction sale in the middle of the street. . . . The temptation to hold a meeting overcame fatigue. I jumped into an automobile nearby and had a most interested crowd until the auctioneer came.”

By 1919, women in many states could vote in state and local elections. Finally, in 1920, the states ratified the **Nineteenth Amendment.** It guaranteed the right to vote for women in all states.

After the 1960s, women won greater civil and economic rights. Federal laws made it illegal to favor men over women in hiring or wages. Women also made gains in politics. In 1981, **Sandra Day O'Connor** became the first woman to sit on the Supreme Court. In 1997, Madeleine Albright became the first woman to serve as Secretary of State.

Lowering the voting age

In March 1971, Congress passed the Twenty-sixth Amendment. It guaranteed the right to vote to citizens age 18 or older.

At the time the amendment was submitted, 18-year-olds were allowed to fight and die in the Vietnam War but were not allowed to vote. The amendment won strong support, and it was ratified in less than four months.

Connections With Arts

In 1997, the Lilith Fair toured the United States. A series of concerts celebrated women's achievements in music. Performers ranged from Sheryl Crow and Tracy Chapman to country singers Emmylou Harris and Mary Chapin Carpenter. The tour also raised money for various charities, including shelters for abused women.

★ Customized Instruction ★

Auditory Learners

Reading a speech Refer auditory learners to sources such as *The American Reader,* edited by Diane Ravitch (Harper Perennial, 1991), to find the text of one or more speeches given by Carrie Chapman Catt for woman suffrage. (Other possible sources include the Internet Web site douglass.speech.nwu.edu/catt_a07.htm and the audiocassette *Great American Women's Speeches,* by Eileen Heckart, et al., [Harper Audio, 1995].) Have students choose a short speech or excerpt for presentation to the class. Students should precede their reading with a brief description of the origin of the piece, where and why it was given, and so on. After the speech, the student may answer questions from the class about Catt's message. (*average*)

RESOURCE DIRECTORY

Teaching Resources
Unit 7/Chapter 20
- Biography Flashcards: Belva Ann Bennett Lockwood, p. 7

A Growing Role for Voters

American voters have won wider powers. In some states, citizens can introduce a bill in the state legislature by collecting signatures on a petition. This process is called an **initiative.** In a **referendum,** people can vote directly on a bill. In some states, voters also have the power to remove a person from office in a **recall** election.

The initiative, referendum, and recall were ideas first supported by reformers in the early 1900s. These reformers were called **Progressives.** Progressives also supported primary elections and direct election of senators. In a **primary,** voters from each political party decide who will be their party's candidate in the general election. The creation of primaries meant that political bosses could no longer hand-pick candidates.

The Constitution originally called for senators to be chosen by state legislatures. The Seventeenth Amendment, ratified in 1913, gave voters in each state the right to elect two senators directly.

A More Active Federal Government

As the nation has expanded, the role of the federal government has grown. Often, the government has used its power to help or protect Americans.

Regulating business

In the late 1800s, the growth of industry created large monopolies. Wealthy business leaders sometimes used their influence unfairly to gain favors from the government.

Reformers called on Congress to regulate large businesses and protect ordinary workers and citizens. Congress created the Interstate Commerce Commission, or ICC, in 1887. The ICC investigated complaints and took some big companies to court.

The Great Depression

During the 1900s, the government became increasingly involved in the lives of Americans. One of the major turning points came during the **Great Depression,** which lasted from 1919 to 1941. It was the worst economic crisis in the nation's history. Millions of Americans lost their jobs, farms, or homes.

At the height of the depression, in 1933, **Franklin Roosevelt** became President. Roosevelt reassured suffering Americans:

> "This great nation will endure as it has endured, will revive and will prosper. So, first of all, let me assert my firm belief that the only thing we have to fear is fear itself—nameless, unreasoning, unjustified terror which

Biography Franklin and Eleanor Roosevelt

Franklin D. Roosevelt (FDR) was the only person elected President four times. To combat the effects of the Great Depression, FDR greatly expanded the role of the federal government in the economy. His wife, Eleanor, played an active role in her husband's administration. She used her position as First Lady to speak out on issues ranging from conditions in coal mines, to women's rights, to justice for African Americans. ★ **During the depression, President Roosevelt told Americans that "the only thing we have to fear is fear itself." What do you think he meant?**

Writing Actively

After Reading Have students write a brief paragraph giving evidence to support this topic sentence: American voters today have more control over their government and government leaders than voters had before the Civil War.

Biography

ANSWER

Students might note that fear sets off panicked reactions that in turn create more fear. Also, fear can prevent people from doing what is necessary to help themselves.

★ Background ★

Linking Past and Present

A limited lifespan Established to oversee the railroad industry, the powers of the ICC were expanded to include regulation of trucks (1935), barges (1940), and freight forwarders (1942). Telephone and telegraph communications were included, 1910–1934. (The FCC then took these over.) By the 1980s, many felt the ICC was no longer useful, and in 1995 Congress abolished it.

Technology

AmericanHeritage® History of the United States CD-ROM

- History Makers: Eleanor Roosevelt, Sandra Day O'Connor
- Face the Issues: Women's Suffrage

★ Section 3 Review ★

ANSWERS

1. (a)–(b) p. 510, **(c)** p. 511, **(d)–(e)** p. 512, **(f)–(h)** p. 513, **(i)–(j)** p. 514

2. (a)–(b) p. 510, **(c)** p. 511, **(d)–(g)** p. 513

3. Possible answers: **(a)** the Voting Rights Act of 1965 **(b)** the 1952 law allowing Asian immigrants to become American citizens **(c)** the 19th Amendment

4. (a) He set up government programs to help the unemployed. **(b)** The federal government regulated many areas of American life.

5. worry about the high cost; fear that the federal government has too much power

6. Possible answer: Civil rights have expanded steadily over the past 100 years. Examples include integregated schools and voting rights for women and 18-year-olds.

7. Possible answers: **(a)** Students may mention federal aid to education, military protection, or need to pay federal taxes. **(b)** Accept any reasoned response.

Activity

Guided Instruction
Have students begin by rereading the excerpt from Martin Luther King's speech on pp. 510–511.

ASSESSMENT See the rubrics in the Alternative Assessment booklet in the Teaching Resources.

RESOURCE DIRECTORY

Teaching Resources
Lesson Planner, p. 110
Unit 7/Chapter 21
- Map Mystery: Why Hawaii? p. 16

Unit 8/Chapter 26
- Connecting History and Literature: Hard Times, p. 16

paralyzes needed efforts to convert retreat into advance.”

With the help of Congress, Roosevelt set up many new programs to relieve the suffering of the unemployed. Under Roosevelt's program, known as the **New Deal,** the government also put unemployed people to work on projects such as building dams, schools, and parks.

▲ *1980 Ronald Reagan campaign button*

One major program of the New Deal was Social Security. It set up a system of pensions for older people. It also set up a system of unemployment insurance and gave states money to support dependent children and people with disabilities. The Social Security system remains in effect today.

Debating the role of government

Following the trend begun during the New Deal, the federal government continued to expand its role in American life. The government passed laws that protected consumers from harmful foods and medicines. It inspected shops and factories to ensure that they were safe for workers. In the 1970s, concerns about the environment led Congress to pass laws cleaning up polluted rivers and smog-filled air.

By the 1980s and 1990s, some Americans began to worry about the high costs of government programs. They worried, too, that the federal government had too much power. In 1980, Americans elected **Ronald Reagan** as President. “Government is not the solution to our problem,” Reagan said, “government is the problem.” Reagan promised to cut taxes and spending. He also sought to reduce government regulation, which he said kept businesses from growing. In the 1990s, President Bill Clinton, a middle-of-the-road Democrat, worked with the Republican Congress to cut federal spending while continuing to protect the neediest citizens.

★ Section 3 Review ★

Recall

1. **Identify** **(a)** civil rights movement, **(b)** Martin Luther King, Jr., **(c)** Voting Rights Act of 1965, **(d)** Nineteenth Amendment, **(e)** Sandra Day O'Connor, **(f)** Progressives, **(g)** Great Depression, **(h)** Franklin Roosevelt, **(i)** New Deal, **(j)** Ronald Reagan.
2. **Define** **(a)** integration, **(b)** civil disobedience, **(c)** suffragist, **(d)** initiative, **(e)** referendum, **(f)** recall, **(g)** primary.

Comprehension

3. List one advance in civil rights won by each of the following during the 1900s: **(a)** African Americans, **(b)** Asians, **(c)** women.
4. **(a)** What steps did Franklin Roosevelt take to relieve the Great Depression? **(b)** How did the trend toward big government continue after the New Deal?
5. Why do many Americans today want to reduce the size of the federal government?

Critical Thinking and Writing

6. **Making a Generalization** Make a generalization about the expansion of civil rights in the United States during the past 100 years. Give three examples to support your generalization.
7. **Linking Past and Present** **(a)** Describe three ways in which the federal government directly affects your life today. **(b)** Do you think you are better off or worse off as a result? Explain.

Activity **Writing a Speech** You are a leader of one of the civil rights movements described in this section. Write a speech to inspire other Americans to support your cause.

★ Activity ★

Cooperative Learning

Creating a mural Milton Meltzer's book, *Brother, Can You Spare a Dime?* uses songs and firsthand accounts to tell the story of the Great Depression and New Deal. Share the following songs from the Meltzer book: “Brother, Can You Spare a Dime?,” “I Don't Want Your Millions, Mister,” “Pastures of Plenty,” “Beans, Bacon, and Gravy,” and “Soup Song.” “Discrimination Blues” in *The Ballad of America* can also be used. Divide the class into groups. Have each choose a different song and make a mural about the Great Depression based on its lyrics. Alternatively, the class could choose one song and different groups could illustrate separate verses. *(average)* ELL T

Becoming a World Power

As You Read

Explore These Questions

- Why did the United States become more involved in world affairs?
- What was the Cold War?
- What role does the United States play in the world today?

Define

- imperialism
- annex
- totalitarian state

Identify

- Spanish-American War
- Theodore Roosevelt
- World War I
- Adolf Hitler
- World War II
- Joseph Stalin
- Cold War
- United Nations
- Vietnam War

SETTING the Scene In 1858, Cyrus Field completed the laying of an underwater telegraph cable across the Atlantic Ocean. The cable carried a few messages between England and the United States and then snapped. Field tried again, with an improved cable, in 1866. This time, he succeeded.

In the years after the Civil War, Field's transatlantic cable connected the United States to Europe. At the same time, new oceangoing steamers and improved railroads cut travel times on land and sea. As technology shrank distances between nations, the United States became more involved in world affairs.

Growing Involvement in World Affairs

During its first 100 years, the United States paid relatively little attention to political events in other countries. Washington, Jefferson, and other early Presidents believed that the young nation would be better able to grow and prosper if it did not become entangled in foreign affairs.

Foreign trade

Despite this policy of isolation from the political affairs of other countries, the United States conducted a lively foreign trade. Europe was the most important market. After the Civil War, trade with Asia and Latin America also grew.

In the 1870s, European nations entered an age of imperialism. **Imperialism** is the control by powerful countries of weaker countries or regions. France, Britain, Germany, and other powers colonized the lands of Africa and Asia. They built great empires that increased their power and wealth.

Americans could not ignore Europe's race for colonies. The United States had become a world leader in industry and agriculture. It needed new markets for its goods. In Congress, Senator Albert Beveridge of Indiana urged the United States to look abroad, especially to Asia:

> "Our largest trade henceforth must be with Asia. The Pacific is our ocean. . . . China is our natural customer. . . . That statesman commits a crime against American trade . . . who fails to put America where she may command that trade."

New territories

In 1898, the United States **annexed,** or added, Hawaii, a chain of islands in the Pacific Ocean. With a safe harbor in Hawaii, the United States could more easily open and protect markets in Asia.

★ Background ★

Did You Know?

Apology rendered In 1993, President Bill Clinton signed a formal apology to the Hawaiian people. In it, Congress officially expressed its regret to the Hawaiian people for the part the United States government had played 100 years earlier in the overthrow of the Hawaiian monarchy, which opened the way for annexation.

Section 4 Becoming a World Power

LESSON PLAN

Objectives

★ Explain why the United States became more involved in world affairs.

★ Describe the Cold War.

★ Describe the role the United States plays in the world today.

1 Engage

Warm Up Write this sentence on the chalkboard and challenge students to explain what it means for the nation: "The United States is the world's superpower."

Activating Prior Knowledge Ask students to identify the foreign wars the United States fought between the time the Constitution was adopted and the Civil War. *(War of 1812 and the War With Mexico)* Refer students to Chapter 10, pages 284–289, and Chapter 13, pages 360–364, to review the wars and why they were fought. Note that students will want to compare these wars with later wars as they study the section.

Reading Actively

Before Reading Have students read the Explore questions and take notes that answer them as they read. Have them use their notes to complete the section review.

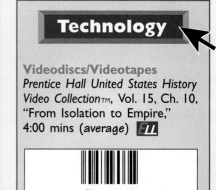

Technology

Videodiscs/Videotapes
Prentice Hall United States History Video Collection™, Vol. 15, Ch. 10, "From Isolation to Empire," 4:00 mins *(average)* ELL

Chapter 10

The **Spanish-American War** of 1898 added other territory to the United States. The war broke out as a result of a dispute over Spain's rule of Cuba. American troops quickly defeated the Spanish. Under the peace treaty, Spain gave the islands of Puerto Rico in the Caribbean, and Guam and the Philippines in the Pacific, to the United States.

Relations With Latin America

The United States also took a more active role in Latin America. In 1901, **Theodore Roosevelt** became President. Roosevelt favored direct action. His motto was "Speak softly, but carry a big stick." By this, he meant that the United States would strive for peace but use force when necessary.

Roosevelt often used the "big stick" in Latin America. For example, Roosevelt wanted to build a canal connecting the Atlantic and Pacific oceans. When Colombia refused to sell the land for the canal, Roosevelt arranged for citizens of Colombia to revolt against the government. The rebels created a new country, Panama. Panama then quickly

The United States in the Caribbean, 1898–1917

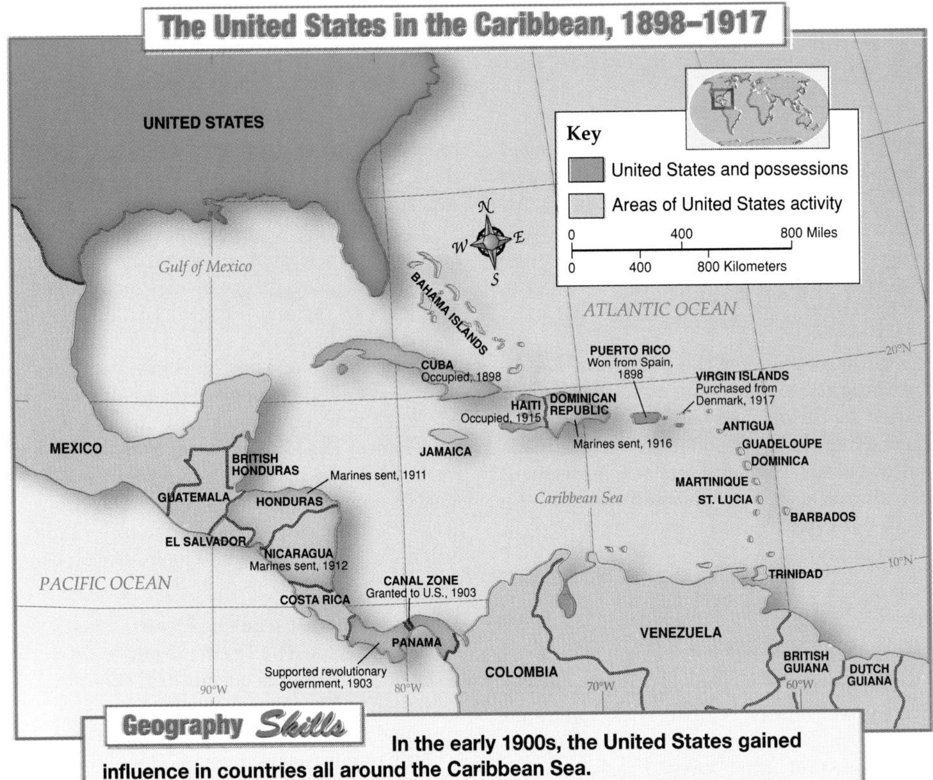

Geography Skills In the early 1900s, the United States gained influence in countries all around the Caribbean Sea.

1. **Location** On the map, locate: **(a)** Colombia, **(b)** Panama, **(c)** Dominican Republic, **(d)** Haiti, **(e)** Honduras, **(f)** Puerto Rico.
2. **Region** What areas shown on the map were governed directly by the United States?
3. **Critical Thinking** Look at the chart on page 618. Which territories shown on this map still belong to the United States?

2 Explore

Have students read the section. For homework, have them find out more about the German Nazis and their goals in the 1930s and early 1940s.

3 Teach

Supply students with an outline map of the world. As you work through the section, have students use numbers or create appropriate map symbols to identify the locations of various foreign wars, conflicts, and other struggles in which the United States has been involved since the Civil War. In the map key, students will name the event, cite the date, and give a brief reason for or description of the conflict. To conclude, call on volunteers to show and explain their maps to the rest of the class.

4 Assess

To close the lesson, have students complete the section review. Or, have students create political cartoons about a war the nation has fought since 1898. Students should take the point of view of an American living at the time of each conflict.

★ ★

Geography Skills

ANSWERS **1.** Review locations with students. **2.** Puerto Rico, Canal Zone, Virgin Islands **3.** Puerto Rico, Virgin Islands

Resource Directory

Teaching Resources
Lesson Planner, p. 113
Unit 7/Chapter 22
- Biography Flashcards: Sergeant York, p. 27

Transparencies
Time Lines
- The United States and the World, 1933–1945, p. E-25

Cause and Effect
- Overseas Expansion, p. F-25
- America's Entry Into World War I, p. F-27

★ Customized Instruction ★

Visual Learners

Reading a map Challenge students to create, exchange, and answer additional questions about the map on this page. Use questions such as the following to get them started: "Which country was not an area of U.S. activity but was bordered only by countries that were?" *(Costa Rica)* "Which country shares a border with the United States?" *(Mexico)*

Next give students notecards and have them write down three additional questions. Have them exchange questions, write answers on the notecards, and return the notecards to the authors. Have the question writers check the responses. *(average)*

ELL T

agreed to let the United States build the Panama Canal.

For most of the 1900s, the United States continued to intervene in Latin America to protect its interests there. President Taft, for example, sent troops into Nicaragua and Honduras. President Wilson intervened in the Dominican Republic and Haiti. President Reagan ordered troops to invade Grenada. President Clinton sent troops to Haiti to oversee elections there.

Over the years, Americans have debated the "big stick" policy. Opponents argue that the United States has made enemies by intervening in the internal affairs of weaker nations. Supporters respond that the United States has a duty to maintain peace and order in Latin America.

Two World Wars

In 1914, **World War I** broke out in Europe. At first, President Woodrow Wilson declared American neutrality. Then, in 1917, the United States entered the war on the side of the Allies—Britain, France, and 22 other nations. The war ended in 1918 with an Allied victory. Afterward, Wilson tried to get the United States to join a League of Nations to prevent future wars. However, Congress refused. Now that the war was over, many Americans sought once more to avoid involvement in foreign affairs.

In the 1930s, the nations of Europe again moved toward war. In Germany, dictator **Adolf Hitler** set up a **totalitarian state,** in which a single party controls the government and every aspect of people's lives. In 1939, war broke out when Hitler invaded neighboring Poland. Italy and Japan sided with Hitler, forming the Axis powers. They fought against the Allies, which included Britain, France, and the Soviet Union.

Again, the United States tried to remain neutral. On December 7, 1941, however, the Japanese launched a surprise attack on Pearl Harbor in Hawaii. Congress quickly declared war on Japan. Days later, Italy and Germany declared war on the United States.

World War II cost millions of lives. The Allies defeated Germany and Italy in April 1945. The war against Japan did not end until August 1945, when American planes dropped atomic bombs on the Japanese cities of Hiroshima and Nagasaki.

Connections With Civics

To honor the dead of World War I, the United States dedicated the Tomb of the Unknown Soldier. In 1921, the body of an unidentified American soldier was brought from an unmarked grave in France to a military cemetery in Arlington, Virginia. Above his grave, a marble monument bears the inscription: "Here rests in honored glory an American soldier known but to God."

The Cold War

After World War II, the United States became concerned about the expanding power of the Soviet Union. The two nations had been allies during the war. Now, however, the Soviets, under **Joseph Stalin,** were setting up communist governments in the countries in Eastern Europe. To contain Soviet influence, the United States and the nations of Western Europe formed the North Atlantic Treaty Organization, or NATO.

Rivalry between the United States and the Soviet Union never erupted into direct armed conflict. With each side pointing nuclear missiles at the other, the prospect of a shooting war was too frightening. Instead, the two superpowers entered a long period of tension and rivalry known as the **Cold War.**

Twice, the United States became involved in regional wars to contain communist expansion. Between 1950 and 1953, American troops battled to turn back an invasion of South Korea by communist North Korea. In the Korean War, Americans fought under the command of the **United Nations,** an international peacekeeping organization set up in 1945.

In the 1960s and 1970s, American soldiers fought against communist rebels in Vietnam. The government argued that, if Vietnam fell to communism, neighboring nations would be threatened. Many Americans, especially young people, protested the war.

Reading Actively

During Reading Have students list evidence supporting this statement: The United States was an imperialist nation by the end of the 1800s.

★ Background ★
Did You Know?

Last but not least Americans were the last of various peoples who tried to build a canal to connect the Atlantic and Pacific oceans. In 1537, Charles I of Spain ordered the first feasibility survey for such a canal. The French began building a canal in 1881 but gave up after they were defeated by bad planning, disease, and charges of fraud.

Technology

AmericanHeritage® History of the United States CD-ROM
- Face the Issues: The Vietnam War

Viewing History ANSWER

Possible answers: On Veterans Day and Memorial Day, many people hang out flags or visit military cemeteries. Some communities and schools hold ceremonies on these holidays. Some communities have war memorials. Individuals in the community can volunteer to work at veterans' hospitals.

Writing Actively

After Reading Have students write two or three sentences summarizing the main ideas of this section. Then have them compare their summaries with the statements for Section 4 in the Epilogue's Review under Sum It Up. Students may revise or expand their statements if appropriate.

Viewing History — Honoring American Veterans

Americans honor those men and women who served in the nation's military. At left, members of the Veterans of Foreign Wars salute a Veterans Day parade in Texas. At right, people visit the Vietnam Veterans Memorial in Washington, D.C. The memorial, designed by Maya Lin, is inscribed with the names of more than 58,000 Americans killed or missing in the Vietnam War. ★ **How does your community honor veterans?**

They said that the conflict was a civil war and that it did not threaten American security. In the early 1970s, American troops finally returned home. More than 57,000 Americans had lost their lives in the **Vietnam War.**

After 1985, superpower tensions eased as Premier Mikhail Gorbachev (mee kah EEL gor buh CHAWF) launched economic and democratic reforms in the Soviet Union. In 1989, countries in Eastern Europe rejected their communist governments. Two years later, the Soviet Union itself broke up. The Cold War was over.

Working for Peace

As the Cold War faded, conflicts in many areas of the globe still threatened the peace. During the 1990s, the United States worked with many nations in an effort to create a more stable, more democratic world.

Presidents George Bush and Bill Clinton used United States influence to help bring stability to war-torn regions such as Bosnia in Eastern Europe. In 1992, American forces led a United Nations mission to Somalia in eastern Africa. The troops helped distribute food during a famine caused by civil war. Two years later, American troops joined a UN mission to Haiti. They forced out military dictators and restored an elected president to the Caribbean island.

The United States also took an active role in the Middle East. The United States supported the peace process between Israel and its Arab neighbors. In 1991, American troops joined a UN force to drive Iraqi invaders out of Kuwait.

RESOURCE DIRECTORY

Teaching Resources

Lesson Planner, p. 122

Unit 9/Chapter 28

- Connecting History and Literature: Hallelujah! p. 6

Interdisciplinary Connections

- Main Idea: Facing the Future, pp. 175–180

Transparencies

Cause and Effect

- End of the Cold War, p. F-33

Skills For LIFE MINI LESSON

CRITICAL THINKING Using a Song as Historical Evidence

1. Provide students with lyrics to Bob Dylan's 1962 song "Blowin' in the Wind." Introduce the skill by explaining that this popular song from the 1960s reflects how some people saw their world.

2. Help students practice the skill by asking what issues Dylan addresses in the first verse *(racism, war)*; second verse *(indifference, social injustice, war)*; third verse *(racism)*. Ask what Dylan meant by "the answer is blowin' in the wind." *(perhaps that the rising tide of protest might bring change)*

3. Have students apply the skill by answering this question: "What might the song reveal about many people in the 1960s?" *(They objected to racism, social injustice, and the war in Vietnam.)*

The United States also used diplomacy to bring about peace. In Northern Ireland, long-standing disputes between Protestants and Catholics had resulted in thousands of deaths. President Clinton sent former Senator George Mitchell to Ireland for peace talks. Mitchell's negotiations helped produce a peace agreement in April 1998.

The Last Superpower

With the Soviet Union gone, the United States became the world's remaining superpower. Some Americans hoped the country would take the opportunity to reduce its role in world affairs. "In the post-Cold War world, we will no longer require our people to carry an unfair burden for the rest of humanity," said Representative Dana Rohrabacher of California.

Others argued that the nation had a responsibility to use its power when needed. "The U.S. must lead, period," declared Newt Gingrich, the Speaker of the House of Representatives. President Bill Clinton told a meeting of foreign policy experts:

> "If we are going to be strong at home and lead abroad, we have to overcome a dangerous and growing temptation in our own land to focus solely on the problems we face here in America. The new isolationists must not be allowed to pull America out of the game."

The Future of a Free People

In this book, you have read about the many individuals, groups, and cultures who helped create the United States. The progress of the republic was never easy. In 1776, the problems facing the United States seemed so great that many believed the new nation would not survive.

What does the future hold? Since 1877, the United States has become a superpower and a model for democratic nations everywhere. It can continue as one only if every American works to preserve the values of life, liberty, and the pursuit of happiness. Your generation holds the power to shape the nation's future.

★ Section 4 Review ★

Recall

1. **Locate** **(a)** Hawaii, **(b)** Puerto Rico, **(c)** Philippines, **(d)** Panama, **(e)** Vietnam.
2. **Identify** **(a)** Spanish-American War, **(b)** Theodore Roosevelt, **(c)** World War I, **(d)** Adolf Hitler, **(e)** World War II, **(f)** Joseph Stalin, **(g)** Cold War, **(h)** United Nations, **(i)** Vietnam War.
3. **Define** **(a)** imperialism, **(b)** annex, **(c)** totalitarian state.

Comprehension

4. Why did the United States become more involved in world affairs in the late 1800s?
5. Why did the United States distrust the Soviet Union after World War II?
6. Give two examples of how the United States used its power to promote democracy and stability after the end of the Cold War.

Critical Thinking and Writing

7. **Making Generalizations** Make a generalization about the role of the United States in world affairs since the late 1800s. Give three examples to support your generalization.
8. **Understanding Alternatives** Review the subsection The Last Superpower, above. **(a)** What alternatives are suggested for the United States in the post–Cold War era? **(b)** Which alternative would you support? Explain.

Activity **Interviewing** Interview someone in your own family or community who served overseas. Think of at least five questions to ask about that person's experiences in the military.

★ Section 4 Review ★

ANSWERS

1. (a), (c), (e) See World Map in the Reference Section. **(b), (d)** See map, p. 516.

2. (a)–(b) p. 516, **(c)–(h)** p. 517, **(i)** p. 518

3. (a)–(b) p. 515, **(c)** p. 517

4. The U.S. needed new markets for its goods.

5. It feared the Soviet Union wanted to spread communism.

6. Possible answers: helped distribute food during a famine caused by civil war in Somalia; helped bring about a peace agreement between Catholics and Protestants in Northern Ireland

7. Possible answer: The U.S. moved from a policy of isolation in the late 1800s to the role of superpower in the late 1900s. Examples: The U.S. acquired new territories in the early 1900s. The U.S. fought in World War I and World War II. After the end of the Cold War, the U.S. worked to create a more stable, democratic world.

8. (a) reduce U.S. role in world affairs or use its power when needed. **(b)** Accept answers that show reasoned thought.

Activity

Guided Instruction
Help students identify people whom they could interview.

ASSESSMENT See the rubrics in the Alternative Assessment booklet in the Teaching Resources.

★ *Activity* ★

Connections With Civics

Taking a poll Have students conduct a poll on these two questions: What are the four most serious problems Americans face today? What do you believe will be the four most serious problems Americans will face in the year 2015? Have students poll people of different ages, compile the data, and identify the top five responses to each question. Then, have them analyze the differences, if any, among age groups and between present and future concerns. Conclude with a discussion of why respondents may have chosen the answers they gave. (*average*) T

Epilogue

Review and Activities

Reviewing the Chapter

Define These Terms

1. b **2.** e **3.** d **4.** a **5.** c

Explore the Main Ideas

1. Most earlier European immigrants were Protestants from Northern and Western Europe. The "new immigrants" were mainly from Southern and Eastern Europe; many were Catholic or Jewish.

2. Railroad construction created a demand for raw materials. The railroads opened up new markets across the nation. New businesses sprang up at rail centers.

3. As a result of increased foreign competition, the U.S. began importing more products from overseas than it exported.

4. Segregation of African Americans was outlawed. The Voting Rights Act of 1965 protected African Americans who registered to vote.

5. The U.S. often intervened in Latin America to protect its interests there. Some Presidents sent troops to Latin American nations.

Geography Activity

1. F **2.** C **3.** A **4.** D **5.** E **6.** B

Region Puerto Rico

Critical Thinking and Writing

1. (a) Many immigrants came to escape poverty or harsh governments in their own countries. **(b)** Yes, immigrants still come to the United States seeking freedom or economic opportunity.

2. (a) railroad, automobile, airplane **(b)** Possible answers: The automobile gave individuals greater freedom to travel where and when they pleased. The airplane was faster than trains or automobiles.

3. Democracy is based on the equality of people under the law. If one group is discriminated against, it endangers democracy.

4. Answers will vary. Students should give reasons for their choices.

Using Primary Sources

(a) They cause conflicts in many countries. **(b)** The United States is using those differences as an advantage rather than as a source of conflict.

Review and Activities

★ Sum It Up ★

Section 1 A Diverse Nation

- Today, as in the past, immigrants from many nations contribute to the rich culture of the United States.
- Since the 1800s, the majority of the population has shifted from farms to cities and suburbs.
- Mass communication has brought many different people closer together.

Section 2 A Changing Economy

- New inventions and business practices sparked tremendous economic growth.
- Today, the United States must compete with many nations in a global economy.

Section 3 A Changing Government

- In the 1900s, women and minorities have fought to secure their full rights under the Constitution.
- The role of the federal government expanded, especially after the Great Depression.
- Today, many Americans want to reduce the size and cost of the government.

Section 4 Becoming a World Power

- The United States has steadily become more involved in world affairs.
- During the Cold War, the United States entered a long rivalry with the Soviet Union.
- Today, Americans debate whether the United States should take a leading role in the affairs of other nations.

For additional review of the major ideas of the Epilogue, see ***Guide to the Essentials of American History*** or ***Interactive Student Tutorial CD-ROM,*** which contains interactive review activities, graphic organizers, and practice tests.

Reviewing the Chapter

Define These Terms

Match each term with the correct definition.

Column 1	Column 2
1. corporation	**a.** system where people vote directly on a law
2. monopoly	**b.** business owned by investors
3. civil disobedience	**c.** control of weaker nations by a stronger nation
4. referendum	**d.** nonviolent protest
5. imperialism	**e.** company that gains control of a certain industry

Explore the Main Ideas

1. How did the "new immigrant" of the late 1800s and early 1900s differ from earlier immigrants?
2. How did railroads spur industrial growth?
3. How did the United States develop a trade deficit?
4. Describe two victories of the civil rights movement.
5. What policy did the United States follow toward Latin America?

Geography Activity

Match the letters on the map with the following places: **1.** United States, **2.** Puerto Rico, **3.** Canal Zone, **4.** Cuba, **5.** Nicaragua, **6.** Dominican Republic. **Region** Which of the above lands became a United States territory as a result of the Spanish-American War?

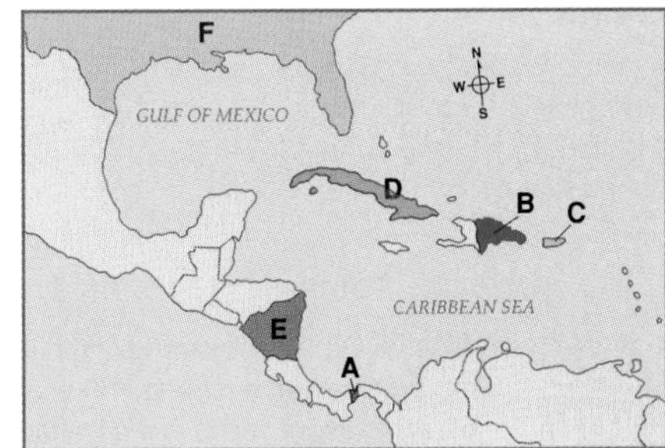

Critical Thinking and Writing

1. **Linking Past and Present** **(a)** Why did many immigrants come to the United States in the late 1800s and early 1900s? **(b)** Do immigrants today come for the same reasons? Explain.
2. **Using Chronology** **(a)** Place the following forms of transportation in their order of invention: airplane; automobile; railroad. **(b)** What advantages did the later forms have?
3. **Analyzing Ideas** Why do you think many people feel it is important for citizens to oppose discrimination even when it does not affect them directly?
4. **Ranking** What would you consider the three most important events described in this chapter? Give reasons for your choices.

Using Primary Sources

In 1996, President Bill Clinton addressed a group of American business leaders:

> "Every day all you have to do is pick up the paper or watch the evening news to see that differences among people—racial, ethnic, religious, and other differences—are tearing the heart out of societies . . . all around the world. In America we're turning all those differences to our advantage. And I think more and more we're getting comfortable with the fact that we are more than ever still a nation of immigrants."

Source: M2 PressWIRE, October 1, 1996.

Recognizing Points of View **(a)** According to Clinton, how do differences among people affect many places in the world? **(b)** How does he say the United States differs from these other places?

Activity Bank

Interdisciplinary Activity

Exploring the Arts Do research on the early days of jazz or rock 'n' roll. Then, prepare a five-minute presentation on a pioneering musician such as Louis Armstrong, or Elvis Presley. Include a recording.

Career Skills Activity

Architects Find out more about the layout and the buildings of a city in the late 1800s. Then, create a model of a city of the period. Include skyscrapers, tenements, stores, theaters, parks, and other features of the city.

Citizenship Activity

Learning About Democracy Does your state allow initiatives or referendums? If so, find out about some recent examples. Working with other class members, prepare for a debate or a panel discussion on one of these issues.

Internet Activity

Use the Internet to find a Web site for a national or local news agency, newspaper, or television station. Report on what kinds of news you can get from that site, and how you can use that site to keep informed about current and future issues.

You are yourself, a young student attending an American school right now. In your EYEWITNESS JOURNAL*, describe three events of the past 25 years that have had the biggest impact on your life. You may write as if you had the ability to go back in time to witness these events.*

Activity Bank

ASSESSMENT To assess the activities on this page, see the rubrics in the Alternative Assessment booklet in the Teaching Resources. You might want to share the rubrics with your students before they begin work.

Interdisciplinary Activity

1. Suggest sources of information, such as periodicals, Internet sites, and old record album covers.
2. Students might prepare overhead transparencies or handouts with lyrics to enrich their presentations.
3. Encourage students to prepare outlines of their presentations to use as they speak, rather than to memorize the speech word for word.

Career Skills Activity

1. Models can reflect the features of a typical city rather than a particular one, but buildings should represent existing architectural styles of the late 1800s.
2. Students can work in groups to complete the project.
3. Display the completed projects in a place where other students can view them.

Citizenship Activity

1. Students could inquire about current initiative or referendum issues at a local town hall or call a nearby chapter of the League of Women Voters.
2. Students can organize their own debate or panel discussion, or invite outside experts to a forum which students moderate.

Eyewitness Journal

1. Have students begin by reviewing the relevant passages of their textbooks.
2. Have students do more research on their selected events before they write.
3. Collect and review the journals, selecting some to read to the class.

Internet Activity

1. Have students go to www.phschool.com, which contains updated information on a variety of topics.
2. Another site you may find useful for this activity is CNN Interactive at http://www.cnn.com.
3. Given the changing nature of the Internet, you may wish to preview this site before sending students to it.

Viewpoints: Source Readings in American History

Historical Documents, Literature, and Eyewitness Accounts

Unit 1 Early Heritage of the Americas

★ Chapter 1 ★

★ 1–1 ★

The Mountains of California (average)

★ ★ ★ ★ ★ ★ ★ ★ ★ ★

Prereading Focus

Have students reread Section 3 of Chapter 1 to review what they have learned about the geography and climate of the Pacific Coast.

Purpose-Setting Question

Ask: "Why is it important to conserve our natural resources and wilderness areas?"

Unit 1 Early Heritage of the Americas

★ Chapter 1 ★ Focus on Geography

★ 1–1 ★ The Mountains of California

Introduction In the late 1800s, Scottish-born naturalist John Muir walked across much of the United States, describing each region. Through his efforts, the government established Yosemite and Sequoia national parks. In 1892, Muir founded the Sierra Club, an organization dedicated to the conservation of American forest lands. This excerpt is from Muir's 1894 book, *The Mountains of California*.

Vocabulary Before you read the selection, find the meanings of these words in a dictionary: **reposing, luminous, celestial, ineffably, adamant, composite, inaccessible.**

★ ★ ★ ★ ★ ★ ★ ★ ★

Making your way through the mazes of the Coast Range to the summit of any of the inner peaks or passes opposite San Francisco, in the clear springtime, the grandest and most telling of all California landscapes is outspread before you. At your feet lies the great Central Valley glowing golden in the sunshine, extending north and south farther than the eye can reach, one smooth, flowery, lake-like bed of fertile soil. Along its eastern margin rises the mighty Sierra, miles in height, reposing like a smooth, cumulous cloud in the sunny sky, and so gloriously colored, and so luminous, it seems to be not clothed with light, but wholly composed of it, like the wall of some celestial city. Along the top, and extending a good way down, you see a pale, pearl gray belt of snow; and below it a belt of blue and dark purple, marking the extension of the forests; and along the base of the range a broad belt of rose purple and yellow, where lie the miner's goldfields and the foot-hill gardens. All these colored belts blending smoothly make a wall of light ineffably fine, and as beautiful as a rainbow, yet firm as adamant.

When I first enjoyed this superb view, one glowing April day, from the summit of the Pacheco Pass, the Central Valley, but little trampled or plowed as yet, was one furred, rich sheet of golden composite, and the luminous wall of the mountains shone in all its glory. Then it seemed to me the Sierra should be called not the Nevada, or Snowy Range, but the Range of Light. And after ten years spent in the heart of it, rejoicing and wondering, bathing in its glorious floods of light, seeing the sunbursts of morning among the ivy peaks, the noonday radiance on the trees and rocks and snow, the flush of the alpenglow, and a thousand dashing waterfalls with their marvelous abundance of irised spray, it still seems to me above all others the Range of Light, the most divinely beautiful of all the mountain-chains I have ever seen.

The Sierra is about 500 miles long, 70 miles wide, and from 7,000 to nearly 15,000 feet high. In general views no mark of man is visible on it, nor anything to suggest the rich-

Background for Understanding

★ ★ ★ ★ ★ ★ ★ ★ ★ ★

Samuel Merrill, Muir's guest at the official founding of the Sierra Club, later recalled Muir's emotions: "He came home jubilant from that meeting . . . I had never seen him so animated and happy before. . . . I venture to say it was the happiest day of his life. . . . In the Sierra Club he saw the crystallization of the dreams and labor of a life-time."

Teaching Alternatives

★ ★ ★ ★ ★ ★ ★ ★ ★ ★

Team Teaching: Language Arts Work with a language arts teacher to present a brief lesson on descriptive prose. Have students review the selection to identify words or phrases that help the reader create visual images from Muir's descriptions. Then have students write a descriptive paragraph about an object, scene, or person.

Yosemite Valley

During the late 1800s, German-born Albert Bierstadt traveled from New York City to the Pacific Ocean. His landscapes, like this one of the Sierra Nevada, show the huge, empty spaces and great beauty of the American west. ★ **What feelings did Bierstadt try to suggest in this painting? How can you tell?**

Albert Bierstadt, *Landscape*

ness of the life it cherishes, or the depth and grandeur of its sculpture. None of its magnificent forest-crowned ridges rises much above the general level to publish its wealth. No great valley or lake is seen, or river, or group of well-marked features of any kind, standing out in distinct pictures. Even the summit-peaks, so clear and high in the sky, seem comparatively smooth and featureless. Nevertheless, glaciers are still at work in the shadows of the peaks, and thousands of lakes and meadows shine and bloom beneath them, and the whole range is furrowed with canyons to a depth of from 2,000 to 5,000 feet, in which once flowed majestic glaciers, and in which now flow and sing a band of beautiful rivers.

Though of such stupendous depth, these famous canyons are not raw, gloomy, jagged-walled gorges, savage and inaccessible. With rough passages here and there they still make delightful pathways for the mountaineer, conducting from the fertile lowlands to the highest icy fountains, as a kind of mountain streets full of charming life and light, graded and sculptured by the ancient glaciers, and presenting, throughout all their courses, a rich variety of novel and attractive scenery, the most attractive that has yet been discovered in the mountain-ranges of the world.

Source: *The Mountains of California,* John Muir, 1894.

Analyzing Primary Sources

1. What first impressed Muir about the Sierra Nevada?
   - **A.** the light
   - **B.** the height of the mountains
   - **C.** the destruction of the land
   - **D.** the mild weather
2. Muir recommends the range to
   - **F.** farmers.
   - **G.** gold miners.
   - **H.** mountain climbers.
   - **J.** painters.
3. **Critical Thinking Recognizing Points of View** What do you think was the main reason that Muir wrote this description?

Historical Critique

Why is Muir's description of the Sierra Nevada an authentic historical document? What facts does Muir include here that could not have come from his own personal observations?

ANSWER

Students might suggest that Bierstadt meant to create a feeling of awe for the landscape by showing the great height of the mountains and size of the valley.

Analyzing Primary Sources

ANSWERS

1. A **2.** H **3.** He wanted to educate people about the beauty of nature and make them aware of the importance of conservation.

Historical Critique He actually saw the Sierra Nevada as they then appeared. Facts that Muir himself did not actually observe include the length, width, and height of the mountains, and possibly the depths of the canyons.

★ 1–2 ★

America the Beautiful (average)

★ ★ ★ ★ ★ ★ ★ ★ ★ ★

Prereading Focus

Have students reread Section 3 in Chapter 1 to review what they have learned about the varied geography of North America.

Purpose-Setting Question

Ask: "What songs or poems celebrating our country have you heard or read?"

ANSWER

the Great Plains or another wheat-growing region

★ 1–2 ★ America the Beautiful

Introduction Katharine Lee Bates was an English professor at Wellesley College in Massachusetts. She wrote many poems and children's books during her long career. However, she is best known for writing the words to "America the Beautiful." Bates wrote the hymn in 1893 and revised it in 1911. Over the years, many people have suggested that this song should become the national anthem of the United States.

Vocabulary Before you read the selection, find the meanings of these words in a dictionary: **amber, strife, alabaster.**

★ ★ ★ ★ ★ ★ ★ ★ ★

O beautiful for spacious skies,
For amber waves of grain,
For purple mountain majesties
Above the fruited plain!
America! America!
God shed His grace on thee
And crown thy good with brotherhood
From sea to shining sea!

O beautiful for pilgrim feet,
Whose stern, impassioned stress
A thoroughfare for freedom beat
Across the wilderness!
America! America!
God mend thine every flaw,
Confirm thy soul in self-control,
Thy liberty in law!

O beautiful for heroes proved
In liberating strife,
Who more than self their country loved,
And mercy more than life!
America! America!
May God thy gold refine,
Till all success be nobleness
And every gain divine!

O beautiful for patriot dream
That sees beyond the years
Thine alabaster cities gleam
Undimmed by human tears!
America! America!
God shed his grace on thee,
And crown thy good with brotherhood
From sea to shining sea!

Source: *America the Beautiful and Other Poems,* Katharine Lee Bates, 1911.

Viewing HISTORY Amber Waves of Grain

This landscape by photographer Adam Jones suggests the "amber waves of grain" described in the song "America the Beautiful." ★ **In what region of the United States might this scene be located? Explain your answer.**

Background for Understanding

★ ★ ★ ★ ★ ★ ★ ★ ★ ★

Katherine Lee Bates wrote the poem *America the Beautiful* after gazing at the awe-inspiring view from Pike's Peak during a visit to Colorado in 1893. Later, the poem was set to music, using the tune of a hymn called "Materna," by American composer Samuel Augustus Ward. The song made its debut in 1910 when the poem and music were first published together.

Teaching Alternatives

★ ★ ★ ★ ★ ★ ★ ★ ★ ★

Team Teaching: Language Arts Work with a language arts teacher to present a lesson on poetry, music, and history. Point out to students that Katherine Lee Bates used poetry that was later set to music to express her love of country and to immortalize the hardships that Americans had overcome. Then have students find and analyze another song that describes or comments on some event in American history.

Analyzing Literature

1. What is the main topic of the song?
   - A. the founding of the United States
   - B. farm life
   - C. city life
   - D. American scenery
2. To what "heroes" does the song refer?
   - F. Pilgrims
   - G. soldiers
   - H. explorers
   - J. farmers
3. **Critical Thinking Synthesizing Information** Briefly list the historical events that the author mentions in the song.

Historical Critique

Patriotic songs are meant to stir feelings of pride in one's country. How does the first verse of "America the Beautiful" encourage feelings of pride?

★ Chapter 2 ★ The First Americans

★ 2–1 ★ The Spider Woman

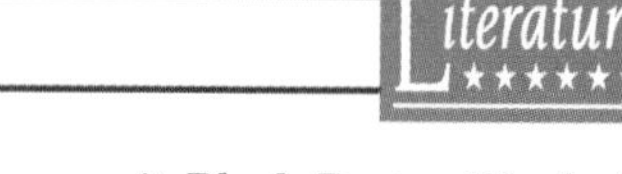

Introduction Weaving is an important part of Navajo culture. The following folk tale tells how Navajo women learned to weave. The Kisani woman, the main character, has been rejected by society because she is considered ugly. She comes upon the Spider Woman sitting in a cave.

Vocabulary Before you read the selection, find the meanings of these words in a dictionary: **abode, hogan, loom.**

★ ★ ★ ★ ★ ★ ★ ★ ★

The Kisani woman climbed down . . . into the abode of the Spider Woman who was weaving something. "Come down and sit here beside me and watch what I do, my grandchild," the old woman said. And the Kisani woman did as she asked.

The Spider Woman was using a stick about a foot long with a hole in one end like a needle, and with this she passed the thread in and out, making a blanket. "What is this that you do, grandmother?" the Kisani girl asked.

"It is a blanket I weave," the old woman replied.

"Does it have a name, my grandmother?"

"I will name it Black Design Blanket." And this became the Black Design Blanket, the first blanket of the Navajo. . . . Then Spider Woman told the girl the sun was low and it would soon be dark. . . .

"It is late and I must be leaving," the girl said.

"Please. Spend the night with me, my grandchild." This the Kisani woman agreed to and began to settle for the night. . . .

Spider Woman made some dumplings out of grass seeds and fed the girl and the next morning started weaving another blanket. She worked so fast that she finished it that day. It was square and as long as her arm and she named this new blanket Pretty Design Blanket. The girl watched her all day and stayed there a second night, and the following morning the Spider Woman started still another blanket. She finished this blanket, which she called White Striped Blanket, that day, and on the fourth morning she began another. This was a "Beautiful Design Skirt" such as Yeibichai dancers and Snake dancers wear, and was white with figures in black.

The next morning the Kisani girl went back to the hogan where she had been

Analyzing Literature

ANSWERS

1. A **2.** G **3.** arrival of the Pilgrims, the American Revolution

Historical Critique It brings to mind the nation's natural resources and beauty. Bates may have wanted to encourage Americans, whom she sees as good, to feel kinship and share their goodness with one another.

★ Chapter 2 ★

★ 2–1 ★

The Spider Woman

(basic)

★ ★ ★ ★ ★ ★ ★ ★ ★ ★

Prereading Focus

Have students reread Section 2 in Chapter 2 to review what they have learned about the early cultures of the Southwest.

Purpose-Setting Question

Ask: "What folk tales do you know that explain how something came to be, such as the story of Johnny Appleseed?"

Background for Understanding

★ ★ ★ ★ ★ ★ ★ ★ ★ ★ ★

Although most Native American cultures produced woven blankets, such as the one shown on p. 528, those of the Navajo are among the best-made and most colorful. The Navajo learned weaving from the Hopi, but they added zigzags and a variety of geometric shapes to the stripes of Hopi blankets. Raising sheep and goats provided a reliable source of wool, which they would wash, spin, and sometimes dye before weaving.

Teaching Alternatives

★ ★ ★ ★ ★ ★ ★ ★ ★ ★ ★

Team Teaching: Language Arts Work with a language arts teacher to present a lesson on folk tales. Explain that folk tales originated as oral traditions, but some were later written down. Most folk tales offer an explanation of a practice, belief, or natural phenomenon. Have students review the reading. Then ask: "What aspect of the Navajo world does this story attempt to explain?"

ANSWER

Hand-woven blankets made long ago are rare, so they are greatly valued. In addition, the careful handiwork is beautiful.

Navajo Blanket

Blanket weaving was a valued tradition among the Navajo people of the Southwest. Designs varied from village to village and were handed down from one generation to the next. The blanket shown here was woven in the late 1800s. ★ **Why are Navajo blankets prized today?**

staying and asked the Navajos for some cotton in three colors—yellow, black, and white. After the cotton had been given to her, she put up a loom, but not like the Spider Woman's loom. She put it up the way Navajo women do now and began a blanket. Her blanket was about half done when another Kisani woman came in and looked at the loom and the design. The girl had made a picture of a bird on both sides of the blanket.

"Where did you learn to do that?" the Kisani woman asked. "I did this on my own thought," answered the girl. "It is called a Black Design Blanket."

She finished it in one day, and the next morning she put up her loom again and asked for more cotton to weave. She made a Beautiful Design Skirt the same day. It was finished when two Kisani men came to see what she was doing and asked to see the blankets she had made. One examined the Beautiful Design Blanket very carefully. The second man observed the Black Design weaving. They then returned to their homes and made looms, copying the designs they had learned. And this is why it is the Kisani men who are known for their beautiful weaving.

The girl only made two blankets and then went back to Spider Woman's house. Spider Woman was now weaving a wicker water jar and after that she wove a big carrying basket such as Navajo women used to carry on their backs. The Kisani girl learned to make the basket and then the water jar. "When I went back," she told Spider Woman, "I showed the people how to make blankets like yours. Now I will go back and make carrying baskets and water jars."

"That is good," said Spider Woman. "I am glad you have taught them. But whenever you make a blanket, you must leave a hole in the middle the way I do. For if you do not, your weaving thoughts will be trapped within the cotton and not only will it bring you bad luck, but it will drive you mad."

The girl went back to her hogan and made a carrying basket and a water jar.

"Where do you learn all these things?" The People asked.

"I just guessed it out," she said.

The Navajo women watched her, and soon they were all making carrying baskets and then they learned to make water jars and blankets too, just like those of the Spider Woman. Unlike the Kisani men, it is the Navajo women who kept on with their blanket weaving. And they always left the spiderhole in the center of a spider web. That keeps them from getting "blanket sickness" of the mind from keeping the weaving patterns inside their heads. Navajo women almost never draw their blanket patterns down but keep them inside as Spider Woman did.

And that's true, even today.

Source: *Sweet Salt: Navajo Folk Tales and Mythology,* edited by Raymond Friday Locke, 1990.

528 ★ Source Readings

Analyzing Literature

1. What distinguishes a blanket woven by a Navajo?
   - **A.** It contains three different colors.
   - **B.** It is made on a loom.
   - **C.** It contains a picture of the sun.
   - **D.** It has a hole in the middle.
2. What is Kisani's obligation to the Spider Woman?
   - **F.** to sell the Spider Woman's blankets
   - **G.** to learn to weave much faster
   - **H.** to take care of the Spider Woman
   - **J.** to teach others how to weave
3. **Critical Thinking Making Generalizations** What role do you think folk tales play in a society?

Historical Critique

This tale was first told in the Navajo language. Also, like many folk tales, it was passed on orally for generations before being written down. How might these two facts affect the authenticity of this version of the story?

★ 2–2 ★ A Description of Montezuma

Introduction Bernal Díaz del Castillo was one of the Spanish soldiers who conquered the Aztec empire in the 1500s. He later settled in Guatemala and wrote his memoirs. In this passage, Díaz describes a visit to the Aztec emperor Montezuma.

Vocabulary Before you read the selection, find the meanings of these words in a dictionary: **proportioned, sparse, fragrant, idol, lavishly, frothy, cacao, stewards, provisioners.**

★ ★ ★ ★ ★ ★ ★ ★ ★

The great Montezuma was about 40 years old, of good height, well proportioned, and slender; he was not very dark but the color natural for an Indian. He did not wear his hair long, only long enough to cover his ears. He had few whiskers, dark and well set and sparse. His face was a little long, but pleasant, while his eyes were attractive, and he showed in his person and in his glance both affection and, when necessary, seriousness. He was most clean, bathing every day, in the afternoon. . . .

There were more than 200 of his main guards in rooms close to his own—not so that they could all talk with him, but only a few at a time. When they went to speak with him, they had to take off their rich clothes and put on others of little value, but they had to be clean. They had to enter barefoot and with their eyes down, and not look at his face. They had to bow three times and say, "Lord, my lord, my great lord," as soon as they reached his presence; and after they told him what they had come for, he attended to them with a few words. They did not turn their backs on him when they left, but kept their faces and eyes directed toward the floor near his feet while they backed from the room.

Let us leave this and return to the way things were served at mealtime. If it was cold, they made a large fire of coals of a wood that did not smoke. The scent of its bark was very fragrant, and so that it would not give off more heat than was wanted, they put in front of it a kind of screen worked in gold and with figures of idols. He [Montezuma] sat at a low stool, soft and rich. The table was also low, and made in the same design as the seats. . . . Four very beautiful and clean women brought water for the hands in things like deep basins called *xicales.* Below, to catch the water, they put a different kind of dish, and they brought him towels while two other women brought him tortillas.

When he began to eat, they placed in front of him a kind of screen of wood lavishly

Analyzing Literature

ANSWERS

1. D **2.** J **3.** Folk tales tell stories that help pass on information about a culture in an entertaining and memorable way.

Historical Critique Words and ideas may have been altered in the translation from one language to another. Also, because it was not originally written down, the story may have changed from the way it was first told.

★ 2–2 ★

A Description of Montezuma

(average)

★ ★ ★ ★ ★ ★ ★ ★ ★ ★

Prereading Focus

You might have students reread Section 3 of Chapter 2 to review what they have learned about the Aztec civilization and the position of the Aztec emperor.

Purpose-Setting Question

Ask: "What details in the excerpt might Spaniards in the late 1500s have found curious?"

Background for Understanding

★ ★ ★ ★ ★ ★ ★ ★ ★ ★

Apparently Díaz felt that historians who had never seen the "New World" had no business describing the adventures of those who risked all to explore strange lands. Díaz decided to tell his own eyewitness story of the conquest of Mexico. He called his account *Verdadera historia de la conquista de la Nueva España,* or *True History of the Conquest of New Spain.*

Teaching Alternatives

★ ★ ★ ★ ★ ★ ★ ★ ★ ★

Team Teaching: Language Arts Work with a language arts teacher to present a lesson on translations. Point out to students that Diaz's memoirs were originally written in Spanish, his native tongue. Ask students to consider how the meaning of his work might have been altered in the translation. If any students in the class are bilingual, ask them to share their knowledge about the sometimes difficult task of accurate translation.

ANSWER

He is clothed in gold and fine fabrics. He wears a headdress that may be a sign of his leadership.

Analyzing Primary Sources

ANSWERS

1. D **2.** F **3.** Díaz viewed Montezuma with respect; his description of him is favorable, and he seems to view the customs and riches of the empire with admiration.

Historical Critique Díaz's memoir is an historical document because it describes an actual time and place in history. Its accuracy is limited by the viewpoint and memory of the author; the memoirs were written years after the events described.

Viewing History **Montezuma, Emperor of the Aztecs**

This oil painting by a later artist gives a fanciful portrait of the last Aztec emperor, Montezuma. From descriptions and sketches of Aztec life, the artist shows how feathers and gold were used as armor and decoration. ★ **How does this portrait suggest that Montezuma was a great leader?**

painted with gold, so he could not be seen eating. The four women stood aside, and at his sides sat four elderly great chiefs, with whom Montezuma spoke from time to time and asked questions. As a great favor he would give to each of them a plate of what he thought was best. It was said that these elders were close relatives, counselors, and judges. . . .

After Montezuma had eaten, all the guards and the house servants had their meal, and it seems to me that they took out more than a thousand plates of food and more than two thousand pitchers of frothy cacao and a countless quantity of fruit. With his women and servants and tortilla makers and cacao makers, how much must it have cost him? Then there were the stewards and the treasurers, the provisioners and the wine cellarers, and those who had charge of the houses where maize was kept. If I tried to tell about each thing by itself, there would be so much to write about that I wouldn't know where to begin. We were astonished at the organization and the quantities of everything.

Source: *The Bernal Díaz Chronicles,* translated by Albert Idel, 1956.

Analyzing Primary Sources

1. What was Díaz describing in the passage above?

- **A.** differences between the Spanish and Aztecs
- **B.** Montezuma's great power and majesty
- **C.** the beauty of Aztec women
- **D.** Montezuma's appearance and eating habits

2. What aspect of Aztec life did Díaz emphasize in this description?

- **F.** the cleanliness of the Aztec emperor
- **G.** Aztec religious practices
- **H.** Montezuma's warlike appearance
- **J.** the abundance of gold and silver

3. Critical Thinking Recognizing Points of View Based on this excerpt, how did Díaz view Montezuma? Explain.

Historical Critique

Why is Bernal Díaz's memoir a historical document? How might its accuracy be limited?

530 ★ Source Readings

★ Chapter 3 ★ A Meeting of Different Worlds

★ 3–1 ★ Two Descriptions of the Middle Passage

Introduction Enslaved Africans were packed onto ships and brought to the Americas on a route known as the Middle Passage. The following two excerpts are the views and observations of men who witnessed it firsthand. John Newton was a former slave ship captain who later became a minister. Dr. Falconbridge was a surgeon who served on a slave ship during the time of the African slave trade.

Vocabulary Before you read the selection, find the meaning of this word in a dictionary: **ensued.**

★ ★ ★ ★ ★ ★ ★ ★ ★

The Reverend John Newton:

The cargo of a vessel of a hundred tons or a little more is calculated to purchase from 220 to 250 slaves. Their lodging rooms below the deck which are three (for the men, the boys, and the women) besides a place for the sick, are sometimes more than five feet high and sometimes less; and this height is divided toward the middle for the slaves lie in two rows, one above the other, on each side of the ship, close to each other like books upon a shelf. I have known them so close that the shelf would not easily contain one more.

The poor creatures, thus cramped, are likewise in irons for the most part which makes it difficult for them to turn or move or attempt to rise or to lie down without hurting themselves or each other.

Dr. Falconbridge:

Some wet and blowing weather. . . having occasioned the port-holes to be shut and the grating to be covered,. . . fever among the Negroes ensued. While they were in this situation, I frequently went down among them till at length their rooms became so extremely hot as to be only bearable for a very short time. . . . The climate was too warm to admit the wearing of any clothing but a shirt and that I had pulled off before I went down; notwithstanding which, by only continuing among them for about a quarter of an hour, I was so overcome with the heat, stench and foul air that I nearly fainted; and it was only with assistance that I could get on deck. The consequence was that I soon after fell sick of the same disorder from which I did not recover for several months.

Source: *Black Cargoes: A History of the Atlantic Slave Trade 1518–1865*, Daniel P. Mannix, 1962.

Viewing History: On Board a Slave Ship

An English officer painted this rare eyewitness picture of a slave ship. Yet it gives only a limited picture of the brutal conditions endured by enslaved Africans. Slave ship captains often crammed people into their cargo holds, knowing that many would die during the Middle Passage. ★ **Why was the death rate so high during the Middle Passage?**

★ Chapter 3 ★

★ 3–1 ★

Two Descriptions of the Middle Passage

(average)

★ ★ ★ ★ ★ ★ ★ ★ ★ ★

Prereading Focus

Have students reread Section 3 of Chapter 3 to review what they have learned about the Atlantic slave trade and the Middle Passage.

Purpose-Setting Question

Ask: "What conditions might captives on slave ships have endured on the voyage from West Africa to the Americas?"

ANSWER

Enslaved Africans were crowded into unhealthy, airless holds, where disease spread quickly.

Background for Understanding

★ ★ ★ ★ ★ ★ ★ ★ ★ ★

Dr. Falconbridge as well as others testified before Parliament on the slave trade, and the secretary recorded his observations of conditions on board slave ships: "[The enslaved] had not so much room as a man in his coffin either in length or breadth. When [Falconbridge] had to enter the slave deck, he took off his shoes to avoid crushing the slaves as he was forced to crawl over them."

Teaching Alternatives

★ ★ ★ ★ ★ ★ ★ ★ ★ ★

Team Teaching: Language Arts Work with a language arts teacher to give a lesson on different ways of conveying information. Point out that Reverend Newton reveals conditions aboard a slave ship by giving factual information. Dr. Falconbridge does so by relating how those same conditions affected him personally. Ask students to consider other ways in which this information might have been conveyed.

Analyzing Primary Sources

ANSWERS

1. B **2.** G **3.** Yes, both portray the Middle Passage as inhumane.

Historical Critique Enslaved Africans had little opportunity to pass such information on: They had been removed from their homes, did not know the language of their captors, and were often unable to live with their families once they were enslaved. They could have told what it was like to experience each day in the holds.

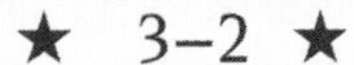

★ 3–2 ★

The Mayflower Compact (challenging)

★ ★ ★ ★ ★ ★ ★ ★ ★ ★

Prereading Focus

Have students reread Section 5 in Chapter 3 to review what they have learned about why the Pilgrims came to the Americas.

Purpose-Setting Question

Ask: "Why would establishing a government be important for people who are settling a new land?"

ANSWER

It suggests that the Pilgrims felt threatened and feared attack in their new environment.

Analyzing Primary Sources

1. What is the main subject of Dr. Falconbridge's account?
   - **A.** bad weather
   - **B.** living conditions on the ship
   - **C.** his illness
   - **D.** the ship's captain
2. According to Captain Newton, what was one of his main jobs as the captain of a slave ship?
   - **F.** to provide a safe and comfortable passage
   - **G.** to load the slave ship to maximum capacity
   - **H.** to keep the crew and passengers healthy
   - **J.** to avoid bad weather
3. **Critical Thinking Recognizing Points of View** Do you think that Dr. Falconbridge and Captain Newton have similar points of view about conditions aboard slave ships?

Historical Critique

Both of these reports, as well as the painting on page 531, are by officers who worked on slave ships. Why do you think there are fewer eyewitness accounts from enslaved Africans on the Middle Passage? What kind of information would an African witness have been able to give that Newton and Falconbridge could not?

★ 3–2 ★ The Mayflower Compact

Introduction Before the *Mayflower* anchored off the coast of what is now Cape Cod, Massachusetts, the 41 male passengers on board the ship signed a binding agreement. The 1620 document established a basis for self-government of their new colony, Plymouth. This agreement, known as the Mayflower Compact, is often considered one of the key documents in American history. Since women had no political rights, the women aboard the *Mayflower* were not asked to sign the document.

Vocabulary Before you read the selection, find the meanings of these words in a dictionary: **sovereign, covenant.**

★ ★ ★ ★ ★ ★ ★ ★ ★

In the name of God Amen, We whose names are underwritten, the loyal subjects of the dread sovereign Lord King James by the grace of God, of Great Britain, France, and Ireland king, defender of the faith, etc.

Pilgrims Go to Church

This painting shows Pilgrim families going to church. It was painted in the 1800s, many years after the Mayflower Compact. Faith in God and study of the Bible were central to Pilgrim life.

★ **What does the fact that the men are carrying weapons suggest about the lives of the Pilgrims?**

Background for Understanding

★ ★ ★ ★ ★ ★ ★ ★ ★ ★

Most passengers on the *Mayflower* were religious dissenters known as Separatists because they wanted to separate from the official Church of England. The *Mayflower Compact* reflected their desire to build a community in which they could practice their faith freely. Before anyone was allowed to leave the ship, all adult males had to sign the document.

Teaching Alternatives

★ ★ ★ ★ ★ ★ ★ ★ ★ ★

Team Teaching: Language Arts Work with a language arts teacher to help students understand the language of the *Mayflower Compact.* Read the second paragraph aloud. Point out that the paragraph has only one sentence but that sentence is made up of many phrases, or parts. Have students work in pairs to analyze and paraphrase each phrase of the paragraph.

Having undertaken for the glory of God, and advancements of the Christian faith and honor of our King and country, a voyage to plant the first colony in the northern parts of Virginia, do by these presents solemnly and mutually in the presence of God, and one of another, covenant and combine ourselves together into a civil body politic; for our better ordering and preservation and furtherance of the ends afore said; and by virtue hereof to enact, constitute, and frame such just and equal laws, ordinances, acts, constitutions, and offices, from time to time, as shall be thought most meet and convenient for the general good of the colony: unto which we promise all due submission and obedience.

In witness whereof we have here under subscribed our names at Cape Cod the 11 of November, in the year the reign of our sovereign Lord King James of England, France, and Ireland, the eighteenth and of Scotland the fifty-fourth Anno Domini 1620.

Source: *The American Reader: Words That Moved a Nation*, edited by Diane Ravitch, 1990.

Analyzing Primary Sources

1. What was the purpose of the Mayflower Compact?
   A. to elect church members
   B. to write a new constitution
   C. to establish a governing body
   D. to honor the English king
2. Where was the document signed?
   F. England
   G. France
   H. Cape Cod
   J. Virginia
3. **Critical Thinking Linking Past and Present** How are the ideas in the Mayflower Compact reflected in the form of government that exists in the United States today?

Historical Critique

Pilgrim men signed the Mayflower Compact while they were still on board ship. What can the document tell us about the government of the Plymouth colony after they landed? What can it not tell us?

★ Chapter 4 ★ The 13 English Colonies

★ 4–1 ★ Attracting Settlers to the Carolinas

Introduction In 1663, King Charles II of England gave eight loyal friends a huge tract of land in North America known as Carolina. These eight Lord Proprietors, as they were called, were eager to attract settlers who would make their land profitable. In 1666, the Lord Proprietors published a pamphlet called *A Brief Description of the Province of Carolina.* The excerpts that follow are taken from this pamphlet.

Vocabulary Before you read the selection, find the meanings of these words in a dictionary: **spacious, magnitude, fowls, thrive, exceedingly, swineherd, sturgeon, plaice, industrious, ingenious, partake, felicities, livelihood, abrogate, subsistence, dowry, civil.**

★ ★ ★ ★ ★ ★ ★ ★ ★

Carolina is a fair and spacious province on the continent of America. . . . The land is of diverse sorts as in all countries of the world. That which lies near the sea is sandy and barren, but bears many tall trees, which make good timber for several uses; and this sandy ground is by experienced men thought

Analyzing Primary Sources
ANSWERS

1. C **2.** H **3.** The ideas of the Mayflower Compact are reflected in the rights of all citizens to vote and participate in government.

Historical Critique It can tell us how the Pilgrims planned to govern but not how they actually did so, nor what laws they enacted.

★ Chapter 4 ★

★ 4–1 ★

Attracting Settlers to the Carolinas
(challenging)

★ ★ ★ ★ ★ ★ ★ ★ ★ ★

Prereading Focus
You might have students reread Section 3 of Chapter 4 to review what they have learned about the settlement of the Southern Colonies.

Purpose-Setting Question
Ask: "What arguments do the proprietors use to encourage people to move to Carolina?"

Background for Understanding

★ ★ ★ ★ ★ ★ ★ ★ ★ ★

South Carolina was inhabited long before the lord proprietors tried to attract settlers to the region. The area was first populated more than 11,000 years ago. Around A.D. 1100, Mississippian peoples moved in; they dominated the area until Europeans arrived. In 1600, South Carolina was home to between 15,000 and 20,000 Native Americans of Siouan, Iroquois, and Muskogean descent; but by the 1770s, these had all but disappeared.

Teaching Alternatives

★ ★ ★ ★ ★ ★ ★ ★ ★ ★

Team Teaching: Language Arts Work with a language arts teacher to present a lesson on descriptive writing. Have students review the excerpt and pick out some of the descriptive words used, such as *sandy, temperate, abundance,* and *wholesome*. Then ask students to write a description of their home, with the purpose of convincing a prospective buyer to purchase the property.

Viewing History ANSWER

Indigo was a cash crop—a product sold or traded primarily to manufacturers in England. It brought British goods and money into the colonies.

Viewing History: Growing Indigo

Early on, indigo plants were introduced to South Carolina and became a successful crop. Indigo produced a blue dye that English manufacturers used in their textiles. This sketch shows a South Carolina indigo plantation in 1773. ★ **How did crops like indigo help colonies to prosper?**

to be one cause of the healthfulness of the place. But up the river about twenty or thirty mile[s], where they have made a town, called Charles Town, there is plenty of as rich ground as any in the world. . . . The woods are stored with deer and wild turkeys, of a great magnitude, weighing many times above 50 lb. a piece, and of a more pleasant taste than in England, being in their proper climate; other sorts of beasts in the woods that are good for food, and also fowls, whose names are not known to them.

This is what they found naturally upon the place; but they have brought with them most sorts of seeds and roots of the Barbados [in the West Indies] which thrive [in] the most temperate clime . . . and they have potatoes, and the other roots and herbs of Barbados, and New England, what they could afford. They have indigo, tobacco, very good, and cotton wool; lime trees, orange, lemon, and other fruit trees they brought, thrive exceedingly. They have two crops of Indian corn in one year, and great increase every crop. Apples, pears, and other English fruit grow there out of the planted kernels.

The marshes and meadows are very large, from 1,500 to 3,000 acres and upwards, and are excellent food for cattle, and will bear any grant being prepared . . . some cattle, both great and small, will live well all the winter, and keep their fat without fodder: hogs find so much mast and other food in the woods that they want no other care than a swineherd to keep them from running wild. The meadows are very proper for rice, rapeseed, linseed, etc., and may many of them be made to overflow at pleasure with a small charge.

Here are as brave rivers as any in the world, stored with great abundance of sturgeon, salmon, bass, plaice, trout, and Spanish mackerel, with many other most pleasant sorts of fish, both flat and round, for which the English tongue has no name. Also, in the little winter they have, abundance of wild geese, ducks, teals, widgeons, and many other pleasant fowl. And (as it is said before) the rivers are very deep and navigable above 100 miles up; also there are wholesome springs and rivulets.

Last of all, the air comes to be considered, which is not the least considerable to the well being of a plantation, for without a wholesome air all other considerations avail nothing. And this is it which makes this place so desirable, being seated in the glorious light of heaven brings many advantages, and His convenient distance secures them from the inconvenience of His scorching beams. . . .

If, therefore, any industrious and ingenious persons shall be willing to partake of the felicities of this country, let them embrace the first opportunity, that they may obtain the greater advantages. . . .

The chief of the privileges are as follows:

First, there is full and free liberty of conscience granted to all, so that no man is to be molested or called in question for matters of religious concern; but everyone to be obedient to the civil government, worshipping God after their own way.

Second, there is freedom from custom for all wine, silk, raisins, currants, oil, olives, and almonds that shall be raised in the province for seven years. . . .

Third, every freeman and freewoman that transport themselves and servants by the 25th of March next, being 1667, shall have for himself, wife, children, and menservants, for each 100 acres of land for him and his heirs forever, and for every womanservant and slave, 50 acres. . . .

Fourth, every manservant at the expiration of their time, is to have of the country 100 acres of land to him and his heirs forever, paying only 1/2D. per acre, per annum, and the women 50 acres of land on the same conditions; their masters also are to allow them two suits of apparel and tools such as he is best able to work with, according to the custom of the country.

Fifth, they are to have a governor and council appointed from among themselves to see the laws of the Assembly put in due execution; but the governor is to rule but three years, and then learn to obey; also he has no power to lay any tax or make or abrogate any law without the consent of the colony in their Assembly.

Sixth, they are to choose annually from among themselves a certain number of men, according to their divisions, which constitute the General Assembly with the governor and his council, and have the sole power of making laws and laying taxes for the common good when need shall require. . . .

Such as are here [in England] tormented with much care how to get worth to gain a livelihood, or that with their labor can hardly get a comfortable subsistence, shall do well to go to this place [Carolina], where any man whatever that is but willing to take moderate pains may be assured of a most comfortable subsistence, and be in a way to raise his fortunes far beyond what he could ever hope for in England. . . .

If any maid or single woman have a desire to go over, they will think themselves in the Golden Age, when men paid a dowry for their wives; for if they be but civil, and under fifty years of age, some honest man or other will purchase them for their wives.

Source: *Historical Collections of South Carolina,* edited by B. R. Carrol, 1836.

Analyzing Primary Sources

1. What idea does this section of the pamphlet emphasize?
   - **A.** need for settlers
   - **B.** healthy air
   - **C.** abundant resources
   - **D.** warm climate
2. What do the proprietors promise settlers?
   - **F.** freedom of religion
   - **G.** freedom of speech
   - **H.** no taxes
   - **J.** all of the above
3. **Critical Thinking Making Inferences** **(a)** For what purpose was this pamphlet issued? **(b)** Do you think people in England in the 1660s would have found the land described in the pamphlet appealing? Explain.

Historical Critique

In 1660s, Europeans knew nothing about South Carolina so they had to rely on pamphlets like these. Why do you think people might have believed what the pamphlet said? Do you think it gives an accurate account of South Carolina? What subjects does it not include? Why?

Analyzing Primary Sources

ANSWERS

1. C **2.** F **3. (a)** to attract settlers to Carolina **(b)** Possible answer: They probably would, because rich woodlands and productive farmland were not readily available to the average person in England.

Historical Critique Those thoroughly unhappy with their current circumstances might be eager to believe a "paradise" was within reach. Yes and no; the description of natural resources seems fairly accurate, if exaggerated, but the pamphlet gives no mention of any of the drawbacks; it does not mention the difficulty of carving out farmland and making a home in a wilderness area, the cost of such an undertaking, or the hot climate; because fewer people would decide to emigrate to Carolina if they knew of the difficulties.

★ 4–2 ★

How I Become a Printer (average)

★ ★ ★ ★ ★ ★ ★ ★ ★ ★

Prereading Focus

Have students reread Section 5 of Chapter 4 to review what they have learned about Benjamin Franklin and the Enlightenment.

Purpose-Setting Question

Ask: "What do you think the job of a printer involved in colonial America?"

ANSWER

Love of reading enabled Franklin to educate himself. He learned to be a printer and manage a newspaper in his brother's shop. These experiences would have helped him succeed with his own newspaper.

★ 4–2 ★ How I Became a Printer

Introduction This excerpt from Benjamin Franklin's autobiography describes his early education and his apprenticeship to his brother James, a printer. Franklin also writes about the role printers played in bringing attention to colonial opposition to British rule.

Vocabulary Before you read the selection, find the meanings of these words in a dictionary: **tithe, censured, admonishing, satire, contrivance.**

★ ★ ★ ★ ★ ★ ★ ★ ★

I was put to the grammar-school at eight years of age, my father intending to devote me, as the tithe of his sons, to the service of the Church. My early readiness in learning to read (which must have been very early, as I do not remember when I could not read), and the opinion of all his friends, that I should certainly make a good scholar, encouraged him in this purpose of his. . . . But my father, in the mean time, from the view of the expense of a college education, which having so large a family he could not well afford . . . took me from the grammar-school, and sent me to a school for writing and arithmetic. . . . At ten years old I was taken home to assist my father in his business, which was that of a tallow-chandler and soapboiler. . . . Accordingly, I was employed in cutting wick for the candles, filling the dipping mold and the molds for cast candles, attending the shop, going of errands etc. . . .

From a child I was fond of reading, and all the little money that came into my hands was ever laid out in books. . . .

This bookish inclination at length determined my father to make me a printer, though he had already one son (James) of that profession. In 1717 my brother James returned from England with a press and letters to set up his business in Boston. I liked it much better than that of my father, but still had a hankering for the sea. To prevent the apprehended effect of such an inclination, my father was impatient to have me bound to my brother. I stood out some time, but at last was persuaded, and signed the indenture when I was yet but twelve years old. I was to serve as an apprentice till I was twenty-one years of age, only I was to be allowed journeyman's wages during the last year. In a little time I made great proficiency in the business, and became a useful hand to my brother.

Viewing History **Ben Franklin, Printer**

In 1723, young Ben Franklin left Boston for Philadelphia. Through hard work, he turned The Pennsylvania Gazette *into a successful newspaper. The* Gazette *allowed Franklin to share his ideas with a large audience.* ★ **How might Franklin's early experiences have helped him make *The Pennsylvania Gazette* prosper?**

Background for Understanding

★ ★ ★ ★ ★ ★ ★ ★ ★ ★

As an apprentice, Franklin struggled for recognition and sought an outlet for his creative talents. So, he wrote an essay about local events under the name "Mrs. Silence Dogood" and submitted it anonymously to his brother. James liked the essay and printed it. Only after he had published 13 more essays from Mrs. Dogood did James discover "her" real identity.

Teaching Alternatives

★ ★ ★ ★ ★ ★ ★ ★ ★ ★

Team Teaching: Language Arts Work with a language arts teacher to present a lesson on newspapers as a form of communication in a community. Have students review the excerpt and write a paragraph on the communications role of James Franklin's newspaper in colonial Boston. Then have them compare the role of a colonial newspaper with that of newspapers today.

Though a brother, he considered himself as my master, and me as his apprentice, and accordingly, expected the same services from me as he would from another, while I thought he demeaned me too much in some he required of me, who from a brother expected more indulgence. Our disputes were often brought before our father, and I fancy I was either generally in the right, or else a better pleader, because the judgment was generally in my favor. But my brother was passionate, and had often beaten me, which I took extremely amiss; and, thinking my apprenticeship very tedious, I was continually wishing for some opportunity of shortening it, which at length offered in a manner unexpected.

One of the pieces in our newspaper on some political point, which I have now forgotten, gave offense to the Assembly, He [James] was taken up, censured, and imprisoned for a month, by the speaker's warrant, I suppose, because he would not discover [reveal] his author. I too was taken up and examined before the council; but, though I did not give them any satisfaction, they contented themselves with admonishing me, and dismissed me, considering me, perhaps, as an apprentice, who was bound to keep his master's secrets.

During my brother's confinement, which I resented a good deal, notwithstanding our private differences, I had the management of the paper; and I made bold to give our rulers some rubs in it, which my brother took very kindly, while others began to consider me in an unfavorable light, as a young genius that had a turn for libeling and satire. My brother's discharge was accompanied with an order of the House (a very odd one), that "James Franklin should no longer print the paper called the New England Courant."

There was a consultation held in our printing-house among his friends, what he should do in this case. Some proposed to evade the order by changing the name of the paper; but my brother, seeing inconveniences in that, it was finally concluded on as a better way, to let it be printed for the future under the name of BENJAMIN FRANKLIN; and to avoid the censure of the Assembly, that might fall on him as still printing it by his apprentice, the contrivance was that my old indenture should be returned to me, with full discharge on the back of it, to be shown on occasion, but to secure to him the benefit of my service, I was to sign new indentures for the remainder of the term, which were to be kept private. A very flimsy scheme it was; however, it was immediately executed, and the paper went on accordingly, under my name for several months.

Source: *Autobiography of Benjamin Franklin,* edited by John Bigelow, 1868.

Analyzing Primary Sources

1. Why did his father decide Benjamin Franklin should become a printer?
   - **A.** He liked books.
   - **B.** He did not do well in school.
   - **C.** His brother was a printer.
   - **D.** He had a large family.
2. Why was James Franklin censured?
   - **F.** He published an offensive political statement.
   - **G.** He refused to pay his taxes.
   - **H.** He beat his brother.
   - **J.** He permitted Benjamin Franklin to run his newspaper.
3. **Critical Thinking Recognizing Points of View** Based on this excerpt, how do you think Benjamin Franklin viewed the British?

Historical Critique

Benjamin Franklin wrote his autobiography when he was around 50 years old. How does an autobiography differ from a diary as a source of historical information?

Analyzing Primary Sources

ANSWERS

1. A **2.** F **3.** Franklin supported his brother. When James was imprisoned, Franklin criticized the king's agents.

Historical Critique Possible answer: An autobiography is based primarily on recollections, while a diary is written when experiences and feelings are fresh. As a source of historical information, a diary is likely to be richer and more accurate in detail.

A Nation Is Born

★ Chapter 5 ★

★ 5–1 ★

Exploring the Ohio Valley (challenging)

★ ★ ★ ★ ★ ★ ★ ★ ★ ★ ★

Prereading Focus

You might have students reread Section 2 of Chapter 5 to review what they have learned about how the British won the Ohio Valley.

Purpose-Setting Question

Ask: "How might the English have used Croghan's journal to attract settlers to the Illinois Territory?"

A Nation Is Born

★ Chapter 5 ★ The Road to Revolution

★ 5–1 ★ Exploring the Ohio Valley

Introduction After the French and Indian War, Britain sent George Croghan to explore the Illinois Territory, part of the region Britain had won from France. Croghan could negotiate with Indians in the area because he knew several Indian languages. The excerpts below are taken from Croghan's journal for 1765.

Vocabulary Before you read the selection, find the meanings of these words in a dictionary: **prospect, dispatched, hoisted, embroiled, breadth, subsistence, clemency.**

★ ★ ★ ★ ★ ★ ★ ★ ★

May 15, 1765. I set off from Fort Pitt with two batteaux [boats] and encamped at Chartier's Island, in the Ohio, three miles below Fort Pitt.

16th. Being joined by deputies of the Seneca, [Shawnee], and Delawares that were to accompany me, we set off at 7 o'clock in the morning.... About a mile below the mouth of the Beaver Creek we passed an old settlement of the Delawares, where the French, in 1756, built a town for that nation. On the north side of the river some of the stone chimneys are yet remaining....

17th. At 6 o'clock in the morning we embarked, and were delighted with the prospect of a fine open country on each side of the river as we passed down. We came to a place called the Two Creeks, about 15 miles from Yellow Creek, where we put to shore; here the Seneca have a village on a high bank, on the north side of the river; the chief of this village offered me his service to go with me to the Illinois, which I could not refuse for fear of giving him offense, although I had a sufficient number of deputies with me already....

20th. At 6 in the morning we embarked in our boats, and proceeded down to the mouth of the Hochocken or Bottle River.... From here I dispatched an Indian to the Plains of Scioto with a letter to the French traders from the Illinois residing there, amongst the [Shawnees], requiring them to come and join me at the mouth of Scioto, in order to proceed with me to their own country, and take the oaths of allegiance to His Britannic Majesty, as they were now become his subjects....

[June] 6th. We arrived at the mouth of the Ouabache [Wabash]... The mouth of this river is about 200 yards wide, and in its course runs through one of the finest countries in the world, the lands being exceedingly rich, and well watered....

9th. An hour before day we set out on our march; passed through thick woods, some highlands, and small savannas, badly watered. Traveled this day about 30 miles.

10th. We set out very early in the morning, and marched through a high country, extremely well timbered.... The remainder of this day we traveled through fine rich bottom, overgrown with reeds, which make the best pasture in the world.... Here is great plenty of wild game of all kinds....

Background for Understanding

★ ★ ★ ★ ★ ★ ★ ★ ★ ★ ★

During the trip, discontented Indians attacked Croghan's party and Croghan was captured. He described the incident to a friend, writing: "I got the stroke of a Hatchet on the Head, but my skull being pretty thick, the hatchet would not enter, so you may see a thick skull is of service on some occasions." Soon after, Croghan was freed and continued his journey.

Teaching Alternatives

★ ★ ★ ★ ★ ★ ★ ★ ★ ★ ★

Team Teaching: Language Arts Work with a language arts teacher to present a lesson on travel writing. Tell students that Croghan's journal is typical of travel writing, as are magazine articles that describe the virtues and drawbacks of places around the world. Ask: "On what aspects of a journey would a modern travel article focus?" "On what aspects of a place?" "How would the focus differ from Croghan's?"

Viewing History: Map of the Ohio River Valley

Fur traders, soldiers, and explorers like George Croghan supplied the information for maps like this one of the Ohio River valley. This early map also shows the southern shore of Lake Erie. ★ **Why did colonists and the British want accurate maps of the Ohio River valley?**

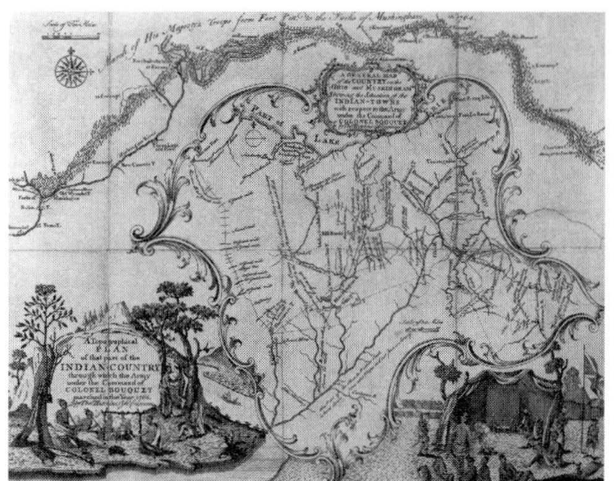

August 1. Within a mile of the Twightwee village, I was met by the chiefs of that nation, who received us very kindly. The most part of these Indians knew me, and conducted me to their village, where they immediately hoisted an English flag that I had formerly given them at Fort Pitt. The next day they held a council, after which they gave me up all the English prisoners they had, then made several speeches, in all which they expressed the great pleasure it gave them, to see the unhappy differences which embroiled the several nations in a war with their brethren, the English, were now so near a happy conclusion, and that peace was established in their country.

17th. In the morning we arrived at the fort, which is a large stockade enclosing about eighty houses; it stands close on the north side of the river, on a high bank, commands a very pleasant prospect for nine miles above and nine miles below the fort; the country is thick settled with French; their plantations are generally laid out about three or four acres in breadth on the river, and eighty acres in depth; the soil is good, producing plenty of grain. All the people here are generally poor wretches, and consist of three or four hundred French families, a lazy idle people, depending chiefly on the [Indians] for their subsistence; though the land, with little labor, produces plenty of grain, they scarcely raise as much as will supply their wants. . . .

In the last Indian war the most part of the French were concerned in it (although the whole settlement had taken the oath of allegiance to His Britannic Majesty); they have, therefore, great reason to be thankful to the English clemency in not bringing them to deserved punishment.

Source: *A History of the Commonwealth of Kentucky,* Mann Butler, 1834.

Analyzing Primary Sources

1. Who accompanied Croghan?
   - **A.** soldiers
   - **B.** settlers
   - **C.** Indians
   - **D.** mapmakers
2. Croghan wants the French traders to
   - **F.** guide him down the river.
   - **G.** take an oath of loyalty to England.
   - **H.** sell him furs.
   - **J.** sign a peace treaty.
3. **Critical Thinking Recognizing Points of View** Based on these excerpts, how did Croghan view the Indians he met on his travels?

Historical Critique

What is Croghan's attitude toward the French people he meets? How do you think recent events may have affected his attitude?

Viewing History ANSWER

Colonists wanted to know where to find the best land to settle; the British wanted to know how much natural wealth the land represented.

Analyzing Primary Sources

ANSWERS

1. C **2.** G **3.** Croghan seems to view the Indians favorably. At the same time, he considers them somewhat dangerous, as he is reluctant to displease them.

Historical Critique Croghan's attitude toward the French is decidedly unfavorable; his attitude is no doubt influenced by the recently fought French and Indian War, in which the French were the enemies of the British.

★ 5–2 ★

Revolutionary Tea

(basic)

★ ★ ★ ★ ★ ★ ★ ★ ★ ★

Prereading Focus

You might have students reread Section 4 of Chapter 5 to review what they have learned about the Tea Act of 1773 and early conflicts between the British and the American colonists.

Purpose-Setting Question

Ask: "Do Americans today use music to protest government actions or social problems? Give an example."

ANSWER

The expensive handiwork of reputable silversmiths in England would have been considered an impressive status symbol in the colonies.

Introduction In 1773, the Tea Act placed a new tax on tea sold in the colonies. The song "Revolutionary Tea," written by an anonymous colonist, reveals how many colonists felt about not only the Tea Act but about their relationship with faraway Britain.

Vocabulary Before you read the selection, find the meanings of these words in a dictionary: **pence, quoth, conveyed, steeped.**

★ ★ ★ ★ ★ ★ ★ ★ ★

There was an old lady lived over the sea.
And she was an Island Queen;
Her daughter lived off in a new country,
With an ocean of water between.
The old lady's pockets were full of gold,
But never contented was she,
So she called on her daughter to pay her
  a tax
Of three pence a pound on her tea,
Of three pence a pound on her tea.

"Now mother, dear mother," the daughter
  replied,
"I shan't do the thing that you ax;
I'm willing to pay a fair price for the tea,
But never the three penny tax."
"You shall," quoth the mother, and red-
  dened with rage,
"For you're my own daughter, you see,
And sure 'tis quite proper the daughter
  should pay
Her mother a tax on her tea,
Her mother a tax on her tea."

And so the old lady her servant called up,
And packed off a budget of tea,
And eager for three pence a pound, she
  put in
Enough for a large family.
She ordered her servants to bring home
  the tax,
Declaring her child should obey,
Or old as she was, and almost woman
  grown,
She'd half whip her life away,
She'd half whip her life away.

The tea was conveyed to the daughter's
  door,
All down by the ocean's side;
And the bouncing girl poured out every
  pound
In the dark and boiling tide.
And then she called out to the Island
  Queen,
"Oh, mother, dear mother," quoth she,
"Your tea you may have when 'tis steeped
  enough,
But never a tax from me.
But never a tax from me."

Source: *Father Kemp's Old Folks Concert Music.*

Viewing History — Colonial Tea Urn

Wealthy colonists took pride in owning silver tea servers. This elegant urn was made in England by a famous silversmith in 1774. It was a wedding present for John P. Custis, son of Martha Washington by her first husband. ★ **Why might colonists want tea services made in England rather than ones made in the colonies?**

Background for Understanding

★ ★ ★ ★ ★ ★ ★ ★ ★ ★

Another song, "The Boston Tea Party," had a more serious air, and ended with the words: "Deep into the sea descended cursèd weed of China's coast; / Thus at once our fears were ended; British rights shall ne'er be lost. / Captains! Once more hoist your streamers, spread your sails and plough the wave; / Tell your masters they were dreamers when they thought to cheat the brave."

Teaching Alternatives

★ ★ ★ ★ ★ ★ ★ ★ ★ ★

Team Teaching: Language Arts Work with a language arts teacher to present a lesson on protest songs. Direct students' attention to the Purpose-Setting Question. Discuss their responses and encourage them to share the lyrics to any protest songs they know. Focus on these questions: "What are some characteristics of a protest song?" "How have protest songs changed since pre-Revolutionary days?"

Analyzing Literature

1. What is the main point of "Revolutionary Tea"?
   - **A.** The colonists will remain loyal to Britain.
   - **B.** The British and the American colonists both love tea.
   - **C.** The American colonists are like disobedient children.
   - **D.** Colonists resent the tax on tea.
2. The "old lady" represents
   - **F.** Massachusetts.
   - **G.** colonial tea merchants.
   - **H.** Britain.
   - **J.** redcoats in Boston.
3. **Critical Thinking Synthesizing Information (a)** What historical event does the last verse of the song describe? **(b)** From whose point of view does it present this event?

Historical Critique

Protest songs like "Revolutionary Tea" expressed the feelings of people at the time. What feeling does the song express? Why do you think colonists might have sung this song and not joined other protests?

★ Chapter 6 ★ The American Revolution

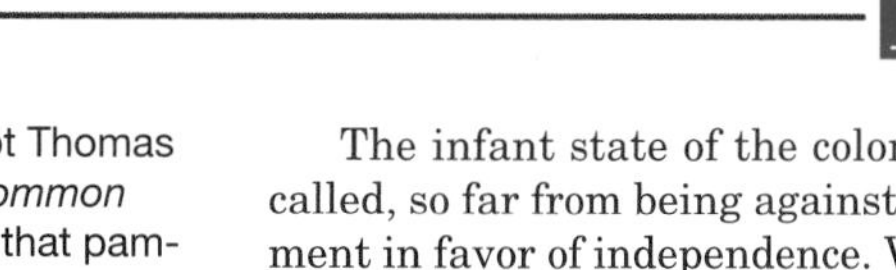

★ 6–1 ★ Common Sense

Historical Document ★★★★★★

Introduction In January 1776, patriot Thomas Paine published a pamphlet called *Common Sense.* In the following passage from that pamphlet, Paine presents several arguments for the 13 colonies to declare their independence from Britain. He also discusses the advantages of representative government.

Vocabulary Before you read the selection, find the meanings of these words in a dictionary: **venture, duplicity, unalterable, concord, posterity, expedience.**

★ ★ ★ ★ ★ ★ ★ ★ ★

Another reason why the present time is preferable to all others, is, that the fewer our numbers are, the more land there is yet unoccupied, which instead of being lavished by the k___ on his worthless dependents, may be hereafter applied, not only to the discharge of the present debt, but to the constant support of government. No nation under heaven hath such an advantage as this.

The infant state of the colonies, as it is called, so far from being against, is an argument in favor of independence. We are sufficiently numerous, and were we more so, we might be less united. It is a matter worthy of observation, that the more a country is peopled, the smaller their armies are. In military numbers, the ancients far exceeded the moderns: and the reason is evident, for trade being the consequence of population, men become too much absorbed thereby to attend to anything else. Commerce diminishes the spirit, both of patriotism and military defense. And history sufficiently informs us, that the bravest achievements were always accomplished in the non-age of a nation. With the increase of commerce, England has lost its spirit. The city of London, notwithstanding its numbers, submits to continued insults with the patience of a coward. The more men have to lose, the less willing are they to venture. The rich are in general slaves to fear, and submit to courtly power with the trembling duplicity of a spaniel.

Analyzing Literature

ANSWERS

1. D **2.** H **3. (a)** The last verse describes the Boston Tea Party. **(b)** The song presents the Boston Tea Party from the point of view of the colonists.

Historical Critique defiance; singing the song was a satisfying way to protest the Tea Act without fear of British reprisals

★ Chapter 6 ★

★ 6–1 ★

Common Sense

(challenging)

★ ★ ★ ★ ★ ★ ★ ★ ★ ★

Prereading Focus

Have students reread Section 2 in Chapter 6 to review what they have learned about how Thomas Paine's writings influenced the course of the American Revolution.

Purpose-Setting Question

Ask: "Is it easier to organize a small or a large group of people to accomplish a common purpose? Why?"

Background for Understanding

★ ★ ★ ★ ★ ★ ★ ★ ★ ★

Because of its content, Paine had trouble finding a printer for *Common Sense*. Once printed, its arguments inspired many to consider independence. Though a poor man, Paine signed over the copyright of the pamphlet to Congress. A million copies were sold at two shillings each, earning a fortune for the Patriot cause.

Teaching Alternatives

★ ★ ★ ★ ★ ★ ★ ★ ★ ★

Team Teaching: Language Arts Work with a language arts teacher to present a brief lesson on persuasive writing. Have students review the excerpt and note how Paine goes about setting out his arguments. How, for example, does he attempt to persuade the reader to agree with him? Have students choose a topic from colonial times or today and write their own persuasive essay.

Viewing HISTORY ANSWER

Yes, Paine supported liberty and believed people had a right to rebel against tyranny.

Viewing HISTORY Raising a Liberty Pole

In this picture by John McRae, Patriots raise a liberty pole, symbol of freedom. Women, men, and children join to show their support for independence from Great Britain. ★ **Do you think Thomas Paine's writings encouraged scenes like this? Explain.**

Youth is the seed time of good habits, as well in nations as in individuals. It might be difficult, if not impossible, to form the continent into one government half a century hence. The vast variety of interests, occasioned by an increase in trade and population, would create confusion. Colony would be against colony. Each being able might scorn each other's assistance: and while the proud and foolish gloried in their little distinctions, the wise would lament that the union had not been formed before. Wherefore, the *present time* is the *true time* for establishing it. The intimacy which is contracted in infancy, and the friendship which is formed in misfortune, are, of all others, the most lasting and unalterable. Our present union is marked with both these characters: we are young, and we have been distressed; but our concord hath withstood our troubles, and fixes a memorable era for posterity to glory in.

The present time, likewise, is that peculiar time, which never happens to a nation but once, [that is] the time of forming itself into a government. Most nations have let slip this opportunity, and by that means have been compelled to receive laws from their conquerors, instead of making laws for themselves. First, they had a king, and then a form of government; whereas, the articles or charter for government should be formed first, and men delegated to execute them afterward: but from the errors of other nations, let us learn wisdom, and lay hold of the present opportunity—to begin government at the right end....

In a former page I likewise mentioned the necessity of a large and equal representation; and there is no political matter which more deserves our attention. A small number of electors, or a small number of representatives, are equally dangerous. But if the number of representatives be not only small, but unequal, the danger is increased....

Immediate necessity makes many things convenient, which if continued would grow into oppressions. Expedience and right are different things. When the calamities of America required a consultation, there was no method so ready, or at that time so proper, as to appoint persons from the several Houses of Assembly for that purpose and the wisdom with which they have proceeded hath preserved this continent from ruin. But as it is more than probable that we shall never be without a Congress, every well wisher to good order, must own, that the mode for choosing

542 ★ Source Readings

members of that body, deserves consideration. And I put it as a question to those who make a study of mankind, whether representation and election is not too great a power for one and the same body of men to possess? When we are planning for posterity, we ought to remember that virtue is not hereditary.

Source: *Common Sense,* Thomas Paine, edited by Isaac Kramnick, 1982.

Analyzing Primary Sources

1. According to Paine, what is one reason to declare independence?
   - **A.** The population of the country is small.
   - **B.** Trade is flourishing.
   - **C.** There is a well-trained military.
   - **D.** Americans have diverse interests.
2. In Paine's view, what is the first step in forming a government?
   - **F.** to write a constitution
   - **G.** to pass laws
   - **H.** to raise taxes
   - **J.** to elect representatives
3. **Critical Thinking Making Inferences** To support what particular cause did Thomas Paine write this document?

Historical Critique

Common Sense was read and discussed throughout the 13 colonies. In evaluating a historical document, why is it important to know how popular and influential the document was?

★ 6–2 ★ Letters on Independence

Introduction John Adams and his wife, Abigail, corresponded through lengthy letters during John's many trips away from home. An avid letter writer, Abigail wrote to her family and friends about her life, including her observations of the political scene. She supported women's rights and opposed slavery. On March 31, 1776, Abigail Adams wrote to her husband while the Continental Congress discussed declaring independence. On April 14, John Adams responded to his wife's concerns.

Vocabulary Before you read the selection, find the meanings of these words in a dictionary: **tyrants, foment, impunity, despotism, oligarchy, ochlocracy.**

★ ★ ★ ★ ★ ★ ★ ★ ★

Abigail to John

. . . . I long to hear that you have declared an independency—and by the way in the new code of laws which I suppose it will be necessary for you to make I desire you would remember the ladies, and be more generous and favorable to them than your ancestors. Do not put such unlimited power into the hands of the husbands. Remember all men would be tyrants if they could. If particular care and attention is not paid to the ladies we are determined to foment a rebellion, and will not hold ourselves bound by any laws in which we have no voice, or representation.

That your sex are naturally tyrannical is a truth so thoroughly established as to admit of no dispute, but such of you as wish to be happy willingly give up the harsh title of master for the more tender and endearing one of friend. Why then, not put it out of the power of the vicious and the lawless to use with cruelty and indignity with impunity? Men of sense of all ages abhor those customs which treat us only as the vassals of your sex. Regard us then as beings placed by providence under your protection and in imitation

Analyzing Primary Sources

ANSWERS

1. A **2.** F **3.** Paine wrote *Common Sense* to persuade Americans to declare independence.

Historical Critique Knowing how a historical document was received helps the reader understand the mood and interests of the people of that time.

★ 6–2 ★

Letters on Independence (average)

★ ★ ★ ★ ★ ★ ★ ★ ★ ★

Prereading Focus

Have students reread Section 2 in Chapter 6 to review the ideas included in the Declaration of Independence.

Purpose-Setting Question

Ask: "How do you think the American Revolution affected women in the late 1700s?"

Background for Understanding

★ ★ ★ ★ ★ ★ ★ ★ ★ ★

A letter from Abigail the previous summer (1775) gave John the news of the Battle of Bunker Hill. She wrote feelingly: "How [many ha]ve fallen we know not—the constant roar of the cannon is so [distre]ssing that we can not Eat, Drink or Sleep. May we be supported and sustained in the dreadful conflict. . . . I cannot compose myself to write any further at present."

Teaching Alternatives

★ ★ ★ ★ ★ ★ ★ ★ ★ ★

Team Teaching: Language Arts Work with a language arts teacher to give a brief lesson on letters as primary source documents. Explain that historians use letters to learn about the past and evaluate the opinions of different individuals. Ask students to write a paragraph in answer to this question: "What concerns about a letter might a historian have when analyzing it as a piece of historical evidence?"

ANSWER

Students might suggest that girls learned the alphabet and numbers by stitching samplers.

Analyzing Primary Sources

ANSWERS

1. B **2.** H **3.** He responds teasingly and suggests that "petticoats" already rule. His response reveals that some men felt women had enough power in the home.

Historical Critique Perhaps—it might reveal how John generally responded to his wife's letters.

Viewing History **An American Sampler**

In colonial times, most well-bred New England women learned to stitch samplers. Mary Richardson stitched this sampler in 1783, when she was 11 years old. ★ **Besides teaching embroidery, how did samplers help educate girls?**

of the supreme being make use of that power only for our happiness.

John to Abigail

....As to your extraordinary code of laws, I cannot but laugh. We have been told that our struggle has loosened the bands of government everywhere. That children and apprentices were disobedient—that schools and colleges were grown turbulent.... But your letter was the first intimation that another tribe more numerous and powerful than all the rest were grown discontented. This is rather too coarse a compliment but you are so saucy, I won't blot it out.

Depend upon it, we know better than to repeal our masculine systems. Although they are in full force, you know they are little more than theory. We dare not exert our power in its full latitude. We are obliged to go fair, and softly, and in practice you know we are the subjects. We have only the name of masters, and rather than give up this, which would completely subject us to the despotism of the petticoat, I hope General Washington, and all our brave heroes would fight. I am sure every good politician would plot, as long as he would against despotism, empire, monarchy, aristocracy, oligarchy, or ochlocracy. A fine story indeed. I begin to think the ministry as deep as they are wicked.... At last they have stimulated the [ladies] to demand new privileges and threaten to rebel.

Source: *The American Reader: Words That Moved a Nation*, edited by Diane Ravitch, 1990.

Analyzing Primary Sources

1. In her letter, Abigail Adams asks her husband, John, to make sure that the new government
- **A.** declares independence.
- **B.** treats women fairly.
- **C.** ends slavery.
- **D.** puts power in the hands of husbands.

2. What does John Adams say about the relationship between men and women in society?
- **F.** Men and women are equal under the law.
- **G.** Men rule over women as tyrants.
- **H.** Men are usually ruled over by women.
- **J.** Men should protect women.

3. Critical Thinking Recognizing Points of View How did John Adams reply to his wife's request? What does his response indicate about his thinking?

Historical Critique

Abigail and John Adams wrote hundreds of letters to each other. Would reading more of their letters help you to evaluate the ones printed above? Explain.

544 ★ Source Readings

★ Chapter 7 ★ Creating a Republic

★ 7–1 ★ Delegates to the Constitutional Convention

Introduction William Pierce of Georgia, one of the delegates to the Constitutional Convention in 1787, wrote character sketches of some of the other delegates. His sketches include information about the age, occupation, war record, and political experience of the men who wrote the United States Constitution.

Vocabulary Before you read the selection, find the meanings of these words in a dictionary: **integrity, perseverance, mercantile, cant, embellish.**

★ ★ ★ ★ ★ ★ ★ ★ ★

Mr. Gerry's character is marked for integrity and perseverance. He is a hesitating and laborious speaker: possesses a great degree of confidence and goes extensively into all subjects that he speaks on, without respect to elegance or flower of diction. He is connected and sometimes clear in his arguments, conceives well, and cherishes as his first virtue, a love for his country. Mr. Gerry is very much of a gentlemen in his principles and manners. He has been engaged in the mercantile line and is a man of property. He is about 37 years of age....

Mr. Sherman exhibits the oddest shaped character I ever remember to have met with. He is awkward, [expressionless], and unaccountably strange in his manner. But in his train of thinking there is something regular, deep, and comprehensive; yet the oddity of his address, the vulgarisms that accompany his public speaking, and that strange New England cant which runs through his public as well as his private speaking make everything that is connected with him grotesque and laughable. And yet he deserves infinite praise,—no man has a better heart or a clearer head. If he cannot embellish he can furnish thoughts that are wise and useful. He is an able politician, and extremely artful in accomplishing any particular object. It is remarked that he seldom fails. I am told that he sits on the bench in Connecticut, and is very correct in the discharge of his judicial functions.... He is about 60....

Colonel Hamilton is deservedly celebrated for his talents. He is a practitioner of the law, and reputed to be a finished scholar. ... Hamilton requires time to think. He inquires into every part of his subject with the searchings of philosophy, and when he comes forward he comes highly charged with interesting matter, there is no skimming over the surface of a subject with him, he must sink to the bottom to see what foundation it rests on. ... He is about 33 years old, of small stature, and lean....

Mr. Lansing is a practicing attorney at Albany, and mayor of that [city]. He has a hesitation in his speech, that will prevent his being an orator of any eminence. His legal knowledge I am told is not extensive, nor his

Viewing History **The Liberty Bell**

The Liberty Bell hung in Philadelphia long before the Revolution. Written on it are words from the Bible: "Proclaim liberty throughout the land. . . ." In the 1800s, the Liberty Bell became an honored symbol of the United States. Because of a crack in the bell, it was no longer rung. ★ **Why is Philadelphia a suitable place for the Liberty Bell?**

★ Chapter 7 ★

★ 7–1 ★

Delegates to the Constitutional Convention (average)

★ ★ ★ ★ ★ ★ ★ ★ ★ ★

Prereading Focus

Have students reread Section 2 in Chapter 7 to review what they have learned about the delegates to the Constitutional Convention.

Purpose-Setting Question

Ask: "What character traits and abilities do you think Americans valued in the late 1780s?"

ANSWER

As the site of the Continental Congress and the Constitutional Convention, Philadelphia was at the center of the American struggle for freedom.

Background for Understanding

★ ★ ★ ★ ★ ★ ★ ★ ★ ★

William Pierce had fought bravely during the Revolution and later received congressional thanks for his valor. His support of the Constitution was pivotal to its approval in Georgia. During this time, he wrote: "I possess ambition ... and the flattering opinion ... of my Friends." Within a short time, however, both his business and health had failed. He died in 1789.

Teaching Alternatives

★ ★ ★ ★ ★ ★ ★ ★ ★ ★

Team Teaching: Language Arts Work with a language arts teacher to give a lesson on using descriptive writing to portray people. Have students review William Pierce's descriptions of individual delegates and list words or phrases that reveal each person whom he is portraying. Then have students choose someone they know and write a descriptive portrait of that person.

education a good one. He is however a man of good sense, plain in his manners, and sincere in his friendships. He is about 32 years of age.

Mr. Patterson is one of those kind of men whose powers break in upon you, and create wonder and astonishment. He is a man of great modesty, with looks that bespeak talents of no great extent, but he is a classic, a lawyer, and an orator; and of a disposition so favorable to his advancement that everyone seemed ready to exalt him with their praises. He is very happy in the choice of time and manner of engaging in a debate, and never speaks but when he understands his subject well. This gentleman is about 34 years of age, of a very low stature. . . .

Dr. Franklin is well known to be the greatest philosopher of the present age; all the operations of nature he seems to understand—the very heavens obey him, and the clouds yield up their lightning to be imprisoned in his rod. But what claim he has to the politician, posterity must determine. . . . He is 82 years old, and possesses an activity of mind equal to a youth of 25 years of age. . . .

Robert Morris . . . [although] not learned, yet he is as great as those who are. I am told that when he speaks in the assembly of Pennsylvania, that he bears down all before him. What could have been his reason for not speaking in the convention I know not—but he never once spoke on any point. This gentleman is about 50 years old.

Source: *The Records of the Federal Convention of 1787,* edited by Max Farrand, 1911.

Analyzing Primary Sources

1. Pierce describes Dr. Benjamin Franklin as a
   - **A.** great philosopher.
   - **B.** man of great modesty.
   - **C.** great politician.
   - **D.** great speaker.
2. Which one of the following men is not a lawyer?
   - **F.** Colonel Hamilton
   - **G.** Mr. Gerry
   - **H.** Mr. Patterson
   - **J.** Mr. Lansing
3. **Critical Thinking Recognizing Points of View** Based on this excerpt, how did William Pierce view these delegates to the Constitutional Convention?

Historical Critique

What information might help you decide if William Pierce's opinions of his fellow delegates are reliable?

★ 7–2 ★ The Federalist Papers

Introduction In 1787, three early American leaders—Alexander Hamilton, James Madison, and John Jay—published a series of essays titled *The Federalist.* The purpose of these essays was to persuade people in the separate states to support the new federal Constitution. Today, the collected essays are known as *The Federalist Papers.* The first passage below is from The *Federalist, Number 1,* written by Hamilton. It introduces the series. The second excerpt is from *The Federalist, Number 10,* written by Madison. In it, Madison discusses what he sees as the many advantages of the proposed system of government.

Vocabulary Before you read the selection, find the meanings of these words in a dictionary: **unequivocal, inefficiency, inducements, philanthropy, solicitude, formidable, diminution, emolument, aggrandize, faction, candid.**

★ ★ ★ ★ ★ ★ ★ ★ ★

Analyzing Primary Sources

ANSWERS

1. A **2.** G **3.** as men of great integrity with superior legal and political expertise

Historical Critique Possible answer: It would be helpful to have information about Pierce's character and political beliefs. If he had serious disagreements with some other delegates, this might have affected his opinion of them.

★ 7–2 ★

The Federalist Papers *(challenging)*

★ ★ ★ ★ ★ ★ ★ ★ ★ ★

Prereading Focus

Have students reread Section 4 in Chapter 7 to review what they have learned about the importance of *The Federalist Papers* in the struggle over ratifying the Constitution.

Purpose-Setting Question

Ask: "If some members of Congress today were trying to convince the people to adopt a new Constitution, what form of communication do you think they would use to present their arguments? Why?"

Background for Understanding

★ ★ ★ ★ ★ ★ ★ ★ ★ ★

The 85 essays written by Hamilton, Madison, and John Jay were all signed "Publius" and soon collected into a book entitled *The Federalist Papers*. The title itself was a clever political move. Using the term "federalist" forced the unwanted term "antifederalist" on their opponents. These opponents highly resented it because it seemed to imply total opposition to any federal government.

Teaching Alternatives

★ ★ ★ ★ ★ ★ ★ ★ ★ ★

Team Teaching: Language Arts Work with a language arts teacher to prepare a lesson on writing to reach an audience. Point out that when *The Federalist Papers* were written, newspapers were one of the few sources of information and entertainment; these essays were thus written to appeal to the reading public. Have students write an essay for a newspaper encouraging today's reader to renew ratification of the Constitution.

Viewing History **Celebrating Ratification**

When the Constitution was ratified, celebrations and parades were common throughout the nation. This parade in New York City featured a float representing the "ship of state." ★ **Why do you think the name *Hamilton* is included on the float?**

ANSWER

As an author of *The Federalist Papers,* Hamilton was one of the strongest supporters of the new Constitution.

Number 1 (Hamilton)

After an unequivocal experience of the inefficiency of the subsisting federal government, you are called upon to deliberate on a new Constitution for the United States of America. The subject speaks its own importance; comprehending in its consequences nothing less than the existence of the UNION, the safety and welfare of the parts of which it is composed, the fate of an empire in many respects the most interesting in the world. It has been frequently remarked that it seems to have been reserved to the people of this country, by their conduct and example, to decide the important question, whether societies of men are really capable or not of establishing good government from reflection and choice, or whether they are forever destined to depend for their political constitutions on accident and force. If there be any truth in the remark, the crisis at which we are arrived may with propriety be regarded as the era in which that decision is to be made; and a wrong election of the part we shall act may, in this view, deserve to be considered as the general misfortune of mankind.

This idea will add the inducements of philanthropy to those of patriotism, to heighten the solicitude which all considerate and good men must feel for the event. Happy will it be if our choice should be directed by a judicious estimate of our true interests, unperplexed and unbiased by considerations not connected with the public good. But this is a thing more ardently to be wished than seriously to be expected. The plan offered to our deliberations affects too many particular interests, innovates upon too many local institutions, not to involve in its discussion a variety of objects foreign to its merits, and of views, passions, and prejudices little favorable to the discovery of truth.

Among the most formidable of the obstacles which the new Constitution will have to encounter may readily be distinguished the obvious interest of a certain class of men in every state to resist all changes which may hazard a diminution of the power, emolument, and consequence of the offices they hold under the state establishments; and the perverted ambitions of another class of men, who will either hope to aggrandize themselves by the confusions of their country, or will flatter themselves with fairer prospects of elevation from the subdivision of the empire into several partial confederacies than from its union under one government.

Source Readings ★ 547

Analyzing Primary Sources

ANSWERS

1. B **2.** F **3.** Both Madison and Hamilton view conflicts of interest as a cause of instability in government.

Historical Critique He claims that many people who oppose the Constitution do so in order to make themselves rich and powerful.

Number 10 (Madison)

Among the numerous advantages promised by a well constructed union, none deserves to be more accurately developed than its tendency to break and control the violence of faction.... The instability, injustice, and confusion introduced into the public councils have, in truth, been the mortal diseases under which popular governments have everywhere perished.... The valuable improvements made by the American Constitution on the popular models, both ancient and modern, cannot certainly be too much admired; but it would be an unwarranted partiality to contend that they have as effectually obviated the danger on this side, as was wished and expected. Complaints are everywhere heard from our most considerate and virtuous citizens, equally the friends of public and private faith and of public and personal liberty, that our governments are too unstable, that the public good is disregarded in the conflicts of rival parties, and that measures are too often decided, not according to the rules of justice and the rights of the minor party, but by the superior force of an interested and overbearing majority.... It will be found, indeed, on a candid review of our situation, that some of the distresses under which we labor have been erroneously charged on the operation of our governments; but it will be found, at the same time, that other causes will not alone account for many of our heaviest misfortunes. . . . These must be chiefly, if not wholly, effects of the unsteadiness and injustice with which a factious spirit has tainted our public administrations.

Source: *Words That Made American History*, Volume 1, edited by Richard N. Current, 1972.

Analyzing Primary Sources

1. What is the main subject of *The Federalist?*
- **A.** the American Revolution
- **B.** the Constitution
- **C.** the Declaration of Independence
- **D.** the Articles of Confederation

2. What does Madison say is the main problem in forming a new government?
- **F.** conflicts between different people
- **G.** holding elections
- **H.** passing new laws
- **J.** choosing a good President

3. Critical Thinking Comparing How does Madison's view of government compare with Hamilton's?

Historical Critique

People often try to win support by attacking their opponents. Give one example of how Hamilton attacks the Antifederalists.

★ Chapter 8 ★

★ 8–1 ★

The Magna Carta
(challenging)

★ ★ ★ ★ ★ ★ ★ ★ ★ ★

Prereading Focus

Have students reread Section 2 in Chapter 8 to review what they have learned about why the framers of the Constitution wanted to limit the power of government.

★ Chapter 8 ★ The Constitution at Work

★ 8–1 ★ The Magna Carta

Introduction On June 15, 1215, King John of England made peace with rebellious barons by agreeing to sign the Magna Carta, or Great Charter. The Magna Carta ensured the barons' rights and limited the king's power. The historic document established the principle that even the king has to obey the law of the land. The Magna Carta became the basis for democratic government in England. Later, in 1787, American leaders used many of the principles found in the Magna Carta when they wrote the Constitution of the United States.

Background for Understanding

★ ★ ★ ★ ★ ★ ★ ★ ★ ★

Nobles benefited most from the Magna Carta. The charter had little effect on commoners, although they made up the majority of England's population. Whereas King John resisted signing the charter, later English rulers abided by it. Over time, it allowed nobles, and later Parliament, to check the power of monarchs.

Teaching Alternatives

★ ★ ★ ★ ★ ★ ★ ★ ★ ★

Team Teaching: Language Arts Work with a language arts teacher to give a lesson on the importance of writing both for government and for society. Ask students to consider, for example, the written documents which set up and define the United States government. Ask: "Could we survive as a nation without such written documents? Why or why not?"

Vocabulary Before you read the selection, find the meanings of these words in a dictionary: **inviolate, compelled, bailiffs, assessment, abbots, counsel, constable, credible, dispossessed, peers.**

★ ★ ★ ★ ★ ★ ★ ★ ★

John, by the grace of God, king of England, lord of Ireland, duke of Normandy and Aquitaine, count of Anjou to the archbishops, bishops, abbots, earls, barons, justiciars, foresters, sheriffs, reeves, servants, and all his bailiffs and his faithful people greeting. . . .

1. In the first place we have granted to God and by this our present charter confirmed for us and our heirs forever that the English church shall be free, and shall hold its rights entire, and her liberties inviolate. . . . We have granted moreover to all free men of our kingdom for us and our heirs forever all the liberties written below, to be held by them and their heirs from us and our heirs forever. . . .

8. No widow shall be compelled to marry, so long as she prefers to live without a husband; provided always that she gives security not to marry without our consent, if she holds of us,* or without the consent of the lord of whom she holds, if she holds of another. . . .

14. And for holding a common council of the kingdom concerning the assessment of an aid [tax] . . . we shall cause to be summoned the archbishops, bishops, abbots, earls, and greater barons . . . we shall cause to be summoned by our sheriffs and bailiffs all others who hold of us in chief, for a fixed date . . . and at a fixed place; and in all letters of such summons we will specify the reason of the summons. And when the summons has thus been made, the business shall proceed on the day appointed, according to the counsel of such as are present, although not all who were summoned have come. . . .

30. No sheriff or bailiff of ours, or other person, shall take the horses or carts of any freeman for transport duty, against the will of the said freeman.

31. Neither we nor our bailiffs shall take, for our castles or for any other work of ours, wood which is not ours, against the will of the owner of that wood. . . .

38. No bailiff for the future shall, upon his own unsupported complaint, put anyone to his "law," without credible witness brought for this purpose.

*To "hold of" meant to live on land granted by the king or by another lord.

The British Parliament Meets

This print shows the House of Commons meeting in London in the 1700s. The British parliamentary tradition was a major influence on the government of the United States. ★ **What branch of the American government is similar to Parliament?**

Purpose-Setting Question

Ask: "What did monarchies expect from their subjects? What did their subjects expect from their rulers?"

ANSWER

the legislature—or Congress

Analyzing Primary Sources

ANSWERS

1. C **2.** G **3.** Possible answer: The reforms listed in the Magna Carta evolved into democratic ideas. These democratic ideas are incorporated into our own Constitution.

Historical Critique If the translation is inaccurate, it may change the meaning of certain words or of the entire document.

★ 8–2 ★

The Volunteer Spirit: Three Views *(average)*

★ ★ ★ ★ ★ ★ ★ ★ ★ ★

Prereading Focus

Have students reread Section 5 of Chapter 8 to review what they have learned about President Kennedy's domestic agenda.

Purpose-Setting Question

Ask: "Why might a President want to set up a national group of volunteers?"

39. No free man shall be taken, or imprisoned, or dispossessed, or outlawed, or banished, or in any way destroyed, except by the legal judgment of his peers or by the law of the land.

40. To no one will we sell, to no one will we deny, or delay, right or justice.

Source: *Readings in European History,* Volume 1, edited by James Harvey Robinson, 1904.

Analyzing Primary Sources

1. What is the purpose of the Magna Carta?

A. to give more rights to the king
B. to write a new constitution
C. to ensure the rights of nobles
D. to give more land for the people

2. What part of the United States legal system is based on article 39?

F. freedom of religion
G. trial by jury
H. election of representatives
J. freedom of speech

3. Critical Thinking Drawing Conclusions Why do you think the Magna Carta is considered one of the key documents of American democracy?

Historical Critique

The Magna Carta was originally written in Latin and has been translated into English. Why is it important to know whether a document has been translated?

★ 8–2 ★ The Volunteer Spirit: Three Views

Introduction The Peace Corps program, started in 1961 by President John Kennedy, gives young people the opportunity to live in another country and teach skills to others. The first two passages below are from Peace Corps volunteers (PCVs) in the Philippines and in Paraguay. In the third account, a fish farmer in Thailand tells how Peace Corps volunteers helped him.

Vocabulary Before you read the selection, find the meanings of these words in a dictionary: **illiteracy, materialistic, atypical.**

★ ★ ★ ★ ★ ★ ★ ★ ★

Dennis Drake:

My first introduction to the [Peace] Corps was via a television advertisement that ran under the slogan, "The toughest job you'll ever love." Perhaps it was partly the slogan that got me thinking about joining or just the chance to change my life and help people at the same time. Really a simplistic view but maybe common thinking for more than just a few volunteers. Just imagine a person thinking he can actually do something about world hunger, poverty, illiteracy, or disease. Those are not "just" problems, but problems the size of mountains, yet the average Peace Corps volunteer believes he can do his part by chipping away at those mountains . . . one person at a time.

Kathleen Maria Sloop:

At the time I received my assignment from Washington, I had just been promoted to a great position as a market analyst in the bank at which I was working. I was a recent college graduate, so it was hard to give up all the things I had recently acquired, like a car, a good job, a nice house that I was sharing with two roommates whom I loved. But, I also knew that I'd learn more as a PCV, and I'd be "richer" as a person, if I lived and ate and shared with people who needed my help and friendship. I saw I was easily slipping into the easy, yet sometimes empty, materialistic life we Americans lead. I wanted to do something that would remind me for the rest of my

Background for Understanding

★ ★ ★ ★ ★ ★ ★ ★ ★ ★

Peace Corps volunteer Robert Burkhardt taught English in Iran from 1962 to 1964. Recalling that time, he said: "Being in the Peace Corps, I felt a part of this incredible pattern going on—in the Philippines, Columbia, Kenya, Iran, Tunisia, and Guatemala—and I was just one little digit in the great wheel of history. It was a great sensation."

Teaching Alternatives

★ ★ ★ ★ ★ ★ ★ ★ ★ ★

Team Teaching: Language Arts Work with a language arts teacher to explore with students what it might be like to work in a country where you are just beginning to learn the language. Have students think of ways they might communicate. Divide the class into small groups, give each group a hypothetical situation, and have them role-play for the class how they might handle that situation.

life that Americans' lifestyles are atypical, not the norm in the world. It was hard to give up the convenience and comfort of the U.S., and I won't say there haven't been times when I wished I could blink and be home again, but I've also never regretted making the decision I did to serve.

Mr. Prakong:

Volunteers have helped me a lot in two different ways: first, with their labor, helping me to run the farm—just proving that they are willing to "get their feet wet" alongside me. They dress in jeans, they put on "farmer pants," sometimes they get diseases or infections, but that's the way they work. The other way they help is that volunteers know something about how to raise fish, the different species, what [food] they need. I never knew anything like that before volunteers came. They taught me induced fish spawning techniques, they helped me build signs on the road to market my fish. . . . If I had to rely on government administrations, I would be starving by now. They work from the top down, they are eager to show off their technical expertise, but they don't know the faces of the people they want to instruct. Peace Corps volunteers work from the bottom up. They have the theory, but they are not afraid to get their feet wet, to work one-on-one with the farmers.

Working this way with Volunteers, a very close relationship develops. I am the "older brother," the Volunteer is the "younger brother or sister." We suffer the same problems together, we sit together, we eat together—sometimes don't eat together if there's no food—joke together. We are family. I cried when the last Volunteer left. I will cry when Ron Rice (my Volunteer coworker) leaves.

Viewing History **A Peace Corps Volunteer in Costa Rica**

This Peace Corps worker is helping students in a school in the Central American nation of Costa Rica. Volunteers do many different kinds of jobs, both in the United States and overseas. ★ **Why do you think many Americans volunteer their time and energy to help other people?**

Source: *Who Cares? Millions Do: A Book About Altruism,* Milton Meltzer, 1994.

Analyzing Primary Sources

1. Where do most Peace Corps volunteers work?
- **A.** in Washington, D.C.
- **B.** on fish farms
- **C.** in foreign countries
- **D.** in Thailand

2. According to Mr. Prakong, what did Peace Corps volunteers teach him?
- **F.** how to read
- **G.** fish farming methods
- **H.** how to stop infections
- **J.** television advertising

3. Critical Thinking **Comparing** Based on this excerpt, what was Mr. Prakong's view of the Peace Corps volunteers?

Historical Critique

Author Milton Meltzer collected these three accounts for a book titled *Who Cares? Millions Do: A Book About Altruism.* (Altruism is unselfish concern for others.) Do you think Meltzer wanted to present a positive or negative view of the Peace Corps? How might this have influenced what he included in his book?

ANSWER

Possible answers: Many Americans are grateful for what they have so that helping others brings a sense of sharing and satisfaction. Religious beliefs, a sense of duty, or a desire to serve may motivate others to help those in need.

Analyzing Primary Sources

ANSWERS

1. C **2.** G **3.** Mr. Prakong thought that the volunteers helped him become a better fish farmer. He respected them for working alongside him.

Historical Critique Possible answer: The word *altruism* shows that Meltzer wanted to present a positive view of the Peace Corps. He would probably not choose to include accounts that gave a negative view.

Unit 3 The Nation Takes Shape

★ Chapter 9 ★

★ 9–1 ★

A Description of George Washington
(average)

★ ★ ★ ★ ★ ★ ★ ★ ★ ★

Prereading Focus
Have students reread Section 1 in Chapter 9 to review what they have learned about George Washington's presidency.

Purpose-Setting Question
Ask: "What personality traits would you expect to find in a person who was a great general and a President of the United States?"

ANSWER
Possible answers: the stars and stripes, the Liberty Bell, George Washington

Unit 3 The Nation Takes Shape

★ Chapter 9 ★ The New Republic Begins

★ 9–1 ★ A Description of George Washington

Introduction Thomas Jefferson, author of the Declaration of Independence, knew all the chief leaders of the Revolution and the new republic. He himself served as third President of the United States. He also wrote on many subjects ranging from philosophy, religion, and science to education and farming. As he grew older, he was often asked about leaders of the Revolutionary era. This excerpt is from a letter Jefferson wrote to Dr. Walter Jones, who had asked about George Washington.

Vocabulary Before you read the selection, find the meanings of these words in a dictionary: **delineate, acute, judiciously, prudence, colloquial, mediocrity, copiousness, fluency, indifferent, constellation, worthies.**

★ ★ ★ ★ ★ ★ ★ ★ ★

I think I knew General Washington intimately and thoroughly; and were I called on to delineate his character, it should be in terms like these.

His mind was great and powerful, without being of the very first order; his penetration [keenness of mind] strong, though not so acute as that of a Newton, Bacon, or Locke; and as far as he saw, no judgment was ever sounder. It was slow in operation, being little aided by invention or imagination, but sure in conclusion. Hence the common remark of his officers, of the advantage he derived [gained] from councils of war, where hearing all suggestions, he selected whatever was best; and certainly no General ever planned his battles more judiciously. But if deranged [upset] during the course of the action, if any member of his plan was dislocated by sudden circumstances, he was slow in readjustment.

Viewing History **Honoring Washington**

An admirer said that George Washington was "first in war, first in peace, first in the hearts of his countrymen." This banner honors the first President. ★ **What symbols of the United States can you identify on this banner?**

Background for Understanding

★ ★ ★ ★ ★ ★ ★ ★ ★ ★

Politician and physician Benjamin Rush wrote that Washington "has so much martial dignity in his deportment that you would distinguish him to be a general and a soldier from among ten thousand people." An English visitor wrote that "Washington has something uncommonly majestic and commanding in his walk, his address, his figure, and his countenance."

Teaching Alternatives

★ ★ ★ ★ ★ ★ ★ ★ ★ ★

Team Teaching: Language Arts Work with a language arts teacher to present a brief lesson on George Washington in literature. Gather descriptions of Washington from both fictional and nonfictional sources, and distribute them to the class. Have students compare the descriptions and develop generalizations about Washington's appearance and temperament.

The consequence was, that he often failed in the field, and rarely against an enemy in station, as in Boston and York.

He was incapable of fear, meeting personal dangers with the calmest unconcern. Perhaps the strongest feature in his character was prudence, never acting until every circumstance, every consideration, was maturely weighed; refraining if he saw a doubt, but, when once decided, going through with his purpose, whatever obstacles opposed....

His heart was not warm in its affections; but he exactly calculated every man's value, and gave him a solid esteem proportioned to it. His person, you know, was fine, his stature exactly what one would wish, his deportment [bearing] easy, erect and noble; the best horseman of his age, and the most graceful figure that could be seen on horseback. Although in the circle of his friends, where he might be unreserved with safety, he took a free share in conversation, his colloquial talents were not above mediocrity, possessing neither copiousness of ideas, nor fluency of words. In public, when called on for a sudden opinion, he was unready, short and embarrassed. Yet he wrote readily, rather diffusely [wordily], in an easy and correct style....

On the whole, his character was, in its mass, perfect, in nothing bad, in a few points indifferent; and it may truly be said, that never did nature and fortune combine more perfectly to make a man great, and to place him in the same constellation with whatever worthies have merited from man an everlasting remembrance.

Source: *The Complete Jefferson,* edited by Saul K. Padover, 1943.

Analyzing Primary Sources

1. What was Jefferson mainly describing in this passage?
- **A.** General Washington's greatest victories
- **B.** the first President's political ideas
- **C.** George Washington's character
- **D.** his long friendship with George Washington

2. In Jefferson's view, what was one of Washington's greatest strengths?
- **F.** his speaking ability
- **G.** his imagination
- **H.** his careful judgment
- **J.** his warmth

3. Critical Thinking Recognizing Points of View Based on this excerpt, does Jefferson think Washington's strengths outweigh his weaknesses? Explain your answer.

Historical Critique

Would you consider Thomas Jefferson to be a reliable source of information about George Washington? Why or why not?

★ 9–2 ★ Farewell Address

Introduction In 1796, after serving two terms as President, George Washington wrote his famous Farewell Address. In it, he announced that he would not seek a third term. As he retired from public service, the outgoing President gave his views on the best policies for the young republic to follow. As the nation's first President, he knew firsthand the great issues of the day. He was especially concerned about the rise of political parties and the danger of the nation becoming involved in European wars. Washington's advice about foreign policy influenced future Presidents for more than a century.The following excerpt is from Washington's Farewell Address.

Vocabulary Before you read the selection, find the meanings of these words in a dictionary: **apprise, baneful, enfeeble, agitate, animosity, foment, facilitate access, enjoin, magnanimous, benevolence, provocation, maxim.**

★ ★ ★ ★ ★ ★ ★ ★ ★

Analyzing Primary Sources

ANSWERS

1. C **2.** H **3.** Yes, students might cite lines such as "his character was, in its mass, perfect" or Jefferson's judgment that Washington deserved to be ranked among the greatest figures of history.

Historical Critique Yes, Jefferson knew Washington personally and professionally over a long period of time.

★ 9–2 ★

Farewell Address

(challenging)

★ ★ ★ ★ ★ ★ ★ ★ ★ ★

Prereading Focus

Have students reread Section 2 in Chapter 9 to review what they have learned about Washington's decision to retire.

Purpose-Setting Question

Ask: "How influential do you think George Washington's advice was in 1796?"

Background for Understanding

★ ★ ★ ★ ★ ★ ★ ★ ★ ★

Historians and contemporaries have lauded Washington for relinquishing the presidency after two terms. "[T]he most important fact about the Farewell Address was that it was made," writes modern author Richard Brookhiser. George III said Washington's retirement "placed him in a light the most distinguished of any man living." After Washington died, Napoleon reputedly said, "They wanted me to be another Washington."

Teaching Alternatives

★ ★ ★ ★ ★ ★ ★ ★ ★ ★

Team Teaching: Language Arts Work with a language arts teacher to present a lesson on the ways that Presidents communicate to the people of the United States. Explain that all Presidents have used speeches, letters or newspapers to convey information to the public. Ask: "What other methods of communication do Presidents use today?"

 ANSWER

Southerners agreed to support Hamilton's economic plan, In return, the nation's new capital was to be built in the South.

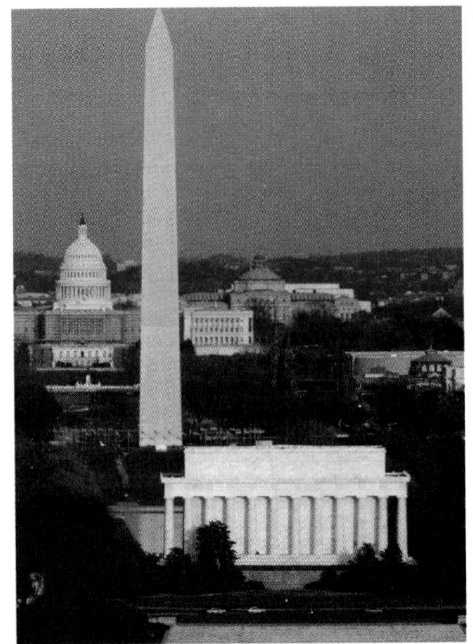

Viewing History **The Nation's Capital**

When George Washington left office in 1797, the new nation's new capital city was still in the planning stages. As a result, Washington was the only President never to live in Washington, D.C. This photograph shows Washington today. The tall white tower is the Washington Monument. ★ **How was the location for the nation's capital chosen?**

FRIENDS AND FELLOW-CITIZENS:

The period for a new election of a citizen, to administer the executive government of the United States, being not far distant . . . , it appears to me proper, . . . that I should now apprise you of the resolution I have formed to decline being considered among the number of those out of whom a choice is to be made. . . .

I have already intimated [suggested] to you the danger of parties in the State, with particular reference to the founding of them on geographical discriminations [bases]. Let me now take a more comprehensive view, and warn you in the most solemn manner against the baneful effects of the spirit of party, generally. . . .

It serves always to distract the public councils and enfeeble the public administration. It agitates the community with ill-founded jealousies and false alarms, kindles the animosity of one part against another, foments occasionally riot and insurrection. It opens the door to foreign influence and corruption, which find a facilitated access to the government itself through the channels of party passions. Thus the policy and the will of one country, are subjected to the policy and will of another. . . .

Observe good faith and justice toward all nations. Cultivate peace and harmony with all. Religion and morality enjoin this conduct and can it be that good policy does not equally enjoin it? It will be worthy of a free, enlightened, and at no distant period, a great nation, to give to mankind the magnanimous and too novel example of a people always guided by an exalted justice and benevolence. . . .

The great rule of conduct for us in regard to foreign nations is, in extending our commercial relations to have with them as little political connection as possible. So far as we have already formed engagements let them be fulfilled, with perfect good faith. Here let us stop.

Europe has a set of primary interests which to us have none, or a very remote relation. Hence she must be engaged in frequent controversies, the causes of which are essentially foreign to our concerns. . . .

Our detached and distant situation invites and enables us to pursue a different course. If we remain one people, under an efficient government, the period is not far off when we may defy material injury from external [outside] annoyance; when we may take such an attitude as will cause the neutrality we may at any time resolve upon to be scrupulously [carefully] respected; when belligerent [warring] nations, under the impossibility of making acquisitions upon us, will not lightly hazard [risk] the giving us provocation; when we may choose peace or war, as our interest, guided by justice, shall counsel. . . .

It is our true policy to steer clear of permanent alliances with any portion of the foreign world, so far, I mean as we are now at liberty to do it; for let me not be understood

554 ★ Source Readings

as capable of patronizing [supporting] infidelity [unfaithfulness] to existing engagements. I hold the maxim no less applicable to public than to private affairs that honesty is always the best policy. I repeat, therefore, let those engagements be observed in their genuine sense. But in my opinion it is unnecessary and would be unwise to extend them.

Taking care always to keep ourselves by suitable establishments on a respectable defensive posture, we may safely trust to temporary alliances for extraordinary emergencies.

Source: *A Documentary History of the United States,* edited by Richard D. Heffner, 1952.

Analyzing Primary Sources

1. What was Washington's view of political parties?
   - **A.** They cost too much money.
   - **B.** They caused dangerous divisions within the nation.
   - **C.** They resulted in the rise of monarchs.
   - **D.** They weakened the system of checks and balances.
2. What advice about foreign policy did Washington give?
   - **F.** Seek trade but avoid other links with Europe.
   - **G.** Have no contact with European countries.
   - **H.** Cancel all treaties with European countries.
   - **J.** Build up a strong army and navy.
3. **Critical Thinking Understanding Cause and Effect** How does Washington think the United States should behave toward other nations? Why does he give that advice?

Historical Critique

Washington himself belonged to no political party. Do you think that fact increases or decreases the effectiveness of what he has to say about parties?

★ Chapter 10 ★ The Age of Jefferson

★ 10–1 ★ Traveling With Lith Lewis and Clark

Introduction A Shoshone woman named Sacajawea, her husband, and her baby son Pomp accompanied Lewis and Clark on their expedition across the Louisiana Territory. As a child Sacajawea had been kidnapped from her village by the Minnetarees, a rival Native American group. She was adopted by a Minnetaree family and lived in their village. Sacajawea met Lewis and Clark when they camped at the Minnetaree village. Years later, Sacajawea told her life story to James Willard Schultz. This passage is from Schultz's book *Bird Woman.* In this passage, Sacajawea refers to Lewis and Clark as Long Knife and Red Hair.

Vocabulary Before you read the selection, find the meaning of this word in a dictionary: **abandon.**

★ ★ ★ ★ ★ ★ ★ ★ ★

Upon my man's return to the fort the boats were all loaded. We had two large ones and six small ones, and we abandoned the fort and headed up river. At the same time that we started, Long Knife and Red Hair sent their very large boat down the river in charge of some of their men. It was loaded with many skins, bones, and other

Analyzing Primary Sources

ANSWERS

1. B **2.** F **3.** The United States should honor its existing commitments and expand trade, but it should have few or no political dealings with European nations because such dealings are "unnecessary" and "unwise."

Historical Critique Possible answers: It increases, because it shows his commitment to what he says and he could be more objective than a party supporter; it decreases, because he has no experience of how a party works from within.

★ Chapter 10 ★

★ 10–1 ★

Traveling With Lewis and Clark (basic)

★ ★ ★ ★ ★ ★ ★ ★ ★ ★

Prereading Focus

Have students reread Section 2 of Chapter 10 to review what they have learned about the Lewis and Clark expedition.

Purpose-Setting Question

Ask: "How might a Native American guide have proved valuable to Lewis and Clark while traveling across the continent?"

Background for Understanding

★ ★ ★ ★ ★ ★ ★ ★ ★ ★

In their book *Sacajawea of the Lewis and Clark Expedition,* authors Ella Clark and Margot Edmonds write that "Sacajawea's major contribution to the Expedition, aside from her ability as interpreter, was her womanly presence with her son—a morale builder in difficult times and a symbol of peace to the Indians everywhere."

Teaching Alternatives

★ ★ ★ ★ ★ ★ ★ ★ ★ ★

Team Teaching: Language Arts Work with a language arts teacher to teach a brief lesson on cultural differences. Have students review the excerpt and point out the passages that show ways in which Sacajawea's background differed from Lewis and Clark's. If the class includes students from other cultures, ask them to relate instances in which they found American culture to be strange or confusing.

ANSWER

Possible answers: Students might include questions about climate, terrain, people, cultures, food and water sources.

Viewing History: Wildlife of the American West

Thomas Jefferson asked Lewis and Clark to explore lands west of the Mississippi. The President also asked them to send back information on the animal life they found. Clark sketched this bird and salmon in his journal. ★ **If you were sending an expedition into an unfamiliar land, what kind of information would you ask for?**

things, presents for the great chief of the whites. Counting in my son, we were thirty-three people in our eight boats. I was given a place in one of the two large ones.

As we went on and on up the river, sometimes making a long distance between the rising and the setting of the sun, I was, at times, I believe, happier than I had ever been in my life, for each day's travel brought me so much nearer my people whom I so much longed to see. Then at other times, whenever I thought of what was before us, I would become very unhappy. I would say to myself that we could not possibly survive the dangers we should be sure to encounter along the way. I may as well say it: my good, kind white chiefs were not cautious; they were too brave, too sure of themselves. From the very start they and their men would foolishly risk their lives by attacking all the mankilling bears that came in sight of us. At night they would build great fires and would be sure to attract to us any wandering war party that might be in the country. After we passed the mouth of the Yellowstone and entered the country of the Blackfeet, I begged my chiefs to be more cautious. I asked them to stop always a short time before dark and build little cooking-fires, and then, after our meal, to put out the fires, and then go on until dark and make camp in the darkness. But they only laughed at me and answered: "We have good guns and know how to use them."

I often said to myself: "Strange are these white men! Strange their ways! They have a certain thing to do, to make a trail to the west to the Everywhere-Salt-Water. Why, then, are we not on horseback and traveling fast and far each day? Here we are in boats, heavily loaded with all kinds of useless things, and when the wind is bad or the water swift, we make but little distance between sun and sun! We could have all got all the horses that we needed from the Earth House tribes, and had we done that, we should long since have arrived at the mountains. Yes, right now I should probably be talking with my own people!"

And those medicine packages of theirs, packages big and little piled all around me in the boat in which I rode, how my chiefs valued them! One day a sudden hard wind struck our sail and the boat began to tip and fill with water. More and more it filled, and the men in it and those on the shore went almost crazy with fear. But I was not afraid. Why should I be when I knew that I could cast off my robe and swim ashore with my little son? More and more water poured into the boat and the medicine packages began to float out of it. I seized them one by one as they were going, and kept seizing them and holding them, and when, at last, we reached the shore, my good white chiefs acted as though I had done a wonderful thing in saving their packages; it seemed as though they could not thank me enough for what I had done. Thinking about it, after it was all over, and when the things had been spread out to dry, I said to myself: "Although I cannot un-

556 ★ Source Readings

derstand them, these little instruments of shining steel and these writings on thin white paper must be powerful medicine. Hereafter, whenever we run into danger, I shall, after my son, have my first thought for their safety, and so please my kind white chiefs."

After leaving the mouth of Little River, or, as my white chiefs named it, Milk River, we went up through a part of the Big River Valley that I had not seen. . . . When we arrived at the mouth of the stream my white chiefs named the Musselshell, some of the men went up it during the afternoon, and, returning, told of a stream coming into it from the plain on the right. My chiefs then told me that it should have my name, as they called it, Sah-ka-já-we-ah.

I asked my man to tell them that I wished they would give it my right name, Bo-í-naiv, Grass Woman.

Source: *Bird Woman,* James Willard Schultz, 1918.

Analyzing Primary Sources

1. Whom did Sacajawea help?
   - **A.** Lewis and Clark
   - **B.** the Blackfeet
   - **C.** the Minnetaree
   - **D.** the Mandan
2. In this excerpt, what transportation did the expedition use?
   - **F.** mules
   - **G.** wagons
   - **H.** boats
   - **J.** horses
3. **Critical Thinking Recognizing Points of View** Why do you think that Sacajawea found the ways of Lewis and Clark strange?

Historical Critique

Sacajawea told her life story to a writer, who did not publish it until 1918. Identify two factors that might affect the reliability of the published account.

★ 10–2 ★ The Pioneers

Introduction James Fenimore Cooper wrote action-filled adventure stories that were very popular. The central character in five of his novels is a wilderness hunter named Natty Bumppo, or Leather-stocking, who lives between the Indian and white worlds. Bumppo has learned the forest skills of the Indians. This selection is from *The Pioneers.* In this scene, Leather-stocking realizes that the wilderness is fast falling to settlers.

Vocabulary Before you read the selection, find the meanings of these words in a dictionary: **species, sapling, gaunt, vain, prodigious, profusion, uneasy, sentiments, indignant.**

★ ★ ★ ★ ★ ★ ★ ★ ★

If the heavens were alive with pigeons, the whole village seemed equally in motion, with men, women, and children. Every species of fire-arms, from the French ducking-gun, with a barrel near six feet in length, to the common horseman's pistol, was to be seen in the hands of the men and boys; while bows and arrows, some made of the simple stick of a walnut sapling, and others in a rude [simple] imitation of the ancient cross-bows, were carried by many of the latter. . . .

Amongst the sportsmen was the tall, gaunt form of Leather-stocking, walking over the field, with his rifle hanging on his arm, his dogs at his heels; the latter now scenting the dead or wounded birds, that were beginning to tumble from the flocks, and then crouching under the legs of their master, as if they participated in his feelings, at this wasteful and unsportsmanlike execution.

The reports of the fire-arms became rapid, whole volleys rising from the plain, as flocks of more than ordinary numbers darted over the opening, shadowing the field, like a cloud; and then the light smoke of a single

Analyzing Primary Sources

ANSWERS

1. A **2.** H **3.** Sacajawea was a Native American. Her culture and way of life were very different from Lewis and Clark's, so it is not surprising that she found their culture strange.

Historical Critique Possible answers: how well Sacajawea remembered events from long ago, how accurately Schultz recorded her recollections.

★ 10–2 ★

The Pioneers *(average)*

★ ★ ★ ★ ★ ★ ★ ★ ★ ★

Prereading Focus

Have students reread Section 4 of Chapter 10 to review what they have learned about westward expansion during Jefferson's presidency.

Purpose-Setting Question

Ask: "How do you think the area where your town is located looked in Jefferson's time?"

Background for Understanding

★ ★ ★ ★ ★ ★ ★ ★ ★ ★

The young James Fenimore Cooper did not seem to be an author in the making. He was expelled from college in his third year for pranks, such as putting a donkey in a professor's chair and using gunpowder to blast open a classmate's door. His sister records that he began writing only after he read a "trashy novel" from England and exclaimed that "I could write a better book … myself."

Teaching Alternatives

★ ★ ★ ★ ★ ★ ★ ★ ★ ★

Team Teaching: Language Arts Work with a language arts teacher to teach a lesson on James Fenimore Cooper's work. Explain to students that Cooper was the first American novelist to win international recognition. He boosted pride in the young nation by writing about American subjects, rather than European ones. Have students review the excerpt and point out ways that it describes a uniquely American situation.

Settlers chopped down trees for fuel, homes, and farms.

piece would issue from among the leafless bushes on the mountain, as death was hurled on the retreat of the affrighted birds, who were rising from a volley, in a vain effort to escape. Arrows, and missiles of every kind, were in the midst of the flocks; and so numerous were the birds, and so low did they take their flight, that even long poles, in the hands of those on the sides of the mountain, were used to strike them to the earth. . . .

So prodigious was the number of birds, that the scattering fire of the guns, with the hurling of missiles, and the cries of the boys, had no other effect than to break off small flocks from the immense masses that continued to dart along the valley, as if the whole of the feathered tribe were pouring through one pass. None pretended to collect the game, which lay scattered over the fields in such profusion, as to cover the very ground with the fluttering victims.

Leather-stocking was a silent, but uneasy spectator of all these proceedings [events], but was able to keep his sentiments to himself until he saw the introduction of the swivel [cannon] into the sports.

"This comes of settling a country!" he said—"here have I known the pigeons to fly for forty long years, and, till you made your clearings, there was nobody to skear [scare] or to hurt them. I loved to see them come into the woods, for they were company to a body; hurting nothing; being, as it was, as harmless as a garter-snake. But now it gives me sore thoughts when I hear the frighty things whizzing through the air, for I know it's only a motion to bring out all the brats in the village. Well! the Lord won't see the waste of his creaters for nothing, and right will be done to the pigeons, as well as others, by-and-by. . . ."

Among the sportsmen was Billy Kirby, who, armed with an old musket, was loading, and, without even looking into the air, was firing, and shouting as his victims fell even on his own person. He heard the speech of Natty, and took upon himself to reply—

"What! old Leather-stocking," he cried, "grumbling at the loss of a few pigeons! If you had to sow your wheat twice, and three times, as I have done, you wouldn't be so massy-fully [mercifully] feeling'd to'wards the divils.—Hurrah, boys! scatter the feathers. This is better than shooting at a turkey's head and neck, old fellow."

"It's better for you, maybe, Billy Kirby," replied the indignant old hunter, "and all them that don't know how to put a ball down a rifle-barrel, or how to bring it up ag'in with a true aim; but it's wicked to be shooting into flocks in this wastey manner; and none do it, who know how to knock over a single bird. If a body has a craving for pigeon's flesh, why! it's made the same as all other creater's, for man's eating, but not to kill twenty and eat one."

Source: *The Pioneers*, James Fenimore Cooper, 1823.

Settling the Wilderness

As they moved westward, settlers had to hack homes out of thick forests. This engraving shows a group of pioneers in the Ohio Valley. Even the smallest child had to work in order for the family to survive. ★ **Based on this picture, identify two reasons settlers chopped down many trees in the frontier forests.**

558 ★ Source Readings

Analyzing Literature

1. Why did Natty Bumppo object to the killing of the pigeons?
   A. He disliked the sound of gunfire.
   B. He felt that eating pigeons was sinful.
   C. He thought the killing was wasteful.
   D. He was afraid people would get shot.
2. Why did the settlers shoot the pigeons?
   F. to sell the feathers
   G. to protect their wheat fields
   H. to show off their hunting skills
   J. to frighten the Indians
3. **Critical Thinking Linking Past and Present** How is Natty Bumppo's conflict with the settlers similar to that between environmentalists and developers today?

Historical Critique

Fiction writers often express their views through the mouths of their characters. Which character do you think expresses Cooper's view: Leather-stocking or Kirby? Give reasons for your answer.

★ Chapter 11 ★ Industry and Growth

★ 11–1 ★ Working in the Lowell Mills

Introduction In 1898, Harriet Hanson Robinson published a book, *Loom and Spindle,* which tells of her experiences working in the Lowell, Massachusetts, textile mills in the 1830s. In the following passage, Robinson describes life in Lowell, and tells about the first strike there.

Vocabulary Before you read the selection, find the meaning of these words in a dictionary: **modes, incendiary, consternation, ardent, irresolute, accede.**

★ ★ ★ ★ ★ ★ ★ ★ ★

In 1831 Lowell was little more than a factory village. Several corporations were started, and the cotton-mills belonging to them were building. Help was in great demand; and stories were told all over the country of the new factory town, and the high wages that were offered to all classes of work-people—stories that reached the ears of mechanics' and farmers' sons, and gave new life to lonely and dependent women in distant towns and farmhouses. Into this Yankee El Dorado,* these needy people began to pour by the various modes of travel known to those slow old days. The stagecoach and the canal boat came everyday, always filled with new recruits for this army of useful people. The mechanic and machinist came, each with his home-made chest of tools, and oftentimes his wife and little ones. The widow came with her little flock and her scanty housekeeping goods to open a boarding-house or variety store, and so provided a home for her fatherless children. Many farmers' daughters came to earn money to complete their wedding outfit, or buy the bride's share of housekeeping articles. . . .

One of the first strikes of cotton factory operatives that ever took place in this country was that in Lowell, in October 1836. When it was announced that the wages were to be cut down, great indignation was felt, and it was decided to strike, *en masse.* This was done. The mills were shut down, and the girls went in procession from their several corporations to the "grove" on Chapel Hill, and listened to "incendiary" speeches from early labor reformers.

One of the girls stood on a pump, and gave vent to the feelings of her companions

*El Dorado refers to a place rich in opportunity to become wealthy.

Analyzing Primary Sources

ANSWERS

1. C **2.** G **3.** Bumppo wanted the wilderness left alone whereas settlers were clearing it to farm. Today, environmentalists want to protect wilderness areas from development.

Historical Critique Leather-stocking, because he is presented sympathetically, even nobly, whereas Kirby is shown as comic and crude.

★ Chapter 11 ★

★ 11–1 ★

Working in the Lowell Mills *(average)*

Prereading Focus

Have students reread Section 2 of Chapter 11 to review what they have learned about the young women and other early factory workers in places such as Lowell, Massachusetts.

Purpose-Setting Question

Ask: "Suppose that you are a young women working in the Lowell mills. You have never been away from home before or worked for wages. How do you think you would react if some of your co-workers went on strike and urged you to join them?"

Background for Understanding

★ ★ ★ ★ ★ ★ ★ ★ ★ ★

The author of this piece, Harriet Hanson Robinson, worked in the Lowell mills until her marriage in 1848. In later years, she, her husband, and her daughter worked for women's suffrage. She and her daughter organized the National Woman Suffrage Association of Massachusetts, and Harriet spoke before a special Senate committee in Washington in 1882 in support of suffrage for women.

Teaching Alternatives

★ ★ ★ ★ ★ ★ ★ ★ ★ ★

Team Teaching: Language Arts Work with a language arts teacher to discuss how authors let readers know they are experts on their subject matter. Have students review the excerpt and point out the ways in which Robinson shows that she is a careful and reliable source of information. Then have students suggest other ways in which authors might establish their credentials.

ANSWER

The cover suggests an idyllic, idealized setting, rather than a real-life factory town.

Analyzing Primary Sources

ANSWERS

1. D **2.** G **3.** The author seems to view the workers sympathetically, seeing their needs but also feeling impatient with their ineffectiveness.

Historical Critique Robinson was part of the first strike, which she remembers vividly; she also worked in the mills so she witnessed factory life. She probably learned from others where they had come from and why they came to Lowell.

Viewing History: The Lowell Offering

The textile mills in Lowell, Massachusetts, employed mostly young, unmarried women. These "Lowell girls" published their own magazine, the Lowell Offering. ★ **What view of life in a factory town does this magazine cover suggest? Explain.**

in a neat speech, declaring that it was their duty to resist all attempts at cutting down the wages. This was the first time a woman had spoken in public in Lowell, and the event caused surprise and consternation among her audience.

Cutting down the wages was not their only grievance, nor the only cause of the strike. Hitherto the corporations had paid twenty-five cents a week towards the board of each operative, and now it was their purpose to have the girls pay the sum; and this, in addition to the cut in wages, would make a difference of at least one dollar a week....

My own recollection of this first strike (or "turn out" as it was called) is very vivid. I worked in a lower room, where I had heard the proposed strike fully, if not vehemently, discussed; I had been an ardent listener to what was said against this attempt at "oppression" on the part of the corporation, and naturally I took sides with the strikers. When the day came on which the girls were to turn out, those in the upper rooms started first, and so many of them left that our mill was at once shut down. Then, when the girls in my room stood irresolute, uncertain what to do, asking each other, "Would you?" or "Shall we turn out?" and not one of them having the courage to lead off, I, who began to think they would not go out, after all their talk, became impatient, and started on ahead, saying, with childish bravado, "I don't care what you do, I am going to turn out, whether any one else does or not"; and I marched out, and was followed by the others....

It is hardly necessary to say that so far as results were concerned this strike did no good. The dissatisfaction of the operatives subsided, or burned itself out, and though the authorities did not accede to their demands, the majority returned to their work, and the corporation went on cutting down the wages.

Source: *Loom and Spindle,* Harriet Hanson Robinson, 1898.

Analyzing Primary Sources

1. Why did the mill workers go on strike?
- **A.** Children had been hired to work in the mills.
- **B.** Factory owners wanted them to work longer hours.
- **C.** Some workers had been fired.
- **D.** Wages were going to be cut.

2. This passage is mainly about
- **F.** transportation in Lowell.
- **G.** working in a cottonmill.
- **H.** women's rights.
- **J.** child labor.

3. Critical Thinking Recognizing Points of View How did the author view the cotton-mill workers?

Historical Critique

How much of what Robinson reports did she witness herself? How much did she learn from other sources?

Historical Document

★ 11–2 ★ The Monroe Doctrine

Introduction In his State of the Union message to Congress in December 1823, James Monroe issued a warning to European powers not to try to extend their influence in the Western Hemisphere. His warning, which has come to be known as the Monroe Doctrine, had immediate implications. At the time, Russia threatened to encroach in the far Northwest, Great Britain showed some interest in acquiring Cuba, and it was thought that the Quadruple Alliance* wanted to help Spain recover its lost American colonies. The following passage includes relevant excerpts from the Monroe Doctrine.

Vocabulary Before you read the selection, find the meaning of these words in a dictionary: **amicable, acceded, solicitude, comport, felicity, candor, *de facto*, eminently.**

★ ★ ★ ★ ★ ★ ★ ★ ★

Annual Message

December 2, 1823

Fellow-citizens of the Senate and House of Representatives:

. . . At the proposal of the Russian Imperial Government, made through the minister of the Emperor residing here, a full power and instructions have been transmitted to the ministers of the United States at St. Petersburg to arrange by amicable negotiations the respective rights and interests of the two nations on the northwest coast of this continent. A similar proposal had been made by His Imperial Majesty to the government of Great Britain, which had likewise been acceded to. The government of the United States has been desirous, by this friendly proceeding, of manifesting the great value which they have invariably attached to the friendship of the Emperor and their solicitude to cultivate the best understanding with his government. In the discussions to which this interest has given rise and in the arrangements by which they may terminate, the occasion has been judged proper for asserting, as a principle in which the rights and interests of the United States are involved, that the American continents, by the free and independent condition which they have assumed and maintain, are henceforth not considered as subject for future colonization by any European powers. . . .

The citizens of the United States cherish sentiments the most friendly in favor of the liberty and happiness of their fellow men on that side of the Atlantic. In the wars of the European powers in matters relating to themselves we have never taken any part, nor does it comport with our policy so to do. It is only when our rights are invaded or seriously menaced that we resent injuries or make preparations for our defense. With the movements in this hemisphere we are of necessity more immediately connected, and by causes which must be obvious to all enlightened and impartial observers. The political system of the allied powers is essentially different in this respect from that of America. This difference proceeds from that which exists in their respective governments; and to the defense of our own, which has been achieved by the loss of so much blood and treasure, and matured by the wisdom of their most enlightened citizens, and under which we have enjoyed unexampled felicity, this whole nation is devoted. We owe it, therefore, to candor and to the amicable relations existing between the United States and those powers to declare that we should consider any attempt on their part to extend their system to any portion of this hemisphere as dangerous to our peace and safety. With the existing colonies or dependencies of any European power we shall not interfere. But with the governments who have declared their independence and maintained it, and whose independence we have, on great consideration and on just principles, acknowledged, we could not view any interposition for the purpose of oppressing them or

* The Quadruple Alliance was a group of European nations that worked together to achieve their goals. It included Britain, Austria, Prussia, and—later—France.

★ 11–2 ★

The Monroe Doctrine

(*challenging*)

★ ★ ★ ★ ★ ★ ★ ★ ★ ★

Prereading Focus

Have students reread Section 4 of Chapter 11 to review what they have learned about why President Monroe decided to issue the Monroe Doctrine.

Purpose-Setting Question

Ask: "Why did the United States want to prevent any European country from recolonizing the Americas in the 1820s?"

Background for Understanding

★ ★ ★ ★ ★ ★ ★ ★ ★ ★

Most major European powers scoffed at the Monroe Doctrine, calling it "blustering," "monstrous," "arrogant," and "haughty." The Russians were especially opposed to it. "The document," said the Russian government, ". . . merits only the most profound contempt." No government, however, protested formally, and the British were prepared to back up Monroes's statement with their powerful navy.

Teaching Alternatives

★ ★ ★ ★ ★ ★ ★ ★ ★ ★

Team Teaching: Language Arts Work with a language arts teacher to present a lesson on diplomatic language. Point out to students that official documents are generally worded carefully to convey their meaning precisely without arousing extreme reactions. review the Monroe Doctrine, noting sentences or phrases in which the language seems to be carefully chosen.

ANSWER

He represents Spanish rule.

Analyzing Primary Sources

ANSWERS

1. B **2.** F **3.** The United States wanted to make clear its determination to prevent any recolonization of the Americas.

Historical Critique Monroe intended his message to reach the American people, European governments, and the new Latin American republics.

Viewing History **The Triumph of Mexico**

This painting uses symbols to celebrate Mexico's struggle for independence. Father Miguel Hidalgo, left, places a victory wreath on the head of a woman representing Mexico. The growth of new nations in Latin America led President James Monroe to issue the Monroe Doctrine. ★ **What do you think the man in the lower left represents?**

controlling in any other manner their destiny, by any European power in any other light than as the manifestation of an unfriendly disposition toward the United States....

Our policy in regard to Europe, which was adopted at an early stage of the wars which have so long agitated that quarter of the globe, nevertheless remains the same, which is, not to interfere in the internal concerns of any of its powers; to consider the government *de facto* as the legitimate government for us; to cultivate friendly relations by a frank, firm, and manly policy, meeting in all instances the just claims of every power, submitting to injuries from none. But in regard to those continents circumstances are eminently and conspicuously different. It is impossible that the allied powers should extend their political system to any portion of either continent without endangering our peace and happiness; nor can anyone believe that our southern brethren, if left to themselves, would adopt it of their own accord. It is equally impossible, therefore, that we should behold such interposition in any form with indifference. If we look to the comparative strength and resources of Spain and those new governments, and their distances from each other, it must be obvious that she can never subdue them. It is still the true policy of the United States to leave the parties to themselves, in the hope that other powers will pursue the same course.

Source: *Words That Made American History,* Volume 1, Richard N. Current, 1972.

Analyzing Primary Sources

1. What is the main point of the Monroe Doctrine?
   - **A.** It recognizes the independent nations in Latin America.
   - **B.** It warns Europe against further colonization in the Americas.
   - **C.** It permits Russia to settle in the Northwest.
   - **D.** It warns Spain against invading Portugal.
2. What policy does the Monroe Doctrine apply to the wars in Europe?
   - **F.** not to interfere in them
   - **G.** to send aid when asked
   - **H.** to help negotiate a peace treaty
   - **J.** not to colonize European countries
3. **Critical Thinking Evaluating Information** Why did the United States issue the Monroe Doctrine?

Historical Critique

Monroe addressed this speech to "Fellow-citizens of the Senate and House of Representatives." What other audience did he intend his message to reach?

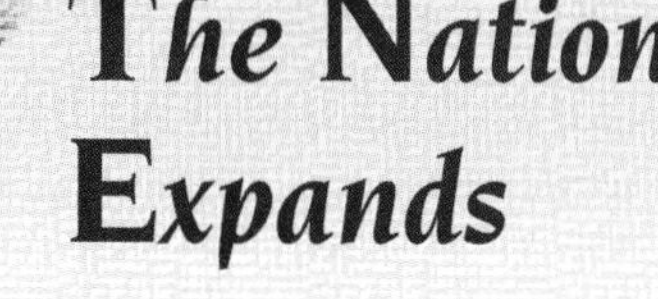

The Nation Expands

★ Chapter 12 ★ Democracy in the Age of Jackson

★ 12–1 ★ Against Nullification

Historical Document

Introduction In 1830, Senator Robert Y. Hayne of South Carolina, representing the southern states, spoke in the Senate in support of states' rights and nullification. Senator Daniel Webster of Massachusetts then replied to Hayne. His dramatic speech, given over two days, became famous throughout the nation. The following excerpt is from Webster's reply to Hayne.

Vocabulary Before you read the selection, find the meanings of these words in a dictionary: **sovereign, construe, interpolated, conscientiously, vigilantly.**

★ ★ ★ ★ ★ ★ ★ ★ ★

If anything be found in the national Constitution . . . which ought not be in it, the people know how to get rid of it. If any construction is established unacceptable to them, so as to become practically a part of the Constitution, they will amend it, at their own sovereign pleasure. But while the people choose to maintain it as it is, while they are satisfied with it, and refuse to change it, who has given, or who can give, to the state legislatures a right to alter it, either by interference, construction, or otherwise? Gentlemen do not seem to recollect that the people have any power to do anything for themselves. They imagine there is no safety for them, any longer than they are under the close guardianship of the state legislatures. . . .

The people of the United States have at no time, in no way, directly or indirectly, authorized any state legislature to construe or interpret *their* high instrument of government; much less to interfere, by their own power, to arrest its course and operation.

Viewing History **Two Nationalist Leaders**

Massachusetts sculptor Thomas Ball created these bronze statuettes of Henry Clay (left) and Daniel Webster (right) in the 1850s. Ball greatly admired Clay and Webster for their efforts to preserve the union. ★ **What impression of Daniel Webster do you get from Ball's sculpture and from Webster's speech?**

The Nation Expands

★ Chapter 12 ★

★ 12–1 ★

Against Nullification

(challenging)

★ ★ ★ ★ ★ ★ ★ ★ ★ ★

Prereading Focus

Have students reread the first half of Section 3 in Chapter 12 to review what they have learned about nullification and states' rights.

Purpose-Setting Question

Ask: What might happen today if a state refused to obey a federal law?"

Viewing History ANSWER

Webster seems to be a determined, powerful, self-confident person with a dramatic flair for speechmaking.

Background for Understanding

★ ★ ★ ★ ★ ★ ★ ★ ★ ★

The Webster-Hayne debates electrified people in Washington, D.C One resident wrote: "Everyone is thronging to the capital to hear Webster's reply. A debate on political principle would have no such attraction. But personalities are irresistible. . . . Every seat, every inch of ground, even the steps were compactly filled."

Teaching Alternatives

★ ★ ★ ★ ★ ★ ★ ★ ★ ★

Team Teaching: Language Arts Work with a language arts teacher to create a lesson on public speaking skills. Point out to students that altering one's tone of voice or inflection can contribute to the impact of a speech. Have students read aloud parts of Webster's speech with anger, indignation, and righteousness. Then discuss how inflection changes or enhances meaning.

Analyzing Literature

ANSWERS

1. B **2.** H **3.** Main ideas include: The people have approved the Constitution and the state legislatures have no right to alter it; the states do not need to protect themselves against the federal government by nullification, but instead the people can ensure that protection through such means as elections, the judiciary, and constitutional amendment; if the Constitution is disregarded, the entire Union would be weakened.

Historical Critique Webster's final words are like a slogan; the sentence has a Biblical rhythm. The words *Liberty* and *Union* had almost sacred meanings. He might have raised his voice and paused after each comma.

If, sir, the people in these respects had done otherwise than they have done, their Constitution could neither have been preserved, nor would it have been worthy preserving. And if its plain provisions shall now be disregarded, and these new doctrines interpolated in it, it will become as feeble and helpless a being as its enemies, whether early or more recent, could possibly desire. It will exist in every state but as a poor dependent on state permission. . . .

But, sir, although there are fears, there are hopes also. The people have preserved this, their own chosen Constitution, for forty years, and have seen their happiness, prosperity, and renown grow with its growth, and strengthen with its strength. They are now, generally, strongly, attached to it. Overthrown by direct assault, it cannot be; evaded, undermined, *nullified,* it will not be, if we, and those who shall succeed us here, as agents and representatives of the people, shall conscientiously and vigilantly discharge the two great branches of our public trust, faithfully to preserve, and wisely to administer it. . . .

While the Union lasts, we have high, exciting, gratifying prospects spread out before us, for us and our children. . . . Liberty *and* Union, now and forever, one and inseparable!

Source: *American Reader: Words That Moved a Nation,* edited by Diane Ravitch, 1990.

Analyzing Primary Sources

1. According to Webster, the liberty of the American people is safeguarded by
   A. Congress.
   B. the Constitution.
   C. state legislatures.
   D. prosperity.
2. In his speech, Webster is supporting
   F. states' rights.
   G. the War of 1812.
   H. preservation of the Union.
   J. succession.
3. **Critical Thinking Identifying Main Ideas** What are the main ideas in Webster's speech?

Historical Critique

In their speeches, politicians often use emotional appeals to rally support for a particular cause. How do Webster's final words appeal to his listeners' emotions? How do you think he used his voice to increase the effect of his words?

★ 12–2 ★

The Cherokee Removal (challenging)

★ ★ ★ ★ ★ ★ ★ ★ ★ ★

Prereading Focus

Have students reread the second half of Section 3 in Chapter 12 to review what they have learned about the Cherokee nation, Indian Removal Act, and Trail of Tears.

Purpose-Setting Question

Ask: "Is a government ever justified in forcing a group of people to leave their homes and move to another area?"

★ 12–2 ★ The Cherokee Removal

Introduction The Indian Removal Act forced the Cherokee, the Creek, the Chickasaw, and the Choctaw to resettle west of the Mississippi. When it came time for the Cherokees to leave their homes in 1838, many resisted. Evan Jones, a Baptist missionary, worked among the Cherokee in North Carolina and joined them on their westward march. The following excerpt is from a series of letters written by Jones.

Vocabulary Before you read the selection, find the meanings of these words in the dictionary: **plunderers, wretches, agitation, consoling, disposition, perpetrated, manifests.**

★ ★ ★ ★ ★ ★ ★ ★ ★

Camp Hetzel, Near Cleveland, June 16

The Cherokees are nearly all prisoners. They have been dragged from their houses, and encamped at the forts and military posts, all over the nation. In Georgia, especially, multitudes were allowed no time to take anything with them, except the clothes they had on. Well-furnished houses were a prey to plunderers, who, like hungry wolves, follow in the train of the captors. These

Background for Understanding

★ ★ ★ ★ ★ ★ ★ ★ ★ ★

Evan Jones was a staunch supporter of the Cherokee people even before their forced march west. When a United States general ordered him to make the Cherokees surrender their guns, Jones refused. He knew the Indians needed their firearms for hunting. Jones was arrested for disobeying orders. After his release, he continued to do what he could to help the Cherokees.

Teaching Alternatives

★ ★ ★ ★ ★ ★ ★ ★ ★ ★

Team Teaching: Language Arts Work with a language arts teacher to examine a writer's choice of words. Ask students to look for words that reveal the author's viewpoint. Explain that these words are descriptive and, while they are not necessary to communicate the facts, they reveal how the author feels about an issue. Ask students to list other such words in the excerpt.

wretches rifle the houses, and strip the helpless, unoffending owners of all they have on earth. . . . The property of many has been taken, and sold before their eyes for almost nothing—the sellers and buyers, in many cases, being combined to cheat the poor Indians. . . . The poor captive, in a state of distressing agitation, his weeping wife almost frantic with terror, surrounded by a group of crying, terrified children, without a friend to speak a consoling word, is in a poor condition to make a good disposition of his property and is in most cases stripped of the whole, at one blow. Many of the Cherokees, who, a few days ago, were in comfortable circumstances, are now victims of abject poverty. Some, who have been allowed to return home, under passport, to inquire after their property, have found their cattle, horses, swine, farming tools, and house furniture all gone. And this is not a description of extreme cases. It is altogether a faint representation of the work which has been perpetrated on the unoffending, unarmed, and unresisting Cherokees. . . .

It is due to justice to say, that, at this station (and I learn the same is true of some others), the officer in command treats his prisoners with great respect and indulgence. But fault rests somewhere. They are prisoners, without a crime to justify the fact. . . .

July 10 and July 11

The work of war in time of peace, is commenced in the Georgia part of the Cherokee nation, and is carried on, in most cases, in the most unfeeling and brutal manner; no regard being paid to the orders of the commanding General, in regard to humane treatment of the Indians. I have heard of only one officer in Georgia (I hope there are

Viewing History **Along the Trail of Tears**

Robert Liudneux painted this view of Cherokee families traveling west on the Trail of Tears. Blue-coated soldiers force Cherokee families to move to Indian Territory. Some families carry their belongings in wagons, but many others must make the journey on foot. ★ **How does the painting suggest the hardships the Cherokees faced?**

ANSWER

People look depressed; women and children are walking; soldiers guard them.

Source Readings ★ 565

Analyzing Primary Sources

ANSWERS

1. A **2.** H **3.** Jones viewed the army's treatment of the Cherokee as brutal and unfair.

Historical Critique No, Jones is also reporting hearsay and giving his own judgments.

more), who manifests anything like humanity, in his treatment of this persecuted people....

The work of capturing being completed, and about 3,000 sent off, the General had agreed to suspend the further transportation of the captives till the first of September. This arrangement, though but a small favor, diffused universal joy through the camps of the prisoners....

On our way, we met a detachment of 1,300 prisoners. As I took some of them by hand, the tears gushed from their eyes. Their hearts, however, were cheered to see us, and to hear a word of consolation. Many members of the church were among them. At Fort Butler, we found a company of 300, just arrived from the mountains, on their way to the general depot, at the agency. Several of our members were among these also.

Source: *The Cherokee Removal: A Brief History With Documents,* edited by Theda Perdue and Michael Green, 1995.

Analyzing Primary Sources

1. Where were the Cherokees living when Jones wrote these letters?
   - **A.** in Georgia
   - **B.** in California
   - **C.** in Texas
   - **D.** in Ohio
2. Where were the Cherokees being taken?
   - **F.** to their homes
   - **G.** to reservations
   - **H.** to forts and military posts
   - **J.** to Cleveland
3. **Critical Thinking Recognizing Points of View** Based on the excerpt, how did Evan Jones view the United States Army's treatment of the Cherokees?

Historical Critique

Did Evan Jones directly witness everything he describes in his letters? Explain.

⋆ Chapter 13 ⋆

★ 13–1 ★

Death Comes for the Archbishop (average)

★ ★ ★ ★ ★ ★ ★ ★ ★ ★

Prereading Focus

Have students reread Section 3 of Chapter 13 to review what they have learned about the Spanish missions and the Southwest in the 1800s.

Purpose-Setting Question

Ask: "Suppose that you are traveling with someone you barely know from another culture. Would you be likely to ask your travel companion question? Why or why not?"

⋆ Chapter 13 ⋆ Westward Expansion

⋆ 13–1 ⋆ Death Comes for the Archbishop

Introduction Many of the novels of Willa Cather focus on pioneer life on the Great Plains. In *Death Comes for the Archbishop,* however, her setting is the American Southwest during the 1850s. The book's main character, Bishop Jean Latour, journeys with his Native American guide, Jacinto, through Arizona and New Mexico. In the following selection, Latour and Jacinto camp for the night during a journey to a distant mission.

Vocabulary Before you read the selection, find the meanings of these words in a dictionary: **firmament, proposition, vehement.**

★ ★ ★ ★ ★ ★ ★ ★ ★

Jacinto got firewood and good water from the Lagunas, and they made their camp in a pleasant spot on the rocks north of the village. As the sun dropped low, the light brought the white church and the yellow adobe houses up into relief from the flat ledges. Behind their camp, not far away, lay a group of great mesas. The Bishop asked Jacinto if he knew the name of the one nearest them.

"No, I do not know any name," he shook his head. "I know Indian name," he added, as if, for once, he were thinking aloud.

"And what is the Indian name?"

"The Laguna Indians call Snow-Bird mountain." He spoke somewhat unwillingly.

"That is very nice," said the Bishop musingly. "Yes, that is a pretty name...."

The Bishop sat drinking his coffee slowly out of the tin cup, keeping the pot near the embers. The sun had set now, the yellow rocks were turning grey, down in the pueblo

Background for Understanding

★ ★ ★ ★ ★ ★ ★ ★ ★ ★

As a child, Willa Cather moved with her family to Nebraska, where their neighbors were often European immigrants and where Cather learned to appreciate people from other cultures. On Sundays, she once wrote, her family might visit a Norwegian, Danish, Swedish, French Catholic or German Lutheran church.

Teaching Alternatives

★ ★ ★ ★ ★ ★ ★ ★ ★ ★

Team Teaching: Language Arts Work with a language arts teacher to present a lesson on descriptive writing. Discuss with students how descriptive writing appeals to the five senses—sight, sound, touch, smell, taste. Have students find examples of descriptive writing in the excerpt and explain how each enhances the story.

the light of the cook fires made red patches of the glassless windows, and the smell of [pine] smoke came softly through the still air.

The whole western sky was the color of golden ashes, with here and there a flush of red on the lip of a little cloud. High above the horizon the evening-star flickered like a lamp just lit, and close beside it was another star of constant light, much smaller. . . .

Viewing HISTORY **A Mission in California**

An unknown California artist painted Oriana Day, Mission Francisco Solano de Sonoma *in the mid-1800s. It shows Native Americans at a mission in northern California. Throughout the Southwest, the Spanish had forced many Indians into missions.* ★ **Study the picture. What seems to be the main building of the mission? Where on the mission grounds did Indians live?**

The two companions sat, each thinking his own thoughts as night closed in about them; a blue night set with stars, the bulk of the solitary mesas cutting into the firmament. The Bishop seldom questioned Jacinto about his thoughts or beliefs. He didn't think it polite, and he believed it to be useless. There was no way he could transfer his own memories of European civilization into the Indian mind, and he was quite willing to believe that behind Jacinto there was a long tradition, a store of experience, which no language could translate to him. A chill came with the darkness. Father Latour put on his old fur-lined cloak, and Jacinto, loosening the blanket tied about his loins, drew it up over his head and shoulders.

"Many stars," he said presently. "What do you think about the stars, Padre?"

"The wise men tell us they are worlds like ours, Jacinto. . . ."

"I think not," [Jacinto] said in the tone of one who has considered a proposition fairly and rejected it. "I think they are leaders—great spirits."

"Perhaps they are," said the Bishop with a sigh. "Whatever they are, they are great. Let us say *Our Father,* and go to sleep, my boy."

Kneeling on either side of the embers they repeated the prayer together and then rolled up in their blankets. The Bishop went to sleep thinking with satisfaction that he was beginning to have some sort of human companionship with his Indian boy. One called the young Indians "boys," perhaps because there was something youthful and elastic in their bodies. Certainly about their behavior there was nothing boyish in the American sense, nor even in the European sense. Jacinto was never, by any chance, [naive]; he was never taken by surprise. One felt that his training, whatever it had been, had prepared him to meet any situation which might confront him. He was as much at home in the Bishop's study as in his own pueblo—and he was never too much at home anywhere. Father Latour felt he had gone a good way toward gaining his guide's friendship, though he did not know how.

The truth was, Jacinto liked the Bishop's way of meeting people; thought he had the right tone with Padre Gallegos, the right tone with Padre Jesus, and that he had good manners with the Indians. In his experience, white people, when they addressed Indians, always put on a false face. There were many kinds of false faces; Father Vaillant's, for

ANSWER

The main building is the church. Indians lived on the edge of the mission grounds.

Source Readings ★ 567

Analyzing Primary Sources

ANSWERS

1. D **2.** J **3. (a)** The Bishop thought the stars might be worlds like his own; Jacinto said they were the spirits of great leaders. **(b)** The Bishop was willing to consider Jacinto's belief; Jacinto rejected the Bishop's idea.

Historical Critique Cather could have read letters, diaries, memoirs, and histories.

example, was kindly but too vehement. The Bishop put on none at all. He stood straight and turned to the Governor of Laguna, and his face underwent no change. Jacinto thought this remarkable.

Source: *Death Comes for the Archbishop,* Willa Cather, 1927.

Analyzing Literature

1. The bishop rarely asked Jacinto about his thoughts and beliefs because
   A. he did not care about Indian beliefs.
   B. he knew Jacinto did not want to talk about his beliefs.
   C. he knew Jacinto did not speak English well.
   D. he did not think Europeans and Indians could fully understand each other.
2. Jacinto came to trust the bishop because the bishop
   F. taught Jacinto how to pray.
   G. always told the truth.
   H. was familiar with the countryside.
   J. never put on a false face.
3. **Critical Thinking Comparing**
   (a) Compare the bishop's and Jacinto's beliefs concerning the stars. **(b)** What did each man think of the other's belief?

Historical Critique

Willa Cather wrote *Death Comes for the Archbishop* in the 1920s—more than 70 years after the novel takes place. What kinds of historical sources could she have used to help her write her novel?

★ 13–2 ★

Trapped in the Sierra Nevada *(average)*

★ ★ ★ ★ ★ ★ ★ ★ ★ ★

Prereading Focus

Have students reread Sections 1 and 5 of Chapter 13 to review what they have learned about what lured people to the West and the hardships travelers faced.

Purpose-Setting Question

Ask: "Suppose that you are part of a rescue crew sent to save people trapped in the wilderness. What emotions might you show in a diary entry describing the rescue?"

★ 13–2 ★ Trapped in the Sierra Nevada

Introduction In 1846, a group of settlers started over the Sierra Nevada on their way to California. They were caught by an early winter snowstorm in what is now called Donner Pass. Of the 79 people in the party, only 45 survived. The following is an excerpt from the diary of H. H. Bancroft about the rescue of the trapped Donner party.

Vocabulary Before you read the selection, find the meanings of these words in a dictionary: **emigrants, intervals, famine, provision, repletion, imperatively.**

★ ★ ★ ★ ★ ★ ★ ★ ★

Foster had told us that we should find the emigrants at or near Truckee Lake, (since called Donner Lake) and in the direction of this we journeyed. Of course we had no guide, and most of our journey was through a dense pine forest, but the lofty peak which overlooks the lake was in sight at intervals, and this and the judgment of our two leaders were our sole means of direction. . . .When we started from the fort, Capt. Sutter assured us that we should be followed by other parties as soon as the necessary preparations could be made. For the guidance of those who might follow us and as a signal to any of the emigrants who might be straggling about in the mountains as well as for our own direction on our return trip, we set fire to every dead pine on or near our trail. . . .

At sunset of the 16th day we crossed Truckee Lake on the ice and came to the spot where we had been told we should find the emigrants. We looked all around but no living thing except ourselves was in sight and we thought that all must have perished. We raised a loud hello and then we saw a woman emerge from a hole in the snow. As we approached her several others made their appearance in like manner coming out of the snow. They were gaunt with famine and I never can forget the horrible, ghastly sight they presented. The first woman spoke in a hollow voice very much agitated and said, "Are you men from California or do you come from heaven?"

Background for Understanding

★ ★ ★ ★ ★ ★ ★ ★ ★ ★

In his recollections, H. H. Bancroft also explained that on the return trip, stores of dried meat had to be guarded to prevent the nearly starved survivors from depleting the stores. Once, when the guard was relaxed, Bancroft reported that the eldest Donner boy ate so much dried meat that he died the following day.

Teaching Alternatives

★ ★ ★ ★ ★ ★ ★ ★ ★ ★

Team Teaching: Language Arts You might work with a language arts teacher to present a lesson on eyewitness accounts. Discuss point of view and explain that students should be aware of the author's point of view when reading an eyewitness account. What is the viewpoint of H. H. Bancroft in the reading? How might that viewpoint affect his reporting of the rescue?

They had been without food except a few work oxen since the first fall of snow, about 3 weeks. They had gathered up the bones of the slaughtered cattle and boiled them to extract the grease and had roasted some of the hides which formed the roofs of their cabins. We gave them food very sparingly and retired for the night having some one on guard until morning to keep close watch on our provision to prevent the starving emigrants from eating them, which they would have done until they died of repletion.

When these emigrants had first been stopped by snow they had built small cabins using skins of the slaughtered oxen for roofs. Storms nearly continuous had caused the snow to fall to the depth of 18 feet so that the tops of their cabins were far beneath the surface. . . .

The morning after our arrival John P. Rhoads and Tucker started for another camp distant 8 miles east, where were the Donner family, to distribute what provisions could be spared and to bring along such of the party as had sufficient strength to walk. They returned bringing four girls and two boys of the Donner family and some others.

The next morning we started on our return trip accompanied by 21 emigrants mostly women and children. John Rhoads carried a child in his arms which died the second night. On the third day, an emigrant named John Denton, exhausted by starvation and totally snow-blind, gave out. He tried to keep up a hopeful and cheerful appearance, but we knew he could not live much longer. We made a platform of saplings, built a fire on it, cut some boughs

Viewing History A Snowy Mountain Pass

The journey to California was long and difficult. Travelers had to navigate narrow passes through the Rocky Mountains and the Sierra Nevada before reaching their destination. This photograph shows Carson Pass in the Sierra Nevada. ★ **If you were a settler heading west in the 1840s, what emotions might you have on seeing this view?**

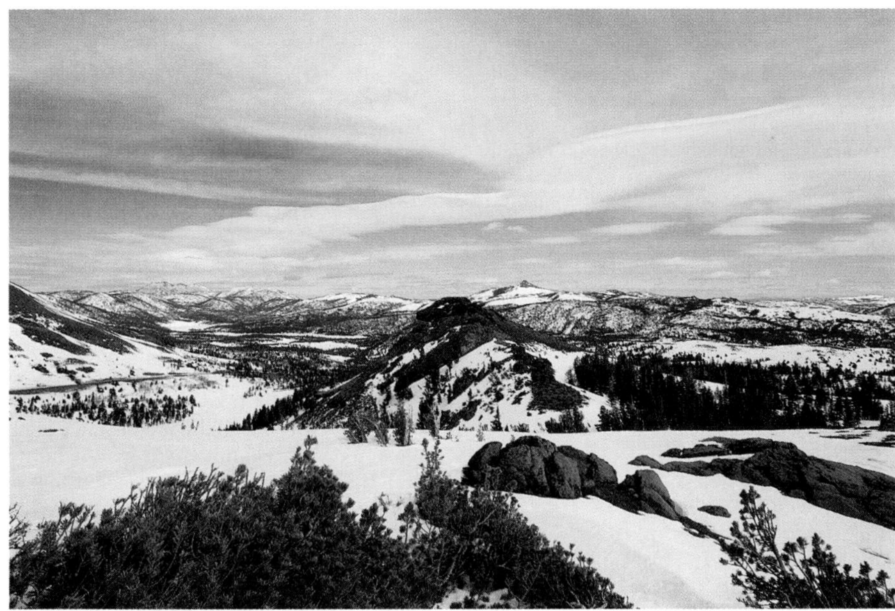

Viewing History ANSWER

Possible answers: awe, dread, fear, anxiety

Source Readings ★ 569

Analyzing Literature

ANSWERS

1. C **2.** H **3.** H. H. Bancroft seemed to view the survivors with both pity and horror.

Historical Critique Bancroft actually witnessed or experienced the trip to Truckee Lake, the death of several people, and the return trip. He heard from others about the snowfall and the travelers' efforts to survive.

★ Chapter 14 ★

★ 14–1 ★

Three Views of Irish Immigration (*average*)

★ ★ ★ ★ ★ ★ ★ ★ ★ ★

Prereading Focus

Have students reread Section 2 of Chapter 14 to review what they have learned about the potato famine in Ireland and the resulting Irish migration to the United States.

Purpose-Setting Question

Ask: "How do you think most people in your community would feel about immigrants who have fled hunger in their homelands?"

for him to sit upon and left him. This was imperatively necessary. The party who followed in our trail from California found his dead body a few days after we had left him, partially eaten by wolves.

Source: *Overland in 1846: Diaries and Letters of the California-Oregon Trail,* edited by Dale Morgan, 1993.

Analyzing Primary Sources

1. At what location were the Donner party survivors found?
- **A.** California
- **B.** a pine forest
- **C.** Truckee Lake
- **D.** Sutter's fort

2. How were the Donner party stranded?
- **F.** They lost their way.
- **G.** Their wagons broke down.
- **H.** There was an early winter snowstorm.
- **J.** They ran out of food.

3. Critical Thinking Recognizing Points of View Based on the excerpt, how do you think H. H. Bancroft viewed the Donner party survivors?

Historical Critique

What information in this selection was Bancroft able to give as an eyewitness? What information did he have to get from members of the Donner party?

★ Chapter 14 ★ *The Worlds of North and South*

★ 14–1 ★ *Three Views of Irish Immigration*

Introduction Under British rule, most farmland in Ireland was used to grow wheat and oats for sale outside of Ireland. Irish peasants depended on the potato for nourishment. Then, in 1845, disease destroyed the potato crop. To escape starvation, thousands of poor Irish families emigrated to the United States. In the first letter below, a young woman in Ireland describes the famine to her parents in Quebec, Canada. The second and third letters were written by new immigrants in New York to their villages back home.

Vocabulary Before you read the selection, find the meanings of these words in a dictionary: **scourge, endeavor, steward, inconceivable, quarries.**

★ ★ ★ ★ ★ ★ ★ ★ ★

Mary Rush:
Ardnaglass, Ireland
September 6, 1846

Dear Father and Mother,

Pen cannot dictate the poverty of this country at present. The potato crop is quite done away all over Ireland. There is nothing expected here, only an immediate famine. If you knew what danger we and our fellow countrymen are suffering, if you were ever so much distressed, you would take us out of this poverty isle. We can only say, the scourge of God fell down on Ireland, in taking away the potatoes, they being the only support of the people. So, dear father and mother, if you don't endeavor to take us out of it, it will be the first news you will hear by some friend of me and my little family to be lost by hunger, and there are thousands dread they will share the same fate. So, I conclude with my blessings to you both....

For God's sake take us out of poverty, and don't let us die with the hunger.

Background for Understanding

★ ★ ★ ★ ★ ★ ★ ★ ★ ★

Kerby Miller, a scholar; and Paul Wagner, a documentary filmmaker; produced a book of letters and photographs about Irish immigrants from which these excerpts are taken. Wagner had earlier made a film called *Out of Ireland* for public television. "Every Irish immigrant's story is unique and intensely personal," the authors note, but the letters "can bring those stories back to life."

Teaching Alternatives

★ ★ ★ ★ ★ ★ ★ ★ ★ ★

Team Teaching: Language Arts Work with a language arts teacher to present a lesson on evaluating letters as primary source documents. Point out to students that letters are written for a specific audience and purpose. Ask students to identify the audience and purpose of each letter in the selection. Discuss how those elements shape each letter's content.

ANSWER

Possible answers: They had heard from friends and relatives about opportunities here; they could buy land or find jobs and escape the desperate poverty of Ireland.

Viewing History **Poverty in Ireland**

Even before famine struck, many Irish peasants lived in desperate poverty. They had to pay high rents to absentee English landlords, who often evicted tenants at will. This print from the later 1800s shows an Irish family thrown off their land with just a few meager possessions. ★ **Why do you think the United States attracted so many Irish immigrants?**

★ ★ ★ ★ ★ ★ ★ ★ ★

Daniel Guiney:
Buffalo, New York
August 9, 1850

Dear Mother and Brothers,

We mean to let you know our situation at present. We arrived here at five o'clock in the afternoon of yesterday, fourteen of us together, where we were received with the greatest kindness and respectability by Matthew Leary and Denis Danihy. When we came to the house we could not state to you how we were treated. We had potatoes, meat, butter, bread, and tea for dinner. . . .

Dear friends, if you were to see old Denis Danihy, he never was in as good health and looks better than he ever did at home. . . . If you were to see Denis Reen when Daniel Danihy dressed him with clothes suitable for this country, you would think him to be a boss or steward, so that we have scarcely words to state to you how happy we felt at present. And as to the girls that used to be trotting on the bogs at home, to hear them talk English would be of great astonishment to you. Mary Keefe got two dresses, one from Mary Danihy and the other from Biddy Matt.

★ ★ ★ ★ ★ ★ ★ ★ ★

William Dever:
New York, New York
September 14, 1848

My dear Uncle and Brothers,

It's inconceivable the thousands that land here every week from all the old countries flying from tyranny and oppression. Wealthy farmers with their whole families are coming here and purchasing farms, some the best land in the whole world. Germans, French, Hollanders are doing this on a large scale.

But most of the Irish come out poor, unable to purchase farms. They work digging quarries, carrying brick and mortar in scorching sun up to the fourth stories of houses, in winter nothing to do, all their money spent. They are despised and kicked about. Many write home they are happy and wealthy, when they are of that class above

Source Readings ★ 571

Analyzing Primary Sources

ANSWERS

1. A **2.** H **3. (a)** Rush might have been even more anxious to leave Ireland after reading Guiney's letter. **(b)** Dever might have said that the letter was full of exaggerations.

Historical Critique Dever claimed that the letters of Irish immigrants often told false stories about their successes.

★ 14–2 ★

The Fires of Jubilee

(average)

★ ★ ★ ★ ★ ★ ★ ★ ★ ★

Prereading Focus

Have students reread Section 4 of Chapter 14 to review what they have learned about life for enslaved African Americans in the South.

Purpose-Setting Question

Ask: "Why did white southerners fear the possibility of slave rebellions?"

mentioned. I heard friends of a young man in this city enquiring if John... was not a banker here, as he wrote home that he was so and persuaded all his relatives to come join him. But what was he, think you? He was sweeper of the office of the bank. They were astonished when told so. And thousands are just like him.

Source: *Out of Ireland: The Story of Irish Emigration to America,* Kerby Miller and Paul Wagner, 1994.

Analyzing Primary Sources

1. Why did Mary Rush send a letter to her parents?
- **A.** She wanted to leave Ireland.
- **B.** She wanted to tell them about life in the United States.
- **C.** She wanted to tell them the latest news from the village.
- **D.** She wanted them to send her money.

2. According to William Dever, unlike German immigrants, the Irish
- **F.** were not good farmers.
- **G.** were treated with great kindness.
- **H.** could not afford to buy land.
- **J.** worked in the banking business.

3. Critical Thinking Recognizing Points of View Explain how you think each of the following might have reacted if they had read Daniel Guiney's letter: **(a)** Mary Rush; **(b)** William Dever.

Historical Critique

How does Dever's letter show why we cannot always take primary sources at face value?

★ 14–2 ★ The Fires of Jubilee

Introduction In 1831, Nat Turner led a group of slaves on an uprising across Southampton County, Virginia. More than 50 white people were killed. Modern writer Stephen B. Oates wrote a dramatic account of this rebellion in *The Fires of Jubilee: Nat Turner's Fierce Rebellion.* The following excerpt describes the reaction of the white community after the rebellion.

Vocabulary Before you read the selection, find the meanings of these words in a dictionary: **pummeled, insurgents, disaffection, dire, commencement, couriers, communiqués, ascertain.**

★ ★ ★ ★ ★ ★ ★ ★ ★

In September, new alarms pummeled upper North Carolina. A man from Murfreesboro, having attended a slave trial in Virginia's Sussex County, reported back that the Southampton insurgents had expected armed slave resistance "from distant neighborhoods," including the large plantations on the Roanoke. Yes, the fellow cried, testimony in the Sussex trial "proved" that a concerted uprising was to have taken place in Virginia and upper North Carolina, where Negro preachers had been spreading disaffection, and that "dire and extensive would have been the slaughter but for a mistake in the day of commencement." The plan, the man said, called for the larger rebellion to begin on the last Sunday in August. But he contended that the Southampton rebels mistook August 21 as the target Sunday, all the while their North Carolina allies were waiting for August 28!

Though no such plan had existed, the report traumatized whites in the northeastern tier of counties, especially in neighborhoods with heavy slave concentrations. Couriers rode for Raleigh to beg for muskets and ammunition. Militia outfits mustered along the Roanoke, chased after imaginary insurgents and... imprisoned... still more innocent blacks. Phantom slave columns marched out

Background for Understanding

★ ★ ★ ★ ★ ★ ★ ★ ★ ★

Stephen B. Oates, who wrote *The Fires of Jubilee,* is also well known as a biographer. He believes that people today are attracted to biography because in our complex and technological society, biography "demonstrates that the individual does count—which is reassuring to people ... who often feel caught up in vast impersonal forces beyond their control."

Teaching Alternatives

★ ★ ★ ★ ★ ★ ★ ★ ★ ★

Team Teaching: Language Arts You might work with a language arts teacher to teach a lesson on journalistic integrity. Explain to students that newspaper are supposed to use reliable sources for the information they print in order to avoid raising false alarms—as was done by reports of slave rebellions in the selection. Ask: "For what other reasons do newspapers need to be as accurate as possible?"

Picking Cotton

The economy of the South depended on cotton, and cotton depended on slavery. This woodcut shows enslaved African Americans picking, baling, and ginning cotton on a plantation.

★ **Compare this picture to the reading. How do they give different pictures of slave life?**

of the Dismal Swamp, only to vanish when militia units rushed out to fight them.

In mid-September came the most shattering alarm of all: couriers reported that a full-scale rebellion had blazed up in southeastern North Carolina, in Duplin and Sampson counties.... Such communiqués were completely false, but frantic whites were now reacting to their own shadows. Militia commanders alerted their troops and sent off exaggerated reports to the governor, which gathered additional frills as express riders bore them to the capital. Meanwhile, mass hysteria gripped the town of Wilmington down near the Atlantic Ocean....

But no slave army appeared. Out of blind vengeance, whites turned on the local Negro population and... forced five hapless blacks into confessing that, yes, they were to meet insurgents from Sampson County....

Raleigh too was in turmoil, as a succession of express riders burst into the city with doomsday reports: slave rebels had allegedly set much of eastern North Carolina afire....

In all the excitement, a few people managed to keep their heads. On September 16, the Raleigh *Star* corrected its initial reports and denied the disturbing news now "circulating through the country." A few days later the Raleigh *Register* admitted that its own account of insurrections in North Carolina had been "highly exaggerated." The storm had passed now, the paper declared, so that it was possible to ascertain the truth. While slaves in the southeastern part of the state had undoubtedly "talked about insurrection," none in fact had transpired.

Source: *The Fires of Jubilee: Nat Turner's Fierce Rebellion,* Stephen B. Oates, 1975.

Analyzing Literature

1. What alarmed the white community ?
   - **A.** the verdict in a slave trial
   - **B.** the burning of Raleigh
   - **C.** the presence of militia in the towns
   - **D.** talk of a slave rebellion
2. Newspapers in Raleigh
   - **F.** supported a slave revolt.
   - **G.** called for an end to slavery.
   - **H.** ignored rumors of a slave revolt.
   - **J.** corrected their earlier reports.
3. **Critical Thinking Distinguishing Fact From Opinion (a)** On what information did the people in North Carolina base their belief that slaves were about to rebel? **(b)** What facts in the selection contradict those beliefs?

Historical Critique

How can you tell that Stephen B. Oates did historical research before writing his book?

Viewing History ANSWER

Possible answers: The picture shows enslaved men and women working in the fields and ginning cotton in a calm and peaceful way, while the reading describes turmoil, rebellion, and fear.

Analyzing Literature

ANSWERS

1. D **2.** J **3. (a)** People's fears were based on the testimony of enslaved African American rebels during their trial. **(b)** The selection later reports that some African Americans were forced to confess they were part of a rebellion, though none had in fact existed.

Historical Critique Oates has collected much detail about where people expected uprisings and how they responded; he also quotes newspaper reports.

★ Chapter 15 ★

★ 15–1 ★

Education of a Slave
(average)

★ ★ ★ ★ ★ ★ ★ ★ ★ ★

Prereading Focus
Have students reread Section 2 of Chapter 15 to review what they have learned about the antislavery movement and Frederick Douglass's part in it.

Purpose-Setting Question
Ask: "How do you think education might add to a person's discontent?"

ANSWER

Douglass wrote and spoke about slavery, thereby "exposing" it.

★ Chapter 15 ★ An Era of Reform

★ 15–1 ★ Education of a Slave

Introduction Frederick Douglass escaped from slavery in 1838 and later became a leading abolitionist. From the money he earned writing and lecturing, Douglass was able to buy his freedom. In 1845, Douglass wrote *Narrative of the Life of Frederick Douglass.* In the following excerpt, Douglass explains why learning to read and write was so important to him.

Vocabulary Before you read the selection, find the meanings of these words in a dictionary: **blighting, impudent, tranquil, irresponsible, commenced, revelation, perplexing.**

★ ★ ★ ★ ★ ★ ★ ★ ★

My new mistress proved to be all she appeared when I first met her at the door—a woman of the kindest heart and finest feelings. She had never had a slave under her control previously to myself, and prior to her marriage she had been dependent upon her own industry for a living. She was by trade a weaver; and by constant application to her business, she had been in a good degree preserved from the blighting and dehumanizing effects of slavery. I was utterly astonished at her goodness. . . . She did not deem it impudent or unmannerly for a slave to look her in the face. The meanest slave was put fully at ease in her presence, and none left without feeling better for having seen her. Her face was made of heavenly smiles, and her voice of tranquil music.

But, alas! this kind heart had but a short time to remain such. The fatal poison of irresponsible power was already in her hands, and soon commenced its infernal work. That

Viewing HISTORY **Frederick Douglass Speaks Out**

In 1845, Frederick Douglass published his Narrative. *The same year, a song celebrating his escape appeared in the North. The photograph (far left) was taken in 1848, the year after Douglass started his antislavery newspaper, the* North Star. ★ **"Expose slavery and it dies," said Frederick Douglass. How did his actions reflect this belief?**

Background for Understanding
★ ★ ★ ★ ★ ★ ★ ★ ★ ★

Douglass's narrative was very popular, selling more than 30,000 copies in five years and becoming a best-seller in both the United States and Europe. Douglass was a brilliant orator. In one memorable speech, he began: "I appear before [you] as a thief and a robber. I stole this head, these limbs, this body from my master, and ran off with them."

Teaching Alternatives
★ ★ ★ ★ ★ ★ ★ ★ ★ ★

Team Teaching: Language Arts Work with a language arts teacher to present a lesson on autobiography. Ask students to find words or passages in the excerpt identifying it as autobiography. In a class discussion, have students focus on the ways that autobiography differs from other types of literature, such as a third-person narrative.

cheerful eye, under the influence of slavery, soon became red with rage....

Very soon after I went to live with Mr. and Mrs. Auld, she very kindly commenced to teach me the A, B, C. After I had learned this, she assisted me in learning to spell words of three or four letters. Just at this point of my progress, Mr. Auld found out what was going on, and at once forbade Mrs. Auld to instruct me further, telling her, among other things, that it was unlawful, as well as unsafe, to teach a slave to read. To use his own words, further, he said, "If... you teach that nigger (speaking of myself) how to read, there would be no keeping him. It would forever unfit him to be a slave. He would at once become unmanageable, and of no value to his master. As to himself, it could do him no good, but a great deal of harm. It would make him discontented and unhappy." These words sank deep into my heart, stirred up sentiments within that lay slumbering, and called into existence an entirely new train of thought. It was a new and special revelation, explaining dark and mysterious things, with which my youthful understanding had struggled, but struggled in vain. I now understood what had been to me a most perplexing difficulty—to wit, the white man's power to enslave the black man. It was a grand achievement, and I prized it highly. From that moment, I understood the pathway from slavery to freedom. It was just what I wanted, and I got it at a time when I the least expected it. Whilst I was saddened by the thought of losing the aid of my kind mistress, I was gladdened by the invaluable instruction which, by the merest accident, I had gained from my master. Though conscious of the difficulty of learning without a teacher, I set out with high hope, and a fixed purpose, at whatever cost of trouble, to learn how to read. The very decided manner with which he spoke, and strove to impress his wife with the evil consequences of giving me instruction, served to convince me that he was deeply sensible of the truths he was uttering. It gave me the best assurance that I might rely with the utmost confidence on the results which, he said, would flow from teaching me to read. What he most dreaded, that I most desired. What he most loved, that I most hated. That which to him was great evil, to be carefully shunned, was to me a great good, to be diligently sought; and the argument which he so warmly urged, against my learning to read, only served to inspire me with a desire and determination to learn. In learning to read, I owe almost as much to the bitter opposition of my master, as to the kindly aid of my mistress. I acknowledge the benefit of both.

Source: *Narrative of the Life of Frederick Douglass, An American Slave*, Frederick Douglass, 1845.

Analyzing Primary Sources

1. Who first taught Frederick Douglass how to read?
   A. Mr. Auld
   B. Mrs. Auld
   C. his mother
   D. another slave
2. According to Douglass, Mrs. Auld changed as a result of her
   F. power over her slaves.
   G. disagreement with her husband.
   H. inability to teach Douglass to read.
   J. fear of a slave revolt.
3. **Critical Thinking Recognizing Points of View** According to the excerpt, how did Frederick Douglass view his master's opposition to educating slaves?

Historical Critique

To gain support for what cause did Douglass write his autobiography? What made him an effective witness?

Analyzing Primary Sources

ANSWERS

1. B **2.** F **3.** Douglass viewed this opposition as revelation. It made him realize the value of education and pushed him to seek ways to learn to read.

Historical Critique He supported abolition; he had experienced slavery so he could explain its horrors to white audiences.

★ 15–2 ★

Declaration of Sentiments (average)

★ ★ ★ ★ ★ ★ ★ ★ ★ ★

Prereading Focus

Have students reread Section 3 of Chapter 15 to review what they have learned about the Seneca Falls Convention and the women's rights movement.

Purpose-Setting Question

Ask: "What arguments might women have used to convince male lawmakers that they deserved equal rights?"

★ 15–2 ★ Declaration of Sentiments

Introduction In 1848, Elizabeth Cady Stanton and Lucretia Mott led a women's rights convention in Seneca Falls, New York. The event marked the beginning of an organized women's rights movement in the United States. The women and men attending the convention adopted the following Declaration of Sentiments and a number of resolutions.

Vocabulary Before you read the selection, find the meanings of these words in a dictionary: **impel, endowed, inalienable, allegiance, prudence, transient, usurpations, evinces, despotism, constrains, tyranny, franchise, facilities, zealous.**

★ ★ ★ ★ ★ ★ ★ ★ ★

Declaration of Sentiments

When, in the course of human events, it becomes necessary for one portion of the family of man to assume among the people of the earth a position different from that which they have hitherto occupied, but one to which the laws of nature and of nature's God entitle them, a decent respect to the opinions of mankind requires that they should declare the causes that impel them to such a course.

We hold these truths to be self-evident that all men and women are created equal; that they are endowed by their Creator with certain inalienable rights; that among these are life, liberty, and the pursuit of happiness; that to secure these rights governments are instituted, deriving their just powers from the consent of the governed. Whenever any form of government becomes destructive of these ends, it is the right of those who suffer from it to refuse allegiance to it, and to insist upon the institution of a new government, laying its foundation on such principles, and organizing its powers in such form, as to them shall seem most likely to effect their safety and happiness. Prudence, indeed, will dictate that governments long established should not be changed for light and transient causes; and accordingly all experience hath shown that mankind are more disposed to suffer while evils are sufferable, than to right themselves by abolishing the forms to which they are accustomed. But when a long train of abuses and usurpations, pursuing invariably the same object, evinces a design to reduce them under absolute despotism, it is their duty to throw off such government, and to provide new guards for their future security. Such has been the patient sufferance of the women under this government, and such is now the necessity which constrains them to demand the equal station to which they are entitled.

The history of mankind is a history of repeated injuries and usurpations on the part of man toward woman, having in direct object the establishment of an absolute tyranny over her. To prove this, let facts be submitted to a candid world.

He has never permitted her to exercise her inalienable right to the elective franchise.

He has compelled her to submit to laws, in the formation of which she had no voice.

He has withheld from her rights which are given to the most ignorant and degraded men—both natives and foreigners.

Having deprived her of this first right of a citizen, the elective franchise, thereby leaving her without representation in the halls of legislation, he has oppressed her on all sides.

He has made her, if married, in the eye of the law, civilly dead.

He has taken from her all right in property, even to the wages she earns. . . .

He has denied her the facilities for obtaining a thorough education, all colleges being closed against her. . . .

Resolutions

Resolved, That all laws which prevent woman from occupying such a station in society as her conscience shall dictate, or which place her in a position inferior to that of man, are contrary to the great precept of nature, and therefore of no force or authority.

Resolved, That woman is man's equal—was intended to be so by the Creator, and the

Background for Understanding

★ ★ ★ ★ ★ ★ ★ ★ ★ ★ ★ ★

Stanton had to overcome the objections of Lucretia Mott and her own husband to include voting rights for women in the Declaration of Sentiments. Mott feared the demand would make them "look ridiculous," while Henry Stanton declared that it would turn the meeting into a farce. Elizabeth Stanton later attributed her resolve to the advice of Irish freedom fighter Daniel O'Connell to claim more than she expected.

Teaching Alternatives

★ ★ ★ ★ ★ ★ ★ ★ ★ ★

Team Teaching: Language Arts Work with a language arts teacher to present a lesson on primary sources. Explain that a document such as the Declaration of Sentiments, as well as such items as diaries, letters, and newspaper accounts, is a primary source. Discuss with students the different kinds of information that historians can glean from various types of primary sources.

Viewing History **Education for Women**

In the early 1800s, American colleges and universities admitted only men. Still, a few women did receive an education at "seminaries for young ladies." This picture by an unknown student shows women studying geography at a seminary, somewhere between 1810 and 1820. ★ **Why did many men think it was not important for women to receive an education?**

highest good of the race demands that she should be recognized as such.

Resolved, That the women of this country ought to be enlightened in regard to the laws under which they live, that they may no longer publish their degradation by declaring themselves satisfied with their present position, nor their ignorance, by asserting that they have all the rights they want....

Resolved, That the speedy success of our cause depends on the zealous and untiring efforts of both men and women....

Source: *Words That Made American History,* Volume 1, edited by Richard N. Current, 1972.

Analyzing Primary Sources

1. What is the main point of this document?
- **A.** Men should have more rights than women.
- **B.** Our laws are unfair to both men and women.
- **C.** Women should have the same rights as men.
- **D.** All men should be allowed to hold public office.

2. According to this document, women did not have the right to
- **F.** work.
- **G.** vote.
- **H.** travel to a foreign country.
- **J.** speak out against injustice.

3. Critical Thinking **Making Inferences** Why do you think that the women at the Seneca Falls Convention used the wording of the Declaration of Independence when they wrote their Declaration of Sentiments?

Historical Critique

For what purpose was this document written? Do you think it was intended to be read primarily by women, by men, or by both?

Viewing History ANSWER

Women were expected to raise their children, look after their husbands, and attend to household matters, all of which were considered their "natural" roles and did not require education.

Analyzing Primary Sources

ANSWERS

1. C **2.** G **3.** The women echoed the greatly admired Declaration of Independence in order to have its protections and rights extended to them.

Historical Critique It was written to draw attention to women's issues and set up a plan of action for the women's rights movement; both, because women as well as men were involved in the issues.

Division and Reunion

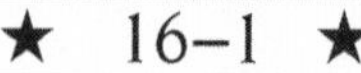

★ 16–1 ★

Caleb's Choice (basic)

★ ★ ★ ★ ★ ★ ★ ★ ★ ★

Prereading Focus
Have students reread Section I of Chapter 16 to review what they have learned about the Fugitive Slave Law and how it divided North and South.

Purpose-Setting Question
Ask: "Suppose that you are living in the South in the 1850s and a runaway slave comes to you for help. How would you respond?"

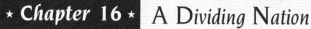

Division and Reunion

★ Chapter 16 ★ A Dividing Nation

★ 16–1 ★ Caleb's Choice

Introduction G. Clifton Wisler's novel *Caleb's Choice* is set in the late 1850s. Young Caleb Delaney goes to northern Texas to live with his grandmother and his cousins Edith and Micah. In Caleb's new home, people are divided over the Fugitive Slave Law. Caleb is not sure how he feels about the law. In the following excerpt, Caleb helps feed two captured fugitives.

Vocabulary Before you read the selection, find the meanings of these words in a dictionary: **shackled, bounty, wretch.**

★ ★ ★ ★ ★ ★ ★ ★ ★

You had to admit that they were good at their work. They captured the two runaways from Waco not a half mile from Spring Creek, and they located three others off a Smith County plantation.

"Already wired their owners," Ulysses boasted. "Mr. Francis Leighton will meet us in Dallas to take delivery of his two. Promised us a fifty-dollar bonus, too. We'll leave the other three with Sheriff Rutherford at McKinney. They're worth two hundred dollars altogether."

I thought about that. Papa needed five hundred dollars, and here the Fitches had earned almost that much capturing runaways! The notion had a powerful pull to it. But when I followed Edith out to the well with some food for the prisoners, I realized that I would never have the heart to be a slave catcher. I recognized the two Waco slaves from the sketches on their posters, but I wasn't prepared for the other three. One was a sad-eyed girl no older than Edith, and the other two were slight-shouldered boys only a little taller than me. Not since departing Dallas had I seen people with such hollow eyes. Their feet were shackled, and their hands were bound with coarse rope that bit into the dark flesh of their wrists. The younger boy bled from the left side of his mouth. Edith gasped when she looked at the backs of the Waco runaways. The Fitches had used a whip on both.

"Fetch some water from the well," Edith told me.

"Already done," Polk Harrison announced, carrying a bucket over. "Spied them on the road."

Edith and Harrison exchanged an odd glance, and I sensed they wanted to say more. The runaways accepted cups of water gratefully, although with downcast eyes. The older ones managed to mumble a thank you when Edith promised to find some salve for their cuts. She placed slices of bread and chunks of ham in their fingers. They ate with considerable difficulty.

"We should notify the sheriff," Edith stormed. "Slaves or not, they don't deserve ill treatment."

"Its not illegal," Harrison argued. "There are slave catchers who do far worse. Fitches know better than to cut off a limb or hamstring a valuable hand. Takes away from the profit."

Background for Understanding

★ ★ ★ ★ ★ ★ ★ ★ ★ ★

G. Clifton Wisler, author of *Caleb's Choice,* admits that he "had a bad habit of daydreaming and showing up late" for school. He credits two teachers with helping him become more conscientious and encouraging his writing. Wisler taught school himself for several years before his first book, *My Brother, the Wind,* was published in 1979.

Teaching Alternatives

★ ★ ★ ★ ★ ★ ★ ★ ★ ★

Team Teaching: Language Arts Work with a language arts teacher to present a lesson on how literature allows the reader to explore moral issues before confronting them in real life. Discuss with students how literature can raise public awareness about issues. Ask how *Caleb's Choice* might have influenced the debate over the Fugitive Slave Law if it had been written in the 1850s.

"They're getting a bonus," I pointed out. "Three hundred and fifty dollars in all."

"A man can always use money," Harrison admitted. "Me, I wouldn't take money earned from another man's bleeding."

"Even a slave?" I asked.

"Especially," Harrison said. "You accept a bounty for a killer, a man likely to hurt somebody else and capable of defending himself, that's one thing. But hunting down some poor wretch who only wants to be left alone?"

"That's pretty strong talk, mister," Ulysses said, walking over, rifle in hand. "You know, it wouldn't surprise me to learn somebody hereabouts hid those older ones. We looked mighty hard for 'em."

"That why you whipped them?" I asked, "To find out?"

"Oh, that was just a little message from Mr. Leighton," Ulysses explained. "Most likely they hid in a slave house at one of the big farms east of here. White men would know better than to help after that trouble on the Colorado River."

"What trouble?" I asked.

"Two years ago the authorities discovered a plot," Harrison told me. "Four hundred slaves were supposed to rise and kill their masters. . . ."

I shivered. Gazing into the eyes of those prisoners, though, I found it hard to imagine myself in much danger. Halfway starved and dressed in rags, they looked more like survivors off a Gulf shipwreck than bloodthirsty killers.

"Don't let 'em fool you, boy," Ulysses said to me in particular. "They hate us. . . ."

"Can't much blame them," Edith said, drawing me away from the well. "Lord knows they've got reason enough."

"I suppose," I said, sighing. "I saw an auction in Dallas. I wouldn't want to be a slave. Desperate like that, they *could* be dangerous, though."

Viewing HISTORY **Human Beings for Sale**

In 1853, British artist Eyre Crowe visited Richmond, Virginia, a leading center of the slave trade. Crowe then painted After the Sale: South From Richmond. *It shows newly sold African Americans in a wagon, waiting to be transported to their new owner. In the lower right, two slave traders argue over the price.* ★ **Identify three details in this painting that create sympathy for the enslaved African Americans.**

Viewing HISTORY ANSWER

Possible answers: The women in the wagon reaching out to a child held by a man suggests a family being separated; the woman in the yellow dress holding her young child while another child sits nearby also suggests family separation; the African American men and women hurrying toward the wagon may be going to say goodbye or may be among those sold to another owner; the presence of the two men at lower right exchanging money reveals that humans are being bought and sold; the man at right with his wrist chained shows lack of freedom; the woman sitting stiffly in the wagon attracts attention as someone who has been sold but maintains her dignity.

Analyzing Literature

ANSWERS

1. A **2.** J **3.** Possible answer: Slave catchers were probably well paid because it was a job that few people would be willing to do, for moral and other reasons.

Historical Critique No, because the novel was written in 1996 and might not reflect views from the 1800s.

★ 16–2 ★

Two Views of the War in Kansas (average)

★ ★ ★ ★ ★ ★ ★ ★ ★ ★

Prereading Focus

Have students reread Section 2 of Chapter 16 to review what they have learned about the battle between proslavery and antislavery groups in Kansas.

Purpose-Setting Question

Ask: "Suppose that you are living in Kansas in 1854. What tactics might you consider using to support your stand on whether or not slavery should be allowed there?"

"I would be," she whispered. "Let's get away from here. I can't bear seeing them that way."

All that afternoon I thought about the slaves. I couldn't get them off my mind. When I sat at the loft table composing letters to my parents for Polk Harrison to carry back south, I tried to free myself from the runaways' ghostly faces. I couldn't.

Source: *Caleb's Choice,* G. Clifton Wisler, 1996.

Analyzing Literature

1. Who were the Fitches?
- **A.** slave catchers
- **B.** Caleb's parents
- **C.** Caleb's grandparents
- **D.** abolitionists

2. Who helped the fugitives?
- **F.** Mr. Leighton
- **G.** Ulysses
- **H.** Sheriff Rutherford
- **J.** Edith

3. Critical Thinking Drawing Conclusions Why do you think that slave catchers were so well paid?

Historical Critique

If you were writing a report about the attitudes of white Texans toward fugitive slaves in the 1800s, could you use *Caleb's Choice* as a historical source? Why or why not?

★ 16–2 ★ Two Views of the War in Kansas

Introduction In 1856, proslavery forces attacked Lawrence, Kansas. An antislavery group led by John Brown attacked Pottawatomie Creek and killed a number of southern settlers. In the following letters, John Lawrie, a northerner, and Axalla John Hoole, a southerner, express their views of the fighting in Kansas.

Vocabulary Before you read the selection, find the meanings of these words in a dictionary: **endeavors, vengeance, propriety, molest.**

★ ★ ★ ★ ★ ★ ★ ★ ★

John Lawrie:

Dear Art,

When I left home on the fifteenth of last June I had no intention of making a home in Kansas. I intended in case I could find any organization ready to take the field against the Missourians [the proslavery settlers], to use my utmost endeavors to change the attitude of the Free-State [antislavery] settlers from a defensive to an offensive warfare. When I reached Leavenworth, I was unable to find any organization of free-state men, and could only tell one when I met him by his hanging head and subdued tone of voice....

Hearing that people held up their heads and spoke what they thought in Lawrence, I started for that point and soon found myself at home as far as a hatred of tyranny and a thirst for vengeance for the insult of the 21st of May was concerned. The people had concluded to try whether there was truth in the Border Ruffian assertion *The... Yankees won't fight!* There was quite a stir among the young men in the way of target fighting and drilling in order to prepare themselves for any emergency that might arise requiring them *to contend with superior numbers,* the only thing that thus far has held them back. I found that arms were really scarce. I expected to find plenty of improved fire-arms, and it was with the greatest difficulty I succeeded in getting an old condemned musket. I was looked upon with distrust by a great many persons in Lawrence, having the appearance of a spy in their eyes. It was complimentary, for my appearance seemed above my position to them; but it was very dis-

Background for Understanding

★ ★ ★ ★ ★ ★ ★ ★ ★ ★ ★

The day before the Kansas-Nebraska Bill passed, Senator William H. Seward gave this impassioned cry: "Come on then, gentlemen of the slave states! Since there is no escaping your challenge, I accept it, in behalf of freedom. We will engage in competition for the virgin soil of Kansas and God give victory to the side that is stronger in numbers, as it is in right."

Teaching Alternatives

★ ★ ★ ★ ★ ★ ★ ★ ★ ★ ★

Team Teaching: Language Arts Work with a language arts teacher to help students analyze these letters. Point out that a letter writer may assume that the person receiving the letter has prior knowledge of what is happening. Review the letters for examples such as Lawrie's reference to Border Ruffians. Have students research the meaning of as many such references as possible.

agreeable. The only military company in town *(the Stubbs)* expected to attend the convention at Topeka on the second and third of July and the opening of the [antislavery] legislature on the Fourth, when it was expected they would be needed to defend the legislature against the Ruffians and troops of the U.S. I applied for admission into the company and was put off with rather evasive answers. I went up to Topeka, however, resolved to prove myself a true man when the trying time came. I found the people discussing the propriety of defending the legislature against all who might attempt to disperse it. . . .

★ ★ ★ ★ ★ ★ ★ ★ ★

Axalla John Hoole:

Dear Sister,

I fear, Sister, that coming here will do no good at last, as I begin to think that this will be made a free state at last. 'Tis true we have elected proslavery men to draft a state Constitution, but I feel pretty certain, if it is put to the vote of the people, it will be rejected, as I feel pretty confident they have a majority here at this time. The South has ceased all efforts, while the North is redoubling her exertions. We nominated a candidate for Congress last Friday—Ex-Gov. Ransom of Michigan. I must confess I have not much faith in him, though he professes to hate the abolitionists bitterly, and I have heard him say that Negroes were a great deal better off with masters. Still, I fear him, but it was the best we could do.

Viewing History **A Violent Abolitionist**

Abolitionist John Brown favored violent solutions to the evil of slavery. In 1856, he and his followers murdered five proslavery settlers in Kansas. Three years later, Brown led a raid on a gun warehouse in Harpers Ferry, Virginia. This painting shows Brown being led to his execution, as northerners imagined the scene. ★ **Why do you think many abolitionists did not support John Brown?**

Source: *America Firsthand,* Volume 1, *From Settlement to Reconstruction*, edited by Robert D. Marcus and David Burner, 1989.

Analyzing Primary Sources

1. The proslavery settlers mentioned in Lawrie's letter were from
   A. Ohio.
   B. Missouri.
   C. Kansas.
   D. Indiana.
2. Free-state settlers were supported by
   F. Border Ruffians.
   G. United States troops.
   H. southerners.
   J. northerners.
3. **Critical Thinking Recognizing Points of View** What was the point of view of each author on the issue of slavery in Kansas?

Historical Critique

Why are both of these letters reliable sources of information, even though they are written from opposing points of view?

Viewing History ANSWER

Many abolitionists considered Brown too violent, too radical, and possibly insane.

Analyzing Primary Sources ANSWERS

1. B **2.** J **3.** Lawrie wanted Kansas to be a free state; Hoole wanted it to be a slave state.

Historical Critique Both were written by eyewitnesses who were involved in the events they describe or expressed their views about the events of their times.

★ Chapter 17 ★

★ 17–1 ★

A Nurse in the Civil War (average)

★ ★ ★ ★ ★ ★ ★ ★ ★ ★

Prereading Focus

Have students reread Section 4 of Chapter 17 to review what they have learned about conditions on the battlefront during the Civil War.

Purpose-Setting Question

Ask: "Suppose that you are a living in 1861, and a call has gone out for volunteers for the war effort. In what capacity might you choose to serve?"

ANSWER

Besides volunteering as nurses, women took over jobs at home, on farms, and in businesses that men left when they went to fight. The women also raised money for medical supplies; a few fought or served as spies.

★ Chapter 17 ★ The Civil War

★ 17–1 ★ A Nurse in the Civil War

Introduction Louisa May Alcott is best known as the author of the classic novel *Little Women.* During the Civil War, Alcott worked at the Union Hospital in the Georgetown area of Washington. She wrote letters home about her experiences as a volunteer nurse. The letters were later published under the title *Hospital Sketches.*

Vocabulary Before you read the selection, find the meanings of these words in a dictionary: **vilest, chronic, premises, fortitude, feebly, comrade, draughts, admonished, tenanted.**

★ ★ ★ ★ ★ ★ ★ ★ ★

The first thing I met was a regiment of the vilest odors that ever assaulted the human nose . . . and the worst of this affliction was, everyone had assured me that it was a chronic weakness of all hospitals, and I must bear it. I did, armed with lavender water, with which I so besprinkled myself and premises, that, like my friend, Sairy, I was soon known among my patients as "the nurse with the bottle.". . . I progressed by slow stages up stairs and down, till the main hall was reached, and I paused to take breath and a survey. There they were! "our brave boys," as the papers justly call them, for cowards could hardly have been so riddled with shot and shell, so torn and shattered, nor have borne suffering for which we have no name, with an uncomplaining fortitude, which made one glad to cherish each as a brother. In they came, some on stretchers, some in men's arms, some feebly staggering along propped on rude crutches, and one lay stark and still with covered face, as a comrade gave his name to be recorded before they carried him away to the dead house. All was hurry and confusion; the hall was full of these wrecks of humanity, for the most exhausted could not reach a bed till duly ticketed and registered; the walls were lined with rows of such as could sit, the floor covered with the more disabled, the steps and doorways filled with helpers and lookers on; the sound of many feet and voices made that usually quiet hour as noisy as noon; and, in the midst of it all, the matron's motherly face brought more comfort to many a poor soul, than the cordial draughts she administered, or the cheery words that welcomed all, making of the hospital a home.

The sight of several stretchers, each with its legless, armless, or desperately wounded occupant, entering my ward, admonished me that I was there to work, not to wonder or weep; so I corked up my feelings, and returned to the path of duty, which was rather

Viewing HISTORY **Nurse and Patient**

This detail is from an engraving honoring the United States Sanitary Commission. It shows a Union nurse comforting a wounded soldier by reading to him. In the Confederacy, too, dedicated women volunteered their time to care for the wounded and the sick. ★ **In what other ways did women help the war effort?**

Background for Understanding

★ ★ ★ ★ ★ ★ ★ ★ ★ ★

Alcott's work as a nurse took a heavy toll on her health, especially when she contracted typhoid. At the time, the standard treatment for typhoid was calomel, a mercury compound that (unknown to people then) caused mercury poisoning. Symptoms included hair loss, mouth sores, anxiety, and delirium. Alcott lay near death for weeks and never fully recovered her health.

Teaching Alternatives

★ ★ ★ ★ ★ ★ ★ ★ ★ ★

Team Teaching: Language Arts Work with a language arts teacher to focus on the life and work of Louisa May Alcott. Remind students that Alcott wrote *Little Women* and many other novels. Have students use library resources to research Alcott, focusing on how experiences such as her volunteer nursing affected her writing. Students may present their findings in oral or written form.

"a hard road to travel" just then. The house had been a hotel before hospitals were needed, and many of the doors still bore their old names; some not so inappropriate as might be imaged, for my ward was in truth a *ball-room,* if gunshot wounds could christen it. Forty beds were prepared, many already tenanted by tired men who fell down anywhere, and drowsed till the smell of food roused them. Round the great stove was gathered the dreariest group I ever saw—ragged, gaunt and pale, mud to the knees, with bloody bandages untouched since put on days before; many bundled up in blankets, coats being lost or useless; and all wearing that disheartened look which proclaimed defeat.... I pitied them so much, I dared not speak to them, though, remembering all they had been through since the roust at Fredericksburg, I yearned to serve the dreariest of them all. Presently, Miss Blank tore me from my refuge behind piles of one-sleeved shirts, odd socks, bandages and lint; put basin, sponge, towels and a block of brown soap into my hands, with these appalling directions:

"Come, my dear, begin to wash as fast as you can. Tell them to take off socks, coats, and shirts, scrub them well, put on clean shirts, and the attendants will finish them off, and lay them in bed."

Source: *Hospital Sketches,* Louisa May Alcott, 1864.

Analyzing Primary Sources

1. What did Miss Blank instruct Louisa May Alcott to do?
   - **A.** make beds
   - **B.** wash patients
   - **C.** change bandages
   - **D.** move patients
2. To handle the terrible odors, Miss Alcott
   - **F.** used lavender water.
   - **G.** opened windows.
   - **H.** washed the floors.
   - **J.** used disinfectant.
3. **Critical Thinking Recognizing Points of View** How did Louisa May Alcott view the soldiers in the hospital?

Historical Critique

Alcott was writing a letter home to her family. Do you think she included all the details of what she witnessed at the hospital? Why or why not?

★ 17–2 ★ The Gettysburg Address

Introduction At the Battle of Gettysburg in July 1863, the Union army lost more than 23,000 soldiers. The Confederates lost 28,000 men. On November 19, 1863, President Abraham Lincoln visited Gettysburg to dedicate the battlefield cemetery. The brief but stirring speech President Lincoln gave on that day became known as the "Gettysburg Address."

Vocabulary Before you read the selection, find the meanings of these words in a dictionary: **score, proposition, consecrate, hallow, detract, vain, perish.**

★ ★ ★ ★ ★ ★ ★ ★ ★

Four score and seven years ago our fathers brought forth on this continent, a new nation, conceived in liberty, and dedicated to the proposition that all men are created equal. Now we are engaged in a great civil war, testing whether that nation, or any nation so conceived and so dedicated, can long endure. We are met on a great battlefield of that war. We have come to dedicate a portion of that field, as a final resting place for those

Background for Understanding

★ ★ ★ ★ ★ ★ ★ ★ ★ ★

Although the Gettysburg Address was so short it fit on a single sheet of paper, public reaction in the North was glowing. The *Chicago Tribune* predicted that the speech would "live among the annals of man." Another newspaper declared it "elegant in every word and comma," while a listener saw it as "an illustration of the difference between oratory and inspiration."

Teaching Alternatives

★ ★ ★ ★ ★ ★ ★ ★ ★ ★

Team Teaching: Language Arts Work with a language arts teacher to have students compare two Civil War documents. Have students locate a speech or letter written by Abraham Lincoln when he first took office or just after the Civil War began. Then ask students to compare that speech or letter, in tone and content, with the Gettysburg Address. Students' work may form the basis for class discussion.

Analyzing Primary Sources

ANSWERS

1. B **2.** F **3.** Alcott viewed the soldiers with pity and respect for their courage and the hardships they had suffered.

Historical Critique Possible answers: Yes, because she needed to share her feelings with them. No, because she did not want them to worry about her.

★ 17–2 ★

The Gettysburg Address (average)

★ ★ ★ ★ ★ ★ ★ ★ ★ ★

Prereading Focus

Have students reread Section 5 of Chapter 17 to review what they have learned about the Battle of Gettysburg and the Gettysburg Address.

Purpose-Setting Question

Ask: "Why do people place great importance on presidential speeches?"

 ANSWER

Union forces drove Confederate troops out of Pennsylvania winning their first victory over Lee.

Analyzing Primary Sources

ANSWERS

1. C **2.** F **3.** Lincoln reminds listeners of the birth of the nation in 1776 and the ideals on which it was founded: that all men are created equal.

Historical Critique Yes, he is trying to rally people to the "unfinished work" of defending freedom.

Viewing History Honoring the Dead

This statue stands at the Gettysburg National Military Park in Pennsylvania. This soldier looks over the now-peaceful field, where a bloody battle took place in July 1863. ★ **What was the outcome of the Battle of Gettysburg?**

who here gave their lives that that nation might live. It is altogether fitting and proper that we should do this. But, in a larger sense, we can not dedicate—we can not consecrate—we can not hallow—this ground. The brave men, living and dead, who struggled here, have consecrated it, far above our poor power to add or detract. The world will little note, nor long remember what we say here, but it can never forget what they did here. It is for us the living, rather, to be dedicated here to the unfinished work which they who fought here have thus far so nobly advanced. It is rather for us to be here dedicated to the great task remaining before us—that from these honored dead we take increased devotion to that cause for which they gave the last full measure of devotion—that we here highly resolve that these dead shall not have died in vain—that this nation, under God, shall have a new birth of freedom—and that government of the people, by the people, for the people, shall not perish from the earth.

Source: *The Annals of America,* Volume 9, *The Crisis of the Union,* 1976.

Analyzing Primary Sources

1. What is this speech mainly about?
- **A.** the Declaration of Independence
- **B.** our nation's founders
- **C.** the Civil War
- **D.** President Lincoln

2. At what occasion was this speech given?
- **F.** the dedication of a cemetery
- **G.** the Battle of Gettysburg
- **H.** President Lincoln's inauguration
- **J.** the end of the Civil War

3. Critical Thinking Analyzing Ideas Give examples of how Lincoln uses this speech to try to remind people of the ideals upon which the United States was founded.

Historical Critique

In addition to honoring the dead, is Lincoln trying to gain support for a particular cause? Explain.

584 ★ Source Readings

★ Chapter 18 ★ The Reconstruction Era

★ 18–1 ★ A Southerner Looks to the Future

Introduction Susan Bradford was the daughter of a Florida planter. In November 1866, she married Nicholas Eppes, who had fought in the Confederate army. His family owned a plantation near Tallahassee. Before her marriage, she kept a diary. Later, Susan Bradford Eppes used her diary and her experiences before and after the war to write books about the South.

Vocabulary Before you read the selection, find the meanings of these words in a dictionary: **fret, invalid, dispatch, proffer, proposition, recoup, impoverished.**

★ ★ ★ ★ ★ ★ ★ ★ ★

January 1st, 1866.—A New Year but a Happy New Year? No indeed. We got up this morning to find ourselves the only occupants of Pine Hill plantation. It was a clean sweep, all were gone.... Not a servant, not one and we unused to work....

January 2nd, 1866.—I have slept well and I feel decidedly better. I am not going to fret because the negroes are gone, nor will I bother my brains as to their whereabouts. I am going to learn to do all these things that need doing and bye and bye I shall do them well....

February 17th, 1866.—The house party is a thing of the past and will be long remembered.... Mrs. Miller is a sweet old lady, a South Carolinian by birth, who married a Northern man. Her invalid son, Lieutenant Charles Miller, excited my pity to such an extent that I have tried to forget his blue [Yankee] uniform and remember only that he suffers. I think the almost constant contact with the sick and wounded soldiers in our own army has automatically made me tender of those who are ill....

Our own boys tease me about my "sick Yankee," but I think it is right or I would not do it....

March 1st, 1866.—Little Diary, I have tried hard to tell you my secret but there are some things too sacred to write about. My Soldier in Gray has held by promise for many months and, before the year is out, we expect to be married....

March 14th, 1866.—Riding horse-back with My Soldier this afternoon I told him ... I had heard Mr. Coolidge [a Yankee officer] was related to him and if that was so I wanted to know why he did not make friends with him? He looked very serious and I was beginning to fear I had hurt him in some unknown way.

At last he spoke, "I have never mentioned my cousin, Sidney Coolidge to you; he came to Florida to visit our family prior to the war.... I loved my cousin Sidney and looked forward to the visit, which he had promised us at some future time.

"The war came on and during the whole four years of war, I was in the thickest of the fighting. After Gettysburg I was promoted and assigned to the Army of the West. One day I was sent to carry a dispatch for my general. Crossing the field of Chickamauga, I was hit by a bullet; ... I was stunned but soon recovered, delivered the dispatch and turned to go. An officer who knew me, laid his hand on my arm and said:

" 'Your cousin, Colonel Coolidge, lies dead in that tent, don't you want to go and look at him?'....

"Now, this young lieutenant you like so much, is probably a relative ... but this is the way I feel about it; if the Confederates had been the victorious army and I had been occupying the conquered country, if, in fact, our positions could be reversed, I should look him up, claim the tie of blood and proffer the hand of friendship. As things stand, he is the conqueror, I am the conquered and if any advances are made they must come from him...."

★ Chapter 18 ★

★ 18–1 ★

A Southerner Looks to the Future (basic)

★ ★ ★ ★ ★ ★ ★ ★ ★ ★

Prereading Focus
Have students reread Section I of Chapter 18 to review what they have learned about the South after the Civil War.

Purpose-Setting Question
Ask: "Suppose that you are a southerner who supported the Confederacy. How might you feel about 'Yankees' after the war? If you kept a diary, what kinds of information would you write in it?"

Background for Understanding

★ ★ ★ ★ ★ ★ ★ ★ ★ ★

Susan Bradford Eppes was a defender of the "Old South." After the Civil War, she regretted the passing of the old ways, railed against Reconstruction, and celebrated the 1876 election that returned southern whites to power. Of her diary, she wrote, "we have adhered ... strictly to the truth ... we deal not in fiction—all is fact."

Teaching Alternatives

★ ★ ★ ★ ★ ★ ★ ★ ★ ★

Team Teaching: Language Arts Work with a language arts teacher to develop a lesson on diary writing. Point out to students that people keep diaries for different reasons. For example, some write only for themselves; others want a record for possible use in the future. Ask students why they think Bradford kept a diary.

ANSWER

The painting's mood is sorrowful, reflecting the South's defeat; Bradford's diary has some sadness and regret but generally seems optimistic about the future.

July 21st, 1866.—This is the anniversary of the Battle of Manassas. How hopeful we were then and it seems ages ago, so much has crowded into life in these last years....

August 26th, 1866.—We have to look ahead and plan for the fall wedding which My Soldier pleads for.... I do not want a grand wedding such as my sisters had; circumstances are so different now. Father's fortune has been swept away by the results of the war. It is true, he still has his land but that is almost valueless at present and it may never bring in anything again as land without labor is a poor proposition.

Father has aged since the surrender and he will never be able to recoup his losses. All this show and expense is wholly unnecessary. What I would like would be a pretty wedding dress, every girl wants that, but I want a quiet wedding with my family and his family present and some of his friends and some of my friends for attendants....

October 5th, 1866.—My dress has been bought....[Mother] has let all our friends know that "no wedding presents must be sent." She says the South is impoverished, there are few who can afford to give a handsome gift and yet almost every one will spend that which they can ill-afford, rather than be outdone in general giving. I am well satisfied with this arrangement....

November 1st, 1866.—My dear little friend... I am telling you goodbye. Whatever the future may bring me of weal or woe will not be recorded. This is MY DAY, my wedding day.

Source: *Through Some Eventful Years,* Susan Bradford Eppes, 1926.

Viewing History: The End of the Confederacy

In Richard Brooke's painting Furling the Flag, *Confederate soldiers weep as they roll up their flag for the last time. The end of the Civil War was a difficult time for southerners. Black and white, they had to adjust to a new world.*

★ **Compare the mood of this painting to the feelings Susan Bradford Eppes expressed in her diary. How are they similar? How are they different?**

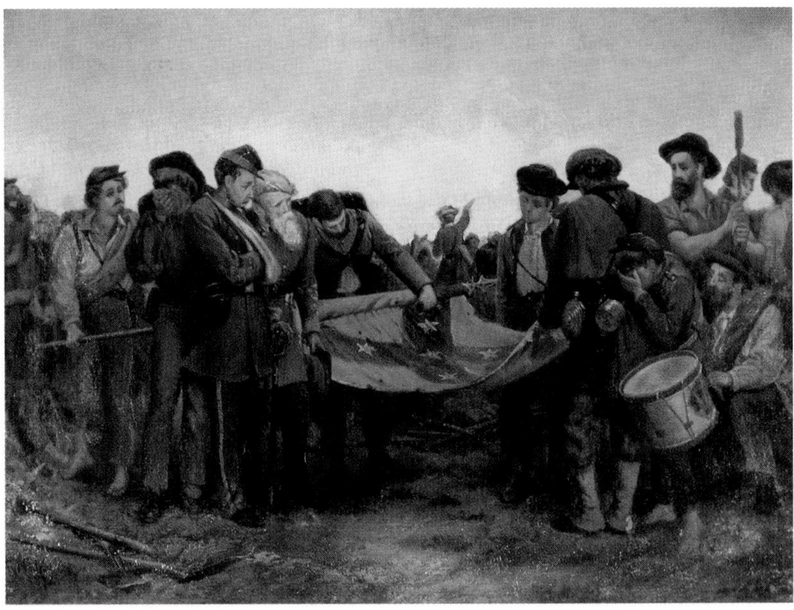

586 ★ Source Readings

Analyzing Primary Sources

1. Why did Susan Bradford Eppes want a simple wedding?
   - **A.** She was marrying a Yankee officer.
   - **B.** She was sad about the South's defeat.
   - **C.** The family's servants had all left.
   - **D.** The war left her family poor.
2. This passage is mainly about the
   - **F.** effects of the Civil War on the author's life.
   - **G.** major battles of the Civil War.
   - **H.** author's plans for her wedding.
   - **J.** conflicts between Yankee and Confederate officers.
3. **Critical Thinking Recognizing Points of View** How does Susan Bradford Eppes reveal her feelings about the South after the war?

Historical Critique

Eppes did not publish her diary at the time it was written. She selected certain passages to include in a book nearly 60 years later. What information would help you judge the reliability of the published diary as a source of information?

★ 18–2 ★ Out From This Place

Introduction *Out From This Place* by Joyce Hansen is a novel about African American life at the start of Reconstruction. In the final chapter, Easter, a freed slave, writes a letter to Miss Grantley, the woman who taught her how to read. Easter describes what she finally decided to do with her life. The letter also describes what life was like for freedmen in a small South Carolina town.

★ ★ ★ ★ ★ ★ ★ ★ ★

March 31, 1866

Dear Miss Grantley,

I hope this letter finds you enjoying the best of health. Please forgive me for taking so long to write to you, but it took me this long to make another decision. First, let me tell you how our town is coming along. We call it New Canaan. We have a church, a school, and we are building a molasses mill and a general store. Some of the people still work for the Williams family to make extra money for the land they purchased.

Miss Fortune moved to the cabin that was built next to the school especially for the teacher. We call it the teacher's house. The men and women take turns keeping guard, though, to make certain that the buckra don't come and burn down our school as they try to do last week. Miss Fortune smelled the smoke and saw the men who set the fire riding away. She say it looked like they was wearing some kind of hood. Thank God we put the fire out before it made much damage. And to think we told her to come and live among us because we thought she would be safer with us than in the cottage near the big house!

Some bad news. Miriam and several other children died from a terrible fever. Brother Thomas still cannot talk and cannot walk by himself. But we pray that one day he'll be better.

Now for my life. I have decided, first, not to marry Julius but to go back to the old Rebel camp and find Mariah and Gabriel. Remember I tell you about them? If Obi is searching for me, he'll go to them because that's where he last left me. I went to the Freedmen's Bureau even though I said I wasn't going again, and I was told that they have a list from a colored regiment. They will write to me when they get more information.

Jason joined a medicine show. I got a letter from him and he says he is happy and fine. I miss him so much.

Now for the big news and decision: I want to go to the school in Philadelphia. We don't

Analyzing Primary Sources

ANSWERS

1. D **2.** F **3.** Bradford refers to the changed circumstances of her family and others, including her father's financial losses and her mother's reasons for saying "no wedding presents." She also notes the anniversary of Manassas.

Historical Critique Possible answer: Having information about her family before and after the war would tell you if her family is typical of southern planters.

★ 18–2 ★

Out From This Place

(basic)

★ ★ ★ ★ ★ ★ ★ ★ ★ ★

Prereading Focus

Have students reread Sections 1 and 3 of Chapter 18 to review what they have learned about Reconstruction and the Freedmen's Bureau.

Purpose-Setting Question

Ask: "Why might attending school be a momentous decision for an African American girl who had once been enslaved?"

Background for Understanding

★ ★ ★ ★ ★ ★ ★ ★ ★ ★

After writing three works of modern fiction, author Joyce Hansen felt like a "trespasser on someone else's property" when she decided to write an historical novel. She did more than a year of research before beginning to write and said that her reading taught her "how complex history is and that it defies any grand, simplistic interpretations."

Teaching Alternatives

★ ★ ★ ★ ★ ★ ★ ★ ★ ★

Team Teaching: Language Arts Work with a language arts teacher to present a lesson on historical novels. Ask students what preparations author Joyce Hansen might have made before writing *Out From This Place*. How could she make the dialogue, setting, and plot of her story authentic? As a class, discuss how this selection supports information in the textbook about Reconstruction.

Viewing History ANSWER

As slaves, African Americans were not allowed to learn to read and write; as freed people, many eagerly chose to get an education.

Analyzing Literature

ANSWERS

1. C **2.** F **3.** Possible answers: that freed slaves were harassed by whites, who tried to burn their school; that disease and illness were a threat; that freed slaves helped one another; and that some had high hopes for the future

Historical Critique No, it is a letter written by a fictional character in a novel written much later.

PRIMARY SCHOOL FOR FREEDMEN, IN CHARGE OF MRS. GREEN, AT VICKSBURG, MISSISSIPPI.

Learning to Read

Many northern teachers, both black and white, went to the South during Reconstruction. Their first task was to teach freedmen to read and write. This engraving shows a classroom in Vicksburg, Mississippi. ★ **Why are there so many adults in this classroom?**

have enough schools or teachers to go around. Our small schoolhouse is full to overflowing, with some of the children coming from the Riverview plantation. Rose and Miss Fortune helped me to make up my mind to go to Philadelphia. Also, Miss Fortune said that I could live with her family while I attended the school. That made me feel less afraid about going. I have a welcome letter from her family already saying that I do not have to worry about my room and board.

So, my dear Miss Grantley, I hope you are happy and excited about my decision as I am. I hope it's not too late for me to attend the school. I saved a little bit of money, and Rose and a few of the other people want to help pay some of the costs too. I look forward to hearing from you soon. I am, as always,

Your Friend and Student,
Easter

Source: *Out From This Place,* Joyce Hansen, 1988.

Analyzing Literature

1. What decision does Easter make about her future?

A. She wants to work for the Freedmen's Bureau.
B. She wants to buy some land.
C. She wants to go to school.
D. She wants to work for the Williams family.

2. Where is Easter planning to go and live?

F. Philadelphia
G. the Williams plantation
H. the Riverview plantation
J. New Canaan

3. Critical Thinking Drawing Conclusions Based on this reading, what impression does the author want to create about freed slaves in the South during Reconstruction?

Historical Critique

Could you use this letter as an authentic historical document about Reconstruction in the South? Why or why not?

588 ★ Source Readings

Reference Section

★ The Declaration of Independence ★

On June 7, 1776, the Continental Congress approved the resolution that "these United Colonies are, and of right ought to be, free and independent States." Congress then appointed a committee to write a declaration of independence. The committee members were John Adams, Benjamin Franklin, Robert Livingston, Roger Sherman, and Thomas Jefferson.

Jefferson actually wrote the Declaration, but he got advice from the others. On July 2, Congress discussed the Declaration and made some changes. On July 4, 1776, it adopted the Declaration of Independence in its final form.

The Declaration is printed in black. The headings have been added to show the parts of the Declaration. They are not part of the original text. Annotations, or explanations, are on the tan side of the page. Page numbers in the annotations show where a subject is discussed in the text. Difficult words are defined.

When in the course of human events it becomes necessary for one people to dissolve the political bands which have connected them with another and to assume, among the powers of the earth, the separate and equal station to which the laws of nature and of nature's God entitle them, a decent respect to the opinions of mankind requires that they should declare the causes which impel them to the separation.

dissolve: break ***powers of the earth:*** other nations ***station:*** place ***impel:*** force

The colonists feel that they must explain to the world the reasons why they are breaking away from England.

The Purpose of Government Is to Protect Basic Rights

We hold these truths to be self-evident, that all men are created equal; that they are endowed by their Creator with certain unalienable rights; that among these are life, liberty, and the pursuit of happiness. That, to secure these rights, governments are instituted among men, deriving their just powers from the consent of the governed; that, whenever any form of government becomes destructive of these ends, it is the right of the people to alter or to abolish it, and to institute a new government, laying its foundation on such principles and organizing its powers in such form, as to them shall seem most likely to effect their safety and happiness. Prudence, indeed, will dictate that governments long established should not be changed for light and transient causes; and, accordingly, all experience hath shown that mankind are more disposed to suffer, while evils are sufferable, than to right themselves by abolishing the forms to which they are accustomed. But when a long train of abuses and usurpations, pursuing invariably the same object, evinces a design to reduce them under absolute despotism, it is their right, it is their duty, to throw off such government and to provide new guards for their future security. Such has been the patient sufferance of these

endowed: given ***unalienable rights:*** so basic that they cannot be taken away ***secure:*** protect ***instituted:*** set up ***deriving:*** getting ***alter:*** change ***effect:*** bring about

People set up governments to protect their basic rights. Governments get their power from the consent of the governed. If a government takes away the basic rights of the people, the people have the right to change the government.

prudence: wisdom ***transient:*** temporary, passing ***disposed:*** likely ***usurpations:*** taking and using powers that do not belong to a person ***invariably:*** always ***evinces a design to reduce them under absolute despotism:*** makes a clear plan to put them under complete and unjust control ***sufferance:*** endurance colonies, and such is now the necessity which constrains them to alter their former systems of government. The history of the present King of Great Britain is a history of repeated injuries and usurpations, all having, in direct object, the establishment of an absolute tyranny over these States. To prove this, let facts be submitted to a candid world:

constrains: forces ***absolute tyranny:*** harsh and unjust government ***candid:*** free from prejudice

People do not change governments for slight reasons. But they are forced to do so when a government becomes tyrannical. King George III has a long record of abusing his power.

Wrongs Done by the King

He has refused his assent to laws the most wholesome and necessary for the public good.

He has forbidden his governors to pass laws of immediate and pressing importance, unless suspended in their operation till his assent should be obtained; and, when so suspended, he has utterly neglected to attend to them.

He has refused to pass other laws for the accommodation of the large districts of people, unless those people would relinquish the right of representation in the legislature; a right inestimable to them and formidable to tyrants only.

assent: approval ***relinquish:*** give up ***inestimable:*** too great a value to be measured ***formidable:*** causing fear

This part of the Declaration spells out three sets of wrongs that led the colonists to break with Britain.

The first set of wrongs is the king's unjust use of power. The king refused to approve laws that are needed. He has tried to control the colonial legislatures.

He has called together legislative bodies at places unusual, uncomfortable, and distant from the depository of their public records, for the sole purpose of fatiguing them into compliance with his measures.

He has dissolved representative houses, repeatedly for opposing, with manly firmness, his invasions on the rights of the people.

He has refused, for a long time after such dissolutions, to cause others to be elected: whereby the legislative powers, incapable of annihilation, have returned to the people at large for their exercise; the state remaining, in the meantime, exposed to all the danger of invasion from without and convulsions within.

depository: storehouse ***fatiguing:*** tiring out ***compliance:*** giving in ***dissolved:*** broken up ***annihilation:*** total destruction ***convulsions:*** disturbances

The king has tried to force colonial legislatures into doing his will by wearing them out. He has dissolved legislatures (such as those of Massachusetts). (See page 90.)

He has endeavored to prevent the population of these States; for that purpose, obstructing the laws for naturalization of foreigners, refusing to pass others to encourage their migration hither, and raising the conditions of new appropriations of lands.

He has obstructed the administration of justice by refusing his assent to laws for establishing judiciary powers.

He has made judges dependent on his will alone for the tenure of their offices and the amount and payment of their salaries.

He has erected a multitude of new offices and sent hither swarms of officers to harass our people and eat out their substance.

endeavored: tried ***obstructing:*** blocking ***naturalization:*** process of becoming a citizen ***migration:*** moving ***hither:*** here ***appropriations:*** grants ***obstructed the administration of justice:*** prevented justice from being done ***judiciary powers:*** system of law courts ***tenure:*** term (of office) ***erected:*** set up ***multitude:*** large number ***swarms:*** huge crowds ***harass:*** cause trouble ***render:*** make

Among other wrongs, he has refused to let settlers move west to take up new land. He has prevented justice from being done. Also, he has sent large numbers of customs officials to cause problems for the colonists.

He has kept among us, in time of peace, standing armies, without the consent of our legislatures.

He has affected to render the military independent of, and superior to, the civil power.

He has combined with others to subject us to a jurisdiction foreign to our Constitution and unacknowledged by our laws, giving his assent to their acts of pretended legislation—

jurisdiction: authority

For quartering large bodies of armed troops among us;

quartering: housing

mock: false

The king has joined with others, meaning Parliament, to make laws for the colonies. The Declaration then lists the second set of wrongs—unjust acts of Parliament.

imposing: forcing ***depriving:*** taking away ***transporting us beyond seas:*** sending colonists to England for trial ***neighboring province:*** Quebec ***arbitrary government:*** unjust rule ***fit instrument:*** suitable tool ***invested with power:*** having the power

During the years leading up to 1776, the colonists claimed that Parliament had no right to make laws for them because they were not represented in Parliament. Here, the colonists object to recent laws of Parliament, such as the Quartering Act and the blockade of colonial ports (page 90), which cut off their trade. They also object to Parliament's claim that it had the right to tax them without their consent.

abdicated: given up ***plundered:*** robbed ***ravaged:*** attacked ***mercenaries:*** hired soldiers ***desolation:*** misery ***perfidy:*** falseness ***barbarous:*** uncivilized ***constrained:*** forced ***brethren:*** brothers ***domestic insurrections:*** internal revolts

Here, the Declaration lists the third set of wrongs—warlike acts of the king. Instead of listening to the colonists, the king has made war on them. He has hired soldiers to fight in America.

oppressions: harsh rule ***petitioned:*** asked ***redress:*** relief ***unwarrantable jurisdiction over:*** unfair authority ***magnanimity:*** generosity ***conjured:*** called upon ***common kindred:*** relatives ***disavow:*** turn away from ***consanguinity:*** blood relationships, kinship ***acquiesce:*** agree ***denounces:*** speaks out against

During this time, colonists have repeatedly asked for relief. But their requests have brought only more suffering. They have appealed to the British people but received no help. So they are forced to separate.

For protecting them by a mock trial from punishment for any murders which they should commit on the inhabitants of these States;

For cutting off our trade with all parts of the world;

For imposing taxes on us without our consent;

For depriving us, in many cases, of the benefit of trial by jury;

For transporting us beyond seas to be tried for pretended offences;

For abolishing the free system of English laws in a neighboring province, establishing therein an arbitrary government, and enlarging its boundaries, so as to render it at once an example and fit instrument for introducing the same absolute rule into these colonies;

For taking away our charters, abolishing our most valuable laws, and altering, fundamentally, the powers of our governments;

For suspending our own legislatures and declaring themselves invested with power to legislate for us in all cases whatsoever.

He has abdicated government here by declaring us out of his protection and waging war against us.

He has plundered our seas, ravaged our coasts, burnt out towns, and destroyed the lives of our people.

He is, at this time, transporting large armies of foreign mercenaries to complete the works of death, desolation, and tyranny already begun with circumstances of cruelty and perfidy scarcely paralleled in the most barbarous ages, and totally unworthy, the head of a civilized nation.

He has constrained our fellow citizens, taken captive on the high seas, to bear arms against their country, to become the executioners of their friends and brethren, or to fall themselves by their hands.

He has excited domestic insurrections amongst us and has endeavored to bring on the inhabitants of our frontiers, the merciless Indian savages, whose known rule of warfare is an undistinguished destruction of all ages, sexes, and conditions.

In every state of these oppressions, we have petitioned for redress in the most humble terms; our repeated petitions have been answered only by repeated injury. A prince whose character is thus marked by every act which may define a tyrant is unfit to be the ruler of a free people.

Nor have we been wanting in attention to our British brethren. We have warned them, from time to time, of attempts made by their legislature to extend an unwarrantable jurisdiction over us. We have reminded them of the circumstances of our emigration and settlement here. We have appealed to their native justice and magnanimity, and we have conjured them, by the ties of our common kindred, to disavow these usurpations, which would inevitably interrupt our connections and correspondence. They, too, have been deaf to the voice of justice and consanguinity. We must, therefore, acquiesce in the necessity which denounces our separation, and hold them, as we hold the rest of mankind, enemies in war, in peace, friends.

Colonies Declare Independence

We, therefore, the representatives of the United States of America, in general Congress assembled, appealing to the Supreme Judge of the world for the rectitude of our intentions, do, in the name and by the authority of the good people of these colonies, solemnly publish and declare, that these united colonies are, and of right ought to be, free and independent states: that they are absolved from all allegiance to the British Crown, and that all political connection between them and the state of Great Britain is, and ought to be, totally dissolved; and that, as free and independent states, they have full power to levy war, conclude peace, contract alliances, establish commerce, and to do all other acts and things which independent states may of right do. And, for the support of this declaration, with a firm reliance on the protection of Divine Providence, we mutually pledge to each other our lives, our fortunes, and our sacred honor.

appealing: calling on ***rectitude of our intentions:*** moral rightness of our plans ***absolved from all allegiance:*** freed from loyalty ***levy war:*** declare war ***contract alliances:*** make treaties

As the representatives of the United States, they declare that the colonies are free and independent states.

The states need no longer be loyal to the British king. They are an independent nation that can make war and sign treaties.

Relying on help from Divine Providence, the signers of the Declaration promise their lives, money, and honor to fight for independence.

★ Signers of the Declaration of Independence ★

John Hancock, President
Charles Thomson, Secretary

New Hampshire
Josiah Bartlett
William Whipple
Matthew Thornton

Massachusetts
Samuel Adams
John Adams
Robert Treat Paine
Elbridge Gerry

Rhode Island
Stephen Hopkins
William Ellery

Connecticut
Roger Sherman
Samuel Huntington
William Williams
Oliver Wolcott

Delaware
Caesar Rodney
George Read
Thomas McKean

New York
William Floyd
Philip Livingston
Francis Lewis
Lewis Morris

New Jersey
Richard Stockton
John Witherspoon
Francis Hopkinson
John Hart
Abraham Clark

Georgia
Button Gwinnett
Lyman Hall
George Walton

Maryland
Samuel Chase
William Paca
Thomas Stone
Charles Carroll

North Carolina
William Hooper
Joseph Hewes
John Penn

Virginia
George Wythe
Richard Henry Lee
Thomas Jefferson
Benjamin Harrison
Thomas Nelson, Jr.
Francis Lightfoot Lee
Carter Braxton

South Carolina
Edward Rutledge
Thomas Heyward, Jr.
Thomas Lynch, Jr.
Arthur Middleton

Pennsylvania
Robert Morris
Benjamin Rush
Benjamin Franklin
John Morton
George Clymer
James Smith
George Taylor
James Wilson
George Ross

★ The Constitution ★ of the United States of America

The Constitution is printed in black. The titles of articles, sections, and clauses are not part of the original document. They have been added to help you find information in the Constitution. Some words or lines are crossed out because they have been changed by amendments or no longer apply. Annotations, or explanations, are on the tan side of the page. Page numbers in the annotations show where a subject is discussed in the text. Difficult words are defined.

Preamble

The Preamble describes the purpose of the government set up by the Constitution. Americans expect their government to defend justice and liberty and provide peace and safety from foreign enemies.

We the people of the United States, in order to form a more perfect Union, establish justice, insure domestic tranquillity, provide for the common defense, promote the general welfare, and secure the blessings of liberty to ourselves and our posterity, do ordain and establish this Constitution for the United States of America.

Article 1. The Legislative Branch

Section 1. A Two-House Legislature

The Constitution gives Congress the power to make laws. Congress is divided into the Senate and the House of Representatives.

All legislative powers herein granted shall be vested in a Congress of the United States, which shall consist of a Senate and House of Representatives.

Section 2. House of Representatives

Clause 1 ***Electors*** refers to voters. Members of the House of Representatives are elected every two years. Any citizen allowed to vote for members of the larger house of the state legislature can also vote for members of the House.

1. Election of Members The House of Representatives shall be composed of members chosen every second year by the people of the several states, and the electors in each state shall have the qualifications requisite for electors of the most numerous branch of the state legislature.

Clause 2 A member of the House of Representatives must be at least 25 years old, an American citizen for 7 years, and a resident of the state he or she represents.

2. Qualifications No person shall be a Representative who shall not have attained to the age of twenty-five years, and been seven years a citizen of the United States, and who shall not, when elected, be an inhabitant of that state in which he shall be chosen.

Clause 3 The number of representatives each state elects is based on its population. An ***enumeration,*** or census, must be taken every 10 years to determine population. Today, the number of representatives in the House is fixed at 435.

This is the famous Three-Fifths Compromise worked out at the Constitutional Convention (page 124). ***Persons bound to service*** meant indentured servants. ***All other persons*** meant slaves. All free people in a state were counted. However, only three fifths of the slaves were included in the population count. This three-fifths clause became meaningless when slaves were freed by the Thirteenth Amendment.

3. Determining Representation Representatives ~~and direct taxes~~ shall be apportioned among the several states which may be included within this Union, according to their respective numbers ~~which shall be determined by adding to the whole number of free persons, including those bound to service for a term of years, and excluding Indians not taxed, three-fifths of all other persons.~~ The actual enumeration shall be made within three years after the first meeting of the Congress of the United States, and within every subsequent term of ten years, in such manner as they shall by law direct. The number of Representatives shall not exceed one for every 30,000, but each state shall have at least one Representative; ~~and until such enumeration shall be made, the state of New Hampshire shall~~

~~be entitled to choose three; Massachusetts, eight; Rhode Island and Providence Plantations, one; Connecticut, five; New York, six; New Jersey, four; Pennsylvania, eight; Delaware, one; Maryland, six; Virginia, ten; North Carolina, five; South Carolina, five; and Georgia, three.~~

4. Filling Vacancies When vacancies happen in the representation from any state, the executive authority thereof shall issue writs of election to fill such vacancies.

Clause 4 ***Executive authority*** means the governor of a state. If a member of the House leaves office before his or her term ends, the governor must call a special election to fill the seat.

5. Selection of Officers; Power of Impeachment The House of Representatives shall choose their Speaker and other officers; and shall have the sole power of impeachment.

Clause 5 The House elects a speaker. Today, the speaker is usually chosen by the party that has a majority in the House. Also, only the House has the power to ***impeach,*** or accuse, a federal official of wrongdoing.

Section 3. The Senate

1. Selection of Members The Senate of the United States shall be composed of two Senators from each state ~~chosen by the legislature thereof,~~ for six years, and each Senator shall have one vote.

Clause 1 Each state has two senators. Senators serve for six-year terms. The Seventeenth Amendment changed the way senators were elected.

2. Alternating Terms; Filling Vacancies Immediately after they shall be assembled in consequence of the first election, they shall be divided as equally as may be into three classes. ~~The seats of the Senators of the first class shall be vacated at the expiration of the second year, of the second class at the expiration of the fourth year, and of the third class at the expiration of the sixth year,~~ so that one-third may be chosen every second year; ~~and if vacancies happen by resignation, or otherwise, during the recess of the legislature of any state, the executive thereof may make temporary appointments until the next meeting of the legislature, which shall then fill such vacancies.~~

Clause 2 Every two years, one third of the senators run for reelection. Thus, the makeup of the Senate is never totally changed by any one election. The Seventeenth Amendment changed the way of filling ***vacancies,*** or empty seats. Today, the governor of a state must choose a senator to fill a vacancy that occurs between elections.

3. Qualifications No person shall be a Senator who shall not have attained to the age of thirty years, and been nine years a citizen of the United States, and who shall not, when elected, be an inhabitant of that state for which he shall be chosen.

Clause 3 A senator must be at least 30 years old, an American citizen for 9 years, and a resident of the state he or she represents.

4. President of the Senate The Vice-President of the United States shall be president of the Senate, but shall have no vote, unless they be equally divided.

Clause 4 The Vice President presides over Senate meetings, but he or she can vote only to break a tie.

5. Election of Senate Officers The Senate shall choose their other officers, and also a president *pro tempore,* in the absence of the Vice-President, or when he shall exercise the office of the President of the United States.

Clause 5 ***Pro tempore*** means temporary. The Senate chooses one of its members to serve as president pro tempore when the Vice President is absent.

6. Impeachment Trials The Senate shall have the sole power to try all impeachments. When sitting for that purpose, they shall be on oath or affirmation. When the President of the United States is tried, the Chief Justice shall preside; and no person shall be convicted without the concurrence of two-thirds of the members present.

Clause 6 The Senate acts as a jury if the House impeaches a federal official. The Chief Justice of the Supreme Court presides if the President is on trial. Two thirds of all senators present must vote for ***conviction,*** or finding the accused guilty. No President has ever been convicted. The House impeached President Andrew Johnson in 1868, but the Senate acquitted him of the charges (page 413). In 1974, President Richard Nixon resigned before he could be impeached.

Clause 7 If an official is found guilty by the Senate, he or she can be removed from office and barred from holding federal office in the future. These are the only punishments the Senate can impose. However, the convicted official can still be tried in a criminal court.

7. Penalties Upon Conviction Judgment in cases of impeachment shall not extend further than to removal from office, and disqualification to hold and enjoy any office of honor, trust, or profit under the United States; but the party convicted shall nevertheless be liable and subject to indictment, trial, judgment, and punishment, according to law.

Section 4. Elections and Meetings

Clause 1 Each state legislature can decide when and how congressional elections take place, but Congress can overrule these decisions. In 1842, Congress required each state to set up congressional districts with one representative elected from each district. In 1872, Congress decided that congressional elections must be held in every state on the same date in even-numbered years.

1. Election of Congress The times, places, and manner of holding elections for Senators and Representatives shall be prescribed in each state by the legislature thereof; but the Congress may at any time by law make or alter such regulations, except as to the places of choosing Senators.

Clause 2 Congress must meet at least once a year. The Twentieth Amendment moved the opening date of Congress to January 3.

2. Annual Sessions The Congress shall assemble at least once in every year, ~~and such meeting shall be on the first Monday in December, unless they shall by law appoint a different day.~~

Section 5. Rules for the Conduct of Business

Clause 1 Each house decides whether a member has the qualifications for office set by the Constitution. A ***quorum*** is the smallest number of members who must be present for business to be conducted. Each house can set its own rules about absent members.

1. Organization Each house shall be the judge of the elections, returns, and qualifications of its own members, and a majority of each shall constitute a quorum to do business; but a smaller number may adjourn from day to day, and may be authorized to compel the attendance of absent members, in such manner, and under such penalties, as each house may provide.

Clause 2 Each house can make rules for the conduct of members. It can only expel a member by a two-thirds vote.

2. Procedures Each house may determine the rules of its proceedings, punish its members for disorderly behavior, and with the concurrence of two-thirds, expel a member.

Clause 3 Each house keeps a record of its meetings. *The Congressional Record* is published every day with excerpts from speeches made in each house. It also records the votes of each member.

3. A Written Record Each house shall keep a journal of its proceedings, and from time to time publish the same, excepting such parts as may in their judgment require secrecy; and the yeas and nays of the members of either house on any question shall, at the desire of one-fifth of those present, be entered on the journal.

Clause 4 Neither house can ***adjourn,*** or stop meeting, for more than three days unless the other house approves. Both houses of Congress must meet in the same city.

4. Rules for Adjournment Neither house, during the session of Congress, shall, without the consent of the other, adjourn for more than three days, nor to any other place than that in which the two houses shall be sitting.

Section 6. Privileges and Restrictions

Clause 1 ***Compensation*** means salary. Congress decides the salary for its members. While Congress is in session, a member is free from arrest in civil cases and cannot be sued for anything he or she says on the floor of Congress. This allows for freedom of debate. However, a member can be arrested for a criminal offense.

1. Salaries and Immunities The Senators and Representatives shall receive a compensation for their services, to be ascertained by law and paid out of the Treasury of the United States. They shall in all cases, except treason, felony, and breach of the peace, be privileged from arrest during their attendance at the session of their respective houses, and in going to and returning from the same; and for any speech or debate in either house, they shall not be questioned in any other place.

2. Restrictions on Other Employment No Senator or Representative shall, during the time for which he was elected, be appointed to any civil office under the authority of the United States, which shall have been created, or the emoluments whereof shall have been increased, during such time; and no person holding any office under the United States shall be a member of either house during his continuance in office.

Clause 2 ***Emolument*** also means salary. A member of Congress cannot hold another federal office during his or her term. A former member of Congress cannot hold an office created while he or she was in Congress. An official in another branch of government cannot serve at the same time in Congress. This strengthens the separation of powers.

Section 7. Law-Making Process

1. Tax Bills All bills for raising revenue shall originate in the House of Representatives; but the Senate may propose or concur with amendments as on other bills.

Clause 1 ***Revenue*** is money raised by the government through taxes. Tax bills must be introduced in the House. The Senate, however, can make changes in tax bills. This clause protects the principle that people can be taxed only with their consent.

2. How a Bill Becomes a Law Every bill which shall have passed the House of Representatives and the Senate shall, before it become a law, be presented to the President of the United States; if he approve, he shall sign it, but if not, he shall return it, with his objections, to that house in which it shall have originated, who shall enter the objections at large on their journal, and proceed to reconsider it. If after such reconsideration two-thirds of that house shall agree to pass the bill, it shall be sent, together with the objections, to the other house, by which it shall likewise be reconsidered, and, if approved by two-thirds of that house, it shall become a law. But in all such cases the votes of both houses shall be determined by yeas and nays, and the names of the persons voting for and against the bill shall be entered on the journal of each house respectively. If any bill shall not be returned by the President within ten days (Sundays excepted) after it shall have been presented to him, the same bill shall be a law, in like manner as if he had signed it, unless the Congress by their adjournment prevent its return, in which case it shall not be a law.

Clause 2 A ***bill,*** or proposed law, that is passed by a majority of the House and Senate is sent to the President. If the President signs the bill, it becomes law.

A bill can also become law without the President's signature. The President can refuse to act on a bill. If Congress is in session at the time, the bill becomes law 10 days after the President receives it.

The President can ***veto,*** or reject, a bill by sending it back to the house where it was introduced. Or if the President refuses to act on a bill and Congress adjourns within 10 days, then the bill dies. This way of killing a bill without taking action is called the ***pocket veto.***

Congress can override the President's veto if each house of Congress passes the bill again by a two-thirds vote. This clause is an important part of the system of checks and balances (page 130).

3. Resolutions Passed by Congress Every order, resolution, or vote to which the concurrence of the Senate and House of Representatives may be necessary (except on a question of adjournment) shall be presented to the President of the United States; and before the same shall take effect, shall be approved by him, or being disapproved by him, shall be repassed by two-thirds of the Senate and House of Representatives, according to the rules and limitations prescribed in the case of a bill.

Clause 3 Congress can pass resolutions or orders that have the same force as laws. Any such resolution or order must be signed by the President (except on questions of adjournment). Thus, this clause prevents Congress from bypassing the President simply by calling a bill by another name.

Section 8. Powers Delegated to Congress

The Congress shall have the power

1. Taxes To lay and collect taxes, duties, imposts, and excises, to pay the debts and provide for the common defense and general welfare of the United States; but all duties, imposts, and excises shall be uniform throughout the United States;

Clause 1 ***Duties*** are tariffs. ***Imposts*** are taxes in general. ***Excises*** are taxes on the production or sale of certain goods. Congress has the power to tax and spend tax money. Taxes must be the same in all parts of the country.

2. Borrowing To borrow money on the credit of the United States;

Clause 2 Congress can borrow money for the United States. The government often borrows money by selling ***bonds,*** or certificates that promise to pay the holder a certain sum of money on a certain date (page 174).

Clause 3 Only Congress has the power to regulate foreign and ***interstate trade,*** or trade between states. Disagreement over interstate trade was a major problem with the Articles of Confederation (pages 117–118).

3. Commerce To regulate commerce with foreign nations, and among the several states, and with the Indian tribes;

Clause 4 ***Naturalization*** is the process whereby a foreigner becomes a citizen. ***Bankruptcy*** is the condition in which a person or business cannot pay its debts. Congress has the power to pass laws on these two issues. The laws must be the same in all parts of the country.

4. Naturalization; Bankruptcy To establish a uniform rule of naturalization, and uniform laws on the subject of bankruptcies throughout the United States;

Clause 5 Congress has the power to coin money and set its value. Congress has set up the National Bureau of Standards to regulate weights and measures.

5. Coins; Weights; Measures To coin money, regulate the value thereof, and of foreign coin, and fix the standard of weights and measures;

Clause 6 ***Counterfeiting*** is the making of imitation money. ***Securities*** are bonds. Congress can make laws to punish counterfeiters.

6. Counterfeiting To provide for the punishment of counterfeiting the securities and current coin of the United States;

Clause 7 Congress has the power to set up and control the delivery of mail.

7. Post Offices To establish post offices and post roads;

Clause 8 Congress may pass copyright and patent laws. A ***copyright*** protects an author. A patent makes an inventor the sole owner of his or her work for a limited time.

8. Copyrights; Patents To promote the progress of science and useful arts by securing for limited times to authors and inventors the exclusive right to their respective writings and discoveries;

Clause 9 Congress has the power to set up ***inferior,*** or lower, federal courts under the Supreme Court.

9. Federal Courts To constitute tribunals inferior to the Supreme Court;

Clause 10 Congress can punish ***piracy,*** or the robbing of ships at sea.

10. Piracy To define and punish piracies and felonies committed on the high seas and offenses against the law of nations;

Clause 11 Only Congress can declare war. Declarations of war are granted at the request of the President. ***Letters of marque and reprisal*** were documents issued by a government allowing merchant ships to arm themselves and attack ships of an enemy nation. They are no longer issued.

11. Declarations of War To declare war, ~~grant letters of marque and reprisal,~~ and make rules concerning captures on land and water;

Clauses 12, 13, 14 These clauses place the army and navy under the control of Congress. Congress decides on the size of the armed forces and the amount of money to spend on the army and navy. It also has the power to write rules governing the armed forces.

12. Army To raise and support armies, but no appropriation of money to that use shall be for a longer term than two years;

13. Navy To provide and maintain a navy;

14. Rules for the Military To make rules for the government and regulation of the land and naval forces;

Clauses 15, 16 The ***militia*** is a body of citizen soldiers. Congress can call up the militia to put down rebellions or fight foreign invaders. Each state has its own militia, today called the National Guard. Normally, the militia is under the command of a state's governor. However, it can be placed under the command of the President.

15. Militia To provide for calling forth the militia to execute the laws of the Union, suppress insurrections, and repel invasions;

16. Rules for the Militia To provide for organizing, arming, and disciplining the militia, and for governing such part of them as may be employed in the service of the United States, reserving to the states, respectively, the appointment of the officers, and the authority of training the militia according to the discipline prescribed by Congress;

17. National Capital To exercise exclusive legislation in all cases whatsoever, over such district (not exceeding ten miles square) as may, by cession of particular states, and the acceptance of Congress, become the seat of government of the United States, and to exercise like authority over all places purchased by the consent of the legislature of the state in which the same shall be, for the erection of forts, magazines, arsenals, dock-yards, and other needful buildings;—and

Clause 17 Congress controls the district around the national capital. In 1790, Congress made Washington, D.C., the nation's capital (page 175). In 1973, it gave residents of the District the right to elect local officials.

18. Necessary Laws To make all laws which shall be necessary and proper for carrying into execution the foregoing powers, and all other powers vested by this Constitution in the government of the United States, or in any department or officer thereof.

Clause 18 Clauses 1–17 list the powers delegated to Congress. The writers of the Constitution added Clause 18 so that Congress could deal with the changing needs of the nation. It gives Congress the power to make laws as needed to carry out the first 17 clauses. Clause 18 is sometimes called the elastic clause because it lets Congress stretch the meaning of its power.

Section 9. Powers Denied to the Federal Government

1. The Slave Trade ~~The migration or importation of such persons as any of the states now existing shall think proper to admit shall not be prohibited by the Congress prior to the year 1808; but a tax or duty may be imposed on such importation, not exceeding $10 for each person.~~

Clause 1 ***Such persons*** means slaves. This clause resulted from a compromise between the supporters and the opponents of the slave trade (page 125). In 1808, as soon as Congress was permitted to abolish the slave trade, it did so. The $10 import tax was never imposed.

2. Writ of Habeas Corpus The privilege of the writ of habeas corpus shall not be suspended, unless when in cases of rebellion or invasion the public safety may require it.

Clause 2 A ***writ of habeas corpus*** is a court order requiring government officials to bring a prisoner to court and explain why he or she is being held. A writ of habeas corpus protects people from unlawful imprisonment. The government cannot suspend this right except in times of rebellion or invasion.

3. Bills of Attainder and Ex Post Facto Laws No bill of attainder or *ex post facto* law shall be passed.

Clause 3 A ***bill of attainder*** is a law declaring that a person is guilty of a particular crime. An ***ex post facto law*** punishes an act which was not illegal when it was committed. Congress cannot pass a bill of attainder or *ex post facto* laws.

4. Apportionment of Direct Taxes ~~No capitation or other direct tax shall be laid, unless in proportion to the census or enumeration herein before directed to be taken.~~

Clause 4 A ***capitation tax*** is a tax placed directly on each person. ***Direct taxes*** are taxes on people or on land. They can be passed only if they are divided among the states according to population. The Sixteenth Amendment allowed Congress to tax income without regard to the population of the states.

5. Taxes on Exports No tax or duty shall be laid on articles exported from any state.

Clause 5 This clause forbids Congress to tax exports. In 1787, southerners insisted on this clause because their economy depended on exports.

6. Special Preference for Trade No preference shall be given any regulation of commerce or revenue to the ports of one state over those of another; nor shall vessels bound to, or from, one state, be obliged to enter, clear, or pay duties in another.

Clause 6 Congress cannot make laws that favor one state over another in trade and commerce. Also, states cannot place tariffs on interstate trade.

7. Spending No money shall be drawn from the Treasury, but in consequence of appropriations made by law; and a regular statement and account of the receipts and expenditures of all public money shall be published from time to time.

Clause 7 The federal government cannot spend money unless Congress ***appropriates*** it, or passes a law allowing it. This clause gives Congress an important check on the President by controlling the money he or she can spend. The government must publish a statement showing how it spends public funds.

Clause 8 The government cannot award titles of nobility, such as Duke or Duchess. American citizens cannot accept titles of nobility from foreign governments without the consent of Congress.

8. Creation of Titles of Nobility No title of nobility shall be granted by the United States; and no person holding any office of profit or trust under them, shall, without the consent of the Congress, accept of any present, emolument, office, or title, of any kind whatever, from any king, prince, or foreign state.

Section 10. Powers Denied to the States

Clause 1 The writers of the Constitution did not want the states to act like separate nations. So they prohibited states from making treaties or coining money. Some powers denied to the federal government are also denied to the states. For example, states cannot pass *ex post facto* laws.

1. Unconditional Prohibitions No state shall enter into any treaty, alliance, or confederation; grant letters of marque and reprisal; coin money; emit bills of credit; make anything but gold and silver coin a tender in payment of debts; pass any bill of attainder, *ex post facto* law, or law impairing the obligation of contracts, or grant any title of nobility.

Clauses 2, 3 Powers listed here are forbidden to the states, but Congress can lift these prohibitions by passing laws that give these powers to the states.

Clause 2 forbids states from taxing imports and exports without the consent of Congress. States may charge inspection fees on goods entering the states. Any profit from these fees must be turned over to the United States Treasury.

Clause 3 forbids states from keeping an army or navy without the consent of Congress. States cannot make treaties or declare war unless an enemy invades or is about to invade.

2. Powers Conditionally Denied No state shall, without the consent of the Congress, lay any imposts or duties on imports or exports, except what may be absolutely necessary for executing its inspection laws; and the net produce of all duties and imposts, laid by any state on imports or exports, shall be for the use of the Treasury of the United States; and all such laws shall be subject to the revision and control of the Congress.

3. Other Denied Powers No state shall, without the consent of Congress, lay any duty of tonnage, keep troops, or ships of war in time of peace, enter into any agreement or compact with another state, or with a foreign power, or engage in war, unless actually invaded, or in such imminent danger as will not admit of delay.

Article 2. The Executive Branch

Section 1. President and Vice-President

Clause 1 The President is responsible for ***executing,*** or carrying out, laws passed by Congress.

1. Chief Executive The executive power shall be vested in a President of the United States of America. He shall hold his office during the term of four years, and together with the Vice-President, chosen for the same term, be elected as follows:

Clauses 2, 3 Some writers of the Constitution were afraid to allow the people to elect the President directly (page 130). Therefore, the Constitutional Convention set up the electoral college. Clause 2 directs each state to choose electors, or delegates to the electoral college, to vote for President. A state's electoral vote is equal to the combined number of senators and representatives. Each state may decide how to choose its electors. Members of Congress and federal officeholders may not serve as electors. This much of the original electoral college system is still in effect.

Clause 3 called upon each elector to vote for two candidates. The candidate who received a majority of the electoral votes would become President. The runner-up would become Vice President. If no candidate won a majority, the House would choose the President. The Senate would choose the Vice President.

The election of 1800 showed a problem with the original electoral college system (page 189). Thomas Jefferson was the Republican candidate

2. Selection of Electors Each state shall appoint, in such manner as the legislature thereof may direct, a number of electors, equal to the whole number of Senators and Representatives to which the state may be entitled in the Congress; but no Senator or Representative, or person holding an office or trust or profit under the United States, shall be appointed an elector.

3. Electoral College Procedures ~~The electors shall meet in their respective states, and vote by ballot for two persons, of whom one at least shall not be an inhabitant of the same state with themselves. And they shall make a list of all the persons voted for, and of the number of votes for each; which list they shall sign and certify, and transmit sealed to the seat of the government of the United States, directed to the president of the Senate. The president of the Senate shall, in the presence of the Senate and House of Representatives, open all the certificates, and the votes shall then be counted. The person having the greatest number of votes shall be President, if such number be a majority of the whole number of electors appointed; and if~~

~~there be more than one who have such majority, and have an equal number of votes, then the House of Representatives shall immediately choose by ballot one of them for President; and if no person have a majority, then from the five highest on the list the said House shall in like manner choose the President. But in choosing the President the votes shall be taken by states, the representation from each state having one vote. A quorum for this purpose shall consist of a member or members from two-thirds of the states, and a majority of all the states shall be necessary to a choice. In every case, after the choice of the President, the person having the greatest number of votes of the electors shall be the Vice-President. But if there should remain two or more who have equal votes, the Senate shall choose from them by ballot the Vice-President.~~

for President, and Aaron Burr was the Republican candidate for Vice President. In the electoral college, the vote ended in a tie. The election was finally decided in the House, where Jefferson was chosen President. The Twelfth Amendment changed the electoral college system so that this could not happen again.

4. Time of Elections The Congress may determine the time of choosing the electors, and the day on which they shall give their votes; which day shall be the same throughout the United States.

Clause 4 By a law passed in 1792, electors are chosen on the Tuesday after the first Monday of November every four years. Electors from each state meet to vote in December.

Today, voters in each state choose ***slates,*** or groups, of electors who are pledged to a candidate for President. The candidate for President who wins the popular vote in each state wins that state's electoral vote.

5. Qualifications for President No person except a natural-born citizen ~~or a citizen of the United States, at the time of the adoption of this Constitution,~~ shall be eligible to the office of the President; neither shall any person be eligible to that office who shall not have attained to the age of thirty-five years, and been fourteen years a resident within the United States.

Clause 5 The President must be a citizen of the United States from birth, at least 35 years old, and a resident of the country for 14 years. The first seven Presidents of the United States were born under British rule, but they were allowed to hold office because they were citizens at the time the Constitution was adopted.

6. Presidential Succession In case of the removal of the President from office, or of his death, resignation, or inability to discharge the powers and duties of the said office, the same shall devolve on the Vice-President, and the Congress may by law provide for the case of removal, death, resignation, or inability, both of the President and Vice-President, declaring what officer shall then act as President, and such officer shall act accordingly, until the disability be removed, or a President shall be elected.

Clause 6 The powers of the President pass to the Vice President if the President leaves office or cannot discharge his or her duties. The wording of this clause caused confusion the first time a President died in office. When President William Henry Harrison died, it was uncertain whether Vice President John Tyler should remain Vice President and act as President or whether he should be sworn in as President. Tyler persuaded a federal judge to swear him in. So he set the precedent that the Vice President assumes the office of President when it becomes vacant. The Twenty-fifth Amendment replaced this clause.

7. Salary The President shall, at stated times, receive for his services, a compensation, which shall neither be increased nor diminished during the period for which he shall have been elected, and he shall not receive within that period any other emolument from the United States, or any of them.

Clause 7 The President is paid a salary. It cannot be raised or lowered during his or her term of office. The President is not allowed to hold any other federal or state position while in office. Today, the President's salary is $200,000 a year.

8. Oath of Office Before he enter on the execution of his office, he shall take the following oath or affirmation:—"I do solemnly swear (or affirm) that I will faithfully execute the office of President of the United States, and will to the best of my ability, preserve, protect, and defend the Constitution of the United States."

Clause 8 Before taking office, the President must promise to protect and defend the Constitution. Usually, the Chief Justice of the Supreme Court gives the oath of office to the President.

★ THE CONSTITUTION ★

Section 2. Powers of the President

Clause 1 The President is head of the armed forces and the state militias when they are called into national service. So the military is under ***civilian,*** or nonmilitary, control.

The President can get advice from the heads of executive departments. In most cases, the President has the power to grant a reprieve or pardon. A ***reprieve*** suspends punishment ordered by law. A ***pardon*** prevents prosecution for a crime or overrides the judgment of a court.

1. Commander in Chief of the Armed Forces The President shall be Commander in Chief of the Army and Navy of the United States, and of the militia of the several states, when called into the actual service of the United States; he may require the opinion, in writing, of the principal officer in each of the executive departments, upon any subject relating to the duties of their respective offices, and he shall have power to grant reprieves and pardons for offenses against the United States, except in cases of impeachment.

Clause 2 The President has the power to make treaties with other nations. Under the system of checks and balances, all treaties must be approved by two thirds of the Senate. Today, the President also makes agreements with foreign governments. These executive agreements do not need Senate approval.

The President has the power to appoint ambassadors to foreign countries and to appoint other high officials. The Senate must ***confirm,*** or approve, these appointments.

2. Making Treaties and Nominations He shall have power, by and with the advice and consent of the Senate, to make treaties, provided two-thirds of the Senators present concur; and he shall nominate, and by and with the advice and consent of the Senate, shall appoint ambassadors, other public ministers and consuls, judges of the Supreme Court, and all other officers of the United States, whose appointments are not herein otherwise provided for, and which shall be established by law; but the Congress may by law vest the appointment of such inferior officers, as they think proper, in the President alone, in the courts of law, or in the heads of departments.

Clause 3 If the Senate is in ***recess,*** or not meeting, the President may fill vacant government posts by making temporary appointments.

3. Temporary Appointments The President shall have power to fill up all vacancies that may happen during the recess of the Senate, by granting commissions which shall expire at the end of their next session.

Section 3. Duties

The President must give Congress a report on the condition of the nation every year. This report is now called the State of the Union Address. Since 1913, the President has given this speech in person each January.

The President can call a special session of Congress and can adjourn Congress if necessary. The President has the power to receive, or recognize, foreign ambassadors.

The President must carry out the laws. Today, many government agencies oversee the execution of laws.

He shall from time to time give to the Congress information of the state of the Union, and recommend to their consideration such measures as he shall judge necessary and expedient; he may, on extraordinary occasions, convene both houses, or either of them, and in case of disagreement between them, with respect to the time of adjournment, he may adjourn them to such time as he shall think proper; he shall receive ambassadors and other public ministers; he shall take care that the laws be faithfully executed, and shall commission all the officers of the United States.

Section 4. Impeachment and Removal From Office

Civil officers include federal judges and members of the Cabinet. ***High crimes*** are major crimes. ***Misdemeanors*** are lesser crimes. The President, Vice President, and others can be forced out of office if impeached and found guilty of certain crimes. Andrew Johnson is the only President to have been impeached.

The President, Vice-President, and all civil officers of the United States, shall be removed from office on impeachment for, and conviction of, treason, bribery, or other high crimes or misdemeanors.

Article 3. The Judicial Branch

Section 1. Federal Courts

Judicial power is the right of the courts to decide legal cases. The Constitution creates the Supreme Court but lets Congress decide the size of the Supreme Court. Congress has the power to set up inferior, or lower, courts. The Judiciary Act of 1789 (page 173) set up district and circuit courts, or courts of appeal. Today, there are 94 district courts and 13 courts of appeal. All federal judges serve for life.

The judicial power of the United States shall be vested in one Supreme Court, and in such inferior courts as the Congress may from time to time ordain and establish. The judges, both of the Supreme and inferior courts, shall hold their offices during good behavior, and shall, at stated times, receive for their services a compensation, which shall not be diminished during their continuance in office.

Section 2. Jurisdiction of Federal Courts

1. Scope of Judicial Power The judicial power shall extend to all cases, in law and equity, arising under this Constitution, the laws of the United States, and treaties made or which shall be made, under their authority; to all cases affecting ambassadors, other public ministers and consuls; to all cases of admiralty and maritime jurisdiction; to controversies to which the United States shall be a party; to controversies between two or more states; ~~between a state and citizens of another state;~~ between citizens of the same state claiming lands under grants of different states, and between a state or the citizens thereof, and foreign states, citizens, or subjects.

Clause 1 ***Jurisdiction*** refers to the right of a court to hear a case. Federal courts have jurisdiction over cases that involve the Constitution, federal laws, treaties, foreign ambassadors and diplomats, naval and maritime laws, disagreements between states or between citizens from different states, and disputes between a state or citizen and a foreign state or citizen.

In *Marbury* v. *Madison,* the Supreme Court established the right to judge whether a law is constitutional (page 197).

2. The Supreme Court In all cases affecting ambassadors, other public ministers and consuls, and those in which a state shall be a party, the Supreme Court shall have original jurisdiction. In all the other cases before mentioned, the Supreme Court shall have appellate jurisdiction, both as to law and fact, with such exceptions, and under such regulations as the Congress shall make.

Clause 2 ***Original jurisdiction*** means the power of a court to hear a case where it first arises. The Supreme Court has original jurisdiction over only a few cases, such as those involving foreign diplomats. More often, the Supreme Court acts as an appellate court. An ***appellate court*** does not decide guilt. It decides whether the lower court trial was properly conducted and reviews the lower court's decision.

3. Trial by Jury The trial of all crimes, except in cases of impeachment, shall be by jury; and such trial shall be held in the state where the said crimes shall have been committed; but when not committed within any state, the trial shall be at such place or places as the Congress may by law have directed.

Clause 3 This clause guarantees the right to a jury trial for anyone accused of a federal crime. The only exceptions are impeachment cases. The trial must be held in the state where the crime was committed.

Section 3. Treason

1. Definition Treason against the United States shall consist only in levying war against them, or in adhering to their enemies, giving them aid and comfort. No person shall be convicted of treason unless on the testimony of two witnesses to the same overt act, or on confession in open court.

Clause 1 Treason is clearly defined. An ***overt act*** is an actual action. A person cannot be convicted of treason for what he or she thinks. A person can be convicted of treason only if he or she confesses or two witnesses testify to it.

2. Punishment The Congress shall have power to declare the punishment of treason, but no attainder of treason shall work corruption of blood or forfeiture except during the life of the person attainted.

Clause 2 Congress has the power to set the punishment for traitors. Congress may not punish the children of convicted traitors by taking away their civil rights or property.

Article 4. Relations Among the States

Section 1. Official Records and Acts

Full faith and credit shall be given in each state to the public acts, records, and judicial proceedings of every other state. And the Congress may by general laws prescribe the manner in which such acts, records, and proceedings shall be proved, and the effect thereof.

Each state must recognize the official acts and records of any other state. For example, each state must recognize marriage certificates issued by another state. Congress can pass laws to ensure this.

Section 2. Privileges of Citizens

1. Privileges The citizens of each state shall be entitled to all privileges and immunities of citizens in the several states.

Clause 1 All states must treat citizens of another state in the same way it treats its own citizens. However, the courts have allowed states to give residents certain privileges, such as lower tuition rates.

Clause 2 Extradition means the act of returning a suspected criminal or escaped prisoner to a state where he or she is wanted. State governors must return a suspect to another state. However, the Supreme Court has ruled that a governor cannot be forced to do so if he or she feels that justice will not be done.

2. Extradition A person charged in any state with treason, felony, or other crime, who shall flee from justice, and be found in another state, shall on demand of the executive authority of the state from which he fled, be delivered up, to be removed to the state having jurisdiction of the crime.

Clause 3 ***Persons held to service or labor*** refers to slaves or indentured servants. This clause required states to return runaway slaves to their owners. The Thirteenth Amendment replaces this clause.

3. Return of Fugitive Slaves ~~No person held to service or labor in one state, under the laws thereof, escaping into another, shall in consequence of any law or regulation therein, be discharged from such service or labor, but shall be delivered up on claim of the party to whom such service or labor may be due.~~

Section 3. New States and Territories

Clause 1 Congress has the power to admit new states to the Union. Existing states cannot be split up or joined together to form new states unless both Congress and the state legislatures approve. New states are equal to all other states.

1. New States New states may be admitted by the Congress into this Union; but no new state shall be formed or erected within the jurisdiction of any other state; nor any state be formed by the junction of two of more states, or parts of states, without the consent of the legislatures of the states concerned as well as of the Congress.

Clause 2 Congress can make rules for managing and governing land owned by the United States. This includes territories not organized into states, such as Puerto Rico and Guam, and federal lands within a state.

2. Federal Lands The Congress shall have power to dispose of and make all needful rules and regulations respecting the territory or other property belonging to the United States; and nothing in this Constitution shall be so construed as to prejudice any claims of the United States, or of any particular state.

Section 4. Guarantees to the States

In a ***republic,*** voters choose representatives to govern them. The federal government must protect the states from foreign invasion and from ***domestic,*** or internal, disorder if asked to do so by a state.

The United States shall guarantee to every state in this Union a republican form of government, and shall protect each of them against invasion; and on application of the legislature, or of the executive (when the legislature cannot be convened) against domestic violence.

Article 5. Amending the Constitution

The Constitution can be ***amended,*** or changed, if necessary. An amendment can be proposed by (1) a two-thirds vote of both houses of Congress or (2) a national convention called by Congress at the request of two thirds of the state legislatures. (This second method has never been used.) An amendment must be ***ratified,*** or approved, by (1) three fourths of the state legislatures or (2) special conventions in three fourths of the states. Congress decides which method will be used.

The Congress, whenever two-thirds of both houses shall deem it necessary, shall propose amendments to this Constitution, or, on the application of the legislatures of two-thirds of the several states, shall call a convention for proposing amendments, which, in either case, shall be valid to all intents and purposes, as part of this Constitution, when ratified by the legislatures of three-fourths of the several states, or by conventions in three-fourths thereof, as the one or the other mode of ratification may be proposed by the Congress; provided that ~~no amendments which may be made prior to the year 1808 shall in any manner affect the first and fourth clauses in the Ninth Section of the First Article; and that~~ no state, without its consent, shall be deprived of its equal suffrage in the Senate.

Article 6. National Supremacy

Section 1. Prior Public Debts

The United States government promised to pay all debts and honor all agreements made under the Articles of Confederation.

All debts contracted and engagements entered into, before the adoption of this Constitution, shall be as valid against the United States under this Constitution, as under the Confederation.

Section 2. Supreme Law of the Land

This Constitution, and the laws of the United States which shall be made in pursuance thereof, and all treaties made, or which shall be made, under the authority of the United States, shall be the supreme law of the land; and the judges in every state shall be bound thereby, anything in the constitution or laws of any state to the contrary notwithstanding.

The Constitution, federal laws, and treaties that the Senate has ratified are the supreme, or highest, law of the land. Thus, they outweigh state laws. A state judge must overturn a state law that conflicts with the Constitution or with a federal law.

Section 3. Oaths of Office

The Senators and Representatives before mentioned, and the members of the several state legislatures, and all executive and judicial officers, both of the United States and of the several states, shall be bound by oath or affirmation, to support this Constitution; but no religious test shall ever be required as a qualification to any office or public trust under the United States.

State and federal officeholders take an oath, or solemn promise, to support the Constitution. However, this clause forbids the use of religious tests for officeholders. During the colonial period, every colony except Rhode Island required a religious test for officeholders.

Article 7. Ratification

The ratification of the convention of nine states shall be sufficient for the establishment of the Constitution between the states so ratifying the same.

During 1787 and 1788, states held special conventions. By October 1788, the required nine states had ratified the Constitution.

Done in convention, by the unanimous consent of the states present, the seventeenth day of September, in the year of our Lord one thousand seven hundred and eighty-seven, and of the independence of the United States of America the twelfth. In Witness *whereof, we have hereunto subscribed our names.*

Attest: William Jackson
Secretary

George Washington
President and deputy from Virginia

New Hampshire
John Langdon
Nicholas Gilman

Massachussetts
Nathaniel Gorham
Rufus King

Connecticut
William Samuel Johnson
Roger Sherman

New York
Alexander Hamilton

New Jersey
William Livingston
David Brearley
William Paterson
Jonathan Dayton

Pennsylvania
Benjamin Franklin
Thomas Mifflin
Robert Morris
George Clymer
Thomas Fitzsimons
Jared Ingersoll
James Wilson
Gouverneur Morris

Delaware
George Read
Gunning Bedford, Jr.
John Dickinson
Richard Bassett
Jacob Broom

Maryland
James McHenry
Dan of St. Thomas Jennifer
Daniel Carroll

Virginia
John Blair
James Madison, Jr.

North Carolina
William Blount
Richard Dobbs Spaight
Hugh Williamson

South Carolina
John Rutledge
Charles Cotesworth Pinckney
Charles Pinckney
Pierce Butler

Georgia
William Few
Abraham Baldwin

★ Amendments to the Constitution ★

The first 10 amendments, which were added to the Constitution in 1791, are called the Bill of Rights. Originally, the Bill of Rights applied only to actions of the federal government. However, the Supreme Court has used the due process clause of the Fourteenth Amendment to extend many of the rights to protect individuals against action by the states.

★ THE CONSTITUTION ★

Amendment 1

Freedoms of Religion, Speech, Press, Assembly, and Petition

Congress shall make no law respecting an establishment of religion, or prohibiting the free exercise thereof; or abridging the freedom of speech, or of the press; or the right of the people peaceably to assemble, and to petition the government for a redress of grievances.

Congress cannot set up an established, or official, church or religion for the nation. During the colonial period, most colonies had established churches. However, the authors of the First Amendment wanted to keep government and religion separate.

Congress may not ***abridge,*** or limit, the freedom to speak and write freely. The government may not censor, or review, books and newspapers before they are printed. This amendment also protects the right to assemble, or hold public meetings. ***Petition*** means ask. ***Redress*** means to correct. ***Grievances*** are wrongs. The people have the right to ask the government for wrongs to be corrected.

Amendment 2

Right to Bear Arms

A well-regulated militia, being necessary to the security of a free state, the right of the people to keep and bear arms shall not be infringed.

State militias, such as the National Guard, have the right to bear arms, or keep weapons. Courts have generally ruled that the government can regulate the ownership of guns by private citizens.

Amendment 3

Lodging Troops in Private Homes

No soldier shall, in time of peace, be quartered in any house, without the consent of the owner; nor in time of war, but in a manner to be prescribed by law.

During the colonial period, the British quartered, or housed, soldiers in private homes without the permission of the owners (page 90). This amendment limits the government's right to use private homes to house soldiers.

Amendment 4

Search and Seizure

The right of the people to be secure in their persons, houses, papers, and effects, against unreasonable searches and seizures, shall not be violated; and no warrants shall issue but upon probable cause, supported by oath or affirmation, and particularly describing the place to be searched, and the persons or things to be seized.

This amendment protects Americans from unreasonable searches and seizures. Search and seizure are permitted only if a judge has issued a ***warrant,*** or written court order. A warrant is issued only if there is probable cause. This means an officer must show that it is probable, or likely, that the search will produce evidence of a crime. A search warrant must name the exact place to be searched and the things to be seized. In some cases, courts have ruled that searches can take place without a warrant. For example, police may search a person who is under arrest. However, evidence found during an unlawful search cannot be used in a trial.

Amendment 5

Rights of the Accused

No person shall be held to answer for a capital, or otherwise infamous, crime, unless on a presentment or indictment of a grand jury, except in cases arising in the land or naval forces, or in the militia, when in actual service in time of war or public danger; nor shall any person be subject for the same offense to be twice put in jeopardy of life and limb; nor shall be compelled, in any criminal case, to be a witness against himself; nor be

This amendment protects the rights of the accused. ***Capital crimes*** are those that can be punished with death. ***Infamous crimes*** are those that can be punished with prison or loss of rights. The federal government must obtain an ***indictment,*** or formal accusation, from a grand jury to prosecute anyone for such crimes. A ***grand jury*** is a panel of between 12 and 23 citizens who deprived of life, liberty, or property, without due process of law; nor shall private property be taken for public use, without just compensation.

decide if the government has enough evidence to justify a trial. This procedure prevents prosecution with little or no evidence of guilt. (Soldiers and the militia in wartime are not covered by this rule.)

Double jeopardy is forbidden. This means that a person cannot be tried twice for the same crime—unless a court sets aside a conviction because of a legal error. A person on trial cannot be forced to testify, or give evidence, against himself or herself. A person accused of a crime is entitled to ***due process of law,*** or a fair hearing or trial. Finally, the government cannot seize private property for public use without paying the owner a fair price for it.

Amendment 6

Right to Speedy Trial by Jury

In all criminal prosecutions, the accused shall enjoy the right to a speedy and public trial, by an impartial jury of the state and district wherein the crime shall have been committed, which district shall have been previously ascertained by law, and to be informed of the nature and cause of the accusation; to be confronted with the witnesses against him; to have compulsory process for obtaining witnesses in his favor, and to have the assistance of counsel for his defense.

In criminal cases, the jury must be ***impartial,*** or not favor either side. The accused is guaranteed the right to a trial by jury. The trial must be speedy. If the government purposely postpones the trial so that it becomes hard for the person to get a fair hearing, the charge may be dismissed. The accused must be told the charges against him or her and be allowed to question prosecution witnesses. Witnesses who can help the accused can be ordered to appear in court.

The accused must be allowed a lawyer. Since 1942, the federal government has been required to provide a lawyer if the accused cannot afford one. In 1963, the Supreme Court decided that states must also provide lawyers for a defendant too poor to pay for one.

Amendment 7

Jury Trial in Civil Cases

In suits at common law, where the value in controversy shall exceed $20, the right of trial by jury shall be preserved, and no fact tried by a jury shall be otherwise re-examined in any court of the United States than according to the rules of the common law.

Common law refers to rules of law established by judges in past cases. This amendment guarantees the right to a jury trial in lawsuits where the sum of money at stake is more than $20. An appeals court cannot change a verdict because it disagrees with the decision of the jury. It can set aside a verdict only if legal errors made the trial unfair.

Amendment 8

Bail and Punishment

Excessive bail shall not be required, nor excessive fines imposed, nor cruel and unusual punishments inflicted.

Bail is money the accused leaves with the court as a pledge to appear for trial. If the accused does not appear for trial, the court keeps the money. ***Excessive*** means too high. This amendment forbids courts to set unreasonably high bail. The amount of bail usually depends on the seriousness of the charge and whether the accused is likely to appear for the trial. The amendment also forbids cruel and unusual punishments such as mental and physical abuse.

Amendment 9

Powers Reserved to the People

The enumeration in the Constitution, of certain rights, shall not be construed to deny or disparage others retained by the people.

People have rights not listed in the Constitution. This amendment was added because some people feared that the Bill of Rights would be used to limit rights to those actually listed.

Amendment 10

Powers Reserved to the States

The powers not delegated to the United States by the Constitution, nor prohibited by it to the states, are reserved to the states respectively, or to the people.

This amendment limits the power of the federal government. Powers that are not given to the federal government belong to the states. The powers reserved to the states are not listed in the Constitution.

Amendment 11

Suits Against States

Passed by Congress on March 4, 1794. Ratified on January 23, 1795.

The judicial power of the United States shall not be construed to extend to any suit in law or equity, commenced or prosecuted against one of the United States, by citizens of another state, or by citizens or subjects of any foreign state.

This amendment changed part of Article 3, Section 2, Clause 1. As a result, a private citizen from one state cannot sue the government of another state in federal court. However, a citizen can sue a state government in a state court.

★ THE CONSTITUTION ★

Amendment 12

Election of President and Vice-President

Passed by Congress on December 9, 1803. Ratified on June 15, 1804.

This amendment changed the way the electoral college voted. Before the amendment was adopted, each elector simply voted for two people. The candidate with the most votes became President. The runner-up became Vice President. In the election of 1800, however, a tie vote resulted between Thomas Jefferson and Aaron Burr (page 189).

In such a case, the Constitution required the House of Representatives to elect the President. Federalists had a majority in the House. They tried to keep Jefferson out of office by voting for Burr. It took 35 ballots in the House before Jefferson was elected President.

To keep this from happening again, the Twelfth Amendment was passed and ratified in time for the election of 1804.

This amendment provides that each elector choose one candidate for President and one candidate for Vice President. If no candidate for President receives a majority of electoral votes, the House of Representatives chooses the President. If no candidate for Vice President receives a majority, the Senate elects the Vice President. The Vice President must be a person who is eligible to be President.

This system is still in use today. However, it is possible for a candidate to win the popular vote and lose in the electoral college. This happened in 1876 (pages 419–420).

The electors shall meet in their respective states, and vote by ballot for President and Vice-President, one of whom, at least, shall not be an inhabitant of the same state with themselves; they shall name in their ballots the person voted for as President, and in distinct ballots the person voted for as Vice-President, and they shall make distinct lists of all persons voted for as President, and of all persons voted for as Vice-President, and of the number of votes for each, which lists they shall sign and certify, and transmit, sealed, to the seat of government of the United States, directed to the President of the Senate; the President of the Senate shall, in the presence of the Senate and House of Representatives, open all the certificates and the votes shall then be counted; the person having the greatest number of votes for President shall be the President, if such number be a majority of the whole number of electors appointed; and if no person have such majority, then from the persons having the highest numbers not exceeding three on the list of those voted for as President, the House of Representatives shall choose immediately, by ballot, the President. But in choosing the President, the votes shall be taken by the states, the representation from each state having one vote; a quorum for this purpose shall consist of a member or members from two-thirds of the states, and a majority of all the states shall be necessary to a choice. And if the House of Representatives shall not choose a President whenever the right of choice shall devolve upon them, before the fourth day of March next following, then the Vice-President shall act as President, as in the case of the death or other constitutional disability of the President. The person having the greatest number of votes as Vice-President, shall be the Vice-President, if such number be a majority of the whole number of electors appointed, and if no person have a majority, then, from the two highest numbers on the list, the Senate shall choose the Vice-President; a quorum for the purpose shall consist of two-thirds of the whole number of Senators, and a majority of the whole number shall be necessary to a choice. But no person constitutionally ineligible to the office of President shall be eligible to that of Vice-President of the United States.

Amendment 13

Abolition of Slavery

Passed by Congress on January 31, 1865. Ratified on December 6, 1865.

The Emancipation Proclamation (1863) freed slaves only in areas controlled by the Confederacy (pages 387–388). This amendment freed all slaves. It also forbids ***involuntary servitude,*** or labor done against one's will. However, it does not prevent prison wardens from making prisoners work.

Section 2 says that Congress can pass laws to carry out this amendment.

Section 1. Neither slavery nor involuntary servitude, except as a punishment for crime whereof the party shall have been duly convicted, shall exist within the United States, or any place subject to their jurisdiction.

Section 2. Congress shall have power to enforce this article by appropriate legislation.

Amendment 14

Rights of Citizens

Passed by Congress on June 13, 1866. Ratified on July 9, 1868.

Section 1 defines citizenship for the first time in the Constitution, and it extends citizenship to

Section 1. Citizenship All persons born or naturalized in the United States and subject to the jurisdiction thereof, are citizens of the United States and of the state wherein they reside. No state shall make or enforce any law which shall abridge the privileges or immunities of citizens of the United States; nor shall any state deprive any person of life, liberty, or property, without due process of law; nor deny to any person within its jurisdiction the equal protection of the laws.

blacks. It also prohibits states from denying the rights and privileges of citizenship to any citizen. This section also forbids states to deny due process of law.

Section 1 guarantees all citizens "equal protection under the law." For a long time, however, the Fourteenth Amendment did not protect blacks from discrimination. After Reconstruction, separate facilities for blacks and whites sprang up (page 423). In 1954, the Supreme Court ruled that separate facilities for blacks and whites were by their nature unequal. This ruling, in the case of *Brown* v. *Board of Education,* made school segregation illegal.

Section 2. Apportionment of Representatives Representatives shall be apportioned among the several states according to their respective numbers, counting the whole number of persons in each state, excluding Indians not taxed. But when the right to vote at any election for the choice of electors for President and Vice-President of the United States, Representatives in Congress, the executive and judicial officers of a state, or the members of the legislature thereof, is denied to any of the male inhabitants of such state, being twenty-one years of age and citizens of the United States, or in any way abridged, except for participation in rebellion, or other crime, the basis of representation therein shall be reduced in the proportion which the number of such male citizens shall bear to the whole number of male citizens twenty-one years of age in such state.

Section 2 replaced the three-fifths clause. It provides that representation in the House of Representatives is decided on the basis of the number of people in the state. It also provides that states which deny the vote to male citizens over age 21 will be punished by losing part of their representation in the House. This provision has never been enforced.

Despite this clause, black citizens were often prevented from voting. In the 1960s, federal laws were passed to end voting discrimination.

Section 3. Former Confederate Officials No person shall be a Senator or Representative in Congress, or elector of President and Vice-President, or hold any office, civil or military, under the United States, or under any state, who, having previously taken an oath, as a member of Congress, or as an officer of the United States, or as a member of any state legislature, or as an executive or judicial officer of any state, to support the Constitution of the United States, shall have engaged in insurrection or rebellion against the same, or given aid or comfort to the enemies thereof. But Congress may, by vote of two-thirds of each house, remove such disability.

This section prohibited people who had been federal or state officials before the Civil War and who had joined the Confederate cause from serving again as government officials. In 1872, Congress restored the rights of former Confederate officials.

Section 4. Government Debt The validity of the public debt of the United States, authorized by law, including debts incurred for payment of pensions and bounties for services in suppressing insurrection or rebellion, shall not be questioned. But neither the United States nor any state shall assume or pay any debt or obligation incurred in aid of insurrection or rebellion against the United States or any claim for the loss or emancipation of any slave; but all such debts, obligations, and claims shall be held illegal and void.

This section recognized that the United States must repay its debts from the Civil War. However, it forbade the repayment of debts of the Confederacy. This meant that people who had loaned money to the Confederacy would not be repaid. Also, states were not allowed to pay former slave owners for the loss of slaves.

Section 5. Enforcement The Congress shall have power to enforce, by appropriate legislation, the provisions of this article.

Congress can pass laws to carry out this amendment.

Amendment 15

Voting Rights

Passed by Congress on February 26, 1869. Ratified on February 2, 1870.

Section 1. Extending the Right to Vote The right of citizens of the United States to vote shall not be denied or abridged by the United States or any state on account of race, color, or previous condition of servitude.

Previous condition of servitude refers to slavery. This amendment gave blacks, both former slaves and free blacks, the right to vote. In the late 1800s, southern states used grandfather clauses, literacy tests, and poll taxes to keep blacks from voting (pages 421–422).

Congress can pass laws to carry out this amendment. The Twenty-fourth Amendment barred the use of poll taxes in national elections. The Voting Rights Act of 1965 gave federal officials the power to register voters in places where there was voting discrimination.

Section 2. Enforcement The Congress shall have power to enforce this article by appropriate legislation.

Amendment 16

The Income Tax

Passed by Congress on July 12, 1909. Ratified on February 3, 1913.

Congress has the power to collect taxes on people's income. An income tax can be collected without regard to a state's population. This amendment changed Article 1, Section 9, Clause 4.

The Congress shall have power to lay and collect taxes on incomes, from whatever source derived, without apportionment among the several states, and without regard to any census or enumeration.

Amendment 17

Direct Election of Senators

Passed by Congress on May 13, 1912. Ratified on April 8, 1913.

This amendment replaced Article 1, Section 2, Clause 1. Before it was adopted, state legislatures chose senators. This amendment provides that senators are directly elected by the people of each state.

Section 1. Method of Election The Senate of the United States shall be composed of two Senators from each state, elected by the people thereof, for six years; and each Senator shall have one vote. The electors in each state shall have the qualifications requisite for electors of the most numerous branch of the state legislatures.

When a Senate seat becomes vacant, the governor of the state must order an election to fill the seat. The state legislature can give the governor power to fill the seat until an election is held.

Section 2. Vacancies When vacancies happen in the representation of any state in the Senate, the executive authority of such state shall issue writs of election to fill such vacancies: *Provided* that the legislature of any state may empower the executive thereof to make temporary appointments until the people fill the vacancies by election as the legislature may direct.

Senators who had already been elected by the state legislatures were not affected by this amendment.

Section 3. Exception ~~This amendment shall not be so construed as to affect the election or term of any Senator chosen before it becomes valid as part of the Constitution.~~

Amendment 18

Prohibition of Alcoholic Beverages

Passed by Congress on December 18, 1917. Ratified on January 16, 1919.

This amendment, known as ***Prohibition,*** banned the making, selling, or transporting of alcoholic beverages in the United States. Later, the Twenty-first Amendment ***repealed,*** or canceled, this amendment.

Section 1. Ban on Alcohol ~~After one year from the ratification of this article the manufacture, sale, or transportation of intoxicating liquors within, the importation thereof into, or the exportation thereof from, the United States and all territory subject to the jurisdiction thereof for beverage purposes is hereby prohibited.~~

Both the states and the federal government had the power to pass laws to enforce this amendment.

Section 2. Enforcement ~~The Congress and the several states shall have concurrent power to enforce this article by appropriate legislation.~~

This amendment had to be approved within seven years. The Eighteenth Amendment was the first amendment to include a time limit for ratification.

Section 3. Method of Ratification ~~This article shall be inoperative unless it shall have been ratified as an amendment to the Constitution by the legislatures of the several states, as provided in the Constitution, within seven years from the date of the submission hereof to the states by the Congress.~~

Amendment 19

Women's Suffrage

Passed by Congress on June 4, 1919. Ratified on August 18, 1920.

Neither the federal government nor state governments can deny the right to vote on account of sex. Thus, women won ***suffrage,*** or the right to vote. Before 1920, some states had allowed women to vote in state elections.

Section 1. The Right to Vote The right of citizens of the United States to vote shall not be denied or abridged by the United States or by any state on account of sex.

Congress can pass laws to carry out this amendment.

Section 2. Enforcement Congress shall have power to enforce this article by appropriate legislation.

Amendment 20

Presidential Terms; Sessions of Congress

Passed by Congress on March 2, 1932. Ratified on January 23, 1933.

Section 1. Beginning of Term The terms of the President and Vice-President shall end at noon on the 20th day of January, and the terms of Senators and Representatives at noon on the 3rd day of January, of the years in which such terms would have ended if this article had not been ratified; and the terms of their successors shall then begin.

The date for the President and Vice President to take office is January 20. Members of Congress begin their terms of office on January 3. Before this amendment was adopted, these terms of office began on March 4.

Section 2. Congressional Sessions The Congress shall assemble at least once in every year, and such meeting shall begin at noon on the 3rd day of January, unless they shall by law appoint a different day.

Congress must meet at least once a year. The new session of Congress begins on January 3. Before this amendment, members of Congress who had been defeated in November continued to hold office until the following March. Such members were known as ***lame ducks.***

Section 3. Presidential Succession If at the time fixed for the beginning of the term of the President, the President-elect shall have died, the Vice-President-elect shall become President. If a President shall not have been chosen before the time fixed for the beginning of his term, or if the President-elect shall have failed to qualify, then the Vice-President-elect shall act as President until a President shall have qualified; and the Congress may by law provide for the case wherein neither a President-elect nor a Vice-President-elect shall have qualified, declaring who shall then act as President, or the manner in which one who is to act shall be selected, and such person shall act accordingly until a President or Vice-President shall have qualified.

By Section 3, if the President-elect dies before taking office, the Vice President-elect becomes President. If no President has been chosen by January 20 or if the elected candidate fails to qualify for office, the Vice President-elect acts as President, but only until a qualified President is chosen.

Finally, Congress can choose a person to act as President if neither the President-elect nor Vice President-elect is qualified to take office.

Section 4. Elections Decided by Congress The Congress may by law provide for the case of the death of any of the persons from whom the House of Representatives may choose a President whenever the right of choice shall have devolved upon them, and for the case of the death of any of the persons from whom the Senate may choose a Vice-President whenever the right of choice shall have devolved upon them.

Congress can pass laws in cases where a presidential candidate dies while an election is being decided in the House. Congress has similar power in cases where a candidate for Vice President dies while an election is being decided in the Senate.

Section 5. Date of Effect ~~Sections 1 and 2 shall take effect on the 15th day of October following the ratification of this article.~~

Section 5 sets the date for the amendment to become effective.

Section 6. Ratification Period ~~This article shall be inoperative unless it shall have been ratified as an amendment to the Constitution by the legislatures of three-fourths of the several states within seven years from the date of its submission.~~

Section 6 sets a time limit for ratification.

Amendment 21

Repeal of Prohibition

Passed by Congress on February 20, 1933. Ratified on December 5, 1933.

Section 1. Repeal of National Prohibition The eighteenth article of amendment to the Constitution of the United States is hereby repealed.

The Eighteenth Amendment is repealed, making it legal to make and sell alcoholic beverages. Prohibition ended December 5, 1933.

Section 2. State Laws The transportation or importation into any state, territory, or possession of the United States for delivery or use therein of intoxicating liquors, in violation of the laws thereof, is hereby prohibited.

Each state was free to ban the making and selling of alcoholic drink within its borders. This section makes bringing liquor into a "dry" state a federal offense.

Section 3. Ratification Period ~~This article shall be inoperative unless it shall have been ratified as an amendment to the Constitution by conventions in the several states, as provided in the Constitution, within seven years from the date of the submission hereof to the states by the Congress.~~

Special state conventions were called to ratify this amendment. This is the only time an amendment was ratified by state conventions rather than state legislatures.

Amendment 22

Limit on Number of President's Terms

Passed by Congress on March 12, 1947. Ratified on March 1, 1951.

Before Franklin Roosevelt became President, no President served more than two terms in office. Roosevelt broke with this custom and was elected to four terms. This amendment provides that no President may serve more than two terms. A President who has already served more than half of someone else's term can serve only one more full term. However, the amendment did not apply to Harry Truman, who had become President after Franklin Roosevelt's death in 1945.

Section 1. Two-Term Limit No person shall be elected to the office of the President more than twice, and no person who has held the office of President, or acted as President, for more than two years of a term to which some other person was elected President shall be elected to the office of the President more than once. ~~But this Article shall not apply to any person holding the office of President when this Article was proposed by the Congress, and shall not prevent any person who may be holding the office of President, or acting as President, during the term within which this Article becomes operative from holding the office of President or acting as President during the remainder of such term.~~

A seven-year time limit is set for ratification.

Section 2. Ratification Period ~~This Article shall be inoperative unless it shall have been ratified as an amendment to the Constitution by the legislatures of three-fourths of the several states within seven years from the date of its submission to the states by the Congress.~~

Amendment 23

Presidential Electors for District of Columbia

Passed by Congress on June 16, 1960. Ratified on April 3, 1961.

This amendment gives residents of Washington, D.C., the right to vote in presidential elections. Until this amendment was adopted, people living in Washington, D.C., could not vote for President because the Constitution had made no provision for choosing electors from the nation's capital. Washington, D.C., has three electoral votes.

Section 1. Determining the Number of Electors The District constituting the seat of Government of the United States shall appoint in such manner as the Congress may direct: A number of electors of President and Vice-President equal to the whole number of Senators and Representatives in Congress to which the District would be entitled if it were a State, but in no event more than the least populous State; they shall be in addition to those appointed by the States, but they shall be considered, for the purposes of the election of President and Vice-President, to be electors appointed by a State; and they shall meet in the District and perform such duties as provided by the twelfth article of amendment.

Congress can pass laws to carry out this amendment.

Section 2. Enforcement The Congress shall have power to enforce this article by appropriate legislation.

Amendment 24

Abolition of Poll Tax in National Elections

Passed by Congress on August 27, 1962. Ratified on January 23, 1964.

A ***poll tax*** is a tax on voters. This amendment bans poll taxes in national elections. Some states used poll taxes to keep blacks from voting. In 1966, the Supreme Court struck down poll taxes in state elections, also.

Section 1. Poll Tax Banned The right of citizens of the United States to vote in any primary or other election for President or Vice-President, for electors for President or Vice-President, or for Senator or Representative in Congress, shall not be denied or abridged by the United States or any state by reason of failure to pay any poll tax or other tax.

Congress can pass laws to carry out this amendment.

Section 2. Enforcement The Congress shall have the power to enforce this article by appropriate legislation.

Amendment 25

Presidential Succession and Disability

Passed by Congress on July 6, 1965. Ratified on February 11, 1967.

If the President dies or resigns, the Vice President becomes President. This section clarifies Article 2, Section 1, Clause 6.

Section 1. President's Death or Resignation In case of the removal of the President from office or his death or resignation, the Vice-President shall become President.

Section 2. Vacancies in Vice-Presidency Whenever there is a vacancy in the office of the Vice-President, the President shall nominate a Vice-President who shall take the office upon confirmation by a majority vote of both houses of Congress.

When a Vice President takes over the office of President, he or she appoints a Vice President who must be approved by a majority vote of both houses of Congress. This section was first applied after Vice President Spiro Agnew resigned in 1973. President Richard Nixon appointed Gerald Ford as Vice President.

Section 3. Disability of the President Whenever the President transmits to the President pro tempore of the Senate and the Speaker of the House of Representatives his written declaration that he is unable to discharge the powers and duties of his office, and until he transmits to them a written declaration to the contrary, such powers and duties shall be discharged by the Vice-President as Acting President.

If the President declares in writing that he or she is unable to perform the duties of office, the Vice President serves as Acting President until the President recovers.

Section 4. Whenever the Vice-President and a majority of either the principal officers of the executive departments or of such other body as Congress may by law provide, transmit to the President *pro tempore* of the Senate and the Speaker of the House of Representatives their written declaration that the President is unable to discharge the powers and duties of his office, the Vice-President shall immediately assume the powers and duties of the office as Acting President.

Thereafter, when the President transmits to the President *pro tempore* of the Senate and the Speaker of the House of Representatives his written declaration that no inability exists, he shall resume the powers and duties of his office unless the Vice-President and a majority of either the principal officers of the executive department or of such other body as Congress may by law provide, transmit within four days to the President *as* of the Senate and the Speaker of the House of Representatives their written declaration that the President is unable to discharge the powers and duties of his office. Thereupon Congress shall decide the issue, assembling within 48 hours for that purpose if not in session. If the Congress, within 21 days after receipt of the latter written declaration, or, if Congress is not in session, within 21 days after Congress is required to assemble, determines by two-thirds vote of both houses that the President is unable to discharge the powers and duties of his office, the Vice-President shall continue to discharge the same as Acting President; otherwise, the President shall assume the powers and duties of his office.

Two Presidents, Woodrow Wilson and Dwight Eisenhower, have fallen gravely ill while in office. The Constitution contained no provision for this kind of emergency.

Section 3 provided that the President can inform Congress that he or she is too sick to perform the duties of office. However, if the President is unconscious or refuses to admit to a disabling illness, Section 4 provides that the Vice President and Cabinet may declare the President disabled. The Vice President becomes Acting President until the President can return to the duties of office. In case of a disagreement between the President and the Vice President and Cabinet over the President's ability to perform the duties of office, Congress must decide the issue. A two-thirds vote of both houses is needed to decide that the President is disabled or unable to fulfill the duties of office.

Amendment 26

Voting Age

Passed by Congress on March 23, 1971. Ratified on July 1, 1971.

Section 1. Lowering of Voting Age The right of citizens of the United States, who are 18 years of age or older, to vote shall not be denied or abridged by the United States or any state on account of age.

In 1970, Congress passed a law allowing 18-year-olds to vote. However, the Supreme Court decided that Congress could not set a minimum age for state elections. So this amendment was passed and ratified.

Section 2. Enforcement The Congress shall have the power to enforce this article by appropriate legislation.

Congress can pass laws to carry out this amendment.

Amendment 27

Congressional Pay Increases

Ratified on May 7, 1992.

No law varying the compensation for the services of the Senators and Representatives shall take effect, until an election of Representatives shall have intervened.

If members of Congress vote themselves a pay increase, it cannot go into effect until after the next congressional election.

★ Presidents of the United States ★

1 George Washington
(1732–1799)

Years in office:
1789–1797
Party:
none
Elected from:
Virginia
Vice President:
John Adams

2 John Adams
(1735–1826)

Years in office:
1797–1801
Party:
Federalist
Elected from:
Massachusetts
Vice President:
Thomas Jefferson

3 Thomas Jefferson
(1743–1826)

Years in office:
1801–1809
Party:
Democratic Republican
Elected from:
Virginia
Vice President:
1) Aaron Burr,
2) George Clinton

4 James Madison
(1751–1836)

Years in office:
1809–1817
Party:
Democratic Republican
Elected from:
Virginia
Vice President:
1) George Clinton,
2) Elbridge Gerry

5 James Monroe
(1758–1831)

Years in office:
1817–1825
Party:
Democratic Republican
Elected from:
Virginia
Vice President:
Daniel Tompkins

6 John Quincy Adams
(1767–1848)

Years in office:
1825–1829
Party:
National Republican
Elected from:
Massachusetts
Vice President:
John Calhoun

7 Andrew Jackson
(1767–1845)

Years in office:
1829–1837
Party:
Democratic
Elected from:
Tennessee
Vice President:
1) John Calhoun,
2) Martin Van Buren

8 Martin Van Buren
(1782–1862)

Years in office:
1837–1841
Party:
Democratic
Elected from:
New York
Vice President:
Richard Johnson

9 William Henry Harrison*
(1773–1841)

Years in office:
1841
Party:
Whig
Elected from:
Ohio
Vice President:
John Tyler

10 John Tyler
(1790–1862)

Years in office:
1841–1845
Party:
Whig
Elected from:
Virginia
Vice President:
none

11 James K. Polk
(1795–1849)

Years in Office:
1845–1849
Party:
Democratic
Elected from:
Tennessee
Vice President:
George Dallas

12 Zachary Taylor*
(1784–1850)

Years in office:
1849–1850
Party:
Whig
Elected from:
Louisiana
Vice President:
Millard Fillmore

***Died in office**

13 Millard Fillmore
(1800–1874)

Years in office: 1850–1853
Party: Whig
Elected from: New York
Vice President: none

14 Franklin Pierce
(1804–1869)

Years in office: 1853–1857
Party: Democratic
Elected from: New Hampshire
Vice President: William King

15 James Buchanan
(1791–1868)

Years in office: 1857–1861
Party: Democratic
Elected from: Pennsylvania
Vice President: John Breckinridge

16 Abraham Lincoln**
(1809–1865)

Years in office: 1861–1865
Party: Republican
Elected from: Illinois
Vice President: 1) Hannibal Hamlin, 2) Andrew Johnson

17 Andrew Johnson
(1808–1875)

Years in office: 1865–1869
Party: Republican
Elected from: Tennessee
Vice President: none

18 Ulysses S. Grant
(1822–1885)

Years in office: 1869–1877
Party: Republican
Elected from: Illinois
Vice President: 1) Schuyler Colfax, 2) Henry Wilson

19 Rutherford B. Hayes
(1822–1893)

Years in office: 1877–1881
Party: Republican
Elected from: Ohio
Vice President: William Wheeler

20 James A. Garfield**
(1831–1881)

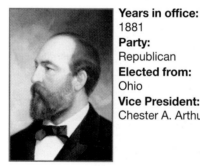

Years in office: 1881
Party: Republican
Elected from: Ohio
Vice President: Chester A. Arthur

21 Chester A. Arthur
(1830–1886)

Years in office: 1881–1885
Party: Republican
Elected from: New York
Vice President: none

22 Grover Cleveland
(1837–1908)

Years in office: 1885–1889
Party: Democratic
Elected from: New York
Vice President: Thomas Hendricks

23 Benjamin Harrison
(1833–1901)

Years in office: 1889–1893
Party: Republican
Elected from: Indiana
Vice President: Levi Morton

24 Grover Cleveland
(1837–1908)

Years in office: 1893–1897
Party: Democratic
Elected from: New York
Vice President: Adlai Stevenson

**Assassinated

25 William McKinley**
(1843–1901)

Years in office: 1897–1901
Party: Republican
Elected from: Ohio
Vice President: 1) Garret Hobart, 2) Theodore Roosevelt

26 Theodore Roosevelt
(1858–1919)

Years in office: 1901–1909
Party: Republican
Elected from: New York
Vice President: Charles Fairbanks

27 William Howard Taft
(1857–1930)

Years in office: 1909–1913
Party: Republican
Elected from: Ohio
Vice President: James Sherman

28 Woodrow Wilson
(1856–1924)

Years in office: 1913–1921
Party: Democratic
Elected from: New Jersey
Vice President: Thomas Marshall

29 Warren G. Harding*
(1865–1923)

Years in office: 1921–1923
Party: Republican
Elected from: Ohio
Vice President: Calvin Coolidge

30 Calvin Coolidge
(1872–1933)

Years in office: 1923–1929
Party: Republican
Elected from: Massachusetts
Vice President: Charles Dawes

31 Herbert C. Hoover
(1874–1964)

Years in office: 1929–1933
Party: Republican
Elected from: California
Vice President: Charles Curtis

32 Franklin D. Roosevelt*
(1882–1945)

Years in office: 1933–1945
Party: Democratic
Elected from: New York
Vice President: 1) John Garner, 2) Henry Wallace, 3) Harry S Truman

33 Harry S Truman
(1884–1972)

Years in office: 1945–1953
Party: Democratic
Elected from: Missouri
Vice President: Alben Barkley

34 Dwight D. Eisenhower
(1890–1969)

Years in office: 1953–1961
Party: Republican
Elected from: New York
Vice President: Richard M. Nixon

35 John F. Kennedy**
(1917–1963)

Years in office: 1961–1963
Party: Democratic
Elected from: Massachusetts
Vice President: Lyndon B. Johnson

36 Lyndon B. Johnson
(1908–1973)

Years in office: 1963–1969
Party: Democratic
Elected from: Texas
Vice President: Hubert Humphrey

***Died in office**
****Assassinated**

37 Richard M. Nixon***
(1913–1994)

Years in office: 1969–1974
Party: Republican
Elected from: New York
Vice President: 1) Spiro Agnew, 2) Gerald R. Ford

38 Gerald R. Ford****
(1913–)

Years in office: 1974–1977
Party: Republican
Appointed from: Michigan
Vice President: Nelson Rockefeller

39 Jimmy Carter
(1924–)

Years in office: 1977–1981
Party: Democratic
Elected from: Georgia
Vice President: Walter Mondale

40 Ronald W. Reagan
(1911–)

Years in office: 1981–1989
Party: Republican
Elected from: California
Vice President: George H.W. Bush

41 George H.W. Bush
(1924–)

Years in office: 1989–1993
Party: Republican
Elected from: Texas
Vice President: J. Danforth Quayle

42 William J. Clinton
(1946–)

Years in office: 1993–
Party: Democratic
Elected from: Arkansas
Vice President: Albert Gore, Jr.

*****Resigned**
******Appointed Vice President in 1973 after resignation of Spiro Agnew**

★ The Fifty States ★

State	Date of Entry to Union (Order of Entry)	Land Area in Square Miles	Population (In Thousands)	Number of Representatives in House	Capital	Largest City
Alabama	1819 (22)	50,750	4,219	7	Montgomery	Birmingham
Alaska	1959 (49)	570,374	606	1	Juneau	Anchorage
Arizona	1912 (48)	113,642	4,075	6	Phoenix	Phoenix
Arkansas	1836 (25)	52,075	2,453	4	Little Rock	Little Rock
California	1850 (31)	155,973	31,431	52	Sacramento	Los Angeles
Colorado	1876 (38)	103,730	3,656	6	Denver	Denver
Connecticut	1788 (5)	4,845	3,275	6	Hartford	Bridgeport
Delaware	1787 (1)	1,955	706	1	Dover	Wilmington
Florida	1845 (27)	53,997	13,953	23	Tallahassee	Jacksonville
Georgia	1788 (4)	57,919	7,055	11	Atlanta	Atlanta
Hawaii	1959 (50)	6,423	1,179	2	Honolulu	Honolulu
Idaho	1890 (43)	82,751	1,133	2	Boise	Boise
Illinois	1818 (21)	55,593	11,752	20	Springfield	Chicago
Indiana	1816 (19)	35,870	5,752	10	Indianapolis	Indianapolis
Iowa	1846 (29)	55,875	2,829	5	Des Moines	Des Moines
Kansas	1861 (34)	81,823	2,554	4	Topeka	Wichita
Kentucky	1792 (15)	39,732	3,827	6	Frankfort	Louisville
Louisiana	1812 (18)	43,566	4,315	7	Baton Rouge	New Orleans
Maine	1820 (23)	30,865	1,240	2	Augusta	Portland
Maryland	1788 (7)	9,775	5,006	8	Annapolis	Baltimore
Massachusetts	1788 (6)	7,838	6,041	10	Boston	Boston
Michigan	1837 (26)	56,809	9,496	16	Lansing	Detroit
Minnesota	1858 (32)	79,617	4,567	8	St. Paul	Minneapolis
Mississippi	1817 (20)	46,914	2,669	5	Jackson	Jackson
Missouri	1821 (24)	68,898	5,278	9	Jefferson City	Kansas City
Montana	1889 (41)	145,556	856	1	Helena	Billings
Nebraska	1867 (37)	76,878	1,623	3	Lincoln	Omaha
Nevada	1864 (36)	109,806	1,457	2	Carson City	Las Vegas
New Hampshire	1788 (9)	8,969	1,137	2	Concord	Manchester
New Jersey	1787 (3)	7,419	7,904	13	Trenton	Newark
New Mexico	1912 (47)	121,365	1,654	3	Santa Fe	Albuquerque
New York	1788 (11)	47,224	18,169	31	Albany	New York
North Carolina	1789 (12)	48,718	7,070	12	Raleigh	Charlotte
North Dakota	1889 (39)	68,994	638	1	Bismarck	Fargo
Ohio	1803 (17)	40,953	11,102	19	Columbus	Columbus
Oklahoma	1907 (46)	68,679	3,258	6	Oklahoma City	Oklahoma City
Oregon	1859 (33)	96,003	3,086	5	Salem	Portland
Pennsylvania	1787 (2)	44,820	12,052	21	Harrisburg	Philadelphia
Rhode Island	1790 (13)	1,045	997	2	Providence	Providence
South Carolina	1788 (8)	30,111	3,664	6	Columbia	Columbia
South Dakota	1889 (40)	75,898	721	1	Pierre	Sioux Falls
Tennessee	1796 (16)	41,220	5,175	9	Nashville	Memphis
Texas	1845 (28)	261,914	18,378	30	Austin	Houston
Utah	1896 (45)	82,168	1,908	3	Salt Lake City	Salt Lake City
Vermont	1791 (14)	9,249	580	1	Montpelier	Burlington
Virginia	1788 (10)	39,598	6,552	11	Richmond	Virginia Beach
Washington	1889 (42)	66,582	5,343	9	Olympia	Seattle
West Virginia	1863 (35)	24,087	1,822	3	Charleston	Charleston
Wisconsin	1848 (30)	54,314	5,082	9	Madison	Milwaukee
Wyoming	1890 (44)	97,105	476	1	Cheyenne	Cheyenne
District of Columbia		61	570	1 (nonvoting)		

Self-Governing Areas, Possessions, and Dependencies	Land Area in Square Miles	Population (In Thousands)	Capital
Puerto Rico	3,515	3,522	San Juan
Guam	209	133	Agana
U.S. Virgin Islands	132	102	Charlotte Amalie
American Samoa	77	52	Pago Pago

Sources: *Department of Commerce, Bureau of the Census, 1997 Information Please Almanac*

★ State Flags ★

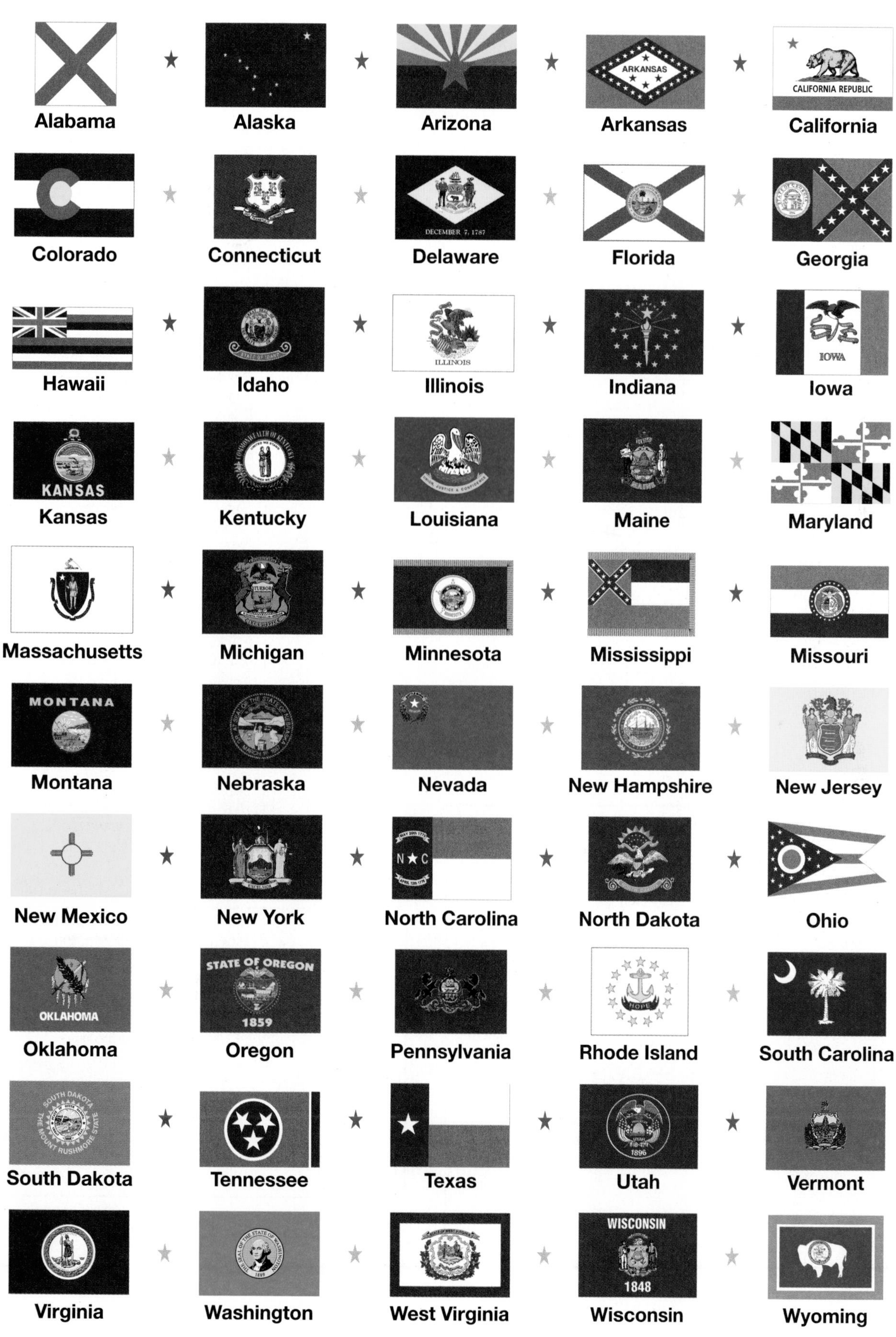
Alabama
Alaska
Arizona
ARKANSAS
Arkansas
CALIFORNIA REPUBLIC
California
Colorado
Connecticut
DECEMBER 7, 1787
Delaware
Florida
Georgia
Hawaii
Idaho
ILLINOIS
Illinois
Indiana
IOWA
Iowa
KANSAS
Kansas
Kentucky
Louisiana
Maine
Maryland
Massachusetts
Michigan
Minnesota
Mississippi
Missouri
MONTANA
Montana
Nebraska
Nevada
New Hampshire
New Jersey
New Mexico
New York
N★C
North Carolina
North Dakota
Ohio
OKLAHOMA
Oklahoma
STATE OF OREGON
1859
Oregon
Pennsylvania
HOPE
Rhode Island
South Carolina
South Dakota
Tennessee
Texas
1896
Utah
Vermont
Virginia
Washington
West Virginia
WISCONSIN
1848
Wisconsin
Wyoming

★ THE FIFTY STATES ★

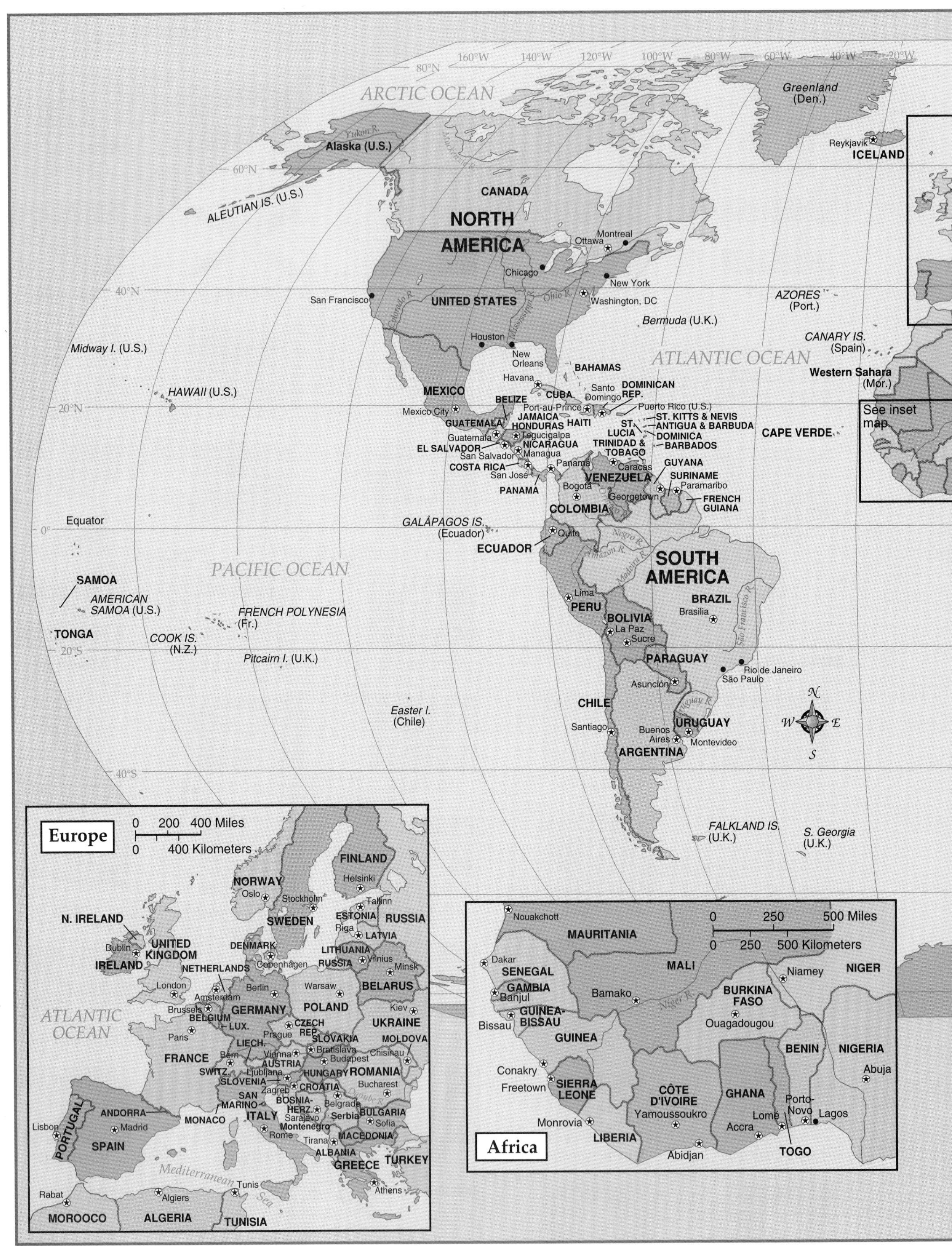

★ GEOGRAPHIC ATLAS ★

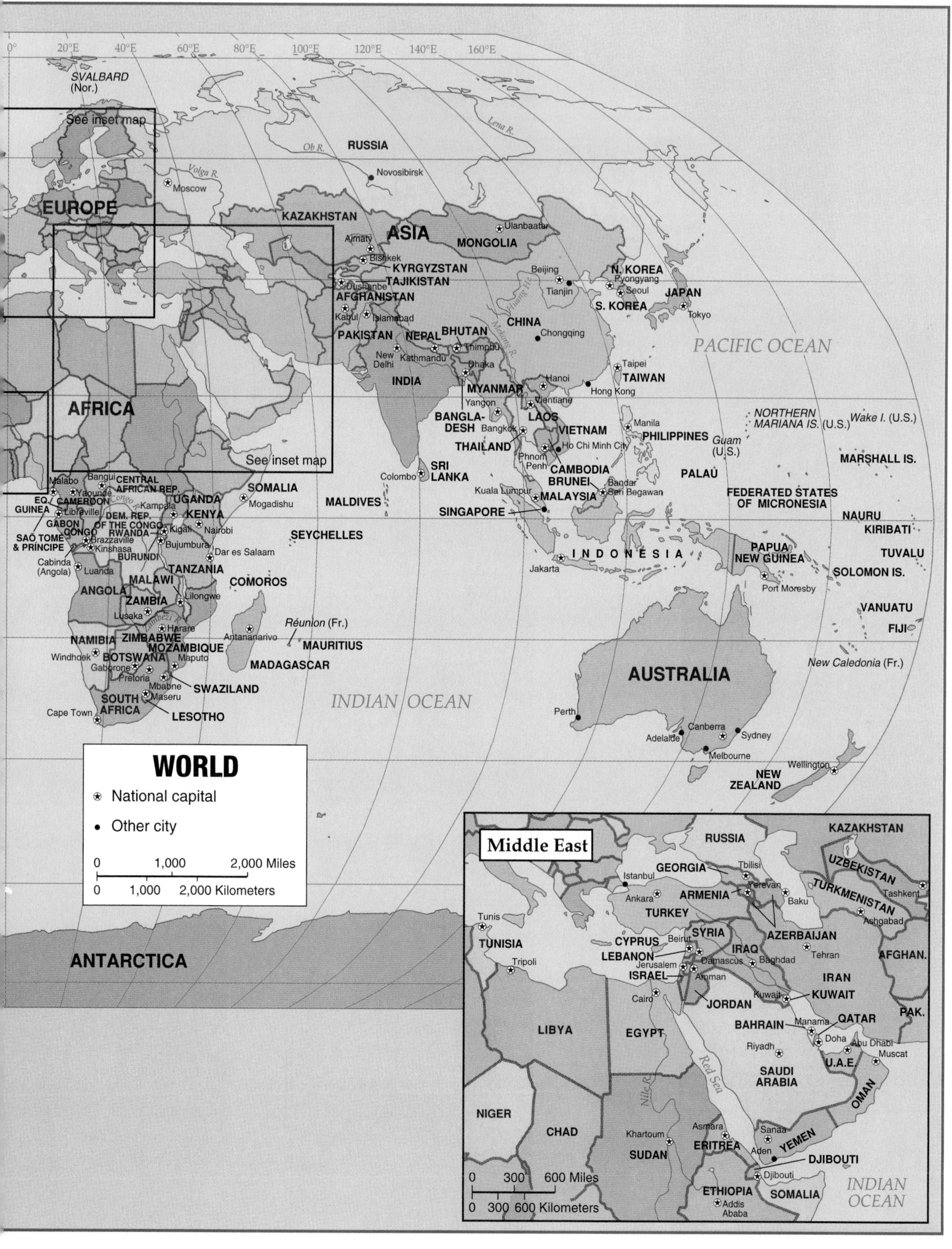

★ GEOGRAPHIC ATLAS ★

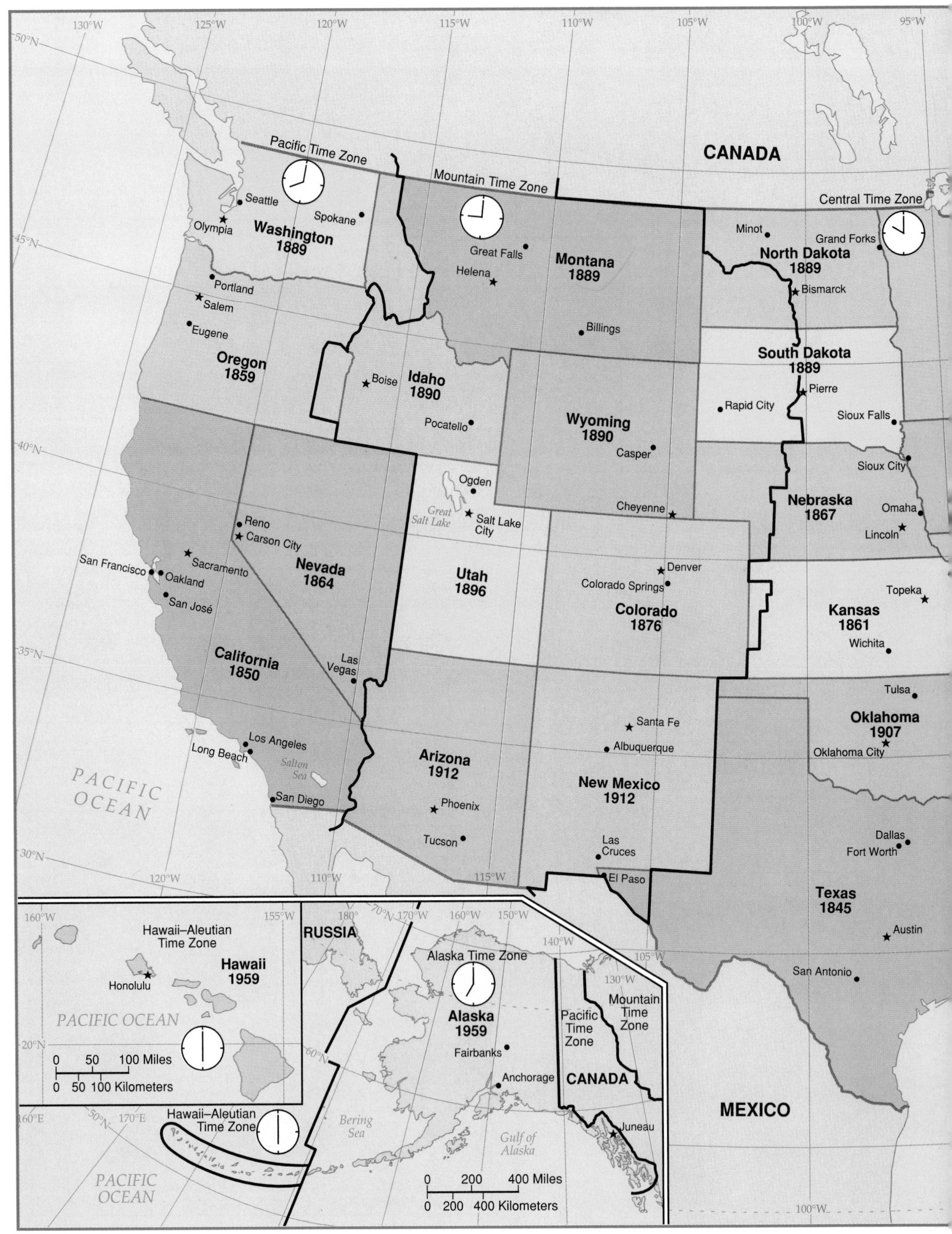

CANADA
Pacific Time Zone
Mountain Time Zone
Central Time Zone
Washington 1889
Seattle
Olympia
Spokane
Oregon 1859
Portland
Salem
Eugene
Idaho 1890
Boise
Pocatello
Montana 1889
Great Falls
Helena
Billings
North Dakota 1889
Minot
Grand Forks
Bismarck
South Dakota 1889
Pierre
Rapid City
Sioux Falls
Wyoming 1890
Casper
Cheyenne
Nebraska 1867
Sioux City
Omaha
Lincoln
California 1850
San Francisco
Oakland
San José
Sacramento
Los Angeles
Long Beach
San Diego
Salton Sea
Nevada 1864
Reno
Carson City
Las Vegas
Utah 1896
Ogden
Great Salt Lake
Salt Lake City
Colorado 1876
Denver
Colorado Springs
Kansas 1861
Topeka
Wichita
Arizona 1912
Phoenix
Tucson
New Mexico 1912
Santa Fe
Albuquerque
Las Cruces
El Paso
Oklahoma 1907
Tulsa
Oklahoma City
Texas 1845
Dallas
Fort Worth
Austin
San Antonio
MEXICO
PACIFIC OCEAN
Hawaii–Aleutian Time Zone
Hawaii 1959
Honolulu
PACIFIC OCEAN
0 50 100 Miles
0 50 100 Kilometers
RUSSIA
Alaska Time Zone
Alaska 1959
Fairbanks
Anchorage
Juneau
Bering Sea
Gulf of Alaska
Pacific Time Zone
Mountain Time Zone
CANADA
Hawaii–Aleutian Time Zone
PACIFIC OCEAN
0 200 400 Miles
0 200 400 Kilometers
130°W
125°W
120°W
115°W
110°W
105°W
100°W
95°W
50°N
45°N
40°N
35°N
30°N

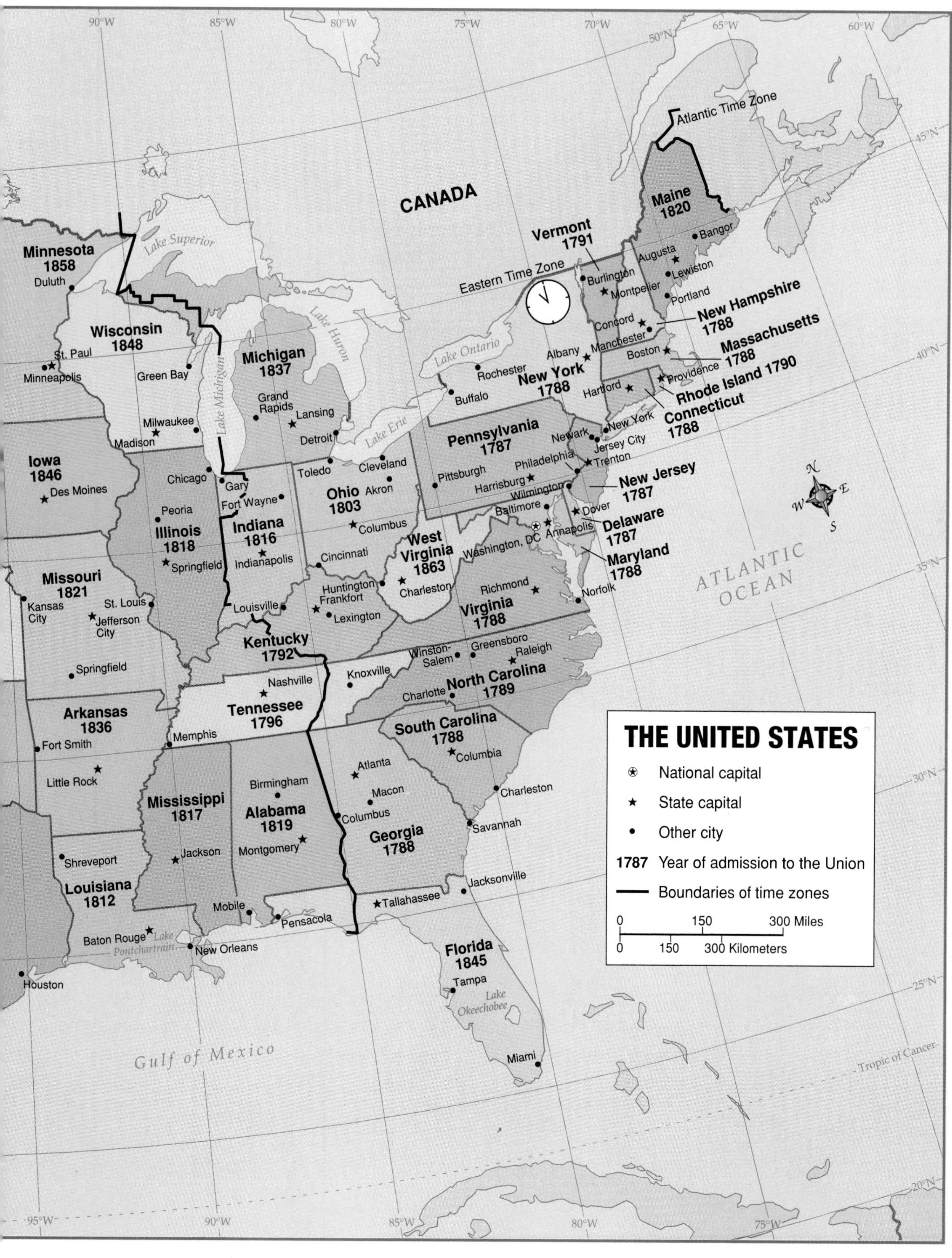
THE UNITED STATES
National capital
State capital
Other city
1787 Year of admission to the Union
Boundaries of time zones
0 150 300 Miles
0 150 300 Kilometers
CANADA
ATLANTIC OCEAN
Gulf of Mexico
Eastern Time Zone
Atlantic Time Zone
Minnesota 1858
Wisconsin 1848
Michigan 1837
Iowa 1846
Illinois 1818
Indiana 1816
Ohio 1803
Missouri 1821
Kentucky 1792
Tennessee 1796
Arkansas 1836
Mississippi 1817
Alabama 1819
Georgia 1788
Louisiana 1812
Florida 1845
South Carolina 1788
North Carolina 1789
Virginia 1788
West Virginia 1863
Pennsylvania 1787
New York 1788
Vermont 1791
Maine 1820
New Hampshire 1788
Massachusetts 1788
Rhode Island 1790
Connecticut 1788
New Jersey 1787
Delaware 1787
Maryland 1788
Washington, DC
Lake Superior
Lake Michigan
Lake Huron
Lake Ontario
Lake Erie
Lake Okeechobee
Lake Pontchartrain
Tropic of Cancer

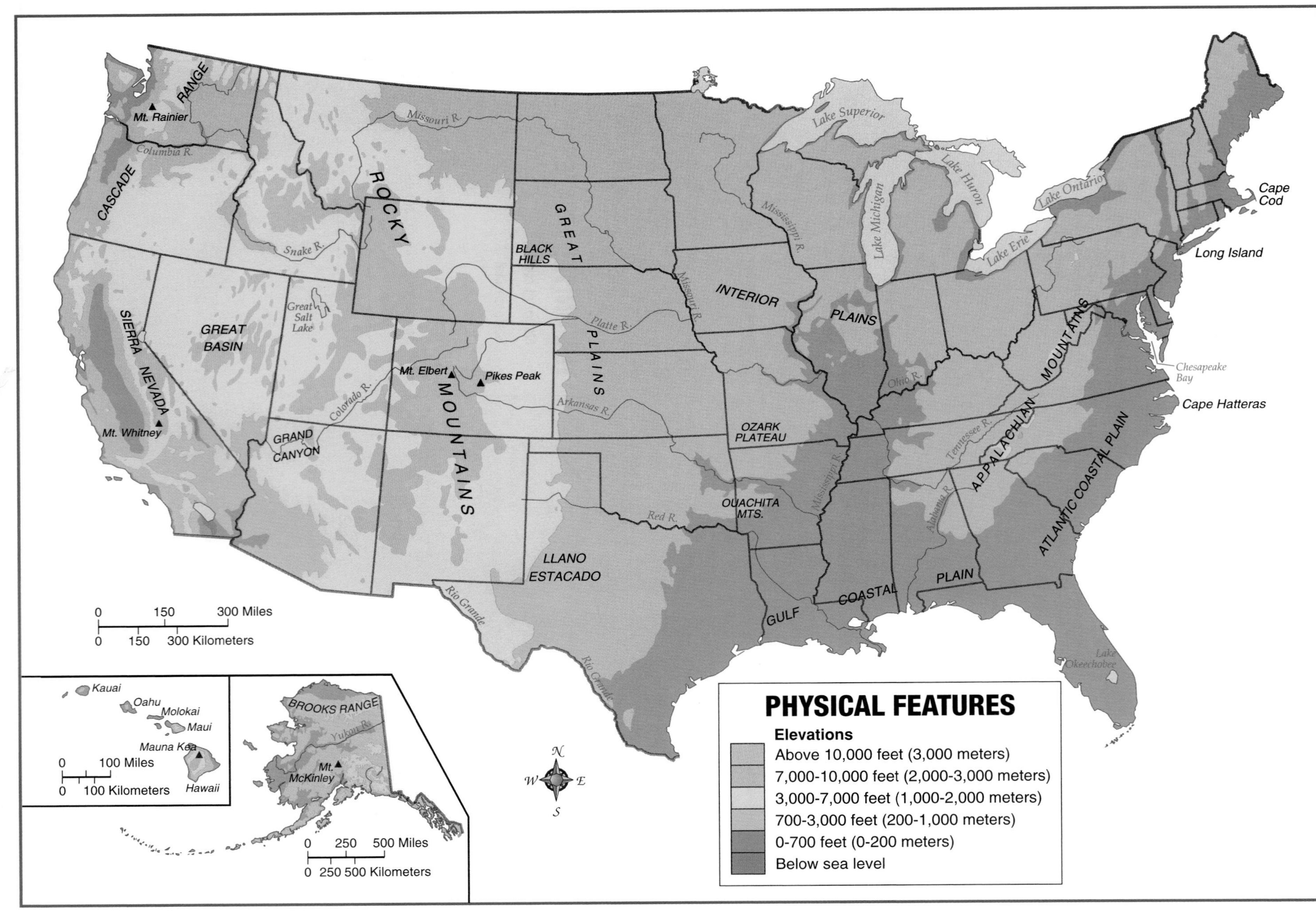
Mt. Rainier
CASCADE RANGE
Columbia R.
Missouri R.
Snake R.
ROCKY MOUNTAINS
Great Salt Lake
GREAT BASIN
SIERRA NEVADA
Mt. Whitney
Colorado R.
GRAND CANYON
Mt. Elbert
Pikes Peak
BLACK HILLS
GREAT PLAINS
Platte R.
Arkansas R.
LLANO ESTACADO
Rio Grande
Red R.
INTERIOR PLAINS
Mississippi R.
OZARK PLATEAU
OUACHITA MTS.
GULF COASTAL PLAIN
Lake Superior
Lake Michigan
Lake Huron
Lake Erie
Lake Ontario
Ohio R.
Tennessee R.
Alabama R.
APPALACHIAN MOUNTAINS
ATLANTIC COASTAL PLAIN
Cape Cod
Long Island
Chesapeake Bay
Cape Hatteras
Lake Okeechobee
0 150 300 Miles
0 150 300 Kilometers
Kauai
Oahu
Molokai
Maui
Mauna Kea
Hawaii
0 100 Miles
0 100 Kilometers
BROOKS RANGE
Yukon R.
Mt. McKinley
0 250 500 Miles
0 250 500 Kilometers
N
W
E
S
PHYSICAL FEATURES
Elevations
Above 10,000 feet (3,000 meters)
7,000-10,000 feet (2,000-3,000 meters)
3,000-7,000 feet (1,000-2,000 meters)
700-3,000 feet (200-1,000 meters)
0-700 feet (0-200 meters)
Below sea level

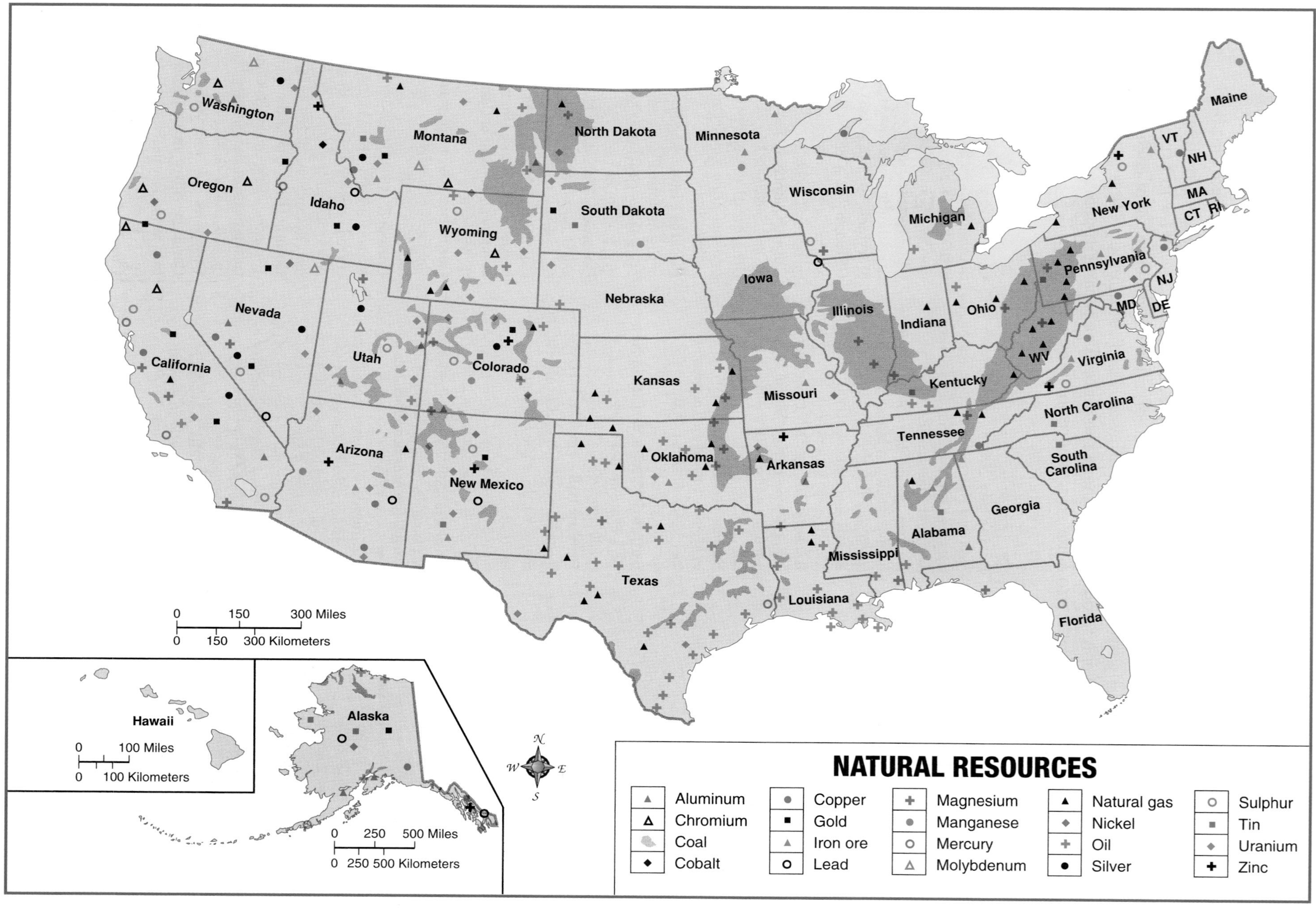
NATURAL RESOURCES
Aluminum
Chromium
Coal
Cobalt
Copper
Gold
Iron ore
Lead
Magnesium
Manganese
Mercury
Molybdenum
Natural gas
Nickel
Oil
Silver
Sulphur
Tin
Uranium
Zinc
Washington
Oregon
California
Nevada
Idaho
Montana
Wyoming
Utah
Arizona
Colorado
New Mexico
North Dakota
South Dakota
Nebraska
Kansas
Oklahoma
Texas
Minnesota
Iowa
Missouri
Arkansas
Louisiana
Wisconsin
Illinois
Michigan
Indiana
Ohio
Kentucky
Tennessee
Mississippi
Alabama
Georgia
Florida
South Carolina
North Carolina
Virginia
WV
Pennsylvania
New York
MD
DE
NJ
CT
RI
MA
VT
NH
Maine
Alaska
Hawaii
N
S
E
W
0 150 300 Miles
0 150 300 Kilometers
0 100 Miles
0 100 Kilometers
0 250 500 Miles
0 250 500 Kilometers

★ Gazetteer of American History ★

This gazetteer, or geographic dictionary, lists places that are important in American history. The approximate latitude and longitude are given for cities, towns, and other specific locations. See text page 10 for information about latitude and longitude. In the Gazetteer, after the description of each place, there are usually two numbers in parentheses. The first number refers to the text page where you can find out more about the place. The second appears in slanted, or *italic,* type and refers to a map *(m)* where the place is shown.

A

Africa Second largest continent in the world. (p. 12, *m10*)
Alabama 22nd state. Nicknamed the Heart of Dixie or the Cotton State. (p. 618, *m622–623*)
Alamo (29°N/99°W) Former mission in San Antonio, Texas, where 255 rebels died during the Texas war for independence. (p. 352, *m352*)
Alaska 49th state. Unofficially nicknamed the Last Frontier. Purchased from Russia in 1867. (p. 618, *m622–623*)
Albany (43°N/74°W) Capital of New York. (p. 171, *m170*)
Andes Rugged mountain chain in South America. (p. 50, *m47*)
Appalachian Mountains Mountain chain that stretches from Georgia to Canada. (p. 16, *m19*)
Appomattox Courthouse (37°N/79°W) Town in Virginia where Lee surrendered to Grant. (p. 473, *m472*)
Argentina Country in South America. (p. 313, *m314*)
Arizona 48th state. Nicknamed the Grand Canyon State. (p. 618, *m622–623*)
Arkansas 25th state. Nicknamed the Land of Opportunity. (p. 618, *m622–623*)
Asia Largest of the world's continents. (p. 12, *m10*)
Atlanta (34°N/84°W) Capital and largest city of Georgia. Burned by Sherman during the Civil War. (p. 472, *m460*)
Atlantic Ocean World's second largest ocean. (p. 14, *m10*)

B

Baltimore (39°N/77°W) Port city in Maryland. (p. 287, *m286*)
Bering Sea Narrow sea between Asia and North America. Scientists think a land bridge was here during the last ice age. *(m31)*
Boston (42°N/71°W) Seaport and industrial city in Massachusetts. (p. 17, *m96*)
Brazil Largest country in South America. (p. 313, *m314*)
Breed's Hill (42°N/71°W) Overlooks Boston harbor. Site of fighting during the Battle of Bunker Hill. (p. 162)
Buena Vista (26°N/101°W) City in Mexico. Site of an American victory in the Mexican War. (p. 362, *m361*)
Buffalo (43°N/79°W) City in New York State on Lake Erie. (p. 307, *m306*)
Bunker Hill (42°N/71°W) Overlooks Boston harbor. Site of first major battle of the Revolution. (p. 162)

C

Cahokia (39°N/90°W) British fort captured by George Rogers Clark during the American Revolution. (p. 174, *m175*)
California 31st state. Nicknamed the Golden State. Ceded to the United States by Mexico in 1848. (p. 618, *m622–623*)
Canada Northern neighbor of the United States. Second largest nation in the world. (p. 141, *m620–621*)
Canadian Shield Lowland region that lies mostly in eastern Canada. (p. 17, *m19*)
Caribbean Sea Tropical sea in the Western Hemisphere. (p. 65, *m67*)
Chancellorsville (38°N/78°W) Site of a Confederate victory in 1863. (p. 458, *m454*)
Charleston (33°N/80°W) City in South Carolina. Site of battles in both the American Revolution and the Civil War. (p. 108, *m107*)
Chesapeake Bay Large inlet of the Atlantic Ocean in Virginia and Maryland. (p. 287, *m286*)
Chicago (42°N/88°W) City in Illinois on Lake Michigan. (p. 5, *m622–623*)
China Country in East Asia. (p. 356, *m620–621*)
Cincinnati (39°N/84°W) City in southern Ohio on the Ohio River. *(m622–623)*
Coastal Plains Region consisting of the Atlantic Plain and the Gulf Plain along the Gulf of Mexico. (p. 17, *m19*)
Colorado 38th state. Nicknamed the Centennial State. (p. 618, *m622–623*)
Colorado River River that begins in the Rocky Mountains and flows into Gulf of California. (p. 18, *m19*)
Columbia River Chief river of the Pacific Northwest. (p. 275, *m273*)
Concord (43°N/71°W) Village in Massachusetts where battle occurred between the British and Americans at the start of the American Revolution. (p. 154, *m162*)
Connecticut One of the original 13 states. Nicknamed the Constitution State or the Nutmeg State. (p. 618, *m622–623*)
Cowpens (35°N/82°W) In South Carolina, site of an American victory in the Revolutionary War. (p. 179, *m179*)
Cumberland Gap (37°N/84°W) Pass in the Appalachian Mountains near the border of Virginia, Kentucky, and Tennessee. (p. 143, *m303*)

Cuzco (14°S/72°W) Capital of the Incan empire. (p. 50, *m47*)

D

Dallas (33°N/97°W) Major city in north central Texas. (*m900–901*)
Delaware One of the original 13 states. Nicknamed the First State or the Diamond State. (p. 618, *m622–623*)
Delaware River Flows into the Atlantic Ocean through Delaware Bay. (p. 82, *m88*)
Detroit (42°N/83°W) Largest city in Michigan. (p. 285, *m286*)
District of Columbia Located on the Potomac River. Seat of the federal government of the United States. (p. 247, *m622–623*)

E

England Part of Great Britain. (p. 78, *m79*)
Equator Line of latitude labeled 0° on maps. Separates the Northern and Southern hemispheres. (p. 10, *m10*)
Erie Canal Linked the Hudson and Mohawk rivers with Buffalo and Lake Erie. Built between 1817 and 1825. (p. 306, *m306*)
Europe World's second smallest continent. (p. 12, *m10*)

F

Florida 27th state. Nicknamed the Sunshine State. (p. 618, *m622–623*)
Fort Donelson (37°N/88°W) Located in Tennessee. Captured by Grant in 1862. (p. 458, *m470*)
Fort Henry (37°N/88°W) Located in Tennessee. Captured by Grant in 1862. (p. 458, *m470*)
Fort McHenry (39°N/77°W) Located in Baltimore harbor. British bombardment there in 1814 inspired Francis Scott Key to write "The Star-Spangled Banner." (p. 287)
Fort Necessity (40°N/79°W) British fort during the French and Indian War. (p. 136, *m138*)
Fort Pitt (40°N/80°W) British fort in the 1700s on the site of present-day Pittsburgh. (p. 140, *m175*)
Fort Sumter (33°N/80°W) Guarded Charleston harbor in South Carolina. First shots of the Civil War fired there in 1861. (p. 443, *m470*)
Fort Ticonderoga (44°N/74°W) Fort at the south end of Lake Champlain. Captured from the British by Ethan Allen in 1775. (p. 140, *m138*)
France Country in Western Europe. (p. 81, *m620–621*)
Fredericksburg (38°N/78°W) Located in eastern Virginia. Site of a Confederate victory in 1862. (p. 457, *m454*)

G

Gadsden Purchase Land purchased from Mexico in 1853. Now part of Arizona and New Mexico. (p. 363, *m363*)
Georgia One of the original 13 states. Nicknamed the Peach State or the Empire State of the South. (p. 618, *m622–623*)
Germany Country in central Europe (p. 381, *m620–621*)
Gettysburg (40°N/77°W) Town in southern Pennsylvania. Site of a Union victory in 1863 and Lincoln's Gettysburg Address. (p. 469, *m454*)
Goliad (29°N//97°W) Texas town where Mexicans killed several hundred Texans during the Texas war for independence. (p. 355, *m355*)
Gonzales (29°N/97°W) City in Texas near San Antonio. Site of the first Texan victory over Mexico in 1835. (p. 352, *m355*)
Great Britain Island nation of Western Europe. Includes England, Scotland, Wales, and Northern Ireland. (p. 135, *m620–621*)
Great Lakes Chain of five lakes in central North America. Lakes Superior, Michigan, Huron, Ontario, and Erie. (p. 18, *m19*)
Great Plains Western part of the Interior Plains. (p. 16, *m19*)
Great Salt Lake (41°N/113°W) Lake in northern Utah with highly saline water. (p. 365, *m366*)
Great Wagon Road Early pioneer route across the Appalachians. (p. 105, *m102*)
Gulf of Mexico Body of water along the southern coast of the United States. (p. 17, *m19*)

H

Haiti Country in the West Indies. The nation won independence from France in the early 1800s. (p. 270, *m620–621*)
Harpers Ferry (39°N/78°W) Town in West Virginia. John Brown raided the arsenal there in 1859. (p. 438, *m454*)
Hawaii Newest of the 50 states. Nicknamed the Aloha State. (p. 618, *m622–623*)
Hawaiian Islands Region in the Pacific Ocean composed of a group of eight large islands and many small islands. (p. 17, *m19*)
Hudson River Largest river in New York State. (p. 78, *m88*)

I

Idaho 43rd state. Nicknamed the Gem State. Acquired as part of the Oregon Territory. (p. 618, *m622–623*)
Illinois 21st state. Nicknamed the Inland Empire. Settled as part of the Northwest Territory. (p. 618, *m622–623*)
Indiana 19th state. Nicknamed the Hoosier State. Settled as part of the Northwest Territory. (p. 618, *m622–623*)
Interior Plains Region of the central United States that stretches from the Rockies to the Appalachians. (p. 16, *m19*)
Intermountain Region Rugged region from the Rocky Mountains to the Sierra Nevada and coastal mountains of the western United States. (p. 15, *m19*)
Iowa 29th state. Nicknamed the Hawkeye State. Acquired as part of the Louisiana Purchase. (p. 618, *m622–623*)
Italy Country in Southern Europe. (p. 502, *m620–621*)

J

Jamestown (37°N/77°W) First successful English colony in North America. (p. 85, *m88*)

K

Kansas 34th state. Nicknamed the Sunflower State. Acquired as part of the Louisiana Purchase. (p. 618, *m622–623*)

Kaskaskia (38°N/90°W) British fort on the Mississippi River captured by George Rogers Clark during the American Revolution. (p. 174, *m175*)
Kentucky 15th state. Nicknamed the Bluegrass State. (p. 618, *m622–623*)
Kilwa (8°S/39°E) East African trading state in the 1400s. (p. 73, *m75*)
King's Mountain (35°N/81°W) In South Carolina, site of an American victory in the Revolutionary War. (p. 178, *m179*)

L

Lancaster Turnpike Road built in the 1790s linking Philadelphia and Lancaster, Pennsylvania. (p. 302, *m303*)
Latin America Name for those parts of the Western Hemisphere where Latin languages such as Spanish, French, and Portuguese are spoken. Includes Mexico, Central America, South America, and the islands of the Caribbean. (p. 312, *m314*)
Lexington (42°N/71°W) Village in Massachusetts. Site of the first clash between minutemen and British troops in 1775. (p. 155, *m162*)
Liberia Country in West Africa. Set up in 1822 as a colony for free African Americans. (p. 403, *m620–621*)
London (51°N/0°) Capital of United Kingdom. (*m898–899*)
Long Island Located in New York. Site of a British victory in the Revolution. (p. 169, *m170*)
Los Angeles (34°N/118°W) City in southern California. First settled by Spanish missionaries. (p. 15, *m67*)
Louisbourg (46°N/60°W) Fort in eastern Canada that played a major role in the French and Indian War. (p. 140, *m138*)
Louisiana 18th state. Nicknamed the Pelican State. First state created out of the Louisiana Purchase. (p. 618, *m622–623*)
Lowell (43°N/83°W) City in Massachusetts. Important site of Industrial Revolution. (p. 296)

M

Maine 23rd state. Nicknamed the Pine Tree State. Originally part of Massachusetts. (p. 618, *m622–623*)
Mali Kingdom in West Africa. Reached its peak between 1200 and 1400. (p. 73, *m75*)
Maryland One of the original 13 states. Nicknamed the Old Line State or the Free State. (p. 618, *m622–623*)
Mason-Dixon Line Boundary between Pennsylvania and Maryland surveyed and marked in the 1760s. (p. 106)
Massachusetts One of the original 13 states. Nicknamed the Bay State or the Old Colony. (p. 618, *m622–623*)
Memphis (35°N/90°W) City in Tennessee on the Mississippi River. Captured by Union forces in 1862. (p. 458, *m470*)
Mexican Cession Lands acquired by the United States from Mexico under the Treaty of Guadalupe Hidalgo in 1848. (p. 363, *m363*)
Mexico Southern neighbor of the United States. Gained independence from Spain in 1821. (p. 312, *m620–621*)
Mexico City (19°N/99°W) Capital of Mexico. (p. 434, *m433*)
Michigan 26th state. Nicknamed the Great Lake State or the Wolverine State. Settled as part of the Northwest Territory. (p. 618, *m622–623*)
Minnesota 32nd state. Nicknamed the Gopher State. Most of it was acquired as part of the Louisiana Purchase from France. (p. 618, *m622–623*)
Mississippi 20th state. Nicknamed the Magnolia State. (p. 618, *m622–623*)
Mississippi River Longest river in the United States. Links the Great Lakes with the Gulf of Mexico. (p. 17, *m19*)
Missouri 24th state. Nicknamed the Show Me State. Acquired as part of the Louisiana Purchase. (p. 618, *m622–623*)
Missouri River Second longest river in the United States. Rises in the northern Rocky Mountains and joins the Mississippi River near St. Louis, Missouri (p. 17, *m19*)
Mogadishu (2°N/45°E) East African trading state in the 1400s. (p. 73, *m75*)
Montana 41st state. Nicknamed the Treasure State. Acquired in part through the Louisiana Purchase. (p. 618, *m622–623*)
Montreal (46°N/74°W) Major city in Canada. Located in the province of Quebec. (p. 141, *m138*)

N

National Road Early road to the West that began in Cumberland, Maryland, and eventually reached Illinois. (p. 303, *m303*)
Nauvoo (41°N/91°W) Town founded by the Mormons in Illinois in the 1840s. (p. 365, *m366*)
Nebraska 37th state. Nicknamed the Cornhusker State. Acquired as part of the Louisiana Purchase. (p. 618, *m622–623*)
Nevada 36th state. Nicknamed the Sagebrush State or the Battle Born State. Acquired at the end of the Mexican War. (p. 618, *m622–623*)
New Amsterdam (41°N/74°W) Town established by Dutch settlers on Manhattan Island in the early 1600s. Renamed New York by the British. (p. 82)
New France Colony established by France in North America. (p. 81, *m79*)
New Hampshire One of the original 13 states. Nicknamed the Granite State. (p. 618, *m622–623*)
New Jersey One of the original 13 states. Nicknamed the Garden State. (p. 618, *m622–623*)
New Mexico 47th state. Nicknamed the Land of Enchantment. Acquired at the end of the Mexican War. (p. 618, *m622–623*)
New Netherland Dutch colony on the Hudson River. Seized by the English and renamed New York in 1664. (p. 82)
New Orleans (30°N/90°W) Port city in Louisiana near the mouth of the Mississippi River. Settled by the French in the 1600s. (p. 82, *m79*)

New Spain Area in the Americas ruled by Spain for some 300 years. Included much of present-day western United States. (p. 68, *m68*)
New York One of the original 13 states. Nicknamed the Empire State. (p. 618, *m622–623*)
New York City (41°N/74°W) Port city at the mouth of the Hudson River. (p. 101, *m102*)
North America World's third largest continent. (p. 14, *m10*)
North Carolina One of the original 13 states. Nicknamed the Tar Heel State or the Old North State. (p. 618, *m622–623*)
North Dakota 39th state. Nicknamed the Sioux State or the Flickertail State. Acquired as part of the Louisiana Purchase. (p. 618, *m622–623*)
Northwest Territory Name for lands north of the Ohio River. Acquired by the Treaty of Paris in 1783. (p. 190, *m191*)
Nueces River Claimed by Mexico in the Mexican War as the southern border of Texas. (p. 361, *m361*)

O

Ohio 17th state. Nicknamed the Buckeye State. Settled as part of the Northwest Territory. (p. 618, *m622–623*)
Ohio River Important transportation route. Begins at Pittsburgh and flows to the Mississippi River. (p. 133, *m133*)
Oklahoma 46th State. Nicknamed the Sooner State. Acquired as part of the Louisiana Purchase. (p. 618, *m622–623*)
Oregon 33rd state. Nicknamed the Beaver State. Acquired as part of the Oregon Territory. (p. 618, *m622–623*)
Oregon Trail Overland route from Independence, Missouri, to the Columbia River valley. (p. 349, *m347*)

P

Pacific Coast Highest and most rugged region of the United States. Includes the Cascades and the Sierra Nevada. (p. 15, *m19*)
Pacific Ocean World's largest ocean. (p. 14, *m10*)
Panama Country on the isthmus separating North and South America. Gained independence from Colombia in 1903. (p. 516, *m516*)
Panama Canal Canal dug through the Isthmus of Panama to link the Atlantic and Pacific oceans. (p. 517, *m516*)
Paris (49°N/2°E) Capital of France. (p. 172, *m619*)
Pennsylvania One of the original 13 states. Nicknamed the Keystone State. (p. 618, *m622–623*)
Petersburg (37°N/78°W) City in Virginia. Union forces kept the city under siege for nine months during the Civil War. (p. 472, *m472*)
Philadelphia (40°N/75°W) Major port and chief city in Pennsylvania. (p. 247, *m102*)
Philippine Islands Group of islands in the Pacific Ocean. Acquired by the United States in 1898. Gained independence in 1946. (p. 516, *m620–621*)
Pikes Peak (39°N/105°W) Mountain located in the Rocky Mountains of central Colorado. (p. 275, *m273*)
Plymouth (42°N/71°W) New England colony founded in 1620 by Pilgrims. (p. 89, *m88*)
Portugal Country in Western Europe. (p. 61, *m75*)
Potomac River Forms part of the Maryland-Virginia border. Flows through Washington, D.C., and into Chesapeake Bay. (p. 455, *m455*)
Prime Meridian Line of longitude labeled 0° on maps. (p. 10, *m10*)
Princeton (40°N/75°W) City in New Jersey. Site of an American victory during the Revolution. (p. 170, *m170*)
Puerto Rico (18°N/67°W) Island in the Caribbean Sea. A self-governing commonwealth of the United States. (p. 516, *m516*)

Q

Quebec (47°N/71°W) City in eastern Canada. (p. 81, *m79*)

R

Rhode Island One of the original 13 states. Nicknamed Little Rhody or the Ocean State. (p. 618, *m622–623*)
Richmond (38°N/78°W) Capital of Virginia. Capital of the Confederate States of America during the Civil War. (p. 453, *m454*)
Rio Grande River that forms the border between the United States and Mexico. (p. 18, *m19*)
Roanoke Island (36°N/76°W) Island off North Carolina. Site of English "lost colony" founded in 1587. (p. 84, *m88*)
Rocky Mountains Mountains extending through the western United States and Canada. (p. 16, *m19*)
Russia Largest country in the world, spanning Europe and Asia. (p. 502, *m620–621*)

S

Sacramento (39°N/122°W) Capital of California. Developed as a gold rush boom town. (p. 367, *m366*)
St. Augustine (30°N/81°W) City in Florida. Founded by Spain in 1565. Oldest European settlement in the United States. (p. 69, *m67*)
St. Lawrence River Waterway from the Great Lakes to the Atlantic Ocean. Forms part of the border between the United States and Canada. (p. 18, *m79*)
St. Louis (38°N/90°W) City in Missouri on the Mississippi River. Lewis and Clark began their expedition there. (p. 272, *m273*)
Salt Lake City (41°N/112°W) Largest city in Utah. Founded in 1847 by Mormons. (p. 366, *m366*)
San Antonio (29°N/99°W) City in southern Texas. Site of the Alamo. (p. 352, *m352*)
San Diego (33°N/117°W) City in southern California. Founded as the first Spanish mission in California. (p. 357, *m366*)

San Francisco (38°N/122°W) City in northern California. Boom town of the California gold rush. (p. 359, *m366*)
Santa Fe (35°N/106°W) Capital of New Mexico. First settled by the Spanish. (p. 69, *m67*)
Santa Fe Trail Overland trail from Independence to Santa Fe. Opened in 1821. (p. 356, *m366*)
Saratoga (43°N/75°W) City in eastern New York. The American victory there in 1777 was a turning point in the Revolution. (p. 172, *m170*)
Savannah (32°N/81°W) Oldest city in Georgia, founded in 1733. (p. 108, *m107*)
Sierra Nevada Mountain range mostly in California. (p. 15, *m19*)
Songhai West African kingdom in the 1400s. (p. 74, *m75*)
South America World's fourth largest continent. (p. 12, *m10*)
South Carolina One of the original 13 states. Nicknamed the Palmetto State. (p. 618, *m622–623*)
South Dakota 40th state. Nicknamed the Coyote State or the Sunshine State. Acquired as part of the Louisiana Purchase. (p. 618, *m622–623*)
Spain Country in southwestern Europe. (p. 61, *m79*)
Spanish Florida Part of New Spain. Purchased by the United States in 1821. (p. 282, *m283*)

T

Tennessee 16th state. Nicknamed the Volunteer State. Gained statehood after North Carolina ceded its western lands to the United States. (p. 618, *m622–623*)
Tenochtitlán (19°N/99°W) Capital of the Aztec empire. Now part of Mexico City. (p. 48, *m47*)
Texas 28th state. Nicknamed the Lone Star State. Proclaimed independence from Mexico in 1836. Was a separate republic until 1845. (p. 618, *m622–623*)
Tikal (17°N/90°W) Ancient Mayan city. (p. 47, *m47*)
Timbuktu (17°N/3°W) City on the Niger River in Africa. (p. 74, *m75*)
Trenton (41°N/74°W) Capital of New Jersey. Site of an American victory in the Revolution. (p. 170, *m170*)

U

Utah 45th state. Nicknamed the Beehive State. Settled by Mormons. (p. 618, *m622–623*)

V

Valley Forge (40°N/76°W) Winter headquarters for the Continental Army in 1777–1778. Located near Philadelphia. (p. 173, *m170*)
Veracruz (19°N/96°W) Port city in Mexico on the Gulf of Mexico. (p. 362, *m361*)
Vermont 14th state. Nicknamed the Green Mountain State.(p. 618, *m622–623*)
Vicksburg (42°N/86°W) City in Mississippi. Site of a Union victory in 1863. (p. 468, *m470*)
Vietnam Country in Southeast Asia. Site of a war involving the United States during the Cold War. (p. 517, *m517*)
Vincennes (39°N/88°W) City in Indiana. British fort there was captured by George Rogers Clark in 1779. (p. 174, *m175*)
Virgin Islands (18°N/64°W) Territory of the United States. Purchased from Denmark in 1917. (p. 896, *m898–899*)
Virginia One of the original 13 states. Nicknamed the Old Dominion. (p. 618, *m622–623*)

W

Washington 42nd state. Nicknamed the Evergreen State. Acquired as part of Oregon Territory. (p. 618, *m622–623*)
Washington, D.C. (39°N/77°W) Capital of the United States since 1800. (p. 287, *m214*)
West Indies Islands in the Caribbean Sea. Explored by Columbus. (p. 62, *m68*)
West Virginia 35th state. Nicknamed the Mountain State. Separated from Virginia early in the Civil War. (p. 618, *m622–623*)
Western Hemisphere Western half of the world. Includes North and South America. (p. 12, *m10*)
Wisconsin 30th state. Nicknamed the Badger State. Settled as part of the Northwest Territory. (p. 618, *m622–623*)
Wyoming 44th state. Nicknamed the Equality State. (p. 618, *m622–623*)

Y

Yorktown (37°N/76°W) Town in Virginia. Site of the British surrender in 1781. (p. 180, *m179*)

★ Glossary ★

This glossary defines all vocabulary words and many important historical terms and phrases. These words and terms appear in blue or boldfaced type the first time that they are used in the text. The page number(s) after each definition refers to the page(s) on which the word or phrase is defined in the text. For other references, see the index.

Pronunciation Key

When difficult names or terms first appear in the text, they are respelled to help you with pronunciation. A syllable printed in SMALL CAPITAL LETTERS receives the greatest stress. The pronunciation key below lists the letters and symbols that will help you pronounce the word. It also includes examples of words using each sound and showing how they would be pronounced.

Symbol	Example	Respelling
a	hat	(hat)
ay	pay, late	(pay), (layt)
ah	star, hot	(stahr), (haht)
ai	air, dare	(air), (dair)
aw	law, all	(law), (awl)
eh	met	(meht)
ee	bee, eat	(bee), (eet)
er	learn, sir, fur	(lern), (ser), (fer)
ih	fit	(fiht)
i	mile	(mīl)
ir	ear	(ir)
oh	no	(noh)
oi	soil, boy	(soil), (boi)
oo	root, rule	(root), (rool)
or	born, door	(born), (dor)
ow	plow, out	(plow), (owt)

Symbol	Example	Respelling
u	put, book	(put), (buk)
uh	fun	(fuhn)
yoo	few, use	(fyoo), (yooz)
ch	chill, reach	(chihl), (reech)
g	go, dig	(goh), (dihg)
j	jet, gently bridge	(jeht), (JEHNT lee), (brihj)
k	kite, cup	(kīt), (kuhp)
ks	mix	(mihks)
kw	quick	(kwihk)
ng	bring	(brihng)
s	say, cent	(say), (sehnt)
sh	she, crash	(shee), (krash)
th	three	(three)
y	yet, onion	(yeht), (UHN yuhn)
z	zip, always	(zihp), (AWL wayz)
zh	treasure	(TREH zher)

A

abolitionist person who wanted to end slavery (p. 404)
absolute power total authority by a ruler over the people (p. 49)
adobe sun-dried clay brick (p. 35)
ally nation that works with another nation for a common purpose (p. 172)
altitude height above sea level (p. 19)
amend to change (p. 208)
amendment formal written change (p. 222)
American System plan proposed by Henry Clay that called for high tariffs and internal improvements (p. 310)
amnesty government pardon (pp. 479, 503)
annex to add on (pp. 355, 515)
Antifederalist person who opposed ratification of the Constitution (p. 205)
appeal to ask that a decision be reviewed by a higher court (p. 231)
apprentice (uh PREHN tihs) person who learns a trade or craft from a master (p. 120)
appropriate to set aside money for a special purpose (p. 226)
aqueduct channel for carrying water (p. 50)
archaeology (ahr kee AHL uh jee) study of evidence left by early people in order to find out about their culture (p. 32)
arsenal warehouse for guns and ammunition (p. 438)
Articles of Confederation first constitution of the United States (p. 189)
artifact (AHRT uh fakt) object made by humans and used by archaeologists to learn about past human cultures (p. 32)
artisan worker who has learned a trade, such as carpentry (p. 379)
assembly line method of production in which workers add parts to a product as it moves along on a belt (p. 507)
astrolabe (AS troh layb) instrument to measure the positions of stars and figure out latitude (p. 61)

B

backcountry area of land along the eastern slopes of the Appalachian Mountains (p. 105)
bill proposed law (pp. 203, 221)

★ GLOSSARY ★

bill of rights list of freedoms that a government promises to protect (p. 116)
Bill of Rights first 10 amendments to the Constitution (p. 208)
black codes laws that severely limited the rights of freedmen after the Civil War (p. 482)
blockade shutting off a port by positioning ships to keep people or supplies from moving in or out (p. 164)
bond certificate that promises to repay money loaned, plus interest, on a certain date (p. 246)
Boston Massacre (1770) shooting of five colonists by British soldiers (p. 148)
Boston Tea Party (1773) protest in which colonists dressed as Indians dumped British tea into Boston harbor (p. 151)
boycott to refuse to buy certain goods or services (p. 144)
buffer land between two other lands that reduces the possibility of conflict between the other two (p. 109)

C

Cabinet group of officials who head government departments and advise the President (pp. 224, 245)
canal artificial channel filled with water to allow boats to cross a stretch of land (p. 305)
capitalist person who invests in a business to make a profit (p. 296)
caravel (KAR uh vehl) ship with a steering rudder and triangular sails (p. 62)
carpetbagger name for a northerner who came south after the Civil War seeking personal gain (p. 486)
cartographer person who makes maps (p. 8)
cash crop crop sold for money (p. 103)
caucus private meeting of political party leaders to choose a candidate (p. 327)
causeway raised road across a stretch of water (p. 48)
cavalry troops on horseback (p. 173)
cede to give up, as land (p. 363)
charter legal document giving certain rights to a person or company (p. 85)
checks and balances system by which each branch of government can check, or control, the actions of the other branches (p. 202)
chinampa Aztec floating garden (p. 49)
city-state town that has its own independent government (p. 73)
civil disobedience nonviolent opposition to a government policy or law by refusing to comply with it (p. 510)
civil rights movement the efforts of African Americans and others who worked for equality (p. 510)
civil war war between people of the same country (p. 428)
civilian person not in the military (p. 463)
civilization advanced culture (p. 46)
clan group of related families (p. 45)
climate average weather of a place over a period of 20 to 30 years (p. 19)
clipper ship fast-sailing ship of the mid-1800s (p. 377)
colony group of people who move to a new land and are ruled by the government of their native land (p. 64)
Columbian Exchange worldwide exchange of goods and ideas that began with Columbus's voyages to the Americas (p. 53)
committee of correspondence group of colonists who wrote letters and pamphlets reporting on British actions (p. 149)
common open field where cattle grazed (p. 98)
compromise settlement in which each side gives up some of its demands in order to reach an agreement (p. 194)
Compromise of 1850 agreement over slavery under which California joined the Union as a free state and a strict fugitive slave law was passed (p. 428)
Confederate States of America nation formed in 1861 by the southern states that seceded from the Union (p. 442)
confederation alliance of independent states (p. 189)
conglomerate giant corporation that owns a large number of smaller companies in different fields (p. 508)
conquistador (kahn KEES tuh dor) Spanish word for conqueror (p. 65)
conservative person who wants to keep conditions as they are or return them to the way they used to be (p. 487)
constituent person who elected a representative to office (p. 228)
constitution document that sets out the laws and principles of a government (p. 188)
Constitutional Convention (1787) meeting of delegates from 12 states who wrote the United States Constitution (p. 193)
Continental Army army established by the Second Continental Congress to fight the British (p. 160)
continental divide mountain ridge that separates river systems flowing toward opposite sides of a continent (p. 274)
Copperheads northerners who opposed using force to keep the southern states in the Union (p. 463)
corduroy road road made of logs (p. 302)
corporation business that is owned by investors (p. 508)
cottonocracy name for the wealthy planters who made their money from cotton in the mid-1800s (p. 388)
coureur de bois (koo ruhr duh BWAH) phrase meaning runner of the woods; trapper or trader in New France (p. 81)
creole person born in Spain's American colonies to Spanish parents (pp. 70, 312)
Crusades wars fought by European Christians in the Middle Ages to gain control of the Middle East (p. 60)
culture entire way of life developed by a people (p. 32)
culture area region in which people share a similar way of life (p. 36)

D

dame school private school for girls in the New England colonies (p. 121)
debtor person who owes money (p. 108)

Declaration of Independence (1776) document stating that the colonies were a free and independent nation (p. 166)
democratic ensuring that all people have the same rights (p. 266)
depression period when business slows, prices and wages fall, and unemployment rises (pp. 192, 338)
discrimination policy or attitude that denies equal rights and treatment to certain groups of people (pp. 381, 461)
dissenting opinion statement explaining why a Supreme Court Justice disagrees with the opinion of the majority (p. 231)
domestic tranquillity peace at home (p. 215)
draft law requiring certain people to serve in the military (p. 464)
drought long dry spell (p. 35)
due process principle that government must follow the same fair rules in all cases brought to trial (pp. 209, 232)
dumping selling of goods in another country at very low prices (p. 310)

E

Elastic Clause section of the Constitution that gives Congress the power to make all "necessary and proper" laws (p. 224)
electoral college group of electors from every state who meet every four years to vote for the President and Vice President of the United States (p. 202)
elevation height above sea level (p. 14)
emancipate to set free (p. 459)
Emancipation Proclamation (1863) President Lincoln's declaration freeing slaves in the Confederacy (p. 460)
embargo ban on trade with another country (p. 350)
encomienda (ehn koh mee EHN dah) right given by Spanish government to Spanish settlers to demand labor or taxes from Native Americans (p. 70)
English Bill of Rights (1689) document guaranteeing the basic rights of English citizens (pp. 116, 199)
Enlightenment movement in Europe in the late 1600s and 1700s that emphasized the use of reason (pp. 121, 199)
Equator imaginary line that lies at 0° latitude (p. 8)
execute to carry out (p. 188)
executive agreement informal agreement made by the President with another head of state (p. 229)
executive branch branch of government that carries out laws (p. 194)
expedition long journey or voyage of exploration (p. 272)
export trade product sent to markets outside a country (p. 112)
extended family close-knit family group that includes grandparents, parents, children, aunts, uncles, and cousins (p. 393)

F

faction group inside a political party or other group (p. 253)
factory system method of producing goods that brought workers and machinery together in one place (p. 296)
famine severe food shortage and starvation (p. 381)
federal having to do with the national government (p. 215)
federalism division of power between the states and the national government (p. 200)
feudalism (FYOOD 'l ihz uhm) rule by lords who owe loyalty to a monarch (p. 60)
First Continental Congress (1774) meeting of delegates from 12 colonies in Philadelphia (p. 154)
foreign policy actions that a nation takes in relation to other nations (p. 251)
forty-niner person who headed to California in search of gold during the Gold Rush of 1849 (p. 367)
freedmen men and women who had been slaves (p. 479)
fugitive runaway (p. 428)

G

general welfare well-being of all the people (p. 216)
gentry highest social class in the 13 English colonies (p. 117)
geography the study of people, their environments, and their resources (p. 4)
Gettysburg Address (1863) speech by President Lincoln after the Battle of Gettysburg (p. 470)
glacier thick sheet of ice (p. 30)
globe sphere with a map of Earth printed on it (p. 8)
Glorious Revolution (1688) movement that brought William and Mary to the throne of England and strengthened the rights of English citizens (p. 116)
grandfather clause law that excused a voter from a literacy test if his grandfather had been eligible to vote on January 1, 1867—protected the voting rights of southern whites but not those of southern blacks (p. 493)
Great Awakening religious movement in the English colonies in the early 1700s (p. 119)
Great Compromise plan at the Constitutional Convention that settled the differences between large and small states (p. 196)
Great Depression (1929–1941) worst period of economic decline in United States history (p. 513)
guerrilla soldier who uses hit-and-run tactics (p. 179)

H

habeas corpus right to have charges filed or a hearing before being jailed (p. 464)
hemisphere half of the Earth (p. 8)
hieroglyphics system of writing that uses pictures to represent words and ideas (p. 47)
hill area of raised land that is lower and more rounded than a mountain (p. 14)
history account of what has happened in the lives of different peoples (p. 4)
hogan house made of mud plaster over a framework of wooden poles (p. 41)
House of Burgesses representative assembly in colonial Virginia (pp. 86, 199)
House of Representatives larger house of Congress, in which each state is represented according to its population (p. 225)

Hudson River School group of American artists who painted landscapes of New York's Hudson River region in the mid-1800s (p. 415)

I

igloo house of snow and ice, developed by the Inuits (p. 37)
illegal alien someone who enters a country without legal permission (p. 503)
immigrant person who enters a country in order to settle there (p. 259)
impeach to bring a formal charge of wrongdoing against the President or another public official (pp. 203, 228, 484)
imperialism policy of powerful countries seeking to control the economic and political affairs of weaker countries or regions (p. 515)
import trade product brought into a country (p. 112)
impressment act of forcing someone to serve in the navy (p. 277)
inauguration ceremony at which the President officially takes the oath of office (p. 244)
income tax tax on people's earnings (p. 466)
indentured servant person who agreed to work without wages for some time in exchange for passage to the colonies (p. 117)
Industrial Revolution process by which machines replaced hand tools, and steam and other new sources of power replaced human and animal power (p. 294)
inflation rise in prices and decrease in the value of money (p. 466)
initiative process by which voters can put a bill directly before the state legislature by collecting signatures on a petition (p. 513)
integration bringing together people of different races or ethnic groups (p. 510)
interchangeable parts identical, machine-made parts for a tool or instrument (p. 299)
interstate commerce trade between different states (p. 311)
intervention direct involvement in another country (p. 315)
Intolerable Acts (1774) laws passed by Parliament to punish colonists for the Boston Tea Party (p. 153)
irrigate to bring water to an area (p. 6)
isthmus narrow strip of land (p. 14)

J

jazz music style that developed from blues, ragtime, and other earlier styles (p. 504)
Jim Crow laws laws that separated people of different races in public places in the South (p. 495)
joint committee congressional committee that includes both House and Senate members (p. 226)
judicial branch branch of government that decides if laws are carried out fairly (p. 194)
judicial review power of the Supreme Court to decide whether acts of a President or laws passed by Congress are constitutional (pp. 224, 269)
justice fairness (p. 215)

K

kachina masked dancer at religious ceremonies of the Southwest Indians (p. 41)
kayak (KI ak) small boat made of animal skins (p. 37)
kinship network close ties among family members (p. 74)
kitchen cabinet group of unofficial advisers to President Andrew Jackson (p. 331)
kiva underground chamber where Pueblo men held religious ceremonies (p. 41)

L

laissez faire (lehs ay FAYR) idea that government should play as small a role as possible in economic affairs (pp. 267, 339)
latitude distance north or south from the Equator (p. 4)
lawsuit legal case brought by one person or group against another to settle a dispute (p. 434)
legislative branch branch of government that passes laws (p. 194)
legislature group of people who have the power to make laws (p. 114)
libel publishing a statement that unjustly damages a person's reputation (p. 123)
liberty freedom to live as you please provided you obey the laws and respect the rights of others (p. 217)
literacy test examination to see if a person can read and write, used in the past to restrict voting rights (p. 493)
locomotive engine that uses steam or another power source to pull a railroad train (p. 376)
long house Native American home built of wood poles and bark (p. 44)
longitude distance east or west from the Prime Meridian (p. 4)
Louisiana Purchase (1803) vast territory west of the Mississippi purchased from France (p. 272)
Loyalist colonist who remained loyal to Britain (p.161)
lynching illegal seizure and execution of someone by a mob (p. 495)

M

Magna Carta (1215) document that guaranteed rights to English nobles (pp. 86, 198)
magnetic compass device that shows which direction is North (p. 61)
majority more than half (p. 324)
Manifest Destiny belief that the United States had the right and the duty to expand to the Pacific (p. 359)
manor district ruled by a lord, including the lord's castle, peasants' huts, and surrounding fields (p. 60)
map projection way of drawing the Earth on a flat surface (p. 8)
Marbury* v. *Madison (1803) Supreme Court decison that established the precedent of judicial review (p. 269)
martial law rule by the army instead of the elected government (p. 448)

★ GLOSSARY ★

martyr person who dies for his or her beliefs (p. 438)
Mayflower Compact (1620) agreement for ruling the Plymouth Colony, signed by Pilgrims before they landed at Plymouth (pp. 88, 199)
McCulloch* v. *Maryland (1819) Supreme Court ruling that states have no right to interfere with federal institutions within their borders (p. 311)
mercantilism (MER kuhn tihl ihz uhm) economic theory that a nation's strength came from building up its gold supplies and expanding its trade (p. 112)
mercenary soldier who fights merely for pay, often for a foreign country (p. 164)
mestizo in Spanish colonies, person of mixed Spanish and Indian background (p. 70)
Middle Ages period of time in European history from about 500 to 1350 (p. 60)
middle class in the 13 English colonies, class that included skilled craftsworkers, farmers, and some tradespeople (p. 117)
Middle Passage ocean trip from Africa to the Americas in which thousands of enslaved Africans died (p. 77)
militia army of citizens who serve as soldiers in an emergency (p. 154)
minuteman colonial volunteer who trained to fight the British (p. 154)
mission religious settlement run by Catholic priests and friars (p. 69)
missionary person who tries to spread certain religious beliefs among a group of people (p. 81)
Missouri Compromise (1819) plan proposed by Henry Clay to keep the number of slave and free states equal (p. 424)
monarch king or queen (p. 60)
monopoly company that controls all or nearly all the business of an industry (p. 508)
Monroe Doctrine (1823) President Monroe's foreign policy statement warning European nations not to interfere in Latin America (p. 315)
mountain high, steep, rugged land, usually at least 1,000 feet (372 m) above the surrounding land (p. 14)
mountain man fur trapper who lived in the western mountains in the early 1800s (p. 347)
mudslinging political tactic of using insults to attack an opponent's reputation (p. 341)

N

national debt total sum of money a government owes (p. 245)
nationalism pride in one's nation (p. 282)
nativist person who wanted to limit immigration and preserve the United States for native-born white Protestants (p. 381)
natural rights rights that belong to all people from birth (p. 168)
neutral not taking sides in a war (pp. 174, 282)
New Deal program of President Franklin D. Roosevelt to end the Great Depression (p. 514)
nominating convention meeting at which a political party chooses a candidate (p. 327)
North American Free Trade Agreement (NAFTA) treaty among the United States, Canada, and Mexico to gradually remove trade barriers (p. 509)
nullification idea that a state had the right to cancel a federal law it considered unconstitutional (p. 333)
nullify to cancel (p. 260)

O

opinion a judge's official statement regarding the laws bearing on a case (p. 231)
ordinance law (p. 190)
override to overrule or set aside (pp. 203, 221)

P

Parliament representative assembly in England (p. 86)
Patriot colonist who supported independence from British rule (p. 161)
patroon owner of a huge estate in a Dutch colony (p. 100)
penal system system of prisons (p. 399)
peninsulare (puh nihn suh LAH ray) person from Spain who held a position of power in a Spanish colony (p. 70)
pet bank state bank in which President Jackson and Secretary of the Treasury Taney deposited federal money (p. 332)
petition formal request to someone in authority, usually written and signed by a group of people (p. 144)
Pilgrims in the 1600s, English settlers who sought religious freedom in the Americas (p. 88)
plain broad area of fairly level land (p. 14)
plantation large estate farmed by many workers (pp. 72, 109)
plateau raised plain (p. 14)
Plessy* v. *Ferguson (1896) Supreme Court ruling that segregation was legal as long as facilities for blacks and whites were equal (p. 505)
poll tax tax required before a person can vote (p. 493)
popular sovereignty idea that the people hold the final authority in government (p. 218), allowing each territory to decide whether to allow slavery (p. 426)
potlatch ceremonial dinner among some Native Americans of the Northwest Coast (p. 38)
preamble opening statement of a declaration, constitution, or other official document (pp. 168, 214)
precedent (PREHS uh dehnt) act or decision that sets an example for others to follow (pp. 224, 244)
precipitation (pree sihp uh TAY shuhn) water that falls as rain, sleet, hail, or snow (p. 19)
predestination belief that God decided in advance which people will gain salvation in heaven (p. 398)
presidio (prih SIHD ee oh) fort where soldiers lived in the Spanish colonies (p. 69)
primary election in which voters choose their party's candidate for the general election (p. 513)
Prime Meridian imaginary line that lies at 0° longitude (p. 8)
profiteer person who takes advantage of a crisis to make money (p. 466)

Progressives reformers who wanted to improve American life in the late 1800s and early 1900s (p. 513)
proprietary colony English colony in which the king gave land to proprietors in exchange for a yearly payment (p. 101)
proprietor owner of a proprietary colony (p. 101)
protective tariff tax on imported goods to protect a country's industry from foreign competition (p. 247)
Protestant Reformation movement to reform the Roman Catholic Church in the 1500s; led to creation of many different Christian churches (p. 79)
public school school supported by taxes (p. 120)
pueblo adobe dwelling of the Anasazis (p. 35); town in the Spanish colonies (p. 69)
Puritans group of English Protestants who settled the Massachusetts Bay Colony (p. 94)

Q

Quakers Protestant reformers who settled in Pennsylvania (p. 101)
quota system system that limited immigration by allowing only a certain number of people from each country to immigrate to the United States (p. 503)

R

racism belief that one race is superior to another (pp. 111, 448)
radical person who wants to make drastic changes in society (p. 482)
ratify to approve (pp. 182, 204)
recall process by which voters can remove an elected official from office (p. 513)
Reconstruction rebuilding of the South after the Civil War (p. 479)
referendum process by which people vote directly on a bill (p. 513)
refugee person who flees his or her homeland to seek safety elsewhere (p. 164)
Renaissance (REHN uh sahns) French word meaning rebirth; burst of learning in Europe from the late 1300s to about 1600 (p. 61)
rendezvous (RAHN day voo) yearly meeting where mountain men traded furs (p. 348)
repeal to cancel or undo (p. 144)
representative government government in which voters elect representatives to make laws for them (pp. 86, 218)
republic nation in which voters elect representatives to govern them (p. 198)
reservation limited area set aside for Native Americans by the government (p. 506)
revival huge meeting held to stir religious feelings (p. 398)
royal colony colony under the control of the English crown (p. 101)

S

Sabbath holy day of rest in some religions (p. 98)
sachem tribal chief of an Eastern Woodlands Native American people (p. 45)
scalawag white southerner who supported the Republicans during Reconstruction (p. 486)
secede to withdraw from membership in a group (pp. 335, 427)
Second Great Awakening religious movement that swept the United States in the early 1800s (p. 398)
sectionalism loyalty to a state or section rather than to the whole country (pp. 310, 425)
sedition stirring up rebellion against a government (p. 259)
segregation separation of people based on racial, ethnic, or other differences (p. 495)
Senate smaller house of Congress, in which each state has two senators (p. 225)
Seneca Falls Convention (1848) meeting at which leaders of the women's rights movement called for equality for women (p. 409)
separation of powers principle by which the powers of government are divided among separate branches (p. 200)
serf peasant who worked for a lord and could not leave without the lord's permission (p. 60)
service industry business in which workers provide a service rather than produce goods (p. 509)
sharecropper person who farms land owned by another in exchange for a share of the crops (p. 490)
Shays' Rebellion (1786) revolt of Massachusetts farmers against increased taxes (p. 192)
siege military blockade of an enemy town or position in order to force it to surrender (pp. 180, 354)
slave code laws that controlled the lives of enslaved African Americans and denied them basic rights (pp. 111, 390)
smuggler person who violates trade laws by illegally taking goods into or out of a country (p. 278)
social reform organized attempt to improve what is unjust or imperfect in society (p. 398)
Sons of Liberty group of colonial men who protested British policies (p. 145)
speculator person who invests in a risky venture in the hope of making a large profit (pp. 246, 338)
spinning jenny machine developed in the 1760s that could spin several threads at once (p. 294)
spoils system practice of rewarding supporters with government jobs (p. 331)
standard time zone one of 24 divisions of the Earth, each an hour apart (p. 12)
standing committee permanent congressional committee assigned to study a specific issue (p. 226)
states' rights idea that states have the right to limit the power of the federal government (p. 333)
stock share in a corporation (p. 508)
strike refusal by workers to do their jobs until their demands are met (p. 379)
suffrage right to vote (p. 326)
suffragist person who campaigned for women's right to vote (p. 512)
Sunbelt name for the southern part of the United States from Florida to southern California (p. 504)
Supreme Court highest court in the United States (p. 231)

surplus an extra amount, more than is needed (p. 50)

T

tariff tax on foreign goods brought into a country (p. 247)
Tariff of Abominatons name southerners gave to the tariff passed in 1828 (p. 333)
telegraph communication device that sends electrical signals along a wire (p. 375)
temperance movement campaign against the sale or drinking of alcohol (p. 401)
tepee (TEE pee) tent made by stretching animal skins on tall poles (p. 42)
terrace level strip of land carved into the side of a hill or mountain for farming (p. 50)
Three-Fifths Compromise agreement at the Constitutional Convention that three fifths of the slaves in any state be counted in its population (p. 196)
toleration willingness to let others practice their own customs and beliefs (p. 96)
total war all-out war that affects civilians at home as well as soldiers in combat (p. 471)
totalitarian state country where a single party controls the government and every aspect of the lives of the people (p. 517)
town meeting session in which citizens discuss and vote on local community issues (p. 98)
trade deficit when a nation buys more goods and services from foreign countries than it sells to them (p. 509)
trade union association of trade workers formed to gain higher wages and better working conditions (p. 379)
Trail of Tears (1838) forced march of Native Americans to lands west of the Mississippi (p. 337)
traitor person who betrays his or her country (p. 166)
transcendentalism belief that the most important truths in life go beyond human reason (p. 413)
transcontinental railroad railroad that stretches across a continent (p. 506)
travois (truh VOI) sled used by Plains people and pulled by a dog or horse (pp. 41, 504)
triangular trade colonial trade route between New England, the West Indies, and Africa (p. 112)
tribe group of Native American people sharing the same customs, languages, and rituals (p. 36)
tributary stream or smaller river that flows into a bigger river (p. 17)
turnpike road built by a private company that charges a toll to use it (p. 302)
tutor private teacher (p. 120)

U

unconstitutional not permitted by the Constitution (pp. 221, 254)
underground railroad network of abolitionists who helped runaway slaves reach freedom in the North or Canada (p. 405)
United Nations international organization formed in 1945 to help solve conflicts between nations (p. 517)
urbanization movement of population from farms to cities (p. 300)

V

veto to reject (pp. 203, 221)
vigilante (vihj uh LAN tee) self-appointed law enforcer who deals out punishment without a trial (p. 368)

W

weather condition of the Earth's atmosphere at any given time and place (p. 19)
Whiskey Rebellion (1794) revolt of farmers to protest the tax on whiskey (p. 249)
women's rights movement campaign to win equality for women (p. 410)
writ of assistance legal document that let a British customs officer inspect a ship's cargo without giving any reason for the search (p. 145)

★ Index ★

Page numbers that are italicized refer to illustrations or quotations. An *m, p, c, g, go,* or *q* before a page number refers to a map *(m)*, picture *(p)*, chart *(c)*, graph *(g)*, graphic organizer *(go)*, or quotation *(q)* on that page.

A

B

★ INDEX ★

C

D

★ INDEX ★

H

I

★ INDEX ★

★ INDEX ★

★ INDEX ★

★ Credits ★

Staff Credits

The people who made up ***The American Nation*** team—representing editorial, editorial services, design services, field marketing, managing editor, market research, marketing services, on-line services/multimedia development, product marketing, production services, and publishing processes—are listed below. Bold type denotes core team members.

Margaret Antonini, Sarah Carroll, Lynda Cloud, Rhett Conklin, Martha Conway, Carlos Crespo, **Jim Doris,** Libby Forsyth, **Annemarie Franklin, Nancy Gilbert,** Holly Gordon, **Dorshia Johnson, Loretta Moe,** Jim O'Shea, Kirsten Richert, Gerry Schrenk, Anne Shea, Annette Simmons, **Marilyn Stearns,** Frank Tangredi, Elizabeth Torjussen

Acknowledgments

Art and Design: Kathyryn Foot, Karen Vignola, Patty Rodriguez, Rui Camarinha, Anthony Barone, Ernest Albanese, Robert Aleman, Penny Baker, Paul DelSignore, Frances Medico, Doreen Mazur **Editorial:** Mary Aldridge, Gaynor Ellis, Marian Manners, Jeremy Naidus, Andrew Roney **Photo Research:** *Photosearch,* Inc., Lashonda Williams, Vicky Menanteaux, Katarina Gavilanes, Diane Alimena

Text Credits

Grateful acknowledgment is made to the following for copyrighted material:

Page 126 From *American Indian Myths and Legends,* edited by Richard Erdoes and Alfonso Ortiz (New York: Pantheon Books, a division of Random House, 1984). Copyright 1984 by Richard Erdoes and Alfonso Ortiz. **Page 238** Excerpts from "Valley Forge" by Maxwell Anderson from *America on Stage*, edited by Stanley Richards. Copyright © 1976. **Page 418** From *Nightjohn* by Gary Paulsen. Copyright © 1993 by Gary Paulsen. Used by permission of Delacorte Press, a division of Bantam Doubleday Dell Publishing Group, Inc. **Page 527** From "Spider Woman Story" from *Sweet Salt: Navajo Folk Tales and Mythology* by Raymond Friday Locke. Copyright © 1990 by Raymond Friday Locke. Reprinted by permission of the author. **Page 550** From *Who Cares? Millions Do...* by Milton Meltzer. Copyright©1994 by Milton Meltzer. Reprinted with permission from Walker and Company, 435 Hudson Street, New York, NY 10014. 1-800-289-2553. All Rights Reserved. **Page 566** From *Death Comes for the Archbishop* by Willa Cather. Copyright 1927 by Willa Cather and renewed 1955 by the Executors of the Estate of Willa Cather. Reprinted by permission of Alfred A. Knopf, Inc. **Page 572** From *The Fires of Jubilee, Nat Turner's Fierce Rebellion* by Stephen B. Oates, Harper and Row, Publishers. Copyright©1975 by Stephen B. Oates. All rights reserved. **Page 578** From *Caleb's Choice* by G. Clifton Wisler. Copyright ©1996 by G. Clifton Wisler. Published by Lodestar Books, an affiliate of Dutton Children's Books, a division of Penguin Putnam Inc. **Page 587** From *Out From This Place* by Joyce Hansen. Copyright©1988 by Joyce Hansen. Reprinted with permission from Walker and Company, 435 Hudson Street, New York, NY 10014. 1-800-289-2553. All Rights Reserved. **Note:** Every effort has been made to locate the copyright owner of material used in this textbook. Omissions brought to our attention will be corrected in subsequent editions.

Illustration Credits

Cover and Title Page Wolfgang Kaehler; Day Williams/Photo Researchers, Inc. **iv** *t The Puritan,* Augustus Saint-Gaudens, All Rights Reserved, The Metropolitan Museum of Art, Bequest of Jacob Ruppart, 1939 (39.65.53); *b* Jerry Jacka Photography **v** *t* Gallery of the Republic; *b* Courtesy, Independence National Historical Park Collection **vi** *t* Rembrandt Peale, *Thomas Jefferson,* detail, Collection of The New-York Historical Society; *bl* O.C. Seltzer, *Lewis and Clark With Sacajawea at the Great Falls of the Missouri,* From the Collection of Gilcrease Museum, Tulsa; *br* American Textile History Museum, Lowell, MA **vii** *t* Museum of Art, Rhode Island School of Design, Gift of Miss Lucy T. Aldrich; *b* Dean Beason, *Settlers' Wagon,* National Gallery of Art, Washington **viii** *t* Photography by Larry Sherer/High Impact Photography, Time-Life Books, Inc.; *mt* Photography by Larry Sherer/High Impact Photography, Time-Life Books, Inc.; *b* Courtesy of the Library of Congress **ix** Courtesy Erie Canal Village **x** ©Robert E. Daemmrich/Tony Stone Images **xi** Lynn Saville **xvi** George Catlin, *LaSalle Claiming Louisiana for France, April 9, 1682,* 1847/1848, Paul Mellon Collection, ©1998 Board of Trustees, National Gallery of Art, Washington **3** NOAA **6** Vito Palmisano/Tony Stone Images **8** Silver Burdett Ginn **12** Map Divison, New York Public Library. Astor, Lenox and Tilden Foundations **14** Daniel J. Cox/Gamma Liaison **15** Jeff Gnass Photography **16** *r* Robert Farber/The Image Bank; *l* ©Francois Gohier/Photo Researchers, Inc. **17** *l* Siegfried Layda/Tony Stone Images; *r* ©Jeff LePore/Photo Researchers, Inc. **18** *r* UPI/CORBIS-BETTMANN; *l* Courtesy National Archives, photo no. NWDNS-79-AA_F09 **20** East Bay Municipal Utility District **21** *l* Duricux/SIPA; *r* Weather Graphics Courtesy of AccuWeather, Inc., 619 West College Avenue, State College, PA 16801, (814) 237-0309; Other Educational Weather Products Available ©1997 **29** Courtesy of the Wheelwright Museum of the American Indian **30** National Museum of American Art, Smithsonian Institution **33** *l* Tom Till/International Stock Photography, Ltd.; *r* Peabody Museum of Archaeology and Ethnology, Harvard University **34** *r* National Park Service; *l* ©Richard J. Green/Photo Researchers, Inc. **35** Jerry Jacka Photography **37** *r* Lee Boltin Picture Library; *l* Grove/ Zuckerman/Index Stock Photography, Inc. **41** *l Kachina Doll,* The Brooklyn Museum, 05.588.7193, Museum Expedition 1905, Museum Collection Fund; *r Butterfly Maiden, Kachina,* Courtesy of the Denver Art Museum, Denver Art Museum, Denver, CO **42** National Museum of American Art, Smithsonian Institution **43** Courtesy of The New York State Museum,

Albany, NY, Lewis Henry Morgan collection **44** Neg./Trans. no. K 10302. Courtesy Department of Library Services, American Museum of Natural History **46** The Granger Collection, New York **48** Laurie Platt Winfrey, Inc. **50** Museo Nacional de Arqueologia, Antropologia E Historia del Peru **51** Loren Mcintyre/Woodfin Camp & Associates **52** © University Museum of National Antiquities, Oslo, Norway. Photo: Eirik Irgens Johnsen **53** The Granger Collection, New York **54** ©Index Stock Photography, Inc. **59** New York Public Library, Rare Book Division; Astor, Lenox and Tilden Foundations **61** Erich Lessing/Art Resource, NY **62** *l* *Christopher Columbus,* Sebastiano del Piombo, All rights reserved, The Metropolitan Museum of Art; *r* The Metropolitan Museum of Art, The Edward C. Moore Collection, Bequest of Edward C. Moore, 1891, Copyright © The Metropolitan Museum of Art **63** Colin Fisher for Prentice Hall **65** Victoria & Albert Museum, London/The Bridgeman Art Library, London **66** *t* The Granger Collection, New York; *b* The Metropolitan Museum of Art, Bashford Dean Memorial Collection, Purchase, 1929. (29.158.142) **69** *t* Luis Castaneda/The Image Bank; *b* ©Brent Winebrenner/International Stock Photography, Ltd. **70** Ampliaciones y Reproducciones MAS (Arxiu Mas) **73** All rights reserved, The Metropolitan Museum of Art, Louis V. Bell and Rogers Funds, 1972 (1972.63ab) **74** *r* Merrit Vincent/PhotoEdit; *l* The Granger Collection, New York **76** *l* Photo Bibliothèque Nationale, Paris; *r* *Sugar Harvest in Louisiana & Texas,* 1856–1860, #65.39.120, Collection: Glenbow Museum, Calgary, Alberta **81** *t* North Wind Picture Archives; *b* Minnesota Historical Society **82** New York Public Library, Rare Book Division; Astor, Lenox and Tilden Foundations **85** detail, National Portrait Gallery, Smithsonian Institution/Art Resource, NY **86** State Capitol, Commonwealth of Virginia. Courtesy The Library of Virginia. **89** Courtesy of the Pilgrim Society, Plymouth, Massachusetts **93** Stephen & Carol Huber **95** *l* Eliot Elisofon/LIFE Magazine©TIME Inc.; *r* *The Puritan,* Augustus Saint-Gaudens, All Rights Reserved, The Metropolitan Museum of Art, Bequest of Jacob Ruppart, 1939 (39.65.53) **97** Courtesy of the Library of Congress **98** *r* Courtesy of the Peabody Essex Museum, Salem, MA. Photo by Mark Sexton; *l* North Wind Picture Archives **100** Museum of the City of New York, Museum purchase, Mrs. Elon Huntington Hooker Fund **101** Collection of The New-York Historical Society **103** *l* Courtesy of the Library of Congress; *r* Kelly Mooney/Corbis **105** New York State Historical Association, Cooperstown **108** The Granger Collection, New York **109** *l* North Wind Picture Archives; *r* The Granger Collection, New York **110** *l* Courtesy, American Antiquarian Society; *r* Gibbes Museum of Art, Carolina Art Association **115** John Lei/Omni-Photo Communications, Inc. for Prentice Hall **117** John Lewis Stage **118** *l* *Mrs. Elizabeth Freake and Baby Mary,* unknown artist, Worcester Art Museum, Worcester, Massachusetts, Gift of Mr. and Mrs. Albert W. Rice; *r* Breton Littlehales © National Geographic Society **120** *George Whitefield,* 1742, John Wollaston, By Courtesy of the National Portrait Gallery, London **121** *l* Yale University Art Gallery; *r* New York Public Library, Rare Book Division. Astor, Lenox and Tilden Foundations **122** *r* Richard T. Nowitz/Corbis **127** Courtesy of W. E. Channing & Co., Santa Fe, NM **128** From the collections of Henry Ford Museum & Greenfield Village, MI/#63.41 **131** detail, The Granger Collection, New York **134** National Gallery of Canada, Ottawa **136** The West Point Museum, United States Military Academy, West Point, New York, Photo by Paul Warchol **137** *l* The Historical Society of Pennsylvania; *r* Giraudon/Art Resource, NY **143** The Granger Collection, New York **145** *l* Courtesy of the Library of Congress; Colorized by Marilynn Hawkridge; *br* Colonial Williamsburg Foundation; *tr* Courtesy of the Library of Congress **146** *t* Chuck Nacke/Woodfin Camp & Associates; *b* Corel Professional Photos CD-ROM™ **147** Bequest of Winslow Warren, Courtesy, Museum of Fine Arts, Boston **148** Courtesy American Antiquarian Society **149** *Samuel Adams,* detail, John Singleton Copley. Deposited by the City of Boston. Courtesy Museum of Fine Arts, Boston **151** *l* Courtesy of the Library of Congress; *r* Courtesy of The Bostonian Society Old State House **152** National Museum of American History, Smithsonian Institution, Photo No. 86-4091 **154** *r* Ivan Massar/Black Star; *l* Kevin Fleming/Corbis **159** *Surrender of Lord Cornwallis at Yorktown,* John Trumbull, Yale University Art Gallery **161** Fort Ticonderoga Museum **163** *t* *Attack on Bunker's Hill, with the Burning of Charles Town,* Gift of Edgar William and Bernice Chrysler Garbisch, ©Board of Trustees, National Gallery of Art, Washington; *b* Courtesy of The Bostonian Society Old State House **165** Boston Athenaeum **166** United States Capitol Historical Society **167** ©Darryl Heikes/Stock South, 1992/PNI **169** West Point Museum Collections, United States Military Academy, West Point, New York **171** The Historical Society of Pennsylvania **176** *l* Fraunces Tavern Museum, New York City; *r* ©Les Stone/Sygma **178** Copyright © 1996 By the Metropolitan Museum of Art **180** Collections of The Virginia State Historical Society, Richmond, VA **183** Gallery of the Republic **187** Architect of the Capitol **188** *The National Archives of the United States* by Herman Viola. Publisher, Harry N. Abrams, Inc. Photograph by Jonathan Wallen **190** *l* The Granger Collection, New York; *b* The Granger Collection, New York **193** Leif Skoogfors/Woodfin Camp & Associates **194** Yale University Art Gallery, gift of Roger Sherman White, B. A. 1859, M.A. **195** Courtesy, Independence National Historical Park Collection **196** *l* Leif Skoogfors/Corbis; *r* Michael Bryant/Woodfin Camp & Associates **199** Bulloz/Art Resource, NY **205** Courtesy of the Library of Congress **206** The Granger Collection, New York **207** *l* John Ficara/Woodfin Camp & Associates; *r* Pat & Tom Leeson/Photo Researchers, Inc. **208** *l* Virginia Historical Society, Richmond, VA; *r* Alan Klehr/Tony Stone Images **213** Mark Hess/The Image Bank **214** Joseph Sohm/ChromoSohm, Inc./Corbis **216** Food and Drug Administration **218** ©Copyright 1997 PhotoDisc, Inc. **219** George Hall/Woodfin Camp & Associates **225** U.S. House of Representatives **228** *t* C.L. Chryslin/The Image Bank; *b* Corel Professional Photos CD-ROM™ **229** *r* Wally McNamee/Woodfin Camp & Associates; *l* Dirck Halstead/Gamma Liaison **230** Collection, The Supreme Court of the United States, courtesy The Supreme Court Historical Society. Photo by Richard Strauss, Smithsonian Institution **232** Corbis **233** *m* ©Alon Reininger/Contact/Stock Market; *l* Jack Bender/Waterloo Courier/Rothco; *r* ©Alon Reininger/Contact/The Stock Market **234** PEOPLE weekly ©1997 Andrew Kaufman **239** Courtesy of The Valley Forge Historical Society **240** John Lewis Krimmel, *Election Day in Philadelphia,* 1815, Courtesy, The Henry Francis du Pont Winterthur Museum **243** Courtesy, The Henry Francis du Pont Winterthur

Museum **245** *t* Private Collection; *b* The Museum of American Political Life, University of Hartford; photo by Sally Anderson-Bruce **246** Courtesy of the Art Commission of the City of New York **248** David Young Wolff/Tony Stone Images **251** *t* Giraudon/Art Resource, NY; *b* Roger Viollet **252** Courtesy of The Mount Vernon Ladies' Association **254** *l* Unknown, American, Pennsylvania, *He That Tilleth His Land Shall be Satisfied,* detail, Philadelphia Museum of Art: The Edgar William and Bernice Chrysler Garbisch Collection; *r* John Neagle, *Pat Lyon at the Forge,* Henry M. and Zoë Oliver Sherman Fund, Courtesy, Museum of Fine Arts, Boston **255** Corel Professional Photos CD-ROM™ **259** *r* The Granger Collection, New York; *l* The Huntington Library, San Marino, California **260** *r* *John Adams,* c. 1800, James Sharples, The Museum of Fine Arts, Houston; The Bayou Bend Collection, gift of Miss Ima Hogg; *m* Gilbert Stuart, *Abigail Smith Adams* (Mrs. John Adams), detail, Gift of Mrs. Robert Homans, ©1997 Board of Trustees, National Gallery of Art, Washington, Photo by: Richard Carafelli; *l* National Park Service, Adams National Historic Site **265** *Lewis and Clark on the Lower Columbia,* Charles M. Russell, 1905, 1961.195, gouache, watercolor and graphite on paper, Amon Carter Museum, Forth Worth **267** *r* Rembrandt Peale, *Thomas Jefferson,* detail, Collection of The New-York Historical Society; *l* Robert Llewellyn Photography **268** *t* Silver Burdett Ginn; *b* ©Junebug Clark/Photo Researchers, Inc. **270** Missouri Historical Society, St. Louis **271** Chicago Historical Society **274** *l* John Woodhouse Audubon, *Antelope Americana,* detail, Neg./Trans. no._3267 (2)(Photo by: P. Hollembeak/ Bauer) Courtesy Department of Library Services, American Museum of Natural History; *r* O.C. Seltzer, *Lewis and Clark with Sacajawea at the Great Falls of the Missouri,* From the Collection of Gilcrease Museum, Tulsa **276** The Granger Collection, New York **279** Ohio State Historical Society, Jim Roese, photographer, courtesy Historic Waynesborough **280** Collection of Cranbrook Institute of Science, #CIS 2207. ©Robert Hensleigh, Photographer **281** *r* Courtesy of the Library of Congress; *l* The Field Museum, Neg.# A93851.1c, Chicago **283** Courtesy Scott Baker, Ohio Society War of 1812 **285** U.S. Navy Photos **287** *l* From the collection of Mac G. and Janelle C. Morris; *r* Ted Baker/The Image Bank **288** Courtesy of the Library of Congress **293** Leon Pomarede, *View of St. Louis,* 1835, The Saint Louis Art Museum, Private collection of Dorothy Ziern Hanon & Joseph B. Hanon **295** *r* James Higgins; Use courtesy of Lowell National Historical Park **297** American Textile History Museum, Lowell, MA **298** Reprinted with permission of the News-Press of Fort Myers **301** Dean Beason, *Settlers' Wagon,* National Gallery of Art, Washington **302** Pavel Petrovich Svinin, *Travel by Stagecoach near Trenton, New Jersey,* All rights reserved, The Metropolitan Museum of Art, Rogers Fund, 1942. (42.95.11) **304** Silver Burdett Ginn and Colonial Williamsburg Foundation **305** *l* Courtesy Erie Canal Village; *r* Courtesy Erie Canal Museum **309** *l* Architect of the Capitol; *m* Francis Alexander, *Daniel Webster,* 1835, Hood Museum of Art, Dartmouth College, Hanover, New Hampshire; gift of Dr. George C. Shattuck, Class of 1803; *r* Charles Bird King, *John Caldwell Calhoun,* National Portrait Gallery, Smithsonian Institution, Transfer from the National Gallery of Art; Gift of Andrew W. Mellon, 1942 **313** *t* Anne S.K. Brown Military Collection; *b* Coleccion Museo Nacional de Colombia, Bogotá **319** John Quidor, *Return of Rip Van Winkle,* 1829, Andrew W. Mellon Collection, ©1998 Board of Trustees, National Gallery of Art, Washington **320** Scotts Bluff National Monument **323** George Caleb Bingham, *The County Election,* 1851–52, oil on canvas, The Saint Louis Art Museum **326** Eunice Pinney, *Two Women,* c. 1815, New York State Historical Association, Cooperstown **327** *l* Courtesy of the Library of Congress; *r* D. Walker/Gamma Liaison **329** Anna Claypoole Peale, *Andrew Jackson,* Yale University Art Gallery **331** The Granger Collection, New York **333** Courtesy of Salem Maritime NHS **334** Lynn Saville **335** Courtesy of the Library of Congress **339** Becker Collection, Division of Political History, National Museum of American History, Smithsonian Institution, #564-97 **340** © Robert E. Daemmrich/Tony Stone Images **345** Courtesy of Bexar County and The Witte Museum, San Antonio, Texas **348** Alfred Jacob Miller, *Fort Laramie,* 1837, Walters Art Gallery, Baltimore **349** *t* Handtinting by Ladleton Studio/Culver Pictures, Inc.; *b* Courtesy of the Lane County Historical Museum **351** Courtesy Local History Programs **353** Corel Professional Photos CD-ROM™ **354** *l* Courtesy of the Texas Memorial Museum; *r* Archives Division, Texas State Library **357** *r* Courtesy of The Oakland Museum History Department; *l* Jim Zuckerman/West Light **360** Bill Pogue/The Stockhouse, Inc. **361** Courtesy of the Costume Department, Chicago Historical Society, 1920.38 **364** *Nuestra Senora del Rosario / Our Lady of the Rosary,* by Santo Nino Santero, New Mexico, 1830–60. Gesso, cloth, tin, wood, and water soluble paint. H: 40 1/2 inches. Courtesy Museum of New Mexico Collections at the Museum of International Folk Art, Santa Fe. Photo by Blair Clark. **368** *l* North Wind Picture Archives; *r* California State Library **373** *b* The Warner Collection of Gulf States Paper Corporation, Tuscaloosa, Alabama; *t* American Steel Foundries **374** National Museum of History and Technology, Smithsonian Institution, Photo No. 90-4210 **379** *l* State Historical Society of Wisconsin; *r* American Textile History Museum, Lowell, MA **380** Michael Newman/PhotoEdit **382** Aaron E. Darling, *John Jones,* 1865, Chicago Historical Society, #1904.0018 **383** National Museum of American History, Smithsonian Institution, Photo No. 73-11287 **384** ©Robert Finken/Photo Researchers, Inc. **387** The Old Print Shop **389** *t* D. Donne Bryant Stock Photography; *b* Courtesy Rosedown Plantation and Historic Garden **391** *t* Maynard Frank Wolfe/Globe Photos; *b* Bob Daemmrich/Stock, Boston/PNI **392** John Antrobus, *Plantation Burial,* 1860, The Historic New Orleans Collection, Museum/Research Center, Acc. No. 1960.46 **397** Museum of Art, Rhode Island School of Design, Gift of Miss Lucy T. Aldrich **399** Courtesy of the Library of Congress **400** Tony Freeman/PhotoEdit **401** *r* Winslow Homer, *Homework,* 1874, watercolor, Canajoharie Library and Art Gallery, Canajoharie, New York; *b* Victor R. Boswell, Jr./National Geographic Society; *m* Richard Nowitz; *l* Richard T. Nowitz, 1991 **403** The Trustees of the Wedgwood Museum, Barlaston, Staffordshire, England **404** *t* Southworth and Hawes, *William Lloyd Garrison,* All Rights Reserved, The Metropolitan Museum of Art, Gift of I.N. Phelps Stokes, Edward S. Hawes, Alice Mary Hawes, Marion Augusta Hawes, 1937 (37.14.37); *b* Courtesy of the Massachusetts Historical Society **405** Sophia Smith Collection, Smith College **406** C.T. Webber, *The Underground Railroad,* Cincinnati Art Museum,

Subscription Fund Purchase **409** *l* Library of Congress/Corbis; *r* Sophia Smith Collection, Smith College **411** Photograph courtesy of the American Medical Women's Association, photograph by Silver Burdett Ginn **413** *l* Culver Pictures, Inc.; *r* The Kobal Collection **414** The Warner Collection of Gulf States Paper Corporation, Tuscaloosa, Alabama **419** Illustration from the cover of the book NIGHTJOHN copyright © 1993 by Jerry Pinkney. Written by Gary Paulsen. Published by Delacorte Press. All rights reserved. Used with permission. **420** Winslow Homer, *Prisoners from the Front,* 1866, All rights reserved, The Metropolitan Museum of Art, Gift of Mrs. Frank B. Porter, 1922 (22.207) **423** Theodor Kaufmann, *On to Liberty,* 1867, All rights reserved, The Metropolitan Museum of Art, Gift of Erving and Joyce Wolf, 1982/95 (1982.443.3) **425** *l* Edwin Taylor, *American Slave Market,* 1852, Chicago Historical Society, 1954.15; *r* Sovfoto/Eastfoto **428** *r* North Wind Pictures; *l* State Historical Society of Wisconsin **432** *r* Anne S.K. Brown Military Collection; *l* Kansas State Historical Society **433** Missouri Historical Society (S-126 E) **435** Ontario County Historical Society **436** Courtesy of the Illinois State Historical Library **437** Carolyn Schaefer/Gamma Liaison **439** CORBIS-BETTMANN **442** *t* Emory Kristoff/National Geographic Society; *b* Fort Sumter National Monument **447** Winslow Homer, *A Rainy Day in Camp,* All Rights Reserved, The Metropolitan Museum of Art, Gift of Mrs. William F. Milton, 1923. (23.77.1) **448** North Carolina Museum of History **453** Chicago Historical Society **455** E.B.D Julio, *The Last Meeting of Lee and Jackson,* detail, The Museum of the Confederacy, Richmond, Virginia, Photography by Katherine Wetzel **457** Courtesy of the Library of Congress **459** Chicago Historical Society **460** Courtesy of the Library of Congress **461** *Attack at Battery Wagner* © 1993 Tom Lovell © 1993 The Greenwich Workshop, Inc. Courtesy of The Greenwich Workshop, Inc., Shelton, Ct **463** Photography by Larry Sherer/High Impact Photography, Time-Life Books, Inc. **464** Cook Collection Valentine Museum, Richmond, Virginia **465** *t* Courtesy National Archives; *b* Courtesy of the American Red Cross. All Rights Reserved in all Countries. Photo by Silver Burdett Ginn **466** Architect of the Capitol **469** *l* ©The Stock Market/Lance Nelson; *r* John Elk III/Stock, Boston **473** Appomattox Court House NHP, National Park Service, USDI **477** Dennis Malone Carter, *Lincoln's Drive Through Richmond,* Chicago Historical Society, Gift of Mr. Philip K. Wrigley, 1955.398 **479** *l* Courtesy of the Library of Congress; *r* Richard T. Nowitz /Virginia Division of Tourism **480** Moorland-Spingarn Research Center, Howard University **481** Culver Pictures, Inc. **483** Courtesy of the Library of Congress **486** The Children's Museum of Indianapolis **487** detail, Chicago Historical Society, P&S-1904.0018 **488** *t* The Granger Collection, New York; *b* Old Court House Museum, Vicksburg, Photo by Bob Pickett **489** New York Public Library, Print Collection. Miriam and Ira D. Wallach Division of Art, Prints and Photographs; Astor, Lenox and Tilden Foundations **490** Brown Brothers **493** The Granger Collection, New York **494** Courtesy of Jim Osborn **499** West Point Museum Collections, United States Military Academy, West Point, New York **501** Tsing-fang Chen, *Liberty States,* Chen Foundation/Lucia Gallery **502** Bancroft Library, University of California **504** CORBIS-BETTMANN **507** From the collections of Henry Ford Museum & Greenfield Village **511** *l* Porterfield/Chickering/Photo Researchers, Inc.; *r* UPI/CORBIS-BETTMANN **512** *l* CORBIS-BETTMANN; *r* Sally Andersen-Bruce **513** UPI/CORBIS-BETTMANN **514** National Museum of American History, Political History Collection, Smithsonian Institution **518** *l* Jack Kurtz/Impact Visuals; *r* Paul Miller/Black Star **523** *l* Collection of The New-York Historical Society; *r* North Wind Picture Archives **525** Albert Bierstadt, *Landscape,* Columbus Museum of Art, Ohio: Bequest of Rutherford H. Platt **526** ©Adam Jones/Photo Researchers, Inc. **528** Courtesy of the School of American Research, Santa Fe, New Mexico: Gift of Mrs. Chandler Hale, Santa Fe, N.M., Catalog Number IAF.T670 **530** All rights reserved, Photo Archives, Denver Museum of Natural History **531** National Maritime Museum, London **532** Collection of The New-York Historical Society **534** Courtesy of Charleston Library Society, Charleston, South Carolina **536** Collection of The New-York Historical Society **539** Library of Congress/Corbis **540** Courtesy of The Mount Vernon Ladies' Association **542** *Raising the Liberty Pole,* John McRae, photo courtesy of the Kennedy Galleries, New York. Whereabouts unknown. **544** Peabody Essex Museum of Salem **545** Leif Skoogfors/Woodfin Camp & Associates **547** Courtesy of the Library of Congress **549** Thomas Rowlandson, *House of Commons,* All Rights Reserved, The Metropolitan Museum of Art Rogers Fund, 1921 **551** Paul S. Conklin **552** *George Washington banner,* c. 1939, Index of American Design, © Board of Trustees, National Gallery of Art, Washington **554** Max Mackenzie ©Uniphoto, Inc. **556** *r* Missouri Historical Society, St. Louis (L/A 188A); *l* Missouri Historical Society, St. Louis (L/A 407) **558** North Wind Picture Archives **560** Courtesy of the Library of Congress **562** Laurie Platt Winfrey, Inc. **563** White House Collection, copyright White House Historical Association **565** Woolaroc Museum, Bartlesville, Oklahoma **567** Unknown artist, *Oriana Day-Mission Francisco Solano de Sonoma,* c. 1838–1886 The Fine Arts Museum of San Francisco, Gift of Eleanor Martin, 37573 **569** Dan Suzio/Photo Researchers, Inc. **571** Mary Evans Picture Library **573** North Wind Picture Archives **574** *l* Chester County Historical Society, West Chester, PA; *r* UPI/CORBIS-BETTMANN **577** Artist Unknown, *Scenes from a Seminary for Young Ladies* (detail), Purchase and Funds Given by Decorative Arts Society 89:1976, The Saint Louis Art Museum (Decorative Arts and Design) **579** Eyre Crowe, *After the Sale: South from Richmond,* Chicago Historical Society, P&S-1957.0027 **581** Thomas Hovenden, *The Last Moments of John Brown,* All Rights Reserved, By the Metropolitan Museum of Art, Gift of Mr. & Mrs. Carl Stoeckel, 1897 **582** Thomas Nast, *Heroes and Heroines of the War,* detail, c. 1863, Chicago Historical Society, Gift of Dr. Otto L. Schmidt, ICHi-22101 **584** National Geographic Society **586** Richard Norris Brooke, *Furling the Flag,* West Point Museum Collections, United States Military Academy, West Point, New York **588** North Wind Picture Archives **589** *bl* Joseph Sohm/ChromoSohm, Inc./Corbis; *br* Courtesy of Bexar County and The Witte Museum, San Antonio, Texas; *t* Pat & Tom Leeson/Photo Researchers, Inc. **614–617** Portrait nos. 1, 2, 4, 5, 6, 9, 10, 12, 14, 15, 18, 20, 21, 25, 26, 27, 35, National Portrait Gallery, Smithsonian Institution/Art Resource, NY; Portrait nos. 3, 7, 8, 11, 13, 16, 17, 19, 22–24, 28–34, 36–42, White House Collection, copyright White House Historical Association

Stop the Presses

Not so long ago, publishers had to stop the presses to get late-breaking information into their books. Today, Prentice Hall can use the Internet to update you quickly and easily on the most recent developments in Social Studies.

Visit Prentice Hall on the Internet at

http://www.phschool.com

for the Prentice Hall Social Studies Update.

There you will find periodic updates in the following areas:

- ★ **United States History**
- ★ **World Studies**
- ★ **American Government**

Each update topic provides you with background information as well as carefully selected links to guide you to related content on the Internet.

T**he most up-to-date, manageable teaching resources on the Internet.**

Prentice Hall Social Studies Internet Support

WWW.PHSCHOOL.COM

Key Features:

- ▶ New information throughout the year
- ▶ Additional content-rich activities
- ▶ Easy-to-use professional and staff development information
- ▶ Access to other educators around the world

The Prentice Hall social studies Website provides you with a structured, online environment that allows you to access curriculum-related resources on the Internet and keeps your Prentice Hall programs up-to-date.

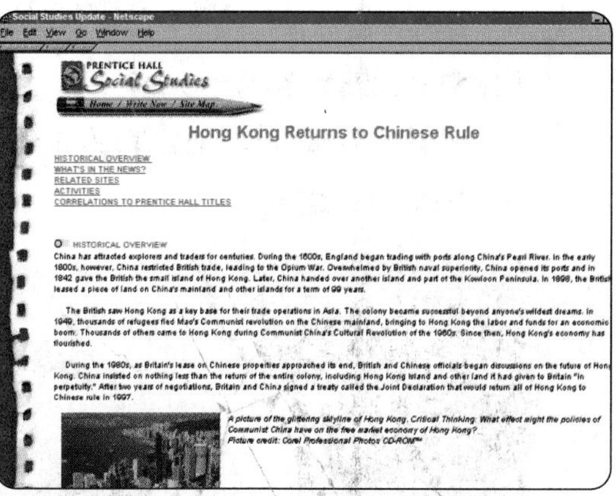

Social studies update

Throughout the year we release up-to-date lesson materials, correlated to your favorite Prentice Hall titles. Each current events update is content-rich and addresses exciting, groundbreaking events in each of the following subject areas: United States History, American Government, and World Studies. Each update topic features:

- Historical Overview
- What's In the News?
- Related Sites
- Activities
- Correlations to Prentice Hall Titles

For Samples, Orders and Information Call **1-800-848-9500**

Title-specific websites

Companion Websites at www.phschool.com contain student activities, teacher resources, and professional development links for many Prentice Hall Social Studies titles. Current events updates and monthly Editor's Picks offer interdisciplinary, curriculum-related links for teachers' use in creating an engaging, interactive atmosphere for learning.

Faculty forum

Share ideas with teachers around the world within the Prentice Hall Website. The Faculty Forum gives you direct access to other educators. Join a discussion group — or start your own. It's a fascinating way to share ideas with educators from around the world.

Regional focus

Now there is customized support for your particular area of the country! Whether you are looking for your sales representative or local Internet activities, the Regional Focus pages have the information you need:

- Local information about Prentice Hall programs
- Materials customized for local curricula
- Resources to help you evaluate Prentice Hall programs
- Schedules of conferences, exhibits, and conventions
- Links to state Departments of Education
- Prentice Hall product information
- Teachers' feedback about Prentice Hall programs

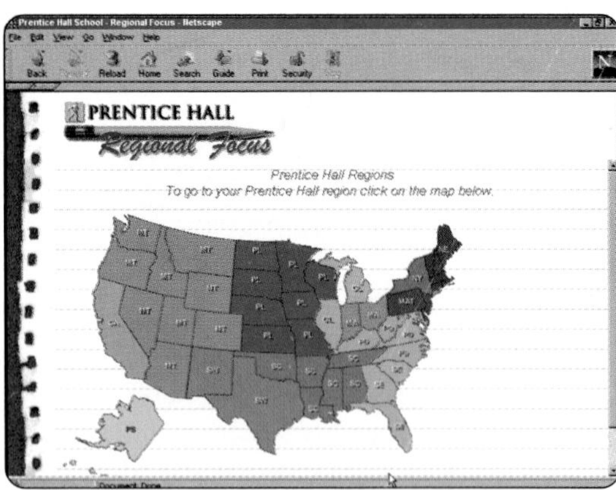

Internet activities

Internet activities enrich instruction in all of our programs. We've carefully constructed Internet explorations on topics throughout the social sciences. Sample lessons cover topics in American History, World History, World Geography, World Cultures, and American Government.

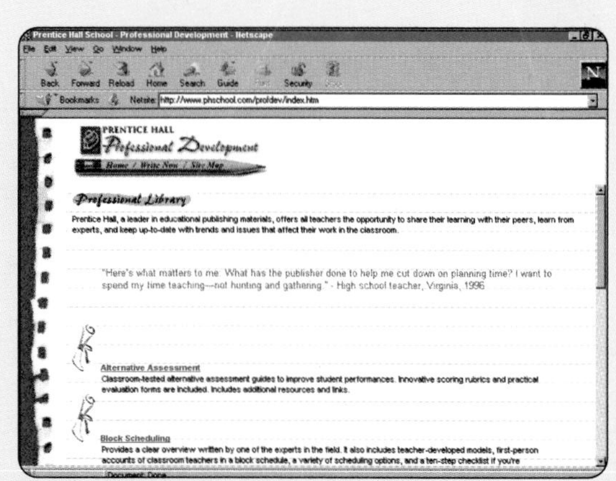

PROFESSIONAL AND STAFF DEVELOPMENT

An organized, professional library of today's educational trends and issues

Simple menus lead to easy-to-use resources covering the topics that interest you most:

- Alternative Assessment
- Block Scheduling
- Career Awareness
- Community Involvement
- The Middle Grades Experience
- Reading in the Content Areas
- Teacher-to-Teacher Activity Network
- Understanding Prejudice
- Using Multimedia Technology
- Using the Internet

The Professional Development area brings you even more:

- Sites for state Departments of Education
- Grant and fellowship information
- Professional organizations